Contemporary Authors®

ISSN 0010-7468

Contemporary Authors®

A Bio-Bibliographical Guide to Current Writers in Fiction, General Nonfiction, Poetry, Journalism, Drama, Motion Pictures, Television, and Other Fields

volume **211**

GALE®

THOMSON

GALE

Detroit • New York • San Diego • San Francisco • Cleveland • New Haven, Conn. • Waterville, Maine • London • Munich

Contemporary Authors, Vol. 211

Project Editor
Scot Peacock

Editorial
Katy Balcer, Shavon Burden, Sara Constantakis, Anna Marie Dahn, Alana Joli Foster, Natalie Fulkerson, Arlene M. Johnson, Michelle Kazensky, Julie Keppen, Joshua Kondek, Thomas McMahon, Jenai A. Mynatt, Judith L. Pyko, Mary Ruby, Lemma Shomali, Susan Strickland, Maikue Vang, Tracey Watson, Thomas Wiloch, Emiene Shija Wright

Research
Tamara C. Nott, Nicodemus Ford, Michelle Campbell

Permissions
Lori Hines

Imaging and Multimedia
Dean Dauphinais, Robert Duncan, Leitha Etheridge-Sims, Mary K. Grimes, Lezlie Light, Dan Newell, David G. Oblender, Christine O'Bryan, Kelly A. Quin, Luke Rademacher

Composition and Electronic Capture
Carolyn A. Roney

Manufacturing
Stacy L. Melson

LIBRARY OF CONGRESS CATALOG CARD NUMBER 62-52046

ISBN 0-7876-6635-1
ISSN 0010-7468

Printed in the United States of America
10 9 8 7 6 5 4 3 2 1

Contents

> **Indexing note:** All *Contemporary Authors* entries are indexed in the *Contemporary Authors* cumulative index, which is published separately and distributed twice a year.
>
> **As always, the most recent Contemporary Authors cumulative index continues to be the user's guide to the location of an individual author's listing.**

Preface

Contemporary Authors (*CA*) provides information on approximately 115,000 writers in a wide range of media, including:

- Current writers of fiction, nonfiction, poetry, and drama whose works have been issued by commercial publishers, risk publishers, or university presses (authors whose books have been published only by known vanity or author-subsidized firms are ordinarily not included)

- Prominent print and broadcast journalists, editors, photojournalists, syndicated cartoonists, graphic novelists, screenwriters, television scriptwriters, and other media people

- Notable international authors

- Literary greats of the early twentieth century whose works are popular in today's high school and college curriculums and continue to elicit critical attention

A *CA* listing entails no charge or obligation. Authors are included on the basis of the above criteria and their interest to *CA* users. Sources of potential listees include trade periodicals, publishers' catalogs, librarians, and other users of the series.

How to Get the Most out of *CA*: Use the Index

The key to locating an author's most recent entry is the *CA* cumulative index, which is published separately and distributed twice a year. It provides access to *all* entries in *CA* and *Contemporary Authors New Revision Series* (*CANR*). Always consult the latest index to find an author's most recent entry.

For the convenience of users, the *CA* cumulative index also includes references to all entries in these Gale literary series: *Authors and Artists for Young Adults, Authors in the News, Bestsellers, Black Literature Criticism, Black Literature Criticism Supplement, Black Writers, Children's Literature Review, Concise Dictionary of American Literary Biography, Concise Dictionary of British Literary Biography, Contemporary Authors Autobiography Series, Contemporary Authors Bibliographical Series, Contemporary Dramatists, Contemporary Literary Criticism, Contemporary Novelists, Contemporary Poets, Contemporary Popular Writers, Contemporary Southern Writers, Contemporary Women Poets, Dictionary of Literary Biography, Dictionary of Literary Biography Documentary Series, Dictionary of Literary Biography Yearbook, DISCovering Authors, DISCovering Authors: British, DISCovering Authors: Canadian, DISCovering Authors: Modules* (including modules for Dramatists, Most-Studied Authors, Multicultural Authors, Novelists, Poets, and Popular/Genre Authors), *DISCovering Authors 3.0, Drama Criticism, Drama for Students, Feminist Writers, Hispanic Literature Criticism, Hispanic Writers, Junior DISCovering Authors, Major Authors and Illustrators for Children and Young Adults, Major 20th-Century Writers, Native North American Literature, Novels for Students, Poetry Criticism, Poetry for Students, Short Stories for Students, Short Story Criticism, Something about the Author, Something about the Author Autobiography Series, St. James Guide to Children's Writers, St. James Guide to Crime & Mystery Writers, St. James Guide to Fantasy Writers, St. James Guide to Horror, Ghost & Gothic Writers, St. James Guide to Science Fiction Writers, St. James Guide to Young Adult Writers, Twentieth-Century Literary Criticism, 20th Century Romance and Historical Writers, World Literature Criticism,* and *Yesterday's Authors of Books for Children.*

A Sample Index Entry:

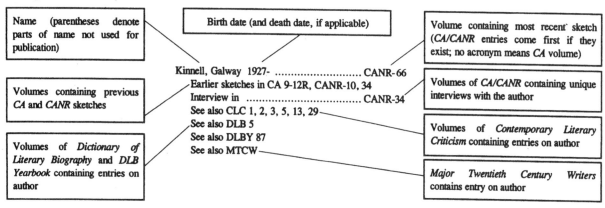

How Are Entries Compiled?

The editors make every effort to secure new information directly from the authors; listees' responses to our questionnaires and query letters provide most of the information featured in *CA*. For deceased writers, or those who fail to reply to requests for data, we consult other reliable biographical sources, such as those indexed in Gale's *Biography and Genealogy Master Index,* and bibliographical sources, including *National Union Catalog, LC MARC,* and *British National Bibliography.* Further details come from published interviews, feature stories, and book reviews, as well as information supplied by the authors' publishers and agents.

An asterisk (*) at the end of a sketch indicates that the listing has been compiled from secondary sources believed to be reliable but has not been personally verified for this edition by the author sketched.

What Kinds of Information Does An Entry Provide?

Sketches in *CA* contain the following biographical and bibliographical information:

- **Entry heading:** the most complete form of author's name, plus any pseudonyms or name variations used for writing

- **Personal information:** author's date and place of birth, family data, ethnicity, educational background, political and religious affiliations, and hobbies and leisure interests

- **Addresses:** author's home, office, or agent's addresses, plus e-mail and fax numbers, as available

- **Career summary:** name of employer, position, and dates held for each career post; resume of other vocational achievements; military service

- **Membership information:** professional, civic, and other association memberships and any official posts held

- **Awards and honors:** military and civic citations, major prizes and nominations, fellowships, grants, and honorary degrees

- **Writings:** a comprehensive, chronological list of titles, publishers, dates of original publication and revised editions, and production information for plays, television scripts, and screenplays

- **Adaptations:** a list of films, plays, and other media which have been adapted from the author's work

- **Work in progress:** current or planned projects, with dates of completion and/or publication, and expected publisher, when known

- **Sidelights:** a biographical portrait of the author's development; information about the critical reception of the author's works; revealing comments, often by the author, on personal interests, aspirations, motivations, and thoughts on writing

- **Interview:** a one-on-one discussion with authors conducted especially for *CA*, offering insight into authors' thoughts about their craft

- **Autobiographical essay:** an original essay written by noted authors for *CA*, a forum in which writers may present themselves, on their own terms, to their audience

- **Photographs:** portraits and personal photographs of notable authors

- **Biographical and critical sources:** a list of books and periodicals in which additional information on an author's life and/or writings appears

- **Obituary Notices** in *CA* provide date and place of birth as well as death information about authors whose full-length sketches appeared in the series before their deaths. The entries also summarize the authors' careers and writings and list other sources of biographical and death information.

Related Titles in the *CA* Series

Contemporary Authors Autobiography Series complements *CA* original and revised volumes with specially commissioned autobiographical essays by important current authors, illustrated with personal photographs they provide. Common topics include their motivations for writing, the people and experiences that shaped their careers, the rewards they derive from their work, and their impressions of the current literary scene.

Contemporary Authors Bibliographical Series surveys writings by and about important American authors since World War II. Each volume concentrates on a specific genre and features approximately ten writers; entries list works written by and about the author and contain a bibliographical essay discussing the merits and deficiencies of major critical and scholarly studies in detail.

Available in Electronic Formats

GaleNet. *CA* is available on a subscription basis through GaleNet, an online information resource that features an easy-to-use end-user interface, powerful search capabilities, and ease of access through the World-Wide Web. For more information, call 1-800-877-GALE.

Licensing. *CA* is available for licensing. The complete database is provided in a fielded format and is deliverable on such media as disk, CD-ROM, or tape. For more information, contact Gale's Business Development Group at 1-800-877-GALE, or visit us on our website at www.galegroup.com/bizdev.

Suggestions Are Welcome

The editors welcome comments and suggestions from users on any aspect of the *CA* series. If readers would like to recommend authors for inclusion in future volumes of the series, they are cordially invited to write the Editors at *Contemporary Authors*, Gale Group, 27500 Drake Rd., Farmington Hills, MI 48331-3535; or call at 1-248-699-4253; or fax at 1-248-699-8054.

Contemporary Authors Product Advisory Board

The editors of *Contemporary Authors* are dedicated to maintaining a high standard of excellence by publishing comprehensive, accurate, and highly readable entries on a wide array of writers. In addition to the quality of the content, the editors take pride in the graphic design of the series, which is intended to be orderly yet inviting, allowing readers to utilize the pages of *CA* easily and with efficiency. Despite the longevity of the *CA* print series, and the success of its format, we are mindful that the vitality of a literary reference product is dependent on its ability to serve its users over time. As literature, and attitudes about literature, constantly evolve, so do the reference needs of students, teachers, scholars, journalists, researchers, and book club members. To be certain that we continue to keep pace with the expectations of our customers, the editors of *CA* listen carefully to their comments regarding the value, utility, and quality of the series. Librarians, who have firsthand knowledge of the needs of library users, are a valuable resource for us. The *Contemporary Authors* Product Advisory Board, made up of school, public, and academic librarians, is a forum to promote focused feedback about *CA* on a regular basis. The seven-member advisory board includes the following individuals, whom the editors wish to thank for sharing their expertise:

- **Anne M. Christensen,** Librarian II, Phoenix Public Library, Phoenix, Arizona.

- **Barbara C. Chumard,** Reference/Adult Services Librarian, Middletown Thrall Library, Middletown, New York.

- **Eva M. Davis,** Youth Department Manager, Ann Arbor District Library, Ann Arbor, Michigan.

- **Adam Janowski, Jr.,** Library Media Specialist, Naples High School Library Media Center, Naples, Florida.

- **Robert Reginald,** Head of Technical Services and Collection Development, California State University, San Bernadino, California.

- **Katharine E. Rubin,** Head of Information and Reference Division, New Orleans Public Library, New Orleans, Louisiana.

- **Barbara A. Wencl,** Media Specialist, Como Park High School, St. Paul, Minnesota.

International Advisory Board

Well-represented among the 115,000 author entries published in *Contemporary Authors* are sketches on notable writers from many non-English-speaking countries. The primary criteria for inclusion of such authors has traditionally been the publication of at least one title in English, either as an original work or as a translation. However, the editors of *Contemporary Authors* came to observe that many important international writers were being overlooked due to a strict adherence to our inclusion criteria. In addition, writers who were publishing in languages other than English were not being covered in the traditional sources we used for identifying new listees. Intent on increasing our coverage of international authors, including those who write only in their native language and have not been translated into English, the editors enlisted the aid of a board of advisors, each of whom is an expert on the literature of a particular country or region. Among the countries we focused attention on are Mexico, Puerto Rico, Germany, Luxembourg, Belgium, the Netherlands, Norway, Sweden, Denmark, Finland, Taiwan, Singapore, Spain, Italy, South Africa, Israel, and Japan, as well as England, Scotland, Wales, Ireland, Australia, and New Zealand. The sixteen-member advisory board includes the following individuals, whom the editors wish to thank for sharing their expertise:

- **Lowell A. Bangerter,** Professor of German, University of Wyoming, Laramie, Wyoming.

- **Nancy E. Berg,** Associate Professor of Hebrew and Comparative Literature, Washington University, St. Louis, Missouri.

- **Frances Devlin-Glass,** Associate Professor, School of Literary and Communication Studies, Deakin University, Burwood, Victoria, Australia.

- **David William Foster,** Regent's Professor of Spanish, Interdisciplinary Humanities, and Women's Studies, Arizona State University, Tempe, Arizona.

- **Hosea Hirata,** Director of the Japanese Program, Associate Professor of Japanese, Tufts University, Medford, Massachusetts.

- **Jack Kolbert,** Professor Emeritus of French Literature, Susquehanna University, Selinsgrove, Pennsylvania.

- **Mark Libin,** Professor, University of Manitoba, Winnipeg, Manitoba, Canada.

- **C. S. Lim,** Professor, University of Malaya, Kuala Lumpur, Malaysia.

- **Eloy E. Merino,** Assistant Professor of Spanish, Northern Illinois University, DeKalb, Illinois.

- **Linda M. Rodríguez Guglielmoni,** Associate Professor, University of Puerto Rico—Mayagüez, Puerto Rico.

- **Sven Hakon Rossel,** Professor and Chair of Scandinavian Studies, University of Vienna, Vienna, Austria.

- **Steven R. Serafin,** Director, Writing Center, Hunter College of the City University of New York, New York City.

- **David Smyth,** Lecturer in Thai, School of Oriental and African Studies, University of London, England.

- **Ismail S. Talib,** Senior Lecturer, Department of English Language and Literature, National University of Singapore, Singapore.

- **Dionisio Viscarri,** Assistant Professor, Ohio State University, Columbus, Ohio.

- **Mark Williams,** Associate Professor, English Department, University of Canterbury, Christchurch, New Zealand.

CA Numbering System and Volume Update Chart

Occasionally questions arise about the *CA* numbering system and which volumes, if any, can be discarded. Despite numbers like " 29-32R," " 97-100" and "210," the entire *CA* print series consists of only 257 physical volumes with the publication of *CA* Volume 211. The following charts note changes in the numbering system and cover design, and indicate which volumes are essential for the most complete, up-to-date coverage.

CA First Revision

- 1-4R through 41-44R (11 books)
  Cover: Brown with black and gold trim.
  There will be no further First Revision volumes because revised entries are now being handled exclusively through the more efficient *New Revision Series* mentioned below.

CA Original Volumes

- 45-48 through 97-100 (14 books)
  Cover: Brown with black and gold trim.
  101 through 211 (111 books)
  Cover: Blue and black with orange bands.
  The same as previous *CA* original volumes but with a new, simplified numbering system and new cover design.

CA Permanent Series

- *CAP*-1 and *CAP*-2 (2 books)
  Cover: Brown with red and gold trim.
  There will be no further Permanent Series volumes because revised entries are now being handled exclusively through the more efficient *New Revision Series* mentioned below.

CA New Revision Series

- CANR-1 through CANR-119 (119 books)
  Cover: Blue and black with green bands.
  Includes only sketches requiring significant changes; **sketches are taken from any previously published CA, CAP, or CANR volume.**

If You Have:	You May Discard:
CA First Revision Volumes 1-4R through 41-44R and *CA Permanent Series* Volumes 1 and 2	*CA* Original Volumes 1, 2, 3, 4 Volumes 5-6 through 41-44
CA Original Volumes 45-48 through 97-100 and 101 through 211	**NONE:** These volumes will not be superseded by corresponding revised volumes. Individual entries from these and all other volumes appearing in the left column of this chart may be revised and included in the various volumes of the *New Revision Series*.
CA New Revision Series Volumes *CANR*-1 through *CANR*-119	**NONE:** The *New Revision Series* does not replace any single volume of *CA*. Instead, volumes of *CANR* include entries from many previous *CA* series volumes. All *New Revision Series* volumes must be retained for full coverage.

A Sampling of Authors and Media People
Featured in This Volume

Kathleen M. Blee

Blee is a sociologist whose work often addresses the relationships of various social factors, including race, class, and gender, and frequently challenges widely held assumptions. *Women of the Klan: Racism and Gender in the 1920s* examines the sense of feminist empowerment felt by women who ironically were working for the oppression of blacks, Jews, and Catholics through their participation in the Ku Klux Klan. In *The Road to Poverty: The Making of Wealth and Hardship in Appalachia,* Blee and coauthor Dwight B. Billings explode some of the stereotypes about the Appalachian region.

Lesley Choyce

Choyce is a prolific and versatile author who incorporates many of his passions—including nature and the environment, surfing, and music—into his fiction, poetry, and nonfiction. Many of Choyce's books appeal to young-adult readers. In his debut YA novel *Skateboard Shakedown,* a group of young skateboard enthusiasts take on a corrupt city government when their favorite skate park is scheduled for development into a shopping area. An autobiographical essay by Choyce is included in this volume of *CA.*

Michael Collins

Born and raised in Ireland, Collins focuses on abusive alcoholics, pious junkies, and doomed IRA renegades in his first collection of short stories, *The Meat Eaters* (published as *The Man Who Dreamt of Lobsters* in the United States). Critics noted in the stories a combination of brutal subject matter and intricate, often philosophical writing. In 2001, Collins' novel *The Keepers of Truth* was shortlisted for the prestigious Booker Prize. He is also the author of *The Resurrectionists,* published in 2002.

P. C. Doherty

A prolific mystery writer, Doherty began his authorial career as a historian, focusing on the early years of the English monarchy. Using a variety of pseudonyms, he has created several different series of mysteries, each distinguished by a strong sense of place and time. Doherty's first novel, *The Death of a King,* explores political intrigue in the reigns of Edward II and III through the eyes of Edward III's clerk. In 1999, Doherty introduced a series of books set in ancient Egypt, starting with *The Mask of Ra.*

Chip Kidd

Kidd, a talented book designer, began working for Alfred E. Knopf in 1986. He has collaborated with Les Daniels on a series of tributes to comic characters Superman, Batman, and Wonder Woman and has demonstrated his superb sense of design on volumes devoted to Plastic Man and the art of "Peanuts" creator Charles M. Schulz. Kidd's debut novel, *The Cheese Monkeys: A Novel in Two Semesters,* was published in 2001 and revolves around a freshman art student on a college campus during the 1950s.

Kelly Link

Link, the author of the short-story collection *Stranger Things Happen,* is also the coeditor of the small-press magazine *Lady Churchill's Rosebud Wristlet,* which publishes works of fiction. She is also co-owner of Small Beer Press, which published her first book. Besides having her first collection named one of *Salon.com*'s Books of the Year, three of Link's short stories included in this book won prestigious awards of their own. "Travels with the Snow Queen," loosely based on the fairy tale, won the James Tiptree, Jr. Award.

Joaquim Monzó

Over the course of his writing career, Monzó has become Catalonia's best-known living author. His sardonic, postmodern novels and books of stories and essays—published under the name Quim Monzó—have sold more than 600,000 copies. Considered part of Spain's Generació dels '70, the group of writers who emerged as the Franco regime withered, Monzó released the short story collection *El millor dels mons* (which means "The Best of Worlds") in 2001.

Lauren Weisberger

In *The Devil Wears Prada,* Weisberger's best-selling first novel, a recent Ivy League graduate lands the job of a lifetime, serving as personal assistant to the editor-in-chief of a famous fashion magazine. However, the assistant quickly discovers the miseries of working for a tyrant. Prior to writing *The Devil Wears Prada,* Weisberger worked as the personal assistant for Anna Wintour, the editor-in-chief of *Vogue,* and the book was widely rumored to be a dishy exposé about working for the notoriously difficult fashion icon.

Acknowledgments

Grateful acknowledgment is made to those publishers, photographers, and artists whose work appear with these authors' essays. Following is a list of the copyright holders who have granted us permission to reproduce material in this volume of *CA*. Every effort has been made to trace copyright, but if omissions have been made, please let us know.

Photographs/Art

Lesley Choyce: All photographs reproduced by permission of the author, except as noted: opening portrait by Jason McGroarthy; portrait of Choyce (in Davy Crockett outfit) by Norma Choyce; portrait of Choyce (as a child, in school uniform) by Suburban Photographers; portrait of Choyce (with musical group) by Cynthia Phillips. All reproduced by permission.

Crawford Kilian: All photographs reproduced by permission of the author.

Dan Wakefield: All photographs reproduced by permission of the author, except as noted: opening portrait © Theresa Mackin; portrait of Wakefield (on boat with Seymour Lawrence) by Gwendolyn Stewart. All reproduced by permission.

A

AKERS, Norman 1958-

PERSONAL: Born October 25, 1958, in Fairfax, OK. *Education:* Kansas City Art Institute, B.F.A., 1982; Institute of American Indian Arts, Santa Fe, NM, certificate of museum training, 1983; University of Illinois—Urbana-Champaign, M.F.A., 1991.

ADDRESSES: Agent—c/o Heard Museum, 2301 North Central Ave., Phoenix, AZ 85004.

CAREER: Museum of Fine Arts, Santa Fe, NM, intern, 1983; Institute of American Indian Arts, Santa Fe, affiliated with collections inventory, 1987; University of Illinois—Urbana-Champaign, visiting assistant professor of art and design, 1991-93; Institute of American Indian Arts, visiting artist, 1993; Bacone College, Pawhuska, OK, adjunct professor. Painter, with work exhibited in group shows throughout the United States, including Pembroke State University, Krannert Art Museum, Tribal Gallery, Los Angeles, CA, Milwaukee Institute of Art and Design, Peace Museum at Maurice Spertus Museum of Judaica, Goshen College of Art, and Jan Cicero Gallery, Chicago, IL; paintings represented in collections at U.S. Department of the Interior, Thomas Gilcrease Museum, Institute of American Indian Arts Museum, Southern Plains Indian Museum and Crafts Center, and White Hair Memorial Resource Center.

AWARDS, HONORS: First place Award, SWAIA Indian Market, 1985; first place, Scottsdale Indian Arts and Crafts Exhibition, 1987.

WRITINGS:

Southern Plains Indian Museum and Crafts Center, [Anadarko, OK], 1986.

Also author (with others) of "6th Native American Fine Arts Invitational" (exhibition booklet), Heard Museum (Phoenix, AZ), 1994.

BIOGRAPHICAL AND CRITICAL SOURCES:

BOOKS

St. James Guide to Native North American Artists, St. James Press (Detroit, MI), 1998, pp. 6-8.

PERIODICALS

Albuquerque Journal, July 28, 1985, John Arnold, "Governor's Gallery Goes American Indian."
Journal North, August 14, 1986, David Bell, "Quality Marks Exhibition of Indian Artists' Work."
New Mexican, August 15, 1985, Michael Roth, "Artist Says, 'Painting Is a Performance.'"
Pasatiempo, April 20, 1984, Deborah Phillips, "Artists Seek out the Spiritual Underpinnings of Life."*

*　　*　　*

ALAMA, Pauline J. 1964-

PERSONAL: Born May 10, 1964, in Belleville, NJ; daughter of Emil Alama (a railway clerk) and Lottie (a teacher; maiden name, Zachai) Alama; married Paul Cunneen (a teacher), August 3, 1996. *Ethnicity:*

"Polish/Italian-American." *Education:* Barnard College, B.A. (English; summa cum laude), 1986; University of Rochester, M.A. (English), 1995, Ph.D., (English), 1998. *Politics:* Green. *Religion:* Catholic.

ADDRESSES: Home—71 Chestnut St., Rutherford, NJ 07070. *E-mail*—PJAlma@excite.com.

CAREER: Writer. Helen Keller International, New York, NY, public relations assistant, 1986-88; New York Mission Society, New York, NY, information officer, 1988-89; New York University, New York, NY, employee development senior project analyst, 1989-91; University of Rochester and Rochester Institute of Technology, Rochester, NY, instructor in English, 1991-99; Teach for America, New York, NY, development associate, 1999-00; New York Foundling, New York, NY, associate director of development, 2000—.

MEMBER: Science Fiction Writers of America, Mythopoeic Society, Science Fiction Association of Bergen County, Phi Beta Kappa.

AWARDS, HONORS: Stains-Berle Memorial Prize in Anglo-Saxon, 1986; W. Cabell Greet Prize for Excellence in English, 1986; Sproull fellowship, 1991-92, 1992-93; second place, Sapphire Award for Short Fiction in Science Fiction Romance, 2001.

WRITINGS:

The Eye of the Night, Spectra (New York, NY), 2002.

Contributor to periodicals and collections, including *Sword and Sorceress,* edited by Marion Zimmer Bradley, DAW, 2001.

WORK IN PROGRESS: The Ghost-Bearers, a novel.

SIDELIGHTS: Pauline J. Alama's first novel, her fantasy *The Eye of the Night,* was called "a beautiful epic" by Harriet Klausner, who reviewed the book for *BookBrowser.* Three central characters drive the story. Jereth leaves the priesthood before taking his vows after his family dies at sea. He wanders until he meets two women with whom he continues his travels as they try to escape the problems that have befallen

their land. Trenara is a beautiful but simple young woman, and Hwyn is a scarred servant girl who carries with her the Eye of the Night, an object shaped like an egg that possesses the ability to bring change.

Alana "richly develops the concept" of the unlikely hero, according to *Booklist* contributor Roberta Johnson. Johnson also noted that the novel is "full of everyday human eccentricity" and is written in accessible language. Liz Zink wrote for *All about Romance* online that *The Eye of the Night* "revolves in some ways around the religion of the land—the worship of the two gods and two goddesses, each with its counterpoint on the Wheel of the years, or corresponding season of the year. This aspect of the plot was well written and descriptive as the companions' journey takes them through all the seasons." *Locus* reviewer Carolyn Cushman said Alama's debut novel is "a little uneven, but is ultimately an enjoyable and pleasantly different fantasy."

Alama told *CA:* "Readers often remark on the religion of the four gods of the World-Wheel in *The Eye of the Night,* and may be surprised to see me identified as Catholic. I think fantasy gives writers and readers a wonderful workshop or play space in which to explore spirituality and discover at a deeper level what we truly believe. That is one of the greatest strengths of the genre."

BIOGRAPHICAL AND CRITICAL SOURCES:

PERIODICALS

Booklist, July, 2002, Roberta Johnson, review of *The Eye of the Night,* p. 1831.
Locus, June, 2002, Carolyn Cushman, review of *The Eye of the Night,* p. 35.

ONLINE

All about Romance, http://www.likesbooks.com/ (August 27, 2002), Liz Zink, review of *The Eye of the Night.*
BookBrowser, http://www.bookbrowser.com/ (May 20, 2002), Harriet Klausner, review of *The Eye of the Night.*

ALBANOV, Valerian Ivanovich 1881-1919

PERSONAL: Born 1881, in Voronezh, Russia; died 1919. *Education:* Naval College of St. Petersburg, graduate, 1904.

CAREER: Navigator and explorer.

WRITINGS:

In the Land of White Death: An Epic Story of Survival in the Siberian Arctic (originally published in Russian in 1917), translation from the French by Alison Anderson, preface by Jon Krakauer, introduction by David Roberts, with additional material from William Barr's translation from the Russian, Modern Library (New York, NY), 2000.

SIDELIGHTS: Valerian Ivanovich Albanov was a Russian explorer who documented his eighteen-month-long ordeal and survival in the Arctic in a diary. The document has been translated into German and French, which finally made its appearance in English as *In the Land of White Death: An Epic Story of Survival in the Siberian Arctic* more than eighty years after its original publication in Russian in 1917. In 1912 Albanov signed on as chief navigation officer of the British-built Russian ship *Santa Anna,* for a 7,000-mile expedition to search for new hunting grounds for the fur trade. The crew of twenty-three included only five sailors, an incompetent captain, Georgi Brusilov, and Yerminiya Zhdanko, a nurse and the only woman on board. They set out from Murmansk in August with insufficient fuel and inadequate charts and soon found themselves imprisoned in an ice floe that took them north in the Kara Sea. Over the next year and a half they drifted. Albanov's diary begins as he makes the decision to leave the ship and seek the safety of distant Franz Josef Land. Leonard Guttridge wrote in the *Washington Post Book World* that "the account gathers true momentum after the transfer of personnel and equipment from the ship's deck to an ice floe, the prelude for a dash to dry land."

Thirteen men joined Albanov, but three eventually returned to the ship. With an inaccurate map torn from a book, Albanov and the ten remaining men began their ninety-day trek, dragging makeshift sledges and kayaks across the ice. They reached land, but only Albanov and one other crew member survived the incredible cold, hunger, scurvy, snow blindness, and threat from dangerous animals as they made their way to an outpost at Cape Flora, where they hoped to be rescued. "The passages describing this death march are among the most hair-raising in the book," wrote Justin Glanville in Chicago's *Tribune Books.* Glanville said that "Albanov's writing is uncannily vivid, pushing the reader into a world of wintry, unrelenting hardship." The two men were finally rescued during the early days of World War I, a conflict of which they had no knowledge. The *Santa Anna* and its remaining crew were never found.

Albanov rewrote the first part of the epic account from memory after his original diary was lost. The second part is the actual log, providing the day-to-day details of their trek. *New York Times Book Review* contributor Caroline Alexander wrote that "Albanov's after-the-fact editing has afforded his narrative a degree of expansiveness that makes his story more accessible to the lay reader and contains passages that capture the men's dreamlike, at times hallucinatory march through the dazzling and improbable landscape." Alexander felt that "missing entirely from Albanov's account is the human drama. . . . Albanov's ten companions remain mostly faceless characters, and there is little sense of their interaction with one another." A French edition includes letters from Brusilov and Zhdanko that indicate that there was friction between members of the crew from the onset. Alexander said that "these tensions of people in close quarters—the record of their deportment among one another in extremis—are what the true adventure classics are all about. The human dynamics are not peripheral or background details to sledging dramas; they are the dramas." *New Scientist* reviewer Gabrielle Walker wrote that in the English edition, "Albanov's storytelling skills more than survive translation." Albanov died two years after his return to Russia.

BIOGRAPHICAL AND CRITICAL SOURCES:

PERIODICALS

New Scientist, November 18, 2000, Gabrielle Walker, "Pole Position," p. 51.
New York Times Book Review, December 10, 2000, Caroline Alexander, "The Second-worst Journey in the World," p. 10.

Tribune Books (Chicago, IL), March 13, 2001, Justin Glanville, "Gripping Tale of Death in the Arctic— From One Who Survived."
Washington Post Book World, December 10, 2000, Leonard Guttridge, "Trapped in a Frozen Sea," p. 3.*

*   *   *

ALEXANDER, Jeffrey C(harles) 1947-

PERSONAL: Born May 30, 1947, in Milwaukee, WI; son of Frederick Charles and Esther Lea (Schlossman) Alexander; children: Aaron, Benjamin. *Education:* Harvard College, B.A., 1969; University of California—Berkeley, Ph.D., 1978. *Politics:* Democrat. *Religion:* Jewish. *Hobbies and other interests:* Photography, tennis, skiing.

ADDRESSES: Office—Department of Sociology, Yale University, New Haven, CT 90024. *E-mail*—jeffrey. alexander@yale.edu.

CAREER: Sociologist, educator, and writer. University of California—Berkeley, lecturer, 1974-76; University of California—Los Angeles, assistant professor, 1976-81, full professor, 1981-2001, chair, sociology department, 1989-92, professor emeritus, beginning 2001; Yale University, professor of sociology, 2001—. University of Bordeaux, France, visiting professor, 1994; Institute for Advanced Studies, Vienna, Austria, visiting professor, 1995.

MEMBER: American Sociological Association, International Sociological Association (founder and co-chair, research Committee on sociological theory, 1990-94), Sociological Research Association.

AWARDS, HONORS: Guggenheim fellow, 1979-80; Ford Foundation, Travel and Study fellow, 1980; Institute for Advanced Studies, Princeton University, fellow, 1985-86; Swedish Colloquium for Advanced Study in the Social Sciences, 1992, 1996; Center for the Advanced Study in the Behavioral Sciences, Stanford University, fellow, 1998-99.

WRITINGS:

Theoretical Logic in Sociology, University of California Press (Berkeley, CA), 1982.

Twenty Lectures: Sociological Theory since World War II, Columbia University Press (New York, NY), 1987.
Action and Its Environments: Toward a New Synthesis, Columbia University Press (New York, NY), 1988.
Structure and Meaning: Relinking Classical Sociology, Columbia University Press (New York, NY), 1989.
Fin de Siecle Social Theory: Relativism, Reduction, and the Problem of Reason, Verso (New York, NY), 1995.
The Meanings of a Social Life: A Cultural Sociology, Oxford University Press (New York, NY), 2003.

EDITOR

Neofunctionalism, Sage Publications (Beverly Hills, CA), 1985.
The Micro-Macro Link, University of California Press (Berkeley, CA), 1987.
Durkheimian Sociology: Cultural Studies, Cambridge University Press (New York, NY), 1988.
(With Seven Seidman) *Culture and Society: Contemporary Debates,* Cambridge University Press (New York, NY) 1990.
(With Paul Colomy) *Differentiation Theory and Social Change: Comparative and Historical Perspectives,* Columbia University Press (New York, NY), 1990.
(With Piotr Sztompka) *Rethinking Progress: Movements, Forces, and Ideas at the End of the 20th Century,* Unwin Hyman (Boston, MA), 1990.
(With Raymond Boudon and Mohamed Cherkaoui) *The Classical Tradition in Sociology: The American Tradition,* Sage Publications (Thousand Oaks, CA), 1997.
Neofunctionalism and After, Blackwell Publishers (Malden, MA), 1998.
Real Civil Societies: Dilemmas of Institutionalization, Sage Publications (Thousand Oaks, CA), 1998.
(With Neil J. Smelser) *Diversity and Its Discontents: Cultural Conflict and Common Ground in Contemporary American Society,* Princeton University Press (Princeton, NJ), 1999.
Mainstream and Critical Social Theory: Classical, Modern, and Contemporary, Sage Publications (Thousand Oaks, CA), 2001.
(With Philip Smith) *The Cambridge Companion to Durkheim,* Cambridge University Press (New York, NY), 2004.

Contributor to books, including *Media, Audience, and Social Structure,* edited by Sandra J. Ball-Rokeach and Muriel G. Cantor, Sage Publications (Newbury Park, CA), 1986.

SIDELIGHTS: American sociologist Jeffrey C. Alexander specializes in the fields of cultural sociology, civil society, and social theory. A contributor to *World of Sociology* noted that Alexander describes his work as "post-Durkheimian" in his approach to sociology and sociological theory. His theories link sociology with literature, political science, and philosophy. For example, *Diversity and Its Discontents: Cultural Conflict and Common Ground in Contemporary American Society,* edited with Neil J. Smelser, examines the American "culture wars" of the late twentieth century. Cultural conflict, Alexander maintains, has always been a part of American society, though it has become more extreme in recent years. This cultural conflict has resulted in significant changes in areas such as family structure, sexual expression, urban lifestyles, and immigration patterns.

Joseph F. Healey, reviewing *Diversity and Its Discontents* in the *Journal of American Ethnic History,* wondered if traditional U.S. values have been "swamped by diversity and moral relativism," and whether U.S. society is in peril of disintegrating at the dawn of the twenty-first century. With *Diversity and Its Discontents,* "Neil Smelser and Jeffrey Alexander have edited a collection of original essays that addresses these questions thoughtfully and provocatively," Healey wrote.

In an overview essay summarizing the numerous issues surrounding diversity and unity in the United States, "Smelser and Alexander argue that the legitimacy of American core values is under attack as never before," Healey observed. Even as the political right asserts that America has lost its traditional values, the political left "agrees with this assessment but celebrates the demise of the oppressive and narrow moral codes of the past," Healey noted. But Smelser and Alexander still feel as though "a broad common culture and consensus on values remains."

The scholars contributing to the book further expand on Smelser and Alexander's views, covering topics such as assimilation experiences of immigrants, new forms and adaptions to diversity in U.S. society, and global perspectives on diversity and related issues.

"This volume is an important contribution to the current discourse on diversity," Healey remarked. "It presents social science at its best: fact-based, careful, and critical scholarship aimed at some of the most significant problems of modern life."

In *Real Civil Societies: Dilemmas of Institutionalization, Social Forces* reviewer Thomas Janoski noted that "Alexander asks the right questions about civil society: What are the problems in establishing and maintaining civil societies as they actually exist?" The volume, edited by Alexander, addresses topics such as uncivil hierarchies that constrain civil society; dichotomies of motives, social relationships, and institutions; and the many-faceted bases of civil society. Although Janoski remarked that he did not believe the book offers "reasonable theoretical answers" to Alexander's questions on civil society, "Nonetheless, this shorter step of examining civil society as a complex variable in different societies is clearly going in the right direction toward 'real' theorizing about civil society."

Fin de Siecle Social Theory: Relativism, Reduction, and the Problem of Reason is Alexander's "response to recent development in sociological (and social) theorizing," wrote Michele Lamont in *American Journal of Sociology.* "In this book, the author tackles everything 'post' and improved (including things modern, 'anti,' and 'neo')." At least half of the book is taken up by Alexander's detailed critique on the work of Pierre Bourdieu. "This is true, genuine, feisty, polemical Alexander, and he takes no prisoners," Lamont observed. "Put very simply," wrote Derek Layder in *Sociology,* "Alexander attacks Bourdieu for producing a failed synthesis which does not recover the actor or the meaningful nature of her world because it does not successfully shake off the influence of the schools of thought from which Bourdieu sought to extricate himself. Thus, Alexander argues that Bourdieu's synthesis is marred by residual imprints of behaviorism, structuralism, and orthodox Marxism." Lamont identified a number of weaknesses in Alexander's critique of Bourdieu, including the fact that Alexander "does not pay sufficient heed to available theoretical critiques and should have been more specific concerning the originality (and limits) of his contribution." However, Lamont concluded that "Alexander's essay can be an important stimulus because, just as Bourdieu's writings have done for so many readers over the past 20 years, it helps foreground questions that have remained muted and unseen to this day."

The purpose of *Differentiation Theory and Social Change: Comparative and Historical Perspectives,* edited by Alexander and Paul Colomy, is "to restore differentiation theory to the high position on the sociological agenda which it enjoyed in the late 1950s and early 1960s," explained Roland Robertson in *Sociology.* Topics covered by contributors to the book include political differentiation in post-Civil War United States, differentiation of the solidary public, and social constitutionalism. Alexander himself "outlines a general theory of the mass news media in society and also provides a stimulating discussion of the relative autonomy of ethnic solidarity which is particularly relevant to the contemporary debate about polyethnicity and multiculturalism."

Despite some flaws in the book, especially "exceedingly little discussion of the history, or the genealogy, of the concept of differentiation," Robertson concluded that *Differentiation Theory and Social Change* "is an interesting and rather important collection, not least because quite a lot of the fifteen chapters involve the systematic weaving together of theory and [U. S.] history"

BIOGRAPHICAL AND CRITICAL SOURCES:

PERIODICALS

Acta Sociologica, April, 1997, Heine Andersen, review of *Fin de Siecle Social Theory: Relativism, Reduction, and the Problem of Reason,* pp. 107-108.

American Journal of Sociology, November, 1988, R. Stephen Warner, review of *Theoretical Logic in Sociology,* Volume 4:, *The Modern Reconstruction of Classical Thought: Talcott Parsons,* p. 644; September, 1989, Toby E. Huff, review of *The Micro-Macro Link,* p. 456; March, 1990, Dennis H. Wrong, review of *Durkheimian Sociology: Cultural Studies,* p. 1358; January, 1998, Michele Lamont, review of *Fin de Siecle Social Theory: Relativism, Reduction, and the Problem of Reason,* p. 1068.

Annals of the American Academy of Political and Social Science, March, 1983, review of *Theoretical Logic in Sociology,* pp. 234-235.

British Journal of Sociology, March, 1989, Mike Gane, review of *Durkheimian Sociology: Cultural Studies,* pp. 166-167; June, 1989, John Holmwood, review of *Action and Its Environments: Toward a New Synthesis,* p. 347; December, 1992, Brian Longhurst, review of *Culture and Society: Contemporary Debates,* p. 681.

Canadian Review of Sociology and Anthropology, February, 1990, Harold Fallding, review of *Twenty Lectures: Sociological Theory since World War II,* p. 125.

Contemporary Sociology, January, 1988, Bryan S. Turner, review of *Twenty Lectures: Sociological Theory since World War II,* pp. 117-118; September, 1988, George Ritzer, review of *The Micro-Macro Link,* p. 703; May, 1990, Gianfranco Poggi, review of *Action and Its Environments: Toward a New Synthesis,* pp. 476-477; July, 1990, Jonathan H. Turner, review of *Durkheimian Sociology: Cultural Studies,* pp. 630-631; July, 1991, Harold J. Bershady, review of *Differentiation Theory and Social Change: Comparative and Historical Perspectives,* p. 635; January, 1999, Ruth A. Wallace, review of *Neofunctionalism and After,* pp. 115-116; January, 2000, Krishan Kumar, review of *Real Civil Societies: Dilemmas of Institutionalization,* pp. 271-272; March, 2002, Philip E. Devine, review of *Diversity and Its Discontents: Cultural Conflict and Common Ground in Contemporary American Society,* pp. 200-201.

Journal of American Ethnic History, winter, 2001, Joseph F. Healey, review of *Diversity and Its Discontents: Cultural Conflict and Common Ground in Contemporary American Society,* p. 122.

Journal of Politics, February, 2001, Margaret Seyford Hrezo, review of *Diversity and Its Discontents: Cultural Conflict and Common Ground in Contemporary American Society,* p. 310.

Law & Society Review, November, 1991, Roger Cotterrell, review of *Durkheimian Sociology: Cultural Studies,* pp. 923-945.

Social Forces, June, 1988, Lawrence E. Hazelrigg, review of *Twenty Lectures: Sociological Theory since World War II,* p. 1122; March, 1990, Douglas D. Heckathorn, review of *The Micro-Macro Link,* p. 940; David E. Woolwine, review of *Durkheimian Sociology: Cultural Studies,* pp. 1006-1007; March, 1991, Thomas J. Fararo, review of *Differentiation Theory and Social Change: Comparative and Historical Perspectives,* pp. 920-921; June, 2000, Thomas Janoski, review of *Real Civil Societies: Dilemmas of Institutionalization,* p. 575.

Social Science Quarterly, June, 1989, James F. Short, review of *Action and Its Environments: Toward a New Synthesis,* pp. 540-541.

Sociological Inquiry, summer, 1991, Brad Bullock, review of *Differentiation Theory and Social Change: Comparative and Historical Perspectives,* p. 397; Donald McQuarie, review of *Structure and Meaning: Relinking Classical Sociology,* p. 412.

Sociological Review, November, 1989, Stiepan G. Mestrovic, review of *Durkheimian Sociology: Cultural Studies,* p. 798.

Sociology, August, 1991, Roland Robertson, review of *Differentiation Theory and Social Change: Comparative and Historical Perspectives,* p. 526; August, 1996, Derek Layder, review of *Fin de Siecle Social Theory: Relativism, Reduction, and the Problem of Reason,* p. 601.*

*   *   *

AL HUSSEIN, Noor 1951-
(Queen Noor)

PERSONAL: Born Lisa Najeeb Halaby, August 23, 1951, in Washington, DC; immigrated to Jordan; daughter of Najeeb Elias (a pilot, director of the Federal Aviation Administration, and chairman of Pan-American Airways) and Doris (a homemaker; maiden name, Lundquist) Halaby; married Hussein bin Talal (King Hussein of Jordan), June 15, 1978 (died, February 7, 1999); children: Hamzah and Hashim (sons), Iman and Raiyah (daughters). *Education:* Princeton University, B.A., 1974. *Hobbies and other interests:* Skiing, water skiing, sailing, horseback riding, reading, gardening, photography.

ADDRESSES: Office—Office of Her Majesty Queen Noor, Bab Al Salam Palace, Amman, Jordan; fax: (962-6) 464 7961. *E-mail*—noor@queennoor.jo.

CAREER: Queen, activist, and architect. Worked as an architect in Australia, Iran, and Jordan; Royal Jordanian Airlines, director of planning; became Queen Noor of Jordan, 1978—. United Nations National Committee for the International Year of the Child, chair, 1979; established Jordan's Royal Endowment for Culture and Education, 1979; convened the first Arab Children's Conference, 1980; affiliated with dozens of organizations, including Seeds of Peace, Refugees International, International Commission on Missing Persons, International Campaign to Ban Landmines, World Conservation Union, World Wildlife Fund International, United World Colleges, United Nations University International Leadership Academy, McGill Middle East Program in Civil Society and Peace Building, Women Waging Peace, International Alert's Women and Peace Building Campaign, International Commission on Peace and Food, SOS-Kinderdorf, International Council of the Near East Foundation, Jordan Society, Mentor Foundation, Journal of Lifetime Trust, Global Committee of the Center for Development and Population Activities, King Hussein Foundation. Founder of in-country organizations and projects, including National Task Force for Children, the King Hussein Cancer Center, Jerash Festival for Culture, the Jubilee School, National Handicrafts Development Project, Noor Hussein Foundation, Children's Heritage and Science Museum, and Mobile Life and Science Museum.

AWARDS, HONORS: Global 500 Award, United Nations, for promoting environmental protection and awareness.

WRITINGS:

(Under name Queen Noor) *Leap of Faith: Memoirs of an Unexpected Life,* Talk Miramax Books (New York, NY), 2003.

SIDELIGHTS: American-born Lisa Najeeb Halaby became Queen Noor al Hussein when she wed Jordan's King Hussein in 1978. During the two decades of their marriage, Noor earned the respect and love of the Jordanian people, who at first suspected the Westerner. She established dozens of programs supporting the health and welfare of her people, the people of the Middle East, and world populations in need. When her husband died of cancer in 1999, Noor stood strong and led the stricken and grieving Jordanians. She also documented the story of her life as queen in *Leap of Faith: Memoirs of an Unexpected Life.*

Noor was the daughter of a Syrian-American father and Swedish-American mother. Her father was a navy test pilot who became director of the Federal Aviation Administration during the Kennedy administration, then chairman of Pan-American Airways. She enjoyed a privileged childhood, attending private schools in Washington, D.C., New York City, and Massachusetts, and she was a member of the first coeducational class at Princeton University. A progressive activist, she protested the Vietnam War and was a member of the Student Nonviolent Coordinating Committee (SNCC). She took a break in her studies to live in Aspen, Colorado, then returned to Princeton to graduate in 1974.

As an architect and urban planner, she first worked in Australia, then in Iran. When the Jordanian government engaged her father to restructure its airline system, he took his daughter along to design a training facility at Arab Air University. She was then offered the position of director of planning and design projects for Royal Jordanian Airlines.

Hussein was mourning the death of his third wife, who had died in a helicopter accident, when he and the young American first met. She was twenty-six, and he, at forty-two, had been king since the age of sixteen. Their friendship developed into love, and when they married in 1978, he renamed her Noor al Hussein, which means "light of Hussein." Noor converted to Islam on the eve of her wedding, but this was considered by many to be an act of expediency, rather than of faith. She was criticized for not following traditional customs, but she ignored such opinion and instead tackled the job of running the royal household and raising the three young children who had lost their mother. The royal couple eventually had four children of their own, and Noor was stepmother to a total of eight other children of the king. King Hussein was the most pro-peace and pro-West voice in the Middle East during the late twentieth century, and at least one dozen assassination attempts were made on his life. Consequently, he and his queen were always surrounded by bodyguards.

The publication of the memoir, scheduled for November 2002, was delayed until March 2003 due to the escalating conflict in the Middle East. In her book, Noor documents her husband's attempts to broker peace, including his meetings with American presidents and Middle Eastern leaders. *Booklist*'s Brad Hooper wrote that "Queen Noor brings a unique perspective to the contemporary history of the region."

In a *Newsweek International* interview with Richard Ernsberger, Jr., Noor said that she wrote the book after her husband's death because she had been asked by many "to share my perspective on living in two differ-

ent cultures. Like my husband, I have a conviction that there is much more that binds culture than separates us. I feel a responsibility to highlight our common ground so that both cultures can work together to resolve conflicts peacefully. My husband is the hero of the book; his search for peace is the central theme, and yet it's not meant to be a definitive historical or political account."

Noor and Hussein were jet-setters who also maintained homes in the United States and England. Julie Salamon wrote in the *New York Times Book Review* that "there are scenes that have the ring of *Roman Holiday*. On her honeymoon, Queen Noor became so overwhelmed by the trappings of royal life that she slipped out to spend the afternoon with a friend." Salamon noted that "while she is candid about the difficulties of marriage, especially marriage to a monarch, she is discreet. No bedroom talk here, beyond this veiled confession: 'I was also deeply attracted to him.'" "That passion clearly extended to the country that made her its queen," continued Salamon; "if only all American ventures in the Middle East could turn out so well."

"The book is not a royal tell-all," wrote Mary Delach Leonard in the *St. Louis Post Dispatch,* "although there are telling glimpses of world figures: During an Arab summit in Amman, Iraq's Saddam Hussein would eat only food prepared by his own staff. Prince Charles was the only British royal not to turn a cold shoulder to Jordan's royal couple during the first Persian Gulf crisis. And, she writes, Barbara Bush once sent a message through an American official that she considered Queen Noor a traitor."

Palm Beach Post critic Leslie Gray Streeter said that Noor is "best summed up in the last pages of the book by King Hussein, in the text of a letter he wrote to the Jordanian people shortly before his death. 'She, the Jordanian, who belongs to this country with every fiber of her being, holds her head high in the defense and services of this country's interest,' Hussein wrote. 'And she, like me, also endured many anxieties and shocks, but always placed her faith in God and hid her tears behind smiles.' And that, it seems, is the most queenly behavior of all."

Profits from the sale of the book went to the King Hussein Foundation, a nonprofit organization that funds health services in the Middle East and education programs that promote peace and democracy. Noor's extensive Web site lists complete information about the nonprofits and other organizations she founded, supports, or with which she is otherwise affiliated.

BIOGRAPHICAL AND CRITICAL SOURCES:

BOOKS

Noor, Queen, *Leap of Faith: Memoirs of an Unexpected Life,* Talk Miramax Books (New York, NY), 2003.

PERIODICALS

Atlanta Journal-Constitution, March 21, 2003, Moni Basu, review of *Leap of Faith: Memoirs of an Unexpected Life,* p. E7.
Booklist, March 15, 2003, Brad Hooper, review of *Leap of Faith,* p. 125.
Boston Herald, March 21, 2003, Rosemary Herbert, review of *Leap of Faith,* p. 51.
Good Housekeeping, April, 2003, Elise O'Shaughnessy, "The American Queen" (interview), p. 125.
Newsweek International, April 7, 2003, Richard Ernsberger, Jr., interview with Queen Noor.
New York Times Book Review, April 13, 2003, Julie Salamon, review of *Leap of Faith,* p. 4.
Palm Beach Post, April 27, 2003, Leslie Gray Streeter, review of *Leap of Faith,* p. 4J.
Publishers Weekly, March 17, 2003, review of *Leap of Faith,* p. 68.
San Francisco Chronicle, March 18, 2003, Leah Garchik, review of *Leap of Faith,* p. D10.
St. Louis Post-Dispatch, March 18, 2003, Mary Delach Leonard, review of *Leap of Faith,* p. E1.

ONLINE

Queen Noor Home Page, http://www.noor.gov.jo/ (May 6, 2003.)*

*   *   *

AMATO, Mary 1961-

PERSONAL: Born January 3, 1961, in Belvidere, IL; married Ivan Amato (a science writer); children: Maxwell, Simon. *Education:* Indiana University, B.S.; Johns Hopkins University, M.A. (creative writing).

ADDRESSES: Agent—c/o Author Mail, Holiday House, 425 Madison Ave., New York, NY 10017. *E-mail*—amato@erols.com.

CAREER: Writer, puppeteer, choreographer, and teacher. Cofounder of Firefly Shadow Theater (puppet company.)

AWARDS, HONORS: Keisler Prize for Poetry, Indiana University; fellowship for Children's Novel-in-Progress, Heekin Foundation; nonfiction book grant and National Magazine Merit Award, both from Society of Children's Book Writers and Illustrators (SCBWI); Arts in Education grant, Target; grant in the Arts, *Washington Post;* visiting artist grant, Arts & Humanities Council of Montgomery County, MD; Highest Quality Titles selection, New England Children's Bookselling advisory council, 2000, for *The Word Eater.*

WRITINGS:

The Word Eater, illustrated by Christopher Ryniak, Holiday House (New York, NY), 2000.
The Riot Brothers (short stories), illustrated by Ethan Long, Holiday House (New York, NY), in press.

Contributor of articles, essays, and poems to periodicals for children and adults, including *Muse, Cicada, Washington Post, Parenting,* and *Mothering.*

SIDELIGHTS: Although she had been a nonfiction writer, puppeteer, and choreographer for some time, in 2000 Mary Amato made her debut as a children's book writer with *The Word Eater,* finally realizing a childhood dream. "I always wanted to be a writer, but it took me a long time to believe that I could actually become one," she told *CA.* "I started writing at the age of seven when my mother handed me a little spiral notebook and told me to keep a journal of our trip to California. I liked the fact that I could record something in my journal and then read it later. My favorite book as a child was *Harriet the Spy* by Louise Fitzhugh because Harriet was a terrific journal keeper."

In *The Word Eater,* Amato portrays a sixth-grade girl named Lerner who discovers Fip, an unusual book worm. Not only does Fip eat words, but when he does, the real objects named by the words disappear permanently. The work caught the attention of reviewers, including *Booklist*'s Susan Dove Lempke, who, despite noticing some unevenness in the narrative, called Amato's "basic idea . . . creative" and observed "some intriguing moments" in the book. Writing in *School Library Journal,* Doris Gebel commended the book's humor, remarking that the plot is full of "clever, if far-fetched events."

Reflecting on her new career, Amato told *CA:* "I love to read, and I love to write. Not all writers love to write. I wake up every morning and can't wait to sit at my dining room table and write. (I write on a laptop computer with a cup of tea nearby.) I especially love to write books for kids ages seven to twelve. I think that's because I needed books when I was a kid. I turned to books when I was lonely or sad or confused or bored. It is extremely fun to think that kids are reading my books."

Believing that "imagination is like a muscle. The more you exercise your imagination, the bigger it is," Amato exercises her imagination by both writing and by continuing her work as a choreographer in musical theater and performing shadow plays with the Firefly Shadow Theater, a company that she cofounded.

BIOGRAPHICAL AND CRITICAL SOURCES:

PERIODICALS

Booklist, October 15, 2000, Susan Dove Lempke, review of *The Word Eater,* p. 437.
Horn Book Guide, spring, 2001, review of *The Word Eater.*
Language Arts, September, 2001, review of *The Word Eater,* p. 79.
Publishers Weekly, July 3, 2000, review of *The Word Eater,* p. 71.
School Library Journal, October, 2000, Doris Gebel, review of *The Word Eater,* p. 155.

*   *   *

AMIOTTE, Arthur (Douglas) 1942-

PERSONAL: Born March 25, 1942, in Pine Ridge, SD; received name Warpa Tanka Kuciyela, 1942; received name Wanbli Hocoka Waste, 1972. *Education:* Northern State College (now University), Aberdeen, SD, B.S., 1964; graduate study at University of Oklahoma, University of South Dakota, and Pennsylvania State University; University of Montana, M.I.S., 1983; also studied at Institute of American Indian Art.

ADDRESSES: Office—c/o Brandon University, Brandon, Manitoba, Canada.

CAREER: Worked as art teacher at public schools and lecturer on art and Lakota history, religion, and culture, 1964-71; U.S. Department of the Interior, director of curriculum development at Aberdeen Area Office, 1971-74; worked as instructor in Lakota studies, 1975-80; Standing Rock Community College, Fort Yates, ND, chair of Lakota Studies Department, 1978-82; Brandon University, Brandon, Manitoba, Canada, professor of Native studies, beginning 1982. Painter, illustrator, and designer of logos, book covers, and posters, 1979—. Smithsonian Institution, curator at Museum of Natural History, 1991; Buffalo Bill Historical Center, Cody, WY, member of board of trustees, 1992; Commission for Indian Memorial, Little Big Horn, MT, member, 1994; National Museum of the American Indian, member of Indian advisory committee, 1995; Institute of American Indian Arts, member, council of regents; member of presidential advisory council for the Performing Arts, Indian Arts and Crafts Board and National Foundation for the Advancement of Arts; Artists at Giverny Program, fellow, 1997. *Exhibitions:* Work represented in dozens of solo and group exhibitions, including Akta Lakota Museum, 1990-91, Los Angeles Craft and Folk Art Museum, 1992-93, American Indian Contemporary Art, San Francisco, CA, 1993-96, National Museum of the American Indian, 1994-95, and at American Art Gallery, New York, NY, Galleria del sol Crafts Gallery, Santa Barbara, CA, Fairtree Crafts Gallery, New York, NY, Hand and the Spirit Crafts Gallery, Scottsdale, AZ, and Via Gambaro Gallery, Washington, DC; work represented in collections throughout the United States, including Haffenreffer Museum, Institute of American Indian Arts Museum, Museum of Natural History, New York Port Authority, and Whitney Gallery of Western Art.

MEMBER: National Native American Art Studies Association (member of board of directors).

AWARDS, HONORS: D.Lakota studies, Oglala Lakota College, 1988; award for outstanding contribution to South Dakota history, Augustana College Dakota History Conference and Center for Western Studies, 1992; Getty Foundation grant, 1993; LL.D., Brandon University, 1994.

WRITINGS:

(Compiler, with Myles Libhart, and contributor) *Photographs and Poems by Sioux Children from the Porcupine Day School, Pine Ridge Indian Reservation, South Dakota,* Tipi Shop, Sioux Indian Museum (Rapid City, SD), 1971.

Contributor to books, including foreword to *The Sacred Pipe: Black Elk's Account of the Seven Rites of the Oglala Sioux,* by Joseph Epes Brown, University of Oklahoma Press (Norman, OK), 1983; *Sioux Indian Religion,* edited by Raymond DeMallie and Douglas Parks, University of Oklahoma Press (Norman, OK), 1985; *An Illustrated History of the Arts of South Dakota,* Center for Western Studies, Augustana College (Sioux Falls, SD), 1989; *I Become Part of It,* edited by D. M. Dooling and Paul Jordan, Parabola Books (New York, NY), 1989; and *Spirit Beings and Sun Dancers: Black Hawk's Vision of the Lakota World,* by Janet Catherine Berlo, George Braziller (New York, NY), 2001. Contributor to periodicals, including *Parabola.*

BIOGRAPHICAL AND CRITICAL SOURCES:

BOOKS

St. James Guide to Native North American Artists, St. James Press (Detroit, MI), 1998, pp. 15-19.
This Path We Travel: Celebrations of Contemporary Native American Creativity, Smithsonian Institution (Washington, DC), 1994.

PERIODICALS

American Indian Art, Volume 10, number 2, 1985, Barbara Loeb, "Arthur Amiotte's Banners."
Christian Science Monitor, August 11, 1987, Hattie Clark, "Art That Spans Two Cultures."
Inside the Black Hills, fall, 1990, Marguerite Mullaney, "Inside Arthur Amiotte."

OTHER

Lakota Sacred Traditions (documentary film), British Broadcasting Corp., 1992.
Museum of Natural History (documentary film), Smithsonian Institution (Washington, DC), 1993.
Somewhere, Sometime: Tribal Arts 1989 (documentary film), South Dakota Public Television, 1989.*

* * *

ANNAQTUSSI TULURIALIK, Ruth 1934-

PERSONAL: Surname is sometimes transliterated as Annaqtusii, Annuktoshe, Annaqtuusi, or Anaktose; born 1934, in Kazan River, Northwest Territories, Canada; daughter of Martha Talerook; adopted daughter of Thomas (an Anglican catechist) and Elisapee Tapatai; married Hugh Tulurialik; children: Barbara Qulaut, Marianne Paunngat, Casey Unurniq.

ADDRESSES: Agent—c/o Author Mail, Oxford University Press, 198 Madison Ave., New York, NY 10016.

CAREER: Painter. Worked as Inuit interpreter at government agencies and retail venues in Baker Lake, Northwest Territories, Canada; Sanavik Cooperative, member and artist. *Exhibitions:* Work represented in solo show, Art Gallery of Windsor, Windsor, Ontario, Canada, and in group shows, including work at Winnipeg Art Gallery, Agnes Etherington Art Centre, Kingston, Ontario, Canada, National Museum of Man, Ottawa, Ontario, Canada, United Nations General Assembly Building, New York, NY, and Macdonald Stewart Art Centre, Guelph, Ontario, Canada.

WRITINGS:

(With David F. Pelly) *Qikaaluktut: Images of Inuit Life,* Oxford University Press (New York, NY), 1986.

BIOGRAPHICAL AND CRITICAL SOURCES:

BOOKS

Jackson, Marion E., and David F. Pelly, *The Vital Vision: Drawings by Ruth Annaqtussi Tulurialik,* [Windsor, Ontario, Canada], 1986.
St. James Guide to Native North American Artists, St. James Press (Detroit, MI), 1998, pp. 25-27.*

ANSARY, Mir Tamim 1948-

PERSONAL: Born November 4, 1948, in Kabul, Afghanistan; son of Mir Amanuddin (a university teacher and administrator) and Terttu (a teacher; maiden name, Palm) Ansary; married Deborah Gale Krant (a conference director), 1981; children: Jessamyn, Elina. *Ethnicity:* "Arab, Mongolian, Finnish." *Education:* Reed College, B.A. (literature), 1970. *Politics:* Liberal. *Religion:* "Secular."

ADDRESSES: Agent—Julie Castiglia, 1155 Camino Del Mar, Ste. 510, Del Mar, CA 92014. *E-mail*—JACLAgency@aol.com.

CAREER: Portland Scribe, Portland, OR, staff writer, 1972-76; The Asia Foundation, San Francisco, CA, assistant editor of *Asian Student,* 1976-78, became editor of development publications, 1979; Harcourt Brace Jovanovich, Orlando, FL, school department editor, 1980-89; freelance writer, educational consultant, and columnist, 1990—.

WRITINGS:

Afghanistan: Fighting for Freedom, Dillon Press (New York, NY), 1991.
Matter: Solids, Liquids, and Gases (part of "Science All Around Me" series), Heinemann Library (Des Plaines, IL), 1996.
Score Booster Handbook: For Reading and Language Arts, Focused Learning (Austin, TX), 2000.
West of Kabul, East of New York: An Afghan American Story (memoir), Farrar, Straus & Giroux (New York, NY), 2002.

Contributor of chapters on Islamic history to *World History: Patterns of Interaction,* McDougal Littell, 1999, and fiction and nonfiction selections to reading anthology *Reach for Literacy,* Rigby, 2002. Development editor of works on reading and geography. Author of column "The Learning Beat" for www.encarta.msn.com.

"CAUGHT READING" SERIES

Carmen's Card, Globe Fearon (Paramus, NJ), 1995.
The Sea House, Globe Fearon (Paramus, NJ), 1995.
Spiders from Outer Space, Globe Fearon (Paramus, NJ), 1995.
The Lost Boy, Globe Fearon (Paramus, NJ), 1995.

"COOL COLLECTIONS" SERIES

Model Cars, Rigby Interactive Library (Crystal Lake, IL), 1997.
Stamps, Rigby Interactive Library (Crystal Lake, IL), 1997.
Dolls, Rigby Interactive Library (Crystal Lake, IL), 1997.
Natural Objects, Rigby Interactive Library (Crystal Lake, IL), 1997.
Insects, Rigby Interactive Library (Crystal Lake, IL), 1997.

"SUPER READERS" SERIES

Mysterious Places, J. Weston Walch (Portland, ME), 1997.
Creepy Creatures, J. Weston Walch (Portland, ME), 1997.
Unbelievable Beasts, illustrated by Carl M. Brand, J. Weston Walch (Portland, ME), 1998.
Baffling Disappearances, illustrated by Carl M. Brand, J. Weston Walch (Portland, ME), 1998.
Great Crime Busters, illustrated by Carl M. Brand, J. Weston Walch (Portland, ME), 1998.

"HOLIDAY HISTORIES" SERIES

Veterans Day, Heinemann Library (Des Plaines, IL), 1999.
Labor Day, Heinemann Library (Des Plaines, IL), 1999.
Martin Luther King, Jr., Day, Heinemann Library (Des Plaines, IL), 1999.
Memorial Day, Heinemann Library (Des Plaines, IL), 1999.
Columbus Day, Heinemann Library (Des Plaines, IL), 1999.
Presidents' Day, Heinemann Library (Des Plaines, IL), 1999.
Earth Day, Heinemann Library (Des Plaines, IL), 2000.
Thanksgiving Day, Heinemann Library (Des Plaines, IL), 2001.
Election Day, Heinemann Library (Des Plaines, IL), 2002.
Independence Day, Heinemann Library (Des Plaines, IL), 2002.

Flag Day, Heinemann Library (Des Plaines, IL), 2002.

Arbor Day, Heinemann Library (Des Plaines, IL), 2002.

"ADVENTURES PLUS" SERIES; EDUCATIONAL COMIC BOOKS

Alien Alert, Focused Learning (Austin, TX), 2000.

Treasure Hunt, Focused Learning (Austin, TX), 2000.

Lost in Time, Focused Learning (Austin, TX), 2000.

Runaway Spaceship, Focused Learning (Austin, TX), 2000.

That's Some Dog, Focused Learning (Austin, TX), 2000.

Case of the Missing Millie, Focused Learning (Austin, TX), 2000.

"NATIVE AMERICANS" SERIES

Plains Indians, Heinemann Library (Des Plaines, IL), 2000.

California Indians, Heinemann Library (Des Plaines, IL), 2000.

Eastern Woodlands Indians, Heinemann Library (Des Plaines, IL), 2000.

Southwest Indians, Heinemann Library (Des Plaines, IL), 2000.

Northwest Coast Indians, Heinemann Library (Des Plaines, IL), 2000.

Great Basin Indians, Heinemann Library (Des Plaines, IL), 2000.

Arctic Peoples, Heinemann Library (Des Plaines, IL), 2000.

Plateau Indians, Heinemann Library (Des Plaines, IL), 2000.

Southeast Indians, Heinemann Library (Des Plaines, IL), 2000.

Subarctic Indians, Heinemann Library (Des Plaines, IL), 2002.

"STATE STUDIES: CALIFORNIA" SERIES

California History, Heinemann Library (Des Plaines, IL), 2002.

All around California: Regions and Resources, Heinemann Library (Des Plaines, IL), 2002.

People of California, Heinemann Library (Des Plaines, IL), 2002.

(With Stephen Feinstein) *Uniquely California,* Heinemann Library (Des Plaines, IL), 2003.

(With Stephen Feinstein) *California Plants and Animals,* Heinemann Library (Des Plaines, IL), 2003.

(With Stephen Feinstein) *California Native Peoples,* Heinemann Library (Des Plaines, IL), 2003.

ADAPTATIONS: West of Kabul, East of New York: An Afghan American Story was produced as a sound recording, Recording for the Blind and Dyslexic (Princeton, NJ), 2002.

SIDELIGHTS: After working as an editor for an educational publisher, Mir Tamim Ansary struck out on his own in 1990. For over a decade, he has been writing juvenile nonfiction, including a handful of series for readers in grades one through five. "Writing nonfiction for very young children is like writing poetry, I have found: every word and all its nuances count," Ansary told *CA.* "It's easy to assume one must sacrifice accuracy to comprehension in order to recount, say, the history of the Industrial Revolution in a book a seven-year-old can read; but to me, that assumption is defeatism. My aim in writing about any given subject has always been to give children a picture that further information will only elaborate and enrich, never falsify."

Born in 1948, Ansary was the son of the first Afghan ever to marry an American woman who was also the first American woman ever to live in Afghanistan as an Afghan. With his father and mother both in education and government administration, Ansary's world was richer in educational opportunities than many of his compatriots. It is thus not surprising that Ansary's love of reading and sharing knowledge came early, as he recalled to *CA:* "Growing up in Afghanistan where TV didn't exist and movies were extremely rare, I found my earliest sources as a writer in the voices of my elders spinning stories in the dark for us children huddled in groups under blankets; and also in the *Book of Knowledge,* a profusely illustrated high-interest, English-language encyclopedia my family had—I used to pore through those volumes every day while the others were at school or work; and then again at night pour back out to them the wonderful things I'd learned that day about elephants and stars."

At age sixteen, Ansary immigrated to the United States. After graduating from Reed College in 1970, he traveled throughout the Islamic world and worked for nine years as an educational editor for Harcourt Brace Jovanovich. In 1990, he began a new career in publishing, that of a freelance writer. Putting this in perspective, Ansary told *CA:* "Now I am an elder myself, spinning stories for an audience I can't physically see, and I'm still that kid, too, trying to tell everyone about the astounding things I've discovered while rummaging through some (metaphorical) Book of Knowledge."

Among Ansary's titles for children are his "Holiday Histories" series, which, in picture book format, explains the significance and origin of major American holidays; the "Cool Collections" series, which gives very basic information on starting collections; and the "Native Americans" series, which presents rudimentary knowledge about the various native tribes that have inhabited the United States. Ansary has also written about his native country in *Afghanistan: Fighting for Freedom,* which includes information that could only be supplied by first-hand experience and the "great warmth" that only a native can bring to the subject, claimed Cynthia Rieben of *Voice of Youth Advocates.*

Elaborating on his desire to give children information that will enrich their lives, Ansary concluded, "As it turns out, that aim drives all my work now, both for children and adults, both in fiction and nonfiction: to get to the essence and deliver it with clarity in my natural speaking voice."

BIOGRAPHICAL AND CRITICAL SOURCES:

PERIODICALS

Booklist, January 1, 1999, Ilene Cooper, reviews of *Labor Day* and *Veterans Day,* p. 880; February 1, 2002, Ilene Cooper, reviews of *Earth Day* and *Election Day,* p. 942.

School Library Journal, March, 1992, Nancy E. Zuwiyya, review of *Afghanistan: Fighting for Freedom,* p. 243; July, 1997, Pamela K. Bomboy, reviews of *Dolls, Model Cars,* and *Stamps,* p. 80; August, 1997, Karey Wehner, reviews of *Insects* and *Natural Objects,* p. 145; February, 1999, Pamela K. Bomboy, reviews of *Columbus Day, Labor Day,* and *Martin Luther King, Jr., Day,* pp. 94-95; January, 2000, Sue Sherif, reviews of *Arctic Peoples* and *Northwest Coast Indians,* pp. 114-

115; January, 2000, Darcy Schild, reviews of *Great Basin Indians* and *Southwest Indians,* p. 115; November, 2000, Dona J. Helmer, reviews of *California Indians* and *Subarctic Indians,* p. 139.

Voice of Youth Advocates, June, 1922, Cynthia Rieben, review of *Afghanistan,* p. 117.

*　　　*　　　*

ANTHONY, Susan B(rownell) 1820-1906

PERSONAL: Born February 15, 1820, in Adams, MA; died March 13, 1906, in Rochester, NY; daughter of Daniel (a teacher and manager of cotton mills) and Lucy Read Anthony. *Education:* Attended a Quaker school in Philadelphia, PA.

CAREER: Activist for women's suffrage and other social reforms; teacher, lecturer, and writer. New York State school system, teacher, 1839-46; Canajoharie Academy, Canajoharie, NY, principal of female department, 1846-49; Woman's State Temperance Society, cofounder, 1852; American Anti-Slavery Society, New York agent, 1856-c. 1863; Women s Loyal National League, cofounder, 1863; *Revolution* (suffragist newspaper), cofounder, 1868, and coeditor, 1868-70; National Woman Suffrage Association, cofounder, 1869; International Council of Women, founder, 1888; National American Woman Suffrage Association (formed through merger of National Woman Suffrage Association and American Woman Suffrage Association), cofounder, 1889, president, 1892-1900; International Women's Suffrage Alliance, founder, 1904.

WRITINGS:

(Editor, with others) *A History of Woman Suffrage,* Fowler & Welles (New York, NY) Volumes 1-3 (with Matilda Joslyn Gage and Elizabeth Cady Stanton) 1881-88, Volume 4 (with Ida Husted Harper), 1903, reprinted, Ayer (Salem, NH), 1985.

Elizabeth Cady Stanton, Susan B. Anthony: Correspondence, Writings, Speeches, edited and with a critical commentary by Ellen Carol DuBois, Schocken Books (New York, NY), 1981, revised as *The Elizabeth Cady Stanton-Susan B. Anthony Reader: Correspondence, Writings, Speeches,* University Press of New England (Boston, MA), 1992.

Failure Is Impossible: Susan B. Anthony in Her Own Words, edited by Lynn Sherr, Times Books (New York, NY), 1995.

The Selected Papers of Elizabeth Cady Stanton and Susan B. Anthony, Volume 1: In the School of Anti-Slavery, 1840-1866, edited by Ann Gordon, Rutgers University Press (New Brunswick, NJ), 1997.

SIDELIGHTS: To many Americans, the name Susan B. Anthony is synonymous with the women's suffrage movement. Anthony came to this cause with experience in campaigns against liquor and slavery. She had been outraged when, at a meeting in 1852, male temperance activists refused to allow women to speak. This led Anthony and her close friend Elizabeth Cady Stanton to form a women's temperance group and to work more and more for women's rights. In her youth, Anthony had seen her mother's personal belongings auctioned off to pay the family's debts—something that convinced her that women should have the right to own and manage property. In 1860, thanks to Anthony and Stanton's work, New York State changed its law to allow married women to own property in their own names and to have a host of other financial rights and responsibilities. Unfortunately, most of the reforms won in New York were repealed within a few years. During the U.S. Civil War, Anthony vigorously campaigned for the abolition of slavery, and she and other supporters of women's rights hoped that after the Union victory, women would be granted the right to vote along with the newly freed slaves. They were disappointed, however, with moderate and liberal men telling them it was "the Negro's hour" and that women would have to wait, and more conservative elements ridiculing the very idea of women voting. Anthony and Stanton responded by forming, in 1869, the National Woman Suffrage Association, which sought a constitutional amendment that would grant women voting rights—a goal finally realized in 1920, fourteen years after Anthony's death. Her years of activism for women's suffrage and other rights saw her arrested for voting in Rochester, New York, in the presidential election of 1872; editing a feminist newspaper, *Revolution;* and speaking and writing extensively in support of her cause.

"Anthony's continuous work and her experience as a newspaper writer and publisher made possible a considerable body of literature," commented a contributor to *Feminist Writers.* Her many contributions include serving as an editor of and contributor to the first four volumes of *A History of Woman Suffrage* (the last two volumes of this six-volume work were published after Anthony's death). Anthony was the "catalyst" for this work, covering the first fifty years of the suffrage movement, the *Feminist Writers* essayist noted, adding that Anthony's efforts as a writer and editor have "longstanding relevance and importance to both women and students of political history, as well as to those wishing to understand women's activism in various reform movements." Doris Yoakum Twitchell, in an essay for *A History and Criticism of American Public Address,* pointed out that Anthony kept up a "voluminous correspondence" all her life, and that "the records of her experiences, which came to fill thirty-three volumes of old ledgers, and her daily journal aided in the writing of *The History of Woman Suffrage.*" Anthony's other writings include suffrage tracts, newspaper stories, and her many speeches. "Miss Anthony spoke to the reason of her listeners and upheld her issues with facts, figures, and examples," Twitchell related. "Her recorded speeches are crowded with statistics and direct quotations from authorities, law, and history." Anthony "excelled in argument," Twitchell continued, and "often spoke of the injustice of allowing any class of people to have control over another. Cruelty and unfairness resulted from allowing the rich to rule the poor, the white to rule the black." She spoke to audiences that were often hostile and sometimes armed, and carried on her work even though she was held up to scorn not only for her ideas but also for her appearance and her unmarried status.

Anthony was at the center of numerous controversies as editor, with Stanton, of the *Revolution,* a newspaper that they published from 1868 to 1870. The paper advocated for women's suffrage and equal rights generally, "championing the right to women to any type of work or education," observed Lynne Masel-Walters in *Journalism Quarterly.* It also supported labor unions, the eight-hour workday, civil service reform, and the abolition of child labor. And the editors dared to discuss abortion and prostitution, both of which they opposed but saw as "a product of bad conditions rather than of bad women," Masel-Walters related. "These conditions would be improved once the female had a more healthful life, an education and enfranchisement." The paper "was considered radical" for addressing these usually taboo subjects. It also made enemies because of its financial backer, George Francis Train, a wealthy eccentric whose favored causes included free trade, currency expansion, and

Irish independence as well as women s rights, but who also was a racist who had sympathized with the South during the Civil War. The paper published Train's writings on financial matters and other features aimed at empowering women to manage money; additional contents outside the strictly political included poetry, fiction, and book reviews. In 1869, Train stopped writing for the *Revolution,* believing his connection with the paper was costing it subscribers and support. He pledged to continue putting money into the paper, but this promise "was never kept," Masel-Walters noted. Finally, in 1870, competition in the form of the better-financed, more conservative suffrage paper *Woman's Journal* forced Anthony and Stanton to give up the *Revolution.* "It was such a short life for such a lively publication," Masel-Walters remarked. "But it was not a life without meaning. . . . The newspaper set down for the first time in a major national forum arguments for women s equality that are still being used."

Likewise, Anthony's writings continue to be published and read nearly a century after her death. In 1997 came the publication of *The Selected Papers of Elizabeth Cady Stanton and Susan B. Anthony, Volume 1: In the School of Anti-Slavery, 1840-1866,* edited by Ann Gordon and inaugurating a projected six-volume series. *New Republic* contributor Christine Stansell called the volume "captivating" and further reported that it illustrates how the two women influenced and complemented each other: "*The Selected Papers* uphold a now common view of Stanton as the brains of the pair and Anthony as the dogsbody organizer, but the book's offerings deepen the meaning of both roles. . . . The friendship had the consequence of attaching some of Stanton's intellectual boldness to Anthony the schoolteacher-organizer, and some of Anthony' s political acumen to Stanton the cerebral housewife. . . . 'In the human soul, the steps between discontent and action are few and short indeed,' she once observed to her abolitionist cousin Gerrit Smith; and it was in large part Anthony who helped her to compress the distance."

BIOGRAPHICAL AND CRITICAL SOURCES:

BOOKS

Anthony, Katharine, *Susan B. Anthony: Her Personal History and Her Era,* Doubleday (Garden City, NY), 1954.

Anthony, Susan B., Matilda Joslyn Gage, Elizabeth Cady Stanton, and Ida Husted Harper, editors, *A History of Woman Suffrage,* six volumes, Fowler & Welles (New York, NY), 1881-1922, reprinted, Ayer (Salem, NH), 1985.

Barry, Kathleen, *Susan B. Anthony: A Biography of a Singular Feminist,* New York University Press (New York, NY), 1988.

Contemporary Heroes and Heroines, Gale (Detroit, MI), 1998.

Dorr, Rheta Childe, *Susan B. Anthony: The Woman Who Changed the Mind of a Nation,* Frederick A. Stokes (New York, NY), 1924.

DuBois, Ellen Carol, editor, *Elizabeth Cady Stanton, Susan B. Anthony: Correspondence, Writings, Speeches,* Schocken Books (New York, NY), 1981, revised as *The Elizabeth Cady Stanton-Susan B. Anthony Reader: Correspondence, Writings, Speeches,* University Press of New England (Boston, MA), 1992.

Encyclopedia of World Biography, second edition, Gale (Detroit, MI), 1998.

Feminist Writers, St. James Press (Detroit, MI), 1996.

Harper, Ida Husted, *The Life and Work of Susan B. Anthony,* three volumes, Hollenbeck Press (Indianapolis, IN), 1898-1908, reprinted, Arno Press (New York, NY), 1969.

Gay and Lesbian Biography, St. James Press (Detroit, MI), 1997.

Gordon, Ann, editor, *The Selected Papers of Elizabeth Cady Stanton and Susan B. Anthony, Volume 1: In the School of Anti-Slavery, 1840-1866,* Rutgers University Press (New Brunswick, NJ), 1997.

Hochmuth, Marie Kathryn, editor, *A History and Criticism of American Public Address,* Volume 3, McGraw (New York, NY), 1955, pp. 97-130.

Historic World Leaders, Gale (Detroit, MI), 1994.

Lutz, Alma, *Susan B. Anthony: Rebel, Crusader, Humanitarian,* Beacon Press (Boston, MA), 1959.

Mason, Gabriel Richard, editor, *Great American Liberals,* Starr King Press (Boston, MA), 1956, pp. 99-108.

Sherr, Lynn, editor, *Failure Is Impossible: Susan B. Anthony in Her Own Words,* Times Books (New York, NY), 1995.

Twentieth-Century Literary Criticism, Volume 84, Gale (Detroit, MI), 1999, pp. 1-59.

Ward, Geoffrey C., *Not for Ourselves Alone: The Story of Elizabeth Cady Stanton and Susan B. Anthony: An Illustrated History,* based on a documentary film by Ken Burns and Paul Barnes, Knopf (New York, NY), 1999.

PERIODICALS

Journalism Quarterly, summer, 1976, Lynne Masel-Walters, "Their Rights and Nothing More: A History of *The Revolution,* 1868-70," pp. 242-251.
New Republic, August 10, 1998, Christine Stansell, "The Road from Seneca Falls: The Feminism of the Mothers, the Feminism of the Daughters, the Feminism of the Girls," p. 26.

OTHER

Not for Ourselves Alone: The Story of Elizabeth Cady Stanton and Susan B. Anthony (documentary film), Florentine Films, 1999.*

*   *   *

APOSTOLOUS, Anna
    See DOHERTY, P(aul) C.

*   *   *

ARMSTRONG, Lance 1971-

PERSONAL: Born September 18, 1971, in Plano, TX; son of Linda Walling; married Kristin Richard, May 8, 1998; children: Luke, Isabelle Rose, Grace Elizabeth.

ADDRESSES: Office—Lance Armstrong Foundation, P.O. Box 13026, Austin, TX 78711.

CAREER: Professional cyclist.

AWARDS, HONORS: Triathlete Rookie of the Year, 1988; World Road-Racing Champion, 1993; U.S. Professional Champion, 1993; winner, Tour DuPont, 1995; Velo New American Male Cyclist of the Year, 1995; winner, Tour de Luxembourg, Rheinland-Pfalz Rundfarht (Germany), and Cascade Classic (Oregon), all 1998; winner, Tour de France, 1999, 2000, 2001, 2002.

WRITINGS:

(With Sally Jenkins) *It's Not About the Bike: My Journey Back to Life,* Putnam (New York, NY), 2000.

(With Chris Carmichael and Peter Joffre Nye) *The Lance Armstrong Performance Program: Seven Weeks to the Perfect Ride,* Rodale (Emmaus, PA), 2000.

ADAPTATIONS: It's Not About the Bike: My Journey Back to Life was made into an audio recording read by Oliver Wyman, Highbridge, 2000.

SIDELIGHTS: Sometimes referred to as the "Golden Boy of American Cycling," Lance Armstrong is a world champion bicycle racer. As a four-time consecutive winner of the most prestigious cycling race, the Tour de France, Armstrong has become one of the most celebrated athletes in the world. But his biggest hurdle in life was not becoming a champion bicyclist. In his autobiography, *It's Not about the Bike: My Journey Back to Life,* Armstrong makes it clear that his toughest fight—and the one that has had the most lasting impact on him—was his battle with testicular cancer.

From a young age, Armstrong showed that he was a natural athlete. By the time he was thirteen years old, he had won the Iron Kids Triathlon, and he turned professional triathlete when he was just sixteen. His unusual success led him to be tested by the Cooper Institute for Aerobic Research in Houston, Texas, where the researchers discovered that the young athletic phenomenon was in the top two percent of all humans in terms of his cardiovascular system and ability to take in oxygen.

Although he was earning nearly $20,000 a year as a triathlete by the time he was seventeen, Armstrong was most drawn to the cycling segment of the triathlon. By the time he reached his senior year in high school, he was devoted to cycling. He quickly rose in the amateur ranks, becoming the U.S. National Amateur Champion in 1991. His switch to professional cycling was not immediately successful, but Armstrong's natural talents and his inner drive soon led him to numerous championships and titles. In 1992, at the age of twenty-one, Armstrong became the youngest cyclist ever to win a stage of the Tour de France. The following year he won the 1993 World Championship.

As Armstrong explains in his autobiography, however, his life was about to be turned upside down. Armstrong began to have pain and swelling in his groin but did not seek medical help because he thought it was related to his long hours on a bicycle during training. But in 1996, at the age of twenty-five, Armstrong woke up one morning to find himself coughing blood, and his right testicle began to swell. A visit to the doctor not only confirmed that he had testicular cancer, but that it had spread to his brain and lungs. He was given only a fifty percent chance of survival. In his book, Armstrong outlines his decision to "fight like hell." Armstrong's emotional turmoil as he faced the diagnosis of cancer and his battle with the disease through chemotherapy and ultimate remission make up the core of his autobiography.

Armstrong readily admits that as an elite athlete he shared many traits with other such athletes, including a sense of arrogance. Because of their self-image of invincibility, Armstrong writes that he and other athletes are not "especially kind, considerate, merciful, benign, lenient, or forgiving, to themselves or anyone around them." However, about the night following his diagnosis, Armstrong writes, "As I sat in my house alone that first night, it was humbling to be so scared. More than that it was humanizing."

Aided by family and friends, Armstrong turned his attention to overcoming his cancer, learning all he could about the disease. Doctors eventually offered him two alternative courses of treatment. A medical doctor from Vanderbilt University who was a bicycling enthusiast had heard about Armstrong's illness. He wrote to tell Armstrong that the standard treatment could scar his lungs, reducing their size and essentially ending any hopes he would have of returning to bicycle racing. Armstrong chose a second chemotherapy regiment that, although more aggressive with more short-term side effects, would have little effect on his lungs.

As his therapy began to take effect, Armstrong once again began thinking about racing and was training a mere five months after his diagnosis. But his comeback wasn't easy. In his autobiography, he writes, "Deep down, I wasn't ready. Had I understood more about survivorship, I would have recognized that my comeback attempt was bound to be fraught with psychological problems." Armstrong notes that he was burdened by "doubt, and some buried resentment, too." Part of the resentment stemmed from his decreased salary and ability to make money through endorsements. "I sarcastically called it an 80-percent cancer tax," Armstrong writes. Although he had been

training and felt that he was in good physical condition, Armstrong found himself uncharacteristically quitting a race when he dropped out of the Paris-Nice competition during a cold day in the pouring rain. Armstrong returned to his home in Austin, Texas, with the intention of never racing again. But a trip to North Carolina with an old riding friend to train for a few "farewell" races, Armstrong's desire to be a champion returned.

Armstrong, who started the Lance Armstrong Foundation to raise cancer awareness and funds for cancer research, soon was not only celebrating a victory over cancer but was "officially" back into professional racing. He went on to win or place in several national events, including winning the Tour de Luxembourg and taking fourth place in the especially grueling three-week Vuelta España. But the best was yet to come. The following year Armstrong became the second American to win the Tour de France, the most prestigious bicycle race in the world. A year after his autobiography was published, Armstrong won his second Tour de France and has since gone on to win the race in 2001 and 2002.

Writing about Armstrong's autobiography in the *Times Literary Supplement,* Graham Robb noted, "Each part of the story—'growing up, fighting cancer and becoming a world-class cyclist'—serves as a metaphor of the others: the hero loses his illusions, develops a more sophisticated approach to cycling and human relationships, and turns his self-destruction to profit." In a review for the *School Library Journal,* Katherine Fitch called the book a "fabulous tribute to the strength of the human spirit" and an "inspiration to everyone." John Maxymuk, writing in the *Library Journal,* called Armstrong's writing style "vibrant and immediate whether he is detailing events from childhood, racing challenges, the demands of cancer treatment, the in vitro fertilization process, or the joy of becoming a father." A *Publishers Weekly* reviewer also noted the book's "disarming and spotless prose style, one far above par for sports memoirs."

Armstrong has continued to be the most accomplished and recognized names in cycling, a feat directly attributable to his reputation for training harder than any of his contemporaries. As for his dedication to cycling, Armstrong explained it succinctly to Michael Hall in *Texas Monthly.* "It's a hard sport," he said. "It isn't basketball, it's not football, it's not baseball. It's five, six hours in the hills and mountains. And you know what? You gotta love it."

BIOGRAPHICAL AND CRITICAL SOURCES:

BOOKS

Armstrong, Lance, and Sally Jenkins, *It's Not About the Bike: My Journey Back to Life,* Putnam (New York, NY), 2000.

PERIODICALS

Biography, fall, 2000, review of *It's Not About the Bike: My Journey Back to Life,* p. 788.
Booklist, May 15, 2000, Brenda Barrera, review of *It's Not About the Bike,* p. 1689; September 1, 2000, Brenda Barrera, review of *The Lance Armstrong Performance Program: 7 Weeks to the Perfect Ride,* p. 48.
Current Health 2, March, 2001, Scott Ingram, "Lance Armstrong: Super Cyclist and Survivor," p. 13.
Library Journal, June 15, 2000, John Maxymuk, review of *It's Not About the Bike,* p. 89.
Publishers Weekly, May 15, 2000, review of *It's Not About the Bike,* p. 106; August 7, 2000, review of *The Lance Armstrong Performance Program,* p. 92.
School Library Journal, January, 2001, Katherine Fitch, review of *It's Not about the Bike,* p. 161.
Sport Illustrated, September 17, 2001, Kelli Anderson, "Return of the Hero: Riding a Surge of American Interest, Lance Armstrong's First U.S. Race in Years Stirred Up a Huge Crowd," p. 3.
Texas Monthly, July, 2001, Michael Hall, "Lance Armstrong Has Something to Get fff His Chest," p. 70.
Times Literary Supplement, December 8, 2000, Graham Robb, "Tour de Force," p. 36.

ONLINE

Lance Armstrong Web site, http://www.lancearmstrong.com/ (May 19, 2003).*

*   *   *

ARTHUR, C. J.
See ARTHUR, Chris

*   *   *

ARTHUR, Chris 1955-
(C. J. Arthur)

PERSONAL: Born 1955, in Ireland. *Education:* University of Edinburgh, M.A., Ph.D., Dip.Ed.

ADDRESSES: Office—Department of Theology, Religious Studies and Islamic Studies, University of Wales, Lampeter, Ceredigion SA48 7ED, Wales. *E-mail*—arthurc@lamp.ac.uk.

CAREER: Essayist, poet, and educator. Worked as a warden on a nature reserve in Lough Neagh in Northern Ireland, TV researcher, and schoolteacher; Department of Theology, Religious Studies & Islamic Studies, University of Wales, Lampeter, senior lecturer in religious studies.

AWARDS, HONORS: Gifford fellow, University of St. Andrews; Akegarasu Haya International Essay Prize; Beverly Hayne Memorial Award for Young Writers.

WRITINGS:

(As C. J. Arthur) *In the Hall of Mirrors: Some Problems of Commitment in a Religiously Plural World,* Mowbray (London, England), 1986.
Biting the Bullet—Some Personal Reflections on Religious Education, Saint Andrew Press (Edinburgh, Scotland), 1990.
(Editor) *Religion and the Media: An Introductory Reader,* University of Wales Press (Cardiff, Wales), 1993.
Globalization of Communications: Some Religious Implications, WCC Publications (Geneva, Switzerland), 1998.
Irish Nocturnes, Davies Group (Aurora, CO), 1999.
Irish Willow, Davies Group (Aurora, CO), 2000.
Religious Pluralism: A Metaphorical Approach, Davies Group (Aurora, CO), 2000.

Contributor of essays to numerous books, including *Rethinking Media, Religion, and Culture,* Sage (London, England), 1997; *The Coming Deliverer,* University of Wales Press, 1997; and *Godly Things: Museums, Objects, and Religion,* Leicester University Press (London, England), 2000. Writings have also appeared in many literary publications, including *American Scholar, Antigonish Review, Centennial Review, Contemporary Review, Dalhousie Review, Descant, Event, Honest Ulsterman, North American Review, Northwest Review, Poetry Ireland Review, Southern Review, Threepenny Review,* and *Wascana Review.*

SIDELIGHTS: As an academician who teaches religious studies, Chris Arthur has written and edited several books about religion, as well as numerous articles and essays. Many of these appeared in his 1990 collection of articles titled *Biting the Bullet—Some Personal Reflections on Religious Education.* More recently, Arthur has reached a much wider audience and critical acclaim with his two books of personal essays titled *Irish Nocturnes* and *Irish Willow.*

Irish Nocturnes, the first of the two volumes to be published, contains eighteen essays. The essays include reflections on his childhood and the beauty of nature, ruminations on the history of linen and its symbolic and metaphorical meanings, thoughts about the word "ferrule," and a description of a frightening midnight walk through a tunnel to an old graveyard. Understandably, many of the essays also touch on religious issues, such as "The Empty Heart." In this essay, Arthur discusses current society's predilection for believing that there is nothing more to life than meets the eye and how religions provide important symbols to help people see the world as a place of mystery and awe.

"I borrow the term nocturnes from the Irish composer John Field to describe a particular type of essay—one written in a pensive, mediative, introspective key," Arthur told Charlotte Austin for an interview on the *Charlotte Austin Review* Web site. "You might also describe the book as creative non-fiction or literary non-fiction."

Irish Nocturnes has received wide critical acclaim. Thomas E. Kennedy, writing in the *Literary Review,* described the the book as "sheer pleasure, a swim through the waters of consciousness of a man clearly fluent and knowledgeable in the essay form, full of information and opinion, fact and personal observation, a book that rewards in many ways, virtually in every sentence." Kennedy also recommended, "Place it on your bed table, take it up at night before you sleep, and read one essay at a time—days, weeks, even months apart—before you shut the light." William Wall, writing a review for the *Local Ireland* Web site, called the collection of essays "an almost overwhelming gift, each a jewel in itself." In the *Boston Irish Reporter,* Thomas O'Grady wrote that the essays "create the impression of impromptu late-night reveries even as they register poignant and, at times, profound perceptions about the human condition."

Arthur's original intent was to publish one large volume of collected essays. But his publisher decided that two smaller volumes was a better approach.

Arthur's second volume of essays, *Irish Willow,* also received stellar reviews. "Arthur's philosophical musings are couched in poetic language and nature images that make for a compelling read," wrote Denise J. Stankovics in *Library Journal.* Writing in the *Los Angeles Times,* Susan Salter Reynolds noted that the "*Irish Willow* is a collection of essays on patterns and meaning and reasons for doing things and different ways of living." She also commented that Arthur's essays meet the test of a good essay in that "there is the feeling of wandering and meeting a conclusion, a lack of effort because meaning is everywhere, if we only tune ourselves perfectly." As an example, in his essay "Willow Pattern," Arthur comes to see his childhood collection of china pieces as part of greater pattern. Writing for *Emigrant Online,* reviewer Pauline Ferrie noted, "These fragments come to represent the different pieces of our lives and the lives of all those who have preceded our existence, as well as the fundamental fragmentation of the author's native Antrim."

"All I know is that I've been moved to express myself in writing for almost as long as I can remember," Arthur told Austin. "I've always been entranced by the beauty and intricacies of language, and still find it amazing what it can be used to convey."

BIOGRAPHICAL AND CRITICAL SOURCES:

PERIODICALS

Boston Irish Reporter, August, 2000, Thomas O'Grady, "A little Night Music, Please."
Contemporary Review, May, 2000, review of *Irish Nocturnes,* p. 277.
Library Journal, January, 2000, Michael W. Ellis, review of *Religious Pluralism: A Metaphorical Approach,* p. 119; spring, 2001, Thomas E. Kennedy, review of *Irish Willow,* p. 80.
Literary Review, spring, 2001, Thomas E. Kennedy, review of *Irish Nocturnes,* p. 602.
Los Angeles Times, March 17, 2002, Susan Salter Reynolds, review of *Irish Willow,* p. R-15.
Scottish Journal of Theology, June, 1993, Adrian Thatcher, review of *Biting the Bullet—Some Personal Reflections on Religious Education,* pp. 249-251; summer, 1996, Alan Main, review of *Religion and the Media,* p. 389.

ONLINE

Charlotte Austin Review Web site, http://collection.nlc-bnc.ca/100/202/300/charlotte/ (September 4, 2002), interview with Chris Arthur.

Emigrant Online, http://www.bookviewireland.ie (September 4, 2002), Pauline Ferrie, review of *Irish Willow.*

Local Ireland Web site, http://www.local.ie (May 29, 2002), William Wall, review of *Irish Nocturnes.**

*   *   *

AVERY, Evelyn 1940-

PERSONAL: Born January 18, 1940, in Brooklyn, NY; daughter of Jack (a grocer) and Fay (a grocer's assistant and homemaker; maiden name, Pittelman) Gross; married Sheldon Avery, June 26, 1960; children: Peter, Daniel. *Ethnicity:* "Jewish." *Education:* Brooklyn College (now of the City University of New York), B.A., 1961; University of Oregon, M.A., 1970, Ph.D., 1976. *Politics:* Independent. *Religion:* Jewish. *Hobbies and other interests:* Biblical study, film viewing and analysis, swimming.

ADDRESSES: Home—Baltimore, MD. *Office*—Department of English, Towson University, 800 York Rd., Towson, MD 21252; fax: 410-704-3999. *E-mail*—eavery@towson.edu.

CAREER: Towson University, Towson, MD, professor of English, 1975—, coordinator of Jewish studies, 1997—. Formerly taught at schools in New York, NY, and in Uganda.

MEMBER: National Association of Scholars (member of board of directors, 1990—), Bernard Malamud Society (coordinator, 1991—).

AWARDS, HONORS: Grant from National Endowment for the Humanities, 1980; fellow of Memorial Foundation for Jewish Culture, 1987; award for outstanding faculty member, Towson Alumni Association, 2002.

WRITINGS:

Rebels and Victims: The Fiction of Richard Wright and Bernard Malamud, Kennikat Press (Port Washington, NY), 1979.

Sex and the Modern Jewish Woman: An Annotated Bibliography, Fresh Meadows Press, 1986.
The Magic Worlds of Bernard Malamud, State University of New York Press (Albany, NY), 2001.

Coeditor, *Malamud Newsletter.*

WORK IN PROGRESS: Editing *Divided Selves: Jewish Women Writers in America.*

SIDELIGHTS: Evelyn Avery told *CA:* "Writing allows me to express distinctive points of view which do not conform to current literary trends such as post-modernism. If successful, I can reach a broader audience and discover like-minded colleagues who also wish to influence literary scholarship and teaching.

"A product of Jewish immigrant culture, I have been influenced by the Hebrew scriptures, Jewish history, and Yiddish and Jewish American literature as well as great European writers such as Fyodor Dostoievsky, Anton Chekhov, and Gustave Flaubert. Having taught in Ugandan and New York City schools and been raised in Brooklyn, I was also attracted to the interaction of ethnic groups, particularly blacks and Jews, about whom Bernard Malamud, the subject of my books, has also written.

"Although I had always considered writing, it was my grandmother's encouragement and Bernard Malamud's fiction that motivated my desire to share my thoughts with others. Malamud's *The Assistant,* which I read at age eighteen, so replicated my life in detail and spirit that I chose to focus on the author for my academic studies. His belief in the possibility of human regeneration is central to Jewish values, and his best works place him inside the Jewish canon of literature.

"Likewise, my grandmother, my *bubbe,* Shenah Pesha, believed in the potential goodness of people until they proved her wrong. And though she experienced horrible anti-Semitism in Poland, she recalled some acts of gentile kindness. She also believed in me and urged me to write about Jewish life. My current work in progress is dedicated to her influence."

B

BAGGOTT, Julianna 1970(?)-

PERSONAL: Born c. 1970; married David G.W. Scott; children: Phoebe, Finneas, Theo. *Education:* University of North Carolina at Greensboro, M.F.A., 1991.

ADDRESSES: Home—Newark, DE. *Agent*—c/o Author Mail, Simon & Schuster, 1230 Avenue of the Americas, New York, NY 10020. *E-mail*—email@julianna baggott.com.

CAREER: Writer and poet.

AWARDS, HONORS: Eyster Prize for short fiction, 1998; fellow, Delaware Division of Arts, Virginia Center for the Creative Arts, Ragdale Foundation, and Bread Loaf Writers' Conference.

WRITINGS:

This Country of Mothers (poetry), Crab Orchard Review and Southern Illinois University Press (Carbondale, IL), 2001.
Girl Talk, Pocket Books (New York, NY), 2001.
The Miss America Family, Pocket Books (New York, NY), 2002.
The Madam: A Novel, Pocket Books (New York, NY), 2003.

Contributor of numerous short stories and poems for literary journals, including *Chelsea, Cream City Review, Ms. Magazine Poetry, Quarterly West,* and *Southern West.* Poems included in *Best American Poetry 2000. Girl Talk* has been translated into five languages.

WORK IN PROGRESS: For the Boy in the Back Row, poems about the art of poetry.

SIDELIGHTS: As a young writer, Julianna Baggott watched as many of her contemporaries headed for the publishing capital of the world, New York City, to make their mark on the literary scene. After receiving her master's degree, however, Baggott and her poet husband headed for a small Delaware city, where she went to work writing short stories and then poetry as she began to raise a family. Baggott wisely wasn't all that interested in the literary scene. "I just wanted to write," she told Dirk Westphal for an article in *Poets & Writers Magazine.* "I didn't want to 'be a writer.'"

The distinction paid off for Baggott. In 2001 at the age of thirty-one, her first two books, a novel and volume of poetry, were published within months of each other. Baggott had arrived on the literary scene whether she liked it or not.

Baggott's novel *Girl Talk,* which appeared in bookstores a month before her collection of poetry titled *This Country of Mothers,* is a mother-daughter, coming-of-age tale in which thirty-year-old Lissy Jablonski, pregnant and unmarried, reflects back to the summer when she was fifteen. That summer, Lissy and her mother took a road trip after Lissy's father had run off with another woman. During the trip, Lissy and her mother engage in nights of "girl talk," and Lissy soon discovers secrets about her mother's past, including the fact that her mother once tried to commit suicide and that her biological father is actually the dwarfish Anthony Pantuliano, who is her mother's only true love.

Writing in the *Washington Post Book World,* Abby Frucht found the novel charming but lacking in substance. Although she described Baggott's novel as "clever," Frucht noted that the novel does not lead "to anything truly persuasive." Most critics, however, praised the book for its serious subject matter , which the author handles with humor and flair. "Baggott's biting, darkly comedic, and brutally honest narrative takes a sardonic look at suburbia and family dysfunction," wrote Carolyn Kubisz in *Booklist.* A *Publishers Weekly* reviewer called the novel a "touching . . . story that delivers more depth than its title might imply." The reviewer went on to note, "Baggott's multilayered, psychological tale is told with a deceptively light tone." Jan Blodgett, writing in the *Library Journal,* commented that the "juxtaposition of stories" between Lissy's present life and her mother's past "turns this first novel . . . from just a thirtysomething coming-of-age tale into a wise look at mother-daughter legacies."

This Country of Mothers is a collection of poems in which Baggott reflects on her experiences as a mother and as a daughter. In her poems, Baggott talks both about love and destruction in a manner that seems entirely personal while, at the same time, embracing universal themes. For example, in her poem "What We Didn't Talk about at Fifteen," Baggott writes about the discovery of a drowned girl who was "found naked and raped." The poem's narrator comments, "Didn't each of our mothers warn it could have been us?"

In her interview with Westphal for *Poets & Writers Magazine,* Baggott related that she turned from focusing solely on fiction to writing poetry, in part, to explore her feelings after giving birth. "I felt kind of betrayed by the animalness of it, and the physicality of [having kids], and the huge emotion of it," she told Westphal. "I wondered why no one had mentioned this to me."

In her second novel, *The Miss America Family,* Baggott once again focuses on a dysfunctional family. She tells her story from the views of two characters: Pixie Kitch, who was crowned Miss New Jersey and longed to become Miss America, and Pixie's sixteen-year-old son Ezra, an awkward teenager who is trying to make sense of a world turned topsy-turvy after his mother shoots her dentist husband and Ezra is sent to stay with his biological father, only to learn that his father is gay. "Baggott takes family dysfunction to a new level," wrote a reviewer in *Publishers Weekly,* noting that Baggott uses "wit and humor" to explore the failings of a seemingly perfect family. Carolyn Kubisz, writing in *Booklist,* called the novel "darkly comedic, and brutally honest." In her *Library Journal* review, Karen Traynos noted that *The Miss America Family* "establishes Baggott's remarkable talent for creating characters who resonate with readers."

As for her own reading preferences, Baggott told Westphal that, although she "fell in love with the novel as a form," she loves reading poetry. "If I'm going to get a book out of the library, I get poems," she said. "Poems have the ability to make me read them for pleasure. They demand it. They say, 'You have to love me.' Whereas other things don't; I read them because I'm taking a clock apart."

BIOGRAPHICAL AND CRITICAL SOURCES:

PERIODICALS

Booklist, November 15, 2000, Michelle Kaske, review of *Girl Talk,* p. 621; February 15, 2002, Carolyn Kubisz, review of *The Miss America Family,* p. 990.
BookPage, April, 2001, review of *This Country of Mothers,* p. 8.
Library Journal, March 15, 2002, Karen Traynor, review of *The Miss America Family,* p. 106.
New York Times Book Review, April 1, 2001, Elizabeth Judd, review of *Girl Talk,* p. 16.
Poets & Writers Magazine, May-June, 2001, Dirk Westphal, "Julianna Baggott, How to Be the Next Big Thing," pp. 32-37.
Publishers Weekly, November 20, 2000, review of *Girl Talk,* p. 43; April 1, 2002, review of *The Miss America Family,* p. 53.
Washington Post Book World, March 4, 2001, Abby Frucht, "Tangled Lives," p. 13.

ONLINE

Julianna Baggott Web site, http://www.juliannabaggott.com (September 7, 2002).
Teenreads, http://aol.teenreads.com (April 29, 2002), review of *Girl Talk.**

BALDWIN, William J. 1937-

PERSONAL: Born September 4, 1937, in Los Angeles, CA; married; wife's name, Judith (a minister). *Education:* University of the Pacific School of Dentistry, D.D.S. 1970; Western University Graduate College of Theology, D.M., 1982; American Commonwealth University, Ph.D., 1988.

ADDRESSES: Home—Enterprise, FL 32725. *Office*—Center for Human Relations, P.O. Box 4061, Enterprise, FL 32725. *E-mail*—Doctorbill@aol.com.

CAREER: Pastoral counselor, Past Lives therapist, hypnotherapist, and international lecturer, trainer, and seminar leader of regression therapy. Dentist, c. 1970-82; Center for Human Relations, Enterprise, FL, co-director and president.

WRITINGS:

Spirit Releasement Therapy: A Technique Manual, Headline Books (Terra Alta, WV), 1991, 2nd edition, 1995.
(With wife, Judith Baldwin) *From My Heart to Yours: A Transformational Guide to Unlocking the Power of Love,* Headline Books (Terra Alta, WV), 1996.
CE-VI: Close Encounters of the Possession Kind, Headline Books (Terra Alta, WV), 1999.
Past Life Therapy: A Technique Manual, Headline Books (Terra Alta, WV), 2003.
Healing Lost Souls, Hampton Roads Publishing (Charlottesville, VA), 2003.

Author of foreword, Louise Ireland-Frey, *Freeing the Captives: The Emerging Therapy of Treating Spirit Attachment,* Hampton Roads Publishing, 1999.

SIDELIGHTS: After receiving his D.D.S. degree in 1970, William Baldwin practiced dentistry for a little over a decade before his career interests took a drastic turn. He became an ordained minister and, nearly twenty-three years after entering the field of dentistry, earned his Ph.D. in clinical psychology. Baldwin has since become co-director of the Center for Human Relations. He has written countless articles and a number of books on the subjects of Spirit Releasement Therapy (SRT) and Past Life Therapy (PLT). The purpose of these two closely-related types of therapy is to detect the underlying reason for problems that physically manifest themselves as illness, disease, or mental imbalances. Baldwin also claims that experiencing SRT or PLT can help resolve conflicts that continually arise in a person's primary relationships.

SRT is based on the idea that a person lives their life on earth with the spirit of someone else—deceased—attached to him or her. Historically, this condition has been labeled spirit possession. Religious history is rife with exorcisms designed to "cast out" the intruding spirit from the living person. Baldwin claims that experts in the field estimate that between 70 percent and 100 percent of the population are influenced by one or more discarnate entities at some time in their lives.

SRT consists of six steps, the first of which is to discover and identify all—Baldwin states there is never just one—attached spirits. The second step is differential diagnosis. Most entities fall into one of three categories, and each type requires specific dialogue, which is step three. Step four actually releases the entity, and again, each type requires a different release process. The fifth step is what Baldwin calls a guided imagery of Light for the client. During this step, the void left by the released being is metaphorically filled. The sixth step is a program of ongoing therapy for the client; it is possible to find and release other attachments during subsequent sessions.

PLT differs from SRT in that it operates on the concept of reincarnation rather than spirit attachment. By regressing through one's past lives, the therapist is able to help the client resolve any accumulated residue that gets carried from one lifetime to another.

Baldwin has written several books on spirit attachment and past life regression. His first, *Spirit Releasement Therapy: A Technique Manual,* was considered by some to a groundbreaking work in the field of psychotherapy. Roger Woolger commented on the *Spirit Releasement* Web site that the manual is a "tour de force whose appearance I am delighted to celebrate. . . . It is a milestone we will all look back to. I predict it will be referred to and argued about for years."

Baldwin and his wife Judith run the Center for Human Relations, where they offer seminars, training courses, and therapy sessions. In addition, they travel the world to lecture and present training classes, and their travels have taken them to Brazil, Switzerland, England, Japan, Israel, and other countries.

BIOGRAPHICAL AND CRITICAL SOURCES:

ONLINE

Spirit Web, http://www.spiritweb.org/ (May 20, 2002), Baldwin, William J., "The Three Faces of Regression Therapy."
Spirit Releasement, http://www.spiritreleasement.org/ (April 22, 2002).

* * *

BALLARD, Guy W(arren) 1878-1939
(Godfré Ray King)

PERSONAL: Born July 28, 1878, in Newton, KS; died December 29, 1939, in Los Angeles, CA; married Edna M. Wheeler (a religious leader), 1916; children: Donald. *Education:* Attended business college.

CAREER: "I AM" Religious Activity, cofounder and leader, beginning 1930s. Cofounder of Saint Germain Foundation and St. Germain Press, Chicago, IL; formerly worked as supervisor of a lead and silver mine in Tucson, AZ. sound recording *Beloved Daddy's Benediction,* released by St. Germain Press (Schaumburg, IL), 1982.

WRITINGS:

(Under pseudonym Godfré Ray King) *Unveiled Mysteries,* St. Germain Press (Chicago, IL), 1934, 4th edition, 1982.
The "I Am" Discourses, by the Ascended Master, Saint Germain, St. Germain Press (Chicago, IL), 1935, 4th edition, 1982.
(Under pseudonym Godfré Ray King) *The Magic Presence,* St. Germain Press (Chicago, IL), 1935, 5th edition, 1982.
(With Edna Wheeler Ballard, writing as Lotus Ray King) *Ascended Master Light, by the Great Cosmic Beings,* St. Germain Press (Chicago, IL), 1938.

The "I Am" Discourses, by the Great Divine Director, St. Germain Press (Chicago, IL), 1942.
(Transcriber) Great Cosmic Being Beloved Mighty Victory, *"I Am" Discourses,* Ascended Master Teaching Foundation (Mount Shasta, CA), 1988.

Author of "The Saint Germain Series," St. Germain Press (Chicago, IL), beginning 1934, and "'I Am' Adorations and Affirmations," St. Germain Press (Chicago, IL), beginning 1935.

BIOGRAPHICAL AND CRITICAL SOURCES:

BOOKS

Encyclopedia of Occultism and Parapsychology, 5th edition, Gale (Detroit, MI), 2001.*

* * *

BANG-CAMPBELL, Monika

PERSONAL: Daughter of Richard H. Campbell (an acoustics engineer) and Molly Bang (an author and illustrator). *Education:* Wheaton College, B.A.; Boston University, M.A. (clinical social work).

ADDRESSES: Agent—c/o Author Mail, Harcourt, 525 B. St., Ste. 1900, San Diego, CA 92101-4495.

CAREER: Sailor and writer.

WRITINGS:

Little Rat Sets Sail, illustrated by Molly Bang, Harcourt (San Diego, CA), 2002.
Little Rat Rides, illustrated by Molly Bang, Harcourt (San Diego, CA), in press.

SIDELIGHTS: A professional sailor, Monika Bang-Campbell joined her mother, well-known author and illustrator Molly Bang, in creating the chapter book *Little Rat Sets Sail.* Bang-Campbell drew on her extensive experience as a sailor to add authenticity to this children's book about the sport, while her mother provided the illustrations. "With a remarkable understanding of childhood feelings," remarked Martha V. Parravano of *Horn Book,* Bang-Campbell tells the story of Little Rat, who is terrified of the water. Unfortunately, her parents have just signed her up for a summer of sailing lessons. Her instructor, Buzzy Bear, allows her to sail with him until her fears subside, and she begins to learn sailing terms and tactics. The more knowledge Little Rat gains about sailing, the less afraid she becomes. Parravano noted that Bang-Campbell "captures the joys of sailing while presenting it from the point of view of a reluctant participant." Also giving *Little Rat Sets Sail* a favorable review, a *Publishers Weekly* critic described Bang-Campbell's debut work as "a breezy junket for aspiring skippers and confirmed landlubbers alike."

Bang-Campbell told *CA:* "I have sailed on boats since I was little and have continued my sailing career into adulthood. I am a professional sailor aboard tall ships that run educational programs for students ranging from middle school to adults.

"I received my master's degree in clinical social work from Boston University. Integrating the art of traditional sail to an educational curriculum enhances the students' learning experience."

BIOGRAPHICAL AND CRITICAL SOURCES:

PERIODICALS

Booklist, April 1, 2002, p. 1326.
Horn Book, July-August, 2002, Martha V. Parravano, review of *Little Rat Sets Sail,* p. 452.
Publishers Weekly, January 7, 2002, *Little Rat Sets Sail,* p. 65.
School Library Journal, June, 2002, p. 80.

ONLINE

Between the Lines, http://www.harcourtbooks.com/ (March 30, 2003), interview with Monika Bang-Campbell.

*   *   *

BARTON, Bruce (Fairchild) 1886-1967

PERSONAL: Born August 5, 1886, in Robbins, TN; died July 5, 1967, in New York, NY; son of William Eleazar (a minister) and Esther Treat (a schoolteacher; maiden name, Bushnell) Barton; married Esther Maude

Randall, October 2, 1913 (died, 1951); children: three. *Education:* Attended Berea College, 1903; Amherst College, graduated, 1907. *Politics:* Republican. *Religion:* Congregationalist.

CAREER: Worked as a time-keeper for a railway company in Montana, c. 1907; *Home Herald,* Chicago, IL, became managing editor; *Continent* (Presbyterian magazine), New York, NY, journalist, 1909; *Collier's,* New York, NY, assistant sales manager, beginning 1912; *Every Week,* editor and editorial writer, 1914-18; Barton, Durstine & Osborn (advertising agency; later known as Batten, Barton, Durstine & Osborn), cofounder, c. 1918, partner and copywriter, 1918-61, chair of board of directors until 1961. U.S. Congress, Republican representative from the state of New York, 1937-41. Also worked as a journalist for *Housekeeper.* Volunteer worker for Salvation Army during World War I; United War Work, publicity chair for fund drive, 1918.

MEMBER: Phi Beta Kappa.

WRITINGS:

The Resurrection of the Soul, 1912.
A Young Man's Jesus, Pilgrim Press (Boston, MA), 1914.
The Women Who Came at Night: Being the Experiences of a Minister, Pilgrim Press (Boston, MA), 1914.
More Power to You: Fifty Editorials from Every Week, Century Co. (New York, NY), 1917.
The Making of George Groton, Doubleday, Page and Co. (Garden City, NY), 1918.
It's a Good Old World: Being a Collection of Little Essays on Various Subjects of Human Interest, Century Co. (New York, NY), 1920.
(With Charles W. Hurd) *Business Correspondence,* Alexander Hamilton Institute (New York, NY), 1921.
Better Days (collected editorials), Century C. (New York, NY), 1924.
The Man Nobody Knows: A Discovery of Jesus, Bobbs-Merrill (Indianapolis, IN), 1925, revised edition published in *The Man and the Book Nobody Knows,* Bobbs-Merrill (Indianapolis, IN), 1956, published as *The Man Nobody Knows: A Discovery of the Real Jesus,* with new introduction by Richard M. Fried, I. R. Dee (Chicago, IL), 2000.

The Book Nobody Knows, Bobbs-Merrill (Indianapolis, IN), 1926, revised edition published in *The Man and the Book Nobody Knows,* Bobbs-Merrill (Indianapolis, IN), 1956.

(With Bernard Lichtenberg) *Advertising Campaigns,* Alexander Hamilton Institute (New York, NY), 1926.

What Can a Man Believe?, Bobbs-Merrill (Indianapolis, IN), 1927.

The Man of Galilee: Twelve Scenes from the Life of Christ, illustrated by Dean Cornwell, Cosmopolitan Book Corp. (New York, NY), 1928.

On the up and Up (essays), Bobbs-Merrill (Indianapolis, IN), 1929.

He Upset the World, Bobbs-Merrill (Indianapolis, IN), 1932.

A Parade of the States, Doubleday, Doran (Garden City, NY), 1932.

Author of shorter works, including pamphlets. Contributor to magazines and newspapers.

Barton's papers are collected at the State Historical Society of Wisconsin, Madison.

BIOGRAPHICAL AND CRITICAL SOURCES:

BOOKS

Encyclopedia of World Biography, 2nd edition, Gale (Detroit, MI), 1998.

Gaebelein, Arno Clemens, *The Christ We Know: Meditations on the Person and Glory of Our Lord Jesus Christ; The Best Answer to the Book "The Man Nobody Knows,"* Bible Institute Colportage (Chicago, IL), 1927.

St. James Encyclopedia of Popular Culture, St. James Press (Detroit, MI), 2000.

PERIODICALS

American Quarterly, fall, 1981, Leo P. Ribuffo, "Jesus Christ as Business Statesman: Bruce Barton and the Selling of Corporate Capitalism."

South Atlantic Quarterly, summer, 1977, James A. Neuchaterlein, "Bruce Barton and the Business Ethos of the 1920s."

OBITUARIES:

PERIODICALS

New York Times, July 6, 1967.*

*   *   *

BATALI, Mario 1960-

PERSONAL: Born September 9, 1960, in Seattle, WA; son of Armandino (an engineer) and Marilyn (a nurse) Batali; married Susi Cahn; children: Benno, Leo. *Education:* Rutgers University, B.A., 1982.

ADDRESSES: Home—New York, NY. *Office*—c/o Babbo Ristorante Enoteca, 110 Waverly Place, New York, NY 10011.

CAREER: Chef, restaurant owner, and author. Po', New York, NY, chef/co-owner, 1993—; Babbo Ristorante Enoteca, New York, NY, chef/co-owner, 1998—; Lupa, New York, NY, chef/co-owner; Esca, New York, NY, chef/co-owner; Italian Wine Merchants, New York, NY, co-owner; The Food Network, New York, NY, television host of *Molto Mario* and *Mario Eats Italy.*

AWARDS, HONORS: D'Artagnan Cervena Who's Who of Food & Beverage in America, lifetime achievement award, 2001.

WRITINGS:

Simple Italian Food: Recipes from My Villages, photographs by Mark Ferri, Clarkson Potter (New York, NY), 1998.

Holiday Food: Family Recipes for the Festive Time of the Year, photographs by Quentin Bacon, Clarkson Potter (New York, NY), 2000.

The Babbo Cookbook, photographs by Christopher Hirscheimer, Clarkson Potter (New York, NY), 2002.

SIDELIGHTS: Although he studied finance and Spanish theatre in college, Mario Batali was drawn to a career as a chef and can trace his culinary inclinations back to his family. "The whole family experience was about food," Batali told a writer for *People* magazine. Batali began his culinary training at the Cordon Bleu school in London, England. Uninspired, he quickly dropped out for a more hands-on experience in a London French restaurant, where he trained for three years under the legendary Marco Pierre White. He returned to the United States in 1984 and began working at the Four Seasons hotel chain until 1989, when he made a daring move and quit his job to work in a family-run restaurant in Borgo Capanne, Italy, population one hundred. Batali received no wages but worked in exchange for lessons in traditional Italian cooking. "It was the most radical thing I ever did," he said in *People*. "And the best thing for my cooking style."

Eventually, Batali returned to the United States and worked for a year upgrading an Italian restaurant in New York City before opening his first restaurant, Po', to stellar reviews in 1993. In 1998 he opened his second restaurant, Babbo, which also received rave reviews from New York food critics. Batali went on to open two more restaurants and a wine shop. He also hosts popular cooking shows on television's Food Network. Batali's success and popularity, coupled with his love of authentic Italian cuisine, has led him to write several renowned cookbooks.

Batali's first book, *Simple Italian Food: Recipes from My Villages,* focuses on the use of pristine ingredients combined with the simple and sensible Italian cooking techniques he learned from his Italian teachers. The cookbook includes more than 200 recipes for pastas and numerous other Italian foods, from classic dishes like baked lasagne with asparagus and pesto to tuna carpaccio with cucumbers, sweet potatoes, and saffron vinaigrette. Writing in *Publishers Weekly,* a reviewer noted, "Batali's first cookbook will surely please those who want Italian easy and quick." Mark Knoblauch, writing in *Booklist,* commented, "Batali emphasizes the essentials of regional Italian cooking, carefully noting the similarities and differences as one travels from one ancient province to another." In a *New York Times Book Review* article, William Grimes called the book "immensely appealing and endlessly useful." He went on to note, "No tricks here, just brilliance."

In *Holiday Food: Family Recipes for the Festive Time of the Year,* Batali once again showcases simple Italian foods, focusing on four complete menus, including the "Feast of Seven Fishes," which is traditionally served in parts of Italy on Christmas Eve. The cookbook includes numerous baking recipes, from traditional Italian recipes to recipes from Batali's own family that he enjoyed as a child. The book includes a discussion by Batali of his own family's holiday meals, in which he notes that "any meals served at our house were mapped out at least a month in advance." In review of *Holiday Food* for *Publishers Weekly,* a reviewer noted, "If you want to enliven your Italian repertoire with authentic, celebratory dishes, this book is invaluable."

Batali's next book, *The Babbo Cookbook,* draws on the widespread fame of his flagship restaurant in New York City's Greenwich Village. Babbo is known as one of the country's most acclaimed Italian restaurants, and the cookbook includes 150 recipes, including Batali's signature dishes of mint love letters with spicy lamb sausage and beef cheek ravioli. The book also takes a look at what has made Babbo such a successful restaurant in a city full of premiere restaurants. Although a reviewer writing in *Publishers Weekly* noted that many of the recipes are "complex" and require "ingredients and equipment" that "will be difficult for lay people to acquire," the reviewer also commented that the "recipes are excellent—clearly written and easy to follow and carefully edited for the home cook."

As for his own cooking style, Batali said in *People,* "Every cook in Italy uses what grows around them. I use local American products, but with the same respect and simplicity Italians do. That's my shtick."

BIOGRAPHICAL AND CRITICAL SOURCES:

PERIODICALS

Art Culinaire, spring, 2001, "Mario Batali," p. 50.
Booklist, October 15, 1998, Mark Knoblauch, review of *Simple Italian Food,* p. 384; October 15, 2000, review of *Holiday Food,* p. 400.
Library Journal, October 15, 1998, review of *Simple Italian Food,* p. 91; October 15, 2000, Judith Sutton, review of *Holiday Food,* p. 96; March 15, 2002, Judith Sutton, review of *The Babbo Cookbook,* p. 103.
New York Times, June 26, 1998, Ruth Reichl, "Babbo," (restaurant review), pp. B42, E44; September 18, 1998, Eric Asimov, "Babbo" (restaurant review),

pp. B39, E42; November 10, 1999, Eric Asimov, "A Clamorous Trattoria, with Food to Match," pp. B16, F12; May 19, 2000, William Griems, "Diner's Journal: Esca," p. B41; December 27, 2000, Joyce Wadler, "A Taste of the Good Life, Served with Gusto," p. B2.

New York Times Book Review, December 6, 1998, William Grimes, review of *Simple Italian Food,* p. 20.

People, November 2, 1998, "Fresh Prince," a profile of Mario Batali, p. 85; November 27, 2000, Max Alexander, review of *Holiday Food,* p. 59.

Publishers Weekly, September 21, 1998, review of *Simple Italian Food,* p. 81; September 4, 2000, review of *Mario Batali Holiday Food,* p. 103; January 21, 2002, review of *The Babbo Cookbook,* p. 83.

Restaurants & Institutions, May 15, 2002, review of *The Babbo Cookbook,* p. 20.

Time, January 15, 2001, John Cloud, "Penne from Heaven," p. 120.*

*   *   *

BATES, Karen Grigsby 1951(?)-

PERSONAL: Born c. 1951; married Bruce Talamon; children: Jordan. *Education:* Wellesley College, B.A., 1973; Yale University Graduate School of Organization and Management, Executive Management Program. *Hobbies and other interests:* Photography.

ADDRESSES: Home—Los Angeles, CA. *Agent*—c/o Carrie Feron, Avon Books/HarperCollins, 10 East 53rd St., New York, NY 10022.

CAREER: Writer, and journalist. *People,* Los Angeles, CA, reporter for West Coast Bureau; *Los Angeles Times,* Los Angeles, CA, contributing columnist; National Public Radio, commentator.

AWARDS, HONORS: Fiction Honor Book award, Black Caucus of the American Library Association, 2002, for *Plain Brown Wrapper: An Alex Powell Novel.*

WRITINGS:

(With Karen Elyse Hudson) *Basic Black: Home Training for Modern Times,* Doubleday (New York, NY), 1996.

Plain Brown Wrapper: An Alex Powell Novel, Avon (New York, NY), 2001.

WORK IN PROGRESS: Chosen People, a second mystery featuring reporter Alex Powell.

SIDELIGHTS: "I've been writing since about age six in one form or another, and I've always gotten in trouble—probably since I was old enough to talk—for having 'Too Many Opinions'!," Karen Grigsby Bates told Gwendolyn E. Osborne in an interview for *Mystery Reader.* Although she grew up on the East coast, Bates lives and works in Los Angeles, California as a journalist and frequent commentator on National Public Radio. A voracious reader, she is also the author of a book on etiquette and a mystery with a heroine who, like Bates, is a black journalist.

In *Basic Black: Home Training for Modern Times,* Bates and coauthor Karen Elyse Hudson present an unusual etiquette book that not only talks about traditional etiquette but also focuses on black American traditions or, as the authors write, "the way our grandmothers, mothers and aunts have taught us for centuries." As a book covering topics like addressing wedding invitations, letter writing, and being a good host, *Basic Black* is universal in its guidelines for good etiquette, regardless of race. However, the book also addresses the concerns of black Americans specifically on topics like black traditions in joining a church, family reunions, and planning a funeral. In addition, Bates and coauthor Hudson go far beyond the boundaries of the typical etiquette book when they instruct black Americans on how to act with dignity, politeness, and assertiveness when faced with bad or unacceptable treatment because of their race. "Each subject is discussed briefly and entertainingly, with solid common sense," wrote Marry Carroll in a review in *Booklist.* A *Library Journal* reviewer called the book a "common-sense approach to etiquette" that "is for everyone, regardless of race."

Bates turned from etiquette to excitement for her next book, the mystery *Plain Brown Wrapper: An Alex Powell Novel.* According to Bates in the *Mystery Writer* interview, the idea for the book came about when she attended a National Association of Black Journalists conference, noting that "it occurred to me that journalists are such interesting and often volatile people, this particular conference would be a perfect setting for a murder." The plot of *Plain Brown Wrapper* centers on the murder of publisher Everett Carson just prior to his receiving a "Journalist of the Year" award from the

National Association of Black Journalists. His friend and former employee, newspaper columnist Alex Powell discovers the body and is soon swept up in the investigation on the orders of her current newspaper employer. A demanding and powerful man who also had a way with the ladies, Carson has numerous enemies. Powell sets off on a two-week cross-country trip with another journalist, Paul Butler, in an investigation that leads them to tangle with the social elite from San Francisco to Martha's Vineyard.

Noting that the book benefits from Bates's "firsthand knowledge" of journalism, a reviewer from *Publishers Weekly* commented that the book has an "easygoing style" with "just the right spark of humor in a fun, suspenseful novel." *Library Journal*'s Rex Klett called the book "Flip and jaunty." Writing in *Black Issues Book Review,* Susan McHenry noted, "The bonus offered by *Plain Brown Wrapper* is a wise and wickedly satirical perspective on today's black media and those of us who will live and die and for it."

BIOGRAPHICAL AND CRITICAL SOURCES:

PERIODICALS

Black Issues Book Review, September, 2001, Susan McHenry, review of *Plain Brown Wrapper,* p. 20.

Booklist, December 15, 1996, Mary Carroll, review of *Basic Black: Home Training for Modern Times,* p. 695; July 21, 2001, Carrie Bissey, review of *Plain Brown Wrapper,* p. 1985.

Essence, August, 2001, review of *Plain Brown Wrapper,* p. 62.

Library Journal, November 1, 1996, Susan B. Hagloch, review of *Basic Black: Home Training for Modern Times,* p. 73; April 15, 1997, review of *Basic Black: Home Training for Modern Times,* p. 37; August, 2001, Rex Klett, review of *Plain Brown Wrapper,* p. 169.

Los Angeles Times, March 21, 1994, "Bates on Farrakhan," p. B6; October 10, 2001, "Sifting through L.A.'s Shadows" (interview with Karen Grigsby Bates), p. E1.

Publishers Weekly, November 18, 1996, review of *Basic Black: Home Training for Modern Times,* p. 73; June 25, 2001, review of *Plain Brown Wrapper,* p. 54.

ONLINE

Mystery Reader Web site, http://www.themysteryreader. com/ (November 9, 2001), review of *Plain Brown Wrapper;* (December 13, 2001) Gwendolyn E. Osborne, "Meet Karen Grigsby Bates."*

*   *   *

BEACH, Edward L(atimer) 1918-2002

OBITUARY NOTICE—See index for *CA* sketch: Born April 20, 1918, in New York, NY; died of cancer December 1, 2002, in Washington, DC. Navy officer and author. Beach was a World War II hero who later became famous for his role as captain of the *Triton,* the first nuclear-powered submarine to travel around the world underwater. The son of a navy captain, Beach followed his father's footsteps and attended the U.S. Naval Academy, where he earned a B.S. in 1939. He immediately went to sea, serving as an ensign on the *Trigger* and making his way up to executive officer while World War II waged in the Pacific. He later served as captain of the submarines *Triton, Piper,* and *Amberjack.* During his years at sea, Beach saw heavy action during which his submarines damaged or sank forty-five Japanese vessels and he was awarded a Navy Cross. After the war, Beach continued to serve at sea until 1953, when he went to Washington, D.C., to work as a naval aide to President Eisenhower. Beach then returned to naval service, captaining the *Salamonie* from 1957 to 1958 and then the nuclear submarine *Triton* from 1958 to 1961. It was in 1960 that he made his famous trip around the world on the *Triton,* a journey that lasted sixty-one days and roughly followed the course Spanish explorer Magellan took centuries before. One of the main purposes of the voyage was to see how a crew would react under such extended conditions underwater. When he returned to the United States, Beach was presented with the Legion of Merit. During the remainder of the 1960s, Beach worked for the Navy Department in Washington, D.C., and as Stephen B. Luce Chair of Naval Service at the U.S. Naval War College in Newport, Rhode Island. He retired from the Navy in 1966, and from 1969 to 1977 he was staff director of the U.S. Senate Republican Policy Committee. Beach recounted his adventures at sea in several books, including *Submarine!* (1952), *Run Silent, Run Deep* (1955), which was adapted as a movie starring Clark Gable in 1958, *Cold Is the Sea* (1978), and his recounting of the *Triton* voyage in *Around the World Submerged* (1962). These books were often praised by critics for the author's admirable powers of description and exciting battle scenes. He also wrote naval histories, such as *The United States Navy: 200 Years* (1986). His last book was the memoir *Salt and Steel: Reflections of a Submariner* (1999).

OBITUARIES AND OTHER SOURCES:

BOOKS

Science and Its Time: Understanding the Social Significance of Scientific Discovery, Volume 7: *1950-Present,* Gale (Detroit, MI), 2000.

PERIODICALS

Chicago Tribune, December 2, 2002, section 1, p. 10.
Los Angeles Times, December 2, 2002, p. B9.
New York Times, December 2, 2002, p. A23.
Times (London, England), December 4, 2002, p. 33.
Washington Post, December 2, 2002, p. B6.

*   *   *

BEAGLEY, Brenda E. 1962-
  (Amy Leigh)

PERSONAL: Born December 24, 1962, in Janesville, WI; daughter of James M. (a water-color artist) and Phyllis (an office assistant) Smith; married Kevin Beagley (a managing director in public relations), May 16, 1986; children: Thomas, Marin. *Ethnicity:* "White." *Education:* Attended University of Missouri, 1981-83; University of Arizona, B.A. (journalism), 1986.

ADDRESSES: Agent—Paige Wheeler, Creative Media Agency, 240 West 35th St., Suite 500, New York, NY 10001. *E-mail*—Bbeagley@aol.com.

CAREER: Writer.

WRITINGS:

(As Amy Leigh) *Chance of a Lifetime* (romance fiction), RFI West, 2001.

*   *   *

BEAMER, Lisa 1969-

PERSONAL: Born 1969, in Albany, NY; daughter of Paul (a research physicist) and Lorraine (a Christian counselor) Brosious; married Todd Morgan Beamer (a software accounts manager), 1994 (died September 11, 2001); children: David, Drew, Morgan Kay. *Education:* Wheaton College, B.A. (business), 1981.

ADDRESSES: Office—c/o Todd M. Beamer Foundation, P.O. Box 32, Cranbury, NJ 08512. *Agent*—c/o Author Mail, Tyndale House Publishers, Inc., 351 Executive Dr., Carol Stream, IL 60188.

CAREER: Founder of Todd M. Beamer Foundation.

AWARDS, HONORS: Named one of the Twenty-five Most Intriguing People of 2001, *People* magazine.

WRITINGS:

(With Ken Abraham) *Let's Roll!: Ordinary People, Extraordinary Courage* (memoir), Tyndale House Publishers (Wheaton, IL), 2002.

SIDELIGHTS: Lisa Beamer was the wife of Todd Beamer, one of a group of passengers who died on September 11, 2001, while attempting to take control of a hijacked commercial airplane that ultimately crashed in a Pennsylvania field, killing all aboard. The twin towers of New York's World Trade Center had been struck by two aircraft and collapsed in flames, and a third aircraft had struck the Pentagon in Washington, D.C. by the time the tragedy that would take the life of Todd Beamer began to unfold. United Airlines Flight 93 was on its way from Newark to San Francisco that morning, when hijackers took control of the plane and rerouted it, perhaps planning to hit a second target in Washington, D.C. Their plans never came to fruition because the plane's passengers, including Oracle software salesman Todd Beamer, banded together to resist.

During the hijacking attempt, many passengers were able to use aircraft phones to contact loved ones. Beamer managed to speak by telephone with Verizon Airfone operator Lisa Jefferson for thirteen minutes. He told her that three people had taken over the plane. Two of the hijackers were armed with knives, and one had a bomb strapped to his waist. The two with knives had locked themselves in the cockpit. As the world reeled in the wake of the collapse of the World Trade towers, it now learned of the new danger posed by Flight 93. While the passengers of the hijacked aircraft headed toward the East Coast, Jefferson told Beamer, "I'll be here as long as you are."

According to *Guardian Unlimited* online contributor Ed Vulliamy, after the conversation between Beamer and Jefferson ended, Jefferson recalled Beamer saying that "he was going to have to go out on faith because they were talking about jumping the guy with the bomb. He was still holding the phone, but he was not talking to me, he was talking to someone else, and I could tell he had turned away. And he said, 'You ready. Okay, let's roll.'" As Beamer and the other passengers of Flight 93 rushed their hijackers the cockpit recorder picked up the sound of fighting and the crash of service trolleys. The pilot lost control of the aircraft at 30,000 feet.

"Lisa Beamer was a national icon within ten days of her husband's death," wrote *Newsweek* contributor Evan Thomas. "She was wearing a borrowed maternity dress and she had not slept in a week when President Bush saluted her before Congress and the nation, and yet she looked calm and radiant. She was whisked from *Good Morning America* to the *Today* show to *Dateline, 20/20,* and *60 Minutes.*" Talk show host Oprah Winfrey even sent her private plane to pick up Beamer for an appearance on her daytime show after the widow expressed her nervousness about flying in the wake of her husband's death in a plane crash. When Beamer appeared on *Oprah* she met Jefferson and heard the telephone operator repeat the final two words she heard Beamer utter. Those words became the title of Lisa Beamer's memoir of her life with the man who had become America's hero: "Let's Roll."

Lisa Beamer was born in Albany, New York and grew up in Shrub Oak, north of New York City, one of three children of Paul and Lorraine Brosious. When she was fifteen, her father, an IBM research physicist, suffered an aneurysm and died. Beamer was raised a Baptist, but her faith was shaken after the loss of her father. She met Todd at Wheaton College, a Christian school near Chicago, and they settled in New Jersey after their marriage. Todd's job required him to do a great deal of traveling, and on the day of the tragedy Lisa wasn't even sure which flight he had taken.

Thomas noted of Beamer's sudden celebrity that at first it was "resented by some of the families of less celebrated victims, particularly those of the flight crew, whose loved ones were too busy trying to do their jobs to call home. But Beamer has soothed ruffled feelings with unfailing graciousness. . . . Still, she does not altogether object to the attention lavished upon her. Deeply religious, she wanted to bear witness she says. Her disarming—and occasionally irreverent—sense of humor gave her crossover appeal to both the religious and the mainstream media."

Beamer delivered her third child, a girl, in January, 2002, and named her daughter Morgan, Todd's middle name. Following Morgan's birth she turned her attention to raising funds for children who had lost their parents, the first being the children whose parents had died in the crash, through a foundation named for her husband. With Ken Abraham, she devoted three months to writing *Let's Roll!: Ordinary People, Extraordinary Courage.* Much of the book is based on interviews Abraham conducted with the couple's family and friends, and some was written by Beamer. With the publication of her book, the widow was again asked to appear on network shows and talk about her book, her life with Todd, and her faith.

Los Angeles Times reviewer Gina Piccalo commented that *Let's Roll* "offers a painfully intimate look at the tragedy from Beamer's perspective." According to her book, while Beamer learned about the details of the crash from a television report that morning, she immediately instinctively knew Todd was on the doomed flight. Completing her book allowed Beamer to work through part of her grief; following its publication she planned to return to the task of raising her three children.

BIOGRAPHICAL AND CRITICAL SOURCES:

BOOKS

Beamer, Lisa, and Ken Abraham, *Let's Roll!: Ordinary People, Extraordinary Courage,* Tyndale House Publishers (Wheaton, IL), 2002.

PERIODICALS

Knight Ridder/Tribune News Service, September 6, 2002, Carolyn Chick, "Lisa Beamer Says She Lives in the Moment, Bolstered by Her Faith," p. K5108.
Los Angeles Times, August 26, 2002, Gina Piccalo, "A Widow's Story," p. E2.
Newsweek, September 9, 2002, Evan Thomas, "Their Faith and Fears," p. 36.
People, January 28, 2002, Patrick Rogers, "Living Legacy," p. 56.

OTHER

Dateline, http://www.msnbc.com/ (August 20, 2002), Stone Phillips, transcript of interview with Beamer.
Guardian Unlimited, http://www.observer.co.uk/ (December 2, 2001), Ed Vulliamy, "Let's Roll."
Modern Reformation, http://www.modernreformation. org/ (September 12, 2002), Ann Henderson Hart, interview with Beamer.*

*   *   *

BEARDSLEE, Karen E. 1965-

PERSONAL: Born June 25, 1965, in New Milford, CT; daughter of Paul William (an innkeeper) and Margaret Mary (Minisce) Beardslee; married Thomas Michael Kwasny, August 1, 2001; stepchildren: Rocky, Stefan. *Ethnicity:* "Italian." *Education:* Shippensburg University, B.A., 1988; East Carolina University, M.A., 1991; Temple University, Ph.D. (American literature), 1998. *Politics:* Independent. *Religion:* Roman Catholic. *Hobbies and other interests:* Guitar, biking, baking.

ADDRESSES: Home and office—2777 Livingston Loop, Virginia Beach, VA 23456; fax: 757-427-2299. *E-mail*—Leejogger@aol.com.

CAREER: Burlington County College, Pemberton, NJ, adjunct professor, 1991-99, lecturer in English, 1999-2002; independent scholar and folklorist, 2002—. Camden County College, adjunct professor, 1992; Rowan College of New Jersey, adjunct professor, 1995; teacher of history and English at a private secondary school in Philadelphia, PA, 1998-99. Moorestown Barnes and Noble Monthly Senior Memoirs Writing Group, co-facilitator, 2000.

MEMBER: Modern Language Association of America, American Folklore Society (chair of folklore and literature section), National Council of Teachers of English, National Women's Studies Association, Popular Culture Association, Society for the Study of Multi-Ethnic Literatures of the United States, American Association of University Women.

WRITINGS:

Literary Legacies, Folklore Foundations: Selfhood and Cultural Tradition in Nineteenth- and Twentieth-Century American Literature, University of Tennessee Press (Knoxville, TN), 2001.

Work represented in anthologies, including *Your Neighborhood of Poems,* edited by Eloise Bradley Fink and John Dickson, Thorntree Press (Winnetka, IL), 1994. Contributor of articles and poetry to periodicals, including *MELUS, Zora Neale Hurston Forum, Reflector, Rebel,* and *Expressions.* Member of editorial advisory board, *Analytical Writer,* 2002.

WORK IN PROGRESS: From San Quentin Gumbo to "Fried Green Tomatoes at the Whistlestop Café": Foodways in Life and Literature, publication by University of Alabama Press expected in 2004; *Translating Tradition: A Family Folklore Reader,* Allyn & Bacon, 2004; and *Variety Shows: An American Family Reader and Writer,* Allyn & Bacon, 2004.

SIDELIGHTS: Karen E. Beardslee told *CA:* "Writing is my primary mode of expression. It has been a part of my life since I was a child. Then, like now, I wrote not only for pleasure, but to pull myself out and into the world. I would have to say that Southern writers—both poets and novelists—influence my work the most. Their works resonate with voices telling stories—the oral tradition—and I am completely lost in narrative when I pick up something by Lee Smith or Robert Morgan, for example.

"I write when I have to—when I am on deadline with a book—and when the occasion calls for it—when experience must become words on paper. The first type of writing is a matter of my profession; the second is a matter of my creative spirit. Together they fill my need to play with words on a daily basis. I am inspired to write the scholarly books I do because of the subject matter they cover: folklore and literature, two of the strongest influences in my life. I also work in poetry and the personal essay, creating pieces that reflect my scholarly interests and seek to record the lives and stories with which I come in contact.

"My experience with my grandparents proved the value of folklore in my own life and became the memoir *Letters to Be Sent: An Epistle Memoir.* I wrote *Literary Legacies, Folklore Foundations: Selfhood and Cultural Tradition in Nineteenth- and Twentieth-Century American Literature* because I wanted others to recognize the role folklore plays in the literature we read and in the lives we lead. Later I was to find folklore a valuable teaching tool, and in order to share this knowledge with others I created *Translating Tradition: A Family Folklore Reader.*"

*　　*　　*

BEER, George L(ouis) 1872-1920

PERSONAL: Born July 26, 1872, in New York, NY; died 1920, in New York, NY; son of Julius (a tobacco importer) and Sophia (Walter) Beer; married Edith Cecilia Hellman, November 11, 1896; children: Eleanor Frances. *Education:* Columbia University, B.A., 1892, M.A., 1893.

CAREER: Historian and author. Columbia University, New York, NY, lecturer, 1893-97; worked in his family's tobacco business, 1893-1903.

AWARDS, HONORS: Loubat Prize, Columbia University, 1913, for *The Origins of the British Colonial System, 1578-1600* and *British Colonial Policy, 1754-1765.*

WRITINGS:

The Commercial Policy of England toward the American Colonies, Columbia University Press (New York, NY), 1893, reprinted, Peter Smith Publisher (Gloucester, England), 1981.

British Colonial Policy, 1754-1765, Macmillan (New York, NY), 1908.

The Origins of the British Colonial System, 1578-1600, Macmillan (New York, NY), 1908.

The Old Colonial System, 1660-1754, Part I: The Establishment of the System, 1660-1688, 2 volumes, Macmillan (New York, NY), 1912.

The English-speaking Peoples; Their Future Relations and Joint International Obligations, Macmillan (New York, NY), 1917.

African Questions at the Paris Peace Conference, with Papers on Egypt, Mesopotamia, and the Colonial Settlement, edited by Louis Herbert Gray, Macmillan (New York, NY), 1923.

Contributor to periodicals, including *Political Science Quarterly, New Republic, Forum,* and *Annals of the American Academy of Political and Social Science.* Beer's diary of his activities immediately before and during the Paris Peace Conference is located at the Rare Book and Manuscript Library of Columbia University; his other papers can be found in various collections at the same library.

SIDELIGHTS: George L. Beer was a versatile scholar, businessman, and revolutionary thinker. Who is regarded as one of the founders of the "imperial school" of early American history. Beer's research into the British Empire and its relationship to its colonies was novel at the time and stood in opposition to prevailing theories. His conclusions, however, have stood the test of time, and were still considered valuable more than a century after he published them in a series of books focusing on the economic history of Great Britain.

Beer came from an affluent family; his father, a German immigrant, managed a successful tobacco importing business. Beer attended the New York public school system and entered Columbia College when he was sixteen years old. Upon completion of his graduate degree, Beer lectured at Columbia and simultaneously worked in the family importation business. He was so financially successful that he was able to comfortably retire in 1903 and devote himself to research and writing.

In 1893 the Columbia University Press published Beer's thesis, *The Commercial Policy of England toward the American Colonies.* This book introduces the theories about the British Empire and colonies that permeate all of Beer's subsequent writings. According to essayist Peter A. Coclanis in the *Dictionary of Literary Biography,* Beer examines in his thesis "the origins and development of English commercial policy toward the colonies from the early seventeenth century to 1763." Beer also describes how the British put their policy into action, and how this policy was received by the colonials. Beer concludes that although British policy may have been a bit harmful to the economic development of the American colonies, it was not intended to be burdensome or manipulative to its subjects.

Another point Beer notes in his thesis is that the colonists did not seem to disagree with the policy or find it questionable until after 1763. Coclanis wrote: "That such sound conclusions were based upon examination of printed sources only and arrived at by so young a scholar underscores the talent and ability with which Beer was blessed."

Upon its publication, *The Commercial Policy of England toward the American Colonies* was very highly regarded. The author was praised by reviewers for his "broad vision, fresh interpretation, and evenhanded treatment of both England and the colonies," Coclanis noted. Beer's book has been reprinted several times, including in 1981, which attests to the fact that his research is still considered valuable and important.

Beer's British Colonial Policy, 1754-1765 was conceived as part of a series of four books describing the origins of the British Empire through the start of the American Revolution. After Beer retired from the tobacco business, he spent fourteen months in London, England, in order to begin his painstaking research. Beer found that he devoted much of his time to reading documents from the Seven Years' War; therefore, he started the series with the declining years of the British Empire. In *British Colonial Policy, 1754-1765* Beer explains that the British were displeased by the

conduct of the American colonists throughout the Seven Years' War and sought, in Coclanis's words, "to restructure the imperial relationship in such a way as to reduce the possibility of similar conduct in the future." Since the colonists disagreed with these changes and considered them harmful to their interests, they resisted and rebelled. Beer maintains that the subsequent revolution was an inevitable outcome of British actions.

British Colonial Policy, 1754-1765 "was something of a classic in its field," according to Samuel Willard Crompton in *American National Biography.* due to the authors use of numerous original sources. Coclanis called *British Colonial Policy, 1754-1765* "unquestionably Beer's greatest work," noting: "Beer's discussions of the considerations involved in British policy-making and the actual manner in which policy was implemented, for example, represented notable contributions to the historiography on the eighteenth century."

The Origins of the British Colonial System, 1548-1660 is the second book in Beer's series on the British system. This book uncovers and examines the roots of the British Empire that may be found in the fertile soil of the Stuart and Tudor periods in England. Coclanis wrote that the book "won unstinting praise," although some reviewers "complained about Beer's arid prose." Coclanis commented that *The Origins of the British Colonial System, 1578-1660* "is not as stimulating or original as [*British Colonial Policy, 1754-1765*] . . . but it is a significant work nonetheless." Crompton stated that despite any that British scholars may have found in the work, Beer "had by this point become the American scholar most fitted to undertake studies of the British Empire."

In 1912 Beer published his third book about the British Empire, *The Old Colonial System, 1660-1754; Part I: The Establishment of the Old System, 1660-1688.* For many years, this book was considered to be "the most complete and authoritative study made on English colonial policy during the period 1660-1688," Crompton noted. "In these long, sober volumes," Coclanis remarked, "Beer attempted nothing strikingly original, being content to extend and expand upon ideas, themes, and arguments from his earlier works."

In 1913 Beer was awarded the Loubat Prize by his alma mater, Columbia University. He was the first to receive the award, which was given to recognize the "best work printed and published in the English language on the History, Geography, Archaeology, Ethnology, Philology, or numismatics of North America during the preceding five years."

With the start of World War I, Beer shifted his focus to international affairs, and thus never completed the fourth book in his series. Instead he published articles in journals such as *Political Science Quarterly* and *New Republic* in which he strongly encouraged the United States to involve itself on the side of the Allied forces. He felt that an alliance of English and American political and strategic forces would prove mutually beneficial. Coclanis remarked that Beer might have been "every bit as skilled at Anglo-American publicity and propaganda as he had been in the scholarly world."

During the war Beer worked as a part of the Inquiry Commission established by President Wilson to prepare a peace program for the United States to abide by at the war's end. Beer later participated in the Paris Peace Conference as a member of the American delegation.

After a long period of ill health, Beer died in 1920 at the relatively young age of forty-eight. He continues to be viewed as a pioneer and forward-thinker. Coclanis wrote: "Beer left a rich legacy both to the historical profession and to modern historiography. . . . [He] helped to revolutionize the study of early American history, rejecting the narrow parochialism that then dominated the field in favor of a much broader interpretive frame."

BIOGRAPHICAL AND CRITICAL SOURCES:

BOOKS

American National Biography, edited by John A. Garraty and Mark C. Carnes, Oxford University Press (New York, NY), 1999, pp. 472-473.
Dictionary of Literary Biography, Volume 47: *American Historians, 1866-1912,* edited by Clyde N. Wilson, Gale (Detroit, MI), 1986, pp. 40-47.*

BEILHART, Jacob 1867-1908

PERSONAL: Born March 4, 1867, in Fairfield, OH; died of peritonitis following surgery November 24, 1908, in Ingleside, IL; son of John (a farmer) and Barbara (Schlotter) Beilhartz; married, 1887. *Education:* Attended Healdsburg College.

CAREER: Farm worker in Kansas, c. 1885; preacher and evangelist in Kansas, beginning c. 1888; worked at a sanitarium in Battle Creek, MI, in the early 1890s; operator of a medical boarding house c. late 1890s; *Spirit Fruit* (magazine), Lisbon (now New Lisbon), OH, founder and publisher, beginning 1899; Spirit Fruit Society (commune; later known as Freedom Hill), founder and leader, 1901-08.

WRITINGS:

Love Letters from Spirit to You, privately printed (Roscoe, CA), 1929, reprinted, New Age Publishing (Los Angeles, CA), 1960.
My Life and Teachings, Quo Vadia? (Geneva, Switzerland), 1932.

Some writings were translated into French and Portuguese.

BIOGRAPHICAL AND CRITICAL SOURCES:

BOOKS

Grant, H. Roger, *Spirit Fruit: A Gentle Utopia,* Northern Illinois University Press (DeKalb, IL), 1988.
Henry, Leroy Freedom Hill, compiler, *Jacob Beilhart: Life and Teachings,* Freedom Hill Pressery (Burbank, CA), 1925.*

* * *

BENDER, Harold S(tauffer) 1897-1962

PERSONAL: Born July 19, 1897, in Elkhart, IN; died September 21, 1962, in Chicago, IL; married Elizabeth Horsch, 1923. *Education:* Goshen College, graduated, 1918; graduate study at Princeton University and Princeton Theological Seminary; University of Heidelberg, Th.D.

CAREER: Hesston College, Hesston, KS, teacher, beginning c. 1918; Goshen College, Elkhart, IN, teacher, beginning mid-1920s, dean, 1931-44, dean of biblical seminary, beginning 1944. Ordained minister of college congregation, Goshen, IN, 1944; member of Mennonite central committee, beginning 1930; Mennonite World Conference, founding member, and president, 1952-62; peaceproblems committee of the Mennonite Church, served as secretary.

MEMBER: American Society of Church History (past president), Mennonite Historical Society (founding member; past president).

WRITINGS:

Two Centuries of American Mennonite Literature: A Bibliography of Mennonitica Americana, 1727-1928, Mennonite Historical Society (Goshen, IN), 1929.

Conrad Grebel: Founder of the Swiss Brethren; Humanist Years, privately printed, 1936, reprinted, Mennonite Historical Society (Goshen, IN), 1950.

These Are My People: The Nature of the Church and Its Discipleship according to the New Testament, Herald Press (Scottsdale, PA), 1962.

(Editor, with Henry C. Smith, and contributor) *The Mennonite Encyclopedia,* four volumes, Herald Press (Scottsdale, PA), 1965-69.

Author of booklets, including "Biblical Revelation and Inspiration," Mennonite Publishing House (Scottsdale, PA), 1959; and "The Anabaptists and Religious Liberty in the Sixteenth Century," Fortress Press (Philadelphia, PA), 1970. Editor of the series "Studies in Anabaptist and Mennonite History," Mennonite Historical Society (Goshen, IN). Contributor to periodicals, including *Church History.* Editor, *Mennonite Quarterly Review,* beginning 1927.

BIOGRAPHICAL AND CRITICAL SOURCES:

BOOKS

Wenger, John Christian, *The Mennonites in Indiana and Michigan,* Herald Press (Scottsdale, PA), 1961.*

BERGER, Samantha (Allison) 1969-

PERSONAL: Born March 21, 1969, in Philadelphia, PA; daughter of David G. Berger (a college professor and author) and Eileen Kitzis (a graduate professor and yoga instructor). *Education:* Temple University, B.A. (English; cum laude), 1991.

ADDRESSES: Agent—c/o Author Mail, Harry N. Abrams, 100 Fifth Ave., New York, NY 10011.

CAREER: City and Country School, New York, NY, teacher, 1994; C.O.L.L.A.G.E. Comics, Philadelphia, PA, designer, editor, and writer, 1994-97; Scholastic, New York, NY, editor and writer, 1997-2000; Nickelodeon, New York, NY, head writer and editorial director of Nickelodeon, Nick Junior, and Nicktoons TV on-air creative group, 2000—.

MEMBER: A.S.I.F.A. (International Animated Film Association).

AWARDS, HONORS: Promax Silver Award, 2002, for *Fairly Odd Parents;* New York Book Show Award, for "Side by Side" readers; Building Language for Literacy Award; Ed Press Award for *Let's Find Out* magazine.

WRITINGS:

Baby Bird, Scholastic (New York, NY), 1999.
Light, Scholastic (New York, NY), 1999.
Honk! Toot! Beep!, illustrated by Gloria Elliott, Scholastic (New York, NY), 2000.
Please Don't Tell about Mom's Bell, illustrated by Rick Brown, Scholastic (New York, NY), 2002.
Spend a Day in Backwards Bay, illustrated by Rick Brown, Scholastic (New York, NY), 2002.
Jan and Stan, illustrated by Rick Brown, Scholastic (New York, NY), 2002.
Ride and Slide, illustrated by R. W. Alley, Scholastic (New York, NY), 2002.
Junior Goes to School, Harry N. Abrams (New York, NY), 2003.

WITH PAMELA CHANKO

Markets, Scholastic (New York, NY), 1998.
Scientists, Scholastic (New York, NY), 1998.

Big and Little, Scholastic (New York, NY), 1998.
School, Scholastic (New York, NY), 1999.
The Boat Book, Scholastic (New York, NY), 1999.
Electricity, Scholastic (New York, NY), 1999.
Festivals, Scholastic (New York, NY), 1999.
It's Spring, illustrated by Melissa Sweet, Scholastic (New York, NY), 2000.

WITH SUSAN CANIZARES

(With Gloria Elliot) *Clay Art with Gloria Elliot,* Scholastic (New York, NY), 1998.
What Do Artists Use?, Scholastic (New York, NY), 1998.
Building Shapes, Scholastic (New York, NY), 1998.
Tedd and Huggly, Scholastic (New York, NY), 1998.
Pelé, the King of Soccer, Scholastic (New York, NY), 1999.
Canada, Scholastic (New York, NY), 1999.
(With the Jim Henson Legacy) *Meet Jim Henson,* Scholastic (New York, NY), 1999.
(With the Jim Henson Foundation) *Puppets,* Scholastic (New York, NY), 1999.
The Voyage of Mae Jemison, Scholastic (New York, NY), 1999.
Tools, Scholastic (New York, NY), 1999.
Restaurant, Scholastic (New York, NY), 2000.
At Home, Scholastic (New York, NY), 2000.

WITH DANIEL MORETON

Why Write?, Scholastic (New York, NY), 1998.
Patterns, Scholastic (New York, NY), 1998.
Then and Now, Scholastic (New York, NY), 1998.
It's a Party, Scholastic (New York, NY), 1998.
Celebrations, Scholastic (New York, NY), 1999.
A Day in Japan, Scholastic (New York, NY), 1999.
Games, Scholastic (New York, NY), 1999.
(With Lisa Eve Huberman) *Junior in the City,* Harry N. Abrams (New York, NY), 2002.
(With Lisa Eve Huberman) *Junior on the Farm,* Harry N. Abrams (New York, NY), 2002.

WITH BETSEY CHESSON

Hello, Scholastic (New York, NY), 1998.
In the Air, Scholastic (New York, NY), 1999.
Apples, Scholastic (New York, NY), 1999.

OTHER

(With Anne Kennedy) *Fifi Ferret's Flute,* Scholastic (New York, NY), 2001.
(With Matt Phillips) *Worm's Wagon,* Scholastic (New York, NY), 2001.
(With Maxie Chambliss) *Hide-and-Seek Hippo,* Scholastic (New York, NY), 2001.

Also involved with television show *Fairly Odd Parents,* "Side by Side" reading series, and *Let's Find Out* magazine.

SIDELIGHTS: Author and illustrator Samantha Berger has written over fifty books for children and has written and illustrated comic books and graphic novels. Many of Berger's books for very young children feature photographs of colorful objects or scenes, and simple descriptive prose. The focus is often on teaching children about their everyday world. Some examples include *At Home,* which shows the many different things one can do at home, and *Celebrations,* which explores a number of occasions for celebration, including birthdays and weddings. *Electricty* has pictures showing how electricity effects everyone's life by contrasting various tasks as they are done with and without electric power, while *Light* explores different sources of illumination, including sunlight, moonlight, lamplight, and candlelight.

Berger's books for slightly older children contain more complicated plot lines, such as *It's Spring,* which features animals in the wild playing a kind of telephone game where they let each other know that the season is upon them. *Junior in the City* and *Junior on the Farm* each star a pig with poor eyesight who has trouble recognizing things without his glasses. A spin wheel allows the reader to select humorous pictures of things Junior thinks he sees—for example, without his spectacles, the sun could be a pumpkin, a fried egg, or even a flower.

In addition to writing, Berger also does voice-overs for animation and is involved in puppeteering.

BIOGRAPHICAL AND CRITICAL SOURCES:

PERIODICALS

Publishers Weekly, August 12, 2002, p. 302.

BERKOVITCH, Nitza 1955-

PERSONAL: Born September 7, 1955, in Israel. *Ethnicity:* "Jewish." *Education:* Tel-Aviv University, B.A. (magna cum laude), 1981, M.A. (magna cum laude), 1986; Stanford University, Ph.D., 1995. *Politics:* "Feminist, left." *Religion:* Jewish.

ADDRESSES: Home—24 Yad Vashem St., Bet See'eem, Beer Sheva, Israel. *Office*—Department of Behavioral Sciences, Ben-Gurion University, Beer Sheva, Israel 84105; fax 97-23-605-0406. *E-mail*—nberko@bgumail.bgu.ac.il.

CAREER: Tel-Aviv University, Tel-Aviv, Israel, visiting lecturer in management and sociology, 1986-88, visiting lecturer in sociology, 1994-95; Stanford University, Stanford, CA, statistical consultant in libraries and information resources, 1991-93, adjunct lecturer in sociology, 1992-94; Ben-Gurion University, Beer Sheva, Israel, lecturer in behavioral sciences, 1995—, co-director of women's studies program, 1996—, head of sociology program, 1997-98. Western Washington University, adjunct lecturer, 1993. Adva Research Institute, member of editorial board of *Lexicon on Inequality,* 1998—; consultant to Israel Science Foundation, Ministry of Science, and Megamot.

AWARDS, HONORS: Grant from Devora Netzer Fund for Research and Promotion of Women in the Community, 1991-92; Morris Ginsberg postdoctoral fellow, Hebrew University of Jerusalem, 1994-95; grants from Ford Foundation, 1999-2001, and Israel Ministry of Science, 1999-2001.

WRITINGS:

From Motherhood to Citizenship: Women's Rights and International Organizations, Johns Hopkins University Press (Baltimore, MD), 1999.

Contributor to books, including *Public Rights, Public Rules: Constituting Citizens in the World Polity and National Policy,* edited by Connie L. McNeely, Garland Publishing (New York, NY), 1998, and *Constructing World Culture: International Non-Governmental Organizations since 1875,* edited by John Boli and George Thomas, Stanford University Press (Stanford, CA), 1996. Contributor of articles and reviews to periodicals in Israel and elsewhere, including *Israeli Sociology, Sociological Perspectives, Theory and Critique,* and *Women Studies International Forum.* Member of editorial board, coeditor of special issue, 1999—.

WORK IN PROGRESS: Globalization, the Textile Industry, and Women's Work, with Uri Ram; *Gender and the Welfare State: The Case of Israel,* with Sara Helam.

*   *   *

BERNSTEIN, Eduard 1850-1932

PERSONAL: Born January 6, 1850, in Berlin, Germany; died December 18, 1932, in Berlin, Germany; son of Jakob Bernstein (a railway engineer). *Politics:* Socialist.

CAREER: Worked as a bank clerk, political organizer for the German Social Democratic Party (SPD), political journalist and editor. Member of the Reichstag (national assembly), 1902-06, 1912-18, and 1920-28.

WRITINGS:

Ferdinand Lassalle as a Social Reformer, translation by Eleanor Marx Aveling, Swan Sonnenschein (London, England), 1893.
(With others) *Geschichte des Sozialismus in Einzeldarstellungen,* J.H.W. Dietz (Stuttgart, Germany), 1895.
Zur Geschichte und Theorie des Socialismus, Edelheim (Berlin, Germany), 1904.
Die Grundbedingungen des Wirtschaftslebens, Buchhandlung Vorwärts, H. Weber (Berlin, Germany), 1906.
Der Streik; sein Wesen und sein Wirken, Literarische Anstalt Rütten und Löening (Frankfurt am Main, Germany), 1906.
Der Geschlechtstrieb, Buchhandlung Vorwärts (Berlin, Germany), 1910.
Aus den Jahren meines Exils, Freidrich Reiss (Berlin, Germany), 1917, translation by Bernard Miall published as *My Years in Exile: Reminiscences of a Socialist,* L. Parsons (London, England), 1921, Greenwood Press (Westport, CT), 1986.

Völkerbund ööder Stätenbund: eine Untersuchung, P. Cassirer (Berlin, Germany), 1919.

Die deutsche Revolution, ihr Ursprung, ihr Verlauf und ihr Werk, Gesellschaft und Erziehung (Berlin, Germany), 1921.

Germanskaia Revoliutsiia, Vostok (Berlin, Germany), 1922.

Die Voraussetzungen des Sozialismus und die Aufgaben der Sozialdemokratie, J. W. Dietz (Stuttgart, Germany), 1899, translation by Edith C. Harvey published as *Evolutionary Socialism,* B.W. Huebsch (New York, NY), 1912, reprinted, Schocken Books (New York, NY), 1961, 1978.

Sozialismus und Demokratie in der Grossen englischen Revolution J. H. W. Dietz (Stuttgart, Germany), 1908, translation by H. J. Stenning published as *Cromwell and Communism: Socialism and Democracy in the Great English Revolution,* G. Allen Unwin (London, England), 1930, A. M. Kelley (New York, NY), 1963.

Also author of a political pamphlets and articles. Coeditor of socialist newspaper *Sozialdemokrat,* 1879-90, published in Zurich until 1888 and afterward in London, England. Edited various other socialist newspapers, magazines, and books.

SIDELIGHTS: German writer, socialist thinker, and politician Eduard Bernstein was the leader of the "revisionist" wing of the German Socialist Democratic Party (SPD) in the early decades of the twentieth century. The author of more than thirty German-language books and political pamphlets, he is remembered today as the author of *Evolutionary Socialism,* a seminal 1899 treatise in which Bernstein reject the inevitability of the apocalyptic class struggle Karl Marx had predicted and offer instead an evolutionary rather than a revolutionary path for socialism.

Bernstein's theories—known as "revisionism," —became the catalyst for a furious debate among leftist intellectuals regarding the essence of socialism and the true nature of capitalist society. "[Bernstein's] intellectual conflicts before the [First World] war with Augustus Bebel, Karl Lautsky and George Plekhanov, 'the giants of orthodox Marxism,' have formed a significant chapter in the history of the development of Socialist thought and modern European politics," the author of Bernstein's 1932 obituary noted in the *New York Times.* "He lived to see his principles

incorporated not only in the official policy of the Social-Democracy of Germany but of other countries of Western Europe and the modern expression of socialism."

Bernstein's ideas also earned him the scorn of orthodox Marxists. Writing in the introduction to a 1963 edition of *Evolutionary Socialism,* Sidney Hook observed: "In Marxist circles to pin the label of 'revisionist' on the ideas of a socialist thinker is comparable to exposing a Christian writer as a 'heretic' or 'atheist' during the heyday of Western religious faith."

Bernstein was the seventh in a family of fifteen children. His father, a railway worker, barely made enough money to put food on the table for the family. Although they were Jewish, the Bernsteins did not follow their religion. According to Peter Gay, in *The Dilemma of Democratic Socialism,* "In this atmosphere young Eduard grew up half believer, half skeptic" and abandoned his faith. However, the writer of the *New York Times* obituary reported, "In his late years . . . he said that he would not do so if he had his life to live over again."

Bernstein was a sickly child and he preferred the world of books to that of sports and physical activity. He had a quick, nimble mind, and an artistic bent. For a time, Bernstein wrote poetry and dreamed of working in the theater either as an actor or a playwright. While he was a good student, money was tight and so Bernstein quit school in 1866 without graduating. To make ends meet, he began a three-year apprenticeship in a Berlin bank. Upon completing his training, Bernstein took a job as a bank clerk, a vocation that he worked at for the next nine years.

Bernstein's political education began early; he absorbed ideas from one of his uncles, an editorial writer for a German Socialist newspaper called *Volkszeitung* "(People's Times)." Bernstein's own political passions were fired by contemporary events, including the Franco-Prussian war of 1870-71 and the persecution of socialist anti-war protesters by Prussian statesman Prince Otto von Bismarck. Bernstein and some friends formed a discussion circle they called "Utopia." It was at a meeting of this group that Bernstein met F. W. Fritzche. Fritzche, a union organizer and SPD supporter, talked about the issues that had split the German socialist movement into two warring factions: the Eisenbachers and the Lassalleans. Inspired by Fritzche's lecture, Bernstein did some reading and decided that he agreed with the Eisenbachers; in February 1872 he joined the SPD. During the next six years, a period Gay quoted Bernstein referring to as his "Social Democratic apprenticeship," Bernstein became a party organizer and an accomplished stump speaker.

German socialists put aside their theoretical differences and united in 1875. This was a time of intense political ferment in Germany, which Bismarck had succeeded in unifying as a country in 1871. Two attempts on the life of Emperor William I by alleged socialist sympathizers gave the "Iron Chancellor" all the excuse he needed in 1878 to push through the Reichstag a law authorizing harsh anti-socialist measures. Around this same time Bernstein went into self-imposed exile, taking a job in Switzerland as secretary to Karl Höchberg, a wealthy young idealist. Höchberg was at odds with Marx and Marx colleague Friedrich Engels, among others in the socialist movement. Bernstein also got heavily involved in the at-times bitter quarrels.

As Bernstein's own political ideas evolved, he found himself drawing closer to Engels. In 1881, at Engels' urging, Bernstein joined the staff of the Zurich-based partisan publication *Sozialdemokrat* ("Social-Democrat"). Thousands of copies of the newspaper were smuggled into Germany. During this period, Bernstein's notions about socialism continued to evolve; in a Bernstein obituary published in the *Nation*, Ludwig Lore noted how Engels, writing in an 1881 letter to Augustus Bebel, had reported, "Bernstein is doing a splendid job. . . . We can hardly find a better man. In his hands the paper is improving from week to week, and he with it."

Incensed by the caustic editorial opinions expressed in *Sozialdemokrat,* Bismarck began pressing the Swiss government to expel the paper's editorial staff. When that happened in April 1888, Bernstein fled to London, where he lived for the next three years. During this period Bernstein met and came to know many of the leaders of the Fabian Society, a British socialist group founded in 1884 that boasted among its members such well-known figures as economist Sidney Webb and his wife, sociologist Beatrice Webb, playwright George Bernard Shaw, novelist H. G. Wells, and politician James Ramsay MacDonald, who in 1924 became Britain's first Labour prime minister.

In 1896 Bernstein wrote a series of articles on the problems of socialism, that were published in *Die neue Zeit* ("The New Times") the newspaper of the German SPD. During his London stay, he absorbed fresh ideas from the Fabians. That group had rejected Marx's revolutionary approach to change, instead advocating an evolutionary approach, which they described as "the inevitability of gradualness." Spurred on by the feedback he had received from his 1896 articles, and by the insights generated by his exposure to the Fabians, Bernstein wrote *Evolutionary Socialism.* This 1899 book, Bernstein's signature work, became the classic statement of socialist "revisionism." In it the author uses scientific analysis to attack the basic tenets of Marx's theories of revolution as the engine of change in capitalist society. Using statistics, Bernstein shows that workers were not becoming inevitably poorer; despite Marx's dire predictions, capitalism was not in imminent danger of collapse.

Writing in the introduction to the first edition of *Evolutionary Socialism,* Bernstein explains, "I set myself against the notion that we have to expect shortly a collapse of the bourgeois economy, and that social democracy should be induced by the prospect of such an imminent, great, social catastrophe to adapt its tactics to that assumption. That I maintain most emphatically." Bernstein goes on to reject the notion of revolution in favor of a moderate, constitutional approach to achieving political power. In order to achieve those ends, he urges the SPD to broaden its political power base by making efforts to appeal to Germany's growing middle class.

The reaction to *Evolutionary Socialism* was swift and intense. A sizeable number of SPD members disagreed with Bernstein's ideas, but many others backed him. Those who did so took to calling themselves "Bernsteinians" or "Revisionists." As a result, when Bernstein returned home to Germany in 1901 after twenty-three years in exile, he discovered that he was a popular figure who was much in demand as a public speaker.

Although voters in the town of Breslau elected Bernstein to the Reichstag in 1902 for the first of three terms, his revisionist views were officially condemned by the SPD. This polarization led to a rift in the party, which split between supporters of Bernstein's evolutionary approach to change and those who continued to advocate armed revolution. The gap of the two factions grew in the wake of the 1917 Bolshevik revolution in Russia and Bernstein's criticisms of Bolshevik leader Vladimir Ilyich Lenin. In addition, Bernstein's opposition to Germany's own war effort led him and other like-minded socialists to split from the SPD to form the Independent Social Democratic Party. When the war ended in November 1918, Bernstein rejoined the SPD, and continued to represent the party in the Reichstag.

After Bernstein retired from political life in 1928 at age seventy-eight, he devoted the last four years of his life to writing. By the time of his death, a scant few weeks before the rise to power of Adolf Hitler and the Nazi party, Bernstein was no longer a leader of the SPD or even an important figure in the party. His ideas were not forgotten, however. "When the [SPD] was reorganized in West Germany after World War II, many of Bernstein's ideas were incorporated in its programs," wrote Christian H. Eismann in a essay in the *Encyclopedia of World Biography.* "The new party gave up its revolutionary theory, emphasized action and reform, and attempted to broaden its political base by cutting across ideological and class lines."

BIOGRAPHICAL AND CRITICAL SOURCES:

BOOKS

Blaug, Mark, *One Hundred Great Economists of the Past,* Humanities Press International (Highlands, NJ), 1986.
Encyclopedia of World Biography, 2nd edition, Gale (Detroit, MI), 1998.
Gay, Peter, *The Dilemma of Democratic Socialism: Eduard Bernstein's Challenge to Marx,* Octagon Books (New York, NY), 1983.
Teed, Peter, editor, *Dictionary of Twentieth-Century History, 1914-1990,* Oxford University Press (Oxford, England), 1992.
World of Sociology, Volume 1, Gale (Detroit, MI), 2001.

PERIODICALS

American Historical Review, June, 1983, R. A. Fletcher, "Cobden as Educator: The Free-Trade Internationalism of Eduard Bernstein, 1899-1914," pp. 561-578.

Journal of Economic Issues, September 9, 1991, Doug Brown, "Thorstein Veblein Meets Eduard Bernstein: Toward An Institutionalist Theory of Mobilization Politics," pp. 689-708.
New Statesman, November 28, 1986, Peter Kravitz, "Between the Lines," p. 44.
Times Literary Supplement, May 6, 1994, Mark Garnett, "The Preconditions of Socialism," p. 27.

OBITUARIES:

PERIODICALS

Nation, January 4, 1933, Ludwig Lore, "Eduard Bernstein," pp. 14-15.
New York Times, December 19, 1932, "Eduard Bernstein, Socialist, Dies, 82," p. 15.
World Tomorrow, January 11, 1933, p. 30.*

                          *   *   *

BIBER, Jacob 1915-
(Ya'akov Biber)

PERSONAL: Born March 15, 1915, in Matzeev (now Lukov), Ukraine; came to the United States, 1947; son of Elkone Dov Konebear "Berka" (a cattle dealer, grocer, and farmer) and Chasia (Gortenstein) Biber; married Eva Cherniak, March 7, 1939; children: Shalom Shakhne (deceased), Chaim Shalom Dov, Ben-Zion, Joseph. *Education:* Attended Jewish religious schools in Matzeev, Ukraine. *Religion:* Conservative Jewish. *Hobbies and other interests:* Reading, poetry, amateur theater.

ADDRESSES: Home—700 South West 128th Ave., Pembroke Pines, FL 33027-1781.

CAREER: Worked on his parents' farm until age 17; grocer from 1932-39; principal and organizer of school in Displaced Persons' (DP) Camp, Föhrenwald, Germany, then head of Teachers' Organization for Bavaria, Germany, DP District, 1946-47. Dairy and poultry farmer in, South Windham, CT, 1948-50; dairy farmer, c. 1950-55; owner of egg production farm and egg distribution service in, Preston, CT, c. 1955-73.

MEMBER: Survivors Club (Pembroke Pines, FL; vice president, 1988-99).

AWARDS, HONORS: Honored by Jewish National Front, 1969; Certificate of Appreciation, New England Crop and Livestock Association, 1974; Certificate of Appreciation, Preston (CT) Historical Society, 1985; honored by the Broward School System for teaching students about the Holocaust, c. 1990s and by a synagogue in Century Village, FL, for his teaching of the Hebrew language; Lion of Israel Award, State of Israel Bonds, 1996; recognized by Holocaust Museum as among outstanding writers in America on the Holocaust.

WRITINGS:

Survivors: A Personal Story of the Holocaust, Star Publishers (New London, CT), 1982, revised edition, Borgo Press (San Bernardino, CA), 1989.

Risen from the Ashes: A Story of the Jewish Displaced Persons in the Aftermath of World War II (sequel to *Survivors*), introduction by Elie Wiesel, Borgo Press (San Bernardino, CA), 1990.

(As Ya'akov Biber) *Bey der Shkieh Fun Lebn: Lider un Poemes Fun a Geratevetn Yid* (title means "At the Twilight of Life: Songs and Poems from a Jewish Survivor"), J. Biber (Pembroke Pines, FL), 1992.

Violence and Devotion: A Novel of the Holocaust, Borgo Press (San Bernardino, CA), 1996.

(Editor) *A Triumph of the Spirit: Ten Stories of Holocaust Survivors,* Borgo Press (San Bernardino, CA), 1994, expanded edition published as *A Triumph of the Spirit: Thirteen Stories of Holocaust Survivors,* 1998.

(As Ya'akov Biber) *Derner un Blumen* (title means "Poems and Flowers"), edited by Alex Silver, J. Biber (Pembroke Pines, FL), 1998.

Work anthologized in *1945: The Year of Liberation: The Guide to the United States Holocaust Memorial Museum,* 1995.

SIDELIGHTS: Jacob Biber is a Holocaust survivor who later moved to the United States, where he wrote and edited several books that strive to preserve Jewish history and the Yiddish language. Biber grow up in the small town of Matzeev, about three hundred miles east of Warsaw, Poland. One-third of the town's 7,500 residents were Jewish, and it was in this community that Biber was educated and married his childhood sweetheart, the granddaughter of the local rabbi. Matzeev was caught up in the many European wars of the first half of the twentieth century, including World War I and the Russian civil war. Biber and his family were nearly killed in April of 1920, during the latter war, when retreating Bolshevik forces set fire to a storage warehouse in the Bibers' neighborhood.

In *Survivors: A Personal Story of the Holocaust* Biber recounts his experiences in World War II. When Nazi Germany invaded the area of Matzeev in the summer of 1941, over three hundred Jewish men and boys, including Biber's brother Ben-Zion, were massacred by the Gestapo, the German secret police. Biber and his wife, Eva, hid in the woods to avoid subsequent shootings by the Germans, but their hiding place was betrayed. As he and Eva ran for their lives, their infant son, Shalom, was shot out of Jacob's arms, and they were forced to abandon his body beneath a bush. Devastated, Jacob and Eva planned to turn themselves in to the Gestapo but were convinced by a friend to reconsider.

Risen from the Ashes: A Story of the Jewish Displaced Persons in the Aftermath of World War II, the sequel to *Survivors,* recounts the Bibers' life in a displaced persons' camp in Germany following the war. Like many of their fellow Jews, they wished to settle in the soon-to-be-realized state of Israel, but the British still controlled the region, and they refused to let the stateless survivors into Palestine. So, for a two-year period, the Bibers lived in Camp Föhrenwald, established and operated by the U.S. during its postwar occupation of Germany. Eventually, their determination to find a new home led them to the United States, where they purchased a farm in Preston, Connecticut.

Biber's anthology of survivors' accounts, *A Triumph of the Spirit: Ten Stories of Holocaust Survivors,* was undertaken after his retirement to Pembroke Pines, Florida. There he and Eva encountered other survivors of the Holocaust and exchanged stories. Biber quickly saw that these people too had a need to share their experiences and to bear witness to future generations. As he explained in his introduction to the book: "It is only through such contemporary reports that the world can be made aware of the acts of insanity a 'civilized and cultured' nation is capable of committing. Their testimonies also bear witness to the great moral and spiritual strength the Jews maintained, even while being subjected to the most horrible conditions, beatings, gruesome brutality, and starvation. They did not waver."

In recent years Biber has begun writing stories and poems in Yiddish, the language of his youth. He also continues to lecture to school audiences and citizen groups on the reality of the Holocaust.

BIOGRAPHICAL AND CRITICAL SOURCES:

PERIODICALS

Day, March 26, 1982; April 19, 1990, p. 4.
Hartford Courant (Hartford, CT), April 4, 1982.
New Haven Register (New Haven, CT), March 14, 1982.
Norwich Bulletin (Norwich, CT), June 4, 1994.
Norwich Bulletin Courier (Norwich, CT), April 27, 1986, p. E1.
Providence Sunday Journal (Providence, RI), February 21, 1982.
Willimantic Chronicle (Willimantic, CT), March 27, 1982.*

                    *   *   *

BIBER, Ya'akov
    See BIBER, Jacob

                    *   *   *

BIDINI, Dave 1963(?)-

PERSONAL: Born c. 1963; married; children: one daughter. *Education:* Attended Trinity College, Dublin. *Hobbies and other interests:* Hockey.

ADDRESSES: Agent—c/o Author Mail, McClelland & Stewart Ltd., 481 University Avenue, Suite 900, Toronto, Ontario, Canada M5G 2E9.

CAREER: Musician, and writer.

WRITINGS:

On a Cold Road: Tales of Adventure in Canadian Rock, McClelland & Stewart (Toronto, Ontario, Canada), 1998.
Tropic of Hockey: My Search for the Game in Unlikely Places, McClelland & Stewart (Toronto, Ontario, Canada), 2000.

Contributor to periodicals, including *Toronto Star,* and *Saturday Night,* and to the anthologies *The Original Six: True Stories from Hockey's Classic Era* and *Maple Leaf Gardens: Memories and Dreams, 1931-1999.*

SIDELIGHTS: A founding member of the Rheostatics, a Canadian rock band, Dave Bidini has been a working musician for more than two decades. Bidini has also been writing for nearly as long, starting with writings that he "scribbled since I was barely into my teens," as he notes on his personal Web site. Budding writers are often told to write about what they know, and Bidini has followed this advice. His first book, *On a Cold Road: Tales of Adventure in Canadian Rock,* chronicles the 1996 tour the Rheostatics made across Canada as openers for the more commercially successful band the *Tragically Hip.* In addition to his own personal stories of the tour, Bidini interweaves the stories of forty-seven older Canadian rockers. Most of them never made it to the big time, but they have plenty of eyebrow-raising stories to tell.

Divided into chapters according to the Canadian provinces the tour goes through, Bidini's book not only throws the spotlight on the mythic aspects of touring in a rock band, such as groupies and drugs, but Bidini's own reflections on both the glamour and dedication required in the music business. In a review on the *eye* Web site, Cindy McGlynn noted that, at times, "Bidini overwrites" especially "when trying too hard to share an experience that obviously moved him." However, she called the book a "cleverly structured and well-written" addition to the Canadian rock canon. Tom Snyders, writing in *Quill & Quire,* called Bidini's writing "well-crafted, personal, and passionate" dubbed book is "candid, Canadian, incisive, and inspirational." On the *Canoe* Web site, Jim Slotek stated that the book's "real joy" is "the Greek chorus of rockers, old and older, who tell their tall tales like boozehounds in a Legion Hall," adding that "Bidini's own tales are told with an honest eye for detail."

In addition to music and writing, Bidini has another passion shared by many Canadians: ice hockey. *Tropic of Hockey: My Search for the Game in Unlikely Places* is a travelogue in which Bidini takes a global odyssey—from China to Russia to the Middle East—in search of people in far-flung places who, unlike the professionals, play for the mere joy of the game. Although Bidini fell out of love with the game for a time, over the years he once again became an avid recreational player. His second book is a humour-filled story of dedicated players with quirky personalities. Bidini also sets forth his views on what is wrong with contemporary hockey, especially on the professional level. "People are always saying you should write about what you know," Bidini told Nicholas Jennings in *Maclean's.* "It's a natural subject for many Canadian musicians because so many of us know hockey. And for a writer, the game really lends itself to poetry and romance."

"Like all good travelogues, Bidini's carries a healthy dose of soul searching," noted a reviewer in *Publishers Weekly,* calling Bidini a "great storyteller" who's "at his best when he stumbles upon revelations about himself or hockey." Larry R. Little, writing in *Library Journal,* called, "Bidini's travelog . . . a humorous cultural exposé of people and how they play the game." Little also commented, "The result is a delightful read that both armchair travelers and aficionados will enjoy." Calling the book "delightful," in her review for *Resource Links,* Margaret Mackey also remarked that, "Laugh-out-loud funny in places, the book has a great deal to offer to hockey fans and others."

BIOGRAPHICAL AND CRITICAL SOURCES:

PERIODICALS

Canadian Book Review, Volume 27, 1998, Jack S. Broumpton, review of *On a Cold Road: Tales of Adventure in Canadian Rock,* p. 50.

Library Journal, March 15, 2002, review of *Tropic of Hockey: My Search for the Game in Unlikely Places,* p. 87.

Maclean's, December 11, 2000, "Rock 'n' Hockey: More and More Artists Are Playing, and Singing about, Canada's Sport," p. 51.

Publishers Weekly, November 27, 2000, D'Arcy Jenish, includes a review of *Tropic of Hockey: My Search for the Game in Unlikely Places,* p. 90; March 15, 2002, review of *Tropic of Hockey: My Search for the Game in Unlikely Places,* p. 56.

Quill & Quire, October, 1998, Tom Snyders, review of *On a Cold Road: Tales of Adventure in Canadian Rock,* p. 31.

Resource Links, October 2001, Margaret Mackey, review of *Tropic of Hockey: My Search for the Game in Unlikely Places,* p. 58.

ONLINE

Canoe Web site, http://www.canoe.ca/ (November 15, 1998), Jim Slotek, review of *On a Cold Road.*

Dave Bidini Home Page, http://www.davebidini.com (September 10, 2002).

Eye Web site, http://www.eye.net/ (October 22, 1998), Cindy McGlynn, "On the Highway to Hull, Canadiana and Guitars in Dave Bidini's *On a Cold Road.*"*

*   *   *

BINNEMA, Theodore 1963-

PERSONAL: Born March 25, 1963, in Red Deer, Alberta, Canada; son of Jacob Hendrik and Hilda (Scholtens) Binnema; married Helena Suzanna Van Harten. *Education:* Calvin College, B.A., 1985; University of Alberta, M.A., 1992, Ph.D., 1998.

ADDRESSES: Home—Prince George, British Columbia, Canada. *Office*—University of Northern British Columbia, Prince George, British Columbia, Canada V2N 4Z9; fax: 250-960-5545. *E-mail*—binnemat@ unbc.ca.

CAREER: University of Northern British Columbia, Prince George, British Columbia, Canada, assistant professor, 2000—.

WRITINGS:

(Editor, with Gerhard Eus and R. C. Macleod) *From Rupert's Land to Canada,* University of Alberta Press (Edmonton, Alberta, Canada), 2001.

Common and Contested Ground: A Human and Environmental History of the Northwestern Plains, University of Oklahoma Press (Norman, OK), 2001.

Contributor to periodicals, including *Canadian Historical Review, American Indian Quarterly, Prairie Forum,* and *Alberta History.*

WORK IN PROGRESS: Research on the history of Canadian Indian policy, on the history of the Northwest Plains, 1806-1880, and on Peter Fidler.

BIOGRAPHICAL AND CRITICAL SOURCES:

PERIODICALS

Canadian Historical Review, March, 2002, R. Douglas Francis, review of *From Rupert's Land to Canada,* p. 124.
Choice, July-August, 2002, J. A. Baughter, review of *Common and Contested Ground: A Human and Environmental History of the Northwestern Plains,* p. 2022.

*　　*　　*

BLANK, Harrod 1963(?)-

PERSONAL: Born c. 1963; son of Les (a filmmaker) and Gail (a ceramic artist) Blank. *Education:* University of California—Santa Cruz, B.A., 1986.

ADDRESSES: Office—2248 Summer St. Berkeley, CA 94709-1428. *E-mail*—harrod@harrodblank.com.

CAREER: Filmmaker, photographer, and author. Producer, director, and editor of the documentary films *Wild Wheels,* produced by PBS, and *Driving the Dream,* part of *National Geographic Explorer* series, 1997.

AWARDS, HONORS: Best Book for Young Adults, American Library Association, c. 1993, for *Wild Wheels.*

WRITINGS:

Wild Wheels, Pomegranate Communications, Inc. (Rohnert Park, CA), 1993.
Art Cars: The Cars, the Artists, the Obsession, the Craft, Lark Books (Asheville, NC), 2002.

WORK IN PROGRESS: I've Got Vision, a book containing photographs of people reacting to their first sighting of the "Camera Van"; *Wild Wheels II,* a documentary.

SIDELIGHTS: Harrod Blank has parlayed his love of "art cars" into a career as a filmmaker and author. It all began when Blank moved from a commune, where he lived with his mother, to downtown Santa Cruz, California, when he was seventeen. While other teenagers may have turned to oddly colored hair and body piercings to express themselves, Blank took a 1965 Volkswagen Beetle and began spray painting it in fluorescent colors. He added a spinning globe to the hood and then planted a television with a skull inside—(a commentary on television violence)—on the roof. More weird and exotic additions soon followed, like plastic baby dolls, which Blank attached as a statement on overpopulation. The reactions he encountered as people saw his car led him to name it "Oh My God!" Several years later, after attending college, Blank set out on a two-year cross-country trip to film a documentary called *Wild Wheels* on the art car scene, which ultimately resulted in a companion book.

The 1993 book *Wild Wheels* includes 100 photographs and descriptions of forty-two art-car aficionados who decorate their cars not only for the attention these vehicles draw but as a personal statement of their beliefs, which are often stranger than fiction. Perhaps the most peculiar of the lot is a man in Alabama who believes he was told by God to "clean up his act" and, as a result, decorated his old Chevrolet with a plethora of faucets. Another participant in this pop-art phenomenon covered his car with grass, of the lawn-type variety. "They're all eccentric but giving," Blank told Janice Min in an article in *People.* "Their cars entertain."

In his second book, *Art Cars: The Cars, the Artists, the Obsession, the Craft.* Blank presents more than 100 new art-car creations, including the Skull Truck, the Cork Car, a car with a working waterfall, and the "Stinkbug!" covered with old cigarette butts. The book also includes an introduction that places the art-car movement within the context of other types of folk art and testimonials by various art-car creators as to why they create art cars and how they achieve their visions. Rebecca Miller, writing in *Library Journal,* commented that the book "could convince even the most stoic skeptics to give it a go with their own wheels." As a result, Blank also includes a how-to section for those that may be inspired to create their own art vehicle.

Another one of Blank's projects developed after he had a dream that he drove around the country in a car covered in cameras to chronicle the reaction people would have to it. Blank began browsing thrift shops for old cameras and asking friends and relatives for their obsolete cameras. He then took a 1972 Dodge van and covered it with more than 1,000 of them. However, hidden among the old broken-down cameras were motorized models that worked via a remote control device installed near the driver's seat. As a result, when people came up to the van to gawk at it, Blank was able to capture their uninhibited reactions. The result was more than 5,000 photographs, which Blank planned to develop into a book titled *I've Got a Vision.* "One of the fringe benefits of doing this," Blank told *People* about his art car passion, "is seeing the smiles, the thumbs-up, the awe in children's eyes."

BIOGRAPHICAL AND CRITICAL SOURCES:

PERIODICALS

Booklist, September 1, 1994, Nancy McCray, review of *Wild Wheels* video, p. 62.
Library Journal, April 1, 2002, Rebecca Miller, review of *Art Cars: The Cars, the Artists, the Obsession, the Craft,* p. 99.
New York Times, August 21, 1992, William Grimes, "No, It's Not a Mad Vision. It's an Art Car. Want a Ride?," p. B3(N), ; August 26, 1995, "A Total of 1,705 Candid Cameras," p. 37.
People, April 18, 1994, Janice Min, "Auto Auteur: Harrod Blank Films Vehicular Fantasies," pp. 57-58.
Publishers Weekly, January 28, 2002, "You Auto See This One!," p. 247.
School Library Journal, December, 1994, Burton H. Brooks, review of *Wild Wheels* (video), p. 61.

ONLINE

Harrod Blank Home Page, http://www.harrodblank. com (September 11, 2002).
Kodak Web site, http://www.kodak.com (May 30, 2002), "Art Cars: Photography by Harrod Blank."*

BLEE, Kathleen M.

PERSONAL: Female. *Education:* Indiana University, B.A. (with highest honors), 1974; University of Wisconsin—Madison, M.S., 1976, Ph.D., 1982.

ADDRESSES: Office—Department of Sociology, 2003 Forbes Quad, University of Pittsburgh, Pittsburgh, PA 15260. *E-mail*—kblee+@pitt.edu.

CAREER: University of Kentucky, Lexington, 1981-96, began as instructor, became professor, director of women's studies program, 1987-89, associate dean of, College of Arts and Sciences, 1989-91, 1992, research professor, 1994-95; University of Pittsburgh, Pittsburgh, PA, professor of sociology and director of women's studies program, 1996—, affiliated appointment with department of history, 1997—.

AWARDS, HONORS: Women of the Klan: Racism and Gender in the 1920s selected as an outstanding book by the Gustavus Myers Center for the Study of Human Rights.

WRITINGS:

Women of the Klan: Racism and Gender in the 1920s, University of California Press (Berkeley, CA), 1991.
(Editor) *No Middle Ground: Women and Radical Protest,* New York University Press (New York, NY), 1998.
(With Dwight B. Billings) *The Road to Poverty: The Making of Wealth and Hardship in Appalachia,* Cambridge University Press (New York, NY), 2000.
(Editor, with France Winddance Twine) *Feminism and Antiracism: International Struggles for Justice,* New York University Press (New York, NY), 2001.
Inside Organized Racism: Women in the Hate Movement, University of California Press (Berkeley, CA), 2002.

SIDELIGHTS: Sociologist Kathleen M. Blee's work often addresses the relationships of various social factors, including race, class, and gender, and frequently challenges widely held assumptions. *Women of the*

Klan: Racism and Gender in the 1920s examines the sense of feminist empowerment felt by women who ironically were working for the oppression of blacks, Jews, and Catholics through their participation in the Ku Klux Klan (KKK). In *Inside Organized Racism: Women in the Hate Movement,* again which deal with the intersection of gender and racial politics, Blee demonstrates that stereotypes of women in racist groups are often inaccurate. *The Road to Poverty: The Making of Wealth and Hardship in Appalachia,* written with Dwight B. Billings, explodes some of the stereotypes about that region.

Women of the Klan deals with a decade in which the Klan regained popularity. The original Klan, which operated in the South in the immediate post-Civil War period, was an all-male organization that carried out violent attacks on blacks ostensibly to protect supposedly defenseless white women. That Klan dissolved in the 1870s; in 1915 a new one was born out of resurgent racism and nativism. During the 1920s many women, newly emancipated by possession of voting rights and relaxation of social strictures, took power into their own hands by becoming active in racist groups that came together in 1923 as Women of the Ku Klux Klan (WKKK). Blee's account includes general information on WKKK activities and a case study of Klanswomen in Indiana. "What is so chilling about Blee's story," commented Dana Frank in the *Nation,* "is that those women did not join just to serve as obeisant handmaidens to their male masters. . . . The 1920s or second Klan appealed to white women in the name of . . . feminism." They saw it, Frank related, as a means "to defend against erosion of their newly won power of the vote by evil, conspiring Catholics, Jews and African-Americans." Some of the women who became Klan members had been activists for suffrage and other progressive social reforms; Blee writes that they had "a facile ability to fold bitter racial and religious bigotry into progressive politics." One of the appeals of the Klan was its antivice crusades, which "shaded easily into fanatic anti-Semitism and especially anti-Catholicism," Frank observed. Barbara Ehrenreich, critiquing for the *Los Angeles Times Book Review,* further explained, "In addition to its familiar ideals of white supremacy, anti-Semitism and so forth, the Ku Klux Klan of the 20s stood for Americanism, temperance, child-welfare measures, good citizenship, morality and militant Christianity."

Robert A. Goldberg, writing in the *Journal of Social History,* called *Women of the Klan* "impressive in several respects," saying, "Blee's insights about Klan culture are fresh and exciting and suggest new areas for research." He saw, however, a lack of data to support some of Blee's statements, such as her estimate of the number of Klanswomen and her assertion that many of them had a feminist bent. "A few Klanswomen at the national level did articulate an equal-rights position," he remarked, "but among the rank and file there seems to have been contentment with traditional gender roles. He did grant that "Blee has pointed scholars in a new and necessary direction." Ehrenreich, who praised the book generally, believed Blee does not draw sufficient distinction between feminist-minded Klanswomen and more typical feminist groups of the era. "Not all civic-minded women of appropriate pigmentation sought sorority within the Women's Klan," Ehrenreich wrote. "Nor did the mainstream feminist organizations, whatever their shortcomings on matters of race and ethnicity, welcome the Klan's support. There is a little space, I would like to think, between prejudice on the one hand and outright hate on the other, but *Women of the Klan* does not explore it." Today's feminist groups, she added, are active in the fight for racial and economic justice. Frank wished Blee had paid more attention to issues of class, but still deemed the book "superb" and its findings, which highlight the "terrifying banality" of racism, "crucial if we are to uncover, and grasp, the depth of white supremacy." A *Publishers Weekly* reviewer thought the book "will prove a revelation to many" and further maintained that "probably no future history of the Ku Klux Klan will be written without reference to this ground-breaking work."

Women's participation in racist groups of the late twentieth century is the topic of *Inside Organized Racism.* For this book, Blee interviewed thirty-four women who are involved in the modern-day KKK, neo-Nazi organizations, the Christian Identity movement, and other white supremacist groups. As in *Women of the Klan,* she contradicts stereotypes of these women, demonstrating that they are better educated and more affluent than generally assumed, that many of them joined racist groups on their own rather than not at the behest of a male partner, and that a substantial proportion of them—more than one-third—come from families with liberal views. They "joined the racist movement casually, socially, without strong racist beliefs and learned racist extremism inside the movement," reported Melanie Kaye/Kantrowitz in *Women's Review of Books.* A *Publishers*

Weekly critic also took note of these findings and commented, "Blee's disquieting account of how everyday racism morphs into extraordinary racism is full of surprises." The critic added that Blee shows uncommon empathy for her subjects, whom she portrays as monstrous, but not monsters. Indeed, Kaye/Kantrowitz wrote, Blee may overstate the "ordinariness of these women," but she also offers 'a message of hope' by asserting that racist groups change people and people can be changed back." The *Publishers Weekly* reviewer summed up the book as "a must-read for its fresh, pertinent scholarship and its riveting prose."

The Road to Poverty is a work of path-breaking scholarship as well, in the opinion of some critics. With a detailed case study of Clay County, Kentucky, Blee and Billings analyze the causes of poverty in Appalachia. They challenge the idea that this poverty resulted from the inherent "backwardness" of Appalachian people, and they argue that local government policies—including governmental relationships with business interests—helped keep people of this region poor. Nineteenth-century Clay County was home to many small farms, but population growth meant that by the end of the U.S. Civil War there were too many farmers for the land to support. "A large population had to out migrate or become wage laborers," related Altina Waller in the *Journal of Social History.* "This economic crisis produced a small group of local elites who allied with outside corporations in a local political system that was coercive, tending to prevent the rise of a middle class while impoverishing most of the population." In the authors' account, according to *American Journal of Sociology* contributor Kathleen Stewart, "the famous Appalachian feuds are shown to be an effect not of an ingrained and timeless sensibility, but of factionalism and schisms among the elites; elite conflicts intruded into public life, paralyzed local political institutions, and eventually erupted into intense violence at the turn of the century, which forced nonelites as well to decide which side they were on."

"One of the strongest features" of *the Road to Poverty*, commented Melissa Latimer in *Social Forces,*. . . "is the emphasis on the role of local state and political development on Appalachian economic development and poverty. . . . The history of capitalist markets, state coercion, and cultural strategies all interacted to shape the road to poverty taken in Clay County, Kentucky. This information should allow us to design more effective antipoverty programs." Several other reviewers noted the broad lessons to be drawn from Clay County. "Billings and Blee have provided a description of the 'road to poverty' that is local in its wealth of detail, yet global in its significance and theoretical sophistication," remarked Allen W. Batteau in the *Journal of the Royal Anthropological Institute.* In a similar vein, Walter observed, "The book is breathtaking in its scope and sophistication of historical and sociological analysis. The authors have probed minute details of one small county and managed to relate that evidence to the most significant theories circulating today regarding the origins and persistence of poverty, wherever it occurs. It should be read and pondered by policy makers everywhere."

BIOGRAPHICAL AND CRITICAL SOURCES:

PERIODICALS

American Journal of Sociology, January, 2001, Kathleen Stewart, review of *The Road to Poverty: The Making of Wealth and Hardship in Appalachia,* p. 1185.

Booklist, September 1, 1999, David Rouse, review of *The Road to Poverty,* p. 38.

Journal of Social History, fall, 1993, Robert A. Goldberg, review of *Women of the Klan: Racism and Gender in the 1920s,* p. 196; winter, 2001, Altina Walter, review of *The Road to Poverty,* p. 468.

Journal of the Royal Anthropological Institute, September, 2001, Allen W. Batteau, review of *The Road to Poverty,* p. 608.

Library Journal, January, 2002, Patricia A. Beaber, review of *Inside Organized Racism: Women in the Hate Movement,* p. 132.

Los Angeles Times Book Review, September 1, 1991, Barbara Ehrenreich, "Another Sisterhood," pp. 1, 5.

Nation, February 17, 1992, Dana Frank, review of *Women of the Klan,* p. 209.

Publishers Weekly, June 7, 1991, review of *Women of the Klan,* p. 49; January 7, 2002, review of *Inside Organized Racism,* p. 59.

Social Forces, September, 2001, Melissa Latimer, review of *The Road to Poverty,* p. 364.

Women's Review of Books, December, 1998, Lois Rita Helmbold, "Action Stations," p. 17; March, 2002, Melanie Kaye/Kantrowitz, "The Banality of Evil," pp. 4-5.

ONLINE

Kathleen Blee Home Page, http://www.pitt.edu/~kblee
(May 8, 2003).*

*   *   *

BLUMENFELD, Laura 1964(?)-

PERSONAL: Born c. 1964; daughter of David (a rabbi) and Norma (an attorney) Blumenfeld ; married Baruch Weiss (a lawyer); children: Daniel and one other child; *Ethnicity:* "Jewish." *Education:* Harvard University, M. A. (international affairs.)

ADDRESSES: Home—New York, NY. *Agent*—c/o Author Mail, Simon & Schuster, 1230 Avenue of the Americas, New York, NY 10020.

CAREER: Journalist. *Washington Post,* Washington, DC, staff writer.

WRITINGS:

Revenge: A Story of Hope, Simon & Schuster (New York, NY), 2002.

ADAPTATIONS: The film rights for *Revenge: A Story of Hope* was bought by Home Box Office (HBO).

SIDELIGHTS: A longtime correspondent for the *Washington Post,* Laura Blumenfeld used her experience as a reporter to hunt down the man who tried to kill her father and to delve into the universal human impulse for revenge when wronged. "I was inhabited by a grandiose thought: My father's injury should not go unanswered," writes Blumenfeld in her book *Revenge: A Story of Hope.* The story begins in 1986 when Blumenfeld's rabbi father, David, visited Israel as part of his effort to create a museum in memory of the Jewish Holocaust of World War II. A member of the rebel faction of the Palestinian Liberation Organization (PLO) shot him but fortunately only grazed his skull. Still for college student Blumenfeld, the incident shattered her sense of security. Shortly afterward, as part of a poetry seminar she was taking at Harvard,

Blumenfeld wrote a poem in which she vowed to find the man who shot her father. "I was not a large person," Blumenfeld writes in her book, "neither ideological, nor heroic, yet for years I was inhabited by a grandiose thought: my father's injury should not go unanswered. The shooting was my first glimpse of the presence of evil the world—someone had tried to murder my father." Over the next thirteen years, Blumenfeld questioned why anyone would want to hurt her father and also considered her desire to seek revenge. In 1998, with a book contract in hand, Blumenfeld took a sabbatical from the *Washington Post* and began her quest.

"I was looking for the shooter, but I also was looking for some kind of wisdom," Blumenfeld writes of her yearlong odyssey. Blumenfeld not only wanted to find and learn more about her father's shooter, but also to delve into her own feelings about revenge and how others view it. "I wanted to master revenge," she writes.

Blumenfeld knew she had her work cut out for her, but the process was to be even more complicated because she had just recently married. As a result, Blumenfeld and her husband went to Israel for an extended honeymoon to coincide with her new project. Before long, Blumenfeld tracked down her father's Palestinian assailant, Omar Khatib, who was serving a twenty-five-year prison term. She also tracked down Khatib's family, introduced herself to them as an objective reporter working on a story about the Palestinian-Israeli conflict, and eventually began a correspondence with Khatib through them. Blumenfeld was initially horrified to hear the Khatib family's seemingly callous view of Omar Khatib shooting "some Jew," which one of Khatib's brothers said "wasn't personal," just "public relations." However, with time, Blumenfeld and the Khatib family became friends, further complicating Blumenfeld's emotional struggles with the idea of revenge and her view of herself as "part journalist, part lonely girl, part cartoon avenger." Blumenfeld also notes that it "was embarrassing" for her not to be able to move on. "It's hard to admit to other people that you have a need to strike back, get even," she writes.

In addition to exploring her own family's association with terrorism and revenge, Blumenfeld explores revenge in a broader cross-cultural context by conducting numerous interviews, including feuding children and relatives, Sicilians who must grapple with vendettas carried on for generations, and an Iranian grand ayatollah. She also talked with Benjamin Netanyahu, a former prime minister of Israel who had an older brother killed by an Arab during an airplane hijacking. In addition, Blumenfeld explores her childhood, her struggles coming to terms with her parents divorce at the time of the shooting, and the strain that her efforts in researching the book put on her own marriage.

In the book's climatic scene, Blumenfeld, after an ongoing correspondence with Khatib that results in the shooter finally renouncing violence as a solution to the Arab-Israeli conflict, finds herself in an Israeli courtroom. The occasion is a hearing to determine if Khatib will be let out on parole. Khatib has asthma and is seeking an early release on medical grounds. During the proceedings, Blumenfeld reveals her true identity to the courtroom and Khatib as she asks the court to grant him parole, noting that Khatib has said he will no longer participate in violence. Although the judges denied the parole until 2010, they asked Blumenfeld why she put herself in such a dangerous position, traveling to Palestine as a Jew. Blumenfeld answered, in part, "You have to take a chance for peace. You have to believe it's possible."

Several reviewers had difficulty with Blumenfeld's personal wish for revenge, pointing out that her father was merely wounded while numerous other families had to move on when their loved ones were much more seriously injured or even killed. They also commented that at times the book is "too personal" in nature to represent a fair look at the issue of revenge. Blake Eskin, writing in the *New York Times,* remarked that the book's focus on the personal "has its advantages: by investing so much energy in the Khatibs, Blumenfeld manages to portray Omar with more subtlety then most descriptions of terrorists." In contrast, Jamie Edwards, in *Bookreporter.com,* wrote that "Blumenfeld's personal obsession" can at times be "irritating in its shortsightedness." Edwards went on to note, "Perhaps, however, that speaks to the intrinsic honesty of her self-examination and the uncomfortable timeliness of the subject at hand." A *Kirkus Reviews* critic called the book "a gripping read," while a reviewer writing in *Maclean's* called the "experiences she shares . . . intimate and haunting." A *Publishers Weekly* reviewer called *Revenge: A Story of Hope* a "remarkable tale" that "is a rite-of passage story, an intense and deeply personal

journey." The reviewer also commented, "The climax is astonishingly powerful—a masterfully rendered scene, crackling with the intensity of which great, life-changing drama is made."

In the end, Blumenfeld sees the story she imparts about revenge as having a silver lining. "I think more than ever it's a story of hope," she told Margaret Warner in an interview on the Public Broadcasting System's *Online NewsHour* Web site, "but it's a story we need to hold on to, because there's a saying in the Middle East, 'When you seek revenge you should dig two graves: One for your enemy and one for yourself.'" Blumenfeld also noted, "There is a spark of hope in my story because it says that the more we can see each other as individuals, the more likely the violence will decline. If we can step way back from the . . . daily hatred and if you can look someone in the eye, it's hard to shoot him in the head."

BIOGRAPHICAL AND CRITICAL SOURCES:

PERIODICALS

Daily Variety, March 11, 2002, Craig Offman, "HBO Exacts Middle East 'Revenge,'" p. 24.

Kirkus Reviews, January 15, 2002, review of *Revenge: A Story of Hope,* p. 81.

Los Angeles times, April 10, 2002, Louise Steinman, "Putting a Face on Hatred," p. E1.

MacLean's, May 6, 2002, "Writing with a Vengeance," p. 52.

New York Times, April 6, 2002, Susan Sachs, "Punishing a Terrorist by Showing Him His Victim's Humanity," p. A19(N), p. ; April 7, 2002, Blake Eskin, "A Slice of the Camel," p. 30.

O, the Oprah Magazine, April, 2002, Cathleen Medwick, "The Best Revenge: In an Urgent, Candid Memoir, an Obsessed Journalist Goes after the Terrorist Who Shot Her Father," p. 190.

People, April 15, 2002, Susan Schindehette, "Settling the Score: After a Terrorist Shoots Her Father, a Reporter Writes Sweet Revenge," p. 129.

Publishers Weekly, March 4, 2002, review of *Revenge: A Story of Hope,* p. 69, and Emily Chenoweth, "PW Talks with Laura Blumenfeld," p. 69.

Washington Monthly, April, 2002, Joshua Hammer, review of *Revenge: A Story of Hope,* p. 59.

ONLINE

Online NewsHour, http://www.pbs.org/newshour/ (April 24, 2002), Margaret Warner, "Conversation: Blumenfeld."

Bookreporter.com, http://www.bookreporter.com/ (March 30, 2002), Jami Edwards, review of *Revenge: A Story of Hope.*

Salon.com, http:www.salon.com/ (April 5, 2002), Susy Hansen, "Her Father's Keeper" (an interview).*

*   *   *

BLUNT, Wilfrid Scawen 1840-1922

PERSONAL: Born August 17, 1840, in Sussex, England; died September 10, 1922, in Sussex, England; son of Francis Scawen and Mary (Chandler) Blunt; married Lady Anne Isabella Noel, June 8, 1869 (died December 15, 1917); children: Judith Anne Dorothea. *Education:* Stonyhurst College, 1852-53, and Attended St. Mary's College, Oxott, 1855-57. *Hobbies and other interests:* Horses.

CAREER: Poet, writer, traveler, and Arabian horse breeder. Worked in diplomatic service as secretary of legation to, Athens, Frankfurt, Madrid, Spain, Paris, Lisbon, Buenos Aires, and Berne, Switzerland, 1858-69.

WRITINGS:

(As Proteus) *Sonnets and Songs,* John Murray (London, England), 1875.

(As Proteus; with Charles Meynell as Amadeus) *Proteus and Amadeus: A Correspondence,* edited by Aubrey De Vere, Kegan Paul (London, England), 1878.

(Editor and author of preface) Lady Anne Blunt, *Bedouin Tribes of the Euphrates,* 2 volumes, Harper (New York, NY), 1879.

(As Proteus) *The Love Sonnets of Proteus,* Kegan Paul (London, England), 1881, Doxey (New York, NY), 1901.

(Editor) Lady Anne Blunt, *A Pilgrimage to Nejd, the Cradle of the Arab Race: A Visit to the Court of the Arab Emir, and "Our Persian Campaign,"* 2 volumes, John Murray (London, England), 1881.

The Future of Islam, Kegan Paul, Trench (London, England), 1882.

The Wind and the Whirlwind, Kegan Paul, Trench (London, England), 1883, Tucker (Boston, MA), 1884.

Ideas about India, Kegan Paul, Trench (London, England), 1885.

Justice and Liberty for Ireland: Extracts from the Speeches of W. S. Blunt to the Electors of Kidderminster, July 1886, British Home Rule Association (London, England), 1886.

Mr. Wilfrid Blunt, Anti-Coercionist Candidate for Deptford: Who Is He? What Has He Done? Why Is He in Prison? National Press Agency (London, England), 1888.

In Vinculis, Kegan Paul, Trench (London, England), 1889.

A New Pilgrimage, and Other Poems, Kegan Paul, Trench (London, England), 1889.

The Love Lyrics and Songs of Proteus, Kelmscott Press (London, England), 1892.

Esther, Love Lyrics, and Natalia's Resurrection, Kegan Paul, Trench, Trübner (London, England), 1892, published as *Esther: A Young Man's Tragedy, Together with the Love Sonnets of Proteus,* Copeland & Day (Boston, MA), 1895, published as *Esther: A Young Man's Tragedy,* Bibelot (Portland, ME), 1905.

Griselda: A Society Novel in Rhymed Verse, Kegan Paul, Trench, Trübner (London, England), 1893.

The Poetry of Wilfrid Blunt, edited by William Ernest Henley and George Wyndham, Heinemann (London, England), 1898.

Satan Absolved: A Victorian Mystery, John Lane (New York, NY), 1899.

The Shame of the Nineteenth Century, [London, England], 1900.

Love Poems of W. S. Blunt, John Lane (New York, NY), 1902.

The Military Fox-hunting Case at Cairo: Mr. Wilfrid Scawen Blunt to the Marquess of Lansdowne . . . A Supplement to the Blue Book Egypt 3, 1901, [London, England], 1902.

Fand of the Fair Cheek: A Three-Act Tragedy in Rhymed Verse, privately printed, 1904.

Atrocities of Justice under British Rule in Egypt, Unwin (London, England), 1906.

To the Rt. Honourable Sir Edward Grey, Bart., M.P., Chiswick (London, England), 1906.

Francis Thompson, Burns & Oates (London, England), 1907.

Secret History of the English Occupation of Egypt: Being a Personal Narrative of Events, Unwin (London, England), 1907, Knopf (New York, NY), 1922.

Mr. Blunt and the "Times": A Memorandum as to the Attitude of the "Times" Newspaper in Egyptian Affairs, privately (London, England), 1907.

The Bride of the Nile: A Political Extravaganza in Three Acts of Rhymed Verse, privately printed, 1907.

The New Situation in Egypt, Burns & Oates (London, England), 1908.

Denshawai Memorial School, [London, England], 1908(?).

India under Ripon: A Private Diary, Unwin (London, England), 1909.

Gordon at Khartoum: Being a Personal Narrative of Events, Swift (London, England), 1911, Knopf (New York, NY), 1923.

The Italian Horror and How to End It, Bonner (London, England), 1911.

The Land War in Ireland: Being a Personal Narrative of Events, Swift (London, England), 1912.

The Poetical Works of Wilfrid Scawen Blunt: A Complete Edition, 2 volumes, Macmillan (London, England), 1914, Scholarly Press (Grosse Pointe, MI), 1968.

The Crabbet Arabian Stud, Whittingham (London, England), c.1915.

History of the Crabbet Estate in Sussex, Chiswick (London, England), 1917.

My Diaries: Being a Personal Narrative of Events, 1888-1914, Secker (London, England), 1919-20, Knopf (New York, NY), 1921.

Poems, edited by Floyd Dell, Knopf (New York, NY), 1923.

Desert Hawk: Abd' el Kader and the French Conquest of Algeria, Methuen (London, England), 1947.

Contributed to Lady Anne Blunt's verse translations from the Arabic. Most of his papers and diaries are housed in the Fitzwilliam Museum, Cambridge, England.

SIDELIGHTS: Wilfrid Scawen Blunt was a nineteenth-century writer whose life and literary works focused on the themes of geography and travel, politics, and love. He was friends with many well-known figures in the literary and political worlds of his day, and earned later admiration from William Butler Yeats and Ezra Pound.

Blunt's father died when Blunt was two years old, whereupon his mother leased the family estate of Crabbet Park and traveled through England and Europe with Blunt and his two siblings. At the age of eighteen Blunt was accepted for diplomatic service in England,

and served for twelve years as an attaché to British embassies and legations around the world. After retiring from diplomatic service in 1869, he married Lady Anne Isabella Noel, Lord Byron's granddaughter, a wealthy aristocrat who shared Blunt's "passion for travel, for literature and for horses," as noted on the *West Sussex Record Office,* Web site.

Blunt and his wife journeyed throughout the world. In the course of their travels they developed a tremendous interest in and deep respect for the Arab world. Their enthusiasm for the desert lands was so great that they established a second home, called Sheykh Obeyd, near Cairo, Egypt. Blunt continued to show his affection for Arabia when he returned to his home in Sussex, England, by wearing the attire of the Bedouin nomads. Along with a love of the Middle East, the Blunts shared a love for horses. They owned a number of prized Arabian horses, one of which they shipped back to their estate in England, where it became known and revered as the Crabbet Arabian stud.

At the time of his marriage to Lady Anne and his retirement from the diplomatic service, Blunt began to dedicate himself to writing; a career he would pursue until the end of his life. Blunt was a champion of the Arab nations, as well as the Indian and Irish peoples in their struggles against British imperialism. He expressed his anti-imperialistic views in such works as *Ideas about India* and *The Land War in Ireland: Being a Personal Narrative of Events.* Blunt wrote in favor of the colonial nations, and spoke negatively about England and its policies. "He is known to historians as a prominent champion of nationalism . . . as an opponent of British imperialism, and as a man willing to go to jail for his political beliefs," observed Donald E. Stanford in the *Dictionary of Literary Biography.*

Alongside his nonfiction and travel books, Blunt also wrote volumes of poetry. It was through this medium that he explored the realm of love. Many of his pieces were dedicated to lovers that he knew before and during his marriage to Lady Anne. Stanford considered Blunt's poetry to be "facile, clichéd, rhetorical, and unconvincing." He noted that the author's work is rarely read today and that "many of his political poems have lost their once interesting topicality." Stafford did feel, however, that Blunt wrote "a few authentic and moving love poems and poems expressing his love for certain areas of rural England." Blunt's poetry, particularly *Esther, Love Lyrics,* and *Natalia's Resur-*

rection and *Sonnets and Songs by Proteus,* exerted influence on younger English poets of his day.

Blunt's *The Love Sonnets of Proteus* includes a sequence of thirty-two sonnets written to "Juliet," who, it is supposed, was actually his lover, Madeline Wyndham. The love affair between Blunt and Wyndham began in 1862 and she terminated it in 1875. After their separation, Blunt wrote the fifteen sonnets titled "Farewell to Juliet" that appear in *The Love Sonnets of Proteus.*

The Future of Islam is a series of essays originally printed in 1881 in the *Fortnightly Review.* These essays address a group of readers Blunt calls "practical Englishmen." He wrote the pieces, noted Syrine C. Hout in the *Dictionary of Literary Biography,* in order to appeal to "an audience that included politicians who might repair some of the damage that Europeans had generally inflicted on Islamic civilization." *The Future of Islam* describes the history and religious beliefs of the Islamic people, and Blunt attempts to reconcile the Eastern and Western worlds by drawing comparisons between Christianity and Islam.

Shortly after the publication of *The Future of Islam,* Blunt was drawn into the Egyptian struggle for nationalism. He supported the Egyptian cause and tried to create an Egyptian lobby within the British government. His plans failed, and the British defeated the militant Egyptian forces. Blunt was able, however, to procure the banishment (rather than the hanging) of Arabi, the Egyptian military leader, by hiring a lawyer to defend him. This incident fueled Blunt's growing anti-imperialistic ideas. In response, he wrote *The Wind and the Whirlwind* in 1883. Stanford observed that this poem "attacks British imperialism in Egypt," noting it is also a personal piece inasmuch as "it was partially inspired by Blunt's affair with Lady Augusta Gregory, who was later to become the patron of William Butler Yeats."

Several years before the downfall of Arabi, Blunt and Lady Anne traveled to India, where they observed firsthand the poverty of the Indian people amid the "forward policy" of the British government. Elizabeth Longford wrote in *A Pilgrimage of Passion* that Blunt left India "with [his] faith in the British Empire and its ways in the East shaken to its foundations." The Blunts' second visit to India in 1883 merely reinforced his discomfort with British policy. As a result, he

published *Ideas about India,* which, as Hout observed, "expresses the growing reservations he felt about the morality of British imperialism." Blunt considered the British Empire to be exploitative and disapproved of the trade and financial agreements between India and Britain.

In 1892 Blunt published a poetry collection titled *Esther, Love Lyrics, and Natalia's Resurrection.* Many of these poems allegedly sprang from his love affair with Catherine Walters—who is called either "Esther" or "Manon" in the poems—and Blunt's subsequent frustration and disillusionment with her affairs with other men. The couple met in 1863, and their love relationship dissolved nearly seven years later. However, they continued a devoted friendship throughout their lives, a feat Blunt managed with many of his former lovers.

Along with his amorous adventures and forays in India and the Middle East, Blunt became interested in Ireland, where the battle for independence from British rule had begun. In 1886 he attended anti-eviction meetings that occurred during the "Land War" "the eviction of the Irish peasantry from lands owned by English landlords." These meetings were banned in September 1887, and when Blunt tried to speak out against the ordinance, he was arrested, convicted, and sent to jail for two months. His book *The Land War in Ireland,* which was not published until 1912, gives an account of his experiences in the battle for Irish independence. In the book, Blunt notes that his prison sentence "deserves to be remembered in Irish history as being the first recorded instance, in all the four hundred years of English oppression, of an Englishman having taken the Celtic Irish side in any conflict, or suffered even the shortest imprisonment for Ireland's sake."

In 1914 *The Poetical Works of Wilfrid Scawen Blunt* appeared. Reviewers, including poet Edward Thomas, positively received the collection. Stanford commented: "Blunt was at his best in a few poems from the early Proteus collections." In a *Poetry* review Maurice Lesemann expressed high praise for Blunt's sonnets, observing that Blunt is able "to write about real people of this world in actual situations and about places he had actually seen."

Upon his death in 1922, Blunt was, by his own orders, given a Bedouin-style funeral. His body was wrapped in an Arabic carpet and he was buried in a grave near Crabbet Park.

BIOGRAPHICAL AND CRITICAL SOURCES:

BOOKS

Longford, Elizabeth, *A Pilgrimage of Passion: The Life of Wilfrid Scawen Blunt,* Knopf (New York, NY), 1980.

Dictionary of Literary Biography, Gale (Detroit, MI),Volume 19: *British Poets, 1880-1914,*1983, pp.29-39, edited by Donald E. Stanford, Volume 174: *British Travel Writers, 1876-1909,* edited by Barbara Brothers and Julia Gergits, Gale (Detroit, MI), 1997, pp. 41-53.

PERIODICALS

Journal of Modern Literature, March, 1971, William T. Going, "A Peacock Dinner: The Homage of Pound and Yeats to Wilfrid Scawen Blunt," pp. 303-310.

Poetry, September, 1923, Maurice Lesemann, "The Passing Aristocracy," pp. 337-341.

ONLINE

West Sussex Record Office Web site, http://www. westsussex.gov.uk/RO/ (June 5, 2002), "The Wilfrid Scawen Blunt Collection."*

*   *   *

BOGLE, Donald

PERSONAL: Born in New York, NY. *Education:* Lincoln University (with honors); attended Indiana University, Harvard University, and Columbia University.

ADDRESSES: Home—New York, NY. *Agent*—c/o Author Mail, Farrar, Straus & Giroux, 19 Union Square W., New York, NY 10001.

CAREER: Historian, editor, and writer. Worked as a staff writer and assistant editor at *Ebony* magazine. Lectured at Lincoln University, University of Pennsylvania, and New York University's Tisch School of the Arts.

AWARDS, HONORS: Theatre Library Association Award, best film book of the year, for *Toms, Coons, Mulattoes, Mammies, and Bucks: An Interpretive History of Blacks in American Films.*

WRITINGS:

Toms, Coons, Mulattoes, Mammies, and Bucks: An Interpretive History of Blacks in American Films, Viking Press (New York, NY), 1973, 4th edition, Continuum (New York, NY), 2001.

*Brown Sugar: Eighty Years of America's Black Female Superstars,*Harmony Books (New York, NY), 1980.

Blacks in American Films and Television: An Encyclopedia, Garland (New York, NY), 1988.

(Editor) *Black Arts Annual 1987/88,* Garland (New York, NY), 1989.

Dorothy Dandridge: A Biography, Amistad (New York, NY), 1997.

Primetime Blues: African Americans on Network Television, Farrar, Straus & Giroux (New York, NY), 2001.

Contributor to *Louis Armstrong: A Cultural Legacy* (essays), edited by Marc Miller, Queens Museum of Art (New York, NY) University of Washington Press (Seattle), 1994.

ADAPTATIONS: Brown Sugar: Eighty Years of America's Black Female Superstars was made into a series by Public Broadcasting Service. Whitney Houston Products purchased the film rights to *Dorothy Dandridge: A Biography.*

SIDELIGHTS: Donald Bogle grew up in Philadelphia, Pennsylvania and, like many American children of the 1960s, spent much of his leisure time going to the movies or, as he says in the introduction to his book *Prime Time Blues: African Americans on Network Television,* "plopped in front of the TV set." As a black American, Bogle was especially drawn to performances by black actors and began pondering the types of characters they played, sensing that a fundamental racism was at work in their stereotypical roles. "Even as a kid," he points out in his introduction, "I often found myself asking all sorts of questions about what I was seeing *and* enjoying."

Bogle's interest in movies and television led him to a career as a writer and a film historian. His first book, *Toms, Coons, Mulattoes, Mammies, and Bucks: An Interpretive History of Blacks in American Films,* takes a comprehensive look at blacks in American films from the silent-movie era on. Bogle places his commentary within the appropriate cultural and social context of the times that the films were made. In addition to discussing the films, Bogle also provides information on the performers' lives. Throughout the book, he discusses the stereotypes that black actors have been forced to play, noting that, even given these stereotypes, these films provided black actors with the opportunity for work. Although reviewer Edward Mapp, writing in the *Library Journal,* felt that "Bogle fails to convince me of the validity of his interpretations," most reviewers found the book to be insightful and important. *Commentary* reviewer Richard Schickel remarked that Bogle "has responded to a complex subject with a complex, non-ideological, aesthetically aware work, infused throughout with a patient humanity and written in a carefully tempered tone." A reviewer in the *New York Times Book Review* commented that Bogle's book "is a model of 'interpretative history,' temperate but shrewd in its judgments . . . well organized, well-written, solidly grounded in historical and biographical fact." The reviewer also called the book "non-ideological, esthetically aware, graceful in tone and humane in its point of view."

Bogle's next book, 1980's *Brown Sugar: Eighty Years of America's Black Female Superstars,* chronicles the lives and works of numerous legendary black female entertainers, from Bessie Smith, Josephine Baker, and Ethel Waters to Diana Ross, Cicely Tyson, and disco queen Donna Summer. Bogle also mentions many lesser-known performers. Writing in *Booklist,* reviewer William Bradly Hooper noted that Bogle writes "with great spirit and earnestness."

In *Blacks in American Films and Television: An Encyclopedia,* Bogle provides critical interpretations of more than 260 films and more than 100 television shows, including commentary on how black characters have evolved since the advent of television. Bogle also presents numerous biographical profiles of black actors and actresses and other blacks involved in movies and television, such as black film directors. As a reference book, *Blacks in American Films and Television* includes a substantial index and bibliography.

However, as a reviewer pointed out in *American Libraries,* "this is no dull merely descriptive encyclopedia." Rather, the reviewer noted, Bogle's "lively and candid style . . . offers insightful interpretations," while Joseph W. Palmer, writing in *American Reference Books Annual,* called it "a meaty volume crammed with facts and strong opinions."

For his book *Dorothy Dandridge: A Biography* Bogle spent several years interviewing family, friends, and associates of the actress, whose success in Hollywood was short-lived and ultimately led to tragedy. The book includes many reminiscences of black entertainers such as Diahann Carroll, Sammy Davis, Jr., and Bobby Short. Bogle recounts how Dandridge rose through the ranks of the entertainment industry, starting out as a child performer and singer in church, vaudeville, and on the "chitlin' circuit," small black nightclubs and "honky tonks" located primarily in the south. Eventually, she began making cameos in mainstream Hollywood movies, like the Marx Brothers film *A Day at the Races,* and then starred in two low-budget "race movies," films produced by black-owned independent film companies. She was then cast in *Carmen Jones* by director Otto Preminger and was nominated for an Oscar for her role. Still, good roles for black actors remained rare. After her role as Bess in the 1959 film *Porgy and Bess,* Dandridge quickly fell from the spotlight. As the press cast aspersions on her for her marriage and affairs with white men and her reputation grew as being "difficult," both her acting and nightclub careers faded. Dandridge died in 1965 from a drug overdose with two dollars and fourteen cents in the bank.

While Bogle focuses on Dandridge in his work, Ed Guerrero, writing in *Cineaste,* pointed out that the author also "vividly charts the professional and evolutionary stages of black entertainment in America" as he tells Dandridge's story. Guerrero also noted that while Bogle clearly delineates "the socially charged performance of race in America", he never "hectors or editorializes." Rather, said Guerrero, Bogle "lets the events and evidence speak for the frank systemic racism of the day that all blacks, from kitchen maids to movie stars, endured." Writing on *BookPage Online,* Robert Fleming noted, "He gives the finest view yet of the gutsy, beautiful black actress fighting to survive in Jim Crow Hollywood despite a flood of slights and tragedies."

Bogle returned to his childhood love of television in his book *Primetime Blues: African Americans on*

Network Television. This comprehensive history of blacks working on network television series begins with the early days of television following World War II through the 1990s. Bogle traces the early stereotypes that blacks were forced to play on such shows as *Beulah,* in which famed black entertainer Ethel Waters played a loyal and not-too-bright maid to a white family, and the infamous *Amos 'n' Andy,* which perhaps epitomized what Bogle calls "parts that were shameless, dishonest travesties of African American life and culture." Nevertheless, says Bogle, many of the performers were able to present portrayals in ways that that allowed the black community to identify with them. Although blacks gained more prominence on network television in the seventies, Bogle points out that ethnic urban comedies like *Sanford and Son* and *Good Times* also presented blacks in a less-than-stellar light. Bogle also analyzes such popular shows in the 1980s at *The Cosby Show* and explores the black-white buddy relationship in programs like *Miami Vice.*

New Republic reviewer John McWhorter found Bogle's fixation on stereotypes to be an "ideological straightjacket." Although John Anderson, writing in the *Nation,* called the history presented in *Primetime Blues* "fascinating," he disagreed with Bogle's seeming emphasis that a "positive image or political message" should be inherent in black acting roles on television. "In this," wrote Anderson, "Bogle skirts the two basic aspects of television's nature. First, that it is craven, soulless and bottom-line fixated. And second that it is aimed at morons." Nevertheless, Anderson and other viewers generally praised Bogle's work as the first comprehensive view of black actors on television. McWhorter called Bogle's chapters focusing on the 1950s and 1960s "masterful." In a review in *Entertainment Weekly,* Ken Tucker called the history "thorough" and "engagingly opinionated." Vanessa Bush, writing in *Booklist,* called *Primetime Blues* "an extensive and even-handed look at how television has mirrored and distorted race images and issues in the premier multiracial society."

BIOGRAPHICAL AND CRITICAL SOURCES:

PERIODICALS

American Libraries, May, 1989, *Blacks in American Films and Television: An Encyclopedia,* p. 410.

American Reference Books Annual, Volume 20, 1989, Joseph W. Palmer, review of *Blacks in American Films and Television: An Encyclopedia,* p. 509.

Black American Literature Forum, winter, 1991, Edward Mapp, review of *Blacks in American Films and Television: An Encyclopedia,* p. 793.

Booklist, June 15, 1980, William Bradley Hooper, review of *Brown Sugar: Eighty Years of America's Black Female Superstars,* p. 1479; July, 1994, review of *Blacks in American Films and Television,* pp. 1966-1967; February 15, 1998, Ray Olson, review of *Dorothy Dandridge: A Biography,* p. 978; January 1, 2001, Vanessa Bush, review of *Primetime Blues: African Americans on Network Television,* p. 896.

Bookwatch, August, 1990, review of *Brown Sugar: Eighty Years of America's Black Female Superstars,* p. 6.

Choice, November, 1973, review of *Toms, Coons, Mulattoes, Mammies, and Bucks: An Interpretive History of Blacks in American Films,* p. 1395; September, 1988, C.A. Larson, *Blacks in American Films and Television: An Encyclopedia,* p. 74.

Cineaste, fall, 1998, Ed Guerrero, review of *Dorothy Dandridge: A Biography,* p. 60.

Commentary, November, 1973, Richard Schickel, review of *Toms, Coons, Mulattoes, Mammies, and Bucks: An Interpretive History of Blacks in American Films,* pp. 90, 92-94.

Encore, August, 1980, "A Talk with Critic Donald Bogle," p. 38.

Entertainment Weekly, March 2, 2001, Ken Tucker, "Color Blind: Donald Bogle Takes an Incisive Look at Small-Screen Depictions of African Americans in *Primetime Blues,*" p. 62.

Journalism & Mass Communication Quarterly, spring, 1998, S. Craig Watkins, review of *Toms, Coons, Mulattoes, Mammies, and Bucks: An Interpretive History of Blacks in American Films,* p. 226.

Library Journal, July, 1973, Edward Mapp, review of *Toms, Coons, Mulattoes, Mammies, and Bucks: An Interpretive History of Blacks in American Films,* p. 2141; June 15, 1980, review of *Brown Sugar: Eighty Years of America's Black Female Superstars,* p. 1405; November 1, 1997, Corinne Nelson, review of *Dorothy Dandridge: A Biography,* p. 75; November 1, 2000, Ann Burns and Emily Joy Jones, review of *Primetime Blues: African Americans on Network Television,* p. 104; January 1, 2001, David M. Lisa, review of *Primetime Blues: African Americans on Network Television,* p. 109.

Los Angeles Times, February 26, 2001, Lynell George, "Tuned in to TV's Racial Divide" (interview), p. E 1.

Nation, April 16, 2001, John Anderson, review of *Primetime Blues: African Americans on Network Television*, p. 28.

New Republic, March 5, 2001, "Gimme a Break! Blacks, Television, and the Decline of Racism in America," p. 30.

New Yorker, August 18, 1997, Hilton Als, review of *Dorothy Dandridge: A Biography*, p. 68.

New York Times Book Review, August 26, 1973, review of *Toms, Coons, Mulattoes, Mammies, and Bucks: An Interpretive History of Blacks in American Films*, p. 8.

Publishers Weekly, November 13, 2000, review of *Primetime Blues: African Americans on Network Television*, p. 91.

ONLINE

BookPage, http://www.bookpage.com/ (March 30, 2002), Robert Fleming, review of *Dorothy Dandridge: A Biography*.

Museum of Television & Radio Web site, http://www.mtr.org/ (September 12, 2002), excerpt from Donald Bogle's introduction in *Prime Time Blues: African Americans on Network Television*.

OTHER

Hollywood and the Black Actor (sound recording), interview with Donald Bogle and others about the portrayal and stereotyping of blacks in American movies, J. Norton Publishers.*

*   *   *

BOHNTINSKY, Dori 1951-

PERSONAL: Surname is pronounced "Bon-*tin*-ski;" born December 17, 1951, in San Jose, CA; daughter of James William Ewart (a teacher) and Dorothy N. Fraser; married Charles L. Bohntinsky (a director of training and development); children: Elise (deceased). *Ethnicity:* "Caucasian." *Education:* California State University—Hayward, B.S., 1974; San Jose State University, M.A., 1976. *Politics:* "Eclectic." *Religion:* "New World."

ADDRESSES: Home—Hayward, CA. *Office*—P.O. Box 20248, Castro Valley, CA 94546. *E-mail*—inwordbound@aol.com.

CAREER: Alameda County Medical Center, manager of department of speech pathology and audiology, 1980-2002; freelance writer and workshop presenter, 2002—. Also affiliated with Consultants for Enhanced Communication.

MEMBER: International Labyrinth Society, American Speech Language Hearing Association, California Speech Language Hearing Association, Northern California Speech Pathology Leadership Forum (chair), Castro Valley Women's Club (chair of home-life committee).

WRITINGS:

Standard American English Pronunciation Training (workbook with audio tapes), Fairview Publishing, 1994.

Pragmatics for Effective Speaking (workbook), Fairview Publishing, 1998.

Once upon a Lunar Eclipse (poetry), International Library of Poetry, 2000.

The Healing Room: Discovering Joy through the Journal (nonfiction), In-Word Bound Publishing, 2002.

WORK IN PROGRESS: Daydreams to Awakening, on "self-discovery through journaling," for In-Word Bound Publishing, completion expected in 2004.

SIDELIGHTS: Dori Bohntinsky commented to *CA:* "As a speech/language pathologist since 1976, my career has focused on helping people communicate. My career began in clinical settings, helping children with delayed language and speech and adults with a wide variety of communication impairments resulting from neurological damage. In the early 1990s I expanded my work by writing a workbook and audio tape program to assist the non-native English speaker in speaking English clearly and effectively. In the late 1990s I expanded my work to training the native English speaker to communicate with greater clarity and effectiveness by writing a workbook on pragmatics. Between 1976 and 2000 my writing was technical and I gave technical workshops.

"In 2000 my life changed. In January, 2000, I lost my fourteen-year-old daughter following a four-month-long illness. During the fourteen months that followed,

I also lost my mother and then my father. I drew upon my clinical experience and writing skills and wrote a journal demonstrating my process of healing from significant loss. During this process I realized that I was writing a book to help people communicate with themselves and to help others communicate with someone going through tragedy. In 2002 I took early retirement after working over twenty years as a manager of speech pathology and audiology at the Alameda County Medical Center. My current motivation is to help people improve their own self-talk and enhance their ability to communicate with themselves. I find it interesting that my career path changed from helping individuals talk to each other to enhancing people's inner dialogue.

"My work has been influenced by free thinkers and writers such as C. W. Leadbeater, Helen Blavatsky, Albert Einstein, Gary Zukav, Wayne Dyer, Deepak Chopra, Betty Bethards, James Van Pragh, Doreen Virtue, and many other lesser-known authors. However, in searching bookstores and the Internet I have found no author except one who wrote with a style similar to mine. The author is Marguerite Porete, who wrote *The Mirror of Simple Souls* in the late 1200s. My style, which is mainly journaling, involves self-disclosure in a unique way. It includes descriptive observation of personal events and then freely flows into insightful prose. Some writing is interspersed with poetry, which is also used as a form of journaling to gain insight. I write to better understand life situations, myself, and to demonstrate to others an approach for enhancing self-awareness through writing. My motivation is to encourage people to touch any pain so they might discover the joy that comes from insight regarding any uncomfortable or painful event. I also teach journaling workshops and use my writings as examples of an ability that I trust all people possess."

*   *   *

BONSIGNORE, Joan 1959-

PERSONAL: Born March 17, 1959, in Chicago, IL; daughter of John (a university professor) and Fenna Lee (a pharmacist; maiden name, Fisher) Bonsignore; children: Catherine. *Ethnicity:* "European descent." *Education:* University of Massachusetts—Amherst, B.A. (English; cum laude), 1982, M.B.A., 1984, Post-B.A., 1989. *Politics:* Democrat. *Religion:* Catholic.

Hobbies and other interests: "Quilting (with focus on design), cooking, baking, crafts of all kinds."

ADDRESSES: Home—6B Graves St., South Deerfield, MA 01373. *Office*—White Brook Middle School, 200 Park St., Easthampton, MA 01027. *E-mail*—bonsignorejEeasthampton.k12.ma.us.

CAREER: Teacher, beginning 1984. Center for Human Resources Development, Northhampton, MA, case manager for adults with developmental disabilities, 1994-99.

WRITINGS:

Stick out Your Tongue!: Fantastic Facts, Features, and Functions of Animal and Human Tongues, illustrated by John T. Ward, Peachtree Publishers (Atlanta, GA), 2001.

WORK IN PROGRESS: Sequels to *Stick out Your Tongue!* on a variety of topics.

SIDELIGHTS: After teaching for around fifteen years, Joan Bonsignore began a new career; she put her experience in the classroom to a new use as a writer of books for children, making her debut in 2001 with the nonfiction *Stick out Your Tongue!: Fantastic Facts, Features, and Functions of Animal and Human Tongues.* Like many children who later become writers and teachers, Bonsignore explored these activities as a child. As she recalled to *CA,* "Teaching and writing are the two endeavors that piqued my enthusiasm from a very young age." The second child in a family of seven, she often taught her younger sisters, using the playroom as a school. "I translated everything to which I was exposed into a simpler format and language suitable for younger minds." So too with writing. "Writing stories for children became a focus from the moment I knew how to read. Creative writing was not encouraged so much in school, but it was something I took great pleasure in at home."

Along with such other creative endeavors as quilting, crafts, and cooking, writing remained a way for Bonsignore to express herself as an adult. While working as a teacher, she enjoyed writing, but she did not attempt to publish her work until after she retired from teaching. Bonsignore explained the genesis of *Stick out Your Tongue!* to *CA:* "The attempt at getting published was really just on a whim. The manuscript then titled *Tongues Aren't Just for Licking Lollypops* had been filed away for years with other stories I had written. I had put the original story in a readable format with my own watercolor sketches of the animals, so that I could read the book to children. It proved to have a wide age appeal, and so I decided eight years after its creation to send it out to a select number of publishers. I was both pleased and surprised when Peachtree Publishers accepted my manuscript." In *Stick out Your Tongue!,* as it ended up being titled, Bonsignore presents examples of how various creatures, such as mammals, reptiles, birds, insects, and fish use their tongues.

Reflecting on her writing plans, Bonsignore told *CA:* "I will continue to write children's stories on a wide variety of topics, and perhaps only a few will ever be sent out to publishers for consideration. It is wonderful to see my name officially in print, but I expect, as before, that the joy of writing will remain a personal pleasure regardless of its acceptance on any wider scale. To write a story for children is for one moment in time to see through the eyes of a child and to regain, if only for that moment, that wonderful innocence belonging only to the young."

BIOGRAPHICAL AND CRITICAL SOURCES:

PERIODICALS

Booklist, August, 2001, Catherine Andronik, review of *Stick out Your Tongue!: Fantastic Facts, Features, and Functions of Animal and Human Tongues,* p. 2124.
Kirkus Reviews, September 1, 2001, review of *Stick out Your Tongue!,* p. 1286.
School Library Journal, November, 2001, Margaret C. Howell, review of *Stick out Your Tongue!,* p. 140.

*   *   *

BOSS, Pauline 1934-

PERSONAL: Born July 11, 1934, in New Glarus, WI; daughter of Paul and Verena (Elmer) Grossenbacher; married Kenneth Boss, December 25, 1953 (divorced, April, 1982); married Dudley Riggs, March 10, 1988; children: (first marriage) David, Ann Boss Sheffels.

Ethnicity: "Swiss-American." *Education:* University of Wisconsin—Madison, B.S., 1956, M.S., 1971, Ph. D., 1975. *Politics:* Independent. *Religion:* United Church of Christ. *Hobbies and other interests:* Theater, concerts, travel.

ADDRESSES: Home—St. Paul, MN. *Office*—Department of Family Social Science, 290 McNeal Hall, University of Minnesota—St. Paul, 1985 Buford Ave., St. Paul, MN 55108; fax: 612-625-4227. *E-mail*—pboss@che.umn.edu.

CAREER: University of Wisconsin—Madison, lecturer, 1973-75, assistant professor, 1975-80, associate professor of child and family studies, 1980-81; University of Minnesota—St. Paul, St. Paul, MN, associate professor, 1981-84, professor of family social science, 1984—, director of marital and family therapy program, 1984-87, director of graduate studies, 1987-91, chair of human subjects committee for behavioral Research, 1982-86, member of Children, Youth, and Family Consortium, 1990—. U.S. Army War College, workshop presenter, 1980-85; University of North Carolina—Greensboro, Mildred Davis Lecturer, 1986; University of Southern California, visiting professor at Andrus Gerontological Center, 1988, special lecturer, 1991; Texas Tech University, guest lecturer, 1993; Harvard University, visiting professor at Judge Baker Children's Center, Harvard Medical School, 1995-96; guest lecturer at Syracuse University, McGill University, University of Pittsburgh, University of Rochester, University of Iowa, University of Connecticut, and other educational institutions; conference speaker in the United States and abroad. Family therapist in private practice, 1976—; Operation de Novo Pre-Trial Diversion Project, clinical staff supervisor for internal systems issues, 1981-83; American Association for Marriage and Family Therapy, director of training program for family therapists, 1981-86; National Council on Family Relations, coordinator and leader of National Family Conceptual Frameworks and Methodology Project, 1987; presenter of seminars and workshops; guest on media programs in the United States and elsewhere, including *Good Morning America* and *20/20;* public speaker. National Task Force on Families of Catastrophe, member, 1980-85; Citizens Ambassador Program, member of people-to-people marriage and family therapy delegation to China, 1988; World Congress on Psychosomatic Medicine, cochair of family section, 1993; volunteer counselor and consultant. Wilhelm Tell Drama Guild, member of board of directors, 1968-78.

MEMBER: American Psychological Association (fellow; member of family psychology division), National Council on Family Relations (fellow; member of board of directors, 1979-81; president, 1996-97), American Association for Marriage and Family Therapy (fellow; clinical member; chair of research committee, 1981-82), American Family Therapy Academy (charter member; research chair, 1995-97), Council on Contemporary Families, Groves Conference on Marriage and Family (national president, 1984-87), Minnesota Association for Marital and Family Therapy, Minnesota Council on Family Relations, Phi Kappa Phi, Phi Upsilon Omicron, Omicron Nu.

AWARDS, HONORS: Grants from Center for Prisoner of War Studies, Department of the Navy, 1974, and National Institute for Aging, 1986-91; Minnesota Friend of Extension Award, Epsilon Sigma Phi, 1986; gold medal, CASE Recognition Competition in Video Feature Programs and Documentaries, 1986, for *A Family's Fall: A Videodrama of a Family in Crisis;* distinguished contribution award, American Family Therapy Association, 1990; grant from Alzheimer's Association, 1993; award of merit, Minnesota chapter, Gamma Sigma Delta, 1994; Bush Foundation sabbatical award, University of Minnesota, 1995-96.

WRITINGS:

(With others) *The Father's Role in Family Systems: An Annotated Bibliography,* University of Wisconsin Press (Madison, WI), 1979.

Family Stress Management, Sage Publications (Newbury Park, CA), 1988, revised edition, 2001.

(Editor, with others, and contributor) *Sourcebook of Family Theories and Methods: A Contextual Approach,* Plenum (New York, NY), 1993.

(Editor) *Family Structures and Child Health in the Twenty-first Century,* Maternal and Child Health Leadership Conference, University of Chicago (Chicago, IL) 1993.

Ambiguous Loss: Learning to Live with Unresolved Grief, Harvard University Press (Cambridge, MA), 1999.

Losing a Way of Life: Ambiguous Loss in Farm Families, Extension, University of Minnesota (St. Paul, MN), 2001.

(With C. Mulligan) *Classic and Contemporary Readings about Family Stress,* Sage Publications (Newbury Park, CA), 2002.

Author of training films and videotapes, including *A Family's Fall: A Videodrama of a Family in Crisis,* Extension Service, University of Minnesota (St. Paul, MN), 1986. Contributor to books, including *Families before and after Perestroika: Russian and U.S. Perspectives,* edited by J. W. Maddock and others, Guilford Press (New York, NY), 1994; *Assessing Family Loss in Wrongful Death Litigation: The Special Roles of Lost Services,* edited by T. Ireland and T. Depperschmidt, Lawyers and Judges Publishing (Tucson, AZ), 1999; *Public Policy through a Family Lens,* National Council on Family Relations (Minneapolis, MN), 2001; *Living in the Presence of Grief,* edited by Dorothy Becvar, Guilford Press, 2001; and *Ambivalences in Intergenerational Relations,* edited by K. Pillemer and K. Luesher, Elsevier/JAL Press, 2002. Author of column "NCFR Reports," 1997. Contributor of articles and reviews to periodicals, including *USA Today, Gerontologist, American Family Therapy Newsletter, Family Therapy Networker, Psychiatry: Interpersonal and Biological Processes,* and *Marriage and Family Review.* Associate editor, *Family Relations,* 1979-86, 1999-2001, *Journal of Marriage and Family,* 1980-86, *Journal of Divorce,* 1981—, *Family Process,* 1982—, *Journal of Psychotherapy and the Family,* 1984-90, and *Journal of Feminist Family Therapy,* 1987—; member of editorial board, *Counseling and Values,* 1989-91, and *Contemporary Family Therapy,* 1991-93; consulting editor, *Journal of Family Psychology,* 1993—; advisory editor, *Journal of Marital and Family Therapy,* 1993—.

Author's books have been translated into Spanish, Chinese, and German.

WORK IN PROGRESS: Family Stress Reader; research on ambiguous loss in families of Alzheimer's disease patients and in families related to the World Trade Towers disaster in 2001.

*   *   *

BOWLES, Samuel 1939-

PERSONAL: Born 1939, in New Haven, CT. *Education:* Yale University, B.A., 1960; Harvard University, Ph.D., 1965.

ADDRESSES: Office—Department of Economics, University of Massachusetts, Amherst, MA 10113;

fax: 413-548-9852; Santa Fe Institute, 1399 Hyde Park Rd., Santa Fe, NM 87501. *E-mail*—bowles@santafe.edu.

CAREER: Economist and writer. Harvard University, Cambridge, MA, assistant professor of economics, 1965-71, associate professor 1971-74; University of Massachusetts at Amherst, professor of economics, 1974—, chair of Department of Economics, 2000, then professor emeritus; Santa Fe Institute, Santa Fe, NM, research associate, 2000—; Research Network on Effects of Inequality on Economic Performance, founder and co-director, 1993—. Visiting professor, University of Siena, 1982—. Has worked as a musician, a high school teacher in Nigeria, and a participant in the civil rights movement.

MEMBER: South African Commission on the Labour Market.

AWARDS, HONORS: Chancellor's Lecture and Bronze Medal, University of Massachusetts, 1979; Guggenheim fellowship, 1980-1981; fellowship of the German Marshall Fund of the United States, 1983; William Fulbright Distinguished Visiting Professor, University of Kyoto and Doshisha University, 1984, University of Siena, 1993; University of Massachusetts Faculty fellowship, 1986; Ford Visiting Professor, University of California—Berkeley, 1988; Museum of Education Book of the Century, 1999, for *Schooling in Capitalist America.*

WRITINGS:

Planning Educational Systems for Economic Growth, Harvard University Press (Cambridge, MA), 1969.
(With David Kendrick, Lance Taylor, and Marc Roberts) *Notes and Problems in Microeconomic Theory,* Markham Publishing. Co. (Chicago, IL), 1970.
(With Herbert Gintis) *Schooling in Capitalist America: Educational Reform and the Contradictions of Economic Life,* Basic Books (New York, NY), 1976.
(With David M. Gordon and Thomas E. Weisskopf) *Beyond the Waste Land: A Democratic Alternative to Economic Decline,* Anchor Press/Doubleday (Garden City, NY), 1983.

(With Richard Edwards) *Understanding Capitalism: Competition, Command, and Change in the U.S. Economy,* Harper & Row (New York, NY), 1985.
(With Herbert Gintis) *Democracy and Capitalism: Property, Community, and the Contradictions of Modern Social Thought,* Basic Books (New York, NY), 1986.
(With Herbert Gintis) *Recasting Egalitarianism: New Rules for Communities, States, and Markets,* edited by Erik Olin Wright, Verso (New York, NY), 1998.
(With David M. Gordon and Thomas E. Weisskopf) *After the Waste Land: A Democratic Economics for the Year 2000,* M. E. Sharpe, Inc. (Armonk, NY), 1990.
Microeconomics: Behavior, Institutions, and Evolution, Princeton University Press (Princeton, NJ), 2003.

EDITOR

(With Hollis B. Chenery) *Studies in Development Planning,* Harvard University Press (Cambridge, MA), 1971.
(With Richard Edwards and William G. Shepherd) *Unconventional Wisdom: Essays on Economics in Honor of John Kenneth Galbraith,* Houghton-Mifflin (Boston, MA), 1989.
(With Richard Edwards) *Radical Political Economy,* Gower Publishing Co. (Brookfield, VT), 1990.
(With Herbert Gintis and Bo Gustafsson) *Markets and Democracy: Participation, Accountability, and Efficiency,* Cambridge University Press (Cambridge, NY), 1993.
(With Thomas E. Weisskopf) David M. Gordon, *Economics and Social Justice: Essays on Power, Labor, and Institutional Change,* Edward Elgar Publishing (Northampton, MA), 1998.
(With Maurizio Franzini and Ugo Pagano), *The Politics and Economics of Power,* Routledge (New York, NY), 1999.
(With Kenneth Arrow and Steven Durlauf) *Meritocracy and Economic Inequality,* Princeton University Press (Princeton, NJ), 2000.

Contributor to periodicals and journals, including *Quarterly Journal of Economics, Journal of Political Economy, American Economic Review, Review of Economics and Statistics, Journal of Economic Perspectives,* and *Boston Review.*

WORK IN PROGRESS: The Foundations of Social Reciprocity, edited with Robert Boyd, Ernst Fehr, and Herbert Gintis; *Intergenerational Inequality,* edited with Gintis and Melissa Osborne, for Princeton University Press/Russell Sage Foundation; *Poverty Traps,* edited with Steven Durlauf and Karla Hoff, for Princeton University Press/Russell Sage Foundation; *Inequality and Environmental Sustainability,* edited with Jean-Marie Baland and Pranab Bardham, for Princeton University Press/Russell Sage Foundation; *Understanding Capitalism: Competition, Command, and Change,* 3rd revised edition, with Frank Roosevelt, for Oxford University Press; *Cooperation, Reciprocity, and Punishment: Experiments from Fifteen Small-scale Societies,* edited with Joe Henrich, Robert Boyd, Colin Camerer, Enrst Fehr, and Gintis.

SIDELIGHTS: Economist, writer, and educator Samuel Bowles was born in 1939 in New Haven, Conneticut. He spent his early childhood in rural areas of New England and lived for a while in India with his parents during the early 1950s. In 1958 Bowles began a two-year tour of Russia as a musician. He also worked for three years as a high school teacher in northern Nigeria. In the early 1960s, he also became active in the civil rights movement.

In 1969 Bowles published his first book, *Planning Educational Systems for Economic Growth,* a revision of his doctoral thesis. His next book, *Notes and Problems in Microeconomic Theory,* written with David Kendrick, was published in 1970. "Both publications were based on the dominant neoclassical understanding of economics of education and microeconomics," wrote a contributor for the *World of Sociology.* "However, by the late 1960s, Bowles had already formed friendships with numerous leftist, radical economists such as Arthur McEwan, Thomas Weisskopf, and Herbert Gintis." Bowles's economic ideas began to evolve, and in 1968 he was a founding member of the Union for Radical Political Economics. In their search for new economic ideas, Marxism became an intellectual influence on Bowles and his contemporaries.

Bowles became an associate professor of economics at Harvard University in 1971, but "his time at Harvard as a faculty member was fairly tumultuous," it was reported in the *World of Sociology* profile. "Deeply involved in the protest against the United States'

involvement in Vietnam and already collaborating with fellow radical economist Gintis, Bowles came into conflict at Harvard as a new professor when he refused to sign an oath of loyalty to the U.S. Constitution. He was fired, but successfully pursued legal action to overturn both the dismissal and the oath requirement." Bowles was denied tenure in 1973. However, he took a position as professor of economics at the University of Massachusetts at Amherst in 1974. In 2000, he became chair of the department of economics there.

Bowles's work continued to approach economics from a Marxist perspective, and he published several papers outlining this outlook. "With the publication of *Schooling of Capitalist America,* cowritten with Gintis, Bowles's rejection of orthodox economics was complete," it was noted in the *World of Sociology* profile. "In this work, Bowles and Gintis explored the relationship between capitalism and the educational system. In so doing, they coined the term 'corresponding principle,' suggesting that school systems tend to adopt a hierarchical structure that mirrors the structure found in the labor market of a capitalist economy. Using this principle, they critiqued liberal educational philosophy, coming to the conclusion that educational reform is incompatible with a capitalist society."

Bowles then collaborated with David Gordon and Weisskopf on a series of papers studying the stagnation of the U.S. economy in the late 1970s and the subsequent expansion of rightist political economic policy. The papers were collected in two volumes, *Beyond the Wasteland* and *After the Waste Land.* His collaborations with Gintis also continued, resulting in books such as *Democracy and Capitalism.* Bowles also continued his study of capitalism from a Marxist perspective during the 1980s and 1990s, and into the 2000s. In 2000, Bowles became a research associate at the Santa Fe Institute in Santa Fe, New Mexico. He was also appointed by South African president Nelson Mandela to serve on South Africa's Commission on the Labour Market, where Bowles helped develop economic policies intended to counter the effects of apartheid.

Markets and Democracy: Participation, Accountability, and Efficiency, edited by Bowles with Herbert Gintis and Bo Gustafsson, "is a large volume, with three editors, twenty-three authors, eighteen separate essays, and a preface," wrote William M. Dugger in *Journal of Economic Issues.* Dugger quoted co-editor Gustafsson in describing the purpose of the book: "Ideally we are in search of an economic system, which combines the flexibility and vitality of modern capitalism with full employment, extensive participation in decision-making, a more egalitarian distribution of income and wealth in firms, and promotion of values oriented toward cooperation and solidarity between people."

In their search for such a system, the editors considered labor-owned and labor-managed firms "as an alternative to the investor-owned and hierarchically managed corporation," Dugger wrote. "The essays ask the right questions, but they use a game-theoretic approach to critique the usual neoclassical economics and its support of the status quo." To Dugger, "A powerful critique it is, but it is still largely hypothetical." However, Dugger observed, "In spite of the analytical gymnastics, several important issues are raised in these essays, and results are often obtained that are the exact opposite of the usual mainstream shibboleths."

In *Recasting Egalitarianism: New rules for Communities, States, and Markets,* Bowles and Gintis edit a volume consisting of a lengthy essay by the editors "advocating a new egalitarian project," wrote Vincent Geoghegan in *Utopian Studies.* Their essay "is followed by a range of responses to the proposal from philosophers, political scientists, and economists." Although Geoghegan found in the book little evidence of "how these egalitarian structures would operate in practice" and how "political forces might hinder or help the introduction of these measures," the broad outlines of the ideas by Bowles and Gintis are "sufficiently present to provide a basis for the lively critical responses in the rest of the volume." *Recasting Egalitarianism* is "a thought-provoking book," Geoghegan concluded. "All the chapters are of a very high quality, and the debates are rigorous and intensely topical."

The springboard essay by Bowles and Gintis "assumes as its starting point that the modern left is bereft of viable models for an efficient egalitarianism," Geoghegan remarked. "It turns its back on the widespread assumption that egalitarianism requires a loss of efficiency, and instead argues that a more equal society can actually provide greater efficiencies than can the inegalitarian capitalism of the modern world."

Meritocracy and Economic Inequality, edited by Bowles, Kenneth Arrow, and Steven Durlauf, approaches issues of economic inequality in contempo-

rary America. "This book . . . argues that economic inequality cannot simply be explained by individual intellectual ability and that social reforms can reduce the extent of inequality and improve the nation's economic well-being," wrote Hiroshi Ishida in *American Journal of Sociology.*

The book contains a chapter by Bowles and Gintis arguing that "schooling increases earnings primarily by transforming individuals' preferences, rather than by enhancing cognitive skills," Ishida observed. Other chapters address issues surrounding intelligence and trends in I.Q. tests; explore relationships among cognitive skill, education, and socioeconomic attainment; provide new economic models for racial inequality; and present simulations showing that wage gaps between high school and college graduates "differ by ability groups," Ishida wrote.

Claudia Goldin, writing in *Journal of Interdisciplinary History,* remarked that although the papers presented in *Meritocracy and Economic Inequality* lack historical evidence, they still "contain revealing research findings and, for those interested in the subject, this collection will be an important stopping point." To Ishida, "this book shows that scientific studies can contribute to tackling one of the most pressing issues confronted by American people: the persistence of economic equality. It should be read not only by the educated public, who will gain a better understanding of the causes of inequality, but also by public policy makers who will learn a great deal about how to craft effective policies to reduce economic equality."

BIOGRAPHICAL AND CRITICAL SOURCES:

BOOKS

Palmisano, Joseph M., editor, *World of Sociology,* Gale (Detroit, MI), 2001.

PERIODICALS

American Journal of Sociology, May, 1987, Robert R. Alford, review of *Democracy and Capitalism: Property, Community, and the Contradictions of Modern Social Thought,* p. 1558; May, 2001, Hiroshi Ishida, review of *Meritocracy and Economic Inequality,* p. 1803.

American Political Science Review, June, 1988, Dickinson McGaw, review of *Democracy and Capitalism: Property, Community, and the Contradictions of Modern Social Thought,* pp. 607-608.

Business Week, August 22, 1983, review of *Beyond the Waste Land: A Democratic Alternative to Economic Decline,* pp. 10-11.

Canadian Journal of Political Science, June, 1989, France Giroux, "La Democratie Post-Liberale: essai politique sur le liberalisme et le marxisme," p. 451.

Center Magazine, July-August, 1986, Donald McDonald, review of *Democracy and Capitalism: Property, Community, and the Contradictions of Modern Social Thought,* pp. 37-38.

Challenge, November-December, 1983, Richard D. Bartel, "The Zero-Sum Illusion" (interview), p. 29.

Choice, June, 2000, J. F. O'Connell, review of *Meritocracy and Economic Inequality,* p. 1863.

Contemporary Sociology, September, 1987, Erik Olin Wright, review of *Democracy and Capitalism: Property, Community, and the Contradictions of Modern Social Thought,* p. 748; May, 2001, George Farkas, review of *Meritocracy and Economic Inequality,* pp. 236-237.

Dollars & Sense, March-April, 1994, Bryan Snyder, "Creating a New World Economy: Forces of Change and Plans for Action," p. 34.

Economic Journal, March, 1986, John Grahl, review of *Understanding Capitalism: Competition, Command, and Change in the U.S. Economy,* p. 272; November, 1991, Walter Eltis, review of *Schools of Thought in Economics,* p. 1602.

Ethics, April, 1987, Michael Wallerstein, review of *Democracy and Capitalism: Property, Community, and the Contradictions of Modern Social Thought,* pp. 684-685.

Foreign Affairs, fall, 1983, William Diebold, Jr., review of *Beyond the Waste Land: A Democratic Alternative to Economic Decline,* p. 215.

Harvard Business Review, January-February, 1984, Timothy B. Blodgett, review of *Beyond the Waste Land: A Democratic Alternative to Economic Decline,* pp. 12-13.

Journal of Comparative Economics, June, 1992, Jeff Frank, review of *After the Waste Land: A Democratic Economics for the Year 2000,* pp. 338-339.

Journal of Economic Behavior & Organization, June, 1987, Michael Barzelay, review of *Democracy and Capitalism: Property, Community, and the Contradictions of Modern Social Thought,* p. 318.

Journal of Economic History, September, 1987, Robert L. Bennett, review of *Democracy and Capitalism: Property, Community, and the Contradictions of Modern Social Thought,* p. 864.

Journal of Economic Issues, March, 1987, Walter C. Wagner, review of *Democracy and Capitalism: Property, Community, and the Contradictions of Modern Social Thought,* p. 549; September, 1994, William M. Dugger, review of *Markets and Democracy: Participation, Accountability, and Efficiency,* p. 946.

Journal of Economic Literature, March, 1989, Dan Usher, review of *Democracy and Capitalism: Property, Community, and the Contradictions of Modern Social Thought,* p. 75; September, 1992, Richard B. du Boff, review of *After the Waste Land: A Democratic Economics for the Year 2000,* p. 1543; March, 1995, Peter Dorman, review of *Markets and Democracy: Participation, Accountability, and Efficiency,* p. 277; March, 2001, Charles Brown, review of *Meritocracy and Economic Inequality,* p. 93.

Journal of Interdisciplinary History, winter, 2001, Claudia Goldin, review of *Meritocracy and Economic Inequality,* p. 431.

Journal of Legislation, summer, 1984, Timothy G. Merker, review of *Beyond the Waste Land: A Democratic Alternative to Economic Decline,* pp. 568-570.

Journal of Management Studies, July, 2001, Michael Rowlinson, review of *The Politics and Economics of Power,* p. 762.

Journal of Sociology & Social Welfare, March, 2000, "Recasting Egalitarianism: New Rules for Communities, States, and Markets," pp. 189-190.

Library Journal, September 1, 1983, Richard C. Schiming, review of *Beyond the Waste Land: A Democratic Alternative to Economic Decline,* p. 1695; May 1, 1986, David Steiniche, review of *Democracy and Capitalism: Property, Community, and the Contradictions of Modern Social Thought,* pp. 122-123; March 1, 1991, Richard C. Schiming, review of *After the Wasteland: A Democratic Economics for the Year 2000,* p. 100.

Nation, July 2, 1983, John McDermott, review of *Beyond the Waste Land: A Democratic Alternative to Economic Decline,* p. 18; July 21, 1984, Norman Birnbaum, review of *Beyond the Waste Land: A Democratic Alternative to Economic Decline,* pp. 58-59.

National Review, August 26, 1991, Alan Reynolds, "Who's on Next? John Kenneth Galbraith Is Still on the Job, after Forty Years as America's Most Urbane Socialist," p. 31.

New Republic, February 13, 1984, Bob Kuttner, review of *Beyond the Waste Land: A Democratic Alternative to Economic Decline,* p. 26.

New York Review of Books, John Kenneth Galbraith, review of *Beyond the Waste Land: A Democratic Alternative to Economic Decline,* p. 3.

New York Times, July 24, 1983, review of *Beyond the Waste Land: A Democratic Alternative to Economic Decline,* p. F2.

New York Times Book Review, July 31, 1983, Peter Passell, *Review of Beyond the Waste Land: A Democratic Alternative to Economic Decline,* pp. 7-8; June 8, 1986, Suzanne Berger, review of *Democracy and Capitalism: Property, Community, and the Contradictions of Modern Social Thought,* p. 31.

Partisan Review, summer, 1990, William Phillips, "Plus ça Change," pp. 337-338.

Political Quarterly, April-June, 1994, Jonathan Boswell, review of *Markets and Democracy: Participation, Accountability, and Efficiency,* pp. 231-232.

Political Studies, September, 1995, Pat Devine, review of *Markets and Democracy: Participation, Accountability, and Efficiency,* pp. 543-544.

Politics & Society, June, 1990, Donald McCloskey, "Their Blackbird, Right or Wrong: A Comment on Contested Exchange," p. 223; John R. Bowman, "Competition and the Microfoundations of the Capitalist Economy: Towards the Redefinition of Homo Economicus," p. 233; John E. Roemer, "A Thin Thread: Comment on Bowles' and Gintis' 'Contested Exchange,'" p. 243; Michael Buraway and Erik Olin Wright, "Coercion and Consent in Contested Exchange," p. 251; Michele Salvati, "When a Mouse Brings Forth a Mountain," p. 267; Frank Thompson, "Bowles and Gintis and Political Economic Explanation," p. 279.

Progressive, December, 1983, J. Patrick Lewis, review of *Beyond the Waste Land: A Democratic Alternative to Economic Decline,* pp. 40-41; August, 1986, J. Patrick Lewis, review of *Democracy and Capitalism: Property, Community, and the Contradictions of Modern Social Thought,* pp. 40-41; July, 1991, John Buell, review of *After the Waste Land: A Democratic Economics for the Year 2000,* p. 40.

Public Interest, summer, 1987, Richard John Neuhaus, review of *Democracy and Capitalism: Property, Community, and the Contradictions of Modern Social Thought,* p. 112.

Publishers Weekly, August 25, 1989, Genevieve Stuttaford, review of *Unconventional Wisdom: Essays on Economics in Honor of John Kenneth Galbraith,* p. 54.

Review of Radical Political Economics, winter, 1987, Raid Seidelman, review of *Democracy and Capitalism: Property, Community, and the Contradictions of Modern Social Thought,* pp. 91-92; winter, 1988, Christing Rider, review of *Understanding Capitalism: Competition, Command, and Change in the U.S. Economy,* p. 98; September, 1994, Ed Ford, review of *Understanding Capitalism: Competition, Command, and Change in the U.S. Economy,* p. 127.

Science & Society, fall, 1987, James N. Devine, review of *Democracy and Capitalism: Property, Community, and the Contradictions of Modern Social Thought,* p. 362.

Socialist Review, April-June, 1990, Jeff Godwin, "Democracy and Capitalism," p. 131.

Southern Economic Journal, January, 1992, Timothy Kroechlin, review of *After the Waste Land: A Democratic Economics for the Year 2000,* pp. 842-843.

Utopian Studies, spring, 2000, Vincent Geoghegan, review of *Recasting Egalitarianism: New Rules for Communities, States, and Markets,* p. 233.

Wall Street Journal, August 25, 1986, William H. Riker, review of *Democracy and Capitalism: Property, Community, and the Contradictions of Modern Social Thought,* pp. 14, 19.

ONLINE

Samuel Bowles Web site, http://www-unix.oit.umass.edu/~bowles (August 15, 2002).*

*   *   *

BREEDLOVE, Lynn 1959(?)-

PERSONAL: Born c. 1959, in Oaktown, CA. *Education:* California State University, Hayward, B.A. (cum laude).

ADDRESSES: Home—San Francisco, CA. *Office*—Harvey Milk Institute, 1800 Market St., Suite Q-31, San Francisco, CA 94102.

CAREER: Musician and writer. Lickety Split All-Girl Courier (delivery service), San Francisco, CA, founder/owner, 1991-c. 2001; Tribe 8, lead singer and songwriter, 1990—; Harvey Milk Institute, San Francisco, CA, teacher. *Military service:* U. S. Army.

WRITINGS:

Godspeed, St. Martin's Press (New York, NY), 2002.

SIDELIGHTS: Although she wrote her first poem when she was in the third grade and had it published in her local paper, Lynn Breedlove didn't began writing in earnest until she was in her thirties. Before that, she was an admitted alcoholic and drug addict who managed to survive, get a college degree, and eventually quit drinking and doing drugs. In the early 1990s the clean-and-sober Breedlove started both a bike delivery service in San Francisco and Tribe 8, a lesbian punk band. By 1993, she had begun writing a novel, finishing it nearly nine years later while on tour with her band. The resulting book, *Godspeed,* is referred to by Breedlove as a *roman à clef* in that it is both autobiographical and based on stories she has been told by her friends in the gay community.

"It's autobiographical in an anachronistic way, with amalgams of characters, so if you recognized yourself, you're probably the head on someone else's body," said Breedlove on the *Tribe 8 Web site.* Breedlove added that she also made up a lot of the novel, including things she'd like to do "like train-hopping and some of the fights."

Godspeed tells the story of "Jim," a butch female bike messenger who loves a stripper/sex-show performer named Ally Cat and shooting up speed. Eventually Jim must choose between her addiction and Ally Cat. Unfortunately, her addiction wins out. Fired from her job, Jim becomes a roadie for a punk all-girl band. The novel graphically describes her ensuing sexual affairs. But Jim still loves Ally Cat and eventually quits doing drugs and returns to San Francisco, only to find that Ally Cat now has her own drug addiction. Calling Breedlove's book "literature as a game of dress-up," a *Kirkus Reviews* critic commented that Breedlove "is actually best at the simple, quiet, yet harrowing moments of life that she actively avoids in favor of hackneyed drug pyrotechnics." A *Publishers Weekly* reviewer noted, "Amid a tornado of activity and attitude, the author builds a small oasis of honest and unvarnished emotion, constructing a touching and nuanced portrait of a 'boy' who has not quite grown up." The reviewer also called the novel an "earnest debut . . . well worth the ride." Whitney Scott, writing in *Booklist,* dubbed the main character Jim the "oddly affecting heroine of an oddly affecting book."

One troubling aspect of the book for the author and, perhaps, for its readers is stated by Scott in her review of *Godspeed* when she noted that "so lyrical does it wax about shooting up and getting high, one almost feels like experimenting." In an interview published on the *Windy City Times* Web site, Greg Shapiro asked Breedlove whether she was concerned about glorifying drug use in the book. Breedlove replied, "Yeah, I was a little. For me, it was a cathartic experience." Breedlove went on to say, "I needed to put myself through that whole experience in order for me to fully say goodbye to that chapter in my life. I'm hoping that people will keep reading past the first couple of chapters and see that it's not that glamorous at all."

BIOGRAPHICAL AND CRITICAL SOURCES:

PERIODICALS

Booklist, March 1, 2002, Whitney Scott, review of *Godspeed,* p. 1089.
Kirkus Reviews, February 1, 2002, review of *Godspeed,* p. 119.
Publishers Weekly, April 29, 2002, review of *Godspeed,* p. 43.

ONLINE

Salon.com, http://www.salon.com/ (September 13, 2002), Amy Benfer, "Dykes on Bikes with Mikes."
Windy City Times Web site, http://www.outlineschicago.com/ (April 24, 2002), Gregg Shapiro, "The Next Chapter: An Interview with Lynn Breedlove."
Tribe 8 Web site, http://www.tribe8.com/ (March 30, 2002), "Lynn Breedlove on Writing *Godspeed.*"*

*   *   *

BRENNAN, Herbie
    See BRENNAN, J(ames) H(erbert)

*   *   *

BRENNAN, J(ames) H(erbert) 1940-
    (Herbie Brennan, Jan Brennan, Maria Palmer, Cornelius Rumstuckle)

PERSONAL: Born July 5, 1940, in County Down, Northern Ireland; son of James (a grocer) and Sarah Jane (a grocer) Brennan; married Helen McMaster,

March 28, 1961 (divorced, 1991); married Jacquie Burgess (a psychotherapist and author), "Summer Solstice, 1993"; children: Aynia, Sian. *Hobbies and other interests:* Studying astronomy, prehistory, history, and philosophy; doing psychical research; watching movies and television.

ADDRESSES: Home—Republic of Ireland. *Agent*—Sophie Hicks, Ed Victor Ltd., 6 Bayley St., Bedford Square, London WC1B 3HB, England; (back catalogue) Georgia Glover, David Higham Associates, 5-8 Lower John Street, Golden Square, London W1R 4HA, England. *E-mail*—herbie@eircom.net.

CAREER: Writer and lecturer. Full-time author, 1973—. Worked variously as a journalist, newspaper and magazine editor, hypnotherapist, counselor, marketer, and director of an advertising firm. Facilitator of seminars on such subjects as spiritual development, psychical research, dream work, sub-nuclear physics, magical training, the astral plane, healing, and reincarnation. Creator of computer software *Tarot: The Teacher* and *Timeship,* Five Star. Developer of boxed games *Man, Myth, and Magic* and *Timeship,* Yaquinto.

MEMBER: Society for Psychical Research.

WRITINGS:

FOR CHILDREN

Marcus Mustard, Bantam (London, England), 1994.
The Mystery Machine, Margaret McElderry Books (New York, NY), 1995.
Blood Brothers, Poolbeg (Dublin, Ireland), 1996.
(As Cornelius Rumstuckle) *The Book of Wizardry: The Apprentice's Guide to the Secrets of the Wizard's Guild,* Llewellyn (St. Paul, MN), 2003.

FICTION; AS HERBIE BRENNAN

Emily and the Werewolf, illustrated by David Pace, Margaret McElderry Books (New York, NY), 1993.
Bad Manners Day, Macdonald (Hemel Hampstead, England), 1996.
Dorothy's Ghost, illustrated by Marie Corner, Heinemann (London, England), 1996.

Little House, illustrated by Stephen Lewis, Macdonald (Hemel Hampstead, England), 1996.
The Thing from Knucker Hole, illustrated by Alex de Wolf, Hippo (London, England), 1996.
Mario Scumbini and the Big Pig Swipe, illustrated by David Simonds, Hamish Hamilton (London, England), 1996.
Kookabura Dreaming, illustrated by Phillip Reeve, Scholastic (London, England), 1997.
Letters from a Mouse, illustrated by Louise Voce, Walker Books (London, England), 1997.
Jennet's Tale: A Story about the Great Plague, Mammoth (London, England), 2000.
Final Victory, A. & C. Black (London, England), 2000.
Zartog's Remote, illustrated by Neil Layton, Bloomsbury (London, England), 2000, Carolrhoda Books (Minneapolis, MN), 2001.
Fairy Nuff: A Tale of Bluebell Wood, illustrated by Ross Collins, Bloomsbury (New York, NY), 2001.
Nuff Said: The New Bluebell Wood Adventure (sequel to *Fairy Nuff*), illustrated by Ross Collins, Bloomsbury (London, England), 2002, published as *Nuff Said: Another Tale of Bluebell Wood,* Bloomsbury (New York, NY), 2002.
Frankenstella and the Video Shop Monster, illustrated by Cathy Gale, Bloomsbury (London, England), 2002, published as *Frankenstella and the Video Store Monster,* Bloomsbury (New York, NY), 2002.
Faerie Wars, Bloomsbury (New York, NY), 2003.

"BARMY JEFFERS" SERIES

Barmy Jeffers and the Quasimodo Walk, Armada (London, England), 1988.
Return of Barmy Jeffers and the Quasimodo Walk, illustrated by David Cobley, Armada (London, England), 1988.
Barmy Jeffers and the Shrinking Potion, Armada (London, England), 1989.

"ICE AGE" SERIES

Shiva: An Adventure of the Ice Age, Collins (London, England), 1989, Lippincott (Philadelphia, PA), 1990.
The Crone: An Adventure of the Ice Age, Collins (London, England), 1990, published as *Shiva Accused: An Adventure of the Ice Age,* HarperCollins (New York, NY), 1991.

Ordeal by Poison, Collins (London, England), 1992, published as *Shiva's Challenge: An Adventure of the Ice Age,* HarperCollins (New York, NY), 1992.

"EDDIE THE DUCK" SERIES; AS HERBIE BRENNAN

Eddie the Duck, illustrated by Ann Kronheimer, Puffin (London, England), 1998.
Eddie and the Bad Egg, illustrated by Ann Kronheimer, Puffin (London, England), 1998.
Eddie and the Dirty Dogs, illustrated by Ann Kronheimer, Puffin (London, England), 2001.

"HORRORSCOPE" SERIES

(As Maria Palmer) *Capricorn's Children,* Mammoth (London, England), 1995.
Cancer: The Black Death, Mammoth (London, England), 1995
The Gravediggers, Mammoth (London, England), 1996.

"SAGAS OF THE DEMONSPAWN" SERIES; FANTASY GAME BOOKS

Demonspawn, Fontana (London, England), 1984.
Fire Wolf, Fontana (London, England), 1984.
The Crypts of Terror, Fontana (London, England), 1984.
Demonstration, illustrated by John Blanche, Fontana (London, England), 1984.
Ancient Evil, illustrated by John Blanche, Fontana (London, England), 1985.
Demondoom, Fontana (London, England), 1985.

"GRAILQUEST" SERIES; FANTASY GAME BOOKS

The Castle of Darkness, illustrated by John Higgins, Armada (London, England), 1984.
The Den of Dragons, illustrated by John Higgins, Armada (London, England), 1984.
The Gateway of Doom, illustrated by John Higgins, Armada (London, England), 1984.
Voyage of Terror, illustrated by John Higgins, Armada (London, England), 1985.
Kingdom of Horror, illustrated by John Higgins, Armada (London, England), 1985.

Realm of Chaos, illustrated by John Higgins, Armada (London, England), 1986.
Tomb of Nightmares, illustrated by John Higgins, Armada (London, England), 1986.
Legion of the Dead, illustrated by John Higgins, Armada (London, England), 1987.

FANTASY GAME BOOKS

The Curse of Frankenstein, illustrated by Tim Sell, Armada (London, England), 1986.
Dracula's Castle, Armada (London, England), 1986.
Monster Horrorshow, Armada (London, England), 1987.
(As Herbie Brennan) *Aztec Quest,* Kingfisher Books (London, England), 1997.
(As Herbie Brennan) *Egyptian Quest,* Kingfisher Books (London, England), 1997.

NONFICTION

Mindpower 1: Succeed at School, Armada (London, England), 1990.
Mindpower 2: Make Yourself a Success, Armada (London, England), 1990.
The Young Ghost Hunter's Guide, Armada (London, England), 1990.
(As Herbie Brennan) *Memory,* Scholastic (London, England, and New York, NY), 1997.
(As Herbie Brennan) *Seriously Weird True Stories,* illustrated by David Wyatt, Scholastic (London, England), 1997.
(As Herbie Brennan) *Seriously Weird True Stories 2,* Scholastic (London, England), 1998.
(As Herbie Brennan) *Alien Contact,* Scholastic (London, England), 1998.
(As Herbie Brennan) *The Internet,* Scholastic (London, England), 1998.
(As Herbie Brennan) *Techno-Future,* illustrated by Jeff Anderson, Puffin (London, England), 2000.
(As Herbie Brennan) *Space Quest: 111 Peculiar Questions Answered,* Faber and Faber (London, England), 2003.
(As Herbie Brennan) *A Spy's Handbook,* Faber and Faber (London, England), 2003.

INFORMATIONAL BOOKS FOR SCHOOLS; AS HERBIE BRENNAN

The Death of the Dinosaurs, illustrated by Chris Brown and others, Pearson Education (Harlow, England), 2001.

Dr. Jenner and the Cow Pox, illustrated by Andrew Quelch and James Sneddon, Pearson Education (Harlow, England), 2001.

How to Remember Absolutely Everything, illustrated by Barbara Vagnozzi, Pearson Education (Harlow, England), 2001.

Leonardo da Vinci: The Greatest Genius Who Ever Lived?, illustrated by Lee Montgomery, Pearsons Education (Harlow, England), 2001.

Why Do Cats Purr?, Pearson Education (Harlow, England), 2001.

PARAPSYCHOLOGY; FOR ADULTS

Discover Astral Projection: How to Achieve Out-of-Body Experiences, Collins (London, England), 1970, published as *The Astral Projection Workbook,* Aquarian/Thorsons (Hammersmith, England), 1989.

Mindreach, Aquarian Press (Wellingborough, England), 1985.

Discover Reincarnation, Aquarian/Thorsons (London, England), 1992, published as *Discover Your Past Lives: A Practical Course,* Sterling Publications (New York, NY), 1994.

ESOTERIC WRITINGS; FOR ADULTS

Astral Doorways, Aquarian Press (Wellingborough, England), 1971, and revised editions, Magis Books (Leicestershire, England), 1991.

Five Keys to Past Lives, Aquarian Press (Wellingborough, England), 1971, revised as *Reincarnation: Five Keys to Past Lives,* Aquarian Press (Wellingborough, England), 1981.

Experimental Magic, illustrated by Helen Brennan and Brendan P. Carey, Aquarian Press (Wellingborough, England), 1972.

Beyond the Fourth Dimension, Futura Publications (London, England), 1975.

The Reincarnation Workbook: A Complete Course in Recalling Past Lives, Aquarian (Wellingborough, England), 1989.

(With Eileen Campbell) *Aquarian Guide to the New Age,* Aquarian (Wellingborough, England), 1990, revised edition as *Dictionary of Mind, Body, and Spirit: Ideas, People, and Places,* Aquarian (London, England), 1994, revised edition, edited by Fran Holt-Underwood, C. F. Tuttle (Boston, MA), 1994.

Nostradamus: Visions of the Future, Aquarian/Thorsons (London, England), 1992.

Ancient Spirit, Warner, 1993.

Magick for Beginners: The Power to Change Your World, Llewellyn (St. Paul, MN), 1998.

(As Herbie Brennan) *The Little Book of Nostradamus: Prophecies for the Twenty-First Century,* Thorsons (London, England), 1999.

The Magical I Ching, Llewellyn (St. Paul, MN), 2000.

(With Dolores Ashcroft-Nowicki) *Magical Use of Thought Forms: A Proven System of Mental and Spiritual Empowerment,* Llewellyn (St. Paul, MN), 2001.

Occult Tibet: Secret Practices of Himalayan Magic, Llewellyn (St. Paul, MN), 2002.

NONFICTION; FOR ADULTS

The Occult Reich, Futura Publications (London, England), 1974.

An Occult History of the World, Volume One Futura Publications (London, England), 1976.

Power Play, Sphere (London, England), 1977.

Getting What You Want: Power Play Techniques for Achieving Success, Stein & Day (New York, NY), 1977, revised as *How to Get Where You Want to Go,* Thorsons (Wellingborough, England), 1991.

The Good Con Guide (humor), Sphere (London, England), 1978.

Getting Rich: A Beginner's Manual, Thorsons (Wellingborough, England), 1988.

A Guide to Megalithic Ireland, Aquarian/Thorsons (London, England), 1994.

Time Travel: A New Perspective, Llewellyn (St. Paul, MN), 1997.

(As Herbie Brennan) *Martian Genesis: The Extraterrestrial Origins of the Human Race,* Piatkus Books (London, England), 1998, Dell (New York, NY), 2000.

(As Herbie Brennan) *The Atlantis Enigma,* Piatkus Books (London, England), 1999, Berkeley (New York, NY), 2000.

(As Herbie Brennan) *The Secret History of Ancient Egypt: Electricity, Sonics, and the Disappearance of an Advanced Civilization,* Piatkus Books (London, England), 2000, Berkeley (New York, NY), 2001.

(As Herbie Brennan) *Death: The Great Mystery of Life,* Carroll & Graf (New York, NY), 2002.

FICTION; FOR ADULTS

The Greythorn Woman Doubleday (Garden City, NY), 1979.

Dark Moon, Michael Joseph (London, England), 1980, Holt (New York, NY), 1981.

(As Jan Brennan) *Dream of Destiny,* Doubleday (Garden City, NY), 1980.

OTHER

Author of *Why Race for Space?,* an informational book for children, Longmans; a radio play, *The Direction of Love,* British Broadcasting Corporation; and *The Ultimate Elsewhere,* a volume of esoteric writing, Futura. Contributor of short stories to collections of science fiction published by Scholastic and Egmont. Contributor to *Flame Angels,* an anthology of Irish writing edited by Polly Nolan. Contributor of science-fiction stories to periodicals, including *Galaxy, Magazine of Fantasy and Science Fiction,* and *Worlds of If.* Contributor of humorous short fiction and romances to periodicals, including *Woman, Woman's Choice, Woman's Own, Woman's Realm,* and *Woman's Way.* Facilitator of *The Way of Laughing,* an online study course in sacred science.

Brennan's books have been published in more than fifty languages, including Finnish, Dutch, Greek, Hebrew, Israeli, Japanese, Korean, Russian, Slovenian, and Turkish.

ADAPTATIONS: Ghosts on Tape, selections drawn from Brennan's stories, was released on audiocassette by HarperCollins, 1993. *The Mystery Machine* was released on audiocassette by American Printing House for the Blind, 1999. *The Black Death* was released on audiocassette by the Reed Group.

WORK IN PROGRESS: A Ghosthunter's Handbook and *An Alienhunter's Handbook,* for Faber and Faber (London, England); *Faerie Wars 2: The Faerie Queen,* for Bloomsbury (London, England).

SIDELIGHTS: A prolific author of fiction and nonfiction for children, young adults, and adults, J. H. Brennan is the creator of a wide variety of works that reflect his interest in psychology, mysticism, the occult,

comparative religions, and quantum physics, among other subjects. Written under several pseudonyms, most of them variations on his given name, his nearly one hundred books have sold over seven million copies. A writer of popular science fiction as well as a pioneering writer of fantasy adventure game books, Brennan is also acknowledged for writing informational books on controversial subjects, works that make provocative statements, backing them up with well-researched documentation. Brennan has written about topics such as magic, reincarnation, time travel, out-of-body experiences, the prophecies of sixteenth-century seer Nostradamus, the existence of Atlantis, and the possibility that the human race was created by extraterrestrial beings. He also has written books on such themes as death, the spiritual practices of Tibet, the unknown history of ancient Egypt, the history of prehistoric Ireland, and the techniques needed to achieve success. Several of Brennan's works of esoteric literature are regarded as classics in their field. Although these books are not directed to young people, some of them have found an audience among young adults.

As a writer for the young, Brennan characteristically blends fantasy and reality in wildly humorous stories, several of which are based around interactions between human children and supernatural creatures. In these works, the author often spoofs well-known genres, such as the detective story, the science-fiction novel, and the horror movie. Although these stories are noted for their riotous antics and broad humor, several of them are underscored with serious subtexts such as prejudice and the relationship between parent and child. As a writer for young adults, Brennan writes realistic and historical fiction as well as works that combine the two. Among his novels is the story of a psychic Cro-Magnon who is accused of murder before becoming a leader of her people; a disabled, fourteenth-century servant girl who is saved from being burned as a witch by the onslaught of the Great Plague; and a German boy who meets his idol, Adolf Hitler, during World War II. Before he is killed, the boy discovers that Hitler is not what he expected. Brennan also has written informational books for young people about such subjects as the evidence for human contact with aliens, how to succeed at school by using your mind, how to use the Internet, and how to be a spy. In addition, he has written two collections of stories featuring weird but true facts, such as a boy who walks on water and nuns who can fly. Brennan also is the creator of several series of fantasy game books, of which the "GrailQuest" series is especially popular. He has also written educational literature for schools, including biographies of inventor Leonardo da Vinci and Dr. Edward Jenner, the creator of the smallpox vaccine.

Brennan fills his fiction and picture books with action, puns, wordplay, and humor, some of it scatological. As a stylist, he sometimes favors literary techniques, such as the creation of parallel plots and the use of alternating chapters with different narrative voices. Several of Brennan's historical books for young adults include author notes that present additional facts about their subjects. Although some critics have noted that Brennan occasionally writes thin texts for children and presents outrageous theories to adults, most observers acknowledge him as an author who combines fantasy, psychology, and science in an arresting manner.

Born in County Down, Northern Ireland, Brennan is the son of two grocers, James and Sarah Jane Brennan. As a small boy, he developed a keen interest in psychology and started to study books on the subject. His research soon led him to other topics, such as hypnosis, and he claims to have hypnotized his first subject, a school friend, at the age of nine. At age eleven, Brennan entered Portadown College, a local prep school, where he stayed until he was eighteen. After graduation, Brennan became a journalist; at twenty-four, he became the youngest newspaper editor in Ireland. Brennan worked as a magazine editor, a hypnotherapist, a counselor, and an advertising director, among other positions, while working on his writing. The success of his first books, *Discover Astral Projection: How to Achieve Out-of-Body Experiences* and *Astral Doorways,* led Brennan to become a full-time writer in 1973. In his subsequent books for adults, the author has continued to explore psychical, psychological, and parapsychological subjects. Brennan has been praised for his examinations of unusual topics in these works, and he is commended for covering both the familiar and the exotic in an insightful and fascinating way. Brennan also has written romantic novels for adults and has contributed humorous and romantic short stories to women's magazines; as well, he has contributed science-fiction stories to anthologies and periodicals.

In 1984, Brennan began producing books for young people. Inspired by role playing in fantasy games, he wrote the first two volumes of his "GrailQuest" and

"Sagas of the Demonspawn," game-books series that include eight and six volumes respectively. The popularity of these series led Brennan to create additional game books. For example, *Egyptian Quest* sends the reader on a journey through ancient Egypt in order to help a pharaoh. Offering players a variety of adventures from which to choose, the volume is filled with plot twists, surprise pitfalls, and humor; it also offers added attractions such as instructions on how to send messages in hieroglyphics.

Brennan's "Ice Age" novel series for young adults, featuring an orphaned Cro-Magnon girl in prehistoric Europe, is among his most well-received. The first book in the series, *Shiva: An Adventure of the Ice Age,* introduces the twelve-year-old title character, who is a member of the Shingu tribe, a society ruled by women and managed by magic. Shiva is saved from an angry wolf by Doban, a Neanderthal boy who is the son of a chief. After Shiva befriends Doban, the boy is imprisoned by the Shingu because the races are mortal enemies. After Shiva frees Doban and takes him to the forest, she puts herself in danger. The Shingu and the "Ogres," as Shiva's tribe calls Doban's people, prepare for war, but because of the understanding between Shiva and Doban—and Shiva's psychic abilities—the pair are able to prevent it. Shiva also discovers the great totem of her tribe, the skull of a saber-toothed tiger, which aids her and Doban in stopping the fight. A writer in *Kirkus Reviews* called the book a "thought-provoking Ice Age adventure" and commented favorably upon Brennan's "sensitivity to different points of view" and his "creation of sympathetic characters on both sides." Writing in *Booklist,* Ilene Cooper wrote that Brennan knows how "to mix history, myth, and adventure," and commended the "book's important messages about similarities and differences."

In *The Crone: An Adventure of the Ice Age,* published in the United States as *Shiva Accused: An Adventure of the Ice Age,* Shiva discovers the murdered body of the Hag, a witch who is the chief wise woman of all the tribes. The Barradik, a rival tribe, accuse Shiva of the murder, an accusation that they use as a ploy in order to take political control when a new Hag is selected. The Barradik capture Shiva, beat her, and condemn her to death by stoning. Shiva is saved when a thousand Ogres—the Neanderthals from the previous book—march out of the forest to act in her defense. Reviewing *Shiva Accused* in *Booklist,* Cooper stated, "By switching from one viewpoint to another,

Brennan provokes readers and holds their attention with the excitement of the tale." Eleanor K. Mac-Donald in *School Library Journal* noted the novel's "real sense of danger and adventure" before concluding that readers "will discover that the use and abuse of power are as old as man (or woman)."

In *Ordeal by Poison,* published in the United States as *Shiva's Challenge: An Adventure of the Ice Age,* Shiva has been chosen to be trained as a Crone, or wise woman. In an initiation ritual, she is commanded to drink from one of six bowls, a traditional "ordeal by poison." She wakes from her drugged sleep in a frozen wasteland and must make her way home in order to prove herself. The story also includes two parallel plots. The first features Thag, the tribal leader of the Ogres. Thag has been challenged in battle by Shil, a jealous warrior who defeats Thag unfairly and banishes him to the frozen forests. The second subplot features Hiram, a Shingu boy who discovers that Shiva has been taken north in her initiation ritual. He enlists the aid of Heft, an Ogre with legendary tracking skills, and sets off to find her. Finally, all of the plot lines come together, and the young people are chosen as tribal leaders. Describing *Shiva's Challenge* as "a good addition to the series," *School Library Journal* critic MacDonald said, "the story moves with a compelling force."

Brennan is also the author of several popular books for younger children. He has written a series of humorous stories about Eddie, a duck that witnesses a bank robbery, is kidnapped (or, as Brennan puts it, "ducknapped"), and, after freeing himself, becomes a "ducktective" in order to bring criminals to justice. Told by the title character in the style of the "hard-boiled" detective stories of the 1940s and 1950s, the "Eddie" stories feature lots of action, witty wordplay, and happy endings. In her review of the first book in the series, *Eddie the Duck,* in *Magpies,* Margaret Phillips concluded, "children will be caught up in the pace and slapstick humour of the story."

Marcus Mustard is a fantasy novel about how the title character, a boy who is apprenticed in a castle that keeps "spinners", large deadly spiders that make silk for the aristocracy, is poisoned by one of the spinners when he becomes trapped in their breeding area. Writing in *School Librarian,* Graham Case noted, "If one of the tests of excellent fantasy has to be 'the willing suspension of disbelief,' than this book has achieved it beautifully!"

In *The Mystery Machine,* young Hubert, a boy who wants to join the circus and become the youngest human cannonball, is catapulted into a shed belonging to his neighbor, the nasty Mrs. Pomfrey-Parkinson. Inside the shed, Hubert discovers a strange machine. When he touches a button, Hubert is transported to a spaceship, where he discovers that his neighbor is part of an alien group that wants to take over the Earth. With the help of his friend Slider and some fireplace soot, Hubert foils the takeover. Writing in *Booklist,* Carolyn Phelan stated, "Not just for science fiction fans, this story has its feet on the ground." Anne Connor of *School Library Journal* concluded, "This fast-paced, madcap, science-fiction spoof will appeal to young adventure lovers."

Aliens also feature in *Zartog's Remote.* A story for primary graders, the book describes how Zartog, an eight-year-old alien with several arms, disobeys his three parents and flies his spaceship to Earth, where he is stranded after he loses his remote control. Eight-year-old Rachel, a black girl with thick glasses who is being bullied by a group of thuggish schoolmates because of her appearance, finds Zartog's remote. Finally, Zartog's computer helps him to get back to his planet by using a time machine. Before he leaves, Zartog, Rachel, and her dog, Lord Percy, use the alien's remote and Rachel's television remote to teach a lesson to the bullies at Rachel's school. Writing in *School Librarian,* Anne Rowe noted, "This is a fast and easy read. . . . It is funny, too, involving Zartog's responses to earthly things and the surreal nature of our language."

With *Frankenstella and the Video Shop Monster,* published in the United States as *Frankenstella and the Video Store Monster*, Brennan made his first contribution to the picture-book genre. In this work, little Stella warns her mother about the monster she sees in the dark corners of the video store they are visiting. However, her mother ignores her and is eaten by the horned creature. Stella transforms herself into a snaggletoothed giant and roars that she is Frankenstella, who eats monsters for breakfast. Before she shrinks back to size, Stella makes the monster burp up her mother before she sends it out to sea (with a life preserver). Even though she is covered in green slime, Stella's mother continues to attribute the monster to Stella's imagination. Calling the book "a riotous creature feature," a reviewer in *Publishers Weekly* noted, "This cathartic book . . . makes good sport of one's inner and outer demons."

Brennan is also the creator of two stories about Fairy Nuff, a young sprite who lives with his parents and his brother and sister, Biggie Nuff and Sweetie Nuff, in a cottage in Bluebell Wood. In *Fairy Nuff: A Tale of Bluebell Wood,* the protagonist is left alone in the family cottage; on his first night, he blows up his home while trying to light a candle with a stick of dynamite on a barrel of gunpowder. This act sends a grenade through the window of the mansion belonging to Widow Jennett Buhiss, a mean witch. The grenade blows up the widow's doghouse and scatters her stock certificates, which are worth billions of pounds. Buhiss sends her troll-like groundskeeper, Orc, to bring Nuff to her. When Orc places Nuff in Buhiss's woodshed, he meets another prisoner: the queen of England. Nuff rescues the queen and thwarts the witch's plan to take over the British Empire. The queen puts Buhiss in the Tower of London and rewards Nuff by making him a knight and giving him the widow's stock certificates. A critic for *Kirkus Reviews* commented that the author's "extravagant puns and over-the-top pacing . . . will give fans. . . more practice in delighted eye-rolling. Fair enuff." Writing in *School Library Journal,* Eva Mitnick predicted, "Kids will relish the broad humor and witty language, but the characters will really win them over."

In *Nuff Said: The New Bluebell Wood Adventure,* appearing in the United States as *Nuff Said: Another Tale of Bluebell Wood,* Nuff throws an enormous garden party at the new castle he has bought with some of the money that he received in the last book. He invites the queen of England and the president of the United States, among other notables, builds a theme park; and gets the Chinese State Circus to entertain his guests. However, he does not plan on the presence of two uninvited guests: Widow Buhiss, who has escaped from the Tower, and her henchman Orc. In addition, Nuff does not know that his contractor, who is dyslexic, has mortared his castle with gunpowder rather than cement. Comparing *Nuff Said* to its predecessor, a writer in *Kirkus Reviews* dubbed the sequel "equally madcap."

In 2002, Brennan produced *Faerie Wars,* a novel noted for its crossover appeal to both children and adults. In this work, young Henry and his friend old Mr. Fogarty become involved with Prince Prygus Malvae, a faerie royal who has been sent from his own world in order to escape the evil Faeries of the Night. The prince, who must get back home to thwart an attack by the treacherous band, convinces Harry and Fogarty to help him. According to *Independent* critic Nicholas Tucker, "Brennan writes with all the dash of an Irish storyteller at the peak of his form. Inventive as Harry Potter, dark as *Gormenghast,* and as intelligently probing as Philip Putnam, here is a title to brighten the dreariest of winter days."

In addition to his career as a writer for children and adults, Brennan has spent much of his professional life as a student and teacher of the mystical arts. He trained in Qabalah, an ancient system of mysticism, with the Society of the Inner Light, and with Helios, the precursors of the Servants of the Light. The latter group runs a Mystery School, the Servants of the Light School of Occult Science, that is headed by Dolores Ashcroft-Nowicki, an author and educator who is the director of studies for the program. Considered one of the most respected esoteric practitioners in the British Isles, Ashcroft-Nowicki collaborated with Brennan on a book for adults, *The Magical Use of Thought Forms.* Brennan has been married twice: his first marriage to Helen McMaster lasted thirty years and produced two children, Aynia and Sian, while his second marriage to Jacquie Burgess, an author and psychotherapist who is considered an expert on the use of crystals and their energies, led to their joint creation of Sacred Science, an informal movement dedicated to the investigation and promotion of the links between modern psychology, physics, and esoteric practice. Brennan is a frequent lecturer on New Age subjects and has traveled internationally to give seminars on such topics as reincarnation, dreams, magic, and sub-nuclear physics.

In an interview with Silence Thayer in *Cyril* magazine online, Brennan explained his attraction to writing: "I discovered years ago I was addicted to writing, much the same way some people get addicted to drugs—and for essentially the same reason. Stephen King somewhere talks about the writing process as a window opening up on the page and the writer passing through it into a whole different world. I know that feeling very well: it's an escape from reality and I love it. That's what gets me writing." After calling himself "a nuts-and-bolts man" who loves to find out how things work, Brennan concluded by discussing his interest in books for children: "I started writing for kids partly because I got interested in role-play gaming and partly because an American publisher told me I'd make lots of money. I kept doing it partly because I discovered I have a very childish mind—what amuses youngsters (bad puns, scatological references, and so on) amuses me as well—and partly because of the feedback. Children are the best critics in the world. They tell you when you're great and they tell you when you're useless. A writer needs that to keep on his toes."

BIOGRAPHICAL AND CRITICAL SOURCES:

BOOKS

Brady, Anne M., and Brian Cleeve, *A Biographical Dictionary of Irish Writers,* St. Martin's Press (New York, NY), 1985.

Dictionary of Irish Literature, 2nd edition, edited by Robert Hogan, Greenwood Press (Westport, CT), 1996.

PERIODICALS

Booklist, December 15, 1990, Ilene Cooper, review of *Shiva: An Adventure of the Ice Age,* p. 855; August, 1991, Ilene Cooper, review of *Shiva Accused: An Adventure of the Ice Age,* pp. 2139-2140; May 1, 1995, Carolyn Phelan, review of *The Mystery Machine,* p. 1571.

Independent, February 13, 2003, Nicholas Tucker, review of *Faerie Wars.*

Kirkus Reviews, October 15, 1990, review of *Shiva,* p. 1453; June 1, 2002, review of *Fairy Nuff: A Tale of Bluebell Wood,* p. 801; October 15, 2002, review of *Nuff Said: Another Tale of Bluebell Wood,* p. 1527.

Magpies, March, 1999, Margaret Phillips, review of *Eddie the Duck,* p. 29.

Publishers Weekly, May 6, 2002, review of *Frankenstella and the Video Store Monster,* p. 58.

School Librarian, November, 1994, Graham Case, review of *Marcus Mustard,* p. 162; winter, 2000, Anne Rowe, review of *Zartog's Remote,* p. 191.

School Library Journal, November, 1991, Eleanor K. MacDonald, review of *Shiva Accused,* p. 116; December, 1992, Eleanor K. MacDonald, review of *Shiva's Challenge: An Adventure of the Ice Age,* p. 108; July, 1995, Anne Connor, review of *The Mystery Machine,* p. 76; August, 2002, Eva Mitnick, review of *Fairy Nuff,* p. 147.

ONLINE

Cyril, http://www.cyrilmagazine.com/ (January 20, 2003), Silence Thayer, interview with Herbie Brennan.

Faerie Wars, http://www.faeriewars.com/ (January 20, 2003).

Herbie Brennan's Bookshelf, http://homepage.tinet.ie/~herbie/ (January 20, 2003).

Herbie Brennan Web Site, http://www.herbiebrennan.com (January 20, 2003).

*   *   *

BRENNAN, Jan
    See BRENNAN, J(ames) H(erbert)

*   *   *

BROCH, Hermann 1886-1951

PERSONAL: Born November 1, 1886, in Vienna, Austria-Hungary (now Austria); died of a heart attack May 30, 1951, in New Haven, CT; married Franziska von Rothermann, December 11, 1909; children: Hermann Friedrich Maria. *Education:* Studied textile engineering at Mulhausen (now Mulhouse, France) and in Alsace; attended University of Vienna, 1925-30.

CAREER: Textile engineer, novelist, poet, and essayist.

AWARDS, HONORS: Literary prize, American Academy of Arts and Sciences, 1942, for *The City of Man: A Declaration on World Democracy.*

WRITINGS:

Die schlafwandler: Eine Romantrilogie, 3 volumes, Rhein (Munich, Germany & Zurich, Switzerland), 1931-1932, translated by Willa and Edwin Muir as *The Sleepwalkers: A Trilogy,* Little, Brown (New York, NY), 1932.

Die imbelammte Grösse: Roman, Fischer (Berlin, Germany), 1933, translated by Willa and Edwin Muir as *The Unknown Quantity,* Viking Press (New York, NY), 1935.

James Joyce und die Gegenwart: Rede zu Joyces 50. Geburstag, Reichner (Vienna, Austria, Leipzig, Germany & Zurich, Switzerland), 1936, translated by Maria and Eugene Jolas as "James Joyce and the Present Age," in *A James Joyce Yearbook*, Transition Press (Paris, France), 1949.

Der Tod des Vergil: Roman, Pantheon (New York, NY), 1945, translated by Jean Starr Untermeyer as *The Death of Vergil*, Pantheon (New York, NY), 1945.

Die Schuldlosen: Roman in elf Erzählungen, Weismann (Munich, Germany), 1950, translated by Ralph Manheim as *The Guiltless*, Little, Brown (Boston, MA), 1974.

Gesammelte Werke, Rhein (Zurich, Switzerland), Volume 1: *Gedichle: Mit 9 Bildern und 2 Handschriftproben des Autors*, edited by Erich Kalher, 1953, Volume 2: *Die Schlafwandler, Romantrilogie*, 1952, Volume 3: *Der Tod des Vergil. Epische Dichtung*, 1952, Volume 4: *Der Versucher: Roman*, edited by Felix Stössinger, 1953, republished as *Demeter*, Suhrkamp (Frankfurt am Main, Germany), 1967, Volume 6: *Dichten and Erkennen: Essays*, edited by Hannah Arendt, 1955, Volume 7: *Erkennen und Handeln: Essays*, edited by Arendt, 1955, Volume 8: *Briefe: Von 1929 bis 1951*, edited by Robert Pick, 1957, Volume 9: *Massenpsychologie: Schriften aus dem Nachlass*, edited by Wolfgang Rothe, 1959, Volume 10: *Die unbekannte Grösse und frühe Schriften*, edited by Ernst Schönwiese, and *Mit den Briefen an Willa Muir*, edited by William Herd, 1961.

Nur das Herz ist das Wirkliche, edited by Ernst Schonwiese, Stiansny (Graz, Austria), 1959.

Die Euts''hnung: Schauspiel, in der Hörspielfassung, edited by Ernst Schoenwiese, Rhein (Zurich, Switzerland), 1961, translated by George E. Wellwarth and Broch de Rotherman as "The Atonement in German Drama Between the Wars," edited by George E. Wellwarth, Dutton (New York, NY), 1972.

Die Heimkehr: Prosa und Lyrik. Auswahl aus dem dichterischen Werk ergänzl durch den Vortrag geist und Zeitgeist, edited by Harald Binde, Fischer (Frankfurt am Main, Germany), 1962.

Der Dichter: Eine Auswahl aus dem dichterischen Werk, edited by Harald Binde, Rhein (Zurich, Switzerland), 1964.

Der Dichter: Eine Auswahl aus dem essayistischen Werk und aus Briefen, edited by Harald Binde, Rhein (Zurich, Switzerland), 1966.

Short Stories, edited by Eric William Herd, Oxford University Press (London, England), 1966.

Die Idea ist ewig: Essays and Briefe, edited by Harald Binde, Deutscher Taschenbuch (Munich, Germany), 1968.

Zur Universitatsreform, edited by Götz Wienold, Suhrkamp (Frankfurt am Main, Germany), 1969.

Bergroman: Die drei Originalfassungen, 4 volumes, edited by Frank Kress and Hans Albert Maier, Suhrkamp (Frankfurt am Main, Germany), 1969.

Gedanken zur Politik, edited by Dieter Hildebrandt, Suhrkamp (Frankfurt am Main, Germany), 1970.

Barbara un andere Novellen: Eine Auswahl aus dem dichterischen Werk, edited by Paul Michael Lutzeler, Suhrkamp (Frankfurt am Main, Germany), 1973.

Völkerbund-Resolution: Das vollst&aouml;ndige politische Pamphlet von 1937 mit Kommentar, Entwurf und Korrespondenz, edited by Paul Michael Lutzeler, Müller (Salzburg, Austria), 1973.

Kommentierte Werkausgabe, 17 volumes, edited by Paul Michael Lutzeler, Suhrkamp (Frankfurt am Main, Germany), 1974-1981, Volume 1: *Die Schlafwandler: Eine Romantrilogie*, 1978, Volume 2: *Die Unbekannte Grösse: Roman*, 1977, Volume 3: *Die Verzauberung*, translated by H. F. Broch de Rothermann as *The Spell*, Farrar, Straus & Giroux (New York, NY), 1987, Volume 4: *Der Tod des Vergil: Roman*, 1976, Volume 5: *Die Schuldlosen: Roman in elf Erzählungen*, 1974, Volume 6: *Novellen; Prosa; Fragmente*, 1980, Volume 7: *Dramen*, 1979, includes *Die Entsühnung,*, Volume 8: *Gedichte*, 1980, Volume 9, *Schriften zur Literatur: Kritik* and *Schriften zur Literatur: Theorie*, both 1975, Volume 10, *Philosophische Schriften: Kritik* and *Philosophische Schriften: Theorie*, both 1977, Volume 11: *Politische Schriften*, 1979, Volume 12: *Massenwahntheorie. Beitraege zu Einer Psychologie der Politik*, 1979, Volume 13: *Briefe 1913-1938, Briefe 1938-1945*, and *Briefe 1945-1951*, all 1981.

Psychische Selbstbiographie, Suhrkamp (Frankfurt am Main, Germany), 1999.

LETTERS

Hermann Broch—Daniel Brody: Briefwechsel 1930-1951, edited by Bertold Hack and Marietta Kleiss, Buchhändler-Vereinigung (Frankfurt am Main, Germany), 1971.

Hermann Broch, Briefe über Deutschland: Die Korrespondenz mit Volkmar von Zühlsdorff, edited by Paul Michael Lutzeler, Suhrkamp (Frankfurt am Main, Germany), 1986.

CONTRIBUTOR

Wiedergeburt der Liebe: Die unsichtbare Revolution, edited by Frank Thiess, Zsolnay (Berlin, Germany), 1931.

Almanach: "Das 48. Jahr," Fischer (Berlin, Germany), 1934.

Patmos: Zwölf Lyriker, edited by Ernst Schönwiese, Johannespresse (Vienna, Austria), 1935.

(Contributor) *The City of Man: A Declaration on World Democracy,* Viking Press (New York, NY), 1940.

On the Iliad, Rachel Bespaloff, translated by Mary McCarthy, Pantheon (New York, NY), 1947.

Frank Thiess: Werk und Dichter. 32 Beiträge zur Problematik unserer Zeit, edited by Rolf Italiänder, Kruger (Hamburg, Germany), 1950.

Contributor to periodicals, including *Brenner, Aktion, Summa, Rettung, Friede, Neue Tag, Neue Rundschau, Prager Presse, Kantstudien, Annalen der Philosophie, Literarische Welt, Frankfurter Zeitung, Berliner Börsen-Courier, Welt im Wort, Weiner Zeitung, Silberboot, Mass und Wert, Saturday Review of Literature, Aufbau, American Journal of International Law, Schweizer Rundschau, Literarische Revue,* and *Hamburger Akademische Rundschau.* Work anthologized in *1860-1920,* University of Chicago Press (Chicago, IL), 1984.

SIDELIGHTS: Poor and relatively unknown outside literary circles, Hermann Broch was nevertheless an influence in philosophy, social studies, and nontraditional writings. Broch may have limited his readership through his use of experimental forms and predilection for philosophy, but these qualities have made his work increasingly significant to scholars since his death in 1951.

While encouraged by his father to study business so he could work at the family textile factory, Broch hoped to study in the humanities. After learning engineering at Mulhausen (now Mulhouse), he traveled to the United States on the premise of uncovering means of producing cotton and returned to become an administrator at the factory in Teesdorf. Having converted to Catholicism, Broch was finally able to marry Franziska von Rothermann in December, 1909. The following October, Franziska gave birth to their only child, Hermann Friedrich Maria. They divorced in 1923, as Franziska's could not adapt to the simple life at Teesdorf.

After his brother, Fritz, joined the Austrian air force, Broch assumed all of the responsibilities of running the family business. Broch then began visiting the literary cafes in Vienna, and in 1918, he published "Eine metholodogische Novell" in *Summa,* a journal of literature. Enrolling at the University of Vienna in 1925, Broch studied mathematics and psychoanalysis, eventually concluding that his instructors were downplaying metaphysical and ethical considerations. Hoping to study these fields in depth, Broch turned his attention to literature.

In 1930 Broch was introduced to Daniel Brody, whose publishing company produced James Joyce's *Ulysses* in a German translation. They planned to publish Broch's novel trilogy *Die Schlafwandler* and came to a contract agreement on *Pasenow oder die Romantik,* the initial installment. Broch's constant revisions forced publishing delays in the book and the following two segments. The book was not available for Christmas, as planned; the reworking did not stop until April 1932, when the final part was at last published. Broch hurt himself financially with these delays, and this trend would continue throughout his literary career.

In *Die Schlafwandler,* translated as *The Sleepwalkers,* Broch illustrates Germany's development in three stages: romantic, anarchistic and objective. Michael Winkler commented in the *Reference Guide to World Literature,* "The Sleepwalkers is a work of high intellectual ambition." Intellectuals liked Broch's work, but the public at large had little exposure to his novels, and the result was a financial disaster. Broch's finances did not improve over time, and in fact worsened as his work drew more literary acclaim. Broch, looking for revenue, began speaking at the Ottakring Adult Education Center in Vienna, where he read several of his essays. Hoping to publish these essays in a compilation, Broch spoke to Brody. Believing the project would not be profitable, Brody denied Broch's request.

Next, Broch tried writing plays. *Die Entsühnung* was his first product, but the play was not performed until March 1934, in Zurich, after the producer eliminated the scene Broch considered most important. When the production was canceled shortly thereafter, Broch continued working on his next play, *Aus der Luft gegriffen.* When this attempt was deemed unsuitable for the stage, Broch turned to writing novels.

Published in 1933, *Die Unbekannte Grösse,* translated as *The Unknown Quantity,* recounts the life of Richard Hieck, a mathematician determined to control life through the rational application of science. Broch himself was dissatisfied with the conclusion of the novel, and it did poorly in Germany and America, although Harald Strauss in a review for the *New York Times* called it "an exquisite and delicate adventure into the distant recesses of the human spirit." Broch then authored poetry, some of which was included in *Patmos: Zwolf Lyriker,* an anthology edited by Ernst Schönwiese. He also produced five shorter novels and made a vain attempt to have these published in a single volume. After writing a screenplay for director Berthold Viertel, Broch adapted *Die unbekannte Grösse* into a screenplay. The film was never produced, and nothing ever came of an offer from Metro-Goldwyn-Mayer to film *The Sleepwalkers.*

Recovering from these disappointments, Broch began working on *Die Verzauberung,* (translated as *The Spell* in 1987) which was published in 1976. Hoping to find peace so he could complete his work, Broch moved to the country, but stopped work on the novel to write "Erwagungen zum Problem des Kultertodes," "Considerations on the Problem of Cultural Death", published in 1936 in *Silberboot.* Returning to work on his novel, Broch finished the initial draft and sent it to Brody in January. Having planned that *Die Verzauberung* would be the first section of a trilogy, Broch never completed the third version, which was published posthumously. The narrator is a doctor who has escaped to a quiet town in the mountains to practice medicine. A stranger, Marius Ratti, comes to the town and disturbs the region's serenity. Ratti, who is modeled after Adolf Hitler, persuades the village to return to the pre-industrial era and open the dormant gold mine. Soon, the entire town is in hysteria, and a young girl is sacrificed. Ratti's nemesis, Mutter Gisson, represents the true order of life, the opposite of Ratti's antiquated, dangerous philosophy. It is thought that Broch's use of a symbolic relationship between the natural and political world was a retort aimed at the National Socialists' support of "Blut-und-Boden"—blood and soil—motif in literature.

In the following years, Broch spent much time attempting to settle his father's estate. Moving to Alt-Aussee in Syria, he continued work on *Die Heimkehr des Vergil,* (*Vergil's Return,* 1973) a short novel he had begun after reading *Vergil: Vater des Abenlandes* by Theodore Hacker. After German soldiers marched into Austria in 1938, Broch was imprisoned after his post-

man reported him for receiving the controversial literary magazine *Das Wort.* Continuing to work on his novella, he was eventually released and ordered to report to the police in Vienna. Instead of following these orders, he stayed in seclusion with friends. Through the help of various acquaintances, Broch received an exit visa and moved to Great Britain. After obtaining an American visa, Broch left for New York, where he met Jean Starr Untermeyer, the poet who would translate his novel about Vergil.

With German novelist Thomas Mann's help, Broch obtained a Guggenheim fellowship stipend until 1941 and continued his research in the psychology of the masses. He also collaborated with Antonio Borgese to compile a book promoting democracy. *The City of Man: A Declaration on World Democracy* was released by Viking Press in 1940. Through this work, Broch was able to obtain further financial support for his study of psychology, a project that was never completed. In 1942, his *Der Tod des Vergil* was awarded a prize from the American Academy of Arts and Sciences, and Broch was able to pay his debts. The novel was finally published in 1945. There were few reviews of the novel in German, but Broch's popularity in the United States had grown and there were more than thirty reviews of the novel in America. Orville Prescott, a critic for the *Yale Review,* wrote "There is a dark beauty in these cloudy pages."

After rejecting a position in literature and psychology at the Friedrich Schiller University in Jena, East Germany, Broch continued to live on a stipend he received each month from well-to-do German exile Wilhelm Roth. Hospitalized for a broken leg, Broch began writing about Hugo von Hofmannsthal. The completed study was published after his death as *Hugo von Hofmannsthal und seine Zeit* in 1975 and was translated as *Hugo von Hofmannsthal and His Time,* in 1984. His next effort was a collection of short stories titled *Die Schuldlosen,* published in 1950, one year after his marriage to Anne Marie Meier-Graefe.

When he died in 1951, Broch had received neither fame nor wealth from his literary achievements. The public overlooked his forthright interpretation of social issues and his experimental writing. In more recent years, however, he has been cited as one of the most astute social critics of his time.

BIOGRAPHICAL AND CRITICAL SOURCES:

BOOKS

Dictionary of Literary Biography, Volume 124: *Twentieth-Century German Dramatists, 1919-1992,* Gale (Detroit), 1992.

Encyclopedia of World Literature in the Twentieth Century, third edition, St. James Press (Detroit, MI), 1999.

Hardin, James, and Donald G. Daviau, editors, *Dictionary of Literary Biography,* Volume 85: *Austrian Fiction Writers after 1914,* Gale (Detroit, MI), 1989.

Henderson, Leslie, editor, *Reference Guide to World Literature,* second edition, two volumes, St. James Press (Detroit, MI), 1995.

PERIODICALS

New York Times, May 12, 1935, p. 7.
Yale Review, autumn, 1945.*

*   *   *

BROSSA, Joan 1919-1998

PERSONAL: Born January 19, 1919, in Barri Sant Gervasi, Barcelona, Spain; died as the result of an accident, December 30, 1998, in Barcelona, Spain; son of an engraver.

CAREER: Poet, dramatist, and visual artist. Worked briefly as an engraver and bookseller.

WRITINGS:

El crim (poetic theater; produced in Barcelona, Spain, 1948), published in *Dau al Set,* 1948.

Sonets de Caruixa, Cobalto (Barcelona, Spain), 1949.

U no és ningú (prose), illustrated by Antoni Tàpies, privately published, 1950, Polígrafa (Barcelona, Spain), 1979.

(With Joan Ponç) *Parafaragamus,* privately printed (Barcelona, Spain), 1950.

Romance del Dragolí, illustrated by Joan Ponç, Dau al Set (Barcelona, Spain), 1950.

Em va fer Joan Brossa (poems), prologue by João Cabral de Melo, Cobalto (Barcelona, Spain), 1951.

Nocturns encontres (poetic theater), published in *Dau al Set,* 1952.

Esquerdes, parracs i enderrocs esberlant figura i La mare màscara (poetic theater), published in *Dau al Set,* 1952.

Poemes civils, Editions R. M. (Barcelona, Spain), 1961.

El bell lloc (poetic theater), Escola d'Art Dramàtic Adrià Gual (Barcelona, Spain), 1962.

Or i sal (poetic theater), prologue by Arnau Puig, Joaquim Horta (Barcelona, Spain), 1963.

El pa a la barca, lithographs by Antoni Tàpies, Sala Gaspar (Barcelona, Spain), 1963.

Cop de poma (performance piece), illustrations by Joan Miró, score by Josep M. Mestres Quadreny, Editions R. M. (Barcelona, Spain), 1963.

Teatre de Joan Brossa (includes *La xarxa, La jugada, Aquí al bosc, Gran guinyol,* and *El bell lloc*), Editions R. M. (Barcelona, Spain), 1964.

Novel.la (poetry), lithographs by Antoni Tàpies, Sala Gaspar (Barcelona, Spain), 1965.

Quadern de poemes, drawing by Antoni Tàpies, Ariel (Barcelona, Spain), 1969.

El saltamartí, Ocnos (Barcelona, Spain), 1969.

Frègoli, lithographs by Antoni Tàpies, Sala Gaspar (Barcelona, Spain), 1969.

Poesia Rasa, prologue by Manuel Sacristán, Ariel (Barcelona, Spain), 1970.

Poemes per a una oda, Montse Ester, Saltar i Parar (Barcelona, Spain), 1970.

Nocturn matinal (poems), illustrated by Antoni Tàpies, Polígrafa (Barcelona, Spain), 1970.

Calç i rajoles (poetic theater), prologue by Pere Gimferrer, Editions 62 (Barcelona, Spain), 1971.

Des d'un got d'aigua fins al petroli, Edició clandestina P.S.U.C. (Mataró, Spain), 1971.

Càntir de càntics, Editions 62 (Barcelona, Spain), 1972.

Vivàrium (prose), Editions 62 (Barcelona, Spain), 1972.

Ahmosis, Amenofis IV, Tutenkhamon; Sord-mut; El gran Francaroli (poetic theater), Estudios escénicos, (Barcelona, Spain), 1972.

Pluja, edited by C. Ameller and others, [Barcelona, Spain], 1973.

Oda a Joan Miró, lithographs by Miró, Polígrafa (Barcelona, Spain), 1973.

Poems from the Catalan (bilingual Catalan/English), introduction by Arthur Terry, Polígrafa (Barcelona, Spain), 1973.

Cinc poemes, etchings by Antoni Tàpies, Filògraf (Barcelona, Spain), 1973.

Cappare (includes *Model de fruita, Dotze sonets a Victòria,* and *Vint-i-set poemes*), Proa (Barcelona, Spain), 1973.

Poesia escènica, four volumes, Editions 62 (Barcelona, Spain), 1973-1980.

La barba del cranc (includes *La porta, Coresforç,* and *Quatre sonets*), Editions 62 (Barcelona, Spain), 1974.

(With Moisès Villèlia) *Cartipàs,* Sala Gaspar (Barcelona, Spain), 1974.

(Translator) Arthur Rimbaud, *Les ungles del guant,* Llibres del Mall (Barcelona, Spain), 1974.

Poemes visuals, Editions 62 (Barcelona, Spain), 1975.

Poemes objecte (postcards), Llibres del Mall (Barcelona, Spain), 1975.

Accions musicals (poetic theater), Llibres del Mall (Barcelona, Spain), 1975.

Oda a Macià i Oda al president Companys, lithographs by Antoni Tàpies, Sala Gaspar (Barcelona, Spain), 1975.

Oda al president Companys, La Humanitat (Barcelona, Spain), 1976.

Maneres, Urgell (Lleida, Spain), 1976.

Oda a Lluís M. Xirinacs, lithographs by Antoni Tàpies, Comissió Lluís Xirinacs (Barcelona, Spain), 1976.

Sextines 76, prologue by Joaquin Molas, Llibres del Mall (Barcelona, Spain), 1977.

Poemes de seny i cabell, prologue by Arthur Terry, Ariel (Barcelona, Spain), 1977.

Striptease català, photography by Ferran Freixa, Mil 69 (Barcelona, Spain), 1977.

(With Joan Miró) *Tres Joans,* Polígrafa (Barcelona, Spain), 1978.

(And photographer) *Poemes objecte,* prologue by Roland Penrose, Servicios Editoriales (Barcelona, Spain), 1978.

(Lyricist) *L'armari en el mar* (score; performed at Festival Internacional de música, 1978), Forum Musical, Teatre Lliure (Barcelona, Spain), 1978.

Cinc poemes visuals, Galeria 491 (Barcelona, Spain), 1979.

Antologia de poemes de revolta, Editions 62 (Barcelona, Spain), 1979.

(With Frederic Amat) *Llibre de la pluja,* Taller Vallirana (Barcelona, Spain), 1979.

Rua de llibres, Ariel (Barcelona, Spain), 1980.

Also author of books *La bola i l'escarbat, La sal i el drac, Catalunya i selva, Trangol, Malviatge, Els entra-i-surts del poeta, Roda de llibres, Striptease,* and *Fogall de sonets.* Contributor to periodicals, including *Tarot, Dau al Set,* and *Els Marges.*

SIDELIGHTS: Considered among the avant-garde throughout his long artistic life, Joan Brossa distinguished himself not only in poetry but in theater and visual arts as well. Brossa's written explorations were conducted in his native language of Catalan and include the stage plays *Nocturn encontres* as well as numerous poems and prose monologues.

Brossa was born in the Barcelona neighborhood of Sant Gervasi, the son of an engraver. At the age of seventeen he enlisted in the Republican Army and fought in the Spanish Civil War, reportedly with a book of Federico García Llorca's poetry in his pocket. Brossa's works from this period were addressed to his companions-in-arms against fascism. They were "half way between a chronicle and apologia," explained Glòria Bordons on the Web site *Lletra.*

While the civil war left its mark on the young Brossa, his work was even more profoundly influenced by two avant-garde Catalan artists whom he met following General Francisco Franco's conquest of Spain. Poet J. V. Foix and painter Joan Miró inspired his interest in both poetry and the surrealist movement then in full bloom. Under the guidance of Foix and Joan Prats, another great Catalan artist of the period, Brossa combined surrealistic imagery with the sonnet form in his first books, *La bola i l'escarbat* and *Fogall de sonets.* The poems in these volumes are "full of dream images, connected one to the other through unconscious associations," commented Bordons. However, Albert Forcadas noted in *World Literature Today* that "the impact of [Brossa's] early readings of Verdaguer, Guimerà and Ignasi Iglèsies and others oozes here and there" within the pages of these first published works.

With his widening circle of avant-gardist Catalan friends, Brossa helped found the influential literary review *Dau al Set* in 1947. About that time, he also began working with new forms, such as prose and theater. In keeping with his surrealistic bent at the time, Brossa's two 1949 "pseudonovels" are non-narrative, and contain odd digressions and leaps into nowhere. One of his first plays, *Sord-mut,* has a similar sardonic obscureness; the play consists entirely of a stage curtain being raised and lowered.

In yet another experiment during the *Dau al Set* period, Brossa began applying surrealist techniques to folk poetic forms like the ode and romancet, and by 1950 he had begun moving in a more political and realistic direction. In the collection *Des d'un got d'aigua fins al petroli* he fashions a clearly patriotic work calling for a Catalonia free of political and religious oppression. The decisive influence in this direction was Brazilian poet João Cabral de Melo, then in Barcelona. Cabral introduced Brossa and his circle to the ideas of Karl Marx. It was shortly after this introduction that Brossa published his landmark *Em va fer Joan Brossa,* in which he abandons the phantasmagoric and absurd to focus entirely upon the ordinary, albeit through a humorous and political lens. The poems were not well received by a Catalan literary establishment which in the 1950s was focused on a more erudite post-symbolism. Critics saw Brossa's new work as less poetic than photographic in its intense ordinariness and simplicity.

Ignoring such criticism, Brossa proceeded in an increasingly political vein. His *Catalunya i selva,* a collection of sonnets, explicitly addresses the plight of Spanish society under the Franco dictatorship, while in *Romancets del Dragolí* he employs mythical subjects appropriate to the medieval poetic form to introduce his political ideas. *World Literature Today* contributor Janet Pérez noted that the poem "Xauxa," with its description of a fantastic land of eternal summer and fruits that tend themselves, "slowly becomes a sociopolitical statement that such countries are worth fighting for."

During the 1960s Brossa became fascinated with the idea of transcending the technical borders of his art. In two books of poetry from the early 1950s, *Trangol* and *Malviatge,* Brossa had experimented with monosyllabic poetry; he now played with the shape of words and even the spaces on the page on which they were written. 1963's *El Saltamartí* marks the beginning of Brossa's "visual poetry": poems that use visual images to convey a poetic meaning. An example from this period is a piece titled "Conscientious Objector," which consists of a rifle barrel topped with a candle snuffer used during the Roman Catholic Mass. Brossa now frequently collaborated with visual artists that included Miró and the internationally renowned Catalan graphic artist Antoni Tàpies.

Meanwhile, Brossa never lost his taste for traditional written poetry. *Els entra-i-surts del poeta* and *Roda de llibres* show Brossa continuing in the style of the Cabral period and creating short, surprising poems full of political and social insight. "The use of everyday language, synthesis, definition, visual games, and especially humor and irony are the principal techniques used in these poems," commented Bordons, adding that the resulting works "are almost jokes of a critical nature."

Brossa found a model for his quasi-theatrical explorations in the "transformist" art of Italian actor Leopoldo Fregoli, who created a kind of early performance art using multiple disguises and other techniques to dramatize his ideas about the continuous change, or transformation, inherent in living beings. Brossa's play 1967 *Striptease* uses Fregoli's ideas in the context of a peep show. The play consists of six girls on a darkened stage. A spotlight roves from one to the next, revealing that each successive girl wears an article less of clothing, but when the stage lights burst forth as the end of the piece the audience realizes that the last girl is not only naked, she is a mannequin. "The superimposed appearances, when eliminated one after the other, do not lead the spectator to a sure knowledge of the naked body, but to another reality," wrote Forcadas. Indeed, he added, Brossa's use of Fregolian techniques "are frequently more fascinating than in Fregoli's own works."

The death of Franco in 1975 ended the decades-long suppression of Catalan language and culture within Spain. For Brossa, this meant opportunities to publish new and old works and reach beyond his small circle of postwar intellectual friends. He charged forward with his avant-garde experiments and won international acclaim. His later work followed two tracks: one poetic and the other "plastic."

In poetry Brossa tried new metrical forms, most notably the complicated Medieval sextina. But his work in non-literary visual arts was what most captured public attention. In the 1980s and 1990s the artist's growing fame resulted in sufficient funding for ever grander projects. As the size of his works and the media used to create them evolved, his themes remained consistent: he retained the critical, almost bitter anti-establishment position he developed in response to the civil war and Franco's long regime. This anti-establishment posture was clearly seen in one of Brossa's major exhibition at the Virreina Palace in Barcelona. One work, "Parasite," consists of a stuffed parrot perched atop a tailor's dummy facing a microphone. The implication is that public speakers are mimics and non-entities, commented Kim Bradley in a review of the exhibition for *Art in America.*

Brossa died as the result of an accident at his Barcelona studio in the Barri d'Horta-Guinardó on December 30, 1998, while preparing for a major exhibition to commemorate his eightieth birthday.

BIOGRAPHICAL AND CRITICAL SOURCES:

PERIODICALS

Art in America, September, 1994, Kim Bradley, review of "Joan Brossa at Virreina Palace," p. 125.
Discurso Literario, Volume 2, number 2, 1985, María A. Salgado, Joan Brossa's *La sal i el drac:* "A Playwright's Reflections on Life, Theatre, Playwrighting," pp. 363-376.
World Literature Today, spring, 1981, Albert M. Forcadas, review of *Antologia poètica (1941-1978),* p. 298; summer, 1981, Janet W. Díaz, review of *Poesía escénica, Volume 4,* p. 445; winter, 1983, Peter Cocozzella, review of *Vint-i-set sextines i un sonet,* p. 88; spring, 1986, Albert M. Forcadas, review of *Fogall de sonets (1943-1948),* p. 298; summer, 1987, Janet Pérez, review of *Romancets del Dragolí,* p. 437; winter, 1992, Albert M. Forcadas, review of *Poemes civils,* p. 118.

OTHER

Escriptors.com, http://www.escriptors.com/ (June, 2002), "Joan Brossa."
Lletra, http://www.uoc.edu/lletra/ (1999), Glòria Bordons, "Joan Brossa."

*   *   *

BROWNSTEIN, Gabriel 1966-

PERSONAL: Born April 13, 1966, in New York, NY; son of Shale (a psychiatrist) and Rachel (a professor) Brownstein; married Marcia Lerner, August 10, 1998; children: Eliza, Lucy. *Education:* Oberlin College, B.A., 1980, Columbia University, M.F.A., 1992.

ADDRESSES: Home—Brooklyn, NY. *Agent*—Paul Cirone, Aaron Priest Literary Agency, 708 Third Ave., 23rd Floor, New York, NY 10017-4103. *E-mail*—gbrownstein@ms.cc.sunysb.edu.

CAREER: Educator and author of short stories. State University of New York at Stony Brook, lecturer in English.

AWARDS, HONORS: PEN/Hemingway award for first fiction, 2002, for *The Curious Case of Benjamin Button, Apt. 3W.*

WRITINGS:

The Curious Case of Benjamin Button, Apt. 3W, W. W. Norton (New York, NY), 2002.

Contributor of short stories to periodicals, including *Zoetrope* and *Literary Review;* contributor of reviews to *Boston Globe* and *New Leader.*

SIDELIGHTS: Gabriel Brownstein's debut collection of short stories, *The Curious Case of Benjamin Button, Apt. 3W,* was partly inspired by characters created by some of literature's most enduring writers. Five of the volume's nine stories are narrated by the teenaged Davey Birnbaum, a resident of an early twentieth-century apartment building on West 89th Street in New York City called the "Old Manse," where he keeps tabs on a cast of misfit tenants. With names, situations, and dialogue lifted straight from the pages of such writers as F. Scott Fitzgerald and Franz Kafka, Brownstein creates "marvelously smooth hybrid tales that prompt readers to think twice about the intersection of life and fiction," according to a *Publishers Weekly* reviewer. Critical praise for *The Curious Case of Benjamin Button, Apt. 3W* was nearly unanimous and garnered Brownstein the 2003 PEN/Hemingway Award for first fiction.

As a child of the 1970s, narrator Davey's mundane concerns include supermodel Cheryl Tiegs and the fantasy role-playing game Dungeons and Dragons, but his favorite pastime is watching the neighbors. His detached observation gives *The Curious Case of Benjamin Button, Apt. 3W* an "achy undercurrent of nostalgia [that] buoys up Brownstein's big themes," according to Mark Rozzo in a review for the *Los Angeles Times.* These big themes include "thorny stuff like assimilation, voyeurism and role-playing," Rozzo added. In the title story, inspired by Fitzgerald's 1922 tale of the same name, a Christian woman gives birth to a full-grown old man, Jewish and bearded, who ages in reverse; save for one central moment, his physical body is perpetually out of sync with his mental state, and he dies a senile infant. According to Amy Reiter of *Salon.com,* the story is about "an immigrant forced to take up foreign customs in a strange land," and, more broadly, about "love, acceptance, openness, [and] growth."

Brownstein is forthright about his generous sampling from other writers; "I have stolen from works of great literature," he admits in the book's preface. Joining Fitzgerald are other authors to which Brownstein pays homage: Kafka inspires the story "A Penal Colony All His Own, 11E," in which a boy creates a living shrine to himself—the "MacMichaelmas Museum of Kevin"—in his dead parents' home; the works of Nathaniel Hawthorne is recalled in "Wakefield, 7E," about a man who leaves his family and spies on them from across the street; W. H. Auden influences the tragic latter-day Icarus tale "Musée des Beaux Arts," in which a misguided proctologist straps wings to his son and pushes him off the roof of an apartment building; and Isaac Bashevis Singer inspires "The Dead Fiddler," about a psychotherapist who loses his faith in science and finds a new faith in religion. Though borrowing so heavily from existing works might make Brownstein open to charges of plagiarism, Jackie McGlone of *Scotland on Sunday* wrote of the title story that the author "has brilliantly fleshed out the character and transmuted the story into something that is surprisingly original, and entirely his own." Similarly, Amy Reiter of *Salon.com* maintained in a review of *The Curious Case of Benjamin Button, Apt. 3W* that "so seamlessly does Brownstein weave these bits and chunks, constructs and conceits into his own quirky, glintingly lively narratives and make them so very much his own that they come off as completely fresh and original."

Garnering comparisons to authors such as J. D. Salinger, Jeffrey Eugenides, and Steven Millhauser, Brownstein's stories evoke an unsettling air, according to Amanda Craig of the London *Times,* which "successfully captures . . . a quintessentially urban air of mystery and strangeness, a willingness to exploit and

manipulate." Four stand-alone stories also included in Brownstein's collection also received good reviews. "Safety" is narrated from beyond the grave by a father who watches his family grieve after he is killed in a car accident; "The Inventor of Love" concerns an abused and orphaned boy who is taken in by two successive gay couples; and "The Bachelor" describes the affair between a Jewish graduate student and the daughter of a Nazi. According to Rob Thomas in a review for Madison, Wisconsin's *Capital Times,* these stand-alone stories "prove that Brownstein can assemble worthy fiction entirely on his own." Thomas also praised the telling of the stories, which he cited as effective due to the fact that the narrators are somewhat removed from the action.

In addition to recalling other works of literature, *The Curious Case of Benjamin Button, Apt. 3W* serves as an ode to New York City, which serves a significant role in the collection. According to Julia LoFaso in *Library Journal,* Brownstein's "stories are infused with a genuine sense of place." The author, a Manhattan native, based the apartment building in his book on the one in which he grew up, and the character of Davey can be read as his alter ego. In an interview with McGlone, he recalled the New York of the 1970s as a "city bankrupt and filthy but full of aspiration. Snowstorm and blackouts and strikes—garbage, transportation, teachers—all this was ordinary, exciting and incomprehensible."

Brownstein told *CA* that his primary motive for writing is the same as it was for twentieth-century writer George Orwell: "Sheer egotism. Beyond that? Habit is a big part of it. I get up in the morning and it's what I expect to do. When I skip a day, I feel it. When I skip several days in a row, I get irritable. Beyond habit, there's pleasure. Of course, there's a lot of frustration involved. And I'm not talking about the pleasure of working, of losing oneself in a task that one feels suited to. In Joan Didion's essay, 'Why I Write,' she says that the time spent writing is the time she feels most herself. I feel that way."

"Everything influences me," Brownstein added. "Anytime I read something, I think, in one way or another: I would (or would not) like to write like that. I wish I could write with a voice as assured and supple as Philip Roth's, with the wit of Lorrie Moore, the inventive geniality of Grace Paley, with the grasp of culture of Don DeLillo, with the authority of a Saul

Bellow or a James Baldwin. I read a story by Alice Munro or Stephen Millhauser and see possibilities, all sorts of things I want to rip off.

"My guess is that most influence happens unintentionally, that you have to distinguish between influence and aspiration. The piles of sword-and-sorcery books I read as a kid must inform my conception of character and narrative and setting, and probably they do so more fundamentally than any more recent reading of Henry James, however much more seriously I studied and considered James. If I had to pick two writers whose sentences shaped mine, they would be Roth and Dashiell Hammett.

"To go back to Joan Didion, she says she writes in order to discover what she is thinking. Maybe writing is a kind of inspiration in itself. You start a sentence and you wonder where it will end. That's not to say I start out with a blank; William Gass compared writing to mixing a martini. I have a vague idea of the martini I want to mix when I start—don't ask me how many parts life and how many parts reading and how many parts stories I have heard (and which one of those is the olive?)—but I am always surprised, and sometimes disappointed, at the kind of drink I end up with. A lot of the pleasure and frustration in writing comes from that gap narrowing, between the hopes for a project and its actualization."

Brownstein described his writing process as "dogged and lazy. I work every day. Sometimes that means writing on my way to work, on the Long Island Railroad. Sometimes that means getting to it very early in the morning. Other times that means lying on my bed and reading the sports pages while my computer hums on the other side of the room. I look out windows. If I've got time, I go get something to eat. I move back and forth from the computer to the page, long hand and notebooks, manuscript and pencil. I like to tinker with sentences. I write a lot of drafts."

BIOGRAPHICAL AND CRITICAL SOURCES:

PERIODICALS

Capital Times (Madison, WI), December 13, 2002, Rob Thomas, "Brownstein's Stories Use Classics Masterfully," p. 11A.

Kirkus Reviews, June 15, 2002, review of *The Curious Case of Benjamin Button, Apt. 3W,* p. 820.

Library Journal, August, 2002, Julia LoFaso, review of *The Curious Case of Benjamin Button, Apt. 3W,* p. 148.

Los Angeles Times, November 10, 2002, Mark Rozzo, "First Fiction," p. R14.

New York Times, September 29, 2002, Sarah Shatz, review of *The Curious Case of Benjamin Button, Apt. 3W,* p. 28.

Publishers Weekly, July 29, 2002, review of *The Curious Case of Benjamin Button, Apt. 3W,* p. 50.

Scotland on Sunday (Edinburgh, Scotland), January 19, 2003, Jackie McGlone, "I'll Take Manhattan by Stealth," p. 6.

Times (London, England), January 15, 2003, Amanda Craig, "Here's Looking at You," p. 18.

OTHER

Salon.com, http://www.salon.com/ (October 10, 2002), Amy Reiter, review of *The Curious Case of Benjamin Button, Apt. 3W.**

*　　*　　*

BURGESS, Mary A(lice Wickizer) 1938-

PERSONAL: Born June 21, 1938, in San Bernardino, CA; daughter of Russell Alger (an attorney and judge) and (Wilma) Evelyn (Swisher) Wickizer; married Floyd Edward Rogers, September 15, 1956 (divorced); married Michael Roy Burgess (also known as Robert Reginald; a writer), October 15, 1976; children: (first marriage) Richard Albert Rogers, Mary Louise Rogers Reynnells. *Education:* San Bernardino Valley College, A.A. (real estate), 1968; California State College (now University), San Bernardino, B.A. (history and English; high honors), 1975; graduate work in history at California State University, San Bernardino, and University of California, Riverside. *Politics:* Democrat. *Hobbies and other interests:* Genealogy, films, travel.

ADDRESSES: Office—Millefleurs Information Services, P.O. Box 2845, San Bernardino, CA 92406-2845. *E-mail*—borgopr@verizon.net.

CAREER: Editor and author. Pacific Bell Telephone & Telegraph Company, San Bernardino, CA, long-distance operator, 1955-56, teletype operator and relief teller for Colton, CA, business office of Pacific Bell, 1956-57; Norton Air Force Base, San Bernardino, data entry operator, 1958; Lynwyck Realty and Investment Company, Inc., San Bernardino, treasurer and real estate broker, beginning 1962; U.S. Post Office, postal clerk, 1969; California State College (now University), San Bernardino, at John M. Pfau Library, as student assistant, then clerical assistant, 1974-76, purchasing agent, 1976-81. Borgo Press, San Bernardino, publisher and editor, 1975-99; *Science Fiction & Fantasy Book Review,* associate publisher, 1979-80; Millefleurs Information Services, co-owner (with husband), 2000—; freelance researcher, 2000—. Has also done freelance indexing for a variety of reference and academic publishers.

WRITINGS:

(With Michael Burgess) *The Wickizer Annals: Wickizer, Wickiser, Wickkiser, Wickkizer, Wickheiser,* Borgo Press (San Bernardino, CA), 1983.

(With Robert Reginald and Douglas Menville) *Futurevisions: The New Golden Age of the Science Fiction Film,* Newcastle Publishing Co. (Van Nuys, CA), 1985.

(With Boden Clarke) *The Work of Katherine Kurtz: An Annotated Bibliography & Guide,* Borgo Press (San Bernardino, CA), 1993.

(With Michael Burgess and Daryl F. Mallett) *The State and Province Vital Records Guide,* Borgo Press (San Bernardino, CA), 1993.

(With Michael Burgess) *The House of the Burgesses: Being a Genealogical History of William Burgess of Richmond (Later King George) County, Virginia, His Son, Edward Burgess of Stafford (Later King George) County, Virginia, with the Descendants in the Male Line of Edward's Sons: Garner Burgess of Fauquier County, Virginia, William Burgess of Stafford County, Virginia, Edward Burgess, Jr. of Fauquier County, Virginia, Moses Burgess of Orange County, Virginia, Reuben Burgess of Rowan (Later Davie) County, North Carolina,* second edition, Borgo Press (San Bernardino, CA), 1994.

(With Michael Burgess, writing as Robert Reginald) *BP 250: An Annotated Bibliography of the First 250 Publications of The Borgo Press, 1975-1996,* Borgo Press (San Bernardino, CA), 1996.

EDITOR

(Editorial associate) Robert Reginald (pseudonym of Michael Burgess), *Science Fiction and Fantasy Literature: A Checklist, 1700-1974,* Gale (Detroit, MI), 1974.

(With Michael Burgess) Burgess McK. Shumway, *California Ranchos: Patented Private Land Grants Listed by County,* Borgo Press (San Bernardino, CA), 1988.

Jacob Biber, *Risen from the Ashes: A Story of the Jewish Displaced Persons in the Aftermath of World War II,* Borgo Press (San Bernardino, CA), 1990.

James Brown Campbell, *Across the Wide Missouri: The Diary of a Journey from Virginia to Missouri in 1819 and Back Again in 1822, with a Description of the City of Cincinnati,* Borgo Press (San Bernardino, CA), 1990.

(With Michael R. Burgess) Rep. William L. Clay, Sr., *To Kill or Not to Kill: Thoughts on Capital Punishment,* Borgo Press (San Bernardino, CA), 1990.

Arnella K. Turner, *Victorian Criticism of American Writers: A Guide to British Criticism of American Writers in the Leading British Periodicals of the Victorian Period, 1824-1900,* Borgo Press (San Bernardino, CA), 1991.

Raymond Z. Gallun, with Jeffrey M. Elliot, *Starclimber: The Literary Adventures and Autobiography of Raymond Z. Gallun,* Borgo Press (San Bernardino, CA), 1991.

Lawrence Estavan, *The Italian Theater in San Francisco, Being a History of the Italian-Language Operatic, Dramatic, and Comedic Productions Presented in the San Francisco Bay Area through the Depression Era, with Reminiscences of the Leading Players and Impresarios of the Times,* Borgo Press (San Bernardino, CA), 1991.

(Editorial associate and contributor) Robert Reginald, *Science Fiction and Fantasy Literature, 1975-1991: A Bibliography of Science Fiction, Fantasy, and Horror Fiction Books and Nonfiction Monographs,* Gale (Detroit, MI), 1992.

Irene Gut Opdyke, with Jeffrey M. Elliot, *Into the Flames: The Life Story of a Righteous Gentile,* Borgo Press (San Bernardino, CA), 1992.

Albert I. Berger, *The Magic That Works: John W. Campbell and the American Response to Technology,* Borgo Press (San Bernardino, CA), 1993.

W. C. Bamberger, *William Eastlake: High Desert Interlocutor,* Borgo Press (San Bernardino, CA), 1993.

(With Jacob Biber) *A Triumph of the Spirit: Ten Stories of Holocaust Survivors,* Borgo Press (San Bernardino, CA), 1994, second edition published as *A Triumph of the Spirit: Thirteen Stories of Holocaust Survivors,* Borgo Press (San Bernardino, CA), 1998.

Mary S. Weinkauf, *Hard-boiled Heretic: The Lew Archer Novels of Ross Macdonald,* Borgo Press (San Bernardino, CA), 1994.

Abigail Ann Martin, *An Irony of Fate: The Fiction of William March,* Borgo Press (San Bernardino, CA), 1994.

Scottie Kimberlin, *The Little Kitchen Cookbook,* Burgess & Wickizer (San Bernardino, CA), 1994.

Hanes Walton, Jr., *Black Women at the United Nations: The Politics, a Theoretical Model, and the Documents,* Borgo Press (San Bernardino, CA), 1995.

Robert Goehlert and Anthony C. Stamatoplos, *The Chinese Economy: A Bibliography of Works in English,* Borgo Press (San Bernardino, CA), 1995.

S. E. Rosenbaum, *A Voyage to America Ninety Years Ago: The Diary of a Bohemian Jew on His Voyage from Hamburg to New York in 1847,* edited by Guido Kisch, newly translated and with an introduction by Nathan Kravetz, Borgo Press (San Bernardino, CA), 1995.

Clark M. Zlotchew, *Voices of the River Plate: Interviews with Writers of Argentina and Uruguay,* Borgo Press (San Bernardino, CA), 1995.

Mary S. Weinkauf, *Murder Most Poetic: The Mystery Novels of Ngaio Marsh,* Borgo Press (San Bernardino, CA), 1996.

Contributor of essays, reviews, obituaries, and bibliographies for various reference works, including *Things to Come: An Illustrated History of the Science-Fiction Film,* by Robert Reginald and Douglas Menville, Times Books, 1977; (with Reginald) *The Encyclopedia of Alternative Medicine and Self-Help,* by Malcolm Hulke, Schocken Books, 1979; (with Reginald) *The Presidential-Congressional Political Dictionary,* by Jeffrey M. Elliot and Sheikh R. Ali, ABC-CLIO, 1984; *The Arms Control, Disarmament, and Military Security Dictionary,* by Reginald and Jeffrey M. Elliot, ABC-CLIO, 1989; *Survey of Modern Fantasy Literature,* five volumes, Salem Press, 1983; *Xenograffiti: Essays on Fantastic Literature,* by Reginald, Borgo Press, 1996; *Twentieth-Century Science-Fiction Authors,* fourth edition, St. James Press, 1996; and the *Contemporary Authors* series.

WORK IN PROGRESS: A history and genealogy of the Campbell family, a second edition of the Wickizer family history, and (with Michael Burgess) *Index Litteratus,* a comprehensive index to the literary publications of Borgo Press and Starmont House.

SIDELIGHTS: Mary A. Burgess is best known in the publishing world for her association with Borgo Press and its associated imprints. Borgo Press, which was founded in 1975 and published its first two books in April of 1976, had published exactly three hundred volumes when it finally closed its doors in 1999. The press focused on the criticism of genre literature and historical research, topics that reflect the personal interests of its founders, Burgess and her husband, Michael Burgess (who writes under the pen name Robert Reginald). Initially, Burgess focused on the business aspects of the enterprise, but she quickly began doing typesetting, indexing, and other production work on the books. By the late 1970s she was doing copy and textual editing, as well as writing back cover and advertising copy for the line. Soon she was extensively reorganizing and reworking the texts of out-of-print volumes reprinted by Borgo Press, and providing rewriting and other editorial services for the press's projects.

Burgess told *CA:* "I have been involved my whole life with books and things literary. I was taught to read by my nursery school teacher, and was subsequently 'skipped' into the third from the first grade because of that fact. I quickly worked my way through all the books in the tiny library which serviced our mountain community grammar school, and moved on to my parents' 'Book-of-the-Month' club offerings, reading such things as *Forever Amber* and *The Kinsey Report* at a very tender age. These things were never censored from me and, as a result, I am a strong believer in allowing children to read what they will, when they will. The important thing is to read, read, read. All else will follow from that.

"I have always been addicted to the study of history. I took up genealogy when just a child, gleaning all the facts I could from our family's collection of such things, and pestering my grandmother for further details. She was born in 1876, and lived to be almost 102 years old, so talking with her was like talking to a time machine. I have spent many hours working on my family histories and, in one of the greatest instances of serendipity I could have imagined, discovered after my second marriage that my husband shared an equal addiction. From that time on, we've spent most of our vacations and free time together researching our genealogies, traveling to small towns across the United States and Canada, investigating old cemeteries, working in court houses, and meeting numerous kinfolk. Sharing this obsession has been a great joy for both of us, and one we could not have predicted.

"My marriage [to Michael Burgess], in fact, has been one of the significant events of my life. Finding another human being who shared such common interests with me has seemed like a continuing miracle. From the day we first met (in the library, of course!), our lives have been centered around books—reading them, researching them, writing them, editing them, indexing them, and publishing them. Our publishing business, in fact, is only a few months older than our marriage. Together we've edited, indexed, and published some three hundred books—not a bad record for twenty-three years, and one which speaks more eloquently for our interests and how we spend our time than even the most detailed essay could.

"My other interests, shared with my husband, include films (watching, critiquing, and writing about them), and travel (usually to do on-site research). But books are still first, and always will be. In spite of all the 'on-line' frenzy these days, there is still nothing so entertaining as settling down to read a good book—and nothing so soul-satisfying as writing or publishing one."

BIOGRAPHICAL AND CRITICAL SOURCES:

BOOKS

Clute, John, and Peter Nicholls, editors, *The Encyclopedia of Science Fiction,* St. Martin's Press (New York, NY), 1993.
Science Fiction and Fantasy Literature, 1975-1991: A Bibliography of Science Fiction, Fantasy, and Horror Fiction Books and Nonfiction Monographs, Gale (Detroit, MI), 1992.

PERIODICALS

Choice, May, 1993, J. A. Adams, review of *Science Fiction and Fantasy Literature, 1975-1991: A Bibliography of Science Fiction, Fantasy, and*

Horror Fiction Books and Nonfiction Monographs, p. 1448; December, 1993, F. R. Levstik, review of *The State and Provincial Vital Records Guide,* p. 580.
Fantasy Newsletter, January, 1981, pp. 18-23, 30.
Towanda Daily Review, June, 1982, "9,000 Miles Later, They Found Her Roots."
Utopian Studies, spring, 1997, Kristine J. Anderson, review of *BP 250: An Annotated Bibliography of the First 250 Publications of the Borgo Press, 1975-1996,* pp. 168-169.

ONLINE

Millefleurs Information Services, http://www.millefleurs.tv/ (March 10, 2003).

*   *   *

BUTCHER, Kristin 1951-

PERSONAL: Born April 23, 1951; married Rob Butcher, August 15, 1970; children: Sara Newton, Dan. *Education:* University of Victoria, teacher certification, 1972. University of Winnipeg, B.A. (education), 1987; attended University of Manitoba, 1989.

ADDRESSES: Home and office—4451 Wilkerson Rd., Victoria, British Columbia V8Z 5C2, Canada. *Agent*—Transatlantic Literary Agency, 72 Glengowan Rd., Toronto, Ontario M4N 1G4, Canada. *E-mail*—kristinbutcher@shaw.ca.

CAREER: Teacher in Manitoba and British Columbia, Canada, 1972-96; Education International, Victoria, Canada, technical writer, 1996-97, author, 1997—. Worked variously as a real estate sales administer, property manager assistant, office manager, item records clerk, tour package organizer, and cashier.

MEMBER: Canadian Society of Children's Authors, Illustrators, and Performers, Children's Writers and Illustrators (liaison/recording secretary of Vancouver Island and Gulf Island branch), Victoria Children's Literature Roundtable, Canadian Children's Book Centre.

AWARDS, HONORS: Silver Birch Award regional winner, Ontario Library Association (OLA), 1998, and Silver Pencil Award (Netherlands), both for *The Runaways;* Great Canadian Short Story Competition runner-up, *Storyteller,* 1999, for "Waltzing Annie Home"; Book of the Year finalist, Canadian Library Association (CLA), 2000, for *The Tomorrow Tunnel,* Best Bet selection, OLA, 2001, Book of the Year for Children shortlist, CLA, Violet Downey Book for Children shortlist, Imperial Order of the Daughters of the Empire, and Our Choice selection, Canadian Children's Book Centre, all 2002, and British Columbia Children's Choice Award shortlist, 2003, all for *The Gramma War;* Best Bet selection, OLA, and Children's Book Award nominee, CLA, both for *Cairo Kelly and the Mann.*

WRITINGS:

The Runaways, Kids Can Press (Toronto, Canada), 1998.

The Tomorrow Tunnel, Thistledown Press (Saskatoon, Canada), 1999.

The Gramma War, Orca Book Publishers (Victoria, Canada), 2001.

Cairo Kelly and the Mann, Orca Book Publishers (Victoria, Canada), 2002.

Summer of Suspense, Whitecap Books (North Vancouver, Canada), 2002.

The Hemingway Tradition, Orca Book Publishers (Victoria, Canada), 2002.

The Trouble with Liberty, Orca Book Publishers (Victoria, Canada), 2003.

Zee's Way, Orca Book Publishers (Victoria, Canada), in press.

Also author of short story "Waltzing Annie Home." Contributor of book reviews to *Canadian Materials* and *Canadian Book Review Annual.*

WORK IN PROGRESS: One Marigold Summer, a coming-of-age novel for adolescents; *After,* an historical novel; *Lions, Spies, and Chocolate Cake; Simon & the Runaway Sock; Ladders Don't Care; Hating Thomas,* a novel for middle readers.

SIDELIGHTS: Kristin Butcher's books for adolescents often feature young characters who have a problem to solve and end up learning much about themselves in the process. Her award-winning 1998 book, *The Runaways,* tells the story of Nick, who is having family troubles. He is confused and upset when his mother tells him she is having a baby with the stepfather Nick dislikes. The young boy decides to run away and finds himself in an old abandoned house—but he is not alone. Another runaway is also seeking shelter in the house. Considered to everyone in town as a just a homeless person, Luther lives on the streets, keeping a secret about his painful past. The two become friends, and Nick soon understands that his life is not so bad when compared to others. While he returns to his family, the teenager does not forget Luther and begins to work on a school report about the poor and homeless in his town. Nick also volunteers at a local soup kitchen and helps Luther in a way no one else had ever been able to. A *Kirkus Reviews* critic called *The Runaways* a "convincing view of the sparking of a young person's social conscience," while Lucinda Lockwood, reviewing the novel for *School Library Journal,* called it "an interesting, sensitive portrayal of homeless citizens."

In *The Gramma War,* Butcher's main character, Annie, has had her life turned upside down. Her grandmother can no longer live alone and must move in with Annie and her family. This means that Annie now has to send her gerbils to the neighbors and share a room with her grumpy older sister. To make matters worse, Gramma is ill and difficult to live with. She picks on Annie and makes demands all day long. When Annie's favorite teacher leaves, she thinks her life is over, but suddenly she develops an interest her ancestors and joins the Junior Genealogical Society. She is able to enlist the help of her grandmother to find out about her family's history, and they soon develop a relationship of their own. Annie learns to deal with a wide range of emotions in this book that Debbie Feulner of *School Library Journal* called a "heartwarming story about change in a young person's life."

Butcher told *CA:* "I've noticed when I read author biographies, that many writers are or have been teachers. I'm not quite sure why that is, but it is—and I'm no exception. For me, teaching was good because it helped me to understand children better. You see, I never really was one myself. Children are active, and I've always been more of a watcher than a doer. Maybe that's why I never learned to swim or skate very well. Perhaps it's also why I was farmed off to the outfield during neighborhood baseball games. I shouldn't give the impression that I was a washout at everything. I could climb trees, though I was even better at falling out of them. And I rode a bike; I even have an assortment of scars to prove it.

"I may not have been overly athletic, but I did have a great imagination and super friends. We put on theatrical extravaganzas, produced magazines, ran detective agencies, held funerals for birds, operated roadside stands of many varieties, and conducted safaris in the woods behind our homes. I always think I grew up in a wonderful era, but perhaps it's all in the way I choose to remember it. But I do remember it—vividly—and that helps me in my writing. It's really not difficult to show a character's thoughts and feelings when you've experienced them yourself.

"I know this sounds crazy, but when I'm writing, I never really know what's going to happen until I write it. I begin with a general idea, and I mull it over for a while to see if it wants to go anywhere. When characters walk into my thoughts, I get to know them. They usually arrive with names. It's like I look at them in my head and they introduce themselves. I might not even like their names, but that's who they are, and I accept them. Then I talk to them. I ask them questions and listen to their answers. I put them in situations and watch what they do. Once I have at least two characters, I note how they interact with each other. I never have to question whether or not they are acting realistically, because I'm not making them do anything. I'm simply recording their thoughts, words, and actions. I think this is probably a lucky thing for a writer.

"For me then, writing is just as exciting as reading—maybe more exciting—because I'm the one doing it and it's still a surprise! Even when I think I know what's going to happen next, the characters can take the plot in a completely different direction than I had intended. And what they do is always better than what I had planned. That's when I look at my pen and wonder if the whole story is inside it or me."

BIOGRAPHICAL AND CRITICAL SOURCES:

PERIODICALS

Booklist, April 15, 1998, p. 1444; October 1, 2001, p. 318.
Bulletin of the Center for Children's Books, January, 2002, p. 166.
Kirkus Reviews, March 15, 1998, review of *The Runaways,* p. 399.
Resource Links, June, 2001, p. 8; June, 2002, p. 10.
School Library Journal, April, 1998, Lucinda Lockwood, review of *The Runaways,* p. 128; September, 2001, Debbie Feulner, review of *The Gramma War,* p. 223.

* * *

BUTLER, Nathan
See SOHL, Jerry

C

CAHILL, Laura

PERSONAL: Born in NJ.

ADDRESSES: Office—c/o Screenwriter Correspondence, Miramax Films, 375 Greenwich St., New York, NY 10013.

CAREER: Playwright and screen and television writer, 1993—. Plays have been produced at Vineyard Theater, New Harmony Project, Naked Angels, and Ensemble Studio Theatre.

WRITINGS:

Hysterical Blindness (two-act play; first produced Off-Off Broadway at Naked Angels, 1993), Dramatists Play Service (New York, NY), 2000, adapted for film by Cahill, Home Box Office (HBO), 2002.
Mercy (two-act play; produced Off-Broadway at Vineyard Theater, 1998), Dramatists Play Service (New York, NY), 2000.

Also author of the plays *Home* and *Jersey Girls Go to the Park.* Work represented in anthologies, including *Marathon 1996,* Smith & Kraus, 1996; *3 by E.S.T.: Three One-Act Plays Presented by Ensemble Studio Theatre,* Dramatists Play Service (New York, NY), 1997; and *Best Short Plays of 1999,* Applause, 2000. Author of pilot script for Warner Brothers Network. Has also adapted plays for film.

WORK IN PROGRESS: Three scripts for Miramax Films.

SIDELIGHTS: Laura Cahill's experiences growing up in northern New Jersey have been translated into comic plays about twenty-something singles trying to wrench meaning from mundane lives. Cahill's best-known work, *Hysterical Blindness,* was produced as a feature film in 2002 after a lengthy gestation as a play, and its themes of loneliness and desperation echo throughout her other works as well. In an interview with *HBO Films,* Cahill said that she is motivated to write about "what people say." She elaborated: "I'm always fascinated with what they really mean to say and what comes out of their mouth, and what people say in, in sort of boring, every day life. . . . These characters are people that I grew up with in New Jersey. They're not real people or any particular people, but they're just sort of the kind of people. They're sort of me and my friends."

Hysterical Blindness is a "small-scale, beautifully made character study about two best friends in their twenties," to quote Caryn James in the *New York Times.* Debby and Beth are working single women who spend their spare time together in bars, looking for men. Beth neglects her ten-year-old daughter, and Debby sometimes quarrels with her mother, with whom she shares a home. The drama follows Debby as she seeks a meaningful relationship with a patently disinterested fellow she has met at the local bar. Her desperation for his approval becomes increasingly pathetic as the story progresses, and ironically, it is her mother who finally achieves a lasting and satisfying romance. Cahill first wrote the work as a play and then adapted it to screen herself at the urging of actress Uma Thurman, who co-produced the feature film and starred in it as Debby.

Cahill said in her HBO interview that she originally intended *Hysterical Blindness* to be a comedy. As adapted to film, however, the story has a disturbing quality as well as subtle humor. In the Bergen County, New Jersey *Record,* Bill Ervolino wrote: "Thurman . . . is a captivating Debby. . . . We root for her because we know she's hurting, we know she's trapped, and, we know things could work out for her if she would just take a long, hard look in the mirror. . . . Filmed in and around the Bayonne area, *Hysterical Blindness* is no one's idea of a feel-good movie, although the ending is vaguely hopeful. It is, however, a wonderfully acted piece that stays with you for days. And it will probably wrench more than a few tears out of you." James likewise felt that Thurman's performance "is deeply felt and eloquent." The critic added: "But while we start off laughing, we come to cringe for Debby and then find her heartbreaking." *Hysterical Blindness* was the centerpiece feature at the 2002 Sundance Film Festival.

Cahill is also the author of *Mercy,* a play in which four characters try to get at life's essential meaning while having dinner in a cluttered urban apartment. The central character is Sarah, a documentary filmmaker, who exhorts the others—mostly fruitlessly—to seek contentment, or at least a gelato and a stroll in the park. *Variety* contributor Matt Wolf faulted the work for its "mannered artificiality of the writing," but nonetheless styled *Mercy* "an ironic comedy of manners whose characters are ill-equipped to fulfill the lives of which they dream."

In the wake of *Hysterical Blindness,* Cahill signed a three-picture contract with Miramax Films.

BIOGRAPHICAL AND CRITICAL SOURCES:

PERIODICALS

Backstage, January 15, 1999, Cindy Nemser, review of *Mercy,* p. 35.
Hollywood Reporter, January 18, 2002, Kirk Honeycutt, review of *Hysterical Blindness,* p. 67.
Newsday (Long Island, NY), August 22, 2002, Noel Holston, "Desperation Isn't Pretty, Even When the Actress Is."
New York Times, August 23, 2002, Caryn James, "Looking for Love, Finding Heartbreak."
Record (Bergen County, NJ), August 25, 2002, Bill Ervolino, "So Wounded She Can't See Straight," p. E1.
Variety, December 21, 1998, Matt Wolf, review of *Mercy,* p. 86.

ONLINE

HBO Online, http://www.hbo.com/ (May 1, 2003), "Hysterical Blindness."*

*   *   *

CAMPBELL-CULVER, Maggie

PERSONAL: Married; husband's name, Michael.

ADDRESSES: Home—Brittany, France. *Agent*—c/o Author Mail, Hodder Headline, 338 Euston Road, London NW1 3BH, England.

CAREER: Ballet Rambert, dancer; lecturer on garden history.

MEMBER: National Council for the Conservation of Plants and Gardens, Garden Trust Movement (founding member), Cornwall Gardens Trust.

AWARDS, HONORS: Garden Writers Guild award shortlist, for *The Origin of Plants.*

WRITINGS:

The Origin of Plants, Headline (London, England), 2001.

SIDELIGHTS: Gardener Maggie Campbell-Culver's book *The Origin of Plants* is a history of plant life in Great Britain, a land that thousands of years ago sported few varieties of foliage, but is now home to more species than almost any other country on the planet. Early settlers to the area imported plants from their native lands, and later on, explorers such as Christopher Columbus introduced varieties of plants from exotic places. Everything from rhododendrons to gladiolus, now considered commonplace, were introduced from lands as far away as China and Brazil.

By 1500, Campbell-Culver states, transcontinental plant-trading became commonplace, as the Dutch, French, and Spanish traded nonindigenous species on the open market. The book features detailed illustrations of many plant varieties and traces how many non-native garden plants came to be transplanted in a country the last ice age left nearly barren. Campbell-Culver also relates the disagreement that exists between experts on the dates of arrival for many species. The history of horticulture is wrapped up in history, and lax record-keeping practices prior to the eighteenth century make it difficult to pinpoint the definitive arrival of plants. Mostly it is a matter of folklore, although she explains that in the future better ways of determining these dates will become available.

The Origin of Plants "is a handsomely produced, well illustrated book," according to Henry Hobhouse in the *Spectator,* who noted that it is also a book "about plant-hunters," especially explorers and European settlers. "The grand Darwinian title is somewhat misleading," stated *Times Literary Supplement* reviewer Alexander Urquhart, "for *The Origin of Plants* is not about evolution but immigration." Urquhart concluded that the book "is nevertheless an impressive work in both scope and detail. The story is a fascinating one."

Campbell-Culver, a former ballet dancer, has studied garden history for many years. As a gardener, she worked on the excavation of Fisbourne Roman Palace in Sussex, England, in the early 1970s, and managed the historic garden at Mount Edgcumbe in Cornwall, England.

BIOGRAPHICAL AND CRITICAL SOURCES:

PERIODICALS

Spectator, September 15, 2001, Henry Hobhouse, review of *The Origin of Plants,* p. 37.
Times Literary Supplement, February 15, 2002, Alexander Urquhart, "Breaking New Ground," p. 36.*

*   *   *

CARAVANTES, Peggy 1935-

PERSONAL: Born April 3, 1935, in Austin, TX; daughter of John Alfred and Dorothy (a china-painting artist; maiden name, Garner) Huddleston; married Ted Caravantes, March 29, 1957 (died June 4, 2001); children: Brian, Susan Richter, Jeffrey. *Ethnicity:* "Anglo." *Education:* Southwestern University, B.A., 1956; Trinity University, M.Ed., 1982. *Religion:* Methodist. *Hobbies and other interests:* Reading, working puzzles, shopping.

ADDRESSES: Home—2518 Silver Ridge, San Antonio, TX 78232. *E-mail*—pcaravantes@satx.rr.com.

CAREER: Worked as an English teacher in several Texas school districts, 1956-82; East Central Independent School District, San Antonio, TX, worked variously as an assistant principal, principal, curriculum director, and deputy superintendent for instruction and personnel, 1982-99. Educational consultant and workshop presenter. Serves on Council of Stewards and Board of Disciples, and as a Stephen Minister at the Coker United Methodist Church.

MEMBER: Texas Middle School Association (member of board of directors), Phi Delta Kappa.

WRITINGS:

Petticoat Spies: Six Women Spies of the Civil War, Morgan Reynolds (Greensboro, NC), 2002.
Marcus Garvey: Black Visionary, Morgan Reynolds (Greensboro, NC), 2003.
O. Henry: William Sidney Porter: Texas Cowboy Writer, Eakin Publications (Austin, TX), 2003.
Sam Houston: No Ordinary Man, Morgan Reynolds (Greensboro, NC), 2004.

Contributor of "Ice to Scream," "Buffalo Soldiers," "The Last Laugh," and "The Silver Ring" to the "Power Up: Building Reading Strength" series by Steck-Vaughn.

WORK IN PROGRESS: Beyond Spellcheck (student activity book), for Holt (New York, NY).

SIDELIGHTS: After forty years of teaching middle-school and high-school English and serving as a school administrator, Peggy Caravantes achieved a long-held dream. When she retired from teaching, she finally had time to write stories and books for children, particularly nonfiction for young adults. While teaching, she told *CA,* "I noticed that many students never found books that interested them. My goal was to write one they enjoyed." Energetically, Caravantes set about making concrete her many book ideas. "To provide readable, enjoyable nonfiction that has a strong, accurate research base," the author told *CA,* she spent "hours poring over resources to find one more detail that might intrigue a young reader." Within three years of beginning her new career, Caravantes had written six and sold four nonfiction books, among them the biographies *Sam Houston: No Ordinary Man, O. Henry: William Sidney Porter: Texas Cowboy Writer,* and *Marcus Garvey: Black Visionary.*

"I write every day—some days I take notes from the research sources," Caravantes told *CA.* While researching American Civil War-era nurses, she discovered Sarah Emma Edmonds, who was both a nurse and a spy. This serendipitous find sparked the idea for *Petticoat Spies: Six Women Spies of the Civil War,* which, according to Patricia Ann Owens of *School Library Journal,* "covers a fascinating aspect of the war." In *Petticoat Spies,* the author tells the story of six women who spied for their governments.

Reflecting on her work habits, Caravantes added, "Other times I write rough drafts, revise, edit, or polish. I work with a critique partner who does not like nonfiction. If I can get her interested in my stories, I feel success!"

Caravantes offered novice writers the following advice: "I stand in awe of the excellent writing in all genres for children and young adults. Despite the competition from television and video games, young people do still read, and the selection has never been better. I encourage new writers not to become discouraged. Good writing is hard work, but perseverance does pay off. Write a few words every day. Talk to other writers; attend writing workshops and institutes. Don't ever give up."

BIOGRAPHICAL AND CRITICAL SOURCES:

PERIODICALS

Booklist, March 15, 2002, Carolyn Phelan, review of *Petticoat Spies: Six Women Spies of the Civil War,* p. 1254.
Children's Bookwatch, August, 2002, review of *Petticoat Spies,* p. 2.
School Library Journal, August, 2002, Patricia Ann Owens, review of *Petticoat Spies,* p. 204.

CARLSON, Keith Thor 1966-

PERSONAL: Born January 11, 1966, in Powell River, British Columbia, Canada; son of John P. and Elizabeth (Wightman) Carlson; married M. Teresa Molina, August 11, 1988; children: William Luis, Benjamin Magnus. *Education:* University of Victoria, B.A., 1988, M.A., 1991; University of British Columbia, Ph. D., 2003. *Religion:* Roman Catholic.

ADDRESSES: Home—102 Smoothstone Cres., Saskatoon, Saskatchewan, Canada S7J 4S8. *Office*—Department of History, University of Saskatchewan, 9 Campus Dr., Saskatoon, Saskatchewan, Canada S7N 5A5.

CAREER: Stó:lō Nation, Churchill, British Columbia, Canada, historian, 1992-2001; University of Saskatchewan, Saskatoon, professor of history, 2001—.

AWARDS, HONORS: Fellow of Social Sciences and Humanities Research Council of Canada, 1996; Roderick Haig Brown Regional Award, British Columbia Book Prizes, 2002.

WRITINGS:

Twisted Road to Freedom, University of the Philippines Press, 1995.
You Are Asked to Witness, Stó:lō Heritage Trust (Chilliwack, British Columbia, Canada), 1997.
I Am Stó:lō (juvenile nonfiction), Stó:lō Heritage Trust (Chilliwack, British Columbia, Canada), 1998.
A Stó:lō-Coast Salish Historical Atlas, University of Washington Press (Seattle, WA), 2001.

WORK IN PROGRESS: Power of Place, Problem of Time, completion expected c. 2003; research on the history of aboriginal identity.

BIOGRAPHICAL AND CRITICAL SOURCES:

PERIODICALS

Oregon Historical Quarterly, spring, 2002, William Wyckoff, review of *A Stó:lō-Coast Salish Historical Atlas,* p. 136.

CARMAN, Dominic

PERSONAL: Married; children: three. *Education:* Attended Durham University.

ADDRESSES: Office—c/o *London Business Review,* Delta House, 175/177 Borough High St., London SE1 1HR, England.

CAREER: Worked in banking, then for News International and Euromoney Publications; IIR (conference company), European head of operations; *London Business Review,* founder and publisher, 2000—.

WRITINGS:

No Ordinary Man: A Life of George Carman, Hodder and Stoughton (London, England), 2002.

SIDELIGHTS: Dominic Carman is both the son and biographer of George Carman, a prominent British lawyer who was perhaps best known for handling libel suits. *No Ordinary Man: A Life of George Carman* describes the public and private sides of the elder Carman, who came from a middle-class family in the north of England. George Carman first became famous in 1979 when he won the acquittal of Jeremy Thorpe, onetime head of Britain's Liberal Party, who had been charged with conspiring to murder a man alleged to have been his lover. Later, Carman won numerous libel suits brought by celebrities, such as singer Elton John, actor Tom Cruise, and publisher Robert Maxwell. Sometimes he crossed to the other side, acting in defense of newspapers against libel claims, and was usually victorious. For all his success in court, however, he had many failings in his personal life, according to his son's account, which was published a year after George Carman's death. Dominic Carman reports that his father was an alcoholic, a reckless gambler, an abusive husband, and a cruel, cold parent. He also believes his father may have been sexually molested as a child—a possible explanation for some of his later behaviors. He further makes the case that George was a repressed homosexual or bisexual who was tormented by the denial of his true nature.

No Ordinary Man "reads strangely . . . albeit grippingly," commented Emma Brockes in the London *Guardian.* She noted that many of George Carman's former associates have denounced his son for the book's negative portrayal, but "in his defence, Dominic says that they saw only one side of his father and that a biography, if it is to be worthwhile, must tell the whole truth." *Spectator* reviewer Jonathan Sumption, though, had a different point of view: "George Carman was not important enough for his personal problems to become public property. There is no need to lie about them, when it is possible to say nothing about them at all." For Sumption, the chapter in which all three of George Carman's wives detail his violence toward them, sometimes committed in front of Dominic, is unnecessary information. *Guardian* critic Alan Rusbridger, however, found this chapter "revelatory" and added, "Uncomfortable though these testimonies are, it is difficult to deny the right—some would even argue duty—of these women, Ursula, Celia and Frances, to tell their stories."

Rusbridger continued, "Many who liked Carman and others who have cause to be grateful to him will find these sections distressing. They will struggle to reconcile the mischievous, gossipy friend and the loyal, tenacious advocate of fond memory with this new and disturbing evidence of a bullying, at times frightening, domestic tyrant. But then that struggle to reconcile the good and the bad, the admirable and the ugly, is at the heart of Dominic Carman's own exploration."

Rusbridger thought the biography "more patchy" in dealing with George Carman's legal career, with the stories of his cases "well told" but offering "few fresh disclosures," except in the portion dealing with Carman's defense of the *Guardian* in a suit brought by former government official Jonathan Aitken. This section features extensive interviews with Aitken, the judge in the case, and other interested parties. *Independent* contributor Robert Verkaik, on the other hand, praised the narratives of certain cases, relating, "Dominic Carman's excellent use of original legal papers provides valuable insight into the case of Ken Dodd, who stood trial for tax evasion. . . . [George] Carman skillfully played on his client's persona as a scatter-brained eccentric, incapable of a complicated act of fraud." Rusbridger summed up the book by saying, "It is, by turns, funny, painful, voyeuristic, Pooterish, muddled, touching, unbalanced, amateurish, painful, racy, angry and—despite it all—affectionate." Meanwhile, Verkaik concluded, "Many have said that Dominic dared not write this book while his father was alive—for fear of being sued. But it remains a painstaking investigation into a life which George Carman had gone to great lengths to hide."

BIOGRAPHICAL AND CRITICAL SOURCES:

PERIODICALS

Daily Mail, January 25, 2002, Tom Bower, "The Guilt of Carman QC," p. 51.

Guardian, January 14, 2002, Paul Kelso, "'Dark Side' of Libel Lawyer Revealed," p. 11; January 25, 2002, Emma Brockes, "Daddy Dearest," p. 4; January 26, 2002, Alan Rusbridger, "Carman v. Carman," p. 9.

Independent, January 24, 2002, Robert Verkaik, "The Demons That Drove the Great Defender," Comment section, p. 5.

Spectator, February 2, 2002, Jonathan Sumption, review of *No Ordinary Man: A Life of George Carman,* p. 31.

Times Literary Supplement, February 8, 2002, Michael Beloff, "Silken Dalliance," p. 27.*

*   *   *

CARRADINE, Beverly 1848-1919

PERSONAL: Born April 4, 1848, in Yazoo County, MS; died 1919; buried in Vicksburg, MS. *Education:* Attended University of Mississippi, 1865-67.

CAREER: Methodist Episcopal Church, South, licensed minister in Vicksburg, MS, c. 1874-76; pastor of congregations in Vernon, Madison, Brandon, and Crystal Springs, MS, between 1876 and 1882; pastor of congregations in New Orleans, LA, 1882-89; declared himself holiness minister, 1889; pastor of congregations in St. Louis, MO, c. 1889-93; itinerant evangelist and writer, beginning 1893.

WRITINGS:

Church Entertainments: Twenty Objections, 1891.

Sanctification, Publishing House of the Methodist Episcopal Church (Nashville, TN), 1891.

A Journey to Palestine, C. B. Woodward Printing (St. Louis, MO), 1891.

Pastoral Sketches, 5th edition, Christian Witness (Chicago, IL), 1896.

The Second Blessing in Symbol, 1893, 3rd edition, 1896.

The Old Man, Pentecostal Publishing (Louisville, KY), 1896.

The Better Way, 2nd edition, M. W. Knapp (Cincinnati, OH), 1896.

Sanctified Life, Office of the Revivalist (Cincinnati, OH), 1897.

Revival Sermons, W. B. Palmore (St. Louis, MO), 1898.

Heart Talks, M. W. Knapp (Cincinnati, OH), 1899.

Soul Help, Christian Witness (Boston, MA), 1900.

Golden Sheaves, J. Gill (Boston, MA), 1901.

Gideon, Pepper Publishing (Philadelphia, PA), 1902.

Beulah Land, Wesleyan Methodist Publishing Association (Syracuse, NY), 1904.

A Church Yard Story (short stories; contains "A Church Yard Story," "The Ballantynes," "A Strange Homestead," "Judge Dalrymple," and "The Two Cronies"), M. A. Donohue and Co. (Chicago, IL), 1904.

Bible Characters, Christian Witness (Chicago, IL), 1907.

Living Illustrations (short stories), Christian Witness (Chicago, IL), 1908.

A Box of Treasure, Christian Witness (Chicago, IL), 1910.

People I Have Met (short stories), Christian Witness (Chicago, IL), 1910.

Graphic Scenes, God's Revivalist Office (Cincinnati, OH), 1911.

Yazoo Stories (short stories; contains "Major Rosser," "Charlie Goodfellow," "Stories around a Camp Fire," "A Conversion in Hades," and "A Misunderstood Man"), Christian Witness (Chicago, IL), 1911.

Revival Incidents, Christian Witness (Chicago, IL), 1913.

Also author of *Pen Pictures,* Christian Witness (Chicago, IL); and "Secret Societies: Are They Right or Wrong? Are They a Blessing or a Curse?" (pamphlet), A. W. Hall (Syracuse, NY), 1891.*

*   *   *

CHASE, Nicholas
See HYDE, Christopher

CHATAWAY, Carol 1955-

PERSONAL: Born December 13, 1955, in England; daughter of John and Mary Morrison (Husthwaite) Harman; married Richard Chataway (a film maker), February 14, 1988; children: Tom, John, Rhys. *Ethnicity:* "Caucasian." *Education:* Flinders University, B.A., 2002.

ADDRESSES: Home and office—9 Cave Ave., Bridgewater, South Australia, 5155. *E-mail*—carol. chataway@bigpond.com.

CAREER: Author. Worked as a school assistant in Salisbury, South Australia, 1975-83, and a school treasurer in Birdwood, South Australia, 1983-88.

MEMBER: Ekidnas (children's book-writing club for published authors and illustrators).

AWARDS, HONORS: Crichton Award shortlist, Children's Book Council of Australia, 2002, for *The Perfect Pet.*

WRITINGS:

The Perfect Pet, illustrated by Greg Holfeld, Working Title Press (Adelaide, Australia), 2001, Kids Can Press (Toronto, Canada), 2002.

WORK IN PROGRESS: Wings, a picture book for Lothian.

SIDELIGHTS: Carol Chataway found that when her three boys, Tom, John, Rhys, were in school all day, she had extra time on her hands. She considered learning to write children's books, because, as she recalled to *CA,* "I had spent many wonderful hours with them reading picture books and hoped one day that I might write one. I always had ideas that I shared with them and they seemed to enjoy my stories. I found that I couldn't tell a story without it becoming funny or absurd in some way. My boys would add their little bit to it and we'd generally end up in hysterics." So she enrolled in a college English program, taking as many creative-writing courses as she could, and in 2001 her first children's book rolled off the press. *The*

Perfect Pet, a "satisfying story," to quote Judith Constantinides of *School Library Journal,* features three pigs, Hamlet, Pygmalion, and Podge, who attempt to find a pet that is just right for all of them. Although they visit Mr. Pinkerton's pet shop with a dog in mind, after trying out several breeds of dogs, they discover another animal suits them better in what *Resource Links* reviewer Evette Signarowski called "a nice twist." Ian Stewart of *Canadian Materials* also recommended this picture book, describing it as "an excellent book" to use in teaching children to solve problems communally.

Reflecting on her creative process, Chataway told *CA:* "My favourite part of writing is when I first get an idea for a story. It consumes me. I write and re-write it in my head for days and can think of nothing else. I am thoroughly happy and so absorbed with it that it is not odd for me to discover I have absentmindedly put my shoes in the fridge. I haven't got as far as preparing them for dinner, thank goodness. Although the way I cook, no one would notice the difference. I think I feel another story coming on!"

BIOGRAPHICAL AND CRITICAL SOURCES:

PERIODICALS

Australian Book Review, October, 2001, Virginia Lowe, "Teaching Tradition," pp. 61-62.
Canadian Materials, May, 10, 2002, Ian Stewart, review of *The Perfect Pet.*
Kirkus Reviews, March 1, 2002, review of *The Perfect Pet,* p. 331.
Resource Links, April, 2002, Evette Signarowski, review of *The Perfect Pet,* pp. 2-3.
School Library Journal, July, 2002, Judith Constantinides, review of *The Perfect Pet,* p. 85.

*   *   *

CHOYCE, Lesley 1951-

PERSONAL: Born March 21, 1951, in Riverside, NJ; son of George (a mechanic) and Norma (a homemaker; maiden name, Willis) Choyce; married Terry Paul (a teacher); children: Sunyata, Pamela. *Education:* Rutgers University, B.A., 1972; Montclair State College, M.A. (American literature), 1974; City University of New York, M.A. (English literature), 1983.

Lesley Choyce

ADDRESSES: Home—83 Leslie Rd., East Lawrencetown, Nova Scotia B2Z 1P8, Canada. *Office*—English Department, Dalhousie University, Halifax, Nova Scotia B3H 3J5, Canada.

CAREER: Writer, publisher, professor, television show host, film director, music performer, and surfer. Referrals Workshop, Denville, NJ, rehabilitation counselor, 1973-74; Bloomfield College, Bloomfield, NJ, coordinator of writing tutorial program, 1974; Montclair State College, Upper Montclair, NJ, instructor in English, 1974-78; Alternate Energy Consultants, Halifax, Nova Scotia, Canada, writer and consultant to Energy, Mines and Resources Canada, 1979-80; Dalhousie University, Halifax, Nova Scotia, Canada, 1981—, began as instructor, became professor of English. Founder of Pottersfield Press. Creative writing instructor, City of Halifax continuing education program, 1978-83; instructor at St. Mary's University, 1978-82, Nova Scotia College of Art and Design, 1981, and Mount St. Vincent University, 1982. Participant in creative writing workshops; public reader and lecturer; freelance broadcaster, 1972—; host of television talk show *Choyce Words* and *Off the Page,* beginning 1985.

MEMBER: International PEN, Atlantic Publishers Association, Canadian Periodical Publishers Association, Association of Canadian Publishers, Literary Press Group, Canadian Poetry Association, Writers' Union of Canada, Writers Federation of Nova Scotia.

AWARDS, HONORS: Canadian Science Fiction and Fantasy Award finalist, 1981; recipient, Order of St. John Award of Merit, 1986; shortlist, Stephen Leacock Medal, 1987; Dartmouth Book Award, 1990, 1995, shortlist, 1991-93; *Event* magazine Creative Nonfiction winner, 1990; Canadian National Surfing Champion, 1993; Ann Connor Brimer Award for Children's Literature, 1994; Manitoba Young Reader's Choice Award finalist, 1994; Authors Award, Foundation for the Advancement of Canadian Letters, co-winner, 1995; finalist, Hackmatack Children's Book Award, 2000, for children's writing; Landmark East Literacy Award, 2000; poet laureate, Peter Gzowski Invitational Golf Tournament, 2000.

WRITINGS:

FICTION

Eastern Sure, Nimbus Publishing (Halifax, Nova Scotia, Canada), 1981.
Billy Botzweiler's Last Dance (stories), Blewointment Press (Toronto, Ontario, Canada), 1984.
Downwind, Creative Publishers (St. John's, Newfoundland, Canada), 1984.
Conventional Emotions (stories), Creative Publishers (St. John's, Newfoundland, Canada), 1985.
The Dream Auditor (science fiction), Ragweed Press (Charlottetown, Prince Edward Island, Canada), 1986.
Coming up for Air, Creative Publishers (St. John's, Newfoundland, Canada), 1988.
The Second Season of Jonas MacPherson, Thistledown (Saskatoon, Saskatchewan, Canada), 1989.
Magnificent Obsessions (photo-novel), Quarry Press (Kingston, Ontario, Canada), 1991.
The Ecstasy Conspiracy, Nuage Editions (Montreal, Quebec, Canada), 1992.
The Republic of Nothing, Goose Lane Editions (Fredericton, New Brunswick, Canada), 1994.
Dance the Rocks Ashore, Goose Lane Editions (Fredericton, New Brunswick, Canada), 1997.
World Enough: A Novel, Goose Lane Editions (Fredericton, New Brunswick, Canada), 1998.

Cold Clear Morning, Porcepic Books (Vancouver, British Columbia, Canada), 2002.

Sea of Tranquility, Dunduin Publishing (Toronto, Ontario, Canada), 2003.

FOR YOUNG ADULTS

Skateboard Shakedown, Formac Publishing (Halifax, Nova Scotia, Canada), 1989.

Hungry Lizards, Collier-Macmillan (Toronto, Ontario, Canada), 1990.

Wave Watch, Formac Publishing (Halifax, Nova Scotia, Canada), 1990.

Some Kind of Hero, Maxwell-Macmillan, 1991.

Wrong Time, Wrong Place, Formac Publishing (Halifax, Nova Scotia, Canada), 1991.

Margin of Error (stories), Borealis Press (Ottawa, Ontario, Canada), 1992.

Clearcut Danger, Formac Publishing (Halifax, Nova Scotia, Canada), 1992.

Full Tilt, Maxwell-Macmillan, 1993.

Good Idea Gone Bad, Formac Publishing (Halifax, Nova Scotia, Canada), 1993.

Dark End of Dream Street, Formac Publishing (Halifax, Nova Scotia, Canada), 1994.

Big Burn, Thistledown Press (Saskatoon, Saskatchewan, Canada), 1995.

The Trap Door to Heaven (science fiction), Quarry Press (Kingston, Ontario, Canada), 1996.

Falling through the Cracks, Formac Publishing (Halifax, Nova Scotia, Canada), 1996.

Couleurs Troubles, [Saint-Laurent, Quebec, Canada], 1997.

The Summer of Apartment X, Goose Lane Editions (Fredericton, New Brunswick, Canada), 1999.

Roid Rage, Harbour Publishing (Madeira Park, British Columbia, Canada), 1999.

Shoulder the Sky, Broadwalk Books (Toronto, Ontario, Canada), 2002.

Refuge Cove, Orca Book Publishers (Custer, WA), 2002.

FOR CHILDREN

Go for It, Carrie, Formac Publishing (Halifax, Nova Scotia, Canada), 1997.

Famous at Last, Pottersfield Press (East Lawrencetown, Nova Scotia, Canada), 1998.

Carrie's Crowd, Formac Publishing (Halifax, Nova Scotia, Canada), 1999.

Far Enough Island, Pottersfield (East Lawrencetown, Nova Scotia, Canada), 2000.

Carrie's Camping Adventure, Formac Publishing (Halifax, Nova Scotia, Canada), 2001.

Carrie Loses Her Nerve, Formac Publishing (Halifax, Nova Scotia, Canada), 2003.

POETRY

Reinventing the Wheel, Fiddle Head Poetry Books (Fredericton, New Brunswick, Canada), 1980.

Fast Living, Fiddle Head Poetry Books (Fredericton, New Brunswick, Canada), 1982.

The End of Ice, Fiddle Head Poetry Books (Fredericton, New Brunswick, Canada), 1982.

The Top of the Heart, Thistledown Press (Saskatoon, Saskatchewan, Canada), 1986.

The Man Who Borrowed the Bay of Fundy, Brandon University (Brandon, Manitoba, Canada), 1988.

The Coastline of Forgetting, Pottersfield Press (Lawerencetown Beach, Nova Scotia, Canada), 1995.

Beautiful Sadness, Ekstasis Editions (Victoria, British Columbia, Canada), 1998.

Caution to the Wind, Ekstasis Editions (Victoria, British Columbia, Canada), 2000.

Typographical Errors, Gaspereau Press (Kentville, Nova Scotia, Canada), 2003.

NONFICTION

Edible Wild Plants of the Maritimes, Wooden Anchor Press (Halifax, Nova Scotia, Canada), 1977.

An Avalanche of Ocean (autobiography), Goose Lane Editions (Fredericton, New Brunswick, Canada), 1987.

December Six/The Halifax Solution, Pottersfield Press (East Lawrencetown), Nova Scotia, Canada), 1988.

Transcendental Anarchy (autobiography), Quarry Press (Kingston, Ontario, Canada), 1993.

Nova Scotia: Shaped by the Sea, Penguin (Toronto, Ontario, Canada), 1996.

The Coasts of Canada: A History, Goose Lane Editions (Fredericton, New Brunswick, Canada), 2002.

EDITOR

The Pottersfield Portfolio, Volumes 1-7, Pottersfield Press (East Lawrencetown, Nova Scotia, Canada), 1971-1985.

Alternating Current: Renewable Energy for Atlantic Canada, Wooden Anchor Press (Halifax, Nova Scotia, Canada), 1977.

Chezzetocook: An Anthology of Contemporary Poetry and Fiction from Atlantic Canada (fiction and poetry), Wooden Anchor Press (Halifax, Nova Scotia, Canada), 1977.

(With Phil Thompson) *ACCESS: Atlantic Canada Community Energy Strategy Sourcebook,* Pottersfield Press (East Lawrencetown, Nova Scotia, Canada), 1979.

(With John Bell) *Visions from the Edge: An Anthology of Atlantic Canadian Science Fiction and Fantasy,* Pottersfield Press (East Lawrencetown, Nova Scotia, Canada), 1981.

The Cape Breton Collection, Pottersfield Press (East Lawrencetown, Nova Scotia, Canada), 1984, new edition, 1989.

(With Andy Wainwright) Charles Bruce, *The Mulgrave Road,* Pottersfield Press (East Lawrencetown, Nova Scotia, Canada), 1985.

Ark of Ice: Canadian Futurefiction, Pottersfield Press (East Lawrencetown, Nova Scotia, Canada), 1985.

(With Rita Joe) *The Mi'kmaq Anthology,* Pottersfield Press (East Lawrencetown, Nova Scotia, Canada), 1997.

Atlantica: Stories from the Maritimes and Newfoundland, Goose Lane (Fredericton, New Brunswick, Canada), 2001.

OTHER

Contributor to more than one hundred magazines and anthologies. Writer/performer on two sound recordings with the Surf Poets, *Long Lost Planet,* Pottersfield Press (East Lawrencetown, Nova Scotia, Canada), 1996, and *Sea Level,* Pottersfield Press (East Lawrencetown, Nova Scotia, Canada), 1998.

ADAPTATIONS: The Republic of Nothing and *Cold Clear Morning* are being developed as feature-length films.

WORK IN PROGRESS: Driving Minnie's Piano, a memoir.

SIDELIGHTS: Lesley Choyce is a prolific and versatile author who incorporates some of his many passions—including nature and the environment, surfing, and music—into his fiction, poetry, and nonfiction. Born in New Jersey, Choyce worked for a time in New York before becoming disillusioned with the greed and indifference he saw as the driving forces behind the city. Attracted in part by the great surf on the north Atlantic coast, he and his wife eventually moved to Nova Scotia and became Canadian citizens.

Many of Choyce's books appeal to young-adult readers. In his debut novel *Skateboard Shakedown,* for example, a group of young skateboard enthusiasts take on a corrupt city government when their favorite skate park is scheduled for development into a shopping area. Writing in *Quill & Quire,* reviewer Norene Smiley said that "this fast-paced novel marks the entrance of a new and refreshing voice for young readers." *Hungry Lizards* features a sixteen-year-old rock band leader who finds that the advantages of winning a performing contract at a local club can be outweighed by the realities of the entertainment business, the conflicting time demands of school and work, and the temptations of a questionable lifestyle. The book is designed for reluctant teen readers, and reviewer Kenneth Oppel concluded in *Quill & Quire* that the book's "tempered view of teenage street life and the rock 'n' roll underworld should appeal to young readers."

Wrong Time, Wrong Place explores racial tensions and social injustice through the story of Corey, a young man with one parent who is black and one who is white. Corey first becomes aware of his status as a biracial youth when he is branded as a troublemaker and rebel and begins to notice how both students and faculty treat lighter-skinned students differently. Through his Uncle Larry's good example and Larry's stories of a black community in Halifax called Africville, Corey comes to identify with his black forebears. As described by *Canadian Children's Literature* reviewer Heidi Petersen, Corey "realizes that he must face injustices himself, and embraces a form of social activism which begins by keeping the past, the truth, alive."

In *Clearcut Danger,* as in *Skateboard Shakedown,* two teenage protagonists take on adult greed, this time in the form of a joint government-business project to build a pollution-prone pulp and paper mill in a job-starved town. Praising Choyce's "strong and interesting" characterization and "good, strong story," reviewer Patty Lawlor concluded in *Quill & Quire* that "booksellers, teachers, and librarians should talk this one up."

In *Dark End of Dream Street,* Choyce takes up the problem of homeless youth in the person of Tara. Tara always considered her friend Janet to be the troubled one, until her own life began spinning out of control. *Quill & Quire* reviewer Fred Boer found the author's subplots—about Tara's friendship with an elderly woman, and both Tara's and Janet's problems with their boyfriends—somewhat distracting, and the absence of swearing oddly cautious. Boer nevertheless praised the book for being "entertaining and readable."

While some of Choyce's young-adult novels are in the high interest/low vocabulary category, *Big Burn* appeals to a more sophisticated audience. Nevertheless, the main plot—two teens against a new incinerator that threatens to poison the atmosphere—is familiar Choyce terrain. In *Quill & Quire,* reviewer Maureen Garvie especially praised the "infectious" quality of the "outrage the author and his characters feel." Other strengths include the portrayal of John's "adolescent darknesses" and the death of a parent.

Downwind is an ecological thriller for a more mature audience. "Choyce's ecological concern is clearly expressed" in this book, according to Allan Weiss in *Dictionary of Literary Biography.* Set in an unspecified near-future, the novel depicts a severe energy crisis and accompanying attempts to establish nuclear power plants in unsafe, environmentally sensitive areas such as Nova Scotia. Weiss called the story "somewhat melodramatic," and added that "its characters are two-dimensional; but it is a well-researched cautionary tale about the dangers of reliance on nuclear power." He concluded that *Downwind* "is at its best when it portrays the landscape and people of Nova Scotia—there are vivid descriptive passages during Warren's periodic hang-gliding excursions."

Discussing *An Avalanche of Ocean* and *Transcendental Anarchy,* his two autobiographies, Choyce once told *CA:* "[Although writing mostly fiction], as time went on I found that some of the facts of my own life were more revealing than the fictional truths I create. This came as a surprise and a shock to me. . . . When I grew into my skin as a writer, I pretended for a while that *what I had to say* really was of importance. After a time, I started believing in the myth, and this convinced me to abandon fiction for awhile and get autobiographical.

"Since my life story would be exceedingly boring, I was forced to edit my personal history ruthlessly until there was something left worth sharing. My first fragmented history of the self came out as *An Avalanche of Ocean,* and I almost thought that I was done with autobiography. What more could I possibly say once I'd written about winter surfing, transcendental wood-splitting, and getting strip-searched for cod tongues in a Labrador airport? But then something happened to me that I can't quite explain. *Avalanche* had set off something in me—a kind of manic, magical couple of years where I felt like I was living on the edge of some important breakthrough. It was a time of greater compressed euphoria and despair than I'd ever felt before. Stuff was happening to me, images of the past were flooding through the doors, and I needed to get it all down. Some of it was funny, some of it was not. Dead writers were hovering over my shoulder, saying, 'Dig deep; follow it through. Don't let any of it go.' And I didn't.

"So again I have the audacity to say that these things that happened to me are worth your attention. . . . In *Transcendental Anarchy* I celebrated the uncompromising passages of a midthirties male, admitting that I would never be an astronaut or a president, and instead finding satisfaction in building with wood, arguing a good cause, or even undergoing a successful vasectomy. Write about what makes you feel the most uncomfortable, a voice in my head told me. So I tackled fear and my own male anger and my biggest failures. And, even more dangerous, I tried writing about the most ordinary of things: a morning in Woolco, an unexceptional day, the thread of things that keeps a life together."

About his writing, Choyce further told *CA:* "Throughout it all, there is, I hope, a record of a search for love and meaning fraught with failure and recovery. Maybe I've developed a basic mistrust of the rational, logical conclusions. I've only had the briefest glimpses beyond the surface, but I've seen enough to know that sometimes facts are not enough. There are times to make the leap, to get metaphysical, and suppose that we all live larger lives than appearances would suggest."

Weiss concluded: "For all its diversity, Choyce's fiction expresses a unified vision of concern for the environment and a need for all people to rediscover their ties to nature. He uses the rationalist genre of science fiction, as well as surrealism, fantasy, and satire, to encourage his readers to see the world in nonscientific ways. For Choyce, humans have suffered—and made their world suffer—for their limited perspective: their utilitarian, selfish, rationalist approach. To be healthy, and to regain the health of the world, they need a more holistic vision, one that recognizes they are part of a larger human and natural universe."

AUTOBIOGRAPHICAL ESSAY:

Lesley Choyce contributed the following autobiographical essay to *CA*:

I was born on the first day of spring, March 21, 1951, the year J. D. Salinger published *Catcher in the Rye*. War was still raging in Korea but at least peace talks had begun towards a cease-fire. The hospital that brought me into the world was in Riverside, New Jersey, and my mother's name was Norma. My father, George Choyce, known as Sonny, drove us all home a few days later to Cinnaminson in his 1946 black Chevy coupe that he had bought when he came home from World War II. It was a pretty snazzy car in its day but by the time I was fourteen, my father was still driving me to the school dances in it and I was scrunched down in the seat, not wanting to be seen in an old rattletrap like that.

I had a brother, Gordon, three years older than me and we all lived in a tiny rounded house trailer that sat up on cinder blocks in a grove of black locust trees, a wedge of land between two country roads that would become virtual highways by the time I became an adult. The world of my youth was exotic rural South Jersey and in the fifties it was a beautiful natural wonderland of fields, streams, forests, farms, and swamps where skunk cabbage bloomed in the spring. As I grew, houses, concrete, shopping centers and asphalt highways swallowed all that good stuff. As my innocence slipped away, bit by bit, so did the pristine natural beauty of South Jersey. Once gone, it never could be resurrected.

I was pretty happy in the trailer, as far as I can tell, and so were Gordy, Norma, and Sonny. My father was a truck mechanic, as he had been during the war. My mother's wartime service had been as a Coast Guard WAC and both had come through the war with few complaints. During my earliest years we didn't have much money. Wages were low but work was steady for my father. He worked for a Ford dealership and, for a long tenure, fixed milk trucks for Millside Farms—those old boxes on wheels where the driver stood up while he drove, no seat belt, no seat, side door wide open so that if he took a turn too fast, he'd fly out onto the curb and the truck would careen into a tree smashing up a hundred glass bottles of non-homogenized milk.

I wore my brother's hand-me-down clothes or something my mother had cobbled out of chicken feed bags. We kept twenty or thirty hens in an old shed my father built and my mom was a whiz at making things out of the white muslin chicken feed bags while my father was off toiling over a milk truck carburetor. Gordy and I rooted around our yard, digging holes with broken shovels, beneath the forty-foot tall locust trees that dropped fragrant, tiny white flowers in the early summer. I don't know why we did so much digging but we did. Maybe we were expecting to find gold or dead bodies. We had a couple of tricycles, I think, and a wagon and sometimes we'd haul the things we'd dug up from one part of the property to another. It didn't get any better than that.

My father and mother were saving every penny as they prepared to build a house for us on the property. Taking the lead from Gordy and me, my dad actually began by digging the basement by hand, one shovelful at a time. He soon grew discouraged of this and blew much of his hard earned money hiring a guy with a bulldozer to finish off excavating the basement so he could get on with the house. Concrete was poured and the whole thing was built from cinder blocks—a substance that puzzled and fascinated me for years to come.

We lived in the trailer all the while my father and mother worked at building the house. Gordy and I had a lot of scrap lumber, nails, and pieces of cinder block to fool around with and that kept us occupied. My mom made a few extra cents by selling chicken eggs. A few years later, when I had entered into the public education system, I actually stole quarters from the chicken egg money to give to a girl named June that I liked very much. I was caught and punished and I believe it was the chicken egg money incident that curtailed any thoughts I might have developed towards a life of crime. When the chickens became slow producers of eggs, my father chopped their heads off with a hand axe and Gordy and I would watch the headless chickens, spurting blood, continue to run frantically around in circles until they gave up on mortality.

Once, the family legend goes, I climbed a ladder and crawled way out on a beam of wood, a joist high above the concrete floor of the unfinished house. I think I was three. My mother and father saw this and were terrified. It was a narrow beam and a long drop below but it was where I wanted to be and my face must have betrayed how proud I was. My mother did not scream (fortunately for me) and my father ascended the ladder and, like a tightrope walker, walked the narrow beam to save me from my ambitions. Ever since they told me this tale and it stuck, I've enjoyed that image of me out there and still like to think that this is who I am. I've climbed the ladder and gone far out on a narrow beam of wood. I'm feeling pretty good about myself and unaware of the dangers. I either stay here, playing intently and happily at whatever childish fantasy fills my head or I lose my balance, fall, and split my head on a hard surface below. Or I await rescue. Whichever comes first.

*

My grandfather on the Choyce side was a George as well (which is why George Jr., was known to everyone as Sonny). He was a World War I vet who fixed farm machinery and he was married to Gertrude, a kind, gentle woman who had raised seven kids through the Depression. Gordy and I called them Mom Mom and Pop Pop. My mother had been a Willis. My grandparents on her side were Eva and Avery, dubbed early on by Gordy as Minnie and Gaga. The two childish names stuck like glue and everyone ended up calling them by those monikers. Minnie worked in Philadelphia as a secretary for Merck Sharpe and Dohme, taking a train into the city each day. Gaga was a carpenter with a hankering to be a gentleman farmer. He bought some farmland in Cinnaminson and set about planting corn and beans and tomatoes and undertaking Herculean battles with farm machinery, baling wire and irrigation piping, all of which refused to operate under the normal parameters of physics.

My father completed building our cinder-block house and we moved in. I found a hand drill and immediately drilled several clever holes in the new linoleum kitchen floor, another feat accomplished with great skill and candor but unappreciated by the adult world. I began going to Sunday school each Sunday at the Palmyra Moravian Church and would eventually receive various certificates and pins for my attendance. I had a hard time with much of the logic of the Old Testament, wherein God seemed to operate somewhat along the same principles as my father dealing with the old hens who had stopped laying eggs. There were not a lot of satisfying answers to my blasphemous questions at Sunday school but it was good place to meet girls.

My earliest girlfriend, met in kindergarten, was Janine Evans. We had a pretty steady thing going and I don't ever really remember breaking up, just becoming more interested in Cub Scouts, where I learned to tie knots, deal with snake bites, and make long-tubed blowguns that shot spit balls across the room. My charm in kindergarten did not go unnoticed and at least one of my contemporaries, Cheryl Lowden, fell off the monkey bars while trying to gain my attention. She broke her arm but continued to have a strong interest in me, yet I never could find the initiative to injure myself in any way as a tribute to her.

I was good at school and had a best friend in Bobby Carr who had several impressive scars from falling out of trees or landing on sharp objects when jumping from the roofs of sheds. He taught me how to jump from garage roofs and together we tied long ropes to high trees to make "Tarzan swings," launching ourselves out over streams and ponds and sometimes roadways. I remember becoming a big fan of rifles and handguns too—all toys, I admit, but there were so many things being killed on television and all the TV ads for toy cowboy six-shooters were so seductive that I soon became part of American gun culture in my youth.

One of my all-time favorite heroes was the Disney version of Davy Crockett. The theme music played over and over in my head. I had a plastic musket and Minnie ripped up part of her 1920s racoon coat to make me a coonskin cap that quickly became my prized possession.

*

Cinnaminson was changing. Housing developments were being built and people pouring out of Philadelphia into the newly minted suburbs. The wilderness

The author as a child, dressed as his hero, Davy Crockett

American flags everywhere. We saluted one in the morning. One blew in the warm breeze above the school and eventually the largest American flag of all would fly above the liquor store built on a parcel of land where my friends and I had once played baseball. I raised pigeons, too, in those days and liked everything about them. Pigeons seemed to make more sense to me than people did. Years later I would still keep a few pigeons even though the hawks of Nova Scotia were ruthless to these gentle birds of beauty.

I can't seem to come up with any significant complaint about my childhood. We didn't have a telephone until I was twelve, I think. My mother always cut my hair in the basement with electric barber shears. She cut it too short and gave no good explanation as to why hair was supposed to be mowed like someone's lawn. By 1972, the pendulum had swung far the other way, and my hair was down to the middle of my back, which will show you what short hair can do to a kid. But no big complaints about my early years. Stewed tomatoes maybe. I was required according to our household rules to eat stewed tomatoes. It seemed pretty cruel at the time but I'm over it now.

Fresh tomatoes were another matter. My father, deep down, was a farmer and we had large gardens where he grew amazing, succulent South Jersey tomatoes and great golden ears of corn. When I was twelve, I would eat a one-pound fresh ripe tomato, picked off the vine in the morning dew. I ate it like religion. Years later, living at Lawrencetown Beach, Nova Scotia, near the shores of the cold North Atlantic, I would grieve over the fact that you couldn't grow a decent tomato here right through to its red intentions. That was my one sacrifice in moving to Canada.

Boy Scouts was a big deal to me. I was a patrol leader, I earned merit badges, did good deeds, tied knots (even taught them to the local Girl Scout troop), went on camping trips into the Jersey Pines. My father took the family to the Jersey Shore in the summer and we all acquired major sunburns. At church camps I made friends and girlfriends with kids from South Philadelphia, a world apart from Cinnaminson.

There was money to be made—big money, relatively speaking—by delivering newspapers. First it was the *Camden Courier Post,* then the *Philadelphia Bulletin.* I delivered all the news to suburban doorsteps—John

around me was vanishing and I knew life would never be the same. I built underground forts with my friends and climbed trees and spent as much time in the dwindling forest as I could. Bobby Carr swung down out of an ill-conceived Tarzan swing onto the windshield of a car passing by but only his pride was injured. We tried smoking the seedpods from catalpa trees—called johnny smokers—with no great satisfaction.

My bicycle gave me considerable freedom. There were pop bottles collected for returns money (two cents each) and nails to be collected from the work site of new homes. Pretty soon, I had a great gaggle of new, mostly unwanted, neighbors and their kids were in my classes at Memorial Elementary School.

In school I discovered I liked to write, and I was weak in math. Teachers taught us all kinds of misleading information about American history and there were

"With Sunday-school pins and bad haircut," c. 1950s

Glenn orbiting the earth, Kennedy assassinated, Johnson bombing North Vietnam, riots in Newark, the Tet offensive, Martin Luther King assassinated, then Bobby Kennedy. If you wanted death and disaster slapped down on your doorstep in Cinnaminson, for over a decade I was your man. Or boy.

Things started to get a little weird around junior high, I think. I lost my naive youthful self-confidence. I didn't like school as much. It was harder to impress girls. Where once, riding my English racer bike downhill without holding onto the handlebars was enough to cause girls to swoon, now, well, something more was required. Merit badges were not enough. I was a Boy Scout, a paperboy, and a kid who raised pigeons. Also, I did not live in a snazzy new suburban home. And my father was still driving me around in his '46 Chevy with significant rust. It all took its toll on my self-esteem.

I survived junior high by the skin of my teeth and then was thrown like a helpless victim into Cinnaminson High School. I was a top-notch English student,

even receiving an award from the American Cancer Society (my first writing award; all the awards before that were for pigeons at the farm fair) for an essay I wrote about curing cancer. I muddled through math and science even though my dream was to be a marine biologist.

Through junior and senior high, my salvation was books. I read voraciously—the *World Book Encyclopedia* cover to cover (well, almost), books about reptiles, books about the sea, but most of all, novels. I was New Jersey's biggest fan of Jules Verne and traveled with him to the center of the earth and to the moon. And I read anything I was told I shouldn't read. *Catcher in the Rye* was de rigor. Most books offered up in school were too tame: *A Separate Peace*, Shakespeare, and *Kim* by Rudyard Kipling, for God's sakes. I decided somewhere in my brainpan that maybe I would be a writer if the marine biology plan didn't pan out.

I fell in and out of semi-relationships with girls. The ones who liked me were of no great interest to me. The ones I fell madly for were interested in someone else—Tim Stack or some other jock. I mooned and moaned privately and honed a great angst like that of other writers before me. My Sunday school attendance diminished, my math grades slipped further, I began to worry about the truth behind those headlines I was delivering in newsprint day after day. Why the hell were we in Vietnam? Why were we building more and more nuclear weapons to blow up the world several times over? The harsher realities of politics and war hit me in a personal way when the brother of Cherie Devlin was killed in Vietnam. I was just beginning a serious relationship with Cherie and didn't quite know how to help her with her grief. Our relationship never did get back on track.

Somewhere in the middle of all that angst, my guess is 1966 or 1967, I was listening to Jan and Dean and the Beach Boys on the radio and decided that I wanted to learn to surf. And did. The Jersey Shore was not the North Shore of Oahu but it was satisfactory for my needs. Surfing carried with it a dream, a vision, a complete mythology and a cachet. I tried bleaching my hair and it turned orange but I bought some baggies, a board, some wax, and I re-imagined myself into a surfer—120 pounds at sixteen years old, pale as a noodle wearing huaraches. I mastered the art of wave riding and began to transform myself into a new me.

Surfing and music mixed well, like 7 UP and ice cream, and I paired up with Jack Parry to learn to play music. We faked it at first. We were just Jack and Les, not much to attract a record label. But then we formed a band, a surf band at first: the Wipeouts. We could play "Wipeout," "Pipeline," "House of the Rising Sun," and the requisite "Louie Louie." Dan Stosuy, Mark Hemphill, and Peter Maerz fleshed out the whole band and there were block parties, school dances, and golden moments of pure heaven when we performed. I played a so-so lead guitar and sang into a mike plugged into my old Silvertone amp. We wrote some of our own material and once even opened the season at a movie drive-in in the distant industrial swampland of South Philadelphia.

*

The year I graduated from high school was 1969. Nixon was president. Kids were smoking marijuana. The music was changing and the Wipeouts and their spin-off groups had tried to keep up. Not long after my graduation, Neil Armstrong stepped on the moon, much to the pleasure of my father, who had been reading about space travel in *Popular Science* for the last thirty years. I don't particularly remember being impressed by it all. The world around me was going to hell. American troops were massacring innocent people in Southeast Asia. I had come to despise so much of what America stood for. Who cared about marine biology if people could be so cruel and if the planet was about to turn into a radioactive cinder?

That summer of 1969 I did not go to Woodstock, though a ride or two was offered. Instead, I worked as a janitor in a nursing home and loved it. I became friends with old people and sick people and women who hallucinated as an escape from the ravages of aging and confinement. In the middle of that summer I met a younger girl named Sharon Green and we fell very much in love.

By fall, however, I was slotted to go away to East Carolina University, three hundred miles to the south. I would study marine biology there; I hadn't planned on falling in love. It was painful to go, but I did and then hitchhiked home every other weekend to continue my relationship with Sharon. At ECU, I read and studied and surfed on occasion, hitchhiking with my friend Steve Mitchell and my surfboard to Nags Head

or Atlantic Beach. I wrote folk songs and I had a show on the on-air campus station, WECU, getting beat up one legendary night while I was on the air. I was giving a long rap about an upcoming war protest when some drunk redneck jocks broke into the station where I was alone. They gave me a lesson in patriotism while my small but loyal listening audience heard them beating the crap out of me.

While in the South, I took part in a major antiwar demonstration at Fort Bragg, where protesters had gone marching inside the army base, led by Jane Fonda. We stood there with our signs, chanting, surrounded by hundreds of soldiers with rifles and I felt a powerful sense of unity with my fellow protesters. I was both scared and proud at the same time to be doing something I believed in.

When I wasn't getting flack for my antiwar sentiments, I loved North Carolina but I felt things were a bit too complacent. Some time around the killing of four Kent State students by Nixon's national guard, I knew I had to get more fully involved. I needed to be back home in the north, both to be near Sharon and also to get closer to the action of shutting down the war and partaking in whatever this revolution was that would change the world forever—or so I believed.

At ECU, John Donne's "Valediction, Forbidding Mourning" interested me more than all the chemistry and biology lab work and I knew I would not be a scientist or get to become the next Jacques Cousteau. Hitchhiking up and down I-95 from Jersey to Carolina and back gave me an even better education and no harm ever came my way.

The summer of 1970 I worked the night shift loading trucks at North Penn Transfer where my father landed me a job. From ten at night until seven in the morning, I hefted everything from light bulbs to 200-gallon barrels of toxic chemicals onto trucks. I was ill-equipped for the job but suffered through until fall. Sometimes after work, at 7 am while some of the boys were headed off to "normalize" their weird work schedule by going to a bar to drink, I would instead join a buddy and head to Long Beach Island to surf. In my spare time I wrote science-fiction short stories, bad poetry, and angst-ridden, politically charged prose about who I was and what I believed.

That fall I went to Livingston College, part of Rutgers University, situated on the old WWII Camp Kilmer (named for the NJ poet who had thought he'd never seen anything as lovely as a tree). I felt out of place at first but soon became supercharged by the atmosphere of radical professors, no grades, creative everything, music and drug-inspired culture. I wrote my brains out—everything and anything. On weekends I went home to work at the nursing home but Livingston radicalized me and I attended major antiwar demonstrations in downtown Manhattan—where I was shoved against the glass walls of the Time Life Building by NYC police horses—and later, attended a massive protest at the Washington Monument in D.C.

At Livingston I met Terry Paul in my human sexuality course and she and I began a tentative relationship that would grow more intense and permanent as the years went by. I read voraciously all the prerequisite authors of the day: Kesey, Hesse, Tolkien, Jung, Baba Ram Dass, Alan Watts and others. Much to my mother's chagrin, my hair just kept getting longer and longer. I applied for conscientious objector status but was turned down. When the draft lottery came into effect I had a lucky number but my brother was at risk. I counseled him on draft dodging if need be—possibly a vacation to Canada. But he never got called.

When school was out, I joined my brother and parents on a journey by truck and camper to Alaska. It was a tough decision because I wanted to move on into my own world but this family odyssey had been in the works for so long. This new month-long absence tested, then severed my relationship with Sharon Green who felt, I think, betrayed by my leaving her yet again. It was a long dusty road from Cinnaminson to Fairbanks and back but I breathed in a good dose of Canada along the way. I read Walt Whitman's *Leaves of Grass* while wandering around, lonelier than Wordsworth's cloud, on a snowy June day in Mt. McKinley National Park. I was enthralled with the north.

Back at school in the fall, Terry and I began a lifetime relationship. We hitchhiked, went to concerts, attended demonstrations, and ended up living in a dorm room together. Surrounded by some totally wonderful and insane fellow students at our experimental college, we probably thought we were the only two normal people in the world. We made art films together—one involving a stuffed alligator and a moose bone I had brought home from Anchorage. Ever restless, though, I decided to leave school and hitchhike around Europe that December of 1972. I flew to Iceland and got stuck

there due to an airline strike. Eventually, I made it to Belgium and caught a ride with some other longhair guys and girls headed to Morocco. I made it as far as Ceuta on Africa's northern coast when it hit me like a ton of bricks that adventuring around the world (I planned to hitchhike across North Africa and on toward India) was something I needed less than what I had left behind—mainly my relationship with Terry.

When I was refused entry into Morocco twice, I took it as sign to go home and I retreated to Luxembourg by train and back to New York by plane, arriving late one night at the Livingston College dorm to surprise Terry, who took me back with no questions asked.

Back in school, I hunkered down to finish up, somehow getting a four-year B.A. in three years, thanks to some independent studies: credits for writing about hitchhiking and working with old people. I had accumulated enough credits to have a major in English. The war had ended while I was writing about my exploits and reading textbooks on abnormal psychology and I think it made me believe that anything—anything at all, was possible. All of our protests had stopped the war. We were on the verge of a glorious future. I wanted to continue to change the world and so did Terry. We had few inhibitions, bold visions, and the psychological tools to do just about anything. One thing was clear to us: we were not motivated by career or money. There is a bluegrass music soundtrack running through that time that had replaced acid rock. Hendrix's "Purple Haze" was overdubbed with Earl Scruggs' "Foggy Mountain Breakdown."

I was a bit confused as to exactly how to change the world, apparently, because I decided to go to graduate school at Montclair State College, not far from Livingston. The college offered me a chance to be a teaching assistant to some English classes and I needed something to do while Terry finished her final year at Livingston. So I took a one-room apartment in Montclair in the same building with some drunk and doped-up neighbors and a young man who punched holes in his walls at night. One evening I tried to defend a disorderly guy from downstairs as the cops battered him around the hallway. High on aftershave, he was whirling a razor blade around him, but I believed him to be a gentle soul becaise he had loaned me his Hank Snow songbooks. I couldn't talk him out of the razor blade waving so the Montclair police hauled him away and the next morning I read in the

Newark Ledger that he was an escaped convict from a North Carolina prison. His conviction had been for murder.

Graduate school was fairly uninspiring. I liked the teaching part though and had a good friend in Anthony Perna, an intense fellow poet who had once had a shot at being a singer in the Four Seasons. I muddled through graduate school and, while ignoring serious scholarly work on John Milton's *Paradise Lost* or John Bunyan's *Pilgrim's Progress,* I was writing fiction and poetry because I wanted to create literature, not just read it.

*

Tired of living in a rented room in a rooming house, my dream was to live on a farm—to get back to the land. The plan was to gather together some friends and rent an old farm somewhere in north Jersey. Terry and I drove around Morris County, New Jersey, until we found an empty farmhouse with a barn. On the barn was painted the words "La Hacienda." A neighbor was kind enough to tell us who owned it, a man named Sabal who was vice president of a chemical company. What the hell. I called him, said I'd like to rent La Hacienda and would be willing to fix it up if he could keep the rent low. We met and when he saw I was a longhair freak, he showed me a hidden photo of himself and Fidel Castro, arm in arm. He and Castro had been good friends before Mr. Sabal sold his soul to capitalism. The farm had been his wife's dream but now they were safely back living in Manhattan, the farm having tested their marriage.

We had a kind of commune I suppose; those of us living there shared expenses and food and La Hacienda became a focal point for parties and music. I remember wasting away far too much time talking about why country life was preferable to city life. I grew some corn and tomatoes in the rocky soil. We bought a male goat and named it Bilbo after Bilbo Baggins. The goat was ornery, but sometimes relaxed by lying down on an old vinyl sofa on the front porch. Someone saw the goat eating an American flag while lounging on the front porch, took offence and sent the police over to check us out. The police held no grudge against us until Bilbo took off one day and walked inside the local high school where summer classes were in session. A teacher got the goat upset by trying to drag it from

the school so the Randolph Township police were called in. The goat didn't like the cop and butted him in the leg a few times, prompting him to pull his gun. Bilbo then attacked the police car, denting in the front fender. The goat would have met his death had not a summer school student recognized Bilbo and come out to smooth things over.

That summer of 1974, I worked as a rehabilitation counselor with people who had various disabilities. I taught a totally blind teenager to drive my VW bug around the parking lot. I learned how to make copper and silver jewelry from Milt Naham, who claimed to have apprenticed with Salvador Dali. I discovered that I liked deaf, blind, and even brain-damaged people more than I liked most academics. It was a grand time until Referrals Workshop went bankrupt, the checks bounced, the farm geese flew away, and a couple of our farm family got arrested for shoplifting.

Although Terry and I stayed with the farm, others moved on and I went back to Montclair State for more graduate school, this time, however, teaching my own English classes. Restless to get on with writing, I also started selling articles to a New York City Tabloid called the *Aquarian.* I wrote long free-form articles about edible wild plants, civil disobedience, hitchhiking, hang gliding, nuclear energy protests, and Timothy Leary's proposal to have his own space station in orbit. I fiddled with writing a novel or two, and created reams of edgy poetry and folk songs. Things were damned good in my life. The only elements lacking were an ocean and a chance to really hunker down and become a writer. I was in denial that surfing and writing were not central to my existence. That must be why we didn't run from New Jersey. Instead, I fumbled my way through my M.A. and logged on for more graduate work at CUNY Grad School—the University of 42nd street as I called it. CUNY gave me a chance to teach at Queens College while doing other part-time teaching work at Montclair, Bloomfield College, and William Patterson College.

Graduate school in the middle of Manhattan took me to the center of something I was trying to avoid: cities. Between seminars on Alexander Pope and Restoration comedy (why was I doing this to myself?) I rambled around the city, a far better education. I was in a book store while it was robbed, attended a free lecture by the Moonies, talked jazz with a street saxophonist, ate my lunch beside a junkie shooting up on the bench beside me in Bryant Park, and chatted with hookers who gave me advice on what to do with my long pony tail. I hauled a derelict that I presumed to be dead out of the sidewalk traffic and sat with him for a while, talking to him until he came back to life and cursed me for trying to help him. One day outside the Port Authority bus terminal, someone shoved me onto a shopping cart full of money being loaded into a Brinks' truck. Guns were pulled and I stared down mortality. Still a little shaken, I had a hard time giving my oral presentation back at the grad school on Jonathan Swift's anal vision.

I convinced Terry that we should spend the summer in Nova Scotia. I'd been there once before with my friend Jack Parry and it had seemed like paradise. We left the farm and headed north in my Volkswagen van. Most of the summer was spent in Inverness, Cape Breton, where Fulty MacPherson had ushered us into a low rent ($40 for the summer) abandoned farmhouse sitting high on a hill above the Gulf of St. Lawrence. We put in some polyethylene windows, gathered some firewood and settled in as bagpipe music drifted our way at sunset. The local community of both fishermen and resident hippies—draft dodgers and meditators and herbal experts—adopted us. I read *Moby Dick* upstairs in an empty room, worked on a novel called *Gypsy Joe and the Silent Rose Man,* and taught Fulty to surf during a major storm at the mouth of the Margaree River. Terry and I became so disconnected from the rest of the world that we refused to believe the gossip that Nixon had resigned back in the States.

Cape Breton Island was a gift to us but we knew we could not live there despite the fact that we had bought a hundred acres of forest land near Alistair MacLeod's hometown of Dunvegan. We began to commute to where the good waves were—Lawrencetown Beach on the Eastern Shore of Nova Scotia. Here we became friends with other surfers and discovered a genuine sense of community. When we found another abandoned house on Petit Lac in West Chezzetcook, for sale for a mere $1500, we bought it and began to fix it up. All this domesticity and good luck must have prompted Terry and me to think about getting married. We'd been living together for a few years and felt a strong commitment but we didn't want a big ceremony and all that complication. A judge in Halifax would do. We had also adopted a puppy and when the van broke down driving to Halifax, we hitchhiked the rest of the way, the three of us, to the Courthouse on Agri-

Performing with the Surf Poets in Halifax

cola Street. It had been built on the ground of the old Mayflower Curling Rink, famed as the place where they stored the bodies gathered up from the sinking of the *Titanic.*

We returned to New Jersey and I held down a gaggle of part-time teaching jobs through the fall and winter at colleges and even at Brookfield Academy, a private high school for rich kids who had been kicked out of other schools. I loved all forms of teaching although I had doubts whether I was succeeding at changing the world or in fact doing anything of significance. I kept writing for *The Aquarian* as I grew more and more discouraged with politics and materialism. I worried that if I stayed put too long, I would be infected by it all, ultimately losing my idealism and my own dreams. I was looking for a way out. Around that time, I went to a small press fair in New York City where I was startled and excited by the endless possibilities of independent publishing—making things happen with words and print.

I had dabbled in self-publishing by producing *Edible Wild Plants of Nova Scotia,* run off on my mother's old Moravian church mimeograph machine. Living in West Chezzetcook during the summer of 1977, I somehow pulled together an anthology of Atlantic Canadian writing called *Chezzetcook,* that included such notables as Alden Nowlan, Harry Thurston, and Gregory Cook. I audaciously included some of my own stuff, even though I clearly only had part-time status. A local bookseller, Elizabeth Eve funded that project and another, *Alternating Currents,* a nonfiction book about solar and wind energy. The world demanded a second edition of *Edible Wild Plants,* whose pages were collated in a backyard shed by volunteers from the community. We called the publishing house Wooden Anchor Press. The vague dream before me was coming into focus: living in Nova Scotia, near waves and wonderful people and all that wilderness, growing a literary press—like all those other wonderfully demented independent presses.

I had published some oddball poems and a sci-fi story or two in small, reckless publications and had even finished *Gypsy Joe,* which kicked off my long career of getting rejected by reputable publishers across North America.

*

By 1978, I was tired of New Jersey, graduate school, and traffic jams outside Yankee Stadium while I tried to get to class. Terry and I would move either to Oregon or British Columbia or best yet, Nova Scotia, where we already had established some roots. I petitioned the Canadian consulate in New York for landed immigrant status and was turned down (just like in publishing) several times until the Canadian bureaucrats grew weary of answering my letters and filing my documents. To avoid further paperwork, they said we could move to Canada and live happily ever after. Which we did.

We packed up as much as we could into the Ford van my brother had turned into a camper and a U-haul trailer, drove north and crossed the border at Calais, Maine. We rented an old house in Seaforth for a few months before discovering an even older house on Leslie Road right at Lawrencetown Beach. No plumbing, minimal electricity, and floors with holes through to the basement—that and a view of the waves I longed to surf. All for $15,000. A dream come true. We moved in and prepared for our first long and intensely demanding Canadian winter. Phil Thompson, a local poet who had been in my *Chezzetcook* anthology, gave me a job as an alternative energy consultant. Before the federal government pulled the plug on low-tech solar and wind energy development, we were working the grassroots with backyard wizards of passive solar and wind generators.

I dug a well by hand, scavenged for firewood, wrote feverishly in a cold, dark room—a novel that would be called *Downwind,* not a particularly good mix of pop thriller and environmental literary novel.

Sunyata, our first daughter, was born October 9, 1979, a month which had coincided with the launching of *The Pottersfield Portfolio,* an annual of writing by Atlantic Canadian writers. Not long after, the Writers Federation of Nova Scotia held a gala event where the new immigrants presented to the world our beautiful new baby and an ongoing literary extravaganza.

Clearly, for me this was the beginning of a golden age. I had decided to abandon my Ph.D. thesis and let City University give me a second M.A. for my work. I had a family, a publishing company, and a head full of books I wanted to write in my cold, dark room. I used to refer to myself as the third or fourth happiest man on the east coast of North America. Even though I still wanted to rail against the bad stuff—nuclear energy, right-wing politics, apathy for the poor—I had somehow wrestled my young, angry, cynical, reckless, loner self into a mid-twenties, starry-eyed surfer poet with a pen in one hand, a wood-splitting axe in the other, and a surfboard tucked under my arm. Add wife and baby and I was truly aware that I had carved out a small republic of euphoria amidst the chaotic clutter of the North American urban wasteland.

I jammed as much of that euphoria as I could (spliced with fragments of the leftover cynic) into a poetry book that Fred Cogswell of Fiddlehead books chose to publish in a moment of weakness. Later, Fred would introduce me to an audience, saying that "Lesley Choyce was not a very good poet but I thought he deserved encouragement." He was referring to that volume called *Re-inventing the Wheel,* published in 1980. My love affair with the crazy, eccentric, and generous people of the Eastern Shore was consummated with the publication of my first collection of short stories, *Eastern Sure,* published by Elizabeth Eve of Nimbus Publishing.

There was part-time teaching to be had over the next few years at St. Mary's University, Mount St. Vincent University, and the Nova Scotia College of Art and Design, as well as the occasional night continuing-ed class where I sometimes carried Sunyata if the responsibilities of motherhood had overwhelmed her mother.

Probably, despite my aversion to people obsessed with their careers and climbing of corporate ladders, I had been infected with a kind of American ambition that I could not shake. It took the form of writing and publishing and I threw myself into both. *The Portfolio* continued and, in 1981, John Bell of Halifax and I had pulled together the second-ever anthology of Canadian science fiction, ours known as *Visions from the Edge,* exclusive to Atlantic writers and including such unlikely luminaries as Spider Robinson, Hugh MacLennan, and Lucy Maud Montgomery, among others.

I landed a part-time teaching gig at Dalhousie University in 1981 and this became a bit more permanent in 1986 when I was honored with a "half time" appointment that included an Intro to Lit class and teaching the English course for the Transition Year Program (TYP) for Black and Native students. TYP proved to be a near-constant source of both frustration and delight for years to come. At Dal, I also made friends with Dr. Malcolm Ross, a man who had helped usher Canadian literature into prominence through his editorial work for McClelland and Stewart and his tutelage of such notable Canadian writers as Margaret Laurence and Adele Wiseman. Malcolm and I could create a wonderful chorus together as we railed against the absurdity and injustices of the world at large. He was a generous and honest critic of my work, suggesting sometimes what to keep and what to throw away. Malcolm and I remained good buddies right up to his death at ninety-one in November of 2002. Having him as a close friend gave me a good intellectual and personal link to a generation well before my time and I needed that.

Fast Living, my second book of poetry, came out with Fiddlehead in 1982 and, after a round of seemingly brutal rejections, *Downwind* found a Newfoundland

publisher called Creative whose editors failed to see the inherent flaws but had the generosity to usher it into print. I saw it as a spinach-and-vodka kind of book—something that's good for you and something that has a kick too.

Terry began a preschool in the community and we traded child-raising tasks. We prided ourselves on living on very little money and we were good at it. We traveled a few times each year to New Jersey and I always breathed a sigh of relief when we passed back into Canada, headed home to the Republic of Leslie Road, a road NOT named after me but the family who had once lived in our two hundred-year-old house.

In 1984 Blewointment Press published a new collection of my stories called *Billy Botzweiler's Last Dance.* The title story drew upon my high school rock-and-roll career. (The motto of the Wipeouts was, "If you can't be good, be loud.") *The Pottersfield Portfolio* had evolved into Pottersfield Press and I edited another anthology, this one of Cape Breton writers (*The Cape Breton Anthology*) as a sort of gift to those incredible people who had nurtured us a few years back. It included Alistair MacLeod and Farley Mowat among others. I was writing a lot of short fiction and poetry, sending them around for literary periodicals and that resulted in another volume of short stories, *Conventional Emotions,* and one of poetry, *The End of Ice,* both in 1985. *The Dream Auditor,* my first collection of science fiction, appeared in 1986, *The Top of the Heart* (poetry) the same year. I think I truly wanted to follow in the footsteps of the SF greats—Verne, Wells, Asimov, Heinlein—but didn't have a clue as to how to fit into the genre I so loved. I would never give up writing SF but never could find my way into the commercial side of it.

Tales of my personal golden age came together in my first autobiographical book, *An Avalanche of Ocean.* I had written about New York and hitchhiking and discovering fool's gold in the backyard where I dug my well. I wrote about winter surfing in Nova Scotia and transcendental wood splitting. And I think I nailed it down—why life was so good and sweet and amazing despite the troubles in the world. It was for this book that the rest of Canada took at least a little notice of me. Peter Gzowski had me on CBC's national radio program, *Morningside* and introduced me as "Nova Scotia's answer to the renaissance man," a term that immediately went to my head.

While most readers reveled in my tongue-in-cheek tales of coastal Canadian life (the book was short-listed for the Stephen Leacock Award), for some there was a mistrust of someone so seemingly productive, happy, self-satisfied, and willing to brave the onslaught of January snowstorms to surf the Atlantic waves. At home in Nova Scotia, I received tremendous support from the Writers Federation of NS, thanks to Gregory Cook and a score of other writers whose own ambitions threaded with my own. We were at the center of our own "renaissance" of Atlantic Canadian writing godfathered, perhaps, by Alistair MacLeod and Thomas Raddall but revved up by younger writers schooled in the sixties and seventies who believed like me that the only way to deal with the world was to make it up as you go along and ignore the naysayers.

I must have been feeling guilty about all the good things in my life and my darker (more responsible) self started chastising the eclectic Whitmanesque surfer-poet to get serious and get back to fixing the world. While driving to New Jersey with Terry and Sunyata, I looked down at the battle grey military ships parked in the river at Portsmouth, New Hampshire, many of them carrying lethal nuclear weapons, and I grew scared. I had read voraciously about how well armed the planet was and was dead certain we were on the road to destroying ourselves, accidentally if not otherwise, with the nuclear arsenals of the East and West. I threw myself into writing a little book called *December Six/The Halifax Solution.* I published it through Pottersfield, breaking my self-imposed rule about not publishing my own books.

Halifax had seen the largest manmade explosion of its day on December 6, 1917, when an ammunition ship blew up in the harbor. Today, Halifax Harbour was the only port in Canada that hosted nuclear-armed ships—Brits and American. Here was my chance to begin cleaning up the planet, one bomb at a time, starting in Nova Scotia and getting others everywhere inspired to join me. In my book, I envisioned living through a nuclear attack on Halifax from my home, twenty-five miles away. In relentless detail, I described what Terry and I would do—hunkered down in our basement with dog and child. I described how we would die. I asked all readers to envision their personal version of this horror and imagine how they would feel. And then they should look up from my book and realize, although nearly imminent, the catastrophe has *not* happened yet. Now go and dedicate part of your life to

make sure it won't happen, I insisted. I offered solutions, including every possible aspect of international cooperation in sports, literature, education, and massive voluntary population displacement between North America and the Soviet Union. (It's bad politics to drop bombs on your own people.) I promoted the idea of passive resistance, protest, and creative alternatives towards disarmament.

I may not have changed the world but I found my way into every niche of the Canadian media with my quixotic quest. Some people still tell me the basement scenario in the book shook them to their roots. By the time the Berlin Wall fell and Soviet Russia began to change forever, my book was becoming hopelessly and happily out of date. But the nuclear arsenals remained. Before the demise of the old Soviet Union, I had been planning a goodwill surfing-literature trip to help foster kinship between Canada and Russia. With the help of the Soviet government's sports offices and a retired pro-disarmament Soviet general, I would have taken some Canadian surfers to the Kamchatka Peninsula on the Pacific to introduce the sport there, garner international media attention, and help promote peace therein. But, before I could get there, the world changed—for the better for once—and I never got to surf Russia.

*

Coming up for Air pulled together more of my short stories in 1988 and a little volume called *The Man Who Borrowed the Bay of Fundy* came out from Brandon University in 1989. More importantly, Formac published my first young adult novel, *Skateboard Shakedown* in 1989. It was clear to me that books changed people's lives in their early teens more than at any other age, and I wanted to be instigating change in those lives. By 1990 I had three other novels in that genre coming out: *Wavewatch* (about surfing, natch) and *Hungry Lizards* from Collier-Macmillan, a story about a teen rock band of that name. A Danish publisher came out with *Skatefreaks og Graesrodder,* a translation of *Skateboard Shakedown.*

But some kind of literary breakthrough happened for me (at least in my own head) with the publication of my novel *The Second Season of Jonas MacPherson,* published by Thistledown Press in Saskatoon. My narrator was a sixty-nine-year-old coast dweller whose wife had died and he was pitted in a psychological battle with death. I was trying to pull into one book my personal battles with global nuclear death, my experiences with old and dying people, my passion for the coast of Nova Scotia, and an ambitious literary quest to write something deeper and more emotionally profound than what had come before.

I was also trying to heal some psychological scars left on me after an attempt to save a woman from drowning at nearby Stoney Beach. On Dominion Day, July 1 of 1984, I had received a call that someone was caught in the river current nearby and being pulled to sea. I arrived on the scene, saw the woman face down, swam out and retrieved her, and began to attempt to revive her with mouth-to-mouth resuscitation until relieved by lifeguards who arrived from a nearby beach. The woman, a mother of three small kids, did not survive, and I took it all very personally. I undertook a very public battle with the province to provide lifeguards at this dangerous beach and made some headway but not enough. For me, as it would be for my fictional Jonas, it was a very real psychological battle against death.

The failed rescue attempt haunted me for many years and the spell wasn't broken until on another occasion, in the year 2000, at the same place, a young fellow surfer and I rescued two kayakers who had swamped in big waves and were caught in the deathtrap of outgoing river current/incoming waves. We paddled them ashore and I felt a weight lifted off my chest.

Jonas won the Dartmouth Book Award. I've always had a love-hate relationship with all the darned literary awards out there and, years later, after sitting on numerous juries including the Governor General's Award, realized that it's the personal taste (and prejudices) of the jurors that determine who wins and why. The award allowed *Jonas* to find a few more readers, however, and that was a blessing so who's to complain?

In 1990 Terry and I adopted a second child, Pamela, who was then four years old and in need of a home. An adopted child presented a whole new range of challenges. I loved being a father, taking my kids to the beach or on hikes in the dense spruce forest behind the house. The world was full of miracles aplenty and Nova Scotia had proven to be the Promised Land. I had built a couple of additions onto my old farmhouse

Appearing on **Off the Page** *television show, c. 1986*

so there was room enough for everybody and for the growth of Pottersfield Press, which produced four to seven books per year—poetry, literary fiction, SF, history, and biography. My publishing ambitions had given me the opportunity to work with a number of writers I greatly admired, including Thomas Raddall, Harry Thurston, Greg Cook, H. R. Percy, Harold Horwood, Susan Kerslake. I published what I believe to be the first screenplay ever to appear in book form in Canada—*The Bay Boy,* by Daniel Petrie, a noted Hollywood director originally from Cape Breton. Nova Scotia has a dynamic black community and I tapped into that large reservoir of talent, producing the first volumes of poetry by George Elliott Clarke, Maxine Tynes, and David Woods.

Mary Jo Anderson and I conspired to produce a TV talk show called *East Coast Authors* and later, *Choyce Words,* for local cable. Mike Boyd at Channel 10 in Halifax put us on air. I was the host and over the years something like three hundred half-hour shows were produced, allowing me to interview in depth regional writers as well as outsiders like William Golding, Allen Ginsberg, prime minister Kim Campbell, John Shelby Spong, Margaret Atwood, David Suzuki, and Timothy Findley. We ran for a while on PBS in Maine and later, nationally on Vision TV. The Vision connection allowed us to continue when cable lost interest so we emerged as an independent production called *Off the Page,* which survived into the next century.

Through the 1990s I juggled (sometimes gracefully, sometimes not) family life with running a publishing company, teaching two courses at university, hosting a weekly TV show, and of course writing. Never able to explain why I was so "ambitious," I was at least happy in my frenetic life, which was rich in diversity and stimulation although not without moments of sheer panic that it would be impossible for me to keep all the balls in the air at once.

I traveled with family to places like Florida, Barbados, California, Ireland, and Portugal, and back to New Jersey and on book tours (some glamorous, some not) to such diverse destinations as Vancouver Island, Labrador, Sudbury, Santa Monica, and Tokyo. Once the YA novels kicked in, there were dozens of school visits a year across Canada and a few in Japan and Scotland.

At home there was hiking, surfing, and pulling the weeds out of my marshland garden in summer to soothe the nerves and plug me back into the planet for rejuvenation. Terry ran her preschool for many years until she decided to move on from that, creating workshops for personal growth for women, a field in which she has proven to be a huge success.

Jonas MacPherson, my attempt at a truly serious literary novel, was followed by its opposite: *Magnificent Obsessions,* a photo-novel that was a spoof autobiography based on a found set of photographs. In 1991 and 1992 three YA novels came out—I was on a roll and loving it, the best of which was probably *Clearcut Danger,* an environmental story about kids up against big forestry business in Nova Scotia. In '92 I pulled together *Ark of Ice: Canadian Future Fiction,* an anthology of Canadian writers whose stories were set in our future. Atwood and Findley were in it, as were W. P. Kinsella, whom I greatly admired, and an array of Canadian SF writers. Judith Merill provided an afterword.

The Ecstasy Conspiracy was my second attempt to produce a novel that was both cerebral yet "popular." It was a murder mystery of sorts about a novelist-English prof. named DeMille. I admired John Fowles' *The Magus* and this was my own attempt to play that sort of complex mind game on a reader. The book came out very late in the publishing season and handily missed its mark.

Transcendental Anarchy was my second autobiographical book, similar in vein to *Avalanche.* In it I told tales of my life of creative anarchy. I wrote about fear, anger, and metaphysical encounters. There were chapters on fights against streetlights, sixties demonstrations, my recent vasectomy, subliminal learning, and love. I also used the book to document the Stoney Beach drowning incident of 1984.

The YA novels *Good Idea Gone Bad* and *Dark End of Dream Street* allowed me to dig a bit deeper into issues like teenage violence and the despair of street kids. The Ann Connor Brimer Award came my way despite the fact I was sure adults would be offended by my *Good Idea Gone Bad* protagonist—a homophobic high school bully who plays drums in an alternative rock band.

Despite absorbing the gloomy news of the early nineties—the Persian Gulf War and the ensuing death of thousands of Iraqi children caused by "our" side, I must have been hatching the next conspiracy in the ragtag empire of my imagination—a mythical chunk of Nova Scotia, part real, part imagined, a separate country of its own that believed in no political ideal. And thus was born *The Republic of Nothing,* the novel that would elicit surprising responses and touch many people deeply. Set on a fictional island on the eastern shore of Nova Scotia, it focuses on an idealistic fisherman and his psychic wife who have a son, Ian, born the same year and same day I was born. Part adventure, part parable, part political treatise, part tall tale, and part experiment, the book had some sparks. I received letters from people far away who said they had read it and had decided to move to Nova Scotia as a result. Years later I would hear from a young woman who said she had suffered an extended depression until she holed up with the *Republic* for three days and was cured. And there were other similar stories. It won the Dartmouth Book Award. The Toronto *Globe and Mail* called it "a triple-decker of a yarn shot through with mythic possibilities." The book would take on a life of its own. A film option was sold but the movie never happened. Although the book never made any bestseller list that I saw, I knew I had done my job well and it would be hard to top.

*

I hiked a thirty-mile section of coastline and wrote an extended poetic narrative called *The Coastline of Forgetting,* trying to get back to the meditative value of being alone in the wilderness and sitting down to write

The author with his wife, Terry, and daughters, Sunyata and Pamela, 2002

ravaged this new world—decimating aboriginals and wildlife, plundering the seas and pouring toxins back in return.

As a blessed escape from the weight of history, music came to my rescue. Doug Barron and Stan Carew convinced me that what the world wanted was spoken word music and thus the Surf Poets were formed. At Deep Nine Recording Studio we produced two CDs with an array of talented performers, my words, and my own limited electric guitar work. We performed before thousands at Halifax's first Word on the Street event and we received some CBC air play. The recording aspect was both unnerving and satisfying. We borrowed heavily from everything: rock, folk, reggae, classical, experimental, hip-hop. On *Long Lost Planet,* we grieved for the loss of the beauty of the natural world and on *Sea Level,* we railed against apathy in a piece called "Best Minds," modeled after Ginsberg's "Howl."

I was lured into writing a series of books for even younger readers with a Black girl named Carrie at the center of the stories. She was a feisty I-can-do-anything girl and kids loved her. Some thought that I was on a cradle-to-grave readership campaign and that was fine by me.

The Surf Poets came in like the tide and moved back out, so I returned my poetry to page with *Beautiful Sadness* and *Caution to the Wind,* both published by a British Columbia publisher I had met at the Paris Book Fair, Richard Olafson at Ekstasis Editions.

World Enough appeared in 1998 as well, a novel about a soul-weary guy who worked at a rehab center quite similar to the one I had worked at years ago in New Jersey. I struggled to find a publisher for the novel that followed, *Cold Clear Morning,* but Beach Holme, another BC publisher, took it on and it finally saw print in 2002. A film option was soon in the works and high hopes running rampant.

Along with Lulu Keating, I produced a half-hour documentary titled *The Skunk Whisperer,* the true-life story of the sixteen skunks that once lived under our house and how I humanely caught them and shuttled them away, one by one, to a new forest home. It was sold to CBC-TV and Animal Planet, and I remain

about it then and there. Thistledown published *Big Burn,* a YA windsurfing-environmental novel. Bob Hilderley of Quarry Press was generous enough to publish my way-out-there SF/fantasy novel, *The Trap Door to Heaven.* It was a time-travel/reincarnation story that begins at the end of humanity and then slips backwards into lives of the past. Bolstered by responses to *The Republic of Nothing,* I must have wanted to make an even more daring leap, but in Canada at least, the science-fiction aspect of the book was the kiss of death.

Cynthia Good at Penguin, having turned down several of my manuscripts, got it in her head that I should write a history of Nova Scotia. Reluctantly I agreed and undertook the dirty work of actual research (and paid a few researchers to help). I cursed myself for having to write facts instead of remaining in my comfortable world of fiction. But the deed was done and *Nova Scotia: Shaped by the Sea* came out in 1996. I was allowed my opinions, however, and raged against how our European ancestors and their descendants had known by many simply as the Skunk Guy for my role in the shoot. Peter Bolkavic helped me do the post-partum on my band with a second mock documentary called *Dead Surf Poet Society,* a digital project shot on a shoestring budget.

Penguin had proposed I do a history of the coastline of Canada—east, north, and west—and I had taken the bait, but in the end it was Goose Lane in New Brunswick who published it in 2002. It had been six years in the works and it spanned several thousand years of history and some of my own trekking around the coast from Newfoundland and Labrador to the outer beaches of Vancouver Island where I kissed my first slug, surfed some fine Tofino waves, discovered my own private Northwest Passage of the heart, and stitched together the history of an enormous chunk of shoreline.

Shoulder the Sky was my attempt to write an unpublishable YA novel. I was getting weary of editors' advice about what I *should* do in my books. I had a protagonist who had a passion for eighteenth-century German philosophers, a shrink who promoted smoking, and enough hairpin turns of plot and character to dissuade any editor looking for a marketable book. But it was the book I wanted to write and ironically, it found a publisher (Dundurn) within three days of being submitted to them by e-mail.

I continue to write novels and poetry and publish other writers' work through Pottersfield Press, including such authors as Bruce Graham, Neil Peart, Budge Wilson, Sheree Fitch, and Joan Baxter.

At this writing, January of 2003, I await *The Sea of Tranquility* to be published in the spring and hope to carve out time to rewrite the rough draft of another novel, *Raising Orion.* Sunyata is twenty-three, a wildlife rehabilitation specialist who occasionally fills our house with orphaned baby racoons, injured blue jays, squirrels, and woodpeckers. Pamela is sixteen and going to Cole Harbour High School. Terry is a Unitarian chaplain and teaches courses on writing and creativity.

My friend Malcolm Ross died in the fall of 2002 and that clearly marked the end of an era in Canadian literature and also a turning point in my life. At fifty-two I feel that I've had a pretty good crack at the things I wanted to do. There will be, I hope, many more books to come. It is the love of writing that fuels the endeavor. I want to be every kind of writer that there is to be. I want to live all those lives of my characters young and old. There are fifty-six titles in print that bear my name. I like to think that I am more concerned with writing a book that has a powerful impact on lives—even a few lives—than one that is commercially successful or created merely for entertainment.

*

Since the wind is light out of the north and I can see the wispy tops of waves blowing high over the dunes, I will finish this task and put on my dry suit—it's winter, after all, here in Canada—and go surfing. As in writing, all I have to do is tap into the natural energy that is surging and work it. Dropping down the sparkling blue face of a North Atlantic winter wave, I will feel the power of the unseen forces, allow it to pick me up and set me on my harrowing but exhilarating path. Beyond that, it's up to my imagination as to what happens next.

BIOGRAPHICAL AND CRITICAL SOURCES:

BOOKS

Choyce, Lesley, *An Avalanche of Ocean,* Goose Lane Editions (Fredericton, New Brunswick, Canada), 1987.

Choyce, Lesley, *Transcendental Anarchy* (autobiography), Quarry Press (Kingston, Ontario, Canada), 1993.

St. James Guide to Young Adult Writers, second edition, St. James Press (Detroit, MI), 1999.

Van Belkom, Edo, *Northern Dreamers: Interviews with Famous Science-Fiction, Fantasy, and Horror Writers,* Quarry Press (Kingston, Ontario, Canada), 1998.

PERIODICALS

Analog Science Fiction & Fact, June, 1993, Tom Easton, review of *Ark of Ice: Canadian Futurefiction,* p. 165; June, 1999, Tom Easton, review of *Trapdoor to Heaven,* p. 134.

Beaver: Exploring Canada's History, February-March, 1997, Christopher Moore, review of *Nova Scotia, Shaped by the Sea: A Living History,* p. 39.

Books in Canada, October, 1995, pp. 49-50; October, 1996, Virigina Beaton, "Surfing the Genres," pp. 11-12.

Canadian Children's Literature, number 62, 1991, pp. 86-88; number 76, 1994, pp. 72-6.

Canadian Forum, December, 1996, review of *Nova Scotia, Shaped by the Sea: A Living History,* p. 36.

Canadian Materials, January, 1991, p. 34; May, 1992, p. 165.

Maclean's, August 15, 1994, John De Mont, "The Surfer Poet," p. 44.

Quill & Quire, March, 1990, p. 22; August, 1990, p. 15; April, 1991, p. 18; May, 1993, pp. 33-34; March, 1995, p. 79; May, 1995, pp. 46-47.

School Library Journal, August, 1999, Cheryle Cufari, review of *Carrie's Crowd,* p. 124.

Wall Street Journal, December 18, 2001, Joel Baglole, "When the Surf's up in Nova Scotia, Who Cares If It's Four Below," p. A1.

ONLINE

Canadian Poets, http://www.library.utoronto.ca/canpoetry/ (January 8, 2003), "Lesley Choyce."

*   *   *

CHURCHILL, Winston 1871-1947

PERSONAL: Born November 10, 1871, in St. Louis, MO; died March 12, 1947, in Winter Park, FL; son of Edward Spaulding (import merchant) and Emma Bell Blaine Churchill; married Mabel Harlakenden Hall, 1895 (died, 1945); children: Mabel, John, Creighton. *Education:* U. S. Naval Academy, received degree, 1894. *Religion:* Episcopalian.

CAREER: Army and Navy Journal, New York, NY, editor, 1894; *Cosmopolitan,* New York, NY, managing editor, 1895; full-time writer from 1895; Republican member of Cornish, NH, legislature, 1903-05; Republican National Convention, Chicago, IL, delegate from New Hampshire, 1904; Progressive Party candidate for New Hampshire governor; *Scribner's,* New York, NY, writer, 1917-18. *Military service:* Served as naval cadet on the *San Francisco,* New York Navy Yard, 1894.

MEMBER: Authors League of America (president, 1913).

WRITINGS:

The Celebrity: An Episode, Macmillan (New York, NY), 1898.

Richard Carvel, Macmillan (New York, NY) 1899.

The Crisis, Macmillan (New York, NY), 1901.

Mr. Keegan's Elopement, Macmillan (New York, NY), 1903.

The Crossing, Macmillan (New York, NY), 1904.

The Title-Mart: A Comedy in Three Acts, Macmillan (New York, NY), 1905.

Coniston, Macmillan (New York, NY), 1906.

Mr. Crewe's Career, Macmillan (New York, NY), 1908.

A Modern Chronicle, Macmillan (New York, NY), 1910.

The Inside of the Cup, Macmillan (New York, NY), 1913.

A Far Country, Macmillan (New York, NY), 1915.

The Dwelling-Place of Light, Macmillan (New York, NY), 1917.

The Faith of Frances Craniford, Macmillan (New York, NY), 1917.

A Traveller in Wartime; With an Essay on the American Contribution and the Democratic Idea, Macmillan (New York, NY), 1918.

Dr. Jonathan: A Play in Three Acts, Macmillan (New York, NY), 1919.

The Crisis: A Play in Four Acts, S. French (New York, NY), 1927.

The Uncharted Way: The Psychology of the Gospel Doctrine, Dorrance (Philadelphia, PA), 1940.

Contributed to periodical publications *Atlantic, Century, Harper's, North American Review,* and *Yale Review.*

SIDELIGHTS: Winston Churchill (no relation to the British Prime Minister) was best known for his earnest, naive historical romances. Churchill's work exceeded all others in popularity during the early twentieth century, but he gradually turned away from his popular historical romances to approach political and moral questions more directly. He also became increasingly involved with the Republican and Progressive political parties, and eventually took up theological speculation. He set aside the "natural storytelling," which had pleased both critics and audiences early in his career, in favor of political and religious musings. Moreover, as a reviewer in the *Cyclopedia of World Authors* explained: "His is a voice from long ago. He concerned himself, with the exception of his early historical novels, with then current problems of divorce, religion and class relationships, but to these problems he—as a product and endorser of the status quo—had no very compelling answer."

Churchill was born in St. Louis, Missouri, on November 10, 1871. His family was wealthy; Churchill's father, Edward Spalding Churchill, was a successful importer and his mother, Emma Bell Blaine Churchill, was a descendant of Jonathan Edwards. Churchill's mother, however, died soon after his birth, and Louisa and James Gazams, Emma's half-sister and brother-in-law, raised him. His relatives sent him to the Smith Academy in St. Louis as an adolescent; eventually, he went to the U. S. Naval Academy in Annapolis, taking his degree in 1894. But after one year working in the Naval Yard in New York, and a brief stretch as an editor at *Cosmopolitan,* Churchill supported himself by marrying St. Louis iron heiress Mabel Harlakenden Hall. The two settled in New Hampshire and raised three children: Mabel, John and Creighton.

After his marriage, Churchill produced a manuscript version of *The Celebrity: An Episode,* which he left with the Macmillan editors. After much prodding from the publishing house, he eventually finished the novel; immediately, the gentle, satirical novel was a hit. With so much encouragement, Churchill embarked on his most famous historical novel, *Richard Carvel.* The novel describes the adventures of the Carvel family during the years leading up to the American Revolution; as Wade Hall explained in an article for *Dictionary of Literary Biography:* "It is a roomy, epic Victorian novel with a large cast of historical and invented characters, violent encounters, romantic interludes, intriguing entanglements, daring rescues, adventures over land and sea, and comfortable conclusions. The historical personages intermingle convincingly with the fictional characters." The novel was a huge success. Churchill's thorough historical research contributed heavily to his critical success. Larry Olpin, writing for the *Encyclopedia of Romance and Historical Writers,* noted: "Churchill took particular care to be historically accurate in his novels. He always did his homework, reading the historical material available to him and carefully checking historical

facts. He paid special attention to biographies and used them to benefit his fiction." But Olpin also cautioned: "[Churchill's] portrayal of history seems accurate, and he is able to capture the essence of a minor character whether from history or totally from his imagination quickly and effectively. In contrast, his weaknesses are all too glaring to the modern reader. His plotting is loose and episodic and he relies too heavily on coincidence. His handling of romance is sentimental and awkward. He also has difficulty drawing major characters who are almost always entirely virtuous and novel or villainous and ignoble, and what is worse he cannot refrain from making this point repeatedly." Nevertheless, as a writer in *World Authors* pointed out: "The novel was hailed by readers and critics in both Britain and the United States, eventually sold more than a million copies, and was, according to the *New York Times,* 'more widely read and discussed during its first year than had been the case with any other book ever published up to that time.'"

Churchill followed up this success with *The Crisis,* in which he tells the story of Stephen Brice, a Boston lawyer who falls in love with Virginia Carvel, a Confederate soldier's daughter. Virginia decides to marry Clarence Colfax, a like-minded Confederate, but through the dark days of the war Virginia realizes she truly loves Brice. This preceded *The Crossing,* which many consider Churchill's best book. It relates the tale of David Ritchie, who grows up on the Kentucky frontier. The story includes a war, orphanhood, career forays across the United States, and a sentimental romance. The novel suffered from the troubles characteristic of all Churchill's historical romances. Olpin wrote: "Churchill tries to do too much in each novel. His novels are too long and too broad in their scope given his constant repetitions and his penchant for seeing everything through the restricted sense of absolute right and wrong." Hall countered: "Despite its contrived plot, *The Crossing* is a fast-paced, gripping story told in authentic language." When *The Crossing* was published, Churchill was one of the most famous authors of his day. As the *New York Times* explained after Churchill's death in 1947: "there were two Winston Churchills who were somewhat in the news. One was a young Englishman, who had had a dashing career as a correspondent and soldier but who still had to be identified as a son of Lord Randolph Churchill. The other was the author of *Richard Carvel,* an American historical novel which beat all selling records. In 1900, even after the British Churchill had been taken prisoner by the Boers and dramatically escaped, there was no question in this country as to which Churchill was *the* Winston Churchill." But it was noted in the *Cyclopedia of World Authors,* "In the summer of 1899, the novelist received a letter from the British Winston Churchill, who was no relation, explaining that henceforth he would sign his books Winston Spencer Churchill."

Despite his fame as a novelist, Churchill turned from the historical stories that so delighted his audience. He increasingly sought a voice in politics rather than literature. His homely morals, which had seemed pleasantly familiar in a narrative of distant times, now became the focus of Churchill's polemic. From 1903 to 1905 Churchill held a seat in the New Hampshire legislature; in 1906 he ran for—but did not win—the New Hampshire governorship. These experiences gradually found their way into his fiction, notably his tale of political corruption, *Coniston.* In this novel, Jethro Bass seeks power by depraved politicking. His ladylove, Cynthia Ware, snubs him for another, but Bass eventually reconciles with her new family by letting go his political might. The novel ends with Cynthia's daughter getting married. The old-fashioned tone pleased many critics as well as readers. The *New York Times* hailed Churchill as a "born storyteller," adding: "*Coniston* can hardly fail to give its readers food for thought. Well will it be for our government if these readers are many, and if they straightway proceed to run according to the reading." But a *Cyclopedia of World Authors* wrote: "Churchill's later novels have a tone of moral earnestness which gave substance to the questions he chose to present. When he tried to resolve the dilemmas he set forth for himself, however, he fell back upon the genteel and the romantic. His attitude toward the American democratic tradition was dualistic; the wealthy in his novels were usually superior in taste and even morals." Churchill continued to write "message" fiction, notably in both *Mr. Crewe's Career* and *A Modern Chronicle.* Later, however, his novels turned from political to religious moralizing; in *The Inside of the Cup,* Churchill describes St. John's Church, a once godly place now settled by corrupt urbanites. As William Higgins explained in the *Reference Guide to American Writers,* the pastor of the church "comes to see the necessity for preaching a social gospel rather than a purely spiritual one. . . . The novel is less hard-hitting than, say, Charles Monroe Sheldon's *In His Steps.*" Higgins explained, "Churchill's popularity declined gradually after he forsook the historical romance, but in 1920 he found himself almost without an audience." Toward the end

of Churchill's career, he published less, preferring to consider theological and moral questions rather than writing about glamorous, daring figures. Nevertheless, his early novels—and, to some extent, his later books—raised the bar for historical fiction because of Churchill's steadfast insistence on thorough research. Though his stories seem, to many critics, to have wilted through the years, they are still good examples of historical romances that connect with contemporary tastes.

BIOGRAPHICAL AND CRITICAL SOURCES:

BOOKS

Benet's Reader's Encyclopedia of American Literature, HarperCollins Publishers (New York, NY), 1991.
Cyclopedia of World Authors, Salem Press (Pasadena, CA), 1997.
Encyclopedia of World Biography, Gale (Detroit, MI), 1998.
Gale, Robert L., *The Gay Nineties in America,* Greenwood Press (Westport, CT), 1992.
Hart, James D., *The Oxford Companion to American Literature,* Oxford University Press (New York, NY), 1995.
Oxford Companion to English Literature, Oxford University Press (New York, NY), 1996.
Oxford Companion to Twentieth-Century Literature in English, Oxford University Press (New York, NY), 1996.
Reference Guide to American Literature, St. James Press (Detroit, MI), 1994.
Twentieth-Century Romance and Historical Writers, St. James Press (Detroit, MI), 1994.

PERIODICALS

American Literary Realism, summer, 1975.
Midwest Quarterly, January, 1962.
New England Quarterly, December, 1974.*

*   *   *

CIMENT, James D. 1958-

PERSONAL: Born May 12, 1958, in Montreal, Canada; son of Mortimer (an electrical engineer) and Gloria (a businessperson; maiden name, Miller) Ciment. *Education:* University of California—Los Angeles, B.A. (English); City University of New York, Ph.D. (history).

ADDRESSES: Home—2020 De La Vina, Apt. B, Santa Barbara, CA 93105. *Office*—1324 State St., #J280, Santa Barbara, CA 93101. *Agent*—John Thornton, Spieler Agency, 154 West 57th St., New York, NY 10019. *E-mail*—james.ciment@verizon.net.

CAREER: City College of New York, New York, NY, lecturer, 1985-94; freelance writer and editor, 1992-2000; ABC-CLIO, Santa Barbara, CA, acquisitions editor, 2000-01; East River Books, Santa Barbara, CA, president, 2002—.

MEMBER: American Historical Association.

WRITINGS:

Law and Order, Chelsea House (New York, NY), 1995.

Scholastic Encyclopedia of the North American Indian, Scholastic (New York, NY), 1996.

The Kurds: State and Minority in Turkey, Iraq, and Iran, Facts on File (New York, NY), 1996.

Algeria: The Fundamentalist Challenge, Facts on File (New York, NY), 1997.

Angola and Mozambique: Postcolonial Wars in Southern Africa, Facts on File (New York, NY), 1997.

Palestine/Israel: The Long Conflict, Facts on File (New York, NY), 1997.

The Young People's History of the United States, Barnes and Noble (New York, NY), 1998.

(Editor, with Immanuel Ness) *Encyclopedia of Global Population and Demographics,* M. E. Sharpe (Armonk, NY), 1999.

(Editor) *Encyclopedia of Conflicts since World War II,* M. E. Sharpe (Armonk, NY), 1999.

(Editor, with Immanuel Ness) *Encyclopedia of Third Parties in America,* M. E. Sharpe (Armonk, NY), 2000.

(Editor) *Encyclopedia of the Great Depression and New Deal,* M. E. Sharpe (Armonk, NY), 2001.

(Editor) *Encyclopedia of American Immigration,* M. E. Sharpe (Armonk, NY), 2001.

Atlas of African-American History, Facts on File (New York, NY), 2001.

WORK IN PROGRESS: Social Issues: An Encyclopedia of Controversies, History, and Debate, Colonial America: An Encyclopedia of Social, Political, Cultural, and Economic History, and *Postwar America: An Encyclopedia of Social, Political, Cultural, and Economic History,* all for M. E. Sharpe (New York, NY).

SIDELIGHTS: James Ciment is a writer and editor whose work focuses largely on educational reference books and informational texts. His book *Scholastic Encyclopedia of the North American Indian* introduces nearly 150 tribes and groups, offering information about family life, language, and location. Ciment also included facts about contemporary Indian culture and politics, along with photographs and maps, offering a up-to-date account of each tribe's history. John Peters of *School Library Journal* wrote of Ciment's text that the author "is not a dispassionate writer, but he's not a sensationalist either, and he describes traditions and beliefs in ways that clearly bring out each tribe's distinctive flavor." The *Encyclopedia of American Immigration* covers the history of a wide range of immigrants, including Southeast Asians and American Indians. Included in the text are a series of essays written by immigrants and copies of numerous immigration documents. Ciment examines how immigration has continued to change America and discusses such topics as law and legislation, culture, economics, and demographics.

Ciment has also written a number of texts on the subject of politics, both in the United States and abroad. *Encyclopedia of Third Parties in America* examines the role of third-party politicians in American history. The reference book includes biographies of the major leaders in third party movements, discusses the ideological roots of the parties, and examines particular issues around which third parties are often centered. There are also forty maps which detail the vote received by third-party candidates in each county of selected elections. Mary Ellen Quinn of *Booklist* called this text "clearly written, well organized." *Encyclopedia of Conflicts since World War II* researches 172 noteworthy conflicts since World War II, including confrontations during the cold war and other fighting, such as border disputes, coups, and ethnic/religious clashes. There is also a section devoted to the numerous efforts at peacekeeping by members of the North Atlantic Treaty Organization (NATO) and the Organization of Africa, among others. In *Algeria: The Fundamentalist Challenge,* Ciment focuses on the country's second civil war in the twentieth century. The war's direct cause, the termination of the 1992 election, is examined in detail. Gilbert Taylor of *Booklist* noted that "Ciment evenhandedly summarizes the beliefs and positions of the parties to the conflict and the individual histories of their leaders."

Ciment told *CA:* "I am a journeyman editor and writer. As such, and as a book producer, my publishing efforts focus on large reference sets and information handbooks, generally in the social sciences. In a sense, I consider myself as much an artisan as a writer, providing a high-quality product to the consumer, whether they are a reader or a librarian. I want the purchasers of my book to feel they are getting value for the money they spend on my products, money that often comes from shrinking library or limited student budgets. To that end, my guiding principles can be summed up in the acronym ART: accuracy, readability, and thoroughness. I believe in providing as much carefully researched, well-organized, clearly written information as possible within the word-length constraints set by my publishers. To those who see writing as a high art form, these values might seem prosaic. But I see my obligations and goals differently. I am a craftsman, a carpenter or plumber with facts and words, diligent in my work and proud of a job well done."

BIOGRAPHICAL AND CRITICAL SOURCES:

PERIODICALS

American Reference Books Annual, 1998, p. 153.
Booklist, February 1, 1996, p. 924; November 15, 1996, p. 614; March 15, 1997, Gilbert Taylor, review of *Algeria: The Fundamentalist Challenge,* p. 1222; August, 1999, pp. 2104, 2106; January 1, 2000, p. 770; July, 2000, Mary Ellen Quinn, review of *Encyclopedia of Third Parties in America,* p. 2060; November 1, 2001, pp. 512, 516.
Choice, October, 2001, p. 290; November, 2001, p. 486.
Contemporary Review, January, 2001, p. 61.
Library Journal, March 15, 1997, p. 75; March 15, 1999, p. 68; July, 1999, p. 80; April 15, 2000, p. 70; September 1, 2001, p. 164; September 15, 2001, pp. 69-70; November, 2001, p. 86.
School Library Journal, November, 1996, John Peters, review of *Scholastic Encyclopedia of the North American Indian,* pp. 136-137; August, 2000, p. 132; February, 2002, p. 83.

CLYNES, Michael
See DOHERTY, P(aul) C.

* * *

COLE, Stephen A. 1955-

PERSONAL: Born February 13, 1955, in Fall River, MA; son of Alton H. (a banker) and Elizabeth W. (a teacher; maiden name, Wade) Cole; married Linda S. Gifford (an art director), September 12, 1981; children: Phoebe E., Eliza M. Cole. *Ethnicity:* "Caucasian." *Education:* Brown University, B.A., 1977; University of Massachusetts, M.R.P., 1996. *Hobbies and other interests:* Reading, music, canoeing, natural history, tennis.

ADDRESSES: Home—80 Bristol Rd., Damariscotta, ME 04543. *Office*—Coastal Enterprises, MC, P.O. Box 268, Wiscasset, ME 04578. *E-mail*—scole@celmaine. org.

CAREER: Maine State Planning Office (economic and environmental policy development), Augusta, senior planner, 1991-98; CEI (a community development corporation), Wiscasset, ME, project manager, 1998—. Affiliated with Belfast-Northport-Lincolnville Land Trust, 1991—, Maine Arts Commission traditional arts panel, 1994—, and Coastal Transportation Board, 1999—.

WRITINGS:

I Was Content and Not Content, Southern Illinois University Press (Carbondale, IL), 2000.

WORK IN PROGRESS: The Rangeley and Its Region: The Rangeley Boat and the Rangeley Lakes of Maine, 2001; *On the Bogs: Cranberry Culture in Massachusetts,* 2002.

SIDELIGHTS: Stephen A. Cole told *CA:* "My interest is to document traditional life and work in New England and its intersection with modern life. My literary influences are Robert Coles, John McPhee, William Warner and Olive Pierce. Visual influences are Todd Webb and Olive Pierce."

COLGRASS, Michael 1932-

PERSONAL: Born April 22, 1932, in Brookfield, IL; son of Michael C. (a postmaster) and Ann (Hand) Colgrass; married Ulla Dahgaard, November 24, 1966; children: Neal. *Education:* University of Illinois, B.A.

ADDRESSES: Home and office—583 Palmerston Ave., Toronto, Ontario, Canada M6G 2P6. *E-mail*—colgrass@interlog.com.

CAREER: Composer and musician, including appearances with Boston Symphony Orchestra, New York Philharmonic Orchestra, American Ballet Theater, Detroit Symphony Orchestra, Minnesota Orchestra, and Toronto Symphony Orchestra. Performed as a jazz percussionist in and around Chicago, IL, 1944-49; percussion soloist and performer with other musicians, including Dizzy Gillespie; recordings include *Variations for Four Drums and Viola,* MGM Records; *Three Brothers,* Urania Records; and *Percussion Music,* Period Records; appeared in television documentary special *Soundings: The Music of Michael Colgrass,* broadcast by Public Broadcasting Service. Certified trainer in neuro-linguistic programming; presenter of Excellence in Performance workshops throughout North America and around the world; creator of "Deep Listening," a hypnosis technique for musical audiences.

MEMBER: American Society of Composers, Authors, and Publishers.

AWARDS, HONORS: Pulitzer Prize for music, 1978, for "Deja vu"; Emmy Award, National Academy of Television Arts and Sciences, 1982, for documentary program *Soundings: The Music of Michael Colgrass;* Jules Leger Prize for new chamber music, 1988; two Guggenheim fellowships; Fromm Award; Ford Foundation award; first prize from Barlow & Sudler International Wind Ensemble competitions; Rockefeller Foundation grant.

WRITINGS:

My Lessons with Kumi: How I Learned to Perform with Confidence in Life and Work, Real People Press (Moab, UT), 2000.

Musical compositions include "A Flute in the Kingdom of Drums and Bells," 1995; "Urban Requiem," 1996; and "Hammer and Bow," 1997. Author of a column in *Music* (Canadian periodical), 1979-88. Contributor to other periodicals, including *New York Times* and *Christian Science Monitor.*

ADAPTATIONS: Many of Colgrass's musical compositions have been recorded by others.

SIDELIGHTS: Michael Colgrass told *CA:* "A friend described my motivation for writing when he called me an 'escapee.' When I asked him what he meant he said, 'You escaped from Brookfield, Illinois—population 10,000—and escapees often feel compelled to go back and help others escape.'

"The content of my book, *My Lessons with Kumi: How I Learned to Perform with Confidence in Life and Work,* is the result of my studies in neuro-linguistic programming combined with my personal experience as a musician-performer from 1943 to 1967, including an eleven-year career as a freelance percussionist in New York City. Participants in my Excellence in Performance workshops requested that I write my ideas in book form. The workshop resulted from my years of performing experience and the desire to share this experience with others."

BIOGRAPHICAL AND CRITICAL SOURCES:

BOOKS

Dilts, Robert, *Tools for Dreamers,* Meta Publications, 1991.

OTHER

Michael Colgrass Web site, http://www.michaelcolgrass.com (September 24, 2002).

*   *   *

COLLEY, Barbara 1947-
(Anne Logan)

PERSONAL: Born July 26, 1947, in Ringgold, LA; daughter of Charles and Doris (a homemaker; maiden name, Wilson) Logan; married A. David Colley, November 18, 1966; children: April, Charles, Anna

Colley Alford. *Ethnicity:* "Caucasian." *Education:* Attended Louisiana Polytechnic Institute (now Louisiana Tech University), 1965-66, and Nicholls University, c. 1976. *Religion:* Christian—Protestant. *Hobbies and other interests:* Shopping at malls, tennis, sailing, travel, playing with her grandchildren.

ADDRESSES: Home—Louisiana. *Agent*—Evan Marshall Agency, 6 Tristam Pl., Pinebrook, NJ 07058-9445. *E-mail*—adcoiii@aol.com.

CAREER: Minden Press & Herald, Minden, LA, classified advertisement receptionist, 1966-67; Sperry Rand Corp., Minden, line dispatcher, 1967-68; Ebasco Services, Taft, LA, receptionist and filing and dispatch clerk, 1977-78; temporary clerical worker, Norco, LA, 1984-85; Ormond Country Club, Destrehan, LA, secretary and receptionist, 1985-87, 1989-91; temporary clerical worker, Luling, LA, 1987-89. writer, 1991—. Member of Malice Domestic and Bouchercon, 2002.

MEMBER: Romance Writers of America (Kiss of Death Chapter), Mystery Writers of America, Sisters in Crime Writers, Southern Louisiana Romance Writers (charter member; president, 1991).

AWARDS, HONORS: ARTemis Award, Romance Writers of America, 1992; Reader's Choice Award, Oklahoma Romance Writers, 1992; named distinguished artist of Louisiana, 1996.

WRITINGS:

Maid for Murder: A Squeaky Clean Charlotte LaRue Mystery, Kensington Publishing (New York, NY), 2002.
Death Tidies Up, Kensington Publishing (New York, NY), 2003.

ROMANCE NOVELS; UNDER PSEUDONYM ANNE LOGAN

Gulf Breezes, Harlequin Books (Tarrytown, NY), 1992.
Twin Oaks, Harlequin Books (Tarrytown, NY), 1993.
Dial "D" for Destiny, Harlequin Books (Tarrytown, NY), 1994.

That Old Devil Moon, Harlequin Books (Tarrytown, NY), 1996.
Finding Kendall, Harlequin Books (Tarrytown, NY), 1997.
A Dance with the Devil, Harlequin Books (Tarrytown, NY), 1997.

WORK IN PROGRESS: Polished Off, publication by Kensington Publishing expected in 2004; two romance novels.

SIDELIGHTS: Barbara Colley told *CA:* "Do you know how you can tell if a person is from Louisiana? The answer is, if they think purple, green, and gold colors go together and look good, then they have to be from Louisiana. Yes, I'm referring to Mardi Gras, and yes, that was supposed to be a joke.

"But seriously, I am a native of Louisiana. I grew up in the small North Louisiana town of Minden, where I worked on my high school newspaper staff and, later, on the staff of the *Minden Press & Herald.* At that time, though, I never really dreamed of becoming a writer.

"After high school, I attended Louisiana Tech University and Nicholls State University as a music education major. My dream then was becoming a band director. Instead, I fell in love with my husband, David, and I'm still in love with him even after thirty-five years of marriage, three grown children, and five precious grandchildren.

"After college, my husband and I moved to a small suburb of New Orleans. What a change for both of us. Most people don't realize that there is a vast difference in the cultures of North Louisiana and South Louisiana. I truly love living near New Orleans. With its Creole French and Spanish influence, New Orleans is such a unique and interesting city. Strolling through the historical French Quarter and the Garden District is one of my favorite pastimes. The city is well over 200 years old, but each time I visit, I find something new and fascinating.

"So how did I get started writing? A lot of people ask me that question, and the answer is both simple and complex. Simply, I was trying to be a good, conscientious mother. More complex, I've always loved to read and, according to my mother, I've always possessed a healthy dose of imagination as well as the belief that I could do anything I wanted to do if I set my mind to it.

"When my oldest daughter was a young teenager, 'Harlequin Presents' began arriving through the mail. Without my knowledge, my daughter had subscribed, and I decided I should read a few to make sure they were suitable for someone her age. I deemed that they were suitable, but a funny thing happened. The more I read, the more I wanted to read. Then I came to a point when I began to believe that I could write 'one of those'.

"Believing I could write a book was half the battle. Actually writing one and getting published was the other half. Well, I did write one, then I wrote another one, then another, and I'm still writing fifteen years later. But even better, I'm published and get to share my stories with thousands of wonderful readers all over the world. To date, my Harlequin romances have been published in sixteen foreign countries as well as the United States and Canada.

"So how did I go from writing romance novels to writing mystery novels? Actually, it wasn't much of a stretch for me to do so. I've always loved to read mystery and romantic suspense, and all of my romance novels have a thread of mystery running through them.

"I have to give my agent a lot of credit for my decision to switch to writing mysteries. I'd been trying to write mainstream thriller novels for a couple of years, without success, and one day in a phone conversation with my agent, he suggested that I might want to try my hand at writing a cozy mystery series instead. He very gently told me that, though there was nothing wrong with my thriller stories or my writing, most publishers only wanted the big-name authors for the thrillers. He knew there was a market for 'cozies,' and he felt sure that he could sell in that market.

"He and I talked about a possible setting as well as the type of sleuth I might use. He suggested the New Orleans Garden District, and I came up with the idea of using a maid for a sleuth. With his encouragement and support, I wrote a proposal. Within two months, my agent called to let me know that a Kensington edi-

tor was interested in buying my series, but he'd like for the sleuth (my maid) to be older, in her late fifties or early sixties. I said, 'No problem. I can do that.' Well, that Kensington editor did buy the series, and he offered me a three-book hardcover/softcover deal. Thus my maid sleuth, Ms. Charlotte LaRue, was born, and the rest, as they say, is history.

"Besides reading and writing mystery and romance books, there are other fun things I enjoy, too. I love shopping at the malls, tennis, sailing, and traveling. But the most fun thing of all is playing with my sweet grandchildren who range in age from two to nine years old.

"For me, writing is a necessity. It took me six years and four completed manuscripts to get published, but I think I would have kept writing even if I had not gotten published. I love the whole creative process of writing. It's fun, but it's also hard work, and I can't imagine doing anything else."

BIOGRAPHICAL AND CRITICAL SOURCES:

PERIODICALS

Library Journal, January, 2002, Rex Klett, review of *Maid for Murder: A Squeaky Clean Charlotte LaRue Mystery,* p. 157.
Publishers Weekly, January 7, 2002, review of *Maid for Murder,* p. 50.

ONLINE

Barbara Colley-Anne Logan Web site, http://www.eclectics.com/barbaracolley-annelogan (December 3, 2002).

*   *   *

COLLINS, Michael 1964-

PERSONAL: Born 1964, in Limerick, Ireland. *Education:* University of Notre Dame, graduated, 1987, M.A., 1991; University of Illinois, Ph.D.

ADDRESSES: Agent—c/o Author Mail, Simon & Schuster, 1230 Avenue of the Americas, New York, NY 10020.

CAREER: Writer and computer programmer. Northwestern University, Chicago, IL, head of computer lab, creative writing teacher;

AWARDS, HONORS: Winner, Last Marathon in Antarctica, 1997; shortlisted for Booker Prize, 2001, for *The Keepers of the Truth.*

WRITINGS:

The Meat Eaters, Jonathan Cape (London, England), 1992, published as *The Man Who Dreamt of Lobsters,* Random House (New York, NY), 1993.
The Life and Times of a Teaboy, Phoenix House (London, England), 1994.
The Feminists Go Swimming, Phoenix House (London, England), 1996.
The Emerald Underground, Phoenix House (London, England), 1998.
The Keepers of Truth, Scribner, (New York, NY), 2001.
The Resurrectionists, Scribner (New York, NY), 2002.

SIDELIGHTS: Born and raised in Ireland, Michael Collins focused on that troubled land and the harsh lives of its unluckiest inhabitants in his earliest works. Abusive alcoholics, pious junkies, and doomed IRA renegades inhabit his first collection of short stories, *The Meat Eaters.* Critics noted the combination of brutal subject matter and intricate, often philosophical writing. Comparing Collins to earlier Irish writers such as James Joyce, Boyd Tonkin wrote in the *Observer,* he "takes the language of his mentors down to a dank cellar and then thumps the stuffing out of them. He writes exquisitely, but the gore and spleen on show here still have a bookish stink about them." Less complimentary was Nicholas Clee in the *Times Literary Supplement,* who wrote, "Michael Collins's language veers between the febrile and the banal. Every noun must have an adjective." Reviewing the U.S. edition, published as *The Man Who Dreamt of Lobsters,* a *Los Angeles Times* critic wrote, "Indeed for a while it seems that cruelty and a vivid muscular prose style are all that Collins does give us. . . . Only gradually do we sense a counter-theme: the endurance

that has sustained the Irish for centuries." A reviewer for *Studies in Short Fiction* wrote, "It is difficult to read a collection by an Irish writer and not think of Joyce's *Dubliners.* . . . Yet Collins is his own writer, his voice strong, as capable of the lyric as of the harsher tones of a difficult world." Joseph Coates, in the *Chicago Tribune,* felt that "Neither the style nor the material is entirely under control, but their strength is undeniable. A powerful new writer is loose."

For his first novel, *The Life and Times of a Teaboy,* Collins focuses on a young man growing up in Limerick, Ireland, shortly after Irish liberation from England, who is ground down by the poverty, cruelty, and cloying piety of his family. Young Ambrose Feeney grows up to take on civil service jobs that leave him stranded between Irish independence and the old subservience to English customs and attitudes. Gradually, Ambrose slips into madness, unable to work out the contradictions in his own life. There was a certain ambivalence in the reaction of some critics to the novel. Jonathan Dyson in the *Times Literary Supplement* felt that "Despite an often rich, fluid style and many interesting ideas, Michael Collins doesn't quite make it home in this, his first novel. The patness of the madness metaphor is reminiscent of similar failings in his earlier, often brilliant, collection of short stories, *The Meat Eaters.*" David Buckley, in the *Observer,* expressed more mixed feelings: "Collins can be irritatingly clever . . . but much of the time his aim is exact and his effect eerie."

Collins's next work was again a collection of short stories, *The Feminists Go Swimming.* In one story, "The End of the World," the pope is scheduled to open an envelope containing the secret of Fatima, and possibly bringing on the apocalypse. For Kim Bunce, writing in the *Observer,* "Collins's book, once opened, is as irresistible as the secret of the Pope's envelope." Other stories explore coaches who push their students too far, dutiful relatives negotiating canonization for an aged aunt in a convent, and an abusive husband who goes too far and enlists the local priest in his cover-up. For *Times Literary Supplement* critic C.L. Dallet, "in all the stories, the prevailing instinct is to avoid scandal, to cover up anything which might upset the conservative Catholic status quo, and it is in this one strand that Michael Collins may have most accurately identified the crisis in Ireland's struggle with the modern world."

Collins has relocated to the United States, and with *The Keepers of Truth,* so does his fiction. Set in an unnamed, decaying town in the Midwestern Rust Belt, the novel tells the story of Bill, a young man who returns to the town after his father's suicide and takes a job at the local paper, *The Daily Truth*, founded by his grandfather. For awhile he muses about inserting diatribes about deindustrialization into the inoffensive paper's editorials, while carrying on a desultory relationship with a supposed girlfriend that consists of swapping answering machine messages. Then the disappearance of a prominent local citizen, with suspicion focusing on his ne'er-do-well son, captures Bill's attention. *New York Times* contributor Maggie Galehouse found that "as Bill fumbles around the breaking news . . . the reader fumbles along beside him, trying to figure out what kind of a novel Collins has cooking. A thriller? A mystery? A twisted love story? 'The Keepers of Truth' turns out to be all three, and Bill pulls us through with his gift of gab, twisting the plot into unlikely but somehow plausible scenarios." *Atlantic Monthly* reviewer Robert Potts concluded, "This book, in the words of its narrator, is 'an almighty . . . roar of despair'; but it is also intelligent, witty, humane, and utterly haunting."

In 2002 Collins published *The Resurrectionists*, about a man who returns to the town where his parents died in a fire twenty years earlier, seeking the answers to questions about his past.

BIOGRAPHICAL AND CRITICAL SOURCES:

PERIODICALS

Atlantic Monthly, November, 2001, Robert Potts, review of *The Keepers of Truth*.

Los Angeles Times Book Review, June 13, 1993, review of *The Man Who Dreamt of Lobsters*, p. 6.

New York Times Book Review, February 3, 2002, Maggie Galehouse, "Rust Belt Blues," p. 15.

Observer (London, England), August 9, 1992, Boyd Tonkin, "The Hypnotist Takes the Lead," p. 51; June 26, 1994, David Buckley, "A Dab Hand with the Mutton Patties," p. 19; March 17, 1996, Kim Bunce, review of *The Feminists Go Swimming*, p. 16.

Studies in Short Fiction, fall, 1994, Brian McCombie, review of *The Man Who Dreamt of Lobsters*, p. 704.

Times Literary Supplement, May 15, 1992, Nicholas Clee, "At the Assassin's Table," p. 22; July 8, 1994, Jonathan Dyson, "Speaking for Ireland," p. 20; February 9, 1996, C. L. Dallat, review of *The Feminists Go Swimming*, p. 27.

Tribune Books (Chicago, IL), April 18, 1993, Joseph Coates, "The Ferocious Paradoxes of Ireland," pp. 1, 9.*

*   *   *

COLWELL, Eileen (Hilda) 1904-2002

OBITUARY NOTICE—See index for *CA* sketch: Born June 16, 1904, in Robin Hoods Bay, Yorkshire, England; died September 17, 2002. Librarian, storyteller, and author. Colwell was one of the first librarians in England to specialize in children's literature, and throughout her life she was an active force in promoting children's books both in England and abroad. She received her diploma in librarianship from the then-newly opened University College School of Librarianship in 1924, and got her first job as a senior library assistant at the Bolton Public Library that year. When she heard that the library in Hendon was creating a new children's collection, Colwell leaped at the chance to help organize it. Specialized libraries in children's literature were, at the time, a new idea, and Colwell therefore was able to lead the way in establishing a collection for children according to her own preferences. When the library officially opened in 1929, she was appointed its librarian and remained in that job until 1967. Colwell was not only active in Hendon, but also throughout England, working with the Library Association to help encourage others to specialize in children's books and to establish the Kate Greenaway and Carnegie medals. In addition to her work as a librarian, Colwell developed a talent for storytelling, and would regularly regale children with stories of her own invention, often changing them according to suggestions she got from her young audience. Many of the best of these are collected in her *A Storyteller's Choice* (1963); her talents as a storyteller are also evident in her book *How I Became a Librarian* (1956) and her autobiography *Once upon a Time* (2000). Colwell also wrote a book on read-aloud techniques titled *Storytelling* (1980), edited numerous story collections for children, and appeared on the television programs *Playschool* and *Jackanory*. For her groundbreaking work she was made a member of the Order of the British Empire in 1965, received an honorary doctorate of letters in 1975 from Loughborough School of Librarianship, and was presented with the Eleanor Farjeon Award in 1994.

OBITUARIES AND OTHER SOURCES:

PERIODICALS

Independent (London, England), October 18, 2002, p. 20.

Times (London, England), October 4, 2002, p. 34.

*   *   *

COMFORT, Philip W(esley) 1950-

PERSONAL: Born October 28, 1950, in Pittsburgh, PA; married 1971; wife's name, Georgia (a piano teacher); children: Jeremy, John, Peter. *Ethnicity:* "Caucasian." *Education:* Cleveland State University, B.A., 1977; Ohio State University, M.A., 1984; Fairfax University, Ph.D., 1989; University of South Africa, D.Litt., 1997. *Politics:* Independent. *Religion:* Christian. *Hobbies and other interests:* Surfing, soccer, drums, writing poetry.

ADDRESSES: Home—307 Hagley Rd., Pawleys Island, SC 29585.

CAREER: Ohio State University, Columbus, instructor in English, 1983-84; Tyndale House Publishers, Wheaton, IL, senior editor of Bible reference works, 1984— and member, New Testament bible translation committee. College of DuPage, lecturer, 1984-87; Wheaton College, Wheaton, IL, visiting professor, 1987-98; North Park College, visiting professor, 1992-93; Trinity Episcopal Seminary, Pawleys Island, SC, adjunct professor, 1997-2000; Coastal Carolina University, instructor, 1998—; Columbia International University, Columbia, SC, professor, 1999—. International Greek New Testament Project: Gospel of John, American member.

MEMBER: Society of Biblical Literature.

WRITINGS:

(Editor and contributor) *A New Commentary on the Whole Bible,* Tyndale House Publishers (Wheaton, IL), 1990.

Early Manuscripts and Modern Translations of the New Testament, Tyndale House Publishers (Wheaton, IL), 1990, 2nd edition, Baker Book House (Grand Rapids, MI), 1996.

(Translator, with Robert Brown) J. D. Douglas, editor, *The New Greek-English Interlinear New Testament,* Tyndale House Publishers (Wheaton, IL), 1990.

The Complete Guide to Bible Versions, Tyndale House Publishers (Wheaton, IL), 1991, revised edition, 1996.

The Quest for the Original Text of the New Testament, Baker Book House (Grand Rapids, MI), 1992.

(With Georgia Comfort) *Dying to Live,* Tyndale House Publishers (Wheaton, IL), 1992.

(Editor and contributor) *The Origin of the Bible,* Tyndale House Publishers (Wheaton, IL), 1992.

(Editor, with J. D. Douglas, and contributor) *Who's Who in Christian History,* Tyndale House Publishers (Wheaton, IL), 1992.

(With Wendell Hawley) *Opening the Gospel of John,* Tyndale House Publishers (Wheaton, IL), 1994.

I Am the Way: A Spiritual Journey through the Gospel of John, Baker Book House (Grand Rapids, MI), 1994.

(New Testament editor) *New Living Translation,* Tyndale House Publishers (Wheaton, IL), 1996.

(Editor, with David Barrett) *The Complete Text of the Earliest New Testament Manuscripts,* Baker Book House (Grand Rapids, MI), 1999.

The Books of the New Testament, Tyndale House Publishers (Wheaton, IL), 1999.

(Editor, with Dan Partner, and contributor) *The One Year Book of Poetry,* Tyndale House Publishers (Wheaton, IL), 1999.

Essential Guide to Bible Versions, Tyndale House Publishers (Wheaton, IL), 2000.

(Editor, with Walter Elwell, and contributor) *Tyndale Bible Dictionary,* Tyndale House Publishers (Wheaton, IL), 2001.

Selected Poems, Morris Publishing, 2001.

The Text of the Earliest New Testament Greek Manuscripts, Tyndale House Publishers (Wheaton, IL), 2001.

(Editor) *Life Application New Testament Commentary,* Tyndale House Publishers (Wheaton, IL), 2001.

Author (with Eugene Carpenter) of the book *Holman Treasury of Key Bible Words,* Broadman & Holman (Nashville, TN). Editor of book series "Life Application Commentary," Tyndale House Publishers

(Wheaton, IL), 1992-99. Contributor to reference books. Contributor to periodicals, including *Decision, Novum Testamentum, Notes on Translation, New Testament Studies,* and *Bible Translator.*

WORK IN PROGRESS: New Testament Text and Translation; another book of poetry.

SIDELIGHTS: Philip W. Comfort told *CA:* "I write scholarly books to bridge the gap between New Testament textual criticism (including ancient New Testament manuscripts) and modern English translations of the New Testament. It has been my passion to help English readers understand the manuscripts used to make Greek texts and then English translations. My other passion is writing poetry, which I will devote more time to in coming years."

* * *

COMPESTINE, Ying Chang 1963-

PERSONAL: Born March 8, 1963, in Wuhan, People's Republic of China; daughter of Chang Sin Liu (a surgeon) and Xiong Xi Guang (a doctor of Chinese medicine); married Greg M. Compestine (a software engineer), March 5, 1990; children: Vinson Ming Da. *Education:* Central China Normal University, B.A. (English and American literature), 1984; CDR Associates Certified Mediator, 1988; University of Colorado—Boulder, graduate teacher training certificate, 1990, M.A. (sociology), 1990; Asian/Pacific Center for Human Development, victim's assistant training, 1990.

ADDRESSES: Agent—Sheldon Fogelman Agency, Inc., 10 East 40th St. New York, NY, 10016. *E-mail*—yingc@csd.net.

CAREER: Teacher and author of cookbooks and children's literature. Former English teacher and government interpreter in China. Spokesperson for Nestlé's Maggi brand "Taste of Asia."

AWARDS, HONORS: Front Range Community College, Master Teacher Award, 1991-92; International College at Beijing, Master Teacher Award, 2000.

WRITINGS:

Secrets of Fat-free Chinese Cooking, Avery (Garden City Park, NY), 1997.
Cooking with Green Tea, Avery (New York, NY), 2000.
The Runaway Rice Cake, illustrated by Tungwai Chau, Simon and Schuster (New York, NY), 2001.
The Story of Chopsticks, illustrated by YongSheng Xuan, Holiday House (New York, NY), 2001.
The Story of Noodles, illustrated by YongSheng Xuan, Holiday House (New York, NY), 2001.
Secrets from a Healthy Asian Kitchen, Avery (New York, NY), 2002.
The Story of Kites, illustrated by YongSheng Xuan, Holiday House (New York, NY), 2003.
The Story of Paper, illustrated by YongSheng Xuan, Holiday House (New York, NY), 2003.

WORK IN PROGRESS: A middle-grade book of historical fiction based on growing up in China during the Cultural Revolution; *A Culinary Journey along the Yangtze River,* "simple, healthy recipes from region around the Yangtze River along with personal stories and observations that tie together culture, history, and traditions."

SIDELIGHTS: Ying Chang Compestine was born in Wuhan, a city in the People's Republic of China. After earning a degree in English and American literature, she taught English and worked as an interpreter for the Chinese government. After relocating to the United States, Ying earned a master's degree in sociology from the University of Colorado—Boulder. She taught sociology for eight years at colleges and universities in both the United States and China.

By blending her long-time passion for cultural diversity and her interest in cooking, Ying turned her talents toward writing stories for children and cookbooks for adults. Her first picture book, *The Runaway Rice Cake,* is reminiscent of the traditional Western folktale about the gingerbread man. Though they have little food, the Chang family is preparing to celebrate the Chinese New Year with a simple holiday meal. But, as Momma Chang begins to serve the family a single rice cake, the cake springs to life, jumps off the table, and runs away. The rice cake runs through town, laughing and taunting animals and people, until it encounters a starving old woman. The Chang family allows her to eat the entire cake, even though it is their only one, and they are rewarded upon their return home with a feast sent by the Kitchen God. While Linda Perkins of *Booklist* felt that this story "lacks the cohesiveness of folklore," a *Kirkus Reviews* critic called it an "original and upbeat Chinese New Year tale." *School Library Journal* writer Tina Hudak called *The Runaway Rice Cake* "a tale of tenderness and sharing."

The Story of Chopsticks features the three boys in the Kang family who adore eating. The youngest brother, Kuai, however, is always hungry. If he tries to grab food straight from the fire, the youngest brother burns his hands. If Kuai waits for the food to cool, his brothers eat it all before he gets any. Finally, the boy's ingenuity leads him to grab two sticks from the woodpile, using them to lift the hot food out of the fire before anyone else has a chance to eat it. All of family's friends and neighbors are soon using the new utensils. An author's note gives facts about the true history of chopsticks and how to use them. Margaret A. Chang of *School Library Journal* noted that this "story is rooted in Chinese culture and offers American readers an authentic glimpse of its traditions," while a critic for *Kirkus Reviews* believed that Compestine "concocts a delicious blend of fact and fiction."

The Kang brothers return in *The Story of Noodles,* which explains the origin of this favorite Chinese food. This time, the boys have been instructed by their mother to make dumplings. They end up ruining the dough and in an attempt to fix their problem, make strips instead of dumplings. There are author's notes about Chinese eating and manners in this "appetizingly funny story," as described by a *Kirkus Reviews* critic.

The Kang brothers are again featured in *The Story of Kites,* which explains the origin of kites. As the author described the book, "The boys are tired of working in the rice fields, protecting the harvest form the birds. They try everything—they bang pots, blow whistles, and wave their arms. If only they could fly, they'd drive those birds away forever! Then the boys get an idea: if they made wings, they could fly! Using paper, straw, and feathers, the boys try to launch themselves into the sky from the hilltop above the rice fields. Kersplash! Kerplop! Kersploosh! What else can the Kang boys come up with to keep those naughty birds away from their rice?"

Compestine told *CA:* "Growing up during the Chinese Cultural Revolution, a very difficult time in Chinese history, searching for good books to read became a daily struggle. The Red Guard took books from our homes and burned them in the streets. For many years, we were only allowed to read the *Little Red Book* (Mao quotations) and political newspapers.

"The best times in my childhood were when I got hold of non-political books that survived the book burning. At that time, a true measure of friendship was not in exchanging toys at each other's birthday party but in sharing 'underground' books. It took a lot of trust and courage! If the authorities found out, it could result in our parents being jailed, or the whole family being sent to live a harsh life in the countryside.

"I often had to wait days for my turn, and once I got a book, I had to finish it quickly because others were waiting. Many of the books had pages missing, usually at the beginning or the end of the story, for it had passed through so many eager hands. That was when I started my own creative writing. I wrote my own beginnings and endings to complete the books and passed them along to the next child in line. Sometimes I received other children's completions. We spent hours arguing over who had the most believable additions. It was not unusual for one book to have six or eight different versions.

"One day when I was eight years old, the teacher sent for my mother. I was so nervous because I thought I had failed a test. But the teacher explained that a magazine wanted to publish an article I had written and the editor of the magazine wanted to meet me. The editor presented me with a hardcover notebook as an award. I brought that notebook with me from China and I've kept it close by in my office for all of these years.

"I can't describe how excited I was the first time I went to a library in America. The books were so beautiful and complete. I just loved the feel of them! I realized that I would never have to finish any of these books! If I wanted to continue my writing, I'd have to write my own books. Often I wonder if all that practice filling out those incomplete books in China helped me become a writer today.

"When I first came to America, I never dreamt I'd be able to write professionally in my second language, English. I used to be so uneasy about writing even a simple note, let alone a book! I worried about spelling, grammar, and sentence structure. In some ways, writing in English helps me face that fear. I discovered that by making mistakes, I could learn and become a better writer. I challenged myself to write a cookbook in English and sold my first book in less than two months.

"After I lost my parents several years ago, I started writing children's stories that reminded me of life in China. It helped me cope with my loss. Just as importantly, it keeps me close to the country I love. *The Runaway Rice Cake* is my childhood New Year fantasy. It's about sharing, compassion, and celebrating the Chinese New Year. The story tells how the Changs (my Chinese family name) are rewarded for their kindness. As a child, when the New Year was approaching, I always wished we could have all the dishes the Chang family enjoyed at the end of my story, and that my brothers and I could have new clothes for New Year's Day. But those wishes rarely came true. So in this story, I let the Chang boys get everything I wished for.

"Growing up with two older brothers, I often had to outsmart them to get more to eat. That led to the idea behind *The Story of Chopsticks*. After I saw how my young son, Vinson, learned to use chopsticks, I knew I had to write the story.

"Food plays an important part in Chinese culture. Perhaps that's why I have always had a passion for food, and why I began my writing career with cookbooks for adults. It may also explain why food is an important element in my children's stories. I have so many fond memories linking food with life in China. For years, my brothers and I played a game eating noodles in different ways. We ate slowly and waited until our parents left the table, then started our game. Since I was the youngest, I was seldom blamed when we were caught. Not surprisingly, after I showed my son, Vinson, different ways to eat noodles, he invented his own 'cutting the grass,' one of the methods the boys use in *The Story of Noodles*. In this story, the brothers invent noodles through their food play.

"I enjoy losing myself in my stories where I relive my childhood fantasies. As a young girl, I lacked the patience for sewing, needlework, and fan dancing—things girls were expected to do in China at that time. I preferred playing with boys! I allow my boy characters to do all the naughty things I wish I could have done. In the end, my boys are always rewarded for their creativity and inventiveness.

"Beyond writing, one of my greatest pleasures is being with children. They ask the most fascinating questions. I love visiting schools and sharing my stories about growing up in China, along with my joys and struggles writing in a second language. I hope my books will help bridge the two countries I love, America and China.

"My typical workday begins with tai chi sword, a kind of Chinese exercise. Then, after a long walk, I sit down to write. Walking helps me structure my writing. And writing makes me so hungry that I have to go to the kitchen, cook, and eat."

BIOGRAPHICAL AND CRITICAL SOURCES:

PERIODICALS

Booklist, February 1, 2001, Linda Perkins, review of *The Runaway Rice Cake,* p. 1055; January 1, 2002, p. 863.
Childhood Education, spring, 2002, p. 173.
Kirkus Reviews, November 15, 2000, review of *The Runaway Rice Cake,* p. 1613; October 1, 2001, review of *The Story of Chopsticks,* p. 1420; October 1, 2002, review of *The Story of Noodles,* p. 1464.
Natural Health, August, 2002, p. 90.
Publishers Weekly, January 8, 2001, p. 66.
School Library Journal, February, 2001, Tina Hudak, review of *The Runaway Rice Cake,* p. 93; December, 2001, Margaret A. Chang, review of *The Story of Chopsticks,* p. 97.

ONLINE

Ying Chang Compestine Web Site, http://www.csd.net/˜yingc (November 20, 2002).

*   *   *

CONRAD, Margaret R. 1946-

PERSONAL: Born September 14, 1946, in Bridgewater, Nova Scotia, Canada; daughter of Douglas and Gladys L. (Weston) Slauenwhite. *Education:* Acadia University, B.A. (with honors), 1967; University of Toronto, M.A., 1968, Ph.D., 1975.

ADDRESSES: Home—80 Selkirk Cres., Fredericton, New Brunswick, Canada E3A 3R4. *Office*—Department of History, University of New Brunswick, Fredericton, New Brunswick, Canada E3B 5A3; fax: 506-453-5068. *E-mail*—mconrad@unb.ca.

CAREER: Clarke, Irwin Publishing Co., Toronto, Ontario, Canada, editor, 1968-69; Acadia University, Wolfville, Nova Scotia, Canada, member of faculty, 1969-87, professor of history, 1987-2002, department head, 1992-95, founding member of planter studies committee, beginning 1984; University of New Brunswick, Fredericton, New Brunswick, Canada, Canada Research Chair in Atlantic Canada Studies, 2002—. University of Victoria, visiting lecturer, 1979; University of Toronto, visiting scholar at Ontario Institute for Studies in Education, 1981-82; Dalhousie University, adjunct professor, beginning 1991; Mount Saint Vincent University, Nancy Rowell Jackman Chair of Women's Studies, 1996-98. Canadian History in Multimedia, member of editorial board, 1997—; member of advisory board, H-NET CANADA, 1994—, and Canadian History Electronic Resource Centre, 2000—. Speaker at educational institutions including Memorial University of Newfoundland, St. Mary's University, University of Tsukuba, Seisen University, Meiji University, University of Western Sydney, University of Maine—Orono, University of Vermont, and University of Edinburgh. National Archives of Canada, member of advisory board from Atlantic Canada, 1989-92; Historic Sites and Monuments Board of Canada, member from Nova Scotia, 1990-98, chair of Built Environment Committee, 1995-98; HISTOR!CA, council member, 2000—; Parks Canada secretariat, member of minister's round table, 2001. Jury member for history and creative or scholarly writing competitions. Producer of video programs on contemporary Canada and the Atlantic region of Canada; workshop coordinator and presenter; guest on media programs, including *Maritimes Today.*

MEMBER: Royal Society of Canada (fellow; member of executive committee, 1996-99), PEN Canada, Association for Canadian Studies (Atlantic region representative on executive committee, 1981-83), Canadian Historical Association (council member, 1977-80), Canadian Research Institute for the Advancement of Women, Canadian Women's Studies Association, Canadian Committee on Women's History, Canadian Association of Learned Journals (member of executive committee, 1999-2000), Atlantic Association of Historians.

AWARDS, HONORS: Woodrow Wilson fellow, 1967-68; Canada Council fellow, 1972-73; Imperial Order of Daughters of the Empire fellow, 1972-73; Planter scholar, 1997; Alison Prentice Award, Ontario Historical Society, 1997, for *Saturday's Child: The Memoirs of Ellen Louks Fairclough, Canada's First Female Federal Cabinet Minister*; Year of Asia Pacific Award, 1997; grant from Health Canada, 1998; grants from various other agencies, including Social Sciences and Humanities Research of Canada.

WRITINGS:

(With John Ricker) *Twentieth-Century Canada,* Clarke, Irwin (Toronto, Ontario, Canada), 1974.

George Nowlan: Maritime Conservative in National Politics, University of Toronto Press (Toronto, Ontario, Canada), 1986.

(With Toni Laidlaw and Donna Smyth) *No Place like Home: The Diaries and Letters of Nova Scotia Women, 1771-1938,* Formac (Halifax, Nova Scotia, Canada), 1988.

(Editor) *They Planted Well: New England Planters in Maritime Canada,* Acadiensis Press (Fredericton, New Brunswick, Canada), 1988.

(Editor) *Making Adjustments: Change and Continuity in Planter Nova Scotia, 1759-1800,* Acadiensis Press (Fredericton, New Brunswick, Canada), 1991.

(With Alvin Finkel, Cornelius Jaenen, and Veronica Strong-Boag) *History of the Canadian Peoples,* two volumes, Copp Clark Pitman (Toronto, Ontario, Canada), 1993, 3rd edition (with Finkel), Addison Wesley Longman (Toronto, Ontario, Canada), 2002.

(Supervising editor) Judith Ann Norton, compiler, *New England Planters in Maritime Canada, 1759-1800: Bibliography of Sources,* University of Toronto Press (Toronto, Ontario, Canada), 1993.

(Editor) *Intimate Relations: Family and Community in Planter Nova Scotia, 1759-1800,* Acadiensis Press (Fredericton, New Brunswick, Canada), 1995.

(Editor) *Saturday's Child: The Memoirs of Ellen Louks Fairclough, Canada's First Female Federal Cabinet Minister,* University of Toronto Press (Toronto, Ontario, Canada), 1995.

(Editor) *Looking into Acadie: Three Illustrated Lectures,* Nova Scotia Museum (Halifax, Nova Scotia, Canada), 1999.

(With James Hiller) *Atlantic Canada: A Region in the Making,* Oxford University Press Canada (Toronto, Ontario, Canada), 2001.

(Editor and contributor) *Active Engagements: A Collection of Lectures by the Holders of Nancy's Chair in Women's Studies, 1986-1998,* Mount Saint Vincent University (Halifax, Nova Scotia, Canada), 2001.

(Editor, with Barry Moody) *Planter Links: Culture and Community in Colonial Nova Scotia,* Acadiensis Press (Fredericton, New Brunswick, Canada), 2001.

Canada: A National History, Pearson Educational Publishing (Toronto, Ontario, Canada), 2002.

History of Nova Scotia, University of Toronto Press (Toronto, Ontario, Canada), in press.

Contributor to books, including *Rethinking Canada: The Promise of Women's History,* edited by Veronica Strong-Boag and Anita Claire Fellman, Copp Clark Pitman (Toronto, Ontario, Canada), 1986; *Beyond Anger and Longing: Community and Development in Atlantic Canada,* edited by Berkeley Fleming, Acadiensis Press (Fredericton, New Brunswick, Canada), 1988; *The Eastern Borderlands: Four Centuries of Interaction,* edited by Stephen Hornsby and others, Acadiensis Press, 1989; *Myth and Milieu: Atlantic Literature and Culture, 1918- 1939,* edited by Gwen Davies, Acadiensis Press, 1993; and *The Atlantic Provinces in Confederation,* edited by E. R. Forbes and D. A. Muise, University of Toronto Press (Toronto, Ontario, Canada), 1993. Contributor of articles and reviews to professional journals and newspapers, including *Acadiensis, Canadian Women's Studies, Resources for Feminist Research, Dalhousie Review, Second Mile,* and *Journal of Canadian Studies. Planter Notes,* editor, 1989-92, coeditor, 1998—; coeditor, *Atlantis,* 1977-85 and fall, 2000, and *Canadian Historical Review,* 1997-2000; member of editorial board, *Historical Papers* of the Canadian Historical Association, 1988-91.

WORK IN PROGRESS: Editing the letters and diaries of the McQueen family of Pictou County, with others; research on Canadian historical consciousness in an international context.

BIOGRAPHICAL AND CRITICAL SOURCES:

PERIODICALS

American Historical Review, April, 1988, Welf H. Heick, review of *George Nowlan: Maritime Conservative in National Politics,* p. 531.

Canadian Historical Review, December, 1987, John Stewart, review of *George Nowlan,* p. 650; December, 1993, Kenneth S. Paulsen, review of *Making Adjustments: Change and Continuity in Planter Nova Scotia, 1759-1800,* p. 636; December, 1997, W. G. Goodfrey, review of *Intimate Relations: Family and Community in Planter Nova Scotia, 1759-1800,* p. 665.

English Historical Review, February, 1995, Ged Martin, review of *History of the Canadian Peoples,* p. 435.

*   *   *

COOPER, William
See HOFF, Harry Summerfield

*   *   *

COSSMAN, E(li) Joseph 1918-2002

OBITUARY NOTICE—See index for CA sketch: Born April 13, 1918, in Pittsburgh, PA; died of complications from a stroke December 7, 2002, in Palm Springs, CA. Businessman and author. Cossman was an entrepreneur who was the creator of the ant farm. He also made millions of dollars selling various novelties and conducting sales seminars. He started his career before World War II as a door-to-door salesman. From 1941 to 1945 he served in the U.S. Army, and in 1946 he cofounded his own mail order company, E. Joseph Cossman & Co., with his brother-in-law, Milton Levine. They sold novelty items around the country and also sold soap to customers in Europe. During the 1950s Cossman came up with his ant farm idea, which became an extremely successful product sold to children all across the country. Cossman's other innovation was a fishing lure that smells like meat. Other than these two inventions, the products he sold were invented by others, including items such as fake shrunken heads. Cossman sold his half of the company to Levine in 1965 and embarked on a second career conducting seminars and selling books on how to become rich as an entrepreneur; he also was among the first to use the television infomercial, creating half-hour programs that helped to sell his seminar courses. Cossman was president of Cossman International, Inc., and founder and president of the American Institute of Marketing in Los Angeles. His books include *How I Made $1,000,000 in Mail Order* (1964) and *Making It!: Wealth-building Secrets from Two Great Entrepreneurial Minds* (1994), the latter which he wrote with his son, William A. Cohen.

OBITUARIES AND OTHER SOURCES:

PERIODICALS

Los Angeles Times, December 19, 2002, p. B14.

*　　*　　*

COWELL, Cressida 1966-

PERSONAL: Born April 4, 1966, in London, England; daughter of Michael (chairman of Kew Gardens) and Marcia (an artist and cancer caring center codirector; maiden name, Hare) Blakenham; married Simon Michael Cowell (a business director); children: Maisie, Clementine. *Education:* Oxford University, B.A. (English literature); Brighton University, M.A. (narrative illustration). *Politics:* Labour Party. *Religion:* Church of England.

ADDRESSES: Agent—Caroline Walsh, David Higham Associates Ltd., 5-8 Lower John St., London W1R 4HA, England.

CAREER: Children's author and illustrator.

WRITINGS:

(Self-illustrated) *Little Bo Peep's Library Book,* Hodder (London, England, 1998, Orchard Books (New York, NY), 1999.
(Self-illustrated) *Don't Do That, Kitty Kilroy!,* Hodder (London, England), 1999, Orchard Books (New York, NY), 2000.
What Shall We Do with the Boo-Hoo Baby? illustrated by Ingrid Godon, Scholastic Press (New York, NY), 2000.
(Self-illustrated) *Hiccup, the Viking Who Was Seasick,* Hodder (London, England), 2000, published as *Hiccup, the Seasick Viking,* Orchard Books (New York, NY), 2001.

One Too Many Tigers, illustrated by Andy Ellis, Hodder (London, England), 2002.
Claydon Was a Clingy Child, Hodder (London, England), 2002.
How to Train Your Dragon, Hodder (London, England), 2003.
Super Sue (pop-up book), illustrated by Russell Ayto, Walker (London, England), in press.

What Shall We Do with the Boo-Hoo Baby? has been translated into twenty-one languages, including Welsh, Spanish, Arabic, Bengali, Tamil, Urdu, Chinese, Panjabi, Gujarati, and Farsi.

WORK IN PROGRESS: A sequel to *How to Train Your Dragon,* a novel for older readers featuring the Hiccup character, for Hodder (London, England); ; *Daddy on the Moon; The Queen and the Ghosties.*

SIDELIGHTS: Cressida Cowell writes and illustrates books for young children. In her first book, *Little Bo Peep's Library Book,* she stands the familiar nursery rhyme on its head and sends Little Bo Peep to the library to look for her sheep. Once there, Mother Goose directs her to books that may help her find her friends. There are three smaller books inserted into the pages of *Little Bo Peep's Library Book* and the cover is even decorated with a library sticker and bar code. "Cowell's winning watercolors sparkle with wit," claimed a *Publishers Weekly* critic, who predicted, "kids will want to keep this one in their own personal libraries." Calling the book "outstanding," a *Books for Keeps* reviewer found that the author/illustrator "plunges the reader into a most convincing nursery rhyme world that is wittily contextualized."

Don't Do That Kitty Kilroy! features a character who may be familiar to young readers—a youngster who does not want to listen to her mother. Kitty Kilroy is tired of being bossed around and tells her mother to leave her alone. Her mother grants the wish and Kilroy embarks on a day filled with junk food, messing up the house, and late-night television. Finally, Kilroy, feeling ill from her over-indulgence of food and freedom, realizes that she needs her mother to help her to bed and end the crazy day. Writing in *Publishers Weekly,* a contributor found that books about "pushing a situation . . . to its logical if ultimately silly conclusion always" appeals to young readers, and the author/illustrator "mines the set-up with brio."

Cowell's 2000 book *What Shall We Do with the Boo-Hoo Baby?* allows young children to participate in the animals sounds and baby's humorous bawling. The cow, dog, cat, and duck are desperate for baby to stop crying, trying everything from feeding him, to bathing him to calm him down. They finally put him to bed and he quiets down, only to wake up just as the animals are collapsing from exhaustion. A *Publishers Weekly* critic noted that this tale for toddlers will "have readers hooting and howling." Several reviewers considered *What Shall We Do with the Boo-Hoo Baby?* excellent selections for story hours, with *School Library Journal* contributor Ann Cook remarking "this title is a joy to read aloud."

In *Hiccup, the Seasick Viking,* originally published in England as *Hiccup, the Viking Who Was Seasick,* Cowell's main character is anything but a strong and fearless Viking. Hiccup is tiny and thoughtful, much to his father's disappointment. His dad, Stoick the Vast, is a huge and brave Viking, who insists that real Vikings do not get scared or sick. In order to prove himself to his father, Hiccup sets sail on the family ship, but immediately gets seasick. The other Vikings laugh at him, until a storm arrives and everyone is sick. Hiccup observes his fellow Vikings dealing with their fears and illness, and it gives him strength. He bravely steers the boat out of the storm and into a safe harbor. Children can learn a valuable lesson in this book where "Cowell gives practical advice about facing fears," remarked a reviewer for *Publishers Weekly.* According to a *Books for Keeps* critic, the author/illustrator's "pictures are full of fun and her text is full of invention and wit."

Hiccup continues his adventures in a second book. Cowell told *CA:* "*How to Train Your Dragon,* is Hiccup's own story, written by him for seven- to ten-year-old readers . . . 'translated' from the Old Norse (and also in parts from Dragonese). . . . This book has been bought by Little, Brown for publication in the United States."

"As a child, I spent my summers on an uninhabited island off the west coast of Scotland. There were no roads or other houses. There was no phone, electricity, or television.

"My parents were very young and they knew no fear. My father drove a turquoise boat, more appropriate to flashing around the Thames than braving the gales of the stormy Hebrides. The fact that he had very little experience on the sea did not stop him from being an exceptionally bossy captain. The Stoick the Vast character in *Hiccup* is based upon fond memories of my father barking out orders as he accidentally ran aground, or attempted to tie the boat to a lobster pot instead of an anchored buoy, or steered us into stormy weather while hopelessly overloaded with children or luggage.

"I have since married a Scot with some good Viking blood in him, and I have two intrepid little girls.

"I try to write books that sound wonderful when read aloud and that both children and adults will enjoy reading."

BIOGRAPHICAL AND CRITICAL SOURCES:

PERIODICALS

Booklist, January 1, 2001, p. 967.
Books for Keeps, May, 1999, review of *Little Bo Peep's Library Book,* p. 22; November, 2001, review of *Hiccup, the Viking Who Was Seasick,* p. 23.
Bulletin of the Center for Children's Books, July, 2000, p. 394; February, 2001, p. 219.
Kirkus Reviews, January 15, 2000, p. 119.
Magpies, July, 2001, p. 28.
Publishers Weekly, July 12, 1999, review of *Little Bo Peep's Library Book,* p. 93; March 6, 2000, review of *Don't Do That, Kitty Kilroy,* p. 110; October 2, 2000, review of *Hiccup, the Seasick Viking,* p. 81; November 6, 2000, review of *What Shall We Do with the Boo-Hoo Baby?,* p. 89.
School Library Journal, March, 2000, pp. 190-192; November, 2000, p. 113; March, 2001, Ann Cook, review of *What Shall We Do with the Boo-Hoo Baby?,* p. 205.
Spectator, December 11, 1999, p. 58; December 9, 2000, p. 48; December 8, 2001, p. 53.

*   *   *

CRAIB, Ian 1945-2002

OBITUARY NOTICE—See index for *CA* sketch: Born December 12, 1945, in Croydon, Surrey, England; died of cancer December 22, 2002, in Cambridge, England. Sociologist, psychotherapist, educator, and author. With his unique background in both sociology and psychotherapy, Craib helped bring these two disciplines together with his theories of the central importance of human interaction. He was a graduate of Borough Polytechnic, London, where he earned his B.A. in 1970, and the University of Manchester, where he received hi Ph.D. in sociology in 1973. In 1985 he became a certified psychotherapist and after completing his Ph.D., Craib joined the faculty at the University of Essex as a lecturer in sociology. He was promoted to reader in 1995 and became a professor in 1997. His interest in his two areas of study led him to help create the first master's degree program in England that combined sociology and psychotherapy. Craib's early work focused on sociology, and included such books as *Sociology and Existentialism: A Study of Jean-Paul Sartre* (1976) and *Modern Social Theory: From Parsons to Habermas* (1984). After he was diagnosed with cancer he wrote *The Importance of Disappointment* (1994) in which he exhorts readers not to avoid anxiety and disappointment but to face it head on. Other works by Craib include *Classical Social Theory* (1997), *Experiencing Identity* (1998), and *Psychoanalysis: A Critical Introduction* (2001).

OBITUARIES AND OTHER SOURCES:

PERIODICALS

Independent (London, England), January 24, 2003, p. 18.
Times (London, England), January 31, 2003.

*   *   *

CRICHTON, Elizabeth G. 1946-

PERSONAL: Born May 16, 1946, in Melbourne, Australia; daughter of Ailsa M. (Blackburn) Crichton. *Ethnicity:* "Caucasian." *Education:* Australian National University, B.Sc. (with honors); University of Queensland, D.Phil.

ADDRESSES: Home—5123 Izard St., Omaha, NE 68132. *Office*—Henry Doorly Zoo, 2701 South Tenth St., Omaha, NE 68107.

CAREER: Omaha Zoological Society, Omaha, NE, research scientist at Center for Conservation and Research, Henry Doorly Zoo, 1997—. Teacher at University of Arizona, University of Hawaii, Pennsylvania State University, and University of Adelaide.

MEMBER: International Embryo Transfer Society, Colorado Bat Society.

AWARDS, HONORS: National Science Foundation grant.

WRITINGS:

(Editor, with P. H. Krutzsch, and contributor) *Biology of Reproduction in Bats,* Academic Press (Orlando, FL), 2000.

Contributor to books, including *A Comparative Overview of Mammalian Fertilization,* edited by B. S. Dunbar and M. O'Rand, Plenum Press (New York, NY), 1991. Contributor to scientific journals and national magazines, including *Australian Science.*

WORK IN PROGRESS: Research on various aspects of assisted reproductive techniques for endangered species.

SIDELIGHTS: Elizabeth G. Crichton told *CA:* "My interest in bats—and their unique and variable (according to species) reproductive biology—led to twenty-five years of research on many different species in Australia and North America. My primary motivation for writing is to share information. *Biology of Reproduction in Bats* was conceived as a productive means of utilizing time during a period of elective unemployment; it was inspired by the passing of Dr. W. A. Wimsatt, a scholar in this field, whose dream it was to write such a volume prior to his untimely death. Dr. Wimsatt was a close friend and collaborator of my coeditor and postdoctoral mentor, Dr. P. H. Krutzsch. We conceived this book to fulfill Dr. Wimsatt's vision and produce the first such text—one that would summarize all the available literature to date and be of value to present and future students in the field of reproductive biology."

*   *   *

CROCKER, Lester G(ilbert) 1912-2002

OBITUARY NOTICE—See index for *CA* sketch: Born April 23, 1912, in New York, NY; died October 12, 2002, in New York, NY. Educator and author. Crocker was a noted scholar of eighteenth-century French literature and Enlightenment philosophy. A graduate of

New York University, where he earned his master's degree in 1934, Crocker received his Ph.D. from the University of California in 1936, as well as earning a Certificat de Literature Française from the University of Paris in 1933. Crocker's first academic position was as an assistant professor of Romance languages at Wittenberg University; during the 1940s he also taught languages at Queens College and Sweet Briar College, jobs that were interrupted by a four-year stint as director of production at Eastern Sound Studios in New York City. The 1950s found Crocker teaching at Goucher College in Baltimore; he then moved to Case Western Reserve University, where he taught and was chair of the department of Romance languages from 1960 to 1963, dean of the graduate school from 1963 to 1967, and dean of humanities from 1967 to 1971. The end of his career was spent at the University of Virginia, where he was Kenan Professor of French from 1971 until his retirement as professor emeritus in 1980. Crocker was also chair of the French department and general linguistics at the University of Virginia from 1971 to 1977. As a scholar, he was well known for his insightful interpretations of the writings of Jean-Jacques Rousseau, Denis Diderot, and the Marquis de Sade, and he was the author of such influential books as *The Embattled Philosopher: A Biography of Denis Diderot* (1954) and the two-volume *Jean-Jacques Rousseau* (1968 and 1973). On French philosophy in general he had a lasting impact in academia with his books *An Age of Crisis: Man and World in Eighteenth-Century French Thought* (1959) and *Nature and Culture: Ethical Thought in the French Enlightenment* (1963). Other books by Crocker include *Rousseau's Social Contract: An Interpretive Essay* (1968) and *Diderot's Chaotic Order: Approach and Synthesis* (1974).

OBITUARIES AND OTHER SOURCES:

PERIODICALS

Times (London, England), November 19, 2002.

* * *

CROOKENDEN, Napier 1915-2002

OBITUARY NOTICE—See index for *CA* sketch: Born August 31, 1915, in Chester, England; died October 31, 2002. Military officer, educator, and author. A hero of World War II, during which he participated in

D-Day and the Battle of the Bulge, Crookenden later became a highly respected teacher and commandant at military schools in England. Coming from a long line of military officers, he attended the Royal Military College for a year before being commissioned into the Cheshire Regiment in 1935. During World War II he saw action in France and, as major of the Sixth Air-landing Brigade, on D-Day in 1943 helped to capture strategic bridges using glider planes. He was then put in command of the Ninth Parachute Battalion, leading his men during the Battle of the Bulge, for which service he was awarded a Distinguished Service Order in 1945. After the war, Crookenden began a distinguished career in military training, first as an instructor at the Staff College and then as general staff officer at the School of Land/Air Warfare before being transferred to Malaya in 1952. From 1960 to 1961 he commanded the 16th Parachute Brigade and in 1962 he became qualified to fly helicopters. In 1967 he was made commandant of the Royal Military College of Science for two years. From there, Crookenden became a colonel of his old Cheshire Regiment in 1969 and then colonel commandant of the Prince of Wales Division from 1971 to 1974; and he was lieutenant of the Tower of London from 1975 to 1981. He also served as chairman of the Sailors, Soldiers, Airmen, and Families Association from 1974 to 1985, deputy lieutenant of Kent in 1979, trustee of the Imperial War Museum from 1973 to 1983, and vice president of the Royal United Services Institute for Defense Studies. Crookenden wrote about his wartime experiences in three books: *Drop Zone Normandy* (1976), *Airborne at War* (1977), and *The Battle of the Bulge* (1979).

OBITUARIES AND OTHER SOURCES:

PERIODICALS

Independent (London, England), November 13, 2002, p. 21.
Times (London, England), November 1, 2002, p. 40.

* * *

CRUMMEY, Michael

PERSONAL: Born in Buchans, Newfoundland, Canada. *Education:* Memorial University, St. John's, Canada, B.A.

ADDRESSES: Home—St. John's, Newfoundland, Canada. *Agent*—c/o Author Mail, Random House of Canada, Ltd., One Toronto St., Unit 300, Toronto, Ontario M5C 2V6, Canada.

CAREER: Poet and writer.

AWARDS, HONORS: Bronwen Wallace Award, 1994; Writers' Alliance of Newfoundland and Labrador Literary Award for Poetry, 1996.

WRITINGS:

Arguments with Gravity, Quarry Press (Kingston, Canada), 1996.
Hard Light, Brick Books (Ontario, Canada), 1998.
Flesh and Blood: Stories, Beach Holme Publishing (Vancouver, Canada), 1998.
River Thieves, Doubleday Canada (Toronto, Canada), 2001.
Salvage, McClelland & Stewart (Toronto, Ontario, Canada), 2002.

SIDELIGHTS: Arguments with Gravity, a collection of poems, established Michael Crummey as a writer worth watching. The first part contains poems centered on his own family and the realities of working class life in Newfoundland. Other sections concern politics, gender issues, and travel, including travel to China. "Flash fires of brilliant lines occur throughout. This young writer has voice," wrote John B. Lee in *Quill & Quire,* though he found the political poems too preachy and bombastic. *Canadian Book Review Annual* contributor James Deahl called it "an impressive debut," particularly the section about his home and father, which "splendidly evokes a world of real work, of cod fishing and hardrock mining."

Crummey's next poetry collection, *Hard Light,* focuses more exclusively on the cod fishers and miners of his hometown. The first section is a series of poetic narratives dealing with the tribulations of small-town life. This was followed by a poetic retelling of a diary written by a Captain John Froude, who sailed the seas in the late nineteenth and early twentieth centuries before retiring to Newfoundland. The last section, "A Map of the Islands," is a series of poems contrasting the permanence of the Newfoundland landscape with the changing lives and cultures of its inhabitants. R.G. Moyles in the *Canadian Book Review Annual* wrote, "Crummey is not only clever in his manipulation of materials; he is a brilliant stylist, never obscure and rarely pedantic." Marnie Parsons in the *University of Toronto Quarterly* noted Crummey's connections between the land, the people, and the fish that are so much a part of both. She wrote, "throughout the book, Crummey suggests the congruity between man and fish—the fish, splayed like a man; the man, heart cut out like a fish. The people in this book are of Newfoundland, the land and the sea, with their many variations and complexities." *Canadian Literature* reviewer Claire Wilkshire concluded, "*Hard Light* marks Crummey's emergence as a poet of distinction."

The same year, Crummey also published *Flesh and Blood,* a collection of linked short stories set, like *Hard Light,* in Newfoundland, more specifically in the small mining town of Black Rock. Torn between magical moments and mundane realities, the miners and housewives of Black Rock often have moments of revelation, but without easy transformations. "In all of Crummey's stories, generosity and understanding are never straightforwardly achieved, and fate is as meaningful as prayer and love in his characters' lives," observed *Canadian Literature* reviewer Danielle Fuller. Many of the stories focus on some kind of exile, and while noting that this provided a unity of design, *Canadian Book Review Annual* contributor R.G. Moyles felt that "the repetition of theme, the insistent negativity, and the lack of variety create a monotony that Crummey avoided entirely in . . . *Hard Light.*" More favorably, *Quill & Quire* reviewer Peter Darbyshire wrote, "Crummey's rich language runs through these stories like a vein of precious metal." For Derbyshire, "The everyday world is transformed here, from a desolate and hard place into a fragile, magical one."

Crummey's next venture was the full-length novel *River Thieves,* this time set in Newfoundland's past and centered around an historical incident. In 1810 a British naval officer, David Buchan, is charged to establish relations with a local tribe, the Beothuks, nicknamed the "Red Indians" for their custom of covering their bodies in red ochre. The expedition ends badly, with an exchange of hostages with the Beothuks, who end up killing their captives, and beheading the corpses. A subsequent expedition, led by one of the area's most prominent citizens, leads to the capture of a Beothuk woman and the murder of her husband. Once again, David Buchan is sent to investigate. "Crummey's craftsmanship is masterful," remarked *Maclean's* reviewer Brian Bethune. "As he seamlessly moves between memories and present events, glossing over horrors from one perspective and pinning them to the wall from another, he juxtaposes the mutual incomprehension of whole peoples with the equally profound misunderstandings among the individual characters."

BIOGRAPHICAL AND CRITICAL SOURCES:

PERIODICALS

Canadian Book Review Annual, 1997, James Deahl, review of *Arguments with Gravity,* p. 224; 1998, R. G. Moyles, review of *Flesh and Blood,* p. 208; 1999, R. G. Moyles, review of *Hard Light,* p. 207.

Canadian Literature, autumn-winter, 2001, Danielle Fuller, "Living in Hopes: Atlantic Realities and Realisms," pp. 199-202; spring, 2001, Claire Wilkshire, "Family History," pp. 130-131.

Maclean's, September 17, 2001, Brian Bethune, "Into the Robbers' Den: A Powerful Debut Mines the Rock's Dark History," p. 46.

Quill & Quire, December, 1996, John. B. Lee, review of *Arguments with Gravity,* p. 33; December, 1998, Peter Darbyshire, review of *Flesh and Blood,* p. 32.

University of Toronto Quarterly, winter, 1999, Marnie Parsons, review of *Hard Light,* pp. 43, 62-67.*

D

DANIELS, Karen 1957-

PERSONAL: Born January 21, 1957, in Long Beach, CA. *Education:* Reed College, B.A. (psychology), 1979.

ADDRESSES: Agent—c/o Author Mail, 2 Neptune Road, Poughkeepsie, NY 12601. *E-mail*—kdauthor@aol.com.

CAREER: Novelist.

MEMBER: International Women's Writing Guild.

WRITINGS:

Dancing Sun (book one of "Zaddack Tales"; science fiction), Vivisphere (Poughkeepsie, NY), 2000.
Mentor's Lair (book two of "Zaddack Tales"; science fiction), Vivisphere (Poughkeepsie, NY), 2000.

WORK IN PROGRESS: Mindspark, book three of "Zaddack Tales."

SIDELIGHTS: Karen Daniels told *CA:* "Though my books are classified as sci-fi, they are really spiritual in nature. I consider my first novels a fusion of sci-fi and the metaphysical. I write because I have to."

BIOGRAPHICAL AND CRITICAL SOURCES:

OTHER

Karen Daniels Web site, http://www.karendaniels.com (April 28, 2000).

DANIELS, Lucy
See OLDFIELD, Jenny

*   *   *

DAY, Nancy 1953-

PERSONAL: Born January 6, 1953, in Newark, NJ; daughter of Robert A. (a writer, editor, and educator) and Betty (a librarian; maiden name, Johnson) Day; married Michael Pohuski (divorced); married Joseph B. Sakaduski (a marketing consultant), August 6, 1982; children: (second marriage) Matthew Philip. *Education:* University of Maryland—Baltimore County, B.A. (communications), 1976; Loyola College (Baltimore, MA), M.B.A., 1982.

ADDRESSES: Home—136 Woodbine Ave., Northport, NY 11768. *E-mail*—nancy@sakaduskimarketing.com.

CAREER: Writer and marketing consultant. BBL Microbiology Systems, Cockeysville, MD, advertising manager, 1976-79; M.A. Bioproducts, Walkersville, MD, director of marketing communications, 1979-81; West Company, Phoenixville, PA, business development manager, 1982-83; CooperBiomedical, Malvern, PA, director of marketing communications, 1983-85; freelance marketing consultant, 1985-2000; Sakaduski Marketing Solutions, Northport, NY, president, 2000—.

AWARDS, HONORS: Society of Children's Book Writers and Illustrators Award for Nonfiction, 1995, for article "Mapping the Mind"; Best Social Studies Book of the Year designation, Society of School Librarians International.

WRITINGS:

The Horseshoe Crab, Dillon Press (New York, NY), 1992.

Animal Experimentation: Cruelty or Science? Enslow Publishers (Hillside, NJ), 1994, revised edition, 2000.

Abortion: Debating the Issue, Enslow Publishers (Hillside, NJ), 1995.

Sensational TV: Trash or Journalism? Enslow Publishers (Hillside, NJ), 1996.

Violence in Schools: Learning in Fear, Enslow Publishers (Hillside, NJ), 1996.

Advertising: Information or Manipulation? Enslow Publishers (Hillside, NJ), 1999.

The Death Penalty for Teens: A Pro/Con Issue, Enslow Publishers (Berkeley Heights, NJ), 2000.

Killer Superbugs: The Story of Drug-resistant Diseases, Enslow Publishers (Berkeley Heights, NJ), 2001.

Malaria, West Nile, and Other Mosquito-borne Diseases, Enslow Publishers (Berkeley Heights, NJ), 2001.

Censorship, or Freedom of Expression? Enslow Publishers (Berkeley Heights, NJ), 2001.

Contributor to periodicals, including *Odyssey, Cobblestone,* and *Highlights for Children.* Author of business booklets, articles, and other publications.

"PASSPORT TO HISTORY" SERIES

Your Travel Guide to Renaissance Europe, Runestone Press (Minneapolis, MN), 2001.

Your Travel Guide to Colonial America, Runestone Press (Minneapolis, MN), 2001.

Your Travel Guide to Ancient Greece, Runestone Press (Minneapolis, MN), 2001.

Your Travel Guide to Civil War America, Runestone Press (Minneapolis, MN), 2001.

Your Travel Guide to Ancient Maya Civilization, Runestone Press (Minneapolis, MN), 2001.

Your Travel Guide to Ancient Egypt, Runestone Press (Minneapolis, MN), 2001.

ADAPTATIONS: Animal Experimentation: Cruelty or Science? was recorded by American Printing House for the Blind, 1997.

SIDELIGHTS: Nancy Day has written a number of nonfiction titles focusing on topics of current interest, many of which involve individual ethical positions. Addressing the controversy surrounding abortion in *Abortion: Debating the Issue,* Day tackles the use of the death penalty in cases where juveniles commit particularly brutal crimes in *The Death Penalty for Teens: A Pro/Con Issue.* Her *Animal Experimentation: Cruelty or Science?* broaches a topic close to the hearts of animal welfare activists who object to the practice of testing drugs and medical procedures on laboratory animals in advance of humans. *Booklist* contributor Anne O'Malley praised *Abortion* as a "brisk, well-researched, well-organized, and very well balanced presentation" of the highly emotional issue, while in *Science Books and Films,* reviewer William G. Wisecup commended *Animal Experimentation* for dealing with "a highly emotional and controversial" topic "carefully, and objectively." Reviewing the same work in *Booklist,* O'Malley noted that Day "offers a wealth of information both pro and con," including the purpose of experimentation, alternatives to such experimentation, and the medical advances that have been made possible by this practice.

First Amendment rights are investigated in *Censorship, or Freedom of Expression?,* while the outgrowth of such freedom is the subject of both *Sensational TV: Trash or Journalism?* and *Advertising: Information or Manipulation?* In *Censorship, or Freedom of Expression?* Day begins with a history of censorship extending back to ancient times, then focuses on U.S. court cases that have helped define modern free speech. Praising the book for presenting both sides of the issue, *Voice of Youth Advocates* contributor Vicky Yablonsky noted that Day "provides up-to-date examples that relate directly to young adult concerns in her basic introduction to a very complex and sensitive issue." Critical thinking skills are encouraged in both *Sensational TV* and *Advertising,* as readers are presented with the techniques used by both the media and advertisers to inform the public in order to sway opinion or provoke a desired reaction. Calling Day's approach "fresh and thought-provoking," *Voice of Youth Advocates* reviewer Debbie Earl praised the last chapter of *Sensational TV* for including "clear suggestions to help [teens] . . . become more critical [television] viewers." Similarly, in a review for *School Library Journal*, Jennifer Ralston maintained that *Advertising* would help "young people . . . look at advertising and how the media influenced their decisions in a whole new light."

In her "Passport to History" series for Runestone, Day lets modern-day history buffs take a trip into the past in books designed to present everyday life in a variety of cultures and historical epochs. In *Your Travel Guide to Ancient Greece,* readers learn about climate, currency, where to shop, where to stay, and what tourist sites to see in fifth-century-B.C. Greece, all in an up-close-and-personal approach that even includes quotes from Euripides. *School Library Journal* contributor Cynthia M. Sturgis remarked favorably on the author's inclusion of "a short who's who . . . and some simple activities [that] wrap up this clever, readable volume," while *Booklist* Susan Dove Lempke commended Day for her "delightfully informative tone as she tells young time travelers what they might expect on a trip to ancient Greece." *Your Travel Guide to Ancient Egypt* is highlighted by maps of the Nile and northern Egypt, photographs, and sidebars explaining everything from how the Pharaohs' paper was made to the way goods and services were priced. Similarly, in *Your Travel Guide to Ancient Maya Civilization,* Day provides "fascinating tidbits" of information on many aspects of Mayan culture during the period 600-800 A.D., according to *School Library Journal* reviewer Lana Miles.

BIOGRAPHICAL AND CRITICAL SOURCES:

PERIODICALS

Appraisal, spring-summer, 1993, Edward J. Zielinski, review of *The Horseshoe Crab,* pp. 109-110.

Booklist, November 1, 1994, Anne O'Malley, review of *Animal Experimentation: Cruelty or Science?,* p. 488; August, 1995, Anne O'Malley, review of *Abortion: Debating the Issue,* p. 1937; April 1, 1996, Ilene Cooper, review of *Sensationalist TV: Trash or Journalism?,* p. 1351; June 1, 1996, Anne O'Malley, review of *Violence in Schools: Learning in Fear,* p. 1688; July, 1999, Shelle Rosenfeld, review of *Advertising: Information or Manipulation?,* p. 1942; October 15, 2000, Susan Dove Lempke, review of *Your Travel Guide to Ancient Greece,* p. 458; February 15, 2001, Roger Leslie, review of *The Death Penalty for Teens: A Pro/Con Issue,* p. 1126.

Book Report, March-April, 1995, Pat Royal, review of *Animal Experimentation,* p. 57; January-February, 1996, Margaret Zinz Jantzen, review of *Abortion,* p. 53.

Bulletin of the Center for Children's Books, June, 1996, review of *Violence in Schools,* pp. 329-330.

Choice, September, 1995.

Civil War Times, June, 2001, Brenda Wilt, "A Wartime Guide for Kids," p. 10.

Kirkus Reviews, July 15, 1994, review of *Animal Experimentation,* p. 981.

School Library Journal, March, 1993, Helen Rosenberg, review of *The Horseshoe Crab,* p. 206; April, 1995, Patricia Manning, review of *Animal Experimentation,* p. 160; December, 1995, Claudia Morrow, review of *Abortion,* p. 134; April, 1996, Joan Soulliere, review of *Sensational TV,* p. 161; July, 1996, Carol Fazioli, review of *Violence in Schools,* p. 101; December, 1999, Jennifer Ralston, review of *Advertising,* pp. 147-148; January, 2001, Cynthia M. Sturgis, review of *Animal Experimentation,* p. 142; January, 2001, and Marilyn Fairbanks, review of *Censorship, or Freedom of Expression?,* p. 143; February, 2001, Cynthia M. Sturgis, review of *Your Travel Guide to Ancient Greece,* pp. 130-131; April, 2001, Lana Miles, review of the "Passport to History" series, pp. 157-158; April, 2001, Mary R. Hofmann, review of *The Death Penalty for Teens,* p. 157; May, 2001, Carol Duruseau, review of *Your Travel Guide to Ancient Egypt,* p. 162; January, 2002, Karey Wehner, review of *Killer Superbugs: The Story of Drug-resistant Diseases,* p. 151.

Science Books and Films, May, 1993, Beatrice L. Burch, review of *The Horseshoe Crab,* p. 109; March, 1995, William G. Wisecup, review of *Animal Experimentation,* p. 41.

Voice of Youth Advocates, October, 1995, Barbara J. Walker, review of *Abortion,* p. 244; June, 1996, Debbie Earl, review of *Sensational TV,* pp. 115-116; April, 2001, Vicky Yablonsky, review of *Censorship, or Freedom of Expression?,* pp. 62-63; June, 2001, Pam Carlson, review of *The Death Penalty for Teens,* p. 139.

*   *   *

DENSLOW, W(illiam) W(allace) 1856-1915

PERSONAL: Born May 5, 1856, in Philadelphia, PA; died from pneumonia, March 29, 1915; son of William (a botanist) and Jane Eva Denslow; married Annie McCartney, 1882 (divorced); married Anne Waters

Holden, 1896 (divorced 1903); married Frances Golsen Doolittle, 1903 (divorced c. 1909). *Education:* Attended Cooper Union Institute, 1870-71, and National Academy of Design, 1872-73.

CAREER: Illustrator, cartoonist, poet, re-teller of children's stories, playwright, and designer of posters, costumes, and scenery. Rand, McNally & Co., designer, 1896-98; Roycrofters, East Aurora, NY, designer, 1898; Niagara Lithograph Company, 1909; Rosenbaum Studios, 1913.

WRITINGS:

Denslow's Picture Books for Children: Humpty Dumpty, Little Red Riding-Hood, Three Bears, Mary Had a Little Lamb, Old Mother Hubbard, House That Jack Built, One Ring Circus, Zoo, Five Little Pigs, Tom Thumb, ABC Book, and Jack and the Bean-Stalk, G. W. Dillingham (New York, NY), 1903, republished in two volumes as *Denslow's Humpty Dumpty and Other Stories* and *Denslow's One Ring Circus and Other Stories,* G. W. Dillingham (New York, NY), 1903.

Denslow's New Series of Picture Books: Scarecrow and the Tin-Man, Simple Simon, Animal Fair, Barn-Yard Circus, Mother Goose ABC Book, and Three Little Kittens, G. W. Dillingham (New York, NY), 1904, republished in one volume as *Denslow's Scarecrow and the Tin-Man and Other Stories,* G. W. Dillingham (New York, NY), 1904.

(With Paul West) *The Pearl and the Pumpkin,* G. W. Dillingham (New York, NY), 1904.

(With Dudley A. Bragdon) *Billy Bounce,* G. W. Dillingham (New York, NY), 1906.

When I Grow Up, Century (New York, NY), 1909.

ILLUSTRATOR

I. H. M'Cauley, *Historical Sketch of Franklin County, Pennsylvania,* D. F. Pursel (Chambersburg, PA), 1878.

John F. Cowan, *A New Invasion of the South,* Board of Officers, Seventy-first Infantry (New York, NY), 1881.

J. P. Johnston, *Twenty Years of Husling,* Hallet (Chicago, IL), 1888.

P. T. Barnum, *Dollars and Sense; or, How to Get On,* People's Publishing (Chicago, IL), 1890.

Opie Read, *A Tennessee Judge,* Laird & Lee (Chicago, IL), 1893.

Le Roy Armstrong, *Byrd Flam in Town,* Bearhope (Chicago, IL), 1894.

Opie Read, *An Arkansas Planter,* Rand, McNally (Chicago, Il), 1896.

Will Phillip Hooper, *An Untold Tale,* Home (New York, NY), 1897.

Charles Warren Stoddard, *A Cruise under the Crescent,* Rand, McNally (Chicago, IL), 1898.

Samuel Taylor Coleridge, *Ye Ancient Mariner,* Roycrofters (East Aurora, NY), 1899.

Edward Fitzgerald, *Rubaiyat of Omar Khayyam,* Roycrofters (East Aurora, NY), 1899.

Frank L. Baum, *Father Goose: His Book,* G. M. Hill (Chicago, IL), 1899.

Frank L. Baum, *The Songs of Father Goose,* G. M. Hill (Chicago, IL), 1900.

Frank L. Baum, *The Wonderful Wizard of Oz,* G. M. Hill (Chicago, IL), 1900.

Frank L. Baum, *Dot and Tot of Merryland,* G. M. Hill (Chicago, IL), 1900.

Denslow's Mother Goose, McClure, Phillips (New York, NY), 1901.

Clement C. Moore, *Denslow's Night before Christmas,* G. W. Dillingham (New York, NY), 1902.

Richard Webb, *Me and Lawson,* G.W. Dillingham (New York, NY), 1905.

Isabel M. Johnston, *The Jeweled Toad,* Bobbs-Merrill (Indianapolis, IN), 1907.

Also contributor of illustrations to periodicals, including *Hearth and Home, St. Nicholas, American Agriculturalist, Theatre, Californian Illustrated Magazine, Philistine, Bill Poster, Fra,* and *John Martin's Book.*

SIDELIGHTS: Best known as the illustrator of L. Frank Baum's *The Wonderful Wizard of Oz,* W. W. Denslow was scarcely recognized for his achievements until the late twentieth century. Denslow, nicknamed "Hippocampus Den" because of his sketch of a seahorse along side his signature "Den" that accompanied most of his work, struggled with alcoholism, financial difficulties, and failed marriages. He was especially praised for his clever and often cynical designs, his striking, multicolored posters, his ability to target his illustrations by audience, and for amending popular children's verse to avoid what he considered unnecessary violence and questionable content.

Denslow began his formal training in design and illustration at age fourteen, attending the Cooper Union Institute and the National Academy of Design, both in

New York City. He began selling some of his work at about age twenty, and lived an independent, often bohemian existence, traveling around the country to sell his craft. Denslow is quoted as saying in Douglas Greene and Michael P. Hearn's *W. W. Denslow* in 1894: "I float, as it were, with the steam, enjoying life as I float. I *do* have a good time and no mistake, besides that I work very hard, being at it night and day. . . . Of course, I should like to do something better, but a big salary and solid comfort make one hesitate to lean to something else."

"Color, fun and action," according to J. M. Bowles in *Brush and Pencil,* were Denslow's buzzwords, particularly when color became more readily available at the turn of the twentieth century. He worked for newspapers and periodicals, and his work was noted for its "clean, sharp lines." Even so, he yearned for an opportunity to design books. Denslow designed theatrical costumes and posters in Chicago, earning international acclaim. After living in Denver and San Francisco, Denslow returned to New York and secured a job with Elbert Hubbard's Roycroft studio. Hubbard, a writer and editor, is noted for launching the handicraft movement in America, and Denslow was paid fifty dollars per week to design Roycroft advertising and literature. Denslow was socially active wherever he lived and in 1986 met L. Frank Baum, who at the time barely made a living selling crockery and needed a creative outlet. They began talking about publishing a children's book and collaborated on *Father Goose, His Book.*

A year later, they published *The Wonderful Wizard of Oz,* which soon became an American icon and children's literary breakthrough. Prosperity and critical acclaim greeted the book. Douglas G. Greene wrote in *Dictionary of Literary Biography,* "The final product integrated text and illustration as no earlier American children's book had done. Denslow's more than one hundred illustrations often cut into the words, and sometimes they were even printed over the type. The full-color plates seem flooded with light, and the entire effect is garish and otherworldly—a perfect fairy-tale world." Michael Patrick Hearn, in *American Artist,* hailed its technical virtues, explaining that "not only [was it] one of the earliest extensive uses of color in an American children's book, but [it was also] Denslow's first assignment in full color." According to Greene and Hearn, "An Illinois paper noted that Baum possessed a 'quaint philosophy that fits like a glove to the skilled hand of Denslow. These two artists work together with marvelous felicity and the productions of their meditations are destined to have a permanent place in the child's literature of the world.'"

They only collaborated on one more book, *Dot and Tot of Merryland,* considered Denslow's most purely decorative creation. Some people attribute the bitter separation of the men to Denslow's greed, especially when financial disputes arose after *The Wonderful World of Oz* was transformed into "an immensely popular musical extravaganza." The men disagreed over who owned production rights, Baum later saying: "Denslow was allowed to copyright his pictures conjointly with my claim to authorship . . . and, having learned my lesson from my unfortunate experiences with Denslow, I will never permit another artist to have an interest in the drawings he makes of my described characters, if I can help it."

Denslow then claimed the right to illustrate, rewrite and thus reinterpret some of the most long-standing children's works of the time. The first two he titled *Denslow's Mother Goose* and *Denslow's Night before Christmas.* Never had an artist or writer put his or her name in front of these children's classics. Although this could have damaged his reputation, his changes were perceived as justified. Denslow took issue with many children's works featuring violence, blatant insinuations of abuse and immoral behavior. For example, whereas the original "Old Woman Who Lived in a Shoe" beat her children soundly before putting them to bed, Denslow had her kiss them instead. In *Little Red Riding Hood,* the previously vicious Big Bad Wolf became domesticated, and Grandma lived to see another day. Greene and Hearne quoted Denslow: "I don't always adhere to the text of the familiar nursery rhymes. I believe in pure fun for the children, and I believe it can be given them without any incidental gruesomeness. In my *Mother Goose* I did not hesitate to change the text where the change would give a gentler and clearer tone to the verse. The comic element isn't lost in this way. . . . So when I illustrate and edit childhood classics I don't hesitate to expurgate. I'd rather please the kids than any other audience in the world."

Still, Denslow took his work very seriously. He studied animals and human figures extensively. He became proficient in anatomical design and function, and paid special attention to human and animal faces. Denslow also scrutinized details of the appearance in individual figures, and their arrangement in books and other publications. He supervised the layout and production of his work. In creating the Scarecrow and the Tin Woodman in *The Wonderful World of Oz,* Denslow told an interviewer, as quoted by Greene and Hearn: "I made twenty-five sketches of those two monkeys before I was satisfied with them. You may well believe that there was a great deal of evolution before I got that golf ball in the Scarecrow's ear or the funnel on the Tim Man's head. I experimented and tried all sorts of straw waist-coats and sheet-iron cravats before I was satisfied."

Denslow never reclaimed his early success. His career went mostly downhill after 1905, and he resumed heavy drinking. Denslow, however, did enjoy sporadic prosperity, purchasing an entire island in the Bahamas, which he jokingly referred to as his "sovereign kingdom." The renowned Mark Twain, receiving a copy of *Father Goose* from Denslow's second wife, recognized the start of a new era in children's literature. According to Greene and Hearn, Twain said he would "usurp ambassadorial powers [to thank Baum and Denslow] in the name of the child world for making it. . . . Father Goose has a double chance to succeed: parents will buy him ostensibly for the nursery so that they may privately smuggle him out and enjoy him themselves."

BIOGRAPHICAL AND CRITICAL SOURCES:

BOOKS

Bader, Barbara, *American Picturebooks from Noah's Ark to the Beast Within,* Macmillan (New York, NY), 1976, pp. 2-12.
Children's Literature Review, Volume 15, Gale (Detroit, MI), 1988.
Dictionary of Literary Biography, Volume 188: *American Book and Magazine Illustrators,* Gale (Detroit, MI), 1998.
Greene, Douglas G., and Michael Patrick Hearn, *W. W. Denslow,* Clarke Historical Library (Mount Pleasant, MI), 1976.
Greene, David L., and Dick Martin, *The Oz Scrapbook,* Random House (New York, NY), 1977.
Meyer, Fred M., *The Best of the Baum Bugle,* International Wizard of Oz Club, 1975.

PERIODICALS

American Artist, May, 1973, Michael Patrick Hearn, "W. W. Denslow: The Forgotten Illustrator," pp. 40-45, 71-73.

Brush and Pencil, September, 1903, J. M. Bowles, "Children's Books for Children," pp. 377-387.
Detroit News, September 13, 1903, "A Lover of Children Who Knows How to Make Them Laugh," p. 3.
Journal of Popular Culture, Douglas G. Greene, "W. W. Denslow, Illustrator," pp. 86-96.
New York Times, summer, 1973, December 22, 1906, p. 11.
New York Times Book Review, September 8, 1900, "A New Book for Children," p. 605.*

*   *   *

DOBSON, Jill 1969-

PERSONAL: Born 1969, in Yorkshire, England. *Education:* Melbourne University, B.A. (history, with honors), 1994, B.Litt. (Japanese), 1995; Australian National University, M.A. (international relations), 1996; study at a provincial Japanese university.

ADDRESSES: Agent—c/o Author Mail, University of Queensland Press, P.O. Box 42, St. Lucia, Queensland, Australia, 4067; Sam Boyce, Sheiland Associates Ltd., 43 Daughty St., London WC1N 2LF, England.

CAREER: Author and editor. Worked variously as a vegetarian caterer, kibbutz farmer, volunteer archaeologist, English teacher in Japan and Russia, copyeditor for *The Moscow Times,* and Australian Department of Defence employee.

MEMBER: Australian Society of Authors, United Kingdom Society of Authors.

WRITINGS:

YOUNG ADULT FICTION

The Inheritors, University of Queensland Press (St. Lucia, Australia), 1988.
Time to Go, University of Queensland Press (St. Lucia, Australia), 1991.
A Journey to Distant Mountains, University of Queensland Press (St. Lucia, Australia), 2001.

WORK IN PROGRESS: Two more novels to complete the trilogy begun by *A Journey to Distant Mountains;* an adult novel.

SIDELIGHTS: Despite her life of travel and adventure, Jill Dobson has had one constant—her writing. She was born in Yorkshire, England, and moved to Australia at age five. While growing up in Albury, she was restless and expressed herself in writing, as she recalled to *CA:* "I started writing very young, not long after I started to read. I can't remember ever making a decision to 'be a writer'; it was simply what I did." Inspired by George Orwell's cautionary novel *1984,* Dobson wrote *The Inheritors* when she was sixteen years old. "At that time," the author recalled, "The University of Queensland Press was starting up its young adult fiction list and were trawling for new Australian writers." Dobson's *The Inheritors* rolled off the university's presses in 1988.

While studying history at the University of Melbourne, Dobson wrote her second novel, *Time to Go.* "It is my most autobiographical novel so far," she told *CA,* "based on my experience of being an ambitious, idealistic teenager desperate to leave country town life behind." To satisfy her wanderlust, Dobson went to Japan, where she taught English before studying at a provincial Japanese university. Upon returning to Australia, she earned a second bachelor's degree, this time in Japanese literature, and then a year later, achieved a masters degree in international relations. Dobson worked several years for the Australian Department of Defence, but she discovered that public service was not a good fit for her. Her need to write nagged at her.

Although Dobson had written the first draft of *A Journey to Distant Mountains* while in her early teens, she had "put it aside to concentrate on something more 'serious' than fantasy," she told *CA.* "The idea never left me alone, however, and I knew I'd eventually come back to it." Come back to it she did, and in 2001 *A Journey to Distant Mountains* appeared. In this first novel of a proposed trilogy, young Princess Atlanta of Eddala escapes an arranged marriage by running away to the Distant Mountains with a motley crew of strangers. For her part, Dobson commented, "Not surprisingly, travel and the redefinition of the self in foreign landscapes is a major theme in my work. A reviewer described *Journey* as 'a novel of destiny and embracing one's true nature,' which describes exactly what I was aiming for."

BIOGRAPHICAL AND CRITICAL SOURCES:

PERIODICALS

School Library Journal, October, 2002, Alison Ching, review of *A Journey to Distant Mountains,* p. 161.

*　　*　　*

DOHERTY, P(aul) C. 1946-
(Anna Apostolou, Michael Clynes, Ann Dukthas, C. L. Grace, Paul Harding)

PERSONAL: Born September 21, 1946, in Middlesborough, England; son of Michael and Catherine (Clynes) Doherty; married Carla L. Corbett, April 6, 1973; children: Hugh, Nigel, Vanessa, Alexandra, Michael, Mark, Paul. *Ethnicity:* British. *Education:* Attended Liverpool University, 1968-71; Exeter College, Oxford, B.A. (first class honors), D.Phil., Ph.D., 1977. *Religion:* Roman Catholic. *Hobbies and other interests:* Writing, local history.

ADDRESSES: Home—Trinity, 14 Mornington Rd., Woodford Green, Essex IG8 0TP, England.

CAREER: School headmaster in England, 1981—; writer, 1985—.

MEMBER: Royal College of Arts (fellow), National Association of Headteachers, Royal Overseas Club, London Library, Pall Mall (London).

AWARDS, HONORS: Herodotus Award, Historical Mystery Appreciation Society, 1999, for lifetime achievement.

WRITINGS:

"HUGH CORBETT" NOVELS

Satan in St. Mary's, St. Martin's (New York, NY), 1987.
The Crown in Darkness, St. Martin's (New York, NY), 1988.

Spy in Chancery, St. Martin's (New York, NY), 1988.

The Angel of Death, St. Martin's (New York, NY), 1990.

The Prince of Darkness, St. Martin's (New York, NY), 1993.

The Assassin in the Greenwood, Headline (London, England), 1993, St. Martin's (New York, NY), 1994.

Murder Wears a Cowl, St. Martin's (New York, NY), 1994.

The Song of a Dark Angel, St. Martin's (New York, NY), 1995.

Satan's Fire, St. Martin's (New York, NY), 1996.

The Devil's Hunt, Headline (London, England), 1996, St. Martin's (New York, NY), 1998.

The Treason of the Ghosts, Headline (London, England), 2000.

The Demon Archer, St. Martin's (New York, NY), 2001.

Corpse Candle, Headline (London, England), 2001, St. Martin's (New York, NY), 2002.

"CANTERBURY TALES/NICHOLAS CHIRKE" NOVELS

An Ancient Evil, Being the Knight's Tale, Headline (London, England), 1994, St. Martin's (New York, NY), 1995.

A Tapestry of Murders, Being the Man of Law's Tale, St. Martin's (New York, NY), 1996.

A Tournament of Murders, Being the Franklin's Tale, St. Martin's (New York, NY), 1997.

Ghostly Murders, Being the Priest's Tale, St. Martin's (New York, NY), 1998.

A Haunt of Murder, Headline (London, England), 2003.

"BROTHER ATHELSTAN" NOVELS

(Under pseudonym Paul Harding) *The Nightingale Gallery,* Headline (London, England), 1991, Morrow (New York, NY), 1992.

(Under pseudonym Paul Harding) *The House of the Red Slayer,* Headline (London, England), 1992, published as *Red Slayer,* Morrow (New York, NY), 1994.

(Under pseudonym Paul Harding) *Murder Most Holy,* Headline (London, England), 1993.

(Under pseudonym Paul Harding) *Anger of God,* Headline (London, England), 1993.

(Under pseudonym Paul Harding) *By Murder's Bright Light,* Headline (London, England), 1994.

(Under pseudonym Paul Harding) *House of Crows,* Headline (London, England), 1995.

(Under pseudonym Paul Harding) *Assassin's Riddle,* Headline (London, England), 1996.

The Devil's Domain, Headline (London, England), 1998.

The Field of Blood, Headline (London, England), 1999.

"EGYPTIAN" NOVELS

The Mask of Ra, St. Martin's (New York, NY), 1999.

The Horus Killing, St. Martin's (New York, NY), 2000.

The Anubis Slayings, St. Martin's (New York, NY), 2001.

The Slayers of Seth, St. Martin's (New York, NY), 2002.

UNDER PSEUDONYM MICHAEL CLYNES; "SIR ROGER SHALLOT" NOVELS

The White Rose Murders, Headline (London, England), 1991, St. Martin's (New York, NY), 1993.

The Poisoned Chalice, Headline (London, England), 1992, O. Penzler (New York, NY), 1994.

The Grail Murders, O. Penzler (New York, NY), 1993.

A Brood of Vipers, Headline (London, England), 1994, St. Martin's (New York, NY), 1996.

The Gallows Murders, St. Martin's Press (New York, NY), 1996.

The Relic Murders, Headline (London, England), 1997.

UNDER PSEUDONYM ANN DUKTHAS; "NICHOLAS SEGALLA" NOVELS

A Time for the Death of a King, St. Martin's (New York, NY), 1994.

The Prince Lost to Time, St. Martin's (New York, NY), 1995.

The Time of Murder at Mayerling, St. Martin's (New York, NY), 1996.

In the Time of the Poisoned Queen, St. Martin's (New York, NY), 1998.

UNDER PSEUDONYM C. L. GRACE; "KATHRYN SWINBROOKE" NOVELS

A Shrine of Murders, St. Martin's (New York, NY), 1993.

The Eye of God, St. Martin's (New York, NY), 1994.

The Merchant of Death, St. Martin's (New York, NY), 1995.

The Book of Shadows, St. Martin's (New York, NY), 1996.

Saintly Murders, St. Martin's (New York, NY), 2001.

A Maze of Murders, St. Martin's (New York, NY), 2003.

"ALEXANDER OF MACEDON" NOVELS

The House of Death, Carroll & Graf (New York, NY), 2001.

The Godless Man, Carroll & Graf (New York, NY), 2002.

The Gates of Hell, Carroll & Graf (New York, NY), 2003.

OTHER

The Death of a King, St. Martin's (New York, NY), 1985.

The Masked Man, St. Martin's (New York, NY), 1991.

King Arthur (juvenile biography), Chelsea House (New York, NY), 1987.

The Whyte Harte, St. Martin's (New York, NY), 1988.

The Fate of Princes, Hale (London, England), 1990, St. Martin's (New York, NY), 1991.

The Serpent among the Lilies, St. Martin's (New York, NY), 1990.

The Rose Demon, Headline (London, England), 1997.

(Under pseudonym Anna Apostolou) *Murder in Macedon,* St. Martin's (New York, NY), 1997.

(Under pseudonym Anna Apostolou) *A Murder in Thebes,* St. Martin's (New York, NY), 1998.

The Haunting, Headline (London, England), 1998.

The Soul Slayer, Headline (London, England), 1998.

Isabella and Edward (nonfiction), Carroll & Graf (New York, NY), 2002.

The Mysterious Death of Tutankhamun (nonfiction), Carroll & Graf (New York, NY), 2002.

ADAPTATIONS: Many of Doherty's novels are available as sound recordings. The film rights to the "Canterbury Tales" series have been optioned.

WORK IN PROGRESS: A novel on Pharaoh Akhenaten.

SIDELIGHTS: Prolific mystery writer P. C. Doherty began his authorial career as a historian, focusing on the early years of the English monarchy. His Ph.D. dissertation, about the time of Edward II and Queen Isabella, launched him into a series of over forty-seven historical novels, many set in England, but some set in Scotland, Austria, France, Egypt, and Greece. Doherty has used a variety of pseudonyms and has created a cast of recurring characters that account for several different series of mysteries, each distinguished by a strong sense of place and time.

Doherty's first novel, *The Death of a King,* explores political intrigue in the reigns of Edward II and III through the eyes of Edward III's clerk, Edmund Beche. Beche has been commissioned to investigate the murder of Edward II, under the guise of researching a history of the king, and the adultery and sinister plots he uncovers place him in mortal danger. Readers of *The Death of a King* considered Doherty's debut a ringing success. A *Publishers Weekly* reviewer called the book "nothing less than a tour de force," remarking on the thorough research and beautiful writing. In addition, as Connie Fletcher observed in *Booklist,* Doherty suggests a "convincing solution" to the real-life mystery of the death of Edward II.

Doherty has taken on other historical intrigues in later novels. *The Whyte Harte* follows narrator Matthew Jankyn through his deceit and betrayals in support of Richard II, who has been replaced by Henry the Fourth. The novel *The Fate of Princes* attempts to offer another interpretation of the mystery of the young children of King Edward IV, often supposed to be executed by command of Richard III. Doherty has also explored French history, first in the novel *Serpent amongst the Lilies,* which has Jankyn investigating the phenomenon of Joan of Arc, and in the novel *The Masked Man,* about the identity of the Bastille's famous Man in the Iron Mask. In some instances critics found the works a bit too historically driven—the Chicago *Tribune Books*'s Kevin Moore said that the climax of *Serpent amongst the Lilies* "is revealed with all the panache of a master's thesis in Middle French." Often, however, critics appreciated the atmosphere and accuracy of Doherty's historical mysteries. A reviewer for *Publishers Weekly* called *The Whyte Harte* "riveting" and "vivid," and *Booklist* contributor Margaret Flanagan said *The Masked Man* iss a "tautly woven thriller" and another "tour de force" for Doherty.

One of Doherty's most successful literary creations has been Hugh Corbett, a clerk to Edward I and

Keeper of the Secret Seal. Corbett first appears in *Satan in St. Mary's,* charged with investigating an apparent suicide thought to be a murder; his investigation eventually encounters a Satanist cult and the threat of treason. In further volumes in the series, Corbett goes to Scotland to investigate the death of Scots King Alexander III (*The Crown in Darkness*), to France to discover an informant for Philip IV (*Spy in Chancery*), and all over England to solve murders in a nunnery (*The Prince of Darkness*), the bog lands of Norfolk (*The Song of a Dark Angel*), and in Oxford (*The Devil's Hunt*). Corbett's faithful sidekick, and the novels' comic relief, is the former felon Ranfulf-atte-Newgate; later novels also include Corbett's wife, Maeve. The plotting of the novels is complex, sometimes too complex, according to some reviewers. A *Kirkus Reviews* critic said of *The Devil's Hunt* that the Hugh Corbett series "grows denser and more convoluted with every episode." But a *Publishers Weekly* writer said of the same novel that although the plot develops slowly, readers' "attention to the complex plot will be amply rewarded." Reviewing the next Corbett novel, *The Demon Archer,* another *Publishers Weekly* writer began by calling the book "another masterful English medieval tale" from "the prolific Doherty."

Other detective series created by Doherty include the mysteries of Brother Athelstan, a Dominican friar and a secretary to the king's coroner; the journals of Sir Roger Shallot, investigator for Cardinal Wolsey and King Henry VII (written as Michael Clynes); the Nicholas Segalla series, about a time-traveler who appears throughout Europe in the sixteenth and nineteenth centuries (written as Ann Dukthas); and the tales of Kathryn Swinbrokke, a fifteenth-century Canterbury physician (written as C. L. Grace). In 1994, Doherty also launched a series of mysteries based on Chaucer's *Canterbury Tales,* beginning with *An Ancient Evil: Being the Knight's Tale.* Chaucer's tales are told by day, but Doherty's tales are told by night, the ideal setting for the grim and often ghostly stories of murder, treason, and the supernatural. The knight volunteers to tell the group of pilgrims traveling to Canterbury a story about a murder in Oxford involving devil-worshipper and a female exorcist. Unlike Doherty's other series, the framework of the Canterbury series allows the other pilgrims to comment on the story as it develops, a technique that *School Library Journal* contributor Judy Sokoll said created "good balance, pace, and momentum." Later books in the series feature the Man of Laws (*A Tapestry of Murders*), the Franklin (*A Tournament of Murders*), the Priest (*Ghostly Murders*), and the clerk of Oxford (*A Haunt of Murder*).

In the late 1990s, Doherty branched out beyond England and western Europe. As Anna Apostolou, he wrote *A Murder in Macedonia* and *A Murder in Thebes,* focusing on the historical characters of Phillip II and his son Alexander the Great. He has since begun another series, under his own name, focusing solely on the world of Alexander. In 1999, Doherty introduced a series of books set in ancient Egypt, starting with *The Mask of Ra.* Margaret Flanagan, reviewing the novel for *Booklist,* noted the author's "meticulous" attention to historical details and called the book an "intelligently crafted thriller." The mystery of *The Mask of Ra,* the unexpected death of the Pharaoh Tuthmosis II, is solved by chief judge Amerotke, who reappears in *The Horus Killing* in the court of Tuthmosis II's widow, Hatshepsut. The queen is trying to become the pharaoh, but the priests who support her are slain in succession, and Amerotke is again charged with the task of solving the crime. As in *The Mask of Ra,* Doherty's strength in this historical mystery is in the marriage of "rich period detail and vivid storytelling," according to a *Publishers Weekly* reviewer. Hatshepsut and Amerotke are revived again in *The Anubis Slayings,* as a string of murders threaten the peace that Hatusu (the short form of Hatshepsut) has brought to Egypt. Reviewing the book for the *BookBrowser* Web site, Harriet Klausner wrote that Doherty made "the glory of Ancient Egypt come alive again." The critic concluded: "P. C. Doherty is a wonderful storyteller whose historical mysteries include the awesome Anubis series and crafty Corbett medieval tales, among others, [that] are all worth reading."

Doherty told *CA:* "I enjoy both fictional crime and historical mysteries-yet-to-be-resolved. I am currently working on the murder of Amy Robsart in 1560—it's great to realise you may have unmasked an assassin after more than 440 years!"

BIOGRAPHICAL AND CRITICAL SOURCES:

PERIODICALS

Armchair Detective, winter, 1987, Rosemary Swan, review of *The Death of a King,* pp. 83-84; spring, 1996, Rick Mattos, review of *Song of a Dark Angel,* p. 234; summer, 1996, Peter Kenny, review of *A Tapestry of Murders,* p. 371.

Booklist, December 15, 1985, Connie Fletcher, review of *The Death of a King,* p. 608; December 1, 1988, Margaret Flanagan, review of *The Whyte Harte,* p. 617; April 1, 1989, Ray Olson, review of *Spy in Chancery,* p. 1348; December 15, 1991, Flanagan, review of *The Masked Man,* p. 752; January 1, 1993, Flanagan, review of *The Prince of Darkness,* p. 793; April 1, 1996, Flanagan, review of *A Tapestry of Murders,* p. 1345; November 15, 1996, Flanagan, review of *Satan's Fire,* p. 574; September 1, 1997, Flanagan, review of *A Tournament of Murders,* p. 63; March 15, 1998, Flanagan, review of *The Devil's Hunt,* p. 1204; April 15, 1999, Flanagan, review of *The Mask of Ra,* p. 1471; February 15, 2000, Barbara Bibel, review of *The Horus Killing,* p. 1087.

Kirkus Reviews, November 15, 1985, review of *The Death of a King,* pp. 1204-1205; February 15, 1987, review of *Satan in St. Mary's,* p. 258; April 15, 1988, review of *The Crown in Darkness,* p. 574; November 1, 1988, review of *The Whyte Harte,* p. 1566; April 1, 1989, review of *Spy in Chancery,* p. 503; February 15, 1990, review of *The Angel of Death,* p. 223; August 15, 1990, review of *Serpent amongst the Lilies,* p. 1131; February 15, 1991, review of *The Fate of Princes,* p. 214; October 1, 1991, review of *The Masked Man,* p. 1248; November 15, 1992, review of *The Prince of Darkness,* p. 1407; January 1, 1994, review of *Murder Wears a Cowl,* p. 20; July 15, 1995, review of *The Song of a Dark Angel,* pp. 985-86; February 1, 1996, review of *A Tapestry of Murders,* p. 175; October 1, 1996, review of *Satan's Fire,* p. 1427; September 1, 1997, review of *A Tournament of Murders,* pp. 1340-41; January 15, 1998, review of *The Devil's Hunt,* p. 83; August 1, 1998, review of *Ghostly Murders,* p. 1070; April 1, 1999, review of *The Mask of Ra,* p. 488; January 15, 2000, review of *The Horus Killings,* p. 89.

Library Journal, April 1, 1987, JoAnn Vicarel, review of *Satan in St. Mary's,* pp. 166, 168; January, 1989, Rex E. Klett, review of *The Whyte Harte,* p. 104; April 1, 1990, Klett, review of *The Angel of Death,* p. 140; November 1, 1991, Klett, review of *The Masked Man,* p. 135; August, 1997, Klett, review of *A Tournament of Murders,* p. 140; February 1, 1998, Klett, review of *The Devil's Hunt,* p. 115; May 1, 1999, Klett, review of *The Mask of Ra,* p. 11; March 1, 2000, Klett, review of *The Horus Killings,* p. 128.

New York Times Book Review, April 7, 1991, Marilyn Stasio, review of *The Fate of Princes,* p. 33.

Publishers Weekly, November 15, 1985, review of *The Death of a King,* p. 48; February 20, 1987, review of *Satan in St. Mary's,* p. 74; May 13, 1988, review of *The Crown in Darkness,* p. 267; October 28, 1988, review of *The Whyte Harte,* p. 64; March 17, 1989, review of *Spy in Chancery,* pp. 81-82; February 16, 1990, review of *The Angel of Death,* p. 70; January 25, 1991, review of *The Fate of Princes,* p. 48; October 4, 1991, review of *The Masked Man,* p. 82; November 16, 1992, review of *The Prince of Darkness,* p. 49; February 14, 1994, review of *Murder Wears a Cowl,* p. 82; August 8, 1994, review of *The Assassin in the Greenwood,* p. 392; March 6, 1995, review of *An Ancient Evil,* p. 63; January 29, 1996, review of *A Tapestry of Murder,* pp. 87-88; July 21, 1997, review of *A Tournament of Murders,* p. 188; December 22, 1997, review of *The Devil's Hunt,* p. 41; April 12, 1999, review of *The Mask of Ra,* p. 58; February 28, 2000, review of *The Horus Killings,* p. 66; January 22, 2001, review of *The Demon Archer,* p. 305.

Quill and Quire, October, 1996, Michael McGowan, review of *The Devil's Hunt,* p. 30.

School Library Journal, September, 1994, Mary T. Gerrity, review of *Murder Wears a Cowl,* p. 255; September, 1995, Judy Sokoll, review of *An Ancient Evil,* p. 232.

Tribune Books (Chicago, IL), October 14, 1990, Kevin Moore, "A Cajun Beat and Brit Cool Set the Mood," p. 6.

ONLINE

BookBrowser, http://www.bookbrowser.com/ (April 30, 2001), Harriet Klausner, review of *The Anubis Slayings.*

Crime Time Web site, http://www.crimetime.co.uk/ (August 6, 2001), review of *The Haunting.*

Mystery Guide, http://www.mysteryguide.com/ (August 22, 2001), review of *The Death of a King.*

Scenes of Crime, http://www.fortunecity.co.uk/ (August 22, 2001), Daniel M. Staines, "The Novels of P. C. Doherty."

Stop, You're Killing Me Web site, http://www.stopyoure killingme.com/ (August 22, 2001).

DOUGLASS, Malcolm P(aul) 1923-2002

OBITUARY NOTICE—See index for *CA* sketch: Born August 18, 1923, in Pullman, WA; died of cancer December 29, 2002, in Claremont, CA. Educator and author. Douglass was a noted reading teacher and theorist who was director of the Claremont Reading Conference. After fighting in Europe as a U.S. infantryman during World War II, he earned his B.A. from Pomona College in 1947, followed by an M.A. from Columbia University in 1948 and an Ed.D. from Stanford University in 1954. His teaching career began at public schools in Sacramento and San Lorenzo, California during the late 1940s and early 1950s. From 1950 to 1954 he was also an elementary school principal in San Lorenzo. Douglass began his long career at what is now Claremont Graduate University in 1954 as an assistant professor. He moved up to professor of education from 1963 until his retirement in 1994, and founded the Center for Developmental Studies in Education in 1971, serving as director until 1989. Douglass was also the director the Claremont Reading Conference from 1959 to 1989. As a reading teacher who had researched methods of reading instruction around the world, Douglass was an advocate of the "whole language" approach that says that children learn to read better through exposure to good books rather than by focusing only on grammar and spelling. He wrote about his theories in such books as *The History, Psychology, and Pedagogy of Reading* (1998) and through editing the "Claremont Reading Conference" series for four decades.

OBITUARIES AND OTHER SOURCES:

PERIODICALS

Los Angeles Times, January 5, 2003, p. B14.

*   *   *

DOYLE, Laura 1967-

PERSONAL: Born January 27, 1967, in Huntington Beach, CA; daughter of W. Peter (an X-ray technician) and Maureen (a violinist) Mills; married John Doyle (a videographer), September 30, 1989. *Education:* San Jose State University, B.A. (with honors), 1989.

ADDRESSES: Agent—Jimmy Vines, The Vines Agency, 648 Broadway, Suite 901, New York, NY 10012. *E-mail*—JV@vinesagency.com.

CAREER: Has worked as a marketing director and copywriter; leads workshops and training seminars based on her books.

WRITINGS:

The Surrendered Wife: A Practical Guide to Finding Intimacy, Passion, and Peace with a Man, Simon & Schuster (New York, NY), 2001.

The Surrendered Single: A Practical Guide to Attracting and Marrying the Man Who's Right for You, Simon & Schuster (New York, NY), 2002.

ADAPTATIONS: The Surrendered Wife is available as an audiobook read by the author, Simon & Schuster.

WORK IN PROGRESS: Things Will Get as Good as You Can Stand: A Woman's Practical Guide to Receiving All the Best in Life, Simon & Schuster (New York, NY), 2004.

SIDELIGHTS: Like many spouses, Laura Doyle was experiencing problems in her marriage. Her reaction to these difficulties led her not only to an improved and more satisfying relationship with her husband, but to the *New York Times* Bestseller list, where her book, *The Surrendered Wife: A Practical Guide to Finding Intimacy, Passion, and Peace with a Man* had a home for numerous weeks.

Doyle explained to *Contemporary Authors* how her first book came to be. "I was trying to save my own marriage when I discovered the principles that contribute to intimacy. Once I learned them, I realized that they are simple, predictable, and constant. Now thousands of women write to me and say how helpful it is for them. So we know this stuff works, and it's important for keeping families together."

Not only do women write to her, men do, too. And in every corner of the world, there's a local Surrendered Wife/Surrendered Single workshop or self-help group springing up. In *The Surrendered Wife,* Doyle urges wives to hand over control of the finances to their husbands. Say Yes to sex at least once weekly. Don't tell the man how to drive or where to turn. Resist telling him what to do. Don't correct him. Avoid arguing. She claims that by following her guide, women will find their marriages more fulfilling both emotionally and physically. The men they married will seem more communicative, more open, and more enjoyable to be with.

Despite the book's popularity with its reading audience, it has proven controversial with critics and feminists, who fault its principles as backward and manipulative. Speaking to *Time* contributor Tamala M. Edwards, Philadelphia therapist Michael Broder warned, "What she is saying here is how to manipulate your husband. True intimacy comes from being able to express your true thoughts and feelings." John Gottman, a noted marriage therapist, found Doyle's surrendered wife concept "personally offensive and scientifically unfounded," as he told London *Observer* writer Maureen Freely. Other therapists have remarked that not being true to one's self leads only to resentment, which will not disappear but only fester until it boils over. Doyle, however, told *Washington Times* interviewer Julia Duin that she advocates surrendering control, not individuality. "It is incumbent on us to say what we want and how we feel. . . . Really expressing your desires is part of being able to be in an intimate relationship."

Other reviewers have pointed out that the author offers some useful suggestions in her book. Edwards, for instance, noted that while "some of Doyle's ideas seem demeaning and questionable," there are others that "have the imprint of sanity. . . . There is a lot to be said for apologizing, for walking away rather than escalating an argument." In the London *Independent*, Yasmin Alibhai-Brown admitted that "there are some sections and chapters which are startlingly revealing for anybody in a long-term relationship. Hidden mirrors placed around the pages which catch you out and make you look and see and think differently about how you are behaving and the effect of this on the people you most love in the world." In answer to charges that her philosophy is anti-feminist, the author told Duin that "I see this as the next phase of feminism. That is, acknowledging that what we want at work is different from what we want at home." As the author explained, "At work you have to be able to manage your staff, you have to be able to manage

your projects, but marriage is not about managing your husband. It's about wanting companionship and romance and tenderness. And those are totally different goals and they require different behaviors."

Anna Reynolds of Brisbane, Australia's *Courier-Mail* wasn't impressed with Doyle's second book, *The Surrendered Single: A Practical Guide to Attracting and Marrying the Man Who's Right for You.* "The dictionary definition and the meaning generally understood by the community is the same: to surrender is to 'yield (something) to the possession or power of another.' This is why *The Surrendered Single* is so appalling." Feminist Katha Pollitt read the book and declared "A woman who follows this advice will get the man she deserves," as Sarah Wilson reported in the Melbourne *Sunday Herald Sun.*

Though some people take issue with Doyle's self-help strategies, her own life has become busier and more productive as a direct result of her writing. She told Peggy O'Crowley, reporter for Newark *The Star-Ledger,* "There's a difference between surrender and submission. Sub means below, that one person is inferior and one is superior. Surrender is giving up the illusion that you can control anyone outside of yourself and, if you could, it would make you happy. Surrender is when you're in traffic, you want the cars to move, but you can't make them, so you use the time to listen to music." Despite the criticism from therapists, sociologists, feminists, and reviewers, there is an audience out there eager to surrender.

BIOGRAPHICAL AND CRITICAL SOURCES:

PERIODICALS

Courier-Mail (Brisbane, Australia), June 6, 2002, Anna Reynolds, "Seduction by the Book Is Surrender, but Not Sweet," p. 21.

Daily Post, June 25, 2002, Noreen Barr, "Inside Out: Single? Try Smiling and Keeping Quiet," p. 18.

Independent (London, England), June 21, 2001, Yasmin Alibhai-Brown, "How I Became a Surrendered Wife," p. 5.

Los Angeles Times, July 7, 1999, Patrice Apodaca, "Controlling Wives Are Urged to Take a Back Seat to Their Husbands on Decision-Making," p. 6.

New Yorker, April 2, 2001, Rebecca Mead, review of *The Surrendered Wife: A Practical Guide for Finding Intimacy, Passion, and Peace with a Man,* p. 82.

Observer (London, England), January 28, 2001, Maureen Freely, "So a Fish Does Need a Bicycle: According to a New U.S. Bestseller out Here Soon, There's Only One Way to Keep Mr. Right—Just Don't Tell Him He's Wrong: Love, Honour and—Shampoo. Mr. and Mrs. Doyle Show Us How to Have a Happy Marriage," p. 1.

People, February 26, 2001, "Mister Right: Who's the Boss? Laura Doyle, Author of *The Surrendered Wife,* Says It's Hubby," p. 55.

Publishers Weekly, December 4, 2000, review of *The Surrendered Wife,* January 1, 2001, Julie Mayeda, "Marriage 101: Here We Go Again," p. 31.

Star-Ledger (Newark, NJ), April 8, 2001, Peggy O'Crowley, "Just 'Surrender' to Married Bliss," p. 1.

Sunday Herald Sun (Melbourne, Australia), July 14, 2002, Sarah Wilson, "How to Hook a Husband," p. Z20.

Sunday Times (London, England), April 28, 2002, Sarah Baxter, "Submission Is a Girl's Best Friend," p. 26.

Time, January 22, 2001, Tamala M. Edwards, "I Surrender, Dear: A Controversial New Book Argues That an Acquiescent Wife Is the Key to a Happy Marriage," p. 71.

Washington Times, January 18, 2001, Julia Duin, "Feminist Suggests Swapping Control for Better Marriage" (interview), p. 2.

Writer's Digest, December, 2001, Katie Struckel Brogan, interview with Laura Doyle, p. 26.

ONLINE

Surrendered Wife, http://www.surrenderedwife.com/ (October 2, 2002), author's Web site.

Surrendered Single, http://www.surrenderedsingle.com/ (May 10, 2003).

*   *   *

DRAKE, Timothy A. 1967-
(Lance Haataja, Robert Pierce)

PERSONAL: Born September 13, 1967, in St. Paul, MN; son of Thomas (a mechanic) and Linda (a secretary; maiden name, Kolbeck) Drake; married Mary (a sign language interpreter), July 8, 1989; children: Elias, Isabel, Claire, Elena. *Education:* University of Minnesota—Morris, B.A. (social sciences), 1989; attended Hamline University, 1993-94. *Religion:* Roman Catholic. *Hobbies and other interests:* Autograph collecting, reading, biking.

ADDRESSES: Home—2009 13th Street South, Saint Cloud, MN 56301. *E-mail*—timd@astound.net.

CAREER: Circle Media, North Haven, CT, features correspondent, 1999—, managing editor, 2001—; *Envoy* Magazine, Hebron, OH, contributing editor, 2000—. Spirit '93 Fund, chairman of advisory board, 2001—. Morris Area Crisis Pregnancy Center, member of board of directors, 1998; Birthline, member of board of directors, 2001—; Human Life Action Council, member of advisory board, 2001—.

MEMBER: Catholic Writer's Association.

AWARDS, HONORS: Ida B. Davis Ethnic Heritage Award, University of Minnesota, 1989, for history of First Lutheran Church of Morris; Metro Write for Life Award, Metro Right to Life, 2000, for Op Ed piece; Bestseller Award, 1st Books Library, 2001, for *There We Stood, Here We Stand: Eleven Lutherans Rediscover Their Catholic Roots.*

WRITINGS:

(Editor, with Henry Graham) *Where We Got the Bible,* Catholic Answers (San Diego, CA), 1997.

(Editor, with Cleta Hartman) *Physicians Healed,* One More Soul (Dayton, OH), 1998.

(With Patrick Madrid) *Suprised by Truth 2,* Sophia Institute Press (Manchester, NH), 2000.

(Editor, with Patrick Madrid) *Where Is That in the Bible?,* Our Sunday Visitor (Huntington, IN), 2001.

(With Lynn Nordhagen) *When Only One Converts,* Our Sunday Visitor (Huntington, IN), 2001.

There We Stood, Here We Stand: Eleven Lutherans Rediscover Their Catholic Roots, 1st Books Library (Bloomington, IN), 2001.

Contributor to magazines and publications including *Be, Gilbert, Catholic World Report, Envoy, Columbia, Lay Witness, the National Catholic Register,* and *The Write Stuff.* Also uses pseudonyms Lance Haataja and Robert Pierce.

WORK IN PROGRESS: Saints of the Jubilee, Beautiful Life, and *Signs of Contradiction,* for 1st Books Library (Bloomington, IN); *The Attic Saint,* for Bethlehem Books (Bathgate, ND); *There We Stood, Here We Stand: Eleven Lutherans Rediscover Their Catholic Roots* (revision), for Our Sunday Visitor (Huntington, IN).

SIDELIGHTS: Timothy A. Drake told *CA:* "My conversion to Catholicism in 1995 had a profound impact on my writing. Suddenly, it seemed to me that there was nothing else worth writing about other than Christ and His Church. Such a decision provided the necessary voice that my previous writing lacked. To date, everything I have written is influenced by a Catholic world view. To others, such a decision might seem limiting, but I have discovered it to be expanding. The more one learns about the Church, the more one realizes what intense depth and beauty and richness there is to it, and the more that one needs to learn. A colleague once described the work of a religion writer as 'missionary work,' because one never knows whom one might influence with a given piece. This has continued to be my motivation, particularly with my journalistic work with the national Catholic weekly the *National Catholic Register.*"

* * *

DRUCKER, Henry M(atthew) 1942-2002

OBITUARY NOTICE—See index for *CA* sketch: Born April 29, 1942, in Patterson, NJ; died October 30, 2002, in London, England. Political scientist, fundraiser, educator, and author. Drucker is credited with changing the practice of philanthropy in England, particularly through his groundbreaking work as a fundraiser for Oxford University. He received his undergraduate degree from Allegheny College in 1964 before moving to England and earning his Ph.D. in political philosophy from the London School of Economics and Political Science in 1967. He then joined the faculty at the University of Edinburgh as a lecturer, serving as senior lecturer in politics from 1978 to 1986. During this time, he wrote several important books on politics, including *The Political Use of Ideology* (1974), *Breakaway: The Scottish Labour Party* (1978), and, with Gordon Brown, *The Politics of Nationalism and Devolution* (1980). Drucker got his first experience as an administrator in

university development working as the director of development at Edinburgh. This made him the most desirable candidate when he was hired by Oxford University as its director of development in 1987. At the time, fundraising for universities was a new concept in England, and Drucker had to start his campaigns from scratch. He did so with outstanding success, raising some £341 million from private and corporate donors between 1988 and 1993. Drucker believed, correctly, that universities could benefit greatly from financial support outside the government, and that corporations and philanthropists would also find advantages and personal satisfaction through their donations. In 1993 he left Oxford to found the consultant company Oxford Philanthropic, for which he was managing director until 1999 and chairman from 1999 to 2002. Other activities included his membership in the Political Studies Association, the Institute of Charity Fund-raising Managers, and the British Museum Development Trust. He was widely consulted by organizations throughout England for his expertise in fundraising.

OBITUARIES AND OTHER SOURCES:

PERIODICALS

Financial Times, November 8, 2002, p. 4.
Times (London, England), November 6, 2002, p. 30.

* * *

DRUMMOND, Edward H. 1953-

PERSONAL: Born June 23, 1953, in Portland, ME; married Amy S. Feitelson (a psychiatrist), May 16, 1982; children: Michael, Rose. *Ethnicity:* "Irish-American." *Education:* Tufts University, B.A. (magna cum laude), M.D.

ADDRESSES: Home—43 Pine St., Rye, NH 03870. *Office*—Seacoast Mental Health Center, 1145 Sagamore Ave., Portsmouth, NH 03801. *Agent*—Jan Miller, Dupree, Miller & Associates, 100 Highland Park Village, Suite 350, Dallas, TX 73205. *E-mail*—tedd@ seacoastmentalhealth.org.

CAREER: Seacoast Mental Health Center, Portsmouth, NH, associate medical director, 1986—.

WRITINGS:

Overcoming Anxiety without Tranquilizers: A Ground-breaking Program for Treating Chronic Anxiety (also published as *Benzo Blues*), Dutton (New York, NY), 1997.

The Complete Guide to Psychiatric Drugs: Straight Talk for Best Results, John Wiley (New York, NY), 2000.

WORK IN PROGRESS: Two works of fiction.

SIDELIGHTS: Edward H. Drummond told *CA:* "I have long been troubled that, although there is a great deal of information about mental-health issues in the media, much of it is one-sided, distorted, or just plain wrong. My purpose in writing is to educate readers about psychiatric problems and treatments so that they are better able to make sensible choices about their care. I have focused my books on the issues involved in using psychiatric drugs because tens of millions of people are using them and need accurate information. My books fall into the self-help genre: they provide the pros and cons of medications and how to use them to best advantage."

BIOGRAPHICAL AND CRITICAL SOURCES:

PERIODICALS

Publishers Weekly, August 18, 1997, review of *Overcoming Anxiety without Tranquilizers: A Groundbreaking Program for Treating Chronic Anxiety,* p. 87.

*   *   *

DUKTHAS, Ann
    See DOHERTY, P(aul) C.

*   *   *

DUNCAN, Alexandra
    See MOORE, Ishbel (Lindsay)

E-F

ELLIS, Reuben 1955-

PERSONAL: Born April 19, 1955, in Oceanside, CA; son of Joseph (a nursery employee) and Ione (a schoolteacher) Ellis; married Brenna Ryan, August 13, 1977 (divorced, 2000); married Linda Dove, May 21, 2001; children: Isaac, Daniel. *Education:* Western State College of Colorado, B.A., 1977; University of Idaho, M.A., 1985; University of Colorado—Boulder, Ph.D. (English), 1990. *Hobbies and other interests:* Mountaineering, archaeology.

ADDRESSES: Office—Prescott College, 301 Grove Ave., Prescott, AZ 86301. *E-mail*—rellis@prescott. edu.

CAREER: Teikyo Lorretto Heights University, Denver, CO, assistant professor of English, 1991-94; Hope College, Holland, MI, associate professor of English, 1994-99; Prescott College, Prescott, AZ, associate professor of English, 1999—.

MEMBER: Modern Language Association of America, American Society for Aesthetics, Western Literature Association, Mary Hunter Austin Society.

WRITINGS:

Beyond Borders, Southern Illinois University Press (Carbondale, IL), 1996.
Stories and Stone, Pruett Publishing, 1997.
Vertical Margins, University of Wisconsin Press (Madison, WI), 2001.

WORK IN PROGRESS: Dangerous Man, a novel; *Word Ruins: Representing Prehistory in Southwestern American Literature.*

SIDELIGHTS: Reuben Ellis told *CA:* "My primary interest is how humans interact with the natural world, responding to it, adapting to it, and often riding roughshod over it, constructing it within the framework of their own limited cultural contexts.

"The American Southwest provides a remarkable laboratory for trying to understand all this, and my scholarly work with the writing of Mary Hunter Austin, one of the twentieth century's first important western regionalist thinkers, is designed to suggest frameworks for how we might use literature to better understand our relationship with place. Similarly, my work with literary representations of prehistoric cultures and archaeological sites in the Southwest undertakes to ask how our understanding of the past in relationship to specific natural environments might help us make better choices for the future.

"My interest in mountaineering literature comes from my love of the wilderness, particularly mountain places, and my instinct that mountaineering, like virtually all cultural practices, is bound up in a complex network of political and ideological forces that make what most of us think of as a 'sport' in fact a much richer and more complicated experience that actually speaks to how we impact the natural world and interact with other peoples on a global scale."

ENRIGHT, D(ennis) J(oseph) 1920-2002

OBITUARY NOTICE—See index for *CA* sketch: Born March 11, 1920, in Leamington, Warwickshire, England; died December 31, 2002, in London, England. Educator and author. Enright was a poet famous for his minimalist, colloquial style and themes about ordinary life. He earned his master's degree from Downing College, Cambridge, in 1946, and after he had bad luck looking for a university job in England, he moved to Alexandria, Egypt, where he obtained his Ph.D. at what is now the University of Alexandria in 1949. After lecturing at Alexandria for three years and back home at the University of Birmingham for another three, Enright embarked on a long career teaching at foreign universities. He taught at Koonan University in Japan from 1953 to 1956, the Free University of Berlin for the next year, Chulalongkorn University in Thailand from 1957 to 1959, and the University of Singapore from 1960 to 1970. His desire to have an open and free curriculum in Singapore caused him to run into some trouble with the restrictive government there, but he was beloved by his students. Many of his early poetry collections concern his experiences in Japan and Singapore, including *The Laughing Hyena* (1953) and *Bread rather than Blossoms* (1956). He also drew on his experiences in Egypt for his novel *Academic Year* (1955). In 1970, Enright returned to England to become coeditor of the literary magazine *Encounter* for two years, followed by a productive eight years at the publishing house Chatto & Windus and a five-year stint, from 1975 to 1980, as an honorary professor of English at Warwick University. Sometimes associated with the Movement, a school of poetry in England during the 1950s and 1960s that was a reaction to the more ornate language of poets such as Dylan Thomas, Enright wrote movingly about subjects such as poverty and his childhood in simple, usually unrhymed verses in collections such as *The Terrible Shears: Scenes from a Twenties Childhood* (1973). In addition to some two dozen poetry collection, he wrote or edited eleven novels, including three for children, completed fourteen essay collections, edited thirteen other books, and translated books by Colette Portal and Marcel Proust. Toward the end of his life, he completed the memoirs *Interplay: A Kind of Commonplace Book* (1995) and *Play Resumed: A Journal* (1998), as well as his *Collected Poems* (1998) and *Signs and Wonders: Selected Essays* (2001). At the time of his death, Enright had just finished another autobiographical book, *Injury Time* that was scheduled for publication in 2003. For his poetic achievements, Enright was awarded the Cholmondeley Award for Poetry from the British Society of Authors in 1974 and the Queen's Gold Medal for Poetry in 1981; he was also named to the Order of the British Empire in 1991.

OBITUARIES AND OTHER SOURCES:

BOOKS

Contemporary Poets, seventh edition, St. James (Detroit, MI), 2001.

PERIODICALS

Chicago Tribune, January 7, 2003, section 2, p. 8.
Los Angeles Times, January 7, 2003, p. B11.
New York Times, January 13, 2003, p. A23.
Times (London, England), January 1, 2003.

*   *   *

FERNÁNDEZ CUBAS, Cristina 1945-

PERSONAL: Born May 28, 1945, in Arenys de Mar, Spain. *Education:* Graduated from law school; studied Arabic in Egypt.

ADDRESSES: Agent—Tusquets Editores, Cesare Cantú, 8, 08023, Barcelona, Spain.

CAREER: Writer; journalist in Peru and in Barcelona.

WRITINGS:

Mi hermana Elba (also see below), Tusquets Editores (Barcelona, Spain), 1980.
El vendedor de sombras (fairy tales; see also below), illustrated by Montserrat Clavé, Argos Vergara (Barcelona, Spain), 1982.
Los altillos de Brumal (also see below), Plaza & Janés Editores (Barcelona, Spain), 1983.

El año de Gracia (novel), Tusquets Editores (Barcelona, Spain), 1985.

Cris y cros; El vendedor de sombras, Alfaguara (Madrid, Spain), 1988.

El ángulo del horror, Tusquets Editores (Barcelona, Spain), 1990.

Mi hermana Elba; y Los altillos de Brumal, Tusquets Editores (Barcelona, Spain), 1988.

Con Agatha en Estambul (short stories), Tusquets Editores (Barcelona, Spain), 1994.

El columpio, Tusquets Editores (Barcelona, Spain), 1995.

Hermanas de sangre, Tusquets Editores (Barcelona, Spain), 1998.

Los altillos de Brumal; En el hemisferio sur, Plaza & Janés Editores (Barcelona, Spain), 1998.

Cosas que ya no existen, Lumen (Barcelona, Spain), 2001.

Contributor to *Doce relatos de mujer,* edited by Ymelda Navajo, Alianza Editorial, 1982. Author of an adaptation of an unfinished novel by Edgar Allan Poe titled *El faro.*

ADAPTATIONS: Los altillos de Brumal was made into a film in 1988.

SIDELIGHTS: Cristina Fernández Cubas began her writing career as a journalist, but has become best known for her "unsettling" and "disquieting" fiction, as it is often termed by reviewers. At a young age, her interest in supernatural tales was sparked by her brother's retellings of Edgar Allen Poe and by her nanny's scary stories. Another hallmark of her work, her fascination with enclosed spaces such as attics, drawers, and trunks, has also been with her since childhood.

Although Fernández Cubas does not like the label "Gothic," it is often applied to her work. "Her fiction reflects some of the main preoccupations of Gothic literature, such as an interest in the divided self and in the 'unspeakable,' a term that encompasses the unreadable, the incomprehensible, and the unknowable," Kathleen M. Glenn wrote in *Encyclopedia of World Literature.*

El año de Gracia, one of Fernández Cubas's early novels, is full of this sense of the unspeakable. Daniel, a young man, leaves the seminary and is given a "year of grace"—a year for traveling, free of obligations—by his sister. With this period of freedom, he heads out into the world in search of adventure. Having read *Robinson Crusoe* and similar action tales, he thinks he can find it by becoming a sailor, but he soon finds more adventure than he had bargained for when he is shipwrecked on an isolated island in the Hebrides. This island, which was contaminated by experiments with chemicals during World War II, is home to only a flock of deformed sheep and a mentally and physically troubled shepherd named Grock. Since Grock speaks an eclectic language composed of mixed Celtic and English, Daniel cannot talk to him, but they eventually find other methods of communication. A year later, Daniel is rescued by a group of scientists who kill Grock, destroy Daniel's manuscript, and forbid him ever to tell anyone about the island.

One of Fernández Cubas's best-known works is the short story collection *Con Agatha en Estambul,* which includes the story "Mundo." The word "mundo" can mean both "trunk" and "world" in Spanish, and both senses of the word are intended. The story is narrated by Carolina, an elderly woman who was sent into a convent against her will at the age of fifteen after she accidently caught her family's housekeeper having affairs with her father and with the local priest. Carolina brings into the convent with her a carved trunk, full of things for which she no longer has any use—including her mother's wedding dress, which she will never get to wear—and of secret compartments. The nuns within the convent have their own secrets as well, especially the supposedly mute Madre Perú. "Fernández Cubas highlights female creativity and the art of storytelling," Glenn wrote in *Hispania,* "as the nuns embroider table linen, sheets, wedding gowns, and christening dresses for the use of others, Madre Perú carves into the surface of a calabash her life history, and the aged Madre Carolina narrates hers to us."

BIOGRAPHICAL AND CRITICAL SOURCES:

BOOKS

Encyclopedia of World Literature, St. James Press (Detriot, MI), 1999.

Perez, Janet, *Contemporary Women Writers of Spain,* Twayne (Boston, MA), 1988.

PERIODICALS

Anales de Literatura Española Contemporanea, Volume 13, number 3, 1988, Mary Lee Bretz, "Cristina Fernández Cubas and the Recuperation of the Semiotic in *Los altillos de Brumal,*" pp. 177-188; Volume 18, number 2, 1993, Kathleen M. Glenn, interview with Fernández Cubas, pp. 355-363.

Explicacion de Textos Literarios, Volume 22, number 1, 1993-94, Catherine G. Bellver, "*El año de Gracia:* El viaje como rito de iniciacion," pp. 3-10; Volume 24, numbers 1-2, 1995-96, Janet Perez, "Fernandez Cubas, Abjection, and the 'Retorica del Horror'," pp. 159-171.

Hispania, May, 1995, Kathleen M. Glenn, review of *Con Agatha in Estabul,* p. 311; December, 1995, Kathleen M. Glenn, review of *El columpio,* p. 118; March, 1996, Phyllis Zatlin, "Amnesia, Strangulation, Hallucination, and Other Mishaps: The Perils of Being Female in Tales of Cristina Fernández Cubas," pp. 36-44.

Hispanofila, January, 1998, Janet Perez, "Cristina Fernández Cubas: Narrative Unreliability and the Flight from Clarity; or, The Quest for Knowledge in the Fog," pp. 29-39.

Insula, April, 1994, Fernando Valls, "De las certezas del amigo a las dudas del heroe: Sobre 'La ventana del jardin,' de Cristina Fernández Cubas," pp. 18-19.

Journal of Interdisciplinary Studies, Volume 7, number 1, 1995, Catherine Bellver, "Robinson Crusoe Revisited: *El año de Gracia* and the Postmodern Ethic," pp. 105-118; Volume 7, number 2, 1995, Robert C. Spires, "Postmodernism/Paralogism: *El angulo del horror* by Cristina Fernández Cubas," pp. 233-245.

Journal of Narrative Techniques, winter, 1997, Robert C. Spires, "Discursive Constructs and Spanish Fiction of the 1980s," pp. 128-146.

Letras Femininas, Volume 8, number 2, 1982, Catherine G. Bellver, "Two New Women Writers from Spain," pp. 3-7; spring-fall, 1989, Lynn K. Talbot, "Journey into the Fantastic: Cristina Fernández Cubas' *Los altillos de Brumal,*" pp. 37-47; summer, 1992, p. 177.

Letras Peninsulares, spring, 1995, Susan Lucan Dobrian, "Echo's Revenge in Three Spanish Narratives by Women," pp. 169-179.

Library Journal, July, 1996, Norma Montero, review of *El columpio,* p. 94.

Mester, fall, 1991, interview with Fernández Cubas, pp. 157-165.

Monographic Review/Revista Monografica, Volume 3, numbers 1-2, 1987, Phyllis Zatlin, "Tales from Fernández Cubas: Adventure in the Fantastic," pp. 107-118; Volume 4, 1988, p. 460; Volume 8, 1992,

Kathleen M. Glenn, "Gothic Indecipherability and Doubling in the Fiction of Cristina Fernández Cubas," pp. 125-141, Julie Gleue, "The Epistemological and Ontological Implications in Cristina Fernández Cubas's *El año de Gracia,*" pp. 142-156, Jose Ortega, "La dimension fantastica en los cuentos de Fernández Cubas," pp. 157-163; 1996, Kay Pritchett, "Cristina Fernández Cubas' 'Con Agatha en Estambul': Traveling into Mist and Mystery," pp. 247-257.

Revista Canadiense de Estudios Hispanicos, winter, 2000, Jessica Aileen Folkart, "Desire, Doubling, and Difference in Cristina Fernández Cubas's *El angulo del horror,*" pp. 343-362.

Romance Languages Annual, Volume 2, 1990, Kathleen M. Glenn, "Authority and Marginality in Three Contemporary Spanish Narratives," pp. 426-430; Volume 4, 1992, pp. 460-465; Volume 9, 1997, Kathleen M. Glenn, "Narrative Designs in Cristina Fernández Cubas's 'Mundo'," pp. 501-504.

Siglo XX/Twentieth Century, Volume 11, numbers 1-2, 1993, John B. Margenot, "Parody and Self-Consciousness in Cristina Fernández Cubas's *El año de Gracia,*" pp. 71-87.

Studies in Twentieth-Century Literature, summer, 1992, Catherine G. Bellver, "*El año de Gracia* and the Displacement of the Word," pp. 221-232.

World Literature Today, spring, 1995, Kay Pritchett, review of *Con Agatha in Estabul,* p. 327.*

*   *   *

FERNÁNDEZ FLÓREZ, Wenceşlao 1885-1964

PERSONAL: Born 1885, in La Coruña, Spain; died 1964.

CAREER: Novelist, playwright, and essayist. *El Parlamento,* editor.

MEMBER: Royal Spanish Academy of the Language.

AWARDS, HONORS: Fine Arts Circle prize, 1917, for *Volvereta;* Premio Mariano Cavia, 1922.

WRITINGS:

La tristerza de la paz, Artistica Española (Madrid, Spain), 1910.
Volvereta, Viudo de Pueyo (Madrid, Spain), 1917, reprinted, Cátedra (Madrid, Spain), 1999.

Silencio, Viudo de Pueyo (Madrid, Spain), 1918.

Acotaciones de un oyente, Viuda de Pueyo (Madrid, Spain), c. 1918.

Las gafas del diablo (title means "The Devil's Glasses"), General de Ediciones (Madrid, Spain), 1918, reprinted, Espasa-Calpe (Madrid, Spain), 1980.

Luz de luna (title means "Moonlight"), Los Contemporáneos (Madrid, Spain), 1919.

El espejo irónico, Renacimiento (Madrid, Spain), c. 1920.

Ha entrado un ladrón (title means "A Thief Has Entered"), Viuda de Pueyo (Madrid, Spain), c. 1920.

La procesión de los días, Viuda de Pueyo (Madrid, Spain), c. 1921.

La caza de la mariposa, Sucesores de Rivadeneyra (Madrid, Spain), 1922.

Tragedías de la vida vulgar, Atlántida (Madrid, Spain), 1922.

La familia Gomar, Gráfica (Madrid, Spain), 1922.

El ilustre Cardona, Sucesores de Rivadeneyra (Madrid, Spain), 1923.

Huella de luz, Sucesores de Rivadeneyra (Madrid, Spain), 1924.

Unos pasos de mujer (title means "A Woman's Footsteps"), Sucesores de Rivadeneyra (Madrid, Spain), 1924.

El fantasma, Sucesores de Rivadeneyra (Madrid, Spain), 1924.

Visiones de neurastenia, Atlántida (Madrid, Spain), 1924.

El calma turbada, Artística de Sáez Hermanos (Madrid, Spain), 1925.

Por qué te engaña tu marido, Sucesores de Rivadeneyra (Madrid, Spain), 1925.

La casa de la lluvia (contains "Luz de luna," "La familia Gomar," and "Aire de muerto"), Sociedad general de publicaciones (Madrid, Spain), 1925.

Mi mujer, Sucesores de Rivadeneyra (Madrid, Spain), 1925, reprinted, Almarabu (Spain), 1985.

La seducida, Artística de Sáez Hermanos (Madrid, Spain), 1925.

El secreto de Barba-Azul (title means "Bluebeard's Secret"), Atlántida (Madrid, Spain), 1925, reprinted, Espasa-Calpe (Madrid, Spain), 1972.

Las siete columnas (title means "The Seven Pillars"), Atlántida (Madrid, Spain), 1926, reprinted, Espasa-Calpe (Madrid, Spain), 1979, translation by Sir Peter Chalmers Mitchell, Macmillan (London, England), 1934.

Frente al dictador, Biblioteca Internacional (Madrid, Spain), 1926.

Una aventura del cine (screenplay), 1927.

Ella y la otra, Artística de Sáez Hermanos (Madrid, Spain), 1927.

Relato inmoral, Atlántida (Madrid, Spain), 1927, reprinted, Mascarón (Barcelona, Spain), 1981.

El pais de papel (title means "The Country of Paper"), Talleres Poligráficos (Madrid, Spain), 1929.

El ladrón de glándulas, Viuda de Pueyo (Madrid, Spain), 1929, reprinted, Peninsula (Barcelona, Spain), 1998.

Fantasmas, Compania Ibero-Americana de Publicaciones (Madrid, Spain), 1930, translated by Henry Baerlein published as *Laugh and the Ghosts Laugh with You,* British Technical and General Press (London, England), 1952.

Los que no fuimos a la guerra (novel), Compania Ibero-Americana de Publicaciones (Madrid, Spain), 1930.

El malvado Carabel (title means "The Wicked Carabel"), Renacimiento (Madrid, Spain), 1931, reprinted, Temas de Hoy (Madrid, Spain), 1998.

Acotaciones de un oyente e impresiones políticas de un hombre de buena fe (title means "A Listener's Notes and Political Impressions of a Man of Good Faith"), in *Obras Completas (1945-1950),* Volumes 7-8, Renacimiento (Madrid, Spain), 1931, reprinted, Espasa-Calpe (Madrid, Spain), 1962.

La conquista del horizonte, Viuda de Pueyo (Madrid, Spain), 1932.

El hombre que compró un automóvil, Pueyo (Madrid, Spain), 1932, reprinted, Anaya (Madrid, Spain), 1990.

Aventuras del caballero Rogelio de Amaral, Viuda de Pueyo (Madrid, Spain), 1933.

Odio (screenplay), 1934.

Los trabajos del detective Ring, Viuda de Pueyo (Madrid, Spain), 1934.

Mis mejores cuentos (stories; contains "Luz de luna," "La familia Gomar," and "El calor de la hoguera"), Prensa Popular (Madrid, Spain), 1934.

Una isla en el mar rojo, Ediciones Españoles (Madrid, Spain), 1939.

Visiones de neurastenia, Librería General (Zaragoza, Spain), 1939.

Los novelas del espino en flor (contains "El secreto de Barba-Azul," "Las siete columnas," and "Relato inmoral"), Ediciones Españoles (Madrid, Spain), 1940.

La novela número 13, Librería General (Zaragoza, Spain), 1941, reprinted, Espasa-Calpe (Madrid, Spain), 1971.

Nube enjaulada, Librería General (Zaragoza, Spain), 1944.

Afan-Evu (screenplay), 1945.

Obras completas, M. Aquilar (Madrid, Spain), 1945, reprinted, 1968.

El toro, el torero y el gato (title means "The Bull, the Bullfighter, and the Cat"), M. Aquilar (Madrid, Spain), 1946.

El bosque animado (title means "The Lively Forest"), Nacional (Madrid, Spain), 1947, reprinted, Espasa-Calpe (Madrid, Spain), 1996.

El sistema pelegrín, Librería General (Zaragoza, Spain), 1949.

De portería a portería, Prensa Española (Madrid, Spain), 1949.

Las maletas del más allá, Alfil (Madrid, Spain), 1952.

Fuego artificiales, Planeta (Barcelona, Spain), 1954.

Mis páginas mejores, Gredos (Madrid, Spain), 1956.

Yo y el ladrón, y otros cuentos, Oxford University Press (New York, NY), 1957.

Antología del humorismo en la literatura universal, Labor (Barcelona, Spain), 1957.

La vaca adúltera, Taurus (Madrid, Spain), 1958.

Filozofio de fantomo, Hispaña Esperanto Federacio (Zaragoza, Spain), 1959.

Impresiones de un hombre de buena fe: 1920-1936, Espasa-Calpe (Madrid, Spain), 1964.

Obras selectas, Caro Roggio (Barcelona, Spain), 1979.

Also author of *El hombre que quiso matar* and *Un cadáver en el comedor.* Contributor to periodicals, including, *Maraña, Diario de Galicia, Tierra Gallega, Imparcial, Ilustración Española e Hispanoamericana,* and *ABC.*

ADAPTATIONS: Novels by Fernández Flórez that have been adapted into film include *El malvado Carabel,* 1935; *Unos pasos de mujer,* 1941; *Un cadáver en el comedor,* 1942; *El hombre que quiso matar,* 1943; *El bosque animado,* 1943; *La casa de la lluvia,* 1943; *El fantasma,* 1944; *Ha entrado un ladrón,* 1950; *El sistema pelegrín,* 1952; *Luz de luna,* 1959; *Los que no fuimos a la guerra,* 1962; *Por qué te engaña tu marido,* 1969; and *Volvereta,* 1976.

SIDELIGHTS: Novelist Wenceşlao Fernández Flórez, according to the *Columbia Dictionary of Modern European Literature,* was "above all a humorist who in his best works offers a desolate and bitter vision of life and of the world that is both personal and universal." He was very successful with writing social and national satire and much of his work contains brash humor and deep irony.

Robert Zaetta, writing in *Kentucky Romance Quarterly,* observed that Fernández Flórez "began writing under the influence of Realism and Naturalism, and his early novels follow the literary conventions of literary schools." Zaetta proposed that *Volvereta, Ha entrado un ladrón,* and *Unos pasos de mujer* are three novels that exemplify Fernández Flórez's early stage of narration. Zaetta stated, "the reader can soon predict their course of action because the protagonists seem programmed to go on committing the same errors."

Delfín Carbonell, writing in *Cuadernos Hispanoamericanos,* insisted that Fernández Flórez "expresses the angst of existence through the medium of vulgarity [ironic humor and caricature], daily. He proves capable of painting two facets of existence: the humorist face and the tragic-humorist. His world is a world of laughter and tears that proves a deep preoccupation with the fundamental heartfelt problem or the significance of existence. He presents examples of vulgar persons . . . men profoundly mortified by the accident of circumstances they do not understand, or are unable to rise above."

Published in 1925, *El secreto del Barba-Azul* "marks the start of the second stage in the development of Fernández Flórez's comic technique," according to Zaetta. "This novel shows a sharp departure from earlier realistic works as the characters become caricatures and the places become symbolic." Another "development" in Fernández Flórez's technique can be seen in *Relato inmoral.* As Zaetta observed, "closely allied to the theme of love and sex is that of the mores of Spanish society," making *Relato inmoral* "a burlesque of the 'novela erótica' . . . in which the character always seems to find sexual gratification. The protagonist in *Relato inmoral* is comic because he anxiously attempts to satisfy his sexual urge, but is constantly thwarted by the taboos of Spanish society." Francisco López, writing in *Insula,* called *El secreto del Barba-Azul* "a significant novel with symbolism, [that] from a distance the precedence of its style can be counted upon. But in *El secreto del Barba-Azul* there are other secrets, [namely] multiple scenes in multiple succession, all a continuous procession of illusion and caricatures that exist in the disconcerting world."

An example of Fernández Flórez's absurdity can be found in *El sistema pelegrín*. As Zaetta commented in *Romance Notes*, "the mind wavers from fact to fiction, from the illogical to the logical, when the dual roles of the protagonist come into rational conflict." Zaetta concluded that Fernández Flórez "employs the comic technique of crowning absurdity by heaping nonsense upon nonsense throughout which culminates in an illogical conclusion that on the surface seems to have a grain of logic. . . . Fernández Flórez's message is clear: man's efforts will always be tinged by his folly."

Another aspect of Fernández Flórez's career was his relationship with cinema. According to Thomas Deveny in *Romance Languages Annual*, that relationship "began in the 1920s, but the period of greatest collaboration was the 1940s and 1950s." His screenplay *El bosque animado*, Deveny said, "provides a pantheistic vision of a forest in Galicia, in northwestern Spain." According to Deveny, film director José Luis Cuerda "captures [the] poetic quality of the narrative from the opening frames of the film" and "has created a film narrative that is different from the original, but which captures the poetic spirit of the novel." Lopéz offered this observation: "*El bosque animado* can be seen as a complex result of two variants that unite existence in the world: the occult and the visible."

BIOGRAPHICAL AND CRITICAL SOURCES:

BOOKS

Bede, Jean-Albert, and William B. Edgerton, editors, *Columbia Dictionary of Modern European Literature*, Columbia University Press (New York, NY), 1980.

Fleischmann, Wolfgang Bernard, editor, *Encyclopedia of World Literature in the Twentieth Century*, Frederick Ungar (New York, NY), 1967.

PERIODICALS

Cuadernos Hispanoamericanos, 1967, Delfín Carbonell, "Unas notas sobre Fernández Flórez: humorismo y tragedia," pp. 577-586.

Dusquesne Hispanic Review, 1966, Reyes Carbonell, "El contraste en los cuentos de Wenceşlao Fernández Flórez," pp. 63-74.

Insula, February, 1967, José-Carlos Mainer, "Una revision: Wenceşlao Fernández Flórez," pp. 1, 10; September, 1985, Francisco López, "Acotaciones sobre una novelística olvidada," pp. 14-15.

Kentucky Romance Quarterly, 1970, Robert Zaetta, "Wenceşlao Fernández Flórez: The Evolution of His Technique in His Novels," pp. 127-137.

Papeles de son Armadans, July, 1971, José-Carlos Mainer, "W. Fernández Flórez, un noventayocho olivado," pp. 23-42.

Revista de Estudios Hispanicos, May, 1972, Robert Zaetta, "The 'Burla' in the Novels of Wenceşlao Fernández Flórez," pp. 283-292.

Romance Language Annual, 1991, Thomas Deveny, "Recuperation of a Novel: The Screen Adaptation of *El bosque animado*," pp. 416-419.

Romance Notes, winter, 1973, Robert Zaetta, "Wenceşlao Fernández Flórez's Comic Technique in *El sistema pelegrín*," pp. 234-237.

OTHER

El poder de la palabra, http://www.epdlp.com/ (April 22, 2002), "Wenceşlao Fernández Flórez."*

*　　　*　　　*

FIELDING, Kate
See OLDFIELD, Jenny

*　　　*　　　*

FISCHER, Gretl Keren 1919-
(Gretl Kraus Fischer)

PERSONAL: Born April 18, 1919, in Olomouc, Czechoslovakia (now Czech Republic); immigrated to Canada, 1951; daughter of Arnošt and Anny (Diamant) Kraus; married Hugo Fischer (a lawyer), September, 1940 (died, 1978). *Education:* University of British Columbia, B.A., 1956; Carleton University, M.A., 1961; McGill University, Ph.D. (English literature), 1972. *Politics:* "Left of center." *Religion:* "Reform Judaism and Reconstructionist; science-based naturalistic theology." *Hobbies and other interests:* Reading, music, theater, square-dancing, swimming, hiking.

ADDRESSES: Agent—c/o Writers' Union of Canada, 40 Wellington St. E., 3rd Floor, Toronto, Ontario, Canada M5E 1C7.

CAREER: Worked as maid and shop assistant in England during World War II; United Nations Intergovernmental Organization, library assistant, 1944-45; United Nations secretariat, assistant in visual information section, 1946; Association of Special Libraries and Information Bureau, librarian and editor, 1947-49; British Transport Commission, library assistant, 1950-51; Imperial Oils Public Relations Library, Toronto, Ontario, Canada, library assistant, 1951; Canadian Bechtel, Inc., Vancouver, British Columbia, Canada, file clerk, 1952-53; Pacific Fisheries Experimental Station, librarian, summers, 1954-56; University of British Columbia, Vancouver, lecturer in German, 1956-58; Algonquin College, Ottawa, Ontario, Canada, English teacher, 1969-76; Carleton University, Ottawa, sessional lecturer in English, 1976-79. Community activist on environmental and human-rights issues.

MEMBER: Writers Union of Canada, Institute on Religion in an Age of Science.

WRITINGS:

(Under name Gretl Kraus Fischer) *In Search of Jerusalem: Religion and Ethics in the Writings of A. M. Klein,* McGill-Queen's University Press (Montreal, Quebec, Canada), 1975.

(Under name Gretl Kraus Fischer) *Skeptics* (trilogy of one-act plays), produced in Ottawa, Ontario, Canada, 1986.

An Answer for Pierre (novel), Borealis Press (Ottawa, Ontario, Canada), 1999.

Work represented in anthologies, including *British Columbia Centennial Anthology,* McClelland & Stewart, 1958; and *Refugees: An Anthology of Poems and Songs,* edited by Brian Coleman, privately printed (Ottawa, Ontario, Canada), 1988. Contributor of short stories, poetry, and essays to periodicals, including *Queen's Quarterly, Dalhousie Review, Fiddlehead, Edge, Canadian Literature, Canadian Forum,* and *Romanquelle.* Editor, *ASLIB Book List,* 1947-49. Writings prior to 1999 appeared under the name Gretl Kraus Fischer.

WORK IN PROGRESS: Slaves of Liberty and Other Stories.

SIDELIGHTS: Gretl Keren Fischer told *CA:* "I consider *An Answer for Pierre* by far the most important of my writings. This novel records Jacob Harald's passionate struggle for a world view. A central aspect of his quest is his refusal to accept the idea (so widespread at the close of the millennium) that good and evil, right and wrong, objectively seen, are nothing but a matter of social orientation or individual preference. When he is confronted with fathomless corruption, he is driven to search for an ethical standard beyond human opinion. He looks to the exciting new teachings of mainstream science for help. Can an ethic based on science be reconciled with his Jewish faith? Gradually his own conclusions emerge in a synthesis: he believes that the basic life-protecting and life-enhancing ethic of Leviticus (such as the Love Commandments or the Ten Commandments) translates into human language an ethical imperative that seems to be rooted in the very depth of the cosmos. Jacob faces many objections that can be raised against his view. It is my hope that his defense will be considered a valid one. We see Jacob's struggle against a background of human relationships. I wanted to express the ideas not just as an academic statement, but to show also their deeply personal impact. Though Jacob fails in his attempt to ease his friend Pierre's spiritual distress, his effort leads to the attainment of his own inner peace."

*   *   *

FISCHER, Gretl Kraus
   See FISCHER, Gretl Keren

*   *   *

FITZPATRICK, Deanne

PERSONAL: Born in Placentia, Newfoundland, Canada; daughter of William P. and Anne Marie Fitzpatrick; married Robert Mansoni, 1992; children: two. *Education:* Acadia University, M.Ed., 1990.

ADDRESSES: Home—R.R.5, Amherst, Nova Scotia, Canada B4H 3Y3. *E-mail*—hookingrugs@ns.sympatico.ca.

CAREER: Fiber artist, with work represented at Canadian Museum of Civilization, Art Gallery of Nova Scotia, Art Galley of Newfoundland and Labrador, and Nova Scotia Art Bank.

MEMBER: Rug Hooking Guild of Nova Scotia.

WRITINGS:

Hook Me a Story: The History and Method of Rug Hooking in Atlantic Canada, Nimbus Publishing (Halifax, Nova Scotia, Canada), 2000.

Contributor to periodicals. Member of editorial board, *Rug Hooking.*

*   *   *

FLOOD, Pansie Hart 1964-

PERSONAL: Born May 20, 1964, in Wilmington, NC; daughter of Sammie (a carpenter) and Zelene (a teacher; maiden name, Wallace) Hart; married Merrill Patrick Flood; children: two. *Ethnicity:* "African American." *Education:* East Carolina University, B.A. (school and community health education), 1986. *Religion:* Baptist.

ADDRESSES: Office—P.O. Box 20614, Greenville, NC 27858. *E-mail*—floodpan@earthlink.net.

CAREER: Bertie County Schools, Windsor, NC, school health educator, 1986-87; Wake County Schools, Raleigh, NC, middle school and high school teacher, 1987-88; Pitt County Schools, Greenville, NC, middle school teacher, 1988—.

MEMBER: Society of Children's Book Writers and Illustrators, North Carolina Association of Educators, North Carolina Writer's Network.

AWARDS, HONORS: East Carolina University African-American Firsts award, 2002; Honor Book, Society of School Librarians International, 2003, for *Sylvia and Miz Lula Maye.*

WRITINGS:

Sylvia and Miz Lula Maye, illustrated by Felicia Marshall, Carolrhoda Books (Minneapolis, MN), 2001.
Secret Holes, illustrated by Felicia Marshall, Carolrhoda Books (Minneapolis, MN), 2003.

WORK IN PROGRESS: September Smiles, Carolrhoda Books (Minneapolis, MN), 2004; *Tiger Turcotte and the Trouble with Tests,* Carolrhoda, 2004; *Tiger Turcotte and the Argument with D.O.,* Carolrhoda, 2005; and *Tiger Turcotte Isn't Wet with Sweat,* Carolrhoda, 2006.

SIDELIGHTS: Middle-school teacher Pansie Hart Flood grew up in Wilmington, North Carolina, where as the youngest of seven children, she was immersed in the activities of family life. For her, one of these activities was writing, as she recalled to *CA:* "As an elementary school kid, writing for fun was something that I acquired naturally. Writing about whatever was going on in my day-to-day life (journal writing) became a habit. For as long as I can remember, I've always enjoyed expressing myself in the written form." Thus, it is not surprising that she should draw upon her home life for subject matter. As she explained to *CA,* "The existence of my 108-year-old grandmother inspired me to write my first novel, *Sylvia and Miz Lula Maye.*" "When my grandmother turned one hundred years old, I was just totally fascinated with that idea, because I had never met anyone who turned one hundred," she elaborated on the *Public Radio East* Web site. "Then my grandmother turned 101, 102, 103, 104, 105, 106, 107, and 108. She just kept on living and living, and it just became even more fascinating. Every year we had a birthday party for my grandmother, and everybody just couldn't believe the condition she was in . . . her spicy and vivacious character, her personality."

Set in South Carolina in the late 1970s, *Sylvia and Miz Lula Maye* revolves around Sylvia, a "spirited, sassy girl, with a strong, engaging voice," to quote *School Library Journal*'s Barbara Auerbach. Part of this authentic voice is due to Sylvia's realistic speech, which even incorporates such grammatical flaws as "she's gots lots of cousins" and "where your peoples from." Sylvia and her single mother have recently moved from Florida, and the ten-year-old girl tells how she befriends Miz Lula Maye, the nearly one-hundred-year-old woman who lives next door. Much to the surprise of the girl's mother, the friendship proves mutually rewarding for the two, for though separated by ninety years in age, they have much in common. According to *Booklist*'s Ilene Cooper, Flood writes with an "authentic voice that captures" the 1978 setting and the friendship between the elderly and young characters, while in *Kirkus Reviews* a commentator noted that overall, the girl's narrative is "delightful."

Flood continued to hone her skills, writing such novels as *Secret Holes, September Smiles,* and the "Tiger Turcotte" chapter-book series for emerging readers. As before, Flood looked to her own family for ideas. She told *CA,* "My own children inspired me to write stories that evolved into the 'Tiger Turcotte' book series of chapter books. Because of my family, I have lots of stories to write.

"I hope that more kids will become encouraged to read books about African Americans and multi-cultures. Diversity in literature is very important on all levels, as well as, ages."

To would-be writers she offered this advice, "I encourage aspiring writers to take a close look at what they know best (family, community, religion, career, hobby, culture, etc.). Stories live all around you and are anxiously waiting to be told. Be patient, persistent, and have perseverance!"

BIOGRAPHICAL AND CRITICAL SOURCES:

PERIODICALS

Booklist, February 15, 2002, Ilene Cooper, review of *Sylvia and Miz Lula Maye,* p. 1032.
Kirkus Reviews, February 15, 2002, review of *Sylvia and Miz Lula Maye,* p. 255.
Publishers Weekly, January 28, 2002, review of *Sylvia and Miz Lula Maye,* p. 291.
School Library Journal, April, 2002, Barbara Auerbach, review of *Sylvia and Miz Lula Maye,* p. 148.

ONLINE

Pansie Flood Web site, http://www.pansieflood.com (April 3, 2003).
Public Radio East Web site, http://www.publicradioeast.org/lifestyle/ (January 15, 2003), review of *Sylvia and Miz Lula Maye.*

*   *   *

FOLGER, Henry Clay 1857-1930

PERSONAL: Born June 18, 1857, in New York, NY; died June 11, 1930, in Brooklyn, NY; son of Henry Clay (a wholesale milliner) and Eliza Jane (Clark) Folger; married Emily C. Jordan, October 6, 1885. *Education:* Attended Adelphi Academy, Brooklyn, NY; Amherst College, A.B., 1879; Columbia University, LL.B. (cum laude), 1881. *Religion:* Congregationalist.

CAREER: Industrialist and book collector. Pratt & Co. (oil company), began as clerk c. 1879, became secretary and then chairman of the manufacturing committee; Standard Oil Co., director in New Jersey, beginning 1908, then director in New York, president, beginning 1911, became chairman of board of directors.

AWARDS, HONORS: Litt.D., Amherst College, 1914.

WRITINGS:

A Tribute to the Memory of Charles Pratt: An Address at Pratt Institute, on Founder's Day, October 2, 1903, privately printed, 1903.
A Unique First Folio, photographs by George Dupont Pratt, Outlook (New York, NY), 1907.

SIDELIGHTS: During his senior year at Amherst College, Henry Clay Folger heard a lecture that would change his life. It was one of Ralph Waldo Emerson's last public lectures, "Superlative or Mental Temperance." It inspired Folger to read Emerson's essays on Shakespeare, including "The Tercentenary of Shakespeare's Birth," and Shakespeare's works enthralled him thereafter. As soon as he could, he began collecting books by and about the poet and dramatist. The result was the Henry Clay Folger Shakespeare Library, the largest Shakespeare library in the world. John Quincy Adams, the Folger's first librarian, was quoted by William Baker in the *Dictionary of Literary Biography* as having once said, "Here . . . in almost unbelievable fullness and richness, we assembled books, pamphlets, documents, manuscripts, relics, curios, oil-paintings, original drawings, watercolors, prints, statues, busts, medals, coins, miscellaneous objects of art, furniture, tapestries, playbills, prompt-books, stage properties, actors' costumes, and other material designed to illustrate the poet at his times. The library is thus more than a mere library; it is also a museum of the Golden Age of Elizabeth, and a memorial to the influence that Shakespeare has exerted upon the world's culture."

Folger, raised Congregationalist, attended Adelphi Academy in Brooklyn before enrolling at Amherst College. During his junior year his father's business failed, and Henry had to attend the College of the City of New York. His childhood friend and Amherst classmate Charles Pratt, and another classmate, William M. Ladd, guaranteed the funding needed for him to continue his studies at Amherst. Folger graduated from Amherst with an A.B. and was elected Phi Beta Kappa in 1879. He then studied law at Columbia University, supporting himself through school with a job at Pratt's father's oil business. In 1885, four years after he graduated from Columbia, he married another Shakespeare enthusiast, Vassar College graduate Emily C. Jordan. She became a vital partner in Folger's collection of Shakespearean works, and helped purchase books and catalogued the collection.

Folger remained with Pratt & Co. following his graduation. He advanced from clerk to secretary and eventually chairman of the manufacturing committee. As chairman he worked with the management of one of the company's big plants, the Standard Oil Co. In 1908 Folger was elected director of the Standard Oil Co. of New Jersey, and the next year director of the Standard Oil Co. of New York. When the Standard Oil trust dissolved in 1911 he helped reorganize it, and became president of the New York company. During his years with Standard Oil its original capital of $5,000,000 grew to $450,000,000 by 1927. By 1928 its net income was $39,645,228 and it owned the entire outstanding stock of several other companies, including the Tank Storage and Carriage Co. Ltd. of Great Britain, the Standard Transportation Co., the Lotus Oil and Distributing Corp. and the Magnolia Co. of Texas. Five years after becoming chairman of the board of directors, Folger left his job to dedicate himself to his Shakespearean library.

Folger had begun purchasing Shakespearean works shortly after he graduated, starting with the Handy Volume Edition of Shakespeare, published by Routledge. For the rest of his life, and throughout his travels, he always kept at least one of the thirteen volumes by him. He competed directly with Henry E. Huntington and another collector, known as the "dean" of Shakespeare collectors, William A. White. White and Huntington, however, collected in other areas while Folger only collected Shakespearean-related materials. Dealers knew this, and often made their first offers to Folger. His first major purchase was a Halliwell-Phillipps edition of Shakespeare's first folio in reduced facsimile. At that time, he had no intentions of starting a collection; he simply wanted to learn more about Shakespeare. But as he studied the edition and discovered the remarkable differences between the first folio text in his facsimile and the contemporary edition, he felt compelled to study more original editions. By the time he completed his collection he had every known issue, but one, of each of the four Shakespeare folios. His collection also included some of the first and rarest of the quartos, including a rare copy of "Titus Andronicus" (1594) purchased from the Lund library in Sweden, and the Gwynn volume, the only known copy of a collected edition of nine plays, which Thomas Pavier and William Jaggard brought out in 1619. Another significant purchase was the Vincent copy of the first folio, brought out in 1623 and still with the original bindings and uncut leaves.

The Folgers took several trips to England to add to the collection, combing auction houses and book catalogues. When he could not travel, Folger had agents search and bid for him. Collecting became the childless couple's obsession, and they lived simply to better fund their collection. As quoted by Baker, by 1889 Folger described his collection in a letter to a friend as "a modest library." Later he wrote that he had "been signally fortunate . . . quite beyond my greatest hopes and have made a collection of material illustrating Shakespeare which I believe will soon be notable." By 1909 his vision for his library had expanded. He wrote that he had "found the means of adding to my collection of Shakespeareana until it is the largest and finest in America, perhaps the world. That is really saying a great deal, for collecting Shakespeareana has been the life-work of many students during the past hundred years." Amherst College awarded Folger with an Litt.D., in 1914.

Once the Folgers realized they had the finest Shakespearean collection in America, if not the world, they started plans to construct a building for it in Washington, D.C. Folger wanted to create a building whose exterior would match the classic architecture of the nearby Library of Congress and U.S. Supreme Court buildings, and whose interior would reference Elizabethan England. The library had room for 150,000 volumes, a study room, a reading room, an exhibition gallery, reception and administration rooms and an auditorium based on a Shakespearean theater. Though Folger died before the building was completed, he lived to see the cornerstone laid on May 28, 1930, less than two weeks before his death. The library was left in the trust of Amherst College trustees with an endowment for maintenance and expansion.

The Henry Clay Folger Shakespeare Library opened in 1931. It had 80,000 volumes, including those owned by other well-known authors, scholarly works on Shakespeare, prompt books, and manuscripts. There were 1,400 different copies of Shakespeare's collected works, with seventy-nine copies of the first folio, fifty of the second folio, and twenty-four of the third folio. Among Shakespeare's poetic works are two copies of the sonnets from their first printing in 1609, and ten copies of the first collected edition, published in 1640. Folger had written several monographs on Shakespearean subjects. These have a place in the library, as do Tudor and Stuart histories. As Adams noted, the library also holds art works, furniture, and other related artifacts.

BIOGRAPHICAL AND CRITICAL SOURCES:

BOOKS

Adams, Joseph Quincy, *The Folger Shakespeare Memorial Library: A Report on Progress, 1931-1941,* Trustees of Amherst College (Amherst, MA), 1942.
Catalog of the Manuscripts of the Folger Shakespeare Library, [Boston, MA], 1971.
Catalog of Printed Books in the Folger Shakespeare Library, [Boston, MA], 1970.
Dictionary of American Book Collectors, Greenwood Press (New York, NY), 1986.
Dictionary of Literary Biography, Volume 140, *American Book-Collectors and Bibliographers,* Gale (Detroit, MI), 1994.
The Folger Shakespeare Library Washington, Trustees of Amherst College (Amherst, MA), 1933.
Henry C. Folger, 18 June 1857-11 June 1930, privately printed (New Haven, CT), 1931.
Wright, Louis B., *The Folger Library: A Decade of Growth 1950-1960,* Folger Shakespeare Library (Washington, DC), 1960.
Wright, Louis B., *The Folger Library: Two Decades of Growth: An Informed Account,* University Press of Virginia (Charlottesville, NC), 1968.

PERIODICALS

Outlook, November 23, 1907.*

FORD, Charles Henri 1908-2002

OBITUARY NOTICE—See index for *CA* sketch: Born February 10, 1908, in Hazlehurst, MS; died September 27, 2002, in New York, NY. Artist, editor, and author. Ford was a surrealist poet, photographer, and painter best known as the editor of the influential literary publication *Blues: A Magazine of New Rhythms* and the art and literature magazine *View.* Ford was interested in editing from an early age, creating his first broadside when he was in grammar school. After reading the magazine *The Exile,* edited by Ezra Pound, he decided to starts his own magazine, *Blues,* in 1929. Though he only edited the publication for a year, within its pages Ford was able to publish the early works of such renowned writers as Erskine Caldwell, Gertrude Stein, and William Carlos Williams, an impressive feat for a young man who was still living with his parents at the time. Moving to New York, then Paris, and then back to the United States, Ford led a peripatetic life, socializing within his literary circle of friends and establishing himself as a poet in his own right. He caused a stir in 1933 when he cowrote the novel *The Young and Evil* with Parker Tyler. The book was published in Paris, but its gay themes caused it to be banned in the United States until the 1960s. During the 1940s Ford founded and edited *View,* and in the 1950s he became increasingly interested in photography and film. He is credited by some with introducing Andy Warhol to underground movies; Ford wrote the screenplay *Johnny Minotaur,* released in 1973. He exhibited his photographs in the United States and Europe, with his final showing as part of the "Poem Posters" exhibit in New York City in 1999, and was also interested in the artform of collage. Though much of his poetry is surrealistic in nature, late in his writing career he explored haiku, a poetic form that captured his interest following a trip to Katmandu. Among Ford's thirteen collections of poems are *Silver Flower Coo* (1968), *Secret Haiku: Om Krishna 111* (1982), and *Out of the Labyrinth: Selected Poems* (1990). Ford was also the author of the autobiographical *I Will Become What I Am* and *Water from a Bucket: A Diary, 1948-1957* (2001).

OBITUARIES AND OTHER SOURCES:

BOOKS

Contemporary Poets, seventh edition, St. James Press (Detroit, MI), 2001.

PERIODICALS

Los Angeles Times October 4, 2002, p. B15.
New York Times, September 30, 2002, p. A31.
Times (London, England), October 1, 2002.
Washington Post, October 1, 2002, p. B7.

*   *   *

FORWARD, Robert L(ull) 1932-2002

OBITUARY NOTICE—See index for *CA* sketch: Born August 15, 1932, in Geneva, NY; died of brain cancer September 21, 2002, in Seattle, WA. Physicist and author. Forward was an acclaimed author of "hard", or technically factual science-fiction novels. After earning a B.S. degree from the University of Maryland in 1954, he served in the U.S. Air Force for two years, reaching the rank of captain. A graduate fellowship permitted him to study physics at the University of California at Los Angeles, where he earned a master's degree in applied physics in 1958 while working at Hughes Research Laboratories. While working his way up the ranks at Hughes, Forward completed his Ph.D. at the University of Maryland in 1965. After becoming a senior scientist at Hughes in 1974, Forward began work on his first science-fiction novel, *Dragon's Egg* (1980), which, as with all his later books, is a story based on scientific fact. Forward retired from Hughes in 1987 in order to spend more time on his writing, impressing reviewers and readers alike with his fantastically imaginative world-building. His books include tales about aliens and civilizations existing on neutron stars, closely orbiting binary planets, and in the clouds above the surface of Saturn. However, at times he was criticized for thin plotlines and shallow characterizations that some felt critics took second place behind his scientifically accurate settings. Nevertheless, Forward found many fans with such novels as *Timemaster* (1992), *Camelot 30K* (1993), and his last book, *Saturn Rukh* (1997). The year he left Hughes, Forward founded his own company, Forward Unlimited, a consulting firm specializing in innovative space propulsion systems and "exotic physics." In 1992 he also founded Tethers Unlimited, which made tethers for the U.S. Air Force and the National Aeronautics and Space Administration. Forward was a brilliant scientist who held twenty patents and whose gravitational radiation antenna—which detects gravity waves—was the first device of its kind; it is currently on display in the Smithsonian Institute. As a physicist, Forward was fascinated by gravity and felt that it was possible to invent an anti-gravity machine; he was also interested in the possibilities of time travel and of warping space-time in order to cross vast distances through the universe. In addition to his works of science fiction, Forward also published over 150 scientific papers and the nonfiction books *Future Magic* (1988) and *Indistinguishable from Magic* (1995), which speculate on the scientific advances of the future. He was also the author, with Joel Davis, of *Mirror Matter: Pioneering Antimatter Physics* (1988).

OBITUARIES AND OTHER SOURCES:

PERIODICALS

Chicago Tribune, September 26, 2002, section 2, p. 9.
Los Angeles Times, September 24, 2002, p. B11.
New York Times, September 28, 2002, p. B15.
Times (London, England), September 30, 2002.
Washington Post, October 9, 2002, p. B6.

ONLINE

Science Fiction and Fantasy Writers of America Web site, http://www.sfwa.org/ (September 26, 2002).

*   *   *

FOX, John O. 1938-

PERSONAL: Born October 6, 1938, in Los Angeles, CA; married, 1964; wife's name Gretchen G. (an art historian); children: Joseph A., Margaret E. *Education:* Harvard University, A.B., 1960; attended London School of Economics and Political Science, 1960-61; University of California—Berkeley, LL.B., 1964; Georgetown University, LL.M., 1967.

ADDRESSES: Home—90 Fearing St., Amherst, MA 01002. *E-mail*—jofox@attbi.com.

CAREER: Sherman, Fox, Meehan & Canton, Washington, DC, founding partner, 1968-84, counsel, 1984-2000. Mount Holyoke College, South Hadley, MA, visiting lecturer, 1985—. Commission on Institutes of Higher Education, public member.

WRITINGS:

If Americans Really Understood the Income Tax: Uncovering Our Most Expensive Ignorance, Westview Press (Boulder, CO), 2000.

WORK IN PROGRESS: Research on the central role of housing in poverty.

SIDELIGHTS: John O. Fox told *CA:* "The book *If Americans Really Understood the Income Tax: Uncovering Our Most Expensive Ignorance* is an examination of the social and economic consequences of federal income tax policy, with proposals for significant reforms, written for the non-expert as well as the policy analyst."

BIOGRAPHICAL AND CRITICAL SOURCES:

PERIODICALS

Booklist, May 1, 2001, Mary Carroll, review of *If Americans Really Understood the Income Tax: Uncovering Our Most Expensive Ignorance,* p. 1646.
Tax Notes, February 25, 2002, Charles Davenport, review of *If Americans Really Understood the Income Tax,* pp. 1049-1053.
Wall Street Journal, April 16, 2001, David R. Henderson, review of *If Americans Really Understood the Income Tax,* p. A16.
Washington Monthly, April, 2001, David Cay Johnston, review of *If Americans Really Understood the Income Tax,* p. 54.

G

GALA (y VELASCO), Antonio (Ángel Custodio) 1936-

PERSONAL: Born October 2, 1936, in Córdoba, Spain; son of Luis Gala Calvo and Adoración Velasco. *Education:* Universidad de Seville, earned law degree; advanced degrees from Universidad de Madrid.

ADDRESSES: Home—Calle Macarena No. 16, 28016 Madrid, Spain. *Agent*—c/o Coreo Autor, Editorial Planeta, Córega 273-277, 08008 Barcelona, Spain.

CAREER: Poet, playwright, and novelist. Worked as a bricklayer's assistant, c. late 1950s; taught religion, art history, and philosophy in secondary schools in Madrid, Spain, c. 1959. Speaker at conferences.

MEMBER: Associación de Amistad Hispano-Árebe (president, 1981).

AWARDS, HONORS: Honorable mention, Premio Adonais de Poesía, 1959, for *Enemigo íntimo;* Premio las Albinas, 1963; Premio Nacional Calderón de la Barca, 1963, for *Los verdes campos del Edén;* Premio Ciudad de Barcelona, 1965; Premio Nacional de Literature, 1973, for *Anillos para una dama;* Premio de Periodismo González Ruano, 1976, for article "Los ojos de Troylo"; D.H.C., Universidad de Córdoba, 1982; named Andaluz Universal, Junta de Andalucía, 1983; Premio Léon Felipe, 1989, for community activism; Premio Planeta, 1990, for *El manuscrito carmesí;* Hidalgo prize; many other awards.

WRITINGS:

PLAYS

Los verdes campos del Edén (two-act; produced in Madrid, Spain, 1963), Escelicer (Madrid, Spain),

1964, published with *Anillos para una dama,* Edaf (Madrid, Spain), 2001, translation published as *The Green Fields of Eden* in *The Contemporary Spanish Theatre: The Social Comedies of the Sixties,* SGEL (Madrid, Spain), 1983.

(Translator) Paul Claudel, *El zapato de raso,* Escelicer (Madrid, Spain), 1965.

El sol en el hormiguero (two-act; produced in Madrid, Spain, 1966), published with *El caracol en el espejo* and *Noviembre y un poco de yerba,* Taurus (Madrid, Spain), 1970.

Noviembre y un poco de yerba (title means "November and a Bit of Grass"; produced in Madrid, Spain, 1967), published with *El sol en el hormiguero* and *El caracol en el espejo,* Taurus (Madrid, Spain), 1970.

Píldora nupcial; Corazones y diamantes; El "Weekend" de Andrómaca; Vieja se muere la alegría (television plays), Escelicer (Madrid, Spain), 1968.

Esa mujer (screenplay), Proesa (Madrid, Spain), 1968.

(Adaptor) Edward Albee, *Un delicado equilibrio,* produced in Madrid, Spain, 1969.

Spain's Strip-tease (produced in Madrid, Spain, 1970), published in *Obras escogidas,* Aguilar (Madrid, Spain), 1981.

Los buenos días perdidos (three-act; produced in Madrid, 1972), Primer Acto (Madrid, Spain), 1972, translation published as *The Bells of Orleans* in *Estreño* (University Park, PA), 1992.

Anillos para una dama (title means "A Ring for a Lady"; produced in Madrid, Spain, 1973), Júcar (Madrid, Spain), 1974.

¡Suerte, campeón! (produced in Madrid, Spain, 1973), published in *Teatro musical,* Espasa-Calpe (Madrid, Spain), 2000.

Canta, gallo acorralado (adaptation of a play by Sean O'Casey), produced in Madrid, Spain, 1973.

Cantar de Santiago para todos (television play), MK (Madrid, Spain), 1974.

Las cítaras colgadas de los árboles (title means "Zithers Hung in the Trees"; produced in Madrid, Spain, 1974), published with *¿Por qué corres, Ulises?* Espasa-Calpe (Madrid, Spain), 1977, 2nd edition, 1981.

Cuatro Conmemoraciones: Eterno Tuy; Auto del Santo Reino; Oratorio de Fuenterrabía; Retablo de Santa Teresa (television plays), Adra (Madrid, Spain), 1976.

Petra Regalada (produced in Madrid, Spain, 1980), MK (Madrid, Spain), 1980.

La vieja señorita del Paraíso (produced in Madrid, Spain, 1981), MK (Madrid, Spain), 1981.

El cemeterio de los pájaros (title means "The Bird Cemetery"; produced in Madrid, Spain, 1982), MK (Madrid, Spain), 1980.

Trilogía de la libertad (includes *Petra Regalada, La vieja señorita del Paraíso,* and *El cemeterio de los pájaros*), Espasa-Calpe (Madrid, Spain), 1983.

Obras escogidas, Aguilar (Madrid, Spain), 1981.

Paisaje Andaluz con figuras (title means "Andalusian Landscapes with Figures"; television play), two volumes, Andaluzas Unidas (Andalucía, Spain), 1984, 2nd edition published as *Paisaje con figuras,* 1985.

Samarkanda (produced in Madrid, Spain, 1985), MK (Madrid, Spain), 1985.

El hotelito (title means "The Little Family Manor"; produced in Madrid, Spain, 1985), published with *Samarkanda,* Espasa-Calpe (Madrid, Spain), 1985.

(With Enrique Jiménez) *El sombrero de tres picos,* Léon (Madrid, Spain), 1986.

Seneca, o el beneficio de la duda (produced in Madrid, Spain, 1987), Espasa-Calpe (Madrid, Spain), 1987.

Carmen Carmen (musical; produced in Madrid, Spain, 1988), Espasa-Calpe (Madrid, Spain), 1988.

Cristóbal Colón (opera; produced in Madrid, Spain, 1989), music by Leonardo Balada, Beteca Music (Pittsburgh, PA), 1989.

La truhana (musical; produced in Madrid, Spain, 1992), published in *Teatro musical,* Espasa-Calpe (Madrid, Spain), 2000.

Los bellos durmientes, Espasa-Calpe (Madrid, Spain), 1994.

Troneras, 1993-1996, Temas de Hoy (Madrid, Spain), 1996.

Teatro musical (contains *¡Suerte, Campeón! Spain's Strip-tease, Carmen Carmen,* and *La truhana*), Espasa-Calpe (Madrid, Spain), 2000.

Author of screenplays, including (with Miguel Rubio and Mario Camús) *Digan lo que digan,* 1968; *Esa mujer,* 1968; (with Luis Lucia) *Pepa Doncel,* 1969; and (with Rubio) *Los buenos días perdidos* (based on his own play), 1975; adaptor for television (with Camús and others) of works by William Shakespeare, Molière, and Euripides, c. 1968. Author, with others, of television series *Si las piedras hablaran,* Iniciativas Culturales de España, 1980.

Gala's plays have been published in numerous editions and anthologies.

NOVELS

El manuscrito carmesí (title means "The Crimson Manuscript"), Planeta (Barcelona, Spain), 1990.

La pasión turca, Espasa-Calpe (Madrid, Spain), 1993.

Más allá del jardín, Planeta (Barcelona, Spain), 1995.

Si las piedras hablaran, Espasa-Calpe (Madrid, Spain), 1995.

La regla de tres, Espasa-Calpe (Madrid, Spain), 1996.

Café cantante, Espasa-Calpe (Madrid, Spain), 1997.

El corazón tardío, Espasa-Calpe (Madrid, Spain), 1998.

Las manzanas del viernes, Espasa-Calpa (Madrid, Spain), 1999.

POETRY

Enemigo íntimo, RIALP (Madrid, Spain), 1960.

Testamento Andaluz, Publicaciones Obra Social y Cultural Cajasur (Córdoba, Spain), 1998.

El águila bicéfala: textos de amor, Espasa-Calpe (Madrid, Spain), 1993.

Poemas de amor, Planeta (Barcelona, Spain), 1997.

Cuaderno de Amor (anthology), Esfera de los Libros (Madrid, Spain), 2001.

OTHER

Córdoba para vivir, Publicaciones Españolas (Madrid, Spain), 1965.

Vicente Vela (criticism), Rayuela (Madrid, Spain), 1975.

Barrera-Wolff: enero 1976 (catalogue), Galeria Kreisler (Madrid, Spain), 1975.

Texto y pretexto, Sedmay (Madrid, Spain), 1977.

Teatro de hoy, teatro de mañana, Ateneo de Almería/ Univers (Almería, Spain), 1978.

Charlas con Troylo (essays; title means "Conversations with Troylo"), Espasa-Calpe (Madrid, Spain), 1981, enlarged edition published as *Charlas con Troylo y desde entonces,* 1998.

En propia mano (essays), Espasa-Calpe (Madrid, Spain), 1983.

Cuaderno de la dama de otoño (essays; originally published in *El País,* 1983), El País (Madrid, Spain), 1985.

Dedicado a Tobías (essays), Planeta (Barcelona, Spain), 1988.

Guía de los vinos españoles = Spanish Wines Guide (nonfiction), Iberia (Madrid, Spain), 1990.

La soledad sonora (essays), Planeta (Barcelona, Spain), 1991.

La Granada de los nazaríes, Planeta (Barcelona, Spain), 1992.

Proas y troneras, Akal (Madrid, Spain), 1993.

Córdoba de Gala, edited by Ana María Padilla Mangas, Caja Provincial de Ahorros de Córdoba (Córdoba, Spain), 1993.

Andaluz, Espasa-Calpe (Madrid, Spain), 1994.

Carta a los herederos, Planeta (Barcelona, Spain), 1995.

El don de la palabra, Espasa-Calpe (Madrid, Spain), 1996.

A quien va conmigo (essays), Planeta (Barcelona, Spain), 1997.

La casa sosegada, Planeta (Barcelona, Spain), 1998.

(Author of text) *Andalucía eterna,* photographs by José Luis Otermin, Otermin (Málaga, Spain), 1998.

Ahora hablaré de mí (autobiography), Planeta (Madrid, Spain), 2000.

Sobre la vida y el escenario (biography), Martínez Roca (Barcelona, Spain), 2001.

Teatro de la historia, Espasa-Calpe (Madrid, Spain), 2001.

El imposible olvido, Planeta (Madrid, Spain), 2001, 2nd edition, 2001.

Los invitados al jardín, Planeta (Madrid, Spain), 2002.

Contributor of column to *Sábado Gráfico,* beginning 1973; author of columns, including "Verbo Transitivo," to *El País,* beginning 1978. Contributor to *El Mundo.*

Gala's work has been translated into several languages, including French.

Gala's manuscripts are included in the theater collection at the Biblioteca Nacional, Madrid, Spain.

ADAPTATIONS: Poetry by Gala has been set to music by various composers, including *Cántico de "La pietá"* (chorus), music by Antón García Abril, Bolamar, 1992; and *Tientos,* music by Lorenzo Palomo, Música Española Contemporanea, 1993. *Más allá del jardín* was adapted as a motion picture, directed by Pedro Olea, Sogete/Lola Films, 1996.

SIDELIGHTS: A noted writer who focuses on the history and landscape of his native Andalusia within his works, award-winning Spanish writer Antonio Gala is credited with penning a number of popular productions for stage and screen as well as novels, poems, and essays. Achieving widespread celebrity status early in his career as a result of his television series *Paisaje con figuras*—which ceased broadcast in 1976 upon orders of Spanish President Arias Navarro—as well as his popular—and sometimes equally controversial—columns, which have appeared in major Spanish newspapers since the early 1970s, Gala has also gained critical praise for the novels he has written beginning in 1990. Noting his tendency to focus on social and political issues, *Contemporary World Writers* essayist Phyllis Zatlin wrote of Gala that his plays "blend . . . sparkling surface humor with an underlying tragic reality" while evidencing "a strong concern for individual freedom." His essay collections, which include *Charlas con Troylo, Dedicado a Tobías,* and *La soledad sonora,* are varied in scope, ranging in subject matter from politics to faith to tradition to sex. "Following in the footsteps of great writers such as Larra and Azorín," maintained Catherine G. Bellver in a *World Literature Today* review of *Dedicado a Tobías,* "Gala uses the print medium not in the common journalistic manner, for the dissemination of information, but for reflection, moral comment, and social testimony."

Born in Cordoba, Spain in 1936, Gala enrolled at the University of Seville at the age of fifteen. After earning a degree in law as well as advanced degrees in both political science and economics, the young man moved to Madrid, intending to follow the wishes of his father and begin a career as a government lawyer. However, the critical acclaim he received for his first book of poetry, *Enemigo íntimo,* convinced Gala to embark upon a career as a writer, and he worked as a laborer while continuing his literary endeavors. By the early 1960s he had earned a number of notable literary awards, most importantly for his first play, *Los verdes campos del Edén,* which was produced in Madrid in 1963. More importantly, he had become a popular playwright, capturing the interest and enthusiasm of his audience.

Since beginning his career in the Madrid theater in the early 1960s, Gala has produced both musicals and dramas, and has incorporated folkloric, historical, and allegorical elements into his plots. Noting that Gala combines spoken dialogue with song in his plays, Hazel Cazorla noted in an essay in *La Chispa '95:* "As an 'andaluz'[—a native of the southern region of Andalusia—], Gala is attuned to that special brand of natural poetry to be found in the speech of down-to-earth, ordinary folk" and possesses a "fine ear for the music of speech on several levels." He has produced three lavish musicals, *Carmen Carmen, Cristóbal Colón,* and *La truhana,* all period pieces employing rich sets and costumes, choreography, and a lush musical score. He also incorporates humor within his stage works. Commenting on *La truhana,* the story of a beautiful seventeenth-century actress who is forced to flee the attentions of the Spanish king, Cazorla noted: "Gala invites us to laugh at the unchanging, yet ever-changing, spectacle of the human comedy, while reminding us, as the original picaresque writers did, that laughter is, after all, the best technique for survival in a world which, for so many, now as then, is only too often a vale of tears."

In addition to musicals, Gala has also produced dramatic plays, such as the highly lauded *Los buenos días perdidos* and 1973's *Anillos para una dama,* which recalls the works of Spanish epic hero El Cid in the person of Gala's protagonist, Rodrigo de Vivar. First recorded in the twelfth-century *Poema de mio Cid,* the legend of Cid focuses on a Christian knight, loyal to Spain, who risks all for king and country. In his play, Gala focuses, not on Cid himself, but on the wife, Jimen, that he leaves behind at his death, his purpose, according to *Romance Quarterly* reviewer Isabel Torres "the demythification of . . . Spain's most revered epic hero. . . . [in order to] illuminate the human cost of heroism, . . . to free his society from the myths which bind and immobilize it." Noting the play's grounding in the history of Spain, *Modern Language Review* contributor John Lyon maintained that *Anillos para una dama* "is firmly anchored in . . .

a clearly-defined human conflict between an individual criterion of love and happiness and the obligations imposed by an alliance of collective tradition, religious morality, and political expediency."

Gala's first full-length novel, *El manuscrito carmesí,* is a work of historical fiction that focuses on the recapture of Spain from the Ottoman Turks in the late fifteenth century by presenting the fictional journal of Boabdil, the last sultan of Granada. "While the first-person account does not ignore factionalism among the Moorish leaders or Arab acts of violence and deceit," commented Zatlin, "the perspective of the Andalusian king tends both to demythify the image of the Catholic victors and to create a greater appreciation for Moorish culture." Gala's subsequent novels, such as *La pasión turca* and *Más allá del jardín,* explore other social issues within a fictional guise and feature what *Hispania* reviewer David K. Herzberger described as "off-beat characters who must overcome compelling social difficulties," such as homosexuality, racism, and political repression.

BIOGRAPHICAL AND CRITICAL SOURCES:

BOOKS

Contemporary World Writers, 2nd edition, St. James Press (Chicago, IL), 1993.

Halsey, Martha T., and Phyllis Zatlin, editors, *Contemporary Spanish Theater: A Collection of Critical Essays,* University Press of America (Lanham, MD), 1988.

Hispanic Literature and Politics, Indiana University of Pennsylvania (Indiana, PA), 1976.

Paolini, Claire J., editor, *La Chispa '95: Selected Proceedings,* Tulane University (New Orleans, LA), 1995.

Quintero, Jesús, *Trece noches* (interview with Gala), Planeta (Barcelona, Spain), 1999.

PERIODICALS

Estreño, Volume 2, number 2, 1976, Farris Anderson, "From Protest to Resignation"; Volume 11, 1985; Volume 18, number 2, 1992, Robert Louis Sheehan, "Antonio Gala's *Cristóbal Colón.*"

Hispania, summer, 1987, Wilma Newberry, "Antonio Gala's *El cemeterio de los párajos* and the Problem of Freedom," p. 431; December, 1994, David K. Herzberger, review of *La pasión turca,* p. 836.

Hispanic Review, summer, 1991, Patricia W. O'Connor, review of *Los buenos días perdidos* and *Anillos para una dama,* pp. 357-358.

Kentucky Romance Quarterly, Volume 24, 1977, Phyllis Zatlin, "The Theater of Antonio Gala: In Search of Paradise," pp. 175-183.

Modern Language Review, July, 1990, John Lyon, review of *Los buenos días perdidos* and *Anillos para una dama,* p. 772.

Romance Studies, autumn, 1995, Isabel Torres, "The Cid in the Shade in Gala's *Anillos para una dama,"* pp. 77-97.

World Literature Today, winter, 1990, Catherine G. Bellver, review of *Dedicado a Tobías,* p. 82; summer, 1992, David Ross Gerling, review of *La soledad sonora,* p. 488.

OTHER

Verdemente, http://www.verdemente.com/ (April 22, 2002), Pepa C. Belmonte, "Entrevista a Antonio Gala."*

*   *   *

GAMMEL, Irene 1959-

PERSONAL: Born 1959. *Education:* McMaster University, M.A., 1988; Ph.D., 1992; attended Universitat des Saarlandes, Saarbrucken, Germany, 1987; Queen's University, Ontario, DAAD visiting student; Sorbonne, University of Paris, auditor libre (comparative literature).

ADDRESSES: Office—Department of English, University of Prince Edward Island, 550 University Avenue, Charlottetown, Prince Edward Island, Canada C1A 4P3. *E-mail*—lgammel@upei.ca.

CAREER: University professor and writer. McMaster University, Toronto, Ontario, Canada, lecturer in English and comparative literature, 1992-93; University of Prince Edward Island, Charlottetown, Prince Edward Island, Canada, assistant professor, 1993-97, associate professor, 1997-2000, professor of English, 2000—. Visiting professor at Friedrich-Schiller-Universitat (Canadian studies) and Jena und Erfurt Universitat (spring term, 2001), both in Germany.

MEMBER: Canadian Comparative Literature Association (president, 1992-93).

AWARDS, HONORS: Buchanan Book Prize for Humanities, McMaster University, 1988; Government of Canada (WUSC) Award for international students in Canada, 1989-91; Award for Outstanding Scholarly Achievement, University of Prince Edward Island, 1995; SSHRC grant, three-time recipient.

WRITINGS:

Sexualizing Power in Naturalism: Theodore Dreiser and Frederick Philip Grove, University of Calgary Press (Calgary, Alberta, Canada), 1994.

(Editor, with Elizabeth Epperly), *L. M. Montgomery and Canadian Culture,* University of Toronto Press (Toronto, Ontario, Canada), 1999.

(Editor) *Confessional Politics: Women's Sexual Self-Representations in Life Writing and Popular Media,* Southern Illinois University Press (Carbondale, IL), 1999.

Baroness Elsa: Gender, Dada, and Everyday Modernity: A Cultural Biography, MIT Press (Cambridge, MA), 2002.

Contributor of numerous articles to literary journals, including *Faulkner Journal, Canadian Review of Comparative Literature,* and *Canadian Literature.* Also contributed chapters to scholarly books, including *Interfaces: Visualizing and Performing Women's Lives,* edited by Sidonie Smith and Julia Watson, University of Michigan Press (Ann Arbor, MI), 2002.

SIDELIGHTS: Specializing in the literature and culture of the modern era from 1900 to 1930, Irene Gammel is an English professor who also speaks and reads German, French, and intermediate Latin. Gammel often writes about women in literature and art from a feminist point of view. Her first book *Sexualizing Power in Naturalism: Theodore Dreiser and Frederick*

Philip Grove, came from her doctoral dissertation in English literature. Gammel points out in the book that her primary purpose is "to provide a revisionary—gender-critical—reading of twentieth-century American and Canadian naturalism." As noted by reviewer Judy Dudar, writing in *Canadian Literature,* publishers often caution that "doctoral dissertations do not necessarily make good books." Dudar commented that Gammel's book does contain "Information Overload." However, she also remarked that Gammel's book "adds depth and insight" into Grove's work and the "events and the individuals" that may have inspired some of the characters in Dreiser's novels. In the *Canadian Book Review Annual,* Paul Hjartarson felt the book "makes a promising beginning on an important topic and will leave readers wanting more."

Gammel is also the author of *Baroness Elsa: Gender, Dada, and Everyday Modernity: A Cultural Biography.* The work represents the first full biography of a woman whose outrageous lifestyle ultimately overshadowed her efforts as a poet, sculptor, and painter. Gammel provides readers with a look at Baroness Elsa's humble beginnings as Else-Hildegard Plötz, the German daughter of a harsh middle-class father and a mother who went insane. The baroness eventually ran away from her small hometown in the Baltic to Berlin, where she survived largely off the largesse of her various lovers. She eventually ended up in America with her second husband, who left her. She then married German Baron Leopold von Fretyag-Loringhoven, who later committed suicide and left his wife with only a title and no money.

Living in New York, the baroness became part of the dada art scene. The name dada comes from a French word meaning "hobbyhorse." Dada art usually contains unconventional forms and is produced using unconventional methods. It uses everyday objects like bicycles and urinals and often reflects the cynicism of the period following World War I. The central theme is that there is no purpose and no meaning to art or, in the larger context, to life. The baroness's art included portraits and sculptures made from everyday materials, as well as costumes. Gammel points out that the baroness, who once shaved her head and painted it red, became one of the first practitioners of body art. Her experimental poetry features odd syntax and phonetic sounds. The baroness, however, was never able to support herself financially. She also alienated many people

with her anti-Semitism and homophobia, although she was bisexual herself. In the end, she returned to Europe and died destitute in Paris in 1926 from gas poisoning. No one is sure whether it was deliberate or accidental.

Although noting that Gammel at times seems to excuse the baroness's often erratic behavior as part of her art, a reviewer writing in *Publishers Weekly* called Gammel's book "large, detailed, and well-researched." Holland Cotter, writing in the *New York Times,* noted, "The Baroness could not have asked for a more thoughtful and engaged monument" than Gammel's book. Although he called the work "flat-footed" stylistically, Cotter commented that "what carries the day" is that Gammel "is clearly for her subject." He added, "All the baroness's faults and absurdities are noted in detail, but so is her role as a pathfinder in transgressive sexuality, and as an artist." The result, noted Cotter, is "a dense, passionate book."

BIOGRAPHICAL AND CRITICAL SOURCES:

PERIODICALS

Ariel, October, 1995, E. D. Blodgett, review of *Sexualizing Power in Naturalism: Theodore Dreiser and Frederick Philip Grove,* pp. 171-174; July, 2000, Danielle Fuller, review of *L. M. Montgomery and Canadian Culture,* p. 180.

Booklist, April 1, 2002, Donna Seaman, review of *Baroness Elsa: Gender, Dada, and Everyday Modernity: A Cultural Biography,* p. 1297.

Canadian Book Review Annual, Volume 33, 1994, Paul Hjartason, review of *Sexualizing Power in Naturalism,* p. 251; Volume 28, 1999, Patricia Morley, review of *L. M. Montgomery and Canadian Culture,* p. 258.

Canadian Literature, winter, 1996, Judy Dudar, *Sexualizing Power in Naturalism,* pp. 133-135.

Children's Literature Association Quarterly, spring, 2001, Raymond E. Jones, review of *L. M. Montgomery and Canadian Culture,* p. 54.

Choice, March, 2000, review of *L. M. Montgomery and Canadian Culture,* p. 1300.

English Literature in Transition, 1880-1920, spring, 2000, review of *Confessional Politics: Women's Sexual Self-Representations in Life Writing and Popular Media,* pp. 250-251.

New York Times, May 19, 2002, "The Mama of Dada," p. 50.

Publishers Weekly, April 8, 2002, review of *Baroness Elsa,* p. 221.

Quill & Quire, July, 1999, Deborah Dundas, review of *L. M. Montgomery and Canadian Culture,* p. 47.*

*   *   *

GARCIA, Jerry 1942-1995

PERSONAL: Born August 1, 1942, in San Francisco, CA; died from a heart attack August 9, 1995, in Forest Knolls, CA; son of Jose (a musician) and Ruth (a nurse) Garcia; married Sarah Katz (divorced) married Carolyn Adams (divorced); married Deborah Koons, February 14, 1994; children: (first marriage) Heather; (second marriage) Annabelle, Trixie.

CAREER: Musician, composer, and performer. Performed and recorded as a founding member with the Grateful Dead band and with numerous other artists. Albums include the *Grateful Dead,* 1966; *American Beauty,* 1970; *Garcia,* 1972, *Virgin Beauty,* 1988; and *Jerry Garcia Band,* 1991. *Military service:* U.S. Army, 1959.

AWARDS, HONORS: Inducted into Rock & Roll Hall of Fame, Cleveland OH, 1994, as a member of the Grateful Dead.

WRITINGS:

Jerry Garcia: Paintings, Drawings, and Sketches, edited by David Hinds, Celestial Arts (Berkeley, CA), 1992.

Harrington Street (autobiographical), Delacorte Press (New York, NY), 1995.

(Illustrator) *Jerry Garcia's Amazing Grace,* HarperCollins (New York, NY), 2001.

(With Charles Reich and Jann Wenner) *Garcia,* Da Capo Press (New York, NY), 2003.

Songwriter with Grateful Dead on albums, including *American Beauty, Skeletons from the Closet,* and *In the Dark.*

Also composer and performer with David Grisman of audio recordings accompanying books illustrated by Bruce Whatley, including *The Teddy Bears' Picnic,* and *There Ain't No Bugs on Me,* both HarperCollins (New York, NY), 1999, and *What Will You Wear, Jenny Jenkins?* HarperCollins (New York, NY), 2000.

SIDELIGHTS: A legendary guitar player and the leading force behind the Grateful Dead band, Jerry Garcia might have been a piano player. However he never quite took to his mother's lessons, and his possibility of every becoming a virtuoso pianist ended when his older brother accidentally chopped off the middle finger of Garcia's right hand while cutting firewood. Garcia's mother eventually bought him his first guitar when he was fifteen. The rest, as they say, is history. After dropping out of high school, Garcia had a short stint in the U.S. Army, which discharged him after he went AWOL several times. He then began honing his musical expertise on the banjo and playing with various bluegrass bands, primarily in the San Francisco Bay area. But he soon gravitated to the electric guitar and with Ron McKernan started a band called the Warlocks, which evolved into the Grateful Dead. As the band gained popularly in the late 1960s, they soon became synonymous with the "hippie" era of free love and drugs. For Garcia, drug use would be an ongoing struggle for the rest of his life.

Over the years Garcia and the Grateful Dead produced numerous albums, and Jerry also created music as a solo artist and with various other musicians. As for the Grateful Dead, they only had one top-ten single during their thirty-year history. Nevertheless, as a touring band they were enormously successfully, earning more than $162 million in 1992. For "Dead Heads," rabid followers of the band who often traveled the country attending their concerts, Garcia was regarded with the same esteem as a spiritual leader. He rejected this role, insisting that all he ever wanted to do was play his guitar in a band. Nevertheless, Garcia became a cultural icon.

Before the Grateful Dead was formed, Garcia briefly studied painting at what would later become the San Francisco Art Institute. Throughout his life he dabbled in drawing and painting. This talent led to projects outside of music, such as a line of Jerry Garcia ties and several book projects, including the 1992 publication of *Jerry Garcia: Paintings, Drawings, and Sketches.* Another book, *Jerry Garcia's Amazing Grace,* was published posthumously and also features a selection of Garcia's artwork, as well as a CD recording of the traditional song performed by Garcia and his longtime friends David Grisman and Tony Rice. Garcia and Grisman recordings are also included with the two children's books, *The Teddy Bears' Picnic* and *There Ain't No Bugs on Me.* "Little Deadheads will enjoy this jaunty rendition," wrote Ilene Cooper in *Booklist* of *There Ain't No Bugs on Me.*

Garcia was also working on an autobiographical book with drawings when he died at the age of fifty-three in 1995. The book, titled *Harrington Street,* was completed by his third wife, Deborah Koons Garcia, and published in that same year. The book, which includes drawings by Garcia, focuses on the musician's life and the world around him as he grew up in the 1940s and 1950s. "Always closer to whimsy than introspection, Garcia nonetheless deals with some emotionally ripe tableaux in the book," wrote Chris Willman in an *Entertainment Weekly* review. In the book, Garcia talks about how he watched his dad drown in a river when Garcia was only five years old. He also discusses being brought up by his maternal grandparents and their strained relationship. Rossiter T. Drake, writing in *People,* called the book an "autobiography in the very loosest sense," pointing out that it is made up of short narrative segments enlivened by "colorful drawings." Nevertheless, Drake called Garcia's tale "fascinating" and noted that the artwork is "a mix of blissful visions and darker, more confusing images—a contrast embodied by the man himself."

BIOGRAPHICAL AND CRITICAL SOURCES:

BOOKS

George-Warren, Holly, and editors of *Rolling Stone,* editors, *Garcia,* Little, Brown & Company (Boston, MA), 1999.
Jackson, Blair, *Garcia: An American Life,* Penguin (New York, NY), 2000.

PERIODICALS

Booklist, November 1, 1992, Ray Olson, review of *Garcia: Paintings, Drawings, and Sketches,* pp. 477-478; August, 1999, Ilene Cooper, review of *There Ain't No Bugs on Me,* p. 2060.
Children's Book & Play Review, March, 2001, Lori Krupke, review of *The Teddy Bear Picnic,* p. 10.
Children's Book Review Service, August, 1996, review of *The Teddy Bear's Picnic,* p. 158.
Entertainment Weekly, December 8, 1995, Chris Willman, "A Deadhead Reckoning: A Rock Legend's Childhood Reminiscence Is Completed by His Widow," p. 60.

New York Times, August 13, 1995, J. Peder Zane, "A Look into Jerry Garcia's Future," p. E4.
People, May 6, 1996, Rossiter T. Drake, review of *Harrington Street,* p. 35.
Publishers Weekly, July 29, 1996, review of *The Teddy Bears' Picnic,* p. 41; May 10, 1999, review of *There Ain't No Bugs on Me,* p. 67.
School Library Journal, January, 1997, Martha Topol, review of *The Teddy Bears' Picnic,* p. 84; July, 1999, Jane Marino, review of *There Ain't No Bugs on Me,* p. 85.
Wall Street Journal, August 17, 1995, Micah Morrison, "A True Original," p. A12(L), p. A10(E).

ONLINE

Hotshotdigial.com Web site, http://www.hotshotdigital.com/ (June 3, 2002), biography of Garcia.

OBITUARIES:

PERIODICALS

Guitar Player, December, 1995, Stephen Cripe, and John Sievert, "Jerry Garcia," p. 56.
Los Angeles Times, August 10, 1995, Steve Hochman, "Jerry Garcia, Grateful Dead Founder, Dies," p. A1.
New York Times, August 11, 1995, "Grateful," p. A14(N).
People, August 21, 1995, Steve Dougherty, "What a Long, Strange Trip: Jerry Garcia Raised the Dead to Joyous Heights, but Bad Habits Finally Silenced the Truckin' Troubadour," p. 64.
Time, August 21, 1995, Richard Corliss, "The Trip Ends: Jerry Garcia, the Pied and Tie-dyed Piper of the Grateful Dead, Dies at 53," p. 60.
Times, August 11, 1995, p. 19.
Variety, August 14, 1995, p. 68.*

*   *   *

GARGAN, Edward A. 1950-

PERSONAL: Born June 19, 1950, in Boston, MA; son of Edward and Bernadette (Praetz) Gargan. *Education:* University of Wisconsin, B.A., 1975, M.A., 1975; Ph.D. work in medieval studies at University of California—Berkeley.

ADDRESSES: Office—Newsday 7.1.133, Jianguomen-wai, Beijing, China 100600.

CAREER: Journalist and author. *New York Times,* bureau chief, La Côte d'Ivoire, 1985-86, Beijing, China, 1986-89, New Delhi, India, 1991-94, Hong Kong, 1995—; *Newsday,* Asia bureau chief, 2000—.

MEMBER: Association for Asian Studies.

AWARDS, HONORS: Edward R. Murrow fellow, 1989-90.

WRITINGS:

China's Fate: A People's Turbulent Struggle with Reform and Repression, 1980-1990, Doubleday (New York, NY), 1991.
The River's Tale: A Year on the Mekong, Knopf (New York, NY), 2002.

Contributing editor to *Los Angeles Times Magazine* and *Opinion.*

WORK IN PROGRESS: "A book on borders, the politics, and the social meaning and implications of boundaries."

SIDELIGHTS: Longtime journalist Edward A. Gargan has written two books based largely on his experiences reporting from several Asian countries, including China. Although Gargan studied Chinese history at the University of Wisconsin and planned on working in academia, he turned to journalism after his college years. Gargan made a mark for himself working as a bureau chief for the *New York Times,* first in Africa, and later in China, India, and Hong Kong. Fluent in several languages, including Chinese, French, and Italian, Gargan spent much of the late 1980s stationed in China, where he witnessed several tumultuous events, including Chinese soldiers massacring student demonstrators in Tiananmen Square in 1989. His first book, *China's Fate: A People's Turbulent Struggle with Reform and Repression, 1980-1990,* includes vivid descriptions of these events. Gargan wrote the book while serving as an Edward R. Murrow fellow in 1989-90, a period he took off from his reporting duties. In 1991, he returned to the *New York Times* and continued

with the publication for the remainder of the decade. In 2000, Gargan joined the staff of *Newsday* to serve as the magazine's Asia bureau chief. Gargan's second work, the critically lauded *The River's Tale: A Year on the Mekong,* is a first-hand account of the 3000-mile-long journey he took down the entire length of the Mekong, southeast Asia's longest river. Along the way, Gargan visited numerous countries bordering the river, including Tibet, China, Laos, Cambodia, and Vietnam. The book contains Gargan's thoughts about the region's recent past, especially how it has been affected by incursions of the Western world. "A perceptive account of regions infrequently visited by westerners," critic Gilbert Taylor of *Booklist* wrote of the book.

In *China's Fate,* Gargan portrays communist China as a nation that denies its citizens basic human rights. While in the country, Gargan witnessed countless examples of political persecution and repression, such as the Tiananmen incident and the thousands of arrests made in its aftermath. Gargan offers a number of opinions on the state of China, as well as U.S. policies toward the nation. Gargan is highly critical of both the Reagan and Bush administrations, because, in his opinion, they ignored the evidence of China's human rights abuses. Throughout his time in China, Gargan interviewed many villagers, as well as city dwellers, including prostitutes and cabbies. He also talked with dissident students and writers clamoring for more freedom in Chinese society. Gargan devotes the last section of the book to the events of Tiananmen Square and China's armed takeover and hostile subjugation of Tibet.

While *China's Fate* did receive a number of positive reviews, critical opinion of it was somewhat mixed. According to Gayle Feldman, who reviewed the book for the *New York Times Book Review,* Gargan's work is a good start for readers unfamilar with recent Chinese history. "For readers who have not perused many other works on the subject, his book provides an informative, accessible overview," Feldman wrote. Feldman especially enjoyed the book's final section dealing with Tibet and Tiananmen Square, feeling it was where "the book really comes alive." Chris Goodrich, who reviewed the book for the *Los Angeles Times Book Review,* enjoyed Gargan's observations about the Chinese people, but not his political analysis of the country. "The most interesting sections deal with the country's people rather than its politics," Goodrich wrote. Judith Shapiro of the *Washington Post Book World* was also critical of Gargan's socio-political opinions. "Gargan is often just enough off the mark to be disconcerting," Shapiro wrote. "There is a tendency to simplify complex questions and omit important descriptions of how China operates; much of what he writes has been better and more thoroughly stated elsewhere. . . . Gargan's strength lies in description rather than analysis."

According to Gargan, one of the main reasons he took a year to travel the Mekong and subsequently write *The River's Tale* was to give himself the time and luxury to strike out and find Asia on his own terms, something tight newspaper deadlines never allowed him to do. As he writes in the book, he wanted to "weave together my passion for Asia with a longing to travel at my own speed, to wander as I wished, to find a river that would pull me through Asia. . . . That river is the Mekong." The Mekong was a natural choice for such a trip, because it meanders through so much of Southeast Asia. The trip gave Gargan the time to fully digest his many years of covering the area for the *New York Times*. However, it also gave him time to come to grips with his more distant past. Gargan was sent to a federal prison in the early 1970s, when he was twenty-one and living in Boston, because he refused to serve in the Vietnam War, which he thought was an unjust conflict. According to Gargan, he wrote the book to "lend some substance and meaning" to the two years he spent in a Kentucky prison. Gargan began his trip in Tibet, where the Mekong's headwaters converge to form the river. As in his first work, Gargan discusses the effects Chinese rule has had on the ancient Tibetan culture, and what its prospects are for the future. From there he traveled south through several countries, including Laos, Cambodia, and Vietnam, each of which was tremendously impacted by the Vietnam War. In Cambodia, for example, he talked to many people who survived the country's horrific Khmer Rouge period, when the communists massacred millions of Cambodians for political reasons. According to Gargan, nearly everybody he spoke with had lost a loved one to the Khmer Rouge. "Almost every conversation I had pivoted on memory and mourning," Gargan writes.

Ultimately Gargan's journey took him to Vietnam, where the Mekong empties into the South China Sea. There, he confronted his personal past and gives an account of the communist nation's progress since the end of the war, which ended in 1975. A number of critics lauded *The River's Tale*. According to Margaret W. Norton, who reviewed the book for *Library Journal,* Gargan provides "a highly informed account." Norton concluded that the author "is clearly well versed in the history and customs of traditional Asia." Alex Frater of the *New York Times Book Review* felt the book to be "a remarkable story, grittily told."

BIOGRAPHICAL AND CRITICAL SOURCES:

BOOKS

Gargan, Edward A., *The River's Tale: A Year on the Mekong,* Knopf (New York, NY), 2002.

PERIODICALS

Booklist, December 15, 2001, p. 700.
Library Journal, January, 2002, p. 135.
Los Angeles Times Book Review, January 27, 1991, p. 6.
New York Times, January 30, 2002, p. B8.
New York Times Book Review, February 3, 1991, Gayle Feldman, review of *China's Fate: A People's Turbulent Struggle with Reform and Repression, 1980-1990,* pp. 16-17; February 10, 2002, Alexander Frater, review of *The River's Tale: A Year on the Mekong,* p. 18.
Publishers Weekly, December 14, 1990, p. 57.
Time International, April 1, 2002, p. 54.
Washington Post Book World, February 17, 1991, p. 8.

OTHER

Newsday, http://www.newsday.com/ (August 1, 2002), "Newsday on the Scene: Edward A. Gargan."

*   *   *

GARRATT, James E. 1954-

PERSONAL: Born May 18, 1954, in Toronto, Ontario, Canada; son of Richard and Rita (Ryan) Garratt; married Verna Lockyer; children: Brant. *Education:* Sir Sandford Fleming College, degree (forest technician). *Hobbies and other interests:* Sailing, wilderness travel, astronomy.

ADDRESSES: Home—4864 Major Mackenzie Dr., Woodbridge, Ontario, Canada L4L 1A6. *Office*—32 Greendowns Dr., Scarborough, Ontario, Canada M1M 2G7.

CAREER: Scanlon Creek Outdoor Education Centre, Bradford, Ontario, Canada, environmental instructor for ten years; Kortright Center for Conservation, Woodbridge, Ontario, Canada, employed in operations for thirteen years. Save the Rouge Valley System, chair; Boyd North stewardship committee, member.

WRITINGS:

The Rouge River Valley: An Urban Wilderness, Natural Heritage Books (Toronto, Ontario, Canada), 2000.

Contributor to periodicals, including *Northward Journal, Nature Canada, CVII, Waves,* and *Brick.*

WORK IN PROGRESS: Northern Euphonia, a novel about the North; *Scarborough Bluffs: Another Urban Wilderness; Oak Ridges Moraine: Life on the Edge.*

SIDELIGHTS: James E. Garratt told *CA:* "My primary motivation for writing is to preserve the natural environment. My writings are usually based upon direct field experience. They communicate my experiences in the outdoors, as well as alternative viewpoints with respect to humanity's interactions with 'wild nature'. My writings are influenced by such authors as Henry Thoreau, Edwin Way Teal, Ray Bradbury, R. Carson, Ann Zwinger, and Charles de Lint."

*   *   *

GAUSE, Damon J. 1915(?)-1944

PERSONAL: Born c. 1915, in GA; died in a flight training accident March 9, 1944, in Beaulieu, England; buried in Cambridge American Cemetery in England; married Ruth Carter, 1941; children: Damon Jr.

CAREER: Army Air Corps fighter pilot.

WRITINGS:

The War Journal of Major Damon "Rocky" Gause, introduction by son, Damon L. Gause, Hyperion (New York, NY), 1999.

SIDELIGHTS: The War Journal of Major Damon "Rocky" Gause "sounds like a movie pilot," wrote Jana Adams in the *Jackson Herald.* During World War II, "Gause escaped his Japanese captors in the Philippines by killing a sentry and swimming three miles toward safety, only to be recaptured. He escaped again, this time into the jungle with another prisoner, and sailed in a native boat 3,200 miles to safe harbor in Australia." Indeed, film rights to the work were secured as of 1999 with Miramax Films.

The *War Journal* "presents that story in [Major Damon's] . . . own words as he wrote it shortly after he returned to the United States. . . . The tale he's left us has the feel of that moment when America was desperate for heroes, and reading it now is as much a trip back in time as it is a journey across the dark Sulu sea," wrote Christopher Dickey in the *New York Times Book Review.* The journal was reportedly found in a foot locker by Damon's son, Damon L. Gause, Jr., and was published on Veteran's Day, 1999. Gause was killed in a training accident in 1944.

"The author's repeated reference to 'japs' and 'nips' and his description of the Japanese conquerors as 'victorycrazed sadistic devils' may offend readers of a more ethnically sensitive era," noted a *Publishers Weekly* critic, "but despite these lapses and his merely workmanlike prose, the drama of the events described will hold readers' attention." "[W]hat a book," claimed Mike Buffington in the *Jackson Herald.* "Although I first read the raw journal about 15 years ago, I was still amazed when I read the book again. . . . It is a story of courage and survival set against the backdrop of the century's greatest conflict. . . . On its face, the book is one man's story, but at a deeper level it also reflects much about this nation and its struggles during the last 100 years." Dickey concluded: "What really drove Rocky Gause? We're not going to know. But one thing's for sure. He'd be just the kind of man you'd want around if you were hoping to try a great escape."

BIOGRAPHICAL AND CRITICAL SOURCES:

PERIODICALS

Jackson Herald, May 13, 1998, Jana Adams, "Bidding Battle: Gause's War Journal Sought by Publishers"; February 17, 1999, "Gause's 'War Journal'

Headed for Silver Screen"; October 20, 1999, Angela Gary, "Gause's Book to be Available Veteran's Day"; November 10, 1999, Mike Buffington, "Gause Book Is a Veteran's Day Tribute."

New York Times Book Review, January 23, 2000, Christopher Dickey, "The Great Escape," p. 25.

Publishers Weekly, October 25, 1999, review of *The War Journal of Major Damon "Rocky" Gause,* p. 60.

ONLINE

University of Georgia Web site, http://www.uga.edu/ (October 24, 2002), "Against All Odds."*

*   *   *

GELTMAKER, Ty 1952-

PERSONAL: Born March 7, 1952, in Peoria, IL; son of Eugene and Milly (Darling) Geltmaker; companion of James Rosen (an architect and furniture designer). *Ethnicity:* "German-Irish-English." *Education:* Trinity College, Hartford, CT, B.A., 1974; attended Università per Stranieri, 1975-76; New York University, M.A., 1986; University of Southern California, Ph.D., 1994. *Politics:* "Democratic Socialist." *Religion:* "Atheist (raised Roman Catholic)." *Hobbies and other interests:* Dogs, gardening, European film.

ADDRESSES: Home—Los Angeles, CA. *Agent*—c/o Author Mail, Peter Lang Publishing, Inc., 275 Seventh Ave., 28th Floor, New York, NY 10001. *E-mail*—echobamboo@sbcglobal.net.

CAREER: Peoria Journal Star, Peoria, IL, reporter and copy editor, summers, 1972-73; *Rome Daily American,* Rome, Italy, copy editor, feature writer, and page layout technician, 1976-77; *International Daily News,* Rome, Italy, editor, political writer, page layout technician, and typesetter, 1977-79; United Press International, New York, NY, editor at international and foreign desks, 1979-81; freelance writer and editor, 1981—. English teacher in Rome, 1976-78; Cerritos Community College, instructor, 1989; University of Southern California, instructor, 1994, visiting lecturer in Italian, 2001; California Institute of the

Arts, Valencia, CA, instructor in history, 1993-95; Bronx Community College of the City University of New York, adjunct assistant professor, 1993-95.

MEMBER: American Historical Association.

WRITINGS:

Tired of Living: Suicide in Italy from National Unification to World War I, 1860-1915, Peter Lang Publishing (New York, NY), 2002.

Contributor to books, including *Negative Capability,* edited by Eugene Walter, [Mobile, AL], 1981; and *Queers in Space,* edited by Gordon Brent Ingram, Bay Press (Seattle, WA), 1997. Contributor to periodicals, including *Society and Space* and *Journal of the History of Sexuality.*

WORK IN PROGRESS: Anni di Piombo: My Years of Lead, a "fictional autobiography" set in Rome in the 1970s; research on passion plays in twentieth-century Los Angeles.

SIDELIGHTS: Ty Geltmaker told *CA:* "I am primarily a fiction writer (of little success) whose works of historical nonfiction have been published. I am committed to historical narrative which incorporates theoretical perspectives without 'fetishizing' theory or letting theory drown out the voices of my historical sources. I am an intellectual, but wary of the academic life, as I fit best somewhere between the academy's essential conservatism and the rough and tumble of journalism. Though I see myself as American to the core, I've always felt most at home in Rome and Berlin (socially and politically). Not surprisingly, Nathaniel Hawthorne is my favorite American writer. Los Angeles is my favorite United States city; it has Rome's insouciance and Berlin's edginess.

"My history of suicide in Italy was an accident. I discovered the topic while reading Italian newspaper reports on the infamous 'Futurist Evenings' of 1909-15 (performances exalting violence ending in mock riot). I've written on AIDS and gay issues with a critical eye on my own experience.

"I write (whether fiction or nonfiction) because the solitary act of doing so makes me feel good—whether or not it gets published."

GENERAL, David 1950-

PERSONAL: Born May 31, 1950, in Oshweken, Ontario, Canada; married; wife's name, Mary; children: Miles, Aisha, Sara, Megan. *Education:* Attended Wilfrid Laurier University and Hamilton Teacher's College.

ADDRESSES: Agent—c/o Jenkins Showler Gallery, 1539 Johnston Rd., White Rock, Canada V4B 3Z6; fax: 604-531-4232.

CAREER: Sculptor and painter. Department of Indian and Northern Affairs, Ottawa, Ontario, Canada, senior cultural development officer; also worked as elementary school teacher and steel worker. National Indian Artist Symposium, member of advisory committee; McMichael Canadian Art Collection, member of board of trustees. *Exhibitions:* Work exhibited in solo and group shows, including exhibitions at Koffler Gallery, Intuit Gallery, Thunder Bay National Exhibition Centre and Centre for Indian Art, Woodland Indian Cultural Educational Centre, Queens Museum in New York, and Jenkins Showler Gallery, White Rock, Canada; work represented in numerous collections, including those of Canadian Museum of Civilization, Canadian Standards Association, Dunlop Art Gallery, North American Indian Travelling College, and Yukon Permanent Art Collection.

MEMBER: Society of Canadian Artists of Native Ancestry (cofounder; past chair).

AWARDS, HONORS: Grants from Department of Indian and Northern Affairs and Ontario Arts Council.

WRITINGS:

Indian Art '76, Woodland Indian Cultural Educational Centre (Brantford, Ontario, Canada), 1976.
Contemporary Art of Iroquoia, MacDonald Gallery, Ministry of Intergovernmental Affairs (Ottawa, Ontario, Canada), 1980.

Contributor to periodicals, including *Native Perspective* and *Artscrafts.*

BIOGRAPHICAL AND CRITICAL SOURCES:

BOOKS

Dinniwell, Norma, and Tom Hill, *Transformation: The Art of David General,* Woodland Indian Cultural Education Centre (Brantford, Ontario, Canada), 1982.
St. James Guide to Native North American Artists, St. James Press (Detroit, MI), 1998, pp. 181-183.

PERIODICALS

Brantford Expositor, September 19, 1982, Laura Ramsay, "General's Exhibition Title Appropriate"; March 7, 1987, Rose Simons, "General Escapes Bonds of 'Native Art.'"
Native Perspective, Volume 3, number 2, 1978, Melissa Lazore, "David General: Exploring Avenues."
Sherbrooke Record, April 2, 1986, "General Is an Artist, Not an Indian Artist."

ONLINE

David General: New Imageries (documentary television special), Canadian Broadcasting Corp. (Toronto, Ontario, Canada), 1994.
Kluane Art Expedition (documentary film), [Whitehorse, Yukon, Canada], 1993.
Lacrosse, the Creator's Game (documentary film), Ken Murch Productions (London, Ontario, Canada), 1993.*

*   *   *

GINER de los RÍOS, Francisco 1839-1915

PERSONAL: Born November (some sources say October) 10, 1839, in Ronda, Spain; died February 17 (some sources say 18), 1915, in Madrid, Spain; son of Francisco Giner de la Fuente and Bernarda de los Ríos Rosas. *Education:* Studied law and philosophy at the universities of Barcelona and Granada; University of Granada, degree in law; University of Madrid, doctorate in law and international law, 1863.

CAREER: Educator, philosopher, and essayist. University of Madrid, chair of philosophy of law, 1868-98; founded Institución Libre de Enseñanza, 1867.

WRITINGS:

Estudios literarios, Imprenta de R. Labajos (Madrid, Spain), 1866.

Estudios jurídicos y politicos, Librería de V. Suarez (Madrid, Spain), 1875, reprinted, Espasa-Calpe (Madrid, Spain), 1921.

Estudios de literatura y arte, Librería de V. Suarez (Madrid, Spain), 1876, reprinted, Lectura (Madrid, Spain), 1919.

Estudios filosóficos y religiosos, Librería de F. Góngora (Madrid, Spain), 1876, reprinted, Espasa-Calpe (Madrid, Spain), 1921.

Encyclopedia jurídica; o, Exposición orgánica de la ciencia del derecho y el estado, Librería de V. Suarez (Madrid, Spain), 1878.

Estudios jurídicos, Aribau (Madrid, Spain), 1878.

Compendio de la historia del derecho romano, Librería de V. Suarez (Madrid, Spain), 1879.

Compendio de estética, Librería de V. Suarez (Madrid, Spain), 1883, reprinted, Verbum (Madrid, Spain), 1995.

Estudios sobre educación, [Madrid, Spain], 1886, reprinted, Julio Cosano (Madrid, Spain), 1922.

Portugal, impresiones para server de guía al viajero, Imprenta Popular (Madrid, Spain), 1888.

Estudios sobre artes industriales, Librería de José Jorro (Madrid, Spain), 1892, reprinted, Lectura (Madrid, Spain), 1926.

La persona social; estudios y fragmentos, Librería de V. Suarez (Madrid, Spain), 1899.

Estudios y fragmentos sobre la teoria de la persona social, E. Rojas (Madrid, Spain), 1899.

Filosofía y sociología, Henrich (Barcelona, Spain), 1904.

Pedagogía universitaria; problemas y noticias, Sucesores de Manuel Soler (Barcelona, Spain), 1914.

Ensayos sobre educación, Ediciones de la Lectura (Madrid, Spain), 1915, reprinted, Editorial Losada (Buenos Aires, Argentina), 1945.

La universidad española, Imprenta Clásica española (Madrid, Spain), 1916, reprinted, Civitas (Madrid, Spain), 2001.

Obras completas de Don Francisco Giner de los Ríos, Espasa-Calpe (Madrid, Spain), 1916, reprinted, Lectura (Madrid, Spain), 1989.

Principios de derecho natural, [Madrid, Spain], 1916.

Obras completas, Lectura (Madrid, Spain), 1916.

Lecciones sumarias de psicología, Clásica Española (Madrid, Spain), 1920.

Educación y enseñanza, Julio Cosano (Madrid, Spain), 1925.

Resumen de filosofía del derecho, Espasa-Calpe (Madrid, Spain), 1926.

Estudios sobre artes industriales y cartas literarias, Espasa-Calpe (Madrid, Spain), 1926.

Ensayos menores sobre educación y enseñanza, Espasa-Calpe (Madrid, Spain), 1927.

Informes del Comisario de Educación de los Estados Unidos, Espasa-Calpe (Madrid, Spain), 1928.

Acerca de la función de la ley, [Madrid, Spain], 1932.

Arqueología artistica de la peninsula, Espasa-Calpe (Madrid, Spain), 1936.

Poesía española, Editorial Signo (Mexico City, Mexico), 1945.

El pensamiento vivo de Giner de los Ríos, Editorial Losada (Buenos Aires, Argentina), 1949.

Tres ensayos, [Mexico City, Mexico], 1960.

Ensayos y cartas, Ediciones Tezontle (Mexico City, Mexico), 1965.

Notas a la enciclopedia jurídica de Enrique Ahrens, Editorial Tecnos (Madrid, Spain), 1965.

La cuestión universitaria, Editorial Tecnos (Madrid, Spain), 1967.

Giner: visito por Galdós, Unamuno, A. Machado, J. Ramón Jiménez, Alfonso Reyes, etc., Instituto Luis Vives (Mexico City, Mexico), 1969.

Sanz del río, 1814-1869, Editorial Tecnos (Madrid, Spain), 1969.

Ensayos, Alianza (Madrid, Spain), 1969.

Unamuno "agitador de espíritus" y Giner de los Ríos, Universidad de Salamanca (Salamanca, Spain), 1976.

Antología pedagógica de Francisco Giner de los Ríos, Santillana (Madrid, Spain), 1977.

El don de consejo: espistolario de Joaquín Costa y Francisco Giner de los Ríos, Guara (Zaragoza, Spain), 1983.

Semblanza de una amistad: epistolario de August G. de Linares a Francisco Giner de los Ríos, Delegación de Cultura del Excmo. Ayuntamiento de Santander (Santander, Spain), 1986.

Escritos sobre la universidad española, Espasa-Calpe (Madrid, Spain), 1990.

Jornadas homenaje a Giner de los Ríos, Universidad de Jaén (Jaén, Spain), 1999.

SIDELIGHTS: Francisco Giner de los Ríos was well known during his lifetime as an author, educator, and philosopher. He was a man of diverse interests; this is evident in his books, as they deal with subjects of art, education, law, literature, religion, and sociology. His subjects are broad in nature, but what they "all have in common [is] a philosophical spirit and a deep social consciousness." Giner de los Ríos was not content, however, simply to write books to expound his ideas. He moved from the philosophical to the practical realm by founding the Institución Libre de Enseñanza, a private nondenominational school. Through this deed, Giner de los Ríos became "the guiding spirit of the educational and intellectual renaissance of modern Spain." His school had a far-reaching influence, and the students and teachers of the Institución included such illustrious figures as Leopoldo Alas, Ortega y Gasset, Américo Castro, Federico García Lorca, Antonio Machado, Joaquín Costa, Juan Ramón Jiménez, Luis Buñuel, Salvador Dalí, Gregorio Marañon, and Miguel de Unamuno.

Giner de los Ríos was born on November 10, 1839, in Ronda, Spain. Due to his father's position as a government employee, the family traveled around the country. Giner de los Ríos studied law and philosophy at the University of Barcelona and finally received a law degree from the University of Granada. During his university studies, he was able to develop his interests in the fields of painting and music, and began his writing career by publishing his first literary and political articles in the magazine *Meridional*. In 1863 Giner de los Ríos moved to Madrid to complete his doctoral studies and became acquainted with Julián Sanz del Río. This teacher introduced him to the ideas of Karl Krause, a German philosopher who reconciled the ideas of theism and pantheism by proposing that God is neither the physical world, nor is He exclusively separated from it, but that this divine being contains the world in Himself and, at the same time, transcends it. Giner de los Ríos was deeply affected by Krause's ideas; they would influence his deeds and thoughts throughout the remainder of his lifetime.

In 1868 Giner de los Ríos became a law professor and served as the department chair at the University of Madrid; he held these positions for more than thirty years. His career was interrupted in 1875, however, when he was imprisoned for protesting against the restoration government's intervention in the academic freedom of public education. Giner de los Ríos was released a year later, and he emerged with the determination to found a school free of political,

religious, or philosophical constraints that would contribute toward "the general progress of education."

He accomplished this goal in the Institución Libre de Enseñanza, which quickly gained national and international renown. The school was originally conceived as a center for university level studies, but soon expanded into primary and secondary schools. Its goal was remarkably radical for the time: to encourage young men and women in becoming balanced human beings through a strong moral, scientific, physical, artistic, and intellectual education. Schooling took place not only in the classroom, but also in art museums and in the natural world. Exams based upon rote memorization of facts and traditional textbooks were not a part of this educational system. Instead, "independent study and free thinking" were encouraged in both male and female students.

In 1881 Giner de los Ríos was reinstated in his position at the University of Madrid, but he continued with his work with the Institución and with his writing. Although Giner de los Ríos's books about pedagogy, literature, sociology, and religion are great contributions to the Spanish intellectual world, perhaps his most influential work is *Resumen de filosofía del derecho,* which describes the philosophy of law.

Estudios de literatura y arte, published in 1876, discusses the topics of epic poetry, music as an expression of esthetics, the basic principles of literature, and which genre of poetry was most appropriate for that time. *Estudios filosóficos y religiosos* investigates Giner de los Ríos's ideas about the Spanish Church, Catholics and the contemporary spirit, comparative psychology, and the scientific doctrine. In *Filosofía y sociología* the author speaks about the history of Plato's methodology of thought, Marx and Engel's so-called historical materialism, and nature and the human spirit.

"The Institución was Giner's greatest work," stated a *Columbia Dictionary of Modern European Literature* contributor. The article noted that the Institución's outstanding quality was based upon the founder's "vibrant personality and glowing spirit" that influenced so many of Spain's leading contributors to the fields of art, politics, science, social work, and literature.

BIOGRAPHICAL AND CRITICAL SOURCES:

BOOKS

Azcárate, Pablo, *La cuestión universitaria, 1875. Epistolario de Francisco Giner de los Ríos, Gumers-*

indo de Azcárate y Nicolás Salmerón, Editorial Tecnos (Madrid, Spain), 1967.

Columbia Dictionary of Modern European Literature, Columbia University Press (New York, NY), 1980.

PERIODICALS

Bailierem, February 22, 1961, Pablo Azcárate, "Don Francisco y Azcárate."

Journal de Genève, April 30, 1916, M. Aguilera, "Un gran educador español."

Nuevo Mundo, March 6, 1915, Eduardo Gómez de Baquero, "Giner de los Ríos," pp. 659-660.

País, April 18, 1915, A. Aguilera y Arjona, "El mejor homenaje," April 18, 1915, Leopoldo Alas y Argüelles, "Nuestro don Francisco."

Vida Nueva, July, 1922, A. Albornoz, "Don Francisco Giner de los Ríos y la Institución Libre de Enseñanza."

ONLINE

Andalucia ADN Web site, http://www.isocanda.org/ (April 24, 2002).

Don Francisco Giner de los Ríos Web site, http://www.giner.drago.net/ (June 30, 2002).

Fundación Francisco Giner de los Ríos Web site, http://www.funaciongi
ner.org/ (April 24, 2002).*

*   *   *

GOLDSTEIN, Leon J. 1927-2002

OBITUARY NOTICE—See index for *CA* sketch: Born February 6, 1927, in Brooklyn, NY; died May 24, 2002, in Binghamton, NY. Educator and author. Goldstein was a philosophy professor at the State University of New York at Binghamton. After serving in the U.S. Army, he graduated from Brooklyn College (now of the City University of New York), where he received his bachelor's degree in 1949; he then attended Yale University's graduate school and completed a doctorate there in 1954. During the late 1950s Goldstein taught at several universities, including Brandeis University, the University of Maryland, and City College of the City University of New York. In 1959 he joined the faculty at the State University of New York at Binghamton, first as a lecturer, and, after 1966, as

professor of philosophy. He was about to be named Bartle Professor of Philosophy at Binghamton when he passed away. Goldstein was the author of three books: *Politics in a Pluralistic Democracy* (1963), which he cowrote with Lucy S. Dawidowicz, *Historical Knowing* (1976), and *The What and the Why of History: Philosophical Essays* (1996). He was also a former editor of *International Studies in Philosophy.*

OBITUARIES AND OTHER SOURCES:

BOOKS

Marquis Who's Who, Marquis (New Providence, NJ), 2001.

ONLINE

Inside Binghamton University, http://inside.binghamton.edu/ (June 20, 2002).

*   *   *

GRACE, C. L.
See DOHERTY, P(aul) C.

*   *   *

GREATOREX, Wilfred 1921(?)-2002

OBITUARY NOTICE—See index for *CA* sketch: Born May 27, 1921 (one source says 1922), in Blackburn, England; died of renal failure October 14, 2002, in Taplow, England. Author. Greatorex was a writer of popular British television series. At the age of eighteen he joined the Royal Air Force to serve in a bomber squadron. After World War II, instead of enrolling at a university, he started a career in journalism, working for a local paper in Blackburn, England, and then for the *Reynold's News* in London. Greatorex's career in television began in the 1960s when he took a job with Associated Television and began writing scripts for such programs as *Danger Man* and *Man in a Suitcase.* His first big success came with the popular drama series *The Plane Makers,* which later became *The Power Game,* and *Front Page Story.* In the 1970s he provided scripts for such programs as *The Frighteners* and *Hine,* as well as creating his own series, *Secret Army;* the last series he worked on was *Airline,* which aired in 1982. In addition to television work, Greatorex wrote film screenplays, among them *Nobody Runs Forever* and the coauthored screenplay for *The Battle of Britain.* He also wrote the novels *The Freelancers* (1975), *Crossover* (1976; published as *Three Potato, Four,* 1977), and *The Button Zone* (1984).

OBITUARIES AND OTHER SOURCES:

BOOKS

Clute, John, and Peter Nicholls, editors, *The Encyclopedia of Science Fiction,* St. Martin's Press (New York, NY), 1993.

PERIODICALS

Times (London, England), October 21, 2002, p. 8.

*   *   *

GREEN, Christine

PERSONAL: Born in Luton, England.

ADDRESSES: Home—Wolverhampton, England. *Agent*—c/o Author Mail, Walker and Company, 435 Hudson St., New York, NY 10014.

CAREER: Mystery novelist. Worked as a nurse in Hampstead, England and the Royal National Throat, Nose, and Ear Hospital in London, England. Worked as a teacher and midwife.

WRITINGS:

"CHIEF INSPECTOR CONNOR O'NEILL AND DETECTIVE SGT. FRAN WILSON" SERIES

Death in the Country, 1994.
Die in My Dreams, 1995.
Fatal Cut, Severn House (New York, NY), 1996.

"KATE KINSELLA" SERIES

Deadly Errand, Walker (New York, NY), 1992.
Deadly Admirer, Walker (New York, NY), 1993.
Deadly Practice, Walker (New York, NY), 1995.
Deadly Partners, Walker (New York, NY), 1996.
Deadly Bond, Severn House (New York, NY), 2002.
Deadly Echo, Severn House (New York, NY), 2003.

"DETECTIVE INSPECTOR THOMAS RYDELL AND SERGEANT DENISE CALDECOTE" SERIES

Fire Angels, Severn House (New York, NY), 2001.
Vain Hope, Severn House (New York, NY), 2002.

OTHER

Coronation Street: The Way to Victory, Andre Deutsch (London, England), 2000.
Coronation Street: The War Years, Andre Deutsch (London, England), 2001.

SIDELIGHTS: British mystery novelist Christine Green has published numerous books, beginning in 1991 with *Deadly Errand,* the first installment in her "Kate Kinsella" series. In a *Nursing Times* review, Richard Morris referred to Green, a longtime nurse, as "a household name among fans of the stiletto knife and mortuary slab." After receiving her medical training in London, Green started her nursing career at a hospital north of the city and subsequently spent thirty years in the profession before turning her full attentions to writing in 1998. Much of her writing is based on her experiences during the years she spent as a nurse, and most of her novels are set in hospitals or other medical facilities. In the *Nursing Times* article, Green told Morris that she encountered all types of bizarre characters and situations during her days nursing, which she was able to draw upon when writing. "I've used my experiences of atmospheres and various problems people suffer several times in my books," she told Morris. "If I hadn't had a background in nursing I would definitely have found it harder to write mystery books." Green has said that mystery novels always intrigued her. Her own writings fall within the police procedural genre. "Crime holds a fascination for people," she told Morris.

During her career, Green has developed three series of novels. Most of her books, including *Deadly Errand,* feature protagonist Kate Kinsella, a English nurse turned private detective who solves crimes of a medical nature. In *Deadly Errand,* the thirty-something Kinsella is hired to solve the murder of nurse Jacky Byfield, who is stabbed to death while working at an English hospital. In addition to being lauded by the Crime Writers' Association, the book received its share of positive critical reviews. For example, a contributor for *Publishers Weekly* called it a "lively and impressive debut." Other books in the "Kinsella" series include *Deadly Admirer, Deadly Practice, Deadly Partners,* and *Deadly Bond.* Many literary critics felt the fourth installment in the series, *Deadly Partners,* was one of Green's strongest novels. The story finds Kinsella running the Medical and Nursing Investigation Agency, but having trouble paying the rent. She accepts a case in which she must solve the disappearance of Nigel Carter, a rich hotel owner, who is despised by many and missed by few. Referring to the book as one of Green's "best works," Harriet Klausner wrote in *Armchair Detective* that, along with the series, the novel works because Kinsella isn't the typical methodical, suave detective. "A prime reason the Kate Kinsella series is such a success is that the female protagonist knows that she is a bumbling sleuth who makes many mistakes," Klausner wrote.

Although less successful, Green's other major series includes three installments beginning with *Death in the Country,* featuring Detective Sergeant Fran Wilson and Chief Inspector Connor O'Neill. The pair is an unlikely duo: Irishman O'Neill is a veteran and likes his libations, whereas Wilson is young and toes the line. Other novels in the series, include *Die in My Dreams* and *Fatal Cut.*

With her 2001 effort, *Fire Angels,* Green began a new series featuring Detective Inspector Thomas Rydell and Sergeant Denise "Denni" Caldecote, who work together to solve a series of rapes in a rural English village. Although the book received mixed reviews, critic Jenny McLarin of *Booklist* called it "another in a long line of successful British procedurals starring mismatched but oddly complementary cops."

BIOGRAPHICAL AND CRITICAL SOURCES:

BOOKS

Detecting Women 2, Purple Moon (Dearborn, MI), 1996.

PERIODICALS

Armchair Detective, spring, 1997, p. 240.
Booklist, January 1, 1997, pp. 824-825; August, 2001, p. 2096.
Kirkus Reviews, May 15, 1992, p. 638; October 15, 1993, p. 1294; April 15, 1995, p. 513; November 15, 1996, p. 1635; December 1, 1999, p. 1848.
Library Journal, July, 1995, p. 127; January, 2000, p. 159; March 1, 2002, p. 144.
Los Angeles Times Book Review, January 9, 1994, p. 8.
Nursing Times, July 23, 1997, pp. 44-45.
Publishers Weekly, June 15, 1992, pp. 88-89; November 1, 1993, p. 70; June 19, 1995, p. 53; November 11, 1996, p. 60; August 6, 2001, p. 65; February 18, 2002, p. 79.

ONLINE

Christine Green Homepage, http://www.christine-green.co.uk (August 2, 2002).

*   *   *

GREEN, Ricky K(enneth) 1958-

PERSONAL: Born March 4, 1958, in Albuquerque, NM; son of David and Edith (Williams) Green. *Ethnicity:* "Black." *Education:* California State University—Sacramento, B.A., 1990; University of California—Santa Barbara, M.A., 1993, Ph.D., 1998.

ADDRESSES: Home—8285 Preston Way, Sacramento, CA 95828. *Office*—Department of Ethnic Studies, California State University—Sacramento, 6000 J St., Sacramento, CA 95819-6013. *E-mail*—greenr@csus.edu.

CAREER: University of California—Santa Barbara, lecturer in political science, 1998; California State University—Sacramento, assistant professor of ethnic studies and government, 1998—.

MEMBER: American Political Science Association, National Association of Ethnic Studies.

WRITINGS:

Democratic Virtue in the Trial and Death of Socrates: Resistance to Imperialism in Classical Athens, Peter Lang Publishing (New York, NY), 2000.

WORK IN PROGRESS: Between Achievement and Resistance; research on democratic theory and black political morality.

SIDELIGHTS: Ricky K. Green told *CA:* "I am an assistant professor at California State University—Sacramento. Currently I teach in the ethnic studies department and the government department. My areas of research include culture and ethics of the black diaspora, democratic thought, and ancient political thought. For the most part my writing is centered around those research interests. My first work, *Democratic Virtue in the Trial and Death of Socrates: Resistance to Imperialism in Classical Athens,* came out of my interest in ancient Greek political philosophy and democracy. My current work is a combination of my interests in African-American culture and political experience and democratic thought. I credit James Baldwin, Richard Wright, Chester Himes, and Maya Angelou with influencing not only my writing style but my subject matter."

*   *   *

GRIMSLEY, Will (Henry) 1914-2002

OBITUARY NOTICE—See index for *CA* sketch: Born January 27, 1914, in Monterey, TN; died October 31, 2002, in East Meadow, NY. Journalist and author. Grimsley was an acclaimed sports writer who enjoyed a long career with the Associated Press and published books on a wide variety of sports. Hired at age eighteen, his first job was writing for the *Evening Tennessean* during the 1930s and early 1940s. He joined the Associated Press in 1943 while still at the newspaper and was transferred to New York City in 1947. Until his retirement in 1984 as a national sports columnist, Grimsley covered many of the world's major sporting events, including the Olympics. His books include *Golf: Its History* (1966), *Football: The Greatest Moments in the Southwest Conference* (1968),

Tennis: Its History, People, and Events (1971), and *Sports Immortals* (1973), along with editing and contributing to other works and writing articles for periodicals such as *Readers Digest* and *Golf World.* Grimsley was active in a number of professional associations and from 1985 to 1986 was president of the National Sportscasters and Sportswriters Association. He was honored with many awards in the field, including a Bronze Hugo award for a documentary on the Olympics, the Eternal Torch from the Chicago International Film Festival in 1974, the 1987 Red Smith Award from Associated Press Sports Editors, and was named National Sportswriter of the Year by the National Sportscasters and Sportswriters Association in 1978, 1980, 1981, and 1983. In 1987 Grimsley was inducted into the Sportscasters and Sportswriters Hall of Fame in Salisbury, North Carolina.

OBITUARIES AND OTHER SOURCES:

PERIODICALS

New York Times, November 6, 2002, p. C13.

*   *   *

GUELBENZU, José María 1944-

PERSONAL: Born April 14, 1944, in Madrid, Spain. *Education:* Studied law.

ADDRESSES: Agent—c/o Alfaguara, Torrelaguna 60, Madrid 28043, Spain.

CAREER: Novelist, poet, and essayist. Worked in publishing beginning in 1964; Taurus Publishing Company, managing editor beginning 1977; Alfaguara Editions, editorial director beginning 1982. Madrid film club, Imagen, codirector. Full-time writer, 1988—.

AWARDS, HONORS: Premio de la Crítica, 1981, for *El río de la luna;* Premio Plaza & Janés, 1991, for *La tierra prometida.*

WRITINGS:

El mercurio, Seix Barral (Barcelona, Spain), 1968.
Antifaz, Seix Barral (Barcelona, Spain), 1970.

El pasajero de ultramar, Galba Edicions (Barcelona, Spain), 1976.

La noche en casa, Alianza Editorial (Madrid, Spain), 1977.

El río de la luna, Alianza Editorial (Madrid, Spain), 1981.

El esperado, Alianza Editorial (Madrid, Spain), 1984.

La mirada, Alianza Editorial (Madrid, Spain), 1987.

La tierra prometida, Plaza & Janés (Barcelona, Spain), 1991.

Ver Madrid, photographs by Ramon Manent, Ediciones Destino (Barcelona, Spain), 1991.

El sentimiento, Alianza Editorial (Madrid, Spain), 1995.

Cuentos populares españoles, Ediciones Siruela (Madrid, Spain), 1996.

Un peso en el mundo, Alfaguara (Madrid, Spain), 1999.

No acosen al asesino, Alfaguara (Madrid, Spain), 2001.

Guelbenzu also authored prologues and introductions for collections of works by José Emilio Pacheco, Gustavo Adolfo Bécquer, Horacio Quiroga, Rudyard Kipling, and Albert Camus.

SIDELIGHTS: José María Guelbenzu is considered among the most creative novelists in modern Spain. With the publication of his first novel, *El mercurio,* in 1968, he is credited with breaking with the prevailing social realism of the time and creating a purely aesthetic style which corresponded to the spirit of Spanish youth coming of age at the end of Francisco Franco's fascist dictatorship.

Guelbenzu was born in Madrid in 1944 and took his Bachillerato with the Jesuits and began to study law and business administration before leaving the university for a career in the publishing business in 1964. He worked first for the literary journal *Cuadernos para el diálogo* and was the co-director of the influential Madrid film club Imagen.

While working both as a contributor and editor Guelbenzu completed his first novel, *El mercurio,* which was a finalist for the Premio Biblioteca Breve and was critically well received. In 1979 Guelbenzu moved to the Taurus publishing company where he became managing director in 1977. For six years beginning in 1982 he was editorial director of the prestigious Alfaguara Editions in Madrid.

Although *El mercurio* showed some of the rough spots of first novels and was perhaps too influenced by his literary hero James Joyce, it covered new ground in the Spanish novel. A reviewer for *Times Literary Supplement* wrote, "It was welcomed then as a break from the grey and earnest social realism of his seniors, but was spoiled by adolescent nihilism and literary pose." David Herzberger, writing in *Hispania,* noted, "Guelbenzu's first novel, *El mercurio,* was immediately recognized as an important vanguardist experiment. The work consists of a potpourri of innovative techniques and stylistic complications derived in a large part from Joyce, Beckett, and Cortázar, and modified to fit the particular requisites of Guelbenzu."

Guelbenzu's second novel, *Antifaz,* follows the same general pattern of experimentation, though the author mitigates some of the excesses and fragmentation in favor of a tightly structured ordering of events and alternating presentation of characters. The three principal characters are the same age as those of *El mercurio,* and they exhibit the same problems: no sense of purpose, aimless wandering through Madrid, and lack of identity. A writer for *The Oxford Companion to Spanish Literature* wrote that "based on the mystery of a love relationship, [*El mercurio*] is an experiment in novelistic creation, with the complexity typical of any work written as a literary search."

El pasajero de ultramar is a development away from the fragmented and experimental style of Guelbenzu's previous novels toward a more incisive analysis of character. Herzberger commented, "[Guelbenzu] examines his protagonist in the Britanic tradition of E. M. Forster. . . . *El pasajero* shows authorial concern for elements of narrative other than language."

La noche en casa portrays a young man and woman, each pursuing a different means of fulfillment. The author reintroduces some of the characters from earlier novels, including Chéspir, a thirty-four-year-old lawyer and part-time poet who undertakes a covert mission. He travels to San Sebastián to deliver a message. Herzberger noted, "*La noche en casa* presents more forcefully and explicitly what is only implied in

Guelbenzu's previous novels; that the characters (all of whom are in their early thirties) are products of the philosophical, political, and moral sterility of postwar Spain. The sterility has not only deprived the postwar generation of values and ideal, but has imposed an inflexible norms that engenders the fundamental loss of identity of Spanish youth. . . . With *La noche en casa* Guelbenzu approaches the thematic traditions of existential narrative in the vein of Camus, Sartre, and Kafka, of Delibes and Martin Santos in Spain."

El río de la luna, which won Spain's critic's prize in 1981, is a love story divided into five sections of seemingly unrelated narrative. The ineffectiveness of the protagonist to express feelings for anyone but themselves is mirrored in the "New Spain" that has overturned the traditional values of Catholic hierarchy and a national mythology. The eventual decision forced on the protagonist, not unlike Raymond of Camus's *L'etranger,* is to face the dilemma of choosing or denying a creative life for its own sake.

Guelbenzu's sixth novel, *El esperado,* conveys dialogue and settings realistically, creating a narrative about family intrigue in the aftermath of the Spanish Civil War. In a review for *World Literature Today* James Abbott added, "allusions to Greek mythology and to Christianity imply a meaning beyond the plotting of events and episodes."

La tierra prometida again reflects the impossibility of a personal relationship living up to the unreachable expectations of a society that places success above all else and assumes anything less is tantamount to failure. The story begins with a chance encounter in a German airport between two old college friends who are both entering middle age. The liberating setting of an anonymous airport allows a free-flowing introspection of two individual who are fully aware of being consumed by the society they live in.

In 2001 Guelbenzu wrote *No acosen al asesino,* a police thriller that is a sub-genre generally denigrated in the world of Spanish letters. Lacking the enduring popularity and often very high quality of the French *polar noir,* the Spanish versions of this genre have never taken the high road with the uniquely American hard-boiled detective story. The story in this case is relatively simple. Magistrate Mariana de Marco is as-

signed to investigate the death of fellow magistrate Celso Medina. His body is found in his home and no apparent motive is found. De Marco solves the case in record time; in four days, with the help of a wonderful analytical world, inspired intuition, and a talent for the job, she has the murderer. A *Terra Cultura* contributor wrote, "José María Guelbenzu gracefully leads us out of this strange beginning which could have been a quick ending with his protagonist Carlos Sastre, who committed the crime for revenge. . . . The real mystery turns out to be something else again: How we come to learn Sastre's real identity is what makes the book a real page turner."

Conte wrote in *Quimera,* "Guelbenzu is, more than any other writer, a true reflection of his generation. . . . The generation, for better or worse, that was formed by May of '68; an historical touchpoint that heightened the concept of the individual at the expense of mass movements, militancies or membership in artistic vanguards."

In addition writing novels, Guelbenzu is a regular columnist in the "Opinion" and "Literature" sections of *El País.*

BIOGRAPHICAL AND CRITICAL SOURCES:

BOOKS

Bédé, Jean-Albert, and William Edgerton, editors, *Columbia Dictionary of Modern European Literature,* Columbia University Press, (New York, NY), 1980.

Landiera, Ricardo, and Luis T. Gonzalez del Valle, editors, *Nuevos y novísimos,* Society of Spanish-American Studies (Boulder, CO), 1987.

Mechtild, Albert, *Vencer no es convencer: literatura e ideologia del fascimo español,* Vervuet (Frankfurt, Germany), 1998.

Ward, Philip, *The Oxford Companion to Spanish Literature,* Oxford University Press (Oxford, England), 1978.

PERIODICALS

Booklist, May 15, 1984, Erwin Buttler, review of *El río de la luna,* p. 1335.

Cuadernos Hispanoamericanos, June, 1989, Maria Altisent, "El erotismo en la actual narrativa española," p. 128.

Hispania, September, 1981, p. 367.

Letras Peninsulares, winter, 1988, Robert C. Spires, review of *El río de la luna,* p. 285.

Quimera, March, 1988, interview with José María Guelbenzu, p. 128.

Times Literary Supplement, May 28, 1971, review of *Antifaz,* p. 610.

World Literature Today, winter, 1997, Luis Larios Vendrell, review of *El sentimento,* p. 126; winter, 1986, James H. Abbott, review of *El esperado,* p. 75.

ONLINE

Terra Cultura, http://www.terra.es/cultura/ (July 30, 2002), review of *No acosen al asesino.**

H

HAATAJA, Lance
See DRAKE, Timothy A.

*   *   *

HAMMOND, Mason 1903-2002

OBITUARY NOTICE—See index for *CA* sketch: Born February 14, 1903, in Boston, MA; died October 13, 2002, in Cambridge, MA. Historian, educator, and author. Hammond was a scholar of Latin and of Roman history who for many decades was a fixture at Harvard University. He was a graduate of Harvard in 1925 and earned his B.Litt. from Balliol College, Oxford in 1930. Although he had teaching stints at Radcliffe College and the American Academy in Rome during the 1930s, 1940s, and 1950s, Hammond spent most of his academic life at Harvard, where he began as an instructor in 1928, moving up to Pope Professor of Latin Language and Literature from 1950 to 1973. His only major interruption to his service to Harvard occurred during World War II, when he was an army intelligence officer assigned to locate art treasures stolen by the Nazis. For this service he achieved the rank of lieutenant colonel and was awarded the Bronze Star and Legion of Honor. A highly regarded expert on Roman history, Hammond was the author of several enduring works on the subject, including *The Augustan Principate* (1933; enlarged edition, 1968) and *City State and World State in Greek and Roman Political Theory to Augustus* (1951). Interested in the history of Harvard University, he was also the author of *Revolutionary Harvard Today: A Walking Tour with Mason Hammond, 1775-1776, 1975-1976* (1976). A former Rhodes scholar, Hammond could also count among his many academic honors the 1987 Harvard Medal of the Harvard Alumni Association and an honorary D.H.L. from the university, the last which he received in 1994.

OBITUARIES AND OTHER SOURCES:

BOOKS

Directory of American Scholars, tenth edition, Gale (Detroit, MI), 2002.

PERIODICALS

New York Times, October 21, 2002, p. A21.

*   *   *

HANNITY, Sean 1961-

PERSONAL: Born 1961, in Franklin Square, NY; married Jill Rhodes (an editor and homemaker), 1993; children: Patrick, Merri. *Education:* Attended college for two years. *Politics:* Conservative. *Religion:* Catholic.

ADDRESSES: Office—The Fox Entertainment Group, 1211 Avenue of the Americas, New York, NY 10036.

CAREER: Journalist. House painter and building contractor, 1982-91; WVNN Radio, Huntsville, AL, talk show host, 1991-92; WGST Radio, Atlanta, GA, talk show host, 1992-96; Fox News, New York, NY, co-host of *Hannity & Colmes,* 1996—; WABC Radio, New York, NY, host, *The Sean Hannity Show,* 1997—, syndicated, 2001—.

AWARDS, HONORS: Voted talk personality of the year by readers of *Radio & Records* magazine.

WRITINGS:

Let Freedom Ring: Winning the War of Ideas in Politics, Media, and Life, Regan Books (New York, NY), 2002.

SIDELIGHTS: Conservative commentator Sean Hannity has forged dual careers in radio and television and is considered by some critics to be the national heir-apparent to Rush Limbaugh. Hannity can be heard daily on syndicated radio on a talk show that originates at WABC Radio in New York City. In the evenings he is co-host of *Hannity & Colmes,* a "point-counterpoint"-style television show on the Fox News channel. In both cases Hannity is a voice for the conservative agenda and an outspoken critic of liberalism as embodied by certain Democrats and former Democratic presidents. Although extremely candid in his remarks, Hannity maintains an affable demeanor that has won him the allegiance of a large audience. He told a *Time* magazine contributor: "One of the things I think works for me is, I am passionate about my belief system but I try never to forget the human side of the debate. I don't take it personally, and I don't make it personal. You can play golf with liberals, be neighbors with them, go out to dinner. I just don't want them in power."

Born on Long Island, New York, Hannity grew up in a household that encouraged hard work and debate. His father was a family court probation officer, his mother a homemaker. He attended college for two years but dropped out when he could no longer afford the tuition. Instead he opened his own house painting business in Rhode Island and within three years saved enough money to travel to the West Coast. He was living in Santa Barbara, California and working as a building contractor when he began to attract attention by his frequent telephone calls to radio talk shows. His ardent opinions about the Iran-Contra arms sales in 1987 won him a brief unpaid position as a talk show host

for a radio station run by the University of California— Santa Barbara. He got his first full-time job in radio in 1991, when a Huntsville, Alabama station responded to a "Job Wanted" advertisement he ran in *Radio & Records* magazine.

Hannity quickly rose through the ranks in talk radio, moving from Huntsville to Atlanta, Georgia in 1992 and on to New York City in 1996. Although he had never been on television before, he was signed to the *Hannity & Colmes* show on the fledgling Fox News network. Conceived as a "point-counterpoint"-style talk show with guests and commentary, *Hannity & Colmes* began to steal a significant market share of cable television news viewers in the nine o'clock p.m. time slot. In 1997 Hannity returned to radio in tandem with his television work, and his syndicated radio program, *The Sean Hannity Show* was heard on more than two hundred stations nationwide by 2003.

The terrorist bombing of the World Trade Center on September 11, 2001 was for Hannity a watershed moment. Always outspoken about the virtues of a strong military and the necessity of a viable international espionage force, Hannity decided to write a book about the dangers liberal thinking poses to American freedoms and the safety of U.S. citizens. *Let Freedom Ring: Winning the War of Ideas in Politics, Media, and Life* was published in 2002 and quickly rose to the *New York Times* nonfiction bestseller list—a significant accomplishment for a first-time author who admitted he was too busy to read many books. Hannity wrote the work by dictating passages into a tape recorder while commuting to work from his home on Long Island. Later, he transcribed his notes and polished them into manuscript form. The book is an unapologetic diatribe against liberalism, exposing its flaws in logic and posing questions about the outcome of its agenda for Americans.

In his *People* review of *Let Freedom Ring,* Todd Seavey called Hannity "an amusing tour guide of an imaginary Museum of Modern Left-Wing Lunacy" and noted that Hannity's "outrage is entertaining." *Washington Times* correspondent Jennifer Harper noted that Hannity "celebrates the cachet of clear conservatism and does not cozy up to centrist territory or the poll du jour." Martha Zoller in the *Atlanta Journal-Constitution* maintained that the book "is essentially an extension of the Hannity broadcast phenomenon. His writing style is much like his talking style—direct, passionate, and respectful. And he has discovered the key to winning debates: getting your opponent to think of issues in a different way."

By all accounts Hannity is a hard-working individual who considers himself fortunate to have such interesting work and to have achieved so much recognition in less than a decade. He told *Time:* "I really don't map out my life. There's no big plan. . . . If I were doing what I do today 30 years from now, I'd be happy."

BIOGRAPHICAL AND CRITICAL SOURCES:

PERIODICALS

Atlanta Journal-Constitution, April 29, 2002, Jill Vejnoska, "Hoppin' Hannity: Whirlwind of a Talk Show Host Expands from TV and Radio to Upcoming Book," p. C1; August 23, 2002, Martha Zoller, "Radio Talker Hannity Pushes Hot Buttons," p. E1.

People, February 11, 2002, Michael A. Lipton and Jennifer Frey, "The (Far) Right Stuff: Fishing's Fun, but Talk Show Host Sean Hannity Would Rather Bait Large-Mouth Liberals," p. 117; September 16, 2002, Todd Seavey, review of *Let Freedom Ring: Winning the War of Ideas in Politics, Media, and Life,* p. 43.

Time, November 11, 2002, Pames Poniewozik, "Ten Questions for Sean Hannity," p. 8.

Variety, April 23, 2001, Paula Bernstein, "Fox Finds a Sleeper Hit," p. 14.

Washington Times, August 19, 2002, Jennifer Harper, "New Hannity Book Maps Defeat of the Left," p. A6.

ONLINE

Sean Hannity Official Home Page, http://www.hannity. com (May 2, 2003).*

* * *

HARDING, Paul
See DOHERTY, P(aul) C.

HAREVEN, Tamara K(ern) 1937-2002

OBITUARY NOTICE—See index for *CA* sketch: Born May 10, 1937, in Cernauti, Rumania (now Chernivsti, Ukraine); died of kidney disease October 18, 2002, in Newark, DE. Historian, educator, and author. Hareven was a social historian who was interested in how family structures change through time. She was a graduate of Hebrew University in Jerusalem, where she earned her B.A. in 1960, followed by a master's degree in 1962 from the University of Cincinnati and a doctorate from Ohio State University in 1965. After completing her degrees, she was an assistant professor of history at Dalhousie University from 1965 to 1967, and then a faculty member at Harvard University. Beginning in 1969, she spent the next twenty years at Clark University in Worcester, Massachusetts, where she taught history and was a research associate at the Center for Population Studies. In 1988 she was hired as Unidel Professor of Family Studies and History at the University of Delaware and held joint appointments in public policy and urban affairs. Hareven's main research interest was in how the course of history has changed families both in America and other countries, especially with regard to the effects of industrialization. Her research helped to disprove the idealized image many Americans have of families in the past where three generations lived happily together in one home. Instead, Hareven showed, it was rare before modern times for people to live long enough to see their grandchildren born. She also wrote about how people commonly rented out rooms in their homes to lodgers until increased economic prosperity and a greater desire for privacy in America largely ended that practice, thus contributing to social isolation. In addition to her studies of American families, Hareven also did research into family dynamics in such countries as Japan, China, France, and Austria, focusing on how knowledge of trades and other skills were passed down from generation to generation. Among her books regarding family structures are *Family Time and Industrial Time* (1982), *Family Time and Industrial Time: The Relationships between the Family and Work in a New England Industrial Community* (1993), and *Families, History, and Social Change: Life Course and Cross-cultural Perspectives* (2000). Hareven also edited numerous books in the field of social history, was the founding editor of the *Journal of Family History,* and was founder and coeditor of *The History of the Family: An International Quarterly.*

OBITUARIES AND OTHER SOURCES:

PERIODICALS

Los Angeles Times, November 7, 2002, p. B25.
New York Times, November 6, 2002, p. C13.

*   *   *

HARPER, John C(arsten) 1924-2002

OBITUARY NOTICE—See index for *CA* sketch: Born July 17, 1924, in Winthrop, MA; died of a heart attack September 13, 2002, in Washington, DC. Minister and author. Because Harper was the rector of St. John's Episcopal Church, which is located near the White House and often referred to as the "Church of Presidents," he came into prominence as the minister to eight different U.S. presidents, though he also did much to change the mission of his church. The son of an Episcopal minister, Harper graduated from Harvard University in 1946 and earned his degree in divinity in 1953 from Episcopal Theological School, the same year he was ordained. During World War II he served in the U.S. Navy and after the war became an English teacher at Taft School, a private boys' school in Watertown, Connecticut. He was a curate in Providence, Rhode Island, in the early 1950s and a rector in Foxboro, Massachusetts, from 1954 to 1957 and in Bedford, New York, from 1957 to 1963. He was made rector of St. John's Church in 1963, where he remained until his retirement in 1993. While at St. John's, Harper preached to U.S. presidents Kennedy, Johnson, Nixon, Ford, Carter, Reagan, Bush, and Clinton. More importantly, however, he transformed his church from a "social church," where Washington, D.C.'s elite went to pray and paid fees for renting pews, into a church that was much more involved in the community. Harper opened St. John's Church to the public and created programs to help the poor and provide counseling to alcoholics and those with other problems. During the protests of the 1960s he allowed St. John's to be a refuge for those seeking shelter from teargas bombs. Harper wrote about his experiences in two books: *Sunday: A Minister's Story* (1974) and *Fifty-two Windows on Lafayette Square* (1978).

OBITUARIES AND OTHER SOURCES:

PERIODICALS

Los Angeles Times, September 17, 2002, p. B11.
New York Times, September 16, 2002, p. A19.
Times (London, England), September 24, 2002.
Washington Post, September 15, 2002, p. C6.

*   *   *

HICOK, Bob 1960-

PERSONAL: Born 1960.

ADDRESSES: Office—Department of English, Western Michigan University, 1903 West Michigan Ave., Kalamazoo, MI 49008-5433. *E-mail*—bob.hicok@ wmich.edu.

CAREER: Poet. Western Michigan University, Kalamazoo, visiting instructor in English, 2002—. Automotive die designer and computer systems administrator in Ann Arbor, MI.

AWARDS, HONORS: Notable Book of the Year award, American Library Association, and Felix Pollak Prize in Poetry, University of Wisconsin, 1995, both for *The Legend of Light;* National Endowment for the Arts fellow, 1999; two Pushcart Prizes; National Book Critics Circle Award for poetry nomination, 2002, for *Animal Soul.*

WRITINGS:

POETRY

Bearing Witness, Ridgeway Press, 1991.
The Legend of Light ("Felix Pollak Prize in Poetry" series), University of Wisconsin Press (Madison, WI), 1995.
Plus Shipping ("American Poets Continuum" series), BOA Editions (Rochester, NY), 1998.
Animal Soul ("Contemporary Classics Poetry" series), Invisible Cities Press (Montpelier, VT), 2001.

Contributor of poems to periodicals, including *New Yorker, American Poetry Review, Poetry, Iowa Review, Southern Review, Kenyon Review, Prairie Schooner,* and *Ploughshares.* Work represented in annual volumes of *Best American Poetry.*

SIDELIGHTS: Bob Hicok is a Michigan-based, prize-winning poet whose collection *The Legend of Light* was awarded the Felix Pollak Prize in Poetry. In reviewing the collection in *American Book Review,* Al Maginnes noted that these poems "concern themselves less with description than with the poet's reactions to the things this world places before him. . . . Hicok is an ambitious poet."

The first poem, "Killing," is about a boy who clubs insects and frogs and who wishes he had a real weapon so that he could go after bigger game, and of his adult resistance to killing any living thing after seeing his own violence reflected in the face of another person. Other poems are observations of violence, such as in "Waiting," wherein a child is being beaten by his father in a car outside a laundry, and the observer does nothing, but merely thinks someone should. In this poem, Hicok reminds us that our failure to act can be as damnable as the most evil of our own deeds. Insanity, incarceration, sexual awakening, persecution, and AIDS are other issues central to his poems. In "530 Lakewood" the poet visits a house where his family had lived and which is now adorned with a swastika. He remembers his mother watching him walk away from the house and her own inevitable leaving. Maginnes, who called this entry "stunning," said that "the mother cannot remain in place any more than the speaker of the poem can." Maginnes said that he was "most drawn" to this collection "in these moments, small and keenly observed, yet cognizant of the larger implications of all that our lives amount to."

Other poems in *The Legend of Light,* portray a doctor covered with blood, a group of foundry workers exchanging small talk, a class of Montessori students discussing an eight-year-old rapist, and an old man approaching death. Elizabeth Gaffney wrote in the *New York Times Book Review* that Hicok's talents fall "somewhere between those of the surgeon and the gods of the foundry and convalescent home: seamlessly, miraculously, his judicious eye imbues even the dreadful with beauty and meaning." A *Publishers Weekly* contributor called the volume a "collection of accomplished, un-self-conscious work." *Choice* reviewer W. V. Davis said Hicok's poems "add up to more than a sum of their parts. . . . Several of these poems will long burn in memory."

Plus Shipping contains poems that reflect Hicok's understanding of the working man, the man who is down on his luck, and the man who is addicted or oppressed. The title poem reflects his outrage at the exploitation of Native-American culture, and in "Watching Welles" he is disheartened by the physical and professional decline of the great actor/director. A *Kirkus Reviews* contributor, comparing Hicok's voice to that of Raymond Carver, said that "Hicok's strength is in his portraiture (a mugging victim, a young prostitute, a snake-handler) and in his at times unsparing view of family."

In reviewing *Animal Soul* for *Boston Review* online, Ethan Paquin noted that Hicok "is armed with a full quiver. Anyone unfortunate enough to fall within his sightlines will bear the brunt of a humorous yet insistent and incisive probing of USA, c. 2001." In this collection, Hicok targets the banality of contemporary culture, and his subjects range from mad cow disease to junk food. Paquin also noted that the small publisher, Invisible Cities Press, produced *Animal Soul* with a heavy cover, contemporary fonts, and luxurious paper, resulting in what Paquin called "a triumph of startling vision."

BIOGRAPHICAL AND CRITICAL SOURCES:

PERIODICALS

American Book Review, June, 1996, Al Maginnes, review of *The Legend of Light,* p. 21.
Choice, May, 1996, W. V. Davis, review of *The Legend of Light,* p. 1478.
Kirkus Reviews, November, 1998, review of *Plus Shipping,* p. 1562.
New York Times Book Review, January 21, 1996, Elizabeth Gaffney, review of *The Legend of Light,* p. 21.
Poetry, March, 1997, Leslie Ullman, review of *The Legend of Light,* p. 345.
Publishers Weekly, November 27, 1995, review of *The Legend of Light,* p. 67.

ONLINE

Boston Review Web site, http://bostonreview.mit.edu/ (July 29, 2002), Ethan Paquin, review of *Animal Soul.**

HILL, Richard W., Sr. 1950-
(Rick Hill)

PERSONAL: Born 1950, in Buffalo, NY. *Education:* Attended School of the Art Institute of Chicago, 1968-70; State University of New York—Buffalo, M.A., 1980.

ADDRESSES: Agent—c/o Author Mail, Abbeville Press, 22 Cortlandt St., New York, NY 10007.

CAREER: Worked for museums of the Buffalo Historical Society and Turtle (Iroquois cultural center), Niagara Falls, NY, in 1970s; Department of Northern Affairs, Ottawa, Ontario, Canada, manager of Indian art collections and exhibitions, 1982-85; Institute of American Indian Arts Museum, Santa Fe, NM, director and exhibition curator, 1990-94. Painter, carver, photographer, and basket weaver. Consultant to National Museum of the American Indian, Smithsonian Institution. Also employed as iron and construction worker in the 1960s. *Exhibitions:* Represented in solo and group shows, including exhibitions at Natural History Museum of the Smithsonian Institution, John F. Kennedy Center for the Performing Arts and Via Gambaro Gallery, both Washington, DC, American Indian Art Gallery, New York, NY, and American Indian Contemporary Arts, San Francisco, CA; work represented in many collections, including those of the Canadian Museum of Civilization, Indian Arts and Crafts Board of U.S. Department of the Interior, International Center of Photography, New York, NY, Seneca-Iroquois National Museum, and Woodland Indian Cultural Education Centre.

AWARDS, HONORS: Fellowships from New York State Historical Society, 1971, and Creative Artists Public Service, 1976; America the Beautiful Fund, photography award, 1972, fellowship, 1973.

WRITINGS:

(As Rick Hill) *Creativity Is Our Tradition,* Institute of American Indian Arts Museum (Santa Fe, NM), 1992.

(With Tom Hill) *Creation's Journey: Native American Identity and Belief,* Smithsonian Institution Press (Washington, DC), 1994.

(With Clara Sue Kidwell) *Treasures of the National Museum of the American Indian: Smithsonian Institution,* Abbeville Press (New York, NY), 1996.

Gifts of the Spirit, Peabody Essex Museum (Salem, MA), 1997.

Contributor to exhibition catalogs, including *Our Land/Ourselves: American Indian Contemporary Artists,* University Art Gallery, State University of New York—Albany (Albany, NY), 1990. Contributor to periodicals, including *Indian Artist.* Some writings appear under the name Rick Hill.

BIOGRAPHICAL AND CRITICAL SOURCES:

BOOKS

St. James Guide to Native North American Artists, St. James Press (Detroit, MI), 1998, pp. 224-228.

PERIODICALS

Albuquerque Journal, August 19, 1990, William Clark, "Indian Art—Indian Voices."

New Times, July 20, 1983, Zoe Tolone, "The Native American Artist: Caught between Culture and Commerce."

Santa Fe Reporter, August 15, 1990, Rowena Dickerson, "Indian Art through Indian Eyes."

Southwest Art, June, 1992, Jacqueline M. Pontello, "Museum Directions: Reclaiming Authority" (interview).

Turtle, winter, 1983, Tim Johnson, "New Directions in Iroquois Photography."*

*   *   *

HILL, Rick
See HILL, Richard W., Sr.

*   *   *

HILL, Ronald C. 1937-

PERSONAL: Born May 13, 1937, in Oak Park, IL; son of Clyde C. (a professor of English) and Fern L. (a teacher) Hill. *Education:* University of Denver, B.A., 1959, J.D., 1962. *Politics:* Republican. *Religion:* Methodist. *Hobbies and other interests:* Photography, bicycling, travel.

ADDRESSES: Home—Denver, CO. *Office*—Anstine, Hill, Richards & Simpson, 899 Logan St., Suite 406, Denver, CO 80203.

CAREER: Anstine & Hill (after 1996 Anstine, Hill, Richards & Simpson), Denver, CO, attorney, 1969—. Colorado Railroad Historical Foundation, president, 1981-94; Rocky Mountain Cancer Centers Foundation, member. *Military service:* U.S. Army, 1962-64; became captain; received Commendation Medal.

MEMBER: Colorado Bar Association, Defense Lawyers Association of Colorado, National Railway Historical Society (president of Intermountain chapter, 1970-71), National Society of the Scabbard and Blade (commander, 1971-75).

WRITINGS:

(With Jeffrey T. Brouws) *Railroading West*, Rail Graphics, 1975, 2nd edition, Darwin Publications, 1979.

Rio Grande in the Rockies, Colorado Railroad Museum, 1977, 2nd edition, 1979.

(With Dave Stanley) *Rails in the Northwest*, Colorado Railroad Museum, 1978.

(With R. H. Kindig) *Union Pacific 8444*, Colorado Railroad Museum, 1978.

(Editor, with R. H. Kindig) *Locomotive 346: The First One Hundred Years*, Colorado Railroad Museum, 1981.

Rio Grande West, Colorado Railroad Museum, 1982.

(With William E. Botkin and R. H. Kindig) *Union Pacific 3985*, Colorado Railroad Museum, 1985.

(With William E. Botkin and Victor Hand) *Union Pacific—Mainline West*, Colorado Railroad Museum, 1986.

Mountain Mainlines of the West, Colorado Railroad Museum, 1988.

Colorful Colorado Railroads in the 1960s, Colorado Railroad Museum, 1992.

(With Al Chione) *The Railroad Artistry of Howard Fogg*, Cedco Publishing (San Rafael, CA), 1999.

Creator of *Those Magnificent Planes* (annual calendar), Cedco Publishing (San Rafael, CA), 1985—. Contributor to books; contributor of articles and photographs to periodicals, including *Airliners.*

SIDELIGHTS: Ronald C. Hill told *CA:* "My primary motivation for writing is to share knowledge with others who have similar interests. I am particularly influenced by history and transportation, especially railroads and airlines. Ordinarily, I form some sort of rough outline—either written or mental—and then write and rewrite a rough draft in longhand with a fountain pen before typing the manuscript in final form. Sometimes subjects on which I am well versed simply occur to me, and at other times an editor will ask me to submit an article on a subject about which I have knowledge. I have a large research library at my disposal, and that is very helpful, of course."

* * *

HILTON, Joni 1956-

PERSONAL: Born 1956, in San Diego, CA; married Bob Hilton (a television news anchor), August 22, 1986; children: Richie, Brandon, Cassidy, Nicole. *Education:* California State University—Northridge, B.A. (journalism; summa cum laude), 1978; University of Southern California, M.F.A. (summa cum laude), 1981. *Hobbies and other interests:* Recipe and cooking contests.

ADDRESSES: Home—831 Morris Way, Sacramento, CA 95864; fax: 916-485-5678. *E-mail*—jonihilton@mstar2.net.

CAREER: Journalist and broadcaster. *Hour Family* (syndicated television specials), cohost; host of daily television program in Los Angeles, CA, for four years; guest on radio programs; national spokesperson for various corporations.

WRITINGS:

Braces, Gym Suits, and Early-Morning Seminary: A Youthquake Survival Manual, Covenant Communications (Salt Lake City, UT), 1985.

Five-Minute Miracles: 373 Quick Daily Projects for You and Your Kids to Share, Running Press, 1992.

Guilt-free Motherhood: How to Raise Great Kids and Have Fun Doing It, Covenant Communications (American Fork, UT), 1996.

Honey on Hot Bread and Other Heartfelt Wishes, Covenant Communications (American Fork, UT), 1997.

Family Fun Book: More than 400 Amazing, Amusing, and All-around Awesome Activities for the Entire Family!, Running Press (Philadelphia, PA), 1998.

The Once-a-Week Cooking Plan: Th Incredible Cooking Program That Will Save You Twenty Hours a Week (and Have Your Family Begging for More!), Prima Publishing (Rocklin, CA), 1999.

Housekeeping Secrets My Mother Never Taught Me, Prima Publishing (Roseville, CA), 2001.

Cooking Secrets My Mother Never Taught Me, Prima Publishing (Roseville, CA), 2001.

Author of screenplays, television episodes, film treatments, adaptations, and stage plays. Contributor of articles to periodicals, including *Family Circle, Saturday Evening Post, McCall's, Family Fun, Ladies' Home Journal,* and *Woman's Day.*

NOVELS

Dating: No Guts, No Glory (for teens), Covenant Communications (Salt Lake City, UT), 1989.

As the Ward Turns, Covenant Communications (American Fork, UT), 1991.

Around the Ward in Eighty Days, Covenant Communications (American Fork, UT), 1993.

Scrambled Home Evenings, Covenant Communications (American Fork, UT), 1994.

That's What Friends Are For (for teens), Covenant Communications (American Fork, UT), 1997.

Stop the Ward: I Want to Get Off!, Covenant Communications (American Fork, UT), 1999.

WORK IN PROGRESS: *The Art of Prayer,* for Covenant Communications; a novel.

SIDELIGHTS: Joni Hilton told *CA:* "My writing process consists of snatching a few minutes here and there as I raise four active children. I cannot afford the luxury of waiting for inspiration; I just sit down and 'force-write.' Luckily, this seems to work.

"Most of my writing is humorous, although some have argued. I write for two audiences: mainstream and Mormon. In both cases, I try to help us laugh at ourselves and thus retain sanity. Many of my magazine pieces reflect this same goal."

HOFF, Harry Summerfield 1910-2002
(William Cooper)

OBITUARY NOTICE—See index for *CA* sketch: Born August 4, 1910, in Crewe, Cheshire, England; died September 5, 2002, in London, England. Civil servant, educator, and author. Hoff will be most remembered as the author of the novel *Scenes from Provincial Life* (1950), the first of his novels written under the William Cooper pseudonym. Educated at Christ's College, Cambridge, where he earned a master's degree in 1933, he was a school master in Leicester before World War II. During the war he served in the Royal Air Force and was promoted to squadron leader. He then embarked on a long career in the civil service, where he remained even after becoming a successful novelist. Hoff held various jobs as a civil servant, including as an assistant commissioner in the 1940s and 1950s, personnel consultant to the Atomic Energy Authority from 1958 to 1971 as well as to the Central Electricity Generating Board, and as an assistant director to Civil Service Technical Services in the early 1970s. From 1975 to 1977 he was a member of the board of Crown agents and personnel consultant to Millbank Technical Services. The last years of his career, from 1977 to 1990, were spent as a lecturer in English literature at Syracuse University. Hoff's writing career began with several undistinguished novels written under his own name. When he published *Scenes from Provincial Life,* however, he felt that its sometimes frank sexual content should not be attributed to the pen of a civil servant, so he had the book published pseudonymously. This novel, in which he tried to realistically portray working-class people in England, was widely praised by critics and author colleagues alike. Hoff followed this accomplishment with several more books that followed the main character in *Scenes,,* Joe Lunn, whose experiences are loosely based on the author's own; unfortunately, none of these sequels were as successful as his most admired novel. Though his later novels never won substantial acclaim, several gained critical praise, among them *The Struggles of Albert Woods* (1952), *Disquiet and Peace* (1956), and *Memoirs of a New Man* (1966). Hoff's last book to be published was the eighth in the "Scenes from Life" series featuring Lunn, *Scenes from Death and Life* (1999).

OBITUARIES AND OTHER SOURCES:

PERIODICALS

Independent (London, England), September 6, 2002, p. 20.

Times (London, England), September 9, 2002, p. 7.

HOLZMAN, Franklyn Dunn 1918-2002

OBITUARY NOTICE—See index for *CA* sketch: Born December 31, 1918, in Brooklyn, NY; died from complications from a stroke September 1, 2002, in Clifton, NJ. Economist, educator, and author. Holzman was an expert on the economy of the former Soviet Union and a critic of President Ronald Reagan's defense budget. He was a graduate of the University of North Carolina, where he earned his A.B. in 1940. During World War II he served with the Army Air Corps in the Ukraine, and it was here that he first became interested in studying the Soviet economy. After the war, Holzman went on to complete his doctorate at Harvard University in 1948. He was an economist for the U.S. Department of the Treasury for three years before joining the faculty at the University of Washington, where he taught until 1961. He then moved on to Tufts University, where he was a professor at the Fletcher School of Law and Diplomacy until retiring in 1992. As a researcher and author, Holzman revealed flaws in the Soviet economy, such as in his *Soviet Taxation: The Fiscal and Monetary Problems of a Planned Economy* (1955) in which he showed that tax laws in the USSR ran counter to the Communist idea of fair distribution of wealth. In the 1980s Holzman argued that the Soviet Union could not sustain its military budget, which was actually far less than it was believed to be. He felt, furthermore, that President Reagan inflated figures for Soviet spending in order to gain approval for his own military budget. Holzman was later proved correct when the Soviet Union collapsed and some of its records were made public. Some of Holzman's other writings about the Soviet economy include *Financial Checks on Soviet Defense Expenditures* (1975), *The Soviet Economy: Past, Present, and Future* (1982), and *The Economics of the Soviet Bloc Trade and Finance* (1987). He was also an expert on foreign trade and inflation.

OBITUARIES AND OTHER SOURCES:

PERIODICALS

New York Times, September 7, 2002, p. A13.
Washington Post, September 9, 2002, p. B6.

* * *

HOTSCHNIG, Alois 1959-

PERSONAL: Born October 3, 1959, in Carinthia, Austria.

ADDRESSES: Home—Innsbruck, Austria. *Agent*—c/o University of Nebraska Press, 312 North 14, P.O. Box 880484, Lincoln, NE 68588-0484.

CAREER: Freelance writer, 1989—.

AWARDS, HONORS: Preis des Landes Kärnten, 1992; Anna Seghers Prize, 1993; Robert Musil scholarship, 1999-2000.

WRITINGS:

Aus: Erzählung (title means "Out"), Luchterhand (Frankfurt, Germany), 1989.
Eine Art Glück (title means "One Kind of Luck"), Luchterhand (Frankfurt, Germany), 1990.
Aus; Eine Art Glück: zwei Erzählungen, Luchterhand (Hamburg, Germany), 1992.
Leonardos Hände, Luchterhand Literaturverlag (Hamburg, Germany), 1992, translation and foreword by Peter Filkins published as *Leonardo's Hands,* University of Nebraska Press (Lincoln, NE), 1999.
Absolution: Ein Stück in drei Akten (play), Kiepenheuer & Witsch (Cologne, Germany), 1994.
Ludwigs Zimmer: Roman, Kiepenheuer & Witsch (Cologne, Germany), 2000.

SIDELIGHTS: Austrian writer Alois Hotschnig has been acclaimed for strong narrative and rhythmic prose in his fiction, as well as his ability to conjure up complex reality unblinkingly, and without flinching from the harshest truths. One of his first novellas, *Eine Art Glück,* tells the story of a boy born without legs who grows up full of self-loathing, keenly aware of his parents' and indeed the world's disappointment in him. "A plot of this kind is sufficiently horrible, painful, and hopeless by itself, but Hotschnig's writing makes it all the more inescapable. . . [the reader becomes] a victim of the author's magnetism. It is indeed a proof of highest craft and enormous talent," wrote Erich Wolfgang Skwara in *World Literature Today.*

Hotschnig's first full-length novel, *Leonardos Hände* (translated as *Leonardo's Hands*) is considered his most important work to date. In this grim tale, a young man named Karl kills an elderly couple in a car accident that leaves their twenty-four-year-old daughter Anna in a coma. Racked by guilt for fleeing the scene of the accident, Karl visits Anna in the hospital and befriends her when she comes out of the coma a year later, helping her to piece her life back together. Eventually, Karl must face the difference between the Anna he imagined and the real Anna he comes to know. Told through multiple perspectives, journal entries, news articles, and other devices, the novel often leaves the characters without much in the way of real information.

Through these methods, "Hotschnig . . . gives us a literary signal of the postmodern century to come. Perception and existentialism are thrown into question in a manner similar to the way surface 'reality' was attacked at the start of our century," wrote Robert Dassanowsky in the *American Book Review.* "Hotschnig's. . . . novel is a compelling depiction of the struggle to span the unbridgeable linguistic gap between perception and expression," wrote Tess Lewis in *World Literature Today.* According to a *Publishers Weekly* reviewer, "Hotschnig's true subject ultimately reveals itself to be consciousness—or, at least, the process of finding and losing one's identity."

Hotschnig followed up *Leonardo's Hands* with a play that once again explored the nature of reality and the limits of perception. In *Absolution: Ein Stück in drei Akten,* an estranged couple, Ernst and Ria, reunites for the funeral of their son, Ludwig, an apparent suicide who had been estranged from both his parents. His brother George and an elderly relative named Berta complete the cast. Questions soon arise as to whether this is really a suicide, an accident, a drug overdose, or even a complex hoax since only a closed coffin is seen throughout most of the play. Reviewing the play in *World Literature Today,* Reinhold Grimm wrote that Hotschnig "is definitely quite capable of composing deft and subtle if subdued dialogue." According to Peter Filkins, in his forward to *Leonardo's Hands,* "Reading Hotschnig . . . one cannot help but feel that Austrian literature continues to hold genuine promise. For here is a writer at last able to meld the difficult with the pleasurable, as well as the philosophical with the immediacy of pure intrigue."

BIOGRAPHICAL AND CRITICAL SOURCES:

PERIODICALS

American Book Review, January-February, 2000, Robert Dassanowsky, "Austrian PoMo," p. 30.

Publishers Weekly, January 25, 1999, review of *Leonardo's Hands,* p. 73.
World Literature Today, summer, 1991, Erich Wolfgang Skwara, review of *Eine Art Glück,* p. 477; winter, 1994, Tess Lewis, review of *Leonardos Hände,* pp. 113-114; spring, 1995, Reinhold Grimm, review of *Absolution,* pp. 352-353.

ONLINE

Austria Kultur Web site, http://www.austriaculture.net/ (February 24, 2000), Peter Filkins, "Remembrance of Things Imagined."*

*   *   *

HUDLER, Ad 1965(?)-

PERSONAL: Born c. 1965; married; wife's name, Carol (a publisher); children: Haley Joy. *Education:* Graduate of the University of Nebraska. *Hobbies and other interests:* Kayaking, gardening, cooking, reading, tennis.

ADDRESSES: Agent—c/o Author Mail, Random House, 1540 Broadway, New York, NY 10036. *E-mail*—ad@adhudler.com.

CAREER: Writer. *Fort Myers News-Press,* Fort Myers, FL, journalist.

WRITINGS:

Househusband, Ballantine (New York, NY), 2002.

SIDELIGHTS: Ad Hudler casts himself as the title character of his debut novel, *Househusband.* Hudler moved to Macon, Georgia, when his wife took a job as a publisher, and he chose to care for their daughter and their home while she pursued her career. A former journalist, Hudler had already begun one book, but paused to begin and finish this one, in which he sprinkles recipes throughout the story of alterego Linc Menner and his househusbandly life. A *Kirkus Reviews* contributor wrote that the novel's "self-impressed narrator takes on househusbanding with a vengeance and makes a better wife and mother than any woman could."

Linc and his wife, Jo, move from California to Rochester, New York, when Jo accepts a job as a hospital administrator. Linc, a former landscape architect of the gardens of the West Coast rich and famous, agrees to stay at home with their small daughter, Violet. Linc is a superdad—cleaning, cooking, and filling the house with plants. He finds no daytime friends with the stay-at-home moms, except for Marilyn, the attractive neighbor whose child-rearing techniques—allowing her children to eat junk food and watch a lot of television—sharply contrast with Linc's own stricter methods. But Linc and Marilyn become friends, drinking and cooking together, and complaining to each other. Eventually, when the other women are able to get over their fear of having their children be alone with a man, they also warm up to Linc, whose cooking and horticultural talents they admire.

A *Publishers Weekly* reviewer noted that while Link tries to be the perfect father and husband, his mother Carol "provides an alternate voicing of desire and longing through her on-the-road e-mails to her son." Carol Menner breaks free from her uncommunicative used-car-salesman husband by stealing one of his cars and taking a road-trip adventure. In reviewing the novel for *BookReporter.com*, Anita Bunn commented that "although [Carol] . . . often indulges herself with revealing too much personal information to her son, and she might not have always been the best parent, Linc does credit her with teaching him to understand women. Carol Menner is also the one to remind her son to relax with his duties as a househusband and to enjoy his daughter more, not to think of her as just another job."

Hudler, in an interview for *BookReporter.com*, was asked whether any of the characters are based on real people and why he chose to use the mother character. Hudler replied, "Linc, of course. And Violet. Linc's mother is also my mother. Though my mom has never run away from home, it is her spirit that resides in the character of Carol. . . . She's my favorite character in the book. I needed a device to help set a time structure for the book, and the mother's e-mails came to mind. . . . I thought the mother would be an interesting counterbalance to Linc's situation. He suddenly finds himself stuck in the life of domestic servitude that she has decided to flee.

"*Househusband* is the story of a man struggling to make it in a woman's world. Linc Menner's masculin-ity and pride are under fire every day. His journey shows that many of the hazards associated with being a stay-at-home mom—low self-esteem, a sagging sex drive, and a feeling that no one appreciates all his hard work—are not female-specific."

Library Journal's John Charles wrote that *Househusband* provides "a genuine glimpse at the guilt and joy that only other stay-at-home parents really understand."

BIOGRAPHICAL AND CRITICAL SOURCES:

PERIODICALS

Kirkus Reviews, February 1, 2002, review of *Househusband*, p. 127.
Library Journal, May 1, 2002, John Charles, review of *Househusband*, p. 133.
Publishers Weekly, February 25, 2002, review of *Househusband*, p. 37.

ONLINE

Ad Hudler Home Page, http://www.adhudler.com (July 9, 2002).
BookReporter.com, http://www.bookreporter.com/ (July 9, 2002), Anita Bunn, review of *Househusband*, and interview with Hudler.*

*   *   *

HUNTER, Kim 1922-2002

OBITUARY NOTICE—See index for *CA* sketch: Original name, Janet Cole; born November 12, 1922, in Detroit, MI; died of a heart attack September 11, 2002, in New York, NY. Actress and author. Hunter was an award-winning actress best known for her role as Stella Kowalski in the 1951 film *A Streetcar Named Desire*. A somewhat lonely child growing up in Florida, she turned to her imagination and acting for comfort. She acted in school and made her professional debut at the age of seventeen in a Miami Women's Club production of *Penny Wise*. Her only formal training was between 1938 to 1940, when she studied acting in Miami with Charmine Lantaff Camine. She then moved to California, where a talent scout saw her in a production of *Arsenic and Old Lace.* Her film debut came in 1943 with the horror movie *The Seventh Victim.* In 1947 she starred as Stella in the stage version of *Streetcar,* for which she won a New York Drama Critics Circle award, and in 1950 she toured with a road production of *Two Blind Mice.* Trouble came in the 1950s, however, when Hunter learned that she had been put on the black lists of the television networks for her involvement in a peace rally. Although she won an Academy Award and a Golden Globe Award for playing Stella in the 1951 film adaptation of *Streetcar,* she was blackballed by television networks and movie studios for several years. Hunter finally reemerged in 1956 in the movie *Storm Center.* Despite this unjust treatment, she did not hold a grudge, and continued to work on stage, in movies, and in all kinds of television shows, including two years on the soap opera *Edge of Night,* and in series such as *Marcus Welby, M.D.* and *Ironside.* Besides the role of Stella, Hunter is probably best remembered for playing Dr. Zira alongside Charlton Heston in the 1968 film *The Planet of the Apes* as well as in its sequels. Other important stage productions Hunter acted in include *The Lion in Winter* (1975), *Death of a Salesman* (1983), *The Cocktail Hour* (1992), and *The Gin Game* (1994). Some of her other films include *A Canterbury Tale* (1949), *Bermuda Affair* (1957), *Midnight in the Garden of Good and Evil* (1997), and, most recently, *The Hiding Place* (2000), *Abilene* (2000), and *Old Hats* (2000). Hunter was also the author of two books: *Kim Hunter: Loose in the Kitchen* (1975) and *Jesus Died on the Electric Chair* (2001).

OBITUARIES AND OTHER SOURCES:

BOOKS

Contemporary Theatre, Film, and Television, Volume 29, Gale (Detroit, MI), 2000.
Pickard, Roy, *The Oscar Stars from A-Z,* Headline (London, England), 1996.

PERIODICALS

Chicago Tribune, September 12, 2002, section 2, p. 9.
Los Angeles Times, September 12, 2002, p. B13.
New York Times, September 12, 2002, p. C11.
Washington Post, September 12, 2002, p. B10.

HYDE, Christopher 1949-
(Nicholas Chase, joint pseudonym)

PERSONAL: Born May 26, 1949, in Ottawa, Ontario, Canada; son of Laurence (an author, illustrator, and producer) and Bettye Marguerite (a child psychologist; maiden name, Bambridge) Hyde; married Mariea Sparks, July 23, 1975; children: Noah Stevenson Sparks, Chelsea Orianna Sparks. *Hobbies and other interests:* Travel, reading, clubs.

ADDRESSES: Agent—c/o Author Mail, Douglas and McIntyre, 2323 Quebec St., Suite 201, Vancouver, British Columbia V5T 4S7, Canada.

CAREER: Writer. Freelance broadcaster for Canadian Broadcasting Corporation (CBC), Ottawa, Ottawa, Ontario, Canada, 1966-68, CBC Vancouver, Vancouver, British Columbia, Canada, 1969, 1973-75, CJOH-TV Ottawa, 1970-71, and CBC, Canadian Television (CTV), and Ontario Educational Communications Authority (OECA), 1971-72; full-time writer, 1977—. Ripping Yarns, Inc., president; Nicholas Chase Productions, partner; Plain Brown Wrapper Puzzles, owner.

MEMBER: Young Men's Christian Association.

WRITINGS:

Temple of the Winds, illustrated by Joseph Cellini, World Publishing (Cleveland, OH), 1965.
The Wave, Doubleday (Garden City, NY), 1979.
The Icarus Seal, Houghton Mifflin (Boston, MA), 1982.
Styx, Severn House (London, England), 1982, Playboy Press (Chicago, IL), 1983.
The Tenth Crusade, Houghton Mifflin (Boston, MA), 1983.
(With brother, Anthony Hyde, under joint pseudonym Nicholas Chase) *Locksley,* Heinemann (London, England), 1983.
Echo Drive, 1983.
Maxwell's Train, Villard Books (New York, NY), 1985.
Jericho Falls, Avon Books (New York, NY), 1986.
Whisperland: A Chilling Tale of Dynastic Evil, Hutchinson (London, England), 1987.
Holy Ghost, 1987.

Crestwood Heights, Avon Books (New York, NY), 1988.

Egypt Green, Simon & Schuster (New York, NY), 1989.

White Lies, Simon & Schuster (New York, NY), 1990, published as *Hard Target,* Morrow (New York, NY), 1991.

Abuse of Trust: The Career of Dr. James Tyhurst, Douglas & McIntyre (Vancouver, British Columbia, Canada), 1991.

Black Dragon, Morrow (New York, NY), 1992.

The Paranoid's Handbook, Key Porter Books (Toronto, Ontario, Canada), 1993.

A Gathering of Saints, Pocket Books (New York, NY), 1996.

The Second Assassin, Onyx (New York, NY), 2002.

Wisdom of the Bones, Onyx (New York, NY), 2003.

SIDELIGHTS: Christopher Hyde is a successful Canadian novelist who worked for a number of media outlets before becoming a full-time writer. His first novel, *The Wave,* called "an epic of eco-disaster" by *Maclean's* writer Margaret Cannon, is a doomsday book with the plot revolving around the failure of the largest dam in the world, located on the Columbia River. It is also about human failure and greed. Heavy rains weaken the surrounding mountain causing a mud slide, and when the dam cracks the resulting wave of water takes out every dam in the chain, with the last being the Grand Coulee Dam, on the other side of which is a nuclear reactor. A U.S. government engineer works to avoid the disaster, and at the same time evade unidentified agents—possibly CIA or FBI—who are out to stop him. Hyde spent three years researching the story, his warning of a disaster that could be. "Readers will love every gruesome, cliff-hanging minute," wrote Judith T. Yamamoto in *Library Journal.* Newgate Callendar noted in the *New York Times Book Review* that Hyde blends "ecology, conspiracy, and nuclear disaster in a heady mixture."

Joseph P. Levy wrote in the *West Coast Review of Books* that Peter Coffin, the protagonist of Hyde's *The Icarus Seal,* has an intellect and wit "sharper than that of James Bond. . . . Above all, Coffin has guts." Peter is an investigative reporter who is contacted by his friend, Sam Underwood, about an international plot. Sam is to fly from England and meet Peter in Toronto, but the flight on which he is to arrive disappears. John North noted in *Quill & Quire* that the book "contains a serious underlying message about the morality of national governments and the safety of the flying public."

As they try to find Sam, Peter and Sam's beautiful sister Georgina are pursued across England, France, and Canada by an international cartel that is using chartered planes for dangerous purposes. Mary Jo Campbell wrote in *School Library Journal* that the story contains "some almost unbelievable coincidences . . . but the book is so good that the reader goes along willingly." *Library Journal*'s Robert H. Donahugh felt that "with plenty of surprises and smart dialogue, this is a superior thriller."

In *Styx,* a team of archeologists is trapped in a cave in Yugoslavia after an earthquake shuts off their means of escape. They follow an underground river, hoping it will lead them out, and as time passes, they undergo a number of horrific events, included waking one night to find a female member of the group being eaten alive by large centipedes. Ann Vanderhoof, who interviewed Hyde for *Quill & Quire,* said, "One wonders what sort of individual conceives of nastiness such as this." Hyde told her, "I'm a psycho-neurotic. My books are about paranoias." Hyde said that his former father-in-law had turned the lights out while they were in an underground cave. "Do you have any idea how dark it is forty feet below ground?" he said.

The Tenth Crusade, noted Vanderhoof, "is based on more sophisticated paranoias: fear of control by organizations or individuals, fear of elimination of freedom of choice, rather than simple fears like hydrophobia and aviophobia (fear of flying)." Vanderhoof wrote that *The Tenth Crusade* grew out of one of the axes Hyde has to grind: the idea that some fundamentalist religious groups exert control over their members, and as "very vocal and very rich minorities, they can exert control over society at large as well." In the book, Hyde's religious group uses a symbol much like the Nazi swastika. Hyde originally planned to include fifteen pages of appendices of factual material on church-sponsored organizations that were indicted under the U.S. Treason Act for fronting Nazi groups in the 1930s, but the publisher was afraid of lawsuits. "Even without the appendices," said Vanderhoof, "*The Tenth Crusade* is far from a flattering profile of a fundamentalist organization. The plot involves terrorist acts, sexual torture, and brainwashing, and implies collusion by U.S. government officials and the military."

Spectator reviewer Harriet Waugh called *The Tenth Crusade* "sufficiently convoluted to keep the reader guessing." In the novel, photographer Philip Kirkland spends time with former lover Heather, now a member of a fundamentalist cult. Philip is then knocked unconscious and finds Heather gone when he comes to. He teams up with Sarah Logan, the daughter of a senator who committed suicide after being slandered by a conservative lobby, and they cross the country trying to prevent its takeover. Hyde integrates an account of how parachurch groups use money to achieve political goals. He also refers to celebrities such as Jesse Helms and Jerry Falwell as examples of how the religious right has attained power and influence. A *Publishers Weekly* contributor said Hyde "has written a cool, smooth thriller with a difference." *Los Angeles Times Book Review* writer Nick B. Williams called the novel "a terrifying yarn of semireligious fanaticism running amok."

Library Journal's Barbara Conaty wrote that with *Maxwell's Train,* Hyde's "crossbreeding of the heist genre and political suspense has produced a vigorous hybrid." Harry Maxwell is a former drifter and drug dealer spending his later years cleaning trains. He decides to pull one last job when he discovers that $35 million in new currency is being shipped from the Bureau of Engraving in Washington to New York and Boston federal reserve banks on an Amtrak train called the Night Owl. Harry assembles a group of cohorts with the intention of pulling off the job with no violence and no one getting hurt, but a heavily armed band of terrorists called the World People's Army beats them to it.

A *Publishers Weekly* contributor wrote of *Maxwell's Train* that "although improbable toward the end, the novel delivers some genuine excitement and thrills." "Hyde's fascination with trains is evident in this fast-paced thriller," noted George Cohen in *Booklist.*

In reviewing *Jericho Falls* for *Quill & Quire,* North called Hyde "a writer of well-researched, eminently readable thrillers. When his themes describe man's attempt to control some aspect of nature, however, his writing seems to acquire an additional edge." While passing through the small New Hampshire town of Jericho Falls, a vehicle carrying a biological warfare material is involved in an accident. The chemical agent, QQ9, kills its victims either instantly or by causing them to develop rapidly growing cancers.

Hyde writes in the book that such a material actually exists and is being studied by the military. *Publishers Weekly* contributor John Mutter called *Jericho Falls* "a frightening and engrossing read."

Whisperland: A Chilling Tale of Dynastic Evil is a story of espionage primarily set in Bermuda, site of the Whisperland Hotel, to which an American draft dodger and fisherman is called by a wealthy uncle who wants him to take over the family's businesses. Louise Griffith wrote in *Canadian Review of Materials* that the story "moves swiftly from one interesting location to another. . . . The vivid description of these locales adds to the glamour of the book."

A *West Coast Review of Books* writer called *Crestwood Heights* "a neat high tech thriller that'll leave you feeling like you just shot the rapids in the Colorado River." Kelly Rhine, an illustrator in New York, inherits a house and movie theater in Crestwood Heights, North Carolina, and, frustrated by the hassle of her life, she leaves New York and moves to the idyllic town where technology makes the lives of its inhabitants easy and peaceful. There is no crime, poverty, or pollution in Crestwood Heights. The owner of the town's newspaper and best friend of her deceased uncle tries to tell Kelly that something sinister is happening in the town, and he soon ends up dead. Kelly attempts to unravel the mystery of the technological manipulation of Crestwood Heights's citizens with the help of Robin Spenser, a resident and former marine. The *West Coast Review of Books* writer noted that "Hyde's crisp writing style will keep you turning the pages right up through the unique double climax ending."

Egypt Green is manipulation on a much bigger scale. The governments of the world are considering kidnapping the brightest children and protecting them in a special environment while that release a plague that would end Earth's overpopulation problem.

Abuse of Trust: The Career of Dr. James Tyhurst is about a boy whose father is murdered and who is then trained by the CIA, with the use of mind-altering drugs, to become a psychiatrist. When he goes into practice, he sexually exploits and humiliates a number of his female patients. The man about whom Hyde writes actually became head of the University of British Columbia's psychiatry department and was charged by patients with taking them to an isolated island where Tyhurst enslaved them, chaining them and forcing them into ritualistic and sexual acts. *Books in Canada*'s Michael Coren said that "Hyde's description of the perversion and pain involved in all of this is seldom prurient and never insensitive, but it is inevitably voyeuristic. It could really be no other way."

In *Hard Target* first published as *White Lies,* the actual Romulus plan, which was created for the purpose of assassinating the dying President Roosevelt, is resurrected to end the life of a young president who has been diagnosed with early senile dementia. A group of Washington establishment people hire a killer with the intention of taking out both the president and the vice president, who has an independent streak and who they know they will not be able to manipulate. A number of secret agencies, including the CIA, KGB, GRU, and FBI, learn of the plan, but drop the ball. Conaty called the resolution "a whizzer of a conclusion." Hyde's message is a questioning of the safety of world leaders if someone really wants them dead. North wrote that "the non-stop pace of the story and the pleasant complexity of the plot are sufficient to keep the pages turning." Frederick Busch commented in Chicago's *Tribune Books* that the story is "elaborately structured, and its suspense is bolstered by a wealth of persuasive details." *Publishers Weekly* contributor Sybil Steinberg wrote that the novel ends with a "powerful resolution and a final stunning surprise."

In *Black Dragon,* the military advisor to the president's drug czar is murdered on the yacht of a senator where the parties involved indulged themselves with opium. The Defense Department wants to get to the bottom of the crime but also wants to keep the whole incident quiet. They bring Colonel Phillip Dane out of retirement to investigate, and he soon finds the trail leading to a Chinese gang who itself seems to be a target of the drug trade bosses. A *Kirkus Reviews* contributor called the story "smooth, literate, and thoroughly cynical. Well done." A *Publishers Weekly* reviewer wrote that Hyde's "dark, stately style suits his characters well, and the sheer multitude of pieces he fits into his puzzle inspires awe."

A Gathering of Saints was called "a baroque, delightfully gruesome serial-killer whodunit," by a *Kirkus Reviews* contributor, who added that the book is "well-researched, relentlessly grim, and remarkably evoca-

tive of its time and place." *Library Journal*'s Andrea Lee Shuey felt that "the book is not for everyone, but it is well done." The story is set in World War II London, where a serial killer known as Queer Jack stalks, kills, and positions the bodies of his victims in such a way as to indicate where the next bombings will occur. Detective Inspector Morris Black discovers that the killer is one of a small group of intelligence officers who broke the Nazi Enigma radio code and could understand their secret messages. Other characters include a psychiatrist who is also a Nazi spy and an American female spy masquerading as a journalist. Hyde refers to real people in this thriller, including Ian Fleming, Guy Burgess, and C. P. Snow. *Booklist*'s George Needham called *A Gathering of Saints* "a fascinating story but definitely not for the squeamish." A *Publishers Weekly* reviewer wrote that the conclusion contains "images of gore and tormented madness that can't soon be forgotten. Readers who relish the raw truth of human, and inhuman, history will find here what they are looking for."

Like *A Gathering of Saints, The Second Assassin* is also steeped in historical detail. The year is 1939, and the United States is on the verge of entering World War II. There are those who would do anything to prevent this from happening, including assassinating Britain's King George on U.S. soil to divide the two countries, thus severing America's obligation to protect and defend England. Thomas Barry is the London detective and Jane Todd the gritty freelance photographer who together pursue professional assassin John Bone. A *Publishers Weekly* reviewer called the novel "a rousing political thriller that bursts with nonstop action, rapid-fire dialogue, and eminently likable characters."

BIOGRAPHICAL AND CRITICAL SOURCES:

BOOKS

St. James Guide to Horror, Ghost, and Gothic Writers, St. James Press (Detroit, MI), 1998.

PERIODICALS

Booklist, March 1, 1985, George Cohen, review of *Maxwell's Train,* p. 927; July, 1996, George Needham, review of *A Gathering of Saints,* p. 1808.

Books in Canada, March, 1992, Michael Coren, review of *Abuse of Trust: The Career of Dr. James Tyhurst,* p. 44.

Canadian Review of Materials, May, 1988, Louise Griffith, review of *Whisperland: A Chilling Tale of Dynastic Evil,* p. 88.

Kirkus Reviews, June 1, 1992, review of *Black Dragon,* p. 687; May 1, 1996, review of *A Gathering of Saints,* p. 624.

Library Journal, August, 1979, Judith T. Yamamoto, review of *The Wave,* p. 1589; September 15, 1982, Robert H. Donahugh, review of *The Icarus Seal,* p. 1769; January, 1984, review of *The Tenth Crusade,* p. 111; January, 1985, Barbara Conaty, review of *Maxwell's Train,* p. 100; December, 1990, Barbara Conaty, review of *Hard Target,* p. 164; June 15, 1996, Andrea Lee Shuey, review of *A Gathering of Saints,* p. 91.

Los Angeles Times Book Review, February 26, 1984, Nick B. Williams, review of *The Tenth Crusade,* p. 6.

Maclean's, October 29, 1979, Margaret Cannon, review of *The Wave,* p. 52; June 14, 1982, Margaret Cannon, review of *The Icarus Seal,* p. 53; April 25, 1983, review of *The Tenth Crusade,* p. 58.

Necrofile, fall, 1991, review of *Egypt Green,* p. 21.

New Scientist, June 16, 1988, Judith Perera, review of *Jericho Falls,* p. 74.

New York Times Book Review, September 16, 1979, Newgate Callendar, review of *The Wave,* p. 26.

Publishers Weekly, September 16, 1983, Barbara A. Bannon, review of *Locksley,* p. 116; January 8, 1988, John Mutter, review of *Crestwood Heights,* p. 75; review of *The Tenth Crusade,* p. 89; December 21, 1984, review of *Maxwell's Train,* p. 83; October 31, 1986, John Mutter, review of *Jericho Falls,* p. 60; November 16, 1990, Sybil Steinberg, review of *Hard Target,* p. 46; June 1, 1992, review of *Black Dragon,* p. 52; May 27, 1996, review of *A Gathering of Saints,* p. 66; February 25, 2002, review of *The Second Assassin,* p. 48.

Quill & Quire, July, 1982, John North, review of *The Icarus Seal,* p. 61; April, 1983, Ann Vanderhoof, "Thrilling the Public Is Nothing to Hyde" (interview), pp. 28-29; January, 1985, John North, review of *Maxwell's Train,* pp. 23-24; February, 1987, John North, review of *Jericho Falls,* p. 17; March, 1991, John North, review of *Hard Target,* p. 60.

School Library Journal, January, 1983, Mary Jo Campbell, review of *The Icarus Seal,* p. 90; March, 1984, Mary Mills, review of *The Tenth Crusade,* p. 178.

Spectator, July 21, 1984, Harriet Waugh, review of *The Tenth Crusade,* p. 29.

Tribune Books (Chicago, IL), January 20, 1991, Frederick Busch, review of *Hard Target,* p. 10.

West Coast Review of Books, November, 1982, Joseph R. Levy, review of *The Icarus Seal,* p. 30; Volume 13, issue 5, 1988, review of *Crestwood Heights,* p. 28.*

J-K

JAMES, Brian 1976-

PERSONAL: Born January 7, 1976, in Portsmouth, VA; son of Nicholas Masino and Anita Uhl; married Sarah Vischer (a photographer), March 16, 2002. *Education:* New York University, B.A.

ADDRESSES: Home—1380 Riverside Dr., Apt. 6B, New York, NY 10033. *E-mail*—brianjamespush@hotmail.com.

CAREER: Writer.

WRITINGS:

Pure Sunshine (young adult novel), Scholastic (New York, NY), 2002.
The Shark Who Was Afraid of Everything, illustrated by Bruce McNally, Scholastic (New York, NY), 2002.
The Spooky Hayride, Scholastic (New York, NY), 2003.
Tomorrow, Maybe (young adult novel), Scholastic (New York, NY), 2003.

"SUPERTWINS" SERIES

The Supertwins: Bad Dogs from Space, illustrated by Chris L. Demarest, Scholastic (New York, NY), 2003.
The Supertwins: The Terrible Tooth Snatcher, illustrated by Chris L. Demarest, Scholastic (New York, NY), 2003.

The Supertwins: Meet the Dangerous Dinobots, illustrated by Chris L. Demarest, Scholastic (New York, NY), 2003.
The Supertwins: Meet the Sneaky, Slimy Bookworms, illustrated by Chris L. Demarest, Scholastic (New York, NY), 2004.

WORK IN PROGRESS: A beginning-reader series titled "Catkid," with illustrations by the author; a third young adult novel; an adult novel.

SIDELIGHTS: Budding novelist and children's book author Brian James made a mark for himself at the age of twenty-four with the publication of his first young-adult novel, *Pure Sunshine.* As James told *CA,* "There are stories that need to be told, characters that say 'Hi, how are you doing?' I make them say more, let them speak and tell their story. Hopefully that story will mean something special to those who read it. That's how I approach everything I write, from my novels to my children's books."

In *Pure Sunshine,* readers are introduced to a shy teen-aged drug user named Brendon, as he realizes that his habit is beginning to take over his life. During the two days covered in James's novel, Brendon drifts through a day of school, the time in between spent tripping on LSD, going clubbing with his burnout friends Will and Kevin, and wandering the streets of Philadelphia. Noting that James's "language is raw and gritty," *School Library Journal* contributor Debbie Stewart maintained that Brendon's character rings true, adding: "the conclusion may not be grounded in reality, but sustains the mood and plot." Dubbing the novel a literary "acid trip," a *Publishers Weekly* reviewer cited James for his "airy, hallucinogenic imagery and nonjudgmental portraits of teen behavior," but cautioned that *Pure Sunshine* contains "no clear anti-drug message."

In addition to his novel, James has authored the 'Supertwins' series, a four-book beginning-reader set illustrated by Chris L. Demarest, and has also collaborated with illustrator Bruce McNally on a picture book titled *The Shark Who Was Afraid of Everything.*

BIOGRAPHICAL AND CRITICAL SOURCES:

PERIODICALS

Publishers Weekly, December 10, 2001, review of *Pure Sunshine,* p. 71.
School Library Journal, July, 2002, Debbie Stewart, review of *Pure Sunshine,* p. 120.

*   *   *

JOHNSON, Chester L. 1951-

PERSONAL: Born March 30, 1951, in Jackson, TN; son of Fred Johnson (a minister) and Bebee Jones-Johnson (a registered nurse); married Shirley Mormen (divorced); children: Chester, Shanna A. *Education:* California State University, Hayward, B.A. (sociology); attended Los Angeles SouthWest College, 1976; Don Martin School of Radio and Television Arts and Sciences, A.A., 1971. *Politics:* Democrat. *Religion:* Baptist. *Hobbies and other interests:* Writing, photography.

ADDRESSES: Home—440 29th St., Richmond, CA 94804. *Office*—C. Johnson Enterprises Ltd.com, 440 29th St., Richmond, CA 94804. *Agent*—The Associates, 8961 Sunset Blvd., Suite B., Los Angeles, CA 90069. *E-mail*—CBebee510@aol.com.

CAREER: Entrepreneur, broadcaster, and writer. CEO and founder, C. Johnson Enterprises Ltd.com (business consultants), Richmond, CA, 1995—; Naval Aviation Depot, Alameda, CA, security supervisor, 1985-95; KCMO/KC95 FM Radio, Fairway, KS, master control operator, announcer, and writer, 1983-85; KACE FM Radio, Los Angeles, CA, announcer/operator, 1977-82; KCMJ Radio (CBS 1010), Palm Springs, CA, announcer/operator and music director, 1974-77. *Military service:* U.S. Marine Corps.

AWARDS, HONORS: Gold records from Stax Records/KPOP/KPIP FM Radio, and Polydor Records/KPOP/KPIP FM Radio, both 1973, both for music direction.

WRITINGS:

Wisdom (poetry), self-published, 1998.
(And editor) *White Man Brown, a Failure of the American Dream* (noir fiction), Xlibris Corp., 2001.

Also author of television script for *Banachek* series, produced 1973.

WORK IN PROGRESS: White Man Brown, the Hip-Hop Godfather; research on the analysis of organizational programs.

SIDELIGHTS: Chester L. Johnson told *CA:* "At a young age, I began picking up the books with lurid covers that I found scattered around my brother's bedroom. Science fiction, mystery and detective novels—I soon devoured them all, but even as a youngster, I wondered: Why aren't any of these characters black like me? Years later, I discovered there were a handful of African-American noir writers from the '40s and '50s known as the 'old school' of black detective fiction. I read some Chester Himes and picked up *In the Heat of the Night,* whose character Virgil Tibbs is black, even though the author wasn't. But other than that, there weren't any, and I didn't understand why. I thought the field could use some people of color. So I decided to one day write my own. What I'm doing has a historical root that goes all the way back to the Harlem Renaissance writers of the 1930s—more known for poetry and lofty prose than hard-boiled fiction—represented by Rudolph Fisher, who penned the 1932 classic *The Conjure-Man Dies,* the first detective novel, to my knowledge, to feature a black protagonist.

"There's no clear rule on how to write. Sometimes it comes easily and perfectly. Sometimes it's like drilling rock and then blasting it out. Once you get the idea of writing, you realize the object is to convey everything, every sensation, feeling, sight, place, and emotion to the reader. My experience as an announcer in radio helped me a great deal in this area. We're all fascinated with evil and wrongdoing and seeing people brought to justice, but for African Americans that sense of seeing wrongs righted is very powerful because, historically, we haven't always seen that happen in our lives. Where else can I tell all these tales of political corruption and racial animus but in the mystery novel?

"When I start a book, whether it's poetry and lofty prose or a suspense novel such as *White Man Brown,* I attempt to create a mood, to write one true sentence and go from there. It's easy then, because there's always one true sentence that I know, or have seen, or have heard someone say. If I start writing elaborately, or like someone introducing or presenting something, I find that I need to stop the nonsense, toss it out, and start over again with the very first declarative sentence I've written. This seems to always work for me."

*   *   *

JONES, Jerry W. 1964-

PERSONAL: Born December 10, 1964, in Wilmington, CA; son of Jerry and Vay Jean Jones; married December 26, 1988; wife's name Marie L. (an administrative audit assistant); children: Evan Thomas. *Education:* Ambassador University, B.A., 1988; Texas A & M University, M.S., 1992; University of North Texas, Ph.D., 1995. *Hobbies and other interests:* Outdoor sports.

ADDRESSES: Office—Tarleton University Center, 1901 South Clear Creek Rd., Killeen, TX 76549. *E-mail*—jjones@tarleton.edu.

CAREER: University of Central Texas, Killeen, assistant professor of history, 1996-99; Tarleton State University, Killeen, assistant professor of history, 1999—.

MEMBER: Society for Military History, United States Naval Institute.

WRITINGS:

U.S. Battleship Operations in World War I, Naval Institute Press (Annapolis, MD), 1998.

WORK IN PROGRESS: Research on the Fourth Infantry Division in Vietnam.

SIDELIGHTS: Jerry W. Jones told *CA:* "Although teaching is my primary emphasis as a university professor, I intend to contribute further to the scholarship of my profession. My hope is to produce a work that is both scholarly and accessible to general readers."

*   *   *

KARETZKY, Stephen 1946-

PERSONAL: Born August 29, 1946, in Brooklyn, NY; son of Harry (a commissioner for labor relations) and Lillian (a homemaker; maiden name, Abrams) Karetzky; married Deborah Ann Shaw, April, 1970 (divorced, July, 1972); married Joanne Ballestrasse (a librarian and author), March 17, 1985. *Ethnicity:* "Jewish." *Education:* Queens College of the City University of New York, B.A., 1967; Columbia University, M.L.S., 1969, D.L.S., 1978; California State University—Dominguez Hills, M.A., 1991. *Politics:* "Conservative/populist." *Religion:* Jewish. *Hobbies and other interests:* Collecting books.

ADDRESSES: Office—Felician College Library, 262 South Main St., Lodi, NJ 07644. *E-mail*—karetzkys@ felician.edu.

CAREER: Brooklyn Public Library, Brooklyn, NY, librarian, 1969-70; State University of New York—Buffalo, assistant professor of library and information studies, 1974-76; State University of New York—College at Geneseo, assistant professor of library and information studies, 1977-78; Haifa University, Haifa, Israel, associate professor of library and information studies, 1978-81; Shapolsky/Steimatzky Publishers, New York, NY, senior editor, 1981-82; San Jose State University, San Jose, CA, associate professor of library and information studies, 1982-85; Shapolsky Publishers, New York, NY, senior editor, 1985-86; Felician College, Lodi, NJ, associate professor of library and information studies and director of library, 1986—. Americans for a Safe Israel, executive director, 1985-86.

MEMBER: Authors Guild, American Historical Association, Organization of American Historians, Historians of American Communism, American

Society for Information Science and Technology, Association for Library and Information Science Education, National Association of Scholars.

WRITINGS:

Reading Research and Librarianship: A History and Analysis, Greenwood Press (Westport, CT), 1982.
The Cannons of Journalism, O'Keefe Press, 1984.
(Editor and contributor) *The Media's War against Israel,* Shapolsky/Steimatzky Publishers (New York, NY), 1985.
(Editor and contributor) *The Media's Coverage of the Arab-Israeli Conflict,* Shapolsky Publishers (New York, NY), 1989.
Not Seeing Red: American Librarianship and the Soviet Union, 1917-1960, University Press of America (Blue Ridge Summit, PA), 2002.

Contributor of articles and reviews to periodicals, including *Catholic Library World, Midstream, New Jersey Libraries,* and *College and Research Libraries News.*

SIDELIGHTS: Stephen Karetzky told *CA:* "My books have been on a wide variety of subjects, but they are united by a common concern: how can democratic countries maintain their free societies by successfully countering aggressive totalitarian nations and by opposing domestic utopian zealots bent on transmogrifying them? I have been particularly interested in assessing the extent to which professionals—like librarians, journalists, and educators—have helped or hindered the cause of freedom. My findings on the roles played by these professions have not been favorable.

"My first work, *Reading Research and Librarianship: A History and Analysis,* describes the attempt by earnest scholars to transform librarianship into a social science during the turbulent 1930s. I was interested in seeing how a body of social-science knowledge is developed, used, and misused. I was very pleased that the book was accorded an honorable mention by the American Society for Information Science in its Best Book of the Year competition, the sole time ever done in the history of this award.

"Living in Israel for three years led directly to my next book, *The Cannons of Journalism.* While there, it became clear to me that Western journalists were do-

ing a poor job of covering events in the region, an unconscionable failure that became more egregious after my return to the United States. It seemed to me that the American people could not make wise decisions concerning their government's foreign policies even if they were getting their information from those newspapers widely touted as the best. The ignorance, sloth, and bias in the journalism profession appalled me, so I decided to document this using the *New York Times* as my example. I also constructed a typology of poor reporting that could be used by others in their research. I was particularly pleased that the Israeli Foreign Office purchased two dozen copies of this slim paperback and made it required reading for many of its officials and staff members.

"This work was followed by a larger book on the same theme. *The Media's War against Israel* includes an introduction by Jack Kemp, essays by Norman Podhoretz, Edward Alexander, and others, as well as the text of *The Cannons of Journalism.* Three years later, there was yet again a need to describe the misreporting in that region, so *The Media's Coverage of the Arab-Israeli Conflict* appeared. The most comprehensive of the three works, it includes not only my original *Cannons* essay, but contributions from Irving Kristol, Ruth R. Wisse, and Jeane Kirkpatrick.

"My most recent book, *Not Seeing Red: American Librarianship and the Soviet Union, 1917-1960,* describes how American librarians and educators—as well as those in Great Britain—responded to the USSR from its inception through its fall. Also treated in this book is a critique of how today's historians view the subject area. It reveals that the leaders of a profession ostensibly devoted to democratic principles failed to criticize the USSR and communism while energetically opposing those who did. While it bears positive blurbs from prominent political scientists and historians, it has—as I predicted in the book—drawn some wild criticism from within the library profession."

BIOGRAPHICAL AND CRITICAL SOURCES:

PERIODICALS

Australian Library Journal, August, 2002, Russell Cope, review of *Not Seeing Red: American Librarianship and the Soviet Union, 1917-1960,* p. 239.

KATO, Shidzue 1897-2001

PERSONAL: Born March 2, 1897, in Japan; died of respiratory failure, December, 22, 2001, in Tokyo, Japan; married Keikichi Ishimoto (a baron and mining engineer; divorced); married Kato Kanju (a trade union leader), 1944 (died, 1978); children: (first marriage) two sons, (second marriage) one daughter. *Education:* Graduate of the Peeresses School. *Politics:* Socialist.

CAREER: Feminist and activist. Founder of Women's Research Institute and Birth Control Consultation Centre, Tokyo, Japan, 1932; elected to Japanese diet, 1946, and House of Councillors (senate), 1950-74. Cofounder and president of Family Planning Federation of Japan, 1954; Japanese Organization for International Cooperation in Family Planning, president.

AWARDS, HONORS: United Nations Population Award, 1988; Avon Grand Award, 1990; Shidzue Kato Award created in her honor by the Japanese Organization for International Cooperation in Family Planning, 1996, to recognize achievements by women in the fields of population and reproductive health.

WRITINGS:

East Way, West Way: A Modern Japanese Girlhood (autobiography), illustrated by Fuji Nakamizo, Farrar and Rinehard (New York, NY), 1936, published as *Facing Two Ways: The Story of My Life,* Stanford University Press (Stanford, CA), 1984.
The Face of Women in Japanese History, 1953.
Straight Road (autobiography), 1956.
A Fight for Women's Happiness: Pioneering the Family Planning Movement in Japan, Japanese Organization for International Cooperation in Family Planning (Tokyo, Japan), 1984.
Kato Shidzue Hyakusai (autobiography; title means "Kato Shidzue at Age 100"), Fujin Gahosha, c. 1997.

SIDELIGHTS: Kato Shidzue was a Japanese feminist who pioneered for women's rights for more than seventy years. She was persecuted and imprisoned, but she prevailed in her fight for reproductive rights and was recognized for her achievements by the United Nations and Japanese groups.

Kato was born Hirota Shidzue into a privileged samurai family. Her father was a mining engineer, and her mother, who had been educated at a missionary school, brought Western ideas into their home during the period in which Japan was changing from a feudal to a more contemporary society. Although women were afforded equality under the law, in reality, their lives had not changed significantly.

After graduating from an exclusive school, Kato married Baron Keikichi Ishimoto, like her father, a mining engineer. She was appalled on viewing the small mining town to which they relocated—the poverty and the unhealthy conditions under which people were living. She and her husband worked for social reform and to improve the lives of the laborers who spent twelve hours a day in the mines, and particularly the women, who then went home to care for their large families.

In 1919 Kato came to the United States and enrolled in secretarial school in order to acquire the skills that would make her independent. While here, she met Margaret Sanger, founder of this country's family planning movement. This first meeting inspired Kato to bring birth control to Japan, but on her return, she caused a great stir for being a woman of the samurai class involved in social causes. Birth control was an unpopular idea, as the country wanted higher birth rates to produce the boys and men needed for war.

Kato also owned a woolen shop and sold clothes and held knitting classes. This, too, was unheard of—a woman of her class being involved in the mercantile trade. But her movement within communities gave her the opportunity to promote the idea of birth control to Japanese women. In 1922 Kato hosted Sanger's visit to her country, made possible by the press coverage that overrode government policy. The Japan Birth Control Study Group resulted, which published a Japanese-language version of *Family Limitation,* Sanger's controversial pamphlet on contraception.

The earthquake of 1923 destroyed Kato's shop, but the movement was growing rapidly, and she established the Women's Research Institute, which studied women's issues. She was, as yet, unable to offer methods of contraception, and so she spent time in the United States and studied under Sanger. In 1932 she founded the Birth Control Consultation Centre, which was staffed with doctors and nurses, and which stocked with contraceptive creams and jellies, the manufacture and distribution of which she personally arranged.

Now an international figure dubbed the "Margaret Sanger of Japan," Kato was asked by American publishers to write her first autobiography, which was published in 1935. It became a bestseller, and following World War II, it was used by the American occupation forces as a textbook on Japanese culture. The right-wing Japanese government arrested Kato in 1937 for her promotion of "dangerous thoughts," and she spent two weeks in prison. The records of the Birth Control Consultation Centre were confiscated and the clinic shut down, temporarily ending the birth control movement in Japan until after World War II.

Over the next years, Kato divorced her husband and lost a son. She remarried, and in an effort to take an active leadership role, she ran for and was elected to the lower house of the Japanese Diet, or Parliament, in 1946, the year after women were given the right to vote and the right to hold political office. Her husband, Kanju Kato was also elected, although they represented different wings of the Socialist Party. In 1947, at the age of forty-eight, Kato gave birth to her third child, and first daughter. Kato was elected to the upper house, or senate, in 1950, where she served until her retirement in 1974.

In 1950 Japan legalized the manufacture and sale of contraceptive drugs, and family planning was encouraged by the Ministry of Health and Welfare. Sanger visited Japan in 1952. In 1954, Kato cofounded the Family Planning Federation of Japan, which became affiliated with the International Planned Parenthood Federation. Tokyo hosted the International Conference on Planned Parenthood in 1955, which supported the movement in Japan and the idea of smaller families.

Kato's leadership was not limited to family planning. "By the mid 1950s," noted the writer of Kato's obituary in the London *Times,* "Japan had still not resumed normal relations with countries it had occupied during the war. At a conference in the Philippines in 1957, Kato and Niro Hoshijima, chairman of the Japan-Korea Society, won the confidence of Korean delegates by apologizing for Japan's harsh treatment of their country during more than thirty years' occupation. On their return to Tokyo, they persuaded Nobusuke Kishi, the prime minister, to revoke Japanese claims on Korea, paving the way for fresh negotiations towards a peace treaty between the two countries." As a member of the Senate Foreign Affairs Committee, Kato offered opposition support to Kishi if he would

apologize on behalf of the Japanese people as he traveled to other countries promoting trade. Kato herself apologized to England and The Netherlands when she visited London in 1971.

After her husband's death in 1978, Kato left the Socialist Party so that she could speak more independently, and she was active in public life until she was 100 years old. She published *Kato Shidzue Hyakusai,* another autobiography, in her centennial year. A writer for *Asahi Shimbun* noted that Kato was born in the Meiji Era and was a young woman and wife during the Taisho Era, during which signs of democracy were evident. Her most active period was during the turbulent Showa Era, and her later and more settled life was during the present Heisei Era. The writer said that "she strikes me as someone who fed on the best part of each of these eras she passed through, even in the worst times." The writer noted that in this last book Kato writes about losing her second son to tuberculosis when he was a young man. Kato said that after recovering from his death, her own advice to herself was, "In a sad moment, let yourself be saddened deeply. In a joyous moment, let yourself explode in celebration."

Kato died in 2001 at the age of 104. Her life was itself a celebration of the power to make change. In an obituary at the Web site of the International Planned Parenthood Federation, the writer noted that her efforts "have continued to bear fruits for Japanese society, bringing down the number of abortions, infant mortality, and maternal death rates, while increasing contraceptive usage to 80 percent. Japan's family planning model has been so successful that it attracts attention from other countries as a working model."

In a message of condolence, Alexander Sanger said, "Madame Kato has now joined her good friend and my grandmother, Margaret Sanger, in eternity; together . . . they worked for the betterment of the status of women in Japan, America, and around the world."

BIOGRAPHICAL AND CRITICAL SOURCES:

BOOKS

Kato Shidzue, *East Way, West Way: A Modern Japanese Girlhood,* illustrated by Fuji Nakamizo, Farrar and Rinehard (New York, NY), 1936, published as *Facing Two Ways: The Story of My Life,* Stanford University Press (Stanford, CA), 1984.

Kato Shidzue, *Straight Road,* 1956.
Kato Shidzue, *Kato Shidzue Hyakusai,* Fujin Gaho-sha (Tokyo, Japan), c. 1997.

PERIODICALS

WIN News, summer, 1997, "Japan: Pioneer Feminist Lawmaker Still a Leader at 100," p. 58.

OBITUARIES:

PERIODICALS

Asahi Shimbun, December, 24, 2001, "Kato Worked for Women," and "Centenarian May Have Meiji Women to Thank."
Times (London, England), January 1, 2002, p. 15.

ONLINE

International Planned Parenthood Federation, http://www.ippf.org/ (July 11, 2002).*

*   *   *

KATZENBACH, Jon R. 1932-

PERSONAL: Born August 26, 1932, in Billings, MT; son of R. H. (a banker) and Della (a homemaker; maiden name, Bischoff) Katzenbach; married Linda Gilbert, November 28, 1970; children: Douglas, Ray, Samuel, Daniel, Michael. *Education:* Stanford University, B.A., 1954; Harvard University, M.B.A., 1959. *Hobbies and other interests:* Golf, boating.

ADDRESSES: Office—Katzenbach Partners LLC, 381 Park Ave., New York, NY 10016. *Agent*—Rafael Sagalyn, The Sagalyn Agency, 4825 Bethesda Ave., Suite 302, Bethesda, MD 20814.

CAREER: McKinsey & Company, New York, NY, director, 1959-98; Katzenbach Partners LLC, New York, NY, senior partner, 1998—. *Military service:* U.S. Navy, 1954-57.

WRITINGS:

(With Douglas Smith) *The Wisdom of Teams: Creating the High-Performance Organization,* Harvard Business School Press (Cambridge, MA), 1993.
Teams at the Top: Unleashing the Potential of Both Teams and Individual Leaders, Harvard Business School Press (Cambridge, MA), 1996.
(With others) *Real Change Leaders: How You Can Create Growth and High Performance at Your Company,* Random House (New York, NY), 1997.
(Editor) *The Work of Teams,* Harvard Business School Press (Cambridge, MA), 1998.
Peak Performance: Aligning the Hearts and Minds of Your Employees, Harvard Business School Press (Cambridge, MA), 2000.
(With Douglas Smith) *The Discipline of Teams: A Mindbook-Workbook for Delivering Small Group Performance,* John Wiley & Sons (New York, NY), 2001.
Why Pride Matters More: The Power of the World's Greatest Motivational Force, Crown Publishers (New York, NY), 2003.

SIDELIGHTS: Jon R. Katzenbach is a business writer who has drawn on his own experiences as an executive to produce a series of books on team-building and effective management within organizations. He is the author, coauthor, or editor of seven books.

In *The Wisdom of Teams* Katzenbach and coauthor Douglas Smith define a team as "a small number of people with complementary skills who are committed to a common purpose, set of performance goals, and approach for which they hold themselves accountable." Karen L. Spencer noted in a review of that book for *Academy of Management Executive* that "despite the culture of individualism in most organizations, the stories the authors relate clearly support the assertion that teams outperform individuals acting alone or in larger organizational groupings, especially when their performance requires multiple skills, judgments, and experiences." She summarized her review by calling *The Wisdom of Teams* a "superb book" and a "required addition to the library of anyone who wishes to support the development of teams in his or her organization." The authors, according to Montgomery van Wart in *Public Administration Review,* "argue that team learning is the most important kind, and that 'the same team dynamics that promote performance also support learning and behavioral change.'" The authors analyze "what makes some teams productive and others not," noted von Wart, and stress that top executives need to "consider whether they are willing to undergo the requisite discipline to become a real or high-performing team."

Sue Gibson observed in *Industry Week* that Smith and Katzenbach in *The Wisdom of Teams* "provide . . . specific recommendations for establishing teams, overcoming obstacles, leading with wisdom, and responding to the inevitable changes engendered by successful teams." In the *Columbia Journal of World Business,* William M. Moore wrote that *The Wisdom of Teams* is "well written, undoubtedly timely, and maintains it focus, choosing to concentrate on teams within American organizations and their impact upon performance."

John Turner in *Personnel Psychology* commented that "peak performance" is defined in Katzenbach's book of the same name as "achieving performance that is '. . . better than the norm, better than expected, better than competition, better than similar workforces, uniquely and constantly.'" In writing *Peak Performance,* Katzenbach studied organizations such as Home Depot, Avon, First USA, the U.S. Marine Corps, and National Aeronautics and Space Administration. "Katzenbach's conclusion is that these organizations are able to sustain high performance levels because they achieve the emotional commitment of their workforces," observed Turner. The book is largely dedicated to describing the actions these organizations take to achieve such commitment. Katzenbach breaks down these actions into five approaches: mission, values and pride path; process and metrics path; entrepreneurial spirit path; individual achievement path; and recognition and celebration path. John Hodge in *HRMagazine* called *Peak Performance* "an excellent overview of strategies organizations may follow to enhance employee motivation and productivity." Both Turner and Hodge identified the greatest strength of *Peak Performance* to be its emphasis on discipline.

Discipline is a concept Katzenbach stresses in most of his books. Mary Whaley observed in a review of *Teams at the Top* for *Booklist,* "The author advises discipline to energize rather than stifle initiative and performance among top executives." *The Discipline of Teams,* remarked a reviewer in the *Houston Business Journal,* "provides . . . guidance that will help any team in any organization set and achieve performance goals."

In order to initiate change within an organization, Katzenbach believes "change leaders" must be employed. Katzenbach explained in an interview with Stratford Sherman for *Forbes* that change leaders are middle managers who tend to be more diverse in gender and race than ordinary middle managers, as well as "in the 25 to 40 age range," "more flexible than ordinary general managers, and much more people oriented. You need them when you are going for dramatic performance increases in speed, productivity, or profits."

Polly LaBarre praised Katzenbach's *Real Change Leaders* in *Industry Week* as a "compelling study of an emerging breed of movers and shakers." LaBarre noted that "real experiences, insights, and dilemmas of managers" are utilized through case histories of such companies as Mobil, Compaq Computer, the New York City Transit Authority, and AT&T. A *Publishers Weekly* reviewer concluded, "This book is highly recommended to all corporate executives who want to learn about effective leadership in large organizations."

BIOGRAPHICAL AND CRITICAL SOURCES:

PERIODICALS

Academy of Management Executive, August, 1993, Karen L. Spencer, review of *The Wisdom of Teams,* p. 100.

Booklist, January 1, 1996, Barbara Jacobs, review of *Real Change Leaders,* p. 765; January 1, 1998, Mary Whaley, review of *Teams at the Top,* p. 755.

Chemistry and Industry, July 19, 1999, Mike Woods, review of *Teams at the Top,* p. 556.

Columbia Journal of World Business, fall, 1993, William M. Moore, review of *The Wisdom of Teams,* p. 104.

Electronic Business, January, 1999, Susan Mulcahy, "On the March to Interdependence," p. 81.

Financial Times, April 12, 1996, Peter Herriot, review of *Real Change Leaders,* p. 10.

Fortune, December 11, 1995, Stratford Sherman, "Wanted: Company Change Agents," p. 197.

Houston Business Journal, June 1, 2001, review of *The Discipline of Teams,* p. 21.

HRMagazine, August, 2000, John Hodge, review of *Peak Performance,* p. 163.

Industry Week, January 22, 1996, Polly LaBarre, review of *Real Change Leaders,* p. 17; March 15, 1993, Sue Gibson, review of *The Wisdom of Teams,* p. 21.

Personnel Psychology, spring, 2001, John Turner, review of *Peak Performance,* p. 206.

Public Administration Review, November-December, 1994, Montgomery von Wart, review of *The Wisdom of Teams,* pp. 577-579.

Publishers Weekly, December 4, 1995, review of *Real Change Leaders,* p. 49.

Tampa Tribune (Tampa, FL), March 15, 1999, "When Building a Team, Take It from the Top," p. 12.

*   *   *

KAUFMAN, Moises

PERSONAL: Born in Venezuela.

ADDRESSES: Office—Tectonic Theater Project, 204 West 84th Street, New York, NY 10024. *E-mail*—info@thelecturebureau.com.

CAREER: Tectonic Theater Project, New York, NY, founder, artistic director; 42nd Street Collective, directing teacher. Director of plays, including *Women in Beckett, In the Winter of Cities, The Nest,* and *Marlowe's Eyes.*

MEMBER: Thespis.

AWARDS, HONORS: Lucille Lortel Award for Best Play, Outer Critics Circle Award for Best Off-Broadway Play, Garland Award for Best Play, Carbonell Award for Best Play, Circle Award for Direction, Bay Area Theater Critics, GLAAD Media Award for New York Theater, and Joe A. Callaway Award for Direction, Society of Stage Directors and Choreographers, all for *Gross Indecency;* Artist of the Year, Casa del Artista, 1999; Guggenheim fellowship in playwriting, 2002.

WRITINGS:

Gross Indecency: The Three Trials of Oscar Wilde, Vintage Books (New York, NY), 1998.

The Laramie Project, Vintage Books (New York, NY), 2001.

ADAPTATIONS: The Laramie Project was adapted for film for HBO.

SIDELIGHTS: Moises Kaufman is a playwright, director, and founder of the Tectonic Theater Project. In his first published book, *Gross Indecency: The Three Trials of Oscar Wilde,* Kaufman tells the story of well-known British playwright Oscar Wilde's trials, resulting from his homosexuality. In 1895 Wilde was arrested, went through three trials, and was imprisoned for two years for what was called the gross indecency of sodomy. When he was released from prison he was shunned by many in his community and died shortly after. *Time* contributor Richard Zoglin called the book "A surprise success." *Gross Indecency* "rivals the best work of the season," observed Greg Evans in a *Variety* review.

The Laramie Project, a play by Kaufman that was later adapted as an Home Box Office (HBO) film, is set in Laramie, Wyoming. It is an reenactment of interviews Kaufman and the members of Tectonic Theater Project conducted with the people of Laramie a month after twenty-one-year-old gay student Matthew Shepard was murdered in 1998 by two local men. *Hollywood Reporter* contributor Kirk Honeycutt concluded, "*The Laramie Project* achieves an intimacy that is heartfelt and deeply unsettling." *Backstage.com* contributor Victor Gluck called *The Laramie Project* "the most ambitious and powerful new American play of the past year."

BIOGRAPHICAL AND CRITICAL SOURCES:

PERIODICALS

Advocate, March 3, 1998, Luis Alfaro, "Oscar in America," p. 62; August 14, 2001, "Moises Kaufman," p. 81.

American Theatre, November, 1997, Jesse McKinley, "As Far as He Could Go," p. 24.

Back Stage, September 30, 1994, Dan Isaac, review of *The Nest,* p. 44; March 3, 2000, Sandra C. Dillard, "Denver," p. 44; June 2, 2000, Victor Gluck, review of *The Laramie Project,* p. 56; February 2, 2001, Sandra C. Dillard, "Denver," p. 49.

Back Stage West, June 14, 2001, Jean Schiffman, "Audience Rating," p. 6; August 16, 2001, Charlene Baldridge, review of *The Laramie Project,* p. 16.

Booklist, September 1, 2001, Jack Helbig, review of *The Laramie Project,* p. 43.

Daily Variety, January 14, 2002, Dennis Harvey, review of *The Laramie Project,* p. 13; March 11, 2002, Bill Higgins, Lily Oei, "High Drama from HBO," p. 35.

Gay & Lesbian Review Worldwide, fall, 2000, Allen Ellenzweig, "Current Event Theater," p. 64.

Hollywood Reporter, January 14, 2002, Kirk Honeycutt, review of *The Laramie Project,* p. 20; March 14, 2002, "Moises Kaufman Has Signed with ICMW," p. 24.

Lambda Book Report, January, 2002, Krandall Kraus, "Reality TV Comes to the Stage," p. 23.

Library Journal, September 1, 2001, Howard Miller, review of *The Laramie Project,* p. 179.

Nation, July 28, 1997, Laurie Stone, review of *Gross Indecency: The Three Trials of Oscar Wilde,* p. 34.

New Leader, June 2, 1997, Stefan Kanfer, review of *Gross Indecency,* p. 22.

New Republic, July 7, 1997, Robert Brustein, review of *Gross Indecency,* p. 28; June 19, 2000, Robert Brustein, "On Theater—The Staged Documentary," p. 29.

New York Times, November 22, 1991, Mel Gussow, "Listen to the Women of Beckett," p. C17.

School Library Journal, November, 2001, Emily Lloyd, review of *The Laramie Project,* p. 194.

Time, June 16, 1997, Richard Zoglin, review of *Gross Indecency,* p. 75.

Variety, June 9, 1997, Greg Evans, review of *Gross Indecency,* p. 88; May 22, 2000, Charles Isherwood, review of *The Laramie Project,* p. 37; January 14, 2002, Dennis Harvey, review of *The Laramie Project,* p. 49.

ONLINE

HBO Web site, http://www.hbo.com/ (June 4, 2002), "Moises Kaufman Writer/Director"; review of *The Laramie Project.*

Tectonic Theater Project, Inc., http://www.tectonictheaterproject.org/ (June 4, 2002).

Time Web site, http://www.time.com/ (June 4, 2002), "Q & A: Moises Kaufman."*

*   *   *

KELLY, Clint 1950-

PERSONAL: Born March 12, 1950, in Portland, OR; son of Clinton Russell and Rita Belle (Willhite) Kelly; married Cheryll Doreen Inman (a tax accountant), September 11, 1971; children: Stephanie, Shane, Amy Holowaty, Nathan. *Education:* Clatsop Community College, A.S. (forest technology), 1969. *Politics:* Republican. *Religion:* Protestant. *Hobbies and other interests:* Humor, cryptozoology (the study of mystery animals), public speaking.

ADDRESSES: Home—504 51st St. SW, Everett, WA 98203. *Office*—Seattle Pacific University, 3307 Third Ave. W, Seattle, WA 98119. *Agent*—Steve Laube, Literary Group, 270 Lafayette St., Ste. 1505, New York, NY 10012. *E-mail*—ckelly@spu.edu.

CAREER: Seattle Pacific University, Seattle, WA, communications specialist, 1988—. Writing instructor for Discover U and for writer's conferences; codirector of Seattle Pacific University Christian Writers Weekend; Presbyterian elder and teacher.

MEMBER: Writers Information Network, International Society of Cryptozoology, Fellowship of Merry Christians, American Christian Writers.

AWARDS, HONORS: Faculty Member of the Year, Florida Christian Writers Conference, 2000; Christy Award finalist (international historical category), 2000.

WRITINGS:

FICTION

The Landing Place ("Reg Danson Adventure" series), Thomas Nelson (Nashville, TN), 1993.

The Lost Kingdom ("Reg Danson Adventure" series), Thomas Nelson (Nashville, TN), 1994.

The Aryan ("Reg Danson Adventure" series), Thomas Nelson (Nashville, TN), 1995.

Deliver Us from Evil ("In the Shadow of the Mountain" series), Bethany House (Minneapolis, MN), 1998.

The Power and the Glory ("In the Shadow of the Mountain" series), Bethany House (Minneapolis, MN), 1999.

Escape Underground (juvenile novel), Bethany House (Minneapolis, MN), 2001.

Also author of the picture book *Bruce the Spruce and the Christmas Goose.*

NONFICTION

The Fame Game: How You, Too, Can Become the Greatest, Performance Press (Everett, WA), 1984.

(With Cliff Bottemiller) *The Everett Cartoon and Trivia Book,* Performance Press (Everett, WA), 1985.

(With John H. Hampsch) *The Key to Inner Peace,* Performance Press (Everett, WA), 1985.

Me Parent, You Kid! Taming the Family Zoo, Honor Books (Tulsa, OK), 1993.

How to Win Grins and Influence Little People, Honor Books (Tulsa, OK), 1996.

Dare to Raise Exceptional Children: Give Your Kids a Sense of Purpose, a Sense of Adventure, and a Sense of Humor, Albury Press (Tulsa, OK), 2001.

Contributor to anthologies, including *The Walker Within,* Lyons Press (New York, NY), 2000. Contributor to periodicals, including *American History Illustrated, Catholic Digest, Child Life, Christianity Today, Family Circle, HomeLife, Mothering, New Man, Reader's Digest, Writer,* and *Writer's Digest.*

WORK IN PROGRESS: Ongoing research in cryptozoology, most particularly Bigfoot, in hopes of writing a fictional account.

SIDELIGHTS: Clint Kelly is an author whose fiction and nonfiction are inspired by his religious faith. Among his novels for young adult readers is *The Lost Kingdom,* the story of adventurer Reg Danson and his son as they go in search of a mysterious creature roaming the African rainforest. Kelly told *CA:* "The idea of 'ordinary heroes' has long fascinated me. I consider parents to be ordinary heroes and so I have written books for parents. These are parent-to-parent breakfast conversations in which we look together at the pain and the triumph of raising a family. There is an exchange of ideas and we leave feeling better and less alone in our impossible task. The task is still there, but the urge to panic has passed.

"In fiction, too, I have sought out the flawed and the heroic in characters who bleed and grow weary and despair of making the world better than they found it. And always the adventure element, that life itself even when difficult is a wonderful gift of adventure from an adventurous God. And always hope. My books all end on a note of hope to say we have not been left to our own devices, but are fearfully and wonderfully made for a higher purpose. To explore that in my books is the greatest privilege.

"I have written of the Armenian people, people of the Book, descendants of Noah the Patriarch, who during World War I were hounded by the Turks and made the scapegoats for government shortcomings. Nearly 1.5 million Armenians were slaughtered in the first genocide of the twentieth century. They are heroes for what they endured and for how they have persisted. Though they came close to annihilation, they live on. I have tried in my stories to give them the voice they were once denied.

"I've written of persecuted Christian children of the first century, of the very real possibility of dragons having once roamed the Earth, and of the continuing dangers of neo-Nazism. I am fascinated by unsolved mysteries and often send my characters in quest of answers. The search for Noah's Ark was the subject of my first novel; Bigfoot is likely to walk tall in a novel to come.

"Nothing, of course, is more mysterious than the human condition and to explore that will consume authors, myself included, for as long as we are given to write.

"In a recent national survey, [television talk show host] Oprah Winfrey was named the most influential woman in America. With all due respect, I must disagree. My mother, a winsome storyteller, was among the most influential women I know. Rita Kelly showed me the great pleasure in producing movies of the mind, heart, and soul. Her original 'Beetle Boy' and 'Buzz Buzz' stories were like honey to a bee. I am so glad she saw me published before she went home to the Great Storyteller.

"Another influential woman is my wife, Cheryll. She does my taxes and helps me resolve plot problems whenever I paint myself into a corner. She accepts me and appreciates me no matter how many editors may reject me. She is my sweet oasis.

"My first adult piece was published in *Mothering* magazine in the summer of 1979. It taught me that nay-sayers are a dime a dozen. Because I would not limit myself by conventional advice, I have been published in women's publications, children's periodicals, and major national magazines, and have written on topics I once knew little about, including rats, blood, and space exploration. I even sold installments of a comic strip I invented, despite the fact that I cannot draw! Lesson learned: Never take too narrow a view of what you can do. Be fresh, creative, and open to the possibilities and stand amazed at where the chips fall.

"Following this advice has led me to teaching opportunities and I have enjoyed conducting writing workshops coast to coast. Today I codirect the Seattle Pacific University Christian Writers Renewal and enjoy the give-and-take that makes any good writer's conference. My first children's picture book, *Bruce the Spruce and the Christmas Goose,* is a work commissioned by a local Christian conference and retreat center for sale in their holiday gift shops. It is a good life and one made so much the richer by the wonder of stories and the making of books."

Kelly offered *CA* his advice to aspiring writers: "First, remember that the editor is your partner, not your enemy. Second, never burn your bridges with an editor as the publishing world is a tight community and you will meet again. Third, think of writing as a giant smorgasbord of opportunity and do not too narrowly define the type of writing you can do. Fourth, challenge yourself each year to pick a new market or genre and give it a try. We receive not because we ask not. Fifth, write for magazines as well as pursue books; each feeds off the other. Sixth, say thank you and say it often. Gratitude begets gratitude, thank you, God."

BIOGRAPHICAL AND CRITICAL SOURCES:

PERIODICALS

Inspirational Resources, October-November, 2001, review of *Escape Underground,* p. 9.
Voice of Youth Advocates, August, 1994, Libby Bergstrom, review of *The Lost Kingdom,* p. 147.

*   *   *

KELLY, Fiona
    See OLDFIELD, Jenny

KIDD, Chip 1964-

PERSONAL: Born 1964, in Shillington, PA; partner of J. D. McClatchy (a poet and editor of the *Yale Review*). *Education:* Graduate of Pennsylvania State University, 1986.

ADDRESSES: Office—Design Dept., Alfred E. Knopf, 201 East 50th St., New York, NY 10022.

CAREER: Graphic designer and writer. Alfred E. Knopf, New York, NY, book designer, 1986—; *Paris Review,* consultant, 1995—; Pantheon, New York, NY, associate editor of comics division. Taught at the School of Visual Arts, New York, NY.

MEMBER: Alliance Graphique Internationalle.

AWARDS, HONORS: Two Best-of-Category Packaging Awards, named one of the top forty designers in the United States, and Design Distinction Award, all from *ID,* for *Batman Collected;* award for use of photography in graphic design, International Center of Photography, 1997; two Eisner Awards, 1998, for *Batman Animated.*

WRITINGS:

Batman Collected, photographs by Geoff Spear, Bulfinch Press (Boston, MA), 1996, expanded edition, Watson-Guptill Publications (New York, NY), 2001.
(With Paul Dini) *Batman Animated,* HarperEntertainment (New York, NY), 1998.
(With Les Daniels) *Superman, the Complete History,* Chronicle Books (San Francisco, CA), 1998.
(With Les Daniels) *Batman: The Complete History,* Chronicle Books (San Francisco, CA), 1999.
(With Les Daniels) *Wonder Woman: The Life and Times of the Amazon Princess,* Chronicle Books (San Francisco, CA), 2000.
(With Les Daniels) *Wonder Woman: The Golden Age,* Chronicle Books (San Francisco, CA), 2001.
(Author of commentary) Charles M. Schulz, *Peanuts: The Art of Charles M. Schulz* Pantheon Books (New York, NY), 2001.

(With Art Spiegelman) *Jack Cole and Plastic Man: Forms Stretched to Their Limits,* Chronicle Books (San Francisco, CA), 2001.

The Cheese Monkeys: A Novel in Two Semesters, Scribner (New York, NY), 2001.

Work featured in *Vanity Fair, New Republic, Time, New York Times, Graphis, New York,* and *ID;* contributor of articles to periodicals, including *Vogue, New York Times, New York Observer, Entertainment Weekly, Details, Arena, 2WICE, New York Post, ID,* and *Print.*

WORK IN PROGRESS: Two novels, one a sequel to *The Cheese Monkeys.*

SIDELIGHTS: Chip Kidd has been creating designs to enhance the books of a long list of popular authors since he began working for Alfred E. Knopf after graduation from Pennsylvania State University in 1986. Kidd was born in the small town of Shillington, Pennsylvania, also the hometown of John Updike, where Updike's father taught Kidd's father math. Several years into his career, Kidd was designing an Updike novel.

The influence of the great masters of comic-book art is evidenced by Kidd's own books, beginning with *Batman Collected,* were called "a virtual love letter to the Dark Knight Detective" by Jonathan Wilson in the London *Observer. Entertainment Weekly'*s Steve Daly said Kidd documents the marketing and promotional aspects of the caped crusader with "a curator's zeal and a social historian's insight." Geoff Spear provides the nearly 500 photographs of the stunning array of memorabilia bearing the image of the crime fighter who first appeared in 1939, with young Bruce Wayne witnessing the vicious murder of his parents.

Included are photographs of wallpaper, bedding, lamps, toothpaste, towels, noodle soup, a bat-shaped tortilla chip, and more. "*Batman Collected* is easy to enjoy, an obvious labor of love by someone who has kept in close contact with his inner kid (pun not intended)," commented Michael Dooley in *Print.* "The author displays a genuine enchantment with, and enthusiasm for, his material."

In *Batman Collected,* Kidd mentions the 1950s congressional investigation led by Senator Estes Kefauver on the relationship between comics and juvenile delinquency, "but," wrote Dooley, "steers clear of psychiatrist Frederic Wertham, who gained notoriety at that time by claiming that the Batman books were 'psychologically homosexual.' Likewise, discussion of the current Batman films avoids any explicit reference to their overt fetishism. Considering Bulfinch Press and DC Comics are both subsidiaries of Time Warner, it's surprising to see even a few hints at the kinkier subtext of the Batman mythology."

In 1998 Kidd was tapped by agent Andrew Wylie to design the reissues and new books of crime writer Elmore Leonard in trade paperback and mass market formats for two publishers, Morrow and Dell. Jonathan Bing wrote in *Publishers Weekly* that "in a marketplace dominated by superstores, in which brand identity depends on sophisticated visual packaging across multiple titles, it's not surprising that Wylie would enlist Kidd to design both series. His often cheeky and urbane jacket art, more MTV than mass market, is more in line with Leonard's developing hipster image, recently enhanced by Quentin Tarantino's adaptation of Leonard's 1992 movie *Rum Punch* for his film *Jackie Brown.*" Wylie felt Kidd's designs would appeal to a younger reader.

Kidd and Les Daniels collaborated on a series of tributes to Superman, Batman, and Wonder Woman published by Chronicle Books, and Kidd worked on another honoring Charles M. Schulz, creator of *Peanuts.* With Art Spiegelman, he collaborated on a biography of the creator of "Plastic Man," *Jack Cole and Plastic Man: Forms Stretched to Their Limits.* Cole led a colorful life. He cycled 7,000 miles across the United States and wrote about it for *Boys Life,* and he became a professional cartoonist after taking a mail-order course. Cole created the types of horror and crime comics that resulted in the anti-comics sentiment of the 1950s, but he also drew for Hugh Hefner's *Playboy.* Cole is most well known, however, for his creation of Plastic Man, the cartoon figure who could stretch every part of his body in order to reach the criminals he pursued. In 1958, with no warning, and for reasons that have never been explained, Cole shot and killed himself. A *Publishers Weekly* contributor said this plastic-bound volume "is an excellent memorial to an innovative American cartoonist."

Calvin Reid, who interviewed Kidd for *Publishers Weekly,* noted that Kidd credits the increasing interest in book-jacket art to the record industry's shift from vinyl to CDs. Kidd told Reid, "The book cover became the last vestige for graphic designers to have a place to play." Reid wrote that "most of us would be happy to succeed at just one of the many creative areas of art and publishing in which Chip Kidd seems to thrive. . . . A lifelong fan and serious student of American comics, he is also an editor at Pantheon, acquiring and overseeing a series of graphic novels by the likes of such previously underground comix artists as Chris Ware and Dan Clowes. He's designer about town, with a high-profile agent . . . hobnobs with the best and the brightest . . . and he's as much in demand as a party guest, raconteur, and genial wit as he is as designer and editor. And as if that weren't enough, the ebullient Kidd is now also a novelist."

Kidd's debut novel is *The Cheese Monkeys: A Novel in Two Semesters.* It is set in the 1950s on a campus much like Pennsylvania State University, the author's alma mater, and revolves around freshman art student Happy, his bold, whiskey-drinking, free-spirited female friend Himillsy Dodd, and Winter Sorbeck, their brilliant but abrasive design teacher. In reviewing the book for *Flakmagazine* online, James Norton called it "a firestorm. The personalities of its three main characters collide, combine, clash, and tear each other apart, using graphic design as the fuel for their varied expressions of interpersonal passion, contempt for society, and artistic questioning. . . . It's also funny. *Very* funny."

By setting the novel in the 1950s, Kidd was able to write the dialogue without using the words fuck or cool, which he favored doing, "not because I'm a prude, but because they've become such a cliché." Norton commented that *The Cheese Monkeys* "dodges clichés like oil companies dodge federal income taxes. What begins as a wacky-but-conventional coming-of-age struggle at a big, faceless university quickly becomes a book that rips into the source code of Kidd's fascinations: visual art, complicated human relationships, and the dastardly trade of teaching. Throughout the book, Sorbeck takes teaching both more lightly and more seriously than any fictional instructor since Professor Henry Higgins. Kidd's fascination with the mechanics of teaching—and the sublime art of teaching well—springs from experience."

Thomas Hine wrote in the *New York Times Book Review* that this is "the book on graphic design that people have probably been urging Kidd to write.

Rather than discourse on theory, Kidd has embedded his belief in the old, universally appealing stories of maturity, finding your calling in life, and being inspired by, and loving, a demanding, serious, and highly eccentric teacher."

"Sorbeck is a demanding pedagogue," said a writer for *Complete Review* online. "Unconventional teaching methods are immediately put to use to winnow out those that are unfit. . . . And he challenges those students that remain with the tasks he assigns (and the generally devastating critiques he then unleashes). When something knocks his socks off—as very rarely happens—he'll be the first to admit it, but most of the time the students don't live up to his high expectations. But Sorbeck is a true teacher. He gets to students. He arouses their passions. He forces them to go far beyond what they had ever thought themselves capable of."

Kidd told *Library Journal*'s Wilda Williams that writing *The Cheese Monkeys* took six years. He wrote evenings and weekends and often put it away for weeks before returning to it. He admitted that it is somewhat autobiograhical and said that the character of Sorbeck is loosely based on Paul Rand, the designer who created the logo for IBM. Kidd also acknowledged the positive criticism and editing of his partner, J. D. McClatchy, poet and editor of *Yale Review.* Kidd told Williams he set the novel in 1957 because "the mid-1950s were ground zero for design education in America on a mass scale. Commercial or applied art, as it was called then, really started at Yale in the late 1940s and would have spread to the state school level by the mid-fifties. Because the novel is concerned with the fundamentals of graphic design, setting it in that period seemed to make sense."

A *Kirkus Reviews* contributor called *The Cheese Monkeys* "sheer charm most of the way." In a *Los Angeles Times* review, Mark Rozzo called Kidd's writing "as meticulous and energized as his book jackets. . . . Like the provocative Sorbeck, Kidd, in this comic gem, teaches us a thing or two about how to look at the world."

BIOGRAPHICAL AND CRITICAL SOURCES:

PERIODICALS

Advocate, September 17, 1996, Glen Helfand, review of *Batman Collected,* p. 55.

Booklist, September 1, 2001, John Green, review of *The Cheese Monkeys: A Novel in Two Semesters,* p. 51.

Entertainment Weekly, March 27, 1992, Kelli Pryor, "Designer Chip Kidd: Jacket Required," p. 68; November 1, 1996, Steve Daly, review of *Batman Collected,* p. 64; September 28, 2001, review of *Jack Cole and Plastic Man: Forms Stretched to Their Limits,* p. 68.

Kirkus Reviews, August 1, 2001, review of *The Cheese Monkeys,* p. 1053.

Library Journal, October 1, 2001, Wilda Williams, "Judging This Author by His Covers," p. 142.

Los Angeles Times, October 21, 2001, Mark Rozzo, review of *The Cheese Monkeys,* p. 10; February 3, 2002, Adam Bresnick, "Long before *South Park; Peanuts: The Art of Charles M. Schulz,* edited by Chip Kidd," p. R12.

New York, September 17, 2001, Derek de Koff, "Captain Kidd," p. 42.

New York Times Book Review, October 14, 2001, Thomas Hine, review of *The Cheese Monkeys,* p. 7.

Observer (London, England), November 24, 1996, Jonathan Wilson, review of *Batman Collected,* p. 18.

Print, September-October, 1997, Michael Dooley, review of *Batman Collected,* p. 28.

Publishers Weekly, February 23, 1998, Jonathan Bing, "Elmore Kidds Around; Knopf's Chip Kidd Gives New Look to First-ever Trade Paperbacks of Leonard's Backlist, from Dell and Morrow," p. 18; August 7, 2000, John F. Baker, "Kidd's Cover: First Novelist," p. 14; September 3, 2001, review of *Jack Cole and Plastic Man,* p. 67; October 29, 2001, Calvin Reid, "Designer-Man Wields Pen!" p. 31.

Village Voice Literary Supplement, winter, 1996, review of *Batman Collected,* p. 20.

ONLINE

Flakmagazine, http://www.flakmag.com/ (July 13, 2002), James Norton, review of *The Cheese Monkeys.*

Complete Review, http://www.complete-review.com/ (July 13, 2002), review of *The Cheese Monkeys.**

KIESLER, Charles A(dolphus) 1934-2002

OBITUARY NOTICE—See index for *CA* sketch: Born August 14, 1934, in St. Louis, MO; died of a heart attack October 11, 2002, in San Diego, CA. Psychologist, educator, and author. Kiesler is best remembered as an effective university administrator and officer of the American Psychological Association and the American Psychological Society. He was educated at Michigan State University, where he received his M.A. in 1960, and Stanford University, where he earned his Ph.D. in 1963. After graduating, he worked briefly as an assistant professor at Ohio State University before joining Yale University, where he taught until 1970. During the early 1970s Kiesler was a professor of psychology and chairman of the department at the University of Kansas, and for the remainder of the decade was executive director of the American Psychological Association, where he is credited with resolving the organization's financial crisis. Joining Carnegie-Mellon University in 1979, he was a psychology professor and then head of the department until 1983, when he became dean of the College of Humanities and Social Sciences. Kiesler's administrative talents were put to use again in 1992 when he became chancellor at the University of Missouri. The university was suffering from low enrollment at the time, and Kiesler turned the institution around by offering student tuition incentives, especially to minority students. He increased the number of black students by fifty-seven percent during his tenure, before arguments with the board of curators led to Kiesler's removal in 1996. Kiesler was also the founder of the American Psychological Society, as well as the author of several books, including *The Psychology of Commitment: Experiments* (1971), *Mental Hospitalization: Myths and Facts about a National Crisis* (1987), and *The Unnoticed Majority in Psychiatric Inpatient Care* (1993).

OBITUARIES AND OTHER SOURCES:

BOOKS

Sheehy, Noel, Antony J. Chapman, and Wendy A. Conroy, editors, *Biographical Dictionary of Psychology,* Routledge (London, England), 1997.

Who's Who in America, 56th edition, Marquis (New Providence, NJ), 2001.

PERIODICALS

Los Angeles Times, October 16, 2002, p. B10.
Washington Post, October 21, 2002, p. B7.

*   *   *

KILIAN, Crawford 1941-

PERSONAL: Born February 7, 1941, in New York, NY; naturalized Canadian citizen, May, 1973; son of Victor William Cosgrove (a writer and engineer) and Verne (a teacher; maiden name, Debney) Kilian; married Alice Hayes Fairfax (a teacher), April 8, 1966; children: Anna Catherine, Margaret Cathleen. *Education:* Columbia University, B.A., 1962; Simon Fraser University, M.A., 1972. *Politics:* New Democratic Party.

ADDRESSES: Office—4635 Cove Cliff Rd, North Vancouver, British Columbia, Canada V7G 1H7. *E-mail*—ckilian@thehub.capcollege.bc.ca; crof@shaw.ca.

CAREER: Freelance writer, 1962-63; Lawrence Radiation Laboratory, Berkeley, CA, library clerk, 1965-66, technical writer and editor, 1966-67; Vancouver City College, Vancouver, British Columbia, instructor, 1967-68; Capilano College, North Vancouver, British Columbia, Canada, instructor in English, 1968—, coordinator of Communications Department, 1975-83; writer-in-electronic-residence, 1990-92, 1995. School trustee in North Vancouver, 1980-82. Guangzhou Institute of Foreign Languages, Canton, People's Republic of China, foreign expert, 1983-84. Chair, Summer Pops Youth Orchestra Board, 1989-91; member of board, Canadian Institute of the Arts for Young Audiences, 1990-91; patron, Friends of the Library, North Vancouver, 1996—. *Military service:* U.S. Army, 1963-65.

WRITINGS:

Wonders, Inc. (juvenile; also see below), illustrated by John Larrecq, Parnassus (Berkeley, CA), 1968.
The Last Vikings (juvenile), illustrated by David Simpson, Clarke, Irwin (Toronto, Ontario, Canada), 1975.

Crawford Kilian

Go Do Some Great Thing: The Black Pioneers of British Columbia (nonfiction), University of Washington Press (Seattle, WA), 1978.
The Empire of Time (novel), Del Rey (New York, NY), 1978.
Icequake (novel), Douglas & McIntyre (Vancouver, British Columbia, Canada), 1979, Bantam (New York, NY), 1980.
Eyas (novel), Bantam (New York, NY), 1982.
Exploring British Columbia's Past (nonfiction), Douglas & McIntyre (Vancouver, British Columbia, Canada), 1983.
Tsunami (novel), Bantam (New York, NY), 1983.
Brother Jonathan (novel), Ace Books (New York, NY), 1985.
School Wars: The Assault on B.C. Education (nonfiction), New Star (Vancouver, British Columbia, Canada), 1985.
Lifter (novel), Ace Books (New York, NY), 1986.
The Fall of the Republic: A Novel of the Chronoplane Wars, Del Rey (New York, NY), 1987.

Rogue Emperor: A Novel of the Chronoplane Wars,
   Del Rey (New York, NY), 1988.
Gryphon (novel), Del Rey (New York, NY), 1989.
Greenmagic (novel), Del Rey (New York, NY), 1992.
Redmagic (novel), Del Rey (New York, NY), 1995.
2020 Visions: The Futures of Canadian Education,
   Arsenal Pulp Press (Vancouver, British Columbia,
   Canada), 1995.
(With Leslie Savage, Azza Sedky, and Martin Wittman)
   *The Communications Book: Writing for the Work-
   place,* 1996, revised edition published as *Writing
   for the Electronic Workplace,* 2001.
Writing Science Fiction and Fantasy, Self-Counsel
   Press, 1998.
Writing for the Web, Self-Counsel Press, 1999,
   "Geeks" edition, 2000.

RADIO PLAYS

A Strange Manuscript Found in a Copper Cylinder
   (adaptation of the novel by James De Mille),
   Canadian Broadcasting Corp. (CBC), 1972.
Little Legion, CBC, 1972.
Generals Die in Bed (adaptation of the novel by
   Charles Yale Harrison), CBC, 1973.
Wonders, Inc. (adaptation of his own book), CBC,
   1973.
Senator Connor's Big Comeback, CBC, 1974.
The Mob Has Got the Bomb, CBC, 1976.

Also author of the e-books *Bring the Jubilee: A
Decade in Computer Education* and *Work in Progress:
Collected Essays, 1972-2002.*

Contributor of articles and book reviews to *Journal of
Canadian Fiction, Dalhousie Review, Georgia Straight,
Vancouver Sun, Globe & Mail, Western Living, Quill
& Quire, B.C. Teacher, Step, Vancouver Forum, Van-
couver Review, Home & School, Internet World, In-
fobahn, Educom Review, Technos, Education Digest,*
and *Office@Home.* Education columnist, *Vancouver
Province,* 1982-94; author of column "The Online
Writer," *Content Spotlight,* 1999-2001. Contributing
editor, *Editorial Eye,* 2001-02.

SIDELIGHTS: Crawford Kilian mingles his teaching
career with his writing career. He has written about
the process of education in his adopted country,
Canada, and has adapted several novels for radio

broadcast by the Canadian Broadcasting Corporation.
He is perhaps best known, however, for his work as a
science fiction and fantasy writer. His works range
from an exploration of alternate histories on parallel
Earths to a grim vision of a future in which the fate of
individuals is controlled by multinational corporations.
"As with any civilized pleasure, that of science fiction
can turn into a vice," Kilian wrote in the *St. James
Guide to Science-Fiction Writers.* "Its persistent theme
is power: over nature, over others, over oneself. And
that power is most often used not to enhance and
expand the capabilities of its wielders but to win for
them only a return to Eden, to some primitive and
unspoiled state of life. Hence so many stories about
Galactic Empires based on European models from
Rome to the Raj, and the fondness for interstellar
societies firmly founded on the technology and
economy of ninth-century France."

Speaking to Paige Hess in an interview for the *Rest
Stop Writers' Newsletter,* Kilian explained: "*The
Empire of Time* was my first published novel, and it
was really a kind of scrapbook of science fiction ideas,
picked up in a dozen places: old James Bond novels,
pop science books, and various time-travel tales. Selling it only made me want to write more—and in fact,
I'd written and re-written another novel more or less
at the same time, which came out about six months
later. That was *Icequake,* whose financial success was
much greater, and which ensured I'd keep plugging
away at writing fiction."

Kilian's favorite of his novels, he revealed to Hess, is
"*Eyas* (1982), about family life in British Columbia
ten million years from now. I really did get the idea
while walking the dog, and wrote my first couple of
novels to teach myself the craft I knew I'd need. It
was going to be a Tolkienesque science-fantasy; it
turned into a domestic novel about a family gained,
lost, and regained. Despite several re-issues, the novel
never did very well—though it got some lovely
reviews."

One of Kilian's best-known works is the novel *Brother
Jonathan,* an exploration of a juvenile psyche caught
in a moral dilemma. "Jonathan is an athetoid, a young
cripple with little control over his ruined body,"
explained the *St. James Guide to Science-Fiction Writers* contributor George Kelley. "He is taken to the
secret laboratories of Dr. Duane Perkin, whose medical team is working with spastics to restore their

mobility through the use of new polydendronic computers that simulate nerve tissue." Jonathan's implant not only gives him control over his body, it also invests him with psionic powers. When the laboratory that funds Perkin's research is destroyed by a rival company, Jonathan and his fellow experiment subjects are forced to take refuge underground. "The rest of the book," Kelley stated, "explores the implications of these superhuman powers, the destruction of the corporate world government, and some satiric asides about juveniles and nationalism."

Critics largely celebrated Kilian's success in *Brother Jonathan. Fantasy Review* contributor W. D. Stephens noted that, although the novel has "a promising story line. . . it fails to live up to [its] promises." "Although a good story," opined Hal Hoover in *Voice of Youth Advocates,* who called the story "fascinating," "it also presents moral issues: medical experiments, corporate ethics, and classified societies." "*Brother Jonathan* is a challenging novel for young adult readers," declared Joanne Findon in *Quill & Quire,* "but Kilian makes this alien future world accessible. . . . [Any] teacher looking to engender discussion about the nature of power would find this a very useful book."

Lifter, Kilian's next novel, also looks at the empowerment of young adults. It is the story of a young man, Rick Stevenson, who suddenly discovers that he has developed the ability to fly. Kilian concentrates the story on the ways Stevenson uses his capabilities: to play tricks on his friends, to impress his girlfriend. "Romance, humor, football, UFO's, military spies, philosophy and the pangs of growing up," explained Muriel Becker in *Fantasy Review,* combine to form an entertaining novel. "Predictable and simple minded," a reviewer for *Science Fiction Chronicle* stated, but "also a lot of fun."

Kilian's interest in writing science fiction led him in 1998 to pen the instructional text *Writing Science Fiction and Fantasy,* a book that Sally Laturi in *Writer* described as being "geared for beginning writers," because it "covers the process of writing a sci-fi or fantasy novel from start to finish." Kilian has also written books aimed at those who hope to write for business and the Internet: *Writing for the Electronic Workplace* and *Writing for the Web.* When writing for the Web, Kilian believes, a writer must keep his prose direct, concise, and short. He also gives tips on how to design a Web site to appeal to the reader who is surf-

ing through and may leave quickly. Reviewing *Writing for the Web* on the *Technical Editors' Eyrie* Web site, Jean Weber deemed it to be "a useful addition to the bookshelf of inexperienced web writers and editors, anyone who teaches or trains writers, or anyone who consults or negotiates with clients or non-writer team members over the content of a website." According to Marc Anderson in the *Writer, Writing for the Web* is "a must-read for anyone thinking of plying their writing trade in cyberspace." Deanna Fay in *Black Enterprise* concluded: "If you're looking for no-nonsense advice, Kilian's book is like encouragement from a good friend."

Kilian once told *CA:* "I write fiction because it's fun, a grown-up form of 'Let's Pretend.' 'Serious fiction' to me is a contradiction in terms no matter how grim the subject matter or earnest the author. A novelist who thinks that writing a story will heal a social evil, or improve its readers, is self-deceiving. A better use of the time and effort would be to call the cops, or run for political office, or to write nonfiction.

"This issue began to clarify for me when I started planning a book about the black pioneers who came to British Columbia in the 1858 gold rush. It seemed at first like a great topic for a slam-bang historical epic, a black western. But the more I learned about the pioneers, the more clearly I saw that forcing their experience into a fictional straitjacket would demean and trivialize that experience. These were real people struggling to make a new life, not puppets pretending to live and die just to amuse someone for a few hours.

"My fiction has, of course, plenty of political and social comment explicit and implicit. People in the world around me are influenced by social pressures and political events; I could hardly tell a plausible lie about the twenty-first century if my characters weren't similarly influenced. Inevitably the concerns and anxieties of the moment turn up in my work: *The Empire of Time* is about a super CIA and was written in the early seventies when Chile and Watergate and Operation Chaos were in the news. *Eyas* is in a sense a novel of parental anxiety and hope, and was planned and written as my wife and I raised our two daughters. But my work reflects general experience rather than particular incident; autobiographical fiction bores and embarrasses me.

"Perhaps the most disastrous thing to happen to a writer in North America is to be able to make a living from writing. In India and Latin America writing is something done as a sideline by chemical engineers, civil servants, and businessmen—people very much involved in their world. Our writers scrape along on academic welfare schemes, or crank out formula work, or make some huge score in best-sellerdom. None of these fates is attractive, because all of them tend to exclude the writer from the surrounding community.

"Even worse, such fates rob the writer of much of the pleasure of writing. Judging by what our serious writers say, writing for them is torture, and life after hours isn't much fun either. The industrious hacks tend to write the same story over and over, changing the color of the heroine's eyes. The blockbuster novelists know they're only one book away from being has-beens.

"So an apprentice writer would be wise to stay away from graduate programs as well as Harlequin and Hollywood. Better to get married, settle down in a community, raise kids, and write exactly what you want to write, what you enjoy writing. If it sells, great. If it doesn't, so what? You and your spouse and the kids won't starve because you've got some kind of productive job. Better to be bored selling insurance than bored writing for money. If that happens, somebody will own your inner life and dictate your dreams. It won't be you."

AUTOBIOGRAPHICAL ESSAY:

Crawford Kilian contributed the following autobiographical essay to *CA*:

BECOMING A WRITER IN JUST SIXTY YEARS

I owe my life to Adolf Hitler and the U.S. State Department. And while writing is a notoriously solitary craft, I owe my career as a writer to a host of friends and mentors—and students.

My parents met in Los Angeles in the late 1930s at meetings of the Hollywood Anti-Nazi League. My mother, then Verne Debney, was a petite blonde knockout, active at UCLA in an organization called Veterans of Future Wars. My father, Victor William Cosgrove Kilian ("Mike" to everyone, including his sons), had tried to get to Spain to join the International Brigades, foreigners fighting in support of the elected Loyalist government. But the State Department had

picked up the guy who was supposed to get Mike overseas, so he was stuck in Los Angeles, dropping anti-Nazi leaflets from airplanes on picnics held by the German-American Bund. Had Mike actually reached Spain, he would likely have been killed. He certainly wouldn't have met and married Verne, and I wouldn't be here to tell you about it.

My parents were what the FBI later called "premature anti-fascists," and they paid a high price for their membership in the Communist Party: FBI harassment, blacklisting, and general stress, which helped break up their marriage. But their politics also shaped me as a writer.

Mike came from a family of German radicals and Yankee revolutionaries. On his father's side he was descended from a line of socialists; his grandfather Heinrich Kilian had immigrated to the United States in 1888 and was soon working with Eugene Debs in the American Socialist Party. On his mother Daisy's side he was descended from William Williams, a signer of the Declaration of Independence, and Jonathan Trumbull, George Washington's quartermaster general and the antecedent (as "Brother Jonathan") of Uncle Sam. He was intensely proud of both lineages.

Verne's family was much less political. Her father, Fred Debney, was an immigrant from Danzig, a tinsmith; Veronica, her mother, a peasant girl from Slovakia. Fred and Veronica had met in Milwaukee, and sometime soon after World War I they had driven out to Los Angeles where Fred had built a house in East Hollywood. Verne's brother Lou had gone to work for Walt Disney as an animator; Verne had gone to UCLA and become a teacher—the first and only university graduate in the family until me.

Mike's father, Victor Sr., was an actor who had appeared in many of Eugene O'Neill's original productions as well as routine Broadway plays. After Vic and Daisy's marriage ended in the early 1930s, Mike chose to stay with his father. He had experienced a bohemian childhood. Daisy had kept him out of school until fifth grade because she couldn't find a school good enough for him, and he left school after tenth grade. But he had also grown up surrounded by intelligent, articulate people: artists, writers, actors. The family alternated between apartments in Manhattan and a cabin in Free Acres, New Jersey, an odd little community that attracted unusual people. Invariably the house was full of visitors or relatives, and invariably everyone talked. So Mike picked up a lot just by listening. I was to be named after one of his Free Acres mentors, an artist named Will Crawford.

In the early 1930s Mike, at age sixteen, worked as a radio operator on a tramp steamer to Scandinavia. Almost as soon as he was back, he and Vic returned to Europe as members of the cast of a Broadway play headed for London. And soon after that, Mike and Vic landed in Hollywood, where Vic was to work in well over a hundred movies. (Mike did some bit parts too, where his height and dark good looks got him cast as "young heavies"—cops and doctors.)

Political activism, however, was my father's real occupation in the late 1930s. Hence his activities with the Anti-Nazi League. He also helped drive a convoy of ambulances across the United States, raising money for the Spanish Loyalists, and then chauffeured Dr. Norman Bethune around New England; the Canadian doctor had just returned from Spain and was fundraising for the Loyalists also, before leaving for China to work with Mao's Eighth Route Army.

Mike and Verne were married on September 16, 1939, just two weeks after the start of World War II. It was not an auspicious time, but they managed. The marriage had to be kept secret at first, because Verne was teaching and in those days a married female teacher would be fired—better to give the job to an unmarried woman or to a married man. Before long they moved to New York, where I was born on February 7, 1941.

Sometime late in the summer of 1941 the family moved back to Los Angeles, where Mike passed the tests for air traffic controller with the highest grades ever recorded. He was to work at Burbank Airport through most of the war, when it was the busiest airfield in the world. In 1944 he left the job and tried to join the armed forces—but, by then the father of two children, he was rejected. He settled for a job as radio operator in the Merchant Marine, perhaps the most hazardous job in the service that suffered the most casualties during the war.

Some of my earliest memories are of Mike in his uniform. I can recall being in the back seat of our Packard late at night while my parents necked in the

Father, Mike Kilian

front; we were at a dock somewhere and he was about to leave for sea. And I recall his return from one voyage, and my pride that I was now tall enough for my head to reach his belt buckle.

Even for toddlers in a Los Angeles suburb, the war was a presence: searchlights swept the skies during air-raid alerts, shopping at the supermarket required ration stamps, and on one April day in 1945 I asked Verne why she was crying: "President Roosevelt just died."

That summer, when I was four years old, I walked my little brother Lincoln (age three) to the corner of our block on Burbank Boulevard in North Hollywood. We could hear car horns blaring in the distance, and I began to spin a story about the reason: a tree had fallen across the road, a car had hit it, and its horn had stuck. Then Mrs. Hunt, who lived in the house on the corner, called out from the door: "Hey, kids! Did you hear the war is over?"

We ran back home and somehow heard that a huge celebration was going on down in Hollywood. We badgered Verne into taking us, and I still have a fragmentary memory of noise and crowds on Hollywood Boulevard as our car crawled through traffic.

*

Life in postwar Los Angeles now looks almost idyllic. The neighborhood was full of kids. We had a nice house with a big back yard for playing in, and an undeveloped park on the banks of a dry wash just a few houses down the street. (When I revisited the neighborhood in 1977, the pepper trees on Burbank Boulevard had vanished and the dry wash was now a freeway.)

Verne taught in our school when I was still in first and second grade; she left to have a third son, Starr, in 1948. Thereafter, we walked the half-mile to school, unescorted. Sometimes on weekends we'd stay with Verne's parents, and then take the streetcar all the way home . . . again unescorted. The dangerous, hard-boiled Los Angeles of Raymond Chandler was somewhere else.

It wasn't all idyllic, of course. There were frequent quarrels between Mike and Verne, frictions with Verne's father (who had mysteriously converted early in the war from left-winger to Nazi sympathizer), and illness. In the fall of 1948 I came down with polio, and spent a week or so in hospital. It was a light case, and after a couple of months' recuperation I was back in school. For a year or so I also had back massages, and suffered no long-term consequences from a disease that now seems as ancient as the Black Death.

The tradition of endless conversation continued, rich with family stories, explanations of science, and history. We liked to speculate on when the first men would reach the moon and whether a human could be cloned. Talk and reading dominated the household, even though we had one of the first TV sets in the neighborhood (Mike had become a TV engineer after the war). On some evenings all the neighbors would come in to watch Hopalong Cassidy; Kukla, Fran, and Ollie; or Shirley Dinsdale and Judy Splinters, a ventriloquism act. Before long we were also watching baseball games, televised live by a remote crew led by Mike. Despite the TV, reading was the preferred entertainment for Linc and me, and our parents ensured we had lots of books to read—Paul Bunyan, American history, Booth Tarkington's "Penrod" stories, *Tom Sawyer.* I loved trips to the library.

Verne, a determined bargain hunter, took us into all kinds of secondhand stores. Their stock often included shelves of old pulp magazines—especially science fiction. I could usually get her to buy me two or three (at ten or fifteen cents each, they were a bargain compared to ten-cent comic books). So my shelves at home filled up with *Startling Stories, Thrilling Wonder, Planet,* and *Astounding Stories.* I loved them, and got an undeserved classroom reputation as a brain because I'd picked up scraps of astronomy and physics from them. And writers now forgotten were major figures in my education: Edmond Hamilton, Sam Merwin, Henry Kuttner—not to mention the big names like Robert Heinlein, Isaac Asimov, and Ray Bradbury.

One reason for my love of SF was that it was literally escapist, and I needed some escape because Mike and Verne's marriage was not a happy one. So I could disappear into interplanetary space for a while, until things calmed down. Linc, when he got a year or two older, took refuge in the past, becoming a Civil War buff owning dozens of books about it.

Television brought us the news of the invasion of South Korea in June 1950, and it was around this time that our parents told us we were moving to New York, where Mike would have a job in another TV station. The house was soon sold, and we got a new Ford station wagon. Our possessions went into a trailer, we said good-bye to our classmates, and left Los Angeles in October.

Not until we were nearly in El Paso did our parents suggest we might want to visit Mexico on our way to New York. Eventually I realized that the "New York job" had been a cover story. Expecting a subpoena from the House Un-American Activities Committee, Mike had found a job with a Mexican TV station. So just before Halloween we rolled into Mexico City, and after a few days in a hotel we settled into a new home in an apartment building in Colonia Nueva Anzures, on Calle Lafayette just around the corner from Calle Shakespeare (pronounced "shock ess pay AW ray").

*

I haven't seen Mexico City in almost half a century, but I recall it as a mostly beautiful place of clear skies, exciting summer thunderstorms, and very nice people. Linc and I picked up Spanish quickly, at least enough to get around with, and while we were a visible minority we rarely had any trouble with other kids. We never thought twice about hopping a bus or streetcar across town to school or a friend's house or a movie—and this when we were aged ten and nine.

Our first school was a brand-new British-run private school, Greengates. It exposed me to a very different kind of teacher from the ones I'd known in North Hollywood: these were young expatriates from England, Gibraltar, and South Africa. (In the second year, Verne taught there also, in exchange for free tuition for Linc and me.) The students were a mix of Brits, Mexicans, and Americans. The school was a converted old house of some size, but with no yard; sports had to wait for twice-weekly trips to a run-down country club, where we learned soccer and played baseball with a cricket bat.

This was a much more intensive education than I'd ever had before: English, French, Spanish, and Latin, plus literature, history, and math. At one point I was pretty good at converting pounds and pence into shillings and half-crowns. More importantly, I was reading very widely, everything from English verse to boys' stories like *Biggles in Spain,* plus Ray Bradbury's *The Martian Chronicles.* And we'd discovered that in the Thieves' Market downtown we could buy not only six-shooters and cavalry sabers, but piles of old American magazines—especially the pulp SF that I'd acquired a taste for in those LA secondhand shops.

At some point in the year and a half I was at Greengates, I stood up in front of my class and told a story. It wasn't much, just an improvisation, and I confess I ended it with ". . . and then I woke up," but the class liked it. And I had liked telling it.

Not long after, Verne got a job at the American School: not only free tuition for us, but an actual salary as well. We moved to a nice house right across the street from the walled campus of the school, but our neighborhood was a slum of tar-paper shanties and open drains. As we walked to the school gate every morning, limousines from the Lomas and other rich districts rolled past us to deliver our classmates.

The move to the American School brought us into contact with the Butler and Trumbo families, who had arrived in Mexico City a few months after we had.

Like us, they were there to try to make a living despite the blacklist. Hugo and Jean Butler and Dalton Trumbo were Hollywood writers who could no longer get work under their own names. But in Mexico they could live well while writing scripts and selling them (at bargain rates) under false names to American film producers. Occasionally they could also sell to a local producer-director like Luis Buñuel.

I met Michael Butler in my first day at the American School in July 1952, and soon knew Chris Trumbo as well. That led to renewed contact between our parents, who'd known each other in the Party during the war. (Verne and Cleo Trumbo, Chris's mother, had even known each other in high school.) We were now in a little community of exiles—writers, artists, business people—who seemed to meet every Saturday morning at the Butlers' for a game of softball in the empty lot next door. After the game, everyone sat down to a big lunch where the adults talked politics and gossiped, and the kids listened or gossiped among themselves.

Sometime in late 1952 or early 1953, I began writing stories. First they were in pencil, with illustrations; soon, though, I was pecking them out on Verne's portable typewriter. They were space operas, mostly, or stories about mutants with superhuman powers, or people revived after being frozen for thousands of years. Not an original idea in the batch, but my parents and teachers (and friends) were greatly impressed and urged me to keep writing. So I did.

It helped that my friends' parents were working writers. For many novices, writing is something done by mysterious beings, probably mutants with superhuman powers. I knew writing was done by ordinary people who (even blacklisted) made pretty decent livings from it. So I kept at it, and within a few months had even written a couple of SF novelettes of eighty pages or so. Dalton Trumbo read one of them and offered me a dollar for it, which I foolishly spurned; a year or two later I burned the manuscript, compounding my foolishness. When I look at the stories that survive from my first years, I'm struck (and appalled) by how little my basic writing style has changed. The pulp authors must have been powerful models.

I suspect I imagined that writing would give me entry to some kind of society of like-minded people. The blacklisted screenwriters and their families were tightly linked by profession, by predicament, and by friendship. The other exiles were less united, and my own family was stressed and fragmented by my parents' quarrels. The Mexicans regarded us as foreigners, as of course we were—just another batch of political exiles, like the Spaniards from the doomed Republic and the ex-Nazi and his family who'd lived downstairs from us in one apartment building. Much as we loved and enjoyed Mexico, we knew it wasn't really our world. Neither was the Cold War U.S.A. In college, writing a story about those years, I invented a term to describe our situation: "discultured," not really belonging anywhere.

But somewhere out there was a world of published writers, loved by their readers and respected by their colleagues and editors. Even at age twelve or thirteen, I had some hazy sense of the American writers of the 1920s—Fitzgerald, Dos Passos, Hemingway—who had not only been friends and rivals, but who had created a magical world of their own.

In my case, however, I didn't imagine myself partying in the south of France or dodging bulls in Pamplona; I imagined going to the science-fiction conventions I read about in *Startling Stories* and *Astounding Science Fiction.* I vividly recall reading about the SF author L. Sprague de Camp at one such convention, sporting "tendrils" on his head like those of the people on his fictional planet Krishna. Loving de Camp's humor and erudition, I longed to see him, tendrils and all. Many years later we did meet, at a convention in Calgary, where he had no tendrils but was a wonderfully attractive, articulate, and likable octogenarian. Alas, most of the conventions I have attended were far less interesting than those I'd imagined in the early 1950s.

Somehow, then, writing was going to bring me in from the isolation of the blacklist, and perhaps help make the larger society a more humane one (propaganda in good causes being a hallmark of "progressive" literature). That didn't happen. Instead I was to rusticate in a suburb of a Canadian city, grading papers and occasionally publishing a novel or nonfiction book. Even more occasionally, someone would write or phone or e-mail to say they'd liked something of mine. And that was about it. I would certainly have a lively social and political life, but it would include almost no writers except for a few of my students.

*

By the age of fourteen or fifteen, I was the author of several novelettes and many short stories. Thereafter,

Mother, Verne Kilian

except for some bad years in college, I would always be working on some kind of writing project. This not only got me some attention and encouragement, but also insulated me a bit from the pain of my parents' breakup. They had separated in 1952. Some months after that, the TV station fired Mike; he had trained everyone and was therefore no longer needed. Mike had to return to the United States for work, but the FBI kept chasing him out of jobs; he ended up working in a Tijuana TV station, but when he returned to Mexico City to get his passport renewed at the U.S. embassy, it was taken from him. He now had no choice but to return to the United States and stay there.

Just before Christmas 1954, Verne brought us back to Los Angeles also. It was too hard to live on her small salary in Mexico, and she seized the chance to teach in a school in Malibu. We settled in Santa Monica in a beachfront apartment. This was a blessing because we were upwind of the horrendous Los Angeles smog, which Mexico City in those days had none of.

Reentry brought "disculture" shock: classes reciting the Pledge of Allegiance, teachers conducting impromptu atomic-bomb drills, and air-raid sirens going off on the last Friday of every month. I had a strong sense that this was a dangerous country—not only because of my parents' unpopular politics, but because it might be blown up at any moment. Those who have grown up since the late 1980s have little understanding of the pervasive anxieties of the Cold War—especially for unpopular radicals and their kids. We knew that one false step, one tactless remark, might mean the loss of Verne's job, or a visit from the FBI, or a beating from patriotic louts.

The other kids in junior high were shocked that I said "sir" and "ma'am" to the teachers, and it didn't help that I spoke pretty good Spanish. Still, I got used to life in a strange world where fighter planes' sonic booms bulged the panes in the classroom windows, tar blobs floated in onto the beach, and no one knew (or cared) anything about Mexico.

Life got better in high school, where I soon met a number of bright nonconformists. We had gravitated to a writing club, the Penpushers, and before long were swapping stories and poems, falling in and out of love, and generally behaving like any other clique. It was around this time, 1956, that I read the first volume of *The Lord of the Rings*; it was just out, little known to anyone outside the small world of science-fiction and fantasy lovers. I'd read stories about mythical worlds before (and even created a couple), but this was of course extraordinary. I happily set to work on a plagiarism of it, a novelette titled "The Year of the Bat," in which my friends and I played major roles under thinly disguised names.

I wrote the novelette on an Optima portable typewriter, a Christmas present from Mike. By the standards of today's laptops, it was a bulky, heavy object, but I loved it. On the back it said: "Made in Germany," with a stamped addendum: "Soviet Occupied." My communist typewriter was sometimes hard to get serviced in those Cold War years, but it was a rugged and durable machine that I was to use for a quarter-century. I still have it.

The high school years were punctuated with two summer trips to Mexico, in the second of which I stayed with the Butler family. Jean Butler actually sat down and read "The Year of the Bat" and commended it. That judgment probably set me permanently on my course as a writer.

Meanwhile, Mike had formed a partnership with Pauline Sopkin, a blacklisted ex-radio writer. Together, under false names, they broke into TV writing; between Pauline's skills with a script, and Mike's knowledge of the technical end of TV, they formed a good team. It was a golden age of TV drama, and for several years they did quite well; Loretta Young was an especially good market. Mike and Pauline won a few awards—notably for a script about the pornography industry and its effect on teenagers wanting to learn about sex. During the times when Linc and I lived with Mike and Pauline, I was again immersed in a household where writing was just the way people made a living. To outsiders, though, it must have seemed a very dysfunctional household: Mike and Pauline worked in their bedroom-office, Pauline at the typewriter and Mike in his easy chair, with each shouting lines of dialogue to the other. To people in the front of the house, it sounded like a raging quarrel.

My own writing in high school consisted mostly of SF and fantasy stories, with one novelette of teen angst—the result of being too impressed with the James Dean movie *Rebel without a Cause*. None of it was really publishable, though one short story nearly saw print in *Ellery Queen's Mystery Magazine*. But they wanted first world publication, and I naively told them the story had appeared in the Penpushers' little student magazine.

After I'd done well on some standardized test in twelfth grade, Mike suggested I apply to Columbia as well as to the obvious local schools like UCLA. He wanted me to experience New York, so I obligingly sent off the application. To my astonishment, they not only accepted me but also offered a meal job and a scholarship.

The rest of that senior year whirled by, and after graduation I flew back to New York with Mike and Linc—courtesy of Vic, who was succeeding on Broadway again after six or seven years on the Hollywood blacklist. (Vic had been subpoenaed in 1951, gone to Washington, and been promptly labeled an "unfriendly witness." He didn't work again in Hollywood until the 1970s.) So we saw him in *Look Homeward, Angel*, enjoyed a number of other Broadway plays, and had a pretty good time.

I also met Stanley Ellin, a notable mystery writer, his wife Jean, and their daughter Susan, with whom I'd been corresponding for a couple of years. Jean and Verne had been pen pals since taking the same maternity class back in 1940, and somehow I'd starting writing to Susan. Her father was another writer-mentor; he gave me serious criticism that made his praise all the more valuable, and it was he who'd passed along one of my stories to *Ellery Queen's*. I greatly enjoyed the times I spent with the Ellins on Clarkson Street in Brooklyn.

Mike and Linc flew home and I stayed in New York. Vic found me a non-paying job as an apprentice in a summer-stock company in Woodstock, New York. (This was a decade before Woodstock became the symbol of a generation.) I spent the summer building sets and doing bit parts in a different play every week. It was fun, but it cured me of any desire to follow in the family profession.

*

Columbia in the fall of 1958 was enhanced by the presence of my old Mexico friends Michael Butler and Chris Trumbo, who had also been admitted. We soon made more friends, and dedicated ourselves to playing poker and hanging out in the West End Bar and Grill.

I wasn't a very good student. Only seventeen when I arrived on campus, I could have used a couple of years in the army just to grow up. So while I did all right, and often enjoyed my courses, I didn't get as much out of the experience as I might have with a little more maturity. It was great to take courses from the likes of Lionel Trilling, F. W. Dupee, and Eric Bentley (not to mention the honor of being flunked in physics by Leon Lederman, who would later win a Nobel Prize).

But my favorite teacher at Columbia was an old ex-sportswriter named George Nobbe, who gave a course in writing short stories. He would sit at the end of the seminar table, beaming at the dozen of us callow youths and resembling Dr. Samuel Johnson minus the wig. Each week he'd assign a topic for next week's story, which we'd read to our classmates. The criticism, from both him and the class, was wonderful—

and it taught me a lot about how to teach the writing of fiction. It was in that class that I wrote the Mexico story about disculturation. It was the first time, but not the last, that my own writing taught me something.

But that was almost all the fiction writing I did in four years. I worked on the *Columbia Review,* our undergraduate literary magazine, and published a couple of minor items there, but made no real progress as a writer. My courses trained me to be a critic, not a writer, so I was too quick to judge and condemn my own work. During one dull Christmas break, a friend and I wrote 20,000 words of a war novel, but we never finished it. Classes resumed and we were back writing essays on De Quincey and Brecht.

In some ways, my real Columbia education took place in the West End and a coffee shop on Broadway called Riker's. I hung out in those places with my friends, gossiping about the profs, preparing for exams, and debating politics. And I learned as much from those conversations as I had as a little kid back in North Hollywood.

I was still in the blacklist community as well. Through Chris and Michael, I got to know Ring Lardner, Jr., and his family. Ring had been one of the Hollywood Ten along with Dalton Trumbo; he and his family now lived in an apartment on West End Avenue, where we often visited. I still recall the wall of bookshelves in the living room—and, on the bottom shelf, an Oscar statuette serving as a bookend. Occasionally Dalton Trumbo or Hugo Butler would swing through town and take us out to dinner, renewing the old ties to Mexico while bringing us up to date on the movie business. I still remember the delight I felt when a story in the *New York Times* reported that Trumbo was the author of the screenplay for Kirk Douglas's epic *Spartacus*. Trumbo had already won an Oscar in the 1950s under a phony name, thereby embarrassing the industry; this only enhanced his glory.

Despite these connections, I wasn't active politically; Columbia in those days was notorious for its political apathy. Many years later I was to see my FBI file, which reported that I was unknown to the FBI informants in the New York Communist Party. That was almost all I learned from the file; most of it had been blacked out to protect the FBI sources' privacy. I sometimes wonder whom the FBI spoke to, and what they learned that had been worth putting into the file.

Not until I was back in Los Angeles for good in the fall of 1962 did I start trying to write again. Mike and Pauline wanted me to get a start as a writer, and supported me for a year. This enabled me to write a large chunk of an autobiographical novel about Columbia. Like the Christmas-break war novel, it was written very quickly, and very badly. A college friend read it and wrote a long, accurate, and devastating critique. It would be a long time before I tried autobiographical fiction again.

The missile crisis of October 1962 gave us a few bad days. As everyone waited to see if war would erupt between us and the Soviets, the Los Angeles civil defense office urged everyone to have two weeks' supply of food on hand. Next day Pauline went up to Ralph's supermarket on Sunset Boulevard to get a bag of birdseed, and found pandemonium as our neighbors tried to push multiple cartloads of groceries through the checkout stands. When the crisis was over, most people tried to return their emergency supplies. That was the funny part. The less-funny part was the announcement on TV that if war did break out, the FBI would promptly throw all subversives into camps already set up for the purpose.

With the missile crisis over, life settled back to normal. I spent my non-writing time hanging out with friends, dating girls, talking politics (and writing) with my parents, and getting involved with the Congress of Racial Equality (CORE). The murder of Medgar Evers in Mississippi seemed to me to demand some kind of action, so I joined CORE and attended a few meetings in the summer of 1963. I even went on a march through South Central LA, where the Watts riots would rage in a couple of years. But my political engagement was brief; I knew the draft would get me eventually, so I volunteered for it. Sometime in September I received my induction notice (and since I'd registered in New York, the notice came with a New York subway token taped to it). Late in October 1963 I was sworn in and took a train to Fort Ord, near Monterey.

My hitch was what we called "good duty." Basic training was about fighting Korea again and doing it right this time. It was still a peacetime army, and didn't especially care about my political background as long as I didn't need a security clearance. After basic, I was assigned to HQ Company right at Ord, where my self-taught typing got me a job cutting orders. My comrades in arms were mostly young paper-pushers

who'd done some business courses or worked as management trainees. No one was eager to show how tough he was.

Off duty, I could hang out in Monterey, or catch a bus to Berkeley, or do an overnight on the Greyhound to LA and spend a weekend at home. I could discuss the growing threat of Vietnam with my parents, but until 1965 it was not a major issue. In '64 you had to work hard to get to Vietnam, and you were far more likely to end up in Germany or Korea. The army fed us some stupid propaganda movies about what a great job we were doing with counter insurgency in general and Vietnam in particular. No one gave a noticeable damn. The guys who volunteered for Vietnam were just looking for rapid promotion and some overseas pay.

For a long stretch I was on night shift, which meant I could sleep late, spend the day doing what I liked, show up for work at 4:30, and knock off when everyone's orders had been typed up. When my fellow typists left for the night, I would stay late, using my electric typewriter to work on my first novel. *The Winter after the War* was an SF war novel about a chunk of central California being run by the army after a brief nuclear/bacteriological World War III.

It was pretty bad, but at least I'd proved that I could write a book-length story. I sent it to just one publisher, who wrote back rejecting it very kindly. After that, it sat on my shelf for decades until I donated it, with a lot of other manuscripts, to the Special Collections of the library at the University of British Columbia.

*

I'd never had any illusions that I could make a living from my writing alone. That was possible for the Butlers and Trumbos, perhaps, and Mike and Pauline had done so for a while, but by the mid-'60s they were scrambling to find work in a market that just wanted scripts where bodies fell out of closets. I certainly didn't expect to get rich writing screenplays, which didn't interest me at all. So I applied to San Francisco State's teacher-training program, thinking that a high school teaching career would be fun while giving me time to write on the side.

The army gave me an early release to enroll at SF State, and I quickly found an apartment in Berkeley with a congenial roommate—a Japanese guy named

The author's wife, Alice

Allen Say who was a brilliant artist and photographer. He wanted to illustrate children's books, so in the fall of 1965 I put together a story, *Wonders, Inc.*, about a factory that built abstractions: a line assembly that built hairlines and timberlines, a space mill that cranked out closet space and elbow room. But I was mostly concerned with education courses that bored me silly.

One of my classmates, however, was a good-looking young woman named Alice Fairfax. I started dating her, and before long Allen was dating her roommate. One thing led to another, and before I knew it I was out of the teacher-training program and working in the library of the Lawrence Radiation Laboratory up on the hill above Berkeley. Alice and I were living together in a little duplex on the north side of Berkeley, and a few months later we were married.

The library job wasn't very challenging (I'd replaced an eighteen-year-old going into the navy), and I was on the verge of quitting. Then Parnassus Press, a small children's publisher in Berkeley, said they wanted to publish *Wonders, Inc.*, which I'd submitted to them months before. (They didn't want Allen Say's illustra-

tions, but he went on to write and illustrate his own superb children's books—and to win a Caldecott for one of them.)

The news of my impending publication somehow got me promoted into the Technical Information Division, where I became an apprentice tech writer/editor. My weak background in science was a disadvantage, but I could translate technical writing into reasonably clear English. So I adapted a lot of reports into terms understandable to our "ideal" reader: a first-term congressman on the House Atomic Energy Committee.

I also learned that Cold War politics were alive and well at the Rad Lab. Its founder, Ernest O. Lawrence, had been a major force in the building of the first atomic bombs. Lawrence had died in 1958, but his spirit still ruled the place: When I found a photo of Robert Oppenheimer attending a Lab conference, I included it in the draft of an annual report. Oppenheimer had since died, and I thought it would make a quiet tribute to a great scientist. But Lawrence had fallen out with Oppenheimer during the hearings that cost Oppenheimer his security clearance. The photo disappeared from the final report.

Meanwhile, Alice had acquired her teaching credential and landed a job teaching in Richmond, just north of Berkeley. We moved into a bigger place, got a dog, and seemed to be settling into young-married life with a circle of friends and colleagues.

But Vietnam now hung over us all. We went on marches, snarled about LBJ, and read *Ramparts* Magazine—including an anti war article by a Special Forces sergeant I'd been greatly impressed by at Fort Ord. One afternoon my brother Starr phoned from UC Santa Cruz, where he and his buddies had decided they should move to Canada before the war got any worse. Would I please call the Canadian consulate in San Francisco and get the information on how to emigrate? I did, but my brother never left; Alice and I did.

We realized we were doing well in jobs we didn't enjoy all that much, and feeling politically and culturally out of step. Berkeley in the mid-'60s was very hip, and if you went to the anti war demos in San Francisco, you saw thousands of people equally opposed to the war. But we decided it was time for a change. One evening, as we listened to the news of yet more B-52s bombing Vietnam, Alice said: "Why don't *we* go to Canada?"

And why not? We'd both lived out of the country before. We had nothing tying us down. My middle brother Linc had spent some time in British Columbia and thought we'd do fine. Like most Americans, we knew almost nothing about Canada except that draft dodgers and deserters were beginning to go there (a step that had been literally unthinkable when I was drafted in 1963). So with very little hassle we wrapped up our jobs, got our immigration papers, and shipped our few belongings to Vancouver. We drove up from Berkeley in three or four days, arriving at the border on August 2, 1967. Less than a week later we had a little house in North Vancouver and were looking for work.

In some ways Canada was more exotic than Mexico. It was a kind of parallel world, one in which the American Revolution hadn't been fought. British cars filled the streets: Cambridges, Austins, Rovers. People paved their driveways with "ashfault" and the post office trucks said "Royal Mail" above the Queen's coat of arms. Most of the other immigrants were Brits or Germans or Dutch. You could buy canned goods from Red China in any grocery store: I felt as if I were trading with the enemy.

By dumb luck, I stumbled into a job at Vancouver Community College and discovered I loved teaching. After a year I moved to a new college, Capilano, and also began taking courses towards a master's degree. I wanted to stay in teaching, so an M.A. was essential. And with some maturity and a clear purpose to my studies, I enjoyed my courses far more than I had at Columbia.

For one course I had to read Northrop Frye's *Anatomy of Criticism,* which I'd never heard of at Columbia. Maybe I wouldn't have responded to it as a callow youth, but now it had the effect reported by many of Frye's students at the University of Toronto: it felt like the top of my head was coming off. Frye made literature make sense. He traced the connections, the conventions, the symbols. Every story or poem or essay was a contribution to an ongoing, centuries-long conversation. As a writer you might be ignorant of most of what had been said before (I certainly was), but your work would be a lot better if you did know, and if you therefore framed your own comments as a response—not just as an imitation. Literature itself is a society in conversation, in which the dead still speak to the living.

I was to correspond occasionally with Frye, and I sent him some of my books—especially *Icequake,* in which a nuclear-reactor engineer, "Herman Northrop," is described as keeping the whole operation going. He took it as I hoped he would, as an affectionate joke. His death in 1991 felt like losing a father.

*

I'd started writing SF and fantasy because I liked the stories in those genres. Now I began to understand how those genres had arisen, what they'd borrowed from, why they relied on some conventions and not on others. I could apply Frye's ideas to the books I was studying—especially to a Canadian classic, *A Strange Manuscript Found in a Copper Cylinder,* by the nineteenth-century writer James de Mille. And I could begin to apply them to my own work as well—not just as a literary critic finding fault with amateurishness, but as an apprentice craftsman finally learning how to use his tools.

By the time I finally received my M.A., I was thirty-one and now truly settled: my job was secure, Alice and I had a daughter, and we'd even bought a house. While working on my M.A. thesis, I'd developed a routine in which a good block of time was available for writing. So with the thesis done, I began to explore some possibilities.

Radio drama was the unlikely first choice. A friend working for the CBC gave me a wildly inflated idea of how much the CBC would pay for a script, but by the time I found out, I'd sold one and was on the way to selling more. That first script was an adaptation of *A Strange Manuscript,* and it worked quite well as a tongue-in-cheek radio fantasy. Success also triggered a lot more ideas. Five more scripts followed in the next few years, including some originals as well as adaptations. My master's thesis had been on early Canadian novels of World War I, and one radio play was based on *Generals Die in Bed,* a tough and brilliant portrait of trench warfare. I was to return to World War I almost thirty years later in my novel *Deserters.*

The author with his daughter, Anna, and grandfather, Victor Kilian, 1977

In the early 1970s I'd also written a kind of social studies text in the form of a story about the last Vikings in Greenland. Looking around for similar topics, I'd discovered accounts of the black pioneers who came to British Columbia in the 1858 gold rush, and I wrote—on spec—a history of them. (As with the CBC scripts, I plunged into this project with a mistakenly optimistic idea of how much money it might make.) A small Vancouver publisher, Douglas & McIntyre, brought it out in 1978, and it did very well. The reviews were excellent and sales were good; the book is still in print. I was beginning to feel I had a career, not just a couple of lucky breaks.

Around this time I began to think about *Eyas,* a story set in Canada ten million years in the future. It would be a big, sprawling story, and I knew I was nowhere near capable of tackling it yet. But some other projects would, I hoped, teach me enough about the craft of fiction to let me gamble on *Eyas.*

In the late 1960s I'd tried another SF novel, *The Empire of Time,* but after ninety pages had run into serious outline trouble. Now I dug it out and saw both its problems and their solutions. But after just a few months' work on *Empire,* another idea occurred to me and I instantly started *Icequake.* Once finished, *Icequake* made the rounds of some New York publishers but didn't find a home. Neither did *Empire of Time.*

I showed them to Scott McIntyre of Douglas & McIntyre. He saw some potential in *Icequake,* and I heavily revised it. Meanwhile, less drastic revisions

made *Empire of Time* salable to Del Rey Books. Encouraged by these successes, I got into *Eyas* in the summer of 1977 and saw it develop as I'd hoped it would.

By the summer of 1979 I was not just published, I was making some surprising money. *Icequake* had sold to Futura, a British house, for 5,000 pounds; Bantam Books bought the North American paperback rights for $20,000, with another $20,000 for a sequel, *Tsunami.* And Bantam then offered $15,000 for *Eyas,* which I'd recently finished.

All these books had strong social and political elements. *Empire of Time* drew on the CIA scandals of the 1950s and '60s (and my desire to satirize the James Bond novels, which had been a guilty pleasure in college). It was also an attempt to respond to my brother Linc's withering comment: "All your heroes are so cool." My time-traveling hit man, Jerry Pierce, was a jerk. *Icequake* and *Tsunami* envisaged a right-wing, isolationist America in which the choice is between surviving as individuals or as members of a group. *Eyas* was about empire and oppression, and the power of the weak when they unite against the strong. These themes continued through all my novels, but I hope I avoided preachiness. I certainly sympathized with my villains, who were just trying to do what seemed right to them; they just didn't know, or care, how their use of power was hurting people.

But the success was mixed with family grief. In 1979 Vic was assaulted and killed by someone who broke into his Hollywood apartment intent on theft. At eighty-seven he was still a working actor, though very frail. The insurance enabled Mike and Pauline to get out of Los Angeles and buy a house in Vermont, where Pauline's older daughter had settled. But soon after they moved, Mike was diagnosed with pancreatic cancer. He fought it with amazing courage and good cheer, and died, in February 1981, with most of his family around him. He was only sixty-four, and I wish he had lived to see the rest of the century. He would have been appalled by the Reagan and Bush years, but he'd have loved fighting them—and using the Internet to do so. A lifelong ham radio operator, he would have taken to e-mail and the Web with huge interest and enjoyment.

In my less dramatic way, I was following in Mike's activist footsteps. I'd joined the New Democratic Party in 1972 when it won the BC provincial election, and spent years as a constituency-association foot soldier. In 1980 I ran for our local school board and won. It was a great experience to see how a school district operates, and I learned a lot. But BC was slipping into a recession, and one result of that was a sharp polarization between right and left. The right was all for cutting school spending and going back to some mythical Golden Age of low-paid teachers and obedient students. The left was trying to hang on to the gains made for teachers and students in the 1960s and '70s. When I ran for re-election in 1982, I was soundly whipped.

It may have been the single best thing that ever happened to my writing career. Like any other discredited politician, I went to the media. I'd already published a few items in the Vancouver *Province* newspaper, and now I approached them with a proposal for a weekly education column. They took me on, and the job was to last until 1994—well over five hundred columns. This was a wonderful experience that took me all over western Canada and led to a 1985 book, *School Wars.* A decade later I wrote another column-based book, *2020 Visions: The Futures of Canadian Education.* The column eventually changed into a more general one, enabling me to write about science, politics, the environment—whatever took my interest.

The column went into suspension in 1983, when Alice and I took our two daughters (then aged twelve and eight) to southern China. We spent five months at the Guangzhou Institute of Foreign Languages (now the Guangdong University of Foreign Studies) teaching English and experiencing a hell of a case of culture shock—not least when we took the hovercraft down the Pearl River to Hong Kong, which was like time-traveling between the nineteenth and twenty-first centuries.

But we made good friends and gained new perspectives not only on China but also on our own country. We loved the students, hated the *waiban* (foreign office) that looked after us, and saw just how grubby and forlorn a communist society could be—even one rapidly converting to "capitalism with Chinese characteristics." I gained high status from the students when I told them how my father had driven Norman Bethune—a huge hero in China—around New England in the late 1930s, raising money for the Spanish Loyalists. My status with the institute administration was less good (I was a complainer), and our students

were advised not to correspond with us after we returned home. Some did anyway, however, and I managed to get Capilano College to send the institute surplus textbooks every year until Tiananmen Square.

On our return in early 1984 I tried to write a political thriller about a violent change of government after the death of Deng Xiaoping, but after sixty pages I realized how little I'd really learned about China, and went back to science fiction and my education column.

During the mid-1980s I also wrote a social studies textbook about BC history, and a textbook on workplace writing that eventually became the commercially published *Communications Book.* It had started as a collection of handouts, and gradually grew into a full-length book. My colleagues and I revised it every couple of years, adding new material and dropping whatever no longer worked.

That was the most obvious link between teaching and writing, but not the only one. In many cases, my classes gave me ideas for writing, and the writing in turn became course material. Around 1980, I started teaching a course in freelance article writing, though I hadn't done many such articles. But to enhance my own credibility as a teacher, I did more freelancing, and sold most of what I wrote. These articles led in turn to the education column, and to other articles; I could draw on that experience in teaching my students. I also created and taught a course in "Marketing Commercial Fiction" (we had to call it marketing because the English department thought *writing,* as such, was their turf). This course required me to think in a more organized fashion about the craft of fiction, which I applied to my own work even while I taught it to my students.

In both courses I included an element as much for my own needs as for my students': every class would start with a "progress report" in which each of us had to describe what we'd written since the previous class. This was surprisingly effective at prodding everyone (including me) into putting something down on paper: a query letter, a couple of pages of a draft article, a few pages on the current novel-in-progress.

I had an ulterior motive in teaching these courses, though at first I didn't understand it myself. I was trying to find talented students and give them a boost and a direction, just as the Butlers and Trumbos and Ellins had helped me. It was as if I were seeking some kind of vindication for my own choice of career—to see others pursue writing as a career and not just a hobby. If that was what I was seeking, I guess I found it. Several of my students did go into journalism, or into writing fiction. One of them, Grace Green, has published over twenty novels, many of them translated into Spanish, German, Greek, and Dutch. If I could not join an existing society of writers, I could at least create such a society by training apprentices in the craft.

But the real society of writers arrived in a different form from what I had imagined. Starting in the late 1980s, I started serving as a "writer-in-electronic-residence" for students scattered from Toronto to the Arctic. I was fascinated by what my students sent me, but also by the nature of this new medium and what it could teach us about writing itself. By the mid-1990s I'd created and taught my own online writing course. I was also getting involved informally with a host of writers connected through the Internet. Without realizing it, I was becoming part of a "community of practice"—a voluntary association of people sharing interests.

Much of that community formed, ironically, because I couldn't run my commercial fiction course any more; in an age of budget cutbacks, it had become a luxury my college couldn't afford.

So I gathered the course handouts into a booklet and gave a one-day version: an introduction to the craft and business. I also posted them on the Internet. The handouts eventually went onto a Web site as the Fiction Writer's Page, and it began to attract writers from around the world. Many of them wrote to thank me, and I was soon reading pieces of their work and offering advice, just as Dalton Trumbo and the Butlers and Ellins had read and criticized my work. I had my society of writers: a librarian in Australia, an office clerk in Johannesburg, an ex-FBI agent in Ohio. I didn't make a cent from this work (and didn't want to), but it has been extraordinarily rewarding.

*

As the 1980s went on, I kept publishing novels—but with decreasing financial success. *Eyas,* which I still consider my best work, did very poorly with Bantam.

My next novel, *Brother Jonathan,* didn't interest Bantam at all, and it ended up with Ace at a fraction of the advances I'd made on my first novels. The same was true of *Lifter.* In the mid-1980s I was able to escape from Ace back to Del Rey, where a sympathetic editor republished *Eyas* and published two more novels based on *Empire of Time,* plus a space opera, *Gryphon.* When those novels did poorly, I pitched Lester del Rey on a fantasy novel, *Greenmagic.* It was fun to write, but like so many of my books it too failed to earn out its advance.

By 1990 I was eager to break out of genre. I tried a historical western based on California's Modoc War of 1872; it went nowhere. I tried a crime thriller with SF overtones, and it too failed to find a publisher. A Canadian house republished *Brother Jonathan* and *Lifter* as young adult titles, but sloppy editing allowed embarrassing numbers of typos; I wasn't too proud of them.

I had this consolation: I was writing what interested me, and most of it, after all, was getting into print. The only book I'd written for money, *Tsunami,* had been an unpleasant experience: two years of forcing a story into shape instead of writing a story that wanted to tell itself. *Redmagic,* a sequel to my first fantasy novel, turned out to be more sorcery than I was happy with, but it did pose some interesting technical challenges. I wasn't making money, or finding a large audience, but I was having fun.

In the mid-1990s, my career changed direction. The *Province* dropped my column in 1994. Much as I'd enjoyed writing it, I'd felt increasingly out of place in a tabloid moving sharply to the political right. A Vancouver weekly, the *Georgia Straight,* gave me opportunities to write much longer pieces on everything from charter schools to global warming.

After the publication of *Redmagic* in 1995, I couldn't seem to interest publishers in more fiction. I was also trying to keep up with the impact of computers in my own courses. So for several years I concentrated on journalism and articles about online education. Then, in 1997, Self-Counsel Press asked me for a book on writing science fiction and fantasy, and I used the Fiction Writer's Page materials (much expanded, revised, and adapted) as the basis for that book. It also contained much that I had learned from my online apprentices.

Meanwhile I had created a course in Web writing, which forced me to research the field and to think hard about this new medium. I was also drawing on the resources of the Web, and on professional Web writers—another community of practice. And again the course materials and the community of practice helped me to write another how-to book, *Writing for the Web*. It appeared first in 1999, and then in a second "Geeks'" edition in 2000. If it takes a village to raise a child, it also seems to take a community to create a book. That community can be very extensive: In September 2002, I gave a workshop in Web writing to seventy Brazilians in São Paulo. Even with the awkwardness of simultaneous translation, it was an enlightening experience—and some of the participants offered valuable insights that I hope to incorporate in a third edition of the book.

My experience with the Self-Counsel books, for which online research had been critical, got me thinking about print and electronic media in new ways. As I began to understand how hypertext works, I began to think about a hypertext version of *Deserters,* a novel I'd been working on for years—a novel about a Vietnam veteran who is experiencing flashbacks to various critical moments in his life. Rather than yank my hero arbitrarily backward and forward in time, I thought, I could let the reader explore his life in any sequence desired. Once the print version of the novel is complete, I hope to adapt it to hypertext.

That novel, *Deserters,* is only one of many projects I'm entangled in. Others include a revision of *The Communications Book* into a multimedia text; a collection of essays and articles about my online-education experiences; another collection of general essays and articles; and at least a couple of science-fiction novels.

Commercial publication of these books would be nice, but that's not the point. The essay collections are giveaways—I'm publishing them on my own Web site, free for the taking. I hope *Deserters* finds a commercial publisher, and the textbook, because they should reach wider audiences than I can achieve on my own site. I have other projects in mind as well: a science fiction novel about nanotech, another revision of the crime thriller, maybe a full-scale family history.

Has it been worth it? Well, I tell my students that writing is its own reward. It helps rewire your brain so that you see things better, you get interested in more

The author with his daughters Maggie (left) and Anna, Hong Kong, 1984

things, you articulate your thoughts more clearly, and therefore you live better. It's like walking your dog, I tell them. The dog benefits from the exercise and so do you. If you happen to find a quarter in the street while you're doing it, that's very nice. But if you go out again and you don't find another quarter, that doesn't mean you're a failure as a dog-walker.

In the summer of 2001, Michael Butler held a kind of reunion. He and his wife now lived in British Columbia, on Saltspring Island. They invited friends and relatives from across North America to celebrate the eighty-fifth birthday of Michael's mother Jean . . .

who had recently published her own memoir of the blacklist, *Refugees from Hollywood.* I saw my brother Linc for the first time in many years, Chris Trumbo, and most of the Butler sisters. (Chris and Michael became screenwriters, like their parents.) With these and other friends, some of whom I hadn't seen in forty years, the conversation resumed as if it had never been broken off. Jean was as bright and effervescent as ever, full of memories of our childhoods. She remembered reading "The Year of the Bat" in that long-ago Mexican summer.

And I had the rare joy of thanking her for setting me on my course.

BIOGRAPHICAL AND CRITICAL SOURCES:

BOOKS

St. James Guide to Science-Fiction Writers, St. James Press (Detroit, MI), 1996.

PERIODICALS

Analog Science Fact/Science Fiction, February, 1988, pp. 186-187; April, 1990, pp. 178-181.
Black Enterprise, June, 2001, Deanna Fay, "Of Prose and Code," p. 82.
Books in Canada, January, 1979; August-September, 1979.
Fantasy Review, January, 1985, p. 16; June, 1985, p. 27; October, 1986, Muriel Becker, review of *Lifter,* p. 31.
Quill and Quire, May, 1995, p. 48; August, 1995, p. 27.
Science Fiction Chronicle, March, 1987, review of *Lifter,* p. 43; May, 1988, p. 45; October, 1989, p. 43.
Science Fiction Review, November, 1985, p. 38.
Voice of Youth Advocates, October, 1985, Hal Hoover, review of *Brother Jonathan,* p. 268; October, 1992, p. 240.
Writer, May, 2001, Marc Anderson, review of *Writing for the Web,* p. 47; June, 2002, Sally Laturi, review of *Writing Science Fiction and Fantasy,* p. 55.

OTHER

Crawford Kilian's Home Page, http://www.capcollege.bc.ca/dept/cmns/crofpers.html/ (October 28, 2002).
Freelance Writing Web site, http://www.freelancewriting.com/ (October 28, 2002), interview.

Rest Stop Writers' Newsletter, http://www.geocities.com/rsw-news/kilian.html/ (January, 1999), Paige Hess, "Interview at the *Rest Stop* with Crawford Kilian."
Technical Editors' Eyrie Web site, http://www.jeanweber.com/books/kilian.htm/ (October 28, 2002), Jean Weber, review of *Writing for the Web.**

* * *

KIM, Myung Mi 1957-

PERSONAL: Born December 6, 1957, in Seoul, Republic of Korea; immigrated to the United States; daughter of Yong Ok and Soo Bok Kim; married Kevin Magee, June 18, 1988; children: Malcolm Song-ok. *Education:* Oberlin College, B.A., 1979; Johns Hopkins University, M.A., 1981; University of Iowa, M.F.A., 1986.

ADDRESSES: Office—Department of Creative Writing, School of Humanities, San Francisco State University, 1600 Holloway Ave., San Francisco, CA 94132-1722.

CAREER: Poet and educator. Chinatown Manpower Project, New York, NY, English-as-a-second-language (ESL) teacher, 1981-82; Stuyvesant High School, New York, NY, English teacher, 1983-84; University of Iowa, teaching-writing fellow, 1984-86; Luther College, director of student support services, 1987-91; San Francisco State University, San Francisco, CA, assistant professor, 1991—.

AWARDS, HONORS: Faculty affirmative action awards, San Francisco State University, 1992, 1993; Djerassi resident artist, 1993; Gertrude Stein Award for innovative North American Poetry, Sun & Moon Press, 1993, 1994; Edelstein-Keller writer-in-residence, University of Minnesota; Fund for Poetry award.

WRITINGS:

Under Flag (poems), Kelsey Street Press (Berkeley, CA), 1991.
The Bounty (poems), Chax Press (Minneapolis, MN), 1996.

Dura (poems), Sun ' Moon Press (Los Angeles, CA), 1998.

Commons (poems), University of California Press (Berkeley, CA), 2002.

Contributor to anthologies, including *Forbidden Stitch: An Asian American Women's Anthology,* Calyx Press, 1989, and *Anthology of Asian American Writing,* 1994, and to literary journals, including *Antioch Review, Ironwood, Hambone, Avec, Sulfur,* and *Conjunctions.*

SIDELIGHTS: Korean-born poet Myung Mi Kim's first collection, *Under Flag,* reflects the memories of hunger, violence, loss of self-esteem, and displacement she experienced during the U.S. occupation of Korea. The book focuses on her life before she immigrated to the United States at the age of nine, "old enough," said Karl Young in *American Book Review,* "to have a good sense of her native language and culture and the modes of thinking they impose; young enough to become proficient in her new language, but never quite at home in it or its correlative mindset. This gives rise to the major technique of the book, a careful modulation between degrees of fluency and difficulty of articulation." A number of Kim's poems are set in the United States.

Minnesota Review contributor Patricia A. Sakurai wrote that Kim's poems "are often marked by powerful understatement and haunted by irrecoverable loss and grief. Rather than rely solely on graphic detail, she uses the subtle and unexpected image to convey the landscape of war and penetrate the reader's conscience. . . . Her poems are a telling, though the act of telling is itself subject to doubt, emphasizing further the themes of transience and a shaken sense of certainty."

In *Multicultural Review,* Joseph Donahue commented that throughout *Under Flag* "historically specific scenes are interwoven with hallucinatory fragments, reminding us of poetry's oldest concerns with destruction, diaspora, and the preservation of the human figure from oblivion."

Kim's other collections include *The Bounty* and *Dura,* the latter a long poem divided into parts titled "Cosmography," "Measure," "Labors," "Chart," "Thirty and Five Books," "Progress in Learning," and

"Hummingbird." Portions of the book first appeared in literary journals. A *Publishers Weekly* reviewer said that in this experimental collection, Kim "finds ways to make her very personal relationship to issues of immigration and cultural severing inclusive."

"Some words strike this reader as unusual," commented Edgar C. Knowlton, Jr., in *World Literature Today,* "such as sept, trillium, burin, and motility, although they all are found in the English lexicon. One can only be favorably impressed by the eagerness with which this poet must have learned to control the mighty riches contained in English dictionaries."

Voice Literary Supplement contributor Ed Park, however, found the issue of language more problematic. "The anxiety of speech reaches near neurotic proportions in Kim's work," he wrote. "Her first book, *Under Flag,* charged the letters of her second language with doubt and possibility. . . . *Commons* begins with an 'Exordium,' a preparation for speech—but its relative order dissipates in the next section ('Lamenta'), a slow-motion explosion of mysterious numbers, anatomy lessons, and punctuation, unfolding in acres of white space." Park said that the final section, "Pollen Fossil Record," "shows Kim doing the critic's job of framing the fragments that have preceded it."

BIOGRAPHICAL AND CRITICAL SOURCES:

PERIODICALS

American Book Review, June, 1993, Karl Young, review of *Under Flag,* p. 21.

Minnesota Review, spring, 1992, Patricia A. Sakurai, review of *Under Flag,* pp. 97-101.

Multicultural Review, April, 1992, Joseph Donahue, review of *Under Flag,* p. 75.

Publishers Weekly, August 31, 1998, review of *Dura,* p. 69.

Voice Literary Supplement, May, 2002, Ed Park, review of *Commons.*

World Literature Today, spring, 1999, Edgar C. Knowlton, Jr., review of *Dura,* p. 389.*

*   *   *

KING, Godfré Ray
   See BALLARD, Guy W(arren)

KING, Lester S(now) 1908-2002

OBITUARY NOTICE—See index for *CA* sketch: Born April 18, 1908, in Cambridge, MA; died of heart failure October 6, 2002, in Chicago, IL. Physician, educator, and author. King made a name for himself as the author of books about the history and philosophy of medicine. A graduate of Harvard University, he studied both philosophy and medicine there, earning his M.D. in 1932. He then taught at Harvard and during the late 1930s was an assistant at the Rockefeller Institute for Medical Research. From 1940 to 1942 he worked as a pathologist at a Connecticut hospital while also teaching the subject at Yale University. During World War II he continued to work as a pathologist for the U.S. Army. After the war King spent the remainder of his career in Chicago, where he was a pathologist at Illinois Masonic Hospital until 1963 and a professor at the University of Illinois Medical Center until 1964. From 1963 to 1973 he was on the staff of the *Journal of the American Medical Association* as a senior editor, continuing as a contributing editor until 1978. As a writer, King was noted for his insistence on clear prose, and his desire to teach other physicians how to write more effectively led to his book *Why Not Say It Clearly? A Guide to Scientific Writing* (second edition, 1991). He was also the author of *The Growth of Medical Thought* (1963), *The Road to Medical Enlightenment, 1650-1695* (1970), *Medical Thinking: A Historical Preface* (1982), and *Transformations in American Medicine: From Benjamin Rush to William Osler* (1991), among other works.

OBITUARIES AND OTHER SOURCES:

PERIODICALS

Chicago Tribune, October 10, 2002, section 2, p. 8.

*   *   *

KING, Stella (Lennox) 1919-2002

OBITUARY NOTICE—See index for *CA* sketch: Born January 6, 1919, in Birmingham, England; died following a stroke October 29, 2002, in Watford, England. Journalist and author. King is best remembered as a writer for the diary page of the London *Evening Standard* and as a biographer. Educated at the Southern College of Art in Bournemouth, England, she was about to start a job as fashion correspondent for the *Bournemouth Times* when World War II began. She joined the Army Transport Services, where she became a captain defending her country from German bombs, and after the war married an air force officer, whom she would divorce in 1953. After her divorce she was hired by the *Evening Standard* to write for the diary page. In this position, King was noted for the contacts she built with politicians, royalty, and other journalists. She later moved to other papers, including the *Daily Express* and *Sunday Express*. While at the former, she wrote her first book with her second husband, the biography *Once upon a Time* (1960), which is about Antony Armstrong-Jones. Quitting her regular job, King became a freelancer for newspapers such as the *New York Times,* and she wrote two more biographies, *Princess Marina: Her Life and Times* (1969) and *Jacqueline, Pioneer Heroine of the Resistance* (1989), which is about French Resistance agent Yvonne Rudellat. In her later years King continued to quench her thirst for knowledge by studying law, learning how to fly an airplane, and becoming an expert fly-fisher.

OBITUARIES AND OTHER SOURCES:

PERIODICALS

Times (London, England), November 19, 2002, p. 34.

*   *   *

KINSELLA, Sophie

PERSONAL: Female.

ADDRESSES: Home—England. *Agent*—c/o Author Mail, Transworld Publishers Ltd./Black Swan, 61-63 Uxbridge Road, Ealing, London W5 5SA, England.

CAREER: Novelist. Former financial writer and journalist.

WRITINGS:

The Secret Dreamworld of a Shopaholic, Corgi (London, England), 2000, published as *Confessions of a Shopaholic,* Bantam Dell/Delta (New York, NY), 2001.

Shopaholic Abroad, Black Swan (London, England), 2001, published as *Shopaholic Takes Manhattan,* Dell (New York, NY), 2002.

Shopaholic Ties the Knot, Black Swan (London, England), 2002, Bantam Dell/Delta (New York, NY), 2003.

SIDELIGHTS: British novelist Sophie Kinsella is the creator of Rebecca "Becky" Bloomwood, the shopping-obsessed protagonist of a series of best-selling novels that began with *The Secret Dreamworld of a Shopaholic,* published in the United States as *Confessions of a Shopaholic.* Kinsella began her career as a financial journalist, a profession practiced by Bloomwood in the series. That is not the only similarity between the Kinsella and her leading lady, in fact.

Discussing *Confessions of a Shopaholic* in a 2000 interview with Lucy Dibdin for *Virgin.net,* Kinsella summarized the similarities: "It's not an autobiography, but there's a lot of Becky in me, and me in her," Kinsella told Dibdin. "I was a financial journalist, I used to sit at my desk dreaming of clothes when I should have been writing—and I do love shopping." Kinsella went on to tell Dibdin that shopping is "the ultimate power. . . . It's like the pursuit of pleasure." Kinsella may have had that philosophy in mind as she developed Bloomwood, whose obsession with shopping leads to tremendous credit difficulties. In fact, much of the plot in *Confessions of a Shopaholic* involves the twenty-five-year-old Bloomwood maneuvering through her world of debt. Bloomwood's problems largely stem from her insistence on upscale living in a fashionable London neighborhood. Although she is respected and admired by her peers because of her position as a financial writer for the London magazine *Successful Savings,* the job does not pay very much, and not enough to support Bloomwood's extravagant lifestyle. As a result, she hides bills rather than pay them. Kinsella injects humor into the tale, as Bloomwood tries a number of get-rich-quick schemes to compensate, including trying to marry several of London's richest bachelors. "Readers will have mixed feelings about *Confessions of a Shopaholic* as the story line is well written and has its amusing moments. The problem is that Becky has no depth," wrote Harriet Klausner of *BookBrowser.com.* Wanting to see a bit more substance in the plot, Suzanne Young in *Booklist* thought the story "would be more compelling if Becky were even slightly more self-aware."

The plot of *Shopaholic Takes Manhattan* is similar to the first work, except Bloomwood, who travels to America with her love interest, shops in the department stores of New York City rather than the boutiques of London. In this story, Bloomwood's spending problems threaten to derail a significant publishing opportunity, her new job as a television journalist, and her relationship with Luke Brandon, a rich advertising executive whom she hopes to marry. A contributor for *Kirkus Reviews* considered the book "a rehash" of the first installment in the series. "Kinsella creates some winning characters, but the credit card and shopping bag action is wearing dangerously thin," wrote a contributor for *Publishers Weekly.* The third installment of the series, *Shopaholic Ties the Knot,* was published in 2002.

BIOGRAPHICAL AND CRITICAL SOURCES:

PERIODICALS

Booklist, January 1, 2001, Suzanne Young, review of *Confessions of a Shopaholic,* p. 918.

Kiplinger's Personal Finance Magazine, June, 2001, review of *Confessions of a Shopaholic,* p. 28.

Kirkus Reviews, November 15, 2001, review of *Shopaholic Takes Manhattan,* p. 1570.

Money, July 1, 2001, review of *Confessions of a Shopaholic,* p. 121.

People, February 12, 2001, Victoria Balfour, review of *Confessions of a Shopaholic,* p. 41.

Publishers Weekly, December 18, 2000, review of *Confessions of a Shopaholic,* p. 53; December 10, 2001, review of *Shopaholic Takes Manhattan,* p. 49; March 11, 2002, Daisy Maryles and Dick Donahue, "12-Step Program Available? (Behind the Bestsellers)," review of *Shopaholic Takes Manhattan,* p. 18.

ONLINE

BookBrowser, http://www.bookbrowser.com/ (January 31, 2001), Harriet Klausner, review of *Confessions of a Shopaholic.*

Virgin.net, http://www.virgin.net/ (December 10, 2000), Lucy Dibdin, "It's Time to Lock up Your Credit Cards," review of *The Secret Dreamworld of a Shopaholic.**

KISMARIC, Carole 1942-2002

OBITUARY NOTICE—See index for *CA* sketch: Born April 28, 1942, in Orange, NJ; died of pancreatic cancer November 19, 2002, in New York, NY. Editor and author. Kismaric was an innovative editor of photography books and magazines and a curator of photography exhibitions. Although she studied psychology at Pennsylvania State University, where she earned her bachelor's degree in 1964, she decided to go into journalism after college. After working a few years as a reporter for United Press International and *Reporter* in Columbus, Ohio, and as a writer for magazine publisher Conde Nast, she joined the staff of Time-Life in 1969 as a picture researcher. She became an associate editor in 1973 and working on Time-Life's photography series. When she moved to Aperture in 1976, the publisher was still creating photography books in the old style in which one photo was displayed per page with no accompanying captions and surrounded by a frame, as if it were in a museum. Kismaric developed a more loosely structured, magazine-like format for the books she edited. She also edited *Aperture,* the publisher's quarterly magazine, until she left the company in 1985. In addition to her work as an editor, Kismaric was involved in a number of photography exhibitions in which her creative flair was also evident. In one exhibition, for example, photographs were accompanied by recording of people talking about how the photos had influenced them. She was especially active with exhibitions in the 1990s, and was co-curator of such traveling shows as "Forced out in Time," "Talking Pictures," and "Fame after Photography". In 1990 Kismaric founded, with Marvin Heiferman, the companies Lookout and Lookout Books, which produced photography books and exhibitions. In addition to the books she worked on for Time-Life and Aperture, Kismaric wrote and edited such works as *The Photography Catalogue* (1976) and the photography books *Forced Out: Refugees on the Move* (1988) and *Forced Out: The Agony of the Refugee in Our Time* (1989). As the wife of the late children's author and illustrator Charles Mikolaycak, Kismaric was also the coauthor of a number of books for children, including *The Boy Who Tried to Cheat Death* (1971), *Cinderella* (1993), and *The Mysterious Case of Nancy Drew and the Hardy Boys* (1998). More recently, she was the author of *The Art of the X-Files* (1998) and *Big Dogs, Little Dogs* (1998).

OBITUARIES AND OTHER SOURCES:

BOOKS

Who's Who in America, 56th edition, Marquis (New Providence, NJ), 2001.

PERIODICALS

Los Angeles Times, November 24, 2002, p. B16.
New York Times, November 20, 2002, p. A21.

*   *   *

KITA, Joe

PERSONAL: Male; married; children: two. *Education:* Lehigh University, B.A. (journalism), 1981.

ADDRESSES: Home—Lehigh, PA. *Agent*—c/o Rodale Press, 33 East Minor Street, Emmaus, PA 18098. *E-mail*—jkita1@rodalepress.com.

CAREER: Author and motivational speaker. Executive writer, *Men's Health,* Emmaus, PA.

WRITINGS:

(Editor) *Bicycling Magazine's Training for Fitness and Endurance,* Rodale (Emmaus, PA), 1990.
(With Lam Kam Chuen) *Wisdom of Our Fathers: Timeless Life Lessons on Health, Wealth, God, Golf, Fear, Fishing, Sex, Serenity, Laughter, and Hope,* Rodale (Emmaus, PA), 1999.
The Father's Guide to the Meaning of Life: What Being a Dad Has Taught Me about Hope, Love, Patience, Pride, and Everyday Wonder, Rodale (Emmaus, PA), 2000.
(Author of foreword) *Five Minutes to Orgasm Every Time You Make Love: Female Orgasm Made Simple,* by D. Claire Hutchins, JPS Publishing (Grand Prairie, TX), 2000.
Another Shot: How I Relived My Life in Less than a Year, Rodale (Emmaus, PA) 2001.
Accidental Courage: Finding out I'm a Bit Brave after All, Rodale (Emmaus, PA), 2002.

Also author of numerous articles on men's health.

ADAPTATIONS: Another Shot has been optioned by Turtleback Productions. Author's works have been recorded on audio cassette.

SIDELIGHTS: As executive writer for *Men's Health,* Joe Kita has been in a perfect position to offer advice. In his work for the magazine he has covered a variety of subjects pertinent to men's physical and emotional well-being, including an illustrated article on scars and the effect of bicycle seats on male fertility. But it was, in large part, the advice of someone else who put him in his present position. "The best advice I ever got," Kita told editor-in-chief David Zinczenko of *Men's Health,* "came after I had resigned the editorship of another magazine to take a lowly writing job at *Men's Health.* Many people interpreted it as a backward career step. But, as my friend Pat told me, you always want to be riding the train with the most momentum, even if you're in the caboose. Now I have no doubt it was the right move."

About three years after his father's death, Kita wrote *Wisdom of Our Fathers: Timeless Life Lessons on Health, Wealth, God, Golf, Fear, Fishing, Sex, Serenity, Laughter, and Hope* with Lam Kam Chuen. Kita interviewed 200 fathers across the country ranging in age from forty to ninety-two, some of them famous, some of them "ordinary dads." *Los Angeles Times* reviewer Shari Roan commented, "Perhaps the moral of the story for men is that Dad does know best. Just ask him."

In *The Father's Guide to the Meaning of Life: What Being a Dad Has Taught Me about Hope, Love, Patience, Pride, and Everyday Wonder,* Kita articulates the often transcendent experiences of being a father in order to offer guidance to other fathers. In distilling the lessons his two children have taught him, Kita comes up with accessible topics such as Play, Secrets, and God. "[T]his little guide is packed with food for thought and poignant moments that will be appreciated by fathers young and old," wrote a *Publishers Weekly* reviewer.

Despite his confidence and his avowed contentment with his life, Kita is a writer who looks back. In doing so he reassesses the choices he had made and helps direct his future. When he turned forty, "rather than shrugging off the past," wrote Jim Burns in *Library Journal,* "he made a list of twenty lingering disap-pointments and sought to set things right." The result was his book *Another Shot: How I Relived My Life in Less than a Year.* His regrets are both trivial (losing his hair) and profound (spending too little time with his children), but there are lessons to be learned throughout this journey. In revisiting the disappointment of being cut from his high school basketball team, Kita trains for six weeks before trying out for the team with kids half his age. And wanting to be a better partner to his wife of fifteen years, the couple attend a sex-therapy workshop. Kita engages a private detective to locate his first car, a 1979 Chevy Camaro. He hires a psychic to communicate with his father, who died suddenly, without giving Kita the chance to say farewell.

Some of his experiences remaking his life are more successful than others, but all in all, "Kita pulls it off with wit and aplomb," a *Publishers Weekly* contributor wrote of the essays. The book itself, however, has been a decided success. *Another Shot* sold for six figures, and the movie rights were optioned by Turtleback Productions. "It's a midlife crisis transformed into a parade of humorous, lively, and sometimes poignant opportunities," wrote Michael Reid in *Hope* magazine, adding that Kita proves "the power of its central premise: we can find ways to build a better life out of an imperfect past."

BIOGRAPHICAL AND CRITICAL SOURCES:

PERIODICALS

Kirkus Reviews, May 15, 1999, review of *Wisdom of Our Fathers: Timeless Life Lessons on Health, Wealth, God, Golf, Fear, Fishing, Sex, Serenity, Laughter, and Hope,* p. 790.

Library Journal, June 1, 2001, Jim Burns, review of *Another Shot: How I Relived My Life in Less than a Year,* p. 174.

Los Angeles Times, July 19, 1999, Shari Roan, review of *Wisdom of Our Fathers,* p. 6.

Men's Health, March, 1999, "Hired Gun," "The Whoopee Cushion," p. 61; May 2001, "A World of Hurt," p. 14; June, 2002, David Zinczenko, "The Son Also Advises," p. 20; July 2001, "Decisions, Decisions," p. 12; September, 2001, "Redford, Casanova, and Me," p. 16.

Publishers Weekly, May 29, 2000, review of *The Father's Guide to the Meaning of Life: What Being a Dad Has Taught Me about Hope, Love,*

Patience, Pride, and Everyday Wonder, p. 74; April 16, 2001, John F. Baker, "PB, Movie Deals for Kita," p. 16; April 23, 2001, review of *Another Shot* p. 67.

ONLINE

Hope, http://www.hopemag.com/ (December 31, 2001).
Joe Kita Web site, http://www.joekita.com (May 7, 2003).*

*   *   *

KITANO, Harry H(aruo) L. 1926-2002

OBITUARY NOTICE—See index for *CA* sketch: Born February 14, 1926, in San Francisco, CA; died of a stroke October 19, 2002, in West Los Angeles, CA. Sociologist, educator, and author. Kitano was an expert in race relations in America, especially with regard to the Japanese-American experience. During World War II he and his family were among the many Japanese Americans who were unjustly sent to internment camps by the U.S. government. After the war he worked for a time as a farm hand and musician before enrolling at the University of California at Berkeley, where he earned degrees in social work and sociology before receiving his doctorate in education and psychology in 1958. He then joined the staff of the University of California at Los Angeles (UCLA) as an assistant professor, eventually becoming a professor of social welfare and sociology. At UCLA he also served twice as the acting director of the Asian-American Studies Center. Kitano first gained national attention in 1969 with his book *Japanese Americans: The Evolution of a Subculture,* which was the first book to discuss the Japanese-American experience from a sociological point of view. He was also the author of several other books, including *Race Relations* (1974; Kitano was working on the sixth edition when he died), and *Generations and Identity: The Japanese American* (1993). Most recently, he coauthored the 1999 book *Achieving the Impossible Dream: How Japanese Americans Obtained Redress.*

OBITUARIES AND OTHER SOURCES:

BOOKS

Notable Asian Americans, Gale (Detroit, MI), 1995.

PERIODICALS

Los Angeles Times, October 24, 2002, p. B15.

*   *   *

KOSHIRO, Yukiko

PERSONAL: Female. Born in Yokohama, Japan; immigrated to United States. *Education:* Tokyo University of Foreign Studies, B.A.; University of Tokyo, M.A.; Columbia University, Ph.D. (history).

ADDRESSES: *Office*—Department of History, Pettengill Hall, Bates College, Lewiston, ME 04240. *Agent*—c/o Columbia University Press, 61 West 62nd St., New York, NY 10023. *E-mail*—ykoshiro@bates.edu.

CAREER: Williams College, Williamstown, MA, visiting assistant professor; East Asian Institute at Columbia University, New York, NY, visiting scholar, 2001-02; University of Notre Dame, Notre Dame, IN, assistant professor of history; Vassar College, Poughkeepsie, NY, visiting professor; Bates College, Lewiston, ME, visiting professor in department of history, 2002-03.

AWARDS, HONORS: Fulbright scholarship; Social Science Research Council postdoctoral fellowship; Association for Asian Studies research travel grant; Japan Foundation research fellowship; Masayoshi Ohira Memorial Prize for *Trans-Pacific Racisms and the U.S. Occupation of Japan.*

WRITINGS:

Trans-Pacific Racisms and the U.S. Occupation of Japan, Columbia University Press (New York, NY), 1999.

Also associate editor, *American-East Asian Relations.*

SIDELIGHTS: Yukiko Koshiro's *Trans-Pacific Racisms and the U.S. Occupation of Japan* attempts to analyze race as an important factor in U.S.-East Asian relations, specifically during the post-World War II American occupation of Japan from 1945 to 1951. Yuki Ichioka in *Pacific Historical Review* described the Japanese racial framework from which Koshiro writes as one of a "dual racial identity . . . within a Western-centered racial hierarchy" Ichioka explained, "the Japanese acknowledged and accepted this racial hierarchy. On the other hand, Japanese racism placed the Japanese people as superior to other Asians and colored people." Within this racial framework Koshiro presents a series of case studies illustrating what she terms the "codependence" of these racial identities and how they played out during the occupation.

Ichioka articulated Koshiro's motivation for such a study by writing, "only if we recognize our mutual racisms and how they have played out in U.S.-Japanese relations can we ever hope to transcend them and relate to each other on the basis of genuine equality and real mutual trust." And *Choice* reviewer J. C. Perry echoed the significance of addressing these issue: "Although the book focuses on the occupation period (1945-1951), its subject relates to a much broader sweep of experience."

BIOGRAPHICAL AND CRITICAL SOURCES:

PERIODICALS

Choice, November, 1999, J. C. Perry, review of *Trans-Pacific Racisms and the U.S. Occupation of Japan,* p. 603.

Pacific Affairs, fall, 2000, E. Patricia Tsurumi, review of *Trans-Pacific Racisms and the U.S. Occupation of Japan,* p. 442.

Pacific Historical Review, February, 2001, Yuji Ichioka, review of *Trans-Pacific Racisms and the U.S. Occupation of Japan,* p. 162.

ONLINE

Bates College Web site, http://www.bates.edu/ (May 7, 2003).

Columbia University Press Catalog Web site, http://www.cc.columbia.edu/cu/cup/catalog/ (February 9, 2000).*

L

LADD, Linda

PERSONAL: Married; husband's name, Bill; children: Laurel, Bill.

ADDRESSES: Home—MO. *Agent*—c/o Author Mail, Doubleday Book Club, 401 Franklin Ave., Garden City, NY 11530-5945. *E-mail*—lindaladd@pbmo.net.

CAREER: Writer.

WRITINGS:

Wildstar, Avon (New York, NY), 1984.

Moonspell, Avon (New York, NY), 1985.

Fireglow, Avon (New York, NY), 1986.

Dream Song, Avon (New York, NY), 1988.

Frost Fire (first novel in "Fire Trilogy"), Avon (New York, NY), 1990.

Midnight Fire (second novel in "Fire Trilogy"), Avon (New York, NY), 1991.

Dragon Fire (third novel in "Fire Trilogy"), Avon (New York, NY), 1992.

White Lily (first novel in "White Flower Trilogy"), Topaz (New York, NY), 1993.

White Rose (second novel in "White Flower Trilogy"), Topaz (New York, NY), 1994.

White Orchid (third novel in "White Flower Trilogy"), Topaz (New York, NY), 1995.

Lilacs on Lace, Topaz (New York, NY), 1996.

Forever, My Love, Topaz (New York, NY), 1997.

A Love So Splendid, Topaz (New York, NY), 1997.

A Love So Fine (sequel to *A Love So Splendid*), Topaz (New York, NY), 1999.

Running Scared, Doubleday Book Club (Garden City, NY), 2000.

Also author of *Midnight Fire* and *Silverswept.*

SIDELIGHTS: Linda Ladd is the author of historical romance novels. Her first, *Wildstar,* is set in the 1800s, it is the story of Starfire (Elizabeth), a blonde girl raised by Cheyenne Indians after the wagon train in which she was traveling was raided, leaving her the only survivor. On the night of her wedding to Lone Wolf, Wildstar is kidnapped by Logan "Tracker" Cord, who has been hired by her wealthy grandparents in St. Louis to find her. *West Coast Review of Books* contributor Suzy Nelson wrote that "this is a fun, romantic story that is easy to read and quite enjoyable." In a *Los Angeles Times Book Review* article, Kristiana Gregory called it "fun, but predictable."

Frostfire is set in 1871, and is the first novel of the "Fire Trilogy." Tyler MacKenzie travels to Chicago to recover what is rightfully hers. Railroad magnate Gray Kincaid's union regiment had trashed Rose Point, the family plantation, and as a result of his bankruptcy, her father had committed suicide. Gray bought Rose Point, and Tyler's plan is to swindle enough of his money to buy it back. Instead, Gray offers it to her as a wedding present, and Tyler, who marries him grudgingly, finally accepts that he is not only rich, but charming. Penny Kaganoff of *Publishers Weekly* reviewed the opener, saying that the story "is packed with subplots and supporting characters that keep the action percolating."

Ladd also wrote the "White Flower Trilogy," beginning with *White Lily,* which takes place during the U.S. Civil War. The Lily of the story is Lily Courtland, an Australian who is rescued from white slavers by Union spy Harte Delaney. Lily is on a search for her brother, Derek, who is working for the Confederacy as a blockade runner, helping bring supplies into the war-torn South, and who Harte is also trying to locate in order to imprison him. Lily is a clairvoyant, and she has been seeing visions of Harte for years, but she does not see his true reason for helping her. A *Publishers Weekly* contributor felt that "attitudes towards the people of color in this book go beyond historical accuracy to offensiveness."

Derek appears in *White Rose,* the heroine of which is Cassandra Delaney, an anthropologist working for the Smithsonian and also as a Confederate spy. When Derek is captured by Union soldiers, Cassandra plans his escape to the Caribbean, and her brother, a Yankee agent, arranges for her to be kidnapped by Derek and taken back to Australia to keep her out of trouble. Cassie is furious when she learns that they are not going to South Carolina as Derek had told her. However, her professional curiosity is aroused at each of the exotic ports of call at which they stop, and she and Derek become attracted to each other on the trip to Australia. A *Publishers Weekly* reviewer wrote that "the plot tends not to hang together in many places, dialogue is often stilted, and Derek is rather a cardboard hero, but their bizarre adventures do keep the pages turning."

In *White Orchid,* British Anjelica Blake and Nicholas Sedgwick have been married by proxy since they were ten. Now twenty, Anjelica, who has lived in India for the entire time, is about to be rescued from the court of a boy maharajah who has pronounced her a man so that she can be his advisor. Her rescuer is Stuart Delaney, a former Confederate agent who has been hired by the Sedgwicks to bring her back to England. By the time they convince the young ruler to let her go, the couple are in love, but because of Anjelica's married status, they remain separate for nearly two years.

Lilacs on Lace is set in seventeenth-century Scotland, where Ainsley Campbell is labeled a witch because of her powers and her unusual eyes. After her parents were murdered, her guardian, Hugh Campbell, placed the child Ainsley in a convent where she was educated.

Now a young woman, she is taken from the convent by the handsome Rodric MacDonald, who she first believes has been sent to bring her to meet the man to whom she has been betrothed, but who she soon discovers is a member of an enemy clan believed to have been responsible for the death of her parents. Rodric tells Ainsley that her father is actually alive and that he has promised her hand in marriage to him. She doesn't believe his story but soon finds out that she is the connection between the two clans. A *Publishers Weekly* contributor called *Lilacs on Lace* "a rousing story filled with vivid emotion, plot twists, memorable characters, and period color."

BIOGRAPHICAL AND CRITICAL SOURCES:

PERIODICALS

Los Angeles Times, June 10, 1984, Kristiana Gregory, review of *Wildstar,* p. 6.
Publishers Weekly, February 23, 1990, Penny Kaganoff, review of *Frostfire,* p. 213; July 12, 1993, review of *White Lily,* p. 74; May 9, 1994, review of *White Rose,* p. 68; March 20, 1995, review of *White Orchid,* p. 55; May 20, 1996, review of *Lilacs on Lace,* p. 255.
West Coast Review of Books, September, 1984, Suzy Nelson, review of *Wildstar,* p. 55.

ONLINE

Romance Reader, http://www.theromancereader.com/ (December 27, 1998), Meredith Moore, review of *A Love So Fine.**

*   *   *

LAÍN ENTRALGO, Pedro 1908-2001

PERSONAL: Born February 15, 1908, in Urrea de Gaén, Spain; died 2001; married Milagro Martínez Prieto, 1934. *Education:* Attended universities of Zaragoza, Valencia, Madrid, and Vienna.

CAREER: Medical historian, essayist, playwright, and anthropologist. Madrid University, Madrid, Spain, professor of the history of medicine, beginning 1942, rector of the university, 1951-56.

MEMBER: Royal Spanish Academy, Royal National Academy of Medicine, Royal Academy of History, Akademy der Wissenschaften (Heidelberg, Germany).

AWARDS, HONORS: Premio Nacional de Teatro, 1970; Premio Montaigne, 1975; Gran Cruz de la Orden Civil de Alfonso X el Sabio, 1978; Gran Cruz de la Orden Civil de Sanidad, 1980; Premio Aragón, 1984; Premio Internacional Menéndez Pelayo, 1991; Premio Internacional de Ensayo Jovellanos, 1999, for *Qué es el hombre: evolución y sentido de la vida*; honorary professor, University of Santiago, Chile, Université de Toulouse, and Universidad de San Marcos, Peru.

WRITINGS:

Medicina e historia, Escorial (Madrid, Spain), 1941.

Los valores morales del nacionalsindicalismo, Editora Nacional Madrid (Madrid, Spain), 1941.

Estudios de historia de la medicina y de antropología médica, Escorial (Madrid, Spain), 1943.

La generación del noventa y ocho, [Madrid, Spain], 1945, 2nd edition, Espasa-Calpe (Madrid, Spain), 1997.

Vestigios: ensayos de crítica y amistad, Ediciones y Publicaciones Españolas (Madrid, Spain), 1948.

España como problema, Aguilar (Madrid, Spain), 1949.

La universidad en la vida española, Publicaciones de la Universidad de Madrid (Madrid, Spain), 1951.

Menéndez Pelayo, Espasa-Calpe (Buenos Aires, Argentina), 1952.

Sobre la universidad hispánica, Cultura Hispánica (Madrid, Spain), 1953.

Menéndez Pelayo: historia de sus problemas intelectuales, Taurus (Madrid, Spain), 1954.

El libro como fiesta, Instituto de España (Madrid, Spain), 1955.

La espera y la esperanza: historia y teoría del esperar humano, Alianza (Madrid, Spain), 1957.

La curación por la palabra en la antigüedad clásica, Revista de Occidente (Barcelona, Spain), 1958, translation by L. J. Rather and John M. Sharp published as *The Therapy of the Word in Classical Antiquity,* Yale University Press (New Haven, CT), 1970.

Ejercicios de comprensión, Taurus (Madrid, Spain), 1959.

Grandes medicos, Salvat (Barcelona, Spain), 1961.

Enfermedad y pecado, Toray Barcelona (Barcelona, Spain), 1961.

Miguel Angel y el cuerpo humano, Magisterio Español, (Madrid, Spain), 1964.

La relación médico-enfermo: historia y teoría, Revista de Occidente (Madrid, Spain), 1964, translation by Frances Partridge published as *Doctor and Patient,* McGraw-Hill (New York, NY), 1969.

Una y diversa España, Edhasa (Barcelona, Spain), 1967.

Entre nosotros: comedia dramática (play), Espasa-Calpe (Madrid, Spain), 1969.

El problema de la universidad: reflexiones de urgencia, Cuadernos para el Diálogo (Madrid, Spain), 1967.

Gregorio Marañón: vida, obra y persona, Espasa-Calpe (Madrid, Spain), 1969.

A qué llamamos España, Espasa-Calpe (Madrid, Spain), 1971.

Historia de la medicina, Salvat (Barcelona, Spain), 1973.

Descargo de conciencia (1930-1960), Seix Barral (Barcelona, Spain), 1976.

La aventura de leer, Espasa-Calpe (Madrid, Spain), 1964.

Antropología de la esperanza, Guadarrama (Madrid, Spain), 1978.

Mas de cien españoles, Planeta (Barcelona, Spain), 1981.

La medicina actual, Dossat Madrid (Madrid, Spain), 1981.

Teoría y realidad del otro, Alianza Editorial (Madrid, Spain), 1983.

Antropología médica para clínicos, Salvat (Barcelona, Spain), 1984.

Teatro del mundo, Espasa-Calpe (Madrid, Spain), 1986.

Ciencia, técnica y medicina, Alianza Universidad (Madrid, Spain), 1986.

El cuerpo humano: Oriente y Grecia Antigua, Espasa-Calpe (Madrid, Spain), 1987.

La medicina hipocrática, Alianza Editorial (Madrid, Spain), 1987.

La antropología en la obra de Fray Luis de Granada, Consejo Superior de Investigaciones Científicas (Madrid, Spain), 1988.

Cuerpo y alma: estructura dinámica del cuerpo humano, Espasa-Calpe (Madrid, Spain), 1991.

Tan sólo hombres, preface by Ricardo Doménech, Espasa-Calpe (Madrid, Spain), 1991.

El cuerpo humano: teoría actual, Espasa-Calpe (Madrid, Spain), 1991.

Esperanza en tiempo de crisis: Unamuno, Ortega, Jaspers, Bloch, Marañón, Heidegger, Zubiri, Sartre, Moltmann, Galaxia Gutenberg (Barcelona, Spain), 1993.

Creer, esperar, amar, Galaxia Gutenberg (Barcelona, Spain), 1993.

Sobre la amistad, Círculo de Lectores (Barcelona, Spain), 1994.

Teatro y vida: doce calas teatrales en la vida del siglo XX, Galaxia Gutenberg (Barcelona, Spain), 1995.

Alma, cuerpo, persona, Galaxia Gutenberg (Barcelona, Spain), 1995.

Idea del hombre, Galaxia Gutenberg (Barcelona, Spain), 1996.

El problema de ser cristiano, Galaxia Gutenberg (Barcelona, Spain), 1997.

Hacia la recta final: revisión de una vida intellectual, Galaxia Gutenberg (Barcelona, Spain), 1998.

La historia clínica: historia y teoría del relato patográfico, Triacastela (Madrid, Spain), 1998.

Ensayistas Hispánicos: Españoles de tres generaciones, Real Academia de la Historia (Madrid, Spain), 1998.

Qué es el hombre: evolución y sentido de la vida, Nobel (Oviedo, Spain), 1999.

Author of numerous prefaces and forewords; provided editorial assistance in the fields of the history of medicine, ethics, theater, philosophy, and the nature of Spanish culture.

SIDELIGHTS: Spanish physician and medical historian Pedro Laín Entralgo contributed much to the study of medicine and the humanities. Although he wrote widely, covering history, philosophy, and culture—and even penning some theatre—"the goal of [Laín Entralgo's] life's work, by his own admission, has consisted of attaining a systematic medical anthropology—a scientific and philosophical cognition of man insofar as he is a healthy being, susceptible to illness, ill, curable, and mortal," Nelson R. Orringer wrote in *Letras Peninsulares.* Over his nearly sixty-year writing career, Laín Entralgo wrote many books in pursuit of this goal, including his first, *Medicina i historia:* others included the work sometimes considered to be his masterpiece, *La historia clínica,* and his massive 1984 publication, the culmination of his years of research titled *Antropología médica para clínicos.*

Laín Entralgo's writings were often influenced by his Catholic faith. In some of his early works, he wrote about the need to Christianize science and to relate traditional Catholic values to modern Spanish culture. One of these books, *La espera y la esperanza,* is a response, from a Catholic viewpoint, to the pessimistic, nihilistic existential philosophies gaining currency in Europe by the mid-twentieth century. A contributor to the *Colombia Dictionary of Modern European Literature* called this work "probably his most profound book."

As a member of the nationalist, right-wing Falange party during the 1936-39 Spanish Civil War, Laín Entralgo was allied with fascist General Francisco Franco. This meant that Entralgo, unlike many of his fellow intellectuals who supported the Spanish monarchy, did not go into exile during or after the war. However, during the 1950s Laín Entralgo broke with Franco's regime and became more politically left-leaning. This progression of thought can be seen in some of his books, including one of his most famous works, *La generación del noventa y ocho,* which was first published in 1945. In this meditation on Spanish culture, while Laín Entralgo has not abandoned his Nationalist and Catholic philosophy, he now draws on the thoughts of more liberal thinkers in making his arguments. In 1954, when students began to protest Franco's regime, Laín Entralgo wrote in support of them, and in 1956 he resigned from his position as rector of the University of Madrid to protest Franco's curtailments of freedom of thought in Spanish universities.

BIOGRAPHICAL AND CRITICAL SOURCES:

BOOKS

Paolini, Gilbert, editor, *La Chispa '89: Selected Proceedings,* Tulane University Press (New Orleans, LA), 1989.

Paolini, Gilbert, editor, *La Chispa '93: Selected Proceedings,* Tulane University Press (New Orleans, LA), 1993.

Fernandez Jimenez, Juan, editor, *Estudios en homenaj e a Enrique Ruiz-Fornells,* Asociacion de Licenciados & Doctores Espanoles en Estados Unidos (Erie, PA), 1990.

PERIODICALS

American Journal of Psychoanalysis, June, 1990, p. 17.

Choice, September, 1970, review of *Doctor and Patient,* p. 882; October, 1970, review of *The Therapy of the Word in Classical Antiquity,* p. 59.

Cuadernos de Investigacion Filologica, May-December, 1983, Gabriel Maria Verd, "'Vestigios,' el libro mas humano de Laín," pp. 183-198.

Cuadernos Hispanoamericanos, Volume 72, 1967, Ricardo Doménech, "Primera cronica del teatro de Laín," pp. 218-233; Volume 269, 1972, Eduardo Tijeras, "El tema de la amistad en Laín Entralgo," pp. 349-352; October, 1983, Diego Gracia Guillen, interview with Laín Entralgo, pp. 11-32; August-September, 1987, Maria Manent, "Como conoci a Laín," pp. 59-60, Agustin Albarracion Teulon, "Pedro Laín Entralgo," pp. 61-77, Franco Meregalli, "Pedro Laín en 1948," pp. 79-86, Elena Hernandez Sandoica, "Laín en la Universidad de Madrid," pp. 87-112, Antonio Buero Vallejo, "Un hombre ante su espejo," pp. 113-126, Francisco Vega Diaz and Pedro Laín Entralgo, "Al cumplirse diez anow de Descargo de conciencia," pp. 127-136, Amancio Sabugo Abril, "Para una antropologia de la otredad," pp. 139-155, Blas Matamoros, "El hombre, esa enfermedad," pp. 165-172, Olegario Gonzalez de Cardedal, "Encuentro memoria, esperanza," pp. 183-194, Mariano Yela, "El conductismo explicativo y comprensive de Laín," pp. 194-201, Francisco R. Adrados, "Laín, los griegos y algunas reflexiones," pp. 203-210, Antonio Tovar, "Pedro Laín y la cultura griega," pp. 211-217, Donald W. Blesnick, "El teatro de Pedro Laín Entralgo," pp. 218-232, Jose L. Abellán, "Laín, filosofo de la cultura espanola," pp. 421-456, Antonio Orozco Acuaviva, "Aprozimacion al hispanoamericanismo de Laín," pp. 457-466, Jose Vidal Bernabeu, "Laín Entralgo y su vision del '98," pp. 467-496; Carlos Alfieri, interview with Laín Entralgo, pp. 17-27.

Insula, April, 1998, Jose M. Jover Zamora, "A que llamamaos España," pp. 17-19, Carlos Seco Serrano, "El mensaje de España como problema," pp. 21-22, Augustin Albarracin Teulon, "La España posible de Pedro Laín," pp. 26-27.

Letras Peninsulares, fall, 1988, Nelson R. Orringer, "Faith, Hope, and Love: Stages of Laín Entralgo's Scientific Evolution," pp. 133-150; winter, 1989, Nelson R. Orringer, "A la luz de Marte," p. 371.

Ometeca, Volume 1, number 1, 1989, Nelson R. Orringer, "Making the Body Human: Ideas Published and Unpublished of Laín Entralgo," pp. 108-141.

Papeles de son Armadans, Volume 56, 1970, "El humanismo de Pedro Laín Entralgo," pp. 101-118.

Razon y Fe, May, 1998, Francisco A. Marcos Marin, "Pedro Laín Entralgo: Mas alla de la experiencia," pp. 501-506.

Revista de Ideas Esteticas, Volume 32, 1974, Fermin de Urmenta, "Sobre estetica Brechtiana," pp. 245-250.

Revista Hispanica Moderna, December, 1992, Carlos Schwalb, "Castilla y una hora de España de Azorin como expresion de la Generacion del '98," pp. 181-192.

Thought, spring, 1970, Thomas Mermall, "Spain's Philosopher of Hope," pp. 103-120.

Times Literary Supplement, February 20, 1969, review of *El problema de la universidad,* p. 193.

Yale Review, June, 1970, review of *The Therapy of the Word in Classical Antiquity,* p. 59.

OTHER

Premio Aragón Web site, http://www.aragob.es/ (April 24, 2002), article about Laín Entralgo.

OBITUARIES:

OTHER

Pais Web site, http://www.elpais.es/ (November 6, 2001).*

*   *   *

LAMB, Patricia Clare 1935-

PERSONAL: Born November 14, 1935, in Houston, TX; daughter of Hugh R. and Margaret (McKeon) Lamb. *Education:* University of St. Thomas, B.A., 1957; graduate study at University of Houston, 1959-65. *Politics:* Democrat. *Religion:* Roman Catholic. *Hobbies and other interests:* Genealogy.

ADDRESSES: Home—3614 Montrose Blvd., #405, Houston, TX 77006-4651.

CAREER: Poet.

MEMBER: Academy of American Poets.

WRITINGS:

POETRY

Why Horatio, Harbottle Press (Houston, TX), 1985.
Dwelling, Harbottle Press (Houston, TX), 1988.

All Men by Nature, Harbottle Press (Houston, TX), 1993.

The Long Love: New and Collected Poems, 1957-1998, Harbottle Press (Houston, TX), 1998.

WORK IN PROGRESS: A collection of new poetry; research on Henry James and other literary topics.

*   *   *

LEIGH, Amy
    See BEAGLEY, Brenda E.

*   *   *

LEVINE, Laura (Sue) 1943-

PERSONAL: Born July 23, 1943 in Brooklyn, NY; daughter of Jacob and Ann (Goldberg) Levine. *Education:* Barnard College, L.B., 1965. *Hobbies and other interests:* Swimming, calligraphy.

ADDRESSES: Office—c/o Kensington Books, 850 Third Ave., New York, NY 10022.

CAREER: Television film script and novel writer. Creator of the characters Count Chocula and Frankenberry for General Mills Cereal Co.

MEMBER: Writers Guild of America West, Society for Calligraphers.

WRITINGS:

(With Dick Chodkowski) *Mr. Wrong, A Guide to the Least-Eligible Bachelors in America,* Pinnacle (New York, NY), 1984.

This Pen for Hire: A Jaine Austen Mystery, Kensington Books (New York, NY), 2002.

Last Writes: A Jaine Austen Mystery, Kensington Books (New York, NY), 2003.

Author of television scripts for various series, including *The Bob Newhart Show, Mary Hartman, Mary Hartman, Three's Company, Laverne and Shirley, The Jeffersons, Good Times,* and others.

SIDELIGHTS: Laura Levine knows what makes people laugh. For years she made audiences laugh with her television comedies, which include episodes and pilots for sitcoms, such as *Three's Company, The Bob Newhart Show,* and *The Jeffersons.* But because she worked behind the scenes, her name was not well known. Even with the publication of *Mr. Wrong: A Guide to the Least-Eligible Bachelors in America,* Levine did not achieve the recognition for which she had the potential. That all changed with the appearance of her debut novel, *This Pen for Hire.*

Levine's foray into the mystery genre—with a comedic twist—has created a solid fan base for the author. The fictional premise lends itself to humor: freelancer Jaine Austen (her mother loved English, but was not so good at spelling) makes her living writing personal ads and commercial brochures as well as love letters. When she gets a request to write a letter from client Howard Murdoch, she accepts, never imagining it will lead to involvement in murder. Geeky Howard longs for a date with the woman of his dreams—a gorgeous fitness instructor named Stacy Lawrence. Much to everyone's surprise, Stacy agrees to a Valentine's Day date. But when Harold arrives for the date, he finds Stacy bludgeoned to death with a ThighMaster.

Jaine feels some responsibility for Harold, who is the primary suspect, so she begins to do some digging. She discovers that, beauty aside, Stacy was not well liked. She appeared to be bisexual. She had affairs with married men. Levine imbues her heroine with a sense of humor that keeps her forging ahead, even when her life is in danger. A *Publishers Weekly* critic praised the novel, noting that "Levine delivers the goods, and readers who appreciate a heroine with wry, self-deprecating humor will hope Jaine soon gets caught up in another murder."

BIOGRAPHICAL AND CRITICAL SOURCES:

PERIODICALS

Kirkus Reviews, March 1, 2002, review of *This Pen for Hire: A Jaine Austen Mystery,* p. 293.

Library Journal, April 1, 2002, Rex E. Klett, review of *This Pen for Hire,* p.146.

Publishers Weekly, March 25, 2002, review of *This Pen for Hire,* p. 44.*

LEVY, Constance 1931-

PERSONAL: Born May 8, 1931, in St. Louis, MO; daughter of Samuel (a clothing store proprietor) and Esther (a homemaker; maiden name, Seigel) Kling; married Monroe D. Levy (a physicist), February 15, 1953; children: Robert, Carol Levy Charles, Kenneth, Donald, Edward. *Education:* Washington University (St. Louis, MO), B.A., 1952, M.A., 1974. *Politics:* Independent. *Religion:* Jewish.

ADDRESSES: Home—58 Frontenac Estates, St. Louis, MO 63131.

CAREER: Webster Groves School District, Webster Groves, MO, teacher, 1952-53; Ritenour School District, St. Louis, MO, teacher, 1953-54; Washington University, St. Louis, MO, supervisor of student teachers, 1974-75; Missouri Arts Council, Writers in the Schools program, St. Louis, children's poet, 1975-81; Harris-Stowe State College, St. Louis, MO, adjunct instructor of children's literature, 1980-82. Freelance poet in schools, 1981-92; member of commission board, Brodsky St. Louis Jewish Library, 1989-93; guest speaker in schools and educational conferences, 1991—.

MEMBER: International Reading Association, Society of Children's Book Writers and Illustrators, American Library Association, National Council of Teacher of English, Authors Guild.

WRITINGS:

I'm Going to Pet a Worm Today and Other Poems, illustrated by Ronald Himler, Macmillan (New York, NY), 1991.
A Tree Place and Other Poems, illustrated by Robert Sabuda, Margaret K. McElderry Books (New York, NY), 1994.
When Whales Exhale, and Other Poems, illustrated by Judy LaBrasca, Margaret K. McElderry Books (New York, NY), 1996.
A Crack in the Clouds and Other Poems, illustrated by Robin Bell Corfield, Margaret K. McElderry Books (New York, NY), 1998.
Splash!: Poems of Our Watery World, illustrated by David Soman, Orchard Books (New York, NY), 2002.
The Story of Red Rubber Ball, illustrated by Hiroe Nakata, Harcourt (San Diego, CA), in press.

Work represented in several periodicals, including *Cricket* and *Instructor,* and anthologies, including *Puddle Wonderful, Twentieth-Century American Poetry,* edited by Jack Prelutsky, *Knock at a Star,* revised edition, edited by X. J. Kennedy, and *Opening Days: Sports Poems,* edited by Lee Bennett Hopkins.

SIDELIGHTS: Like many poets, Constance Levy takes writing poetry seriously; thus her verse for children, published in a handful of collections, reflects both her talent for choosing topics that appeal to young readers and her careful attention to external and internal rhyme, rhythm, alliteration, and assonance. As her book titles suggest, Levy's poems often deal with nature. *A Crack in the Clouds and Other Poems* deals with things a person can observe overhead, while *Splash!: Poems of Our Watery World* treats water in all its guises. Although the topics are commonplace, Levy's treatment is not trite, claim reviewers. By drawing on her own childhood encounters, she re-experiences these things and events through verse in the fresh and exuberant ways that children perceive natural objects and phenomena, often for the first time. Reviewers have consistently praised Levy's poems for their accessible yet creative language. Upon the debut of *I'm Going to Pet a Worm Today and Other Poems,* a *Kirkus Reviews* critic praised Levy for her "clear eye," "fresh voice," and "graceful cadences." *A Tree Place and Other Poems* elicited praise from *Horn Book*'s Nancy Vasilakis, who noted that Levy composes poems "that are accessible without writing down to her young readers," and *School Library Journal*'s Meg Stackpole, who commented positively on the author's "apt metaphors and vivid imagery."

Fireworks, icicles, and comets number among the topics in Levy's *A Crack in the Clouds,* which, according to John Peters of *Booklist,* demonstrates the poet's "consistently distinct voice and . . . lively imagination." Likewise, Margaret Bush, writing in *School Library Journal,* praised the poems' "beauty and humor." With *Splash!,* Levy gives readers reasons to celebrate water in what *Booklist*'s Shelle Rosenfeld dubbed "an accessible, charming collection." Perhaps *School Library Journal*'s Kathleen Whalin summed up the appeal of Levy's verse best in her review of *When Whales Exhale and Other Poems*: "To read Levy is to see the wonder of the everyday world."

About her career as a poet of children's verse, Levy once told *CA,* "I'm both a new author and an old one, a grandmother with a first book published in 1991 and an 'old,' occasionally published poet with poems in teacher's educational journals, *Cricket* magazine, and anthologies.

"I would never have wondered about how I became a poet except that children I meet as a visiting poet frequently ask that question. And the only answer I can provide, for them and for myself, is that I don't really know, but I think I always was. As a child I was drawn to poetry and loved hearing my mother recite poems for me that she learned when she was young. It always seemed that the poem I read or listened to was speaking to me. I could see it and feel it. The words made music and danced and played games with each other and stirred my senses. I have never stopped loving poetry, especially poetry for children. Poems are habit-forming, you know. Once you have a good taste of a flavor that suits you, you want more and more, and the pleasures stay with you always.

"My writing years began, as I recall, the day I was able to write the words, at around age six; I was at my creative best from ages six through ten or eleven. It was so easy then. Poems seemed to turn themselves on and bubble and flow onto the paper. The wonderful feeling of getting a poem 'right' nourished my spirit then as it does now. Through high school and college I enjoyed reading poetry but did little writing. Becoming a primary grade teacher and then a mother helped turn the spigot back on. Of course, it has never again been so easy to please myself or catch the 'flow' as it was in those early years when children all possess that special magic. I work slowly now and I'm a stern editor of my own work, often working and reworking even a small poem until it begs for mercy, and I have to put it aside for another time.

"Many years after that 'magic' time of childhood, when I received my master's degree in education, I was determined to do my part to keep that magic from fading and to use it to enrich the educational process. Instead of becoming a reading specialist as planned, I became a poet in the schools for the Missouri Arts Council and engaged children and teachers in poetry workshops. It was obvious that children of all abilities thrived on this kind of reading, writing, and talking in poetry workshops. Teachers who continued incorporating poetry in the curriculum were enthusiastic and well rewarded for their efforts. After leaving the Arts Council program, I continued as a freelance poet in

the schools, and am continuing to share poetry now as a published poet. I still go into the schools as an author and teach occasional workshops. I sometimes feel that I am a 'Johnny Appleseed' for poetry (a 'Connie' Appleseed?).

"When you read a poet's work, you peek inside her or him, and I am no exception. As a writer I reveal myself in my poems, not intentionally, but because poetry is a natural expression of what the poet thinks, feels, and observes. It is me as silly, thoughtful, wondering, playing, discovering. If curiosity really 'killed', I'd be long gone, because I like to poke around to find the how and why of things, never tire of watching bugs go about their bug business and, yes, I really did 'pet' a worm. I love the out of doors and am constantly discovering and rediscovering it, as children do. I feel a special rapport with children and especially enjoy writing about the kinds of things they respond to, ordinary things that adults sometimes don't really 'see' for all our modern distractions."

Reflecting on the experience of sharing her poetry with children and adult audiences, Levy once told *CA*: "The children (and adults) enjoy the sharing of observations, feelings, and sometimes technique, all of which serves to bring them closer to my poems and how poetry is made, and stimulates them to write their own. My poems are 'me,' and I want them to be 'them' and to feel free to play with ideas and words and join in the 'game' of language."

BIOGRAPHICAL AND CRITICAL SOURCES:

BOOKS

Something about the Author Autobiography Series, Volume 22, Gale (Detroit, MI), 1996.

PERIODICALS

Booklist, September 1, 1994, Carolyn Phelan, review of *A Tree Place and Other Poems,* p. 38; December 15, 1996, Hazel Rochman, review of *When Whales Exhale and Other Poems,* p. 723; January 1, 1999, John Peters, review of *A Crack in the Clouds and Other Poems,* p. 860; April 1, 2002, Shelle Rosenfeld, review of *Splash! Poems of Our Watery World,* p. 1322.

Bulletin of the Center for Children's Books, February, 1992, Betsy Hearne, review of *I'm Going to Pet a Worm Today and Other Poems,* p. 161; March, 1994, Betsy Hearne, review of *The Tree Place and Other Poems,* p. 225.

Horn Book, May, 1994, Nancy Vasilakis, review of *A Tree Place and Other Poems,* pp. 329-330; July, 2002, Roger Sutton, review of *Splash!,* p. 479.

Horn Book Guide, spring, 1997, review of *When Whales Exhale and Other Poems,* p. 153.

Kirkus Reviews, September 1, 1991, review of *I'm Going to Pet a Worm Today,* p. 1162; April 1, 1994, review of *A Tree Place and Other Poems,* p. 481.

School Library Journal, April, 1994, Meg Stackpole, review of *A Tree Place and Other Poems,* p. 140; December, 1996, Kathleen Whalin, review of *When Whales Exhale and Other Poems,* p. 131; December, 1998, Margaret Bush, review of *A Crack in the Clouds and Other Poems,* p. 139; May, 2002, Jane Marino, review of *Splash!,* pp. 139-140.

*　　*　　*

LILIENHEIM, Henry 1908-2002

OBITUARY NOTICE—See index for *CA* sketch: Born March 8, 1908, in Warsaw, Poland; died of respiratory arrest December 12, 2002, in Glencoe, IL. Attorney and author. Lilienheim was a survivor of the Holocaust who later wrote about his experiences in his autobiography. After receiving a master's degree in engineering from the École Superieure in France in 1939, he returned to his native Warsaw and was captured by the Germans after the Nazis invaded Poland. Although he and his wife were released when she faked a pregnancy, they were later imprisoned again and sent to separate concentration camps. After Lilienheim was liberated from Dachau in 1945 and his wife escaped from Magdeburg, they spent several months searching for each other. They found each other later that year and after the war spent four years living in Munich. In 1949 the Lilienheims moved to New York City, where he got a job as a translator for the law firm Langner, Parry, Card & Langner (now Landas & Parry). He was transferred to Chicago in 1956, where he earned his law degree from John Marshall Law School in 1960; he then worked as a patent attorney and translator in Chicago. After his daughter,

Irene, was born, Lilienheim had a desire to share his story about the war with his child. He wrote his tale down, but did not publish *The Aftermath: A Survivor's Odyssey through War-torn Europe* until 1994. His daughter, the filmmaker Irene Angelico, made a documentary about her parents titled *Dark Lullabies* (1985). Lilienheim was also the author of two self-published books: *Friends* and *The Most Interesting Women of All Times,* and was working on two more manuscripts when he passed away.

OBITUARIES AND OTHER SOURCES:

PERIODICALS

Chicago Tribune, December 18, 2002, section 1, p. 13.

*　　*　　*

LINDENMUTH, Kevin J. 1965-

PERSONAL: Born July 10, 1965, in Dearborn, MI; son of John and Nancy (Portugal) Lindenmuth; married Audrey Geyer, October 8, 1998. *Ethnicity:* "Caucasian." *Education:* University of Michigan, B.A. (film and video studies).

ADDRESSES: Home and office—Brimstone Media Productions, 7900 State St., Brighton, MI 48116; fax: 810-225-7796. *E-mail*—Transtill@aol.com.

CAREER: B Productions, Inc., New York, NY, production manager, 1989-98; Brimstone Media Productions, Brighton, MI, owner, 1992—.

MEMBER: Horror Writers Association.

WRITINGS:

(With others) *Addicted to Murder* (screenplay), 1995.
Addicted to Murder 2 (screenplay), 1998.
Making Movies on Your Own: Practical Talk from Independent Filmmakers, McFarland and Co. (Jefferson, NC), 1998.
The Independent Film Experience, McFarland and Co. (Jefferson, NC), 2002.

BIOGRAPHICAL AND CRITICAL SOURCES:

PERIODICALS

Library Journal, October 1, 1998, Tom Wiener, review of *Making Movies on Your Own: Practical Talk from Independent Filmmakers,* p. 90.

*   *   *

LINK, Kelly

PERSONAL: Married Gavin Grant. *Education:* Columbia University, B.A.; University of North Carolina, M.F.A.

ADDRESSES: Home—Brooklyn, NY. *Office*—Small Beer Press, 176 Prospect Ave., Northampton, MA 01060. *E-mail*—info@kellylink.net.

CAREER: Writer. *Lady Churchill's Rosebud Wristlet,* co-editor; Small Beer Press, Northampton, MA, co-owner. Also teaches writing seminars.

AWARDS, HONORS: James Tiptree, Jr. Award, 1997, for "Travels with the Snow Queen;" World Fantasy Award, 1999, for "The Specialist's Hat;" Nebula Award, 2002, for "Louise's Ghost;" *Salon.com* Book of the Year designation, 2002, for *Stranger Things Happen.*

WRITINGS:

Stranger Things Happen (short stories), Small Beer Press (Northampton, MA), 2001.
(Editor) *Trampoline: An Anthology,* Small Beer Press, 2003.

SIDELIGHTS: Kelly Link, the author of the short-story collection *Stranger Things Happen,* is also the coeditor of the magazine *Lady Churchill's Rosebud Wristlet,* which publishes works of fiction. She is also co-owner of Small Beer Press, which published her first book.

Besides having her first collection named *Salon.com*'s Book of the Year, three of Link's short stories included in this book won prestigious awards of their own. "Travels with the Snow Queen" won the James Tiptree, Jr. Award, and is loosely based on the fairy tale by Hans Christian Anderson, but with a slight feminist twist. In Link's version of this story, the heroine is all grown up and is searching for her lover, who has left her for the Snow Queen. In the process of the search, she comprises a list of things that she plans to recite upon finding her lover. This list, as quoted by Chris Barzak's in a review for the online *Strange Horizons,* includes: "I never really liked your friends all that much" and "After you left, I didn't water your plants on purpose. They're all dead." Her boyfriend was last seen by a clerk at a corner store, who relates that the missing lover left with a beautiful woman who was riding in a sleigh pulled by white geese. Along the search for her lover, the young woman meets several bigger-than-life characters and "more talking animals than she would have preferred," wrote Laura Miller in *Salon.com.*

The protagonist decides, by the end of her search, that she doesn't really want her lover to return to her, after all. As a reviewer from *Publishers Weekly* pointed out, the protagonist eventually "reconsiders her fairy-tale romance when she deconstructs the clichés of traditional fairy tales and realizes that their heroines inevitably sacrifice and suffer much more than their heroes do."

Link is not the only writer who has put a feminist twist on old fairy tales, but in her review for *Salon.com,* Miller stated that Link's style is quite different from most other attempts to project contemporary feminist thought on the traditional tales. "Link's writing is cool, controlled and scrupulously spare," Miller wrote; and while other writers have celebrated female desire, "Link prefers to tally up its costs."

Andrew O'Hehir in the *New York Times Book Review* referred to Link's *Stranger Things Happen* as an "often dazzling debut collection" that is "not entirely of this world." Link often mixes reality with fantasy, preferring to keep her readers on guard. In her *Salon.com* interview with Miller, Link admitted: "I like the idea of taking things that are alien and making them seem really very cozy and familiar." Then she added: "On the other hand, what I like about more realistic fiction . . . is the way it looks at familiar things and makes them seem so strange. What I hope to do is to mix those up, so that you're constantly feeling comfortable and unsettled at the same time." *Booklist* reviewer Bonnie Johnston commented on Link's technique by describing her stories as "strange and tantalizing," as she gives her fiction a "fair-tale ambience" as she "boldly weaves myth and fairy tale into contemporary life."

BIOGRAPHICAL AND CRITICAL SOURCES:

PERIODICALS

Booklist, July 2001, Bonnie Johnston, review of *Stranger Things Happen,* p. 1991.
New York Times Book Review, November 11, 2001, Andrew O'Hehir, "Hell's Belles".
Publishers Weekly, June 25, 2001, review of *Stranger Things Happen,* p. 56.

ONLINE

Beatrice, http://www.beatrice.com/ (May 16, 2002), Ron Hogan, "Beatrice Interview with Kelly Link."
Salon.com, http://www.salon.com/books (May 16, 2002), Laura Miller, "Romance and Other Myths" (interview); Laura Miller, review of *Stranger Things Happen.*
Strange Horizons, http://www.strangehorizons.com/ (May 16, 2002), Chris Barzak, "Witnessing Magic: Kelly Link's *Stranger Things Happen.*"*

*　　*　　*

LOGAN, Anne
    See **COLLEY, Barbara**

*　　*　　*

LOHRER, M(ary) Alice 1907-2002

OBITUARY NOTICE—See index for *CA* sketch: Born January 29, 1907, in Chicago, IL; died September 15, 2002, in Chicago, IL. Librarian, educator, and author. Lohrer was a longtime professor of library science at the University of Illinois and was particularly interested in literature for young readers. After receiving her Ph.B. from the University of Chicago in 1928, Lohrer worked for ten years as a high school librarian in

Oak Park, Illinois, and, after earning a bachelor's degree in library science from the University of Illinois in 1937, for another three years in Hinsdale, Illinois. She then joined the University of Illinois as an assistant professor of library science, working in this position during the 1940s and 1950s while earning her master's degree from the University of Chicago in 1945. She remained at the University of Illinois throughout the rest of her career, becoming a professor of library science in 1967 and retiring as professor emeritus in 1974. For her service to the university, she received several honors, including having an award in library sciences named after her. Lohrer was the coauthor of *Planning Guide for the High School Library Program* (1951) and author of *The Identification and Role of School Libraries That Function as Instructional Materials Centers, and Implications for Library Education in the United States.* She was also an editor and contributor to other books in her field.

OBITUARIES AND OTHER SOURCES:

PERIODICALS

School Library Journal, September 30, 2002.

*　　*　　*

LOKI
    See **PEARSON, Karl**

*　　*　　*

LUCAS, Russell 1930-2002

OBITUARY NOTICE—See index for *CA* sketch: Born January 11, 1930, in Bombay, India; died August 11, 2002. Author. Lucas was especially well known for writing novels and stories set in India during the British Raj. After spending his first years of childhood in India, Lucas moved to England with his mother after she divorced and married an Englishman. Too young to enlist during World War II, he nevertheless served in the British Army infantry from 1948 to 1949. Lucas returned to his beloved India, for which he always harbored fond memories, to work as a traveling salesman, but he soon returned to England and a lucrative job as a banking manager and treasury executive at Wauchall Motors to better support his family. He worked for this company from 1956 to 1987 before taking early retirement in order to write fiction. Lucas's short stories and novels, set during the Raj era, are characterized by their satire, black humor, and accounts of sexual exploits, often between Englishmen and Indians, and are flavored by the author's love of India and mistrust of the English occupational forces. His writings include the short story collection *Evenings at Mongini's and Other Stories* (1990), the novels *Lip Service* (1991) and *The Ice Factory* (1992), and the screenplay *Keep Smiling* (1991). He also contributed stories to anthologies and periodicals and won the 1995 Stand International Award for best short story at the Cheltenham Festival of Literature for the story "Space."

OBITUARIES AND OTHER SOURCES:

PERIODICALS

Daily Telegraph (London, England), August 19, 2002.
Times (London, England), September 9, 2002, p. 8.

M

MACHADO (Y RUIZ), Manuel 1874-1947

PERSONAL: Born August 29, 1874, in Seville, Spain; died January 19, 1947, in Madrid, Spain; son of Antonio Machado Alvarez (a journalist) and Ana Ruiz Hernández; married Eulalia Cáceres, 1910. *Education:* Earned a university degree in Seville, c. 1897; attended the University of Madrid.

CAREER: Librarian, poet, dramatist, and translator. Passed librarian exam in 1913; appointed to government university in Santiago de Compostela; transferred to Biblioteca Nacional, Madrid; cofounder of *Revista de la Biblioteca, Archivo de Madrid,* 1924; director of Biblioteca Municipal, beginning 1925; director of Museo Municipal, 1928-44. Worked as translator for Garnier Frères, Paris, France, beginning 1900; served on editorial board of *Electra* and *Juventud,* beginning 1901; *Liberal* (daily newspaper), theater critic, beginning 1916; *Libertad* (newspaper), staffwriter, 1919-34. Co-founded Musa Musae (writers' society), c.1940.

MEMBER: Musa Musae (writers' society).

AWARDS, HONORS: Elected to Real Academia Española, 1938.

WRITINGS:

(With Enrique Paradas) *Tristes y alegres,* Catalana (Madrid, Spain), 1894.
(With Enrique Paradas) *Etcétera,* López Robert (Barcelona, Spain), 1895.
Alma (title means "Soul"), Marzo (Madrid, Spain), 1900.
(With José Luis Montoto de Sedas) *Amor alvuelo: comedia en un acto,* [Seville, Spain], 1904.
Caprichos (title means "Caprices"), Revista de Archivos (Madrid, Spain), 1905.
La fiesta nacional: rojo y negro, Fortanet (Madrid, Spain), 1906.
Poesías escogidas, Maucci (Barcelona, Spain), 1907.
Alma. Museo. Los cantares, Pueyo (Madrid, Spain), 1907.
El mal poema, Gutenburg-Castro (Madrid, Spain), 1909.
Trofeos, Gasso (Barcelona, Spain), 1910.
Alma. Opera selecta, Garnier (Paris, France), 1911.
Apolo. Teatro pictórico (title means "Apollo. Pictorial Theater"), Prieto (Madrid, Spain), 1911.
Cante hondo. Cantares, canciones y coplas, compuestas al estilo popular de Andalucía, Helénica (Madrid, Spain), 1912.
El amor y la muerte: capítulos de novela, Helénica (Madrid, Spain), 1913.
La guerra literaria, 1898-1914: Crítica y ensayos, Hispano-alemana (Madrid, Spain), 1913.
Canciones y dedicatorias, Hispanio-alemana (Madrid, Spain), 1915.
Poesías completas, Residencia de Estudiantes (Madrid, Spain), 1917.
Un año de teatro, Biblioteca Nueva (Madrid, Spain), 1918.
Día por día de mi calendario, Pueyo (Madrid, Spain), 1918.
Sevilla y otros poemas, América (Madrid, Spain), 1918.
Ars moriendi (title means "The Art of Dying"), Mundo Latino (Madrid, Spain), 1921.

Obras completas, five volumes, Mundo Latino (Madrid, Spain), 1922-24.

Poesía: opera omnia lírica (title means "Poetry: Complete Lyric Works"), Internacional (Madrid, Spain), 1924.

La égloga Antonia: una obra inédita de Lope de Vega, Municipal (Madrid, Spain), 1924.

La prima Fernanda, Farsa (Madrid, Spain), 1931.

Cante hondo, Sevilla, Aguilar (Madrid, Spain), 1934.

Phoenix: nuevas canciones, Altolaguirre/Héroe (Madrid, Spain), 1936.

Horas de oro: devocionario poético, Castellana (Valladolid, Spain), 1938.

Antología poética, Zugazaga (Burgos, Spain), 1938.

Antología, Espasa-Calpe (Buenos Aires, Argentina), 1940.

Unos versos, un alma y una época: Discursos leídos en la Real Academia Española, con motivo de la recepcíon de Manuel Machado, Españolas/Diana (Madrid, Spain), 1940.

Ars longa, Garcilaso (Madrid, Spain), 1943.

Cadencias de cadencias: nuevas dedicatorias, Nacional (Madrid, Spain), 1943.

El pilar de la victoria, Nacional (Madrid, Spain), 1945.

Horario: poemas religiosos (title means "Book of Hours"), Nacional (Madrid, Spain), 1947.

Estampas sevillanas, Aguado (Madrid, Spain), 1949.

Poemas de Manuel Machado, Horizonte (Medellín, Colombia), 1963.

Prosa, edited by José Luis Ortiz de Lanzagorta, Universidad de Sevilla (Seville, Spain), 1974.

Antología poética, edited by Margarita Smerdou Altolaguirre, E.M.E.S.A. (Madrid, Spain), 1977.

Poesías, Alianza Editorial (Madrid, Spain), 1979.

Cualquier día en Sevilla, RC Editor (Seville, Spain), 1988.

Manuel Machado para niños, Ediciones del la Torre (Madrid, Spain), 1991.

Poesía de guerra y posguerra, Universidad de Granada (Granada, Spain), 1992.

Cuentos completos, Clan Editorial (Madrid, Spain), 1999.

Impresiones: el modernismo: artíclos, crónicas y reseñas, 1899-1909, Pres-Textos (Valencia, Spain), 2000.

Del arte largo: (antología poética), Editorial Lumen (Barcelona, Spain), 2001.

WITH ANTONIO MACHADO

Poemas de Antonio y Manuel Machado, Cultura (Mexico), 1917.

Desdichas de la fortuna, o Julianillo Valcárcel, Fernando Fé (Madrid, Spain), 1926.

Juan de mañana, Espasa-Calpe (Madrid, Spain), 1927.

Las adelfas, Farsa (Madrid, Spain), 1928.

La Lola se va a los puertos (title means "Lola Goes off to Sea"), Farsa (Madrid, Spain), 1929.

La duquesa de Benamejí, Farsa (Madrid, Spain), 1932.

Teatro completo, two volumes, C.I.A.P. (Madrid, Spain), 1932.

La duquesa de Benamejí, La prima Fernanda y Juan de mañana, Espasa-Calpe (Buenos Aires, Argentina), 1942.

Las adelfas y El hombre que murió en la guerra, Espasa-Calpe (Buenos Aires, Argentina), 1947.

Obras completas, Plenitud (Madrid, Spain), 1947.

La prehistoria de Antonio Machado, Torre/Universidad de Puerto Rico (Río Piedras, Puerto Rico), 1961.

Cartas a los Machado, Diputación Provincial de Sevilla (Seville, Spain), 1981.

Los Machado y su tiempo: exposición itinerante, Sevilla Madrid, Baeza, Segovia, Soria, Barcelona, Collioure, 1987, La Fundación (Madrid, Spain), 1987.

TRANSLATOR

Paul Verlaine, *Fiestas galantes. Poemas saturnianos . . . y otras poesías,* Fortanet (Madrid, Spain), 1910.

(With Antonio Machado and Francisco Villaspesa) Victor Hugo, *Hernani,* Farsa (Madrid, Spain), 1928.

Virgil, *Obras,* Casa Editorial Garnier Hermanos (Paris, France), 1929.

(With Luis de Oteyza) Edmond Rostand, *El aguilucho,* Farsa (Madrid, Spain), 1932.

Contributor to *Documentos ineditos referentes al poeta Garcilaso de la Vega,* 1915, and to periodicals *Helios, Alfar,* and *Indice.*

ADAPTATIONS: Work included in sound recording *Poetas para el cante,* EMI, 1992.

SIDELIGHTS: Early in the twentieth century, Manuel Machado was instrumental in introducing modernism to Spanish poetry. He made his reputation as a poet with later folk and flamenco-influenced writings, but it is Machado's early poetry that continues to be admired by critics. In the *Dictionary of Literary Biography,* Michael L. Perna commented that "at his best [Machado] gives a poem apparently spontaneous, sincere emotion in the midst of musical elegance and verbal finesse." Writing in the *Times Literary Supplement,* Gordon Brotherston called Machado "the salient poet of Spanish Modernism at the turn of the [twentieth] century," but he also noted that Machado's work had not yet been studied properly. Commenting on a 1975 collection of Machado's work, Brotherston pointed to persistent "problems of dating and variants" caused by the author's numerous publications. Machado also worked as a librarian, did translations, and wrote plays with his brother Antonio.

During Machado's early childhood in Seville, his father collected, studied, and published popular flamenco songs, which resulted in the boy's immersion in folk ballads. The family later moved to Madrid, but Manuel and his brother completed high school in Seville. It was during this period that he published his first poetry in two collections written with his friend Enrique Paradas. In 1899 the brothers went to Paris, where Machado worked as a translator. He associated with Spanish and Latin American writers, met famous literary figures, and began his first serious writing. He was influenced by Victor Hugo, the French Parnassians, Nicaraguan writer Rubén Darío, and avant-garde theater, but most importantly became fascinated by the symbolism of Paul Verlaine.

The work Machado started in Paris would be published in the collection *Alma.* Perna described this work as including exotic themes resembling those of the Parnassians, being "fine examples of the modernists' emphasis on the mystery of emotions that cannot be expressed in words." Other poems in *Alma* used traditional Spanish meters but assonance instead of full rhyme and, according to Perna, show an "attitude of rebellion." They earned Machado a reputation as a leading young poet.

Machado returned to Madrid, where he became a part of literary and café society. He became close friends with Darío, with whom he enjoyed drinking and meeting young women. Their pleasures are reflected in the erotic verse of Machado's next collection, *Caprichos.* Subsequent collections from this period include *La fiesta nacional: rojo y negro,* which was inspired by a friend's bullfighting career, and *Alma. Museo. Los cantares,* a reprint of most of the poet's work to 1907.

When Machado's friends commented on the inferior quality of his more recent work, he responded with the collection *El mal poema,* which deals with the lives of prostitutes and criminals. The poet complained that his poverty forced him to write and publish quickly, resulting in "bad poetry."

Following the publication of a long series of poems about paintings, *Apolo. Teatro Pictório,* which included reflections on the work of Peter Paul Rubens, Francisco de Zurbarán, Fra Angelico, and Sandro Botticelli, Machado decided to become a librarian. After attending university and passing the civil service exam, he worked primarily in Madrid at the Bibilioteca Nacional, Biblioteca Municipal, and Museo Municipal. He continued to publish poetry, including *Sevilla y otros poemas.* This collection was described by Perna as nowadays appearing "marred . . . by superficial Andalusianism," but it is also judged as having helped create the atmosphere in which Federico García Lorca developed his more authentic folk presence.

During a turbulent period in Spain, Machado took political changes in stride. He worked happily under the dictatorship of General Miguel Primo de Rivera and collaborated with his brother writing plays, completing about one per year from 1926 to 1932. Their biggest production was *La Lola se va a los puertos* with actress Lola Membrives. He published the collection *Phoenix: Nuevas canciones* on the eve of the Spanish Civil War, which necessarily lessened critical notice of the poems. Machado was on vacation when he found himself caught inside territory controlled by Generalissimo Francisco Franco's Nationalists. Soon he was writing poetry for the new regime's propaganda office. At the same time, his brother was in Madrid supporting the Republic.

Following Franco's victory in 1939, Machado returned to his job in Madrid. He now spoke of himself as "the oldest of the young poets and the youngest of the old." He was sixty-nine years old when he published *Cadencias de cadencias: nuevas dedicatorias.* Perna wrote that this collection "shows he could write in the neoclassical style of the Garcilaso movement, at times as well as any of its younger members. Many of his poems, similar to his earlier approaches to painting and bullfighting, focus on moments in the performing arts." The poet's popularity declined after his retirement from civil service in 1944, after which he made veiled criticisms of Franco's dictatorship in poems published in a Monarchist daily. Machado fell ill early in 1947 and died just a few days later.

BIOGRAPHICAL AND CRITICAL SOURCES:

BOOKS

Dictionary of Literary Biography, Volume 108: *Twentieth-Century Spanish Poets,* Gale (Detroit, MI), 1991.

PERIODICALS

Times Literary Supplement, May, 23, 1975, Gordon Brotherston, review of *Antología,* p. 559.*

*   *   *

MANENT, Marià 1898-1988

PERSONAL: Born 1898, in Barcelona, Spain; died 1988.

CAREER: Literary director for a publisher, poet, translator, and literary critic. *Revista de Poesia,* founder, 1925; *Quaderns de Poesia,* editorial committee member, from 1935.

AWARDS, HONORS: Lletra d'Or, 1968, for *Com un núvol lleuger;* Ensenya de Cavaller de l'Imperi Britànic, 1976, for superior translation of English poetry; Premi Josep Pla, 1974, for *El vel de maia: dietari de la guerra civil (1936-39);* Premi d'Honor de les Lletres Catalanes, 1985.

WRITINGS:

La branca, Poemes (1916-1918), Joan Sallent, (Sabadell, Spain), 1918.
La collita en la boira (1918-1920): elegies, poemes de primavera, odes, La Revista (Barcelona, Spain), 1920, reprinted, Edicions 62 (Barcelona, Spain), 1987.
Marian Manent, prologue by Tomàs Garcés, Lira (Barcelona, Spain), 1923.

L'ombra i altres poemes, Atenes Arts Gràfiques (Barcelona, Spain), 1931, reprinted, 1946.
Notes sobre literatura estrangera, La Revista (Barcelona, Spain), 1934, reprinted, Parcir Edicions Selectes (Manresa, Spain), 1992.
Montseny: Zodíac d'un paisatge, illustrated by Josep Fossas, Atenes Arts Gràfiques (Barcelona, Spain), 1948, published as *Poemes,* prologue by Miquel Desclot, Taller de Picasso (Barcelona, Spain), 1983.
(Selector and author of prologue) Kathleen Raine, *Poemas,* Ediciones Rialp (Madrid, Spain), 1951.
(Selector and author of prologue) *La poesía irlandesa,* José Janés (Barcelona, Spain), 1952.
(Selector and author of prologue) *Llibre de l'Eucaristia,* Editorial Selecta (Barcelona, Spain), 1952.
(Editor) *Antología amorosa,* Editorial Selecta (Barcelona, Spain), 1955.
Obra poètica, Editorial Selecta (Barcelona, Spain), 1956.
(Selector and author of prologue) *La poesía inglesa,* José Janés (Barcelona, Spain), 1958.
Maragall, 1860-1911, Editorial Franciscana (Barcelona, Spain), 1960.
La ciutat del temps: poemes, J. Pedreira (Barcelona, Spain), 1961.
Como nace el poema y otros ensayos y notas, Aguilar (Madrid, Spain), 1962.
A flor d'oblit, prologue by Joan Teixidor, Edicions 62 (Barcelona, Spain), 1968, reprinted, 1986.
Palabra y poesía, y otras notas críticas, Seminarios y Ediciones (Madrid, Spain), 1971.
Poesia, llenguatge, forma: dotze poetes catalans i altres notes critiques, Edicions 62 (Barcelona, Spain), 1973.
El vel de maia, dietari de la guerra civil (1936-39), Edicions Destino (Barcelona, Spain), 1975.
Antologia poètica: homentage al poeta en el seus vuitanta anys, prologue by Pere Gimferrer, Edicions Proa (Barcelona, Spain), 1978.
Notícies d'art, prologue by Albert Ràfols-Casamada, Edicions 62 (Barcelona, Spain), 1981.
L'aroma d'arc: dietari dispers (1919-1981), Edicions Laertes (Barcelona, Spain), 1982.
Llibres d'ara i d'antany, Edicions 62 (Barcelona, Spain), 1982.
A una dama i a tres noise: poemes, Filograf (Barcelona, Spain), 1982.
The Shade of Mist: Selected Poems/Color de boirada: poemas escollits (bilingual edition, English and Catalan), English translation by Sam Abrams, In-

stituto de Estudios Norteamericanos (Barcelona, Spain), 1984.

La muntanya i l'ocell, with four sheets of plates by Gabriel and others, Les Edicions (Barcelona, Spain), 1984.

(Adaptator) *Contes del Japó,* Catalan translation by Jordi Janén, Juventud (Barcelona, Spain), 1985.

(Adaptor) *Vell país natal, de Wang Wei,* literal Catalan translation by Maria Dolors Folch, Edicions Empúries (Barcelona, Spain), 1986.

Poesia completa, 1916-1986, edited by Álex Susanna, Edicions Columna (Barcelona, Spain), 1986.

Las acacias salvajes (bilingual edition; Spanish and Catalan), Spanish translation by José Agustín Goytisolo, edited and with a prologue by Álex Susanna, Edicions del Mall (Barcelona, Spain), 1986.

Rellegint, Edicions 62 (Barcelona, Spain), 1987.

Eight Catalan Poems, translations by John Adlard, Perdix, 1988.

Poesia completa: de La brança, La collita en la boira, L'ombra i altres poemas, La ciutat del temps, El cant amagadís, Edicions Columna (Barcelona, Spain), 1989.

Marià Manent, PPU (Barcelona, Spain), 1989.

Notes de dietari, 1937-1939, Abadia de Montserrat (Barcelona, Spain), 1992.

Vuit cartes a Palau i Fabre, Vèrtex (Mataró, Spain), 1994.

Dietari dispers, 1918-1984, Edicions 62 (Barcelona, Spain), 1995.

(Adaptor) *Cuentos del Japón,* illustrated by Luis Filella, Editorial Juventud (Barcelona, Spain), 1997.

Els millors poemes, Edicions Proa (Barcelona, Spain), 1998.

Dietaris, edited by Sam Abrams, Edicions 62 (Barcelona, Spain), 1999.

Crítica, personatges, confidències: articles inèdits i dispersos, edited by Miquel Batalla, Edicions Columna (Barcelona, Spain), 1999.

Obres completes de Marià Manent, edited by Sam Abrams, Edicions 62 (Barcelona, Spain), 2000.

Poesía catalana contemporánea: selección, con versions métricas en castellano, Edicions Pre-Textos (Madrid, Spain), 1999.

TRANSLATOR

Rudyard Kipling, *El llibre de la jungla. Segon llibre de la jungla,* Edicions Catalana, (Barcelona, Spain), 1923, reprinted, Edicions Selecta (Barcelona, Spain), 1981.

L'aire daurat: interpretacions de poesia xinesa, Atenes Arts Gràfiques (Barcelona, Spain), 1928, reprinted, Edicions Proa (Barcelona, Spain), 1986.

Versions de l'anglès (parallel text in Catalan and English), Edicions de la Residència d'Estudiants (Barcelona, Spain), 1938, published as *El gran vent i les heures: "Versions de l'anglès,"* Editorial Laertes (Barcelona, Spain), 1983.

Jérôme and Jean Tharaud, *Leyendas de la Virgen,* illustrated by Mercedes Llimona, Ediciones Mediterráneas (Barcelona, Spain), 1942.

Kenneth Grahame, *El viento en los sauces,* illustrated by Ernest H. Shepard, Editorial Juventud (Barcelona, Spain), 1945.

(And selector and author of prologue) *La poesía inglesa de los primitivos a los neoclásicos,* Ediciones Lauro (Barcelona, Spain), 1945.

(And selector and author of prologue) *La poesía inglesa: románticos y victorianos,* Ediciones Lauro (Barcelona, Spain), 1945.

Percy Bysshe Shelley, *Epipsychidion,* Helikon (Barcelona, Spain), 1946.

(And selector and author of prologue) *Los contemporáneous,* Ediciones Lauro (Barcelona, Spain), 1948.

(And author of notes) *Poesia anglesa i nordamericana,* Edicions Alpha (Barcelona, Spain), 1955.

(And editor) Emily Dickinson, *Poemas,* Editorial Juventud (Barcelona, Spain), 1957, reprinted 1994, Catalan translation by Manent published as *Poemes d'Emily Dickinson: selecció,* Edicions 62 (Barcelona, Spain), 1979.

Com un núvol lleuger, Edicions Proa (Barcelona, Spain), 1967.

(With Josep Carner) Hans Christian Andersen, *Rondalles de Hans Andersen,* illustrated by Arthur Rackham, Editorial Juventud (Barcelona, Spain), 1969.

Dylan Thomas, *Poemes de Dylan Thomas,* Edicions 62 (Barcelona, Spain), 1974, reprinted, 2001.

William Blake, *Llibres profètics,* Edicions 62 (Barcelona, Spain), 1976.

Espígol blau: poemes anglesos per a infants, Edicions Juventud (Barcelona, Spain), 1980.

20 poemes xinesos, Miquel Plana (Olot, Spain), 1980.

Archibald MacLeish, *Poemes,* Edicions 62 (Barcelona, Spain), 1981.

S. T. Coleridge, *Poema del vell mariner,* Edicions del Mall (St. Boi de Llobregat, Spain), 1982.

Rudyard Kipling, *Precisamente así: historias para los niños y para los que aman a los niños,* illustrated by Ángel Domínguez, Juventud (Barcelona, Spain), 1998.

Randall Jarrell, *Vol de nit,* illustrated by Maurice Sendak, Antoni Bosch (Barcelona, Spain), 1999.

Also translator of the poetry of Keats and Rupert Brooke.

ADAPTATIONS: Manent's texts have been set to music by Alejandro Yagüe and Juan Manau Valor.

SIDELIGHTS: Marià Manent was a publisher, poet, translator, literary critic, and author of memoirs. His literary background is in the period of Noucentisme—a Catalan political and cultural movement founded by Eugenie d'Ors at the beginning of the twentieth century—from which his poetry moved towards symbolism and "pure poetry." He was influenced by Verdaguer, Carner, and Claudel, as well as by Chinese poets, whom he translated in such volumes as *L'aire daurat: interpretacions de poesia xinesa* and *Com un núvol lleuger.* He also translated the work of numerous English and American poets.

Sean Golden, writing in the *Journal of Catalan Studies,* suggested that "a close examination of the prefaces [Manent] wrote for each of his collections could provide us with an insight into his motivations. . . . in the aftermath of the [Spanish] Civil War, a large part of his motivation . . . was a result of his empathy for the plight of classical Chinese poets. Like them, he was in many ways a powerless individual confronted by a system of arbitrary and stifling authority." Golden later continued, "Chinese poets constantly lamented the state of affairs and sought consolation in the world of nature, without ever becoming rebels themselves, as did Manent." Manent's original poetry strived for the same serenity and equilibrium he intuited in Chinese poetry.

Manent's *Dietari dispers, 1918-1984* is of particular interest to scholars, especially its best-known fragment *El vel de maia: dietari de la guerra civil (1936-39),* which corresponds to the period of the Spanish Civil War and which was awarded the 1974 Josep Pla Prize. *Obres completes de Marià Manent* is a complete collection of Manent's poetry. His literary and art criticism, published in reviews and newspapers before and after the Franco dictatorship, is collected in volumes

like *Notícies d'art* and *Rellegint.* Manent strove to make each of the genres with which he worked compatible with the others, resulting in a highly homogenous body of literature.

BIOGRAPHICAL AND CRITICAL SOURCES:

PERIODICALS

Journal of Catalan Studies, 1998, Sean Golden, "Subversive Empathy: Marià Manent in Exile in the Land of Chinese Poetry."

Revista de Estudios Hispanicos, May, 1988, Enric Bou, "El poeta en el museo: pasajes y paisajes (A propósito de Pedro Salinas y Marià Manent)," pp. 63-79.

Revista de Occidente, July, 1996, Jose Munoz Millanes, "Los placers de los diarios: el caso de Marià Manent," pp. 136-146.*

*   *   *

MANGAN, (John Joseph) Sherry 1904-1961
(Terence Phelan, Sean Niall)

PERSONAL: Born July 27, 1904, in Lynn, MA; died June 24, 1961 in Rome, Italy. *Education:* Harvard University, B.A., 1925.

CAREER: Larus, the Celestial Visitor, editor, 1927-28; *Pagany, a Native Quarterly,* assistant publisher, 1930-33; writer from 1930; Paris-based journalist for *Time, Life,* and *Fortune* magazines, 1938-48.

WRITINGS:

Cinderella Married, A & C Boni (New York, NY), 1932.

No Apology for Poetrie and Other Poems Written 1922-31, Bruce Humphries (Boston, MA), 1934.

Salutation to Valediction, Bruce Humphries (Boston, MA), 1938.

OTHER

(Editor as Terence Phelan) Frederick Lang, *Maritime,* Pioneer (New York, NY), 1943.

(Translator) Wolfgang Amadeus Mozart, *Idomeneum, King of Crete,* Juilliard Opera Company (New York, NY), 1955.

Contributor to periodicals, including *Pagany.* Work included in the anthology *Americans Abroad: An Anthology,* edited by Peter Neagoe, Servire (The Hague, Netherlands), 1932. Author, under name Sean Niall, of column "Paris Letter" for *Partisan Review.*

SIDELIGHTS: Sherry Mangan is best known for the European-influenced fiction, essays, and criticism through which he helped introduce American readers to innovative modernism. Though his interest in surrealism at times stifled Mangan's writing career, it enriched his editing career. As Alan Wald wrote in the *Dictionary of Literary Biography:* "A number of Mangan's experimental prose writings were partly inspired by the techniques of the French Surrealists, and Mangan was responsible for introducing work by several Paris-based writers to the American public."

Mangan took honors in classical literature at Harvard University. Soon after graduating, he moved to Paris, where he quickly connected with literary and artistic expatriates. Through Harvard friends such as Virgil Thomson and Maurice Grosser he befriended the likes of Gertrude Stein, Robert McAlmon, and Georges Hugnet. Mangan's stay in Paris introduced him, most importantly, to French surrealist writing and to the experiments of modernism. When he returned to the United States, Mangan edited the small literary journal *Larus, The Celestial Visitor,* and worked under Richard Johns at *Pagany: A Native Quarterly.* In those journals, he published the work of those he had met abroad. According to Wald, Mangan, through his connections, helped publish "The Revolving Mirror" by McAlmon, "Five Words in a Line" by Stein and other works from Paris by Hugnet, Mary Butts, and Bernard Fay.

Mangan also published much of his own creative work during this period; *Cinderella Married,* which Wald called a "highly mannered social satire, stylistically imitative of Ronald Firbank," tells of a modern Cinderella after she marries Prince Charming. Princess Ella, the novel's heroine, is confused during her marriage to the Oxford-educated, riding-boot-wearing prince, but her fairy godmother helps her manage. Reviewers, though praising the book for its wit, were

still lukewarm. A *Bookseller* reviewer wrote: "There is no doubt about Mr. Mangan's cleverness. He is complete with quips, cranks, and wreathed smiles, with winks, innuendoes and ambiguities. If you poured some extract of James Branch Cabell into bottled essence of Anita Loos, shook them up together and, at the last moment, added a drop or two of Hemingway, you could approximate the Mangan punch. You should be warned, however, that too much of this refreshment will put you under the table." However, Mangan's sheer cleverness won over others: "Mangan's poetry and fiction exhibited a remarkable versatility," Wald explained, "but his difficulty in communicating a philosophic vision caused Virgil Thomson to describe him as 'a sterile virtuoso.'"

Critics also brushed off Mangan's poetry as mere clever word trickery; his collection *No Apology for Poetrie and Other Poems Written 1922-1931* was considered technically superior, but lacking in subject matter. John Wheelwright, reviewing it for *Poetry,* said: "Thirty of these poems are in academic styles: epigram quatrains, antique meters, John D. Harvard sonnet (D. standing for Donne). In half of them the pre-cast forms for thought and sound do not let the ideas inside show through. But the bulk of the book (solid beating narrative arguments and ruminations upon sex) is in a counter-academic style, rich in muted metrical variants." A *Boston Transcript* writer, though, still said Mangan's poems seemed empty: "Mr. Mangan is deserving of praise, because he knows how to write good poetry, because of his easy wit, and because he makes himself very much at home with the romanticists in the grand manner. But turning to the substance of his work, one feels that he is rather given to wasting his talent on a type of sensualism and unchecked hedonism that we find not particularly tasteful. In fact, were it not for the wit in the volume, we would be inclined to drop it in the first convenient bucket."

Mangan excelled in journalism more than in poetry or fiction. From 1938 to 1948, after moving to Paris, he wrote for *Time, Life,* and *Fortune* magazines. A Marxist, he helped organize the French unit of the International Federation of Independent Revolutionary Art. He also wrote "Paris Letter," a feature for *Partisan Review* under the pen name Sean Niall. In "Paris Letter," Wald wrote, "he provided unusual information about the French publication of works by Benjamin Peret and Nicholas Calas, and in great detail he described the literary conflicts among radical writers in Paris." After the Nazis occupied Paris, however, Mangan's writing career began to decline. He stayed briefly in Paris as a journalist, but because of his work on behalf of the underground French Trotskyite movement, he was expelled in 1940.

Mangan worked variously as a translator and editor in his later years. "After World War II he drifted into literary obscurity and died penniless and alone in Rome," Wald wrote.

BIOGRAPHICAL AND CRITICAL SOURCES:

BOOKS

Dictionary of Literary Biography, Volume 4: *American Writers in Paris, 1920-1939,* Gale (Detroit, MI), 1980.
Wald, Alan, *The Revolutionary Imagination: The Poetry and Politics of John Wheelright and Sherry Mangan,* University of North Carolina Press (Chapel Hill, NC), 1983.

PERIODICALS

Bookseller, April 17, 1932, review of *Cinderella Married,* p. 15.
Boston Transcript, April 27, 1932, review of *Cinderella Married,* p. 3; January 23, 1935, review of *No Apology for Poetrie,* p. 2.
Poetry, March, 1935, John Wheelwright, review of *No Apology for Poetrie.**

*   *   *

MAQUET, Paul G. J. 1928-

PERSONAL: Born July 17, 1928, in Liège, Belgium; son of René and Mariette (Jansen) Maquet; married Josette Dubois, August 12, 1952; children: Anne Maquet de Vera, Françoise Van Brabant-Maquet, Pierre, Jacqueline. *Education:* Université de Liège, M.D.

ADDRESSES: Home—25 Thier Bosset, B-4920 Aywaille, Belgium; fax: 00-324-384-4079. *E-mail*—paulmaquet@swing.be.

CAREER: Physician. Clinique de l'Espérance, Montegnée Liège, Belgium, orthopedic surgeon. *Military service:* Belgian Army Medical Corps, surgeon, 1959-68; became major.

MEMBER: Société Belge de Chirurgie Orthopédique et de Traumatologie (past president), Société Française de Chirurgie Orthopédique et Traumatologique (honorary member).

AWARDS, HONORS: Honorary doctorate, University of Paris XII; Prix Joncheere.

WRITINGS:

Biomechanics of the Knee, Springer (New York, NY), 1976, 2nd edition, 1984.
Biomechanics of the Hip, Springer (New York, NY), 1985.

TRANSLATOR FROM GERMAN

F. Pauwels, *Biomechanics of the Normal and Diseased Hip: An Atlas,* Springer (New York, NY), 1975.
F. Pauwels, *Biomechanics of the Locomotor Apparatus,* Springer (New York, NY), 1980.
W. Braune and O. Fischer, *On the Centre of Gravity of the Human Body,* Springer (New York, NY), 1985.
J. Wolff, *The Law of Bone Remodelling,* Springer (New York, NY), 1986.
W. Braune and O. Fischer, *The Human Gait,* Springer (New York, NY), 1987.
W. Braune and O. Fischer, *Determination of the Moments of Inertia of the Human Body and Its Limbs,* Springer (New York, NY), 1988.
W. Weber and E. Weber, *Mechanics of the Human Walking Apparatus,* Springer (New York, NY), 1992.

Also translator of books from German into French.

TRANSLATOR FROM LATIN

G. A. Borelli, *On the Movement of Animals,* Springer (New York, NY), 1989.
(With others) T. Kardel, editor, *Steno: Life—Science—Philosophy,* Danish National Library of Science and Medicine, 1994.

William Croone, *On the Reason of the Movement of the Muscles,* American Philosophical Society (Philadelphia, PA), 2000.

Contributor of translations to periodicals.

* * *

MARKOE, Merrill

PERSONAL: Born in New York, NY; daughter of Gerry (a real estate developer) and Ronny (a research librarian) Markoe; *Education:* University of California—Berkeley, M.F.A., 1974.

ADDRESSES: Agent—c/o Author Mail, Random House, 1540 Broadway, New York, NY 10036.

CAREER: Writer, performer, and standup comic. University of Southern California, art teacher, 1970s; *The David Letterman Show* and *Late Night with David Letterman,* head comedy writer, c. 1970s to 1980s; writer for television series, including *Buffalo Bill, Making the Grade, Mary, Moonlighting, Newhart,* and *Sex in the City;* contributor and performer for *Not Necessarily the News* and *TV Nation; Buzz* (magazine), humor columnist; featured performer in Home Box Office and other comedy specials.

AWARDS, HONORS: Four Emmy awards for comedy writing for *The David Letterman Show* and *Late Night with David Letterman;* Writers Guild and Ace performance awards for *Not Necessarily the News.*

WRITINGS:

(Editor) Andy Breckman and others *Late Night with David Letterman: The Book,* Villard (New York, NY), 1985.
What the Dogs Have Taught Me and Other Amazing Things I've Learned, Viking (New York, NY), 1992.
How to Be Hap-Hap-Happy like Me, Viking (New York, NY), 1994.
Merrill Markoe's Guide to Love, Atlantic Monthly Press (New York, NY), 1997.

The Day My Dogs Became Guys (juvenile), illustrated by Eric Brace, Viking (New York, NY), 1999.
It's My F—ing Birthday (novel), Villard (New York, NY), 2002.

Contributor to periodicals, including *Woman's Day* and *New York Woman;* author of scripts for television specials, including *This Week Indoors,* 1987, and *Merrill Markoe's Guide to Glamourous Living,* 1988, both Cinemax.

SIDELIGHTS: Merrill Markoe's specialty is comedy. She has performed it, written it, and received numerous awards for it, particular for her work as head writer for David Letterman, who was both her comedic, and one-time personal partner. Markoe met Letterman in the late 1970s, during a period when she shared the stage with some of the other greats of the time, in places like Los Angeles's Comedy Store. She had unsuccessfully tried writing her offbeat brand of humor earlier in her career, but going into the 1980s, television was finally ripe for the wacky sketches Markoe created for Letterman's show. Markoe has also written for other comedians, including Bob Newhart.

Markoe was editor of *Late Night with David Letterman: The Book,* which features photographs, cartoons, and typical skits. *School Library Journal's* Elizabeth Thurston felt that young adults who stay up late enough to watch the show "will find this is a very funny book."

After leaving Letterman, Markoe wrote for and appeared in a number of television shows, including *Not Necessarily the News* and *TV Nation.* John T. O'Connor reviewed her Cinemax special, *Merrill Markoe's Guide to Glamourous Living,* in the *New York Times,* noting that "Ms. Markoe is all over the place, and television is much the better for it." Joanne Kaufman commented in *People* that Markoe "is one of the most talented comedy writers in the biz, playing a large role in creating the slightly skewed tone of *Late Night.* Hey, she deserves to be in the Comedy Hall of Fame just for thinking up Stupid Pet Tricks."

Beginning in the early 1990s, Markoe wrote a number of books, including *What the Dogs Have Taught Me and Other Amazing Things I've Learned,* which includes many of her essays originally published in

New York Woman. A *Publishers Weekly* contributor called them "the literary equivalent of snack food: they're quickly devoured and difficult to put down." Markoe talks about and through her dogs and discusses male retreats, living alone, and "chick" flicks like *Pretty Woman* in a tone that could be described as feminism lite. *Time*'s Amelia Weiss called the collection "flimsy when she talks about horoscopes and cute guys. But where the dogs reign, Markoe shines." *Booklist*'s Ilene Cooper wrote that Markoe is "as funny as that darn old Dave any day. She can make you fall off the chair laughing without even a Top Ten list to her name." *Library Journal* reviewer Carol Spielman Lezak felt that the book "deserves to be read by men and women alike. . . . Markoe's dog essays are the jewel of this book."

How to Be Hap-Hap-Happy like Me is a collection of thirty-three tips on how to achieve happiness, with everything from pampering, to dining, to taking a class. The class Marcoe takes is with an S & M dominatrix, and she shares a dinner with supermodel Fabio. Her dogs are central to her happiness, as are makeup and screening calls on the answering machine. She parodies Girl Scout cookie drives, home shopping shows, and party-giving in the style of Martha Stewart. A *Publishers Weekly* critic wrote that "Marcoe's brand of chirpy cynicism can grow grating." However, *People*'s Joanne Kaufmann called Markoe "the funniest woman in America and, please, let's have no arguing, okay?" Cooper said, "Markoe's version of life on the wry is not to be missed."

Merrill Markoe's Guide to Love is also about the disappointing methods used to find love, which she thoroughly researched by attending seminars and reading how-to books. A *Publishers Weekly* reviewer felt that her "look at love and sex in the 1990s is often tiresome, sometimes wickedly funny, and occasionally hilarious." Donna Seaman noted in *Booklist* that Markoe "decides that love is simply chemistry gone awry, like an allergic reaction." Chicago *Tribune Books* critic Carolyn Alessio wrote that "in general, Markoe receives advice that is implausible and impractical. But delivered in Markoe's ironic style, the *Guide to Love* is a hilarious, refreshing lampoon of the endless self-help resources on romance and relationships. . . . Ultimately, she realizes that she has learned the most about love and relationships from her four dogs."

Markoe's *The Day My Dogs Became Guys* is a tale for children, with illustrations by Eric Brace that Janice M. Del Negro wrote in *Bulletin of the Center for Children's Books* resemble the "slightly off-the-wall visuals reminiscent of *Ren and Stimpy* cartoons." Carey is the boy of the story, and his dogs are Butch, Dee Dee, and Ed, normal pets until a solar eclipse changes them into the "guys" of the title. They retain their dog personalities, however, and cause all sorts of mischief, then turn back into dogs with the end of the eclipse, just as Carey's mother returns home from work. Susan Dove Lempke noted in *Booklist* that "the basic situation is humorous." A *Kirkus Reviews* contributor felt this story will be embraced by "readers who ever hoped that their pets could become people." A *Publishers Weekly* reviewer observed that Brace's illustrations "will have children of all ages rolling on the floor" and said Markoe's first juvenile work "makes a very droll children's book debut."

It's My F—ing Birthday is Markoe's first novel and consists of the journal entries of a single high school art teacher on seven consecutive birthdays following the end of a relationship. A *Publishers Weekly* reviewer called the book "the perfect gift for all women who face birthdays with grim determination, pepper spray, and sharp fingernail files." Beginning with her thirty-sixth birthday, the unnamed narrator writes an overview of the past year and makes poignant observations about men, such as "Here was a guy who claimed to earn his living as a handyman. . . . But he had no idea at all where anything was on a woman."

The narrator is forced to celebrate every birthday with her parents, who spend the entire time telling her what a loser she is and who give her gifts of incredibly ugly clothing. One of the actions the narrator takes is to refuse to continue this annual torture. In each entry, she takes a stand. On her thirty-sixth birthday she vows not to participate in bad sex. On her thirty-seventh she says no more shopping with her mother. She concludes on her thirty-eighth birthday that it is no big deal that she didn't have a partner that year. "When you have never loved at all, at least you have enough attention span left to get some reading done," is her revelation at thirty-nine. Seaman wrote that "Markoe's hero discovers at age forty what readers knew all along: that she's mighty good company, boyfriend or no boyfriend." "This funny story about jerky men and clueless parents is a great complement to Markoe's nonfiction works," commented Kathy Ingels Helmond in *Library Journal.*

Publishers Weekly's Melissa Mia Hall interviewed Markoe, and asked her if *It's My F—ing Birthday* is autobiographical. Markoe replied, "I was trying to write the voice of the women I've been hanging out with for the past ten years—assorted smart, really neat, great women. And there's this lament I've been listening to and participating in. It's the joint voice of that peer group."

Hall asked Markoe if she thought birthdays should be celebrated or outlawed. Markoe said, "Let's get rid of them. You can have one like every fifteen or twenty years. It's the underlying attitude—it has nothing to do with the birthday. It's the whole way they hammer at us about being nervous about life. To hell with it."

BIOGRAPHICAL AND CRITICAL SOURCES:

PERIODICALS

Book, March-April, 2002, Steve Wilson, review of *It's My F—ing Birthday,* p. 76.

Booklist, May 1, 1992, Ilene Cooper, review of *What the Dogs Have Taught Me and Other Amazing Things I've Learned,* p. 1578; August, 1994, Ilene Cooper, review of *How to Be Hap-Hap-Happy Like Me,* p. 2017; February 1, 1997, Donna Seaman, review of *Merrill Markoe's Guide to Love,* p. 912; February 15, 1999, Susan Dove Lempke, review of *The Day My Dogs Became Guys,* p. 1076; February 1, 2002, Donna Seaman, review of *It's My F—ing Birthday,* p. 922.

Bulletin of the Center for Children's Books, March, 1999, Janice M. Del Negro, review of *The Day My Dogs Became Guys,* p. 248.

Cosmopolitan, January, 1987, Caroline Latham, "Does Anyone Know the Real David Letterman?" p. 68.

Entertainment Weekly, October 28, 1994, Matthew Flamm, review of *How to Be Hap-Hap-Happy like Me,* p. 84.

Kirkus Reviews, January 1, 1999, review of *The Day My Dogs Became Guys,* p. 69.

Library Journal, April 15, 1992, Carol Spielman Lezak, review of *What the Dogs Have Taught Me and Other Amazing Things I've Learned,* p. 90; September 15, 1994, Wilda Williams, review of *How to Be Hap-Hap-Happy like Me,* p. 72; January, 2002, Kathy Ingels Helmond, review of *It's My F—ing Birthday,* p. 150.

Los Angeles Times, March 21, 1997, Irene Lacher, review of *Merrill Markoe's Guide to Love,* pp. E1-E2.

New York Times, June 6, 1988, John J. O'Connor, review of *Merrill Markoe's Guide to Glamourous Living,* p. C18.

O, March, 2002, Lisa Kogan, review of *It's My F—ing Birthday,* p. 128.

People, July 27, 1987, Jeff Jarvis, review of *This Week Indoors,* p. 11; May 23, 1988, Joanne Kaufman, "Merrill Markoe, *Late Night*'s Loss and Cable's Gain, Surfaces in a Glamourous Special All her Own," p. 79; July 25, 1994, Craig Tomashoff, "*TV Nation,*" p. 15; October 24, 1994, Joanne Kaufman, interview, p. 24, review of *How to Be Hap-Hap-Happy like Me,* p. 25.

Publishers Weekly, February 24, 1992, review of *What the Dogs Have Taught Me and Other Amazing Things I've Learned,* p. 35; August 8, 1994, review of *How to Be Hap-Hap-Happy like Me,* p. 408; January 2, 1995, review of *How to Be Hap-Hap-Happy like Me,* p. 42; December 9, 1996, review of *Merrill Markoe's Guide to Love,* p. 54; January 18, 1999, review of *The Day My Dogs Became Guys,* p. 337; January 21, 2002, review of *It's My F—ing Birthday,* p. 64, Melissa Mia Hall, "*PW* Talks with Merrill Markoe,*" p. 65.

School Library Journal, April, 1986, Elizabeth Thurston, review of *Late Night with David Letterman: The Book,* p. 107.

Time, June 1, 1992, Amelia Weiss, review of *What the Dogs Have Taught Me and Other Amazing Things I've Learned,* p. 86; October 3, 1994, Ginia Bellafante, review of *How to Be Hap-Hap-Happy like Me,* p. 87.

Tribune Books (Chicago, IL), February 9, 1997, Carolyn Alessio, review of *Merrill Markoe's Guide to Love,* p. 6.*

*   *   *

MARQUINA, Eduardo 1879-1946

PERSONAL: Born January 21, 1879, in Barcelona, Spain; died as result of a heart attack November 21, 1946, in New York, NY; son of Luis Marquina (a businessman); married Mercedes Pichot, June 18, 1903; children: Luis. *Education:* Attended Universidad Barcelona, 1896.

CAREER: Poet, playwright, and translator. *España Nueva,* correspondent, 1900-01.

MEMBER: Warsaw Conference of Dramatic and Musical Authors (president, 1930), Spanish Royal Academy, Sociedad de Autores Españoles (president, beginning 1932).

AWARDS, HONORS: Premio Piquer, Spanish Royal Academy, 1908, for *Las hijas del Cid,* 1910, for *En Flandres se ha puesto el sol;* Gold Medal from the City of Barcelona, 1946.

WRITINGS:

PLAYS

El pastor (three-act; title means "The Shepherd"; produced in Madrid, Spain, 1902), A. Lopez (Barcelona, Spain), 1902.

Aqua mansa (title means "Still Water"; produced in Madrid, Spain, 1902), Velasco (Madrid, Spain), 1903.

La vuelta del rebaño (title means "The Return of the Flock"; produced in Madrid, Spain, 1903), Velasco (Madrid, Spain), 1903.

Mala cabeza (produced in Madrid, Spain, 1906), Velasco (Madrid, Spain), 1906.

Benvenuto Cellini (four-act; produced in Madrid, Spain, 1906), Sociedad de Autores Españoles (Madrid, Spain), 1906.

Emporium, music by Enrique Morera, F. Giró (Barcelona, Spain), 1906.

(With José Salmerón) *El delfín: zarzuela histórica* (title means "The Dauphin"; produced in Madrid, Spain, 1907), Biblioteca Clasíca (Madrid, Spain), 1908.

La hijas del Cid: leyenda trágica (five-act; title means "The Daughters of the Cid"; produced in Madrid, Spain, 1908), Velasco (Madrid, Spain), 1908.

Doña María la Brava (produced in Madrid, Spain, 1909), Renacimiento (Madrid, Spain), 1909.

En Flandres se ha puesto el sol (title means "The Sun Has Set in Flanders"; produced in Montevideo, Spain, 1910), Renacimiento (Madrid, Spain), 1911.

El último día, produced in Madrid, Spain, 1911.

La alcaidesa de Pastrana (also see below; produced in Madrid, Spain, 1911), Renacimiento (Madrid, Spain), 1911.

La muñeca irromible (for children; produced in Madrid, Spain, c. 1912), Juventud (Barcelona, Spain), 1949.

Las cartas de la monja (also see below), produced in Madrid, Spain, 1912.

El rey trovador (four-act; produced in Madrid, Spain, 1912), Renacimiento (Madrid, Spain), 1912.

El antifaz, produced in Madrid, Spain, 1912.

La muerte en Alba (also see below), produced in Madrid, Spain, 1912.

Cuando florezcan los rosales (three-act comedy; produced in Madrid, Spain, 1913), Sociedad anónima (Madrid, Spain), 1912, translation by Charles Alfred Turrell published as *When the Roses Are in Bloom Again,* in *Contemporary Spanish Dramatists,* R. D. Badger (Boston, MA), 1919.

Por los pecados del rey (three-act; produced in Madrid, Spain, 1913), Renacimiento (Madrid, Spain), 1913.

El gavilán de la espada, produced in Madrid, Spain, 1913.

El retablo de Agrellano (produced in Madrid, Spain, 1913), Renacimiento (Madrid, Spain), 1914.

Cantiga de serrana (anthology), Hispania (Madrid, Spain), 1914.

La hiedra (produced in Madrid, Spain, 1914), Renacimiento (Madrid, Spain), 1914.

La Morisca (produced in Madrid, Spain, 1914), Renacimiento (Madrid, Spain), 1918.

Las flores de Aragon (produced in Madrid, Spain, 1914), Renacimiento (Madrid, Spain), 1915.

Una mujer (three-act; produced in Madrid, Spain, 1915), Velasco (Madrid, Spain), 1915.

Juglarías (includes *El ultimo día* and *Una leyenda*), Libreria Española (Barcelona, Spain), 1915.

El gran capitán: leyenda dramática de amor caballeresco (three-act; produced in Madrid, Spain, 1916), Renacimiento (Madrid, Spain), 1916.

Alondra, produced in Madrid, Spain, 1918.

Dondiego de Noche, produced in Madrid, Spain, 1919.

Alimaña (four-act; produced in Madrid, Spain, 1919), published with *La princesa juega,* Reus (Madrid, Spain), 1921.

La princesa juega (two-act; produced in Madrid, Spain, 1920), published with *Alimaña,* Reus (Madrid, Spain), 1921.

Ebora, produced in Madrid, Spain, 1921.

El pavo real (title means "The Peacock"; produced in Madrid, Spain, 1922), [Barcelona, Spain], 1922.

(With Luis Fernández Ardavín) *Rosa de Francia* (three-act; produced in Madrid, Spain, 1923), Hispania (Madrid, Spain), 1923.

Una noche en Venencia (produced in Madrid, Spain, 1923), Reus (Madrid, Spain), 1923.

El pobrecito carpintero (title means "The Poor Little Carpenter"; produced in Madrid, Spain, 1924), Reus (Madrid, Spain), 1924.

(With Alfonso Hernández Catá) *Don Luis Mejía: comedia legendaria de capa y espada* (four-act; produced in Madrid, Spain, 1925), Reus (Madrid, Spain), 1925.

Fruto bendito (produced in Madrid, Spain, 1927), Reus (Madrid, Spain), 1927.

La ermita, la fuente y el río (three-act; title means "The Hermitage, the Fountain, and the River"; produced in Madrid, Spain, 1927), Reus (Madrid, Spain), 1927.

Sin horca ni cuchillo (three-act; produced in Madrid, Spain, 1927), Reus (Madrid, Spain), 1929.

La vida es más (three-act; produced in Madrid, Spain, 1928), Reus (Madrid, Spain), 1928.

Salvadora: drama rural (produced in Madrid, Spain, 1929), Reus (Madrid, Spain), 1929.

(With Gregorio Martínez Sierra) *El camino de la felicidad,* produced in Madrid, Spain, 1929.

El monje blanco: retablos de leyenda primitiva (title means "The White Monk"; produced in Madrid, Spain, 1930), Estrella (Madrid, Spain), 1930.

Fuente escondida (title means "Hidden Spring"; produced in Madrid, Spain, 1931), Renacimiento (Madrid, Spain), 1931.

Los Julianes (three-act; produced in Madrid, Spain, 1932), Reus (Madrid, Spain), 1932.

Era Una vez en Bagdad (title means "Once upon a Time in Bagdad"; produced in Madrid, Spain, 1932), Reus (Madrid, Spain), 1932.

Pasos y trabajos de Santa Teresa de Jesús (estampas carmelitas) (includes *La alcaidesa de Pastrana, Las cartas de la monja,* and *La muerte en Alba*), Reus (Madrid, Spain), 1933.

(Adaptor) Lope de Vega, . . . *La Dorotea* (comedy), Reus (Madrid, Spain), 1935.

Los que dios non perdona, produced in Madrid, Spain, 1935.

En el nombre del padre (produced in Madrid, Spain, 1935), Reus (Madrid, Spain), 1936.

La bandera de San Martín, produced in Buenos Aires, Argentina, 1937.

La Santa Hermandad (title means "The Holy Brotherhood"), produced in Santiago, Chile, 1937.

El estudiante ediablado (title means "The Devilish Student"; produced in Madrid, Spain, 1942.

María la viuda: poema dramatico (title means "Maria the Widow"; produced in Madrid, Spain, 1943), Españolas (Madrid, Spain), 1943.

El galeón y el milagro: folletin romantica (five-act; produced in Madrid, Spain, 1946), Reus (Madrid, Spain), 1947.

OTHER

(With Guerra Junqueiro) *La musa en ocios,* Atlante (Barcelona, Spain), 1878.

Odas (poetry), Académica de Serra Hnos y Russell (Barcelona, Spain), 1900.

Las vendimias (poetry; title means "The Grape Harvests"), F. Seix (Barcelona, Spain), 1901.

Eglogas (poetry), Rodríguez Serra (Madrid, Spain), 1901.

Elegías (poetry), Renacimiento (Madrid, Spain), 1905.

La caravana (short stories), R. Sopena (Barcelona, Spain), 1907.

Vendimión (long poem), Biblioteca Clasíca (Madrid, Spain), 1908.

Almas anónimas (novel), Casa Editorial Maucci (Barcelona, Spain), 1908.

Canciones del momento (poetry), F. Beltrán (Madrid, Spain), 1910.

Tierras de España (poetry), Renacimiento (Madrid, Spain), 1914.

Brevario de un año, [Madrid, Spain], 1918.

La dos vidas (novel), E. Domenech (Barcelona, Spain), 1919.

El beso en la herida (novel), Estrella (Madrid, Spain), 1920.

El alma de Sixto (novel), Prensa Gráfica (Madrid, Spain), 1921.

La casa cerrada (novel), Prensa Gráfica (Madrid, Spain), 1922.

La poesía de San Francisco de Asís (long poem), Reus (Madrid, Spain), 1927.

Mujeres (1917-1936) (poetry), J. Peuser (Buenos Aires, Argentina), 1936.

Los pueblos y su alma (1917-1936) (poetry), J. Peuser (Buenos Aires, Argentina), 1936.

Mi huerto en la ladera (poetry), J. Peuser (Buenos Aires, Argentina), 1936.

Los tres libros de España (contains *España en ocaso, España miltante,* and *España en albas*), Escelicer (Madrid, Spain), 1941.

Avisos y máximas de Santa Teresa de Jesús (poetry anthology), Betis (Barcelona, Spain), 1942.

La reina mujer (Isabel la Católica) (novel), Betis (Barcelona, Spain), 1942.

Lámparas (poetry), 1943.

Obras completas (includes the novels *Almas anónimas* and *La reina mujer*), 8 volumes, Aguilar (Madrid, Spain), 1944-1951.

Antología poética, compiled by Federico Carlos Sáinz de Robles, Aguilar (Madrid, Spain), 1944.

Spanish Poet Eduardo Marquina Reading from His Work (sound recording), Library of Congress (Washington, DC), 1946.

Maternidad (novel), E. Heras (Barcelona, Spain), 1950.

Eduardo Marquina: sus mejores poesías, edited by F. González Ledesman, Bruguera (Barcelona, Spain), 1954.

Días de infancia y adolescencia: memorias del último tercio del siglo (memoirs), Juventud (Barcelona, Spain), 1964.

La misa azul, Emiliano Escolar (Madrid, Spain), 1980.

Contributor of poems, stories, translations, and essays to periodicals, including *Luz, La Publicidad, Caras y Caretas, El Cuento Semanal,* and *Heraldo de Madrid.* Contributor to anthology *Cancionero de la guerra: versos,* Españoles (Madrid, Spain), 1939. Translator of works from Portuguese, Italian, and other languages.

Marquina's works have been translated into several languages, including Italian.

SIDELIGHTS: Writing many of his plays as his country headed into a period of political upheaval that culminated in violent civil war, prolific Spanish playwright and poet Eduardo Marquina avoided dealing with such political concerns by setting his popular dramas in the past, or in rural areas relatively untouched by war. Wishing to revive poetic drama, he used verse to glorify Spain's triumphant past, and focused on heroic figures and courtly subjects. During the years near his death in 1946 the conservative playwright's concern over morals and faith grew increasingly more pronounced, and his work became redolent of his strong Catholic faith. Among his plays, 1943's *María la viuda* is considered by many critics to be Marquina's best drama, while his long poem *Vendimión* has continued to impress critics with its impassioned philosophical stance and its grandiose presentation since its initial publication in 1909.

Born in 1879 to parents from the Aragon region bordering the Pyrenees of northeastern Spain, Marquina was one of seven children. After attending first a Catholic school run by French monks and then a Jesuit school, he enrolled at the Universidad Barcelona but dropped out after only a few months. Determined to make his living as a poet, he began to contribute to the modernist journal *Luz* and other publications and had some small success when *Luz* editors began to publish his poems in 1897. In 1900 Marquina released his first book of poems, *Odas,* but was forced to find work as a journalist when the volume did not provide him the hoped-for entré into Madrid's literary community.

Marquina's first play, the idealistic *El pastor,* was produced in the winter of 1902 and ran for four days under the patronage of Spanish musician Ruperto Chapí; among its follow-up efforts was 1906's *Benvenuto Cellini,* a biographical work that follows the life of the sixteenth-century Italian sculptor and through which a young, socialist-minded Marquina "exalts the value of art above all utilitarian principles and the right of the artist to create freely," according to Manuel de la Nuez in his *Eduardo Marquina.*

Married and the father of a son, Luis, by 1904, Marquina moved his family to Madrid, then the center of Spanish theater. Spain's theater community was at this point undergoing a transformation, as the influx of young playwrights such as Adelardo López de Ayala began to overshadow the prominence of established writers such as nineteenth-century Nobel Prize-winning playwright José Echegaray. Now a part of this vibrant community, and with the backing of Madrid's influential Guerrero-Mendoza theater company, Marquina entered a more mature phase of his career, and perfected the verse drama form. His five-act play *Las hijas del Cid,* with its focus on traditional Spanish themes and its author-penned dedication to "the future of the mother country" and "the new life of the heroes who died for love and pain for old Castille," proved to be the playwright's first critical success upon its opening in March of 1908. The story of the Cid's attempts to marry off his daughters to honorable nobles, the play draws on the Spanish epic of El Cid, a heroic warrior and defender of the realm on horseback and who was first popularized in a poem dating from the twelfth century. Awarded the Premio Piquer from the Spanish Royal Academy, *Las hijas del Cid* was less warmly embraced by the public and had only a fifteen-day run in Madrid.

After his success with *Las hijas del Cid,* Marquina's subsequent dramatic efforts proved uneven, the unqualified critical success of his historical drama *En Flandes se ha puesto el sol* followed by a series of low-profile plays that culminated with the disappointing *El gran capitán* in March of 1916. Running less than two weeks, *El gran capitán* focuses on the unwanted attentions of a Spanish nobleman toward Queen Isabella; its controversial presentation of the Spanish Crown and the overshadowing of the play's romantic element by a script dense with rhyme caused little excitement among either theatergoers or critics. Acknowledging the lack of depth of such historical dramas, and recognizing the public's unenthusiastic response to the verse drama form, Marquina authored several prose plays set in contemporary Spain, and also traveled to Latin America in 1916 in the company of the touring Guerrero-Mendoza troupe. Although these plays met with a relatively positive reception, the prose style did not suit Marquina, and by the 1920s he had began to once again pen verse dramas. Unlike his previous works of this type, he now focused on glorifying the lives of the rural poor in such plays as *El pobrecito carpintero* and *La ermita, la fuente y el.*

One of several collaborative efforts he undertook during his long career, Marquina joined fellow playwright Alfonso Hernández Catá to produce 1925's *Don Luis Mejía,* which focuses on the legendary lover Don Juan. However, an increasingly conservative Marquina's first religious-themed play, *El monje blanco,* premiered in Madrid in 1930 and marked the beginning of what many critics have viewed as the final phase of his writing career. Following a tour of Austria, Poland, and Czechoslovakia, Marquina returned to Spain and in 1931 was elected to the prestigious Spanish Royal Academy. His subsequent election as president of the Sociedad de Autores Españoles was yet another symbol of Marquina's growing stature within Spain's intellectual community.

When the Spanish Civil War broke out in 1936 and Generalissimo Francisco Franco began—with the help of fellow European dictators Adolph Hitler and Benito Mussolini—his three-year military push to become dictator of all Spain, Marquina was out of the country on a tour of Latin America with his theatre associates. Because of the playwright's known anti-communist sympathies, Marquina's wife and son were forced to go in to hiding and left Spain to join Marquina in Buenos Aires, Argentina. While in Buenos Aires the playwright began work on *La Santa Hermandad,* a play with strong Nationalist undertones that draws connections between the glorious reign of Ferdinand and Isabella and the events of the Spanish Civil War then underway. The opposing forces of Nationalism and Republicanism are personified in the play's two main characters, brothers Blas—the "good" brother, who represents Nationalism—and Martín, who represents the discordant influences of Republicanism. Disappointed in the "simplistic" resolution of the conflict between the two brothers, De la Nuez nonetheless noted that the playwright's "inherent human goodness manifests itself clearly" in *La Santa Hermandad:* "In 1937, in the midst of a bloody civil war, when cries for vengeance were ringing out on both sides, [Marquina] . . . was asking for reconciliation among Spaniards, as both brothers are finally reunited."

In 1938 the Marquina family returned to Spain and settled in Seville because, unlike Madrid, that city was under the protection of Nationalist Movement forces. Due to his extended stay away from Spain, the ongoing political disruption, and because of his increasing participation in the activities of Spain's literary elite, Marquina found his play production declining during the 1930s and 1940s. Interestingly, *Maria la viuda,* which premiered in 1943, is considered by many critics to be his best play, due to its well-rounded portrayal of strong, realistic female characters. 1946's *El galeón y el milagro,* was the last of Marquina's historical dramas to be produced during his lifetime. While traveling in Central and North America in the fall of 1946 as a representative of Spain's literary community, the playwright suffered a series of heart attacks. He died in New York City in November, at the age of sixty-seven.

BIOGRAPHICAL AND CRITICAL SOURCES:

BOOKS

De la Nuez, Manuel, *Eduardo Marquina,* Twayne (Boston, MA), 1976.
Montera Alonso, José, *Vida de Eduardo Marquina,* Nacional (Madrid, Spain), 1965.

PERIODICALS

Circulo, Volume 12, 1984, pp. 55-61.
Cuadernos de Aldeeu, January, 1983, pp. 91-99.
Explicación de Textos Literarios, Volume 12, number 1, 1983-84, pp. 79-85.

Revista de Filologia Española, January-June, 1988, Manuel Alvar, "Un cantarcillo transmitido por Andrés Bernáldez," pp. 141-142.

Salina, November, 1999, Gregorio Torres Nebrera, "*En Flandes se ha puesto el sol:* Teatralidad, contexto histórico y parodia," pp. 111-128.*

*   *   *

MARSDEN, Carolyn 1950-

PERSONAL: Born August 14, 1950, in Mexico City, Mexico; daughter of Wesley Matzigkeit (a minister) and Winifred (a teacher; maiden name, Howell) Marsden; married Panratt Manoorasada (an electrician), August 8, 1987, children: Maleeka, Preeya. *Ethnicity:* "White." *Education:* Attended University of Arizona; University of Colorado, B.A. (philosophy), 1972; Vermont College, M.F.A. (writing for children), 2000. *Religion:* Buddhist.

ADDRESSES: Agent—c/o Author Mail, Candlewick Press, 2067 Massachusetts Ave., Third Fl., Cambridge, MA 02140. *E-mail*—prahathit@aol.com.

CAREER: Has worked variously as a bilingual (Spanish-English) elementary and preschool teacher in Tucson, AZ, Chula Vista, CA, and National City, CA; Arizona Commission on the Arts, writer-in-residence, 1978-85.

MEMBER: Society of Children's Book Writers and Illustrators.

AWARDS, HONORS: Candlewick scholarship to Vermont College, 2000.

WRITINGS:

The Gold-threaded Dress, Candlewick Press (Cambridge, MA), 2002.

Mama Had to Work on Christmas, Viking (New York, NY), 2003.

Silk Umbrellas, Candlewick Press (Cambridge, MA), in press.

WORK IN PROGRESS: The Moon Journal, for Candlewick Press (Cambridge, MA); *The Brightest Place in the Sky: When a Mariachi Sings,* a photographic essay on a blind mariachi singer; *Bird Spring,* a novel about a Navajo boy.

SIDELIGHTS: Poet, short-story writer, and novelist Carolyn Marsden began publishing multiracial children's books in 2002, yet she had long been active in helping children appreciate the wonders of language. She earned a bachelor's degree in philosophy in 1972, from the University of Colorado. She later studied with poet Steve Orlen in the Master of Fine Arts program at the University of Arizona. With the support of the Arizona Arts Commission, she taught poetry writing in classes ranging from kindergarten through high school. The author also studied poetry at the University of Arizona. For Marsden, these were fulfilling activities for as she told *CA,* "I gain inspiration and courage from the children with whom I spend my days."

From a young age, Marsden was also interested in longer works, writing her first book while still a young teen. "I first embarked on the adventure of writing when I was thirteen years old. Inspired by the movie *Twenty-Thousand Leagues under the Sea,* I adapted Jules Verne's classic tale and created my own fantasy set in outer space. Instead of underwater excitement, the crew of my space ship experienced the dangers of a Mars-like planet. While I was writing this story, I made the attic of my house into a spaceship. In my dark blue school uniform, I pretended that I was the gloomy, charismatic captain of the spaceship. In Verne's story, the submarine was elegantly furnished, so I borrowed my mother's fine china and real silverware. She couldn't figure out where it had disappeared to!"

Becoming a parent often influences future children's book writers as well. For Marsden, poetry took on a new form after making up stories for the oldest of her two daughters. She remembered, "I made up bedtime stories about a family of rabbits. My little girl always giggled when the baby rabbit drove the green car very fast! Picture books seemed like another form of poetry and my interest in writing for children grew."

Marsden studied writing for children at Vermont College, earning her M.F.A. in 2000. In this renowned program, she "got to study with the giants of contemporary children's literature," she said, adding, "I also made many close writer friends. We call ourselves 'The Hive' because we are always buzzing with ideas!" Marsden's hard work there paid off in several ways. In 2000 she won the Vermont College Candlewick Scholarship, and shortly after she graduated Candlewick Press bought the rights to her first novel, *The Gold-threaded Dress,* which is geared to middle-grade readers. "I love the form of the middle-grade chapter book," she enthused. "It isn't as lengthy as a full novel and doesn't have the constraints of a picture book. I write intuitively, without much of an outline. I draw upon my past experience and training in poetry for imagery and musicality of language."

In writing *The Gold-threaded Dress,* Marsden borrowed from her personal experiences and those of other people she knew: It "was inspired when my younger daughter was teased about being Chinese at school. I mulled over her situation in my mind. I combined her story with experiences that I had had with a Vietnamese immigrant family when I taught preschool. Also, my husband's brother was considering coming over to the United States to work as a cook." She put her experiences as a classroom teacher to use as well, as she explained, "The making and breaking of friendships, bullying and teasing, and an increasingly diverse United States are all an integral part of school experience." *The Gold-threaded Dress,* which tells the story of Oy, a very shy girl from Thailand who wants acceptance from her classmates, was published to good reviews. In a starred review, *Booklist*'s Carolyn Phelan praised Marsden for her "keen observation" and understanding of school children, as did a *Publishers Weekly* reviewer, who noted that the author deals with the subject matter "squarely and truthfully." Deborah Stevenson noted in a review for the *Bulletin of the Center for Children's Books* that while the topic is common, the use of a Thai family is "unusual" for the middle-grade novel. In addition, several reviewers complimented Marsden's narrative style, including Alison Follos of *School Library Journal,* who described it as having a "natural voice" and Stevenson who praised its "straightforward sweetness." Remarking on the novel's "forceful message," a *Kirkus Reviews* critic believed that children could learn important lessons about friendship from reading it, while a *New York Times* critic summed it up as "a fine novel for newly independent readers."

Marsden has continued to mine her life for story ideas. For example, the act of enjoying brunch at a fancy hotel restaurant on Christmas Day sparked the idea for the short illustrated chapter book *Mama Had to Work on Christmas.* "I became uncomfortable thinking of the families of the people who were working," Marsden recalled. "Drawing upon my knowledge of California Latino culture, I wrote a book from the point of view of a little girl whose mother works in the ladies' restroom of a sumptuous hotel." Another personal experience led to Marsden writing a sports book, a genre in which she had never dreamed of writing. "When my daughter was in fifth grade, she suddenly began to excel in the long jump and fifty-meter sprint. Yet my daughter wasn't a competitor at heart and worried that by jumping too high or running too fast, she would make her athletic friends jealous and lose their friendship." When she combined her daughter's story in journal form with a plot about a sibling conflict, *The Moon Journal,* a chapter book for seven to nine year olds, was the result.

The author told *CA,* "In 1994, while visiting Thailand, I learned of the electronic factories located in the northern part of the country. These factories operate without regulations for the protection of the environment or worker safety. On returning home, I began my first story for children, *Silk Umbrellas.* This book is about a young girl, Noi, whose older sister works in a radio factory. Noi must work against time to fulfil her dream of becoming an umbrella painter, like her grandmother, instead of joining her sister as a factory worker.

"In progress is a sequel to *The Gold-threaded Dress.* The working title is *The Quail Club.* Like *The Gold-threaded Dress,* this story was inspired by events at school involving my young daughter. I transposed the characters of *The Gold-threaded Dress* onto this situation. The main character's friends want her to dance a rock and roll song with them in the talent show, but Oy longs to perform her Thai dance instead. Once again, she is faced with the difficult decision of choosing between friendship and culture."

"I am also beginning a historical-fiction chapter book inspired by my grandmother's childhood in Santa Monica, California, and Ensenada, Mexico, where her father was foreman of a fruit cannery at the turn of the century. The working title is *Alice Fern.*" Marsden is also at work on the photographic essay *The Brightest Place in the Sky: When a Mariachi Sings,* about a teenage Mariachi singer, Jessica Rojas, who is blind.

In the classroom and at home, Marsden finds much to enrich her writing. "I get most of my story ideas from the children in my life," she told *CA*. "I watch and listen closely at home and in the classroom. Sometimes I carry a notebook with me to jot down a description, an interesting thing that a person says, or a conflict I see unfolding. I then use my imagination to shape these bits and pieces into stories."

Marsden's imagination brims with ideas for new books, which will not stay long on the back burner. "Although I work full time, I always have several manuscripts in progress and write every day," she revealed at her personal Web site.

BIOGRAPHICAL AND CRITICAL SOURCES:

PERIODICALS

Booklist, May 1, 2002, Carolyn Phelan, review of *The Gold-threaded Dress,* p. 1521.
Bulletin of the Center for Children's Books, June, 2002, Deborah Stevenson, review of *The Gold-threaded Dress.*
Kirkus Reviews, February 15, 2002, review of *The Gold-threaded Dress,* p. 262.
New York Times, July 14, 2002, Lawrence Downes, review of *The Gold-threaded Dress,* p. 18.
Publishers Weekly, March 4, 2002, review of *The Gold-threaded Dress,* pp. 79-80.
School Library Journal, April, 2002, Alison Follos, review of *The Gold-threaded Dress,* p. 117.

ONLINE

Carolyn Marsden Web site, http//carolynmarsden.com (November 20, 2002).

*   *   *

MARSH, Fabienne 1957-

PERSONAL: Born September 17, 1957, in Schenectady, NY; daughter of Louis V. and Jeanne (Caulet) Marsh; married Aloke K. Mandal (a surgeon), June 22, 1995; children: Paul, Juliette. *Education:* Williams College, B.A., 1979.

ADDRESSES: Agent—Richard Pine, Arthur Pine Associates, 250 West 57th St., New York, NY 10019. *E-mail*—FabInk@aol.com.

CAREER: American Broadcasting Co., New York, NY, researcher for documentary film unit, 1980-84; freelance writer, consultant, and field producer for documentary films, 1984—. Johns Hopkins University, Baltimore, MD, lecturer in creative writing, 1997-2000; University of Minnesota, lecturer, 2001; radio commentator.

AWARDS, HONORS: Woolrich fellow, Columbia University, 1981; Rotary journalism fellow, London School of Economics and Political Science, 1984-85.

WRITINGS:

Long Distances (novel), Simon & Schuster (New York, NY), 1988.
The Moralist of the Alphabet Streets (novel), Algonquin Books of Chapel Hill (Chapel Hill, NC), 1991.
(With Michael Cader) *Dave's World* (humor), Warner Books (New York, NY), 1995.
(Editor and contributor) *Saturday Night Live: The First Twenty Years,* Houghton-Mifflin (Boston, MA), 1994.
Single, White, Cave Man (novel), iUniverse, 2002.

Contributor to magazines and newspapers, including *Poetry Review, Chicago Tribune, Economist, International Herald Tribune,* and *New York Times.*

WORK IN PROGRESS: Cunningham's Last Wish, a novel; a radio series for National Public Radio.

*   *   *

MATALON, Ronit 1959-

PERSONAL: Born 1959, in Ganei Tikva, Israel. *Education:* Attended Tel Aviv University. *Religion:* Jewish.

ADDRESSES: Home—Tel Aviv, Israel. *Agent*—c/o Author Mail, Metropolitan Books, Henry Holt and Company, 115 West 18th St., New York, NY 10011.

CAREER: Journalist, educator, and author. Journalist for Israeli television; currently journalist for Israeli daily *Ha'aretz;* critic and book reviewer. Camera Obscura School of the Arts, Tel Aviv, Israel, literature professor, 1993—. Member, Ministry of Education, Council for Culture and Art, and Van Leer Institute, Culture Forum of Mediterranean Culture.

AWARDS, HONORS: Israeli Prime Minister's Award for Literature, 1994.

WRITINGS:

(With Rut Tsarefati) *Sipur she-mathil be-levayah shel nahash* (juvenile fiction; title means "A Story That Begins with a Snake's Funeral"), Dvir (Tel Aviv, Israel), 1989.

Zarim ba-bayit: sipurim (title means "Strangers at Home"), ha-Kibuts ha-me'uhad (Tel Aviv, Israel), 1992.

Zeh 'im ha-panim elenu, 'Am 'oved (Tel Aviv, Israel), 1995, translation by Marsha Weinstein published as *The One Facing Us,* Metropolitan Books (New York, NY), 1998.

Osher me-ahore ha-'etsim, ha-Arets (Tel Aviv, Israel), 1997.

Sarah, Sarah, 'Am 'oved (Tel Aviv, Israel), 2000.

Kero u-khetov (title means "Read and Write"), ha-Kibuts ha-me'uhad (Tel Aviv, Israel), 2001.

OTHER

(With Avi Mugrabi and Dina Zvi-Riklis) *Sipur she-mathil bi-levayah shel nahash* (screenplay; produced 1989; also released as *Dreams of Innocence*), Keren le-'idud ha-seret ha-Yise'eli (Tel Aviv, Israel), 1993.

(With others) *Ashkenazim, Mizrahiyim, Sefaradim* (screenplay), ha-Rashut ha-sheniyah la-televizyah vela-radyo, 1999.

Author's work has been translated into Dutch and German. Short stories translated and collected in anthologies, including "Photograph", translation by Gal Kedai and Miriyam Glazer, published in *Dreaming of the Actual: Contemporary Fiction and Poetry by Israeli Women Writers,* edited by Miryam Glazer, State University of New York Press (Albany, NY),

2000; and "Little Brother", translation by Marsha Weinstein, in *Keys to the Garden: New Israeli Writing,* edited by Ammiel Alcalay, City Light Books (San Francisco, CA), 1996.

SIDELIGHTS: Ronit Matalon was born in the immigrant town of Ganei Tikva, outside Tel Aviv, Israel. Her early work was published in the 1980s in *Siman Kri'a,* a literary journal, followed by her first collection in 1991. She writes in Hebrew, mixed with Arabic, French, and sometimes English. Her writing has been recognized in English-language anthologies of Israeli writing, such as *Dreaming of the Actual: Contemporary Fiction and Poetry by Israeli Women Writers* and *Keys to the Garden: New Israeli Writing.* Her first translated novel, *Zeh 'im ha-panim elenu,* published in English as *The One Facing Us,* was very well received by a wider audience.

Matalon's works are heavily influenced by her life during Israel's coming of age, and are marked by the confusion and fighting stemming from contemporary events. Her 1984 short story "Little Brother" was inspired by Yitzak Gormezano Goren's description of the death of Shimon Yehoshua. It alludes to a similar circumstance, which is then relived again and again in the psyches of Matalon's characters. In this story, the dreams of life and work at a kibbutz become supplanted by worries of aging and financial troubles. The plot is simple, and Matalon leaves many details unsaid and unexplained though clues are filtered through her haunted characters.

In the novel *The One Facing Us,* an adolescent Esther serves as a mirror to her Levantine family and ancestors, loosely referencing Matalon's own Egyptian-Jewish roots. While staying with her Uncle Sicourelle in Cameroon, Esther searches through family photographs and subjectively retold stories for clues to help define her own identity. Matalon begins each chapter with photographs of the family, who have since dispersed from Egypt to Israel and New York. The initial catalyst for their exodus is Cairo's shattered post-war economy, in which the family is forced to choose between Zionism and communism. Esther learns of the family's struggles with failed marriages, poverty, the experiences of fighting for Israeli independence, and Uncle Sicourelle's own entrepreneurial ventures in Central America. Disappointed by Zionism, the scattered aunts and uncles long for the life they had in Egypt—but Esther finds memory is not necessarily accurate in its portrayal of past events. Bill Ott wrote in *Booklist* that *The One Facing Us* is "a family saga with the texture of reality. Plotless, oblique, but rich in character and filled with irony and guarded affection." It follows lives to find a common root, exposing guiltlessly what Susie Linfield of the *Los Angeles Times* described as the "stupidities, cohesions, ruptures, [and] radically imperfect modes of survival" of the family. *Carpe librum*'s Matthias Kehle saw this premise as trite, but praised Matalon's sense of historical timing.

The family saga related in *The One Facing Us* reinforces the importance of and difficulty in assessing a personal history in Israelis' search for identity and roots, but it also alludes to other historical events. The novel's plot moves effortlessly through time and geography. Far more than a look at the changes in a family over time, it offers an insight into colonization and its echoes in a post-colonial Africa. The novel is further expanded by excerpts from the work of Egyptian-Jewish essayist Jacqueline Kahanoff, an analyst of the Middle East's Westernization and subsequent suppression of intrinsic cultural differences. In keeping a neutral tone to the novel, Matalon offers no personal reply to Kahanoff's criticisms. Instead, as noted by *World Literary Journal*'s Gila Ramras-Rauch, through the use of these appropriated essays, Matalon can successfully "expand the parameters of her novel from personal first-person narrator to an intellectual discourse [which] allows for an escape from sentimentalism and pathos."

The subject of a search for truth is expounded on in Matalon's 1999 short story, "Photograph". In it, a presumably Israeli woman illegally crosses into the Gaza strip to learn about a missing Palestinian friend. In her mission, she is aided by another Palestinian. Matalon challenges the historical rivalry between Palestinians and Israelis by joining the few characters in a common quest for clarity, closure, and finally peace. Though the story pushes the ideas of death and a lack of safety, the narrator's tone seems detached, her actions almost routine. *Dreaming of the Actual* editor Miriyam Glazer viewed this as attributable to Matalon's assignment for *Ha'aretz*, a newspaper covering the Gaza and West Bank from 1985 to 1990. Personal experience, then, is key in creating the realism in all of Matalon's work.

BIOGRAPHICAL AND CRITICAL SOURCES:

BOOKS

Alcalay, Ammiel, editor, *Keys to the Garden: New Israeli Writing,* City Light Books (San Francisco, CA), 1996, p. 205.

Glazer, Miriyam, editor, *Dreaming of the Actual: Contemporary Fiction and Poetry by Israeli Woman Writers,* State University of New York Press (Albany, NY), 2000, pp. 193-194.

PERIODICALS

Booklist, June 1, 1998, Bill Ott, review of *The One Facing Us,* pp. 1725-1726.

Library Journal, June 1, 1998, Molly Abramowitz, review of *The One Facing Us,* p. 154.

New York Times Book Review, August 9, 1998, Elizabeth Gleick, review of *The One Facing Us,* p. 9.

Publishers Weekly, May 4, 1998, review of *The One Facing Us,* pp. 202-203.

World Literature Today, winter, 1996, Dov Vardi, review of *The One Facing Us,* p. 235; spring, 1999, Gila Ramras-Rauch, review of *The One Facing Us,* pp. 387-388.

ONLINE

Carpe librum, http://www.carpe.com/ (September 8, 2002), Matthias Kehle, "Was die Bilder nicht erzählen."

Institute for the Translation of Hebrew Literature Web site, http://www.ithl.org.il/ (September 8, 2002).

Source, http://www.thesourceisrael.com/ (September 8, 2002), biography of Ronit Matalon.*

*   *   *

McCALLY, David 1949-

PERSONAL: Born September 10, 1949, in Pensacola, FL; son of James Dallas (a naval officer) and Betty (maiden name, Malenke; later surname, Thomas) McCally; married Lisa Daughtry, 1982 (divorced, 1986); married Linda Pickrell (a social worker), July, 1986.

Ethnicity: "White." *Education:* University of West Florida, B.A., 1987, M.A., 1991; University of Florida, Ph.D., 1997. *Politics:* Democrat. *Religion:* "Taoist." *Hobbies and other interests:* The natural world.

ADDRESSES: Home—2519 Northwest Fourth Terr., Gainesville, FL 32609. *Office*—Department of History, University of Florida, 203 Keene-Flint, Gainesville, FL 32611. *E-mail*—DavidMcCally@aol.com.

CAREER: Eckerd College, St. Petersburg, FL, visiting assistant professor, 1995-99; University of South Florida, Tampa, visiting professor of history, 1998-99, 2000-01; Bethune-Cookman College, Daytona Beach, FL, visiting professor of history, 1999-2000; University of Florida, Gainesville, adjunct professor of history, 2001-02. *Military service:* U.S. Navy, 1969-73, 1977-79.

AWARDS, HONORS: Rembert Patrick Award, Florida Historical Society, 2000, for *The Everglades: An Environmental History.*

WRITINGS:

The Everglades: An Environmental History, University Press of Florida (Gainesville, FL), 1999.

WORK IN PROGRESS: Ecology of Dreams: Americans in South Florida.

SIDELIGHTS: David McCally told *CA:* "Although I have spent the last several years in college teaching, I came to an academic career rather late in life, not receiving a B.A. until I was thirty-eight. My work concentrates on the development of Florida during the twentieth century. I am particularly interested in the relationship between the nation's mode of development and the environment. As human activity makes the world increasingly finite, it seems to me that we need to question the consumerism that so drives the country, especially when we offer it as a model to the rest of the world. My work in progress will examine the way that pursuit of the American way of life has shaped South Florida into an environment almost solely of human construct.

"I am a native Floridian, born in Pensacola, who has spent a majority of his life in the state—although I have also lived in Houston and New Orleans. Before returning to school I served in the Navy and worked at a variety of jobs, including plumber, longshoreman, and oil field roughneck."

*   *   *

McCAMANT, James D. 1933-
   (Jim McCamant)

PERSONAL: Born October 15, 1933, in Billings, MT; son of Thomas McCamant (a minister); married; wife's name Mary Ann; children: Megan, John, Katherine, Freya. *Education:* Stanford University, B.S., 1955.

ADDRESSES: Home—2799 Piedmont, Berkeley, CA 94705. *Office*—2748 Adeline St., Suite A, Berkeley, CA 94703. *E-mail*—MTSL@bioinvest.com.

CAREER: Medical Technology Stock Letter, Berkeley, CA, editor, 1984-2001, currently editor-at-large. Founder and principal of Shaefer, Lowe & McCamant and San Francisco Investment Corp (brokerage firms). *Military service:* U.S. Marine Corps, 1955-59; became first lieutenant.

WRITINGS:

(Under name Jim McCamant) *Biotech Investing: Every Investor's Guide,* Perseus Publishing (Cambridge, MA), 2002.

BIOGRAPHICAL AND CRITICAL SOURCES:

PERIODICALS

San Diego Business Journal, July 8, 2002, Marion Webb, "Biotech Analyst McCamant Publishers Book for Investors: 'Every Investor's Guide' Seeks to Unravel Complicated Science Issues," p. 8.

*   *   *

McCAMANT, Jim
   See McCAMANT, James D.

McGREGOR, Jon 1976-

PERSONAL: Born 1976, in Bermuda; son of a vicar and a teacher; married, wife's name Alice (a social worker). *Education:* University of Bradford, B.A., 1998.

ADDRESSES: Home—Nottingham, England. *Agent*—c/o Author Mail, Bloomsbury Publishing Plc. 38 Soho Sq., London W1D 3HB, England.

CAREER: Writer. Has worked in restaurants, bakeries, post offices, and a textile factory; also worked as a transcriber of notes for disabled university students.

AWARDS, HONORS: Booker Prize "longlist" citation, and "shortlist" citation for Best First Book category, and Eurasia Region of the Commonwealth Writers Prize, both 2002, both for *If Nobody Speaks of Remarkable Things.*

WRITINGS:

If Nobody Speaks of Remarkable Things (novel), Bloomsbury (New York, NY), 2002.

Contributor of short stories to *Five Easy Pieces* (anthology), Pulp Faction, 1998; and *Granta* magazine.

WORK IN PROGRESS: A new novel.

SIDELIGHTS: Jon McGregor was only twenty-six years old when his first novel, *If Nobody Speaks of Remarkable Things,* made the "longlist" for the Booker Prize. The honor catapulted McGregor to fame in Great Britain, where the receipt of a Booker Prize is considered an outstanding career achievement. The young author was working as a kitchen helper in a vegetarian restaurant when he heard of his debut novel's success. Since then he has been able to support himself as a writer, his dream since his college days. As Claire Bowman put it in the London *Times,* McGregor is "just an ordinary bloke in an ordinary town with an ordinary life—he just happens to have an extraordinary talent."

It was in fact the "ordinary" that inspired McGregor to write *If Nobody Speaks of Remarkable Things.* The novel takes place over a single day in a single street in an unnamed English city, its residents shunning social contact until tragedy strikes. In *BloomsburyMagazine. com,* McGregor described his setting as "an ordinary street where an unordinary thing happens. The story details the lives of the people living in the street, their interactions and lack of interactions, and the impact that this one day has on their lives. It's a story about the importance of the ordinary, the way that the everyday miracles of life and death go unwitnessed in favour of celebrity and sensation, and it's about the difficulty of experiencing community in an increasingly transient society."

McGregor drew the story from his imagination after hearing that a young man in Bolton was murdered at approximately the same time that Princess Diana died. As he watched the publicity surrounding the princess's death, he wondered about the anonymous deaths and tragedies that were simultaneously being mourned in private. Matt Seaton noted in the *Guardian:* "Death, or a death . . . is at the centre of *If Nobody Speaks of Remarkable Things.* From the outset, the reader is aware that something bad is going to happen, although McGregor maintains a degree of suspense about precisely what until the final pages. But it is actually much more a novel about life; the presence of death in the story is counterpointed by the narration of one of the main characters, a young woman who reveals that she is pregnant."

Most members of the British press greeted the novel with enthusiasm. Julie Myerson in the *Guardian* wrote: "This is a clean, bare, sensitive and undoubtedly well-intentioned piece of fiction by someone still in his twenties. It's admirably adventurous." *New Statesman* contributor Abbie Fielding-Smith styled the work "at once an irritating and a moving paean to the small moments in life that often pass unnoticed or go unremarked." Fielding-Smith concluded that *If Nobody Speaks of Remarkable Things* "is a passionate novel by a young writer seeking to unravel the essential mystery of other people, to make us care. . . . McGregor succeeds in what he set out to do: revitalize the commonplace." Claire Bowman commented: "In McGregor's hands, the lives of the neighbours are laid out as a series of snapshots, a literary photo album. In dazzling close-up we are invited into their private worlds to witness their hopes, their fears, and their unspoken despairs. . . . But what shines out as much as the characters and the developing story line is the style of McGregor's writing. In his hands even the prosaic—the sounds of the city, of traffic and pneumatic drills—take on a lyrical energy of their own."

The son of a vicar, McGregor was born in Bermuda and raised in Norwich, England. He studied media technology and production at the University of Bradford but began publishing short stories toward the end of his college years. He has moved frequently within the United Kingdom but prefers not to live in London. McGregor told the London *Times:* "People ask me how I write the way I do, where I get my ideas from, and I don't really have an answer. The most important thing for me is how the words sound; I read them in my head rather than on the page."

BIOGRAPHICAL AND CRITICAL SOURCES:

PERIODICALS

Guardian, August 19, 2002, John Ezard, "Veterans Vie with Newcomer in Booker Prize Stakes," p. 7; August 24, 2002, Julie Myerson, "Woolf at the Door."

New Statesman, August 20, 2002, Matt Seaton, "New Kid on the Block," September 23, 2002, Abbie Fielding-Smith, "The Song of the City," p. 55.

Times (London, England), August 3, 2002, Claire Bowman, "The Word on the Street: Interview," p. 44.

ONLINE

BloomsburyMagazine.com, http://www.bloomsbury magazine.com/ (August 20, 2002), Jenny Parrott, "Speaking of Remarkable Things."

University of Bradford Web site, http://www.bradford. ac.uk/ (August 29, 2002), "Bradford Graduate Longlisted for Booker Prize."*

*   *   *

McMASTER, Gerald 1953-

PERSONAL: Born March 9, 1953, in Red Pheasant, Saskatchewan, Canada. *Education:* Institute of American Indian Arts, A.F.A., 1975; Minneapolis College of Art and Design, B.F.A., 1977; attended Banff School of Fine Arts, 1986; Carleton University, M.A., 1994; Amsterdam School of Cultural Analysis, doctoral study, 1997.

ADDRESSES: Office—Canadian Museum of Civilization, 100 Laurier St., P.O. Box 3100, Station B, Hull, Quebec, Canada J8X 4H2; fax: 819-776-8300.

CAREER: Artist, author, photographer, and illustrator. University of Regina, Saskatchewan Indian Federated College, Regina, Saskatchewan, Canada, head of Indian art program, 1977-81, coordinator of Second National Native Arts Conference, 1979; Canadian Museum of Civilization, Hull, Quebec, Canada, curator of contemporary Indian art, 1981—; Carleton University, Carleton, MN, adjunct research professor, 1981—. Designer of record album covers; creator of murals and installation pieces. With Red Earth Singers, recorded the album *Songs from Bismarck,* Indian Records (Taos, NM), 1976. Inuit Art Foundation, member of board of directors, 1991-93; Ontario Arts Council, member of board of directors, 1991-94; International Council of Museums, member of board of directors of Canada affiliate, 1992-95; Smithsonian Institution, member of board of directors of National Museum of the American Indian, 1995-98. *Exhibitions:* Work represented in solo and group shows, including exhibitions at Ottawa Art Gallery, Intermedia Arts Minnesota, Woodland Indian Cultural Educational Centre, Southern Plains Indian Museum, and Shoestring Gallery, Saskatoon, Saskatchewan, Canada; collections include work at Canadian Museum of Civilization, Guilford Native American Art Gallery, Department of Indian Affairs, Ottawa, Ontario, Canada, Institute of American Indian Arts, and exhibitions in Austria and China.

MEMBER: Canadian Museums Association (member of board of directors, 1991-93), Native Art Studies Association of Canada (vice president, 1987; president, 1988-89).

AWARDS, HONORS: Winner, Scottsdale Annual Indian Art Competition, 1976; first prize, La Loche, 1981, for *Byron and His Balloon.*

WRITINGS:

(Illustrator) David May, *Byron and His Balloon* (juvenile), Tree Frog Press (Edmonton, Alberta, Canada), 1984.

Challenges, de Meervaart Cultural Center (Amsterdam, Netherlands), 1985.

(Editor, with Lee-Ann Martin) *Indigena: Contemporary Native Perspectives,* Douglas & McIntyre (Vancouver, British Columbia, Canada), 1992.

(Author of text) *Edward Poitras Canada: XLVI Biennale di Venezia,* Canadian Museum of Civilization (Hull, Quebec, Canada), 1995.

(Author of text) *Jeffrey Thomas: Portraits from the Dancing Grounds,* Ottawa Art Gallery (Ottawa, Ontario, Canada), 1996.

(Author of text) *Mary Longman: Traces,* Kamloops Art Gallery (Kamloops, British Columbia, Canada), 1996.

(Editor) *Reservation X: The Power of Place in Aboriginal Contemporary Art,* University of Washington Press (Seattle, WA), 1998.

Contributor to books and exhibition catalogs, including *American Visions: Artistic and Cultural Identity in the Western Hemisphere,* edited by Noreen Tomassi, Mary Jane Jacob, and Ivo Mesquita, Allworth Press (New York, NY), 1994; *All Roads Are Good: Native Voices on Life and Culture,* National Museum of the American Indian (Washington, DC), 1994; *Thinking about Exhibitions,* edited by Reesa Greenberg, Bruce W. Ferguson, and Sandy Nairne, Routledge (New York, NY), 1996; and *Twentieth Century Native American Art: Essays on History and Criticism,* edited by W. Jackson Rushing, Routledge (London, England), 1997. Contributor to periodicals, including *Canadian Journal of Native Studies, American Indian Art, European Review of Native American Studies, Cultural Studies, International Journal of Canadian Studies,* and *Fuse.* General editor, *NASAC Newsletter,* 1988-92.

BIOGRAPHICAL AND CRITICAL SOURCES:

BOOKS

St. James Guide to Native North-American Artists, St. James Press (Detroit, MI), 1998, pp. 370-373.

PERIODICALS

Akwe:kon Journal, spring, 1994, "An Interview with Gerald McMaster."

American Anthropologist, December, 1999, Lisa A. Roberts, review of *Reservation X: The Power of Place in Aboriginal Contemporary Art,* p. 824.

Artweek, November 2, 1985, "Beside and beyond the Mainstream."

Border Crossings, Volume 11, number 4, 1992, Charlotte Townsend-Gault, "Stereotypes under De(Construction)."

Canadian Art, winter, 1992, review by Robin Laurence.

Echo, October-November, 1984, Bill White, "Teacher-Artist's Commitment Extends beyond Work as Curator."

Edmonton Journal, April 4, 1980, Jean Richards, "Indian Art Throws off Limitations."

Fuse, July, 1988, Alfred Young Man, "Token and Taboo."

Globe and Mail (Toronto, Ontario, Canada), March 26, 1991, Michael Valpy, "Peeping across Ignorance Barriers."

Library Journal, May 1, 1999, Gay W. Neale, review of *Reservation X,* p. 72.

Ottawa Citizen, October 17, 1981, Nancy Baele, "Native Art Illuminated by Sun's Presence"; September 21, 1989, Nancy Baele, "Baseball as a Mystical Art Form."

Parachute, December-February, 1990, Jacqueline Fry, "Review of Ancients Singing."

Regina Leader Post, November 3, 1979, Lorna Burke, "Exhibits Shouldn't Be Missed."

Talking Stick: First Nations Arts, winter, 1994, "Crossfires of Identity: An Interview with Gerald McMaster."

Toronto Star, February 8, 1991, Christopher Hume, "Native Painter's Criticism Packs Strong Medicine."*

*   *   *

McNALLY, Raymond T(homas) 1931-2002

OBITUARY NOTICE—See index for *CA* sketch: Born May 15, 1931, in Cleveland, OH; died of liver and lung cancer October 2, 2002, in Newton, MA. Educator and author. McNally was a scholar of Slavic and Eastern European cultures who became famous for his books about Vlad Tepes, who, McNally maintained, was the basis for the fictional Count Dracula. After earning his bachelor's degree from Fordham University in 1953, McNally finished his Ph.D. at the Free University of Berlin in 1956 and attended the University of Leningrad for postdoctoral studies in 1961. McNally's first academic position was as an instructor in history at John Carroll University from 1956 to 1958. He spent the rest of his career at Boston College, where in 1964 he founded the Slavic and East European Center and became a professor of history in 1970. In 1995 he helped establish the Balkan Studies Institute, and retired in 2001. McNally, who was interested in East European cultures throughout his life, became fascinated by Dracula after reading the Bram Stoker novel. Because Stoker provided so much factual information in his book, McNally surmised that the character may have been based on an actual person, so he set off to the Transylvania region of Romania to find out. His research led him to conclude that Dracula was based on Vlad Tepes, a nobleman during the fifteenth century known for his savage treatment of the Turks, who he sometimes mounted on spears while supposedly drinking their blood. Vlad's nickname was Draculya, which means "son of the devil." Together with colleague Radu Florescu, McNally wrote about his ideas in the books *In Search of Dracula: A True History of Dracula and Vampire Legends* (1972) and *Dracula: A Biography of Vlad the Impaler, 1431-1476* (1973); he also coauthored *Dracula, Prince of Many Faces: His Life and His Times* (1989) and edited two other books about the Dracula legend. After his initial theories about Vlad were published, McNally heard about a Hungarian woman named Elizabeth Bathory who tortured and killed young girls and then bathed in their blood to preserve her youth. This led McNally to write *Dracula Was a Woman: In Search of the Blood Countess of Transylvania* (1983); he also released a CD-ROM on the subject called *Dracula: Truth or Terror* (1996). These books caused McNally to become a hero among fans of vampire books, and he was often invited to their conventions (he organized one himself in 1997), and he enjoyed wearing a black cape and swooping into rooms dramatically. However, McNally was always a serious scholar; in addition to his books about Dracula, he was the author of two books about writer and philosopher Peter Chaadayev, as well as of the book *In Search of Dr. Jekyll and Mr. Hyde* (2000), which, similar to his Dracula theory, proposed that the Robert Louis Stevenson character was based on a real person, William Deacon Brodie.

OBITUARIES AND OTHER SOURCES:

BOOKS

Who's Who, St. Martin's Press (New York, NY), 2000.

PERIODICALS

Boston Globe, October 5, 2002, p. B7.
Boston Herald, October 6, 2002, p. 41.
New York Times, October 20, 2002, p. A31.

*   *   *

MEACOCK, Heather 1949-

PERSONAL: Born December 12, 1949, in London, England; married Robin Meacock (an electrical engineer), April 24, 1995. *Ethnicity:* "White European." *Education:* West London Institute of Higher Education, University of London, certificate in education (with distinction), 1982, B.A. (with honors), 1990; University of Bristol, Ph.D., 1997. *Politics:* Socialist. *Religion:* "Religious pluralist." *Hobbies and other interests:* Opera, ballet, horseback riding.

ADDRESSES: Home—Flat 9, 39 Bramham Gardens, London SW5 0HG, England.

CAREER: Educator. Teacher in British schools, 1982-86; St. Bernard's Preparatory School, teacher and coordinator of history curriculum, 1986-95, teacher and coordinator of English curriculum, 1997—; Brunel University, Uxbridge, England, senior lecturer in religious studies and religious education, 1995-96; La Sainte Union College of Higher Education, senior lecturer in religious education, 1996-97; Birbeck College, London, part-time lecturer, 2000—.

WRITINGS:

An Anthropological Approach to Theology: A Study of John Hick's Theology of Religious Pluralism toward Ethical Criteria for a Global Theology of Religions, University Press of America (Lanham, MD), 2000.

Contributor to periodicals, including *Religious Studies Journal* and *Scottish Journal of Religious Studies.*

WORK IN PROGRESS: Research on religious pluralism, ethics, and inter-faith dialogue.

SIDELIGHTS: Heather Meacock told *CA:* "My primary motivation in writing is the search for truth in essential issues which concern all people, whether they are religious believers or secular atheists. Does God exist? Why are we here? What is the purpose of life? Is there one true faith, or are there many equally valid paths to God? How can people with opposing religious beliefs engage in fruitful inter-faith dialogue? My work has been particularly influenced by Professor John Hick, the major British theologian and philosopher to represent the pluralist position in theology.

"My writing process involves extensive reading and research, and follows traditional methodology. I read, write, think, redraft, and transcribe by hand before using a word processor.

"I was first inspired to write on my chosen subject by what can only be described as a quest for the truth about life's ultimate meaning."

*   *   *

MEGGS, Philip B(axter) 1942-2002

*OBITUARY NOTICE—*See index for *CA* sketch: Born May 30, 1942, in Newberry, SC; died of leukemia November 24, 2002, in Richmond, VA. Graphic designer, educator, and author. Meggs was an authority on the history of graphic design and wrote the first book in the United States to cover the full history of the graphic arts. He was a graduate of Virginia Commonwealth University, where he earned an M.F.A. in 1971. Meggs began his career as a graphics designer at Reynolds Aluminum in 1965 and from 1966 to 1968 was art director for A. H. Robins Co. When he took a position as an instructor at his alma mater in 1968, Meggs discovered that his students did not understand the history of typography and book design; he therefore created a course that covered everything from the invention of the printing press up to the computer age. The research materials and syllabuses he developed became the core of his landmark book *A History of Graphic Design* (1983; third edition, 1992), which has since become required reading in graphics design courses in the United States. Meggs remained at Virginia Commonwealth University for the rest of his career, becoming professor of communications and arts and design in 1983; he was also dean of the

department from 1974 to 1987. In addition to his influential history, Meggs wrote and edited several other books about printing and graphics design, including cowriting *Typographic Design: Form and Communication* (1985) and coediting *Texts on Type: Critical Writings on Typography* (2001); he was also a regular contributor to *Print* magazine. Beginning in 1993, Meggs lent his experience to the U.S. Postal Service's citizen stamp advisory committee, and his name was in the news for his criticism of the redesign of U.S. currency; he believed that the designs were timid and dated. Meggs was presented an award for excellence in publishing from the American Association of Publishers for his *History of Graphic Design,* and in 2002 was given the Educator Award from the Art Directors Club of New York.

OBITUARIES AND OTHER SOURCES:

BOOKS

Who's Who in American Art, 23rd edition, Marquis (New Providence, NJ), 1999.

PERIODICALS

Los Angeles Times, December 6, 2002, p. B15.
New York Times, December 1, 2002, p. A34.

*   *   *

MICHAEL, Sami 1926-

PERSONAL: Born 1926, in Baghdad, Iraq; immigrated to Iran, 1948, immigrated to Israel, 1949; children: two. *Education:* Attended Haifa University (Israel).

*ADDRESSES: Home—*Haifa, Israel. *Agent—*c/o Author Mail, Pan Macmillan, 20 New Wharf Rd., London N1 9RR, England.

CAREER: Author, translator, and newspaper editor. Ministry of Agriculture, Israel, hydrologist, 1949-74. Oxford Centre for Hebrew and Jewish Studies visiting fellow, 2000; supporter of Center for the Protection of Democracy in Israel. Appears on Israeli radio and television broadcasts.

AWARDS, HONORS: Honorary doctorate from Ben-Gurion University of the Neger, 2000, for contributions to Hebrew literature; Prix WIZO, France, for *Victoria;* Israeli Prime Minister's Prize; Ze'ev Prize; ACUM Award; IBBY Award (Berlin, Germany).

WRITINGS:

Shavim ve-shavim yoter (title means "All Men Are Equal—but Some Are More"), Hotsa'at Bustan (Tel Aviv, Israel), 1974.

Sufah ben ha-dekalim (youth; title means "Palm Trees in the Storm"), 'Am 'oved (Tel Aviv, Israel), 1975.

Hasut, 'Am 'oved (Tel Aviv, Israel), 1977, translation by Edward Grossman published as *Refuge,* Jewish Publication Society (Philadelphia, PA), 1988.

Hofen shel'arafel (title means "A Handful of Mist"), 'Am 'oved (Tel Aviv, Israel), 1979.

(With Dani Kerman) *Pahonim va-halomot* (youth; title means "Shacks and Dreams"), 'Am 'oved (Tel Aviv, Israel), 1979.

Shedim Ba-Martef (title means "Demons in the Basement"), produced at Haifa Theater, 1983.

Bedouins: The Sinai Nomads, photographs by Shlomo Arad, translated by Shoshana Rothschild, Massada (Ramat-Gan, Israel), 1984.

Eleh shivte Yisra'el: shetem esreh sihot 'al ha-she'elah ha-'adatit (title means "These Are the Tribes of Israel: Twelve Interviews about Social Integration in Israel"), Sifiyat po'alim and ha-Kibuts ha-Artsi ha-Shomer ha-Tsa'ir (Tel Aviv, Israel), 1984.

Memories (part of "My Parents' House," Volume III: "Reading and Study Material on Jewish Roots" series), Center for Programming, Department of Development and Community Services, W.Z.O. (Jerusalem, Israel), 1986.

Chatsotsra Ba'waddi [and] *Hatsotstah ba-vadi* (title means "A Trumpet in the Wadi"), 'Am 'oved (Tel Aviv, Israel), 1987.

Teomim (title means "Twins"), produced at Haifa Theater, 1988.

(With Nurit Tsarefati) *Ahavah ben ha-dekalim* (Juvenile; title means "Love among the Palms"), Domino (Jerusalem, Israel), 1990.

Viktoryah, 'Am 'oved (Tel Aviv, Israel), 1993, translation by Dalya Bilu published as *Victoria,* Macmillan (London, England), 1995.

(With Volf Bulbah) *Shedim humim* (youth; title means "Brown Devils"), Yedi'ot aharonot (Tel Aviv, Israel), 1993.

(With Aleks Zehavi and Gil'ad Yisrael) *Ahavah ben ha-dekalim* (fiction) ha-Rashut ha-meshutefet le-hinukh Yehudi Tsiyoni, ha-Mahlakah le-hinukh ule-tarbut Yehudiyim ba-golah, Hadar Ben-Tsiyon (Jerusalem, Israel), 1998.

ha-Kanaf ha-shelishit (title means "Third Wing"), Keter (Jerusalem, Israel), 2000.

(With Rubik Rozental) *Gevulot ha-ruah: sihot 'im Ruvik Rozental* (title means "Unbounded Ideas: Ruvik Rosenthal Talks with Sami Michael"), ha-Kibuts ha-me'uhad (Tel Aviv, Israel), 2000.

Mayim noshkim le-mayim (title means "Water Kissing Water") 'Am 'oved (Tel Aviv, Israel), 2001.

ha-Havayah ha-Yisre'elit (title means "Israeli Experience"), Sifriyat Ma'ariv (Ot Yehudah, Israel), 2001.

Contributor to *Bulletin of the Israeli Academic Center in Cairo;* contributor to *Sleepwalkers and Other Stories: The Arab in Hebrew Fiction,* edited by Ehud Ben-Ezer, Lynne Rienner (Boulder, CO), 1999.

Author's works have been translated into Arabic, Chinese, Dutch, English, French, German, Greek, and Russian.

ADAPTATIONS: Chatsotsra Ba'waddi was adapted for film by Amit Lior, directed by Lina and Slava Chaplin, 2001.

SIDELIGHTS: Israeli novelist Sami Michael was born to a large, extended family (hamila) of Sephardic Jews in Baghdad, Iraq. In the 1940s, he became actively involved with an underground communist group which fought to undermine the Iraqi regime. To escape prosecution, he fled to Iran in 1948, and, facing extradition there, escaped to Israel the following year. In Israel, he fulfilled his obligatory military service and worked for twenty-five years as a hydrologist, surveying water sources along the Syrian border. He began writing early, first in Arabic, then Hebrew, and was first published in 1973. In addition to his own writing, Michael has translated into Hebrew the writings of Egyptian writer Naguib Mahfouz. Only two of Michael's novels have been published in English.

Michael's writing strives to bring into peaceful balance and understanding the opposing forces in the Middle East: the Jews and Arabs, communists and nationalists, men and women. He works to highlight the alienation within a people, bound by common religion, but not ethnic background and custom. The juxtaposed pairing in his novels draws heavily upon his own experiences. As Michael explained to Gershon Shaked during a roundtable discussion transcribed in *Modern Hebrew Literature:* "I am Iraqi and I am also Israeli. These two identities exist in me and I love them both because they are a part of me. Both these rivers flow into my work." A history of dual identity, coupled with a history of war, transpires throughout his stories.

Hasut, published in English as *Refuge,* is set during the aftermath of the 1973 October War (Yom Kippur War). It centers on only a few characters, and all seem to be outsiders, political refugees in forced or voluntary exile. Marduch, a Jewish exile from Iraq, houses Fathki, an Arab poet and fellow communist, during a foreign—presumably Arab—invasion. When Marduch leaves to fight for Israel, Fathki is left alone with his host's wife and retarded son. The situation faces the characters with not only political, but also moral and sexual tension. As a commentor for *Kirkus Reviews* pointed out, the plot is analogous to the Palestinian's "guest" stay in the Israeli state, but the analogy then assigns unfavorable characteristics to the Arab population. According to a review in *Publishers Weekly,* the presentation of the chiefly Israeli-communist characters is not flowery prose, but a social documentation of "a party struggling with hypocrisy and rife with anti-Semitic Arabs and Arab-hating Jews, misogynists and conformists."

Michael's novel *Victoria* tells the triumphant story of love's redemption. In this work set in a family courtyard in Baghdad, the heroine struggles to salvage her marriage to a womanizing sailor, Raphael. Commentor Nitza Ben-Dov set the work in a larger literary context, finding that it "recalls Flaubert's 'Madame Bovary' and Tolstoy's 'Anna Karenina' as well as Amos Oz's 'My Michael'—novels written by men about women who are at the same time outstanding and typical, singular and archetypal." Michael writes of a woman in a patriarchal society and makes no amends for the misogynistic tendencies in the plot. As with his other novels, he allows the characters to speak their thoughts, not his. The novel has a happy end of salvation and victory, which is not achieved through moralizing or pedagogical tone. Michael provides a foil for each character. Victoria is mirrored by her childhood friend, as are all the characters in the book accentuated by their antithesis, a secondary conscience. The reader, through the comparisons, is allowed to objectively judge the decisions of the characters.

Michael's novels are inspired by his struggles with political opposition, and they almost exclusively deal with disappointment in governments and lack of political progress. *Hofen shel'arafel* (title means "A Handful of Mist") describes in an almost autobiographical manner the growing disillusionment of Ramsi, a Jewish communist from Baghdad. Michael's work intends to criticize existing situations, and to increase understanding between warring factions. *Uni-Erlangen* cites the comments of David Grossman, who, in reviewing *Chatsotsra Ba'waddi* (title means "A Trumpet in the Wadi"), described Michael's achievement of transgressing the boundary between "us" and "them" or "Jews" and "non-Jews," as one for Israeli literature and as a daily affirmation. Michael does not over-romanticize or stereotype the opposing social classes he interweaves in his writing. The aim is truth in representation, from which may come understanding and peace in the Middle Eastern region. In *Modern Hebrew Literature,* Ehud Ben Ezer summed up Michael's work as "free of bitterness, imbued with understanding and profound compassion, and this is no mean achievement, when the scene it describes with such astonishing accuracy is as painful and stormy as it is." Michael goes beyond the immediacy of the constant fighting to present a literary mirror, in which all individuals are allowed to see both their justification and their fault.

BIOGRAPHICAL AND CRITICAL SOURCES:

BOOKS

Murphy, Bruce, editor, *Benét's Reader's Encyclopedia,* 4th edition, HarperCollins (New York, NY), 1996.

PERIODICALS

Kirkus Reviews, Volume 56, number 1, 1988, review of *Refuge,* p. 1268.
Library Journal, Volume 113, number 18, 1988, Molly Abramovitz, review of *Refuge,* p. 110.

Los Angeles Times, May 6, 1995, Jordan Elgraby, "Touring Poet, Playwright Promote Mideast Peace: Sami Michael and Salem Jubran Tour U.S. to Promote Peace among Jews and Arabs," p. B5.

Modern Hebrew Literature, winter, 1981, Ezhud Ben Ezer, "Refuge from Baghdad: On Sammy Michael's 'A Handful of Mist,'" pp. 40-43; fall, 1989, Rochelle Furstenberg, "Rochelle Furstenberg interviews Sammy Michael: On the Border, between Two Nations," pp. 25-26; spring-summer, 1993, "Exorcising Demons," pp. 10-11.

Publishers Weekly, Volume 234, number 13, 1988, Sybil Steinberg, review of *Refuge,* pp. 58-59.

OTHER

Carpe liberum, http://www.carpe.com/ (March 21, 2002), Ulrich Larger, review of *Viktoryah.**

*   *   *

MILLMAN, Brock 1963-

PERSONAL: Born 1963. *Education:* Attended University of Western Ontario, London University, and McGill University.

ADDRESSES: Agent—c/o Frank Cass, Crown House, 47 Chase Side, London N14 5BP, England.

CAREER: Historian and educator. University of British Columbia, Banff, BC, Canada, former lecturer in history; instructor at University of Windsor and Royal Military College; University of Western Ontario, currently professor of history.

WRITINGS:

The Ill-made Alliance: Anglo-Turkish Relations, 1934-1940, McGill-Queen's University Press (Montreal, Quebec, Canada), 1998.

Managing Domestic Dissent in First World War Britain, 1914-1918, Frank Cass (London, England), 2000.

Pessimism and British War Policy, 1916-1918, Frank Cass (London, England), 2001.

SIDELIGHTS: An historian with a focus on British policy in the early Twentieth century, Brock Millman published *The Ill-made Alliance: Anglo-Turkish Relations, 1934-1940* to challenge the historical consensus that Turkey was a reluctant alliance partner during World War II. According to Millman, it was Turkey that wanted closer relations with Britain, and the British who missed an opportunity through negligence and a lack of imagination, ultimately letting the alliance collapse in 1939-40, producing Turkish neutrality in World War II.

Millman's 2000 work looks back to World War I and focuses on a little-known aspect of that war. In *Managing Domestic Dissent in First World War Britain,* Millman uses recently uncovered documents to explore trade union unrest, the role of the courts and censorship, and the British government's contingency plans for controlling dissent, particularly violent opposition. "He has consulted a wide variety of manuscript repositories and has presented a solid piece of research to show that one of the war's chief victims was the liberty of the subject," concluded a *Contemporary Review* contributor. Not all were convinced. Writing in the *Times Literary Supplement,* Keith Jeffrey questioned Millman's "rather lurid picture of well-organized and increasingly revolutionary 'dissent' posing a challenge to the state." Similarly, David Woodward in the *Journal of Military History* wrote that the absence of concrete evidence for some of the contingency plans did pose some problems. Still, he concluded "this work deserves a careful reading from anyone interested in World War I in general and British history in particular. The research in the available sources is exceeding thorough and the writing lucid."

BIOGRAPHICAL AND CRITICAL SOURCES:

PERIODICALS

Contemporary Review, June, 2001, review of *Managing Domestic Dissent in First World War Britain,* p. 383.

Journal of Military History, January, 2002, David R. Woodward, review of *Managing Domestic Dissent in First World War Britain,* pp. 217-218.

Times Literary Supplement, September 21, 2001, Keith Jeffery, review of *Managing Domestic Dissent in First World War Britain,* p. 30.

MILLMAN, Isaac 1933-

PERSONAL: Born August 26, 1933, in Paris, France; married 1957; wife's name Jeanine (a bookkeeper); children: Roland, Claude. *Education:* Attended Pratt Institute for four years.

ADDRESSES: Home—249 East 48th St., No. 16B, New York, NY 10017.

CAREER: Illustrator and writer. *Military service:* Served in the U.S. armed forces.

WRITINGS:

SELF-ILLUSTRATED

Moses Goes to a Concert, Farrar, Straus & Giroux (New York, NY), 1998.
Moses Goes to School, Farrar, Straus & Giroux (New York, NY), 2000.
Moses Goes to the Circus, Farrar, Straus & Giroux (New York, NY), 2003.
Moses Sees a Play, Farrar, Straus & Giroux (New York, NY), 2004.

ILLUSTRATOR

Kate Banks, *Howie Bowles, Secret Agent,* Farrar, Straus & Giroux (New York, NY), 1999.
Kate Banks, *Howie Bowles and Uncle Sam,* Farrar, Straus & Giroux (New York, NY), 2000.

SIDELIGHTS: Author and illustrator Isaac Millman draws inspiration for his stories and art from real life. "I enjoy writing and drawing for children because I can really let my imagination go," he was quoted as saying on the *Houghton Mifflin Reading* Web site. Of Polish descent, Millman was born in France. As a teenager he immigrated to the United States, where he eventually became an American citizen.

In addition to illustrating several chapter books by Kate Banks, including *Howie Bowles, Secret Agent* and *Howie Bowles and Uncle Sam,* Millman has created a series of self-illustrated books about a deaf boy, debuting with *Moses Goes to a Concert.* In this "breakthrough picture book," to quote *Booklist*'s Hazel Rochman, Moses and his classmates from a school for the deaf attend a concert, creating a story that, according to a *Publishers Weekly* critic, will likely be a "revelation for readers" who do not realize there is more than one way to appreciate music. The students' teacher gives each child an inflated balloon so that he or she can better feel the vibrations the music creates. The students, noticing that the percussionist performs barefooted, later learn that she, too, is deaf. In this work, Millman employs "delicate watercolors" and inset boxes showing American Sign Language as well as text, a *Kirkus Reviews* contributor remarked. In a review of *Moses Goes to School,* about a typical day at a school for the deaf, Rosalyn Pierini of *School Library Journal* declared the work a success. Overall, she noted that, like other well-written titles about children with disabilities, *Moses Goes to School* is more than a didactic story; instead, it "succeeds as effective storytelling in its own right." Likewise, a *Kirkus Reviews* critic called *Moses Goes to School* an "excellent read-aloud."

BIOGRAPHICAL AND CRITICAL SOURCES:

PERIODICALS

Booklist, April 15, 1998, Hazel Rochman, review of *Moses Goes to a Concert,* p. 1439.
Horn Book, November, 1999, Lauren Adams, review of *Howie Bowles, Secret Agent,* p. 733.
Kirkus Reviews, January 1, 1998, review of *Moses Goes to a Concert,* p. 59; July 1, 2001, review of *Moses Goes to School,* p. 962.
Publishers Weekly, February 23, 1998, review of *Moses Goes to a Concert,* p. 76; October 25, 1999, review of *Howie Bowles, Secret Agent,* p. 81; June 19, 2000, review of *Moses Goes to School,* p. 82.
School Library Journal, April, 1998, Sally R. Dow, review of *Moses Goes to a Concert,* p. 106; October, 1999, Laura Santoro, review of *Howie Bowles, Secret Agent,* p. 102; August, 2000, Rosalyn Pierini, review of *Moses Goes to School,* p. 160; December, 2000, Sharon McNeil, review of *Howie Bowles, Secret Agent,* p. 94.

ONLINE

Houghton Mifflin Reading, http://www.eduplace.com/kids/hmr/ (January 13, 2003), "Meet the Author/Illustrator: Isaac Millman."

MIRIKITANI, Janice 1942-

PERSONAL: Born February 5, 1942, in Stockton, CA; daughter of Ted and BelleAnne (Matsuda) Mirikitani; married Cecil Williams (a minister), 1982; children: Tianne (daughter). *Education:* University of California—Los Angeles, B.A. (cum laude), 1962; University of California—Berkeley, teaching credentials, 1963; attended San Francisco State University.

ADDRESSES: Office—Glide Foundation, 330 Ellis St., San Francisco, CA 94102. *E-mail*—child_youth_family@glide.org.

CAREER: Poet, activist, teacher, choreographer, writer, and editor. Contra Costa Unified School District, Contra Costa, CA, teacher, 1964-65; Glide Church, San Francisco, CA, administrative assistant, 1966-69, Glide Church/Urban Center, program director, 1969—, Glide Dance Group, choreographer and artistic director, 1973—, Glide Foundation, president, 1983—. San Francisco State University, San Francisco, CA, lecturer in Japanese American literature and creative writing, 1972; Asian American Dance Collective, San Francisco, guest choreographer, 1983-85; cofounder of Asian American Publications; member of Third World Communications. Affiliated with Vanguard Foundation, Asian American Media Center, Yerba Buena Cultural Board, California Poets in the Schools, Asian American Theatre Company, Zellerbach Community Arts Distribution Committee (board member), United Tenderloin Community Fund (board of directors), and Haight-Ashbury Free Medical Clinic.

AWARDS, HONORS: American Book Lifetime Achievement Award for Literature; Woman Warrior in Arts and Culture award, Pacific Asian American Bay Area Women's Coalition, 1983; Woman of Words award, Women's Foundation, 1985; with husband, Cecil Williams, Chancellor's Medal of Honor, University of California—San Francisco, 1988; named Woman of the Year by the California State Assembly, 1988; Outstanding Leadership award, Japanese Community Youth Council, 1990; named poet laureate of San Francisco, CA, 2000.

WRITINGS:

POETRY AND PROSE

Awake in the River (poetry and prose), Isthmus Press, 1978.

Shedding Silence: Poetry and Prose, Celestial Arts (Berkeley, CA), 1987.
We, the Dangerous: New and Selected Poems, Celestial Arts (Berkeley, CA), 1995.
Love Works ("Poet Laureate" series), City Lights Foundation (San Francisco, CA), 2002.

OTHER

(Editor) *Third World Women,* 1973.
(Editor, with others) *Time to Greez!: Incantations from the Third World* (poetry), introduction by Maya Angelou, Glide Publications (San Francisco, CA), 1975.
(Editor) *Ayumi: A Japanese American Anthology,* Japanese American Anthology Committee (San Francisco, CA), 1980.
(With husband, Cecil Williams) *Breaking Free: A Glide Songbook,* Glide Word Press (San Francisco, CA), 1989.
(Editor, with husband, Cecil Williams) *I Have Something to Say about This Big Trouble: Children of the Tenderloin Speak Out,* Glide Word Press (San Francisco, CA), 1989.
(Editor) *Watch Out! We're Talking,* 1993.
(With Maya Angelou and Guy Johnson) *A Celebration with Maya Angelou, Guy Johnson, and Janice Mirikitani on the Occasion of Guy Johnson's Fiftieth Birthday* (sound recording), Don't Quit Your Day Job Records (San Francisco, CA), 1996.

Contributor to periodicals and journals.

SIDELIGHTS: Janice Mirikitani is a third-generation Japanese American who spent her infancy in an internment camp in Arkansas. As an adult, she has spoken out against this containment, as well as against continuing racism against Asian Americans and people of color. During the 1960s Mirikitani began working at the Glide Church in San Francisco, where she met and married Cecil Williams, the church's pastor. Mirikitani advanced to become program director of the Glide Church and Urban Center, and in this capacity she oversaw programs that provided food, housing, and health care for the poor and homeless, rape and abuse recovery programs and counseling for women, and job training and counseling services for young people. She became choreographer and artistic director of the church's dance company and was eventually elected president of the Glide Foundation.

Mirikitani has served on a multitude of boards in the Bay area and has choreographed and produced dozens of socially themed dance productions. These include *Who Among the Missing,* in honor of Central Americans who have been tortured, imprisoned, and murdered; *A Tribute to King,* in honor of Martin Luther King, Jr.; *Lonnie's Song,* about the AIDS crisis; and *Revealing Secrets, Releasing Fear,* which deals with incest, addiction, and recovery. Under Mirikitani's leadership, Glide has experienced rapid growth, and in 1999, the number of volunteers who were assisting in these programs reached 35,000. Mirikitani's creative work follows a path similar to that of her community work, and she is committed to helping women artists and writers. She has collected and published women's writings in anthologies and magazines, and her own poetry and writing has been included in anthologies, journals, textbooks, and magazines.

Rowena Tomaneng wrote in *Reference Guide to American Literature* that in Mirikitani's first collection, *Awake in the River,* the poet's "experience of subjugation and racism within her own 'homeland' provided a historical context with which to view other events taking place globally. The trauma of Japanese American internment, the nuclear devastations of both Hiroshima and Nagasaki, and U.S. imperialism in Southeast Asia are painful experiences that have shaped Mirikitani's poetry in *Awake in the River.* In this first collection, Mirikitani has turned her sense of history into a weapon, an active protest against racist ideology in America. The opening poem, 'For My Father,' reveals the dominant concerns and imagery of the rest of Mirikitani's work." Mirikitani portrays her father as both the hero and the antihero of his children. He denies them the strawberries he has grown because he must sell them to earn money. "This poem is powerful in its depiction of the results of oppression," continued Tomaneng. "Mirikitani contrasts the wealthy white world to the isolated, impoverished, and oppressive world of the Japanese Americans." "Tule Lake" describes the experiences of the Japanese Americans who were interned at the most severe desert camp, and the title poem depicts the struggle for survival in the camps. "Loving from Vietnam to Zimbabwe" includes graphic descriptions of American atrocities in Vietnam.

Mirikitani is an editor of *Time to Greez!: Incantations from the Third World,* a collection of poems, prose, and graphic art by Third World writers and artists,

with an introduction by American poet Maya Angelou. A "greeze" is a feast of food, and a *Publishers Weekly* contributor noted that the feast this volume presents consists of contributions that reflect "a righteous rage" or "a weary knowingness," but added that also to be found among the pages is "the joy of identity and guileless humor."

Shedding Silence: Poetry and Prose, a collection of thirty-five poems, several works of prose, and a short play, is divided into four sections. The first, "Without Tongue," contains angry poems about racial discrimination. The works of "It Isn't Easy" are personal and address Mirikitani's marriage and marriage in general. The last two sections, titled "What Matters" and "Reversals", address a variety of issues from the politics of various nations to the pollution of Love Canal. *Kliatt* reviewer Maureen K. Griffin called "When There Is Talk of War" and the play *Shedding Silence* "outstandingly beautiful. The Japanese-American experience is clearly delineated and should be required reading for young Americans."

Two of the poems are intergenerational. "Breaking Tradition" is about the poet's own daughter, who sees herself as being different from her mother, and "Breaking Silence" focuses on the poet's mother, who breaks her silence about her internment and past suffering. Shirley Geok-lin Lim wrote of Mirikitani's writing in *Belles Lettres* that "the theme of breaking taboos, of defying conventions and stereotypes, runs throughout her work."

Mirikitani and her husband collaborated on *I Have Something to Say about This Big Trouble: Children of the Tenderloin Speak Out,* which contains the works of children participating in Glide's writing program. The multiracial Tenderloin district of San Francisco is notorious for it crime, prostitution, and drugs, and in the poems, prose, and drawings of this collection, children speak out about their despair, but also about their hopes and dreams for themselves and their families. Penny Kaganoff wrote in *Publishers Weekly* that "with a primitive urban minimalism both verbal and visual, the children bear witness to the deprivations of their world."

School Library Journal's John Philbrook felt that "although invaluable as a social document and useful in discussions of the current drug wars, there is also some excellent writing to be had here." Philbrook noted the talent of fifteen-year-old Randall Woodruff and said that nine-year-old Tianah Maji's fictional meeting of Latoya Jackson and Roger Rabbit "is deliciously funny."

Mirikitani continues her protest of racial and gender inequality, patriarchy, and oppression with the poems of *We, the Dangerous: New and Selected Poems,* many of which are disturbing, particularly those about child rape, as in "Insect Collection" and "Where Bodies Are Buried." "Many of the poems focus on the violation of the body as both an inescapably physical act of violence, and a metaphor for the silencing and erasure of the marginalized," wrote Traise Yamamoto in *Amerasia Journal.* "As in her previous work, Mirikitani consistently identifies silence with frustrated repression, fear, and powerlessness. Where only speech is recognized as power, the language of silence is no language at all: it does not protest but enables rape, systemic racism, and imperialist aggression."

Ann E. Reuman wrote in an *American Women Writers* profile, "Direct, vitally angry, and politically impassioned, Mirikitani breaks taboos, writing against expectations of her as a woman and as an Asian American to speak decorously. Without apology, diminution, self-deprecation, or conciliation, she validates her voice and places its power, its passion, and its rage in the context of large and violent truths. While some have found her writings too angry and blunt, many have felt empowered by her explosive poetry and prose and her clear political commitment. In all that she does, Mirikitani insists on the collective power of voice and vows to do her part to stop violence."

Mirikitani was named San Francisco's poet laureate in 2000. Tomaneng wrote that "it is Mirikitani's role as both artist and community representative that makes her an indispensable writer in the literary history of Asian Americans."

BIOGRAPHICAL AND CRITICAL SOURCES:

BOOKS

American Women Writers, St. James Press (Detroit, MI), 2000.
Bruchac, Joseph, editor, *Breaking Silence: An Anthology of Contemporary Asian American Poets,* 1983.

Fisher, Dexter, editor, *The Third Woman: Minority Women Writers of the United States,* 1980.
Reference Guide to American Literature, Gale (Detroit, MI), 2000.
Yamamoto, Traise, *Masking Selves, Making Subjects: Japanese-American Women, Identity, and the Body,* University of California Press (Berkeley, CA), 1999.

PERIODICALS

Amerasia Journal, winter, 1996, Traise Yamamoto, review of *We, the Dangerous: New and Selected Poems,* pp. 155-156.
Belles Lettres, May, 1988, Shirley Geok-lin Lim, review of *Shedding Silence: Poetry and Prose,* p. 2.
Kliatt, January, 1988, Maureen K. Griffin, review of *Shedding Silence,* p. 29.
Publishers Weekly, March 10, 1975, review of *Time to Greez!: Incantations from the Third World,* p. 58; July 21, 1989, Penny Kaganoff, review of *I Have Something to Say about This Big Trouble: Children of the Tenderloin Speak Out,* pp. 55, 56.
School Library Journal, December, 1989, John Philbrook, review of *I Have Something to Say about This Big Trouble,* p. 116.
Women's Review of Books, February, 1988, Adrian Oktenberg, review of *Shedding Silence,* p. 12.*

* * *

MOFFEIT, Tony A. 1942-

PERSONAL: Born March 14, 1942, in Claremore, OK; son of Archie and Virginia (Bell) Moffeit; married 1962; wife's name Diana (divorced); children: Miles. *Education:* Oklahoma State University, B.S. (psychology), 1964; University of Oklahoma, M.L.S., 1965.

ADDRESSES: Home—1501 East Seventh, Pueblo, CO 81001. *Office*—University of Southern Colorado Library, 2200 Bonforte Blvd., Pueblo, CO 81001. *E-mail*—moffeit@uscolo.edu.

CAREER: Central State University, Edmond, OK, reference librarian, 1967-71; Oklahoma State University, Stillwater, archivist, 1971-74; Western Kentucky

University, Bowling Green, social sciences librarian, 1974-76; University of Southern Colorado Library, Pueblo, department chair, library services and poet-in-residence, 1976—; Oklahoma Dept. of Libraries, Oklahoma City, field librarian, 1965-67. Board of directors, University Press of Colorado; director, Pueblo Poetry Project.

AWARDS, HONORS: Jack Kerouac Award, Cherry Valley Editions, 1986, for *Pueblo Blues;* National Endowment for the Arts Writer's fellowship, 1992; Thomas Hornsby Ferril Poetry Prize, Denver Press Club, 1997; Provost's Award for Excellence in Scholarship, University of Southern Colorado, 2000.

WRITINGS:

POETRY

Pueblo Blues, Cherry Valley Editions (Cherry Valley, NY), 1986.
Luminous Animal, Cherry Valley Editions (Cherry Valley, NY), 1989.
Poetry Is Dangerous: The Poet Is an Outlaw, Floating Island Publications, 1995.
(With Kyle Laws) *Tango,* Kings Estate Press, 1997.
Midnight Knocking at the Door, Ye Olde Font Shoppe, 1998.
Billy the Kid and Frida Kahlo, Ye Olde Font Shoppe, 2000.

Contributor to periodicals, including *Chiron Review, Poetry Motel, Abbey, Bogg, Bloomsbury Review, Butcher's Block,* and *Atom Mind.*

WORK IN PROGRESS: Outlaw Blues (poetry), Butcher's Block Press.

SIDELIGHTS: Tony A. Moffeit told *CA:* "There is something mystical about being a poet. Something magical and yet ghostlike in creating words which express who and what you are, your inner self, your poetic self. Words, language, rhythms, images are communicated in a kind of ghost language, so that there is a kind of mystical connection between poet and reader. The unconscious comes into play, the dreamlife comes into play, there is a magical transformation of syntax, so that communication takes place between dream-world and dreamworld. It is this talking in ghost language, talking with the ghosts, which is my primary motivation for writing.

"Who or what particularly influences my work? Those poets who write in a kind of ghost language: Federico García Lorca, d. a. levy, Robert Desnos, and Friedrich Nietzsche. The lyricism and rhythms of the blues. Performers of song and poetry: Mick Jagger, Jack Micheline, Elvis Presley. The actor James Dean. Those huge energetic yea-sayers of life: Neal Cassady, Henry Miller, Walt Whitman. Zen Buddhism. Surrealism. The Beats.

"My writing process involves getting in tune with the ghost energy. This may come about through an old blues, through an old movie, or through silence. Getting in touch with the inner depths, a kind of seance. A line from another poet. A song off the radio. The pure connection with the unconscious. A wave of pure electricity so that the poem almost writes itself. The blues, New Orleans, and voodoo have been a supercharged inspiration. Visiting New Orleans, meeting the Chickenman, the oldest and the greatest of the Voodoo Kings, listening to the blues on street corners, soaking in all the mystery and ambience of the French Quarter. I am a blues singer as well as poet, so that the energy of the blues is soaked into my work. The West: Taos, New Mexico, Billy the Kid, the outlaw spirit, independence, wide open spaces, going your own way, all these come from growing up and living in the West. This obsession with liberty is not only American, but a product of the West. Creating one's own laws, creating oneself."

*   *   *

MOGELON, Ronna 1960-

PERSONAL: Born June 10, 1960, in Montreal, Quebec, Canada; daughter of Alex (a writer and producer) and Lila (a producer; maiden name, Brownberg) Mogelon. *Education:* Concordia University, B.F.A., 1982.

ADDRESSES: Home—Ontario, Canada. *Agent*—c/o M. Evans & Co., Inc., 216 East 49th St., New York, NY 10017. *E-mail*—ronna@glen-net.ca.

CAREER: Writer.

WRITINGS:

Freda Pemberton Smith: Her Work in Honour of Her Eightieth Birthday (monograph), Vankleek Gallery, 1982.

Famous People's Cats, St. Martin's Press (New York, NY), 1995.

Wild in the Kitchen (cookbook), M. Evans & Co. (New York, NY), 2001.

*   *   *

MONZÓ, Joaquim 1952-
(Quim Monzó)

PERSONAL: Born March 24, 1952, in Barri Sans, Barcelona, Spain.

ADDRESSES: Office—c/o Author Mail, Quaderns Crema, Ferran Valls I, Taberner 8, Barcelona 8006, Spain.

CAREER: Novelist, journalist, and scriptwriter. Worked as a graphic artist, photo editor, and war correspondent.

WRITINGS:

AS QUIM MONZÓ

L'udol del griso al caire de les clavegueres (novel), Edicions 62 (Barcelona, Spain), 1976.

(With Biel Mesquida) *Self-Service* (short stories), Iniciatives Editoriales (Barcelona, Spain), 1977.

Uf, va dir ell (short stories; title means "Oof, He Said"), Quaderns Crema (Barcelona, Spain), 1978.

Olivetti, Moulinex, Chaffoteaux et Maury (short stories), Quaderns Crema (Barcelona, Spain), 1980, translation by Mary Ann Newman published as *O'Clock,* Ballantine (New York, NY), 1986.

Benzina (novel; title means "Gasoline"), Quaderns Crema (Barcelona, Spain), 1983.

El dia del senyor (articles), Quaderns Crema (Barcelona, Spain), 1984.

L'illa de Maians (short stories), Quaderns Crema (Barcelona, Spain), 1985.

Zzzzzzzz (articles), Quaderns Crema (Barcelona, Spain), 1987.

La magnitud de la tragèdia (novel), Quaderns Crema (Barcelona, Spain), 1989.

La maleta turca (articles; title means "The Turkish Suitcase"), Quaderns Crema (Barcelona, Spain), 1990.

Hotel Intercontinental (articles), Quaderns Crema (Barcelona, Spain), 1991.

El perquè de tot plegat (short stories; title means "The Why of It All"), Quaderns Crema (Barcelona, Spain), 1993.

No plantaré cap arbre (articles; title means "I Will Not Plant Any Tree"), Quaderns Crema (Barcelona, Spain), 1994.

Guadalajara (short stories), Quaderns Crema (Barcelona, Spain), 1996.

Del tot indefens davant dels hostils imperis alienígenes (articles; title means "Completely Defenseless before Hostile Alien Empires"), Quaderns Crema (Barcelona, Spain), 1998.

Vuitanta—sis contes (short stories; contains "Uf, va dir ell," "Olivetti, Moulinex, Chaffoteaux et Maury," "L'illa de Maians," "El perquè de tot plegat," and "Guadalajara"), Quaderns Crema (Barcelona, Spain), 1999.

Tot és mentida (articles; title means "It's All a Lie"), Quaderns Crema (Barcelona, Spain), 2000.

El millor dels mons (short stories; title means "The Best of Worlds"), Quaderns Crema (Barcelona, Spain), 2001.

Contributor to books, including *Relatos urbanos,* Alfaguara (Buenos Aires, Argentina), 1994; *Pep Trujillo: pinturas,* Galeria Maeght (Barcelona, Spain), 1992; and *El lloro, el moro, el mico i el senyor de Puerto Rico,* Editorial Empúries (Barcelona, Spain), 2001. Contributor of column "El Runrún" to *La Vanguardia.* Author of screenplays and radio plays.

Author's works have been translated into Basque, Danish, Dutch, Finnish, French, Galician, German, Hungarian, Italian, Japanese, Norwegian, Russian, Spanish, and Swedish.

TRANSLATOR

Ray Bradbury, *Les cròniques marcianes* (translation of *The Martian Chronicles*), Editorial Proa (Barcelona, Spain), 2000.

J. D. Salinger, *Nou contes* (translation of *Nine Stories*), Editorial Empúries (Barcelona, Spain), 2001.

Thomas Hardy, *Jude, l'obscur* (translation of *Jude the Obscure*), Edicions 62 (Barcelona, Spain), 2002.

Mary Wollstonecraft Shelley, *Frankenstein,* Edicions de la Magrana, 1983.

SIDELIGHTS: Over the course of his writing career, Joaquim Monzó has become Catalonia's best-known living author. His sardonic, postmodern novels and books of stories and essays—published under the name Quim Monzó—have sold more than 600,000 copies.

The Barcelona native began his writing career as a war correspondent in the early 1970s, publishing articles in the Spanish media from locations such as Vietnam, Cambodia, and Northern Ireland. Monzó tackled fiction several years later when he wrote his first novel, *L'udol del griso al caire de les clavegueres.* In 1977 he collaborated with fellow—Majorcan—Catalan writer Biel Mesquida on *Self-Service,* a book of short stories. Monzó is considered part of Spain's Generació dels '70, the group of writers who emerged as the Franco regime withered.

Monzó's novel *Benzina* was published in 1983, following his extended stay in New York City. Not surprisingly, the book is set in New York, and concerns a pair of up-and-coming artists, each successively married to the same woman, a modern art promoter. Although both men owe their meteoric ascensions to stardom to their capable wife, when poised to reap the benefits of their success they confront an existential crisis in the form of impotence and an inability to create new work. In *Forum for Modern Language Studies,* contributor Josep-Anton Fernández related the theme of the novel to a demographic fact: that writers and readers of books in Catalan are increasingly women. Monzó's novel articulates "certain anxieties of male authorship in a period of definitional crisis, affecting both hegemonic masculinity and the Catalan cultural field," the critic conjectured.

While *Benzina* uses the phenomenon of impotence to examine the postmodern male predicament, excessive potency is the problem in Monzó's next book, 1989's *La magnitud de la tragèdia.* In this novel an otherwise ordinary middle-aged man suddenly finds himself with a permanent erection. After enjoying his new potency for some weeks, the protagonist reluctantly visits a doctor at the urging of his lover. The diagnosis: "Sciamscia syndrome," a rare degenerative disease that will kill the man within two months. In an interview with a Spanish newspaper, Monzó claimed the protagonist's priapic erection to be "an emblem of the human condition, of the thirst for life" and its inevitable frustration. In a review of the book on the online *Lletre,* Manel Ollé praised the novel for its elegant writing "from a savage joy, from a lucid pessimism, not at all masochistic."

Monzó has affirmed his preference for the short story form, which dominates his body of work. His stories, collected in several books, plumb the neurotic, erotic, and absurd. For instance, a story collected in the 1980 anthology *Olivetti, Moulinex, Chaffoteaux et Maury* concerns a nasty "Dear John" letter within which an ex-girlfriend details the great sex life with her new man and mockingly reminds her jilted lover of his pledge to commit suicide. The letter is delivered to a man who has just killed himself. In his review of Monzó's 1996 short-story collection *Guadalajara* in *World Literature Today,* Mark Juditz explained that the writer "has given intense thought to all the ways human beings can fail to communicate and the ways he can communicate that failure."

Some of Monzó's stories reflect his taste for the metafiction of his literary idols Robert Coover and Donald Barthelme. "Monarquia," collected in 2000's *Vuitanta—sis contes,* is a fractured postscript to the Cinderella fairy tale. Here the former Prince Charming neglects his beautiful queen and turns his attentions to men with "big shoes" (homosexuals).

Beside writing his own fiction, Monzó has translated several classic English-language novels into Catalan, including Thomas Hardy's *Jude the Obscure* and Ray Bradbury's *The Martian Chronicles.* He has also worked extensively on scripts for radio and television and become a minor media personality in the process. The most regular forum for Monzó is the column he writes for the Spanish-language daily *La Vanguardia* in Barcelona. The column, "El Runrún," serves as a bully pulpit for the writer's views on topics ranging from politics to art to the frustrations of daily life in Catalonia. They are often written with a sarcastic tone, a fact that has earned the author his share of controversy.

Monzó has repeatedly expressed his doubts about the survival of the Catalan language. "It's in full agony," he told Jim Blake in an interview for the *Barcelona*

Review. "At times I think that the Yiddish writers, like [Isaac Bashevis] Singer must have felt something like I feel: that under my feet the country is disappearing."

BIOGRAPHICAL AND CRITICAL SOURCES:

PERIODICALS

Forum for Modern Language Studies, July, 1998, Josep-Anton Fernández, "My Tragedy Is Bigger than Yours: Masculinity in Trouble and the Crisis of Male Authorship in Quim Monzó's Novels," pp. 262-273.

Los Angeles Times Book Review, June 15, 1986, Jonathan Kirsch, review of *O'Clock,* p. 9.

Publishers Weekly, February 28, 1986, review of *O'Clock,* p. 121.

World Literature Today, spring, 1987, Albert M. Forcadas, review of *O'Clock,* pp. 269-270; autumn, 1997, Mark Juditz, review of *Guadalajara,* p. 772; spring, 2000, Albert M. Forcadas, review of *Vuitanta-sis contes,* pp. 452-454.

OTHER

Association of Writers in the Catalan Language Web site, http://www.escriptors.com/ (June, 2002), "Quim Monzó."

Barcelona Review, http://www.BarcelonaReview.com/ (May, 1997), Jim Blake, interview with Quim Monzó.

Lletra, http://www.uoc.edu/lletra/ (August 28, 2002), Manel Ollé, "Quim Monzó."*

*   *   *

MONZÓ, Quim
   See MONZÓ, Joaquim

*   *   *

MOORE, Ishbel (Lindsay) 1954-
   (Alexandra Duncan)

PERSONAL: Born December 13, 1954, in Glasgow, Scotland; daughter of James Turnbull (an automobile mechanic) and Ishbel MacLean (a nurse; maiden name, Lindsay) Turnbull; married Grant Buckoski, July 9, 1977 (divorced, 1984); married Michael Leigh Moore (a biomedical technician), July 25, 1986; children: Brad, Ishbel, Elizabeth. *Ethnicity:* "Scottish." *Education:* Studied English and music at the university level; earned medical transcriptionist certificate from Herzing Career College (Winnipeg, Canada). *Hobbies and other interests:* Golf, needlepoint, singing, horseback riding, gardening, walking the dog, reading, eating M & M's, caring for five fish, five finches, two cats, a dog, and two horses.

ADDRESSES: Home—1086 Peel St., St. Andrews, Manitoba RW1 3W5, Canada. *E-mail*—ilmoore@mb. sympatico.ca.

CAREER: Author. Speaker at schools, libraries, and workshops. Worked variously as a medical transcriptionist, piano teacher, playground supervisor, drug store clerk, and aide to students with disabilities.

MEMBER: Canadian Authors Association (Manitoba Branch president, 1995-97; vice president for Manitoba and Saskatchewan Branches, 1997-99, 2000-02; and president), Canadian Society of Children's Authors, Illustrators, and Performers, Manitoba Writers Guild, Saskatchewan Writers Guild, Writers' Collective, Writers' Union of Canada, Lovers Knot (founding member), Penhandlers, Canadian Children's Book Centre, Children of the Quill (president and founding member), Blue Pencil Critiquing Service (founder).

AWARDS, HONORS: First prize, adult short fiction contest, Canadian Authors Association—Manitoba branch, 1993, 1994; first prize for fiction, Nell Anderson Competition, 1994, 1995; third prize, Canadian Authors Association Poetry Contest, 1995; named YM-YWCA Woman of Distinction, 1995; ten most notable books of Canadian fiction selection, 1995, for *The Medal;* second prize for nonfiction, Nell Anderson Competition, 1997; Kathleen Strange Memorial Award, Canadian Authors Association—Manitoba Branch, 1998, for distinguished service; Young Adult Book of the Year shortlist, Canadian Library Association, 1998, for *Dolina May;* McNally Robinson Books for Young People Award shortlist for *Annilea;* Ontario regional winner and finalist, Red Maple Award (Canada), 2001, for *Daughter;* second prize for fiction, Nell Anderson Competition, 2001; Alan Sangster Memorial Award, Canadian Authors Association, 2001, for dedicated voluntary service.

WRITINGS:

The Summer of the Hand, Roussan Publishers (Montreal, Quebec, Canada), 1994.

The Medal, Roussan Publishers (Montreal, Quebec, Canada), 1994.

Branch of Talking Teeth, Roussan Publishers (Montreal, Quebec, Canada), 1995.

Xanthe's Pyramid, Roussan Publishers (Montreal, Quebec, Canada), 1998.

Daughter, Kids Can Press (Toronto, Ontario, Canada), 1999.

Annilea, Roussan Publishers (Montreal, Quebec, Canada), 2000.

Kitchen Sink Concert, BeWrite Books (Bristol, England), 2002.

"DOLINA" TRILOGY

Dolina May, Roussan Publishers (Montreal, Quebec, Canada), 1997.

Dolina's Grad, Roussan Publishers (Montreal, Quebec, Canada), 1998.

Dolina's Decision, Roussan Publishers (Montreal, Quebec, Canada), 2000.

OTHER

Creator of "Music for Its Own Sake," a text for the Winnipeg Philharmonic's 75th anniversary, 1997, and author of *Rock of Ages,* an adult romance cowritten with Maureen Branningan under the pseudonym Alexandra Duncan, in print-on-demand format through Books for Pleasure (Canada). *Dolina May* was translated into German; *Daughter* has been translated into Norwegian and Swedish.

SIDELIGHTS: Children's author Ishbel Moore began putting her stories to paper at an early age. As a teenager, she started writing realistic short stories and what she supposed were historical romances, but, as she recalled at the *Kids Can Press* Web site, they were "so bad that my friend called them 'hysterical' romances." She studied English, music, and art at a university but quit college to get married. Later, she divorced and, needing a way to support herself and her son, pursued several other careers, including as a classroom aide, musician, and medical transcriptionist.

Finally, while working other jobs part-time, Moore returned to writing. She did not intend to become a writer of children's books, yet she found writing for young adults exciting, producing a handful of novels as well as the "Dolina" trilogy in six years. "I am addicted to writing, to the magic of the creation process, [to] the discipline of working through the story to the joy of publication," Moore wrote at the *Manitoba Author Publication* Web site. "I am inspired by billions of things, but primarily by little-known historical (and sometimes medical) facts."

Moore published her first juvenile novels, the time-travel adventures *The Summer of the Hand* and *The Medal,* and *Branch of the Talking Teeth* in quick succession in the mid-1990s. The last reflects Moore's childhood dream of becoming an archeologist and was partly inspired by the 1973 discovery of a 7,000-year old grave site on Labrador coast. This novel, set in prehistoric times, is organized around the curved stick to which six human teeth have been attached. Each tooth is a talisman and mnemonic device for the tribe's storyteller, Moonhead, who, as a castaway and newcomer to the tribe, tries to make a place for himself. As Helen Norrie explained in *Canadian Materials,* the tales Moonhead carries "emphasise the power stories have on our consciousness, which is the underlying theme of the novel."

When asked what she likes most about writing for children, Moore replied at the *Kids Can Press* Web site, "Kids' books are fun, even when they deal with sad stuff." She continued, "Kids will go on crazy adventures without asking any questions. Kids demand energy and movement in their books, and that makes writing them an exciting challenge. Also in teen books I get the opportunity to explore the wild and wonderful hormonal years of zits, boyfriends, and coming of age all over again." For example, in *Xanthe's Pyramid,* Moore depicts one week in the life of sixteen-year-old Xanthe, who is grounded by her parents when they discover that she is infatuated with Colton, whom they have decided is the "wrong kind" of boy. As a *Quill & Quire* reviewer noted, the "increasingly adept and confident" Moore "skillfully rendered" Xanthe's emotions as Colton's behavior becomes more and more erratic.

In similar fashion, Moore delves into the mind of her Dolina character, which she enjoyed so much that she wrote a trilogy about her in a little over three years:

Dolina May, Dolina's Grad, and *Dolina's Decision.* In the debut, readers meet seventeen-year-old Dolina, who suddenly finds herself stranded in rural Manitoba after an argument in the car with her abusive boyfriend, Mitch. Then when the feisty, independent young woman seeks help at a farmhouse, she is surprised by what she encounters there. In the second novel, Dolina is back at home with her divorced mother, but she has graduation, romance, and the identity of her absentee father on her mind. Finally, in the third volume, Dolina meets her father and must make some important decisions about her life. Like the author, several reviewers offered warm words for the character of Dolina. Sally M. Tibbetts, in a review of *Dolina's Decision* for *Kliatt,* called Dolina a "wonderful character," while a *Quill and Quire* critic poetically described Dolina, in a review of *Dolina May,* as a "he-rione who has been force-bloomed from a sodden and prickly weed to a quite splendid dandelion."

Moore mined her store of medical knowledge to write the novels *Daughter* and *Annilea.* As she explained to *Kids Can Press,* "After I get an idea, I glean information from the Internet or books, other people's stories, medical files. Then I sit and read, read, read, until one magical day the story 'sets' itself in my brain, even if I don't realize it." In *Daughter,* fourteen-year-old Sylvie finds her divorcée mother acting stranger and stranger. Finally, the teenager must seek help to cope with her mother, who in her forties is diagnosed with an early onset case of Alzheimer's disease. Several reviewers commented on Moore's characterizations. In the opinion of Kathleen Isaacs of *School Library Journal,* Moore's description of the mother "grips readers in horrified fascination," and in *Reading Time,* a critic called the characters "strongly established" and liable to elicit empathy from readers. Moreover, a *Kirkus Reviews* contributor particularly praised the "often heart-stopping" confusion from which Sylvie initially suffers, dubbing Moore's overall portrayal of Sylvie "fairly convincing." For its "solid theme, believable situations, and realistic young characters," *Booklist's* Roger Leslie recommended *Daughter* as a "good selection."

While the general reading public is likely unaware that Alzheimer's disease can affect the middle-aged and not just the elderly, the topic of Moore's other "medical" novel, *Annilea* is even more obscure. In this novel, the fourteen-year-old hockey-playing protagonist strives to overcome the repercussions of Moebius syndrome, a congenital defect in which some facial muscles are missing. At the end of each of her "medical" novels, Moore provides information on research and support groups for people affected by the ailment in question.

Moore believes in the value of peer-support groups for authors and in addition to working with the existing Canadian societies, has started several critique groups of her own, including the Blue Pencil Critiquing Service geared to aiding isolated writers. For her dedication, Moore's peers recognized her in 2001 by awarding her the Alan Sangster Memorial Award for dedicated voluntary service to the national Canadian Authors Association.

When not on the road promoting her novels and writing in general, Moore works at her computer in her Winnipeg home. After enough thought, "Away I go into my own little world until the story is done," she told *Kids Can Press.* "My family always knows when that is happening. For instance, [when] I'm eating at the table with them but I'm not really there."

BIOGRAPHICAL AND CRITICAL SOURCES:

PERIODICALS

Booklist, November 15, 1999, Roger Leslie, review of *Daughter,* p. 614.

Books in Canada, February, 2000, review of *Daughter,* pp. 36-37.

Canadian Children's Literature, summer, 1996, review of *Summer of the Hand,* pp. 89-93; spring, 2001, review of *Daughter,* p. 143.

Canadian Materials, October, 1994, review of *Summer of the Hand,* p. 180; June 16, 1995, Helen Norrie, review of *Branch of the Talking Teeth.*

Childhood Education, spring, 2002, Elsa Geskus and Jeanie Burnett, review of *Daughter,* p. 174.

Kirkus Reviews, October 1, 1999, review of *Daughter,* p. 1582.

Kliatt, September, 2001, Sally M. Tibbetts, review of *Dolina's Decision,* p. 19.

NeWest Review, April-May, 1998, review of *Dolina May,* p. 31.

Prairie Fire, fall, 1998, review of *Xanthe's Pyramid,* pp. 127-128, review of *Dolina May,* p. 157.

Quill and Quire, April, 1997, review of *Dolina May,* p. 38; May, 1998, review of *Xanthe's Pyramid,* p. 34; September, 1999, review of *Daughter,* p. 71.

Reading Time, November, 2002, Jo Goodman, review of *Daughter,* p. 35.

Resource Links, June, 1996, review of *Branch of the Talking Teeth,* pp. 231-232; April, 1999, review of *Dolina's Grad,* pp. 25-26; December, 1999, review of *Daughter,* pp. 28-29; October, 2000, review of *Dolina's Decision,* p. 29; June, 2001, Krista Johansen, review of *Annilea,* p. 10.

School Library Journal, November, 1999, Kathleen Isaacs, review of *Daughter,* p. 161; August, 2001, Angela J. Reynolds, review of *Dolina's Decision,* p. 186.

Times Educational Supplement, September 14, 2001, Linda Newbery, p. 9.

ONLINE

Ishbel Moore Web site, http://www3.mb.sympatico.ca/~ilmoore/pobbles.htm/ (February 19, 2003).

Kids Can Press Web site, http://www.nelvana.com/kidscanpress/ (February 19, 2003), "Author: Ishbel Moore."

Manitoba Author Publication Index, http://www.mbwriter.mb.ca/ (February 19, 2003), "Ishbel Moore."

*　　*　　*

MORRISSEAU, Norval 1932-

PERSONAL: Native American name, Copper Thunderbird; born March 14, 1932, in Sand Point Reserve, Ontario, Canada; grandson of Moses and Vernique Nanakonagas; married Harriet Kakegamic, 1957 (marriage ended); children: six. *Education:* Attended Indian boarding school in Fort William (now Thunder Bay), Ontario, Canada. *Religion:* Christian; Eckankar.

ADDRESSES: Home—British Columbia, Canada. *Agent*—c/o Kinsman Robinson Gallery, 108 Cumberland St., Toronto, Ontario M5R 1A6, Canada.

CAREER: Writer; painter, printmaker, and illustrator. *Exhibitions:* Work exhibited in many solo and group shows, beginning 1962, including exhibitions at Kinsman Robinson Galleries, Toronto, Ontario, Canada, Native American Center for the Living Arts, Niagara Falls, NY, Thunder Bay Art Gallery, Southwest Museum, Los Angeles, CA, Department of Indian and Northern Affairs, Ottawa, Ontario, Canada, and Pollock Gallery, Toronto, Ontario, Canada; collections include work at Winnipeg Art Gallery, Royal Ontario Museum, Montreal Museum of Fine Art, Canadian Museum of Civilization, and Canada Council ArtBank.

MEMBER: Royal Canadian Academy of Art.

AWARDS, HONORS: Member, Order of Canada, 1978; LL.D., McMaster University, 1980; honored by Assembly of First Nations, 1995.

WRITINGS:

(And illustrator) *Legends of My People: The Great Ojibway,* edited by Selwyn Dewdney, Ryerson Press (Toronto, Ontario, Canada), 1965, McGraw-Hill Ryerson (New York, NY), 1977.

(Illustrator) Herbert T. Schwarz, *Windigo and Other Tales of the Ojibways,* McClelland & Stewart (Toronto, Ontario, Canada), 1969.

(With Donald Robinson) *Norval Morrisseau: Travels to the House of Invention,* Key Porter Books (Toronto, Ontario, Canada), 1997.

BIOGRAPHICAL AND CRITICAL SOURCES:

BOOKS

McLuhan, Elizabeth, and Tom Hill, *Norval Morrisseau and the Emergence of the Image Makers,* Methuen (New York, NY), 1984.

Morrisseau, Norval, *Legends of My People: The Great Ojibway,* edited by Selwyn Dewdney, Ryerson Press (Toronto, Ontario, Canada), 1965.

Notable Native Americans, Gale (Detroit, MI), 1995.

St. James Guide to Native North-American Artists, St. James Press (Detroit, MI), 1998, pp. 396-398.

Sinclair, Lister, and Jack Pollock, *The Art of Norval Morrisseau,* foreword by Norval Morrisseau, Methuen (New York, NY), 1979.

PERIODICALS

Art, summer, 1974, Tom Hill, "Canadian Indian Artist's Death and Rebirth" and interview by James Stephens; summer, 1976, Nancy-Lou Patterson, "Shaking Tents and Medicine Snakes: Traditional Elements in Contemporary Woodland Art."

Artwest, May, 1983, Jamake Highwater, "North American Indian Art: A Special Way of Seeing."

Canadian Art, January-February, 1963, Selwyn Dewdney, "Norval Morrisseau."

Canadian Forum, December, 1989, Jack Pollock, "Meeting Morrisseau," p. 784.

London Free Press, September 29, 1962, Lenore Crawford, "Self-taught Ojibway Artist Finds Fame Overnight."

Maclean's, March 5, 1984, Gillian MacKay, "Salute to a Vibrant Revolutionary," p. 62.

New York Times, March 16, 2001, Holland Cotter, "Draw and Tell: The Transformative Lines of Norval Morrisseau/Copper Thunderbird," p. B35.

Time, September 28, 1962, "Myths and Symbols"; August 25, 1975, "Fierce Clarity and Sophistication."

Toronto Daily Star, June 12, 1962, Bill Brown, "Cooper Thunderbird: An Ojibway Paints His People's Past."

OTHER

The Colours of Pride (documentary film), National Film Board of Canada, 1974.

The Originals: Norval Morrisseau (documentary film), City Television (Toronto, Ontario, Canada), 1990.

The Paradox of Norval Morrisseau (documentary film), National Film Board of Canada, 1974.

"Spirits Speaking Through: Canadian Woodland Artists" (documentary program), *Spectrum* (television series), Canadian Broadcasting Corp., 1982.*

* * *

MORSELLI, Guido 1912-1973

PERSONAL: Born April 15, 1912, in Bologna, Italy; committed suicide July 31, 1973; son of Giovanni Morselli, (a pharmaceutical company manager) and Olga Vincenzi. *Education:* University of Milan, law degree, 1935.

CAREER: Novelist, essayist, philosopher, newspaper writer, and farmer. *Military service:* Italian Army; served during World War II.

WRITINGS:

Proust o del sentimento (title means "Proust or Concerning Sentiment"), Garzanti (Milan, Italy), 1943.

Realismo e fantasia (title means "Realism and Imagination"), Bocca (Milan, Italy), 1947.

Roma senza papa: cronache romane di fine secolo ventesimo (title means "Rome without a Pope: Roman Chronicles at the End of the Twentieth Century"), Adelphi (Milan, Italy), 1974.

Contro-passato prossimo: Un'ipotesi retrospettiva, Adelphi (Milan, Italy), 1975, translated by Hugh Shankland as *Past Conditional: A Retrospective Hypothesis,* Chatto and Windus (London, England), 1989.

Divertimento 1889, Adelphi (Milan, Italy), 1975, translated by Hugh Shankland, Dutton (New York, NY) 1986.

Il comunista (title means "The Communist"), Adelphi (Milan, Italy), 1976.

Dissipatio H.G. (title means "The Dissolution of the Human Race"), Adelphi (Milan, Italy), 1977.

Fede e critica (title means "Faith and Criticism"), [Milan, Italy], 1977.

Un dramma borghese (title means "A Bourgeois Drama"), Adelphi (Milan, Italy), 1978.

Incontro col comunista (title means "Encounter with a Communist"), Adelphi (Milan, Italy), 1980.

Diario, edited by Valentina Fortichiari, Adelphi (Milan, Italy), 1988.

La felicità non è un lusso, edited by Valentina Fortichiari, Adelphi (Milan, Italy), 1994.

SIDELIGHTS: Guido Morselli's death defines him as much as the detailed intellectual terseness of his literary efforts. Morselli's fame has largely been posthumous following thirty years of constant publishing rejection and his suicide at age sixty-one. Morselli saw only two of his works published.

His mother's death in 1924, when Morselli was twelve, may have had, as Charles Fantazzi suggested in the *Dictionary of Literary Biography,* "far-reaching effects on his already introverted character." A classical education at a Jesuit preparatory school and a law degree from the University of Milan did little to encourage him to enter Italian society. Instead of starting a legal practice, Morselli toured Europe, honing his command of European cultures and languages. During military service in World War II, Morselli spent three enforced, isolated years in Calabria, on Italy's southwest coast. In a cruel twist, Morselli's first book, *Proust o del sentimento,* was published while he was cut off from the main currents of Italian culture. Fittingly, the work concerns a struggling writer whom the Italian literary mainstream has neglected.

After the war Morselli returned to Varese, his affluent family's new home, and spent the following decade writing for various newspapers. The second and last book he would see published came out during this period. *Realismo e fantasia* is a philosophical text covering a range of subjects from religion to art. In 1958 Morselli moved to an isolated area at Sasso di Gavirate, near Lake Maggiore. He spent the next twenty-five years of his life in a house he built and named Santa Trinita. Though he faced numerous publishers' rejections, he continued writing and spent time horseback riding and tending to his small farm. Morselli moved back to the more urban surroundings of Varese in 1973. Several months and two returned manuscripts later he killed himself.

Morselli's work began to gain popularity shortly after his death, when his small circle of friends, led by critic Dante Isella, began promoting his works. Morselli's isolation, more than anything, may have contributed to his publishing failures. Although his writings are deeply philosophical, and about scholarly subjects, they are also rooted in Morselli's world. As Fantazzi wrote, "Morselli considered . . . [a philosopher] any individual endowed with good sense. His goal was not to offer solutions to transcendental inquiries, but to capture philosophical thought in its nascent state."

Morselli's obsession with religion and sexuality, for instance, would most certainly have appealed to a mid–twentieth-century European public, while his more specific inquiries about post–World War II communism and the de-Stalinization of Europe in the 1950s raised political hackles even in the 1970s, when they were eventually published. Italian critics cited these successes as they pointed an accusing finger at the publishing world of Morselli's time.

Un dramma borghese involves a recovering father and daughter—he from rheumatism, she from an appendectomy—landing in the same hospital room. Their interaction raises the danger of incest, prompted by the eighteen-year-old girl's blossoming sexual passions, and suicide, introducing a Browning pistol which surfaces later in Morselli's work and which the author used to kill himself eleven years later.

Il comunista is a political novel about an elected official wrestling with his party allegiance. Walter Ferranini, an up-and-coming Communist party member of the 1958 Rome parliament, finds himself opposing contemporary Marxist doctrine. The party investigates and sanctions him for his careful study of Marx and Engels, and the man/party philosophical split.

In *Roma senza papa* Morselli composes a satire about the condition of papal Rome thirty years into the future, in 1997. Confessionals are computerized, the papal residence is a motel complex, and the Vatican has allied with the Soviet government to oppose secularized schools and divorce while advocating birth control, euthanasia, and the mystical use of drugs. The pope himself is characterized as a snake-charmer, illustrating the deterioration of the religious hierarchy by claiming that "God is not a priest. And not even a friar." He actually holds court at one point with Jacqueline Kennedy. In *Roma senza papa,* Fantazzi wrote, Morselli clearly believes "religion belongs to the common man and not to age-old institutions."

Morselli looks backward in his next two efforts. *Contro-passato prossimo,* set in the war-ravaged Europe of 1915, sees the Allied victory as illogical. In *Divertimento 1889* Umberto I, the reluctant second king of Italy, is followed to the Alps where he hopes to quietly abdicate his throne and have romantic affairs along the way. As the title suggests, Morselli offers the piece as essentially a mind-settling exercise in which he claims to "have found pleasure."

The manuscript for Morselli's *Dissipatio H. G.* was returned to the author shortly before his suicide. The text is somewhat autobiographical, following the suicide efforts of its protagonist and his discovery of a world without humanity. Morselli suggests that the end of all creation will, and should, happen peacefully.

Morselli, according to Fantazzi, could have succeeded more in his lifetime had he written in a more Italian style. "He had always been averse to the excesses of rhetoric and bombast, which he regarded as the chief bane of Italian writing, and was the fierce enemy of all forms of exaggerated romanticism and idealism." Morselli himself once claimed "Art stylizes reality, it does not reproduce it; it wants unity or concentration, while life by its very nature is many sided and disparate." Later critics have cited his intellect and diversity, adding that the snubbing he received while alive was unjustified.

BIOGRAPHICAL AND CRITICAL SOURCES:

BOOKS

Dictionary of Literary Biography, Volume 177: *Italian Novelists since World War II,* Gale (Detroit, MI), 1997.
Encyclopedia of Science Fiction, St. Martin's Press (New York, NY), 1993.*

*   *   *

MOUNTJOY, Roberta Jean
See SOHL, Jerry

*   *   *

MULGREW, Ian 1957-

PERSONAL: Born February 4, 1957, in Dumbarton, Scotland; son of Edward and Marion (Harper) Mulgrew; married; children: Christopher, Deanna, Paul. *Education:* Attended Simon Fraser University and York University. *Religion:* Roman Catholic. *Hobbies and other interests:* Sailing, skiing, reading, chess.

ADDRESSES: Home—1-2531 Pt. Grey Rd., Vancouver, British Columbia V6K 1A1, Canada. *Office*—*Vancouver Sun,* 200 Granville St., Suite 1, Vancouver, British Columbia V6C 3N3 Canada. *E-mail*—imulgrew@pacpress.southam.ca.

CAREER: Journalist and author. Thomson Newspapers, Ltd., 1977-80; *Globe and Mail,* Toronto, Ontario, Canada, 1980-85; *Province,* city editor, 1985-89; *Vancouver Sun,* Vancouver, British Columbia, Canada, senior feature writer, columnist; *Toronto Star,* Toronto, book critic. Taught journalism at Kwantlen College, Richmond, British Columbia, Canada. Producer and/or host of numerous television programs, including *Forum, Canada AM, As It Happens, Western Voices, Beyond the News,* and *Hooked on the Blues.*

AWARDS, HONORS: B'nai Brith award; Best Limited Series award, 1989, for *Forum.*

WRITINGS:

Unholy Terror: The Sikhs and International Terrorism, Key Porter Books (Toronto, Ontario, Canada), 1988.
Final Payoff: The True Price of Convicting Clifford Robert Olson, Seal Books (Toronto, Ontario, Canada), 1990.
(Ghostwriter) Jack Webster, *Webster! An Autobiography of Jack Webster,* Douglas & McIntyre (Vancouver, British Columbia, Canada), 1991.
Who Killed Cindy James, Seal Books (Toronto, Ontario, Canada), 1991.
(With Colin Angus) *Amazon Extreme: Three Men, a Raft, and the World's Most Dangerous River,* Stoddart Publishing Co. (Toronto, Ontario, Canada), 2001, Broadway Books (New York, NY), 2002.
(With Colin Angus) *Lost in Mongolia: Rafting the World's Last Unchallenged River,* Stoddart Publishing Co. (Toronto, Ontario, Canada), 2002.

Host of *Forum,* Canadian Broadcasting Corporation.

SIDELIGHTS: Ian Mulgrew is a Canada-based journalist and author whose *Unholy Terror: The Sikhs and International Terrorism* is a study of a siege that occurred in 1984, the history that led to it, and its aftermath. In June of that year, Prime Minister Indira Ghandi of India ordered the military attack on the Golden Temple of Amritsar in the Punjab. The site is the religious center of the Sikh faith and was the place at which fundamentalist leader Sant Jarnail Singh Bhindranwale was killed, making him a martyr who died without creating his dream of a separate Sikh land to be called Khalistan. Hundreds of Sikh pilgrims were killed in the attack, called Operation Bluestar, and approximately 1,500 people were arrested. Following the destruction at the temple, Ghandi herself was assassinated by her Sikh bodyguards.

On June 23, 1985, Sikhs were implicated in two bombings that took the lives of more than 300, most of them Canadian citizens of Indian ancestry. An Air India flight traveling from Canada to London crashed off the coast of Ireland, and a suitcase being transferred from a Canadian Pacific plane to a connecting Air India flight exploded, killing two. Other acts of violence continued across Canada, which has a large Indian population, with both Sikhs and Hindus being harassed and killed. *Books in Canada* contributor Bruce Serafin noted that "the more moderate Sikhs, those for whom Canada is home, have been cowed: with a few exceptions, they are afraid to speak out, afraid of reprisals within their community." Serafin called Mulgrew's *Unholy Terror: The Sikhs and International Terrorism* "a factual, prosaic piece of journalism: it doesn't interpret events, and it doesn't take sides. As such, it is a necessary book, but only a beginning."

Serafin noted that Canada is a "multicultural" country, but that the downside of this is that problems within specific communities are largely ignored until serious violence erupts, for example in connection with Asian gangs and triads. Serafin said the reason is that Canada, like other homogenous societies, is racist. "If people aren't like us, we ignore them. We don't build bridges to them. They live in their cell; we live in ours. So that we don't pay attention to the shameful treatment of newly arrived Canadian Asian and Indian women, for instance, just as we don't pay attention to the intimidation of Asian and Sikh communities by the thugs in their midst. Our standards, we say aren't theirs: let them work it out. This is our 'tolerance.' But this 'tolerance' is merely a subtle form of racism. And in the case of the Sikhs it has backfired." Serafin noted that in his book, Mulgrew provides the history and the details, and added that "it is up to us to go on from there."

Jane O'Hara wrote in a review of *Unholy Terror* for *Maclean's* that Mulgrew "was unable to infiltrate the province's tightly knit fundamentalist Sikh community: most of his own interviews are conducted with Westernized moderates who shed little light on Sikh extremism." O'Hara conceded, however, that Mulgrew's book "succeeds as a primer on Sikh politics and religion."

Quill & Quire's Philip Plews wrote that "even when Mulgrew does interview the right people, he fails to ask the right questions or isn't pushy enough. He allows his subjects to spout party dogma and, rather than challenging them at the time to get their reaction, comments on it months later while writing the book. Mulgrew's strengths lie in behind-the-scenes investigation and the ability to connect events with people who, in the past, have been superficially treated in the press." Plews specifically noted Mulgrew's profile of Talwinder Singh Parmar, a Sikh militant leader living in exile in British Columbia who was suspected but never convicted of his participation in the explosion aboard Air India 182. Parmar rose within the ranks from a laborer to a priest, with his sole purpose in life being the establishment of Khalistan. "With portraits like this," commented Plews, "Mulgrew immerses the reader in a subculture within a subculture, whose members live above the law."

Final Payoff: The True Price of Convicting Clifford Robert Olson is Mulgrew's account of the man who went on a killing spree in British Columbia in 1980 and 1981, and who was paid $100,000 for naming the location of his victims' corpses. *Quill & Quire*'s Ted Mumford felt that *Final Payoff* "works reasonably well," but wondered why Mulgrew did not raise the questions of why Olson committed these crimes and whether or not the police were ethically and morally responsible in making the deal. Mumford called "commendable" the fact that Mulgrew does not go into detail about the murders themselves, "but it is less wise to skim over the killer's upbringing. Mulgrew calls him a 'pathetic nutcase' and leaves it at that." Mumford concluded by saying that "it's too bad [the book] didn't ask 'why' more often."

In a *Books in Canada* review, David Wilson called *Final Payoff* "a thoroughly researched and highly readable book," and added that Mulgrew "in his trademark rapid-fire style . . . manages to piece together perhaps the most detailed and forthright examination yet of the entire Clifford Olson saga."

Cindy James went missing for two weeks before her body was found in Richmond, British Columbia on June 8, 1989. A black stocking was wrapped around her neck, and another was used to hog-tie her hands and legs behind her back. The eventual finding by the coroner's jury was that the cause of her death could not be determined. James had been threatened and assaulted many times over the previous seven years, and she had been institutionalized twice. It could not be ascertained whether she was a victim of an undiscovered assailant or of herself. *Quill & Quire*'s Peter Robinson noted that in *Who Killed Cindy James*, "though Mulgrew is critical of both the police and the psychiatric establishment for failing her, he argues that she manipulated the authorities into believing her tales of terror in order to get attention." Mulgrew also felt many of the men involved became "infatuated" with James, but that the female officers never trusted her.

Ultimately, the source of James's suffering could never be discovered.

Mulgrew collaborated with British Columbian adventurer Colin Angus in writing the account of Angus's travels with Ben Kozel of Australia and Scott Borthwick of South Africa. *Amazon Extreme: Three Men, a Raft, and the World's Most Dangerous River* is the story of the first group ever to raft the entire length of the Amazon, which they accomplished in five months in 1999 in a rubber raft. The young men ducked gunfire and suffered dehydration and dangerous rapids, but they also were privy to some of the most beautiful landscape and abundant wildlife in the world. "Included is interesting historical background on the Amazon and the mystery and mythology surrounding this awesome river," wrote a writer for the *Boating Channel* online. "There have been many explorers who leave in search of finding the true source of this river and return with only a possible theory. The question has yet to be answered."

Library Journal's Joseph L. Carlson wrote of *Amazon Extreme*: "Sure, the information about the Amazon is fascinating, but what lingers is the sensation that we have completed the voyage with the authors." "These pages don't feature a lot of introspection," commented a *Kirkus Reviews* critic, "but they're also refreshingly free of portentousness, favoring slam-bang episodes of suicidal behavior laced with doses of humor."

Angus and Kozel teamed up with Canadian Remy Quinter and Australian Tim Cope for a similar trek across Outer Mongolia and Siberia in 2001. Mulgrew and Angus documented this adventure in *Lost in Mongolia: Rafting the World's Last Unchallenged River.*

BIOGRAPHICAL AND CRITICAL SOURCES:

PERIODICALS

Books in Canada, November, 1988, Bruce Serafin, review of *Unholy Terror: The Sikhs and International Terrorism,* p. 36; November, 1990, David Wilson, review of *Final Payoff: The True Price of Convicting Clifford Robert Olson,* pp. 43-44.
Kirkus Reviews, January 1, 2002, review of *Amazon Extreme: Three Men, a Raft, and the World's Most Dangerous River,* p. 26.

Library Journal, March 15, 2002, Joseph L. Carlson, review of *Amazon Extreme,* p. 100.
Maclean's, July 11, 1988, Jane O'Hara, review of *Unholy Terror,* p. 48.
Quill & Quire, September, 1988, Philip Plews, review of *Unholy Terror,* p. 74; October, 1990, Ted Mumford, review of *Final Payoff,* p. 20; March, 1991, Peter Robinson, review of *Who Killed Cindy James?,* p. 63.

ONLINE

Boating Channel, http://www.boatingchannel.com/ (June 6, 2002), review of *Amazon Extreme.**

*   *   *

MUMAW, Barton 1912-

PERSONAL: Born 1912, in Eustis, FL. *Education:* Attended Rollins College; studied at Denishawn New York School of Dance, 1930.

ADDRESSES: Agent—c/o Author Mail, Wesleyan University Press/University Press of New England, 23 South Main St., Hanover, NH 03755.

CAREER: Denishawn (dance company), began as chauffeur and dresser, became ensemble dancer, 1931-32; Ted Shawn's Men Dancers, Becket, MA, lead dancer, 1933-40; dancer on stage in New York, NY, 1948-58, including appearances in *Annie Get Your Gun* and Broadway productions of *The Golden Apple* and *My Fair Lady;* Jacob's Pillow, Becket, MA, dancer, choreographer, and teacher. Also taught at Springfield College, Springfield, MA. *Military service:* U.S. Armed Forces, entertainment specialist, 1942-46; served in Europe; became sergeant.

WRITINGS:

(With Jane Sherman) *Barton Mumaw, Dancer: From Denishawn to Jacob's Pillow and Beyond,* Dance Horizons (New York, NY), 1986, with new foreword by David Gere, Wesleyan University Press (Hanover, NH), 2000.

BIOGRAPHICAL AND CRITICAL SOURCES:

BOOKS

International Dictionary of Modern Dance, St. James Press (Detroit, MI), 1998.

PERIODICALS

Dance, November, 2000, Merrill Leigh, review of *Barton Mumaw, Dancer: From Denishawn to Jacob's Pillow and Beyond,* p. 85.*

*   *   *

MUSTOE, Anne 1933-

PERSONAL: Born May 24, 1933; daughter of H. W. Revill; married Nelson Edwin Mustoe (died, 1976). *Education:* Girton College, Cambridge, B.A., 1955, M.A., 1958, diploma, IPM, 1959. *Hobbies and other interests:* Cycling, music.

ADDRESSES: Home—12 Melcombe Court, Dorset Square, London NW1 6EP, England.

CAREER: Educator, travel writer, and lecturer. Keen & Nettlefolds Ltd., guest, 1956-60; Francis Holland School, head of classics, 1965-69; independent travel agent, 1969-73; Cobham Hall, Kent, England, deputy headmistress, 1975-78; St. Felix School, Suffolk, England, 1978-87. Girls' Common Entrance Examinations, member of board of managers, 1983-86; Girls' Schools Association, president, 1984-85; International School in Switzerland, chairman, 1986-87. Governor of Hethersett Old Hall School, 1981-86, Cobham Hall, 1986—, James Allen's Girls' School, 1991-99, and Thornton College, 1992-97, served as magistrate and member of Final Selection Board for the UK Foreign Office and Home Civil Service.

WRITINGS:

Escaping the Winter, Robert Hale (London, England), 1993.
A Bike Ride: 12,000 Miles around the World, Virgin (London, England), 1991.

Lone Traveller: One Woman, Two Wheels, and the World, Swan Hill (Shrewsbury, England), 1998.
Two Wheels in the Dust: From Kathmandu to Kandy, Virgin (London, England), 2001.
Cleopatra's Needle: From the Thames to the Nile by Bicycle, Virgin (London, England), 2003.

SIDELIGHTS: In 1987 Anne Mustoe left her position as headmistress of St. Felix School in England to travel extensively, and then went on to write and speak about her adventures. She had developed tours during the years she worked in the travel business, but the mode of transportation Mustoe chose was the bicycle. Mustoe rode around the world twice, and her lecture topics cover everything from the Turkish empires, to traveling the Silk Road, to the pioneer trails and Pony Express of the United States.

A Bike Ride: 12,000 Miles around the World documents Mustoe's fifteen-month journey, at the age of fifty-four, through Europe, India, Thailand, Malaysia, the Far East, and the Americas. *Lone Traveller: One Woman, Two Wheels, and the World* follows her east-to-west trip around the globe. Mustoe admitted to Les Woodland of *Bycycle* that she doesn't train and also doesn't know how to fix a flat. She said that she only experienced three punctures in her round-the-world travels, and added that "every time there was somebody there happy to do it for me."

In *Lone Traveller,* Mustoe writes about cycling solo, dealing with authorities, traveling over rugged terrain, and how to follow maps that are missing whole mountain ranges. She relates how Brazilians were perplexed by an older woman riding alone, how she was arrested in China, and how the athletic citizens of Australia celebrated her achievements.

Mustoe was in her early sixties when in 1992 she began a trip that would take her from Nepal to Sri Lanka, following the Sanskrit path of the Ramayana through the Indian subcontinent. In *Two Wheels in the Dust: From Kathmandu to Kandy* she combines travel with history and religion, retelling the tale of Rama and his encounters with the vulture king and the monkey god. Her starting point, Nepal, was the home of Rama's wife, Sita. Mustoe's own adventures revolve around India's geography and people and follows the unfolding of the Hindu saga. A *Publishers Weekly* contributor felt that Mustoe's stories, taken together, provide "a vivid travelogue . . . from the perspective of a sympathetic outsider who observes how the nation's deeply rooted faith and social practices make it a unique paradox of ancient and modern."

"Like the bike, the book goes at an amiable pace," wrote Trevor Fishlock in the London *Daily Telegraph.* Mustoe writes that when her patience was tested, the teacher in her surfaced. In one instance, three policemen burst into her room in Nepal and she said to them authoritatively, "I am a headmistress," upon which they quickly retreated. Mustoe admits to seeking out a beer or enjoying a joint with backpackers during her more relaxed moments.

Chapters of the book begin with literary quotations from authors, including Shakespeare, Robert Burns, and Rudyard Kipling, and there is a picture of Mustoe's bike, named Condor. A London *Independent Sunday* reviewer feared that because of Mustoe's background as a headmistress, the book would read like the work of a Victorian eccentric. But the reviewer, who called *Two Wheels in the Dust* "a compelling read," found that Mustoe's style "is unassuming, and the story is made up of basic day-to-day observations, 'the stuff of our lives.'"

In 2003 Mustoe published *Cleopatra's Needle: From the Thames to the Nile by Bicycle.*

BIOGRAPHICAL AND CRITICAL SOURCES:

PERIODICALS

Daily Telegraph (London, England), November 17, 2001, Trevor Fishlock, review of *Two Wheels in the Dust: From Kathmandu to Kandy.*
Independent Sunday (London, England), June 21, 1998, review of *Lone Traveller: One Woman, Two Wheels, and the World,* p. 10.
M2 Best Books, March 28, 2002, "Trilogy of Travel Books on Bicycle Trips around the World."
Publishers Weekly, November 12, 2001, review of *Two Wheels in the Dust,* p. 54.

OTHER

Bycycle, http://www.bikereader.com/ (June-July, 2000), Les Woodland, "Just Do It."

N

NIALL, Sean
   See MANGAN, (John Joseph) Sherry

*   *   *

NOLLEN, Scott Allen 1963-

PERSONAL: Born April 2, 1963, in Harlan, IA; married; wife's name, Michelle. *Education:* University of Iowa, B.A., 1988, M.A., 1989. *Hobbies and other interests:* Cinema, literature, British history and culture, Celtic and jazz music.

ADDRESSES: Home—Iowa City, IA. *Agent*—c/o Author Mail, McFarland & Co., Box 611, Jefferson, NC 28640. *E-mail*—snollen@hoover.nara.gov.

CAREER: Author, musician, and editor. Formerly producer and audiovisual archivist at presidential library of the National Archives and Records Administration; producer of musical soundtracks for film.

WRITINGS:

The Boys: The Cinematic World of Laurel and Hardy, foreword by John McCabe, McFarland & Co. (Jefferson, NC), 1989.

Boris Karloff: A Critical Account of His Screen, Stage, Radio, Television, and Recording Work, foreword by Ray Bradbury, McFarland & Co. (Jefferson, NC), 1991.

Robert Louis Stevenson: Life, Literature, and the Silver Screen, McFarland & Co. (Jefferson, NC), 1994.

Sir Arthur Conan Doyle at the Cinema, foreword by Nicholas Meyer, McFarland & Co. (Jefferson, NC), 1996.

Robin Hood: A Cinematic History of the English Outlaw and His Scottish Counterparts, McFarland & Co. (Jefferson, NC), 1999.

Boris Karloff: A Gentlemen's Life: The Authorized Biography, foreword by Sarah Jane Karloff, Midnight Marquee Press (Baltimore, MD), 1999.

Jethro Tull: A History of the Band, 1968-2001, foreword by Ian Anderson, afterword by David Pegg, McFarland & Co. (Jefferson, NC), 2002.

SIDELIGHTS: Scott Allen Nollen worked for ten years at a presidential library, where he wrote, produced, and directed several video programs showcasing exhibits. His topics included the U.S. Civil War, the American frontier, U.S.-China relations, the 1950s, American women, and life in the White House.

On his Internet home page, Nollen says his interests are "nonfiction and cultural history, particularly Golden-Age Hollywood and British film, Victorian literature, Scottish history, and traditional and jazz music." Nollen also names his heroes, among them a number of people about whom he has written entire volumes.

In *The Boys: The Cinematic World of Laurel and Hardy,* Nollen studies the comedy duo who entertained audiences from the time of silent movies to the early 1950s. He points out that the pair had a close and complex relationship and that Stan, who appeared on screen as the more empty-headed of the two, was actually the one who wrote most of their skits. Nollen looks at their routines, camera techniques, and how their on-screen characters related to each other, as well as their individual work. *Choice* contributor T. Lindvall called *The Boys* "a solid albeit casual, prosaic, and conventional work." A reviewer for *Films in Review* said the filmography, "rated in a discerning, cult-be-damned attitude," was particularly enjoyable.

Boris Karloff: A Critical Account of His Screen, Stage, Radio, Television, and Recording Work contains facts about Karloff's career, his films, and his nonfilm work. *Library Journal*'s Anne Sharpe wrote that "much of the 'critical' portion of this book involves Nollen's opinions about Hollywood filmmaking and the horror genre." *Choice* reviewer B. Grant noted that Nollen does not provide the dates of Karloff's recordings, but called the volume "useful for the production histories it does provide, and the bibliography and numerous appendixes are well done."

Robert Louis Stevenson: Life, Literature, and the Silver Screen commemorates the centennial anniversary of Stevenson's death and is a review of his life and work. Nollen studies film adaptations of the nineteenth-century British author's novels and short stories, including *The Body Snatcher, Treasure Island, The Strange Case of Dr. Jekyll and Mr. Hyde, The Black Arrow, Kidnapped, The Master of Ballantrae,* and *The Wrong Box.* Fourteen appendixes list all Stevenson-related materials, including films, television and radio adaptations, programs about the author, and sound recordings. *Choice* contributor J. Belton called the volume "a useful reference."

Sir Arthur Conan Doyle at the Cinema reviews film adaptations of the Doyle's work, including his Sherlock Holmes successes and others like *The Lost World.* Nollen's history spans 100 years and is a study of films back to the silents.

In *Robin Hood: A Cinematic History of the English Outlaw and His Scottish Counterparts,* Nollen provides a long introduction to the character of Robin Hood, plus those of Rob Roy and other English and Scottish bandits. He then studies the film version of the legendary robber from 1908. Anthony J. Adam noted in *American Reference Books Annual* that Nollen does not include television versions, of which there were at least five, nor does he discuss foreign films. "However," stated Adam, "Nollen does examine Sinatra's *Robin and the Seven Hoods* (1964), for an interesting take on the story."

Nollen, a Jethro Tull fan and friend, spent the ten years leading up to his completion of *Jethro Tull: A History of the Band, 1968-2001* collecting interviews with former members and the British band's leader, flutist Ian Anderson, and documenting the band's career. Anderson wrote the foreword and members Glenn Cornick, Jeffery Hammond, Dave Pegg, Barrie Barlow, and others provide anecdotes going back to Tull's first public performance, when they shared the stage at the Sunbury Jazz and Blues Festival with Eric Clapton and Ginger Baker.

The book is divided into thirty-one chapters, one for each of Tull's albums. Nollen notes who the members were for each, how each album ranked on the charts, and he scores and provides a critical analyses for all. *Library Journal*'s Lloyd Jansen wrote that Nollen "parlays his friendship with the band into an engaging biography." *Booklist* contributor Mike Tribby called the book "a welcome addition to comprehensive music collections." "If there was ever a question of their status, *Jethro Tull* has provided the proof that this was, and is, a band with versatility and staying power," wrote Kate Brown for *Green Man Review* online. Brown called the volume "a must for any serious collector or Tull fan."

BIOGRAPHICAL AND CRITICAL SOURCES:

PERIODICALS

American Reference Books Annual, 2000, Anthony J. Adam, review of *Robin Hood: History of the English Outlaw and His Scottish Counterparts,* p. 562.

Booklist, February 1, 2002, Mike Tribby, review of *Jethro Tull: A History of the Band, 1968-2001,* p. 915.

Choice, February, 1990, T. Lindvall, review of *The Boys: The Cinematic World of Laurel and Hardy,* p. 958; October, 1991, B. Grant, review of *Boris Karloff: A Critical Account of His Screen, Stage, Radio, Televison, and Recording Work,* p. 292;

March, 1995, J. Belton, review of *Robert Louis Stevenson: Life, Literature, and the Silver Screen,* pp. 1086-1087.

Films in Review, March, 1990, review of *The Boys,* p. 185.

Library Journal, May 1, 1991, Anne Sharpe, review of *Boris Karloff,* p. 78; June 1, 2001, Michael Rogers, review of *The Boys,* p. 226; March 15, 2002, Lloyd Jansen, review of *Jethro Tull,* p. 84.

Reference & Research Book News, May, 1997, review of *Sir Arthur Conan Doyle at the Cinema,* p. 131.

Variety, February 7, 1990, review of *The Boys,* p. 186.

ONLINE

Green Man Review, http://www.greenmanreview.com/ (June 6, 2002), Kate Brown, review of *Jethro Tull.*

Scott Allen Nollen Home Page, http://www.authorpoint. com/Scott_Allen_Nollen (June 6, 2002).*

*   *   *

NORDHAUS, Jean 1939-

PERSONAL: Born November 14, 1939, in Baltimore, MD; daughter of Herbert Lee (in business) and Minna (a homemaker; maiden name, Cantor) Friedberg; married Robert Riggs Nordhaus (an energy and environmental lawyer), June 27, 1964; children: Ronald Edward, Hannah Elizabeth. *Ethnicity:* "Jewish." *Education:* Barnard College, B.A., 1960; Yale University, Ph.D., 1969.

ADDRESSES: Home—623 East Capitol St. S.W., Washington, DC 20003. *E-mail*—jnordhaus@att.net.

CAREER: University of Maryland—College Park, assistant professor of German, 1964-65; University of the District of Columbia, assistant professor of English, 1971-73; Folger Shakespeare Library, programs coordinator for poetry, 1980-83, 1991-92, coordinator of PEN/Faulkner Award for Fiction, 1982-83; freelance writer and poet. Writer's Center, Bethesda, MD, presenter of poetry workshops, 1986—; also seminar and workshop presenter at George Mason University, 1984, St. Mary's College of Maryland, 1987, Bread Loaf Writer's Conference, summers, 1992-94, American University, 1995, and Taos Institute

of the Arts, 1998; gives readings from her works; guest on media programs. Poetry Committee of Greater Washington, executive director, 1980-83, 1991; Washington Writers' Publishing House, president, 1989-94.

MEMBER: Poetry Society of America, Academy of American Poetry.

AWARDS, HONORS: Bread Loaf Writers' Conference, William Raney Scholar, 1984, Meralmikjen fellow, 1987; first prize, *Yankee* Poetry Awards, 1987; Colladay Prize, 1991, for *My Life in Hiding;* Consuelo Ford Award (corecipient), Poetry Society of America, 1995; Edward Stanley Award, *Prairie Schooner,* 1996; Kinloch Rivers Chapbook Contest winner, 1998, for *A Purchase of Porcelain.*

WRITINGS:

A Language of Hands (poetry chapbook), SCOP (College Park, MD), 1982.

A Bracelet of Lies (poetry), Washington Writers' Publishing House (Washington, DC), 1987.

My Life in Hiding (poetry), Quarterly Review of Literature (Princeton, NJ), 1991.

A Purchase of Porcelain (poetry chapbook), Poetry Society of South Carolina, 1998.

The Porcelain Apes of Moses Mendelssohn (poetry), Milkweed Editions (Minneapolis, MN), 2002.

Work represented in anthologies, including *American Classic: Car Poems; Anthology of Magazine Verse and Yearbook of American Poetry,* 1981; *Natives, Tourists, and Other Mysteries,* Watershed Tapes, 1985; *Her Face in the Mirror: Jewish Women on Mothers and Daughters,* Beacon Hill Press, 1994; and *Best American Poetry 2000.* Contributor of poetry, articles, essays, and reviews to periodicals, including *American Poetry Review, Centennial Review, Greenfield Review, Poet Lore, Plowshares, Prairie Schooner, Washingtonian, Kansas Quarterly, Southern Poetry Review,* and *Yankee.*

Some of Nordhaus's poems have been translated into Hebrew.

WORK IN PROGRESS: Dinner on the Fault Line, a poetry collection.

BIOGRAPHICAL AND CRITICAL SOURCES:

PERIODICALS

Booklist, March 1, 2002, Ray Olson, review of *The Porcelain Apes of Moses Mendelssohn* p. 1079.

*　　*　　*

NORDHOFF, Charles Bernard 1887-1947

PERSONAL: Born February 1, 1887 in London, England; died of a heart attack April 11, 1947, in CA; father a correspondent for the *New York Times;* married Vahime Tua Tearae Smidt, 1920 (divorced); married Laura Whiley, 1941; children: (first marriage) seven; (with Tahitian mistress) three. *Education:* Harvard University, B.A., 1909.

CAREER: Novelist, short story writer, essayist, and historian. Worked on a Sugar plantation in Mexico, 1909-11; Tile and Fine Brick Company, California, secretary and treasurer, 1911-16. *Military service:* Enlisted in the French Ambulance Corps in 1916; later joined the French Foreign Legion and the Lafayette Flying Corps; transferred to the United States Air Service after the United States entered World War I, where he served as a lieutenant.

WRITINGS:

The Fledgling, Houghton Mifflin (Boston, MA), 1919.
The Pearl Lagoon, Atlantic Monthly Press (Boston, MA), 1924.
Pícaro, Harper (New York, NY), 1924.
The Derelict: Further Adventures of Charles Selden and His Native Friends in the South Seas, Little, Brown (Boston, MA), 1928.

WITH JAMES NORMAN HALL

(Editor) *The Lafayette Flying Corps,* 2 vols., Houghton, Mifflin (Boston, MA), 1920.
Faery Lands of the South Seas, Harper (New York, NY), 1921.

Falcons of France A Tale of Youth and the Air, Little, Brown (Boston, MA), 1929.
The Island Wreck, Methuen (London, England), 1929.
Mutiny on the Bounty, Little, Brown (Boston, MA), 1932, published as *Mutiny!* Chapman & Hall (London, England), 1933.
Men against the Sea, Little, Brown (Boston, MA), 1934.
Pitcairn's Island, Little, Brown (Boston, MA), 1934.
The Hurricane, Little, Brown (Boston, MA), 1936.
The Dark River, Little, Brown (Boston, MA), 1938.
No More Gas, Little, Brown (Boston, MA), 1940.
Botany Bay, Little, Brown (Boston, MA), 1941.
Men without Country, Little, Brown (Boston, MA), 1942.
The High Barbaree, Little, Brown (Boston, MA), 1945.

Contributor to periodicals, including *Atlantic Monthly* and *Harper's.*

ADAPTATIONS: Mutiny on the Bounty was adapted for film in 1935, in 1962, and, as *The Bounty,* in 1984; *Men without Country* was filmed as *Passage to Marseilles; The Hurricane* was filmed in 1937 and 1979; *No More Gas* as *The Turtles of Tahiti* in 1942; *High Barbaree* in 1947; and *Botany Bay* in 1952.

SIDELIGHTS: A biographical essay on Charles Bernard Nordhoff cannot be written without immediately mentioning James Norman Hall, Nordhoff's writing partner of nearly thirty years. Though Nordhoff did in fact author several books, articles, and essays on his own, he is most well known and acclaimed for his collaboration with Hall on their legendary trilogy: *Mutiny on the Bounty*, *Men against the Sea*, and *Pitcairn's Island.* In *Romance and Historical Writers* Joan McGrath called the duo's efforts "a landmark work of fiction in which a sordid mutiny against authority in the person of a petty tyrant won for both captain and mutineers alike a place in the annals of courage, endurance, and adventure." The American reading public wholeheartedly embraced the abounding themes of courage, greed, and man against nature. Hollywood immortalized *Mutiny on the Bounty* in a film version in 1935, again in 1962, and yet again as *The Bounty* in 1984, making the incredible account of a nearly forgotten true story accessible to millions more people than had already read the books. McGrath called the trilogy "the result of a coming together of well-matched talents perfectly suited to the subject matter; their bold, distinctly masculine style of prose was exactly right for the story they had to tell."

Nordhoff's was born in London in 1887 to American parents. He spent his childhood on ranchlands owned by his parents in both California and Mexico. Apparently intellectually gifted, he was accepted by Harvard University and graduated with a B.A. in 1909. After working on a sugar plantation in Mexico for two years and then for five years in California as secretary and treasurer for a company that manufactured tile and bricks, Nordhoff decided to join the French Ambulance Corps in 1916. He later joined the French Foreign Legion and the Lafayette Flying Corps, but after the United States entered World War I he transferred to the U.S. Air Service, in which he served in the capacity of lieutenant. It was his mother who launched his writing career, as she is responsible for sending Nordhoff's descriptive accounts of his ambulance driving and piloting experiences to the *Atlantic Monthly*. These letters home appealed to the public as true-life war tales, and coincidentally appeared with wartime essays written by Hall. The letters were gathered in whole and were published as *The Fledgling*.

By 1918 both Nordhoff and Hall were decorated pilots and published writers. The two men were introduced that year and asked to collaborate on an official history of the Lafayette Flying Corps, of which they had both been members. This collaboration was published in 1920, and by its end the men decided they were through with civilization. They solicited *Harper's* magazine for a cash advance in exchange for a proposed series of articles on the South Seas, and they sailed to Papeete, Tahiti. The articles became the essay collection *Faery Lands of the South Seas,* which was published in 1921. According to the essayist in *Twentieth-Century Literary Criticism,* "the men later recalled that their initial meeting was uncongenial, promising nothing of the close friendship that was to follow."

Obviously, the writing team eventually discovered that they in fact had quite a lot in common, and were thrilled at the ease of their mutual efforts and the complementary strengths of their writing habits. McGrath describes Nordhoff as "ambitious, sceptical, handsome" and Hall as "more of the plain, homespun dependable sort," and the two consequently "created what neither could accomplish on their own." In the 1920s Nordhoff was approached by his publisher to write a sequel to an adventure novel he had written for children, and he invited Hall to share the assignment. The result, *Falcons of France: A Tale of Youth and the Air,* was a commercial success, and compelled the authors to consider their next project. Both had been consistently intrigued by one of the island's favorite stories about a mutiny that happened aboard a British ship in 1789. Strangely, only two attempts had been made to recount the amazing tale—a factual account by Sir John Barrow published in 1831 and a fictionalized children's book that was published in 1845. They amassed as much research as possible, pouring through mutineers' diaries, accounts recorded by the ship's infamous Captain Bligh, interviews with the only surviving mutineer and transcripts of the eventual trial. The ambitious men spent the next three years sorting through their research, ordering the stories, recreating events to the best of their abilities, and editing each others' work. The result is described in *Twentieth-Century* as "one of the most finely integrated collaborative efforts in literature."

In *Mutiny on the Bounty,* the authors tell the tale through Captain Roger Byam, who was a lowly midshipmen under Captain Bligh. The *New York Times* hailed the result, proclaiming: "The book is a superb achievement in its genre. It is truly romantic—not sentimental. The writing is remarkable in its fidelity to eighteenth-century flavor and refreshing in its charm and beauty. . . . The story marches from chapter to chapter with never a let-down. Here is what the historical novel should be—a bit of history brought to life in a book." E. F. Edgett of the *Boston Transcript* wrote that Nordhoff and Hall "have made it not merely a tale of the sea; they have made it a tale of life itself, of the varying aspects of good and bad in humanity." The authors were applauded for their creative restraint and literary discipline in the face of such an incredulous historical event.

Similar compliments were bestowed upon Nordhoff and Hall for their fine work on the second book in the trilogy, *Men against the Sea*. It is the story of Captain Bligh and the eighteen men who sailed with him in an open boat, traveling 3,600 miles from the Friendly Islands in the South Pacific to the Dutch colony of Timor in the East Indies. The *Boston Transcript* reviewer stated: "Of the manner in which the tale is told too much cannot be said in praise. . . . On every page it bears evidence of its truth; in every word it has the actual semblance of events that have happened." The review in the *Nation* celebrated the work for paying homage to pioneering seaman, citing that the book "reveals . . . the hardships seamen were forced to undergo not many generations back. It reveals, too, what heights of courage and fortitude men can reach when the demand is put upon them. . . . As for the sea, its say has been said in this new masterpiece." Amazingly, *Men against the Sea* was written in only two months, during which time the authors stopped work on what would be their next novel, *Pitcairn's Island.*

The final installment of the trilogy, *Pitcairn's Island,* received favorable reviews despite the fact that the authors had to utilize conflicting accounts and incomplete information. Archie Binns wrote in the *Saturday Review of Literature:* "Where they had to guess and reconstruct they guessed and reconstructed well. . . . Out of the available sources—sometimes sketchy and sometimes luxuriant with divergent accounts—they have built a plausible, three-dimensional human story of great depth and terror and beauty."

Nordhoff and Hall ultimately collaborated on six more novels, most of which faired well, arguably in large part because of their solid reputation. Nordhoff's productivity tapered off as a result of marital problems and his abusive relationship with alcohol. He eventually abandoned his island paradise—as well as four children from his first marriage and three children from a relationship with his Tahitian mistress—and moved back to California with two of his daughters, and he remarried. Nordhoff was ill for most of the decade before he died of a heart attack in 1947. Although the end of his life was plagued by pain and frustration, Nordhoff will always be remembered for his contribution to some of the most famous and celebrated sea adventure stories of all time.

BIOGRAPHICAL AND CRITICAL SOURCES:

BOOKS

Benet's Reader's Encyclopedia of American Literature, Edition 1, 1991, p. 744, 780.
Dictionary of Literary Biography, Volume 9: *American Novelists, 1910-1945,* Gale (Detroit, MI), 1981.
Twentieth-Century Literary Criticism, Volume 23, Gale (Detroit, MI), 1987.
Twentieth-Century Romance and Historical Writers, third edition, St. James Press (Detroit, MI), 1994.

PERIODICALS

Boston Transcript, October 1, 1932; January 12, 1934.
Nation, February 14, 1934.
New York Times, October 16, 1932.
Saturday Review of Literature, November 3, 1934.*

O

OLDFIELD, Jenny 1949-
(Lucy Daniels, Kate Fielding, Fiona Kelly)

PERSONAL: Born August 8, 1949, in Harrogate, England; children: Kate Sioban, Eve Helen. *Education:* University of Birmingham, B.A. (with honors), 1970, M.A., 1972, Ph.D., 1976.

ADDRESSES: Home—Ash Tree House, 124 Skipton Rd., Ilkley LS29 9BQ, England. *Agent*—Caroline Sheldon, Thorley Manor Farm, Thorley, Yarmouth PO41 0SJ, England.

CAREER: Teacher and children's book writer. Edgbaston High School, Birmingham, England, English teacher, 1972-74; Wroxton College, Fairleigh Dickinson University, Banbury, England, lecturer in English, 1976; King Edward's High School for Girls, Edgbaston, England, English teacher, 1977; taught English in schools and colleges throughout England to 1993; writer, 1977—.

AWARDS, HONORS: World Book Day selection, 2003, for *Tough It out, Tom.*

WRITINGS:

Tomorrow Shall Be My Dancing Day, Heinemann (London, England), 1975.
Mr. Hardisty's Kind Offer, Heinemann (London, England), 1975.
Secret of the Seasons, Heinemann (London, England), 1976.
Jane Eyre and Wuthering Heights: A Study Guide, Heinemann (London, England), 1976.
Fancy That! illustrated by Jake Tebbit, E. J. Arnold (Leeds, England), 1979.
Going Soft, illustrated by Jake Tebbit, E. J. Arnold (Leeds, England), 1979.
Yours Truly—, illustrated by Jake Tebbit, E. J. Arnold (Leeds, England), 1979.
The Terrible Pet, illustrated by Jake Tebbit, E. J. Arnold (Leeds, England), 1979.
Fitzwilliam Frog: His Problem at the Pool, E. J. Arnold (Leeds, England), 1986,
Said the Blind Man (adult novel), Macmillan (London, England), 1986.
Vincent Viper, illustrated by Alan Chatfield, Arnold-Wheaton (Leeds, England), 1987.
Ricardo Rat, illustrated by Alan Chatfield, Arnold-Wheaton (Leeds, England), 1987.
Leonardo Lizard, illustrated by Alan Chatfield, Arnold-Wheaton (Leeds, England), 1988.
Smile Please, illustrated by Clare Herroneau, E. J. Arnold (Leeds, England), 1989.
Bad Company, Macdonald (London, England), 1989.
January's Child, Macdonald (London, England), 1989.
Misfits and Rebels: Short Stories, Virago (London, England), 1990, Virago (New York, NY), 1991.
Rings on Her Fingers, Learning Disabilities Association (Wisbech, England), 1992.
Camping Paradiso, illustrated by Francis Scappatacci, Longman (Harrow, England), 1994.
The Hidden Tomb, Hippo (London, England), 1995.
Pardise Court, Macmillan (London, England), 1995.
After Hours, Macmillan (London, England), 1995.
Deadline, Severn House (New York, NY), 1996.

All Fall Down, Macmillan (London, England), 1997.

Extra Time, illustrated by Maggie Downer, Barrington Stoke (Edinburgh, Scotland), 1999.

Off-Side, illustrated by Maggie Downer, Barrington Stoke (Edinburgh, Scotland), 2001.

Silver Cloud ("Dreamseeker" trilogy), Hodder (London, England), 2002.

Iron Eyes ("Dreamseeker" trilogy), Hodder (London, England), 2002.

Bad Heart ("Dreamseeker" trilogy), Hodder (London, England), 2003.

Also author of *The True Loves of Tannockburn,* 1980, and *Rough Remedies,* 1981. Has also published under the pseudonyms Fiona Kelly, Lucy Daniels, and Kate Fielding.

"ANIMAL ALERT" SERIES

Abandoned, Hodder (London, England), 1997.

Killer on the Loose, Hodder (London, England), 1997.

Quarantine, Hodder (London, England), 1997.

Intensive Care, Hodder (London, England), 1997.

Skin and Bone, Hodder (London, England), 1998.

Living Proof, Hodder (London, England), 1998.

Blind Alley, Hodder (London, England), 1998.

Grievous Bodily Harm, Hodder (London, England), 1998.

Running Wild, Hodder (London, England), 1998.

Lost and Found, Hodder (London, England), 1999.

Heatwave, Hodder (London, England), 1999.

"ONE FOR SORROW" SERIES

One for Sorrow, Hodder (London, England), 1999.

Two for Joy, Hodder (London, England), 1999.

Three for a Girl, Hodder (London, England), 1999.

Four for a Boy, Hodder (London, England), 1999.

Five for Silver, Hodder (London, England), 2000.

Six for Gold, Hodder (London, England), 2000.

Seven for a Secret, Hodder (London, England), 2000.

Eight for a Wish, Hodder (London, England), 2000.

Nine for a Kiss, Hodder (London, England), 2000.

"HOME FARM TWINS" SERIES

Speckle: The Stray (also see below), illustrated by Kate Aldous, Hodder (London, England), 1996.

Solo: The Homeless, illustrated by Kate Aldous, Hodder (London, England), 1996.

Susie: The Orphan, illustrated by Kate Aldous, Hodder (London, England), 1996.

Snip and Snap: The Truants, illustrated by Kate Aldous, Hodder (London, England), 1996.

Spike: The Tramp, illustrated by Kate Aldous, Hodder (London, England), 1996.

Sinbad: The Runaway (also see below), illustrated by Kate Aldous, Hodder (London, England), 1996.

Home Farm Twins (contains *Speckle: The Stray* and *Sinbad: The Runaway*), Hodder (London, England), 1997.

Sunny: The Hero, illustrated by Kate Aldous, Hodder (London, England), 1997.

Stevie: The Rebel, illustrated by Kate Aldous, Hodder (London, England), 1997.

Sampson: The Giant, illustrated by Kate Aldous, Hodder (London, England), 1997.

Scruffy: The Scamp, illustrated by Kate Aldous, Hodder (London, England), 1997.

Socks: The Survivor, illustrated by Kate Aldous, Hodder (London, England), 1997.

Skye: The Champion, illustrated by Kate Aldous, Hodder (London, England), 1998.

Stanley: The Troublemaker, illustrated by Kate Aldous, Hodder (London, England), 1998.

Sorrel: The Substitute, illustrated by Kate Aldous, Hodder (London, England), 1998.

Sultan: The Patient, illustrated by Kate Aldous, Hodder (London, England), 1998.

Sugar and Spice: The Pickpockets, illustrated by Kate Aldous, Hodder (London, England), 1998.

Sophie: The Show-Off, illustrated by Kate Aldous, Hodder (London, England), 1998.

Smoky: The Mystery, illustrated by Kate Aldous, Hodder (London, England), 1998.

Silky: The Foundling, illustrated by Kate Aldous, Hodder (London, England), 1999.

Stalky: The Mascot, illustrated by Kate Aldous, Hodder (London, England), 1999.

Shelley: The Shadow, illustrated by Kate Aldous, Hodder (London, England), 1999.

Spot: The Prisoner, illustrated by Kate Aldous, Hodder (London, England), 1999.

Scott: The Braveheart, illustrated by Kate Aldous, Hodder (London, England), 1999.

Samantha: The Snob, illustrated by Kate Aldous, Hodder (London, England), 1999.

Star: The Surprise, illustrated by Kate Aldous, Hodder (London, England), 1999.

Maisie Wants Her Mum, illustrated by Kate Aldous, Hodder (London, England), 2000.

Home Farm Friends: Short Story Collection, illustrated by Kate Aldous, Hodder (London, England), 2000.

Short Story Collections Snapshots, Hodder (London, England), 2000.

Mitch Goes Missing, illustrated by Kate Aldous, Hodder (London, England), 2000.

Smarty: The Outcast, illustrated by Kate Aldous, Hodder (London, England), 2000.

Mac Climbs a Mountain, illustrated by Kate Aldous, Hodder (London, England), 2000.

Titch Plays Tricks, illustrated by Kate Aldous, Hodder (London, England), 2001.

Tess Gets Trapped, illustrated by Kate Aldous, Hodder (London, England), 2001.

Toby Takes the Plunge, illustrated by Kate Aldous, Hodder (London, England), 2001.

"HORSES OF HALF MOON RANCH" SERIES

Wild Horses, illustrated by Paul Hunt, Hodder (London, England), 1999.

Midnight Lady, illustrated by Paul Hunt, Hodder (London, England), 1999.

Crazy Horse, illustrated by Paul Hunt, Hodder (London, England), 1999.

Johnny Mohawk, illustrated by Paul Hunt, Hodder (London, England), 1999.

Rodeo Rocky, illustrated by Paul Hunt, Hodder (London, England), 1999.

Third-Time Lucky, illustrated by Paul Hunt, Hodder (London, England), 1999.

Navaho Joe, illustrated by Paul Hunt, Hodder (London, England), 2000.

Jethro Junior, illustrated by Paul Hunt, Hodder (London, England), 2000.

Danny Boy, illustrated by Paul Hunt, Hodder (London, England), 2000.

Hollywood Princess, illustrated by Paul Hunt, Hodder (London, England), 2000.

Little Vixen, illustrated by Paul Hunt, Hodder (London, England), 2000.

Gunsmoke, illustrated by Paul Hunt, Hodder (London, England), 2000.

Golden Dawn, illustrated by Paul Hunt, Hodder (London, England), 2000.

Starlight, illustrated by Paul Hunt, Hodder (London, England), 2000.

Moondance, illustrated by Paul Hunt, Hodder (London, England), 2001.

Skylark, illustrated by Paul Hunt, Hodder (London, England), 2001.

Steamboat Charlie, illustrated by Paul Hunt, Hodder (London, England), 2001.

Lady Roseanne, illustrated by Paul Hunt, Hodder (London, England), 2001.

Silver Spur, illustrated by Paul Hunt, Hodder (London, England), 2001.

Eagle Wing, illustrated by Paul Hunt, Hodder (London, England), 2001.

El Dorado, Hodder (London, England), 2001.

Santa Ana, Hodder (London, England), 2001.

Chiquita, Hodder (London, England), 2001.

Diamond Charm, Hodder (London, England), 2002.

"DEFINITELY DAISY" SERIES

You're a Disgrace, Daisy! illustrated by Lauren Child, Hodder (London, England), 2001.

Just You Wait, Winona! illustrated by Lauren Child, Hodder (London, England), 2001.

You Must Be Joking, Jimmy! illustrated by Lauren Child, Hodder (London, England), 2001.

I'd Like a Little Word, Leonie! illustrated by Lauren Child, Hodder (London, England), 2001.

Not Now, Nathan! illustrated by Lauren Child, Hodder (London, England), 2001.

What's the Matter, Maya? illustrated by Lauren Child, Hodder (London, England), 2001.

Dream on, Daisy! illustrated by Lauren Child, Hodder (London, England), 2001.

"TOTALLY TOM" SERIES

Tell Me the Truth, Tom! illustrated by Neal Layton, Hodder (London, England), 2002.

Watch out, Wayne, illustrated by Neal Layton, Hodder (London, England), 2002.

Get Lost, Lola! illustrated by Neal Layton, Hodder (London, England), 2002.

Keep the Noise down, Kingsley, illustrated by Neal Layton, Hodder (London, England), 2002.

Drop Dead, Danielle, illustrated by Neal Layton, Hodder (London, England), 2002.

Don't Make Me Laugh, Liam, illustrated by Neal Layton, Hodder (London, England), 2002.

Tough It Out, Tom, illustrated by Neal Layton, Hodder (London, England), 2003.

When Ellie Cheated, Hodder (London, England), 2002.
When Scott Got Lost, Hodder (London, England), 2002.
When Geri and I Fell Out, Hodder (London, England), 2002.
When Dad Went on a Date, Hodder (London, England), 2002.
When I Won a Prize, Hodder (London, England), 2002.
When Shah Went Weird, Hodder (London, England), 2002.

SIDELIGHTS: A former English teacher in her native England, Jenny Oldfield is a prolific author who has produced a large selection of accessible fiction books in the "Animal Alert," "Definitely Daisy," and "Horses of Half Moon Ranch" series, to name a few. In the "Definitely Daisy" books, readers meet the rambunctious heroine as she ignores the advice and wishes of the adults in her life to go her own way. Books such as *Blind Alley,* part of the "Animal Alert" series, focus on the veterinarians and animal welfare experts who intervene in cases of animal cruelty and injury, as well as those who train and work with animals. Reluctant or dyslexic readers in the middle grades are the target of several lighthearted novels penned by Oldfield, among them *Extra Time,* about a teen soccer player named Danny who has girl-trouble off the playing field, and its sequel, *Off-Side.* In a review of *Off-Side* for the *Times Educational Supplement,* Linda Newbery praised the book as being attractive to its intended audience due to its "well-spaced text and . . . lively illustrations."

Although most of her titles fall into the mass market category, Oldfield has made a reputation as a skilled young adult novelist. *Tomorrow Shall Be My Dancing Day,* published in 1975, tells the story of a girl caught up in the magic and drama of a group of otherworldly dancers who appear near her home at night. Oldfield's first novel, *Tomorrow Shall Be My Dancing Day,* prompted a *Junior Bookshelf* reviewer to remark that the "delicate but happy" work "shows great promise." The reviewer noted that the book's strong ending "gives hope and expectancy for more work of some distinction" from Oldfield. Praising Oldfield for her *fine sense of style,* another *Junior Bookshelf* contributor enjoyed her next novel, *Mr. Hardisty's Kind Offer,* a Victorian-era melodrama about a street-smart Cockney girl and the adults out to bamboozle her.

Continuing to write for a young audience through the 1980s, Oldfield hit her stride with teen problem novels such as *Bad Company* and *January's Child.* In *January's Child,* fifteen-year-old Justine runs away from her foster home and attempts to care for her younger brother while living on the street. The love of a boyfriend finally provides Justine with the ability to pull her life together in a novel that "has a good plot and deals well with the feelings of the protagonists," according to *School Librarian* contributor Valerie Caless. An abused teen is the focus of *Bad Company,* and as in *January's Child,* Oldfield makes a romance with a caring young man the catalyst through which the young protagonist learns to confront her problems. Calling *Bad Company* a novel with more to recommend "than merely a good storyline," *School Librarian* contributor Elizabeth Finlayson noted that Oldfield provides readers with a text that is both "clear-sighted [and] perceptive." A *Books for Keeps* reviewer also had praise for *Bad Company,* noting that readers are kept intrigued by its realistic characters and "detached but confidential tone."

Oldfield described herself to *CA* as "a frequent visitor to the United States, especially Colorado, the inspiration for many of my books." Her "Horses of Half Moon Ranch" and the "Dreamseeker" trilogy are both inspired by her interest in the American West and its history.

BIOGRAPHICAL AND CRITICAL SOURCES:

PERIODICALS

Booklist, July, 1991, Hazel Rochman, review of *Misfits and Rebels,* p. 2040.
Books for Keeps, January, 1990, Jessica Yates, review of *Bad Company* and *January's Child,* pp. 10, 11; September, 1990, review of *Misfits and Rebels,* p. 15; May, 1999, review of *Extra Time,* p. 25.
British Book News, September, 1986, Jessica Mann, review of *Said the Blind Man,* pp. 514, 516.
Growing Point, April, 1975, review of *Tomorrow Shall Be My Dancing Day,* p. 2597.
Junior Bookshelf, June, 1975, review of *Tomorrow Shall Be My Dancing Day,* p. 202; February, 1976, review of *Mr. Hardisty's Kind Offer,* p. 52; December, 1976, review of *Secrets of the Season,* p. 351; August, 1990, review of *Misfits and Rebels,* p. 199.

Listener, December 7, 1989, Joanna Porter, review of *Bad Company,* p. 28.

School Librarian, August, 1989, Valerie Caless, review of *January's Child,* p. 116; May, 1990, review of *Bad Company,* p. 78; autumn, 1998, Lucinda Fox, review of *Blind Alley,* p. 148; autumn, 1999, Frances Ball, review of *Extra Time,* pp. 134-135; summer, 2000, Sandra Bennett, review of *Four for a Boy,* p. 101; summer, 2001, Prue Goodwin, review of *You're a Disgrace, Daisy!,* p. 76; winter, 2001, Andrea Rayner, review of *Off-Side,* p. 192.

Times Educational Supplement, October 27, 1995, Tom Deveson, review of *The Hidden Tomb,* p. S11; July 6, 2001, Linda Newbery, review of *Off-Side,* p. 23.

Times Literary Supplement, April 4, 1975, Rosamond Faith, review of *Tomorrow Shall Be My Dancing Day,* p. 361; December 5, 1975, Ann Carter, review of *Mr. Hardisty's Kind Offer,* p. 1455; July 16, 1976, Ann Evans, review of *Secrets of the Seasons,* p. 880.

*   *   *

O'LEARY, Patrick G. 1952-

PERSONAL: Born September 13, 1952, in Saginaw, MI; son of Dennis (a railroad site engineer) and Katherine (a teacher and principal; maiden name Glynn) O'Leary; married Claire Varieur (an activist), May 20, 1977; children: Lochlan Dennis, Colin Joseph. *Education:* Wayne State University, B.A. (English), 1974.

ADDRESSES: Home—2701 Douglas Dr., Bloomfield Hills, MI 48304. *Office*—Campbell-Ewald, 30400 Van Dyke, Warren, MI 48093. *Agent*—Susan Ann Protter, 110 West 40th St., New York, NY 10018. *E-mail*—patrickoleary@comcast.net.

CAREER: Writer and poet. Campbell-Ewald, Warren, MI, associate creative director, 1975—.

AWARDS, HONORS: Best Book of 1995 citation, *Publishers Weekly,* for *Door Number Three.*

WRITINGS:

Door Number Three, Tor (New York, NY), 1995.
The Gift, Tor (New York, NY), 1997.

Other Voices, Other Doors (collection), Fairwood Press, 2001.
The Impossible Bird, Tor (New York, NY), 2002.

Contributor to periodicals, including *Talebones, Iowa Review, Poetry East, New York Review of Science Fiction, Crawdaddy,* and *Phoenix,* and to Web sites, including *Scifiction.com.*

SIDELIGHTS: Science-fiction writer Patrick O'Leary's debut novel, *Door Number Three,* was called "brilliant" by *Booklist*'s Carl Hays, who wrote, "Striking and insightful, this is one of the year's finest sf novels, deserving of widespread recognition beyond the genre." Psychotherapist John Donnelly's new female patient claims an alien heritage. Donnelly begins to accept the truth when the patient's former therapist is murdered and his own life turns bizarre, not only in his dreams, but also in reality. A *Publishers Weekly* reviewer compared O'Leary's novel to the writings of Philip I. Dick and the early works of Kurt Vonnegut, and called it "a highly appealing mix of skilled writing and zany imaginings."

In *The Gift,* King Simon and young Tim, the deaf son of a woodcutter, must search out and destroy the evil Usher of the Night and are aided in their quest by a series of magical creatures and the gift of power bestowed on Tim. The story is a tale within a tale, told to a group of shipboard sailors. In a *Booklist,* review, Roland Green credited O'Leary with "creative world building, superior handling of characters." A *Publishers Weekly* contributor commented that the story "moves gracefully back and forth between its nautical frame and the adventures of its youthful protagonists."

As the story opens in *The Impossible Bird,* two estranged brothers, literature professor Daniel Glynn and his director brother Mike, die in different locations but are unaware of this fact. They enter a virtual world, and each is charged with finding the other by persons claiming to be government agents. They become drawn into the intrigue created by two alien groups with opposing purposes in which hummingbirds are used as data-collecting devices. In reviewing the book for *BookPage* online, Gavin Grant said that "it's almost impossible to talk about *The Impossible Bird* without giving away the huge secrets at the heart of the novel. There are conspiracies within conspiracies, so that what starts off as a relatively simple chase novel quickly becomes a multi-level tale where reality may not be all it's cracked up to be." *Locus* reviewer Bill Sheehan noted that in addition to being a science fiction tale, *The Impossible Bird* "is a persuasive, deeply felt examination of some fundamental human issues."

In the novel, two brothers begin to recollect his childhood and deal with the issues each has put aside. "O'Leary develops an intriguing story as he slowly fills in gaps in their memories," commented *Booklist*'s Bryan Baldus. A *Publishers Weekly* contributor wrote that "a zany premise, coupled with realistic characters drawn into a confusing reality, results in a tour de force that handles themes of death, loss, and love with panache and a dash of humor."

BIOGRAPHICAL AND CRITICAL SOURCES:

PERIODICALS

Analog Science Fiction and Fact, January, 1996, review of *Door Number Three,* p. 273.

Booklist, October 15, 1995, Carl Hays, review of *Door Number Three,* p. 389; October 1, 1997, Roland Green, review of *The Gift,* p. 312; January 1, 2002, Bryan Baldus, review of *The Impossible Bird,* p. 825.

Kirkus Reviews, August 15, 1995, review of *Door Number Three,* p. 1148; August 1, 1997, review of *The Gift,* p. 1165; November 1, 2001, review of *The Impossible Bird,* p. 1523.

Kliatt, May, 1997, review of *Door Number Three,* p. 15; January, 1999, review of *The Gift,* p. 19.

Library Journal, October 15, 1997, Susan Hamburger, review of *The Gift,* p. 98; January, 2002, Jackie Cassada, review of *The Impossible Bird,* p. 159.

Locus, September, 1999, Patrick O'Leary; February, 2002, Bill Sheehan, review of *The Impossible Bird,* p. 31.

Magazine of Fantasy and Science Fiction, May, 1996, review of *Door Number Three,* p. 47; October, 1997, review of *The Gift,* p. 40.

New York Times Book Review, November 12, 1995, review of *Door Number Three,* p. 65; February 1, 1998, review of *The Gift,* p. 22.

Publishers Weekly, September 25, 1995, review of *Door Number Three,* p. 47; September 8, 1997, review of *The Gift* p. 63; November 26, 2002, review of *The Impossible Bird,* p. 44.

Science Fiction Chronicle, April, 1997, review of *Door Number Three,* p. 65; May, 2001, review of *Other Voices, Other Doors,* p. 41.

Voice of Youth Advocates, June, 1998, review of *The Gift,* p. 132.

ONLINE

BookPage, http://www.bookpage.com/ (February, 2001) Gavin Grant, review of *The Impossible Bird.*

Patrick O'Leary Web site, http://mywebpages.comcast. net/patrickoleary/newindex.html (June 20, 2003).*

*   *   *

OLIANSKY, Joel 1935-2002

OBITUARY NOTICE—See index for *CA* sketch: Born October 11, 1935, in New York, NY; died of heart failure July 29, 2002, in Los Angeles, CA. Director and author. Oliansky was an award-winning director of television programs and movies, many of which he also wrote. A 1959 graduate of Hofstra University, where he earned a bachelor's degree, and Yale University, where he received an M.F.A. in 1962, Oliansky worked for a few years as playwright-in-residence at Yale before moving to California in 1964. In Hollywood he launched a prosperous career directing episodes of such television series as *Kojak, Alfred Hitchcock Presents,* and *Quincy.* Despite becoming a respected director, however, Oliansky was even more highly regarded as a writer. He was honored with an Emmy award for his script for *The Senator* (1970) and with Writers Guild awards for *The Law* (1979) and *Masada* (1981). He was also the author of the play *Bedford Forrest* and of the novel *Shame, Shame on the Johnson Boys* (1966). Oliansky's more recent work includes writing and directing *The Competition* (1980), writing *Bird* (1988), which drew on his extensive knowledge of jazz music, and directing *In Defense of a Married Man* (1990).

OBITUARIES AND OTHER SOURCES:

PERIODICALS

Los Angeles Times, August 1, 2002, p. B13.
New York Times, August 5, 2002, p. A12.
Washington Post, August 3, 2002, p. B7.

ORLÉANS, Marion (de Bourbon) d' 1941-

PERSONAL: Born September 4, 1941, in Santiago, Chile; daughter of James and Mercedes (Devia) Gordon-Orr; married Prince Thibaut Louis Denis Humbert de Bourbon d'Orléans (Comte de La Marche), September 23, 1972 (died, 1983); children: Robert Benoit Paul Henri James Marie, Louis-Philippe Albert François Marie (deceased).

ADDRESSES: Agent—c/o Editions André Balland, 33 Rue Saint André des Arts, 75006 Paris, France 06.

CAREER: Novelist. Comtesse de La Marche by virtue of her husband's title.

WRITINGS:

"LES PRINCES DU SANG" SERIES; WITH HUSBAND, THIBAUT D'ORLÉANS

Un château de Bavière (title means "A Castle in Bavaria"; also see below), Editions André Balland (Paris, France), 1973.
Le Témps des aventuriers (title means "The Time of Adventurers"; also see below), Editions André Balland (Paris, France), 1973.
L'Ombre de la guerre (title means "The Shadow of the War"), Editions André Balland (Paris, France), 1974.
Le Sort des armes (title means "The Fate of the Arms"), Editions André Balland (Paris, France), 1974.
A Castle in Bavaria: A Novel (abridged and revised combination of *Un Château de Bavière* and *Le Témps des aventuriers*), translated by Helen Weaver, Simon and Schuster (New York, NY), 1975.

SIDELIGHTS: Princess Marion d'Orléans and her husband, Prince Thibaut d'Orléans, the fifth and youngest son of the current Bourbon pretender to the throne of France, used their connections to the major royal houses of Europe to create a four-volume saga that follows one fictional royal family, the Hartburgs, through the political turmoil that continent experienced in the years between World War I and World War II.

The political upheavals of November 1918 resulted in the deposition of the twenty-four reigning royal families of the German Empire, as well as Emperor Karl I of Austria-Hungary and King Nikola I of Montenegro (later part of Yugoslavia). The Russian Emperor Nikolai II had already been toppled from his throne some eighteen months earlier, and the Ottoman Sultan Mehmet VI would follow suit within four years. Also affected were the many German and Austrian nobles who did not possess sovereign status, but who still occupied the highest rungs of society. These high-born princes suddenly found themselves being blamed for the devastation of World War I, and for the severe economic depression that followed in 1929.

In the Orléans' novels, the Hartburgs, former grand chamberlains and political advisers to the elderly Ludwig III, last king of Bavaria, have branches naturalized in England (the earls of Hardcastle), Austria, and France. This places them in four major capitals in postwar Europe, making them perfect observers of the European political scene. The story begins in the final days of World War I, on November 7, 1918, with Prince Gottfried von Hartburg advising the old king, his boyhood playmate, that the socialist revolutionaries gathering in the streets of Munich are indeed serious, and that they threaten not only the monarch's seat of power, but also his life as well. By evening the throngs of people in the streets have exceeded one hundred thousand, and by the following day, Kurt Eisner has deposed the monarchy and erected a socialist republic. The king and his children flee to the countryside, where they will be better protected.

Meanwhile, Prince Gottfried's eldest son and heir, Prince Ruprecht, is with Germany's Kaiser Wilhelm II at army headquarters, where Ruprecht witnesses the vacillation of the emperor over his decision about whether or not to abdicate. Finally, Wilhelm receives word that his last chancellor, Prince Max of Baden, has taken the ultimate step on his own, leaving him with no choice but to flee with his family to the safety of the Netherlands. In Austria, Ruprecht's younger brother, Prince George von Hartburg-Daranyi, provides a firsthand account of the devolution of the Austrian monarchy into chaos and communist revolution. In each of these scenarios, the Hartburgs represent the conservative status quo, except for the absent Princess Maria Radzinski, Prince Ruprecht's wife, who abandons her family and runs off with revolutionary painter Frederic Rosen, by whom she ultimately bears an illegitimate child.

The second novel in the series advances the timeline to the beginning of the Depression era, with the forces of National Socialism (the Nazi Party) on the rise in Germany. *Le Témps des aventuriers* ends with the death of Prince Gottfried in 1929. The third novel, *L'Ombre de la guerre,* deals with the rise to power of Adolf Hitler, and the effects of his pernicious philosophy and political tyranny on western and central Europe. The final book in the series, *Le Sort des armes,* puts the Hartburgs into the maw of World War II.

In all of these books, the sections which seem truest to life are those dealing with the titled families of Europe at the close of World War I. Clearly, Prince Thibaut and his wife visited the palaces, castles, and settings described, and knew something of the relationships involved. Both the Bavarian and French royal families, being Catholic, have intermarried at various times in the past two centuries. For this reason, *A Castle in Bavaria* and its French-language sequels remain interesting reading as a study of princely life by the royals themselves.

BIOGRAPHICAL AND CRITICAL SOURCES:

BOOKS

Burke's Royal Families of the World, Volume I: *Europe and Latin America,* Burke's Peerage Ltd. (Stokesley, England), 1977.

PERIODICALS

Booklist, June 1, 1977, p. 1483.
Library Journal, April 15, 1977, p. 947.
Publishers Weekly, February 21, 1977, p. 66.*

OWEN, W(arwick) J(ack) B(urgoyne) 1916-2002

OBITUARY NOTICE—See index for *CA* sketch: Born May 12, 1916, in Aukland, New Zealand; died November 20, 2002. Educator and author. Owen was a noted scholar of poet William Wordsworth. Educated at the University of Aukland where he received a master's degree in 1938, he was an assistant lecturer in English there for a year before moving to England to study at Oxford University. At Oxford he earned another master's degree in 1946, and at the University of Wales he completed his doctorate in 1955. During World War II Owen served with the British Army's Royal Army Ordnance Corps and the Royal Electrical and Mechanical Engineers, seeing action in North Africa and Italy and attaining the rank of captain. Beginning in 1946 he was a lecturer in English at University College, Bangor, in North Wales, leaving for Canada in 1965 to teach at McMaster University. At McMaster Owen was a professor of English until his retirement in 1981. Fascinated by English poet William Wordsworth, all of Owen's published books focus on this subject, among them *Wordsworth as Critic* (1969) and the edited works *Lyrical Ballads, 1798* (1967; second edition, 1969) and *The Fourteen-Book Prelude* (1985).

OBITUARIES AND OTHER SOURCES:

BOOKS

Lumley, Elizabeth, editor, *Canadian Who's Who,* Volume 36, University of Toronto Press (Toronto, Ontario, Canada), 2001.

PERIODICALS

Times (London, England), December 26, 2002.

P

PACKARD, William 1933-2002

OBITUARY NOTICE—See index for *CA* sketch: Born September 2, 1933, in New York, NY; died of heart disease November 3, 2002, in New York, NY. Editor, educator, and author. Packard was a poet and fiction writer best remembered as the founding editor of the poetry magazine *New York Quarterly*. He was a graduate of Stanford University, where he earned a bachelor's degree in 1956 and attended graduate courses in 1960 and 1961. Packard then embarked on a writing career, mostly consisting of plays and poetry, interspersed with several teaching jobs, including at the Institute for Advanced Studies in the Theatre Arts in New York City in 1965, at the Clark Center for the Performing Arts at New York University, at the New School for Social Research, and at Cooper Union. He founded *New York Quarterly* in 1969, which he edited until 1996, when he suffered a stroke that caused the journal to suspend publication. He recovered enough to return to the magazine in 2002, editing the fall issue just before his death. Packard's poetry collections include such works as *To Peel an Apple* (1963), *What Hands Are These?* (1977), and *The American Experience* (1979), and he wrote several plays, including *In the First Place* (1958), *On the Other Hand* (1963), and *From Now On* (1964). He was also the author of several books on writing, among them *The Poet's Dictionary: A Handbook of Prosody and Poetic Devices* (1989), *The Art of Poetry Writing* (1992), and *The Art of the Playwright: Creating the Magic of Theatre* (1997).

OBITUARIES AND OTHER SOURCES:

PERIODICALS

New York Times, November 16, 2002, p. A16.
Washington Post, November 20, 2002, p. B6.

PALANDRI, Enrico 1956-

PERSONAL: Born 1956, in Venice, Italy.

ADDRESSES: Home—England. *Agent*—c/o Author Mail, Giangiacomo Feltrinelli Editore, via Andegari 6, Milan, Italy 20121. *E-mail*—E.Palandri@ucl.ac.uk.

CAREER: Novelist, radio and film writer, journalist, translator, and professor. University College, London, England, writer-in-residence, 2002.

WRITINGS:

Bologna marzo 1977, Bertani (Verona, Italy), 1977.
Boccalone, L'erba voglio (Milan, Italy), 1979.
Le pietre e il sale (title means "The Rocks and the Salt"), Garzanti (Milan, Italy), 1986, translation published as *Ages Apart,* Collins Harvill (London, England), 1989.
La via del ritorno, Bompiani (Milan, Italy), 1990, translation published as *The Way Back,* Serpent's Tail (London, England), 1993.
Allegro fantastico, Bompiani (Milan, Italy), 1993.
Le colpevoli ambiguità di Herbert Markus, Bompiani (Milan, Italy), 1997.
Angela prende il volo, Giangiacomo Feltrinelli (Milan, Italy), 2000.

Also author, with Marco Bellocchio, of the screenplay *Diavolo in corpo* (title means "Devil in the Flesh").

Contributor to Italian and English radio and television as well as to several Italian newspapers.

SIDELIGHTS: Born in Venice in 1956, Enrico Palandri has established himself as one of the most important Italian fiction writers of his generation. His books have a post-modern feel and demonstrate the influence of other Italian masters such as Italo Calvino and Umberto Eco. In addition to his books, Palandri has collaborated on projects for cinema, radio, and television. Palandri has worked in Covent Garden as a language instructor for opera singers, a writer for *Unità* and *Diario della Settimana,* and as a writer-in-residence at University College, London.

Palandri initially made his mark as one of the first Italian writers of the Seventies Generation to write in a more traditional narrative style, departing from the avant-garde experimentation and disillusion of the late sixties and early seventies. His first important work was *Boccalone,* published in 1979. The novel deals with the lives of a group of young activists involved in the student/autonomist movement in Bologna in 1977. The book presents issues important to the younger generation but also tells an entertaining story marked by unique linguistic invention. Palandri's next book, *Le pietre e il sale,* appeared in 1986 and solidified his reputation as a talented, inventive writer.

In 1990, *La via del ritorno* was published and once again showed Palandri's skill in presenting ordinary people dealing with personal situations. The book focuses on the feelings and sensations of Davide, an Italian psychologist living in England. Returning to Rome with his Scottish singer girlfriend, he recalls the key events that have led him to that moment in his life. There are memories of his Polish-Jewish mother who fled to Italy during the war while the rest of her family perished in a concentration camp, school, his participation in radical leftist groups during the turbulent 1970s, and finally his new life in England. Arriving in Italy triggers memories of Livio, a childhood friend whose family's wealth, elegant home, and material advantages contrasted so much with his own humble origins. Davide's dilemma is one of identity; he feels Italian yet will undoubtedly return to the life he has carved out in England. At times, the book, which is more a parade of memories and images than a unified story, seems to represent the experiences of the generation that came of age in the 1970s, a generation that Palandri sees as decimated by both drugs and the dark cloud of political terrorism. Once again, Palandri's linguistic abilities and turns of phrase tie together the book's powerful recollections.

During the 1990s, Palandri published two books. The first was *Allegro fantastico,* published in 1993, a seamless collection of thirteen short stories, each under twenty pages, in which there is little distinction made between reality, dreams, and fiction. Subjects such as the power of television, a credit card to prove one's identity, and dreams take the reader on a literary voyage where a change of characters or stories is not always immediately apparent. *Le colpevoli ambiguità di Herbert Markus* appeared in 1997 and deals with solitude and an intellectual's attempt to break out of it. Once again, the book mirrors Palandri's generation and its problems entering middle age in a changing world. There are three basic themes within the novel, the first of which is the disillusion of the left following the fall of the Berlin Wall. Where positions and ideals once seemed clearly defined, there is now a confusing array of options and a world where right and wrong seem relative. Markus, once a staunch communist, now can only carry on without a defined ideology. It is this individual solitude that makes up the book's second theme. A generation that was once dedicated to the idea of collectivism now finds itself dealing with a rapidly changing world as detached individuals. Romantic matters, a favorite subject of Palandri, raise their head with Markus loving Zdena, who may be a spy. The couple's complicated, tormented relationship seems to advance the idea that there are no longer reference points in the construction of stable, fulfilling relationships. The book's third theme is the need to recapture a sense of place and day-to-day life amid one's seemingly banal existence. Markus clearly needs this, though there are no easy answers and even he cannot clearly express what his idea of "normal" would now be. The book concludes on a positive note as Markus begins to rise above his fears and existential emptiness.

Angela prende il volo, published in 2000, centers on a sixteen-year-old girl who is trying to overcome emotional burdens while finding herself in a world where she is practically alone. The story begins with her getting off a plane—the title literally translated means "Angela Takes the Plane"—and going to visit her father, who has remarried and now has another family. Never having accepting her father's new status, Angela finds such meetings—as well as general relationships with the opposite sex—difficult and has been forced to grow up faster than most girls her age. Her father is a physicist who speaks often and only about his work, laboratory, and experiments with space/time displacement. With the dreams of a sixteen year old, Angela envisions being able to build a time machine. Leaving Olmo, a friend of her father's who helps the girl with her time-machine research and eventually becomes more than just a friend, she finally meets her first true love, a foreigner named Thomas, on the train. Olmo, who also narrates the story, seems to have a romantic obsession with the young girl but in reality what he desires and envies is her youth and freedom. He knows both of these have passed him by. Time, whether in the form of dreams of a time machine or in the inevitable effects of its passing, is a central element in the book. In the end Angela, who at the beginning of the story is a frightened lonely child, overcomes her fears and achieves a lightness of being that Palandri tells us is the sign of true maturity. With each book, Palandri has impressed both readers and critics.

BIOGRAPHICAL AND CRITICAL SOURCES:

PERIODICALS

Booklist, March 15, 1994, John Shreffler, review of *The Way Back,* p. 1328.
Kirkus Reviews, February 1, 1994, review of *The Way Back,* p. 92.
New Statesman, March 27, 1987, Luca Fontana, "Italy, the Names and the Prose," pp. 39-40.
Observer (London, England), April 11, 1993, p. 59.
Publishers Weekly, February 28, 1994, review of *The Way Back,* p. 80.
World Literature Today, summer, 1994, Rocco Capozzi, review of *Allegro fantastico,* pp. 545-546.*

*   *   *

PALMER, Maria
    See BRENNAN, J(ames) H(erbert)

*   *   *

PALMQUIST, Peter E. 1936-2003

PERSONAL: Born 1936, in Oakland, CA; died after being struck by a car January 11, 2003.

CAREER: Photographer, historian, and writer. North Atlantic Treaty Organization (NATO), Europe, member of staff; Humboldt State University, staff photographer, 1960-89. *Military service:* U.S. Army, served as photographer.

MEMBER: National Stereoscopic Association.

WRITINGS:

With Nature's Children: Emma B. Freeman, 1880-1928—Camera and Brush, Interface California Corporation (Eureka, CA), 1977.
Lawrence & Houseworth/Thomas Houseworth & Co, a Unique View of the West 1860-1886, National Stereoscopic Association (Columbus, OH), 1980.
Carleton E. Watkins: Photographer of the American West, University of New Mexico Press/Amon Carter Museum (Albuquerque, NM), 1983.
(With Lincoln Kilian), *The Photographers of the Humboldt Bay Region 1870-1875,* Eureka Printing Company (Eureka, CA), 1986.
A Bibliography of Writings by and about Women in Photography 1850-1950, Peter E. Palmquist (Arcata, CA), 1990.
Shadowcatchers: A Directory of Women in California Photography before 1901, Peter E. Palmquist (Arcata, CA), 1990.
(Editor) *Photographers: A Sourcebook for Historical Research,* Carl Mautz Publishing (Nevada City, CA), 2000.
(With Thomas R. Kailbourn) *Pioneer Photographers of the Far West: A Biographical Dictionary,* Stanford University Press (Palo Alto, CA), 2000.
(Photographer) Peter Johnstone, editor, *Giants in the Earth: The California Redwoods,* Heyday Books (Berkeley, CA), 2001.

Contributor to books, including *Capturing Light: Masterpieces of California Photography, 1850 to the Present,* edited by Drew Heath Johnson Oakland Museum of California/W.W. Norton (New York, NY), 2001. Founding editor of *Daguerreian Annual.*

SIDELIGHTS: Peter E. Palmquist was a self-taught scholar and prolific historian of photography, especially western photography. Born in Oakland, California, in 1936, Palmquist lived the majority of his life in rural Humboldt County, California. "His childhood education included a one-room school house with eight students; without electricity or running water," wrote a biographer at the *Women Artists of the American West* Web site. "His high school graduating class totaled twenty-seven students." Palmquist taught himself photography at age twelve, served five years as a photographer in the U.S. Army, and worked for twenty-eight years as a photographer for Humboldt State University before retiring in 1989. He was an independent historian of photography from 1971, until his death in 2003.

"Much about Palmquist is unorthodox—from his academic credentials (he has none) to his collection of more than 100,000 photographs, the bulk of which would be deemed of little value by many collectors," wrote Myriam Weisang Misrach at the *Women Artists of the American West* Web site. "Still, the soft-spoken . . . man [was] . . . considered a leading photography expert by prominent auction houses and museums and . . . served as advisor on a plethora of books and exhibits. He . . . curated important shows" in addition to writing more than twenty books.

Among Palmquist's books are *With Nature's Children: Emma B. Freeman, 1880-1928—Camera and Brush,* "Despite the condescending title, this is a gem of a book about a remarkable woman," wrote Mary Mallory in *Library Journal.* Freeman, a free-spirited and flamboyant artist and photographer, was known for her romanticized portraits of local Klamath and Hupa Indians—images that were often highly artistic but culturally inaccurate. "Though her Indian portraits were finely crafted and sold well, Palmquist warns that they will not provide anthropologists with 'new and significant insights,'" wrote Ann Marie Cunningham in *Ms.* "Emma viewed her subjects through a lens clouded by mysticism and romance—a distorted perspective which she shared with most of her contemporaries."

Palmquist's 1980 book, *Lawrence & Houseworth/ Thomas Houseworth & Co, a Unique View of the West 1860-1886,* provides a history and catalogue of the Houseworth company, a California dealer in optics that also sold stereoscopes and stereoscopic viewers, along with stereoscopic photographs of subjects in California and the American West. Palmquist provides "painstaking research into the history of the Houseworth firm," wrote a reviewer in *American West.* A reviewer in *AP Bookman's Weekly* noted that "Palmquist's work sheds light on the firm's business activities, on the steroscopic branch of photography,

and on life in the west." In *Carleton E. Watkins: Photographer of the American West,* Palmquist provides "a good comprehensive biography of one of the foremost photographers of the American West," remarked a reviewer in *Choice.* "Palmquist's thorough scholarship, expansive bibliography, chronology, and listing of collections" make *Carleton E. Watkins* a "very significant addition" to collections focused on photography or history, wrote Ann Copeland in *Library Journal.* Jessica Reichman, writing in *Journal of the West,* called Palmquist's *Photographers of the Humboldt Bay Region 1870-1875,* "an entertaining, well-written volume that is packed with information." In addition, "The Era of ingenious nineteenth-century photographers is vividly portrayed in this volume," Reichman commented.

Among Palmquist's more ambitious projects is *Shadowcatchers: A Directory of Women in California Photography before 1901.* The book provides "a comprehensive list of women active in photography in California in the nineteenth century," wrote Judy Dykl in *American Reference Books Annual.* "Palmquist has collected an unpretentious alphabetical listing of over seven hundred women who were involved in photography and its related occupations," wrote Angela Howard Zogby in *Journal of American History.* Although Zogby remarked that "the organization of the material obstructs quick scanning of all the entries for readily listed demographic data," she also said that "the wealth of detail in Palmquist's entries will be useful to historians as well as photographers interested in the region and the era." Dykl concluded that "Since most histories of women photographers deal only with the major figures, the comprehensiveness of this narrowly focused directory will prove useful to anyone doing research in this area."

Photographers: A Sourcebook for Historical Research, edited by Palmquist, provides "a framework and good advice for novices and experienced researchers alike," wrote L. L. Scarth in *Choice.* The "highly informative" book includes instructional essays "on the theory and techniques of regional research," along with a bibliography of directories of photographers, compiled by Richard Radisill, wrote Ron Polito in *AB Bookman's Weekly.* "Archivists who fail to appreciate this volume apparently have no one but themselves to blame," remarked a reviewer in *American Archivist.*

Pioneer Photographers of the Far West "exhibits many of the virtues and some of the faults to be expected from a lifelong obsession, which, according to the preface, it appears to have been," wrote Benjamin Markovits in the *Times Literary Supplement*. "Browsing through the dictionary itself feels slightly like walking through a military cemetery: disparate people have been bunched together according to a common cause that may have meant much or little to each," Markovits observed. "The entries themselves resemble a kind of elaborate headstone, rich in dates and places, marriages and births, but occasionally short on the lives between. Still," Markovits wrote, "the book has the fascination of a graveyard, as indeed to the photographic portraits interspersed." Jonathan Kirsch, writing in *Los Angeles Times*, noted that "like every well-written and well-produced dictionary, it's possible to open the book at random and find something fascinating, illuminating, or funny, and sometimes all of them at once."

In his work with photography, Palmquist's intent was "to interpret each photograph in order to understand the times in which it was taken, the person who shot it, the people who appear in it," Misrach wrote. "He [was] . . . interested in weaving a vast tapestry of California's past through the lens of as many photographers as possible." To Palmquist, who studied advanced amateur photographers as intently as well-known professionals, "a print worth twenty-five cents can thus be as valuable as one that may cost a thousand dollars," Misrach observed. "Anything that allow[ed] . . . him to 'perceive the fingerprints of the artist' is of importance, be it a landscape or family portrait."

On January 11, 2003, Palmquist was struck and killed by a hit-and-run driver while walking his dog.

BIOGRAPHICAL AND CRITICAL SOURCES:

PERIODICALS

AB Bookman's Weekly, January 24, 1983, review of *Lawrence & Houseworth/Thomas Houseworth & Co., a Unique View of the West 1860-1886,* pp. 513-514; March 16, 1992, Ron Polito, review of *Photographers: A Sourcebook for Historical Research,* p. 1028.

American Archivist, summer, 1992, review of *Photographers: A Sourcebook for Historical Research,* p. 510.

American Reference Books Annual, 1992, Judy Dykl, review of *A Bibliography of Writings by and about Women in Photography 1850-1950* and *Shadowcatchers: A Directory of Women in California Photography before 1901,* pp. 387-388.

American West, January-February, 1978, review of *With Nature's Children: Emma B. Freeman, 1880-1928—Camera and Brush,* p. 56; January-February, 1982, review of *Lawrence & Houseworth/Thomas Houseworth & Co., a Unique View of the West 1860-1886,* p. 64; June, 1990, review of *Photography in the West,* p. 32P.

Choice, September, 1983, review of *Carleton E. Watkins: Photographer of the American West,* p. 80; February, 2001, L. L. Scarth, review of *Photographers: A Sourcebook for Historical Research,* p. 1058; September, 2001, P. D. Thomas, review of *Pioneer Photographers of the Far West: A Biographical Dictionary, 1840-1865,* p. 86; September, 2001, W. A. McIntyre, review of *Capturing Light: Masterpieces of California Photography, 1850 to the Present,* p. 106.

Journal of American History, March, 1992, Angela Howard Zogby, review of *Shadowcatchers: A Directory of Women in California Photography before 1901,* p. 1551.

Journal of the West, April, 1988, Jessica Reichman, review of *The Photographers of the Humboldt Bay Region 1870-1875,* p. 91.

Library Journal, June 15, 1977, Mary Mallory, review of *With Nature's Children: Emma B. Freeman, 1880-1928—Camera and Brush,* p. 1369; July, 1983, Ann Copeland, review of *Carleton E. Watkins, Photographer of the American West,* p. 1357.

Los Angeles Times, August 8, 2001, Jonathan Kirsch, "Turning Curious Eyes on a Rough-Edged Frontier," pp. E1, E3.

Ms., June, 1977, review of *With Nature's Children,* p. 86.

Times Literary Supplement, February 8, 2002, Benjamin Markovits, "How the West Was Shot," p. 7.

Washington Post Book World, May 22, 1983, Michael Dirda, review of *Carleton E. Watkins: Photographer of the American West,* p. 13.

ONLINE

Women Artists of the American West Web site, http://www.sla.purdue.edu/WAAW/ (May 8, 2002), Myriam Weisang Misrach, "Through the Lens of Time."

OBITUARIES:

PERIODICALS

Los Angeles Times, January 20, 2003, "Peter Palmquist, 66; Photography Historian," p. B-11.

ONLINE

NCCN.net, http://www.nccn.net (April 29, 2003), "In Memoriam: Peter E. Palmquist, 1936-2003."*

*   *   *

PANCOL, Katherine 1954-

PERSONAL: Born 1954, in Casablanca, Morocco; immigrated to France, c. 1959; children: Charlotte.

ADDRESSES: *Agent*—c/o Editions Albin Michel, 22 Rue Huyghens, 75014 Paris, France.

CAREER: Journalist and novelist.

WRITINGS:

Moi d'abord, Editions Points-Seuil (Paris, France), 1979.
Le barbare, Editions Points-Seuil (Paris, France), 1981.
Scarlett, si possible, Editions Points-Seuil (Paris, France), 1985, translation by Suzanne White published as *Call Me Scarlett,* Bergh Publishing Group (New York, NY), 1986.
Les hommes cruels ne courent pas dans les rues, Editions Points-Seuil (Paris, France), 1990.
Vue de l'exterior, Editions Points-Seuil (Paris, France), 1993.
Une si belle image, Editions Points-Seuil (Paris, France) 1995.
Encore une danse, Editions Fayard (Paris, France), 1998.
J'etais la avant, Editions Albin Michel (Paris, France), 1999.
Et monter lentement dans un immense amour, Editions Albin Michel (Paris, France), 2001.

SIDELIGHTS: Katherine Pancol was pursuing a career in journalism with *Paris Match* and *Cosmopolitan* when Parisian editor Robert Lafont suggested that she try her hand at writing novels. In 1979 she published her first novel, *Moi d'bord,* which focuses on a modern French woman and reminds readers that the feminist movement of earlier decades is no longer only a specific political movement: its liberating ideas have become an integral part of French culture. The novel was surprisingly successful, and Pancol explained on her Web site that she fled to New York to get over it. However, she continued writing as she lived in New York and was soon being heralded as "the Françoise Sagan of the 1980s."

Scarlett si possible, Pancol's third novel, was published in English as *Call Me Scarlett.* This "sassy, fast-paced novel," as a reviewer for *Publishers Weekly* described it, is set in late 1960s Paris. Three girls from rural France have moved to Paris in search of careers and love, although their successes in both fields are mixed. One falls in love with a thief and dreams of going to America. Another sleeps with her editor to ensure her advancement at the newspaper where she works, even though she is in fact in love with another reporter, while the third agrees to become the paid mistress of the owner of the concrete company for which she works after she falls in love with an unemployed actor.

BIOGRAPHICAL AND CRITICAL SOURCES:

PERIODICALS

Express International, December 22, 1994, Martine de Rabaudy, interview with Katherine Pancol, p. 65; May 27, 1993, Sophie Grassin, review of *Vue de l'exterior,* p. 74.
Kirkus Reviews, March 1, 1986, review of *Call Me Scarlett,* p. 333.
Publishers Weekly, March 28, 1986, review of *Call Me Scarlett,* p. 48.

OTHER

Cyberpresse, http://www.cyberpresse.ca/ (October 21, 2001), Guilaume Bourgault-Côte, interview with Katherine Pancol.

Express Livres, http://livres.lexpress.fr/ (February 28, 2002), Roland Mihail and Antoine Silber, interview with Katherine Pancol.

Katherine Pancol's Home Page, http://www.katherine-pancol.com (February 28, 2002).

Lire, http://www.lire.fr/ (February 28, 2002), Gabrielle Rolin, review of *Encore une danse.*

Nouvel Observateur Online, http://www.nouvelobs.com/ (February 28, 2002), Françoise Xenakis, review of *J'etais la avant.**

* * *

PAPES, Robert 1943-

PERSONAL: Born October 30, 1943, in Chicago, IL; married Katheryne Palubicki, June 12, 1965; children: Kimberly Papes Trenck, Leah, Sabrina. *Ethnicity:* "Polish/Czech." *Education:* Bellarmine University, B.A., 1966.

ADDRESSES: Home—3241 Pimlico Blvd., Stow, OH 44224. *E-mail*—rpapes1030@aol.com.

CAREER: Employed by General Electric Co., 1966-85; James River, Greenville, SC, general manager, 1986-90; International Paper, Richmond, VA, general manager, 1990-92; General Services Industry, Nashville, TN, general manager, 1992-95; American P & Ds Paper, general manager in Buffalo, NY, and Chicago, IL, 1995-98; ITW, Twinsburg, OH, general manager, 1998-2002.

MEMBER: Turnaround Management Association, Ohio Manufacturing Association.

WRITINGS:

Turnaround, Cypress Publishing, 2002.

SIDELIGHTS: Robert Papes told *CA:* "My career in general management didn't start out to have a focus of turning around businesses, but my teams engineered four consecutive turnarounds of Herculean proportions. These turnarounds were in three different industries.

"In my book, *Turnaround,* I share my real-life experiences. Many books and seminars tell the audience what to do. My book not only tells the reader what to do, but how to do it as well. It is truly one of a kind.

"My inspiration for writing the book is a result of my strong desire to see manufacturing in our country survive against the threat of foreign goods. I believe that our economy depends upon our ability to produce the goods we need.

"My book is for anyone undertaking the daunting task of trying to save a business. It is suited for business majors, people with M.B.A. degrees, owners, general managers, chief operating officers, and chief executive officers. It is an easy read, as each chapter is short and tightly focused. It also has a workbook at the end of each chapter."

* * *

PARILLO, Mark P. 1955-

PERSONAL: Born February 7, 1955, in Youngstown, OH; son of Anthony J. (an advertising executive) and Anne Mabel (Sherock) Parillo; married Marcella Zetts, August 6, 1977; children: Donata Terese Parillo Pemberton, Domenica Anne, Alexis Joe-Claire, Taryn Elaine. *Education:* University of Notre Dame, B.A., 1978; Ohio State University, M.A., 1981, Ph.D., 1987.

ADDRESSES: Office—Department of History, Kansas State University, Manhattan, KS 66506.

CAREER: Kansas State University, Manhattan, associate professor of history, 1992—.

WRITINGS:

The Japanese Merchant Marine in World War II, Naval Institute Press (Annapolis, MD), 1993.

(Editor) *We Were in the Big One: Experiences of the World War II Generation,* Scholarly Resources (Wilmington, DE), 2002.

BIOGRAPHICAL AND CRITICAL SOURCES:

PERIODICALS

Historian, summer, 1994, Charles Yates, review of *The Japanese Merchant Marine in World War II,* p. 772.

PEARSON, Karl 1857-1936
(Loki)

PERSONAL: Given name originally Carl; born March 27, 1857, in London, England; died of cardiac failure April 27, 1936, in Coldharbour (one source says London), Surrey, England; son of William (a lawyer) and Fanny (Smith) Pearson; married Maria Sharpe, 1890 (died, 1928); married Margaret V. Child, 1929; children: (first marriage) Egon, Sigrid, Helga. *Education:* King's College, Cambridge, B.S. (with honors), 1879, LL.D., 1881, M.S., 1882.

CAREER: University College, London, London, England, Goldsmid Professor of Applied Mathematics and Mechanics, 1884-91, Gresham College Professor of Geometry, 1891-1911, Galton Professor of Eugenics, 1911-33, head of Francis Galton Laboratory for National Eugenics, 1906; writer.

AWARDS, HONORS: Rudolf Virchow Medal, Anthropological Society of Berlin, 1933; honorary degree, University of London, 1934.

WRITINGS:

(Under pseudonym Loki) *The New Werther* (novel), 1880.

The Trinity (play), 1882.

The Ethic of Freethought: A Selection of Essays and Lectures, Fisher Unwin (London, England), 1888.

(Editor, with Richard Charles Rowe) William Kingdom Clifford, *The Common Sense of the Exact Sciences,* Appleton (New York, NY), 1888.

The Grammar of Science, Walter Scott, 1892.

The Chances of Death, and Other Studies in Evolution, Edward Arnold (New York, NY), 1897.

(With Alice Elizabeth Lee) *Tables of F and H Functions,* Offices of the Association (London, England), 1899.

National Life from the Standpoint of Science (speech), A. & C. Black (London, England), 1901.

(With L. W. Atcherley) *On the Graphics of Metal Arches,* Dulau (London, England), 1905.

On Torsional Vibrations in Axles and Shafting, Dulau (London, England), 1905.

On the General Theory of Skew Correlation and Nonlinear Regression, Dulau (London, England), 1905.

A Mathematical Theory of Random Migration, Dulau (London, England), 1906.

Treasury of Human Inheritance, Dulau (London, England), 1909.

(With Amy Barrington) *A Preliminary Study of Extreme Alcoholism in Adults,* Dulau (London, England), 1910.

(With David Heron and Gustav A. Jaederholm) *Mendelism and the Problem of Mental Defect,* Dulau (London, England), 1913.

(Editor) *Tables for Statisticians and Biometricians,* Cambridge University Press (Cambridge, England), 1914.

On the Handicapping of the First Born (lecture), Dulau (London, England), 1914.

The Life, Letters, and Labours of Francis Galton (biography), Cambridge University Press (Cambridge, England), Volume 1, 1914, Volume 2, 1924, Volume 3, 1930.

The Relative Strength of Nurture and Nature, University of Chicago Press (Chicago, IL), 1915.

(With Andrew W. Young and Ethel M. Elderton) *On the Torsion Resulting from Flexure in Prisms with Cross Sections of Uni-axial Symmetry Only,* University of Chicago Press (Chicago, IL), 1918.

The Function of Science in the Modern State, Cambridge University Press (Cambridge, England), 1919.

On the Construction of Tables and on Interpolation, University of Chicago Press (Chicago, IL), 1920.

(Editor) *Tables of the Incomplete Gamma Function,* Department of Scientific and Industrial Research (London, England), 1922.

On the Relationship of Health to the Psychical and Physical Characters in School Children, Cambridge University Press (Cambridge, England), 1923.

(Editor) *Tables of the Incomplete Beta Function,* Office of Biometrika, (London, England), 1934.

(Editor) *Tables of the Incomplete Y Function,* Office of Biometrika (London, England), 1934.

Early Statistical Papers, Cambridge University Press (Cambridge, England), 1948.

E. S. Pearson, editor, *The History of Statistics in the Seventeenth and Eighteenth Centuries against the Changing Background of Intellectual, Scientific, and Religious Thought* (lectures), Griffin (London, England), 1978.

Contributor to periodicals, including *Nature, Proceedings of the Royal Society* and *Philosophical Transac-*

tions of the Royal Society. Founding editor, *Annals of Eugenics,* 1925-33; editor, *Biometrika,* 1901-35.

SIDELIGHTS: Karl Pearson is considered a pioneer in the development of statistics as a science. In *Notable Scientists: From 1900 to the Present,* he is credited with "developing ways to analyze and represent scientific observations," achievements considered "the groundwork for the development of the field of statistics . . . and its use in medicine, engineering, anthropology, and psychology."

Pearson received his education at King's College, Cambridge, where he distinguished himself in mathematics and jurisprudence. During the course of his education in Cambridge, Pearson regularly traveled to Germany, where he indulged his passions for philosophy and socialism. During this period, Pearson produced his first published books, including a novel, *The New Werther,* which he wrote under the pseudonym Loki, and a passion play, *The Trinity.* The novel was later described by George Levine, writing in *Victorian Studies,* as "curious."

In 1888 Pearson returned to England and became Goldsmid Professor of Applied Mathematics and Mechanics at University College, London. That same year, he also published *The Ethic of Freethought: A Selection of Essays and Lectures* and teamed with Richard Charles Rowe in editing William Kingdom Clifford's *The Common Sense of the Exact Sciences.*

By the early 1890s, Pearson had already begun exploring the nature of correlation between events, and through the application of mathematical concepts he undertook the development of a statistical method for evaluating the likelihood of correlation. He devised graphs representing the likelihood of correlation, and developed the concept of standard deviation as a means for measuring variance. He also determined randomness through application of the chi-square test, which is described in *World of Scientific Discovery* as Pearson's "most significant finding." Ian Hacking, writing in *Science,* found the chi-square test useful "for hypotheses and data where observations naturally fall into discrete categories that statisticians call cells," and Boris Mirkin, in an *American Statistician* essay, acknowledged chi-squared as "most popular among the contingency coefficients."

Pearson continued to teach at University College until 1933, when he retired after twenty-two years as Galton Professor of Eugenics. Three years later, he died

from cardiac failure. His posthumous publications include *Early Statistical Papers,* which appeared in 1948, and *The History of Statistics in the Seventeenth and Eighteenth Centuries against the Changing Background of Intellectual, Scientific, and Religious Thought,* which followed thirty years later.

BIOGRAPHICAL AND CRITICAL SOURCES:

BOOKS

Notable Scientists: From 1900 to the Present, Gale (Detroit, MI), 2001.
World of Scientific Inquiry, Gale (Detroit, MI), 1999.

PERIODICALS

American Statistician, May, 2001, Boris Mirkin, "Eleven Ways to Look at the Chi-aquared Coefficient for Contingency Tables."
History of Science, March, 1999, M. Eileen Magnello, "Rival Forms of Laboratory Work in Karl Pearson's Career at University College, London."
Science, November, 1984, Ian Hacking, "Trial by Number: Karl Pearson's Chi-square Test."
Victorian Studies, autumn, 2000, George Levine, "Two Ways Not to Be a Solipsist: Art and Science, Pater and Pearson."*

*   *   *

PEDULLÀ, Walter 1930-

PERSONAL: Born 1930, in Siderno, Calabria, Italy. *Education:* University of Messina, graduated 1958.

ADDRESSES: *Office*—Università de Roma "La Sapienza," Piazzale Aldo Moro 5, Rome 00185, Italy.

CAREER: University of Rome "La Sapienza," professor of modern and contemporary Italian literature, 1958—; Istituto Universitario Orientale, Naples, Italy, professor of literature and Italian language; magistero di Salerno, professor of cricitism; literary critic for *Mondo nuovo,* 1959-61; literary critic for *L'Avanti,* 1961—; journalist.

WRITINGS:

(With Elio Pagliarani) *I maestri del racconto italian,* Rizzoli (Milan, Italy), 1964.

La letteratura del benessere, Libreria Scientifica Editrice (Naples, Italy), 1968.

La rivoluzione della letteratura, Ennese (Rome, Italy), 1970.

L'estrema funzione: la letteratura degli anni Settanta svela i propri segreti, Marsilio (Venice, Italy), 1975.

Il morbo di Besedow ovvero dell'avanguardia, Lerici (Cosenza, Italy), 1975.

(With Silvana Castelli and Stefano Giovanardi) *La letteratura emarginata: i narratori giovani degli anni '70,* Lerici (Rome, Italy), 1978.

Alberto Savinio scrittore ipocrita e privo di scopo, Lerici (Cosenza, Italy), 1979.

Miti, finzioni e buone manier di fine millennio, Rusconi (Milan, Italy), 1983.

Il ritorno dell'uomo di fumo: viaggio paradossale con Palazzeschi in un paese allegro e innocente, Marsilio (Venice, Italy), 1987.

Lo schiaffo di Svevo: giochi, fantasie, figure del novecento italiano, Camunia (Milan, Italy), 1990.

Alberto Savinio, Editoriale Fabbri (Milan, Italy), 1991.

Le caramelle di Musil, Rizzoli (Milan, Italy), 1993.

Sappia la sinistra quello che fa la destra, Rizzoli (Milan, Italy), 1994.

(With Corrado Alvaro and Mario Strati) *Scritti dispersi, 1921-1956,* Bompiani (Milan, Italy), 1995.

(With Italo Svevo) *Italo Svevo,* Istituto Poligrafico e Zecca dello Stato (Rome, Italy), 1995.

Carlo Emilio Gadda: il narratore come delinquente, Rizzoli (Milan, Italy), 1997.

(With Nino Borsellino) *Storia generale della letteratura italiana,* Motta (Milan, Italy), 1999.

I titoli: Landolfi, Gadda, Savinio, Impronte degli Uccelli (Rome, Italy), 1999.

(With Nino Borsellino) *Letteratura italiana del Novecento,* Rizzoli (Milan, Italy), 2000.

Le armi del comico: narratori italiani del Novecento, Mondadori (Milan, Italy), 2001.

SIDELIGHTS: Walter Pedullà is a literary critic and professor of Italian literature. He has published a number of books on literature and has been an active contributor to a number of magazines and other publications on the subject.

Pedullà was born in Siderno, Calabria, in 1930. He earned his degree in letters in Messina under Giacomo Devenedetti, who made him an assistant professor at the University of Rome "La Sapienza" in 1958. He became a professor at the same university in the faculty of letters, teaching modern and contemporary Italian literature. He also became a professor of literature and Italian language at the Oriental University Institute in Naples and of the history of criticism in Salerno.

As a professional journalist, Pedullà worked on a number of publications and magazines. From 1959 to 1961, he was the literary critic for *Mondo nuovo.* In 1961, he became the literary critic for the daily *L'Avanti.* He contributed to *Il Mattino* in Naples, *Il Messaggero* in Rome, and *Italia Oggi* in Milan. He worked as an advisor for Radio Italia from 1975 until 1992, when he was elected president. He has sat on the editorial boards of a number of magazines, including *Il cavallo di Troia, Tempo presente,* and *Lettera internazionale.* He has also been president of the Teatro di Roma.

Pedullà has worked on several compilations of literary series. He collaborated with Nino Borsellino on *Storia della letteratura italiana.* He has also written a number of books on Italian literature.*

*   *   *

PEPPERPOD, Pip
    See STODDARD, Charles Warren

*   *   *

PHELAN, Terence
    See MANGAN, (John Joseph) Sherry

*   *   *

PHILLIPS, William 1907-2002

*OBITUARY NOTICE—*See index for *CA* sketch: Born November 14, 1907, in East Harlem, NY; died of pneumonia September 13, 2002, in New York, NY. Editor, educator, and author. Phillips was a cofounder and editor of the literary magazine *Partisan Review.* He did his undergraduate work at what is now the City College of the City University of New York, where he earned a B.S. in 1928, and completed his master's degree at New York University two years later; he also attended graduate courses at Columbia

University from 1930 to 1931. His first job was as an English instructor at New York University from 1929 to 1932. Phillips was interested in literary criticism and modernist writers, and his intellectual pursuits led him to Communism and the John Reed Club, a Greenwich Village-based group that supported the Communist Party. It was there that he met Philip Rahv, with whom he founded *Partisan Review* in 1934. The purpose of the magazine was to publish stories, literary criticism, and philosophical and political essays by the day's most brilliant intellectuals, combining new radicalism with modernism in what the editors hoped would inspire a new literary movement. Within the first issues of *Partisan Review* appeared essays and stories by such writers as Delmore Schwartz, Wallace Steven, and Lionel Abel. With the rise of Stalinism in Russia, Phillips and Rahv, who were stoutly against the dictator, had a falling out with the John Reed Club and split from the group in 1937. They managed to find financial support and to gain enough readers to keep the magazine going, continuing to publish such now-famous writers as Lionel Trilling, Meyer Schapiro, Albert Camus, Norman Mailer, Simone de Beauvoir, Jean Paul Sartre, and Clement Greenberg. *Partisan Review* was at its most influential in the years immediately preceding and following World War II. The partnership between Phillips and Rahv was contentious, however, and when the editorial board chose Phillips to be editor-in-chief, Rahv fought to regain control. Despite being granted the right to continue to review manuscripts, Rahv resigned his editorship in 1969. By this time, the magazine was in decline, having lost its influence to other rising literary magazines. Phillips managed to get financial support from Rutgers University, where he was also granted a post as professor in 1963. When Rutgers withdrew support of the magazine in 1978, Phillips moved *Partisan Review* to Boston University and was also a professor here. Even into his nineties, Phillips continued to read manuscript submissions for his magazine, though he had by then relinquished much of the editorial control to others. During his editorial career Phillips was also an associate professor at Columbia in 1945 and at New York University in the early 1960s. He edited several essay and fiction collections, including, with Rahv, *The Partisan Reader, 1934-1944* (1946), *The New Partisan Reader, 1945-1953* (1953), *Partisan Review: The Fiftieth Anniversary Edition* (1985), and *Sixty Years of Great Fiction from Partisan Review* (1996), and was the author of *A Sense of Present* (1967) and the memoir *A Partisan View: Five Decades of Literary Life* (1984).

OBITUARIES AND OTHER SOURCES:

PERIODICALS

Chicago Tribune, September 14, 2002, section 1, p. 23.
Los Angeles Times, September 14, 2002, p. B20.
New York Times, September 14, 2002, p. A26.
Times (London, England), September 18, 2002.
Washington Post, September 15, 2002, p. C6.

* * *

PIERCE, Robert
    See DRAKE, Timothy A.

* * *

PLAIT, Philip C. 1964(?)-

PERSONAL: Born c.1964; married, May 27, 1995; wife's name, Marcella; children: Zoe. *Education:* University of Virginia, Ph.D., 1994.

ADDRESSES: Office—Sonoma State University, Department of Physics and Astronomy, 1801 East Cotati Ave., Rohnert Park, CA 94928. *E-mail*—badastro@ badastronomy.com.

CAREER: Astronomer, programmer, journalist, and columnist. Department of physics and astronomy, Sonoma State University, Rohnert Park, CA, astronomer. Has worked as an astronomer at Goddard Space Flight Center and as a teacher of introductory astronomy classes at the University of Virginia.

WRITINGS:

Bad Astronomy: Misconceptions and Misuses Revealed, from Astrology to the Moon Landing "Hoax," John Wiley & Sons (New York, NY), 2002.

Contributor to periodicals, including *Frankfurter Allgemeine Zeitung* and *Astronomy.* Writer of monthly column for *astronomy.com* Web site.

SIDELIGHTS: Philip C. Plait calls himself "The Bad Astronomer," not because he performs poorly at his chosen vocation, but because he devotes a significant portion of his professional life to identifying and correcting bad astronomy and incorrect science in movies, books, television, the media, or anywhere else that astronomical misinformation may be found.

Plait maintains the *Bad Astronomy* Web site, an online resource dedicated to rooting out misinformation about science and astronomy. "Sometimes this information is just plain silly," Plait wrote on the site, "but many times it makes just enough sense that people believe it. Sometimes the news media help spread these ideas (like the one that you can spin or stand an egg on end during the Vernal Equinox), sometimes it's TV and sometimes it's plain old word of mouth, but the misinformation does get around. I feel obliged to right these wrongs when I can."

A professional astronomer and programmer with a Ph.D. in astronomy from the University of Virginia, Plait worked on a number of skygazing projects, including the Cosmic Background Explorer, where he helped calibrate instruments designed to detect infrared light from the beginning of the universe. He has also worked at NASA's Goddard Space Flight Center on the space telescope imaging spectrograph, a camera installed on the Hubble space telescope. In the course of his career, Plait has conducted independent research, and has been "involved with many interesting projects," he wrote on the *Bad Astronomy* Web site, including activities such as taking images of such celestial events and objects as "stars being born, stars dying, galaxies, quasars, black holes, asteroids and a number of other things." His other accomplishments include assisting in the analysis of the first brown dwarf ever discovered—("A brown dwarf is an object that is too small to be a star but too big to be a planet," Plait explained)—and working on analyses of images and spectra taken of a exploding star in 1987. An active science writer, Plait is also a frequent lecturer and presenter of topics in astronomy, including speaking to students about careers in the field. However, Plait admits on his Web site, sometimes in answer to the curious, "when people ask me what astronomers do, I tell them 'They *astronom!*'"

With his book *Bad Astronomy: Misconceptions and Misuses Revealed, from Astrology to the Moon Landing "Hoax,"* Plait takes his mission from the Web to print. He describes—and corrects—twenty-four common misconceptions and fallacies about astronomy, including such notions that planetary alignments can cause disasters on earth, that stars can be seen in the daytime from the bottom of a well, and that raw eggs can be balanced on end only during the vernal equinox. "The author sharply and convincingly dismisses astrology, creationism, and UFO sightings and explains the principles behind basic general concepts," wrote Jeffrey Beall in *Library Journal.*

Plait's explanations not only clear up fallacies, they also provide a solid foundation in the basics of astronomy, observed a reviewer in *Publishers Weekly.* "With avuncular humor, he points out the ways advertising and media reinforce bas science and pleads for more accuracy in Hollywood storylines and special effects," the reviewer wrote.

Among the worst instances of bad astronomy, Plait said in an interview with *VirginiaOnlineMag,* is "a resurgence in the idea that NASA faked the moon landings." One of the examples used by those who believe this idea is the fact that there are no stars in pictures taken on the moon when they believe the black lunar sky should be full of them. However, Plait explained, "those pictures were taken of a fully sunlit landscape, of astronauts standing in the Sun. The exposure times used in the pictures were far too short to see stars. If you went out at night here on Earth and took a picture using the same settings, you'd see a blank, black sky too, even if it were blazing with stars to your eye."

"As television and movies have become better and better at shaping our views of the world, it is becoming more and more important that we understand what it means to be scientific," Plait observed on the *Bad Astronomy* site. "Like it or not, those that understand science and technology will always have the advantage over those that don't. If everyone had even a basic grasp of scientific principles, this planet would be a better place."

BIOGRAPHICAL AND CRITICAL SOURCES:

PERIODICALS

Library Journal, March 15, 2002, Jeffrey Beall, review of *Bad Astronomy: Misconceptions and Misuses Revealed, from Astrology to the Moon Landing "Hoax,"* p. 105.

Natural History, July, 2001, Robert Anderson, review of *Bad Astronomy* Web site, p. 78.

Publishers Weekly, February 25, 2002, review of *Bad Astronomy,* p. 52.

Science News, April 6, 2002, review of *Bad Astronomy,* p. 223.

ONLINE

Bad Astronomy Web site, http://www.badastronomy. com/ (August 9, 2002).

VirginiaOnlineMag, http://www.virginiaonlinemag.org/ (May 8, 2002), interview with Philip C. Plait.*

* * *

PONTIGGIA, Giuseppe 1934-

PERSONAL: Born September 25, 1934, in Erba, Italy; married Lucia Magnocavallo, 1963; children: Andrea. *Education:* Graduated from Catholic University of Milan, 1959.

ADDRESSES: Agent—c/o Author Mail, Mondadori, Via Mondadori, 20090 Segrate, Milan, Italy.

CAREER: Novelist and translator. Worked in a bank while attending college. Taught Italian language and literature for twenty years.

AWARDS, HONORS: Premio Selezione Campiello, 1978, for *Il giocatore invisible;* Premio Strega, 1989, for *La grande sera.*

WRITINGS:

FICTION

La morte in banca: Cinque racconti e un romanzo breve, Rusconi e Paolazzi (Milan, Italy), 1959, enlarged as *La morte in banca: Un romanzo breve e undici racconti,* Mondadori (Milan, Italy), 1979, enlarged as *La morte in banca: un romanzo breve e sedici racconti,* Mondadori (Milan, Italy), 1991.

L'arte della fuga (title means "The Art of Fleeing"), Adelphi (Milan, Italy), 1968.

Il giocatore invisibile: romanzo, Mondadori (Milan, Italy), 1978, translation by Annapaola Cancogni published as *The Invisible Player,* Eridanos Press (Hygiene, CO), 1988.

Chichita la scimmia parlante, Lisciani & Zampetti (Teramo, Italy), 1979.

Il raggio d'ombra, Mondadori (Milan, Italy), 1983.

La grande sera, Mondadori (Milan, Italy), 1989, translation by Sacha Reabinovitch published as *The Big Night,* Halban (London, England), 1991.

Le sabbie immobili, Mulino (Bologna, Italy), 1991.

Vite di uomini non illustri, Mondadori (Milan, Italy), 1993.

L'isola volante (title means "The Flying Island"), Mondadori (Milan, Italy), 1996.

OTHER

(With Marco Forti) *Almanacco dello specchio, n. 2-1973,* Mondadori (Milan, Italy), 1973.

(Editor) Leonardo Snisgalli, *L'ellisse: poesie 1932-1972,* Mondadori (Milan, Italy), 1974.

Il giardino delle Esperidi, Adelphi (Milan, Italy), 1984.

(Translator, with Leo Lionni) Decimus Magnus Ausonius, *La Mosella,* Verba (Italy), 1984.

(Editor, with Guido Bezzola) *Manzoni europeo,* Cassa di Resparmio delle Provincie Lombarde (Milan, Italy), 1985.

(With Roberto Fedi) *Le Donne, i cavallier, l'arme, gli amori: viaggio per viali e sentieri della letteratura italiana percorsi e ripercorsi a suo tempo fino agli esami e lungo i quali la memoria nostalgica e un po'ironica ama riandare,* Mursia (Milan, Italy), 1986.

(With Franco Della Peruta) *Il tramanto di un regno: il Lombardo-Veneto dalla restaurazione al risorgimento, 1814-1859,* Cassa di Risparmio delle Provincie Lombarde (Milan, Italy), 1988.

(Translator, with Maria Corti) Bonvesin da la Riva, *De magnalibus Mediolani = Le meraviglie di Milano,* Bompiani (Milan, Italy), 1974.

(With Achille Bonito Oliva and Alberto Vacca) *Radici* (exhibition catalogue), Prearo (Milan, Italy), 1991.

(With Giovanni Francesio) *L'officina del racconto, conversazioni con Giuseppe Pontiggia, Paola Capriolo, Michele mari, Aurelio Picca, Vincenzo Pardini, Nico Orengo, Carlo Fruttero, Andrea De Carlo, Vincenzo Cerami, Luca Doninelli,* Nuova Compagnia Editrice (Forlì, Italy), 1996.

(Editor, with Marco Manzoni) *I Volti di Hermann Hesse: atti del Convegno, Milano 27 marzo 1992,* Fondazione Arnoldo e Alberto Mondadori (Milan, Italy), 1993.

I contemporanei del futuro, Mondadori (Milan, Italy), 1998.

(Translator, with Alberto Cavaglion) Isaac Bashevis Singer, *Racconti,* Mondadori (Milan, Italy), 1998.

(With Daniela Marcheschi) Francesco Guicciardini, *Francesco Guicciardini,* Istituto Poligrafico e Zecca dello Stato (Rome, Italy), 1999.

Nati due volte: romanzo, Mondadori (Milan, Italy), 2000.

Edited Carlo Collodi's *I racconti delle fate* (title means "Fairy Tales").

Contributor to *Corriere della Sera.*

Works have been translated into French, Spanish, English, and Czech.

SIDELIGHTS: Italian novelist Giuseppe Pontiggia stands out among his contemporaries for having followed his own distinctive literary style during a period dominated by Neorealism. Influenced by French writer René Daumal, Pontiggia has crafted novels that address existential questions and point out destructive human behavior. In an essay for the *Dictionary of Literary Biography,* Daniela Marcheschi commented, "Pontiggia believes that the quest for truth sustains literature." She also described him as an exceptional writer: "He has shown the ability to reach a balance between fresh creativity and intellectual depth, between irony and emotion, humor and sadness, elegant prose and wealth of meanings. . . . Pontiggia has given his readers a significant picture of Italian society in the twentieth century." One of the author's best-known works is *Il giocatore invisible,* in which he uses the psychological thriller format to show that ethics are an essential base for intellectual endeavors. A former teacher of language and literature, Pontiggia has published numerous other books, including translations of works by other writers.

Pontiggia's childhood growing up outside of Como, Italy was punctuated by tragedy. In 1943 his father was murdered amidst civic unrest. After the family moved to Milan, his sister committed suicide. Pontiggia earned a degree from the Catholic University of Milan and wrote a thesis on the work of Italo Svevo. His interest in literature was shared by his brother Giampiero, who became a poet writing under the name Giampero Neri.

Having worked at a bank while attending university, Pontiggia used the experience as a basis for his first novel, which was originally collected with short stories as *La morte in banca: Cinque racconti e un romanzo breve.* The novel's eighteen-year-old protagonist Carabba is dramatically changed by his time spent working in a bank, where he loses his optimistic outlook under the influence of his aggressive, hate-filled co-workers and the office's mechanized routine. Pontiggia repeatedly and sometimes explicitly presents Carabba as an element in a chess game, an analogy he uses again in other works. This game ends with Carraba's maturation or psychological death and rebirth. The story allows Pontiggia to develop themes including the negative, violent effects of industrialization and the importance of facing reality and accepting life as a mystery.

In a review for *World Literature Today,* Cecilia Ross called *La morte in banca* "a fine psychological study" in which "the reader looks at the struggle through a fine mesh; the talented narrator brings out only the high points." The accompanying six short stories in the enlarged 1979 edition earned even higher praise. Ross said that they "reveal the pen of a writer of distinction." Her brief appraisal noted that they use "few paragraphs, occasionally 'brusque' syntax, masterly dialogue, fast action."

In *L'arte della fuga* Pontiggia experimented with a mostly plotless fictional account focusing on violent crime. The avant-garde work is heavy with symbolism. It features two contrasting central characters, a dogmatic clerk and a writer of cultural criticism. Numerous murders and flights take place, with the clerk and writer interacting with many, often anonymous, figures. According to Marcheschi, the book reflects social pressures to "collectivize" the individual and reveals that "any effort to eschew individual destiny . . . is not only vain but also tragic and absurd because it has to end inevitably in death." Marcheschi described the work as one of Pontiggia's most successful books, but also as having been critically ignored until some twenty years after its publication.

While *Il giocatore invisible* treats many of the same issues found in *L'arte della fuga,* Pontiggia adopted a more conventional format for this novel. It is a psychological thriller that Marcheschi likened to the work of Carlo Emilio Gadda. Marcheschi judged that in this novel, "seeking a middle road between simplicity and complexity, between clarity and enigma," Pontiggia "lays bare the mediocrity and pettiness of his characters who speak hypocritically of truth and sincerity even though they are contradicted at every turn by events around them." The story begins with the central figure, a nameless college professor, being criticized in a professional journal for his assertion that he can confirm the origins of the word "hypocrite." The professor sets out to find this anonymous writer, who shows a real hatred for him. In the process, he begins to look at his wife, his lover, and his colleagues in a new and often unflattering light. When he eventually uncovers the identity of the critic, it has little importance compared to his growing personal problems, which are fueled by his being deceived and deceiving.

The novel's translation as *The Invisible Player* by Annapaola Cancogni was Pontiggia's U.S. debut. Reviews of this version stressed its intellectual qualities and sometimes presented it as difficult to read. A *Publishers Weekly* critic noted that the professor's search is "tediously protracted" and that "readers will find it difficult to muster empathy for him." While the reviewer enjoyed the satirical treatment of academic characters, the novel remains "an earnest performance rather than an enthralling story." A writer for *Kirkus Reviews* was amused by *The Invisible Player* but advised that it is best suited to "an erudite audience." The reviewer said that the plot "seems more like an elaborate joke stretched into a novel . . . than like a credible story, but satirical set-pieces and the development of a psychological love-triangle save it." Lois E. Nesbit reviewed the novel for *American Book Review,* where she described it as an imperfect but still rewarding book. "It is Pontiggia's gift for creating and portraying these idiosyncratic figures with humor and poignancy that saves this book, with its familiar theme and unambitious form, from ordinariness," Nesbit commented. In particular, she admired Pontiggia's dialogue, which she said is "deftly rendered and matches the novel's thesis that all language is lies and deception."

An actual 1927 incident involving the escape of a political prisoner provided the basis for Pontiggia's novel *Il raggio d'ombra*. A doctor without strong political interests is persuaded to take in a fugitive named Losi, who in the end proves to be an informer

assigned to help orchestrate the arrest of others. However, it is the doctor who will receive the worst punishment. A subsequent search for Losi ends in the cemetery where his grave is located. Thus, the pressing question of why he acted as he did remains unanswered. *World Literature Today* reviewer Charles Fantazzi called *Il raggio d'ombra* "a gripping spy story, narrated in a quiet, rapid, unsensational manner." Fantazzi pointed out both the novel's absurd qualities and standard elements of an espionage story, such as secret meetings and dramatic locations. He concluded, "the narrative is suffused with a subdued irony and elusive melancholy that may be construed as a veiled allegory of the political betrayals and moral ambiguities of contemporary Italy."

Pontiggia's best-selling *La grande sera* is a consistently antirealistic novel about a man who abandons his family, friends, and career because he is tired of them. He leaves to create a new life, but the novel stays focused on the lives of the people left in his wake. Marcheschi has likened this approach to "a carousel with strange figures rotating around a hidden pivot" and said of the secondary characters, "they share a gray, unhappy life devoid of meaning and purpose." In a review for *World Literature Today,* Gaetano A. Iannace explained that the novel "tells a story which evolves in an atmosphere of decaying values and the breakdown of such cherished human institutions as marriage and the family." Iannace was strongly critical of what he perceived as the author's liberal use of facts, violence, and sex to create commercial appeal. The critic also was unhappy with Pontiggia's use of satire and humor, which he said "might have been intended as a satire of the human condition," but instead left the reader "hopelessly confused and dissatisfied."

The author uses yet another unconventional approach in *Vite di uomini non illustri,* a fictional encyclopedia of eighteen "non-illustrious" people. Parodying Plutarch's classical model of reviewing famous lives, it instead details the experiences of ordinary people. Their lives are often unhappy and marked by self-deception, with exceptional happiness appearing as a rare occurrence. Describing it as being filled with sarcasm as well as compassion, "informed by caustic intent" as well as stocked with comic relief, Marcheschi called *Vite di uomini non illustri* one of Pontiggia's "most accomplished books."

BIOGRAPHICAL AND CRITICAL SOURCES:

BOOKS

Dictionary of Literary Biography, Volume 196: *Italian Novelists since World War II, 1965-1995,* Gale (Detroit, MI), 1999.

PERIODICALS

American Book Review, May-June, 1990, Lois E. Nesbit, review of *The Invisible Player,* pp. 25-26.
Kirkus Reviews, December 1, 1988, review of *The Invisible Player,* p. 1701.
Publishers Weekly, December, 9, 1988, review of *The Invisible Player,* p. 58.
World Literature Today, spring, 1980, Cecilia Ross, review of *La morte in banca,* p. 266; spring, 1984, Charles Fantazzi, review of *Il raggio d'ombra,* p. 252; spring, 1990, Gaetano A. Iannace, review of *La grande sera,* p. 292.*

*   *   *

POWER, Samantha 1970-

PERSONAL: Born 1970, in Ireland; moved to the United States, 1979. *Education:* Attended Yale University and Harvard Law School.

ADDRESSES: Home—Winthrop, MA. *Office*—Carr Center for Human Rights Policy, Harvard University, 79 J. F. Kennedy St., Cambridge, MA 02138. *E-mail*—samantha_power@harvard.edu.

CAREER: Journalist and educator. *U.S. News and World Report* and *Economist,* reporter, 1993-96; International Crisis Group, political analyst, 1996; Carr Center for Human Rights Policy, John F. Kennedy School of Government, Harvard University, adjunct lecturer in public policy and executive director.

AWARDS, HONORS: Nation Book Critics Circle Award; Pulitzer Prize, 2003, for *A Problem from Hell: America and the Age of Genocide.*

WRITINGS:

Breakdown in the Balkans: A Chronicle of Events, January 1989 to May, 1993, Preface by Morton Abramowitz, Carnegie Endowment for International Peace (Washington, DC), 1993.
(Editor, with Graham Allison), *Realizing Human Rights: Moving from Inspiration to Impact,* St. Martin's Press (New York, NY), 2000.
A Problem from Hell: America and the Age of Genocide, Basic Books (New York, NY), 2002.

Contributor to publications such as *New Republic* and *Atlantic Monthly.*

SIDELIGHTS: In *A Problem from Hell: America and the Age of Genocide,* Irish-born author Samantha Power offers a detailed account of U.S. reactions to international cases of genocide. Power, an adjunct lecturer in public policy at Harvard University, "expertly documents American passivity in the face of Turkey's Armenian genocide, the Khmer Rouge's systematic murder of more than a million Cambodians, the Iraqi regime's gassing of its Kurdish population, the Bosnian Serbian Army's butchery of unarmed Muslims and the Rwandan Hutu militia's slaughter of some 800,000 Tutsi," wrote Laura Secor in *New York Times Book Review.* Other "massacres of similar and larger scale" in countries such as Burundi, Bangladesh, Nigeria, and East Timor are mentioned only briefly due to space limitations in the book, Secor noted.

To Secor, *A Problem from Hell* is "a vivid and gripping work of American history [that] doubles as a prosecutor's brief: time and again, Power recounts, although the United States had the knowledge and the means to stop genocide abroad, it has not acted. Worse, it has made a resolute commitment to not acting. Washington's record, Power ruefully observes, is not one of failure, but success."

Power, a former reporter for *U.S. News and World Report* and *Economist,* has seen first-hand the effects of war as a correspondent in Yugoslavia. Much of her professional work has focused on issues of politics and human rights. She has served as a political analyst for the International Crisis Group (ICG), as the executive director of the Carr Center for Human Rights Policy at Harvard's John F. Kennedy School of

Government, and as the editor of volumes such as *Realizing Human Rights: Moving from Inspiration to Impact,* edited with Graham Allison. In addition, she has taught such classes at Harvard as "Human Rights and U.S. Foreign Policy." It is this deep level of expertise that Power brings to *A Problem from Hell,* a book which the author describes on the *Perseus Books Group Web site* as "an effort to understand why," despite symbolic steps such as Holocaust remembrance, "the United States has never intervened to stop genocide."

Power focuses her expertise on a systematic and historical examination of genocide in *A Problem from Hell.* She sets the theme for the book with a detailed account of the Turkish killings of Armenians during World War I, "what is commonly considered the first modern instance of genocide," wrote an online reviewer for the *Complete Review.* "Despite receiving considerable media attention, the United States took essentially no action that might have limited the killings, a type of nonresponse that, as Power writes, 'established patterns that would be repeated.'" Similar cases of post-World War II genocide face the same level of inaction by the United States.

Power devotes a substantial portion of *A Problem from Hell* to Raphael Lemkin, a Polish attorney born near the turn of the twentieth century who coined the term "genocide." Lemkin's interest in the issue began in 1921 when, while a student at the University of Lvov, he read a news report about a young Armenian survivor of the Turkish massacres, Soghomon Tehlirian, who assassinated Talaat Pasha, a former Turkish minister of the interior. Lemkin wondered why Talaat could not have been held accountable for the massacre. He "was told there was no law under which [Talaat] could have been tried," wrote Brian Urquhart in *New York Review of Books.* Lemkin could not understand why the Armenian could be charged with killing one man while someone responsible for killing hundreds of thousands could not be held accountable. "'It is a crime for Tehlirian to kill a man, but it is not a crime for his oppressor to kill more than a million men?' Lemkin asked. 'This is most inconsistent.' Lemkin transferred to the Lvov law school and spent the rest of his life searching for a way to correct this inconsistency," Urquhart wrote. Lemkin was instrumental bringing the term and concept of "genocide" to a mass audience. "Gaunt, shabby, his pockets brimming over with notes and papers, he was the most indefatigable

and relentless of lobbyists" of the United Nations, Urquhart wrote. "Diplomats, politicians, officials, and correspondents, busy with their own affairs, tried to shake him off, but in Lemkin's single-minded determination there was a heroic quality, an indomitable cheerfulness and sweetness that compelled busy people, often reluctantly, to pay attention to his cause."

In 1948, Lemkin's persistence paid off with the passing of the UN's Convention on the Prevention and Punishment of the Crime of Genocide. "Theoretically, once the convention was ratified states committing genocide would no longer have a legal right to be left alone," Urquhart said. "Genocide, in principle at least, would henceforth be the world's business."

But if genocide became the world's business, *A Problem from Hell* suggests that the world largely ignored it. "Power's book is largely documentary rather than accusatory, but the facts alone are enough to condemn almost all American responses (and lack thereof) to some of the most Heinous and outrageous acts perpetrated over the past hundred years," the *Complete Review* critic wrote. "Because it is a book primarily about the United States and genocide, other countries get off rather lightly," Urquhart observed. "Power's underlying assumption seems to be that only United States leadership could ensure successful action."

Power "presents a superb analysis of the U.S. government's evident unwillingness to intervene in ethnic slaughter," a contributor wrote in *Kirkus Reviews.* A *Publishers Weekly* reviewer noted that Power "offers an uncompromising and disturbing examination of 20th-century acts of genocide and U.S. responses to them." *A Problem from Hell* examines recorded instances of genocide case by case and country by country. "It is depressing, frustrating, and sometimes sickening reading," the *Complete Review* critic remarked. U.S. involvement and intervention "need not always have been military," the *Complete Review* critic wrote. "Financial, political, and other pressure could have also helped in each of these situations. But the U.S. largely simply stood aside."

Despite her stance on U.S. non-intervention, however, Power "gives us a Washington that is vibrant, complex, and refreshingly human," commented Secor. "Within it, she finds an unlikely, bipartisan collection of men and women whose courage and moral commitment she admires." Among those who attempted to influence the government's stance on genocide were Henry Morgenthau, Madeline Albright, Robert Dole, a number of junior State Department officials who resigned in protest over America's lack of action in Bosnia, and Senator William Proxmire, who "regaled the senate with a 'speech a day' for twenty years urging that the United States become a party to the Genocide Convention," Secor wrote.

However, the Washington in Power's book, Secor observed, remains "a place of defeatism, inertia, selfishness, and cowardice. Warnings pass up the chain and disappear. Intelligence is gathered and then ignored or denied. The will of the executive remains steadfastly opposed to intervention; its guiding assumption is that the cost of stopping genocide is great, while the political cost of ignoring it is next to nil."

"In some cases, the stories of genocide were not believed because they were so extreme," the *Complete Review* critic observed. "Power repeatedly notes that many accounts were simply not thought to be credible because the outrages were on such an incredible scale and of such obscene callousness and violence (and often served no remotely rational purpose)."

Throughout *A Problem from Hell*, "Power manages—astonishingly—to keep her emotions largely in check," the *Complete Review* critic observed. "She recounts with some passion, but she never loses her objectivity. For the reader it might be harder going; the events recounted here are as unpalatable and disturbing as it gets. The book is, literally, a terrible one, telling truths that few people probably want to hear."

Despite the book's harsh honesty, it is considered "a well-researched and powerful study that is both a history and a call to action," wrote a *Publishers Weekly* reviewer. A *Kirkus Reviews* critic called *A Problem from Hell* "a well-reasoned argument for the moral necessity of halting genocide wherever it occurs, and an unpleasant reminder of our role in enabling it, however unwittingly." For the *Complete Review* critic, "there is no doubt the book is an impressive accomplishment. This is one of those truly 'important books.' One hopes that it will lead readers to try and influence their elected representatives and help get America to assert some moral leadership in the world. It clearly shows idly standing by is simply not acceptable."

Power's *Realizing Human Rights: Moving from Inspiration to Impact*, edited with Graham Allison, also tackles fundamental human rights issues. Contributors include such well-known public figures as Jimmy Carter and Kofi Annan, academics such as Louis Henkin, and U.S. government officials such as Morton Halperin and John Shattuck. Power and Allison "have gathered an eclectic collection of authors to address the issue of how best to impalement international standards on human rights," wrote D. P. Forsythe in *Choice*. The book offers basic information on human rights combined with "the views of official who have had some practical experience," Forsythe remarked.

BIOGRAPHICAL AND CRITICAL SOURCES:

BOOKS

Power, Samantha, *A Problem from Hell: America and the Age of Genocide*, Basic Books (New York, NY), 2002.

PERIODICALS

Canadian Slavonic Papers, September-December, 1995, Anto Knezevic, review of *Breakdown in the Balkans: A Chronicle of Events, January 1989 to May, 1993*, pp. 552-554.

Choice, May, 2001, D.P. Forsythe, review of *Realizing Human Rights: Moving from Inspiration to Impact*, pp. 1691-1692.

Chronicle of Higher Education, November 12, 1998, "A Hands-on Approach to Human Rights," p. A9.

Economist, March 23, 2002, "How to Stop the Killing: Genocide."

Kirkus Reviews, February 1, 2002, review of *A Problem from Hell: America and the Age of Genocide*, pp. 167-168.

Los Angeles Times, April 7, 2002, Jacob Heilbrunn, review of *A Problem from Hell*, p. R-7.

New Yorker, March 18, 2002, review of *A Problem from Hell*, p. 145.

New York Review of Books, April 25, 2002, Brian Urquhart, review of *A Problem from Hell*, pp. 12-14.

New York Times Book Review, April 14, 2002, Laura Secor, review of *A Problem from Hell*, p. 9.

Publishers Weekly, February 25, 2002, review of *A Problem from Hell*, p. 52.

ONLINE

Complete Review Web site, http://www.complete-review.com/ (May 8, 2002), review of *A Problem from Hell: America and the Age of Genocide.*

Conversation with History, http://globetrotter.berkeley.edu/ (May 2, 2003), interview with Samantha Power.

Perseus Books Group Web site, http://www.perseusbooksgroup.com/ (May 8, 2002), author's comments on *A Problem from Hell: America and the Age of Genocide.*

Samantha Power Web page, http://ksgnotes.harvard.edu (May 2, 2003).*

*   *   *

PRATOLINI, Vasco 1913-1991

PERSONAL: Born October 19, 1913, in Florence, Italy; died January 12, 1991, in Rome, Italy; married Cecilia Punzo (an actress), 1941.

CAREER: Novelist, short-story writer, and essayist. Founder and editor, with Alfonso Gatto, of the literary review magazine *Campi di Marte.*

AWARDS, HONORS: Libera Stampa prize, 1947, for *Cronache di Poveri Amanti;* Viareggio prize, 1955, for *Metello;* Premio Nazionale Feltrinelli (equivalent to the Italian Nobel Prize), Accademia dei Lincei, 1957, for entire body of work; Charles Veillon International prize, 1960, for *Le Scialo.*

WRITINGS:

Il tappeto verde, Vallecchi (Florence, Italy), 1941, reprinted, 1978.

Cronache dal Giro d'Italia (maggio-giugno 1947), Lombardi (Milan, Italy), 1945, reprinted, 1992.

Via de' Magazzini, Vallecchi (Florence, Italy), 1942.

Le amiche, Vallecchi (Florence, Italy), 1943.

Il quartiere, Nuova Biblioteca Editrice (Milan, Italy), 1944, reprinted, Mondadori (Milan, Italy), 1973, translation by Peter Duncan and Pamela Duncan published as *The Naked Streets,* Wyn (New York, NY), 1952, and as *A Tale of Santa Croce,* Peter Owen (London, England), 1952.

Cronaca familiare, Vallecchi (Florence, Italy), 1947, reprinted, Mondadori (Milan, Italy), 1973, translation by Barbara Kennedy published as *Two Brothers,* Orion (New York, NY), 1962, translation by Martha King published as *Family Chronicle,* Italica Press (New York, NY), 1988.

Cronache di poveri amanti, Vallecchi (Florence, Italy), 1947, reprinted, Mondadori (Milano, Italy), 1971, translation published as *A Tale of Poor Lovers,* Viking (New York, NY), 1949, reprinted, Monthly Review Press (New York, NY), 1988.

Mestiere da vagabondo, Mondadori (Milan, Italy), 1947, reprinted, Mondadori (Milan, Italy), 1978.

Un eroe del nostro tempo, Bompiani (Milan, Italy), 1949, reprinted, Mondadori (Milan, Italy), 1972, translation by Eric Mosbacher published as *A Hero of Our Time,* Prentice-Hall (New York, NY), 1951, and as *A Hero of Today,* Hamilton (London, England), 1951.

Le ragazze di San Frediano (title means "The Young Women of San Frediano"), Vallecchi (Florence, Italy), 1949, reprinted, Mondadori (Milan, Italy), 1975.

Gli uomini che si voltano. Diario di villa Rosa, Atlante (Rome, Italy), 1952.

Il mio cuore a Ponte Milvio (title means "My Heart at Ponte Milvio"), Edizioni di Cultura Sociale (Rome, Italy), 1954.

Metello (first novel in trilogy), Vallecchi (Florence, Italy), 1955, reprinted, Mondadori (Milan, Italy), 1989, translation by Raymond Rosenthal published as *Metello,* Little, Brown (Boston, MA), 1968.

Diario sentimentale (title means "Sentimental Diary"), Vallecchi (Florence, Italy), 1956, reprinted, Mondadori (Milan, Italy), 1992.

Lo scialo (second novel in trilogy; two volumes; title means "The Waste"), Mondadori (Milan, Italy), 1960, revised edition (three volumes), 1976.

La costanza della ragione, Mondadori (Milan, Italy), 1963, reprinted, 1987, translation by Raymond Rosenthal published as *Bruno Santini,* Little, Brown (Boston, MA), 1964.

Allegoria e derisione (third novel in trilogy; title means "Allegory and Derision"), Mondadori (Milan, Italy), 1966, reprinted, 1985.

La mia città ha trent'anni (poetry; title means "My City is Thirty Years Old"), Scheiwiller (Milan, Italy), 1967.

Diario del '67, Mondadori (Milan, Italy), 1975.

Calendario del '67. Lettera agli amici salernitani, Catalogo (Salerno, Italy), 1978.

Il mannello di Natascia, Catalogo (Salerno, Italy), 1980, republished as *Il mannello di Natascia e altre cronache in versi e in prosa (1920-1980),* Mondadori (Milan, Italy), 1985.

La lunga attesa. Lettere a Romano Bilenchi, 1933-1972 (title means "The Long Wait: Letters to Romano Bilenchi"), Bompiani (Milan, Italy), 1989.

La carriera di Nini (serial story originally published in eleven installments in *Il Contemporaneo*), Riuniti, 1997.

OTHER

(Editor) Mario Pratesi, *L'eredità,* Bompiani (Milan, Italy), 1942, reprinted, 1965.

(Author of introduction) Victor Hugo, *Cose viste,* Einaudi (Turin, Italy), 1943.

(Editor, with Luigi Incoronato) *Quello che scoprirai: Antologia per la scuola media,* Vallecchi (Florence, Italy), 1953.

(Editor, with Paolo Ricci) Raffaele Viviani, *Poesie,* Vallecchi (Florence, Italy), 1956.

(Editor, with Carlo Bernari) Giagni Giandomenico, *Il confine,* Basilicata (Matera, Italy), 1976.

(Editor, with Sergio Checconi and Franco Mollia) *Il portolano: antologia di letture interdisciplinari,* Calderini (Bologna, Italy), 1983.

Collaborator on several film productions, including *La viacca/The Love Makers,* 1962; *Les mauvais chemins,* 1993; and *Rocco and His Brothers* 1960.

Also contributed articles of political and literary commentary, short stories, and prose to numerous magazines. Author of produced plays *La Domenica della povera gente* (with G. D. Giagni) and *Lungo Viaggio di Natale.* Translator of French fiction into Italian. Works have been translated into many languages including French, German, and Chinese.

SIDELIGHTS: Vasco Pratolini has been heralded as one of the most important Italian fiction writers of the twentieth century. This self-taught author left a valuable legacy to the literature and culture of his generation. In an essay for *Dictionary of Literary Biography,* Anthony Costantini commented: "Few writers in the twentieth century have provoked such intense and conflicting reactions as has Pratolini. . . . His narratives always deal with social and historical

reality even when, as in his early works, he gives lyrical expression to his personal life. Pratolini remained faithful to his vision of the novel as an enduring quest for truth marked by social and moral concerns."

Pratolini was born into a poor working-class family in a Florence tormented by war, in which the harsh realities of survival left no time for intellectual or aesthetic luxuries. Raised from early childhood by his maternal grandmother after his mother's death, Pratolini left home at the age of thirteen, supporting himself through various jobs. Encouraged by friends such as painter Ottone Rosai and writer Elio Vittorini, he studied works by Dante, Giovanni Boccaccio, Franco Sacchetti, Aldo Palazzeschi, and Mario Pratesi (with whom Costantini said he shared a "spiritual affinity and strong social commitment"). He also studied foreign writers such as Charles Dickens, Theodore Dreiser, and Fyodor Dostoyevsky.

Pratolini's political, social, and moral consciousness influenced all his works. The disillusionment that deeply affected Italian society following World War I affected Pratolini as well. According to Frank Rosengarten, writing for *MLN,* Pratolini embraced fascism as a "movement that would vindicate the rights of the poor and the oppressed through a program of national regeneration . . . Mussolini's regime represented to him at once the triumph of order and social discipline over capitalist exploitation. . . . the enfranchisement of Italian youth, and the possibility of a great rebirth of artistic and literary endeavor." He was invited by the editor of *Il Bargello,* the official publication of the Florentine fascist movement, to contribute articles to the paper, and began doing so in 1932 at the age of nineteen. Thus began his literary career.

In 1935 Pratolini developed tuberculosis. He spent two years in sanitariums, where he became deeply introspective. In the 1954 preface to *Diario di Villa Rosa,* Pratolini wrote: "They were two decisive years in every sense. I was violent; I became submissive; I learned to fear death, to respect life—above all, the life of other people, because I had learned to value my own."

During a brief visit to Florence in 1936, Pratolini met Vittorini, the first intellectual in Florence to break with fascism. Rosengarten commented that "The friendship between the two writers was much more than literary in character, and it proved to be of crucial importance to Pratolini's intellectual and moral development." This relationship, and, as Costantini noted, Pratolini's "proletarian consciousness," led to a shift in his social and political perspective, a shift that would lay the foundation for the rest of his literary career.

Costantini called Pratolini's early works "tentative and amorphous in structure, reflecting the themes, style, and even the language of the authors he was reading." After founding the literary review *Campo di Marte* with poet Alfonso Gatto in 1938, however, his writing became more refined and focused. Rosengarten observed that both the tone and content suggested a "marked advance in his emotional and intellectual development," while his most interesting entries in the review concerned literary themes. "He felt a moral obligation to defend the ideal of literature as an instrument of human communication against the encroachments of propaganda, bombast, and sentimentality," wrote Rosengarten.

In a brief article posted on the *Italica Press* Web site following Pratolini's death, the contributor noted that *Campo di Marte* was heavily criticized for "being out of phase with the real needs of our times," and the ultimate suppression of its publication should have been no surprise to its editors. Perhaps not surprised but obviously affronted, Pratolini wrote that this had been "the last dispassionate attempt to initiate a dialectical exchange of views on a common and revolutionary level. . . . In the course of our work . . . we were besieged by the blasphemous assaults of all those who in the name of the established order attacked us, not with plausible reasons, but with vulgar invective and insults."

Pratolini moved to Rome in 1940, worked briefly for the Ministry of Culture, and then began writing a regular column for the literary review *La Ruota,* which encouraged greater realism in literature. His contribution to this and other magazines clarified his intense concern with social issues. By the beginning of World War II, Pratolini was vehemently anti-fascist. Joining the Resistance in 1943, he quickly emerged as a leader. Mario B. Mignone, writing for the *Encyclopedia of World Literature in the Twentieth Century,* commented that after this experience, and with the newfound political freedom in Italy during post-war reconstruction, Pratolini "advanced beyond the restricted dimensions of the autobiographical short story and delicate

prose poem, giving a predominantly social character to his works." Mignone added that the author was "able to convey a strong confidence in man's capacity to change and to shape his own destiny." His Resistance activities were also highly influential in the composition of his book *Il mio cuore a Ponte Milvio.*

Pratolini decided to stay in Rome after the war, and lived there for the rest of his life, devoting himself to his writing. *Cronaca familiare,* written in one week of almost continuous effort following his brother's serious illness and subsequent death, is virtually a conversation with his dead brother that delves into the difficult relationship between the siblings, who barely knew each other. Costantini noted that the work is characterized by "emotional intensity and willful exclusion of fictional elements that would diminish or falsify the relationship."

Mignone observed that, in writing *Il quartiere* and *Cronache di poveri amanti* (the latter having more than fifty characters who collectively form a single protagonist), Pratolini "wove social and personal relationships with larger, historical events," thereby carrying the reader into the working-class world of Florence and exposing life under Mussolini's dictatorship as full of suffering and evil.

The success of *Cronache di poveri amanti* encouraged Pratolini to begin a trilogy, "Una Storia Italiana," in 1950. An ambitious work comprised of *Metello, Lo Scialo,* and *Allegoria e derisione,* the trilogy paints a lengthy portrait of Italian society from 1875 to 1945. Pratolini combines social realism and historical facts to portray what Costantini called "the slow progress toward economic prosperity of the lower classes, the loss of freedom during Fascism, and the failure to realize the yearnings for social justice nurtured by Italians since the unification of the country in 1864."

Mignone observed that Pratolini's major works portray the struggle against exploitation and a desire for solidarity and independence. "It is, indeed, primarily his moral and political commitment and the psychological insight with which he portrays his characters that distinguish Pratolini's work," Mignone wrote.

Pratolini remained relatively silent from 1966 to his death in 1991, publishing several books of poems and letters exchanged with Roman Bilenchi. Costantini called Pratolini an "innovative writer: he did not rewrite the same book but evolved from early lyricism to his neorealistic chronicles to his own version of realism. For the most part, critics have been unwilling to recognize his process of constant renewal. Since the 1980s a new generation of critics, less tied to partisan ideology, has attempted to reassess Pratolini's work, and his integrity as an artist has begun to be appreciated."

BIOGRAPHICAL AND CRITICAL SOURCES:

BOOKS

Bede, Albert, and William B. Edgerton, editors, *Columbia Dictionary of Modern European Literature,* 2nd edition, Columbia University Press (New York, NY), 1980.

Dictionary of Literary Biography, Volume 177: *Italian Novelists since World War II, 1945-1965,* Gale (Detroit, MI), 1997.

Encyclopedia of World Literature in the Twentieth Century, 3rd edition, St. James Press (Detroit, MI), 1999.

Seymour-Smith, Martin, editor, *Novels and Novelists,* St. Martin's Press (New York, NY), 1980.

PERIODICALS

Choice, January, 1989, review of *Family Chronicle,* p. 811.

Contemporary Review, November, 1970, Paul Tabori, "An Interview with Vasco Pratolini," pp. 253-257.

Italian Culture, 1981, Janice M. Kozma, "Functions of Metaphor in Pratolini's *Cronache di poveri amanti:* Maciste and the Signora," pp. 87-102.

Italica, March, 1963, Frank Rosengarten, "Vasco Pratolini's *Una Storia Italiana* and the Question of Literary Realism," pp. 62-72.

MLN, January, 1964, Frank Rosengarten, "A Crucial Decade in the Career of Vasco Pratolini (1932-1942)," pp. 246-268.

Observer (London, England), November 10, 1991, review of *Family Chronicle,* p. 58.

Small Press Review, May, 1989, Robert Hauptman, review of *Family Chronicle,* p. 12.

ONLINE

Italica Press Web site, http://www.italicapress.com/ (June 4, 2001), "Vasco Pratolini."*

PRUTER, Hugo R.
　See PRÜTER, Karl

* 　 * 　 *

PRÜTER, Karl 1920-
　(Hugo R. Pruter)

PERSONAL: Original name, Hugo Rehling Prüter; born July 3, 1920, in Poughkeepsie, NY; son of William Karl (a janitor) and Katherine (Rehling) Prüter; married Nancy Lee Taylor, September 4, 1943 (deceased); children: Hugo Rehling Jr., Robert, Nancy Goodman, Karl, Stephen, Maurice, Katherine. *Education:* Northeastern University, B.A., 1944; Lutheran Theological Seminary, M.Div., 1946; Roosevelt University, M.A. (education), 1963; Boston University, M.A. (history), 1965.

ADDRESSES: Office—Cathedral of the Prince of Peace, P.O. Box 63, Highlandville, MO 54669. *E-mail*—bishopkarl@juno.com.

CAREER: Congregationalist minister, 1946-63; guest lecturer in Landerziehungsheim, Stein, Germany, 1964-65; ordained a priest of Christ Catholic Church, 1965; Church of the Transfiguration, Boston, MA pastor, 1965-70; Christ Catholic Church, presiding archbishop, 1967-91; suffragen bishop, 1991—. Serves the Cathedral of the Prince of Peace, Christ Catholic Church, Highlandville, MO. Also involved, with St. Willibrord's Press and later Cathedral Books, in the publishing and retailing of mail-order books for the religious market, in New Hampshire, New Mexico, Chicago, and Highlandville, MO.

WRITINGS:

(As Hugo R. Pruter) *A Divine Liturgy for the Free Church,* Brownist Press (Berwyn, IL), 1948.

(As Hugo R. Pruter) *Neo-Congregationalism,* Brownist Press (Berwyn, IL), 1957, new edition, Borgo Press (San Bernardino, CA), 1985.

(As Hugo R. Pruter) *The Theology of Congregationalism,* Brownist Press (Berwyn, IL), 1957, reprinted, Borgo Press (San Bernardino, CA), 1985.

The Teachings of the Great Mystics, St. Willibrord's Press (Goffstown, NH), 1969, reprinted, Borgo Press (San Bernardino, CA), 1985.

A History of the Old Catholic Church, St. Willibrord's Press (Scottsdale, AZ), 1973, expanded edition published as *The Old Catholic Church: A History and Chronology,* Borgo Press (San Bernardino, CA), 1996.

The People of God, St. Willibrord's Press (Scottsdale, AZ), 1974.

The Priest's Handbook, St. Willibrord's Press, 1974, second edition, Borgo Press (San Bernardino, CA), 1996.

St. Willibrord, 658-739, St. Willibrord's Press, 1982.

(With J. Gordon Melton) *The Old Catholic Sourcebook,* Garland Publishing (New York, NY), 1983.

A Directory of Autocephalous Anglican, Catholic and Orthodox Bishops, St. Willibrord's Press (Highlandville, MO), 1985, eighth edition published as *A Directory of Autocephalous Bishops of the Churches of the Apostolic Succession,* St. Willibrord's Press (San Bernardino, CA), 1996.

Bishops Extraordinary, St. Willibrord's Press (Highlandville, MO), 1985.

The Strange Partnership of George Alexander McGuire and Marcus Garvey, St. Willibrord's Press (Highlandville, MO), 1986.

Jewish Christians in the United States: A Bibliography, Garland Publishing (New York, NY), 1987.

The House Church Movement, St. Willibrord's Press (Highlandville, MO), 1989.

One Day with God: A Guide to Retreats and the Contemplative Life, St. Willibrord's Press (Highlandville, MO), 1990, revised edition, Borgo Press (San Bernardino, CA), 1991.

The Catholic Priest: A Guide to Holy Orders, edited by Paul David Seldis, Borgo Press (San Bernardino, CA), 1993.

The Story of Christ Catholic Church, St. Willibrord's Press (San Bernardino, CA), 1993, third edition, 1996.

Rufus, St. Willibrord's Press (San Bernardino, CA), 1994.

The Mystic Path, St. Willibrord's Press (San Bernardino, CA), 1997.

AS EDITOR

Rev. Fr. Alexey Young, *The Russian Orthodox Church outside Russia: A History and Chronology,* Borgo Press (San Bernardino, CA), 1993.

Lawrence Barringer, *The American Carpatho-Russian Orthodox Greek Catholic Diocese: A History and Chronology,* Borgo Press (San Bernardino, CA), 1995.

Archpriest Antony Gabriel, *The Ancient Church on New Shores: Antioch in North America,* Borgo Press (San Bernardino, CA), 1996.

Editor of the journal *Pastoral Counseling;* editor and sometimes author of two continuing series of books, *St. Willibrord's Studies in Philosophy and Religion* and *The Autocephalous Orthodox Churches,* both published by Borgo Press; editor and publisher of the periodical, *St. Willibrord Journal.*

SIDELIGHTS: Bishop Karl Prüter is the founder of Christ Catholic Church, one of several Old Catholic denominations in the United States. The Old Catholics retain the ancient practices and sacraments of the original, undivided Catholic Church, including allowing priests to marry, and deny the authority and infallibility of the pope. Since 1983 Prüter has run the Cathedral of the Prince of Peace, in Highlandville, Missouri, which at fifteen-by-seventeen feet is listed in *The Guinness Book of World Records* as the world's smallest cathedral.

Prüter attended a Lutheran seminary and began his career as a Congregationalist minister, but from the early part of his ministry, in the 1940s, Prüter was involved in the Free Catholic movement. The Free Catholics, not connected to the Roman Catholic Church, maintain much of the Catholic liturgy and ritual but allow followers greater freedom to follow their own consciences and to interpret Scripture more freely than the Roman Catholic Church does. When the Congregational Church merged with the Evangelical and Reformed Church in the late 1950s, Prüter found that the ritually oriented, liturgical style of worship favored by the Free Catholic movement was out of place in the newly created church. Prüter left his Congregational ministry in 1963, and late in 1965 he was ordained by an independent Orthodox bishop of the Orthodox Catholic Patriarchate of America. Two years later Prüter was consecrated as an independent Catholic bishop, and shortly thereafter he began to create his own denomination under the name Christ Catholic Church.

As he moved about the country, building his church, Prüter wrote several books about theology and church history. Many of these books were published by Prüter's own press, St. Willibrord's. He also regularly publishes a directory of the names and addresses of independent bishops, which is a useful sourcebook for a decentralized church with few other ways of finding fellow believers. Prüter retired as archbishop of Christ Catholic Church in 1991, but he has remained active in publishing and has continued to teach and spread the gospel through his publications and book distribution network. He has also written a personal project, *Rufus,* which gives an autobiographical account of his many journeys to various independent congregations throughout the United States with his beloved dog and companion of that name.

BIOGRAPHICAL AND CRITICAL SOURCES:

BOOKS

Religious Leaders of America, second edition, Gale (Detroit, MI), 1999.

Ward, Gary, Bertil Persson, and Alan Bain, editors, *Independent Bishops: An International Directory,* Apogee Books, 1990.

PERIODICALS

American Reference Books Annual, 1988, p. 573.
Choice, January, 1984, p. 718; September, 1987, p. 92.

ONLINE

Salina Journal (Salina, KS), http://www.saljournal. com/ (March 7, 2003), Doug Johnson, "Curious Cathedral: Small Missouri Church Seats Only Fifteen but Has a Magnetic Appeal."*

Q-R

QUEEN NOOR
See Al HUSSEIN, Noor

*   *   *

RALEIGH, Debbie 1961-

PERSONAL: Born April 14, 1961, in Casper, WY; daughter of Jim and Carol Hays; married David Raleigh (an administrator of special education), September 29, 1984; children: Chance, Alexander. *Education:* Truman State University, B.A., 1984.

ADDRESSES: Home—Ewing, MO. *Agent*—c/o Author Mail, Kensington Publishing Corp., 850 Third Ave., New York, NY 10022. *E-mail*—djraleigh@hotmail. com.

CAREER: Lewis County C-1 School District, Ewing, MO, bookkeeper, 1999—.

MEMBER: Romance Writers of America, Beau Monde, Rising Stars.

WRITINGS:

NOVELS

Lord Carlton's Courtship, Zebra/Kensington Publishing (New York, NY), 2000.
Spring Kittens Anthology, Zebra/Kensington Publishing (New York, NY), 2000.

Lord Mumford's Minx, Zebra/Kensington Publishing (New York, NY), 2000.
A Bride for Lord Challmond, Zebra/Kensington Publishing (New York, NY), 2001.
Valentine Rogues Anthology, Zebra/Kensington Publishing (New York, NY), 2001.
A Bride for Lord Wickton, Zebra/Kensington Publishing (New York, NY), 2001.
A Bride for Lord Brasleigh, Zebra/Kensington Publishing (New York, NY), 2001.
Christmas Eve Kittens, Zebra/Kensington Publishing (New York, NY), 2001.
The Christmas Wish, Zebra/Kensington Publishing (New York, NY), 2001.
The Valentine Wish, Zebra/Kensington Publishing (New York, NY), 2002.
The Wedding Wish, Zebra/Kensington Publishing (New York, NY), 2002.
Only with a Rogue, Zebra/Kensington Publishing (New York, NY), 2002.
A Taste of Christmas Anthology, Zebra/Kensington Publishing (New York, NY), 2002.
A Proper Marriage (first novel in trilogy), Zebra/Kensington Publishing (New York, NY), 2002.
A Convenient Marriage (second novel in trilogy), Zebra/Kensington Publishing (New York, NY), 2002.

WORK IN PROGRESS: A Scandalous Marriage, the third novel in a trilogy; *Mother's Day Anthology, Bewitching Season Anthology,* and *One Night with a Rogue Anthology,* all for Zebra/Kensington Publishing (New York, NY), completion expected 2003.

SIDELIGHTS: Debbie Raleigh told *CA:* "My love for writing began at a very young age and was influenced heavily by writers such as Jane Austen, Georgette Heyer, and George Bernard Shaw. Their clever wit and ability to capture the foolishness of human vanity has always fascinated me. To be able to capture characters that transcend generations is a goal I am always striving to meet. Such writers also influenced my decision to write during the Regency period. I love the drawing-room comedies that can make a reader laugh at the same time they can help a reader to consider the changes that have occurred in both political and social norms. My trilogy, *A Convenient Marriage, A Proper Marriage,* and *A Scandalous Marriage,* deals with the expected roles of women in marriage during the early 1800s as well as the social reactions to strong-willed women who dare to step out of the traditional mold."

*   *   *

REED, Barry C(lement) 1927-2002

OBITUARY NOTICE—See index for *CA* sketch: Born January 28, 1927, in San Francisco, CA; died July 19, 2002, in Norwood, MA. Attorney and author. Reed was a highly respected trial lawyer who gained national attention as the author of the bestselling novel *The Verdict* (1980). Earning his bachelor's degree from Holy Cross College in 1949 after serving in the U.S. Army during World War II, Reed went on to receive his law degree from Boston College in 1954 and was admitted to the Massachusetts Bar the following year. Entering into practice in Boston, Reed earned a solid reputation as an attorney specializing in medical malpractice, personal injury, and civil litigation cases. For his outstanding legal work, he was honored with the Clarence Darrow Award for trial excellence. Reed was also a former president of the Massachusetts Trial Lawyers Association, cofounder of the American Society of Law and Medicine, and one-time governor of the Massachusetts Academy of Trial Lawyers. Before he gained literary fame with *The Verdict,* Reed was the coauthor of *The Heart and the Law: A Practical Guide to Medicolegal Cardiology* (1968) and *The Law and Clinical Medicine* (1970). The success of his first novel, which was adapted as the 1982 Academy Award-winning film of the same title, encouraged Reed to publish three more works of fiction: *The Choice* (1991), *The Indictment* (1994), and *The Deception* (1997).

OBITUARIES AND OTHER SOURCES:

PERIODICALS

Chicago Tribune, July 22, 2002, section 2, p. 7.
Los Angeles Times, July 22, 2002, p. B9.
New York Times, July 23, 2002, p. A17.
Washington Post, July 23, 2002, p. B6.

*   *   *

REINHOLD, Meyer 1909-2002

OBITUARY NOTICE—See index for *CA* sketch: Born September 1, 1909, in Brooklyn, NY; died July 1, 2002, in Nashville, TN. Historian, educator, and author. Reinhold was a scholar of the classics and worked to popularize Greek and Roman literature. He received his A.B. from the City College of the City University of New York in 1929 and his doctorate from Columbia University in 1933; he then studied in Rome for two years as a fellow of the American Academy. From 1938 to 1955 Reinhold taught classical languages and literature at Brooklyn College, but he was fired when, during the McCarthy era, he refused to reveal any of his political affiliations to the government (the college later apologized to him and others for these unjust dismissals). In need of work, he joined his brother's advertising firm, Richmond Advertising Services, where he was vice president for ten years. Reinhold returned to academia as an associate professor of Greek, Latin, and ancient history at Southern Illinois University, moving on to the University of Missouri at Columbia in 1967 as professor of classical studies. Promoted to Byler Distinguished Professor of Classical Studies in 1976, Reinhold left the university as emeritus professor in 1980. However, he did not retire from teaching, and went on to found the Institute for the Classical Tradition at Boston University, where he was a visiting professor until 1995. Reinhold was also founder and coeditor of the *International Journal of the Classical Tradition.* As a teacher, he went against tradition in his belief that the classics should be taught in translation so that those who could not read Greek or Latin could also appreciate these ancient works. Among his publications, many of which have remained in use in U.S. colleges, are some two dozen authored and edited books, including *The Classical Drama* (1959), *Es-*

sentials of Greek and Roman Classics: A Guide to the Humanities (1971), and *Studies in Classical History and Society* (2001).

OBITUARIES AND OTHER SOURCES:

PERIODICALS

New York Times, July 5, 2002, p. A19.
Tennessean, July 4, 2002, p. B3.

*   *   *

RENÉE, Janina 1956-

PERSONAL: Born March 4, 1956, in Detroit, MI; children: Tom, Alyn (sons). *Ethnicity:* "White." *Education:* Chapman College, B.A. (anthropology), 1977; postgraduate work in American studies, Michigan State University. *Politics:* "Political moderate." *Religion:* "Buddhist eclectic."

ADDRESSES: Agent—c/o Author Mail, Llewellyn Publications, P.O. Box 64383, St. Paul, MN 55164-0383.

CAREER: Writer.

MEMBER: Autism Society of Michigan.

AWARDS, HONORS: Best Self-Help Book Award, Coalition of Visionary Retailers (COVR), 2000, for *Tarot: Your Everyday Guide: Practical Problem Solving and Everyday Advice;* Best General Interest Title Award, COVR, 2001, for *Tarot for a New Generation.*

WRITINGS:

Tarot Spells, illustrated by Robin Wood, Llewellyn Publications (St. Paul, MN), 1990.
Playful Magic, Llewellyn Publications (St. Paul, MN), 1994.
Tarot: Your Everyday Guide: Practical Problem Solving and Everyday Advice, Llewellyn Publications (St. Paul, MN), 2000.
Tarot for a New Generation (for young adults), Llewellyn Publications (St. Paul, MN), 2001.

WORK IN PROGRESS: By Candlelight: Rites for Celebration, Blessing, and Prayer, for Llewellyn Publications (St. Paul, MN); "Research on the use of ritualism in nature writing and in material culture; the role and subject position of high-functioning autistic people in history, literature, and culture."

SIDELIGHTS: The author of two adult books on tarot published a decade apart, in 2001 Janina Renée published *Tarot for a New Generation,* which is geared to young adults. In it, she explains how to interpret the tarot card deck. Reflecting on her works about tarot, she told *CA:* "I am not a writer of children's books per se, as *Tarot for a New Generation* is the only one of my books that is specially aimed at a young audience. I wrote this book because there are (to my knowledge) no other tarot manuals addressing young people's concerns, even though shop owners tell me that large numbers of teenagers buy tarot cards, and many of them actually collect different decks."

Renée continued to *CA,* "I have been concerned because so many teenagers and other young people don't seem to have any dreams or plans for the future, but I believe the tarot's vast collection of images can ignite their imaginations and ambitions by highlighting many paths of possibility. The tarot interpretations which I provide cover many areas of life, but they consistently advocate a strong ethical code and sense of responsibility.

"Also, as the mother of a child with Asperger's syndrome (a form of autism spectrum disorder) and a person who suffers myself from many Asperger's-type symptoms, I have a long-standing interest in learning disabilities. For this reason, *Tarot for a New Generation* includes a chapter which touches on different learning styles and discusses how tarot imagery can be used to aid memory and inspire homework projects. As part of my continuing research, I am exploring ways that other areas of folk wisdom can be applied to learning challenges. I am also researching different ethnic and traditional means of blessing children and developing their self-esteem, moral character, work ethic, and the like."

BIOGRAPHICAL AND CRITICAL SOURCES:

PERIODICALS

School Library Journal, January, 2002, Sheryl Fowler, review of *Tarot for a New Generation,* pp. 172-173.

RIDDLES, Libby 1956-

PERSONAL: Born April 1, 1956, in Madison, WI; daughter of Willard P. (a college professor) and Mary Reynolds (an educator and homemaker) Riddles.

ADDRESSES: Office—P.O. Box 15253, Fritz Creek, AK 99603.

CAREER: Author and lecturer, 1985—; also worked as a sled dog racer, television commentator, and sled dog wrangler. Arctic Winter Games International, board member, 1990-97.

MEMBER: Iditarod Trail Committee.

AWARDS, HONORS: First woman to win the Iditarod Race, 1985; Leonard Sepella Humanitarian Award, Alaska Airlines, 1985; Professional Sports Woman of the Year, Women's Sports Foundation, 1985; Victor Award for Excellence in Sports; Best Books for Young Adults selection, American Library Association, 1988, for *Race across Alaska.*

WRITINGS:

(With Tim Jones) *Race across Alaska: First Woman to Win the Iditarod Tells Her Story,* Stackpole Books (Harrisburg, PA), 1988.
(With Shelley Gill) *Danger, the Dog Yard Cat* (with audiocassette), Paws IV (Homer, Alaska), 1989.
Storm Run, Paws IV (Homer, Alaska), 1996, published as *Storm Run: The Story of the First Woman to Win the Iditarod Sled Dog Race,* 2002.

SIDELIGHTS: Libby Riddles is an author and champion sled dog racer who lives in Alaska. In 1985, she became the first woman ever to win the Iditarod, a thousand mile dog sled race across Alaska. Coauthored with Tim Jones, Riddles' book *Race across Alaska: First Woman to Win the Iditarod Tells Her Story* recounts her grueling race along some of Alaska's roughest country. The book also includes details of her life in Alaska with her fifty dogs, how she became interested in dog sledding, and how she trained. Riddles retells her story for a younger audience in the 1996 title *Storm Run.* Riddles is also the coauthor,

with Shelley Gill, of *Danger, the Dog Yard Cat,* published in 1990. Also for young readers, *Danger* features the story of Riddles' cat in real life, who seems to want to lead a dogsled team.

As a writer, Riddles did not always feel as confident as she does with her dogs. She told *NASA Quest,* "I was a natural writer, even as a child, but didn't have much confidence. That came with experience, and by being successful with smaller goals." When asked about living her dream, she responded, "I think it's important for young people to spend those years being kids and finding out what kinds of things they like without having to worry too much about their future. If you have the chance to explore and see what things there are to do out there and then follow where you feel the most passion, the future tends to take care of itself."

Riddles told *CA:* "I started writing journals when I was twelve—writing seemed like a natural form of expression to me. I moved to Alaska when I was sixteen, ready for a life of adventure. Twelve years later, after becoming the first woman to win the 1,000 mile Iditarod Sled Dog Race, I wrote my first book, *Race across Alaska.* I wanted to share the experience, as so many people had written to me, fascinated by the story. A lot of my racing fan mail came from children, so it seemed natural to write a book for kids. *Danger* is the almost true story of my cat who lives with fifty-seven sled dogs. It is a collaboration with Shelley Gill and illustrator Shannon Cartwright. We made a cassette tape to go along with it, with songs and the text narrated. I hoped to show kids our Alaskan lifestyle in a fun way and encourage them to be anything they want to be.

"*Storm Run* is my race story, but for children. This book is more educational with maps and gear information.

"My writing habits are not so great, as I still have about forty sled dogs, so my writing doesn't always get priority. Having deadlines helps me get with the program. It gives me a great sense of accomplishment to have become an author. Being a strong reader was key to my having enough imagination to find such a unique lifestyle for myself. I hope through my writing to inspire people to reach for their own adventures."

BIOGRAPHICAL AND CRITICAL SOURCES:

BOOKS

Encyclopedia of Women and Sports, ABC-CLIO (Santa Barbara, CA), 1996.
Women's Firsts, Gale (Detroit, MI), 1997.

PERIODICALS

Booklist, March 15, 1989, p. 1280; March 1, 2002, p. 1148.
People Weekly, May 7, 1990, p. 45.
Publishers Weekly, February 25, 2002, p. 69.

ONLINE

Libby Riddles Web site, http://www.alaska.net/~riddles (November 20, 2002).
NASA Quest, http://quest.arc.nasa.gov/ (November 20, 2002), interview with Libby Riddles.*

*　　*　　*

ROSOW, Jerome M(orris) 1919-2002

OBITUARY NOTICE—See index for *CA* sketch: Born December 2, 1919, in Chicago, IL; died October 11, 2002, in Bronx, NY. Business manager, government adviser, and author. Rosow was an expert in employee productivity and personnel management, and is most remembered as the founder of the Work in America Institute. He was a graduate of the University of Chicago, where he earned a bachelor's degree in 1942 before working for the federal government for ten years in personnel and policy. He took his knowledge of personnel issues with him when he was hired by several oil companies, including Creole Petroleum, Exxon, and Esso, during the 1950s and 1960s. After working for two years as assistant secretary of labor for the U.S. Department of Labor, he returned to Exxon as a manager in public affairs and planning. In 1975 he founded the Work in America Institute in Scarsdale, New York. The institute, for which Rosow was also chairman, was a think tank for businesses to develop better ways to increase employee productivity.

One of the major conclusions arrived at was that employees who have a say in company policies that affect them are more productive. Rosow, who had also served as an advisor to three U.S. presidents, wrote several authoritative books about employees, management, and productivity in the United States, including *New Work Schedules for a Changing Society* (1981), *Employment Security in a Free Economy* (1984), and *Made in America* (1984); he also edited such works as *The Worker and the Job* (1974), *Productivity Prospects for Growth* (1981), and *The Global Marketplace* (1988).

OBITUARIES AND OTHER SOURCES:

BOOKS

Who's Who in America, 56th edition, Marquis (New Providence, NJ), 2001.

PERIODICALS

New York Times, October 21, 2002, p. A21.
Washington Post, October 22, 2002, p. B6.

*　　*　　*

ROTE, Kyle 1928-2002

OBITUARY NOTICE—See index for *CA* sketch: Born October 27, 1928, in San Antonio, TX; died of cardiopulmonary complications from pneumonia August 15, 2002, in Baltimore, MD. Professional athlete, sportscaster, and author. Rote was a star football player for the New York Giants during the 1950s and early 1960s. He attended Vanderbilt University and then transferred to Southern Methodist University, where his obvious talents led to his nomination for the Heisman Trophy in 1950. In 1951 he joined the Giants, where he played running back and split end positions for eleven seasons, captaining the team for ten. While playing for the Giants, his team appeared in four national championships and won the title against the Chicago Bears in 1958. After he retired, Rote was inducted into the Football Hall of Fame in 1964. His post-football career consisted of work as a broadcaster for NBC television and, during the 1960s, as director of sports and community relations for WNEW-Radio in New York City. He also served as national sports director for the National Foundation for Neuromuscular Disease and the Society for the Prevention of Juvenile Delinquency. Rote was the author of three books about football, including *The Language of Pro Football* (1966), and two books on soccer, including *Wilson Guide to Soccer* (1994), written with Donn Risolo.

OBITUARIES AND OTHER SOURCES:

BOOKS

Hickok, Ralph, *A Who's Who of Sports Champions,* Houghton (Boston, MA), 1995.

PERIODICALS

Los Angeles Times, August 16, 2002, p. B13.
New York Times, August 16, 2002, p. A17.

*   *   *

ROWER, Ann 1938-

PERSONAL: Born 1938.

ADDRESSES: Home—60-82 60th Dr., Maspeth, NY 11378-3536. *Office*—School of Visual Arts, 209 East 23rd St., New York, NY 10010.

CAREER: Writer. School of Visual Arts, New York, NY, member of faculty.

WRITINGS:

If You're a Girl, Semiotext(e) (Brooklyn, NY), 1990.
Armed Response, Serpent's Tail (New York, NY), 1996.
Baby, Serpent's Tail, (New York, NY), 2002.
Lee and Elaine, Serpent's Tail (New York, NY), 2002.

Contributor to periodicals such as *BOMB, Journal of Contemporary Fiction,* and *High Risk 2.*

WORK IN PROGRESS: Biography of her uncle, singer Leo Robin.

SIDELIGHTS: Author Ann Rower "has a word for the fiction/nonfiction crossover: transfiction," wrote Regina Weinreich in *American Book Review,* noting that it is an attractive word, because of the combination of the words transfix and trance, and the inherent pun on the word "transfixion." Rower's 1990 book, *If You're a Girl,* is such a fiction/nonfiction hybrid, Weinreich wrote, an "experiment in how to write about what actually occurred," Weinreich observed. Among the segments of the book are transcriptions of an interview with Rower conducted by the Wooster Theater Group, in which she describes in detail her early days as a babysitter for Timothy Leary's kids—and frequently, for his distinguished visitors. "Especially poignant are her descriptions of relationships, so full of a resigned tone," Weinreich wrote. "I'm not sure if it was supposed to be like this, but this is the way it is anyway."

Rower's 1996 book, *Armed Response,* is a "bitterly funny novel about death, personal space, and home-security systems in L.A.," wrote Glen Helfand on the *Guardian Lit* Web site. "In this hauntingly bitchy book the city is a glittering upscale necropolis. It's filled with European sports cars, circular Wilshire Boulevard condominiums, lavish, never-used swimming pools, and the chic air-conditioned eateries."

The book's narrator, Ann, is a New York writer who must make regular trips to the west coast to attend funerals and death-watches for soon-to-expire relatives. The story revolves around Ann, her aunt Cherrie, and Cherrie's daughter Lainie's family. "They're an entertaining, tragic lot," Helfand observed. Though deteriorating physically, Cherrie maintains her own dignity as well as a grip on the dignity of old Hollywood. Lainie, on the other hand, lives in high-class but repressive suburban luxury. Lainie's husband Rocky is a lout and her daughter Candee is a depressed aspiring actress. In *Armed Response* "Rower gives entertainingly sociological insight into her ironically regional characters," Helfand wrote. To someone with little direct experience with L.A., Rower's characters may seem like stereotypes, Helfand remarked. "But take it from a native—this stuff is for real."

"As she scratches the surface of this shiny landscape," Helfand noted, "Rower reveals aspects of the city's inherent alienation and unique social boundaries." This includes a type of claustrophobic panic that ultimately leads Candee to commit suicide by ingesting rat poison; her funeral is an exercise in the banal, another aspect of L.A. life illuminated by the novel. "Rower taps into highly universal themes and draws not-so-unlikely connections between the genuine pain you feel when a favorite auntie passes away and what you feel when you find out that she didn't will you the Jag."

In Rower's 2002 novel *Lee and Elaine*, the unnamed narrator, a painter and art teacher in New York, is jolted into a midlife crisis by the death of an old friend. While visiting the Green River Cemetery in the Hamptons, the narrator happens upon the graves of Lee Krasner and Elaine de Kooning—wives of famed painters Jackson Pollock and Willem de Kooning. She becomes convinced that there is a connection between the two wives; she decides to write a book reimagining the wives as close friends and lesbian lovers. "*Lee and Elaine* is the saga of her not writing this book," wrote Carol Anshaw in *Advocate*.

The narrator, which Anshaw called "one of the most self-absorbed protagonists in modern fiction," uses the research as "a way for the narrator to avoid her own failed career, her fears of aging, and the disintegration of a 20-year relationship with her live-in boyfriend," wrote a *Publishers Weekly* reviewer. The narrator engages in a lesbian relationship with Iris, one of her students, and has liaisons with other younger women when the affair with Iris dissolves. Her sporadic research on Lee and Elaine reveals that the women were not only straight, but didn't seem to like each other much at all. "The upshot: she doesn't have much of a story, and neither do we," wrote a *Kirkus Reviews* critic.

"There is something hugely irritating but nonetheless riveting about the childlike way this character views life—all of it—as something that's essentially about her," Anshaw commented. "Perhaps many people feel this way; they're just too embarrassed to admit it, except perhaps to their journals. Reading *Lee & Elaine* offers precisely something of this guilty pleasure, like picking up a stranger's diary off a bus seat."

BIOGRAPHICAL AND CRITICAL SOURCES:

BOOKS

A Dictionary of American Poets and Fiction Writers, 1999-2000 edition, Poets & Writers, Inc. (New York, NY), 1998.

PERIODICALS

Advocate, Carol Anshaw, April 2, 2002, review of *Lee and Elaine,* p. 75.
Booklist, February 15, 2002, Whitney Scott, review of *Lee and Elaine,* p. 994.
Kirkus Reviews, August 15, 1995, review of *Armed Response,* p. 1139; February 1, 2002, review of *Lee and Elaine,* p. 141.
Publishers Weekly, October 9, 1995, review of *Armed Response,* p. 82; February 25, 2002, review of *Lee and Elaine,* p. 43.
Village Voice Literary Supplement, June, 1991, review of *If You're a Girl,* p. 29.

ONLINE

Guardian Lit Web site, http://www.sfbg.com/ (May 9, 2002), Glen Helfand, "Forever L.A.; Death, Space, and Home-Security Systems in Los Angeles," review of *Armed Response.*
Advocate Web Site, http://www.advocate/com (May 9, 2002), Carol Anshaw, "Narcissistic Sister."*

*   *   *

RUDDICK, James 1923-

PERSONAL: Born June 11, 1923, in Elmira, NY; son of James H. and Mary Cordelia (Litzelman) Ruddick. *Education:* Fordham University, 1940-44; Woodstock College, A.B., 1946, Ph.L., 1947, S.T.L., 1956; St. Louis University, M.S., 1950, Ph.D., 1952. *Religion:* Roman Catholic.

ADDRESSES: Office—Canisius College, 2001 Main St., Buffalo, NY 14208. *E-mail*—ruddick@canisius. edu.

CAREER: Writer, journalist, and educator. Joined Society of Jesus, 1940; ordained Roman Catholic priest, 1955. St. Peter's College, Jersey City, NJ, instructor in physics, 1947-48; Canisius College, Buffalo, NY, assistant professor of physics, 1957-64, associate professor of physics, 1964—, director, seismology station, 1969—. Jesuit Community, rector, 1971—; Senate Priests, Buffalo Diocese, vice president, 1973-74; St. Peter's College, Jersey City, JN, trustee, 1970-76; Canisius College, Buffalo, NY, trustee, 1971—.

MEMBER: New York Academy of Sciences, American Physics Society, Optical Society of America, American Association of Physics Teachers, Sigma Xi.

WRITINGS:

Lord Lucan, the Truth about the Century's Most Celebrated Murder Mystery, Headline (London, England), 1994.
Death at the Priory: Love, Sex, and Murder in Victorian England, Atlantic Monthly Press (New York, NY), 2001.

SIDELIGHTS: A murder mystery more than 125 years old is the focus of James Ruddick's *Death at the Priory; Love, Sex, and Murder in Victorian England.* The 1876 poisoning of prominent attorney Charles Bravo has long puzzled sleuths; even Agatha Christie declared it "one of the most mysterious poisoning cases ever recorded," wrote Paul Collins in *New York Times Book Review.* In *Death at the Priory,* Ruddick presents new evidence and detailed investigation which, he believes, points directly to the obvious culprit in the murder.

Ruddick is an ordained Roman Catholic priest and a lifelong journalist and educator. In *Death at the Priory,* Ruddick covers in detail the fatal poisoning of barrister Charles Bravo. "The sensational 1876 domestic poisoning," wrote a *Publishers Weekly* reviewer, is highlighted by "archetypal mystery elements, including a gloomy south London mansion, inscrutable servants, rejected lovers, a despicable victim, and a protagonist embodying her era's tortured sexual politics." The murder and the resulting inquest, which revealed sexual indiscretions on the part of Florence Bravo, generated as much public interest and notoriety as the Whitechapel murders of Jack the Ripper twelve years later.

The story begins with Florence Campbell, "an uncommonly independent young woman," wrote Mike Snyder at the *HoustonChronicle.com* Web site, Yet Florence "was the proverbial bird in the gilded cage," wrote Mary Ann Gwinn in a review at the *Seattle Times* Web site. "A young and beautiful daughter of a famous industrialist, she was raised in a 10-bedroom mansion surrounded by 3000 acres of parkland," Gwinn noted. However, Victorian England imposed considerable restrictions on young women of the time, barring them from education and professional work, forcing them into arranged marriages, and widely denying them rights that are taken for granted in modern society.

Florence married Alexander Ricardo but left him seven months after their marriage, after discovering he was an abusive, philandering alcoholic. However, she was ordered to return to him by her father. Instead, her mother arranged a stay at a sanatorium for Florence to recover before attempting a reconciliation with Ricardo.

The sanatorium Florence attended, called the Hydro, was managed by Dr. James Gully, a noted physician who had attended notables such as Dickens, Darwin, Gladstone, and Disrali. Gully, over forty years Florence's senior, "was kind and solicitous," Synder remarked, "and his attitudes about women were beyond progressive for his time." Florence finally left Ricardo for good, and he died shortly thereafter, leaving Florence a considerable fortune. But soon it was revealed that Gully and Florence had been engaged in an extended affair, before and after Ricardo's death, and the affair ended bitterly with an abortion, a lurid scandal, and Florence's social humiliation and ostracization.

Then Florence met Charles Bravo, "a socially respectable lawyer of her own age, and managed—with the help of her housekeeper, Mrs. Cox—to attract a marriage proposal from him despite her damaged reputation," Snyder wrote. Florence's wealth "was no doubt a major factor," Snyder observed. Charles Bravo turned out to be just as unpleasant and domineering as Ricardo, seizing control of Florence's fortune and abusing her psychologically and sexually. Bravo soon began indiscriminately dismissing Florence's servants at their south London mansion, the Priory. At risk of firing and attendant poverty was Mrs. Cox, "fiercely loyal to her mistress and facing the prospect of dismissal at Bravo's hands," Snyder wrote, and George Griffiths, a former coachman "publicly bitter about his recent sacking by Bravo," wrote Jackson.

One night in July, 1876, someone slipped a lethal dosage of poison into Bravo's bedside drinking water. In the "fifty-five excruciating hours" it took Bravo to die, wrote Thomas Jackson in *Forbes FYI,* his physicians had plenty of time to determine that he had been deliberately poisoned—but neither they, nor Bravo himself, could say who had done it.

The list of suspects, however, was lengthy. At first, suspicion focused on Mrs. Cox, because she seemingly provided misleading information to doctors and investigators in the case. Following the sensational inquest that revealed all the details of Florence Bravo's indiscretions, it was concluded that there was insufficient evidence to name a murderer. British authorities never solved the crime. Jane Cox eventually settled in Jamaica, and Florence Bravo, after the ordeal of the inquest, "drank herself to death," Snyder wrote.

Death at the Priory "is as full of dastardly villains and ladies in distress as any bodiceripper, but it also maintains a scholarly meticulousness," wrote a *Kirkus Reviews* critic. "Masterful detective work and storytelling keep the suspense high through the final pages."

More than a century and a quarter later, Ruddick "has uncovered fresh evidence, and he believes he's got the mystery licked," Jackson wrote. Following a trail of evidence across the Americas, Europe, and Australia, "Ruddick has done much admirable sleuthing," remarked Collins, and Snyder observed that "His research was impressively thorough—he reviewed original investigative documents, interviewed descendants of the principal characters, and traveled to Jamaica, where Jane Cox had settled after Bravo's death."

Nicola Upson in *New Statesman* wrote, "True crime can license greater flights of the imagination than fiction, but *Death at the Priory* has its feet refreshingly on the ground, and what Ruddick lacks in style he makes up for with exhaustive research . . . and, most importantly, considerable social and historical awareness to produce a solution that is not just plausible, but inevitable."

In addition to primary sources, original documents, and descendants of participants, Ruddick also had access to evidence previously inaccessible to other researchers of the Bravo case. This new evidence, including unpublished letters and family papers, provided "a rather surprising detail about Mrs. Cox that arguably cracks the case," Jackson wrote.

Although critics generally believed Ruddick's investigation to be exhaustively thorough and his conclusions effectively presented, some still questioned his solution to the mystery. "Ruddick's evidence is certainly persuasive, if not conclusive," Snyder remarked. A *Kirkus Reviews* contributor observed that Ruddick's work had produced a satisfactory solution with considerable support by the evidence, although it is a solution that is "not, perhaps, airtight." To Upson, "Ruddick's conclusions are hardly shattering, and the final twist, the moment of realization, never quite happens." Robert C. Jones, writing in *Library Journal,* remarked that Ruddick "has produced a book that is both murder mystery and social history," but further concluded that *Death at the Priory* "is not convincing in either capacity." Snyder remarked that "Ruddick's investigation is essentially a distraction from the far more interesting story of Florence Campbell, who defied the rigid social conventions that amounted to the enslavement of women in Victorian England."

Still, "Ruddick is extraordinarily good at dissecting a woman, her marriage, and society," Upson wrote. "The order and 'normality' demanded of Victorian women came at a dreadfully high price," Gwinn observed, concluding that "Ruddick traces, with precise logic, forces that dictated that Florence Bravo's ordeal would end with blood on the drawing-room floor."

BIOGRAPHICAL AND CRITICAL SOURCES:

PERIODICALS

Armchair Detective, spring, 1996, S. M. Tyson, review of *Lord Lucan, the Truth about the Century's Most Celebrated Murder Mystery,* p. 250.

Forbes FYI, March 4, 2002, Thomas Jackson, review of *Death at the Priory: Love, Sex, and Murder in Victorian England,* p. 84.

Kirkus Reviews, October 15, 2001, review of *Death at the Priory,* p. 1472.

Legal Times, February 25, 2002, Beth Johnston, review of *Death at the Priory,* p. 25.

Library Journal, October 15, 2001, Robert C. Jones, review of *Death at the Priory,* p. 93.

Los Angeles Times, January 21, 2002, Merle Rubin, "Fabled Murder Case Gets a Retelling—and a New Ending," p. E3.

New Statesman, October 8, 2001, Nicola Upson, "Who Killed Bravo?" p. 53.

New York Times Book Review, February 10, 2002, Paul Collins, review of *Death at the Priory,* p. 23.

Publishers Weekly, October 22, 2001, review of *Death at the Priory,* p. 59.

ONLINE

HoustonChronicle.com, http://www.chron.com/ (May 9, 2002), Mike Snyder, "A Victorian Murder."

Seattle Times Web site, http://seattletimes.nwsource.com/ (May 9, 2002), Mary Ann Gwinn, "Victorian Murder Mystery Reveals the Dark Side of the British Class System."*

*   *   *

RUMSTUCKLE, Cornelius
See BRENNAN, J(ames) H(erbert)

S

SALISACHS, Mercedes (Rovilralta) 1916-

PERSONAL: Born September 18, 1916, in Barcelona, Spain; married, 1935; children: five. *Education:* Attended School of Commerce, Barcelona. *Hobbies and other interests:* Interior decorating, travel.

ADDRESSES: Agent—c/o Author Mail, Plaza y Janés Editor, Enric Granados 86-88, Barcelona 8008, Spain.

CAREER: Novelist and short story writer. Interior decorating firm, partner.

AWARDS, HONORS: City of Barcelona prize, 1960, for *Una mujer llega al pueblo;* Premio Planeta, 1975, for *La gangrena.*

WRITINGS:

Fohen, c. 1940, revised and published as *Adán Helicóptero,* Editorial AHR (Barcelona, Spain), 1957.
Los que se queden, Juventud (Barcelona, Spain), 1942.
Primera mañana, última mañana, Liberia de Caralt (Barcelona, Spain), 1955, reprinted, Plaza y Janés (Barcelona, Spain), 1999.
Carretera intermedia, Libreria de Caralt (Barcelona, Spain), 1956, reprinted, Plaza y Janés (Barcelona, Spain), 1999.
Más allá de los raíles, Libreria de Caralt (Barcelona, Spain), 1957.
Una mujer llega al pueblo (title means "A Woman Comes to Town"), Planeta (Barcelona, Spain), 1957, reprinted, Plaza y Janés (Barcelona, Spain), 1999, translation by Delano Ames published as *The Eyes of the Proud,* Harcourt Brace (New York, NY), 1960.

Pasos conocidos, Pareja y Borrás (Barcelona, Spain), 1958.
Vendimia interrumpida, Planeta (Barcelona, Spain), 1960.
La estación de las hojas amarillas, Planeta (Barcelona, Spain), 1963, reprinted, Plaza y Janés (Barcelona, Spain), 1999.
El declive y la cuesta, Planeta (Barcelona, Spain), 1966.
La última aventura, Planeta (Barcelona, Spain), 1967.
La decoración, Nauta (Barcelona, Spain), 1969.
Adagio confidencial, Planeta (Barcelona, Spain), 1973.
La gangrena, Planeta (Barcelona, Spain), 1975.
Viaje a Sodoma, Planeta (Barcelona, Spain), 1977.
El proyecto y otros relatos, Planeta (Barcelona, Spain), 1978.
La presencia, Argos Vergara (Barcelona, Spain), 1979.
Derribos, Argos Vergara (Barcelona, Spain), 1981.
La sinfonía y las moscas, Planeta (Barcelona, Spain), 1982.
Los volumen de la ausencia (title means "The Volume of Absence"), Planeta (Barcelona, Spain), 1983.
La danza de los salmones: una fábula novelada, Planeta (Barcelona, Spain), 1985.
Bacteria mutante, Planeta (Barcelona, Spain), 1996.
El secreto de las flores, Plaza y Janés (Barcelona, Spain), 1997.
La voz del árbol, Plaza y Janés (Barcelona, Spain), 1998.
Los clamores del silencio, Plaza y Janés (Barcelona, Spain), 2000.

Contributor to anthologies, including *El Interrogante de Garabandal* and *She Went in Haste to the Mountain.*

Works have been translated into English, French, German, Italian, Portuguese, Swedish, and Finnish.

SIDELIGHTS: Mercedes Salisachs is one of Spain's most successful contemporary authors. Her early works, including *La mujer llega al pueblo* and *La gangrena,* garnered both critical attention and awards. Throughout Salisachs' literary career she has written about such issues as adultery, homosexuality, alcoholism, and drug addiction, but always with a keen eye focused on the style, structure, and content of her work.

La mujer llega al pueblo centers around the love triangle of Eulalia, Joanet, and José Mendía. Such an "arrangement" results in nothing but tragedy when suppositions of the paternity of Eulalia's unborn child combine with suppressed emotions to lead Joanet to murder. According to Phyllis Zatlin in *Letras Femeninas,* "underlying the facile use of caricatures and a surface level of comedy, there is an undercurrent of friction between the Catalan-speaking *pueblo* and the wealthy Mendías and their cosmopolitan friends, as well as a resentment of the tourist invasion in spite of the money it brings." The critic added: "Salisachs' point, of course, is that martyrdom is still in style for young women like Eulalia who may be victimized simultaneously by the immorality of the upper classes and the self-righteousness of most representatives of the lower classes."

Salisachs' novel *Adagio confidencial* concerns the reunion of a couple after a twenty-year separation, while *Derribos* is a memoir of the author's childhood. Elena Olazagasti-Segovia, reviewing *Derribos* in *Letras Femeninas,* noted that the novelist "recognizes the great weight of the past in any individual's life, for [Salisachs'] opinion is: 'The neutral and realistic recollection of the roots that time allows us . . . can open large avenues to have us compress not only our present but our future, without external behaviors we arrive at collisions and disappointment.'" According to Olazagasti-Segovia, "Salisachs accepts the connection between life and work: 'Surely I have not written a single page without, mixing the fiction, [life] is strained [like liquid] in the part of my [work] that happens to liberate the one who falls behind.'"

Los volumen de la ausencia, according to a contributor in *Modern Women Writers,* "tells the story of a middle-aged woman who has just been told that she has a terminal disease." The contributor explained that the 1983 novel is considered among the author's best, "especially in its psychological portrayal." *La sinfonia de las moscas* is the tragic story of a family living in Barcelona during the middle part of the twentieth century. Salisachs' *Los clamores del silencio* touches upon the incredible grief she experienced after the death of her son Miguel in 1958.

BIOGRAPHICAL AND CRITICAL SOURCES:

BOOKS

Robinson, Lillian S., editor and compiler, *Modern Women Writers,* Continuum Publishing (New York, NY), 1996.

PERIODICALS

Booklist, March 1, 1975, Earle M. Gladden, review of *Adagio confidencial,* p. 675; August, 1983, Erwin Butler, review of *Derribos,* p. 1451; May 15, 1984, Erwin Butler, review of *La sinfonía de las moscas,* p. 1335.
Letras Femeninas, spring, 1990, Phyllis Zatlin, "Childbirth with Fear: Bleeding to Death Softly," pp. 37-44; spring-fall, 1992, Elena Olazagasti-Segovia, "'En busca del tiempo perdidio': Tres novelistas españolas cuentan su historia," pp. 64-73.*

*   *   *

SAMUEL, Vivette 1919-

PERSONAL: Born May 21, 1919, in Paris, France; daughter of Nahum (a journalist) and Rachel (a journalist; maiden name, Spirt) Herman; married Julien Samuel, 1942; children: Françoise Samuel Elbaz, Jean Pierre, Nicole Samuel Guinard. *Education:* Attended Sorbonne, University of Paris. *Religion:* Jewish.

ADDRESSES: Home—44 rue de la gare de Reuilly, 75012 Paris, France.

CAREER: Association pour le déportés internés de la resistance, Paris, France, social worker, c. early 1940s; Union Mondiale pour la Protection de la Sante des Populations Juives et Oeuvres de Secours aux Enfants, Paris, assistant director and director; retired.

WRITINGS:

Sauver les enfants, [Paris, France], 1995, translation by Charles B. Paul published as *Rescuing the Children: A Holocaust Memoir,* foreword by Elie Wiesel, University of Wisconsin Press (Madison, WI), 2002.

Samuel's book was also published in German.

SIDELIGHTS: Vivette Samuel told *CA:* "My primary motivation for writing was to offer a testimony about the children in camps in France during World War II. The account was based on my own writings from 1943 and by interviews of children. In 1992 I started working with my granddaughter, Judith Elbaz, who was twenty-two years old, just the age I had been during my work in rescuing children. It was important for both of us. When the book was published in France, Judith wrote the first preface. In the English edition, Elie Wiesel, who was one of the children we helped, wrote the second preface. A long introduction for the translation was written by Charles B. Paul, He and his sister were also among the children described in the book."

BIOGRAPHICAL AND CRITICAL SOURCES:

PERIODICALS

Publishers Weekly, April 29, 2002, review of *Rescuing the Children: A Holocaust Memoir,* p. 59.

*   *   *

SANCHEZ, Patrick 1970-

PERSONAL: Born February 9, 1970, in Fort Leonardwood, MO; son of Guillermo (a physician) and Patricia (a nurse) Sanchez. *Ethnicity:* "Hispanic." *Education:* George Mason University, B.A., 1992.

ADDRESSES: Home—2513-A South Walter Reed Dr., Arlington, VA 22206. *Agent*—Deborah Schneider, 250 West 57th St., New York, NY 10107. *E-mail*—patrick@erols.com.

CAREER: Value Options Managed Healthcare Co., Falls Church, VA, director of proposals, 1993—.

WRITINGS:

Girlfriends (fiction), Kensington Publishing (New York, NY), 2001.

*   *   *

SAPIR, Edward 1884-1939

PERSONAL: Born January 26, 1884 in Louenburg, Pomerania (now Poland); died from coronary thrombosis February 4, 1939 in New Haven, CT; immigrated to the United States, 1889; son of Jacob David (a cantor) and Eva (Sigel) Sapir; married Florence Delson, 1911 (deceased), married Jean Victoria McClenaghan, 1926; children: (first marriage) Herbert, Helen, Philip; (second marriage) Paul, James. *Education:* Columbia College (now University), B.A., 1904, M.A., 1905, Ph.D., 1909.

CAREER: University of Pennsylvania, instructor of anthropology, 1908-10; Canadian National Museum, Ottawa, Ontario, Canada, Division of Anthropology of the Geological Survey, chief of anthropology, 1910-25; University of Chicago, Chicago, IL, professor, 1925-31; Yale University, New Haven, CT, Sterling Professor of Anthropology and Linguistics, 1931-39.

MEMBER: Linguistic Society of America (president, 1933), National Academy of Sciences, American Philosophical Society, American Anthropological Association (president, 1938).

AWARDS, HONORS: Honorary degrees from Columbia University and Yale University.

WRITINGS:

Takelma Texts, University Museum (Philadelphia, PA), 1909.
(Editor) *Wishram Texts/Wasco Tales and Myths,* collected by Jeremiah Curtin, E. J. Brill (Leyden, Netherlands), 1909, reprint AMS Press (New York, NY), 1974.

Yana Texts, with Yana myths collected by Roland B. Dixon, University of California Press (Berkeley, CA), 1910.

The Takelma Language of Southwestern Oregon, U.S. Government Printing Office (Washington, DC), 1912.

Notes on Chasta Costa Phonology and Morphology, University Museum (Philadelphia, PA), 1914.

A Sketch of the Social Organization of the Nass River Indians, Canadian Government Printing Bureau (Ottawa, Canada), 1915.

Noun Reduplication in Comox, a Salish Language of Vancouver Island, Canadian Government Printing Bureau (Ottawa, Ontario, Canada), 1915.

Time Perspective in Aboriginal American Culture: A Study in Method, Canadian Government Printing Bureau (Ottawa, Ontario, Canada), 1916.

The Position of the Yana in the Hokan Stock, University of California Press (Berkeley, CA), 1917.

Dreams and Gibes, Poet Lore (Boston, MA), 1917.

Yana Terms of Relationship, University of California Press (Berkeley, CA), 1918.

Language: An Introduction to the Study of Speech, Harcourt, Brace (New York, NY), 1921.

(With Leslie Spier) *Wishram Ethnography,* University of Washington Press (Seattle, WA), 1930.

Totality, Waverly Press (Baltimore, MD), 1930.

The Southern Paiute Language, three volumes, American Academy of Art and Sciences (Boston, MA), 1930-31.

(With Herbert N. Shenton and Otto Jesperson) *International Communication: A Symposium on the Language Problem,* Paul, Trench, Trübner (London, England), 1931.

The Expression of the Ending-Point Relation in English, French, and German, edited by Alice V. Morris, Waverly (Baltimore, MD), 1932.

(With Leslie Spier) *Notes on the Culture of the Yana,* University of California Press (Berkeley, CA), 1943.

Selected Writings in Language, Culture and Personality, edited by David G. Mandelbaum, University of California Press (Berkeley, CA), 1949.

(With Morris Swadesh) *Yana Dictionary,* edited by Mary R. Haas, University of California Press (Berkeley, CA), 1960.

Letters from Edward Sapir to Robert H. Lowie, edited by Luella Cole Lowie, privately publsihed (Berkeley, CA), 1965.

(With Harry Hoijer) *The Phonology and Morphology of the Navaho Language,* University of California Press (Berkeley, CA), 1967.

Edward Sapir's Correspondence, edited by Louise Dallaire, National Museums of Canada (Ottawa, Ontario, Canada), 1984.

The Southern Paiute Language, AMS Press (New York, NY), 1984.

The Sapir-Kroeber Correspondence, edited by Victor Golla, University of California Press (Berkeley, CA), 1984.

The Psychology of Culture: A Course of Lectures, reconstructed and edited by Judith T. Irvine, Mouton de Gruyter (Hawthorne, NY), 1994.

The Collected Works of Edward Sapir, fourteen volumes, Mouton de Gruyter (Hawthorne, NY), 2001.

SIDELIGHTS: Edward Sapir is remembered as an anthropologist and linguist whose studies were still current more than a half-century after their original publication. He is among the founders of the science of linguistics, particularly ethno-linguistics—(the study of the relationship of culture to language)—and structural linguistics, which analyzes actual speech to learn about the language's underlying structure. Sapir and his pupil, Benjamin Lee Whorf, studied the effect that the structure and vocabulary of a language have on a language speaker's perception of the world and developed what later became known as the Sapir-Whorf hypothesis. Through his other activities, Sapir demonstrated his interest in music, poetry, and psychology, as well. To quote Regna Darnell in *New Perspectives in Language, Culture, and Personality,* "Sapir's genius was that while other people stayed in their boxes, he refused to be bound by such limits. This protean scholarly and artistic activity became the hallmark of his intellectual style."

A bright student, Sapir won a scholarship to Columbia University, where he studied Germanics, until he met the famous anthropologist and linguist Franz Boas. Under Boas's supervision, Sapir studied Native American languages, earned his doctorate, and embarked on a college teaching career. Boas encouraged him to document Native American languages before they became extinct. Thus during these early years as a student and teacher, Sapir conducted field work among the Chinook, Takelma, Yana, and Paiute tribes, collecting data that he would later analyze and publish in numerous works.

Among Sapir's most productive years were those fifteen he spent as chief of the Division of Anthropology of the Geological Survey of the Canadian National

Museum in Ottawa. In addition to writing numerous articles on Native American languages and theoretical topics, he published his major works: *Time Perspective in Aboriginal American Culture: A Study in Method* and *Language: An Introduction to the Study of Speech.* The first, a special commission, deals with methods for reconstructing cultural history. In *Language* Sapir explains for a lay readership the structure of languages and proposes his six-unit classification system of Native American languages.

Unknown to many, Sapir was also a poet. In his verse he expressed a part of himself that was not fulfilled by his work as a scientist, including his emotions over the mental illness and eventual death of his first wife, Florence Delson. Of his verse, only *Dreams and Gibes* was published, and that volume's lukewarm reviews cooled his desire to publish further verse. His wife's illness also sparked Sapir's interest in psychology, an interest that lasted until the end of his life.

J. David Sapir, Sapir's son and an anthropologist himself, reminisced about his father's passion for his work to the audience at the centenary session of the American Anthropological Association, which was later published in *Language and Society:* "Edward Sapir devoted an extraordinary amount of time to his grammatical and comparative studies. And he loved every minute of it—the crammed notebooks and the shoe boxes full of unending slips of paper. . . . My mother always said that he would confess (perhaps a little guiltily) to his delight in the abstract play of linguistic form. He was to return continually to his phonology, his grammar, and comparative notes when 'weary of life's considerations'—as Robert Frost put it." With his love of his subject and his keen intellect, Sapir ranged far and wide from the then narrowly defined subjects and techniques of his profession. "Language did not provide Sapir with a systematic dogma," J. David Sapir continued. "For Sapir, language, especially the form of language and the varieties that form took, was an absorbing and fascinating subject. Because language was a subject and not a dogma or moral imperative, he could easily move from topic to topic without feeling in the least constrained. Grammar, phonology, comparative linguistics, poetics, poetry, culture, the individual, the unconscious, all came naturally, for Sapir's mind 'ran on many levels,' and all that was necessary was that each topic should run into the other, that each should in some way imply the other."

Another less-biased observer made a similar assessment. In a personal letter to Jean McClenaghan Sapir dated 1956, David Mandelbaum, editor of the *Selected Writings,* remarked on Sapir's particular genius as a renaissance man: "Science and art were combined in Sapir in unusual degree. He was a meticulous linguist. . . . Yet he was a humanist and artist as well. He was a poet. . . . His essays in music and literature show not only a perceptive, creative intelligence but also reveal the joy he found in those arts."

BIOGRAPHICAL AND CRITICAL SOURCES:

BOOKS

Cowan, William, Michael K. Foster, and Konrad Corner, editors, *New Perspectives in Language, Culture, and Personality: Proceedings of the Edward Sapir Centenary Conference,* John Benjamin Publishing Company (Philadelphia, PA), 1986, pp. 553-588.

Darnell, Regna, *Edward Sapir: Linguist, Anthropologist, Humanist,* University of California Press (Berkeley, CA), 1990.

Dictionary of Literary Biography, Volume 92: *Canadian Writers, 1890-1920,* Gale (Detroit, MI), 1990.

Observers Observed: Essays on Ethnographic Fieldwork, edited by George W. Stocking, Jr., University of Wisconsin Press, 1983, pp. 208-231.

Corner, Konrad, editor, *Edward Sapir: Appraisals of His Life and Work,* John Benjamin Publishing Company (Philadelphia, PA), 1984.

Maidhood, Madeleine, editor, *Ethnolinguistics: Boas, Sapir, and Whorf Revisited,* Mouton Publishers (The Hague, Netherlands), 1979.

Twentieth-Century Literary Criticism, Volume 108, Gale (Detroit, MI), 2001.

PERIODICALS

American Anthropologist, March, 1998, Lars Rodseth, "Distributive Models of Culture: A Sapirian Alternative to Essentialism," pp. 55-69; June, 1998, Regan Darnel, "Camelot at Yale: The Construction and Dismantling of the Sapirian Synthesis, 1931-39," pp. 361-362.

American Ethnologist, November, 1995, Kenneth M. George, "The Psychology of Culture: A Course of Lectures," pp. 1002-1003.

American Indian Quarterly, fall, 1992, Margaret Langdon, review of *The Collected Works of Edward Sapir,* Volume 5, pp. 566-568.

Anthropological Linguistics, summer, 1996, Alexis Manaster Ramer, "Sapir's Classifications: Haida and Other Na-Dene Languages," pp. 179-105; winter, 1996, Philip K. Bock, "The Psychology of Culture: A Course of Lectures," pp. 745-747; summer, 1999, David W. Dinwoodie, "Textuality and the 'Voices' of Informants: The Case of Edward Sapir's 1929 Navajo Field School," pp. 165-192.

Anthropological Quarterly, January, 1989, Richard Handler, "Anti-romantic Romanticism: Edward Sapir and the Critique of American Individualism," pp. 1-13.

Essays on Canadian Writing, summer, 1989, Susan Lynne Knutson, "Bowering and Melville on Benjamin's Wharf: A Look at Indigenous-English Communication Strategies," pp. 67-80.

Ethnology, October, 1989, A. E. M. J. Pans, "Levirate and Sororate and the Terminological Classification of Uncles, Aunts, and Siblings' Children," pp. 343-258.

History of Anthropology, Volume 1, 1983, Richard Handler, "The Dainty and the Hungry Man: Literature and Anthropology in the Work of Edward Sapir," pp. 208-231; Volume 4, 1986, Regan Darnel, "Personality and Culture: The Fate of the Sapirian Alternative," pp. 156-183; Volume 4, 1986, Richard Handler, "The Vigorous Male and Aspiring Female: Poetry, Personality and Culture in Edward Sapir and Ruth Benedict," pp. 127-155.

Journal of the Royal Anthropological Institute, March, 1996, Nigel Rapport, review of *The Collected Works of Edward Sapir,* pp. 183-185.

Language: Journal of the Linguistic Society of America, September, 1981, Yakov Malkiel, "Drift, Slope, and Slant: Background of, and Variations upon, a Sapirian Theme," pp. 535-537.

Philosophy of the Social Sciences, September, 1996, Robert McMillan, "The Psychology of Culture: A Course of Lectures," pp. 387-397.

Poetics Today, summer, 1982, Augusto de Campo, "The Concrete Coin of Speech," pp. 167-176.

Psychiatry: Interpersonal and Biological Processes, spring, 2001, Laurence J. Kirmayer, "Commentary on 'Why Cultural Anthropology Needs the Psychiatrist': Sapir's Vision of Culture and Personality," p. 23.*

SCHWARTZ, Gary E. 1944-

PERSONAL: Born June 14, 1944, in Mineola, NY; son of Howard and Shirley Schwartz; married Jeanne Iris Gross, June 13, 1965. *Education:* Cornell University, Ithaca, NY, A.B., 1966; Harvard University, A.M., 1969, Ph.D., 1971.

ADDRESSES: Office—University of Arizona, Tucson, AZ 85721. *E-mail*—gschwart@u.arizona.edu.

CAREER: Psychologist, educator, and writer. Harvard University, assistant professor of psychology, 1971-75; Yale University, associate professor, and Yale University School of Medicine, assistant professor of psychiatry, 1976-79; Yale University, professor of psychology and psychiatry, 1980-87; Human Energy Systems Laboratory, University of Arizona, professor of psychology, medicine, neurology, psychiatry, and surgery, and director, 1988—. University of British Columbia, visiting associate professor of psychology, 1975-76; University of California Medical School, San Francisco, CA, visiting associate professor of psychiatry, 1976. Member, Personality and Cognition Study Section, National Institute of Mental Health, 1972-76; National Heart, Lung, and Blood Institute, consultant, 1976—; National Institutes of Health, ad hoc behavior medicine study section, member, 1977—.

MEMBER: American Psychological Association, American Association for the Advancement of Science, Biofeedback Society of America (president, 1974-75), Society for Psychophysiological Research (director, 1975-78), Academy of Behavioral Medicine Research, Claude Bernard Club, Phi Beta Kappa, Sigma Xi, Psi Chi, Alpha Epsilon Pi.

AWARDS, HONORS: Young Psychologist Award, American Psychological Association, 1972; Young Investigator Award, Stress Program, Roche Psychiatric Service Institute, 1975; Early Career Award, American Psychological Association, 1978.

WRITINGS:

(Editor, with David Shapiro) *Consciousness and Self-Regulation: Advances in Research,* Volume 1, Plenum Press (New York, NY), 1976.

(Editor, with Jackson Beatty) *Biofeedback, Theory and Research,* Academic Press (New York, NY), 1977.

(Editor, with Leonard White and Bernard Tursky) *Placebo: Theory, Research, and Mechanisms,* foreword by Norman Sartorius, Guilford Press (New York, NY), 1985.

(With Linda G. S. Russek) *The Living Energy Universe: A Fundamental Discovery That Transforms Science and Medicine,* Hampton Roads (Charlottesville, VA), 1999.

(With Suzy Smith and Linda G. S. Russek) *The Afterlife Codes: Searching for Evidence of the Survival of the Soul,* Hampton Roads (Charlottesville, VA), 2000.

(With William L. Simon) *The Afterlife Experiments: Breakthrough Scientific Evidence of Life after Death,* foreword by Deepak Chopra, Pocket Books (New York, NY), 2002.

Associate editor, *Biological Physiology* and *Biofeedback and Self-Regulation,* 1976—, *Psychophysiology,* 1978—.

SIDELIGHTS: The search for proof of life after death is a quest long undertaken by science and religion as well as parapsychology. The question of an afterlife has been pondered since ancient cultures, by average people profoundly affected by the loss of loved ones and the deepest thinkers of the ages, concerned with humankind's purpose and destiny. The strongest claims to knowledge of an afterlife remained confined to the deeply felt tenets of religion and the assertions of psychics, mediums, and ghost hunters. Yet despite the earnest claims of faith, science, or pseudoscience, there exists little tangible, reproducible evidence of life after death. In *The Afterlife Experiments: Breakthrough Scientific Evidence of Life after Death,* Gary E. Schwartz and coauthor William L. Simon approach the issue with the rigor of science. In the process, they provide "astonishing answers to a timeless question," wrote a reviewer on the *Lanternlight Traveller Book Corner* Web site: Is there an afterlife?

The Afterlife Experiments delves into Schwartz's longtime interest in the possibility of the survival of human consciousness after death. The results obtained in the experiments provide some support for Schwartz's theories. "This riveting narrative, with its electrifying transcripts, puts the reader on the scene of a breakthrough scientific achievement: contact with the beyond under controlled laboratory conditions," wrote the *Lanternlight Traveller Book Corner* reviewer.

In carefully regulated and controlled experiments, a number of well-known mediums made attempts to contact deceased friends and relatives of volunteer "sitters." These sitters could not be seen during the experiments, and they did not communicate to provide any cues to the mediums. The mediums were able provide information that they otherwise would not have known, including messages about a son's suicide; the statements a deceased father wanted to make before he died, but which he was prevented from saying due to a coma; and the "forecast" of a spouse's death. The results of the experiments, wrote William Beatty in *Booklist,* "showed definite examples of precognition and surprisingly accurate observations by the mediums." However, to a *Publishers Weekly* reviewer, "the story comes off like high-grade magic or a splendid infomercial."

Despite any misgivings by critics, "*The Afterlife Experiments* should provoke considerable discussion," Beatty observed, and it "should be of value for further investigation in this controversial field." Even the *Publishers Weekly* reviewer concluded that Schwartz possesses "an admirable passion for curious knowledge."

Schwartz also addressed a similar theory in *The Living Energy Universe: A Fundamental Discovery That Transforms Science and Medicine,* written with Linda G. S. Russek. "This is a book about a big idea: 'Everything is alive and remembers,'" wrote Rupert Sheldrake in *Journal of Parapsychology.* The book, Sheldrake said, "combines ideas, autobiography, and Linda's quest to find out if the death of her father meant the extinction of his consciousness, or whether he in some sense survived. It is refreshing to find a book about ideas written in such a personal way, and with such obvious excitement and enthusiasm."

Schwartz's theory, Sheldrake wrote, is based on the idea that if two components of a coupled system (designated A and B) influence each other in some way, the system will include not only their interactions but a memory of the interactions. "For example," Sheldrake observed, "if A and B are similar tuning forks, if A is set vibrating, B will be respond to A by vibrating in resonance; but then B's vibrations will affect A, and these changes in A will in turn affect B, and so on. This argument is quite general and applies to any coupled systems." Schwartz and Russek's "systemic memory hypothesis," could account for otherwise speculative or metaphysical events, including life after death, "cosmic evolution, past lives, karma, love, eternal life, the memory of water, cold fusion," and more, Sheldrake wrote.

While critics of the systemic memory hypothesis might agree that interactions leave a memory within the system, "these traces would seem too weak to make much difference," Sheldrake observed. To overcome this limitation, Schwartz and Russek rely on Erwin Lazlo's ideas of the vacuum of space itself as the place where everything is connected. Thus, "the vacuum itself is invoked as a locus of memory," Sheldrake said. "When we add the systemic memory process to Laszlo's logic, the vacuum of space itself becomes eternal, alive, and evolving." To Sheldrake, "*The Living Energy Universe* contains little new evidence for the ideas contained within it." Despite some speculations that he found "over the top," however, "the idea of memory in nature seems both attractive and plausible."

Schwartz, a professor of psychology, medicine, neurology, psychiatry, and surgery, and directory of the Human Energy Systems Laboratory at the University of Arizona, is no stranger to championing ideas that exist outside those widely accepted by the scientific mainstream. His 1977 book *Biofeedback: Theory and Research*, edited with Jackson Beatty, addresses what was then a very new and highly controversial field. However, to a reviewer writing in *Choice*, "it is refreshing to see a publishing attempt of this kind undertaken." The book focuses on four areas: theoretical and applied issues, the autonomic nervous system, the central nervous system, and skeletal musculature, with each chapter written by a practicing researcher in the field. Chapters include literature reviews, author and subject indexes, and detailed bibliographies.

Reviewer B. M. Shmavonian, writing in *Contemporary Psychology*, remarked favorably on many aspects of the book. "The most exquisite chapter in the theoretical section, perhaps in the entire book, is the chapter by Jasper Brener entitled 'Sensory and Perceptual Determinants of Voluntary Visceral Control.' This chapter epitomizes the rigorous experimental approach as well as considerations of the involvement of the central nervous system and the brain." Similarly, Shmavonian commented that "the chapter by Taub entitled 'Self-Regulation of Human Tissue Temperature' is particularly well done and should be required reading for those who do temperature regulation without taking into consideration the problems Taub discusses."

Shmavonian's praise wasn't universal, however, as he wrote that the book has "uneven contributions." However, he concluded that *Biofeedback: Theory and Research* is nonetheless "a very useful book, both for researchers and practitioners, particularly those practitioners who practice with ignorance of the pitfalls and shortcomings of many of the techniques described in this text."

Schwartz's *Consciousness and Self-Regulation: Advances in Research*, edited with David Shapiro, offers "a scholarly forum for discussing the integration of the diverse areas represented in consciousness and self-regulation," wrote Timothy J. Teyler in *Contemporary Psychology*. "They attempt this by presenting some of the best research and theory," presenting nine chapters with an overall "strong biological slant," Teyler observed. Despite a strong presentation, "the major liability of the volume is in its failure to provide a framework for the chapters or to provide a smooth transition from one to another." Still, Teyler remarked, "the editors have done an admirable job of assembling a wide variety of contributions from competent people."

BIOGRAPHICAL AND CRITICAL SOURCES:

PERIODICALS

Booklist, February 15, 2002, William Beatty, review of *The Afterlife Experiments: Breakthrough Scientific Evidence of Life after Death*, p. 973.

Choice, October, 1977, review of *Biofeedback: Theory and Research*, p. 1127.

Contemporary Psychology, May, 1978, Timothy J. Teyler, review of *Consciousness and Self-Regulation: Advances in Research*, Volume 1, pp. 292-294; May, 1979, B.M. Shmavonian, review of *Biofeedback: Theory and Research*, pp. 401-402.

Journal of Parapsychology, March, 2000, Rupert Sheldrake, review of *The Living Energy Universe: A Fundamental Discovery That Transforms Science and Medicine*, p. 101.

Publishers Weekly, February 25, 2002, review of *The Afterlife Experiments: Breakthrough Scientific Evidence of Life after Death*, p. 52.

Afterlife Experiments Web site, http://www.openmind sciences.com/ (May 9, 2002).

Lanternlight Traveler Book Corner, http://lantrav bookcorner.com/ (May 9, 2002), review of *The Afterlife Experiments: Breakthrough Scientific Evidence of Life After Death.**

*   *   *

SCIANNA, Ferdinando 1943-

PERSONAL: Born July 4, 1943, in Bagheria, Sicily, Italy; married Carmela Bologna, 1966; married Paola Bergna, 1983; children: (first marriage) Francesca, Fernanda; (second marriage) Eleonara. *Education:* University of Palermo, 1962-65.

ADDRESSES: Home—6 via Giannone, 20154 Milan, Italy. *Agent*—Magnum Photos, 19 Rue Hegesippe Moreau 75018 Paris, France.

CAREER: Freelance photographer and journalist. *L'Europeo* (magazine), Milan, Italy, Paris correspondent, 1974-83; journalist for *Le Monde Diplomatique,* 1976, and *La Quinzaine Littèraire.* Member of Magnum Photos agency, Paris, and Milan, 1983—; established studio in Milan, 1983—. *Exhibitions:* Individual exhibitions include *Feste in Sicilia,* Circolo di Cultura, Bagheria, Sicily, 1962; *Feste in Sicilia,* Biblioteca Comunale, Milan, Italy, 1963; *Glorioso Alberto,* at SICOF, Milan, 1973; *Gitans,* at SICOF, Milan, 1975; *Les Siciliens,* Institut Culturel Français, Naples, Italy, 1977; *I Siciliani,* Institut Culturel Italien, Paris, France, 1977; *Sicilia e dintorni,* Galleria Il Diaframma, Milan, 1979; Galleria Arte al Borgo, Palermo, Sicily, 1980; Landesbildstelle Württemberg, Stuttgart, Germany, 1981; *Kami,* Musée de l'Elysée, Lausanne, Switzerland, 1989; *Le Forme del Caos,* Château d'Eau, Toulouse, France, 1992; and Villa Medicis, Rome, Italy, 1992. Selected group exhibitions include *Third World Exhibition of Photography,* Pressehaus Stern, Hamburg, Germany, 1973; *La Photographie Italienne Rencontres Internationals de Photographie,* Arles, France, 1978; *The Italian Eye,* Alternative Center for International Arts, New York, 1978; *Fotografia Italiana,* Biennale, Venice, Italy, 1979; *Ten European Photographs,* P.S.1, New York, NY, 1980; and *Italian Photography,* Beijin Museum, China, 1982. Work is in permanent collections, including Bibliothèque Nationale and Fonds National de la Photographie, both Paris and Salford University, Lancashire, England.

AWARDS, HONORS: Prix Nadar, (France, 1966).

WRITINGS:

(Photographer) Leonardo Sciascia, *Feste Religiose in Sicilia* (title means "Religious Festivals in Sicily"), [Bari, Italy], 1965.

(Photographer) Leonardo Sciascia, *Il Glorioso Alberto* (title means "The Glorious Albert"), [Milan, Italy], 1971.

La Villa dei mostri (title means "The Villa of the Monsters"), introduction by Leonardo Sciascia, [Turin, Italy], 1977.

(Photographer) Dominique Fernandez and Leonardo Sciascia, *Les Siciliens* (title means "The Sicilians"), [Paris, France], 1977.

I Grandi fotografi: Ferdinando Scianna, introduction by Leonardo Sciascia, [Milan, Italy], 1983.

Il Grande libro della Sicilia (title means "The Big Book of Sicily"), [Milan, Italy], 1985.

Ferdinando Scianna: L'instante e la forma (title means "The Instant and the Form"), 1987.

(Photographer) *Kami* (exhibition catalogue), [Milan, Italy], 1988.

(Photographer) Leonardo Sciascia, *Ore di Spagna* (title means "Spanish Hours"), note by Natale Tedesco, Pungitopo (Marina di Patti, Italy), 1988.

Città del mondo (title means "Cities of the World"), 1988.

(Photographer) *Le Forme del caos* (title means "Shape of the Chaos," exhibition catalogue), [Udine, Italy], 1989.

Leonardo Sciascia Fotografato da Ferdinando Scianna (title means "Sciascia Photographed by Ferdinando Scianna"), 1989.

Marpessa, [Milan, Italy], 1993.

Altrove: Reportage di moda (title means "Fashion Reportage"), 1995.

Viaggio a Lourdes (title means "Travel to Lourdes"), 1996.

Scianna: Dormire, forse sognare, edited by Roberta Valtorta, Arte (Italy), 1997.

Altre forme del caos, Contrasto (Rome, Italy), 2000.

(Photographer) Dacia Maraini, *Sicilia Ricordata,* Rizzoli (Milan, Italy), 2001.

Obiettivo ambiguo, Rizzoli (Milan, Italy), 2001.

SIDELIGHTS: Ferdinando Scianna, photographer, photojournalist, and writer, initially made his reputation chronicling the culture of his native Sicily. His first book, *Feste Religiose in Sicily,* was published when he was only twenty-one years old; it won the Prix Nadar in 1966. In it, Scianna portrays people celebrating their religious ceremonies, caught up in the exotic mixture of Christian and pagan influences. He returned to the subject again in 1977 with *Les Sicilians.* According to a *Contemporary Photographers* writer, the book "provided Scianna with the ideal space in which to construct an organic assemblage of photographs which fleshed out striking stories and combined to form part of his long visual romance with the land and people of Sicily. . . . [he] avoided the facile picturesque approaches to local folklore or pretty Mediterranean landscapes . . . [he] strove in his images to represent people in their daily life—never as the sublime or romantic beings that photography had so often tried to make them." In these books depicting a region both held fast by strong traditions and religious beliefs and open to modern ways, Scianna followed the style of 1940s Italian neorealists, dramatically incorporating light and dark shadows.

In 1966, Scianna moved to the Italian mainland city of Milan, and a year later started as a staff photographer for the weekly magazine *L'Europeo;* moving to Paris, France, to be a Paris correspondent for the publication in 1974; and continuing his career as a journalist for *Le Monde Diplomatique* in 1976 and then *La Quinzaine Littèraire.* He met Magnum Photos cofounder Henri Cartier-Bresson in 1977, was a Magnum nominee in 1982, and began pursuing stories around the world, becoming a Magnum member in 1989.

Scianna made his foray into fashion photography in 1987 when Italian designers Dolce and Gabbana, at the time comparatively unknown, asked him to photograph their clothing in Sicilian settings for a catalogue. "The two designers wanted Scianna to apply his skills at recording reality to the capricious, illusory world of fashion," remarked an *American Photo* writer; "Scianna responded with evocative images of the model Marpessa . . . strolling down sunblanched streets and pouting in local shops. The campaign was

a hit." Scianna said of the project to Carol Squires in *American Photo,* "I made the pictures trying to find my memory of what the women were like when I was a child." Squires concluded, "Scianna was able to use his journalist's eye to recast the streets of Sicily into a setting for beauty and glamour."

The success of this campaign put Scianna in constant demand for fashion photography, leading to work in the French, Italian, and Spanish *Vogue,* Italian *Vanity Fair, Stern, Marie Claire,* and many other European magazines. However, he did not intend to give up his other photographic and photojournalist interests. He told Squires in *American Photo,* "I don't believe in specialists. I think you have good photographers and bad photographers." And Squires reflected, "Scianna is clearly one of the good ones."

Said Henri Cartier-Bresson of Scianna's work in *Aperture,* "Ferdinando Scianna is one of those photographers who has the visual gift we call in French 'l'oeil de peintre.'"

BIOGRAPHICAL AND CRITICAL SOURCES:

BOOKS

Contemporary Photographers, 3rd edition, St. James Press (Detroit, MI), 1996.

PERIODICALS

American Photo, March, 1992, Carol Squires, "The Europeans: As the World Looks to Them in the '90s, They Look for New Ways to See Themselves," pp. 46-47, 49; March, 1992, "Italy, Ferdinando Scianno," p. 49; March, 1992, Russell Hart, "Scianna's Body Count," p. 106.
Aperture, spring, 1998, Henri Cartier-Bresson's comments, p. 34.

ONLINE

Magnum Photos Web site, http://www.magnumphotos.com/ (August 7, 2002).*

SHEA, Suzanne Strempek

PERSONAL: Born in MA; married; husband's name, Tommy (a columnist for the *Springfield Union-News* [MA]). *Education:* Graduated from the Portland School of Art (now Maine College of Art). *Hobbies and other interests:* Playing the accordion.

ADDRESSES: Home—P.O. Box 468, Thorndike, MA 01079. *E-mail*—heavenmail@aol.com.

CAREER: Author, 1994—. Formerly staff writer for *Springfield Newspapers,* Springfield, MA and the *Providence Journal-Bulletin,* Providence, RI.

AWARDS, HONORS: New England Booksellers Association chose *Hoopi Shoopi Donna* for the "Discovery of the Month", June, 1996; Oskar Halecki Prize, Polish American Historical Association, for depiction of the Polish experience in the United States; New England Book Award for Fiction, New England Booksellers Association, 2002, for contribution to New England literature.

WRITINGS:

Selling the Lite of Heaven, Pocket Books (New York, NY), 1994.
Hoopi Shoopi Donna, Pocket Books (New York, NY), 1996.
Lily of the Valley, Pocket Books (New York, NY), 1999.
Around Again, Pocket Books (New York, NY), 2001.
Songs from a Lead-lined Room; Notes—High and Low—from My Journey through Breast Cancer, Beacon Press (Boston, MA), 2002.

Contributor to periodicals, including *Yankee, Boston Globe Magazine, Philadelphia Inquirer,* and *New England Monthly.*

SIDELIGHTS: Suzanne Strempek Shea works in both fiction and nonfiction. She began her writing life in journalism as a staff writer for various newspapers in New England, among them the *Providence Journal-Bulletin* and the *Springfield Newspapers.* In 1994 her first novel, *Selling the Lite of Heaven,* was published. Her novels are generally considered to be character-

driven, revolving around a young woman who lacks a clear sense of herself or her direction in life. To this end, the author employs a device by which the protagonist brushes against something unexpected and powerful that propels her into a process of self-discovery. Shea has been recognized for her realistic portrayals of ordinary life in the Polish-American community.

Shea's debut novel, *Selling the Lite of Heaven,* concerns a young woman, well ensconced in her small Polish-American community, who decides to sell her engagement ring after her fiancée chooses a life in the Church. Her contact with the prospective buyers stimulates some reflection on the course of her life and it is clear by the end of the book that some changes will be made. Shea uses the realistic details of everyday life and gentle humor to create a portrait of a young woman beginning to seek her place in the world. A *Kirkus Reviews* contributor wrote, "A promising debut that with shrewdness and a lively display of humor reminds us just how much drama there can be in the everyday."

Hoopi Shoopi Donna is set in a Polish-American community and again revolves around a young girl who comes to establish herself by means of an accident that resulted in a misunderstanding and a painful break with her father. The culture of Polish-American life plays a larger role in this book—(the title is the American pronunciation of a Polish polka)—than it did in the previous title. *Hoopi Shoopi Donna* was chosen by the New England Booksellers as its "Selection of the Month" for June, 1996. In January, 1998, the Polish American Historical Society awarded this novel the Oskar Halecki Prize for its contribution to research on the Polish experience in America. *Library Journal* contributor Barbara Maslekoff noted that *Hoopi Shoopi Donna* "captures the agonies and ecstasies of ordinary and extraordinary family life."

In *Lily of the Valley,* the author continues her practice of character-driven novels in a story of an ambitious young woman from a small town in Massachusetts. Lily Wilk knew at an early age that she wanted to be an artist. She declares her ambition by saying, "Someday, I will make something that people will stand in line for hours just to look at and study and be struck by. Then satisfied beyond belief, they will travel all the way home in stunned silence, reflecting how they have been changed in some vital way by the sight of a thing made by my own right hand." She draws and paints ceaselessly, but without gaining the fame she desires, until one day she receives a commission for a group portrait. As this picture comes to life, Lily achieves a clearer understanding of her world, her family and herself. All of the reviews agree that Shea's attention to the details of ordinary life make this an engaging, if sentimental, novel.

Finding oneself through adversity also drives the action of Shea's fourth novel, *Around Again.* This time the protagonist is a woman in her forties whose involvement as a teenager with two other people created a summer of confusion and fear. The characters meet again in middle age, endure another episode that mirrors the first one, but resolve the mysteries and mature.

Notes from a Lead-lined Room: Notes—High and Low—from My Journey through Breast Cancer is an account of Shea's radiation treatment for breast cancer. The memoir begins with her diagnosis at age forty-one and continues through to the completion of her treatment. With her customary attention to everyday detail, she describes the emotional highs and lows, the psychological changes, and the response of friends and family. The result is a very complete picture of a harrowing experience. Shea is frank in the expression of her outrage at the diagnosis; after all, she was someone who "liked [her life] the way it was." She wrote this book to encourage and give comfort to women in similar circumstances.

BIOGRAPHICAL AND CRITICAL SOURCES:

PERIODICALS

Booklist, May 15, 1994, Mary Carroll, review of *Selling the Lite of Heaven,* p. 1664; August 1999, GraceAnne A. DeCandido, review of *Lily of the Valley,* p. 2029; June 1, 2001, Joanne Wilkinson, review of *Around Again,* p. 1849.
Christian Science Monitor, July 1, 1996, Yvonne Zipp, review of *Hoopi Shoopi Donna, p.*15.
Kirkus Reviews, April 15, 1994, review of *Selling the Lite of Heaven,* p. 503; April 1, 1996, review of *Hoopi Shoopi Donna,* p. 483; June 15, 1999, review of *Lily of the Valley,* p. 908; May 15, 2001, review of *Around Again,* p. 695.

Knight-Ridder/Tribune News Service, October 5, 1994, Tanya Barrientos, review of *Selling the Lite of Heaven.*
Library Journal, April 15, 1996, Barbara Maslekoff, review of *Hoopi Shoopi Donna,* p. 124; July, 1999, Nancy Pearl, review of *Lily of the Valley,* p. 136; June 1, 2001, Ellen R. Cohen, review of *Around Again,* p. 218; April 1, 2002, Bette-Lee Fox, review of *Songs from a Lead-lined Room: Notes—High and Low—from My Journey Through Breast Cancer and Radiation,* p. 132.
Publishers Weekly, April 8, 1996, review of *Hoopi Shoopi Donna,* p. 54; July 5, 1999, review of *Lily of the Valley,* p. 59; July 9, 2001, review of *Around Again,* p. 46; March 18, 2002, review of *Songs from a Lead-Lined Room: Notes—High and Low—from My Journey through Breast Cancer,* p. 86.

ONLINE

Capital Times (Madison, WI), http://www.madison.com/ (June 7, 2002).
EducETH, http://www.educeth.ch/ (June 7, 2002).
SR Web site, http://www.ruf.rice.edu/ (June 7, 2002).
Suzanne Strempek Shea Web site, http://www.suzanne strempekshea.com (June 7, 2002).*

*   *   *

SHEFFIELD, Charles 1935-2002

OBITUARY NOTICE—See index for *CA* sketch: Born June 25, 1935, in Hull, England; died of brain cancer November 2, 2002, in Rockville, MD. Physicist and author. Sheffield was a Hugo and Nebula Award-winning science-fiction novelist. He was educated at St. John's College, Cambridge, where he earned his master's degree in 1961 before coming to the United States to earn his doctorate at American University in 1965. He then embarked on a career as a physicist, working as chief scientist and board member for the Earth Satellite Corp. beginning in 1971, and as a consultant to the National Aeronautic and Space Administration. Sheffield's life took a dramatic turn after his first wife died in 1977. He turned his grief inward and decided to write down the stories dwelling within his mind. Sheffield began to write science fiction of the "hard" variety, meaning his stories were all based on scientific fact; one reason he turned to this genre was that he felt there was very little good science fiction available at the time. Sheffield was rewarded for his efforts with a large readership and he won several important science-fiction awards, including the John W. Campbell Award in 1992 for *Brother to Dragons* and the Hugo and Nebula awards in 1994 for his novella *Georgia on My Mind*. Over the course of his career he completed over two dozen novels, including *My Brother's Keeper* (1982), *Godspeed* (1993), *Tomorrow and Tomorrow* (1997), and *The Spheres of Heaven* (2001), as well as books in the "Behrooz Wolf" and "Heritage Universe" series and the juvenile series "Jupiter." Sheffield also published many short-story collections and works of nonfiction. Although for much of his later life Sheffield was despondent over the death of his first wife, and his second marriage ended in divorce, the last five years of his life were joyous due to his marriage with fellow science-fiction writer Nancy Kress.

OBITUARIES AND OTHER SOURCES:

PERIODICALS

Chicago Tribune, November 10, 2002, section 4, p. 11.
Independent (London, England), November 6, 2002, p. 16.
New York Times, November 9, 2002, p. A30.
Washington Post, November 3, 2002, p. C10.

*   *   *

SHEINBERG, Marcia 1943-

PERSONAL: Born March 10, 1943, in Brooklyn, NY. *Education:* Rutgers University, B.A., 1965; New York University, M.S.W., 1970; Ackerman Institute for the Family, postgraduate certificate in family therapy, 1979.

ADDRESSES: Office—Ackerman Institute for the Family, 149 East 78th St., New York, NY 10021.

CAREER: Children's Aid Society, Buffalo, NY, staff member, 1970-71; part-time social worker for public schools in Princeton, NJ, 1972-82; Ackerman Institute for the Family, New York, NY, clinical faculty member, 1980—, cofounder of Ackerman Violence and Gender Project, 1984-89, director of clinical service, 1987-92, founder and director of Ackerman Sex Abuse Project, 1988—, director of training, 1992—, director of training and clinical services, 1998—. Private practice of psychotherapy, 1980—; New York State Child Advocacy Resource and Consultation Center, member of board of advisors; participant in workshops in the United States and abroad; consultant to New York City Hospital Chaplains.

MEMBER: American Family Therapy Association, American Association of Marriage and Therapy.

AWARDS, HONORS: Grants from Squib, Doris Jones Stein Foundation, Ms. Foundation, Seth Sprague Foundation, NIFTI Foundation, Frances and Edwin Cummings Foundation, Educational Fund of America, Ronald McDonald Children's Charities, Henry and Lucy Moses Foundation, New-Land Foundation, and Michael Charles Foundation.

WRITINGS:

(With Peter Fraenkel) *The Relational Trauma of Incest: An Integrated Family-based Approach to Treatment,* Guilford Press (New York, NY), 2000.

Contributor to books, including *The Family Therapist as System Consultant,* edited by L. Wynne, T. Weber, and S. H. McDaniel, Guilford Press (New York, NY), 1985. Contributor to periodicals, including *Psychotherapy Networker, Journal of Systemic and Strategic Therapy, Journal of Marital and Family Therapy,* and *Family Systems Medicine.* Member of advisory editorial board, *Family Process* and *Journal of Feminist Family Therapy.*

*   *   *

SILL, John 1947-

PERSONAL: Born November 22, 1947, in St. Pauls, NC; son of Charles Frank (an artist) and Mary Louise (a homemaker; maiden name, McGoogan) Sill; married Cathryn Powell (a teacher and author), March 16, 1975. *Education:* North Carolina State University, B.S. *Religion:* Christian.

ADDRESSES: Home—North Carolina. *Agent*—c/o Author Mail, Peachtree Publishers, 1700 Chattahoochee Ave., Atlanta, GA 30318.

CAREER: Author and illustrator. Viking Penguin, New York, NY, bird calendar artist, 1978—; *South Carolina Wildlife* magazine, Columbia, SC, illustrator, 1991—; freelance author and illustrator, 1987—. *Exhibitions:* Birds in Art, Leigh Yawkey Woodson Art Museum (Wausau, WI), 1992, 1993.

AWARDS, HONORS: First-place awards in North Carolina and Georgia art shows.

WRITINGS:

ILLUSTRATOR

Peter C. Alden and Roger Tory Peterson, *A Field Guide to the Birds Coloring Book,* Houghton Mifflin (Boston, MA), 1982.
A Guide to Bird Behavior, Volume 2, Little, Brown (Boston, MA), 1983.
Cathryn Sill, *About Birds: A Guide for Children,* Peachtree (Atlanta, GA), 1991.
Cathryn Sill, *About Mammals: A Guide for Children,* Peachtree (Atlanta, GA), 1997.
Lang Elliott, *Backyard Bird Walk* (with audiocassette or compact disc), Northwood Audio, 1998.
Cathryn Sill, *About Reptiles: A Guide for Children,* Peachtree (Atlanta, GA), 1999.
Richard K. Walton and Robert W. Lawson, *Birding by Ear: Western North America* (with audiocassette or compact disc), Houghton Mifflin (Boston, MA), 1999.
Cathryn Sill, *About Amphibians: A Guide for Children,* Peachtree (Atlanta, GA), 2000.
Cathryn Sill, *About Insects: A Guide for Children,* Peachtree (Atlanta, GA), 2000.
Cathryn Sill, *About Fish: A Guide for Children,* Peachtree (Atlanta, GA), 2002.
Cathryn Sill, *About Arachnids: A Guide for Children,* Peachtree (Atlanta, GA), 2003.

Also illustrator of the National Fish and Wildlife Foundation's 1998 Migratory Bird Day poster.

ADULT HUMOR

(With wife, Cathryn Sill, and brother, Ben Sill; and illustrator) *A Field Guide to Little-Known and Seldom-Seen Birds of North America,* Peachtree (Atlanta, GA), 1988.

(With Ben Sill and Cathryn Sill; and illustrator) *Another Field Guide to Little-Known and Seldom-Seen Birds of North America,* Peachtree (Atlanta, GA), 1990.
(With Ben Sill and Cathryn Sill; and illustrator) *Beyond Birdwatching: More than There Is to Know about Birding,* Peachtree (Atlanta, GA), 1993.

SIDELIGHTS: Illustrator and author John Sill has collaborated with his wife, author and educator Cathryn Sill, on several books for young naturalists that each focus on a specific part of the natural world. From birds to reptiles to spiders and other creepy-crawlies, books by the Sills have been praised by critics as "inviting, informative, and eye-catching," to quote *School Library Journal* critic Patricia Manning in her review of *About Amphibians: A Guide for Children.*

Complementing his wife's simple, direct text and a selection of black-and-white photos, Sill's water-color paintings take center stage in each of the "Guide for Children" books. Karey Wehner praised the full-page illustrations in *About Insects: A Guide for Children* as "bright, attractive, and nicely varied in composition" in a favorable *School Library Journal* review, while *Booklist*'s Gillian Engberg described Sill's artwork as "beautiful" and "naturalistic." "The artwork shows a sensitivity to young children's interests," observed Carolyn Phelan in a review of *About Mammals: A Guide for Children* for *Booklist.*

Sill once told *CA:* "I truly enjoy birds. Their beauty, their songs, and their behavior are a continual source of both pleasure and inspiration." He added: "I was very fortunate to have been able to learn a great deal from my father, whose main love was watercolor." Sill and his wife make their home in the mountains of North Carolina, where he was raised. In addition to book illustrations, his non-commissioned work has appeared on calendars, posters, and at numerous juried art shows. The National Fish and Wildlife Foundation's 1998 Migratory Bird Day poster was designed and painted by Sill.

BIOGRAPHICAL AND CRITICAL SOURCES:

PERIODICALS

Birder's World, February, 1999, "The Artist behind the Paintings: John Sill," p. 52.

Booklist, June 1, 1997, Carolyn Phelan, review of *About Mammals: A Guide for Children,* p. 1714; June 1, 1999, Carolyn Phelan, review of *About Reptiles: A Guide for Children,* p. 1835; February 1, 2000, Gillian Engberg, review of *About Insects: A Guide for Children,* p. 1026.

Childhood Education, spring, 2000, Emily A. Johnson, review of *About Reptiles,* p. 172.

School Library Journal, June, 1997, Susan Oliver, review of *About Mammals,* p. 113; July, 1999, Karey Wehner, review of *About Reptiles,* p. 90; June, 2000, Karey Wehner, review of *About Insects,* p. 98; June, 2001, Patricia Manning, review of *About Amphibians: A Guide for Children,* p. 141; June, 2002, Jean Pollock, review of *About Fish: A Guide for Children* p. 126.*

*   *   *

SIMPSON, (Bessie) Wallis Warfield (Spencer) 1896(?)-1986

PERSONAL: Original name, Bessie Wallis Warfield; born June 19, 1896 (some sources say 1895), in Blue Ridge Summit, PA; naturalized British citizen; died April 24, 1986, in Paris, France; daughter of Teackle Wallis and Alice (Montague) Warfield; married Earl Winfield Spencer, Jr., November 8, 1916 (divorced, 1927), married Ernest Aldrich Simpson, July 21, 1928 (divorced, 1937), married Edward, Duke of Windsor, June 3, 1937. *Religion:* Episcopalian.

CAREER: First woman governor of the American Hospital, Paris, France, beginning 1972.

AWARDS, HONORS: Named *Time* magazine's woman of the year, 1937.

WRITINGS:

Some Favorite Southern Recipes of the Duchess of Windsor, Charles Scribner's Sons (New York, NY), 1942.

The Heart Has Its Reasons: The Memoirs of the Duchess of Windsor, Michael Joseph (London, England), 1956.

(With Edward, Duke of Windsor) *Wallis & Edward: Letters, 1931-1937: The Intimate Correspondence of the Duke and Duchess of Windsor,* edited by Michael Bloch, Summit Books (New York, NY), 1986.

SIDELIGHTS: Wallis Warfield Simpson and her husband, the former King Edward VIII of England, had what has often been considered to be one of the most romantic love affairs of the twentieth century. When Edward's father, George V, died on January 20, 1936, Prince Edward became king at the age of forty-one. However, unbeknownst to much of the British public, the new, unmarried king had been carrying on an affair with Simpson for several years.

Simpson was at the time married to her second husband, London-based shipbroker Ernest Aldrich Simpson. Simpson was born into an old, venerable Southern family, but her father died of tuberculosis only a few months after she was born, and for most of Simpson's childhood she and her mother survived on the charity of Simpson's wealthy uncle, Solomon Warfield. At the age of twenty, Simpson married her first husband, a Navy lieutenant named Earl Winfield Spencer. Their marriage did not go well, and they eventually divorced. Only months after the divorce became final, Simpson, with no other means of support, married her second husband.

It was through her second husband that Simpson was presented at court and met the future King Edward VIII. Although their relationship was widely reported in the foreign press and certainly known to many upper-class Britons, the British press maintained a policy of not reporting on the private lives of their royalty, so the mass of the British population was not aware of it. However, when Edward did not break off the affair when he ascended to the throne, their relationship became legitimate news, as well as a cause of great consternation to certain members of the British ruling class. Edward, as king, was also head of the Church of England, and it was thought that the head of a church ought to display a higher standard of morality.

The scandal became a crisis when Simpson's husband granted her a divorce in the fall of 1936, to become official in the spring of 1937. When Edward was informed of this, he told the prime minister that he was going to marry Simpson. The prime minister told Edward that as the head of the Church of England he could not marry a divorcee, and the rest of the royal family, not to say the majority of the British public, agreed. Faced with such opposition, on December 10, 1936, Edward gave up his crown rather than give up the woman he loved.

The couple were married the following summer, and became the Duke and Duchess of Windsor, the title conferred on the ex-monarch by his brother and successor, the new King George VI. They settled at a villa in France, and although the two were forced to live abroad, mostly in the Bahamas, for the duration of World War II, they would spend most of the rest of their lives living and entertaining in France. Edward died in 1972, and within a few years Simpson's own health began to decline. She lived to be ninety, but after Edward's death she lived generally out of the public eye.

Her autobiography, *The Heart Has Its Reasons: The Memoirs of the Duchess of Windsor,* received much comment and was a bestseller in its day. It was often compared to her husband's own book, *A King's Story: The Memoirs of H.R.H. the Duke of Windsor,* which was published in 1951. Both books emphasize the romantic elements of their relationship. The year that Simpson died, a collection of letters edited by biographer Michael Bloch, who also penned several volumes about the Windsors, was published. *Wallis & Edward: Letters, 1931-1937: The Intimate Correspondence of the Duke and Duchess of Windsor,* consisted mostly of letters written by the Duchess to her American aunt during the mid-1930s, when the abdication crisis in Britain was at its height, although the book also includes some notes from Edward to Wallis.

BIOGRAPHICAL AND CRITICAL SOURCES:

BOOKS

Alice Countess of Romanoes, *The Spy Went Dancing,* G. P. Putnam's Sons (New York, NY), 1990.

Birmingham, Stephen, *Duchess: The Story of Wallis Warfield Windsor,* Little, Brown (Boston, MA), 1981.

Blackwood, Caroline, *The Last of the Duchess,* Pantheon Books (New York, NY), 1995.

Bocca, Geoffrey, *The Woman Who Would Be Queen,* Rinehart (New York, NY), 1954.

Higham, Charles, *The Duchess of Windsor: The Secret Life,* McGraw-Hill (New York, NY), 1988.

Jardine, Rev. R. Anderson, *At Long Last,* Murray & Gee (Hollywood, CA), 1943.

Lockridge, Norman, *Lese Majesty: The Private Lives of the Duke and Duchess of Windsor,* Boar's Head Books (New York, NY), 1952.

Martin, Ralph G., *The Woman He Loved,* Simon & Schuster (New York, NY), 1974.

PERIODICALS

Atlantic, October, 1956, p. 102.
Booklist, October 1, 1956, p. 68.
Bookmark, October, 1956, p. 8.
Book Review Digest, 1956, p. 1013; 1987, p. 2009.
Chicago Sunday Tribune, October 7, 1956, p. 1.
Christian Science Monitor, September 27, 1956, p. 5.
Cleveland Open Shelf, December, 1956, p. 2.
Library Journal, September 15, 1956, p. 1991; August, 1986, Pat Ensor, review of *Wallis and Edward: Letters, 1931-1937: The Intimate Correspondence of the Duke and Duchess of Windsor,* p. 141.
Los Angeles Times, December 15, 1994, Patricia Ward Biederman, "Icons of Style," p. E1.
Mademoiselle, October, 1986, Barbara Grizzuti Harrison, October, 1986, "Tear Jerks: Looking Back at the Duke and Duchess of Windsor," p. 170.
New Leader, December 1, 1986, Ray Alan, "Hanging on Princes' Favors," pp. 16-17.
New Statesman, December 6, 1996, Susan Jeffreys, "Sixty Years Not a Queen," p. 48.
New Statesman & Nation, October 6, 1956, p. 416.
Newsweek, June 16, 1986, p. 72.
New York, January 16, 1989, Leslie Field, "Palais Royal: How the Windsors Lived," pp. 25-26.
New York Herald Tribune Book Review, September 30, 1956, p. 3.
New York Times, September 30, 1956, p. 7; March 16, 1980, Russell Baker, "Pookie and the Duke of Windsor," p. 14; December 15, 1980, Susan Heller Anderson, "An Old Friend Fondly Recalls the Duchess of Windsor," pp. 21, B16; December 13, 1986, A. L. Rowse, "Let's Be Fair to Edward and Wallis," pp. 19, 27; December 21, 1989, Alan Riding, "A House of Windsor Reclaims Its Grace," pp. B1, C1; October 5, 1995, Christopher Mason, "A House Is Coming out of Exile, for One Day," pp. B4, C5; January 30, 2003, Alan Cowell, "A Big Secret Wallis Simpson Kept from her Royal Lover," p. A1.
New York Times Book Review, June 29, 1986, Judith Martin, review of *Wallis and Edward,* p. 12.
People, December 22, 1986, Charlene Bry, "End of an Era," pp. 126-127; February 12, 1996, "The Greatest Love Stories of the Century: King Edward VIII and Wallis Simpson," pp. 66-68.
San Francisco Chronicle, September 30, 1956, p. 19.
Saturday Review, October 6, 1956, p. 28.
Spectator, October 5, 1956, p. 465.
Springfield Republican, October 7, 1956, p. 10C.

Time, January 4, 1937, "Woman of the Year: Mrs. Wallis Warfield Simpson;" October, 1956, p. 94.

Times (London, England), August 24, 2000, Richard Ford, "Domineering Delilah Who Ensnared a King," p. 5.

Times Literary Supplement, October 5, 1956, p. 582; May 16, 1986, p. 527.

Town & Country, April, 1988, Jane Wilkens Michael, "A Love Affair with Style," pp. 160-163.

Women's Wear Daily, September 13, 1999, Keitha McLean, "The Duchess of Windsor: Wallis Simpson on Romance, Clothes and the Pursuit of Happiness," p. 68S.

ONLINE

British Broadcasting Company Web site, http://www.bbc.co.uk/ (January 29, 2003), Chris Jones, "Profile: Wallis Simpson."

OBITUARIES:

PERIODICALS

Los Angeles Times, April 25, 1986, p. 1; April 30, 1986, pp. 5, 10.

New York Times, April 25, 1986, pp. 1, 13, D19; April 30, 1986, pp. 52, B4.*

*   *   *

SLOAN, SUSAN R.

PERSONAL: Born in New York, NY.

ADDRESSES: Home—Bainbridge Island, WA. *Agent*—c/o Author Mail, Warner Books, 1271 Avenue of the Americas, New York, NY 10020. *E-mail*—feedback@sloanbooks.com.

CAREER: Attorney and novelist. Operates animal rescue center, Furrytown Farm.

WRITINGS:

Guilt by Association, Warner Books, (New York, NY), 1995.

An Isolated Incident, Warner Books, (New York, NY), 1998.

Act of God, Warner Books, (New York, NY), 2002.

SIDELIGHTS: Susan R. Sloan was born and educated in New York and spent most of her early life on the East coast. She eventually moved to California where she lived for fifteen years. She now resides in the state of Washington on Bainbridge Island in Puget Sound. In addition to her career as a writer, Sloan is also devoted to rescuing and helping abused and abandoned animals. To this end, she has established Furrytown Farm, a place where such animals can receive medical care and rehabilitation.

Before she began writing, Sloan was a practicing attorney. Her novels always address questions surrounding the role and effectiveness of the law in a civil society and the extent to which justice can be done. To date, all of her novels are built around the exploration of a social issue, such as equality before the law, bigotry, and the abortion controversy.

Sloan's first novel, *Guilt by Association,* revolves around a young woman's rape by a man from a powerful family. The crime was committed in 1962. At that time, a crime such as acquaintance rape was barely acknowledged, much less prosecuted. The book follows the victim through this tumultuous period in America, describing the changes in her life as well as the life of the culture. Thirty years after the event a situation arises that makes it possible for her to bring her experience out into the open. Her decision to speak publicly and the consequences both personally and legally drive the action. The impact of this event on the life of the victim and her instigation of a process of justice change her identity from victim to victor.

In *An Isolated Incident,* the author again finds herself fascinated by a social issue—bigotry, in this case—and the stew of gossip, secrets, destruction that spring from it. The story is set on an island some distance from Seattle, an area that Sloan knows well. Events are set in motion by the murder of a teenage girl, the daughter of one of the notable men of the community. The crime is committed in a town where violence is virtually unknown, or so it seems. The drive for revenge is strong in the wake of this tragedy. One of the larger issues explored in the book is the ability of the law to dispense justice when it is opposed to the wishes of a mob. A *Publishers Weekly* reviewer wrote that *An Isolated Incident* "convincingly portrays the worst consequences of stereotyping."

Terrorism and its wrenching aftermath are explored in Sloan's third novel, *Act of God.* A bomb goes off at an abortion clinic, killing a large number of people. A likely suspect is found and arrested. Is he really the criminal? The attorney assigned to defend him finds herself in the unenviable position of trying to get a fair trial for a man who seems unquestionably guilty. The radical mind-set is explored along with questions about the legal system's ability to discover the truth. A *Publishers Weekly* reviewer called the novel "provocative" and "explosive."

BIOGRAPHICAL AND CRITICAL SOURCES:

PERIODICALS

Booklist, December 1, 1997, Stephanie Zvirin, review of *An Isolated Incident,* p. 611; April 1, 2002, Connie Fletcher, review of *Act of God,* p. 1310.

Kirkus Reviews, October 15, 1994, review of *Guilt by Association,* p. 1368; December, 1997, review of *An Isolated Incident,* p. 1734; March 1, 2002, review of *Act of God,* p. 287.

Law Institute Journal, October, 1995, Peta Kowalski, review of *Guilt by Association,* p. 1050.

Library Journal, October 15, 1997, Mary Ellen Elsbernd, review of *An Isolated Incident,* p. 94; April 1, 2002, Jetta Carol Culpepper, review of *Act of God,* p. 143.

Los Angeles Times Book Review, March 12, 1995, Charles Champlin, review of *Guilt by Association,* p. 6.

Publishers Weekly, November 3, 1997, review of *An Isolated Incident,* p. 65; March 25, 2002, review of *Act of God,* p. 42.

ONLINE

Fortner Books Web site, http://www.fortnerbooks.com/ (June 7, 2002).

Susan R. Sloan Web site, http://www.sloanbooks.com (June 7, 2002).*

*   *   *

SLOCUM, Joshua 1844-1910(?)

PERSONAL: Born February 20, 1844, in Wilmot Township, Nova Scotia, Canada; died c. 1910 (some sources say November 14, 1909), at sea; naturalized U.S. citizen, 1869; son of John (a farmer and bootmaker) and Sarah Jane (Southern) Slocum; married Virginia Albertina Walker, 1871 (died 1884); married Henrietta Miller Elliott, 1886; children: (first marriage) four. *Education:* Attended school until age ten.

CAREER: Sailor and lecturer; sailed around the world alone, 1895-98.

WRITINGS:

Voyage of the Liberdade (also see below), Press of Robinson & Stephenson (Boston, MA), 1890, reprinted, Dover (Mineola, NY), 1998.

Sailing Alone Around the World, illustrated by Thomas Fogarty and George Varian, Century Co. (New York, NY), 1900, reprinted, Regatta Press (Mount Kisco, NY), 2000, published as *Around the World in the Sloop Spray,* Charles Scribner's Sons (New York, NY), 1903.

Sailing Alone Around the World and *Voyage of the Liberdade,* introduction by Arthur Ransome, Hart-Davis (London, England), 1948.

The Voyages of Joshua Slocum, collected and introduced by Walter Magnes Teller, Rutgers University Press (New Brunswick, NJ), 1958, anniversary edition, 1995.

Voyage Around the Horn, Phoenix (London, England), 1995.

Also author of *Voyage of the Destroyer from New York to Brazil . . . ,* 1894.

SIDELIGHTS: Captain Joshua Slocum was a Canadian-born American sailor who spent his life from the age of ten at sea. From the time of his first command in 1869 until 1886, Slocum navigated numerous ships carrying cargo to anywhere from Australia to Brazil. After the age of wind-powered sail boats was largely over, Slocum decided he would navigate a ship he had rebuilt called the *Spray* around the world by himself. His exploits on this trip were published as *Sailing Alone Around the World.* Slocum died c. 1910 after attempting to sail down the Amazon to the sea and back to New England. He left on November 14, 1909 and was never seen again.

Slocum's *Sailing Alone Around the World* was first serialized in *Century* then published as a book in 1900, and is considered a classic of nautical literature.

Slocum's tale of his 46,000-mile journey was a success and enabled him to purchase a farm in Martha's Vineyard. "Slocum's writing is as elegant as his thirty-seven-foot sloop," noted a *New Yorker* critic. "For his gift of graceful expression, his quiet humor and his deep, knowing love of the sea, Captain Slocum stands alone," wrote Bernie Lee in *Sports Illustrated.*

Sailing Alone Around the World has been published in numerous editions since its first appearance and critics have been largely positive in their assessment of the work. Jonathan Raban in the *New York Review of Books* noted that though Slocum was in need of an editor to add the polishing touches to his work, the captain has "a pitch perfect ear for tone and cadence—and he created for himself a written voice of understated eloquence and tinderdry irony. In outline, *Sailing Alone* can easily be misrepresented as solemn. . . . In reality, it is surprisingly funny. . . . If his book resembles *Walden,* it's even more like Mark Twain's *Walden.*" The Joshua Slocum Society International was founded in 1955 to keep the legendary captain's memory alive.

BIOGRAPHICAL AND CRITICAL SOURCES:

BOOKS

Blake, Robert J. *Spray,* Philomel Books (New York, NY), 1996.

Clark, James I., *Three Years on the Ocean,* Raintree Publishers (Milwaukee, WI), 1980.

Fortman, Janis L., *First to Sail the World Alone: Joshua Slocum,* C.P.I. (New York, NY), 1978.

Joyce, Jessie Slocum, *Joshua Slocum, Sailor: A Biography Written by Beth Day, from the Story Told by His Daughter Jessie Slocum Joyce,* Houghton Mifflin (Boston, MA), 1953.

Lasky, Kathryn, *Born in the Breezes: The Voyages of Joshua Slocum,* Orchard Books (New York, NY), 2001.

Lopes, Myra A., *Captain Joshua Slocum: A Centennial Tribute,* RPI Graphics (New Bedford, MA), 1994.

Lopes, Myra A., *Captain Slocum's Life before and after the Spray,* RPI Graphics (New Bedford, MA), 1997.

Roberts-Goodson, R. Bruce, *Spray: The Ultimate Cruising Boat,* Sheridan House (Dobbs Ferry, NY), 1995.

Spencer, Ann, *Alone at Sea: The Adventures of Joshua Slocum,* Doubleday Canada (Toronto, Canada), 1998.

Teller, Walter Magnes, *Joshua Slocum,* Rutgers University Press (New Brunswick, NJ), 1971.

Teller, Walter Magnes, *The Search for Captain Slocum: A Biography,* Scribner (New York, NY), 1956.

PERIODICALS

Cruising World, April, 1995, Phillip Shea, "How He Made Spray 'Pay,'" p. 64.

Maclean's, July 6, 1992, John DeMont, "Sailing Solo," p. 50.

New Yorker, September 7, 1998, review of *Sailing Alone Around the World,* p. 14.

New York Review of Books, April 20, 1995, Jonathan Raban, review of *Sailing Alone Around the World,* p. 21.

Sports Illustrated, September 5, 1988, Bernie Lee, "Around the World Alone," p. 132.

Yachting, June, 1984, Chris Caswell, review of *Sailing Alone Around the World,* p. 30; February, 1995, Barry Pickthall, "The Lonesome Road," p. 72.*

*   *   *

SMEDES, Lewis B. 1921-2002

OBITUARY NOTICE—See index for *CA* sketch: Born August 21, 1921, in MI; died after a fall December 19, 2002, in Arcadia, CA. Minister, educator, and author. Smedes was an evangelical minister and professor who was best known for his teachings and writings on forgiveness. After earning an undergraduate degree from Calvin College in 1947, he completed his M.Div. at Calvin Theological Seminary in 1951 and his Ph.D. at the Free University of Amsterdam; he also took graduate courses at Oxford University and the University of Basel. Smedes' early career consisted of serving as a pastor in the Christian Reformed Church, but most of his career was spent in academia. He was an associate professor of religion at Calvin College from 1957 to 1960 and a professor from 1960 to 1968. He then moved to Fuller Theological Seminary in Pasadena, California, where he joined the faculty as professor of theology and ethics and was chair of the department from 1990 until his retirement in 1995. Smedes was an open-minded theologian who sometimes departed from his evangelical routes. For example, he was more willing to accept other people's homosexuality rather than to condemn it outright. It was for his teachings about forgiveness, however, that he became most noted. Smedes believed that a person should not wait for someone else to apologize for a sin or other transgression but should forgive them as soon as possible. In this way, one could best get on with his or her life and not become lost in destructive hatred. Smedes wrote about this philosophy in his influential book *Forgive and Forget: Healing the Hurt We Don't Deserve* (1985). He also wrote many other spiritual guides, including *Love within Limits: A Realist's View of I Corinthians* (1978), *Shame and Grace: Healing the Shame We Don't Deserve* (1993), and *A Life of Distinction: What It Takes to Live with Courage, Honesty, and Gratitude* (2002), and was the author of the autobiography *My God and I: A Memoir* (2003).

OBITUARIES AND OTHER SOURCES:

PERIODICALS

Chicago Tribune, December 23, 2002, section 1, p. 11.
Los Angeles Times, December 21, 2002, p. B16.
Washington Post, December 23, 2002, p. B5.

* * *

SMITH, Doris Buchanan 1934-2002

OBITUARY NOTICE—See index for *CA* sketch: Born June 1, 1934, in Washington, DC; died August 8, 2002, in Atlanta, GA. Author. Smith was an award-winning author of novels and short stories for young adults. She attended South Georgia College from 1952 to 1953, but never entered the job market. Instead, she was a full-time mother who, over the course of many years, was also a foster mother to over 200 children. Beginning in the early 1970s, she transformed her understanding of children and adolescents into a series of realistic young adult novels that deal with such important issues as death, child abuse, divorce, juvenile delinquency, and eating disorders. She penned seventeen books during her career, including *A Taste of Blackberries* (1973), *Kelly's Creek* (1975), *Last Was*

Lloyd (1981), *Return to Bitter Creek* (1986), and her last novel, *Remember the Red-Shouldered Hawk* (1994). Among her many honors were three Georgia Children's Book Author of the Year awards, which she won in 1974, 1975, and 1982, the 1973 Child Study Association Book of the Year Award for *A Taste of Blackberries,* and the 1986 Parents' Choice Literature Award for *Return to Bitter Creek.*

OBITUARIES AND OTHER SOURCES:

BOOKS

St. James Guide to Young Adult Writers, second edition, St. James (Detroit, MI), 1999.

PERIODICALS

Washington Post, August 16, 2002, p. B6.

* * *

SMITH, Harry E(dmund) 1928-2002

OBITUARY NOTICE—See index for *CA* sketch: Born August 29, 1928, in Austin, TX; died October 24, 2002, in Santa Fe, NM. Minister, college administrator, and author. Smith was a former president of Austin College. He earned a B.A. from the University of Texas in 1950, a bachelor's degree in divinity from Yale University in 1953, and a doctorate from Drew University in 1965. During the late 1950s and 1960s he was campus pastor at the University of North Carolina, Chapel Hill, and served from 1968 to 1969 as chancellor for residential college development there. Before becoming president of Austin College, Smith was an associate professor of religion in higher education at Yale and was executive director of the Society for Values in Higher Education. While serving as Austin College president he worked hard to improve the campus and encouraged students to take foreign languages and study abroad. Smith was the author of *Secularization and the University* (1968).

OBITUARIES AND OTHER SOURCES:

BOOKS

Who's Who in America, 46th edition, Marquis (Wilmette, IL), 1990.

ONLINE

Austin College Web site, http://www.austincollege.edu/ (February 4, 2003).

*   *   *

SNOWDON, David A. 1952-

PERSONAL: Born May 10, 1952, in Redlands, CA. *Education:* California Polytechnic State University, B.Sc., 1974; California State University, M.S., 1976; University of Minnesota, M.Ph., 1977.

ADDRESSES: Office—University of Kentucky, Center on Aging, 303 Sanders-Brown Center 0230, Lexington, KY 40506. *E-mail*—snowdon@uky.edu.

CAREER: Division of Epidemiology, School of Public Health, University of Minnesota, Minneapolis, MN, resident fellow, beginning 1977; Sanders-Brown Center on Aging, University of Kentucky Medical Center, professor of neurology.

MEMBER: Society of Epidemiology Research, American Association of Advanced Sciences, Phi Kappa Phi.

WRITINGS:

Aging with Grace: What the Nun Study Teaches Us about Leading Longer, Healthier, and More Meaningful Lives, Bantam Books (New York, NY), 2001.

SIDELIGHTS: Featured internationally in the media for his research on aging, particularly his work with the School Sisters of Notre Dame, David A. Snowdon has published his findings in a book titled *Aging with Grace: What the Nun Study Teaches Us about Leading Longer, Healthier, and More Meaningful Lives.* Snowdon's "nun study," as his research is popularly known as, focuses on the story of a group of nuns between the ages of seventy-five and 106, studying their medical histories and their lifestyles to gain clues about the onset of aging and Alzheimer's disease. Snowdon launched his research with the nuns in 1986 and focused on this group of subjects because of the similarity of their diets, lifestyle and other characteristics. Although he has published some of his findings in *Aging with Grace,* Snowdon continues to work on the study at the University of Kentucky. In the meantime, his book has been published to critical acclaim, with reviewers praising Snowdon for his delicate balance of science and story. For example, John McCrone wrote in the *Guardian* that *Aging with Grace* is a "rare book" because of "the way it combines cutting-edge science with an inside view of how that knowledge is being won." Similarly, Jodith Janes said in the *Library Journal* that Snowdon has written an "inspirational and fascinating" book that melds "personal histories with scientific fact" in an extraordinary manner.

BIOGRAPHICAL AND CRITICAL SOURCES:

PERIODICALS

America, October 8, 2001, Myles N. Sheehan, "The Nun Study," p. 30.
Guardian, August 18, 2001, John McCrone, "Sisters of Mercy."
Library Journal, June 15, 2001, Jodith Janes, review of *Aging with Grace: What the Nun Study Teaches Us about Leading Longer, Healthier, and More Meaningful Lives,* p. 96.
Prevention, November, 2001, Michele J. Morris, "Smile and Your Body Smiles with You," p. 1S36.
Publishers Weekly, May 7, 2001, review of *Aging with Grace: What the Nun Study Teaches Us about Leading Longer, Healthier, and More Meaningful Lives,* p. 239.
Time, May 14, 2001, "The Nun Study: How One Scientist and 678 Sisters are Helping Unlock the Secrets of Alzheimer's," p. 54.*

*   *   *

SOHL, Jerry 1913-2002
(Nathan Butler, Roberta Jean Mountjoy, Sean Mei Sullivan)

OBITUARY NOTICE—See index for *CA* sketch: Born December 2, 1913, in Los Angeles, CA; died November 4, 2002, in Thousand Oaks, CA. Journalist and author. Sohl was best known as a science-fiction novelist and contributor to the television series *Twilight Zone* and *Star Trek.* He attended the Central College of Arts and Sciences in Chicago, but dropped out in 1934 to pursue a career in journalism. Serving in the U.S. Army Air Force during World War II, he returned home to join the staff at the *Daily Pantagraph* in Bloomington, Illinois, where he worked as a photographer, reporter, and critic until 1958. Even before leaving the newspaper, he had embarked on a career writing for television, contributing scripts to such series as *Alfred Hitchcock Presents* and *Route 66,* as well as to science-fiction programs. He also began writing novels, the first of which was *The Haploids* (1952). Most of Sohl's work was in the genre of science fiction, but he also occasionally wrote mysteries, horror, or adventure novels. Sohl completed over two dozen novels, some pseudonymously, and three screenplays, including *Twelve Hours to Kill* (1960) and *Die, Monster, Die* (1963). His last novels, *Death Sleep* and *Black Thunder,* appeared in 1983.

OBITUARIES AND OTHER SOURCES:

BOOKS

St. James Guide to Science-Fiction Writers, fourth edition, St. James Press (Detroit, MI), 1996.

PERIODICALS

Chicago Tribune, November 11, 2002, section 1, p. 13.
Independent (London, England), November 12, 2002, p. 18.
Los Angeles Times, November 10, 2002, p. B18.
Washington Post, November 20, 2002, p. B6.

*   *   *

SOLOMON, Ezra 1920-2002

OBITUARY NOTICE—See index for *CA* sketch: Born March 20, 1920, in Rangoon, Burma (now Myanmar); died of a stroke December 9, 2002, in Stanford, CA. Economist, educator, and author. Solomon was a founding director of Stanford University's International Center for the Advancement of Management Educa-

tion and a former economics advisor to President Richard M. Nixon. Born in what is now Myanmar, he received his bachelor's degree from the University of Rangoon just before the World War II Japanese invasion in 1940. Fleeing to India, he joined the British Royal Navy and became a gunboat captain during the war. When he received a graduate school fellowship in 1947, he moved to the United States to attend the University of Chicago, where he earned his doctorate in 1950 and became a naturalized U.S. citizen. He was also a professor there until 1960, when he moved to Stanford University to teach. He was the university's first Dean Witter Professor of Finance from 1965 until 1971. In 1963 Solomon published his influential book *The Theory of Financial Management,* which helped establish his reputation as a prominent economic theorist. This influential work led to a post, from 1971 to 1973, on President Nixon's Council of Economic Advisors, which supported the decision to abandon the gold standard and put limits on the U.S. money supply. He then took on a number of consulting jobs, including to the U.S. Secretary of the Treasury from 1973 to 1975, to the government of Manitoba, Canada, and to a number of U.S. agencies and institutions. Solomon was the author or editor of thirteen books, including *The Anxious Economy* (1976) and *International Patterns of Inflation* (1984). For his work at Austin College, he was awarded the college's most prestigious award, the Founder's Medal, in 1994.

OBITUARIES AND OTHER SOURCES:

BOOKS

Who's Who in America, 56th edition, Marquis (New Providence, NJ), 2001.

PERIODICALS

Los Angeles Times, December 21, 2002, p. B17.
New York Times, December 19, 2002, p. A29.

*   *   *

SOMERVILL, Barbara A(nn) 1948-

PERSONAL: Born July 28, 1948, in New Rochelle, NY; daughter of Harold P. (a plumbing and heating contractor) and Hope (a secretary and bookkeeper; maiden name, Hayden) Klesius; married Michael O. McWilliams, June 10, 1972 (divorced, July 10, 1986);

married Charles F. Somervill (a chemist), June 30, 1990; children: Scott, Matthew (first marriage); Seth, Taylor (second marriage). *Education:* St. Lawrence University, B.A. (English), 1970. *Religion:* Episcopalian. *Hobbies and other interests:* Bridge, needlework, reading, theater.

ADDRESSES: Agent—c/o Author Mail, Morgan Reynolds, 620 South Elm St., Ste. 223, Greensboro, NC 27406. *E-mail*—Somervill@aol.com.

CAREER: Author, editor, and video scriptwriter. Karastan/Bigelow, Greenville, SC, public relations manager, 1986-88; PYA/Monarch, Greenville, SC, editor of trade publication, 1988-94; Somervill, Inc. (advertising agency), Simpsonville, SC, president, 1994—.

MEMBER: Society of Children's Book Writers and Illustrators, NAFE.

WRITINGS:

The Best Guide to Success: How to Get Ahead in Your Career, Renaissance Books (Los Angeles, CA), 1999.
Historical Case Studies: The Great Migration (text and teacher's guide), Globe Fearon Educational (Upper Saddle River, NJ), 2000.
(With Lewis Parker) *Survival Guide for Computer Literacy: Making Your Way in the World of Computers* (text and teacher's guide), Globe Fearon Educational (Upper Saddle River, NJ), 2000.
Pacemaker United States History: Critical Thinking Exercises (workbook and teachers' guide), Pearson Educational (Upper Saddle River, NJ), 2001.
Ida M. Tarbell: Pioneer Investigative Reporter, Morgan Reynolds (Greensboro, NC), 2002.
Franklin Pierce, Compass Point Books (Minneapolis, MN), 2002.
Votes for Women!: The Story of Carrie Chapman Catt, Morgan Reynolds (Greensboro, NC), 2003.
Enchantment of the World: Iceland, Children's Press (New York, NY), 2003.
Andrew Jackson, Compass Point Books (Minneapolis, MN), 2003.
James K. Polk, Compass Point Books (Minneapolis, MN), 2003.

Backstage at a Newscast, Children's Press (Danbury, CT), 2003.
Scott O'Grady: Behind Enemy Lines, Children's Press (Danbury, CT), 2003.
Wolverines, Child's World (Chanhassen, MN), 2003.
Australia, Child's World (Chanhassen, MN), 2004.
Mary McLeod Bethune: African-American Educator, Child's World (Chanhassen, MN), 2004.

Also author of student work books.

"SEA TO SHINING SEA" SERIES

Florida, Children's Press (New York, NY), 2001.
Alaska, Children's Press (New York, NY), 2002.
Maryland, Children's Press (New York, NY), 2003.
Pennsylvania, Children's Press (New York, NY), 2003.
West Virginia, Children's Press (New York, NY), 2003.
Mississippi, Children's Press (New York, NY), 2003.

"SPIRIT OF AMERICA" SERIES

Massachusetts, Child's World (Chanhassen, MN), 2003.
New York, Child's World (Chanhassen, MN), 2003.
The Rhode Island Colony, Child's World (Chanhassen, MN), 2003.

ADAPTATIONS: The Best Guide to Success was adapted as an audiobook, Renaissance Books (Los Angeles, CA), 1999.

WORK IN PROGRESS: Warren G. Harding, Compass Point Books (Minneapolis, MN), 2004; "Our Living World" series, Traditions Publishing, 2004; *Biography of a Biome: Praries* and *Biography of a Biome: The Sahara,* Millbrook Press (Brookfield, CT), 2004; *Mary McLeod Bethune, Australia, New York, Massachusetts,* and *Rhode Island,* Child's World (New York, NY), 2004; *Scott O'Grady: Behind Enemy Lines,* Rosen (New York, NY), 2004.

SIDELIGHTS: Barbara A. Somervill worked for many years in the business world, using her writing talent to promote businesses through company publications and other forms of advertising. In 2000, she began a second career as the author of children's nonfiction books, researching and organizing a multitude of facts into easily accessible formats for students. Among her many titles are biographical accounts of several U.S. presidents and noted late-nineteenth-century figures of history. *Ida M. Tarbell: Pioneer Investigative Reporter* follows the career of the muckraking journalist from her youth in west Pennsylvania oil country to her work as a biographer and her well-known 1904 exposé on millionaire John D. Rockefeller and the Standard Oil Company. The life of a noted early feminist is recounted in Somervill's *Votes for Women!: The Life of Carrie Chapman Catt,* which discusses Catt's work as a prominent prohibitionist and vocal advocate of the Nineteenth Amendment to the U.S. Constitution that guaranteed women the right to vote.

Somervill credits being laid off from an editorial staff job as "the best thing that ever happened to my writing career. . . . My severance pay funded eleven months of freedom, during which I started my freelance writing company. I've never looked back. I've never been happier."

Since beginning her career, Sovervill has admittedly "written some strange stuff: a brochure about caskets, a video script about a hospital bed with a potty in it, a safety script about laying asphalt, and a dozen scripts about tires. I've even written a magazine article about cowboy hats and how they're made. I've written about states and presidents, the environment, and a couple of gutsy ladies from the 1900s.

"If anyone had told me ten years ago that I would end up writing children's nonfiction books—and loving it—I wouldn't have believed it. I have a strong business background and figured that was the direction I'd head.

"The best part of my job is talking to professionals from all over the world about what they do. I've interviewed salmon experts, walrus commissioners, condor savers, and some delightful Icelandic citizens. In writing about states, I've heard from residents of Florida, Illinois, Alaska, and Pennsylvania. Hopefully, I was able to convey their pride in their culture."

Somervill's advice to budding writers: "Read, read, read. I'm never without a book—even when I go out to dinner or to a movie. There's always time to finish a page or start a new chapter. I generally have favorite authors rather than favorite books. I've read everything written by Jane Austen, Ken Follett, Jack Higgins, Maeve Binchy, and Elizabeth Peters. Yes, they are VERY different authors—but who wants to read the same thing all the time?

"Among children's books, I love *Ellen Tebbits, The Wind in the Willows, Bunnicula,* and *Charlotte's Web. The Midwife's Apprentice* really impressed me as a children's book with a mature approach to a difficult topic. Future writers—don't discount children's authors as poor or weak writers. They're not! It is much harder to write well using a third-grader's vocabulary than it is to babble on and on for adults.

"Every published author provides writing lessons for his or her readers. Look for the 'golden moments' in every writer's work. A careful eye will uncover a brilliantly written phrase, a superb description, or something emotionally moving. I discovered my first golden reading moment when I was seven, reading *Charlotte's Web:* 'She [Charlotte] was in a class by herself. It is not often that someone comes along who is a true friend and a good writer. Charlotte was both.'"

BIOGRAPHICAL AND CRITICAL SOURCES:

PERIODICALS

Booklist, March 15, 2000, Nancy Spillman, review of *The Best Guide to Success: How to Get Ahead in Your Career,* p. 1396; March 1, 2002, Gillian Engberg, review of *Ida M. Tarbell: Pioneer Investigative Reporter,* p. 1145; November 15, 2002, GraceAnne A. DeCandido, review of *Votes for Women!: The Story of Carrie Chapman Catt,* p. 599.
Children's Bookwatch, January, 2003, review of *Votes for Women!: The Story of Carrie Chapman Catt,* p. 4.
School Library Journal, June, 2002, Carol Fazioli, review of *Ida M. Tarbell,* p. 169; January, 2003, Lisa Dennis, review of *Votes for Women!,* p. 171.

*   *   *

SOTO, Lourdes Diáz

PERSONAL: Born in New York, NY; children: Maria Soto Ponton, Daniel E., Deane G. *Ethnicity:* "Puerto Rican." *Education:* Kingston Hospital School of Nursing, R.N. (magna cum laude), 1966; State University of New York—College at New Paltz, B.S., 1970; Hunter College of the City University of New York, M.S. (cum laude), 1974; Pennsylvania State University, Ph.D., 1986.

ADDRESSES: Office—Department of Curriculum and Instruction, 149 Chambers Bldg., Pennsylvania State University, University Park, PA 16802; fax: 814-863-7602. *E-mail*—lcs1@psu.edu.

CAREER: Kindergarten teacher in Mamaroneck, NY, 1970-74; head teacher at a school in Dorado, PR, 1974-78; junior and senior high school teacher of chemistry and health, Toa Alta, PR, 1978-80; teacher of mathematics, science, and language arts at an elementary school, Guaynabo, PR, 1980-82; Florida Atlantic University, Boca Raton, assistant professor of education, 1986-87; Pennsylvania State University, University Park, assistant professor of education, 1987-91, member of executive board of Commission for Women, 1988-91, member of advisory board for Cedar Day Care Center, 1990, and director of Comprehensive Bilingual Early Childhood Project; Lehigh University, Bethlehem, PA, associate professor of education, 1991-95, and coordinator of bilingual education program; Pennsylvania State University, University Park, professor of education, 1995—, and coordinator of bilingual/multicultural education. Columbia University, visiting professor at Teachers College, 2001-02; guest speaker at Costa Rican universities, 1997, and at other institutions, including University of West Virginia. California Tomorrow, member of advisory panel; Commonwealth of Pennsylvania, member of Latino Commission.

MEMBER: National Association for Bilingual Educators (past chair of early childhood special interest group), National Association for the Education of Young Children (chair of bilingual/bicultural caucus), American Anthropological Association (past chair of cultural acquisition and transmission committee), American Educational Research Association, National Association of Early Childhood Teacher Educators, Society for Research in Child Development, American Association of University Women, Pennsylvania Association for Bilingual Education (president, 1992-94), Spanish-Speaking Organizations of the Lehigh Valley (member-at-large of governing board, 1992-94), Phi Kappa Delta.

AWARDS, HONORS: Honorary member of editorial board, *Taboo;* grant from Spencer Foundation.

WRITINGS:

Language, Culture, and Power: Bilingual Families and the Struggle for Quality Education, State University of New York Press (Albany, NY), 1997.
(Editor and contributor) *The Politics of Early Childhood Education,* Peter Lang Publishers (New York, NY), 2000.
Making a Difference in the Lives of Bilingual/Bicultural Children, Peter Lang Publishers (New York, NY), 2001.

Contributor to books, including *Children's Play in Diverse Cultures,* edited by J. Johnson and J. Roopnarine, State University of New York Press (Albany, NY), 1994; *Unauthorized Methods: Strategies for Critical Teaching,* edited by J. Kincheloe and S. Steinberg, Routledge (New York, NY), 1998; *The Post-Formal Reader: Cognition and Education,* edited by J. Kincheloe, Garland Publishing (New York, NY), 1999; *Early Childhood Curriculum: A Review of Current Research,* edited by C. Seefeldt, Teachers College Press (New York, NY), 1999; and *Kidworld: Childhood Studies, Global Perspectives, and Education,* edited by G. Cannella, J. Kincheloe, and K. Anijar, Peter Lang Publishers (New York, NY), 2002. Contributor to academic journals, including *Hispanic Outlook in Higher Education, Insights on Diversity, Young Children, Urban Review, Anthropology and Education Quarterly, Contemporary Psychology Journal, Multicultural Education, Journal of Early Childhood Teacher Education, Contemporary Issues in Early Childhood Education,* and *Journal of Curriculum Inquiry.* Member of editorial board, *Bilingual Research Journal, Wesleyan Review, Early Childhood Research Quarterly,* and *International Journal of Early Childhood Literacy.*

BIOGRAPHICAL AND CRITICAL SOURCES:

PERIODICALS

Childhood Education, summer, 2002, MaryJane Blasi, review of *The Politics of Early Childhood Education,* p. 245.

*　　*　　*

SOUTHERN, Eileen (Jackson) 1920-2002

OBITUARY NOTICE—See index for *CA* sketch: Born February 19, 2002, in Minneapolis, MN; died October 13, 2002, in Port Charlotte, FL. Musicologist, educator, and author. Southern was an authority on African-

American and Renaissance music. She received her master's degree in music from the University of Chicago in 1941, after which she taught music at colleges in Texas, Louisiana, and South Carolina. Moving to New York City in 1954, Southern taught at public schools until she received her Ph.D. from New York University in 1961. During the 1960s she was a professor at Brooklyn College of the City University of New York, followed by several years during the early 1970s as an associate professor at York College of the City University of New York. Her final years in academia were spent at Harvard University, where she was professor of music and Afro-American studies from 1976 to 1987 and headed the department of Afro-American studies from 1975 to 1979. Although very interested in Renaissance music, about which she wrote in her doctoral thesis and in *The Buxheim Organ Book* (1963), the main focus of Southern's research, teaching, and writing was on the contributions African Americans made to the music world. Toward this end, she published numerous works, including *The Music of Black Americans: A History* (1971; third edition, 1997) and, with Josephine Wright, *Images: Iconography of Music in African-American Culture (1770s-1920s)* (2000), and compiled the *Biographical Dictionary of Afro-American and African Musicians* (1982). Southern made a number of breakthroughs in her career. Struggling calmly against racism, she managed to become the first African-American woman to receive tenure at Harvard University, and she founded and edited, along with her husband, the first journal devoted to black music, *Black Perspectives in Music*, which was published from 1973 to 1990; she also edited the journal *Nineteenth-Century African-American Musical Theater*. But Southern not only wrote about music, she was a talented musician herself and made several appearances as a concert pianist. For her many achievements in the area of musicology, she was awarded the Lifetime Achievement Award from the Society of American Music in 2000 and the National Humanities Medal in 2001.

OBITUARIES AND OTHER SOURCES:

BOOKS

Who's Who among Black Americans, eighth edition, Gale (Detroit, MI), 1994.
Who's Who in the East, 29th edition, Marquis (New Providence, NJ), 2001.

PERIODICALS

Los Angeles Times, October 20, 2002, p. B17.
New York Times, October 19, 2002, p. A15.

STEELE-PERKINS, Christopher Horace 1947-

PERSONAL: Born July 28, 1947, in Rangoon, Burma; son of an English military officer and a Burmese mother. *Education:* University of Newcastle upon Tyne, B.Sc., 1970.

ADDRESSES: Home—5 St. John's Buildings, Canterbury Crescent, London SW9 7QB, England. *Agent*—Magnum Photos, 5 Old St., London EC1V 9HL, England. *E-mail*—magnum@magnumphotos.co.uk.

CAREER: Freelance photographer. Worked for numerous publications, including *Fortune, Geo, Newsweek, Observer Magazine, Paris-Match, Stern, Time,* and London *Sunday Times.* Polytechnic of Central London, lecturer in photography, 1976-77. Affiliated with Exit group of photographers, London, England, 1975—; Viva photo agency, Paris, France (associate, 1976-78); Magnum photo agency, London, Paris, New York (nominee, 1979-83; member, 1983—). *Exhibitions:* Individual exhibitions include *The Face of Bengal,* Camerawork Gallery, London, England, 1974; *Film Ends,* Photographers Gallery, Southampton, Hampshire, England (traveling exhibit), 1977; *The Teds,* Camerawork Gallery, London, 1979; *Survival Programmes,* Side Gallery, Newcastle upon Tyne, England, 1982; *Beirut,* Camerawork Gallery, London, 1983; *Lebanon,* Magnum Gallery, Paris, France, 1985; *The Pleasure Principle* (traveling exhibit), 1990; *Afghanistan,* Perpignan Festival, France, 1999. Group exhibitions include *The Inquisitive Eye,* Institute of Contemporary Arts, London, 1974; *Young British Photographers,* Photographers Gallery, London, 1975; *Maritime England,* Photographers Gallery, London, 1982; *The Indelible Image,* Corcoran Gallery, Washington, DC, 1985; *South Africa,* FNAC-Montparnasse, Paris, 1986; *In Our Time,* Magnum Photos world tour, 1990; *A Terrible Beauty,* Artists Space, New York, NY, 1994. Works are in the collections of Victoria and Albert Museum, London; Bibliothèque Nationale, Paris; Arts Council of Great Britain, London; Side Gallery, Newcastle upon Tyne; Photographers' Gallery, London, National Gallery of Victoria, Melbourne, Australia; FNAC, Paris.

MEMBER: Arts Council of Great Britain (member of photography committee, 1976-79).

AWARDS, HONORS: Gulbenkian Foundation Grant, 1975; Oskar Barnak Award—World Press (Netherlands), 1988; Tom Hopkinson Award, Photographers'

Gallery, London, 1988; Robert Capa Gold Medal, ICP New York, 1989; Cooperative Award and One World Award, both 1994, both for film *Dying for Publicity*; World Press Award, 2000.

WRITINGS:

(Photographer) *Young British Photographers* (exhibition catalogue), [London, England], 1975.

(Photographer) Richard Smith *The Teds*, Travelling Light (London, England), 1979.

(Photographer and editor) *About Seventy Photographs*, Arts Council of Great Britain (London, England), 1980.

(Photographer, with Homer Sykes) Wieland Giebel, *Das kurze Leben des Brian Steward: Alltag im irischen Bürgerkrieg*, Elefanten Press (West Berlin, Germany), 1981.

(Photographer) *Survival Programmes* (exhibition catalogue), Open University Press (Milton Keynes, England), 1982.

(Photographer) Selim Nasib and Caroline Tisdall *Beirut Frontline Story*, [London, England], 1982.

(Photographer) Jane Livingston and Frances Fralin, *The Indelible Image* (exhibition catalogue) [New York, NY], 1985.

In Our Time, Magnum Group, Norton (New York, NY), 1989.

The Pleasure Principle, Aperture Foundation (New York, NY), 1990.

St. Thomas's Hospital, [London, England], 1992.

(Photographer) Sayd Bahodine Majrouth, *Afghanistan*, Westzone Publishing, Limited (London, England), 2001.

Fuji, Powerhouse Cultural Entertainment (New York, NY), 2002.

SIDELIGHTS: Photographer Christopher Horace Steele-Perkins was born in Rangoon, Burma, but when he was two years old, his English military officer father deserted his Burmese mother and went back to England with Steele-Perkins in tow. They settled in a small town on the sea coast, where as a mixed-race child, Steele-Perkins felt conspicuous; he later said in the *Eyestorm* Web site, that "there was no ethnic community into which I could retreat . . . I was seen as a Chink." Educated at Christ's Hospital School in Sussex, he then studied chemistry at the University of York for a year, left it for a short stint in Canada, and came back to England and enrolled at the University

of Newcastle Upon Tyne, where he concentrated on psychology. He became a photographer and picture editor for a student magazine, and upon graduating in 1970, he continued this interest as a freelance photographer specializing in theater while lecturing in psychology.

A year later, Steele-Perkins moved to London to pursue a full-time career as a freelance photographer. He has since worked for a variety of publications, including *Fortune, Geo, Newsweek, Observer Magazine, Paris-Match, Stern, Time,* and the London *Sunday Times.* Several relief agencies commissioned him to travel to Bangladesh, and in 1974, these photographs comprised his first individual exhibit, *The Face of Bengal,* at London's Cameraworks Gallery. He also exhibited in a group show, *The Inquisitive Eye,* that same year and was part of *Young British Photographers* in 1975 after becoming involved with the documentary group Exit and working with it on its projects examining inner-city life. Continuing to expand his career, Steele-Perkins became an associate with Viva, a French photographic agency, in 1976, and was a lecturer in photography at the Polytechnic of Central London. Though he had been primarily a photojournalist to this point, in 1977 he collaborated with fellow photographer Mark Edwards on a project of conceptual photography, *Film Ends.* Picking through 5,000 found film rolls, Steele-Perkins and Edwards concentrated on the frames photographers expose to finish out a roll before developing it, and printed forty. "The creative act, obviously, was not in the careless exposing of film ends, but in discovering what a treasure of chance events of significance might be hidden in such photos," described a *Contemporary Photographers* writer of the endeavor.

The Teds was Steele-Perkins' first book, and the photographs also appeared in a traveling exhibition. The series portrayed the final wave of Teddy Boys, an English youth movement born in the 1950s; its adherents dressed in a distinctive style and adopted a distinctive attitude. Observed the *Contemporary Photographers* writer, "In this series, he works in the genre of the journalistic portrait: many of the photos are of Teds' faces. Other photos in the series are 'live,' depicting typical situations from their lives, their amusements. The series as a whole . . . is modern reportage at its best." Steels-Perkins continued to exhibit and publish his photographs; his second book was *About Seventy Photographs,* a collection of photographs he edited for the U.K. Arts Council; his third was *Survival Programmes,* more of his work with the group Exit.

Steele-Perkins left Viva and became first a nominee, in 1979, and then a full member, by 1983, of the Magnum Photo Agency. This allowed him to travel and work abroad in Africa, the Middle East, the Soviet Union, and Central America, photographing famine, wars, and other tragedies. "Previously my work had been focused on particulars of Britain: poverty, subculture. I did not have any parallel reality against which to properly assess my position," he said in *Eyestorm.* He had several exhibits of work from these trips, including *Beirut,* in 1983, *Lebanon,* in 1985, and *Famine in Africa* in 1985. Noted the *Contemporary Photographers* writer, "This honest approach to a difficult subject saved his work from the sensation-seeking effect so commonplace in current journalism, since his aim was not to excite the imagination but to persuade the viewer that the necessary reaction should be more than mere sympathy." In 1989, Steele-Perkins published his first book of color photographs, *The Pleasure Principle.* He said in *Eyestorm* that this collection portraying British society was "in one sense about our hedonism and our search for a better world. In another sense they are about me and the ambiguous feelings I have about England."

In the 1990s, Steele-Perkins went several times to Afghanistan, covering such dramatic events as the civil war and life afterward and the 1998 earthquake, but especially Afghani people going about their daily lives. The resulting book, *Afghanistan,* had text by Afghan poet Sayd Bahodine Majrouh as well as entries from Steele-Perkins' diary. "The stark photographs address destruction and mayhem on the one hand and daily life in the fields and cities on the other. The pictures are allowed to tell their own story . . . Steele-Perkins' diary excerpts provide some context to the overall work and Majrouh's poetry further enhances the impressionistic tone of the work," remarked John R. Riddick in the *Library Journal.* Commended *Spectator* reviewer Philip Hensher, "These astonishingly beautiful photographs are more moving than can be described; they hardly ever dwell on physical brutalities, but on the bleak rubble and desert of the country, punctuated by inexplicable moments of formal beauty, even pastoral bliss . . . the grandeur of the images comes from Steele-Perkins never neglecting the human, the individual face in the great crowd of history."

According to the *Creative Review, Afghanistan* "reveal[s] a tragic country in a new light." Steele-Perkins said in an interview with *Scotland on Sunday* about the book that he was allowed to travel all over the country during the course of his four visits, even on his last trip, when the Taliban controlled most of the country. "I was operating with them [the Taliban]. The majority were just ordinary guys. They would offer you tea and food—they wouldn't have any for themselves, but they would give you theirs," he said. Steele-Perkins also displayed images from his Afghan trips in a traveling exhibition, also called *Afghanistan.* Observed reviewer Nick Redman in the *Evening Standard,* "His work . . . concerns itself with the daily cycles of Afghan lives made austere by civil war, while leaving the fighting out of the frame. . . . While it would be facile to underestimate the awful reality of life under the Taliban regime, Steele-Perkins' work proves there is life beyond that channeled handily through a news-hungry lens." The exhibit drew this comment from Jonathan Jones in the *Guardian,* "Steele-Perkins . . . maintains a tradition of photographic truth-telling that is under threat in an age of digital images."

Moving to a startling different part of the world, Steele-Perkins turned his camera lens on Japan, publishing his photographs in a book, *Fuji,* and collecting them in a traveling exhibition of the same name. He captured a variety of facets of Japanese contemporary life within sight of Mount Fuji, including supermarkets, playgrounds, streetlife, and landscapes, "inspired by the famed 19th century prints of Hokusai and Hiroshige," related a reviewer in the *Daily Post.* "It was a move that demonstrated as effectively as anything the ranginess and flexibility of his approach and his singular openness to all kinds of experience," concluded the *Eyestorm* article of this work.

BIOGRAPHICAL AND CRITICAL SOURCES:

BOOKS

Contemporary Photographers, 3rd ed. St. James Press (Detroit, MI), 1996.

PERIODICALS

Creative Review, December 2000, "Olympus Campaign Asks the Difficult Questions," p. 13; June 2001, review of *Afghanistan,* p. 74.

Daily Post (Liverpool, England), January 11, 2002, "Triple Exhibition," p. 25.

Evening Standard (London, England), April 6, 2001, Nick Redman, "9 to 5, Afghan-Style," p. 67.

Guardian (London, England), August 17, 2000, Jonathan Jones, "The Guide Thursday: Exhibitions: Chris Steele-Perkins," p. 19.

Library Journal, December 2001, John F. Riddick, review of *Afghanistan,* p. 150.

Scotland on Sunday (Edinburgh, Scotland), September 23, 2001, "Witness: The Taliban Are Seen as Extremists, but Photographer Chris Steele-Perkins Has Captured Their Humanity," p. 13.

Spectator, May 19, 2001, Philip Hensher, review of *Afghanistan,* p. 36

ONLINE

Eyestorm Contemporary Art and Photography Web site, http://www.eyestorm.com/ (May 7, 2002).*

*   *   *

STÉFAN, Jude 1930-

PERSONAL: Born 1930, in Pont-Audemer, France.

ADDRESSES: Agent—c/o Gallimard, 5 rue Sebastien-Bottin, Paris 75328, France.

CAREER: Professor of French, Latin, and Greek; writer.

WRITINGS:

Cyprès, Gallimard (Paris, France), 1967.
Libères, Gallimard (Paris, France), 1970.
Vie de mon frère, Gallimard (Paris, France), 1973.
Idylles suivi de Cippes, Gallimard (Paris, France), 1973.
La crevaison: (nouvelles), Gallimard (Paris, France), 1976.
Aux chiens du soir: poèmes en titre, Gallimard (Paris, France), 1979.
Lettres tombales: (ad familiares), Le temps qu'il fait (Cognac, France), 1983.

Suites slaves, Ryôan-ji (Marseilles, France), 1983.
Les accidents: nouvelles (ou variations), Ryôan-ji (Marseilles, France), 1984.
Laures: poèmes, Gallimard (Paris, France), 1984.
Les ogresses, musical score with Luciano Sampaoli, Luisè (Rimini, Italy), 1985.
Gnomiques, ou, De l'inconsolation, Le Temps qu'il Fait (Cognac, France), 1985.
Alme Diane, Le Temps qu'il Fait (Cognac, France), 1986.
Les états du corps: nouvelle (ou Variations II), Champ Vallon (Seyssel, France), 1986.
Faux journal, Le Temps qu'il Fait (Cognac, France), 1986.
Dialogues avec la soeur, Champ Vallon (Seyssel, France), 1987.
Dialogue des figures, Champ Vallon (Seyssel, France), 1988.
À la vieille parque, Gallimard (Paris, France), 1989.
Litanies du scribe, Le Temps qu'il Fait (Cognac, France), 1989.
De Catulle: et vingt transcriptions (translations), Le Temps qu'il fait (Cognac, France), 1990.
Stances, ou 52 contre-haï-ku, Le Temps qu'il fait (Cognac, France), 1991.
La fête de la patronne: nouvelles ou variations III, Champ Vallon (Seyssel, France), 1991.
Xénies, Gallimard (Paris, France), 1992.
Scholies: notes et notules, Le Temps qu'il fait (Cognac, France), 1992.
Le nouvelliste: nouvelles ou variations IV, Champ Vallon (Seyssel, France), 1993.
Epitomé, ou, Chrestomathie à l'usage des débutants en littérature, Le Temps qu'il Fait (Cognac, France), 1993.
Elégiades; suivi de deux méditations: poèmes, Gallimard (Paris, France), 1993.
Senilia, Le temps qu'il fait (Cognac, France), 1994.
Prosopées: poèmes, Gallimard (Paris, France), 1995.
Scènes dernières: "histoires de vie-mort," ou, Variations V, Champ Vallon (Seyssel, France), 1995.
Variété VI: huit entretiens, quatre traductions, trois lettres, deux dialogues, onze notes, Le Temps qu'il Fait (Cognac, France), 1995.
Chronique catoniques, La Table ronde (Paris, France), 1996.
Silles: journal de lettres, Le Temps qu'il Fait (Cognac, France), 1997.
Povrésies, ou 65 poèmes autant d'années, Gallimard (Paris, France), 1997.
PrOsÈMES, L'Instant Perpétuel (Rouen, France), 1997, 1998.

Variations, VI, vie de Saint, Champ Vallon (Seyssel, France), 1998.

Epodes, ou, poèmes de la désuétude, Gallimard (Paris, France), 1999.

Variété VII, Le Temps qu'il Fait (Cognac, France), 1999.

Génitifs: poèmes, Gallimard (Paris, France), 2001.

SIDELIGHTS: Jude Stéfan's interest in classical languages has influenced not only the work he has chosen to do—he has published translations of classics as well as taught these languages—but also the voice in which he speaks through his poetry, fiction, and other writings.

Several themes run through his work, perhaps the most dominant of which is cynicism. As John Taylor pointed out in a piece on Stéfan's *Faux journal* for *Review of Contemporary Fiction,* this is expressed by his warning "in the epigraph to *Faux journal* that all diaries are *faux:* 'false,' 'fake,' 'phony.'" The reviewer continued, "In the 'diary' itself he excoriates 'the unbearable style employed in [them], when the only person concerned notes for others matters which interest him alone ('saw X again, who seemed to have changed a lot,' 'met Z at the reception,' etc)."

Taylor also stressed that Stéfan's writing "is impregnated with classical literature and rhetoric; his experimenting with the French language is all the more intrepid for his learnèd sense of moderation. Rhythm, syntax, diction: these are the elements of style to which Stéfan applies his originality."

In a *Times Literary Supplement* review of Stéfan's *Idylles suivi de Cippes,* Jean Tortel wrote, "A dense and tormented syntax, a diction that has overtones of some previous but timeless century, and an apparently arbitrary but really very carefully calculated method of amputating his lines in mid-phrase, so that they often end on an apostrophe or a hyphen: these are techniques that lend force to his basic themes of rampant Eros and ghoulish Thanatos." The reviewer continued, "Within the limits of his subject-matter M. Stéfan is a powerful poet. It is true that his theme is primal, but one none the less wonders if it is not time for his inspiration to be broadened a little."

John Taylor, writing in *French Review* about *Les états du corps: nouvelle (ou Variations II),* noted, "Jude Stéfan's latest collection of short stories, *Les états du corps,* though organized in its own right around the theme of aging—the narrative or main character is successively twelve, sixteen, twenty, twenty-five, thirty, thirty-five, forty, fifty and seventy years old, before becoming a 'legend'—nonetheless deploys a variety of styles and textual forms, narrates from a variety of perspectives, evokes a variety of emotions, thus suggesting that rich variety of 'bodily states' which come and go in the course of a lifetime."

One of Stéfan's "frequent themes," the reviewer pointed out, "his relationship with his sister, her suicide" is pursued in the story "Histoire de la Muse" from that collection. In it "she tells him one day while he is sitting in the garden", the reviewer wrote, "'Il faudra que tu écrives, plus tard,' (you must write about this later on). 'Mais quoi?' (But why?) the poet asks, to which she replies, 'Toi, nous' or 'you (in the intimate form), us.'"

Writing about *Laures: poèmes* in *French Review,* Carol L. Kaplan commented, "Death lurks most always behind Stéfan's images of woman. Indeed his short poems may be compared to the small, portable mirrors found in Renaissance paintings in which people, especially women, looked at their reflections and were unable to perceived the true state of their corporeal existences, that is, the skeleton behind their temporal beauty."

Reviewing the same volume in *World Literature Today,* John T. Naughton began enthusiastically: "Here is a serious book of poetry. Learned, technically accomplished, wide-ranging and varied in its exploration of human limitation and defeat, Jude Stéfan's *Laures* evokes Western man at the outermost edge of his history—in 'la scène finale.'"

The critic continued, "The title [Laures] gives a sense of the book's complexity and import, for the French word *laure* is both the name of the beloved, lastingly celebrated by Plutarch, and the designation for the secluded sanctuaries of the monasteries of the East. Furthermore, the homophone *l'or* suggests the (alchemical) gold of poetic research, and *laurier* the poet's laurel wreath."

Naughton summed up much of the general critical feeling about the poet's work when he concluded, "Bookish and despairing, Stéfan's poem, with its antecedents in Villon and Scève and in certain dimensions of Baudelaire and Rimbaud, among others, provokes a vivid and memorable example of one of the faces of the present state of poetic expression: aware of its past, conscious of its futility, unresigned to its defeat."

BIOGRAPHICAL AND CRITICAL SOURCES:

PERIODICALS

French Review, number 2, 1986, Carol L. Kaplan, review of *Laures: poèmes,* p. 298; April, 1988, John Taylor, review of *Les états du corps: nouvelle (ou Variations II),* p. 841.
Review of Contemporary Fiction, summer, 1988, John Taylor, review of *Faux Journal,* p. 331.
Times Literary Supplement, June 1, 1973, Jean Tortel, review of *Idylles suivi de Cippes,* p. 610.
World Literature Today, winter, 1986, John T. Naughton, review of *Laures,* p. 70.*

*   *   *

STEPHENSON, Pamela 1950-

PERSONAL: Born December 4, 1950, in Auckland, New Zealand; married, Nicholas Ball, 1979 (divorced); married Billy Connolly, December 20, 1989; children: Daisy, Amy, Scarlett. *Education:* Sydney Church of England Grammar School for Girls, Sydney, New South Wales, Australia; National Institute of Dramatic Arts, Sydney, New South Wales, Australia.

ADDRESSES: Agent—c/o Author Mail, Overlook Press, One Overlook Drive, Woodstock, NY 12498.

CAREER: Licensed psychotherapist, Los Angles, CA. Performed briefly as a stand-up comedian at the Comic Strip, a club in London, England; *Not the Nine O'Clock News,* England, cast member, 1979-82. Has appeared in numerous movies, among them *The Secret Policeman's Other Ball,* 1982, *Superman III,* 1983, and *Scandalous,* 1984. Also appeared on the television show, *Saturday Night Live,* 1984-85.

AWARDS, HONORS: W. H. Smith Book Award for best biography, 2002, for *Billy.*

WRITINGS:

Billy, HarperCollins (London, England), 2001, Overlook Press (Woodstock, NY), 2002.

SIDELIGHTS: Pamela Stephenson has always been known for her irrepressible personality, and proudly notes that she resisted the best efforts of her parents and the Sydney Church of England Grammar School for Girls to subdue her. She studied dance to help recover from polio. Her interest in drama and performance took her to the National Institute of Dramatic Arts in Sydney where she studied until she left Australia in 1975. After some months traveling, Stephenson settled in London, England and began a career in entertainment. She performed as a stand-up comedian at the Comic Strip, a London club. From 1979 to 1982 she appeared regularly with Rowan Atkinson, Griff Rhys Jones, and Mel Smith on the satirical British television show, *Not the Nine O'Clock News.* Stephenson's talents as an impersonator are well recognized. In her prime she could offer up a range of characters as diverse as Barbra Streisand, Margaret Thatcher and Amy Carter. Stephenson has appeared in a number of films, among them John Gielgud's *Scandalous, The Secret Policeman's Other Ball,* and Richard Lester's *Superman III,* where she played Christopher Reeve's romantic interest. *Saturday Night Live* also claimed her as a cast member from 1984 to 1985.

Upon her move to Los Angeles with her husband and children, Stephenson changed careers. She enrolled in a clinical psychology program and is now a practicing psychotherapist in California. The production of her biography of her husband has added the title of author to her resume.

Billy, Stephenson's biography of her husband, Billy Connolly, was published by HarperCollins in 2001 in London. Connolly is a renowned comedian and actor with a reputation for an uncensored and raucous style of humor. His great suffering during childhood, including maternal abandonment and sexual abuse by his father created problems in his adult life. His busy career and family life are the result of having wrestled successfully with the demons of his youth. *Billy* won the W. H. Smith Award in the biography category.

BIOGRAPHICAL AND CRITICAL SOURCES:

PERIODICALS

Herald (Glasgow, Scotland), September 3, 2001, Susan Barr, "Wild-child Ways of Pam the Bam," p. 29.

Independent (London, England), April 10, 2002, Louise Jury, review of *Billy,* p. 6.

M2 Best Books, January 8, 2002, review of *Billy;* March 7, 2002, review of *Billy.*

People, July 25, 1983, Jill Jerome, "Being Bad is Wicked Fun for Superman's Seducer," p. 68.

Spectator, November 10, 2001, Andro Linklater, review of *Billy,* p.76.

Sunday Mail (Glasgow, Scotland), January 7, 1996, Ellen Grehan, "The Changing Face and the Changing Pace of Dr. Pam."

Sunday Times (London, England), November 11, 2001, Lesley White, review of *Billy,* p. 40; March 17, 2002, John Dugdale, review of *Billy,* p. 37.

ONLINE

Best Bits of Britcom Web site, http:// britcom.hispeed. com/ (June 7, 2002).

Stars Online Web site, http://www.stars.com/ (June 7, 2002).*

*   *   *

STODDARD, Charles Warren 1843-1909
(Pip Pepperpod)

PERSONAL: Born August 7, 1843, in Rochester, NY; died April 23, 1909, in Monterey, CA. *Religion:* Roman Catholic.

CAREER: Travel writer, poet, and journalist. *Golden Era,* weekly columnist, 1867; secretary-companion of Mark Twain in England, 1873; Honolulu newspaper, editorial writer, 1880s; University of Notre Dame, South Bend, IN, professor in English and American literature, 1885-86; Catholic University of America, Washington, D.C., chairman of English literature, 1889-1902.

MEMBER: Bohemian Club, 1870s.

WRITINGS:

Poems, Anton Roman (San Francisco, CA), 1867.

South-Sea Idyls, James R. Osgood (Boston, MA), 1873, published as *Summer Cruising in the South Seas,* Chatto & Windus (London, England), 1874, second revised edition, Scribners (New York, NY), 1892.

Mashallah! A Flight into Egypt, Appleton (New York, NY), 1881.

A Trip to Hawaii, Oceanic Steamship Co. (San Francisco, CA), 1885.

A Troubled Heart and How It Was Comforted at Last, J. A. Lyons (Notre Dame, IN), 1885.

The Lepers of Molokai, Ave Maria Press (Notre Dame, IN), 1886.

Hawaiian Life: Being Lazy Letters from Low Latitudes, F. T. Neely (Chicago, IL), 1894.

The Wonder-Worker of Padua, Ave Maria Press (Notre Dame, IN), 1896.

A Cruise Under the Crescent: From Suez to San Marco, Rand McNally (Chicago, IL), 1898.

Over the Rocky Mountains to Alaska, B. Herder (St. Louis, MO), 1899.

Father Damien: The Martyr of Molokai, Catholic Truth Society (San Francisco, CA), 1901.

In the Footprints of the Padres, A. M. Robertson (San Francisco, CA), 1902, revised edition, 1911.

Exits and Entrances: A Book of Essays and Sketches, Lothrop (Boston, MA), 1903.

For the Pleasure of His Company: An Affair of the Misty City, Thrice Told, A. M. Robertson (San Francisco, CA), 1903.

The Island of Tranquil Delights: A South Sea Idyl and Others, Herbert B. Turner (Boston, MA), 1904.

Apostrophe to the Skylark; The Bells of San Gabriel; Joe of Lahaina; Father Damien Among His Lepers; An Appreciation of Charles Warren Stoddard, by George Wharton James, Arroyo Guild Press (Los Angeles, CA), 1909.

Poems of Charles Warren Stoddard, compiled by Ina Coolbrith and Thomas Walsh, John Lane (New York, NY), 1917.

Charles Warren Stoddard's Diary of a Visit to Molokai in 1884, introduction by Oscar Lewis, Book Club of California (San Francisco, CA), 1933.

Cruising the South Seas: Stories by Charles Warren Stoddard, edited by Winston Leyland, Gay Sunshine Press (San Francisco, CA), 1987.

Contributor to periodical publications including *American Literature* and *Huntington Library Quarterly.* Published poems under pseudonym Pip Pepperpod.

SIDELIGHTS: Charles Warren Stoddard was an American poet, educator, and travel writer. His most influential travel book is *South-Sea Idyls.* His account of his conversion to Roman Catholicism, *A Troubled Heart and How It Was Comforted at Last,* is regarded as one of his most outstanding works. Poet and renowned literary figure Ina Coolbrith collected his poems in 1917. With Coolbrith, he coedited the *Overland Monthly.* Stoddard, often disorganized, did not finish his formal education and had a truncated acting career. However, as M. E. Grenander said in *Dictionary of Literary Biography,* "His talents as a good listener and fondness for the bottle contributed to his popularity with a variety of friends, including Ambrose Bierce, Mark Twain, and, in 1870, Joaquin Miller." Grenander believed that with the increased scholarly focus on gay and lesbian studies, Stoddard will receive more critical attention. In addition to almost twenty books, he contributed more than nine hundred articles to periodicals.

Stoddard spent most of his childhood in Rochester, New York. His family tree includes former Vice President Aaron Burr, best known for his duel with Alexander Hamilton, and theologian Jonathan Edwards. In 1855, his family moved to San Francisco, where his father found a job in the shipping industry. Upon returning east, he settled with his maternal grandparents in western New York and continued his formal education. At age fifteen, he returned to San Francisco at his father's request. Stoddard, determined to become a poet, befriended various journalists, took on work as a handyman in a bookstore and studied in San Francisco and Oakland. He contributed poems to Bret Harte's *Golden Era,* under the pseudonym "Pip Pepperpod." He also struggled with his homosexuality, which society then did not understand well.

Stoddard's poor health led a doctor to advise him to go to Hawaii. He went in 1864 and, for six months, immersed himself in native Polynesian culture. He had an affair with a native boy named Kane-Aloha, a relationship Stoddard describes in *The Island of Tranquil Delights: A South Sea Idyl and Others.* This affair, Grenander said, "marked the inception of his interest in the brown-skinned youths he called 'barbarians,' to whose 'instinctual' life his own instincts could respond with delight."

In 1867, Harte edited Stoddard's *Poems,* his first book. Stoddard biographer Carl Stroven, according to Grenander, thought the edition, which was illustrated and stamped in gold, was "the first example of fine book making to be produced in California." That year Stoddard converted to Catholicism, while publishing verse in a new journal called the *Californian.*

Stoddard's sister invited him to visit her in Hawaii in 1868, and he returned for an eight-month stay. The *San Francisco Evening Bulletin* commissioned him to write travel sketches about his experiences there. Upon returning to California, he started writing a weekly column for the *Golden Era.* He helped form the Golden Gate Trinity (also known as the Overland Trinity), a trio of writers that included Harte and Coolbrith. They formed the editorial team of the *Overland Monthly,* a California literary journal Anton Roman founded in 1868. Stoddard and Coolbrith coedited the *Overland* under Harte's direction. For the *Overland,* Stoddard also wrote sketches of Hawaii, especially about youths he met there. In the 1870s, he joined San Francisco's Bohemian Club, over which Coolbrith presided.

Stoddard's fascination with Polynesian and South Pacific culture intensified and, in 1870, he set off to Tahiti on a French ship with a gay crew. Short on funds, he stayed only three months, but the voyage provided him with stories he told in *The Island of Tranquil Delights.* In 1872, he published an article titled "A Prodigal in Tahiti" in the *Atlantic Monthly.*

The following year he departed to Europe as a traveling correspondent, and met literary figures that included Ambrose Bierce, Samuel Clemens (Mark Twain) and Joaquin Miller. Shortly after he arrived, he worked as a secretary-companion for Clemens, during his lecturing throughout England. Stoddard was comfortable with Europe's literary elite. "His lavender elegance was at the opposite end of the spectrum from the Wild West stereotype Miller's roughneck persona was carrying to ridiculous extremes," Genander wrote. Bierce knew the British were less tolerant than Californians about homosexuality. Grenander quoted Bierce, in a warning letter to Stoddard: "You will, by the way, be under the microscope here; your lightest word and most careless action noted down, and commented on by men who cannot understand how a person of individuality in thought or conduct can be other than a very bad man. . . . Walk, therefore, circumspectly . . . avoid any appearance of eccentricity."

That same year, Stoddard's most important travel book, *South-Sea Idyls,* was published. Chatto & Windus in London republished it a year later as *Summer Cruising in the South Seas.* Many important writers, including Robert Louis Stevenson, read the book, with Polynesia becoming a literary trend. Stevenson and Stoddard became friends. Stoddard was later the model for a character in Stevenson's novel *The Wrecker*, in which he was described as a "youngish, good-looking, fellow . . . lively and engaging."

Stoddard then visited the Middle East. He sailed there in 1876 and returned to the United States via Europe the following year. Back in the United States, he borrowed money and relied on friends' generosity, never really working regularly. His next three works reflected his experiences abroad: *Mashallah! A Flight into Egypt, A Cruise Under the Crescent: From Suez to San Marco,* and *Exits and Entrances: A Book of Essays and Sketches.*

In the early 1880s, financially strapped, he became an editorial writer for a newspaper in Honolulu. *The Lepers of Molokai* was based on his visit to the Molokai leper colony. He also had another affair with a young man. In 1885, he began to teach English and American literature at the University of Notre Dame, where he stayed for a year and a half. During that time, he traveled to Alaska with one of the professors, and described the trip in *Over the Rocky Mountains to Alaska.*

After leaving Notre Dame, Stoddard settled in Kentucky, where he had his most important affair, with a youth named Tom Cleary. In 1888, he traveled to Europe with Mrs. Theodore Vail, a rich widow, and her son. The following year he became chairman of English literature at the new Catholic University of America in Washington, D.C. He remained there for thirteen years. Stoddard's health worsened and he moved to Cambridge, Massachusetts, returning after two years to San Francisco in 1905 and settling in Monterey in 1906, where he died three years later.

Stoddard, a well-traveled aesthete and great conversationalist, had many literary elite friends. Grenander called him "an acute observer of superficial details, and he was a master of tropes with a remarkable flair for words." Grenander added, however, "He lacked the powerful shaping imagination." Considered a minor writer today, he enjoyed considerable acclaim during his day. A *New York Times* reviewer said of *Poems,* "There is singularly little that is antiquated about these poems. . . . Stoddard was a supreme artist in verse as in prose, and was well in advance of his time in his entire sincerity and lack of literary pose."

BIOGRAPHICAL AND CRITICAL SOURCES:

BOOKS

Dictionary of Literary Biography, Volume 186: *Nineteeth-Century American Western Writers,* Gale (Detroit, MI), 1997.

Gale, Robert L., editor, *The Gay Nineties in America: A Cultural Dictionary of the 1890s,* Greenwood Press (Westport, CT), 1992.

Hart, James D., editor, *The Oxford Companion to American Literature,* Sixth edition, Oxford University Press (New York, NY), 1995.

Perkins, George, Barbara Perkins, and Phillip Leininger, editors, *Benet's Reader's Encyclopedia of American Literature,* HarperCollins Publishers (New York, NY), 1990.

PERIODICALS

New York Times, November 4, 1917.*

*   *   *

STRIEGEL, Jana 1955-
(Jana Striegel-Wilson)

PERSONAL: Born November 15, 1955, in Oklahoma City, OK; daughter of J. R. and Ollie Virginia Striegel; married Mark Wilson (an entrepreneur), September 28, 1985; children: Tanner. *Education:* University of New Mexico, bachelor's degree (dance, theater arts, and education; with distinction), 1982; earned teaching certificate. *Hobbies and other interests:* Walking, biking, using the gym, studying piano, reading, gardening, and enjoying theater.

ADDRESSES: Home—Albuquerque, NM. *Agent*—c/o Author Mail, Holiday House, 425 Madison Ave., New York, NY 10017; George M. Nicholson, Sterling Lord Literistic, Inc., 65 Bleecker St., New York, NY 10012. *E-mail*—jana@janastriegel.com.

CAREER: Dance instructor; dancer for New Mexico Ballet Company, Ballet del Monte Sol, American Southwest Ballet Company, and Six Flags over Mid-America, St. Louis, MO; choreographer and producer/

director, Albuquerque and New Mexico Junior Miss scholarship program, 1973-82; owner/artistic director, Jana's Academy of Music and Dance, 1982-90; writer, 1990—.

MEMBER: Society of Children's Book Writers and Illustrators, Author's Guild, Southwest Writers.

AWARDS, HONORS: Best Book Honor, language arts—grades seven to twelve novel category, Society of School Librarians International, 2002, for *Homeroom Exercise.*

WRITINGS:

Homeroom Exercise, Holiday House (New York, NY), 2002.

Also contributor to periodicals, including *New York Times* and *Albuquerque Journal,* sometimes under the name Jana Striegel-Wilson.

WORK IN PROGRESS: The Audition, middle-grade fiction.

SIDELIGHTS: Dancing had always been an important part of Jana Striegel's life and it became the subject matter of her second career, writing books for children. As she explained to *CA,* "Writing came to me at a later stage of my life. Although I was an avid reader, I can't say that when I was a child I knew writing was what I had to do. What I've always been is a dancer. From my first recital as a yellow-feathered canary to today, I am a dancer. Now retired from professional dance, my writing has become an extension of that life." In 2002, Striegel made her debut as a novelist with *Homeroom Exercise,* a story about a young dancer for middle-grade readers.

Striegel likens writing novels to choreographing dances, which she did extensively as the owner of a dance studio and participant in ballet and musical theater productions for over a decade. At her dance studio, she also developed a reading readiness class for preschool children in which she used movement and music to prepare young students for academic learning. "Choreography had always been one of my favorite parts of the dance world," she confided to *CA.*

"Creating dances was a way for me to tell stories with bodies, lights, and music; when I started writing, I slipped comfortably into putting stories into words on paper." Working with so many dance students of different ages gave Striegel raw material for characters as well. "My characters emerged as a composite of the young people I have taught: from children of supportive families secure in who they are, to children of dysfunctional families looking to the studio as a place to be safe, happy, and respected."

The main character of *Homeroom Exercise,* Regan is a talented dancer with a supportive family. She plans to pursue dancing as a career and hopes that being selected to host her school's closed-circuit television dance show, called *Homeroom Exercise,* will give her a leg up, figuratively speaking. Suddenly, however, Regan's joints swell and she is feverish, symptoms that lead to a diagnosis of juvenile rheumatoid arthritis, a disease that can cripple. On her personal Web site, Striegel told of the inspiration for this character: "I met a dancer during her senior year of high school who had been diagnosed with juvenile rheumatoid arthritis when she was eleven years old." Although Striegel knew about the adult form of this disease, she was not aware that children could fall prey to it. "As I studied the juvenile form of arthritis," she continued, "I learned it was not that uncommon and read of the courage of young people who deal with this illness. The idea of the strong determined young dancer dealing with a debilitating disease came together and the character of Regan was born."

In the course of the novel, Regan deals emotionally and physically with her illness and relationships with her friends. Several reviewers of *Homeroom Exercise* commented on its medical subject matter, including a *New York Times Book Review* critic, who called Striegel's portrayal of the disease "good medical information." Despite the novel's potentially maudlin topic, *Booklist* contributor Kay Weisman remarked that its subplots "lighten the tone" sufficiently. The outlook for Regan, while not overly optimistic, is at least hopeful and reflects the position that Striegel has had to take in her own life. "Pursuing goals is a theme you will find in my writing," Striegel shared with *CA:* "I am a cancer survivor, diagnosed in 1994, and continue to be a chronic cancer patient but refuse to give up my dreams. In that time, I have started a family and begun my publishing career. I believe the study of dance equipped me to deal with these challenges."

She concluded, "I hope that readers find my books entertaining as well as a place of comfort and encouragement. I strive to share the joy, beauty, and magic of dance, which has graced my life."

BIOGRAPHICAL AND CRITICAL SOURCES:

PERIODICALS

Booklist, March 1, 2002, Kay Weisman, review of *Homeroom Exercise,* p. 1137.

Children's Literature, March 31, 2003, Linnea Hendrickson, review of *Homeroom Exercise.*

Midwest Book Review, June 8, 2002, review of *Homeroom Exercise.*

New York Times Book Review, April 21, 2002, review of *Homeroom Exercise,* p. 24.

School Library Journal, June, 2002, Shilo Halfen, review of *Homeroom Exercise,* p. 146.

ONLINE

Jana Striegel Web site, http://janastriegel.com/ (April 2, 2003).

*   *   *

STRIEGEL-WILSON, Jana
 See STRIEGEL, Jana

*   *   *

STUX, Erica 1929-

PERSONAL: Born November 29, 1929; daughter of Max (a doctor) and Trudy (a homemaker and seamstress: maiden name, Moses) Houser; married Paul Stux, November 19, 1955 (died, July 5, 1984); married William Shore, February 6, 2000; children: (first marriage) Lydia, Ted, Arnold. *Education:* University of Cincinnati, B.S., 1949, M.S., 1950. *Hobbies and other interests:* Conservation, bird-watching, playing bridge, playing accordion, composing songs.

ADDRESSES: Home—10055 Larwin Ave., No. 5, Chatsworth, CA 91311.

CAREER: Poet, novelist, and author. Worked as a chemist in Cincinnati, OH, 1950-56; P.P.G. Industries, Akron, OH, technical writer, 1978-84; University of Akron, Akron, OH, instructor in technical writing, 1988-92. Active in philanthropic and arts-supporting groups in Akron, and, since 1999, in the San Fernando Valley, CA.

MEMBER: Society of Children's Book Writers and Illustrators, California Writer' Club, Sierra Club, Audubon Society, MENSA, Chatsworth Women's Club.

AWARDS, HONORS: Akron Area Manuscript Club award.

WRITINGS:

Landlady (novel), Winston-Derek (Nashville, TN), 1991.

Strobe Lights (poetry chapbook), Plowman (Whitby, Ontario, Canada), 1995.

Eight Who Made a Difference: Pioneer Women in the Arts, Avisson Press (Greensboro, NC), 1999.

Writing for Freedom: A Story about Lydia Maria Child, illustrated by Mary O'Keefe Young, Carolrhoda (Minneapolis, MN), 2001.

Enrico Fermi: Trailblazer in Nuclear Physics, Enslow (Berkeley Heights, NY), 2004.

Contributor of poems and articles to *Grit, Columbus Dispatch, Philadelphia Inquirer, Saturday Evening Post, Wall Street Journal, Reader's Digest, Canto, Maryland Review of Poetry, Lutheran Digest, Scroll, Haiku, Outdoor, Summit, Chicago Daily News,* and *Gentle Survivalist.* Contributor of children's poems and stories to periodicals, including *Climb, Explore, Wee Wisdom, Hopscotch, Adventures in Storytelling, Real Kids, Story Friends, Words of Cheer, Purring in a Pocket, Ohio Woodlands,* and *Young Crusader* and to publications used by the Southern Baptist Sunday School.

Composer/lyricist of popular country songs, including "Too Scared," "How Good You Had It," and "One Good Friend."

MUSICAL PLAYS

Rainbow Days, produced in Akron, OH, 1988.
Let It Out, produced in Akron, OH, 1996.

Rain, produced in Akron, OH, 1996.
From Shepherd to King, produced in Akron, OH, 1997.

SIDELIGHTS: Among the many works Erica Stux has authored during her writing life have been a number of poems and stories for children, as well as several book-length biographies. Her interest in the arts as well as her feminist beliefs have inspired several of these books, among them *Eight Who Made a Difference: Pioneer Women in the Arts* and *Writing for Freedom: A Story about Lydia Maria Child,* the latter Stux's 2000 biography of the courageous nineteenth-century American abolitionist.

Stux's 1999 work *Eight Who Made a Difference* includes short biographies on eight women who excelled in their chosen field and gained fame during the twentieth century because of their talents rather than their gender. The accomplishments of Native-American ballet dancer Maria Tallchief, vocalists Marian Anderson and Beverly Sills, American photojournalist Margaret Bourke-White, artists Mary Cassatt and Louise Nevelson, architect Julia Morgan, and French pianist Nadia Boulanger are each presented by Stux, often incorporating quotations from the subject herself. Praising Stux for setting her subjects against the cultural and social backdrop of their day, *Booklist* contributor Anne O'Malley also commended the author for penning "interesting portraits that stress [each of the women's] . . . challenges and accomplishments."

Stux told *CA:* "I began writing when I had children of my own, first poems and prose pieces for children, then light verse for adults, and finally, longer works. I write about subjects that interest me and would, I hope, interest others.

"I especially like to write for children about animals and the environment, but my dozen or so manuscripts on these topics are still searching for a publisher. I still write poetry for children, both factual and whimsical, and an occasional humorous verse for adults."

BIOGRAPHICAL AND CRITICAL SOURCES:

PERIODICALS

Booklist, February 15, 1999, Anne O'Malley, review of *Eight Who Made a Difference: Pioneer Women in the Arts,* p. 1959.

Kirkus Reviews, December 1, 1998, review of *Eight Who Made a Difference,* p. 1740.
School Library Journal, May, 1999, Marilyn Heath, review of *Eight Who Made a Difference,* pp. 143-144; January, 2001, Jean Gaffney, review of *Writing for Freedom: A Story about Lydia Maria Child,* p. 116.

*　　*　　*

SULLIVAN, Sean Mei
　　See SOHL, Jerry

*　　*　　*

SVARTVIK, Jesper 1965-

PERSONAL: Born December 13, 1965, in Gothenburg, Sweden; son of Jan (a university professor) and Gunilla (a teacher; maiden name, Berner) Svartik; married Lena Bliding (a psychiatrist), September 21, 1985; children: Maria, Mikael. *Education:* University of Lund, M.Th., 1990, Ph.D., 2000; attended Swedish Theological Institute, Jerusalem, Israel, 1990, and Hebrew University of Jerusalem, 1993. *Hobbies and other interests:* Music, travel.

ADDRESSES: *Home*—Nils Lundahls väg 6, SE-224 66 Lund, Sweden. *Office*—Department of Theology and Religious Studies, University of Lund, Allhelgona Kyrkogata 8, SE-223 62 Lund, Sweden; fax: +46-46-222-4426. *E-mail*—jesper.svartik@teol.lu.se.

CAREER: Ordained Lutheran minister, 1991; University of Lund, Lund, Sweden, Swedish Research Council fellow, 2002—. Speaker at educational institutions, including Kristianstad University, Ersta College, and secondary schools in Sweden; guest on media programs.

MEMBER: International Council for Christians and Jews (chair for southern Sweden, 1994-98), Society of Biblical Literature, Uppsala Exegetiska Sällskap.

WRITINGS:

Mark and Mission: Mark 7:1-23 in Its Narrative and Historical Contexts, Almqvist & Wiksell International (Stockholm, Sweden), 2000.

Skriftens ansikten: Konsten att läsa mellan raderna i Bibeln, Arcus (Lund, Sweden), 2001.

(With Bo Frid) *Thomasevangeliet: Med Jesusorden från Oxyrhynchus,* Arcus (Lund, Sweden), 2002.

Author of introductions to videos on New Testament topics. Contributor to books, including *The Concept of God in Global Dialogue,* edited by Werner Jeanrond and Aasulv Lande, Maryknoll Press, 2002. Contributor of articles and reviews to periodicals, including *Christian Compass.* Member of editorial committee, *Svensk teologisk kvartalskrift,* 2002—.

WORK IN PROGRESS: *In the Shadow of the Cross,* on Christians and the Holocaust; *Let My People Go!,* a "mnemohistorical survey of Egypt as metaphor."

SIDELIGHTS: Jesper Svartvik told *CA:* "After my basic training at the University of Lund, I was granted a scholarship for theological studies at the Swedish Theological Institute in Jerusalem. The director of the institute, Dr. Goran Larsson, and his competent staff introduced me to Judaism today, rabbinical theology, and inter-faith dialogue. I returned to Sweden determined to commence doctoral studies after my pastoral theological studies.

"My second book discusses biblical figures central to both Jewish and Christian interpreters. I am happy to see that it has been well received by both Jews and Christians. My third book is a translation of and a commentary on the popular apocryphal Gospel of Thomas."

*   *   *

SWAN, Sharon

PERSONAL: Born in Chicago, IL. *Ethnicity:* "German/Irish." *Education:* Attended DePaul University.

ADDRESSES: *Home*—Mesa, AZ. *Agent*—Pam Hopkins, Hopkins Literary Associates, 2117 Buffalo Rd., Suite 327, Rochester, NY 14624.

CAREER: Writer. Worked as customer service representative, office administrator, and administrative assistant for various firms in and around Chicago, IL, and Phoenix, AZ.

MEMBER: Romance Writers of America.

WRITINGS:

ROMANCE NOVELS

Cowboys and Cradles, Harlequin Enterprises (Don Mills, Ontario, Canada), 2002.

Home-grown Husband, Harlequin Enterprises (Don Mills, Ontario, Canada), 2002.

Husbands, Husbands Everywhere!, Harlequin Enterprises (Don Mills, Ontario, Canada), 2002.

Four-Karat Fiancee, Harlequin Enterprises (Don Mills, Ontario, Canada), 2003.

WORK IN PROGRESS: *Husband by Necessity,* for Harlequin Enterprises (Don Mills, Ontario, Canada).

SIDELIGHTS: Sharon Swan told *CA:* "I credit my mother, who read to me regularly, with prompting an early and lasting affection for the written word. To me, books have always held a magic all their own. Still I never considered a writing career for myself until I moved from Chicago to the Phoenix, Arizona, area and met Pierce Brosnan, the actor, at a local shopping mall. It was a chance meeting that changed my life, because I found myself thinking 'What if?' What if two fictional characters had met in the same way? That formed the basis for my first story, 'Daring Dreams,' which in turn soon led to a cheerful addiction to writing contemporary romance and playing 'What if?'

"Some of my personal heroes in the writing profession are Nora Roberts, Jayne Ann Krentz, and Susan Elizabeth Phillips. I chose the romance genre for my own focus as an author because I truly believe in the power of love. I read about it, write about it, and can't help but be thrilled every time I see it triumph in real life."

T

TALEV, Dimitér 1898 1966

PERSONAL: Born September 1, 1898, in Prilep, Ottoman Empire (now Macedonia); died of stomach cancer October 20, 1966, in Sofia, Bulgaria; son of Tale (a blacksmith) and Donka Petrov Palislamov. *Education:* Studied medicine at University of Zagreb, 1920; studied philosophy at University of Vienna, 1921; studied Slavic philology at University of Sofia after 1925.

CAREER: Writer, 1917-66. *Makedonia* (newspaper), Sofia, Bulgaria, proofreader, 1927-29, member of editorial board, 1929-30, editor-in-chief, 1930-31.

MEMBER: Union of Bulgarian Writers.

AWARDS, HONORS: Dimitrov Prize, 1959; named People's Cultural Worker of Bulgaria, government of Bulgaria, 1966.

WRITINGS:

Sélzite na mama (title means "Mama's Tears: Short Stories and Fairy Tales for Children"), Knizharnitsa "Apolon," Pechatnitsa "Séglasie" (Sofia, Bulgaria) 1925.

Usilni godini (title means "Hard Years"), Book I: *V drezgavinata na utroto* (title means "In the Twilight of the Morning"), Knizharnitsa "Apolon," Pechatnitsa "Séglasie" (Sofia, Bulgaria), 1928, Book II: *Podem* (title means "Uplift"), Izdanie na avtora (Sofia, Bulgaria), 1929, Book III: *Ilinden* (title means "Saint Elija's Day"), Izdanie na avtora (Sofia, Bulgaria), 1930.

Zdravets i Iglika. Sértseto tsvete (title means "Crane's Bill and Primrose: The Flower Heart"), Knizharnitsa Georgi T. Kréstev, Pechatnitsa "Sredets" (Sofia, Bulgaria), 1930.

Proletta e magyosnitsa (title means "Spring Is a Magician"), Knizharnitsa Georgi T. Kréstev, Pechatnitsa P. Ovcharov (Sofia, Bulgaria), 1931.

Pod mrachno nebe (title means "Under a Gloomy Sky"), Séyuz na Makedonskite Kulturno-prosvetni Organizatsii v Bélgariya, Pechatnitsa Ovcharov (Sofia, Bulgaria), 1932.

Zlatniyat klyuch (short stories; title means "The Gold Key"), Pechatnitsa P. Ovcharov (Sofia, Bulgaria), 1935.

Velikiyat tsar (title means "The Great Tsar"), Kazanléshka Dolina (Sofia, Bulgaria), 1937.

Starata késhta (title means "The Old House"), Khemus (Sofia, Bulgaria), 1938.

Igra (title means "A Game"), Séyuz na bélgarskite pisateli, Pechatnitsa "ABV" (Sofia, Bulgaria), 1939.

Na zavoy (title means "At a Turn"), Biblioteka "Zaveti," Pechatnitsa Poligrafiya (Sofia, Bulgaria), 1940.

Gotse Delchev, Biblioteka "Brannik," Pechatnitsa "Izgrev" (Sofia, Bulgaria) 1942.

Grad Prilep. Borbi za rod i svoboda (title means "The Town of Prilep: Struggles for Kin and Freedom"), Ministerstvo na Narodnoto Prosveshtenie (Sofia, Bulgaria), 1943.

Zavréshtane (title means "Return"), Perun (Sofia, Bulgaria), 1943.

Zhelezniyat svetilnik, Bélgarski pisatel (Sofia, Bulgaria), 1952, translated by Marguerite Alexevia as *The Iron Candlestick,* Foreign Languages Press (Sofia, Bulgaria), 1964.

Ilinden (title means "Saint Elija's Day"), Bélgarski Pisatel (Sofia, Bulgaria), 1953, translated by Nadya Kolin as *Ilinden: A Novel of the Macedonian Rebellion of 1903,* Foreign Languages Press (Sofia, Bulgaria), 1966.

Kiprovets véstana (title means "Kiprovets Revolted"), Narodna kultura (Sofia, Bulgaria), 1953.

Prespanskite kambani, Bélgarski Pisatel (Sofia, Bulgaria), 1954, translated by Mihail Todorov as *The Bells of Prespa,* Foreign Languages Press (Sofia, Bulgaria), 1966.

Ilindentsi, Narodna Mladezh (Sofia, Bulgaria), 1955.

Samuil, Narodna Kultura (Sofia, Bulgaria), Book I: *Shtitove kamenni* (title means "Shields of Stone"), 1958, Book II: *Pepelyashka i tsarskiyat sin* (title means "Cinderella and the Prince") 1959, Book III: *Pogibel* (title means "Destruction") 1960, revised edition published as *Samuil. Roman-letopis za kraya na Pérvata bélgarska durzhava,* 3 volumes, Narodna kultura (Sofia, Bulgaria), 1965.

Bratyata ot Struga (title means "The Brothers from Struga"), Bélgarski pisatel (Sofia, Bulgaria), 1962.

Hilendarskiyat monah (title means "The Monk of Hilendar"), Narodna Mladezh (Sofia, Bulgaria), 1962.

Glasovete vi chuvam (title means "Your Voices I Hear"), Bélgarski Pisatel (Sofia, Bulgaria), 1966.

COLLECTED WORKS

Razkazi i povesti. 1927-1960 (title means "Short Stories and Novellas, 1927-1960"), Bélgarski Pisatel (Sofia, Bulgaria), 1962.

Séchineniya, 11 volumes, edited by Stoyan Karolev and others, Bégarski Pisatel (Sofia, Bulgaria), 1972-1978.

Contributor to periodicals, including *Rodina* ("Fatherland"), *Rabotnicheski vestnik* ("Workers' Newspaper"), *Rabotnichesko edinstvo* ("Workers' Unity"), *Léch* ("A Ray"), *Nov pét* ("New Way"), *Makedonska tribuna* ("Macedonian Tribune"), *Vardar, Svoboda ili smért* ("Freedom or Death"), and *Zora* ("Dawn").

SIDELIGHTS: For Dimitér Talev, the contentious history between the Macedonia of his birth and the Bulgaria where he lived would fuel a wealth of literary interpretations. The career of this deeply patriotic Macedonian writer spanned some of the most politically shattering events in the Balkan region, and his first-hand experiences enriched his fiction. Talev was incarcerated for several months when Soviet-style communism took over Bulgaria in 1944. Laboring in mining camps under inhumane conditions weakened his health, and though he was known as a leading Macedonian writer in Bulgaria, he died of cancer in 1966. Talev's numerous historical novels and short stories explored how ethnic prejudices caused regional tensions over generations.

Talev was born in the city of Prilep, when Macedonia had yet to exist as a nation but was instead an ethnic group spread across Bulgaria, Greece and what would later become Yugoslavia. Talev's mother was from Prilep, but had married a newcomer to the town, a peasant who was a blacksmith by trade. When Talev was around five, Macedonians attempted to rid themselves of Ottoman Turk control on "Ilinden," or Saint Elija's Day, 1903. Talev based several fictional works on these events.

Two of Talev's older brothers were politically active in the VMRO, the nationalist Macedonian group at the forefront of the Ilinden uprising, which was quashed. Through them, Talev became involved in the underground resistance movement as a teen, a period he would later portray vividly in some of his stories. When war in the Balkans broke out in 1912, Talev was fourteen, and he was forced to relocate often to finish his education. That war would spiral in just two years, which prolonged his studies.

Talev's first short story was published in a newspaper in Skopje, the Macedonian capital, in 1917. After one final college switch, to Bulgaria's University of Sofia, he graduated with a degree in Slavic philology. He stayed in the capital city the rest of his life. Talev wrote many short stories and essays during this period, and published his first book, *Sélzite na mama.* Most of the publications in which he was published were leftist in ideology, and by 1927 he was working for the newspaper *Makedonia.* He rose from proofreader to editorial board member to editor-in-chief in a few years.

In 1928, part I of Talev's first novel for adults, *Usilni godini,* appeared. This first installment, *V drezgavinata na utroto,* begins with the end of the resolution of

Russo-Turkish War in the Balkans in 1878. The next two parts, *Podem* and *Ilinden,* carry the story through the next crucial three decades. *Usilni godini* won critical acclaim for Talev. According to Ivan Ruskov in *Dictionary of Literary Biography,* it "marks the beginning of the basic issue in his work—the fate of Macedonia identified as a geographic and ethnocultural area, whose status and frontiers are determined by complicated political and ideological factors and are based on various multinational confrontations and the contradictory interests of local Balkan and European entities."

In the early 1930s Talev quit the staff of *Makedonia* to live in Paris. There, he wrote his 1932 drama, *Pod mrachno nebe,* about ethnic tensions between Serbs and Bulgarians. He returned to Sofia to be managing editor of *Makedonia,* but Tsar Boris III established a Bulgarian dictatorship in 1934, and authorities shut the paper down. Talev continued to write and found acceptance in other pro-Macedonian publications such as *Makedonska tribuna* ("Macedonian Tribune") and *Zora* ("Dawn"), which published many of his stories.

Some of those stories were collected in five volumes published in Sofia between 1935 and 1943. These collections included *Zlatniyat klyuch, Velikiyat tsar, Starata késhta, Igra,* and *Zavréshtane.* The works center on life in the countryside and the recent epoch of Macedonian-Bulgarian relations. Y. V. Karageorge, in *Encyclopedia of World Literature in the Twentieth Century,* said that *Zlatniyat klyuch, Starata késhta* and *Zavréshtane* "draw a vivid panorama of the Macedonian ethos, with its patriarchal structures, and celebrate the enduring spirit of the people of greater Bulgaria."

Talev's second novel, *Na zavoy,* is set in Bulgaria during a bleak 1920s era of human-rights abuses. Its hero, Krum Kosherov, begins adult life as a communist, but events steer him to political apathy; his marriage to a well-off young woman establishes his mindset firmly in the middle class. "In his book Talev suggests a way out of the conflicts by showing what turns an individual must make to save himself, his family, and his country," Ruskov said.

In the early 1940s Bulgaria had joined an alliance with Nazi Germany, Boris III died mysteriously after a visit with German chancellor Adolf Hitler in Berlin,

and Soviet troops occupied Bulgaria and established a one-party communist state. Talev's literary career continued apace, however, and he wrote two important nonfiction works: a biography of a martyred VMRO leader, *Gotse Delchev,* and an account of Macedonian nationalism as centered in his hometown with the essay *Grad Prilep. Borbi za rod i svoboda.* During this time he also wrote more short stories and two psychological novellas: "Posledno pétuvane," in which an elderly woman is abandoned by her thoughtless sons, and "Dva miliona," the tale of a well-to-do pharmacist on his death bed and his family's eager anticipation of the inheritance.

World War II had ended for Bulgaria in September 1944 when Soviet troops entered, and Talev's life changed dramatically. His youthful VMRO work, his editorship of *Makedonia,* and his fictional themes, especially in *Na zavoy,* all contributed to Bulgarian Communist authorities viewing him suspiciously. That October, he was jailed for six months, though not charged with any crime, and then released to a labor camp in Bulgaria's mining region for four months.

Another crackdown on those considered potential dissidents occurred in 1947, and Talev was sentenced to forced labor at another mine with equally atrocious living conditions. Five days before Christmas, a coal avalanche completely buried him, and his fellow inmates were lucky to find him. In Sofia, colleagues and longtime friends of Talev's petitioned the government for his freedom. He was released in February, 1948, but later that year his entire family was exiled to Lukovit.

In early 1951, the newspaper *Pirinsko delo* ("Pirin Cause") published an unusual statement from Talev that denounced both the VMRO and some Yugoslavian leaders. (The borders of the recently created Yugoslav republic of Macedonia, Greek Macedonia, and the Macedonian section of Bulgaria would remain a source of political drama well into the 1990s.) "The amateurish language and the redundancy of vulgar ideological clichés indicate that this squib, typical of the Cold War, was dictated by someone other than Talev," Ruskov said. Yet Talev and his family were allowed to return to Sofia, and *Zhelezniyat svetilnik,* what critics consider his most significant work, was published.

Talev had finished *Zhelezniyat svetilnik* in 1946, and its 1952 publication marked a return to a quieter period for him as well as to his status as a leading Macedonian writer. The work, translated into English and published as *The Iron Candlestick,* belongs to a quartet of novels during this period that critics deem the apotheosis of his literary gifts—*Prespanskite kambani, Ilinden* and *Glasovete vi chuvam.* All four novels strive to re-create the saga of contemporary Macedonian history through the ambitions and tragedies in one family, the Glaushevs. "This novel marked the beginning of Talev's recognition and his remarkable writer's career," Ruskov said. "Along with that, however, one notices the growing influence of ideological prescriptions imposed during the 1950s and 1960s."

Zhelezniyat svetilnik begins in the 1830s in Prespa—the literary name for Prilep, the town of Talev's birth—after the end of a devastating plague. The area is under harsh Turkish rule. A young woman, Sultana, belongs to one of the town's oldest families; she shocks many when she marries Stojan Glaushev, a newcomer peasant. Talev based much of the Sultana character's independence and will upon his own mother. She first endures accusations of immoral behavior for her decision to marry the outsider peasant, but helps him rise to affluence through his blacksmith business. Their son, Lazar, grows up to lead a local insurgency movement. But a daughter, Katerina, is involved in a tragic love story with Rafe Klintche, a woodcarver from another region. Talev also had a sister who died in 1935, and "the description of the psychological drama of Sultana, who, torn between maternal love and moral norms, causes the death of her daughter, Katerina, is among the masterpieces of Bulgarian literature," Ruskov said.

In *Zhelezniyat svetilnik* and its sequels, several different plot lines for each main character enhance Talev's credible individuals. Their conflicts even affect their sons' and daughters' lives. *Prespanskite kambani,* which succeeded *Zhelezniyat svetilnik,* was translated into English in 1966 as "The Bells of Prespa," and takes up where the first book ended, at Lazar's marriage. It chronicles the Glaushev family from the 1860s to the 1880s, and in particular concentrates on Lazar's beleaguered wife, Niya, who endures Sultana's disapproval until she finally produces a grandchild.

The Russo-Turkish War of 1877-1878 is important to the novel as well: Macedonia comes under Turkish rule, and Macedonian rebels led by Lazar and a local teacher foment an uprising in Prespa. Like nearly every fictional portrayal of actual demonstrations of Mace-

donian nationalism, this, too, concludes tragically. The teacher is executed and Lazar jailed for three years. *Prespanskite kambani* ends with the death of Lazar's parents, Stojan and Sultana.

Ilinden, the third novel in Talev's collected opus, was actually published before *Prespanskite kambani,* in honor of the fiftieth anniversary of the 1903 uprising of that name. *Ilinden,* a reworking of Book III of *Usilni Godini,* chronicles the events leading to this fateful day, and portrays how Macedonia became a battleground for differing ethnic groups and their ambitions—the Bulgarians, Serbs, and Greeks—regardless of the Macedonians themselves. Lazar and Niya's now-grown son, Boris, leads the uprising, which is brutally suppressed.

In the fourth novel of this cycle, *Glasovete vi chuvam,* Talev, through protagonist Boris, sketches the nine years of strife between the Ilinden uprising and the Balkan War onset. A Greek girl's love for Boris symbolizes hopelessness; since any union between the two nationalities is impossible, she commits suicide. Talev exposes the double-edged sword of patriotism through one character's query: "Isn't the love of your people a hatred of the other one?" The doomed Angelika continues a long line of female heroines in Talev's cycle, and in his other works as well, created as "female Christ-like figures who transform the lives of embittered, hurt, or lost men," Karageorge said.

In between the four novels of his Glaushev family saga, Talev wrote many other shorter works. These included *Ilindentsi,* a children's version of the events in *Ilinden.* Another significant politically themed work for younger readers came in a trio of books with the collective title *Samuil.* Its three parts are *Shtitove kamenni, Pepelyashka i tsarskiyat sin* and *Pogibel.* Samuil was an eleventh-century Bulgarian tsar who battled with a Byzantine empire to predictably tragic results. The more powerful emperor ordered Samuil's 15,000 soldiers to be blinded for their part in the uprising, and when Samuil saw their return, he broke down and died shortly thereafter.

Collections of Talev's fiction were published in *Razkazi i povesti. 1927-1960,* and the eleven-volume *Séchineniya.* Ruskov termed him "one of the most significant Bulgarian novelists in the years after World War II," and "a writer who provided a profound and many-sided portrait of the Macedonian people by evoking their complex and tragic history, their way of life, and their moral and spiritual values."

BIOGRAPHICAL AND CRITICAL SOURCES:

BOOKS

Dictionary of Literary Biography, Volume 181: *South Slavic Writers since World War II,* Gale (Detroit, MI), 1997.
Encyclopedia of World Literature in the Twentieth Century, third edition, St. James Press (Detroit, MI), 1999, p. 289.*

*   *   *

TAMBUTTI, Susana 1947-

PERSONAL: Born October 4, 1947, in Buenos Aires, Argentina; divorced. *Education:* University of Buenos Aires, degree in architecture, 1972; studied dance at the London School of Contemporary Dance and with Martha Graham.

ADDRESSES: Home—Buenos Aires, Argentina. *Office*—c/o University of Buenos Aires, Buenos Aires, Argentina.

CAREER: Choreographer and dancer. Nucleodanza, co-founder and co-artistic director, 1974—; University of Buenos Aires, Buenos Aires, Argentina, dance theory instructor, 1987—.

AWARDS, HONORS: National Choreography Award for the Arts and Sciences, Argentina, 1983; Estrella de mar Award, 1990; Venice Festival Critics' Award, 1995, for choreography in *Tangos: El exilio de gardel;* Fulbright Fiftieth Anniversary Distinguished Fellowship, 1996.

WRITINGS:

Closing in on the Study of the History of Western Dance, [Buenos Aires, Argentina], 1995.

SIDELIGHTS: Susana Tambutti did not become interested in dance and choreography until after she graduated from the University of Buenos Aires with a degree in architecture. While working as an architect she attended a modern dance class taught by Ana Kamien, a well-known choreographer. She recognized her love for dance, and soon after she quit architecture for good to commit her career to dance.

In 1974 Tambutti and Margarita Ball formed the dance group Nucleodanza, which has become the longest running independent contemporary dance company in Argentina. Nucleodanza started touring around the world in the late 1980s. *News & Record* contributor Stephanie Nelson reported, "the company has won international attention and praise for its amalgam of dance and performance art."

Tambutti began her career as a choreographer in the early 1980s, choreographing works for Nucleodanza. Winning Argentina's National Choreography Award for the Arts and Sciences in 1983 brought her more recognition and the chance to choreograph for the prestigious Ballet Contemporaneo del Teatro Municipal General San Martin, the only official modern dance company in Argentina. An *International Dictionary of Modern Dance* contributor noted, "Her work is marked by the permanent search of the internal conflict of the work, in whichever domain this is to be found: movement, emotion, or narrative."

BIOGRAPHICAL AND CRITICAL SOURCES:

BOOKS

International Dictionary of Modern Dance, St. James Press (Detroit, MI), 1998.

PERIODICALS

News & Record, April 4, 1998, Stephanie Nelson, "Nucleodanza Enthralls Local Audience," p. B2B.

OTHER

Nando Times, http://nandotimes.com/ (April 15, 2002), Linda Belans, "International Choreographers July 16, 17."*

TATE, Claudia C. 1946-2002

OBITUARY NOTICE—See index for *CA* sketch: Born December 14, 1946, in Long Beach, NJ; died of lung cancer July 29, 2002, in Princeton, NJ. Educator and author. Tate was a noted scholar of African-American literature. Her 1968 undergraduate degree was from the University of Michigan, and she earned a Ph.D. in English and American literature and language from Harvard University in 1977. Tate then joined the faculty at Howard University as an associate professor of English in 1977; she left Howard in 1989 to become a professor of English at George Washington University until 1997, when she moved to Princeton University. As a scholarly critic of African-American writers, Tate was considered innovative in her approach, which took into account all psychological aspects of the writings she analyzed. Her creativity was also evident in the interviews she conducted in her groundbreaking book *Black Women Writers at Work* (1983). Tate also edited *The Works of Katherine Davis Chapman Tillman* (1991) and was the author of *Domestic Allegories of Political Desire: The Black Heroine's Text at the Turn of the Century* (1992) and *Psychoanalysis and Black Novels: Desire and the Protocols of Race* (1998).

OBITUARIES AND OTHER SOURCES:

ONLINE

Princeton University Web site, http://www.princeton. edu/ (August 30, 2002).

*   *   *

TINLING, Marion (Rose) 1904-

PERSONAL: Born December 17, 1904, in Richmond Hill, NY; daughter of Frank Newton (a contractor) and Nora (a nurse; maiden name, Sale) Goble; married Willis Tinling, 1930 (divorced, 1948); children: Jaime Rose Tinling Watson, Nora Tinling Hughes, Nicholas Graeme. *Education:* Attended Occidental College 1926-27; Keuka College, B.A., 1929. *Politics:* Democrat. *Hobbies and other interests:* History, women's rights.

ADDRESSES: Home—3225 Freeport Blvd., No. 512, Sacramento, CA 95818. *E-mail*—mtinling@ mindspring.com.

CAREER: Huntington Library, San Marino, CA, typist, proofreader, editor, and secretary of publications, 1930-49; California State Department of Education, Sacramento, CA, editor, 1949-54; National Historical Publications Commission, Washington, DC, editor and transcriber of documents, 1954-62; California State Personnel Board, Sacramento, CA, social worker, 1963-70. Member of California State Personnel Board, 1962-63; founder, Meals a la Car, Sacramento, CA.

MEMBER: Renaissance Society, Sacramento Book Collectors, Grandmothers for Peace, Older Women's League (president, 1990), Lewis & Clark Trail Heritage Foundation.

AWARDS, HONORS: Guggenheim fellow, 1960; Woman in History citation, Sacramento History Museum, 1991; Keuka College Alumni Award, 1993.

WRITINGS:

(Editor, with Louis B. Wright) William Byrd, *The Secret Diary of William Byrd of Westover, 1709-1712,* Dietz Press (Richmond, VA), 1941.

(Editor, with Maude Howlett Woodfin) William Byrd, *Another Secret Diary of William Byrd of Westover, 1739-1741,* Dietz Press (Richmond, VA), 1942.

(Editor, with Louis B. Wright) Robert Hunter, *Quebec to Carolina in 1785-1786: Being the Travel Diary and Observations of Robert Hunter, Jr., a Young Merchant of London,* Huntington Library and Art Gallery (San Marino, CA), 1943.

(Editor, with Godfrey Davies) Harry Toulmin, *The Western Country in 1793: Reports on Kentucky and Virginia,* Huntington Library and Art Gallery (San Marino, CA), 1948.

(Editor, with Louis B. Wright) William Byrd, *The London Diary, 1717-1721, and Other Writings,* Oxford University Press (New York, NY), 1958.

(Editor) *The Correspondence of the Three William Byrds of Westover, Virginia, 1684-1776,* two volumes, University Press of Virginia (Charlottesville, VA), 1977.

Women Remembered: A Guide to Landmarks of Women's History in the United States, Greenwood Press (New York, NY), 1986.

(Compiler and editor) *Women into the Unknown: A Sourcebook on Women Explorers and Travelers,* Greenwood Press (New York, NY), 1989.

(Compiler and editor) *With Women's Eyes: Visitors to the New World, 1775-1918,* Archon Books (Hamden, CT), 1993.

Sacajawea's Son: The Life of Jean Baptiste Charbonneau, Mountain Press (Missoula, MT), 2001.

Contributor to journals, including *William & Mary Quarterly* and *Huntington Library Bulletin;* contributor to *Encyclopedia Britannica.*

SIDELIGHTS: A former editor of historic documents, Marion Tinling has made several contributions to the late-twentieth-century field of women's history by compiling and presenting primary documents that reveal the contributions of forward-thinking and energetic women in many walks of life. In addition to such works as *Women into the Unknown: A Sourcebook on Women Explorers and Travelers* and *With Women's Eyes: Visitors to the New World, 1775-1918,* she has also authored a juvenile biography titled *Sacajawea's Son: The Life of Jean Baptiste Charbonneau,* which was published in 2001. Of Tinling's *Women Remembered: A Guide to Landmarks of Women's History in the United States, American Reference Book Annual* contributor Catherine R. Loeb enthused: "This treasure trove of information . . . makes for fascinating browsing, serves as a valuable biographical dictionary, and extends to the women's history buff a tantalizing invitation to travel." *Library Journal* reviewer James Moffet praised the detailed work as "obviously a labor of love for the author."

Born in 1904, Tinling graduated from New York's Keuka College in 1929 before beginning her career as an editor and secretary of publications at San Marino, California's Huntington Library. "Over my nineteen years there, I was privileged to work with leading scholars in the fields of English and American history and literature," Tinling later recalled, "and there I got more education than I received in college."

At the Huntington Library, Tinling worked on scholarly editions of documents, among them several volumes of the collected diaries of eighteenth-century writer William Byrd of Virginia. After her retirement, she found time to pursue her personal interest: the growing area of women's history. "My object was to 'write women back into history,'" Tinling explained, maintaining that "history as taught in high schools and colleges has ignored women's contributions. The result has been that women in our society are considered minor figures of little account and not deserving of equality to men. This attitude must change if civilization is to improve."

Published in 1989, *Women into the Unknown* features writings by such noted women adventurers as nineteenth-century Englishwoman Isabel Bird Bishop and U.S. photojournalist Margaret Bourke-White as well as a host of others, among them Egyptian explorer Florence von Sass Baker and mountaineers Violet Cressy-Marcks, Elizabeth Sarah Mauchelli, and Annie Smith Peck. Covering forty-two world adventurers whose travels spanned both the nineteenth and twentieth centuries, the book was praised by *Library Journal* contributor Olga Wise as a "valuable compilation" due to Tinling's detailed essays and useful list of available resource materials. In a *Choice* review of *Women into the Unknown,* G. J. Martin praised the author for essays that "will variously intrigue, interest, and fascinate readers," while in *Booklist,* contributor Sandy Whiteley found "the description of the fortitude and determination of the women . . . fascinating."

The impressions of British- and European-born world travelers such as Fanny Kemble, Madame de la Tour du Pin, and Theresa Pulszky are just a few of the twenty-six entries included in Tinling's 1993 work, *With Women's Eyes.* Drawing from journals, diaries, and letters home, Tinling collects a diversity of viewpoints which, due to the varied historical epochs and socio-cultural backgrounds of their writers, are "strikingly descriptive and thought-provoking" according to *School Library Journal* critic Susan H. Woodcock. Woodcock also remarked on the "hardiness and independence of these early travelers to North America," an observation echoed by a *Publishers Weekly* contributor who described the writers included as primarily "single, motivated by a strong sense of adventure, inquiry, and reform," and for the most part, staunch social activists.

In more recent years, Tinling has expanded her concern from the field of women's history to "a deeper need of society: to recognize the power of love." As she explained: "I am compiling an anthology of the literature of love: love poetry, love letters, classic love stories, journals, and essays. Love goes beyond the relations between a man and a woman to include relations within families, connections to our fellow creatures, love of the earth, and a recognition that all the world is one, and all people need and deserve to be loved."

BIOGRAPHICAL AND CRITICAL SOURCES:

PERIODICALS

American Literature, November, 1978, J. A. Leo Lemay, review of *The Correspondence of the Three William Byrds of Westover, Virginia, 1684-1776,* pp. 480-481.

American Reference Book Annual, 1987, Catherine R. Loeb, review of *Women Remembered: A Guide to Landmarks of Women's History in the United States,* pp. 333-334.

Booklist, June 15, 1989, Sandy Whiteley, review of *Women into the Unknown: A Sourcebook on Women Explorers and Travelers,* p. 1807.

Choice, September, 1978, review of *The Correspondence of the Three William Byrds of Westover, Virginia, 1684-1776,* p. 941; June, 1989, G. J. Martin, review of *Women into the Unknown: A Sourcebook on Women Explorers and Travelers,* p. 1729.

Journal of American History, March, 1988, Angela Howard Zophy, review of *Women Remembered,* p. 1420.

Library Journal, October 1, 1986, James Moffet, review of *Women Remembered,* p. 88; May 1, 1989, Olga Wise, review of *Women into the Unknown,* p. 75; June 15, 1993, Jenny Presnell, review of *With Women's Eyes: Visitors to the New World, 1775-1918,* p. 85.

Publishers Weekly, April 26, 1993, review of *With Women's Eyes,* p. 67.

School Library Journal, September, 1993, Susan H. Woodcock, review of *With Women's Eyes,* p. 264.

Women's History Review, spring, 2001, Hsu-Ming Teo, review of *With Women's Eyes,* p. 159.

*   *   *

TOFEL, Richard J. 1957-

PERSONAL: Born February 17, 1957, in New York, NY; son of Robert L. (an attorney) and Carol (in education administration; maiden name, Collins) Tofel; married Jeanne Straus (a newspaper executive), 1983; children: Rachel, Colin. *Ethnicity:* "Jewish." *Education:* Harvard College, A.B., 1979, Harvard Law School, J.D., 1983, Kennedy School of Government at Harvard University, M.P.P., 1983. *Politics:* Democrat.

ADDRESSES: Office—Dow Jones & Company, 200 Liberty St., New York, NY 10281. *E-mail*—dick. tofel@dowjones.com.

CAREER: Attorney and publishing executive. Dow Jones & Company/*Wall Street Journal,* New York, NY, assistant general counsel, 1989-92, assistant managing editor of *Wall Street Journal,* 1992-95, director of international development of *Wall Street Journal,* 1995-97, vice president of corporate communications of Dow Jones & Company, 1997-2000, assistant to the publisher of *Wall Street Journal,* 2000-02, assistant publisher of *Wall Street Journal,* 2002—.

WRITINGS:

A Legend in the Making: The New York Yankees in 1939, Ivan R. Dee (Chicago, IL), 2002.

WORK IN PROGRESS: A book on New York City politics, circa 1930.

SIDELIGHTS: A long-time employee with Dow Jones & Company/*Wall Street Journal,* lawyer Richard J. Tofel worked his way from assistant legal counsel to assistant publisher, along the way acting as assistant managing editor of the *Wall Street Journal* and vice president of corporate communications. As a result of his work and interests in baseball, history, and writing, he decided to pen a book of his own. As he explained to *CA,* "I'd been reviewing books on baseball for the *Wall Street Journal* for some years, and had long wanted to write a book. I was inspired by Burt Solomon's *Where They Ain't* on the Baltimore Orioles of the 1890s and then by Rob Neyer and Eddie Epstein's *Baseball Dynasties,* which concludes that the 1939 Yankees were the greatest team of all time—and notes that no one had ever written a book about them."

In his spare time, Tofel researched and wrote *A Legend in the Making: The New York Yankees in 1939,* a look at a crucial year in that franchise's history. While in

1939, the Yankees won a fourth consecutive world championship, becoming eight-time winners in total, they also saw Lou Gerhrig begin to suffer from the effects of amyotrophic lateral sclerosis. Focusing both on player personalities, among them Joe DiMaggio and Ted Williams, and accomplishments on the field, Tofel recounts the season's events in chronological order. Ever the historian, Tofel puts Yankee history in the larger context of baseball history, and baseball history in the larger context of American and world history. When this "sweet, heavily anecdotal account," to quote *Library Journal*'s Paul Kaplan and Robert C. Cottrell, rolled off presses in 2002, it elicited praise from reviewers. While a *Publishers Weekly* contributor praised Tofel's "splendid job of capturing the different personalities" of players, *Booklist*'s GraceAnne A. De-Candido called it a "fine gift for fans."

Tofel continued to *CA*, "I continue to be fascinated by history. My next book . . . is likely to be about politics and corruption in New York City of the late 1920s and early 1930s. This period continues to intrigue me, as it is recent enough to have research materials readily accessible, but sufficiently long ago that even the longest-lived subjects are just past interviewing; since I'm doing my book-work off hours, interviews aren't practical for me. I need to make the subject come alive from contemporary sources, and I think I'm able to do that."

BIOGRAPHICAL AND CRITICAL SOURCES:

PERIODICALS

Booklist, January 1, 2002, GraceAnne A. DeCandido, review of *A Legend in the Making: The New York Yankees in 1939,* p. 793.

Library Journal, February 1, 2002, Paul Kaplan and Robert C. Cottrell, review of *A Legend in the Making,* p. 104.

New York Times Book Review, March 31, 2002, Buster Olney, "Pride of the Yankees: As the 1939 Team Was Playing the Best Baseball Ever (Maybe), Lou Gehrig Was Dying," p. 11.

Publishers Weekly, February 11, 2002, review of *A Legend in the Making,* p. 174.

Wall Street Journal, March 14, 2002, Erich Eichman, "Gehrig, DiMaggio, and a Season to Remember," p. A16.

*   *   *

TRAUB, Charles (Henry) 1945-

PERSONAL: Born April 6, 1945, in Louisville, KY; married Mary Cadden, 1969; children: Aaron. *Education:* University of Illinois, B.A., 1967; attended University of Louisville, 1967-69; Institute of Design, Illinois Institute of Technology, M.S., 1971.

ADDRESSES: Home—39 East 10th Street, New York, NY 10003.

CAREER: Photographer, 1971—; Columbia College, Chicago, IL, instructor in photography, 1971-75, photography department chairman, 1975-78; Center for Contemporary Photography, Chicago, IL, founder and chairman, 1975-78; Light Gallery, New York, NY, director, 1978-80; School of Visual Arts, New York, NY, instructor in photography; International Center of Photography, New York, NY, visiting lecturer, 1978—. *Exhibitions:* Works included in permanent collections at the Museum of Modern Art, New York, NY; International Center of Photography, New York, NY; International Museum of Photography, George Eastman House, Rochester, NY; Visual Studies Workshop, Rochester, NY; Art Institute of Chicago, Chicago, IL; Center for Contemporary Photography, Chicago, IL; and Speed Museum, Louisville, KY. Individual exhibitions include New England School of Photography, Boston, MA, 1974; University of Michigan, Ann Arbor, MI, 1975; Light Gallery, New York, NY; and Jeb Gallery, Providence, RI, 1983. *Military service:* U.S. Army, 1969.

AWARDS, HONORS: Illinois Art Council grant, 1977; Manda grant, 1983; Cornell Kapa Award; Brendan Gill Award, Childrens' Aid Society.

WRITINGS:

Charles Traub: Beach, Horizon Press (New York, NY), 1978.

(With Luigi Ballerini) *Italy Observed in Photography and Literature,* preface by Umberto Eco, Rizzoli (New York, NY), 1988.

(Editor) *An Angler's Album: Fishing in Photography and Literature,* introduction by Charles Kuralt, Rizzoli (New York, NY), 1990.

(With Jonathan Lipkin) *In the Realm of the Circuit: Computers, Art, and Culture,* Prentice Hall (New York, NY), 2003.

SIDELIGHTS: Professional photographer Charles Traub commented in *Contemporary Photographers,* "Photography is the most exciting act I can engage in. I am totally out of myself while I am photographing."

Traub's *An Angler's Album: Fishing in Photography and Literature,* is a collection of photographs of people fishing taken by professional photographers over 150 years, along with corresponding quotes by writers, such as Thoreau, Steinbeck, Izaak Walton, and Shakespeare. *Sports Illustrated* contributor Ron Fimrite noted, "Even if you are not a fisherman . . . this remarkable book can coax a smile from you."

BIOGRAPHICAL AND CRITICAL SOURCES:

BOOKS

Contemporary Photographers, 3rd edition, St. James Press (Detroit, MI), 1996.

PERIODICALS

New York Times, October 9, 2001, Roberta Smith, "Snapshots of Sept. 11: A Gathering of Witnesses," p. E1.
Publishers Weekly, November 2, 1990, Genevieve Stuttaford, review of *An Angler's Album: Fishing in Photography and Literature,* p. 61.
Sports Illustrated, December 24, 1990, Ron Fimrite, review of *An Angler's Album: Fishing in Photography and Literature,* p. 115.

OTHER

Visual Studies Workshop Web site, http://www.vsw.org/ (May 3, 2002), "Gallery Artist: Charles Traub."

TRAVIS, Neal 1940-2002

OBITUARY NOTICE—See index for *CA* sketch: Born April 8, 1940, in Otago, New Zealand; died of cancer August 14, 2002, in New York, NY. Journalist and author. Travis was an admired gossip columnist who gained a wide following of readers in New York City. At the age of sixteen he dropped out of high school and accepted a job with the Dunedin, New Zealand, *Evening Star.* He quickly moved on to other newspapers, including the *Sydney Sun,* Port Moresby, New Guinea's *South Pacific Post,* and the *Sydney Daily Mirror.* In 1966 he traveled to New York City as a correspondent for the Sydney paper and fell in love with the Big Apple, though he would not work there full-time until 1977. In the late 1960s and early 1970s he was an editor for the *Daily Mirror* and *Melbourne Truth,* becoming editor-in-chief of three Australian newspapers owned by Rupert Murdoch. When Murdoch purchased the *New York Post,* Travis found a way to get back to New York City as the editor of the "Page Six" section. He later left the *Post* to edit the "Intelligencer" column for *New York Magazine,* and during the early 1990s he made the leap to television briefly as a producer on the news program *Hard Copy.* In 1993 Travis returned to the *New York Post* to write the gossip column "Neal Travis' New York." In addition to his journalism work, Travis was also the author of six novels, including *Manhattan* (1979), *Castles* (1982), *Palaces* (1983), *Mansions* (1984), *Wings* (1985), and *Island* (1986).

OBITUARIES AND OTHER SOURCES:

PERIODICALS

Los Angeles Times, August 16, 2002, p. B13.
New York Post, August 15, 2002, p. 6.
New York Times, August 15, 2002, p. A21.
Times (London, England), August 17, 2002.

V-Y

VELARDE, Pablita 1918-

PERSONAL: Born September 19, 1918, in Santa Clara, NM; daughter of Herman (a storyteller) and Marianita Velarde; married Herbert Hardin, 1942, (divorced, 1959); children: Helen, Herbert Jr. *Education:* St. Catherine's Indian School, Santa Fe, NM; Santa Fe Indian School, 1932.

ADDRESSES: Agent—c/o Author Mail, Clear Light Publishers, 823 Don Diego, Santa Fe, NM 87501.

CAREER: Artist, lecturer, teacher, illustrator, and author. Muralist, commissioned by the Museum of Fine Arts, Santa Fe, NM, Bandelier National Monument (also artist-in-residence), and Santa Clara Day School.

AWARDS, HONORS: First-place honors, All American Indian Days, Sheridan, Wyoming, Trail of Tears Show, Cherokee National Museum, Tahlequah, Oklahoma; Inter-Tribal Indian Ceremonies, Galiup, New Mexico, (four times), and Indian Market, Santa Fe (seven times, including the Helen Hardin Award); Palmes d'Academiques (France), 1954; New Mexico Governor's Award for Outstanding Achievement in the Arts.

WRITINGS:

Old Father, The Storyteller, Clear Light Publishers (Santa Fe, NM), 1989.

SIDELIGHTS: Pablita Velarde was born into a Pueblo family in Santa Clara, New Mexico in 1918. In 1924, she was sent to an Indian boarding school in Santa Fe, as were most young Indian children during that time period. At the age of fourteen, Velarde began to study at the first art school for Native Americans, which was part of the Santa Fe Indian School. It was there that she realized her talent as an artist. Though separated from her family, Velarde spent summers with her grandmother, a medicine woman. From her, she learned about the traditional customs and art of her people. Her father was a Native storyteller and from him, she learned her people's myths and legends. All of this deeply influenced Velarde's artwork.

After graduating from the Indian School in 1936, Velarde began teaching art at the Santa Clara Day School in her hometown. She was soon commissioned to paint murals, one in Albuquerque, and a collection for the Park Service of New Mexico in the Bandelier National Monument Visitor's Center. Her murals portrayed the daily lives of traditional Pueblo Indians, including religious ceremonies, basket and drum making, divisions of labor and the political aspects of ancient Pueblos.

Though a celebrated and well-known artist, Velarde is best known for the book she wrote and illustrated in 1989, *Old Father, The Storyteller.* It is a collection of her father's tales, complemented by her own artwork.

BIOGRAPHICAL AND CRITICAL SOURCES:

BOOKS

Native North American Artists, St. James Press (Detroit, MI), 1998.

PERIODICALS

Art Journal, spring, 1994, Sally Hyer, interview with Pablita Velarde, p. 61.

Publishers Weekly, November 27, 1995, "Modern by Tradition: American Indian Painting in the Studio Style," p. 61.*

*   *   *

VILEISIS, Ann 1967-

PERSONAL: Surname is pronounced "Vil-*eye*-sis;" born March 18, 1967, in Waterbury, CT; daughter of Peter (a demolition contractor) and Janet Fleming (a nurse; maiden name, Taylor) Vileisis; married Tim Palmer (a writer), August 6, 1994. *Ethnicity:* "Lithuanian/Italian/Irish/German." *Education:* Yale University, B.A. (cum laude), 1989; Utah State University, M.A., 1992. *Hobbies and other interests:* Hiking, white-water boating (canoeing, kayaking, rafting), skiing, drawing, cooking.

ADDRESSES: Home—Box 814, Southbury, CT 06488. *E-mail*—avileisis@yahoo.com.

CAREER: Independent scholar and writer, 1995—. Colorado Outward Bound School, Jensen, UT, course director for educational river expeditions in Colorado, Utah, and Alaska, 1990-95. Lecturer at colleges and universities; public speaker. Canyonlands National Park, volunteer, 1989.

MEMBER: American Society for Environmental History.

AWARDS, HONORS: George Perkins Marsh Prize, American Society for Environmental History, and Herbert Feis Award, American Historical Association, both 1999, both for *Discovering the Unknown Landscape: A History of America's Wetlands;* fellow, National Museum of American History, Smithsonian Institution, 1999.

WRITINGS:

Discovering the Unknown Landscape: A History of America's Wetlands, Island Press (Washington, DC), 1997.

Contributor to books, including *The Piracy of America,* edited by Judith Scherff, Clarity Press, 1998; *Water and Environment since 1945: Global Perspectives,* edited by Char Miller, Manley, 2001; and *Stories of the Wild,* edited by Susan Marsh, Murie Center, 2001. Contributor to periodicals, including *Paddler.*

WORK IN PROGRESS: A book about "how Americans have lost the knowledge that their food comes from nature."

SIDELIGHTS: Ann Vileisis told *CA:* "I write books because I am curious and deeply concerned about the natural world. I want to share my sense of both wonder and grief and my compulsion to understand why Americans love nature but also can't seem to help but use it in destructive ways.

"I was first intrigued by environmental history when I studied with William Cronon as an undergraduate at Yale. His writing and teaching inspired me to look for more stories to explain the seemingly paradoxical and troubling situations we now find ourselves in—stories that involve the interplay of culture and nature, people and land. In my research, I like to find unexpected links between art, science, economics, politics, popular culture, and ecological change and try to make sense of them, but my ultimate aim is to find useful insights that might help us all to gain better understanding. I believe that, when people know stories of the land where they live, they often feel inspired to support and work for its conservation.

"After completing a master's degree in history, I took my research on the road when I married environmental writer Tim Palmer and joined him in a nomadic, bohemian lifestyle. He'd already pioneered the discipline of writing in a van, with a dozen books to show for his eleven years of travels and exploration. We have continued to travel depending on our research, mostly in the western United States, though back in 1993, when I was researching *Discovering the Unknown Landscape: A History of America's Wetlands,* we trekked through the swampy Southeast. While many historians begin and end their work in libraries, travel has enabled me to begin my work on the land, learning what questions to ask by first looking for myself. After this grounding, I gather materials in libraries wherever I go.

"We treasure the simplicity of our van life. We have a desk that doubles as a kitchen table, a bunk, shelves with hundreds of books, boxes of files, two computers, a bike, a guitar, a raft, two pairs of skis, two canoes, and a kayak on top, and all sorts of other things tucked into nooks and corners. It feels cozy, not crowded, and we are always ready for anything. Most important, the solitude and quiet we find permits us to work without interruption and distraction. Time spent outdoors exploring nature balances the long hours at our desk, and the beauty we discover inspires us to continue learning and to share what we learn by writing."

BIOGRAPHICAL AND CRITICAL SOURCES:

PERIODICALS

Environment, September, 1998, Karen Bartlett, review of *Discovering the Unknown Landscape: A History of America's Wetlands,* p. 25.

Library Journal, November 1, 1997, Joan S. Elbers, review of *Discovering the Unknown Landscape,* p. 114.

Publishers Weekly, September 22, 1997, review of *Discovering the Unknown Landscape,* p. 61.

Regional Science and Urban Economics, February, 2001, Stephen Polasky, review of *Discovering the Unknown Landscape,* p. 127.

Sierra, May-June, 1998, Bob Schildgen, review of *Discovering the Unknown Landscape,* p. 80.

Smithsonian, April, 1998, Joyce Wolkomir and Richard Wolkomir, review of *Discovering the Unknown Landscape,* p.142.

*   *   *

WAKEFIELD, Dan 1932-

PERSONAL: Born May 21, 1932, in Indianapolis, IN; son of Ben H. (a pharmacist) and Brucie (Ridge) Wakefield. *Education:* Attended Indiana University, 1950-51; Columbia University, B.A., 1955.

ADDRESSES: Agent—Elaine Markson, 44 Greenwich Ave., New York, NY 10011.

CAREER: Princeton Packet, Princeton, NJ, news editor, 1955; Columbia University, New York, NY, research assistant to Professor C. Wright Mills, 1955; *Nation,* New York, NY, staff writer, 1956-59; free-

Dan Wakefield

lance writer, beginning 1959; *Atlantic Monthly,* contributing editor, 1968-80; National Broadcasting Corporation (NBC), story consultant for TV series *James at 15,* 1977. Staff member, Bread Loaf Writer's Conference, 1964 and 1966; visiting lecturer at University of Massachusetts at Boston, 1965-67, University of Illinois, 1968, University of Iowa, 1972, Boston University, 1974, University of Massachusetts at Boston, 1981-82; writer-in-residence, Florida International University, 1994—.

MEMBER: Authors Guild of America, PEN, Beacon Hill Civic Association, Writers Guild of America East, National Writers Union

AWARDS, HONORS: DeVoto fellowship to Bread Loaf Writers Conference, 1958; Neiman fellowship, Harvard University, 1963-64; Short story prize, National Council of Arts, 1968; Rockefeller Foundation grant in imaginative writing, 1969; National Book Award nomination, 1970, for *Going All the Way;* film version of *Going All the Way* was selected by Sundance Film Festival in 1997.

WRITINGS:

Island in the City: The World of Spanish Harlem (nonfiction), Houghton (Boston, MA), 1959.

Revolt in the South (nonfiction), Grove (New York, NY), 1961.

(Editor) *The Addict: An Anthology,* Fawcett (Greenwich, CT), 1963.

Between the Lines (nonfiction), New American Library (New York, NY), 1967.

Supernation at Peace and War (nonfiction), Atlantic Monthly Press (Boston, MA), 1968.

(Contributor) Robert Manning and Michael Janeway, editors, *Who We Are: An Atlantic Chronicle of the United States and Vietnam,* Atlantic Monthly Press (Boston, MA), 1969.

Going All the Way (novel; also see below), Delacorte (New York, NY), 1970, reprinted, Indiana University Press (Bloomington, IN), 1997.

Starting Over (novel), Delacorte (New York, NY), 1973.

All Her Children, Doubleday (New York, NY), 1976.

Home Free (novel), Delacorte (New York, NY), 1977.

(And coproducer) *The Seduction of Miss Leona* (movie for television), CBS, 1980.

Under the Apple Tree (novel), Delacorte (New York, NY), 1982.

(Adapter) Mark Twain *The Innocents Abroad* (movie for television), PBS, 1982.

Selling Out (novel), Little, Brown (Boston, MA), 1985.

Returning: A Spiritual Journey, Doubleday (New York, NY), 1988.

The Story of Your Life: Writing a Spiritual Autobiography, Beacon Press (Boston, MA), 1990.

New York in the Fifties (also see below), Houghton (Boston, MA), 1992.

Expect a Miracle, HarperSanFrancisco (San Francisco, CA), 1995.

Creating from the Spirit, Ballantine (New York, NY), 1996.

Going all the Way (screenplay), Gramercy Pictures, 1997.

How Do We Know When It's God? Little, Brown (Boston, MA), 1999.

Releasing the Creative Spirit, SkyLight Paths (Woodstock, VT), 2001.

New York in the Fifties (documentary), Sundance Channel, 2001.

Also writer of an episode of *Heartbeat,* ABC, 1984. Short stories included in *Best American Stories of 1966,* and *American Literary Anthology 2;* contributor of numerous articles, essays, reviews, and short stories to *Atlantic, Esquire, Commentary, Playboy, New York Times Magazine, New York Times Book Review, Los Angeles Times Book Review, GQ, Poets and Writers, Theology Today, Modern Maturity, Spirituality and Health,* and other periodicals. *Ploughshares,* guest editor, 1982; *Beliefnet.com,* writer of column "Spiritually Incorrect," 2001-03.

Author's works have ben translated into Italian, Norwegian, and Japanese.

SIDELIGHTS: An *Atlantic* editor once called Dan Wakefield "one of the best of a rare and vanishing breed . . . [and] an independent writer-reporter who finds the delicate balance between head and heart." In his books and numerous published articles, Wakefield has scrutinized his environment in order to "tell it like it is" in what a *Time* reporter called "less an eyewitness report than a very private vision."

Wakefield's first book, *Island in the City,* is the story of the world of Spanish Harlem ("one of the world's worst slums") where he lived for six months in "personal immersion in the major experiences of his subjects," according to A. D. Vidich. In his book, said Elihu Katz, "Wakefield . . . tries (and sometimes too hard) to be poetic and to communicate insight into how it feels to be on the night coach from Puerto Rico, at a spiritualist seance, on a drug cure, in a sweatshop . . . He tries to communicate his sadness over all those who do not understand." According to Harrison Salisbury, "some of the social workers who devote themselves to the Puerto Ricans and some of the sociologists who have made long and elaborate studies . . . may know Spanish Harlem more comprehensively than Mr. Wakefield. But no one—with the possible exception of Christopher Rand— . . . has captured the spirit of the Puerto Rican in New York so warmly and so sensitively."

In his journalistic books, and particularly in *Supernation at Peace and War,* Wakefield continues to be "an entertaining, often rueful, and revealing guide," according to R. R. Lingeman, as "he conducts us through his journalistic quest." Originally an assignment from the *Atlantic,* Wakefield traveled throughout the United States for four months and his article was published in the March, 1968, issue, with the subtitle, "being certain observations, depositions, testimonies and graffiti gathered on a one-man fact-and-fantasy-finding tour of the most powerful nation in the world." Wakefield adopts what David Cort considered "a classical satirical tone: . . . an innocent credulous voice producing effects of deadpan irony." He is concerned with the

U.S.A. in 1968, "at war with itself and with enemies half way round the world." Concerning these "two wars," Wakefield divides U.S. society into three major attitudinal blocks: "Protest, Patriotism, and Pacification." Florence Casey defined these groups as "divided quite naturally [among] the several hundred people interviewed: 1. Those who are 'against' (the war, suburban life, black poverty, Mother, and The Way Things Are); 2. Those who were 'for' (the war, suburbia, black impoverishment, Mother, and The Way Things Are); and 3. Those who were uncertain (about some, or all, of the same items)." A *Time* reviewer commented: "The well-fed, worried face of supernation deserves a better effort." Thomas Laske, however, wrote: "The scenes in this book may not always be familiar, but the arguments will be. They are part of a continuing dialogue going on all over the country. His book is a handy and inviting way of becoming part of it."

Commenting on Wakefield's journalistic style, Robert Phelps wrote: "As one of our very best journalists in the past decade, Dan Wakefield has been conspicuous for two virtues: a novelist's instinct for the right detail . . . and then something even rarer, an intimate, yet never merely egocentric, scale of observation." In a review of Wakefield's first novel, *Going All the Way,* Robert Kirsch noted that the book is "filled with a kind of wry humor and irony which comes not so much from exaggeration as from keen observation of life . . . . But beneath the humor is the sharp sadness of life that is no life at all, bound by bias, crippled by reaction, and which could only bring the desire for flight and escape, for new beginnings." Edgar Z. Friedenberg believed that "although it is not a very good novel, . . . it is nevertheless a very good book. . . . His touch throughout the book is deft and sure, and there is none of the awkwardness of a writer who sets out to do something and fails."

In 1988, Wakefield produced a book that surprised colleagues and readers: *Returning: A Spiritual Journey.* Leonard Kriegel of *Nation* commented in his review, "Having read almost everything [Wakefield] had written, I was surprised when a mutual friend told me that Wakefield had 'returned,'—the word was his—to the Christian faith." Wakefield tells of his journey back to Christianity in *Returning,* and continues on writing about his spiritual development in such books as *Expect a Miracle, Creating from the Spirit,* and *How Do We Know When It's God?* Along with writing

spiritual memoirs, Wakefield has also lead workshops for writers to develop their own spiritual autobiographies. Despite this seeming change in his focus, the books have been well received. A reviewer for *Publishers Weekly* called *Creating from the Spirit* a "potentially life-changing work," and another reviewer for the same magazine considered *Expect a Miracle* "a lively collection filled with honest revelations and searching questions."

Wakefield told Connie Lauerman of *Knight Ridder/ Tribune News Service* that *How Do We Know When It's God?* is "the most revealing thing I've ever done." A writer for *People Weekly* explained that in this spiritual autobiography, Wakefield "continues his deeply personal account of spiritual rebirth and growth in a roller-coaster career that plummeted from literary heights to alcoholic depths, only to rise again." Lawrence S. Cunningham of *Commonweal* praised Wakefield's "honesty, earnestness, and ability to write sinewy, nonsentimental prose" while John Moryl of *Library Journal* commented, "His life story reads like a novel." Even Kriegel, whose first reaction to was *Returning* was to write an essay defending agnosticism (which Wakefield attacks in his book), acknowledged, "for all my reservations, I find myself looking both with approval and a touch of envy on the journey Wakefield has undertaken. I don't know whether such a journey would work for me or for other writers I know. . . . But it has worked for him."

AUTOBIOGRAPHICAL ESSAY:

Dan Wakefield contributed the following autobiographical essay to *CA:*

A WRITING LIFE

GROWING UP WITH STORIES

"Bowser Brent" was the name of the boy hero in the first book I remember reading, *The Bears of Blue River.* It was about pioneers in Indiana, the very place I was born (Indianapolis, 1932) and lived myself, and that made it all the more thrilling. Along with my neighborhood friends and sometimes by myself I searched for arrowheads in the backyard, imagining almost any small, flat rock might have served that purpose. I loved to read about pioneers—my own intrepid ancestors in buckskin, clearing the land now civilized into streets

Father, Ben Wakefield, holding "just-a-few-weeks-old" Danny

with small frame houses—and the Indians who dwelt in the forests before them, possessors of secrets of the wind and stars, the earliest language of life.

My first-grade teacher, Mrs. Roxie Lingle Day, wanted to know if I'd learned to read at home since I took to it so quickly and naturally. I was the first in my class at School 80 to read all the preprimers in the Broad Ripple Branch Public Library around the corner, and get to go on to the primers, but I had no instruction in reading. It came naturally, as if I had known all along and simply had to be told when to begin. I'm sure it came partly out of my love of stories, for I grew up listening to them.

My mother told me stories she made up when I was a child—the one I liked best was about the animals' picnic, which they went to by train, thus combining some of my favorite elements (bears, devilled eggs, and locomotives). My Sunday-school teacher at the

First Presbyterian Church, Amy Frantz, told me stories of Jesus healing the sick and feeding the multitudes—I saw him on the dusty roads, in that land of white stone houses, among the beggars and kings, donkeys and children, in the colored pictures in our family Bible.

My uncle Jim from Louisville talked the way the Bible sounded, in long sentences that moved with the cadence of poetry, the rhythm of deep-down truth that came from the very elements of life, like wind and rain. His brother was the Baptist minister I was named after, William Daniel Wakefield—my grandfather who died in his thirties when my own father was only twelve years old. Will was the minister who saved people's souls at revival meetings in Columbia, South Carolina, and Shelbyville, Kentucky, and Jim seemed to be the black-sheep brother who I heard whispered was a bookie in Louisville, a gambling man who sometimes came up north to small towns in Indiana to bet on cockfights and dropped in to see us. He had been a revenue agent going after bootleggers and moonshiners during Prohibition, a man who carried a gun and knew how to use it, a man of adventures and stories to tell as tall as they were true.

I loved to listen to him speak, for even when he told only tales of ordinary people, his and my own kin, he made them sound like legend. He might have been speaking of Delilah or Scheherazade when he said of his own daughter, my colorful cousin Katherine ("I'm your kissin' cousin, darlin', now don't be shy!" she told me as I shivered in fascinated fright), with a mixture of admiration and mock despair: "That woman would rather climb to the top of a greased pole and tell a lie than stand at the bottom and tell the truth."

Uncle Jim really got going and sounded like a preacher when he spoke of his love of the South, mocking my father for being a turncoat, a lost soul who lived above the Mason-Dixon line. He would get his best cadences moving and throw back his head, speaking like the author of Ecclesiastes when he told of the man from Kentucky who came up north to Indiana and tried to become a city slicker but got so homesick he had to go back and so put an ad in the paper that began, "Wanted to trade—spats for a bullet mold. Lord, I'm comin' home." My father's face would light with joy and I could feel the goose bumps rise along my arms as Uncle Jim began to intone that particular incantation of his homeland: "I can hear the whippoorwills calling and taste the black-eyed peas. . . ." After recounting the joys that awaited the prodigal, perhaps he would throw in a passage of exile from the Psalms, telling how we sat down and wept by the rivers of Babylon, and hung up our harps; and it all seemed of a piece, a story whose narrative stretched from Moses to my father, from Bathsheba to Cousin Katherine, woven with the King James cadence, the rhyme that connected all stories into one continuing, everlasting, ever-changing (and yet the same) *story.* And nothing in the world was more essential, more deeply stirring. The story not only told what we had done, but who we were.

When my mother's grandmother, my great-grandma Stephens, came up to my grandma Irenee's house to die (to live out the last months she knew she had left with family) she told us stories. I was seven or eight years old and I sat at her feet by the rocking chair while she told me of being a little girl, even a year or so younger than I was then—maybe she was six years old—and she saw the flames in the night sky of the burning farms and houses in the Georgia countryside when Sherman marched to the sea. I can hear the cracking of her voice and the creak of the rocking chair that gave the rhythm to the story—a story I would encounter a few years later in history books about the Civil War. But Grandma Stephens' story was better than the history books, because she was there, she saw the flames, and she made me see them too, in my mind's eye. It was magic, this storytelling, whether you made it up or whether you had actually been there—I had pictured the animals at my mother's imaginary picnic just as clearly as the Union soldiers marching down the night roads of Georgia.

The first stories I knew were the ones I heard, was told, and then I learned to read and write and immediately became entranced with that way of telling stories as well. When people ask me when I first knew I wanted to be a writer I explain that it was really back in the first grade, when words and sentences and stories and books seemed to be my natural element, while numbers looked to me like the distorted, mysterious marks of some code I could never crack—nor had I any desire to decipher its mysteries. I liked pictures, but when it came to using my long twenty-five-crayon box of Crayolas I felt awkward and frustrated (I loved "magenta" but more for the sound of the word than the color). I could not transfer from my brain to the paper via the crayons the pictures that flickered in my mind (they came out sticklike, blocky, and crudely

The author with his mother, Brucie Ridge Wakefield, after church, about 1938

uneven), while with words I could convey the stories that ran through my head in adventurous scenarios of cowboys and covered wagons, football players and airplane flights.

I wrote articles, stories, and poems (doggerel verse whose rhyming sounds delighted me) for my grade-school newspaper, the *Rippler,* and went on to the *Shortridge Daily Echo* in high school—the first high-school daily in America, and surely the world. When I said I wanted to grow up and be a writer most people patted me on the head with condescending tolerance ("You'll mature and realize that's unrealistic, young fellow"), but a few nodded seriously and said, "There was this one fella, name of Vonnegut. Sometimes he has stories in the *Saturday Evening Post.*" Kurt Vonnegut had been a Shortridge graduate a decade before me, and I faithfully searched old copies of the *Post* in the barbershop and read them admiringly while I waited for haircuts.

The fact that a guy who went to my own high school had become a "real writer" with stories in one of the great American magazines made the possibility of such a fabulous career seem more possible. (Later I corresponded with Vonnegut, finally met him in Cambridge in 1963 when he was living on Cape Cod and I was a Nieman fellow at Harvard, and he became a friend and supporter whose enthusiastic backing was crucial to the publication and success of my first novel.)

There was another legendary Shortridge grad who had made good as writer in the great world, a woman named Madeline Pugh Davis. She had been a member of the school literary club around the time of Vonnegut, and in the 1940s, after her graduation from college, she set out with another woman friend on a venture that was surely unheard of for females of that era—they got a car and drove to Los Angeles to seek their fortunes. Madeline became a writer of the *I Love Lucy* show, and I met her in Hollywood in 1978 when I was out there working on a TV series I created called *James at 15.* She and a partner had been called in to rescue an ailing sitcom called *Alice* and they raised it to the top of the ratings. I carry in my mind the picture of her as a young woman with her friend, getting into this old Model T Ford (all this was how I elaborated the story in my head) and tossing their suitcases in the rumble seat, chugging courageously out of Indianapolis, and heading west.

The lives of writers seemed wonderfully adventurous to me, for whether they were sitting at home or going out in search of some story they seemed to be always engaged in a kind of quest. I first got hooked on novels because of the thrill I felt on reading the dedication Sinclair Lewis wrote to Paul de Kruif in *Arrowsmith* for helping him do the research that formed the scientific and medical background of the story. I still remember the line that sent the chill of excitement through me, a reminiscence of Lewis's travels with the scientist: "The deck at dawn as we steamed into tropic ports." Oh God. What could be higher or finer, more thrilling, than to be a writer in search of a story, standing on the deck at dawn, steaming into some tropic

As a Cub Scout, 1941

port? It later made me think of Somerset Maugham, another great travelling storyteller, going to the ends of the earth to find in the jungles and remote reaches of empire the most exciting, revealing tales imaginable, in the seemingly humdrum lives of humble natives and bored bureaucrats at the very edges of civilization.

I wanted to move out myself, see the world, leave home and Indiana behind, and go on the great quest, the search for the meaning, the grail, the story. Back in high school I already saw ahead as I lay in my room reading Carl Sandburg, loving my family and friends yet knowing I needed to leave them, like "The Red Son" of the poem who said in language that spoke to my own teenage longing:

> I love your faces I saw the many years
> I drank your milk and filled my mouth
> With your home talk, slept in your house
> And was one of you.
>   But a fire burns in my heart. . . .

The last line of the poem kept going around in my head as I thought of the people of my home whom I loved and at the same time wanted to leave: "You for the little hills and I go away."

The Journalistic Eye

When I went off to college at Columbia in New York City I soon reported for duty at the *Daily Spectator,* the school newspaper. It was what I did. I'd been writing for the school paper since good old School 80, where I got some of my doggerel verse into the *Rippler,* and continued through the glorious years of high school, where I not only had my own sports column but served as editor of the Thursday edition of the *Shortridge Daily Echo.* Being on the school paper was like being in school, and it was a way of connecting with Columbia, of making myself at home in the initially unfamiliar and overwhelming environment of New York City. A good way of learning about where I'd come was to write about it, which was also (though I didn't think of it that way at the time) a good way of dealing with the culture shock of moving from the Midwest to Manhattan as a college student.

Writing for the paper was a kind of socialization process, for I met new friends through the *Spectator* like Jerry Landauer, the chain-smoking investigative reporter who went on to a fine career as Washington correspondent for the *Wall Street Journal.* It was also serious professional training. I wanted to write, and the school paper was an outlet for getting my work in print, and training me to become adept at doing that and responsible for meeting deadlines.

At Columbia, my newspaper writing took on another professional dimension as well. I longed to tell stories in the form of fiction, and as I delved into contemporary literature I saw in Ernest Hemingway an idol and role model as well as a writer of lucid prose whose precision and spareness thrilled and inspired me. I learned that Hemingway had worked for the *Kansas City Star* and used his early reporting assignments as training for his fiction writing, a way not only of honing skills but also of looking hard and close at human experience and learning to examine and know what he really felt instead of what he was supposed to feel. I wanted to do the same, and that purpose gave my newspaper work more meaning. I was not getting "just the facts, ma'am," à la Jack Webb in *Dragnet,* I was training myself to be a fiction writer by being a factual reporter.

After my sophomore year in college I landed a summer replacement job in the sports department of the *Indianapolis Star,* and not only was able to secretly (it wasn't something you went around blabbing about) train myself for fiction writing, but as an extra bonus also got to talk about novels and read new ones suggested by my boss, a witty and well-read young mentor named Bob Collins. Sitting around the sports department talking about books I'd just read by Budd Schulberg and Kenneth Roberts was a special thrill, a kind of initiation into the world of adulthood as well as books.

The stutter of the wire-service teletype machines at the *Star* was a thrilling sound, and the whole newspaper ambience was exciting and rewarding in itself, not just as a private training ground for fiction. I felt a kinship with newspaper people, and working around them was like belonging to some special kind of lodge, one whose members were a little more learned, worldly-wise, and understandingly humane. They had seen it all in the course of their work—death, disaster, corruption, victory—and described what they heard and saw in terse, no-nonsense prose, telling it like it was. I respected and admired them and felt privileged to be among them.

Hoping to gain even more good experience away from home, I wrote to the editors of about forty newspapers throughout America (I gleaned the names and addresses from a copy of *Editor & Publisher* I got from the library) toward the end of my junior year in college, asking for a summer job, and got about four replies, one of which led to my being hired for the vacation as a general assignment reporter by the *Grand Rapids Press.* It was especially thrilling because it was away from home, and it wasn't just sports but "real life"—which turned out to be features on retired couples raising roses, an amateur horse breeder, a collector of rare china, and a veteran of the Korean War who shook so badly when I tried to ask him how he earned his Purple Heart that I didn't have the journalistic guts to continue the interview.

The *Press* reporters were like a welcoming family, taking me home to dinner and buying me beers, a happy relief from the loneliness of the rooming house where I played the *New World* Symphony over and over, brooding by Dvorák's music and trying to compose short stories. I felt the composer had really captured something of the deep-down spirit of the land, and I ached to be able to do the same in words.

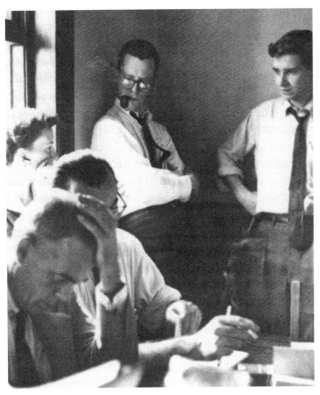

(Far right) Covering the Emmett Till murder for Nation *magazine, Sumner, Mississippi, 1955*

A few years later after graduation from college I brooded and tried to write stories in another rooming house after working on a newspaper all day, this time in Princeton, New Jersey, where I'd gone to work on the *Weekly Packet,* which was owned by Bernard Kilgore, the publisher of the *Wall Street Journal.* Barney Kilgore was an "Indiana boy" and I got an introduction to him through my high-school history teacher, Dorothy Peterson, who had been a classmate of his at DePauw University in Greencastle, Indiana. He was a classic newspaperman who loved ink and print and bought his hometown paper to have the kind of hands-on experience with it he no longer had at the *Journal* from his lofty office with the plush carpet and the Dow-Jones ticker on his desk.

I covered the local hearings on schools and sewers, dashed with my Rolleiflex to photograph as well as report on fires and highway crashes, but my heart wasn't really in it. I longed to get back to the excitement I had already discovered in Greenwich Village, and to see the world as Hemingway had, in far-off exotic places like Barcelona and Paris. The offer of a job as research assistant to my Columbia sociology professor, C. Wright Mills, enabled me to return to

New York and bang away at the fiction while I made reading reports for Mills and picked up extra income doing in-house reviews for the Book Find Club.

In Princeton I had met my journalistic hero Murray Kempton, who wrote a splendid column in the *New York Post* (the kind of elegant prose that made journalism seem worthy to me), and he helped me get my first magazine assignment for the *Nation,* covering the murder trial of two white men in Mississippi accused of murdering Emmett Till, a black teenager from Chicago who had committed the Dixie "crime" of whistling at a white woman. I began to publish other pieces in the *Nation,* which allowed me to write as well as I could without the limitations of daily newspaper journalism. Better still, the new publisher, George Kirstein, took a liking to me and my work, and agreed to back me on a trip to Israel to write a series of articles.

I had been inspired by Arthur Koestler's account of his adventures as a young journalist in Palestine in his autobiographical *Arrow in the Blue* while I restlessly paced my tame, wallpapered room in Princeton. My dream of following in the footsteps of such intrepid writer-reporters (like Hemingway he went on from journalistic apprenticeship to write powerful novels) came true when I sailed on the SS *Israel* from New York to Haifa in January of 1956.

I learned to observe and experience in a much more focussed way in Israel I think. I have a sense that being away from my familiar home, language, and landscape, plunged into totally new social as well as geographical terrain, accentuated and highlighted what I was seeing and doing. I had a sense of seeing more clearly, into the heart of things, as if all emotion and speech and action were brought out in bright, sharp contrast by the very circumstance of being so far away from everything and everyone I knew. There was an excitement in the writing as well as in the events I was writing about, a sense I was really *learning,* gaining some command over my craft.

When I got back to New York I found myself drawn to another "foreign" terrain for the setting and subject of my first book—*The World of Spanish Harlem.* (I moved to 100th Street in East Harlem to begin doing research about the neighborhood in 1957, wrote the following year, and the book was published in 1959.) I

Wakefield with a copy of his first book, Island in the City *1959*

was led there by three young women I met at the Catholic Worker hospitality house in the Bowery, and immediately was drawn to this first of New York's Puerto Rican neighborhoods. The bright colors, the staccato Spanish, the rhythmic Latin music all made a different kind of scene, one that, like Israel, stood out for me because of its very unfamiliarity and somehow because of that seemed more accessible for rendering as journalism. I was still looking, learning (I began to realize there would never come a time when you had finished learning, whether in data or the practice of the craft).

I went south to write about the civil-rights struggle for the *Nation* magazine, from 1955 to 1962, and the articles formed the basis of a book called *Revolt in the South* that Grove Press brought out as a paperback original. Though I hadn't thought of it till now, that subject also led me to an exotic *other* sort of scene with its Dixie accents, Faulknerian settings, and issues outlined and highlighted in black and white.

I wrote a profile for *Esquire* of Adam Clayton Powell, Jr., the suave and controversial Harlem congressman,

which began a productive relationship with that magazine that flourished from 1959 to 1963, when I wrote other journalistic portraits that included William F. Buckley, Jr.; John Dos Passos; and Robert F. Kennedy. It was through my editor at *Esquire*—a generous man named Harold Hayes whom writers loved because he made the business seem exciting and fun—that I applied for and won a Nieman fellowship in journalism that took me to Harvard in 1963-64. I enjoyed the year, and though I didn't fall in love with either Harvard or Cambridge, I discovered Boston as the place I would happily adopt as home for my adult life.

My own coming to Boston on the Nieman coincided with the arrival of another former Nieman, Robert Manning, to take over the editorship of the *Atlantic Monthly*. He published an essay I did on Jack Kerouac and the Beat Generation, and called me into his office to talk about my doing more for the magazine. Through Manning's support as editor and friend I found a home at the *Atlantic* as well as in Boston. I began to do essays for them on literature, journalism, and movies, and was given a desk at the magazine's stately offices at 8 Arlington Street overlooking the Boston Public Garden. In 1967 I was also given the title of contributing editor and a place on the masthead, which lasted until a year or so after Manning's untimely departure in an unhappy wrangle with new ownership in 1980.

My contributions to the magazine had been more commentary than journalism, until one fateful evening when, while drinking martinis and cooking hamburgers over an outdoor grill at the Mannings' house in Cambridge, Bob and I got to talking about the frustration of covering the story that most people were talking about that spring of 1967—America's involvement in the Vietnam War. Bob said the reports from the field with statistics of battles didn't really seem to bring much light to the subject, and perhaps the important thing to be examined was what the effect of the war was on our own country, right here at home. I agreed, and over the next martini, Bob said it might be a good idea to send someone around the country and do that kind of a report. I said it sounded like a fine idea, especially for a magazine with a two-month lead time that couldn't keep up with the daily-news aspect of the story, and then Bob asked if I would like to have such an assignment. I said I could start the first of June, when I finished teaching some classes at the University of Massachusetts at Boston.

I felt that whatever journalistic experience I had was now put to the test, as I travelled into Canada and around the United States for nearly six months, interviewing soldiers and draft resisters, hawks and doves, families of men who had been killed in action and dropouts protesting the war in love-ins, policemen and editorial writers, housewives arid hippies, the whole spectrum of American society as I found it from one coast to the other, ending up with interviews with government people in Washington, D.C., where I wrote what would become the entire March 1968 issue of the *Atlantic,* "Supernation at Peace amid War."

I was proud of "Supernation," and it seemed a kind of fulfillment and culmination of my journalistic career. I must have interviewed several hundreds of people, and when I started to write in Washington I worked from grocery boxes full of notebooks and clippings I had accumulated in my travels. I was drained when I finished, and felt in some way exhausted in particular from my role as reporter. I told friends that I'd had enough of that kind of work, that when I finished "Supernation" I had "OD'd on journalism." I was still a writer, of course. And I still hadn't written the novel. I had made false starts and failed to finish. I had written and published three short stories, but never the novel. At age thirty-six, I decided it was now or never. I took the advance I had got from the book publication of "Supernation" and headed west.

When I was in Los Angeles doing research for "Supernation" I had met up with some old friends who had moved there from New York about the time I had gone to Boston, and they invited me to come out and stay in their house in Hollywood while I looked for a place to live and write for a year. I thought the change of scene—to another exotic, foreign sort of ambience like the ones that had stirred me in Israel and East Harlem—might help me get going on the novel. I felt relaxed and confident, and a popular song of the year ran through my head as I travelled to California: "Goin' where the sun keeps shinin' through the fallin' rain / goin' where the weather suits my clothes. . . ."

To See the Dream

Why did I still think, after all that time, that I could write a novel? I was painfully aware of the hollowness of the clichés that all journalists had a novel "in their desk drawer," that everyone thought they "had a novel

in them," ha-ha, but few really came through. After I'd finished my first book, the journalistic account of Spanish Harlem, I wrote fifty pages of my first "first novel" and my agent sent it to Houghton Mifflin, who had published *Island in the City.* They turned it down flat. They patted me on the head and said they thought very highly of me *as a journalist,* and they wanted very much to publish my next *nonfiction* book. They said if I wanted to try that novel elsewhere, I was free to do so. I was crushed. I took back the pages and scrunched them into some box to get out later. When I did, they seemed flat and failed (they *had* failed, at least with my first publisher). That was in 1959, and in the next nine years I made several more false starts, but could never even get into the novel I wanted to write. Yet here I was whistling my way to California to hunker down and write my novel, completely confident I was going to do it. How come?

I believe it was because I had a dream, and I don't just mean a vision or longing or desire to write a novel. I mean I literally had a dream in the form of a novel. The dream began with a title page, then a story took place, with a character rather like myself but who had another sort of job and identity, and at the end of the adventure a final page said "The End" and the book was closed. When I woke, I felt exhilarated. Even though I knew the story was not the one I would write in my novel, it had a beginning, a middle, and end (not to mention the title and end pages), and since it was my dream, it had come from me, and I had the feeling it was a message from some deeper part of myself assuring my conscious self that I really could do it, that in fact I "had it in me" and would someday be able to write the novel.

I had that dream when I was living in the Village after my publisher had turned down my first attempt at a novel, so it must have been around 1959. Though I tried and failed to write the novel several times in the ensuing nine years, it was that dream that sustained me, that gave me some kind of inner assurance that despite all the exterior evidence I could still do it, I could still write that novel. That was the main hope I had going for me when I found an apartment in Venice, California, on Ocean Front Walk in the summer of 1968 and sat down to do it. I finished in Boston in the fall of 1969, and the novel called *Going All the Way* was published in 1970, became a national best-seller, a dual main selection of the Literary Guild, and was published abroad in England, Italy, Spain, and Japan. I wrote an account of the creation of it called "Novel Bites Man" that came out in the August 1970 issue of the *Atlantic*.

Writing the novel was indeed a fulfillment, a deep satisfaction of some very basic kind. The novels that followed were tremendously satisfying as well (*Starting Over,* 1973; *Home Free,* 1977; *Under the Apple Tree,* 1982; and *Selling Out,* 1985) though none matched the emotional "breakthrough" feeling of the first. To my chagrin and surprise, none of them got any easier to write, either. Unlike most enterprises in life—building a house, for instance—writing a novel does not mean that you learn something in such a way that you can do it faster or better or more efficiently the next time. It's as if each time you begin at the beginning, feeling like a sculptor with a rusty Boy Scout knife facing a gigantic boulder.

In between novels I returned to nonfiction for articles and at least one book, though it was not in the old "hard-journalism" mode of objective inquiry. Rather, my book about the making of a soap opera—*All Her Children,* 1975—was more like "A Fan's Notes" on a show (the daytime serial *All My Children*) and a world I got hooked on, and whose creator, Agnes Nixon, became a significant friend.

A year later, out of the blue, I got a chance to write my own television series—not a daily soap opera, but a weekly prime-time drama. When I actually got the go-ahead from NBC to write a pilot about a teenage boy growing up in America, I frantically asked the executive who had got me involved, "How do I write a TV script? I've never done it before." He gave me the best advice I ever got in that whole field: "Forget you're writing for television," he said, "and simply write the best story you can." I took him at his word. The result was a two-hour movie that served as a pilot for the series *James at 15.*

I had tried to write scripts in the past—had in fact done a rewrite of my novel *Starting Over,* before the book was optioned by a veteran TV writer who wrote his own script that became the feature film. I had also optioned on my own a story called "Dump Gull" by a writer whose work I love named Fanny Howe and wrote a film script, but nothing came of it. Just as I had once been told to "stick to journalism" and not try novels, after writing novels I was told to "stick to

The author with his publisher, Seymour Lawrence, at a party for the novel Starting Over *on a boat in Boston Harbor, 1973*

novels" and not try writing scripts. The TV offer gave me a chance, and it worked. Everything came together in one of the happiest television productions I can imagine, in which everyone involved was proud and pleased (a rare thing for any medium, and especially for television).

David Sontag, then a vice president of television at Twentieth Century-Fox, put together the team of me as writer, Martin Manulis as producer, and Joe Hardy as director, with a cast starring Lance Kerwin as James and Linden Chiles and Lynn Carlin as his parents. It was one of those amazing occurrences when all the elements meshed. The pilot was a hit—number one for the week, and a whopping 42 "share" in the Nielsen Ratings—as well as a big critical success. Watching the show on TV in the Hollywood home of Joe Hardy, with Martin Manulis and other people from the show present, was one of the most "high" points of my life, in terms of pure elation. For a writer to see his work on the air, and know that while he is watching it is also being watched by roughly twenty million people throughout America at the same time, is an incredibly powerful experience, especially when you're proud of the show, as I was of *James.* Jessamyn West once wrote a book about the making of her novel *The Friendly Persuasion* into a movie and titled it *To See the Dream.* That was what the film of *James* was like for me—a dramatization of the script I had written that was true to my own vision of it.

The pressures of a weekly series and the ratings and the edicts from network executives on high soon brought *James* to his untimely demise, just after reaching age sixteen (or rather, the twenty one-hour shows plus the two-hour pilot that made up a full television "season" at that time). I stayed on writing TV movies and getting more and more frustrated and homesick for Boston, finally flying (fleeing) back there in April of 1980.

Returning

It was a welcome relief to return to the novel as well as Boston, and in the autumn of 1980 I settled into my old neighborhood on Beacon Hill and took up writing *Under the Apple Tree,* which I hadn't been able to concentrate on after beginning it in Hollywood the previous spring. I finished in the summer of 1981, and felt I had reestablished myself, in terms of place as well as work. In 1984 I finished a novel based on my experience writing a TV series in Hollywood, called *Selling Out* (it was published in 1985), and felt I had purged myself of the painful downside of that whole period, which had left me feeling like someone at the bottom of "the pit" that people talk about so often in the Psalms.

On the TV talk show *Good Day* in Boston I was interviewed about *Selling Out* by psychologist Tom Cottle, a bright and perceptive man who had actually read the book (a rarity among television interviewers). At one point he asked why I—as opposed to the character "Perry Moss," the New England writer who went to Hollywood and barely survived—had returned to Boston. Wondering how I could sum up such a complex set of circumstances in any brief answer, I blurted out, "The Twenty-third Psalm."

The words of that psalm had come to my mind in one of the dark periods before coming back to Boston, and marked the beginning of my most recent book, *Returning: A Spiritual Journey* (spring, 1988). In 1980 I went to a Christmas Eve service at King's Chapel, a

church near where I live on Beacon Hill, and that began a course that took me back to attending church again for the first time in more than a quarter century, joining in 1982, and becoming an active member. I served as cochair of the adult religious education committee from 1982 to 1986, and was named to be a member of the vestry, 1986-89.

All this had a direct effect on what I was writing. I took a class in "Spiritual Autobiography" given by our minister, the Reverend Carl Scovel, in 1982, and then again as an assistant to the minister in that class in 1985. The ten-page spiritual autobiography that I wrote in the second class was published in the *New York Times Magazine* on December 22, 1985, as "Returning to Church," and republished in newspapers around the country via the *New York Times* syndication service. I received more mail about it than anything I had ever written, from people all over the country who had experienced some kind of "return" similar to my own, or wished they had, or were on a path toward it, or simply wanted to share some of their own thoughts with a person who had struggled with his own demons and been drawn to a different direction in life and touched something deeper in himself as a result.

Several publishers wrote and asked if I would be interested in expanding the article into a book. That was exactly what I wanted to do, though I hadn't anticipated such a project until I had written the essay in the class at King's Chapel. It felt natural, as if it had flowed out of all the other work I had done as a writer, though it wasn't precisely like any of it. I had made some brief autobiographical connections in a collection of articles I published back in 1966 called *Between the Lines,* but I had no plan or desire whatsoever to write "my autobiography." This seemed different though, for what I had begun to do in the article, and what I wanted to do in the book, was write about my experience as seen and understood from a spiritual point of view, as opposed to a psychological, economic, or even literary vantage. In doing so, I felt I might be articulating and maybe even, hopefully, illuminating that course in the lives of many others.

Writing that book, *Returning,* was a different experience than any of the other books I had written. I remembered my old Columbia professor Mark Van Doren speaking of a writer who in his later life seemed to have "tapped some rich vein in himself" that resulted in a particular book. I felt as if, in the writing

With godchildren Jonathan Geller and Michael Wakefield Geller, 1986

of *Returning,* I had gone deeply into myself in a way I had not even done before in my novels, and it was not painful, but rather, seemed like a natural act, a process of being in tune with my own nature and expressing it. I had never so much enjoyed and looked forward to the very act of writing. I don't mean to say it was "easy," but that it was "natural" in a way I had known before only on brief occasions, when a passage or (once) a short story seemed to "flow" as if it were "given."

I look forward to what comes next. At age fifty-five, I feel I have not only "returned," but just begun.

POSTSCRIPT:

Wakefield contributed the following update to *CA* in 2003:

The last of a series of iron-barred doors slammed shut behind me. The place was colder and more grim than I'd imagined. There were guards with guns at each of the doors I was taken through, and men in cages, like animals. This was prison.

Welcome to Sing Sing.

I never dreamed that returning to church would lead me here.

Thankfully, I was not an inmate. I'd come to give a workshop in spiritual autobiography for a group of sixteen prisoners who were studying for a master's degree that would enable them to get jobs as chaplains, ministers, or social workers when they finished serving their terms. I had been invited by the man who founded and was leading the program, Rev. George W. Webber, Dean of the New York Theological Seminary (which he'd also founded). "Bill" Webber was also a founder of the East Harlem Protestant Parish, which I'd written about in my first book, *Island in the City: The World of Spanish Harlem.* Back then I might have more easily believed I would someday be in prison than I'd have believed that I'd ever be giving workshops in spiritual autobiography!

The book *Returning: A Spiritual Journey* led me on a whole new path, giving workshops like the one I'd taken at King's Chapel, at churches, synagogues, adult education centers, health spas, and Sing Sing Prison. I'd traveled around the country and to Northern Ireland and Mexico giving these workshops, which eventually led to a book on "how to do it" called *The Story of Your Life: Writing a Spiritual Autobiography.*

The workshop at Sing Sing was held in a basement room with a coffee pot and a long table with the men sitting around it. They were mostly black, with some Latinos and a few white men, ranging in age from twenties to sixties, imprisoned for crimes ranging from narcotics possession and/or sales to murder. I didn't know or want to know who committed what crime. I only knew I was talking with a group of articulate, intelligent human beings with deep religious faith— most were Christian, some Muslim—who were trying to keep their souls and bodies alive while shut up in cages for years or decades or life.

I always came away from these visits with a sense of uplift and exhilaration. I was awed by the hard faith that sustained these men, and the appreciation they had of any volunteers who came to speak to them and offer some kind of helpful program. I thought of a poster I have by Sister Corita that I've kept for twenty-five years, with a message by Albert Schweitzer that I sometimes forget and that always comes back to me when I try to live by its wisdom: "I don't know what your destiny will be, but one thing I know, the only ones among you who will be really happy are those who have sought and found a way to serve."

*

"Do you now renounce your earlier work?"

For a moment I was speechless. I'd just given a talk at St. Bartholomew's Episcopal Church in New York City, and a young woman in the back of the audience raised her hand and asked this question. No one had ever asked me that before, but I knew what she meant.

In the five novels I'd written—from *Going All the Way* to *Selling Out*—I had dealt frankly with sexuality and used the language appropriate to the situations. I'd never used sex as a subject to shock or offend, but rather to portray real-life situations, and to put in the mouth of my characters the words that such people would really speak. Not only are sexual issues dealt with openly in these works, but religious beliefs are probed and questioned. Sonny Burns, the protagonist of *Going All the Way,* is a young man rebelling against the conformity of middle America in the 1950s, striking out against home, family, church, and God—a God he feels other people are trying to force down his throat.

When the young woman asked if I renounced such work, I answered honestly, "I *embrace* my earlier work." I believe that writing is not necessarily "religious" because it is about religion, but rather, because it comes from the heart, the true understanding of the author in his effort to tell the truth as he or she knows it.

The escort on a book tour for *Creating from the Spirit* told me he had trouble arranging my appearances at some of the stores in his area. He had asked that they have the new book on hand, as well as a recent paperback of my novel *Going All the Way*. A few of the bookstore managers told him that those books were written by different authors: they thought there was one Dan Wakefield who wrote the spiritual books, and another one who wrote the novels. "I had to convince them," the escort said, "that you're the same guy."

I assured the book store managers I was indeed, "the same guy" who wrote the novels as well as the books on spirituality. And I was proud of them all.

*

I found myself back in Sheridan Square, the heart of Greenwich Village, on the eve of my sixtieth birthday (an age I never expected to reach in my hard-drinking

The author (second from right) at a reunion of roommates he lived with in New York City in 1955

youth.) Some of the landmarks of my life in that neighborhood from 1956 to 1963 were gone now. Louis' Tavern—where I took dates to dinner for sixty-five cents for spaghetti with two meatballs and salad—was replaced by a super market.

In spite of the disappearance of some of the old landmarks, I felt the spirit and excitement, the Village ambience, of art and books and music and freedom. Just as in the old days, a sense of relief always came when I got off the Seventh Avenue subway at Sheridan Square after being anywhere else in the city. North of Fourteenth Street you needed to wear a jacket and tie; south of that border you could still relax and be comfortable.

I had started going back to Manhattan from Boston in 1990 to visit old haunts and interview friends for a memoir of *New York in the Fifties*. When the book was published in 1992, nostalgia and restlessness took me back to live in the city again. As a friend told me, "You were seduced by your own book."

Art Cooper, the editor of *GQ,* had inspired the book when he commissioned me to write a memoir of James Baldwin for the magazine. When it appeared, I got a letter from Seymour Lawrence urging me to write a book about the era when I had known Baldwin, and he offered me a contract. For the publication, Sam Lawrence and Art Cooper hosted a party that celebrated both the book and my sixtieth birthday. It was held at the Village Gate, one of my old hangouts of the '50s, and featured music from a jazz group led by David

Amram, a friend of that era who had played with Charlie Mingus and Dizzy Gillespie. I blew out sixty candles on a mammoth cake, while friends from my youth in the Village and later years in Boston looked on and cheered. I could not have imagined a more fulfilling way to hit sixty.

*

I was naked and shivering as two men in blue aprons dunked me into the cold water of a rectangular pool in the small French village of Lourdes—the most popular pilgrimage site in the world. It was there that a shepherd girl named Bernadette had a vision of the Virgin Mary in 1848, and water from the spring she discovered was declared to have healing powers. People from all over the world come there to take the baths, visit the grotto shrine, walk in torchlight processions honoring Mary, and pray. I traveled there from New York in 1993 researching a book called *Expect a Miracle,* and I wanted to experience the ritual immersion in the legendary waters.

The dunking at Lourdes reminded me of my baptism at age eleven, when the minister of the Broad Ripple Christian Church in Indianapolis put a handkerchief over my nose and dipped me under the water of the pool created for the ceremony behind the pulpit. No lightning struck or voices came out of the sky on either occasion, but the trip to Lourdes reaffirmed my faith and my sense of wonder and appreciation.

I witnessed again how service brings fulfillment to the servant as well as the served, for everyone who comes with a physical pain or illness is assigned a volunteer to take them from place to place, to make sure all their needs are met. This service creates a sense of joy, and produces the healing of spirit Lourdes emphasizes, and makes the infirmities of the flesh easier to bear, even if not healed. That's why so many people return.

*

The phone rang in my Village studio shortly after I moved there in '92, and a woman I didn't know asked if I was the writer who gave workshops in spiritual autobiography. When I said I was, she told me she had

With Jill Clayburgh on the set of the movie **Going All the Way,** *1997*

been to her dentist's office that morning. I wondered what in the world that had to do with *me*! Then she explained she had read an article about my workshops in a magazine in her dentist's waiting room, and she wondered if I could come to lead one at her church in Palm Beach, Florida.

It was the first of a cluster of unexpected invitations that took me to a place I never imagined going—South Florida. In the next two years I gave talks and workshops at the Miami Book Fair, the Broward County Library's "Night of Literary Feasts" in Ft. Lauderdale, and the Seaside. From my studio apartment on Horatio Street in the next few years, I traveled on writing assignments from Rancho La Puerta, the legendary health spa in Mexico, to a Writers Conference sponsored by Florida International University (FIU). In January of '94 I was asked to teach in the creative writing graduate program of the University, which led to a regular appointment there as writer-in-residence.

I had to laugh when I took my first dip in the ocean outside my condo in Miami Beach, and thought about how I ended up living there. I certainly didn't set out for it, and yet it soon felt natural. I simply followed a path that seemed to have been laid out for me. I thought back to that first phone call from the woman who read about my workshop in the waiting room of her dentist's office, and a startling question occurred to me: *Where would I be if she'd gone to a different dentist?*

*

Dressed in farmer's overalls, I stood in a country church outside Indianapolis, surrounded by friends from high school in the summer of 1996. We were not there for a revival meeting, but the filming of a scene for the movie being made of my novel *Going All the Way.* I had long ago given up hope of such a movie being made, after four different options had expired and the "property," as it's called in Hollywood, had been pronounced dead by the moguls of moviedom. It was still alive, though, in the dream of a young director who had read the book when he was in high school and vowed to make it his first movie.

Mark Pellington had won an MTV award for best director of a music video, and directed documentaries for PBS as well as television commercials, when he told me he wanted to make my first novel his first feature film. He found independent backing, commissioned me to write a script, and against all odds, turned it into a beautiful film with a great cast, including Ben Affleck, Jeremy Davies, Rose McGowan, Jill Clayburgh, and Lesley Ann Warren. The movie *Going All The Way* was selected for showing at the Sundance Film Festival in 1997 and released in theaters the same year (just before Affleck became a major star with *Good Will Hunting.*)

The movie of *Going All The Way,* like the novel it is based on, stirred outrage as well as appreciation. The reviewer for the *New York Times* viewed its accurate and satiric portrayal of the 1950s mores and morals through the politically correct lens of the 1990s and attacked it with egregious venom, while the *Boston Globe* rated it one of the Ten Best Movies of the Year, praising its "sheer audacity and elegiac beauty." Roger Ebert on his TV show affirmed the vision that director Mark Pellington so powerfully realized:

> I've never seen a film in my life that is closer to the experience in mind and body and in sexuality that I had when I was just getting out of high school and going to college, than this film. In other words, the friendships, the girls, everything reminded me specifically of things I had either seen or gone through.

The author with his goddaughter, Karina Corrales, Christmas 2001

The movie was a commercial failure but, more than a success, a personal fulfillment, and, I truly believe, a work of art, due to the director and his producer partner, Tom Gorai—and what later turned out to be an "all-star cast." It still has a life on cable TV and DVD.

The premiere of the movie in Indianapolis led to another kind of movie being made of one of my books. A young woman who had gone to the same high school as I did, at a much later time, approached me after the party that followed the hometown opening, and said she'd like to make a documentary based on my book *New York in the Fifties.* In the summer of '98 I went back to New York with Betsy Blankenbaker, the talented producer/director who was making the documentary, and we interviewed many of the friends and colleagues from that era whom I'd written about in the book, including Gay and Nan Talese, Joan Didion and John Dunne, Bruce Jay Freidman, Nat Hentoff, and many others. Ms. Blankenbaker created an insightful and moving documentary that premiered at the Santa Barbara Film Festival in 2000, opened theatrically in New York in 2001 to good reviews in the *New York Times,* the *New York Daily News,* and *Newsday,* before being shown on the Sundance Channel and released as a video and DVD the following year.

As well as having good movies made of their books, another common dream of writers is having a column of their own, a place to sound off their personal opinions on issues they feel strongly about. That opportunity came to me when a new Web site called *Beliefnet.com* invited me to be one of their columnists on the subject of spirituality. With great pleasure, I've written for them a column called "Spiritually Incorrect," which has covered everything from the importance of coffee houses as a sanctuary, to the continuing influence of Dorothy Day, the iconoclastic founder of the Catholic Worker movement.

Teaching my writing courses at FIU as well as continuing my workshops in "Spiritual Autobiography" and "Releasing the Creative Spirit" at churches and adult ed centers around the country, gives me more pleasure with each passing year. My teaching has allowed me to write as well, publishing a sequel to *Returning* whose title poses one of the deepest questions for people of faith, whatever that faith may be: *How Do We Know When It's God?*

I haven't discovered any quick or easy answers, but the question itself is a kind of guide, a reminder of the mystery. Michael Murphy, founder of the Esalen Institute, summed up its fascination and power when he told me in an interview: "The great game, the game of games, the story of stories is the unfolding of the Divine."

BIOGRAPHICAL AND CRITICAL SOURCES:

PERIODICALS

America, May 14, 1966.
American Anthropology, December, 1959.
American Journal of Sociology, March, 1960
Atlantic, June, 1966; August, 1970.
Booklist, March 15, 1959; July, 1995, Steve Schroeder, review of *Expect a Miracle: The Miraculous Things That Happen to Ordinary People,* p. 1840; August, 1999, Ray Olson, review of *How Do We Know When It's God?* p. 1995.
Bookmark, February, 1959.
Book Week, May 22, 1966.
Catholic World, June, 1959.
Christian Century, March 25, 1959.
Christian Science Monitor, June 16, 1966; June 13, 1968.
Commentary, 1966.

Commonweal, June 10, 1966; June 12, 1968; September 8, 2000, Lawrence S. Cunningham, review of *How Do We Know When It's God?* p. 40.
Kirkus Reviews, December 1, 1958; April 15, 1968.
Knight Ridder/Tribune News Service, December 29, 1999, Connie Lauerman, "After Years of Intellectual Atheism, Dan Wakefield Finds Spiritual Healing," p. K4628.
Library Journal, March 1, 1988, Elise Chase, review of *Returning: A Spiritual Journey,* p. 70; May 1, 1995, Henry Carrigan, Jr., review of *Expect a Miracle,* p. 104; July, 1996, Henry Carrigan, Jr., review of *Creating from the Spirit: Living Each Day as a Creative Act,* p. 123; May 15, 1997, Michael Rogers, review of *Going All the Way,* p. 107; August, 1999, John Moryl, review of *How Do We Know When It's God?* p. 101.
Modern Maturity, January-February, 2000, Dan Wakefield, "Soul Man," p. 35.
Nation, May 2, 1959, November 11, 1968; December 23, 1996, Leonard Kriegel, review of *Returning: A Spiritual Journey,* p. 30.
National Review, May 17, 1966; July 30, 1968.
New York Herald Tribune Book Review, February 15, 1959.
New York Review of Books, November 5, 1970.
New York Times, August 27, 1992, Richard F. Shepard, "Back in Greenwich Village, Strolling among the Wise," p. C1; September 24, 1993, Michiko Kakutani, "Taking Chances to Stroll Literary Paths to the Past," p. C1.
New York Times Book Review, February 15, 1959; May 1, 1966; June 8, 1968; August 9, 1970; March 6, 1988, David Toolan, review of *Returning,* p. 9; June 7, 1992, Vance Bourjaily, review of *New York in the Fifties,* p. 1; May 29, 1995, Abraham Verghese, review of *Expect a Miracle,* p. 22.
People Weekly, November 15, 1999, "Beyond Belief: Successful Novelist Dan Wakefield Found a Second Career Writing about the Spiritual Rebirth That Changed His Life," p. 231.
Poets & Writers, January-February, 2000, Pamela Gordon, "Getting Clear: Dan Wakefield's Creative Path," p. 14.
Publishers Weekly, February 19, 1988, Genevieve Stuttaford, review of *Returning,* p. 66; March 4, 1988, Judith Rosen, interview with Wakefield, p. 89; April 10, 1995, review of *Expect a Miracle,* p. 30; April 22, 1968; June 3, 1996, review of *Creating from the Spirit,* p. 70; July 12, 1999, review of *How Do We Know When It's God?* p. 91.
Reporter, June 16, 1966.

Saturday Review, March 7, 1959.
Time, February 23, 1968, June 14, 1968.
Washington Post, August 26, 1970.

ONLINE

Dan Wakefield's Home Page: Welcome to Wakespace, http://www.danwakefield.com/ (May 14, 2003).

*   *   *

WALKER, Robert 1945-

PERSONAL: Born June 8, 1945, in Montreal, Quebec, Canada; married Ania Swietlik, 1985. *Education:* Sir George Williams University, B.A., 1969, studied photography at workshops conducted by Lee Friedlander, 1975, Gary Winogrand, 1980.

ADDRESSES: Home—1477 Rue Viau, Montreal, Quebec HIV 3G8, Canada.

CAREER: Independent photographer, Montreal, Quebec, Canada, 1975-77, and New York, NY, 1977—. Galerie Optica, *Camerart* exhibition curator, 1974; International Center of Photography, *Philippe Halsman '79* exhibition curator, 1979. *Exhibitions:* Works included in permanent collections at Musee d'Art Contemporain, Montreal, Quebec, Canada; Canadian Museum of Photography, Ottawa, Ontario, Canada; Canada Council Art Bank, Ottawa, Ontario, Canada; International Center of Photography, New York, NY; Victoria and Albert Museum, London, England; Bibliotheque Nationale, Paris, France; Chiat/Day/Mojo Advertising, New York, NY, and Los Angeles, CA; Ivanhoe Corporation, Montreal, Quebec, Canada. Individual exhibitions include Galerie Optica, Montreal, Quebec, Canada, 1977; Eye Level Gallery, Halifax, Nova Scotia, Canada, 1979; Canadian Cultural Centre, Brussels, Belgium, 1981; International Center of Photography, New York, NY, 1985; and Saidye Bronfman Centre, Montreal, Quebec, Canada, 1991.

AWARDS, HONORS: Arts grant, Canada Council, 1976, 1979, 1980, 1981, 1991; bursary, Ministere de la Culture, 1990.

WRITINGS:

(Editor) *Camerart,* (exhibition catalogue), [Montreal, Quebec, Canada], 1974.
(Editor, with Cornell Capa) *Halsman '79* (exhibition catalogue), [New York, NY], 1979.
New York Inside Out, introduction by William Burroughs, [Toronto, Ontario, Canada], 1984.
Color Is Power, Thames & Hudson (New York, NY), 2002.

SIDELIGHTS: Photographer Robert Walker is known for his extraordinary use of color in his photographs. A *Contemporary Photographers* biographer noted, "Colour is fundamental and crucial to Walker's photography and everything else is subordinate to it: objects, situations, events, and even people." Walker has been influenced by the photography known as street photography, and by other photographers interested in the use of color, such as William Eggleston and Joel Meyerowitz.

BIOGRAPHICAL AND CRITICAL SOURCES:

BOOKS

Contemporary Photographers, 3rd edition, St. James Press (Detroit, MI), 1996.*

*   *   *

WALLACE, Diana 1964-

PERSONAL: Born 1964. *Education:* Lancaster University, B.A., M.A.; Loughborough University, Ph.D.

ADDRESSES: Agent—c/o Author Mail, St. Martin's Press, 175 Fifth Ave., New York, NY 10010. *E-mail*—dwallace@glam.ac.uk.

CAREER: University of Glamorgan, Pontypridd, Wales, lecturer in English literature.

WRITINGS:

Sisters and Rivals in British Women's Fiction, 1914-1939, St. Martin's Press (New York, NY), 2000.

SIDELIGHTS: Diana Wallace combined her interests in literature and women's studies in *Sisters and Rivals in British Women's Fiction, 1914-1939*. During World War I and its aftermath, a "man shortage" and the subsequent importance of women's friendships caught the attention of a number of female novelists. In her study, Wallace focuses on five of these: May Sinclair, Rebecca West, Vera Brittain, Winifred Holtby, and Rosamond Lehmann. "Wallace revisits some themes and concepts central to feminist literary criticism—a female tradition, canonicity, identity, lesbianism, romance—with a fresh eye and from a new angle," according to Tess Cosslett in *Tulsa Studies in Women's Literature*. She covers both the historical context, at a time when women were taking on "men's roles" and blurring gender lines, as well as the influence of Freudian psychology, which raised anxieties about women's friendships as potentially lesbian and "unnatural." Among other subjects, she considers sibling rivalry, including the relationships between fiction and actual sisters. Similarly, she explores the complex friendships and rivalries of her five subjects, and their relationship to the wider literary world, including the more "canonical" writers. "One of her most interesting ideas is that the very 'subject of female homosociality' actively marks 'a text as not canonical,'" noted Tess Cosslett. "The discussions throughout are well-organized, cogent, and nondogmatic," concluded *Choice* reviewer J. E. Steiner.

BIOGRAPHICAL AND CRITICAL SOURCES:

PERIODICALS

Choice, December, 2000, J. E. Steiner, review of *Sisters and Rivals in British Women's Fiction*, p. 711.

Tulsa Studies in Women's Literature, fall, 2001, Tess Cosslett, review of *Sisters and Rivals in British Women's Fiction*, pp. 297-298.*

*   *   *

WANG, Anyi 1954-

PERSONAL: Born 1954, in Nanjing, China; daughter of Ru Zhijuan (a writer). *Education:* Attended University of Iowa International Writing Program, 1983.

ADDRESSES: Agent—c/o Author Mail, New Directions, 80 Eighth Ave., New York, NY 10011.

CAREER: Novelist and author of screenplays and short fiction. Lecturer in China and the United States.

MEMBER: Chinese Association of Writers.

WRITINGS:

Yu, sha sha sha (stories; title means "The Rain Patters On"), Bai hua wen yi chubanshe (Tianjin, China), 1981.

Wang Anyi zhong duan pian xiao shuo ji, Zhongguo qing nian chubanshe (Beijing, China), 1983.

Hei hie bai bai, Shao nian er tong chubanshe (Shanghai, China), 1983.

Weisheng, Sichuan ren min chubanshe (Chengdu, China), 1983.

Yang qi li xiang di feng fan, Zhongguo qing nian chubanshe (Beijing, China), 1983.

Liushi, Sichuan ren min chubanshe (Chengdu, China), 1983, translation by Gladys Yang and others published as *Lapse of Time,* Panda Books (San Francisco, CA), 1988.

69 jie chuzhong sheng, 1984, Zhongguo qing nian chubanshe (Beijing, China), 1986.

Mu nü tong you Meilijian, San lian shu dian Xianggang fen dian (Xianggang, China), 1986.

Xiao Baozhuang, Wen yi chubanshe (Shanghai, China), 1986, translation by Martha Avery published as *Baotown,* Viking (London, England), 1988.

Huanghe gudao ren, Sichuan wen yi chubanshe (Chengdu, China), 1986.

Mu nü man you Meilijian, Shanghai wen yi chubanshe (Shanghai, China), 1986.

Huangshan zhi lian (novel; first in trilogy), 1986, Nan Yue chubanshe (Xianggang, China), 1988, translation by Eva Hung published as *Love on a Barren Mountain,* Renditions (Hong Kong), 1991.

Xiaocheng zhi lian (novel; second in trilogy), 1986, Lin bai chubanshe you xian gong si (Taipei, China), 1988, translation by Eva Hung published as *Love in a Small Town,* Renditions (Hong Kong), 1989.

Junxiugu zhi lian (novel; third in trilogy), [China], 1987, translation by Bonnie S. McDougall and Chen Maiping published as *Brocade Valley,* New Directions (New York, NY), 1992.

Liushui sanshi zhang, 1988, Shanghai wen yi chuban-she (Shanghai, China), 1990.

Pugong ying, Shanghai wen yi chubanshe (Shanghai, China), 1989.

Hai shang fanhua meng, Hua cheng chubanshe (Guangzhou, China), 1989.

Lü De di gushi, Jiangsu wen yi chubanshe (Nanjing, China), 1990.

Shushu di gushi, Ye quiang chubanshe (Taipei, China), 1990.

Shen sheng ji tan, Ren min wen xue chubanshe (Beijing, China), 1991.

Mi Ni (short stories), Jiangsu wen yi chubanshe (Nanjing Shi, China), 1991, published as *Mi Ni: zhang pain xiao shuo jiuan,* Zuo jia chubanshe (Beijing, China), 1996.

Zhu lu zhong jie, Mai tian chuban you xian gong si (Taipei, China), 1992.

(With Zhang Xinxin) *Nan nan nü nü,* Qin yuan chubanshe (Xianggang, China), 1992.

Zhi quing xioa shuo: cuo tuo sui yue yong tan diao, Sichuan wen yi chubanshe (Chengdu, China), 1992.

Jishi he xu gou: Chuang zaoshi jie fang fa zhi yi zhong, Ren min wen xue chubanshe (Beijing, China), 1993.

Wu tuo bang shi pian, Hua yi chubanshe (Beijing, China), 1993.

Bian zou: Nu xing yi duan wen xue, Chun feng wen yi chubanshe (Shenyang, China), 1993.

(With others) *Fu xi he mu xi di shin hua,* Zhejiang wen yi chubanshe (Hangzhou, China), 1994.

Xianggang de qing yu ai, Mai tian chuban you xian gong si (Taipei, China), 1994.

Mei gui zhi men, Shi dai wen yi chubanshe (Zhangchun, China), 1995.

Shangxin Taipingyang, Hua yi chubanshe (Beijing, China), 1995.

Changhen ge, Zuo jia chubanshe (Beijing, China), 1996.

Zi wu, Jin ri Zhongguo chubanshe (Beijing, China), 1995.

Wang Anyi, Ren min wen xue chubanshe (Beijing, China), 1995.

Cheng huo che lü xing, Zhongguo Hua qiao chubanshe (Beijing, China), 1995.

Piao po de yu yan: san wen juan, Zuo jia chubanshe (Beijing, China), 1996.

Hai shang fan hua meng: zhong pian xiao shuo juan (short stories), Zuo jia chubanshe (Beijing, China), 1996.

Xiao cheng zhi lian: zhong pian xiao shuo juan (short stories), Zuo jia chubanshe (Beijing, China), 1996.

Xianggang de qing yu ai: zhong pian xiao shuo juan (short stories), Zuo jia chubanshe (Beijing, China), 1996.

(With Chen Kaige) *Feng yue* (screenplay; produced as *Temptress Moon,* Miramax, 1996), Yuan liu chubanshi ye gu fen you xian gong si (Taipei, China), 1996.

Jishi yu xu gou: Shanghai de gu shi (title means "Reality and Fiction: A Shanghai Story"), Mai tian chuban you xian gong si (Taipei, China), 1996.

Qing jie = Quin jie, Dunhuang wen yi chubanshe (Lanzhou, China), 1996.

Ren shi di chen fu, Wen hui chubanshe (Shanghai, China), 1996.

Zi mie men: Wang Anyi zhong duan pian xiao shuo zi xuan ji (short stories), Hua xia chubanshe (Beijing, China), 1996.

Chenghen ge: chang pian xiao shuo juan (short stories; title means "Song of Everlasting Sorrow"), Zuo jia chubanshe (Beijing, China), 1996.

Wang Anyi zi xuan ji, Zuo jia chubanshe (Beijing, China), 1996.

Chong jian xiang ya ta, Shanghai yuan dong chubanshe (Shanghai, China), 1997.

Wang Anyi xuan jin ren san wen, Shanghai wen yi chubanshe (Shanghai, China), 1997.

Xin ling shi jie: Wang Anyi xiao shui jiang gao, Fu dan da xue chubanshe (Shanghai, China), 1997.

Yi ge gu shi di san zhong jiang fa, Ming tian chubanshe (Jinan, China), 1997.

Du yu, Hunan wen yi chubanshe (Changsha, China), 1998.

Chu nü dan, Mai tian chuban you xian gong si (Taipei, China), 1998.

You shang de nian dai, Mai tian chuban you xian gong si (Taipei, China), 1998.

Jie jin shi ji chu: Wang Anyi san wen xin zuo, Zhejiang wen yi chubanshe (Hangzhou, China), 1998.

Fu Ping, Hunan wen yi chubanshe (Changsha, China), 1998.

Wo ai Bi'er, Jin ri Zhongguo chubanshe (Beijing, China), 1998.

Yin ju di shi dai, Mai tian chuban you xian gong si (Taipei, China), 1999.

Wang Anyi xiao shuo xuan (short stories; in Chinese and English), Zhongguo wen xue chubanshe (Beijing, China), 1999.

Nü ren er shi, Hunan wen yi chubanshe (Changsha, China), 2000.

Qing zhi shang, Zhongguo wen lian chubanshe (Beijing, China), 2000.

Mei tou, Nan hai chuban gong si (Haikou, China), 2000.

Gang shang de shi ji, Yunnan ren min chubanshe (Kunming, China), 2000.

Nan ren he nü ren nü ren he cheng shi, Yunnan ren min chubanshe (Kunming, China), 2000.

Ti du, Nan hai chuban gong si (Haikou, China), 2000.

Mini, Nan hai chuban gong si (Haikou, China), 2000.

Ge xing Riben lai, Bei yue wen yi chubanshe (Taiwan, China), 2000.

San lian = Shan lian, Zhejiang wen yi chubanshe (Hangzhou, China), 2001.

Wen gong tuan: Wang Anyi xiao shuo (short stories), Wen hua yi shu chubanshe (Beijing, China), 2001.

Wo du wo kan, Shanghai ren min chubanshe (Shanghai, China), 2001.

Contributor to *Childhood* magazine.

SIDELIGHTS: Chinese novelist and short-story writer Wang Anyi is notable as a voice for women in the post-Mao era. She has based some of her fiction on her life as a young woman growing up before and during the Cultural Revolution. Wang's mother, Ru Zhijuan, was a noted writer herself, and Wang grew up in a politically charged household. Her father was denounced for his Rightist views, and the controversy interrupted Wang's education. As a teenager she was a member of the "Urban Youth," a back-to-basics movement that sent urbanized young adults to live with and learn from the peasant class. After living in a commune in Anhui, China, Wang at age sixteen got a new assignment: joining a state-sponsored traveling performing-arts troupe as a cellist. By 1976, at age nineteen, Wang began publishing her stories; following the Cultural Revolution and the fall of the Gang of Four she returned to Shanghai to work on the magazine *Childhood.*

Wang's earliest collection of stories, 1981's *Yu, sha sha sha,* focuses on personal experience as seen through the eyes of a writer still in her twenties. A prolific writer, she continued to publish short stories, as well as novellas and novels, throughout the 1980s, and has rarely flagged in the production of books since beginning her career.

A handful of Wang's works have been brought to English-reading audiences. *Baotown* is a short novel about life in a small village much like Anhui, where the author spent her adolescent years. The chapters focus on the different characters who inhabit this town. One of the protagonists is Little Jade, a smart and beautiful girl who is set up to marry what Carolyn See, in a *Los Angeles Times Book Review* article, called "the town lummox. How she gets out of this is an ongoing shaggy-dog tale." In another chapter, a single woman adopts an orphan boy; all is well until the boy grows up and the two engage in a physical relationship that enrages the town. "In a contest among affection, lust and/or family loyalty," noted See, "a series of imaginative arrangements must be made." See called Baotown a "marvelously interesting book," a view shared by Valerie Miner of *Nation.* While expressing some disappointment that "most of [*Baotown*'s] major characters are male," Miner went on to praise the work as "a very satisfying novel—deft, original, tragic, funny."

In one story from her collection *Lapse of Time,* Wang explores "what has become a familiar Chinese theme," according to *New York Review of Books* contributor Jonathan Mirsky: the effect of the Cultural Revolution on everyday people. In this case, Lao Kang is an office worker exiled from the city to the country, "probably because he comes from the upper class," wrote Mirsky, after which "he is pardoned and returns, a suffering, silent wreck." Wang, the reviewer continued, "likes optimistic endings; she finishes with 'the profound and insightful' words of Lao Kang's cheerful old housekeeper that, when you come down to it, life is just breathing in and out—so Lao Kang is not so badly off after all." Scarlet Cheng, writing in *Belles Lettres,* was reminded of Wang's stint as a traveling performer while reading the story "The Stage, a Miniature World." In this tale, a musical troupe designed to enlighten the masses "finds itself stooping to featuring an electric guitarist because audiences crave the new," as Cheng wrote. In fact, the reviewer added, "Change is much of what these stories are about: in the political and social environment, in family fortunes, in the self."

Wang caused something of a scandal in 1980s China when she published a trilogy of novels all containing the word *lien*—"love"; i.e. sex—in the title. "It was regarded at the time either as a daring 'breakthrough' by supporters or an immoral piece of pornography by detractors," explained *Pacific Affairs* critic Michael S. Duke. The three books were published in English as *Love on a Barren Mountain, Love in a Small Town,* and *Brocade Valley. Love on a Barren Mountain* puts political ideals aside, said Fatima Wu, to explore "extramarital relationships in a culturally repressed society." Wu, writing in *World Literature Today,* explained that the novel focuses on two lovers, separated by fate, who are brought together in midlife when both have married and established families. Their union, which ends tragically, said Wu, appeared predestined by the author: "the girl keeps on crying, while the music of the *erhu* seems to be weeping. Wang's gloomy world view, symbolized by the barren mountain, seems to announce that nothing could have prevented or stopped the [lovers'] double suicide."

Love in a Small Town tells of an affair carried on over several years by two members of a rural ballet troupe. The two meet when the boy is sixteen and the girl twelve; Wang has said that the story is based on events she witnessed during her days as a state-sponsored performer. Duke dismissed the tale as "excruciatingly dull," while Russell McLeod of *World Literature Today* had a different reaction. "After years of often dreary 'social realism' and 'revolutionary romanticism,'" he said, "it is refreshing to read a piece of fiction in which the author's only interest is in a universal human impulse."

The third novel in the trilogy, *Brocade Valley* tells of a woman whose daily drudgery of work and housekeeping is broken by a brief extramarital fling. Like *Love in a Small Town, Brocade Valley* was met with mixed critical reaction. The novel "promises drama that it never delivers," according to a *Publishers Weekly* reviewer, who added that the author "makes it difficult [for readers] to care about her unnamed characters." But in a *World Literature Today* piece, Frances La Fleur thought that the author kept a deliberate distance from her characters: She "creates a fairy-tale-like atmosphere in which the heroine escapes from her humdrum existence." LaFleur summed up *Brocade Valley* as "an absorbing story, told with the delicacy and restraint that characterize Wang Anyi's unique style."

In the 1990s, Wang turned to her family's history as a source for her writing, publishing works that combine mythology and history with personal memoirs and fantasies. The author has also published works of journalism, travel writings, and literary criticism. Much in demand as a speaker in China and the United States, she had become something of a symbol of the future of postrevolutionary Chinese literature by 2000. Eva Hung, writing in *Encyclopedia of World Literature in the Twentieth Century,* stated that "While her existing oeuvre will ensure her a prominent place in the history of Chinese literature, there is reason to believe that the imaginative scope of [Wang's] work will continue to grow."

"I firmly believe that an individual, and a people, must possess the insight and courage to engage in self-examination," Wang once said in a speech for the International Conference on Contemporary Chinese Literature that was quoted on the *Kirjasto* Web site. "This spirit of self-examination is what guarantees that individuals will become real human beings, and that a people will develop into a strong and worthy nation."

BIOGRAPHICAL AND CRITICAL SOURCES:

BOOKS

Encyclopedia of World Literature in the Twentieth Century, St. James Press (Detroit, MI), 1999.

PERIODICALS

Belles Lettres, winter, 1989, Scarlet Cheng, "Foreign All Your Life," p. 9.

Booklist, October 15, 1989, review of *Baotown,* p. 425; January 1, 1991, review of *Baotown,* p. 915; November 1, 1992, review of *Brocade Valley,* p. 488; March 1, 1999, review of *You shang de nian dai,* p. 1162.

Choice, April, 1994, Jeffrey Kinkley, "The New Chinese Literature: The Mainland and Beyond," pp. 1249-1265.

Kirkus Reviews, August 1, 1988, review of *Lapse of Time,* p. 1097; October 1, 1992, review of *Brocade Valley,* p. 1213.

Library Journal, September 15, 1989, review of *Baotown,* p. 138.

Los Angeles Times Book Review, January 14, 1990, Carolyn See, "Cultural Revolution," p. 1.

Nation, March 19, 1990, Valerie Miner, review of *Baotown,* p. 389.

New York Review of Books, October 26, 1989, Jonathan Mirsky, "Stories from the Ice Age," p. 27.

Pacific Affairs, fall, 1989, Michael Duke, review of *Love in a Small Town,* pp. 445-446.

Publishers Weekly, August 26, 1988, review of *Lapse of Time,* p. 79; August 18, 1989, review of *Baotown,* p. 49; September 28, 1992, review of *Brocade Valley,* p. 64.

World Literature Today, summer, 1989, Michael Duke, review of *Lapse of Time,* p. 535; winter, 1990, Russell McLeod, review of *Love in a Small Town,* pp. 192-193; summer, 1991, Fatima Wu, review of *Love on a Barren Mountain,* p. 547; autumn, 1993, Frances LaFleur, review of *Brocade Valley,* p. 891.

OTHER

Kirjasto Web site, http://www.kirjasto.sci.fi/ (April 22, 2002), "Wang Anyi."*

*   *   *

WATSON, Jean 1933-

PERSONAL: Born 1933, in Whangarei, New Zealand; daughter of William Albert and Jane (Struthers) Watson; married Barry Crump (a writer).

ADDRESSES: Home—41 Maida Vale Rd., Roseneath, Wellington, New Zealand. *E-mail*—jean@actrix.gen.nz.

CAREER: Novelist.

WRITINGS:

Stand in the Rain, Pegasus (Christchurch, New Zealand), 1965, reprinted, Allen & Unwin/Port Nicholson Press (Wellington, New Zealand), 1986.

The Balloon Watchers, Dunmore Press (Palmerston North, New Zealand), 1975.

The World Is an Orange and the Sun, Dunmore Press (Palmerston North, New Zealand), 1978.

Flowers from Happyever, Voice Press (Wellington, New Zealand), 1980.

Address to a King, Allen & Unwin/Port Nicholson Press (Wellington, New Zealand), 1986.

Karunai Illam: The Story of an Orphanage, Daphne Brasell Associates Press (Wellington, New Zealand), 2001.

Three Sea Stories, Daphne Brasell Associates Press (Wellington, New Zealand), 1994.

SIDELIGHTS: New Zealand novelist and short story writer Jean Watson is best known for her novel *Stand in the Rain,* often referred to as a woman's 'on-the-road' novel. Drawing on Watson's marriage to writer Barry Crump, *Stand in the Rain* relates the story of Sarah, a budding writer, and her husband Abungus, a bushman, as they travel seeking work.

In more recent years Watson has become known for her non-fiction book, *Karunai Illam: The Story of an Orphange.* The story recounts the tale of how Watson and an Indian friend set up a home for the education of children from destitute families in South India. The orphanage continues to flourish and grow, so Watson devotes less time to writing but still works persistently on her craft. *Three Sea Stories,* is sort of a companion to *Karunai Illam* as it is a fictional account of the founding of the children's home.

Watson told *CA:* "My first fiction *Stand in the Rain* and my latest nonfiction *Karunai Illam* have much in common; they are both love stories, the first 'eros' and the last, 'agape.'"

*   *   *

WATSON, Stephen 1953-

PERSONAL: Born 1953, in Cape Town, South Africa. *Education:* Ph.D.

ADDRESSES: Home—Cape Town, South Africa. *Agent*—c/o Author Mail, New Africa Books, 99 Garfield Road, Claremont 7700; or P.O. Box 23408, Claremont 7735, South Africa; fax: (021) 674 3358. *E-mail*—swatson@humanities.uct.ac.za.

CAREER: Poet, writer, critic, and teacher. University of Cape Town, Department of English, South Africa, professor of English.

WRITINGS:

Poems 1977-1982, Bateleur Press (Johannesburg, South Africa, 1982.

In This City: Poems, David Philip (Cape Town, South Africa), 1986.

Sydney Clouts and the Limits of Romanticism, Centre for African Studies, University of Cape Town (Cape Town, South Africa), 1986.

Cape Town Days, and Other Poems, Cecil Skotnes & Clarke's Bookshop (Cape Town, South Africa), 1989.

Selected Essays, 1980-1990, Carrefour Press (Cape Town, South Africa), 1990.

Return of the Moon: Versions from the Xam, Carrefour Press (Cape Town, South Africa), 1991, revised edition, published as *Song of the Broken String: After the /Xam Bushmen: Poems from a Lost Oral Tradition,* Sheep Meadow Press (Riverdale-on-Hudson, NY), 1996.

(Editor) Guy Butler, *Essays and Lectures, 1949-1991,* David Philip (Cape Town, South Africa), 1994.

(Editor) Patrick Cullinan, *Selected Poems, 1961-1994,* illustrations by Judith Mason, Snailpress (Plunstead, South Africa), 1994.

Presence of the Earth: New Poems, D. Philip (Cape Town, South Africa), 1995.

(Editor, with Graham Huggan) *Critical Perspectives on J. M. Coetzee,* St. Martin's Press (New York, NY), 1996.

A Writer's Diary, Queillerie Publishers (Cape Town, South Africa), 1997.

The Other City: Selected Poems, 1977-1999, D. Philip (Cape Town, South Africa), 2000.

Contributor to *Sound from the Thinking Strings: A Visual, Literary, Archeological, and Historical Interpretation of the Finals Years of Xam Life,* edited and etchings by Pippa Skotnes, translated by W. H. I. Bleek and Lucy Lloyd, Axeage Private Press (Cape Town, South Africa), 1991. *Song of the Broken String: After the Xam Bushmen,* the revised version of *Return of the Moon: Versions from the Xam,* has been published in French.

SIDELIGHTS: A teacher in the English Department at the University of Cape Town, Stephen Watson has written several volumes of poetry, as well as numerous critical essays and a book about his experiences as a writer. In the collection *Selected Essays: 1980-1990,* Watson focuses primarily on South African poetry. Writing in *World Literature Today,* reviewer Reed Way Dasenbrock said he was "somewhat confused" about Watson's feelings about contemporary South African English poetry. He also called Watson an "intelligent and careful reader of poetry" and noted that the collection of essays "provide a helpful guide to the contemporary South African poetic situation." Watson is also the author of *Writer's Diary,* in which he explores his own "pre-occupations" as a writer.

Watson, however, is primarily noted for his poetry and has been called Cape Town's definitive poet. Watson's 2000 collection of poems titled *The Other City* contains both new poems and previously published poems from five earlier volumes of poetry, some of which Watson revised. Writing in the *Time Literary Supplement,* Peter Reading called the collection a "soundly-produced edition" and noted, "The five sections of this book all chronicle, in one way or another, the demise of individuals, eras, regions and notions."

BIOGRAPHICAL AND CRITICAL SOURCES:

PERIODICALS

English in Africa, May, 1998, Dirk Klopper, "On the Edge of Darkness: Stephen Watson and the Return of the Romantic Imagination," pp. 87-98.

Research in African Literatures, spring, 1992, Patrick Cullinan, review of *Return of the Moon: Versions from the Xam,* pp. 393-394; winter, 1996, Dominic Head, review of *Critical Perspective on J. M. Coetzee,* pp. 205-207.

Times Literary Supplement, July 27, 2001, Peter Reading, review of *The Other City,* p. 23.

World Literature Today, summer, 1991, Reed Way Basenbrock, review of *Selected Essays 1980-1990,* p. 537.

OTHER

Mondaypaper Web site, http://www.uct.ac.za/general/monpaper/ (July 31-August 7, 2000), "Watson's Poems on Cape Town Draw Acclaim."*

*   *   *

WAYNER, Peter 1964-

PERSONAL: Born 1964.

ADDRESSES: *Agent*—c/o Author Mail, HarperBusiness, 10 East 53rd St., 7th Floor, New York, NY 10022. *E-mail*—p3@wayner.org.

CAREER: New York Times, New York, NY, technology reporter. Teacher of computer science at Cornell University and Georgetown University.

WRITINGS:

Agents Unleashed: A Public Domain Look at Agent Technology, AP Professional (Boston, MA), 1995.
Digital Cash: Commerce on the Net, AP Professional (Boston, MA), 1996.
Disappearing Cryptography: Being and Nothingness on the Net, AP Professional (Boston, MA), 1996.
Digital Copyright Protection, AP Professional (Boston, MA), 1997.
Java and JavaScript Programming, AP Professional (Boston, MA), 1997.
(With others) *The Management of Risks Created by Internet-Initiated Value Transfers,* Internet Council (Herndon, VA), 1997.
Java Beans for Real Programmers, AP Professional (San Diego, CA), 1998.
Compression Algorithms for Real Programmers, AP Professional (San Diego, CA), 1999.
Free for All: How LINUX and the Free Software Movement Undercut the High-Tech Titans, HarperBusiness (New York, NY), 2000.

Also contributor to periodicals, including *Computerworld.*

SIDELIGHTS: Peter Wayner is a technology writer for the *New York Times.* He is also the author of books on computers and the Internet. In *Agents Unleashed: A Public Domain Look at Agent Technology,* Wayner discusses software agents. These are Internet programs that electronically order goods and services. Wayner examines the ins and outs of security, digital cash transactions, and programming tips for these agents. The book comes with a software agent disk. *Digital Cash: Commerce on the Net* is a complete guide to financial transactions on the Internet, including digital checks, digital coupons, divisible cash, and anonymous digital cash. The book also examines the currently available commercial digital cash systems. In *PC* Sebastian Rupley called the book a "treasure trove" for those wanting to use First Virtual technology for on-line selling.

Digital Copyright Protection considers technical methods of protecting data from theft by data pirates, including cryptography, compression, tamper-resistant

features, and commercial products. It also includes discussions of the legal aspects of copyright versus artistic freedom, intellectual property law, and patenting ideas. In the *Australian Library Journal* Richard Pang wrote, "Comprehensive in subject scope, well-structured and in parts extremely detailed, this work avoids becoming a totally abstruse technical exegesis by commencing each chapter with a humorous anecdote."

In *Disappearing Cryptography: Being and Nothingness on the Net,* Wayner examines the use of encryption in computer files, including its pros and cons. On the one hand, encrypted data often attracts attention, letting observers know there is a secret hidden within. Encryption does not protect data from being erased, diverted, or corrupted. On the other hand, the possibilities for hiding encrypted files are endless: data can be disguised as a baseball announcer's game talk, or hidden in a photo of a pet. Each chapter begins with an amusing anecdote or game relevant to its topic, then discusses the technology involved in easy-to-understand terms. This is followed by a more technical and mathematical analysis. *Compression Algorithms for Real Programmers* explains how readers can compress information and create the smallest possible files, so that they can conserve space, time, and money when sending files over the Internet.

In *Free for All: How LINUX and the Free Software Movement Undercut the High-Tech Titans,* Wayner examines the history of the free software movement, and how it continues to threaten the profits of big companies such as Microsoft. The free software movement was begun in 1984 by programmer Richard Stallman, who believed that software should be freely distributed. Linus Torvalds, a University of Helsinki student and follower of Stallman, invented LINUX, an operating system that is reliable, flexible, and free, is now used in over fifty percent of the Web servers on the Internet, and which, Wayner predicts, will eventually overtake Microsoft. A *Publishers Weekly* reviewer called *Free for All* an "intriguing history of the free software movement," while in the *New Yorker* Francine du Plessix Gray deemed *Free for All* an "entertaining, unabashedly partisan chronicle."

BIOGRAPHICAL AND CRITICAL SOURCES:

PERIODICALS

Australian Library Journal, November, 1997, Richard Pang, review of *Digital Copyright Protection,* p. 438.

Booklist, May 1, 2000, David Rouse, review of *Free for All: How LINUX and the Free Software Movement Undercut the High-Tech Titans,* p. 1628.

Inc., June, 2000, review of *Free for All,* p. 145.

Library Journal, June 15, 2000, review of *Free for All,* p. 104.

New Scientist, September 14, 1996, Wendy Grossman, "Collected Works," p. 46.

New Yorker, August 7, 2000, Francine du Plessix Gray, review of *Free for All,* p. 85.

PC, May 28, 1996, Sebastian Rupley, "All the Web's a Wallet—or Soon Will Be," p. 60.

Personal Computer World, September, 1996, Eleanor Turton-Hill, review of *Agents Unleashed,* p. 217; November, 1998, Tim Anderson, review of *Java Beans for Real Programmers,* p. 320.

Publishers Weekly, June 26, 2000, review of *Free for All,* p. 65.

Wall Street Journal, July 26, 2000, Lee Gomes, review of *Free for All,* p. A24.

Washington Post Book World, August 27, 2000, review of *Free for All,* p. 11.

OTHER

Peter Wayner Web site, http://www.wayner.org/ (February 10, 2003).*

*　　*　　*

WEAVER, John D(owning) 1912-2002

OBITUARY NOTICE—See index for *CA* sketch: Born February 4, 1912, in Washington, DC; died December 4, 2002, in Las Vegas, NV. Journalist and author. Weaver was a respected author of historical books, especially on the subject of Los Angeles and the 1906 Black Dreyfus Affair. A graduate of William and Mary College where he earned an A.B. in 1932, he went on to receive his master's degree from George Washington University in 1933. Before World War II he worked for the National Recovery Administration and was a reporter and writer for the *Kansas City Star.* After serving in the Signal Corps during the war, Weaver returned home to work as a freelance writer, authoring such books as *Another Such Victory* (1948) and the young adult book *Tad Lincoln: Mischief-Maker in the White House* (1963). He became interested in the case involving black soldiers who were accused of killing one white man and wounding another near Fort Brown after learning about it from his father, who had been U.S. House of Representative official reporter at the time of the incident. The "Black Dreyfus" case had been ushered quickly through the courts, and all 167 men in the unit had been accused of covering it up, even though there was evidence that rifle shells had been planted at the scene in order to frame them. President Roosevelt ordered the soldiers dishonorably discharged; this decision was upheld by the U.S. Senate. Through his diligent research, Weaver showed that the men were innocent, and the U.S. Army cleared their records of all charges in 1972; he also followed up the story with his 1997 book, *The Senator and the Sharecropper's Son: Exoneration of the Brownsville Soldiers.* In addition to this respected work of history, Weaver was appreciated for his historical writings on the Los Angeles area, including *Los Angeles: The Enormous Village* (1980).

OBITUARIES AND OTHER SOURCES:

BOOKS

Ward, Martha E., and others, editors, *Authors of Books for Young People,* third edition, Scarecrow Press (Metuchen, NJ), 1990.

PERIODICALS

Los Angeles Times, December 7, 2002, p. B22.
New York Times, December 23, 2002, p. A25.
Washington Post, December 9, 2002, p. B7.

*　　*　　*

WEBB, Todd 1905-2000

PERSONAL: Born Charles Clayton Webb, September 15, 1905, in Detroit, MI; died, April 15, 2000, in Lewiston, ME; married Lucille Minqueau, 1949. *Education:* Attended University of Toronto, 1924-25; studied photography at Detroit Camera Club under Ansel Adams, 1940.

CAREER: Stockbroker, 1920s; freelance photographer, 1946-2000; Standard Oil Company, New York, NY, photographer 1947-49; United Nations, New York,

NY, photographer, 1955-69. *Exhibitions:* Works included in permanent collections at the Center for Creative Photography, University of Arizona, Tucson, AZ; International Center of Photography, New York, NY; Westbrook College, Portland, ME; Museum of Modern Art, New York, NY; New York Public Library, New York, NY; Worcester Museum of Art, Worcester, MA; Art Institute of Chicago, Chicago, IL; Amon Carter Museum, Fort Worth, TX; New Mexico Museum, Santa Fe, NM; and Bibliotheque Nationale, Paris, France. Individual exhibitions include Museum of the City of New York, 1946; International Museum of Photography, George Eastman House, Rochester, NY, 1954; Maison de la Tour, St. Restitut, France, 1968; and Nelson-Atkins Museum, Kansas City, MO, 1986. *Military service:* U.S. Navy, 1942-45, South Pacific, photographers mate first class.

AWARDS, HONORS: Guggenheim Fellowship in Photography, 1955, 1956; National Endowment for the Arts photography fellowship, 1979.

WRITINGS:

Gold Strikes and Ghost Towns, Doubleday (New York, NY), 1961.
The Gold Rush Trail and the Road to Oregon, Doubleday (New York, NY), 1961.
Todd Webb: Photographs, Amon Carter Museum (Fort Worth, TX), 1965, 1979.
Texas Homes of the Nineteenth Century, University of Texas (Austin, TX), 1966.
Texas Public Buildings of the Nineteenth Century, University of Texas (Austin, TX), 1974.
Georgia O'Keeffe: The Artist and Her Landscape, Twelvetrees Press (Pasadena, CA), 1984.
Photographs of New York and Paris 1946-1960, Hallmark Cards (Kansas City, MO), 1985.
Looking Back: Memoirs and Photographs, foreword by Michael Rowell, University of New Mexico Press (Albuquerque, NM), 1991.

SIDELIGHTS: Before becoming a photographer Todd Webb was a stockbroker. When he lost his earnings due to the stock market crash, he set off for California in 1929, and later to Panama, in search of gold. In Panama he became interested in photography. His interest continued when he returned to the United States, and in 1938 he joined the Detroit Camera Club and studied photography under Ansel Adams. Webb's first exhibition was in 1946 at the Museum of the City of New York, which brought him much popularity.

Webb took photographs all over the world, but he is mostly known for his photographs of New York City, Paris, and the American Southwest. He began keeping a journal in 1946, the same year of his first exhibit, and in his book *Looking Back: Memoirs and Photographs* he shares some of his journal entries and photographs. Included are daily activities, problems he encountered as a photographer, and personal stories about close friends such as Georgia O'Keeffe, Harry Callahan, and Nancy Newall. A *PSA Journal* contributor commented, "Through a lifetime dedicated to his medium, Todd Webb has achieved a prominent place in the history of American photography with his unique vision and universal appeal."

BIOGRAPHICAL AND CRITICAL SOURCES:

BOOKS

Contemporary Photographers, 3rd edition, St. James Press (Detroit, MI), 1996.

PERIODICALS

Library Journal, June 1, 1997, Rosemary Arneson, review of *Honest Vision: A Portrait of Todd Webb,* p. 171.
PSA Journal, February, 1992, review of *Looking Back: Memoirs and Photographs,* p. 7.

OTHER

Todd Webb Photographs Web site, http://www.toddwebbphotographs.com/ (May 2, 2002), "About Todd Webb."*

OBITUARIES:

PERIODICALS

Art in America, June, 2000, p. 142.

WEISBERGER, Lauren 1977-

PERSONAL: Born 1977. *Education:* Cornell University, B.A., 1999.

ADDRESSES: Home—New York, NY. *Agent*—Deborah Schneider, Gelfman & Schneider Literary Agents, 250 West 57th St., Suite 2515, New York, NY 10107.

CAREER: Vogue magazine, New York, NY, personal assistant, c. 2001; *Departures* magazine, New York, NY, staff writer, c. 2003.

WRITINGS:

The Devil Wears Prada, Doubleday (New York, NY), 2003.

ADAPTATIONS: The Devil Wears Prada was optioned for film by Fox Searchlight Pictures.

SIDELIGHTS: In *The Devil Wears Prada,* Lauren Weisberger's first novel, recent ivy league graduate Andrea Sachs lands the job of a lifetime as the personal assistant to Miranda Priestly, the tough-as-nails Prada-wearing editor-in-chief of *Runway* magazine, the country's leading fashion publication. As Andrea simmers through the menial and demeaning tasks that comprise her days, she dreams of a more fulfilling career as a staff writer for the *New Yorker* and hopes that her current job will be the stepping stone to the next one. Even though she is constantly reminded that "millions of girls would kill for her job," she finds it hard to be grateful for the opportunity to be humiliated in public by her boss, even if she gets free designer shoes in the process. At the bottom of the publishing pecking order, Andrea's hours are long, recognition is nonexistent, and the boss keeps her on call twenty-four hours a day. Her exciting life in New York City leaves her no time for her friends and family and makes her suspect that her college education was a waste of time. The biggest names in the fashion world—Hilfiger, de la Renta, Versace, et al—serve as the backdrop.

When *The Devil Wears Prada* was published in the spring of 2003, it became a bestseller as much for *what* it was about as for *who* it was about. Prior to

writing the book, Weisberger worked as the personal assistant for Anna Wintour, the editor-in-chief of American *Vogue,* and the book was widely rumored to be a dishy exposé about working for the notoriously difficult fashion icon. Interest in the book even before it was finished led to a bidding war and a high-profile deal that also gained Weisberger a lucrative deal for the film rights.

Like her heroine, Weisberger graduated from an ivy league school in 1999 and quickly landed her job at *Vogue,* where she was launched head first into the fashion world with little preparation or experience. She quit after a year, and when her next job left her enough time to enroll in a writing seminar, she compiled a collection of vignettes based on her work experiences that her instructor urged her to submit to an agent. The agent, Deborah Schneider, generated lots of advance buzz about the book, and by the time it was published expectations were high. As Kate Betts noted in the *New York Times,* "does it even matter what's actually on the page when everybody is reading between the lines?"

The fashion-unconscious Andrea has only taken the *Runway* job because she hopes that Miranda will recommend her to the *New Yorker.* She arrives at the office wearing Nine West shoes, and soon enough a kind soul gives her a makeover, raiding the office's vaunted "closet" in the process, which wields her a pair of thousand-dollar Gucci pants that no one else can wear because they are a hefty size six. Add a pair of Jimmy Choo stilettos, and Andrea's fashion consciousness starts to revive. But Miranda makes her life too miserable for her to enjoy playing dress-up. The boss is an overbearing size zero who eats bacon, steak, and ice cream and throws her clothes away after she wears them twice. She makes unreasonable demands: Andrea must not eat in her presence; Andrea must pack her travel clothes in velvet; Andrea must locate copies of the yet-to-be-published Harry Potter book to ship to Miranda's children in Paris.

The pressure prompts Andrea to indulge in revenge fantasies. "You don't want her to die," she thinks, "because if she does, you lose all hope of killing her yourself. And that would be a shame." Andrea blows off steam over late-night drinks with her friends, but she regretfully finds herself losing touch with her childhood friend, whose drinking habit is verging out of control. Also neglected is Andrea's boyfriend, Alex, a fourth-grade teacher of disadvantaged kids, who is perennially disappointed over having to take a back seat to his girlfriend's career. Apart from the magazine, her career plan involves attracting the attention of Christian Collinsworth, a literary *wunderkind* whose first book was hailed "as one of the most significant literary achievements of the 20th century." With encouraging words from him under her belt, Andrea musters the nerve to confront Miranda at a Paris fashion show that becomes a showdown.

Critics reacted to the story's tell-all nature with varying shades of amusement, with many of them comparing the book to other recent muckraking chick-lit novels, such as *The Nanny Diaries.* Stacy Alesi of *Library Journal* called *The Devil Wears Prada* a "fast-paced black comedy [that] has enough dirt to please any fashionista." A reviewer for *Publishers Weekly* said the book has "plenty of dead-on assessments of fashion's frivolity and realistic, funny portrayals of life as a peon," and a *Kirkus Reviews* contributor deemed it an "on-the-money kiss-and-tell debut."

Other critics took issue with the character of Andrea, pointing out that her reason for wanting to write for the *New Yorker*—they have witty cartoons—is a bit naïve. Some found Andrea's small-fish-in-a-big-pond attitude toward New York patronizing; she stereotypes East Indians for their love of curry and expresses surprise over surviving her first subway ride. The "book's sour, sarcastic, self-involved heroine is too much of a pill to be endearing," wrote Janet Maslin in the *New York Times.* Furthermore, Maslin stated, "the book's way of dropping names, labels and price tags while feigning disregard for these things is another of its unattractive qualities." Betts also noticed some of Andrea's hypocritical tendencies and said that "Andrea's aura of self-importance is almost enough to make you sympathize with the Prada-wearing devil herself." A number of critics failed to see the devil in Miranda at all. According to Jenny McCartney of the London *Sunday Telegraph,* "to seize power in the fashion world, players need to transform themselves into an instantly-recognisable brand," which is exactly what Wintour (and Miranda) do.

In interviews, Weisberger distanced the character of Miranda from her former boss and discouraged comparisons between *Runway* and *Vogue.* Miranda "is certainly not modeled after Anna," she told David D. Kirkpatrick of the *New York Times.* On the contrary,

she continued, "there was something amazing about getting to work for and see this incredibly bright, powerful woman." Furthermore, Weisberger believes the scope of the novel is broader than critics have deemed it. "I think it goes beyond the fashion industry," she told Lynn Andriani of *Publishers Weekly.* "It's a year in the life of this girl: her relationships, and what it's like to be right out of college and living in New York. . . . You're in so far over your head, you have no idea of up from down." Furthermore, she stated that the narrative "is composed of stories from my friends. . . . And a lot of it is my slightly overactive imagination." But not everyone was convinced. "*The Devil Wears Prada* is a roman a clef of the unsubtlest sort," wrote Diane Roberts of the *Atlanta Journal-Constitution,* "maybe more a roman a vengeance." Summarizing the wide-ranging opinions of many critics, Lisa Lockwood of *Women's Wear Daily* wrote that "the book is far from a literary masterpiece, but its in-depth knowledge of the inner workings and absurdities of the fashion magazine world should keep both outsiders and insiders chuckling through the breathless sentences."

BIOGRAPHICAL AND CRITICAL SOURCES:

BOOKS

Weisberger, Lauren, *The Devil Wears Prada,* Doubleday (New York, NY), 2003.

PERIODICALS

Atlanta Journal-Constitution, April 25, 2003, Diane Roberts, "Devil Skewers Fashion Maven," p. E1.
Booklist, April 1, 2003, Kathleen Hughes, review of *The Devil Wears Prada,* p. 1355.
Kirkus Reviews, February 15, 2003, review of *The Devil Wears Prada,* p. 268.
Library Journal, April 1, 2003, Stacy Alesi, review of *The Devil Wears Prada,* p. 132.
Newsweek, April 28, 2003, Cathleen McGuigan, "Prada, Yada, Yada: A Wintour's Tale," p. 60.
New York Observer, March 31, 2003, Alexandra Jacobs, "The Underling's Revenge, by Conde Nast's Whistleblower," p. 11.
New York Times, May 27, 2002, David D. Kirkpatrick, "An Insider's View of Fashion Magazines," p. C6; April 14, 2003, Janet Maslin, "Elegant Magazine, Avalanche of Dirt," p. E1.

New York Times Book Review, April 13, 2003, Kate Betts, "Anna Dearest," p. 30.

Publishers Weekly, March 17, 2003, Lynn Andriani, "The Devil Wears Prada, and the Writer Wears . . . Dior?," p. 53; March 17, 2003, review of *The Devil Wears Prada,* p. 53.

Sunday Telegraph (London, England), March 9, 2003, Jenny McCartney, "In the Fashion Business, It's Cool to Be Cruel."

Women's Wear Daily, May 24, 2002, Lisa Lockwood, "What's in Vogue for 2003," p. 13.

ONLINE

Bookreporter.com, http://www.bookreporter.com/ (May 12, 2003), Carlie Kraft, review of *The Devil Wears Prada.*

Readers Read, http://www.readersread.com/ (May 12, 2003), interview with Lauren Weisberger.*

*   *   *

WEISS, David 1909-2002

OBITUARY NOTICE—See index for *CA* sketch: Born June 12, 1909, in Philadelphia, PA; died from thrombophlebitis and complications from a fall November 29, 2002, in La Jolla, CA. Author. Weiss built a reputation as a historical novelist writing about various artists. He received a B.Sc. from Temple University in 1933 and attended the New School for Social Research from 1942 to 1945, but he never decided on a single course of study suitable for a career. He worked in various unrelated jobs, including swimming instructor, actor, welfare worker, stevedore, and, most notably, as a story editor for film producer David O. Selznick. Nevertheless, throughout his life he maintained an abiding interest in music and the arts, and was particularly fond of Mozart, about whom he wrote two fictionalized accounts: *Sacred and Profane: A Novel of the Life and Times of Mozart* (1968) and *The Assassination of Mozart* (1970). Weiss wrote a dozen books in all, including *Naked Came I: A Novel of Rodin* (1963), *Myself, Christopher Wren* (1974), and *I, Rembrandt* (1979).

OBITUARIES AND OTHER SOURCES:

PERIODICALS

Los Angeles Times, December 12, 2002, p. B15.

WEITZ, John 1923-2002

OBITUARY NOTICE—See index for *CA* sketch: Born May 25, 1923, in Berlin, Germany; died of cancer October 3, 2002, in Bridghampton, NY. Fashion designer and author. Weitz was a renowned clothing designer who was particularly notable for his clothes for active men, but he also made a name for himself later in life as an author of novels and nonfiction. The son of a World War I hero who was a clothing manufacturer, Weitz learned from his father and also from fashion modernist Edward Molyneaux in London. After attending schools in London, he and his family moved to the United States in the late 1930s. During World War II Weitz served with the Office of Strategic Services in Germany. He then returned to New York City and worked as a designer of women's sportswear. Weitz gained experience at various clothing companies before founding John Weitz Designs in 1954, where he built a reputation for designing active wear for men and introduced the "European cut" dress shirt. With a keen sense of marketing, Weitz also was the first designer in the United States to aggressively license his company's name to products such as men's cologne, housewares, and even sewing patterns. Winning the Coty Award, the most prestigious prize in the fashion industry, in 1974, Weitz felt he had brought his company far enough along that he no longer had to actively run the business. He stepped back to let others take charge while he turned his attention to writing books. His first published work was the novel *The Value of Nothing* (1970), which was followed by several more books, including works about Nazi Germany such as *Hitler's Diplomat: The Life and Times of Joachim von Ribbentrop* (1992) and *Hitler's Banker: Hjalmar Horace Greeley Schacht* (1997). At the time of his death Weitz was finishing a rewrite of a novel about German boxer Max Schmeling.

OBITUARIES AND OTHER SOURCES:

BOOKS

Contemporary Designers, third edition, St. James Press (Detroit, MI), 1997.

Who's Who in America, 56th edition, Marquis (New Providence, NJ), 2001.

PERIODICALS

Chicago Tribune, October 8, 2002, section 2, p. 9.

Los Angeles Times, October 5, 2002, p. B21.

New York Times, October 4, 2002, p. C21.
Times (London, England), November 16, 2002.
Washington Post, October 6, 2002, p. C10.

*   *   *

WELCH, Ann Courtenay (Edmonds) 1917-2002

OBITUARY NOTICE—See index for *CA* sketch: Born May 20, 1917, in London, England; died December 5, 2002. Aviator and author. Welch was a major contributor to sport and recreational aviation in England and was highly respected internationally for her flying achievements. She left school at the age of sixteen in order to pursue her interest in flying, obtaining her license at the age of seventeen. From there she pursued more training with the Anglo-German Fellowship in 1937 and in 1939 founded the Surrey Gliding Club. During World War II Welch was part of the Air Transport Auxiliary, a group of amateur pilots who flew planes to airfields for air force pilots. She could fly any aircraft made, and often did, including Spitfires, Wellingtons, and Hurricanes. After the war she became increasingly interested in glider planes and was made manager of the British gliding team in 1948, winning a number of international competitions. In the 1970s, as flying became more and more expensive for amateurs to pursue, she became an advocate of hang-gliding and paragliding. Welch was involved in many flying organizations, including the Fédération Aéronautique International (FAI), the British Gliding Association, for which she served as vice chairperson, the British Women Pilots' Association, and the British Hang-Gliding and Paragliding Association, for which she served as president beginning in 1991. Welch received numerous awards for her aeronautic achievements, which included setting a national glider goal flight record in 1961. These honors include the Jean Lennox-Bird pendant for lifetime achievement from the British Women Pilots' Association, an international silver badge in 1946 and a gold badge in 1969, the Lilienthal Medal from the FAI in 1973, and an FAI Gold Air Medal in 1980; in 1997 she was made an honorary fellow of the Royal Institute of Navigation. Named to the Order of the British Empire in 1966, Welch was the author of several books on aviation, including *Glider Flying* (1963), *Complete Soaring Guide* (1986), and the autobiography *Happy to Fly* (1983).

OBITUARIES AND OTHER SOURCES:

BOOKS

Welch, Rosanne, *Encyclopedia of Women in Aviation and Space,* ABC-CLIO (Santa Barbara, CA), 1998.

PERIODICALS

Daily Telegraph (London, England), December 7, 2002, p. 38.
Times (London, England), December 12, 2002, p. 37.

*   *   *

WENGER, Etienne 1952-

PERSONAL: Born 1952. *Education:* University of California at Irvine, Ph.D. *Hobbies and other interests:* Piano, guitar.

ADDRESSES: Office—P.O. Box 810, North San Juan, CA 95960. *E-mail*—Etienne@ewenger.com.

CAREER: Consultant on knowledge management; formerly affiliated with the Institute for Research on Learning. Teacher.

WRITINGS:

Artificial Intelligence and Tutoring Systems: Computational and Cognitive Approaches to the Communication of Knowledge, Morgan Kaufmann Publishers (Los Altos, CA), 1987.
(With Jean Lave) *Situated Learning: Legitimate Peripheral Participation,* Cambridge University Press (New York, NY), 1991.
Communities of Practice: Learning, Meaning, and Identity, Cambridge University Press (New York, NY), 1998.
(With Richard McDermott and William Snyder) *Cultivating Communities of Practice: A Guide to Managing Knowledge,* Harvard Business School Press (Boston, MA), 2002.

SIDELIGHTS: Etienne Wenger was initially interested in the field of artificial intelligence, earning a Ph.D. in the subject and writing a book on its relation to learning, *Artificial Intelligence and Tutoring Systems: Computational and Cognitive Approaches to the Communication of Knowledge.* Gradually, he moved away from the study of artificial intelligence but maintained a strong interest in the communication of knowledge. In 1991 he coauthored a study on the social aspects of learning titled *Situated Learning: Legitimate Peripheral Participation.* Focusing on the apprenticeship aspects of learning, Wenger and coauthor Jean Lave stress the integration between learning and group participation. "In developing this argument, Lave and Wenger highlight a number of important phenomena that are routinely ignored by the 'learning is something that happens in the head' perspective. They demonstrate, for example, that learning is happening all the time, not just in pedagogical settings," noted Edwin Hutchins in *American Anthropologist.* For Wenger and Lave, the development from novice to expert is closely bound up with the transition from newcomer to veteran within the community. To demonstrate this, they study not only the apprenticeships of Yucatec midwives and Liberian quartermasters, but also the members of Alcoholics Anonymous. *MAN* reviewer Maurice Bloch commended *Situated Learning* as "a thought-provoking book, very clearly written, which will be useful in teaching and convincing anthropologists of the crucial importance of constructing rigourous theories for studying the transmission of knowledge in society." Similarly, *American Ethnologist* contributors Eugene Matusov, Nancy Bell, and Barbara Rogoff wrote, "We expect that this book will be a landmark in showing the way to reconceptualize individual participation as constituting communities of practice, which at the same time constitute individual participation and attendant learning."

In Wenger's next book, he focuses on communities of practice. *Communities of Practice: Learning, Meaning, and Identity* identifies ways in which corporations can go beyond teams to develop real communities of practitioners who will nourish each other's creativity. For Wenger, the key ingredients are a shared area of expertise, periodic face-to-face interactions, and shared development of practices over time. In this sense, "a community of practice is more than a mere community of interest," he told *Information Outlook* interviewer Jeff De Cagna. While teams are very task-oriented and tend to dissolve when the task is completed, communities of practice are ongoing, long-term groups

built around a shared interest. "You can see why the concept of community of practice is very powerful because, at its core, it is a group of practitioners who have taken on the responsibility of managing knowledge in their domain," Wenger told de Cagna.

In 2002 Wenger coauthored *Cultivating Communities of Practice: A Guide to Managing Knowledge,* in which he "moves from theory to practice, and argues that communities of practice—when managed correctly—can be the key driver of organizational success," in the words of a *Research-Technology Management* contributor. The book introduces a number of real-world examples drawn from Wenger's work with the World Bank, DaimlerChrysler, Royal Dutch/Shell Group, and other large organizations. "Although some of the concepts and structures presented are more complex than necessary . . . the book is inspiring," wrote *Technology & Development* reviewer Amy Newman.

BIOGRAPHICAL AND CRITICAL SOURCES:

PERIODICALS

American Anthropologist, September, 1993, Edwin Hutchins, review of *Situated Learning,* pp. 743-744.
American Ethnologist, November, 1994, Eugene Matusov, Nancy Bell, and Barbara Rogoff, review of *Situated Learning,* pp. 918-919.
Information Outlook, July, 2001, Jeff De Cagna, interview with Etienne Wenger, p. 6.
MAN, June, 1994, Maurice Bloch, review of *Situated Learning,* p. 487.
Research-Technology Management, March-April, 2002, review of *Cultivating Communities of Practice,* p. 60.
Training & Development, February, 2002, Amy Newman, review of *Cultivating Communities of Practice,* p. 83.*

*   *   *

WESLEY, Mary (Aline) 1912-2002

OBITUARY NOTICE—See index for *CA* sketch: Born June 24, 1912, in Engfield Green, England; died December 30, 2002, in Totnes, England. Author. Wesley was a late-blooming bestselling novelist who did not published her first adult novel until she was seventy years old. Because her parents did not believe in education for girls, Wesley received no formal schooling, although she did learn to speak German, French, and Italian by following her parents during their European travels. She was married off to a baron, the second Lord Swinfen, in 1937 and during World War II worked for British intelligence deciphering code. Her marriage ended in 1944, and she remarried in 1952. When Wesley's second husband died, she had no means for supporting herself and her children, so she decided to turn to writing. Although she had published two children's books in 1969—*Speaking Terms* and *The Sixth Seal*—she had not tried anything since. After many efforts, she published a third children's book, *Harnessing Peacocks,* in 1983, but found even greater success with her first adult novel, *Jumping the Queue* (1983). Her second book, *The Chamomile Lawn* (1984), was an even bigger hit. Soon she found herself publishing a novel a year, adeptly blending middle-class morals with sex scenes that titillated audiences who could not believe that a septuagenarian could write such steamy prose. Her books were often set during World War II, and many of the characters belonged to royalty—something Wesley was familiar with, having been married to a baron. She wrote ten novels in all, including *Not That Sort of Girl at All* (1987), *A Dubious Legacy* (1992), and her final book, *Part of the Furniture* (1997). Many of Wesley's books were adapted as popular television miniseries.

OBITUARIES AND OTHER SOURCES:

BOOKS

Contemporary Novelists, seventh edition, St. James Press (Detroit, MI), 2001.
Dictionary of Literary Biography, Volume 231: *British Novelists since 1960,* Gale (Detroit, MI), 2001.

PERIODICALS

Chicago Tribune, January 1, 2003, section 1, p. 11.
Los Angeles Times, January 6, 2003, p. B9.
New York Times, January 1, 2003, p. C10.
Times (London, England), January 1, 2003.
Washington Post, January 5, 2003, p. C10.

WHITLEY, Peggy 1938-

PERSONAL: Born September 3, 1938, in Wycaff, NJ; daughter of John (a minister) and Ethel (a homemaker; maiden name, Lant) Kroeze; married Gilmer S. Whitley; children: Brette, Penn, Maggie. *Education:* Southern Methodist University, B.A. (education), 1961; Sam Houston University, M.L.S. *Hobbies and other interests:* Teaching "mystery novel" courses.

ADDRESSES: Home—58 Cobble Hill, The Woodlands, TX 77381. *Office*—Kingwood College, 20000 Kingwood Dr., Kingwood, TX 77339. *E-mail*—pwhitley@ nhmccd.edu.

CAREER: Educator and librarian. Kingwood College, Kingwood, TX, dean of educational services.

MEMBER: American Library Association, Texas Library Association.

AWARDS, HONORS: Teacher Excellence Award.

WRITINGS:

(With Catherine Olson and Susan Williams Goodwin) *Ninety-nine Jumpstarts to Research: Topic Guides for Finding Information on Current Issues,* Libraries Unlimited (Englewood, CO), 2001.
(With Susan Williams Goodwin) *Ninety-nine Jumpstarts for Kids: Getting Started in Research,* Libraries Unlimited (Englewood, CO), 2003.

SIDELIGHTS: Longtime teacher and librarian Peggy Whitley has been part of the late-twentieth-century information revolution. She reflected on the changes in librarianship caused by this revolution, telling *CA,* "With the advent of the Internet and the many electronic databases available online, today's libraries are moving outside their walls. Librarians must be prepared to do so, too. Students and library patrons are now inundated with too much information. It has become the role of the librarian to teach users 'information literacy' or how to select the best sources and evaluate the information they find."

To help meet this need, Whitley teamed up with Catherine Olson and Susan Williams Goodwin to write *Ninety-nine Jumpstarts to Research: Topic Guides for*

Finding Information on Current Issues. This work, which *School Library Journal* reviewer Mary Lankford called "timely, practical" and "useful . . . for developing good research habits," provides a plethora of information. The work is divided alphabetically into two-page sections by such topics as abortion, politics, gun control, immigration, medicine, and crime, among many others. Each topic contains information on library search terms, relevant questions, agencies to contact, and sources of information from the print media and from Web sites.

As an adjunct to her information services work, Whitley, dean of educational services at Kingwood College, has also co-created and taught the "Whodunit Series." These college literature classes focus on mystery literature and have examined the development of the mystery as a genre, British historical and regional mysteries, and American historical and regional mysteries. "It is always exciting to renew our friendship with participants from earlier classes and meet new mystery readers," Whitley told a *Houston Chronicle* reporter.

BIOGRAPHICAL AND CRITICAL SOURCES:

PERIODICALS

Houston Chronicle, October 11, 2001, "Kingwood College Offers New 'Whodunit' Series," p. 11.
School Library Journal, March, 2002, Mary Lankford, review of *Ninety-nine Jumpstarts to Research: Topic Guides to Finding Information on Current Issues,* p. 263.

*　　*　　*

WILKINSON, Bruce H. 1947-

PERSONAL: Born 1947, in Kearney, NJ; married Darlene Wilkinson, 1969; children: David, Jennifer, Jessica. *Education:* Northeastern Bible College, B.A.; Dallas Theological Seminary, M.A., 1974; Western Conservative Baptist Seminary, Portland, OR, D.D.

ADDRESSES: Home—Johannesburg, South Africa. *Agent*—c/o Author Mail, Multnomah Publishers, P.O. Box 1720, Sisters, OR 97759.

CAREER: Walk Thru the Bible Ministries, founder and president, c.1977-2002; writer.

AWARDS, HONORS: Gold Medallion Book Award in Christian Living, for *The Prayer of Jabez: Breaking Through to the Blessed Life,* 2001; Christian Book of the Year, Evangelical Christian Publishers Association, 2001, 2002.

WRITINGS:

(With others) *The Daily Walk Bible with 365 Devotional Helps to Guide You Through the Bible in One Year,* Tyndale (Wheaton, IL), 1987.
(Editor, with Kenneth Boa) *Talk Thru the Bible,* Thomas Nelson (Nashville, TN), 1990.
How to Teach Almost Anything to Practically Anyone, Multnomah (Sisters, OR), 1992.
(With others) *A Closer Walk,* Zondervan (Grand Rapids, MI), 1992.
(Editor) *Almost Every Answer for Practically Any Teacher: A Resource Guide for All Who Desire to Teach for Lifechange,* Multnomah (Sisters, OR), 1992.
(With Gene A. Getz) *Nehemiah: Becoming a Disciplined Leader,* Broadman & Holman (Nashville, TN), 1995.
(With others) *Family Walk Devotional Bible,* Zondervan (Grand Rapids, MI), 1996.
(Editor, with others) *NIV Youthwalk Devotional Bible,* Zondervan (Grand Rapids, MI), 1997.
(Editor, with others) *Closer Walk New Testament,* Walk Thru the Bible Ministries (Atlanta, GA), 1997.
Personal Holiness in Times of Temptation, Harvest House, 1998.
(Editor) *Thirty Days to Experiencing Spiritual Breakthroughs,* Multnomah (Sisters, OR), 1999.
Experiencing Spiritual Breakthroughs: The Powerful Principle of the Three Chairs, Multnomah (Sisters, OR), 1999.
The Prayer of Jabez: Breaking Through to the Blessed Life, Multnomah (Sisters, OR), 2000.
(With David Kopp) *The Prayer of Jabez Devotional,* Multnomah (Sisters, OR), 2001.
(With David Kopp) *Secrets of the Vine: Breaking Through to Abundance,* Multnomah (Sisters, OR), 2001.
(With David Kopp) *The Prayer of Jabez for Teens,* Multnomah (Sisters, OR), 2001.

The Prayer of Jabez for Kids, illustrated by Dan Brawner, Thomas Nelson (Nashville, TN), 2001.

(With Melody Carlson) *The Prayer of Jabez for Little Ones,* Thomas Nelson (Nashville, TN), 2001.

The Prayer of Jabez Devotions for Kids Living Big for God, illustrated by Rob Suggs, Thomas Nelson (Nashville, TN), 2001.

(With David Kopp) *Experiencing Spiritual Breakthroughs,* Multnomah (Sisters, OR), 2002.

(With David Kopp) *Secrets of the Vine Devotional,* Multnomah (Sisters, OR), 2002.

Secrets of the Vine for Kids, Thomas Nelson (Nashville, TN), 2002.

(With Melody Carlson) *Secrets of the Vine for Little Ones,* Thomas Nelson (Nashville, TN), 2002.

Secrets of the Vine for Young Hearts, illustrated by Rob Suggs, Thomas Nelson (Nashville, TN), 2002.

(With Mack Thomas) *A Life God Rewards for Guys Only,* Multnomah (Sisters, OR), 2002.

(With Mack Thomas) *A Life God Rewards for Kids,* Multnomah (Sisters, OR), 2002.

(With David Kopp) *A Life God Rewards for Teens,* Multnomah (Sisters, OR), 2002.

(With Mack Thomas) *A Life God Rewards: Girls Only,* Multnomah (Sisters, OR), 2002.

(With David Kopp) *Reflections from A Life God Rewards,* Multnomah (Sisters, OR), 2002.

(With Mack Thomas) *A Life God Rewards for Little Ones,* Multnomah (Sisters, OR), 2002.

(With Kenneth Boa) *The Wilkinson and Boa Bible Handbook: The Ultimate Guide to Help You Get More Out of the Bible,* Thomas Nelson (Nashville, TN), 2002.

(With David Kopp) *Secrets of the Vine for Teens,* Multnomah (Sisters, OR), 2003.

Set Apart: Discovering Personal Victory Through Holiness, Multnomah (Sisters, OR), 2003.

ADAPTATIONS: The Prayer of Jabez for Teens Cards, Hay House; *The Prayer of Jabez for Young Hearts,* audiocassette, Thomas Nelson; *Secrets of the Vine Cards: Breaking Through to Abundance,* Hay House; *Wilkinson Bible Handbook,* Thomas Nelson.

SIDELIGHTS: Born into a devout Christian home, Bruce H. Wilkinson seemed destined to forge a career in religious work. After earning his doctorate of divinity, Wilkinson established the Walk Thru the Bible Ministries, utilizing a study method he had developed while still a graduate student. This nondenominational group, wrote John Blake in the *Atlanta Journal-*

Constitution, now has "an annual budget of about $17 million, conducts biblical training seminars in 52 countries and publishes 11 Christian magazines."

Among Wilkinson's many works is a book that has become an international best-seller: *The Prayer of Jabez: Breaking Through to the Blessed Life.* Jabez, the thirty-fifth son of Judah, had a favorite prayer that Wilkinson discovered more than thirty years ago in 1 Chronicles 4:10: "Oh, that you would bless me indeed, and enlarge my territory, that your hand would be with me, and that you would keep me from evil, that it may not grieve me!" Wilkinson made the prayer a part of his daily life. Laura Dempsey, writing in the *Dayton Daily News,* commented, "Wilkinson liked the fact that Jabez wasn't afraid to ask God to bless him indeed and to broaden his borders." A reviewer in the *Christian Science Monitor* stated that Wilkinson "believes that when this prayer is used daily, it opens the doors to God's blessing."

The publication of *The Prayer of Jabez* has been met with a certain amount of controversy. Erin McClam, writing in the *Memphis Commercial Appeal,* noted that "one camp of theologians believes *Jabez* is stunning in its selfishness." Wilkinson told McClam, however, that because of *The Prayer of Jabez,* "millions of people are discovering prayer." Judith Cebula, writing in the *Indianapolis Star,* commented that, with millions of copies sold since its release, *The Prayer of Jabez* "has catapulted an obscure character from the most obscure part of the Bible into the prayer lives of evangelical Christians nationwide." Jim Jones, writing for the *Knight-Ridder/Tribune News Service,* stated, "A part of the prayer's appeal is that Jabez, whose name means 'pain' in Hebrew, is not one of the heroes of the Bible. He's an ordinary person like you and me. Yet God blesses him greatly."

Although the controversy endures, several religious leaders find that the book is personally satisfying, while at the same time it encourages their congregations to seek prayer. Charles Austin, writing in the *Bergen County Record,* asked a number of leaders why they thought the book had such appeal. One pastor replied, "Because there's this thirst out there for spiritual things." Sherice L. Shields, writing for the *Knight-Ridder/Tribune News Service,* summed up *The Prayer of Jabez* phenomenon: "A tiny blessing prayer in a tiny book is having a mighty impact nationwide."

Wilkinson continues to fulfill his religious calling by writing books, giving speaking engagements—he has addressed 350,000 men across America in three years—producing video seminars based on his conferences, and teaching.

BIOGRAPHICAL AND CRITICAL SOURCES:

PERIODICALS

Atlanta Journal-Constitution, April 28, 2001, John Blake, "Bruce Wilkinson Truly Believes in the Power of Prayer," p. B1.

Christian Science Monitor, July 26, 2001, "The Monitor's Guide to Religious Bestsellers," p. 21.

Commercial Appeal (Memphis, TN), June 17, 2001, Erin McClam, "Prayer of Jabez: God's Will or Guide for Greed?" p. E1.

Dallas Morning News, April 7, 2001, Berta Delgado, "A Simple Prayer with Awesome Answers," p. 1G.

Dayton Daily News, May 24, 2001, Laura Dempsey, "Salesman's Prayer Answered," p. 1C.

Indianapolis Star, May 26, 2001, Judith Cebula, "Does 'Bless Me' Mean 'Gimme'?: Prayer by Jabez Raises Questions about Asking for Prosperity," p. F1.

Knight-Ridder/Tribune News Service, May 16, 2001, Sherice L. Shields, "New Book *Prayer of Jabez* Is Igniting Spirits and Sales," p. K1290; May 23, 2001, Jim Jones, "Is it Selfish or Valid?: Prayer Stirs Debate," p. K5067.

Palm Beach Post (West Palm Beach, FL), May 26, 2001, Elizabeth Clarke, "Book: Prayer Will Change Your Life in Month," p. 8D.

Record (Bergen County, NJ), July 9, 2001, Charles Austin, "'Always-Answered' Prayer Sparks Questions in Some," p. A1.

Virginia Pilot, August 12, 2001, James W. H. Sell, "*Jabez* Touts the Gospel of Greed," p. J1.*

* * *

WILLIAMS, Mark London 1959-

PERSONAL: Born June 19, 1959, in Sacramento, CA; son of William R. (a journalist) and Deborah R. (an administrator) Williams; married; wife's name, Catherine (a midwife); children: Elijah, Asher. *Education:* University of California—Berkeley, A.B. (drama), 1981; University of Southern California, M.P.W., 1994. *Politics:* "Transformative." *Religion:* "Questioning."

ADDRESSES: Office—P.O. Box 4381, North Hollywood, CA 91617. *Agent*—Ruth Cohen, P.O. Box 2244, La Jolla, CA 92038. *E-mail*—scribe@dangerboy. com.

CAREER: Journalist, editor, and freelance writer. Instructor, California State University—Northridge Extension and Learning Tree University.

MEMBER: Society of Children's Book Writers and Illustrators, PEN West.

AWARDS, HONORS: Golden Duck Award nominee for excellence in children's science fiction, for *Ancient Fire.*

WRITINGS:

Ancient Fire ("Danger Boy" series), Tricycle Press (Berkley, CA), 2001.

Dino Sword ("Danger Boy" series), Tricycle Press (Berkley, CA), 2001.

Contributor of articles and poetry to periodicals, including *L.A. Business Journal, Los Angeles Times, Variety,* and *L.A. Times Online.* Script writer for Piranha Press and Mojo Press, both publishers of comics.

WORK IN PROGRESS: More installments in "Danger Boy" series; a fable; a picture book; research on passenger train lines and California Indian history.

SIDELIGHTS: During his varied literary career, Mark London Williams has scripted comics, published poetry, written reviews for *Variety* and the *Los Angeles Times* column "Meta Hollywood," produced plays nationally and internationally, and written his own series of children's books. When one day Williams's son Elijah blurted out "I'm Danger Boy!" he unknowingly sparked the idea for his father's "Danger Boy" series for middle-grade readers, which first rolled off the presses in 2001 with *Ancient Fire.* In the debut novel, main character Eli, who lives in the year 2019, is a regular kid until his mother disappears during a time-travel experiment. Then Eli must go back in time to the ancient Egyptian city of Alexandria, where he teams up with Clyne, a highly evolved dinosaur from another planet, and Thea, the daughter of the last librarian of Alexandria, to save the world and rescue Eli's mother. The tale is told in the first person, with chapters alternating between the three characters. Upon returning to his present time, Eli earns the moniker "Danger Boy." In the second installment in the "Danger Boy" series, *Dino Sword,* Eli and his companions from the first book team up again to tackle the "Fifth Dimension."

Both novels were popular with readers, reaching the *Los Angeles Times* best-seller list of children's books, and *Ancient Fire* was nominated for a children's science fiction award. A *Publishers Weekly* reviewer praised Williams for being able to write clearly about complicated ideas, predicting that *Ancient Fire,* an "inventively twisted" story, will give readers a "rewarding excursion." Furthermore, *School Library Journal* contributor Mara Alpert predicted that the first volume in the "Danger Boy" series "will leave readers awaiting the next installment."

BIOGRAPHICAL AND CRITICAL SOURCES:

PERIODICALS

Publishers Weekly, March 26, 2001, review of *Ancient Fire,* p. 94.
School Library Journal, April, 2001, Mara Alpert, review of *Ancient Fire,* p. 152.

ONLINE

Danger Boy Web site, http://dangerboy.com/ (March 30, 2003).
SciFan, http://www.scifan.com/ (January 14, 2003), "Mark London Williams."*

*   *   *

WILSON, Lyle (Giles) 1955-

PERSONAL: Born 1955, in Butedale, British Columbia, Canada. *Education:* Attended University of British Columbia, 1976-79, B.Ed., 1987; Emily Carr College of Art and Design, diploma in printmaking, 1986.

ADDRESSES: Office—Museum of Anthropology, University of British Columbia, Vancouver, British Columbia, Canada.

CAREER: University of British Columbia, Vancouver, British Columbia, Canada, curatorial assistant and artist-in-residence at Museum of Anthropology, 1987—. Sculptor, graphic artist, and printmaker, including work commissioned by Expo 1992, First Nations House of Learning at University of British Columbia, Canadian National Institute for the Blind, Canadian consulate in Osaka, Japan, and British Columbia Sports Hall of Fame. *Exhibitions:* Solo exhibitions at Regional Art Gallery, London, Ontario, Canada, Philbrook Art Center, Tulsa, OK, Inuit Gallery, Vancouver, British Columbia, Canada, and elsewhere; work collected at Burnaby Art Gallery, Vancouver, British Columbia, Canada, Toronto Dominion Bank, Royal British Columbia Museum, and Canada Council Art Bank.

WRITINGS:

(With Allene Drake) *Eulachon: A Fish to Cure Humanity* (exhibition catalog), Museum of Anthropology, University of British Columbia (Vancouver, British Columbia, Canada), 1992.

BIOGRAPHICAL AND CRITICAL SOURCES:

BOOKS

St. James Guide to Native North American Artists, St. James Press (Detroit, MI), 1998, pp. 633-635.

PERIODICALS

American Indian Quarterly, Volume 18, number 4, 1994, Charlotte Townsend-Gault, "Northwest Coast Art: The Culture of the Land Claims."
University of British Columbia Museum of Anthropology Museum Notes, number 28, 1989, Karen Duffek, "Lyle Wilson: When Worlds Collide."*

*   *   *

WOLFLE, Dael (Lee) 1906-2002

OBITUARY NOTICE—See index for *CA* sketch: Born March 5, 1906, in Puyallup, WA; died of congestive heart failure December 26, 2002, in Seattle, WA. Psychologist, administrator, educator, and author. Wolfle is best remembered for his service as longtime head of the American Association for the Advancement of Science. A graduate of the University of Washington, where he earned his master's degree in 1928, he went on to earn a Ph.D. in experimental psychology in 1931. During the 1930s and 1940s he taught at several universities, including Ohio State, the University of Mississippi, and the University of Chicago; the years during World War II saw Wolfe as a civilian training administrator for electronics for the Army Signal Corps, and he also worked for the Office of Scientific Research and Development as a technical aide. Wolfle left academia in 1946 to become executive secretary of the American Psychological Association, followed by a position as director of the Commission on Human Resources and Advanced Training from 1950 to 1954. Wolfle was fascinated by the study of science, and so his next appointment, as executive officer of the American Association for the Advancement of Science, was a perfect fit. He directed the AAAS until 1970 and was the editor of its journal, *Science.* In 1970 Wolfle returned to teaching, joining the faculty of the University of Washington as a professor of public affairs—policy issues were also a great interest of his—until his retirement in 1996. In addition to his teaching and administrative posts, Wolfle served on committees for the National Science Foundation, the National Academy of Sciences, and the American Council on Education. He was also the author, coauthor, or editor of over a dozen books, including *Science and Public Policy* (1959), *The Uses of Talent* (1971), and *Renewing a Scientific Society: The American Association for the Advancement of Science from World War II to 1970* (1989). Wolfle received several honors for his contributions, including two honorary degrees and, in 1979, the Alumnus Summa Laude Dignatus award from the University of Washington.

OBITUARIES AND OTHER SOURCES:

PERIODICALS

Seattle Times, January 3, 2003, p. B5.
Washington Post, January 10, 2002, p. B5.

*   *   *

WOLFSON, Susan J. 1948-

PERSONAL: Born 1948. *Education:* University of California, Berkeley, A.B., 1970, M.A., 1972, Ph.D., 1978.

ADDRESSES: Home—64 Stony Brook Lane, Princeton, NJ 08544-7512. *Office*—Department of English, 222 McCosh Hall, Princeton University, Princeton, NJ 08544-1016; fax: 609-258-1607. *E-mail*—wolfson@princeton.edu.

CAREER: Rutgers University, New Brunswick, NJ, assistant professor, 1978-84, chair of sophomore English, 1984-85, associate professor, 1984-90, chair of English honors program, 1984-86, 1987-88, professor, 1990-91, chair of graduate admissions, 1990-91; Princeton University, Princeton, NJ, visiting fellow, 1988-89, 1989-90, professor of English, 1991—. University of California, Los Angeles, visiting fellow, 1986-87.

MEMBER: North American Society for the Study of Romanticism (advisory board member), Modern Language Association (division executive committee, 1988-92, chair, 1991), North East Modern Language Association (division committee, 1983, chair, 1984), Keats-Shelley Association of America, Byron Society, Association of Literary Scholars and Critics, Berkeley Foundation, Wordsworth-Coleridge Association of America (president, 1985), Phi Beta Kappa.

AWARDS, HONORS: Woodrow Wilson fellow, 1970-71; Keats-Shelley Association, prize for distinguished essay, 1988, Distinguished Scholar Award, 2001; Rutgers University Faculty of Arts and Sciences Distinguished Teaching Award, 1990; Guggenheim Foundation fellowship, 1990; National Endowment for the Humanities fellowship, 1995-96; American Conference on Romanticism, Jean-Pierre Barricelli Prize for outstanding book of 1997, for *Formal Charges: The Shaping of Poetry in British Romanticism.*

WRITINGS:

The Questioning Presence: Wordsworth, Keats, and the Interrogative Mode in Romantic Poetry, Cornell University Press (Ithaca, NY), 1986.
(Author of introduction and coeditor with Barry V. Qualls) *The Strange Case of Dr. Jekyll and Mr. Hyde,* Washington Square Press (New York, NY), 1995.
(Coeditor and preface with Peter J. Manning) *Lord Byron: Selected Poems,* Penguin Books (New York, NY), 1996.

Formal Charges: The Shaping of Poetry in British Romanticism, Stanford University Press (Stanford, CA), 1997.

(Coeditor with Peter J. Manning) *The Romantics and Their Contemporaries,* Longman (New York, NY), 1999.

(Editor) *Felicia Hemans: Selected Poems, Letters, and Reception Materials,* Princeton University Press (Princeton, NJ), 2000.

(Coeditor with Peter J. Manning) *Selected Poems of Thomas Hood, Winthrop Mackworth Praed, Thomas Lovell Beddoes,* Penguin Classics (New York, NY), 2000.

(Editor) *The Cambridge Companion to Keats,* Cambridge University Press (Cambridge, MA), 2001.

(Coeditor with Elizabeth Fay) *The Siege of Valencia, by Felicia Hemans: The 1823 Publication and the Manuscript,* Broadview Press (Peterborough, Ontario, Canada), 2002.

(Editor) *Mary Shelley's Frankenstein,* Longman Publishers (New York, NY), 2002.

(Author of introduction and coeditor with Claudia L. Johnson) *Jane Austen's Pride and Prejudice,* Longman Publishers (New York, NY), 2003.

Contributor to books, including *Cambridge History of Romanticism,* edited by James Chandler, 2002; *The Cambridge Companion to Mary Wollstonecraft Shelley,* edited by Esther Shore, 2002; *Encyclopedia of the Romantic Era, 1760-1860,* 2002; *The Cambridge Companion to William Blake,* edited by Morris Eaves, 2002; *Felicia Hemans: Reimagining Poetry in the Nineteenth Century,* edited by Nanora Sweet and Julie Melnyck, 2001; *Romanticism and Women Poets: Opening the Doors of Reception,* edited by Stephen C. Behrendt and Harriet Kramer Linking, 1999; *The Lessons of Romanticism: A Critical Companion,* edited by Thomas Pfau and Robert F. Gleckner, 1998, and *A Companion to Romanticism,* edited by Duncan Wu, 1997. Contributor to journals, including *PMLA, Wordsworth Circle, Modern Language Quarterly, Romanticism on the Net, European Romantic Review, Romantic Praxis, Studies in Romanticism, Eighteenth-Century Life,* and the *Keats-Shelley Journal.* Member of the editorial boards of the *Keats-Shelley Journal, Romanticism, Nineteenth-Century Contexts, Nineteenth-Century Literature, Romanticism on the Net,* and *Wordsworth Circle.*

WORK IN PROGRESS: Figures on the Margin: The Language of Gender in British Romanticism, for University of Pennsylvania Press; *Selected Poetry of Walter Scott,* for Penguin English Poetry.

SIDELIGHTS: Susan J. Wolfson has been a professor of English at Princeton University since 1991. She has written, edited, and contributed to many books and publications on the topic of the British Romantic era and its poetry.

In *Formal Charges: The Shaping of Poetry in British Romanticism* Wolfson analyzes British poetry and six poets of the Romantic era. In her analysis Wolfson concentrates on formalism's cultural and historical aspects and its current relationship to British Romantic poetry. As Mark Kipperman noted, writing for *Studies in Romanticism,* "Susan Wolfson attempts to navigate these treacherous shoals and return formal study to the center of a sophisticated and historically sensitive analysis of romantic poems . . . calling, in effect, for a New Formalism." *Notes and Queries* contributor Chris Jones concluded, "Readers of all levels of expertise will benefit from these accomplished readings that restore to the poetry the subtle, self-situating irony which has most often been turned against it." In a review for the *Journal of English and Germanic Philology,* Theresa M. Kelley called *Formal Charges* a "well reasoned defense of formalist criticism" which "emphasizes the inner complexity of form as a medium of poetic agency." *ANQ* reviewer L. J. Swingle felt that "the primary value of Wolfson's book . . . is the precision and intensity of her focus on formal issues in the poetry."

Wolfson also edited a book about Felicia Hemans, a leading female poet in England and the United States during the Romantic era. *Felicia Hemans: Selected Poems, Letters, and Reception Materials* contains five of her major works; letters written by Hemans that reveal her thoughts on her poetry and the poetry of others, information about her publishers, her celebrity status, and more; and letters written about Hemans by individuals, such as Lord Byron and Walter Scott. According to *Wordsworth Circle* reviewer Duncan Wu, "Wolfson has assembled in compact form the various materials that may be considered essential to a critical appreciation of her life and work." "Wolfson's edition is useful not only as a good introduction to Hemans's poetry, but also for charting the poet's particularly 'erratic reception history,'" noted *Times Literary Supplement* contributor Clare Pettitt, while Stephen C. Behrendt, in a review for *Criticism,* commented, "It is one of the great triumphs of Susan Wolfson's fine new edition that she enables us to see so clearly and with such an unencumbered view the work of one of the greatest of British Romantic poets. This edition sets— and then meets—high standards for textual editing, for circumspect biography, and for intellectual, aesthetic, and cultural sensitivity."

BIOGRAPHICAL AND CRITICAL SOURCES:

PERIODICALS

ANQ, spring, 1999, L. J. Swingle, review of *Formal Charges: The Shaping of Poetry in British Romanticism,* p. 53.

Criticism, spring, 2002, Stephen C. Behrendt, review of *Felicia Hemans: Selected Poems, Letters, and Reception Materials,* p. 217.

Journal of English and Germanic Philology, January, 2000, Theresa M. Kelley, review of *Formal Charges,* p. 146.

Nineteenth-Century Literature, June, 1998, Paul D. Sheats, review of *Formal Charges,* p. 111.

Notes and Queries, September, 1998, Chris Jones, review of *Formal Charges,* p. 393.

Romantic Circles, January, 2001, review of *Formal Charges,* p. 393.

Studies in Romanticism, fall, 2000, Mark Kipperman, review of *Formal Charges,* p. 53.

Times Literary Supplement, July 20, 2001, Clare Pettitt, review of *Felicia Hemans,* p. 33.

Wordsworth Circle, fall, 2001, Duncan Wu, review of *Felicia Hemans,* p. 255.

OTHER

Princeton University Press Web site, http://pup.princeton.edu/ (April 1, 2003).

Romantic Circles Praxis Series, http://www.rc.umd.edu/ (April, 2002), "Re-reading *Box Hill:* Reading the Practice of Reading Everyday Life."

University of Pittsburgh Press Web site, http://www.pitt.edu/ (April 1, 2003).*

*   *   *

WOOD, Margaret 1950-

PERSONAL: Born January 23, 1950, in Parker, AZ; married; children: two sons. *Education:* Arizona State University, B.A., 1971; University of Denver, M.A., 1973.

ADDRESSES: Office—Native American Fashions, Inc., P.O. Box 44802, Phoenix, AZ 85064.

CAREER: Schoolteacher for Window Rock School District, 1971-72; Navajo Community College, director of library services, 1973-74; librarian in Phoenix, AZ, 1975-78; Heard Museum, Phoenix, AZ, intern and lecturer, 1986; Native American Fashions, Inc., owner. Waverly Fabric Corp., lecturer, 1986. Atlatl (service organization for Native American arts), volunteer executive director, 1990-92; education consultant. Textile artist, with work collected at Wheelwright Museum of the American Indian; *Exhibitions:* Held solo exhibition at MARS Artspace, Phoenix, AZ; work included in group shows across the United States, including exhibitions at American Indian Community House Gallery and Museum, New York, NY, Hand and the Spirit, Mesa Southwest Museum, California Craft Museum, and Hunter Museum of Art, Chattanooga, TN.

AWARDS, HONORS: Heard Museum Guild Indian Fair Market, award for best of quilting division, 1993.

WRITINGS:

Native American Fashions: Adaptations of Traditional Designs, Van Nostrand Reinhold (New York, NY), 1981, 2nd revised edition, Native American Fashions, Inc. (Phoenix, AZ), 1997.

Contributor to periodicals, including *Akwe:kon Journal.*

BIOGRAPHICAL AND CRITICAL SOURCES:

BOOKS

St. James Guide to Native North American Artists, St. James Press (Detroit, MI), 1998, pp. 635-636.

PERIODICALS

Blair & Ketchum's Country Journal, June, 1982, Lee Pennock Huntington, review of *Native American Fashions: Adaptations of Traditional Designs,* p. 89.

Library Journal, December 1, 1981, review of *Native American Fashions,* p. 2306.

Native Peoples, Volume 9, number 2, 1996, "In Profile: Margaret Wood."

PHX Downtown, February, 1993, "Alter-Native: Offerings to Our Heritage."

Publishers Weekly, November 20, 1981, Sybil Steinberg, review of *Native American Fashions,* p. 51.

Santa Fe New Mexican, July 2, 1993, "Margaret Wood's Quilts, Soft Sculptures Open New Show."*

*   *   *

WRIGHT, Vinita Hampton 1958-

PERSONAL: Born 1958, in KS; married a photographer, 1990. *Education:* Wheaton College, M.A.

ADDRESSES: Home—Chicago, IL. *Office*—Loyola Press, 3441 North Ashland Ave., Chicago, IL 60657.

CAREER: Writer, editor, and compiler. Harold Shaw Publishers, editor; Tyndale House, editor; Loyola Press, Chicago, IL, editorial director of trade books division, currently senior book editor.

WRITINGS:

(Compiler, with Carol Plueddemann) *World Shapers: A Treasury of Quotes from Great Missionaries,* H. Shaw Publishers (Wheaton, IL), 1991.

(Compiler, with Carol Plueddemann) *Prayers around the Family Table: Dinner-time Discussion and Prayer,* H. Shaw Publishers (Wheaton, IL), 1992.

(Editor) *Prayers across the Centuries: Abraham, Jesus, St. Augustine, Martin Luther, Susanna Wesley,* H. Shaw Publishers (Wheaton, IL), 1993.

(Compiler, with Mary Horner) *Women's Widsom through the Ages: Timeless Quotations on Life and Faith,* Testament Books (New York, NY), 1994.

(Compiler, with Carol Plueddemann) *Family Prayers for All Occasions,* H. Shaw Publishers (Wheaton, IL), 1995.

(Compiler, with Keith Call) *A Dickens Christmas Collection,* H. Shaw Publishers (Wheaton, IL), 1995.

Grace at Bender Springs: A Novel, Broadman & Holman (Nashville, TN), 1999.

Velma Still Cooks in Leeway (novel), Broadman & Holman (Nashville, TN), 2000.

Simple Acts of Moving Forward: A Little Book about Getting Unstuck, Shaw Books (Colorado Springs, CO), 2003.

WORK IN PROGRESS: A novel about a family enduring an Iowa farm crisis and the changing character of rural life.

SIDELIGHTS: Born and raised in a small town in Kansas, Vinita Hampton Wright was intending to pursue a career in music education and performance when she traveled in her early twenties to Jordan to teach English and music in a Baptist school. While she was working there, however, she realized that she wanted to become a writer.

Inspired to write a story about grace after viewing the film *Miss Firecracker,* Wright sat down and began *Grace at Bender Springs,* which also drew from the experiences of her youth in Kansas. Although the initial Christian publishing house halted publication of the novel at the eleventh hour, within the following year Wright had landed an agent and a three-book contract with another Christian publisher, Broadman & Holman.

Wright honed what was originally a collection of short stories into a novel. *Grace at Bender Springs: A Novel* uses the metaphor of a drought to explore a "community's spiritual dryness." In the end, grace "haltingly, mysteriously flows through the parched town." In his *Booklist* review, John Mort noted that "seldom is Christian fiction so well informed and potent" as Wright's novel. Called "cross-over" fiction, *Grace at Bender Springs* has appealed to a broad audience. Reviewing *Grace at Bender Springs* in *Publishers Weekly,* Jana Riess called the book "a deeply resonant novel about healing."

According to interviewer Lauren F. Winner, writing in *Christianity Today,* Wright's second novel, *Velma Still Cooks in Leeway,* "also tackles a theological theme, this time forgiveness." The narrator is Velma, a short-order cook at her own restaurant. Again the story unfolds through a series of points of view. John Mort, writing in *Booklist,* considered Wright's story of an aging widow in a town in need of forgiveness "a worthy successor to her fine debut novel." A reviewer in *Publishers Weekly* described *Velma Still Cooks in Leeway* as "a cosmic drama of divine grace" and "an extraordinary, character-driven novel."

Interviewing the author for *Publishers Weekly,* Jana Riess asked Wright whether her novels "fill a need in the world of Christian fiction." Wright responded: "What I want to do is present real Christians in my books. I think these people are worth knowing and they're worth knowing, just the way they are. They're learning things about themselves and other people, and they're learning how faith works and who God is in ever-changing situations." In her *Publishers Weekly* review, Riess noted that *Velma Still Cooks in Leeway* "is driven . . . by the quiet dignity of ordinary people weathering extraordinary trials." In Wright's own observation: "Spirituality is just very interesting, and I love exploring that with characters. A character without that spiritual dynamic is just as flat as a character without a sexual dynamic."

One of Wright's challenges is finding enough time to write. She told Riess that she "takes two weeks of paid and two weeks of unpaid vacation each year to write full-time." The remainder of the year she works as an editor of nonfiction at Loyola Press and makes room for writing time during evenings and weekends.

BIOGRAPHICAL AND CRITICAL SOURCES:

PERIODICALS

Booklist, October 1, 1999, John Mort, review of *Grace at Bender Spring: A Novel,* p. 326; October 1, 2000, John Mort, review of *Velma Still Cooks in Leeway,* p. 304.
Christianity Today, April 23, 2001, Lauren F. Winner, "The Wright Stuff," p. 84.
Publishers Weekly, August 30, 1999, Jana Riess, review of *Grace at Bender Springs,* p. S15; July 24, 2000, review of *Velma Still Cooks in Leeway,* p. 66; September 18, 2000, Jana Riess, "Vinita Hampton Wright: A Life of Quiet Grace," p. 82.*

*   *   *

YOUNG, Dean 1955-

PERSONAL: Born 1955, in Columbia, PA; married Cornelia Nixon (a writer).

ADDRESSES: Home—Berkeley, CA; and Chicago, IL. *Office*—Loyola University Chicago, 6525 North Sheridan Rd., Chicago, IL 60626. *E-mail*—dyoung1@luc.edu.

CAREER: Teacher and writer. Loyola University Chicago, Chicago, IL, currently associate professor of English; University of Iowa Writers' Workshop, Iowa City, visiting faculty member, 1997-98, 2001. Has also taught at the University of Wisconsin.

AWARDS, HONORS: Fellowship, Fine Arts Work Center; Stegner fellowship, Stanford University; National Endowment for the Arts fellowship; Colorado Poetry Prize, 1995, for *Strike Anywhere.*

WRITINGS:

Design with X, Wesleyan University Press (Middletown, CT), 1988.
Beloved Infidel, University Press of New England (Hanover, NH), 1992.
Strike Anywhere, Center for Literary Publications, Press of Colorado (Niwot, CO), 1995.
First Course in Turbulence, University of Pittsburgh Press (Pittsburgh, PA), 1999.
Skid, University of Pittsburgh Press (Pittsburgh, PA), 2002.

Has also produced audio recordings of his poetry for the Library of Congress. Contributor of poetry to numerous periodicals and anthologies, including *Ploughshares, Gettysburg Review, Pushcart Prize XXI: Best of the Small Presses, Threepenny Review,* and many others.

SIDELIGHTS: Described as one of the standard bearers of modern surrealism, poet Dean Young has been the recipient of a variety of fellowships and awards, acknowledgement that he is being read and heard. Young's first book of poetry, *Design with X,* was published in 1988, followed by *Beloved Infidel* in 1992. *Publishers Weekly* reviewed *Beloved Infidel* and praised it. "Like many of the 'language poets,' Young seems interested in issues of form vs. formlessness and the tradition of indeterminate language, yet the work remains coherent." *Ploughshares* contributor Diann Blakely Shoaf similarly remarked on how Young uses the "slightly cracked and wavy but nonetheless serviceable mirror of contemporary language" to comment on modern life, and concluded that *Beloved Infidel* is "a book that's a winner of hearts."

Young's poetry has been described as witty, exhilarating, and urgent by readers and critics alike. As Charles Simic noted in a remark quoted on the *University of Iowa Web site:* "The language, the invention, the imagination and the sheer fun of his poems is astounding." *Strike Anywhere,* Young's third collection, won the Colorado Poetry Prize in 1995. Judged Don Revell of the book, according to the *University of Iowa Web site:* "In this, the most beautiful of his three collections, Dean Young enlarges the project of North American Surrealism, gifting it with an entirely new intimacy and equally new range."

After 1999's *First Course in Turbulence,* Young's 2002 collection, *Skid,* received high marks. As the author remarked on the *University of Iowa Web site* about the poems in his fifth book: "I think they're very much about misunderstanding. I think to tie meaning too closely to understanding misses the point." *Booklist*'s Ray Olson wrote, "There are now so many things and ideas in the world that it addles even the best-intentioned mind. . . . Surrealism seldom seems as much like real life as in Young's hilarious and cautionary poems."

Young himself acknowledges a subtle evolution in his poetry, as he observed on the *University of Iowa Web site:* "I think my first two books were relatively austere. In the following books, I tried to work toward celebration and joy and goofiness. But life conspires against you, hand you tragedy, proves that nothing can last. I think all of that is more apparent in *Skid* than it was in *First Course in Turbulence.*"

BIOGRAPHICAL AND CRITICAL SOURCES:

PERIODICALS

Antioch Review, summer, 1993, James Harms, review of *Beloved Infidel,* p. 57.

Booklist, February 15, 2002, Ray Olson, review of *Skid,* p. 986.

Boston Book Review, June, 199, review of *First Course in Turbulence,* p. 32.

Ohio Review, spring, 1993, Tony Hoagland, review of *Beloved Infidel,* p. 468.

Ploughshares, fall, 1993, Diann Blakely Shoaf, review of *Beloved Infidel,* pp. 250-51.

Publishers Weekly, June 1, 1992, review of *Beloved Infidel,* p. 57; February 25, 2002, review of *Skid,* p. 58.

Threepenny Review, summer, 1990, review of *Design with X,* p. 21.

Virginia Quarterly Review, summer, 1996, review of *Strike Anywhere,* p. 100.

ONLINE

Loyola University Web site, http://www.luc.edu/ (July 24, 2002), excerpt from *First Course in Turbulence.*

University of Iowa Web site, http://www.uiowa.edu/ (July 24, 2002).

Colorado State University Web site, http://www.colostate.edu/ (July 24, 2002), "Center for Literary Publishing."*

*   *   *

YOUNG MAN, Alfred 1948-

PERSONAL: Also known as Eagle Chief; born April 12, 1948, in Browning, MT. *Education:* Institute of American Indian Arts, postgraduate diploma, 1968; Slade School of Fine Arts, B.F.A., 1972; University of Montana, M.A., 1973; Northern Montana College, teacher's certificate, 1974-75; attended Flathead Valley Community College, 1977-85; Rutgers University, doctoral study, 1989.

ADDRESSES: Office—Department of Native American Studies, University of Lethbridge, Lethbridge, Alberta, Canada.

CAREER: Teacher, author, painter, and curator. Elementary school art teacher, 1973-74, and teacher of remedial reading and art, 1975; Flathead Valley Community College, media specialist and instructor in educational television, 1976-77; University of Lethbridge, Lethbridge, Alberta, Canada, assistant professor, 1977-92, associate professor of Native American studies, 1992—, member of faculty exchange program with University of Leeds, 1985, and Hokkai Gakuen University, 1992. *Exhibitions:* Solo shows at Long Gallery, University of London, and Museum of the Plains Indian, University of Montana; participant in group shows, including exhibitions at Wallace Gallery, Calgary, Alberta, Canada, Yakima Cultural Center, Gallery of the American Indian Community House, New York, NY, University of California—Davis, Amon Carter Museum, Fort Worth, TX, and traveling exhibitions in South America and Switzerland; work represented in collections, including those of the Canadian Department of Indian and Northern Development, Indian Association of Alberta, Institute of American Indian Arts Museum, and Universidae Collection of Native Art.

WRITINGS:

(Editor) *Networking: National Native Indian Artists Symposium IV,* [Lethbridge, Alberta, Canada], 1988.

(Editor) *A Dominican Experience: Three Aboriginal Artists of Canada in the Dominican Republic,* Om niiak Native Arts Group (Ottawa, Ontario, Canada), 1989.

(With Bryce Kanbara and Ingo Jessel) *Visions of Power* (exhibition catalog), York Quay Gallery/Leo Kamen Gallery (Toronto, Ontario, Canada), 1991.

(With others) *Indigena: Contemporary Native Perspectives,* [Ottawa, Ontario, Canada], 1992.

North American Indian Art: It's a Question of Integrity, Kamloops Art Gallery (Kamloops, British Columbia, Canada), 1998.

Contributor to books, including *New Territories 350/500 Years After,* abridged edition, Vision Planetaire (Montreal, Quebec, Canada), 1992; and *Canadian Music: Issues of Hegemony and Identity,* edited by Beverly Diamond and Robert Witmer, Canadian Scholars' Press (Toronto, Ontario, Canada), 1994. Contributor of articles and reviews to periodicals, including *Fuse, Parallelogramme, Remote Control, Talking Stick: First Nations Arts, Studies in Critical Practices, American Indian Culture and Research Journal, American Indian Quarterly,* and *Prairie Forum: Journal of the Canadian Research Center.*

BIOGRAPHICAL AND CRITICAL SOURCES:

BOOKS

St. James Guide to Native North American Artists, St. James Press (Detroit, MI), 1998, pp. 639-642.

PERIODICALS

Albuquerque Journal, November 4, 1990, "Indian Artists Shrug off Stereotypes to Express Defiant Spirits."

American Indian Art, spring, 1995, John Anson Warner, "New Visions in Canadian Plains Painting."

American Indian Quarterly, summer, 1994, Larry Abbott, "Contemporary Native Art: A Bibliography."

Christian Science Monitor, June 30, 1981, Mary S. Cowen, "An Art of Seeking and Finding," p. 20.

Journal of Inquiry and Research, January, 1994, John Anson Warner, "Ideology and Native American Nationalism: A Case Study."

Lethbridge Herald, October 27, 1984 and October 29, 1984, "Face to Face: The Herald's Joanne Helmer Chats with Alfred Young Man on Nicaragua."

OTHER

The Primal Mind (documentary film), broadcast by Public Broadcasting Service, 1986.*